$500

AFSCME Iowa

Bankers Trust Co.

Galin and Carol Berrier

Mr. and Mrs. Cox B. Birkholm

Burlington Kiwanis Club

Celebrating African-American

    Culture Class

Lynda M. Chase

Clarke County Development

David P. Close

DMACC – Student Action

Dubuque Co. Historical Soci

John and Elaine Estes

Fayette County Historical So

Federal Home Loan Bank

Robert and Ann Fleming

Fort Des Moines Memorial

    Park and Education Cer

Friends of Iowa Civil Rights

Alex and Catherine Chase Gross

Hawkeye Elks Lodge #160

Iowa Bankers Association

Iowa Federation of Labor AFL–CIO

Iowa State University

Iowa Public Television

Iowa – Colorado Club. Inc.

$100

A.A.U.W. – Indianola Branch

Alpha Kappa Alpha – Des Moine

Alpha Phi Alpha Fraternity

    – Des Moines

deration of Teachers

acqueline Blank

Dee Buchanan

Burrell

Black Trade Unionist

rs-Chapman

elia Chase

beard

ley Cunningham

aney

Theta

, Inc. – Des Moines

EA

QWL

t Dwyer

Marvin and Lillian Eivins

Lynn Engen

Estherville Abstract Company

Estherville Rotary Club

Linda and David Fobian

Judith M. Gordon-Omelka

David and Hannah Gradwohl

Renee Hardman

Rose Hoffman-Toubes

I'll Make Me A World In Iowa

Iowa Civil Rights Commission

Iowa Commission on the Status of

    African-Americans

tions

och Bridgford

e

ds

Mr. and Mrs. George W. Sullivan

Jack & Florence Thomas

David and Judy Trask

Lynda Walker-Webster

Ann Wolf

OUTSIDE IN

African-American History in Iowa

1838–2000

OUTSIDE IN

African-American History in Iowa 1838–2000

Bill Silag
Editor

Susan Koch Bridgford
Designer

Hal Chase
Coordinator

Published by the State Historical Society of Iowa

First edition, 2001
International Standard Book Number: 0-89033-013-1
Project coordination: Hal Chase
Editing: Bill Silag
Proofreading: Shellie Jo Orngard
Index: Randy Jedele
Design and Production: Paul F. and Susan Koch Bridgford
Cover design: ©Paul Bridgford 2001
Photoconversion: Mussetter's Graphics
Printing and Binding: Tru-Art Color Graphics, Iowa City IA 52240
Published by the State Historical Society of Iowa, Des Moines IA 50319

Special thanks to Tom Morain, former administrator, State Historical Society
of Iowa, for his support of *Outside In.*

Library of Congress Cataloging-in-Publication Data

Outside In: African American History in Iowa, 1838–2000 / edited by Bill Silag.
        p. cm.
Includes bibliographical references and index.
ISBN 0-89033-013-1 (alk. paper)
    1. African Americans--Iowa--History. 2. Iowa History. I. Bill Silag, 1946-

E185.93.I64 098 2001
977.700496073--dc21

                                                                2001049015

"Unriddle this riddle of outside in, of white men's children in black men's skin."

— *Georgia Douglas Johnson, 1925*

John Chapman and family in Buxton, c. 1910 (courtesy Mary Collier Graves)

Roger Saunders and army buddy, early 1950s (courtesy Meredith Saunders)

James Hoffa Jr., president, and Ron McClain of Des Moines, trustee, International Teamsters (courtesy Ron McClain)

Table of Contents

Young boy with Housing Council sign in Des Moines (courtesy Margaret Garrison)

Friends spar in Colfax (courtesy Robert Weesner)

Sweet Beulah Court #7 (courtesy Paul Jackson / Josephine Boykin)

Foreword

The Negro Renaissance in Iowa

by Leola Nelson Bergmann

Lulu Merle Johnson became the first black woman to be granted a doctorate by the University of Iowa, as well as the first in the United States to receive that degree in history. However . . . the doors to the white *academic world had not yet opened.*

Lulu M. Johnson (courtesy John Jackson)

"What prompted you to write *The Negro in Iowa* in 1948?" is a question I have been asked rather frequently since the inception of *Outside In.* The answer is simple. My association with its origin began in Iowa City a half-century ago in the library of the State Historical Society of Iowa. I was then a part-time editorial assistant on the staff of the society. Five years earlier I had received a degree in American Civilization at the University of Iowa after writing a thesis dealing with Norwegian immigrants, their settlements on farms and in small towns, mainly in the Midwest. By the second and third generation they were contributing to American life from a wide variety of professions. I was thus on familiar research turf when I was asked by the editor of the *Iowa Journal of History and Politics,* the quarterly publication of the society, to collect and write a history of the African-Americans in Iowa. Up to that time (1946–47) only a handful of articles existed, scattered in various books, journals, and newspapers. The time had come to assemble this data and probe for untapped sources.

My interest in taking on this daunting new research might well have had its beginnings some years earlier when, in a seminar on the history of the South, I became acquainted with a black graduate student, Lulu Merle Johnson, from an Iowa farm community. At that time Negro students were a rarity in the humanities, especially at the graduate level. However, as I recall, there was no sign of discrimination among our colleagues. Lulu's intellectual clarity and lively personality easily fit into our small group of hopefuls climbing the academic ladder. She became the first black woman to be granted a doctorate by the University of Iowa, as well as the first in the United States to receive that degree in the field of history. However, it must be noted that the doors to the *white* academic world had not yet opened. In succeeding years Dr. Lulu Johnson taught at the university for black students in West Virginia and later at Pennsylvania's Cheney State College where she was also dean.

By the end of 1947 the manuscript for "The Negro in Iowa" was ready for publication and appeared — slightly cut to conform to the format of the *Journal* — in the January 1948 issue. Read principally by subscribers to the *Journal,* the article, I suspect, lived a dusty shelf life for the next 20 years.

Nevertheless, major social changes were taking place during this time span. More and more migrations of peoples from war-torn countries were reaching American shores and the interior of the continent. Cities ballooned, racial tensions flared. Leading figures in government and industry, in universities, in "think tanks" and humanitarian organizations fostered programs to make the wheels of the nation function more smoothly. Ethnic groups found their voices, adding their special talents to the pulsing energy of mid-century America. Thus came about — somewhat hesitantly at first — the entrance into academia of ethnic studies. This trend is what gave new life to *The Negro in Iowa,* making clear the need to finish an unfinished task.

So it came to pass that in the seventh decade of the twentieth century — 1968 — the director of the State Historical Society of Iowa, Dr. William J. Petersen — in response to a growing demand for more recent history of the Negro in Iowa — planned to reprint the article as a separate monograph, and proposed that I write a new foreword. Unfortunately, during the intervening decades I had moved gradually out of the field of immigration history and into the world of fine arts, which demanded all my time. But I was pleased that Dr. Petersen was willing to marshal what information he had at his disposal and to publish a brief editorial addendum.

This new publication rather quickly reached a wider audience, for occasionally in the 1970s I received requests from college and high school teachers in states far distant from Iowa for additional material on some specific topic touched upon in both the 1948 and 1968 printings. This did not surprise me, knowing that the study of multi-national and racial groups was by now firmly established in the American lexicon.

The spark that ignited the desire to round out the century with fresh knowledge of how the Negro in Iowa became the African-American in Iowa is best told by the historians who in the spring of 1996 organized an epochal exhibit of *Patten's Neighborhood* at the State Historical Society of Iowa in Des Moines. That event and, also in 1996, the publication of Dr. Dorothy Schwieder's *Iowa: The Middle Land,* in which she called for a history of African-Americans in Iowa, spurred the group into action.

With vision and courage the group's members began to lay plans for what they knew would be a formidable undertaking. It was during this exploratory period that I was contacted by Dr. Hal Chase and invited to meet in Iowa City with a few of these people. I was impressed then by their earnestness and determination and, in the following years as a bystander, watched with growing admiration the evolution of the volume you see today. With vigor and infectious enthusiasm Dr. Chase recruited a bevy of scholars and able writers for the 20 chapters needed to resurrect the stories of Iowa's African-Americans that had remained buried during the 50-year lacuna. Diligently they collected, wrote, and rewrote drafts, giving freely of their time and resources. Meanwhile Dr. Chase, in presentations at schools and organizations, carried the message throughout the state to gain the attention, interest, and support of legislators, corporations, and philanthropists.

Through the years of the entire enterprise the State Historical Society of Iowa, with the valuable assistance of its administrator, Dr. Tom Morain, became a focal point of activity not only for the researchers but also as a venue for progress-report meetings and special public presentations.

The culmination of the project came at an April 2000 gathering held in conjunction with an Iowa History Forum at the Iowa Historical Building. Through the all-day session, discussions ranged from the content of the chapters to technical problems of publication and design. Later in the day and evening, at the home of Hal and Avril Chase, discussions continued, problems probed, questions asked and answered, suggestions made. Editor Bill Silag and designer Susan Koch Bridgford presented their solutions for producing an attractive, readable book, bearing in mind that it would be used by school children throughout Iowa, thanks to the appropriation by the state legislature for that purpose.

These countless planners, writers, and contributors deserve the thanks of every Iowan for shouldering the immense task of preserving for future generations the history of African-Americans in Iowa and the gratitude of all readers who wish to follow the fascinating story of these unique people.

Born and educated in the Midwest, Leola Nelson Bergmann received her B.A. (1937) at St. Olaf College and her M.A. (1939) and Ph.D. (1942) at the University of Iowa. In 1964, she returned to the University of Iowa to study printmaking and later established her own studio.

Dr. Bergmann's classic work, The Negro in Iowa, *appeared originally in the* Iowa Journal of History and Politics *in 1948 and was reprinted as a book publication of the State Historical Society of Iowa in 1969. Her book publications also include* Music Master of the Middle West *(University of Minnesota Press, 1944) and* Americans from Norway *(J.B. Lippincott, 1950).*

Leola Bergmann was married to Gustav Bergmann, now deceased. She is the mother of Iowa City attorney Hanna B. Weston.

Students at Grant Elementary School, Waterloo, 1949–50 (courtesy Reasby family)

Preface
All of Our Stories Are Bound Together

by Spencer R. Crew

The stories comprising the rich tapestry of our nation's heritage come from a multitude of sources. They are stories not just about the deeds of great men and women or about the major events of the past. The lives of ordinary women and men have also shaped who we are as a people and as a nation. Ultimately all of our stories are bound together in the narrative of American history. Unfortunately, we have not always acknowledged the ties that bind us together as Americans. Too often it has been easier to highlight differences or to ignore the role played by less prominent groups than to take the time to understand the relevance of their contributions. The risk in this approach is that diminishing the accomplishments of one group impairs one's understanding of the full breadth and power of the whole.

When Dr. Leola N. Bergmann published "The Negro in Iowa" in 1948, she understood the importance of uncovering stories previously untold. She sought to show how African-Americans had settled in Iowa and worked like other residents to develop a vibrant state, a place where they could raise their families and fulfill their dreams. It was an archetypical American experience, but one that few people in Iowa or anywhere else knew or understood. Dr. Bergmann believed her publication would help rectify this oversight. She also hoped it would encourage stronger bonds between African-Americans and other Iowa residents.

Dr. Bergmann's views paralleled the vision of another scholar, Dr. Carter G. Woodson. Born in Virginia in 1875, Woodson earned a Ph.D. in history from Harvard University. While there, he developed a lifelong dedication to the history of African-Americans. Woodson's energy in this regard was spurred in part by his Harvard professors' doubts about the importance of the role of African-Americans in the development of the nation. They felt Woodson was wasting his time, but he persisted and wrote his doctoral dissertation on African-American history. His first publication, *The Education of the Negro Prior to 1861*, was just one of many volumes he would write describing the black experience in America. In 1915 Woodson founded the Association for the Study of Negro Life and History, an organization dedicated to promoting African-American history. The primary publication of the association, the *Journal of Negro History,* regularly printed articles examining the historical contributions of African-Americans. Individuals from all walks of life participated in the association's activities, reflecting Woodson's commitment to democratizing the study of history.

Woodson also created Negro History Week to increase awareness of African-American history within the black community. He felt that African-Americans did not know enough about their past and that greater knowledge would result in heightened self-respect. Woodson chose the second week of February for the celebration — to commemorate the birthdays of Frederick Douglass and Abraham Lincoln, both of which occurred during that seven-day period. The idea caught on and became a regular event in African-American communities across the nation. As it grew in popularity, Negro History Week came to include parades with costumed figures from black history, breakfasts, banquets, speeches, lectures, exhibits, poetry readings, and special presentations. The genealogical research, oral-history interviews, and community studies encouraged by Negro History Week organizers suggested new ways of learning about the past and encouraged everyone, not just those with formal academic training, to think of themselves as historians. Over time Negro History Week, which later evolved into Black History Month, served as a catalyst for people all over the country to reflect on the African-American past.

The work of Leola Bergmann was in many ways a legacy of these efforts of Carter G. Woodson. While Woodson's desire was

The lives of ordinary women and men have also shaped who we are as a people and as a nation. Ultimately all of our stories are bound together in the narrative of American history.

to promote greater knowledge on a national level, Bergmann sought to accomplish similar goals on the state and local levels. "The Negro in Iowa" brought together stories of numerous black men and women who made Iowa their home, describing how they shaped the history of their state. Included were people like George H. Woodson, who founded the Iowa Negro Bar Association and later the National Negro Bar Association and served as the first president of each organization. And Gertrude Rush, who established the Charity League, which provided social services for people of color, and was the first African-American woman to pass the Iowa bar. Published on the eve of the civil rights movement, Dr. Bergmann's profiles of George Woodson, Gertrude Rush, and others undoubtedly encouraged African-Americans and their supporters across Iowa to agitate for a fuller role in the social and civic life of their state. An understanding of black contributions to Iowa's development added power to demands that African-Americans receive the same treatment and rights accorded to the state's other residents.

Histories focused on the contributions of African-Americans had a similar impact on efforts throughout the U.S. as the civil rights movement gained momentum. The writings of John Hope Franklin, Kenneth Stampp, Benjamin Quarles, Herbert Aptheker, and others encouraged pride in black culture. While this renaissance of black historical studies was not the only factor spurring civil rights efforts, it was certainly an important contributor to the cultural awareness upon which these activities were based.

While black histories written during the civil rights era pointed up the distinctiveness of the African-American experience, they also illustrated how closely bound all Americans were to one another, despite entrenched traditions of segregation and discrimination. They revealed how, as Americans, people shared many basic values and beliefs. They wanted the same things for themselves and their families. They were willing to put in the time and energy necessary to improve their lives. In times of crisis, they stood ready to defend their country and make the ultimate sacrifice on its behalf. And in some instances they even shared a common bloodline and heritage. Research uncovered story after story of individuals who worked around or through the obstacles placed in their path — to improve their living conditions, to provide a better future for their children, and to work with others who shared their hopes and dreams for a good life.

The burgeoning interest in black history since Dr.

Bergmann's study first appeared in 1948 recently prompted Dr. Dorothy Schwieder to call for a more complete history of African-Americans in Iowa. In her book *Iowa: The Middle Land,* Dr. Schwieder noted that published works to date had only scratched the surface of Iowa's African-American history. Her own book added to the published information about the African-American experience in Iowa, but it hardly filled the void in the historical record. Much more research was needed, wrote Dr. Schwieder.

The authors writing in *Outside In* see their research as a first effort to fill the void. What they have produced here is in fact a monumental achievement, particularly in light of the historical sources available to them. The people brought to life in these pages probably never expected to have their stories told. Surely they did not see their stories in the same category as those of the politicians, scientists, and other public figures they read about in newspapers or history books. Most were people focused on earning a living, some literally just surviving the challenges that faced them on a daily basis. Creating a record of their lives — saving precious documents or cultural artifacts — was not very high on their list of things to do. But the authors of *Outside In* have rescued their stories, thousands of them, from oblivion. As a result, we now have a better sense of their lives — the jobs they held, the homes and churches they built, the men and women they chose to lead their organizations, and the issues that moved them to political action.

Both individual and collective endeavors are highlighted throughout *Outside In.* The story of Thomas C. Motts, who established several successful businesses in Muscatine, offers one example. So does the story of Dorothy Mae Neal Collier's family, living in the Gobbler's Nob area of Buxton, the interracial community that flourished in the early 1900s. The majority of Buxton's population was African-American, which meant that many of the town's black residents held positions of responsibility they could not have attained in other places. Since the town no longer exists, African-American accomplishments are not well known today except in the memories of former residents like Mrs. Collier, whose story is told in detail in *Outside In.* The book also describes the collaborative efforts of black and white Iowans who participated in the Underground Railroad, which gave runaway slaves an escape route to freedom.

Seen in isolation, *Outside In's* stories of courage and commitment might be considered singular acts of achievement,

While black histories written during the civil rights era pointed up the distinctiveness of the African-American experience, they also illustrated how closely bound all Americans were to one another. . . .

heroic tales set against the backdrop of tremendous challenges. Yet seen in the context of many generations of men and women, such individual acts reflect the strength of African-American culture as a whole. *Outside In* shows that black Iowans did not passively accept what life sent their way but actively worked to shape what happened to them and to the communities in which they lived. No aspect of Iowa's African-American past better exemplifies this self-reliance than the struggle to extend educational opportunity. Stretching back to Alexander Clark's successful fight in 1867 against segregation in public education, these struggles continued well into the twentieth century. A similar ongoing effort, dating from the territorial period, marked the struggle for full citizenship rights for African-Americans in Iowa.

While not as prolonged as the struggles for educational and legal rights, the collective efforts of social and cultural organizations to strengthen the African-American community constitute another important dimension of black history in Iowa. African-American churches have provided not only spiritual guidance but moral, cultural, and political leadership as well. Social, fraternal, cultural, and civic organizations — including among their members lawyers, business people, physicians, educators, and other professionals — have often supplied the resources to help the less fortunate and to push against the barriers facing the black community as a whole. Another significant dimension of black history in Iowa involves the literary, artistic, and sports figures whose achievements — and the personal examples they set — are critical to how African-Americans see themselves and how others see African-Americans. The authors of *Outside In* address all of these topics, and more, in their coverage of the multifaceted history of African-Americans in Iowa.

Carter G. Woodson would get great satisfaction from the publication of *Outside In*. Woodson believed that history belongs to all of us — not just professionally trained historians but anyone with a passion for studying and writing about the past. Like the historical figures they write about, the authors of *Outside In* come from many walks of life. Some are professors of history, others are community leaders. Some have been active participants in the stories they tell, while others were born generations after the events they describe. What they all hold in common is their commitment to sharing with their readers a fervent interest in Iowa's African-American history. Woodson would also be pleased by the wealth of information they have

extracted from public records, newspapers, family papers, and personal memories, and the way the authors have brought to life people and events that might otherwise have been forgotten or lost. And Woodson would no doubt agree that reading *Outside In* is an extremely enriching experience, important not just for African-Americans but for all Americans, in Iowa and throughout the nation. Through their research and writing, the authors of *Outside In* have taken a major step in showing us how our stories are joined together in the complex tapestry of American experience that is our collective history.

Spencer R. Crew was appointed director of the Smithsonian Institution's National Museum of American History in 1994, after serving two years as the museum's acting director.

Dr. Crew joined the staff of the National Museum in 1981. He became a curator in the museum's Division of Community Life in 1987 and was named chair of the Department of Social and Cultural History in 1991. Among the exhibitions he has curated at the museum is "Field to Factory: Afro-American Migration, 1914–1940," a permanent exhibition.

Before coming to the Smithsonian, Dr. Crew was assistant professor of African American History and American History at the University of Maryland, Baltimore County. He is a 1971 graduate of Brown University and holds M.A. and Ph.D. degrees from Rutgers University.

Freedom Train color guard, Burlington, c. 1950
(from Verla Lewis's scrapbook courtesy Laura Baker)

THE MASON CITY METHODIST

NEW MEMBERS: Pictured above are the new members received into our church from Union Memorial on July 11th. Back row: Dr. Carl, Mr. and Mrs. Glenn Gilbert (Chairmen of the Commission on Membership and Evangelism) Mr. and Mrs. Felix Parker, Rev. Squire, Mr. and Mrs. Roy McAlister, Dr. Kindred (District Superintendent), Center row: Mrs. Carl, Mrs. Kindred, Mrs. Grace Woolery, Mrs. O. E. Blanks, Miss Madelyn Walls, Mr. A. G. Moore, Denise Moore, Mrs. A. G. Moore, Virgil Fisher. Front row: Mrs. Maude Brewton, Mrs. Marie Maddocks, Mr. and Mrs. Wayne, Mrs. Will Solomon, Mrs. E. S. Walls, Mr. and Mrs. Virgil Warren, Mr. and Mrs. Charles Williams, Mrs. Ruth Cabell. A complete list of names and addresses appeared in the July 9th MASON CITY METHODIST.

Mason City's Union Memorial Methodist and First Methodist churches merged in 1965. (Mason City Globe-Gazette)

Introduction

OUTSIDE IN: A Book for All Iowans

by Tom Morain

"No man is an island."[1] The human family is a family, and what affects one member affects all. Rules for children shape roles for parents. Changing norms for women affect men. What consumers want creates new challenges and opportunities for producers. And the story of African-Americans in Iowa is the story of all Iowans.

I learned an important lesson about this aspect of social wholeness when I was involved in the writing of an Iowa history textbook for elementary school students. It was a lesson about the impact of passive verbs that denote an action without saying by whom it was said or done. The book was left on the table. (By whom?) The money was given secretly. (By whom?)

In the case of the textbook, one of the authors had written a section about ethnic groups from eastern and southern Europe who began migrating to Iowa in sizable numbers in the late nineteenth and early twentieth centuries. She included a discussion about the forms of discrimination these groups had to overcome because they had been stereotyped as "lazy or spendthrift." (Stereotyped by whom?) A committee of teachers reviewing the book objected to that chapter because they feared students would associate these attributes with the ethnic groups as if they were true, forgetting the context about inaccurate and unfair stereotypes.

What occurred to me sometime later was that the reality of those stereotypes was part of the history of both the newly arrived groups and the older stock Iowans who held them. One could have organized that same material into a chapter headed "Erroneous Beliefs of Northern European Caucasians." Included in such a collection could have been the once firmly held convictions that you'll get cramps if you go swimming less than an hour after you eat, that you get warts from toads, and that strenuous sports are not healthy for girls. (I vote to include the notion that Brussels sprouts are edible.) It could also have listed assumptions about the intellectual superiority of certain races or the male gender. It would have been a chapter devoted to mistaken beliefs but focused on the people who believed those fallacies, not on those about whom the assumptions were made.

Race is a part of all Americans' history because we all have assumptions about race that affect how we relate within and across racial lines. For that reason, *Outside In* is a book for all Iowans, not just African-Americans. For most of us, whatever our race, the information in these chapters will be new. I grew up in an Iowa small town that had no African-American residents. I remember no Hispanics or Asians either. Had we been asked if there was racial discrimination in Iowa, we would have responded in good conscience that segregation was the practice in southern states but did not occur in the North. We believed it. For those of raised in such innocence, *Outside In* will be startling and disturbing.

Perhaps because their numbers have been so small, there has been little written about African-Americans in Iowa. Leola Bergmann's work, "The Negro in Iowa," was ground breaking when it appeared in 1948, and it is fitting that the authors of *Outside In* recognize the significance of her work. This collection builds and expands upon her original efforts. Like Bergmann, these authors have chosen to make Iowa their common focus and to organize their research on a statewide basis. Iowans are indeed fortunate that this was the decision, and we owe a tremendous vote of thanks to the authors and others who have made *Outside In* a reality.

Because this is such a pioneering work, many of these authors are the only ones so far who have attempted first to locate and then to organize their subject information. They could not expand upon the works of previous historians because so little history about these topics exists. Some of them have had to build their accounts from facts gleaned from oral histories or snippets of newspaper

Race is a part of all Americans' history because we all have assumptions about it that affect how we relate within and across racial lines. For that reason, Outside In is a book for all Iowans, not just African-Americans.

articles or an occasional census record. On other topics the primary and secondary materials are more plentiful. For all of these authors, however, the difficulties in piecing together scattered bits of information are both the glory and the burden of their explorations. None of the essays is the final word on the subject; future historians will expand upon these chapters just as these authors drew when they could from Dr. Bergmann's account. Yet like DNA from our distant ancestors, the primary data in these chapters — names, incidents, accomplishments — will appear over and over as future historians add to the record and rework individual facts into new patterns of understanding.

Outside In opens with two chapters that take radically different approaches to the African-American experience in Iowa. Dr. Willis Goudy's statistical overview of the demographic characteristics of the state's black population is juxtaposed with Gradwohl and Johnsen's focus on the experience of one family in Buxton, Iowa's multi-racial coal community. The two together remind us that the history of the group is the sum of the histories of the individuals who compose it.

Part Two explores the legal definition of race in Iowa's 160 years as a territory and state. Unable to resolve the tension between its philosophical commitment to equality and its anxieties about full racial integration, the Iowa majority left an inconsistent record in legislative, administrative, and judicial proceedings. Sometimes

Depression-era workers at Kruidenier Cadillac in Des Moines (Des Moines Pioneer Club)

denying blacks the basic rights of citizenship but sometimes taking progressive stands far ahead of the times, Iowa laws reflect the struggles of a people uncertain about the significance of skin color. As the first "free" state west of the Mississippi, created in the bitter sectional conflicts preceding the Civil War, Iowans were forced to confront the slave issue in the persons of runaway slaves and in the Kansas-Nebraska Act of 1854, which opened the prospect of slavery on Iowa's western border. The Civil War abolished the institution of slavery but not legal distinctions based on skin color. In the courts, the military, and the schools in the years since that gruesome conflict, Iowans have grappled with what Gunnar Myrdal terms "the American dilemma."

Part Three examines the economic realities of African-Americans in the state. On farms, professional offices, and factories, blacks have struggled for a slice of the pie. They have fought to overcome educational barriers to enter the professions. They have been denied membership in professional organizations. They have faced barriers in unions created to advance the interests of labor. These chapters, however, focus more on achievements than on restrictions. When the cameras of the world documented the arrival of the McCaughey septuplets in 1997, were we surprised that the co-captains of the army of health care workers in the delivery room were two calm and competent African-American obstetricians, Dr. Paula Mahone and Dr. Karen Drake? Through that and thousands of less spectacular moments, African-Americans in Iowa have marked their progress toward equality in the work force, overcoming racial barriers unknown to whites.

Voluntary organizations are a major part of the American social fabric, a fact noted as early as the 1840s by the French commentator Alexis de Tocqueville. African-Americans in Iowa have also created strong networks of formal and informal associations, within and across racial lines. Political parties, the church, civic organizations, and social clubs promote causes and enrich the lives of their members. Often excluded from white organizations, African-Americans have sometimes created a parallel system of associations. African-American churches have been an especially powerful voice on political and social issues as well as religious matters. Because African-American Iowans have been so few in number, the same individuals often figure prominently in several different chapters. Understanding this interconnectedness provides an important insight into the mobilization of the African-American community on key issues.

Nowhere is the contribution of African-Americans more evident than in entertainment and the arts. Black athletes, male and female, today compete successfully in all sports. Jazz and gospel music amalgamate traditional and modern harmonies and rhythms to create uniquely American idioms. Black authors and artists enrich our understanding of the human experience. Part Five shares the stories of African-American Iowans who have contributed to these rich traditions.

Iowans take great pride in the strength of our cities, towns, and neighborhoods. Hometown loyalties run strong. "We" are the residents of my town; "they" are from the town down the road. While "we" may be organized internally into different religious congregations, political parties, or business interests, it is our families and hometowns that have traditionally commanded Iowans' primary loyalties.

We Iowans seem to have been able to overcome every division except one — race. No matter how large the city or how small to village, we have never fully escaped the racial divide. On either side of line, we have continued to see the world as "we" and "them." Even as we begin the twenty-first century, we struggle to put aside distorted and antiquated formulations that mandate social and legal distinctions based on skin color. The dark side of community is that our sense of belonging can become stronger by focusing on who is excluded rather than the common interests of those within the circle. Like wearing shoes too small, we also suffer when our definitions of community are too small.

The State Historical Society of Iowa is proud to publish *Outside In* and present it to the people of Iowa and beyond. Do we offer this collection as a tribute to the history of a state that has been a paragon of racial tolerance? No, these essays reveal our shortcomings. Do we expect discrimination and suspicion to melt away when people read these accounts? No, these works reveal how persistent the problems are.

Yet we also inherit from the past a simple faith in a revolutionary proposition — "that all men and women are created equal and endowed by their Creator with certain inalienable rights." If in our history we see our faults, from the past we also inherit the standard by which we measure how far we have fallen short. It is our hope that with the publication of *Outside In* we will move together, as one people indivisible by race or skin color, a little closer to the promised land: "Iowa — a place of trust in a time not to be trusted." [2]

Tom Morain received his Ph.D. in American Civilization at the University of Iowa in 1974. After teaching history for 5 years at Iowa State University, he became director of history at Living History Farms in Urbandale, a position he held for 13 years. In 1995, he was appointed administrator of the State Historical Society of Iowa. Now he is Dean of the Liberal Arts College at Graceland University in Lamoni, Iowa. He has published 3 books on Iowa history and served for 6 years on the Iowa Commission on the Status of Women.

Notes

1. John Donne, Meditation 17, "Devotions Upon Urgent Occasions."

2. Paul Engle, "Heartland," *The World Comes to Iowa* (Ames: Iowa State Univ. Press, 1987).

Editorial Note

by Bill Silag

Outside In's authors have improved access to the African-American historical record for all of us. But there is still plenty to do. The work of collection and preservation must continue if future historians are to build on the strong foundation established here.

Outside In: African-American History in Iowa, 1838-2000, is the result of a unique collaboration involving academic scholars, local historians, archivists, museum curators, and community leaders. Each of the book's 20 topical chapters has been written by an expert in the field. Some chapters have been written by professional practitioners — doctors, lawyers, and journalists — who are establishing for the first time a framework for future research in their respective fields. Other chapters build on research published since 1948, when Leola Bergmann's pathbreaking "The Negro in Iowa" appeared in the *Iowa Journal of History and Politics.* But every chapter of *Outside In* marks a major step forward in our knowledge about the black experience in Iowa and about Iowa history in general.

Those of us involved in the publication of *Outside In* — designers, editors, and proofreaders — are grateful to the authors for their diligence in researching their topics, sharing their findings with one another, and helping us locate and identify photographs for inclusion in the book. We are thankful also for the authors' patience with the prolonged process of editing and production required by a book as big as *Outside In*. We hope the authors and their readers are pleased with the results.

In copyediting we have followed the *Chicago Manual of Style (CMS)*, 14th ed. (Chicago: Univ. of Chicago Press, 1993), though the variety of historical material drawn upon by the authors of *Outside In* has prompted some deviations from *CMS* prescripts. For example, we have adopted the style of Harvard University Press and the *New York Times* in hyphenating *African-American*, whether the term is used as a noun phrase or as an adjective.

We have also looked for ways to streamline the presentation of references at the ends of chapters. Full citations are given for a source at first mention in each chapter; subsequent citations for the source typically list just the source's author and the appropriate page number(s). The titles of three frequently cited publications have been abbreviated throughout the notes: *Annals of Iowa (AI), Iowa Journal of History and Politics (IJHP)*, and *Des Moines Register (DMR).* The complete name of the *Bystander,* the source cited most often in *Outside In,* appears each time the nespaper is cited so as to include the slight variations in its name over time.

Regarding full citations, references to government publications are listed with the basic information needed to access the document. Books, scholarly journal articles, mass media, news publications, and yearbooks and other ephemeral literature are listed with as much publication data as was available to the authors. In a small number of cases, where for example a newspaper reference includes "n.d." (no date) or a book reference includes "n.p." (no publication data), a library or archival collection is usually listed to locate the source. Much of the material cited in *Outside In* is archived at the State Historical Society of Iowa (SHSI). In most SHSI citations, Iowa City and Des Moines holdings have been distinguished. Unless otherwise indicated, all interviews were conducted by the authors of the chapters in which the interviews are cited.

In their respective chapters, authors Kathi Neal and Lynda Walker-Webster urge us to step up our efforts to preserve the historical record pertaining to the black experience in Iowa. *Outside In* has already had a positive impact in this respect, for in the act of researching — examining manuscripts, conducting interviews, and organizing photograph collections — the book's authors have improved access to the African-American historical record for all of us. Journals, letters, interviews, reminiscences, records of businesses and social organizations — as well as legal documents, newspapers, and other published — sources have been identified and their contents described. But as our authors remind us, there is still plenty to do. The work of collection and preservation must continue if future historians are to build on the strong foundation established here.

Waterloo YMCA, c. 1930 (Grout Museum)

Bill Silag received his Ph.D. at the University of Iowa in 1979. Subsequently he served as editor of The Palimpsest; *managing editor and editor-in-chief at Iowa State University Press; and program coordinator at Iowa State University. He has taught history at the University of Pittsburgh, the University of Iowa, and Iowa State University. His articles and reviews have appeared in the* Annals of Iowa, *the* Journal of American History, American Quarterly, *and the* Western Historical Quarterly.

In addition to his work as a historical writer and editor, in recent years Silag has worked in program evaluation and organizational development for colleges and universities in Iowa, Nebraska, and California.

Some of Iowa's earliest African-American residents came as steamboat laborers on the Mississippi and Missouri Rivers. (Dubuque Historical Society)

PART ONE

Two perspectives on the black experience in Iowa

[1] The Buxton Wonders baseball team, George Neal standing at right (courtesy Dorothy Neal Collier)

"A Kind of Heaven to Me"

The Neal Family's Experience in Buxton, Iowa

by David Mayer Gradwohl and Nancy Osborn Johnsen

[2] Dorothy Neal Collier and her son, William, in 1981 (ISU Archaeological Laboratory)

In this chapter, we discuss the former settlement of Buxton, Iowa, drawing upon the central theme and the spirit of this book's title, *Outside In: African-American History in Iowa*. Having never lived in Buxton and, indeed, having been born after the community ceased to exist, we are admittedly outsiders. Our interest and perspective in studying Buxton stem from our grounding in anthropology, and in particular the subfield of historical archaeology. In essence, we are students of material culture (the structures and portable objects made by human beings), the historical and cultural contexts of those physical things, and the people who made and used those artifacts in their everyday lives.

The central voice in this essay, however, is that of Dorothy Mae Neal Collier (see illustration [2], this page), a woman who was born in Buxton, whose childhood there molded her intellect and world view, and who transmitted her family's proud historical tradition and values from her grandparents and parents to her 7 children, 20 grandchildren, and many great grandchildren.[1]

In that sense, the Neal family's experience in Buxton extends across six generations. Beyond that realm, Dorothy actively sought to share this heritage with others, across lines of race, gender, age, and religion. In this capacity, she advised and informed us as we explored the archaeology of the Buxton townsite.

Following a framework often used in anthropology, Dorothy, as a primary informant, provided an *emic* or insider's understanding and perspective of life in Buxton. As social scientists, we brought an *etic* or outsider's viewpoint and approach to the data given our training in historical archaeology.[2] On September 27, 1995, Dorothy Neal Collier passed away; but she left a fortune to her family and all Iowans in her accumulated knowledge and resource materials regarding Buxton.

Through Dorothy's recollections, documents, and photographs, she was able to put a face on Iowa's African-American history and to illuminate many topics, including demography, economic and occupational opportunities, the church, education, sports, and the roles of women.

Although the Neal family's experience was certainly not unique, it is highlighted in this chapter to exemplify the generally good life African-Americans enjoyed in Buxton and the manner in which the memory of that community still shapes the lives of people today.

The Neal family's experience in Buxton extends across six generations. Beyond that realm, Dorothy actively sought to share this heritage with others, across lines of race, gender, age, and religion.

[3] George Neal (right) in his Coopertown tailor shop, November 1914 (courtesy Dorothy Neal Collier)

[4] George and Alice Neal with their children, Dorothy and Harry, and the family dog, Kid, c. 1910 (courtesy Dorothy Neal Collier)

Dorothy Neal (Collier) was born on December 18, 1906. She was delivered by a midwife in her parents' home on Gobbler's Nob, a residential neighborhood within the town of Buxton, a community situated on the northern edge of Monroe County, Iowa. Her father, George Lawrence Neal [3], worked as a tailor in a shop a few blocks away from the Neal home in an area of Buxton called Coopertown that was actually located in Mahaska County. George Neal was also rather famous as a player on the Buxton Wonders baseball team. (See illustration [1], page 2.) Dorothy's mother was Alice Mobilia Snead Neal [4], a housewife and part-time cook at a hotel and at a lunchroom near a coal mine. Several years after Dorothy was born, her parents had another child named Harry. And the family had a pet dog named Kid. In recalling the days of her childhood, Dorothy once commented that Buxton "was kind of heaven to me, in a way of speaking, 'cause the memories were so nice."[3]

So far, this scenario and its actors are not particularly unusual. One could replicate them easily in many other locales across Iowa and elsewhere in the American prairies and plains during the early twentieth century. Taking a closer look, however, one notes that the Neal family is African-American, that Gobbler's Nob was a racially integrated residential neighborhood, and that Buxton had a population of something over 5,000 people within which blacks apparently outnumbered whites. Furthermore African-Americans intermarried with Euro-Americans there and held various professional and commercial positions within the community as well as in the town's mining and railroading ventures. The Ku Klux Klan marched in neighboring towns, but its members did not show their white sheets in Buxton. These facts, and others discussed in this chapter, make both the scenario and its actors unusual if not unique in the American midlands.

The purpose of this essay is to describe the Neal family's home and yard lot within the socio-cultural context of the Buxton community [7]. To accomplish this objective, as historical archaeologists we employ what is called the *ethnoarchaeological* approach in understanding the experience of African-Americans in one Iowa locality, now an abandoned town site consisting of farm fields and pastures [8]. This approach enables a view of individual and family behavior systems, as well as the larger group cultural patterns typically considered in archaeology. The resulting information is of potential use in museology in addition to archaeological theory. The immediate objective of this chapter in

this book, however, is to elucidate the experience that many African-Americans had in Buxton as a part of their history in Iowa. This ethnoarchaeological synthesis, we hope, reflects the rich cultural history of Iowa and will contribute to greater appreciation of the varied ethnic heritages and traditions that have influenced our society in the American Midwest and will continue to do so well into the twenty-first century.

Background and Methodology

Only a few salient facts about Buxton will be summarized here, since the community has been described extensively elsewhere. In 1900 the Consolidation Coal Company, a subsidiary of the Chicago and North Western Railroad, established the town as a base of operations for its pit mines in northern Monroe and southern Mahaska counties [6]. Buxton was set out and buildings quickly constructed according to a pre-conceived and detailed plan [5]. As discussed below, the Consolidation Coal Company constructed many public facilities for the use of Buxton residents; some of these amenities are not available in many Iowa towns today.

At its peak, Buxton had a population numbering between 5,000 and 6,000 people, the majority of whom were black. Among the whites were people of Swedish, English, Welsh, Italian, German, and Czechoslovakian national origin. In Buxton there were African-American doctors, dentists, druggists, lawyers, mine engineers, music teachers, school teachers, school principals, merchants, farm owners, newspaper editors, and ministers, in addition to railroad workers, coal miners, midwives, cooks, seamstresses, farmers, hair dressers, teamsters, and blacksmiths. African-Americans were active members of the United Mine Workers of America union — as recorded not only in archival documents but also verified by an inscription on a gravestone in the Buxton cemetery.

Among Buxton's African-American population were veterans of the U.S. Army, at least one of whom was buried in Buxton's cemetery in a grave marked by a military headstone. While Buxton was in existence, the town's high quality of life was particularly extolled in the black news media — for example, the *Iowa State Bystander*, an African-American newspaper published in Des Moines, and the *Southern Workman*, a journal published at Hampton Institute in Virginia. After the abandonment of Buxton in the mid-1920s, the town's history was briefly summarized in articles appearing in several Iowa journals.[4]

[5] *Plat map of the town of Buxton, Iowa, drawn in 1919. The area shown is Section 4 — the main part of town owned by Consolidation Coal Company — and the north part of Section 9 with some of the outlying settlements. (Geo. A. Ogle and Co., 1919)*

[6] *View to the west of the depot and tracks of the Chicago and North Western Railroad in Buxton, Iowa (courtesy Wilma Stewart)*

[7] *Residential Buxton looking southeast from the top of the water tower — note the uniform construction details of company-owned frame houses, the layout of the quarter-acre lots, and the structures such as outhouses, coal sheds, cisterns, and fences (courtesy Wilma Stewart)*

[8] *Overview of the Buxton townsite, looking southeast from Mahaska County in 1980 (ISU Archaeological Laboratory)*

[9] ISU archaeological crew opening excavations at the Buxton townsite (ISU Archaeological Laboratory)

[10] Shovel skimming to explore a former house lot

[11] Excavating a trash-filled outhouse pit

Between 1980 and 1982 an interdisciplinary group from Iowa State University conducted a study of the Buxton townsite and the community's former residents under a grant from the Heritage Conservation and Recreation Service (HCRS; now part of the National Park Service) via the Iowa State Historical Department. We were in charge of the archaeological explorations of the town site. These investigations included reconnaissance surface survey and sub-surface test excavations [9, 10, 11]. Results of the archaeological investigations were submitted to the National Park Service as a contract completion report in 1982 and led to the placement of the Buxton townsite on the National Register of Historic Places in 1983. A revised version of the report was formally published as a book, *Exploring Buried Buxton: Archaeology of an Abandoned Coal Mining Town with a Large Black Population*, in 1984.[5] In 1986 we also published a videotape on our investigations at Buxton titled *Blacks and Whites in Buxton: A Site Explored, A Town Remembered*.[6] The results of archival studies and scheduled interviews with 75 former Buxton residents conducted by historians and sociologists were published separately in 1987 in a book titled *Buxton: Work and Racial Equality in a Coal Mining Town*, by Dorothy Schwieder, Joseph Hraba, and Elmer Schwieder.[7]

After 1982 and the termination of research funds, we continued our analysis of the archaeological inventory and our association with Dorothy Neal Collier as a primary historical and ethnographic informant. Although we had both general and specific topics in mind for investigation, we intentionally eschewed formal scheduled interviews in favor of informal and less structured discussions without strict time frames. Information was collected during taped discussions at Dorothy's house in Des Moines and informal conversations via the telephone or over food at restaurants and receptions, plus some written correspondence. In addition, Dorothy visited the Iowa State University campus on several occasions to make class presentations and to observe Buxton artifacts in the ISU Archaeological Laboratory.[8]

As indicated above, this discussion of Buxton uses the

ethnoarchaeological perspective. In a nutshell, ethnoarchaeology is "the study of contemporary cultures with a view to understanding the behavioral relationships that underlie the production of material culture."[9] The theoretical basis and methodological procedures that we employ in our ethnoarchaeological scheme are essentially those articulated by William H. Adams in his study of Silcott, Washington, a community occupied contemporaneously with Buxton.[10] In our methodological approach to analyzing Buxton's past, we simultaneously use data bases derived from archaeology, history, and ethnology in the sense that those disciplines are traditionally understood.

Our archaeological base consists of the artifacts and evidence for structural remains that we obtained through survey and sub-surface testing at the Buxton townsite during the summers of 1980 and 1981. Among the primary and secondary historical sources at our disposal are old photographs, plat maps, gazetteers, architectural plans, newspaper articles, correspondence, census data, and previously published journal essays. The ethnographic corpus includes the above-mentioned information from scheduled interviews conducted by sociologists and historians in addition to our own non-scheduled interviews and conversations with former Buxton residents over a period of 15 years.

The ethnoarchaeological approach is, in many ways, distinctive in terms of the source materials studied and, above all, the kinds of interpretation to which those data are subjected. The perspective here derives from training in holistic anthropology as opposed to traditional approaches in history and sociology or, for that matter, the knowledge of material culture used by informed antique dealers. Our database extends well beyond the bits of china, glass, and metal we collected at the Buxton townsite. As anthropologists, we used photographs as additional primary sources for soliciting data from informants and validating their comments in regard to settlement patterns and spatial relationships of buildings within the town.

Photographs could be used to date the sequence of construction and abandonment of structures within the town — for example, the presence or absence of certain buildings on a particular block, the height of trees in the town, and the size of landscaping plants around individual houses or company buildings. Photographs also documented the location and nature of the White House Hotel and the mine superintendent's home, which were not shown on the 1919 plat map of Buxton. That map did show, however, the location of the high school, which had burned down in 1907, as well as the entire grid system of streets, the town reservoir, and the principal buildings in Buxton's downtown district.

The plat map was an important document for the anthropologists, although its internal accuracy had to be critically evaluated. In terms of our interest in material culture, we asked Dorothy many questions about family heirlooms she had from Buxton (for example, her mother's and grandmother's china and crystal) and how the rooms in the Neal family's house were used. Some of these questions admittedly bordered on matters that were personal and private. Although Dorothy reported to us that she thought some of these topics posed by other researchers were "nosey" and inappropriate (adjectives people too often associate with the stereotypical pith-helmeted anthropologist studying the "natives"), she proceeded to discuss the same matters with us in great detail and to share other information that was of a personal nature. In addition, she allowed us to open up her china cupboard, remove objects to photograph, and record manufacturers' marks. She understood perfectly *our* bizarre behavior and invited us back to record more information at another time.

Dorothy Neal Collier as Principal Informant

Since Dorothy Neal Collier was our key informant in this study, it would be in order to provide some biographical information that will establish the extent of her recollections about Buxton and the reliability of her data. Dorothy completed primary grades in racially integrated classes at the Fifth Street Elementary

School [12, 13], which was located across the street from the house of her grandmother Sally James Snead Reasby. Mrs. Reasby was a dressmaker and ran a boarding house. The Neal family attended religious services at Mount Zion Baptist Church [14], which was located not far from the Fifth Street Elementary School near the center of Buxton.

It should be noted that the Consolidation Coal Company, as a part of its plan to establish a comfortable and harmonious community, had built the Fifth Street Elementary School and the Mount Zion Baptist Church along with several other schools and churches, a bank, a company store, a hotel for visiting sales people and entertainers, and two YMCA buildings (one for adults, the other for youth) that housed a gymnasium, a swimming pool, facilities for dancing and roller skating, a library, an auditorium, and meeting rooms for social and fraternal organizations [15, 16].

In 1916 the Neal family moved to Cedar Rapids, Iowa, but returned to Buxton often to visit Mrs. Reasby and other relatives. Dorothy went to junior and senior high schools in Cedar Rapids, except for two terms at a black Catholic boarding school in Normandy, Missouri. In 1926, just short of high school graduation, Dorothy married Clyde Collier and moved to Des Moines. In addition to raising seven children, Dorothy worked with her husband as a furrier and also as a part-time cleaning lady and cook. At age 60, Dorothy finished high school by completing her General Equivalency Degree (GED).

Dorothy's endeavors as a lay historian were particularly impressive. She had an extensive collection of photographs, postcards, newspaper articles, and other memorabilia from Buxton.

[14] *Mount Zion Baptist Church (SHSI Des Moines)*

[15] *Two YMCA buildings, shown in 1907 (Iowa State Bystander, December 6, 1907)*

[16] *Downtown Buxton (below), showing two YMCA buildings, a second company store, and house lots, after 1911 (courtesy Wilma Stewart)*

[12] *Mt. Zion Baptist Church, Fifth Street Elementary School, and the high school on the horizon (SHSI Des Moines)*

[13] *Fifth Street Elementary School class, c. 1912, Dorothy Neal stands in the back row, fourth from left. (courtesy Dorothy Neal Collier)*

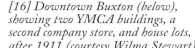

She was one of the co-founders of the Buxton, Iowa Club, Inc., a nationwide organization of former Buxton residents. Club members exchange information about the abandoned town, host annual Labor Day picnics and banquets with guest speakers, participate in various Black History Month events, and hold public information meetings. Dorothy was one of three persons appointed by the Buxton Club to serve as liaisons with ISU faculty on the grant from the Heritage Conservation and Recreation Service.

In 1980, it was Dorothy's son, William Collier, who introduced us to the Buxton townsite [17] and shared with us stories told to him by his mother, who could not accompany us to the field because of a recent hip operation. Dorothy helped the sociologists and historians contact other former Buxton residents and assisted with their formal interviews. She spent hours peering into microfilm readers in an attempt to gather census statistics. She ferreted out old Buxton photographs and memorabilia from a variety of sources, studied them, and identified people and buildings. When she could not identify items, she called on others for assistance and recorded their information.

On one occasion, after the grant period, she called upon us to research the medal and ribbon of an African-American fraternal sodality (Order of Calanthe) that a friend from Buxton had given her. When we jokingly reminded her that there were no longer grant funds to underwrite research, she caught our intended humor but responded, in essence, "Yeah, yeah, yeah, but go find out what this medal is!"

At another time, she and her daughter, Mary Jane Graves, tape recorded *us* tape recording *them* as we discussed Buxton. And on another occasion Dorothy loaned us a cassette tape because we

had run out — we had only taken two hours of recording tapes with us to Des Moines. She was almost obsessed with the necessity of having her recollections of Buxton recorded while she was still in sound health and mind. During one long session when we were recording information ultimately for use in this essay, we suggested that we stop and continue our work at another time. Dorothy quickly retorted, "No. Now! My mind might be gone next time." She laughed, but the insistence was there; so we continued. Dorothy was a perfectionist — a stickler for small details. When she could not think of something immediately, she typically chastised herself saying, "I'm just wool gathering now." Dorothy also realized that some of her comments might contradict what she had told us before. So she advised us, "Just be sure you keep it recorded, 'cause it might be a little different next time I think of something." In essence, Dorothy Neal Collier was indefatigable in her pursuit of Buxton's past. It is our observation that she had an appreciation for the relevance of minute details and an awareness of the encompassing big picture that surpass those capacities in many professional academicians with advanced degrees.

Where Was Gobbler's Nob?

Unfortunately, among Dorothy's extensive collection of photographs, there were none of the Neal family home or, so far as can be identified, the immediate neighborhood. Early on in our research on Buxton, we asked Dorothy where the Neal family home had been located within the town. She responded, "We lived on Gobbler's Nob," but she was unable to further specify the location. We then handed her an enlargement of the 1919 plat map, confident that she would point immediately to the street and

[17] Archaeologists' initial visit to the townsite in 1980 (below left) was guided by William Collier, member of the Buxton, Iowa Club, Inc. Artifacts were observed along the edge of Bluff Creek. (ISU Archaeological Laboratory)

[18] (Center) View to the north of the Monroe Mercantile Company's second store building on East 1st Street, after 1912 — note one auto and two carriages parked in front of the store. (courtesy Wilma Stewart)

[19] (Right) View to the north-northeast along northern entry road, in front of Armstrong's Meat Market. The First Methodist Church and the African Methodist Episcopal Church are in the background. (courtesy Donald Gaines)

particular block where her family had lived. She just stared at the map and could not relate to the drawing, which she had not seen before the inception of the project.

We were disappointed, of course, but had learned a lesson that the informant perceived the town as remembered houses, stores, streets, bridges, and the like — not as an abstract map. For example, Dorothy remembered well the company store [18]. So we asked her to describe the route she and her mother took there from their house. She responded immediately: "To go to the company store, we'd take a short cut, go down across the wagon bridge, and up the cinder road, round the corner past the stables, and the ice house, the meat market, and then the company store."[11]

Later we brought out a photograph taken along 1st Street showing the meat market, ice house, stables, and other structures [19]. She recognized this as part of the route she had previously described, and commented, "you know, a lot of things come back to you when you see the pictures." Gobbler's Nob, however, was not shown on that photograph — or on any others so far as we have been able to ascertain.

We next tried to learn the location of the "cinder road" to which Dorothy had referred. She said the road was next to a ravine:

"The ravine ran north and south. . . . The [cinder] road was on the west side of the ravine. . . . Our house was east of the ravine." Having conducted a surface reconnaissance of most of Section 4 of Bluff Creek Township, we were aware of the large ravine to which Dorothy referred. It appeared from her description that Gobbler's Nob would have been in the townsite portion we had designated Site Survey Unit C-4.[12]

On a different occasion, and quite unexpectedly, our assumption was proved correct. Dorothy had pulled out a big box of photographs and was telling us about her father's exploits on the Buxton Wonder's baseball team. She showed us a picture postcard sent to her father from the manager of a Chicago baseball team desirous of taking on the Buxton Wonders [21].

We turned the postcard over and noted, with a good deal of excitement, that the communication was addressed to George Neal at *34 East 4th Street*. Curiously, Dorothy had handled the postcard many times but had never taken particular notice of the address. That address corresponded to a lot number on the 1919 plat map, was precisely where we had hypothesized Gobbler's Nob to be, and provided a key for fixing all other specific addresses in Buxton [20].

[20] (Left) Plat map detail showing location of the George Neal residence at 34 East 4th Street, Buxton (Geo. A. Ogle and Co., 1919)

[21] (Right) George Neal's street address in Buxton on a postcard sent to him as manager of the Buxton Wonders baseball team (courtesy Dorothy Neal Collier)

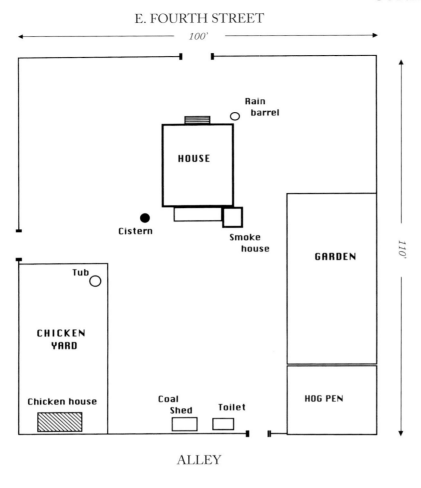

[22] Neal family house lot, a quarter-acre of heaven for the young Dorothy Neal. Drawn by the authors from information provided by Dorothy Neal Collier

E. FOURTH STREET

100'

Rain barrel

HOUSE

Cistern

Smoke house

GARDEN

110'

Tub

CHICKEN YARD

Chicken house

Coal Shed

Toilet

HOG PEN

ALLEY

[23] View of the coal conveyor along Buxton's Main Street at the top of Coal Chute Hill (courtesy Wilma Stewart)

Yard Space and Outbuildings

Having ascertained the location of the Neal residence in Buxton, we asked Dorothy if she could draw a plan of her house and yard since she had, on several occasions, described them in considerable detail. She claimed that she could not draw, but she agreed to guide us if we would sketch the location of items as she described them. So we proceeded according to her suggestion. We drew as she talked; we erased as she corrected us; and we submitted the results for her final review [22]. As with the plat map, Dorothy had more difficulty interpreting the drawing than a photograph. But she did, however, understand the representation enough to evaluate its accuracy and suggest some further modifications.

Dorothy described her house yard as follows: "They had pretty good-sized yards [in Buxton]. I guess a quarter of an acre is pretty good size! Our yard was fenced in. Just an ordinary wire fence. Up on Gobbler's Nob most of the houses were fenced in."[13] Dorothy subsequently indicated there were three entrances through the fence into the yard. A back gate off the alley was made from metal and wire; the "wagon gate" on the west was wooden; but the entrance to the front yard may not have had a gate.[14] She continued: "In the front yard was grass. You had to cut that with a sickle. [In back] on the alley, we had a chicken house, a coal shed, and the toilet [also referred to as the 'air conditioned bathroom']. Everybody had the same thing. One half of the coal shed would open into the alley. We brought in little buckets of coal and put them in the coal box by the stove.

"The chicken yard was to the west. In our yard the chicken yard was fenced off. The chicken house was up on blocks; it was big enough you could walk into it. We had some guinea chickens. I didn't know that they ate 'em. We probably ate 'em, but I didn't know it. I thought they kept 'em to let you know people was coming up the hill! . . .

"On the east end [of the yard] was the garden and that was fenced. [Mama grew] corn, potatoes, peas, beans, greens, onions, carrots, cucumbers, and peppers. I remember peppers, because she used to make piccalilli and stuffed peppers. . . . We had some flowers. Irises — we called 'em 'flags.' Grandma had flags, bouncing Betties, and pansy bushes. . . .

"We had a hog pen at the end of the lot. The neighborhood men would come and butcher. And then they'd hang [the hog] up with sticks inside for it to drain, I guess. They might have made a frame to hang the hog on, I don't know. I can't remember no tree in the yard, 'cause I used to climb the one outside the yard going down to the ravine. A big oak tree. I used to climb up in there and hide. I don't think we had a tree in the yard. They must have built a rack, you know, to hang the hog on. [Then] they'd make a fire. I remember their making a fire in the yard to heat the water. Then they'd put it in a barrel. The barrel was kind of tipped. They'd put real hot bricks in there. Then they'd push the hog in there and pull him out and scrape him. Ah . . . boy! Now they'd just put you in jail! . . . And then we had a little smokehouse right next to the house, east of the porch. That's where they smoked the pigs when they killed them. . . . We played in the open yard. Of course, there was no grass. Mama would sweep the [back] yard every morning."

At this point in the discussion, the ethnoarchaeologists could not resist an observation about what they would find — or *not* find — if they could excavate the Neal family house yard. One of us commented: "That means that we don't get to find anything, because you've swept it all away." Dorothy Collier, perceptively understanding the archaeological potential of her information, responded, "Well, it might be there around the coal house or somewhere. I don't know. You'd have to *dig* for it, I guess!"

Sources of Water Used in the House

In response to our questions about the sources of water used in the house, Dorothy provided more information about the layout of the Neal yard: "We didn't have no water on the inside. We didn't have a pump. Some people who were a little better off had pumps. . . . We had a cistern. It had a little part and a big part. The water would go in the little part and filter through a brick wall into the big part. We took water out of the big part. We used to get water from the company water tank. They'd bring the water. . . . We didn't have an icebox. We hung butter and things like that in a basket in the cistern. . . . I know we [also] had a rain barrel."[15]

In a later conversation, Dorothy indicated that the cistern was located in back of the house, a short distance from the porch, between the house and the wagon gate. The rain barrel was located at the northeast front corner of the house.[16]

Description of the Neal's House

Although Dorothy did not have a photograph of the house at 34 East 4th Street in Buxton, she had seen photographs of other houses in the town, and she could picture her childhood home in very vivid and precise terms: "It was a regular company house. Our house was painted white or light gray. There was one window in each room and two in the living room. There was a little transom over the front door and, I think, over the back door too. We had one of those fancy screen doors with a white porcelain handle and the little curlicues in the corner." Here Dorothy referred to gingerbread woodwork similar to that shown on the photo of Dr. Carter's office door. She continued: "The back door was plain. Not everybody had screen doors. On the front of the house there

[24] Historic view to the southeast of Main Street, also known as Coal Chute Hill (SHSI Des Moines)

were just stairs that went down. There was no porch, just the stairs. I would say about six or seven stairs. You could almost walk up under the front part of the house. We played under there."[17]

Dorothy indicated that she kept her sled and other toys under the raised part of the house. The sled and Coal Chute Hill, shown as Main Street on the 1919 plat map, figured large in Dorothy's memories of Buxton: "Oh, we used to slide down Coal Chute Hill on sleds [23, 24]. We'd come up from the top of the hill where the coal chute was . . . clear down to the railroad track where the train with a hopper on would load the little car, pulled it up to the top of the hill, and the wagons would back in and they'd load 'em and take 'em, you know, wherever you would want 'em."[18]

N

[25] Plan for the first floor of the Neal house, as described by Dorothy Neal Collier

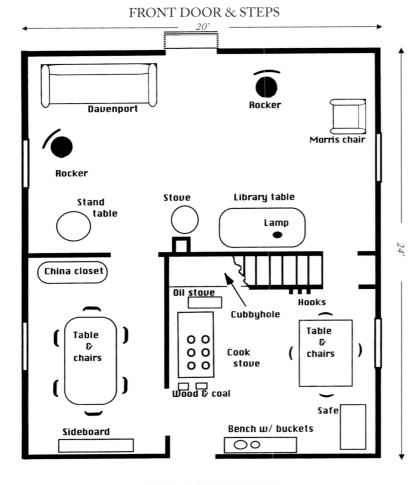

FRONT DOOR & STEPS

20'

24'

Davenport

Rocker

Morris chair

Rocker

Stand table

Stove

Library table

Lamp

China closet

Oil stove

Cubbyhole

Hooks

Table & chairs

Cook stove

Table & chairs

Wood & coal

Safe

Sideboard

Bench w/ buckets

BACK DOOR & PORCH

"We had a porch

on the back. . . .

A big porch, you know.

Open. . . .

We made kraut in

the great big crocks.

It smelled

to high heaven!

Mama kept it outdoors

on the porch."

— **Dorothy Neal Collier**

Back Porch

In her recollections, Dorothy took us onto the back porch and into the Neal's house through the kitchen, which was the door the family normally used: "We had a porch on the back. It was kind of level with the ground [25]. A big porch, you know. Open. It just had a roof on it; that's all. We made kraut in the great big crocks. It smelled to high heaven! Mama kept it outdoors on the porch. Pickles, apple butter, and stuffed peppers were [also] stored in crocks . . . that was tied with a cloth cover over it, you know. My aunt had a farm and kept [them] in a cave; but we never had a cave."[19]

Kitchen

"The kitchen door would be facing south. We [always] used the kitchen door. And as you went in the door, on the east we had a bench, and it had two buckets of water on it. One was for drinking and one was for cooking. Above that [the bench] was a shelf that held the [kerosene] lamps. There was no window on the south wall.

"And then right in that corner of the house there was a 'safe.' Now they'd call it a cupboard. The back of it would be to the east wall. It had two [glass] doors at the top, and then a long drawer across that, and two doors at the bottom. And then there was a window. Mama had a big table across that window. A kitchen table. A big square table. There were four chairs around the table. There was four of us; but mostly Papa was traveling, so there were just three of us around the table: Mama, my brother, and I. Uh-huh, now I'm going around the wall. Right on going to the north there was a door that went upstairs or straight through into the living room. The stairs went up to the west, between the living room and the kitchen. And now I'll go around on the other side of the wall.

"Next to the stair wall there was a door up under the stairs where the men would put their mining clothes." Dorothy indicated that George Neal kept his baseball clothes in there too. And along that wall there were also hooks for the children's coats. She continued: "That was the cubbyhole — where the 'bad man' was. I was scared to death of that hole!

"Then there was the stove on the west wall. We had a cook stove. It had a reservoir, you know, for hot water. . . . And behind it I can remember a salt box [crock] and a [metal] match box on the wall." Dorothy recalled that the stove had six burners. In addition, she remembered that her mother had hung iron skillets on the wall behind the stove.

Dorothy finished her description of the kitchen as follows: "Then further on, where you could reach them, next to the stove, there was a coal box and a wood box toward the dining room door. That's all there was in the kitchen, you know, because the door would open against the wall. . . . In the later years when we got the new dining room table, Mama bought a two-burner oil stove. And that was next to the wall where the cubbyhole was. We were into the money then, I guess! It was just a two-burner stove that had a tank somewhere on the side. I don't remember Mama ever cooking on the oil stove. She always cooked on the cook stove."[20]

Dining Room

From the kitchen, Dorothy's tour of the Neal house continued into the dining room: "In the dining room, let's see now, we had a sideboard and a long [oval] table kind of close to the window. We had one window in the dining room almost across from the kitchen window. I think we had six chairs in there. Near the corner was an old-fashioned china closet. Maybe you've seen it. It stood up, but each corner glass was rounded and the middle door was flat glass that opened. . . . We used [the dining room] mostly on holidays. Usually it was closed off. We did everything right there in the kitchen 'cause it was big and warm."

Living Room

Dorothy's remembered journey through her childhood home then continued into the living room via a connecting door from the dining room. To the left of the door: "We had a little stand table with claws and a glass ball in the claws. . . . The living room was the whole width of the house with a window at each end [on the east and the west]. And the outside door was in the middle of the house. There was a little transom window over the front door. We had a big green davenport that let back into a bed. And the arms, they were wide, and where you'd pull it was the head of a lion." With a little laughter, Dorothy recalled that as a child she used to put her hands on the arms of the davenport and then slide her fingers down into the lion's mouth.

She continued, "The davenport was against the northwest corner, just straight against the wall. And then we had a big black Morris chair. It was like what they call a lounger, you know. It had notches in the back. You take an iron rod and let it down. That set to the northeast corner. We had two wooden rockers. One set on the north wall between the door and the Morris chair; the other was by the davenport, by that west window. . . . The stove was on the other side of the door in the living room, kind of in the middle of the [south] wall. It was kind of round and had a lot of metal — I can [still] see the nickel around the bottom and on the sides. It had what they call 'isinglass' in the door and an ornament on the top. That was a good looking stove, I guess. We had an oblong library table to the east of the stove. And the table had a lamp on it. I'd call it an Aladdin lamp. You'd have to pump it up and then light it. It had Tiffany [glass] — it looked like yellow and white marble at the top, and it had little strings of beads that hung all around. It had two mantles. That was only for Sunday."

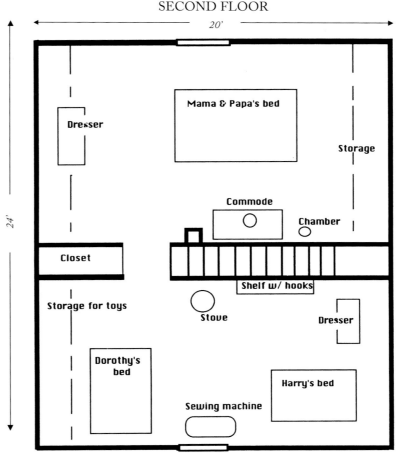

SECOND FLOOR

N

[26] Plan for the second level of the Neal house, as described by Dorothy Neal Collier

"They kept those doors shut. We lived mostly in the kitchen and upstairs. Sundays, [Mama] she'd take a shovel of coal and start the fire in the living room. We'd set in there and play. Of course it was all carpeted, you know. We had wall-to-wall carpeting. The carpeting was kind of like tapestry. Mama said they put straw underneath — to make it soft and keep the air out — and tacked it down."[21] Dorothy recalled that on the living room walls there were pictures of her father and the Buxton Wonders baseball team, in addition to a milk glass dish-like plaque with owls.

Upstairs

Next Dorothy took us to the landing between the living room and kitchen and then up the stairs to the second floor [26]: "There were two rooms upstairs. One would be north and one would be

"We lived mostly in the kitchen and upstairs. Sundays, [Mama] she'd take a shovel of coal and start a fire in the living room. We'd sit in there and play."

— Dorothy Neal Collier

south. There was a big closet right straight at the head of the stairs. They had a curtain over it. I don't remember what they kept in there; just nothing particular."

Dorothy and Harry's Bedroom

"Our bedroom would be on the south. The stove was in that room. It was on the side where you come in the bedroom door. It was a little round stove. There were no closets in the rooms. There was a shelf where they store [things]. A board was tacked to the wall on the side that you go down the stairs. And it had hooks on it where you hung your clothes. We didn't have too many clothes in those days."

"In our bedroom there were two beds. They were high, curlicue [brass] beds, so one end hit the side of the slanting roof. The walls slanted, you know, so the beds couldn't go to the outside. There was room behind [for storage]. At the foot of the bed on the west wall was a shelf where the stairs come in; there was a little place in there kind of under the eaves. It wasn't blocked off. Mama had a shelf in there where she kept some of her canning stuff."

Dorothy also recalled that she and her brother kept their toys in this area. She remembered especially her doll and doll buggy and Harry's little "movie projector" — apparently a lantern slide viewer. She reminded us that we had seen the picture of her doll and doll buggy [27].

Her description then went on: "But on the other side was the little bed and a dresser. There was a big bed and a little bed —

we didn't call them double beds or twin beds. I had the big bed and my brother had the little bed, 'cause when Papa was away, Mama would come in and she'd sleep with me. There was one window on the [south] end. Mama had her sewing machine across the window."[22]

"We used to take a bath upstairs. Can you imagine? Carrying water upstairs! Taking a bath in a big round galvanized tub with handles on the side! It was kept on the back porch. Sometimes we would bathe in the kitchen."

Mama's Bedroom

On the other side of the upstairs floor was the bedroom used by Dorothy's parents: "In Mama's room the window was on the north. It seemed like Mama's room was bigger than our room. Her bed would be north and south to the right side in the middle of the room. It was a big brass bed [with large knobs on top]. At the head of the bed, Papa kept fruit jars full of his money. On the wall next to the stair was a commode. It had a little door and two drawers, and on top of it there was a big porcelain pitcher and a bowl. And something came up on each side and had a rod across it for towels. It had a china soap dish and something else, but I don't know. The china pieces were blue and white."

"On the other side, on the west wall, was a dresser. And, of course, we had a chamber [pot]. That was kept by the side of the commode. And we had slop jars. They were *heavy* white porcelain and the chamber was too. The chamber was low, and the slop jar was about like that [gesturing a taller form and laughing]. Yeah, Mama made crochet covers to go over the top of the slop jar. It had a lid, you know. Just fancy, so it would be sitting out in the room and you wouldn't know what it was [continuing her laughter]."

Cross-check on the Reliability of Dorothy's Recollections

Throughout our association with Dorothy Collier, we had numerous opportunities to cross-check the validity of her recollections of Buxton. We were able to ask her the same questions and compare the answers. Almost invariably the information was the same. Only on rare occasions were there contradictions — although new details might occur to her as she went through her thought processes again. The details she summarized for us on October 23, 1988, for example, paralleled very closely the data we had obtained in interviews conducted on March 19, 1982, and December 1, 1983. As a side note, it should be pointed out that

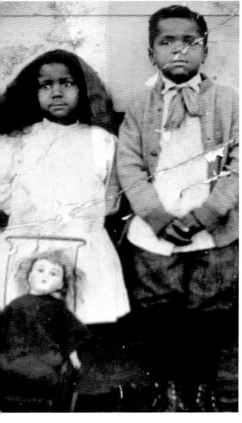

[27] Dorothy and her brother, Harry — note Dorothy's doll and buggy (courtesy Dorothy Neal Collier)

[28] A company-owned miner's house in Buxton — location and resident(s) not identified — much like the Neal's residence (SHSI Des Moines)

"We used to take

a bath upstairs.

Can you imagine?

Carrying water

upstairs!

Taking a bath in a

big round galvanized

tub with handles

on the side!

It was kept on the

back porch."

— **Dorothy Neal Collier**

Dorothy had been hospitalized for a short time early in October 1988 for a "slight stroke." When we offered to postpone our meeting in Des Moines, she rejoined quickly: "No, come on down. It didn't get my mind!"

The general data Dorothy Collier provided on her home and yard lot in Buxton are also substantiated by information gleaned from scheduled interviews that the sociologists and historians conducted with other former Buxton residents. As further corroborating material, we also have the transcript of an informal interview with Dorothy Collier obtained by the late Dr. Charles C. Irby, former chair of the Department of Ethnic and Women's Studies at California State Polytechnic University in Pomona. This transcript was especially helpful as a cross-check against racial bias since both the interviewer and interviewee were African-Americans. Although none of the former Buxton residents, so far as we know, has provided the wealth of details regarding yard lots, house layouts, and family furniture as recollected by Dorothy Collier, both the general pattern and the variations selected by individual families are readily apparent.

As indicated above, historical photographs of general Buxton scenes and, in particular, the exterior of company houses provided a valuable tool for substantiating Dorothy Collier's descriptions [28, 29]. Particularly striking are the correspondences on the size of yards, presence and placement of specific outbuildings, location of vegetable and flower gardens, and structural details of the houses, including the placement of porches and windows and the decoration of screen doors.

Unfortunately there are few if any photographic views of the interiors of Buxton homes, although such are available for the company store, a blacksmith shop, the Granberry Brothers' tailor shop in which George Neal worked, and the studios of several professional photographers.

Fortunately, and quite unexpectedly, a crucial substantiating document came to our attention subsequent to the HCRS grant period and after we had obtained our initial descriptions of the interior of the Neal home from Dorothy Collier. This evidence consisted of a packet of architectural drawings that was turned over to the Iowa State Historical Department by the firm of

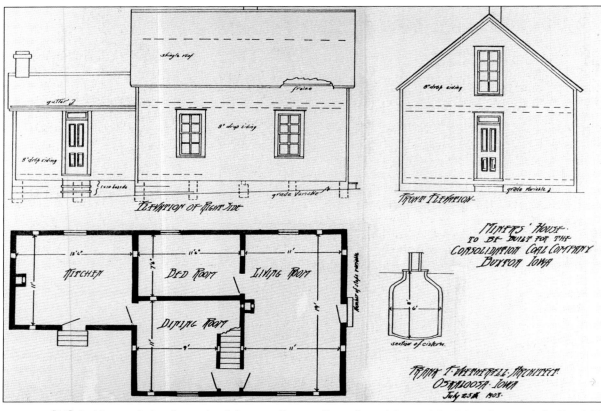

[30] *Architectural plan for a miner's house at Buxton. Reconfigured from original drawings made by Frank E. Wetherell, then of Oskaloosa, Iowa, between 1901 and 1904. The original drawings were donated to the Iowa State Historical Museum by the architectural firm of Wetherell, Ericson and Leusink of Des Moines. (SHSI Des Moines)*

Wetherell and Ericsson Architects of Des Moines. The packet had been drafted between 1901 and 1904 by the late Frank E. Wetherell, then of Oskaloosa, at the request of the Consolidation Coal Company. The drawings included plans for the African Methodist Episcopal Church, the Mount Zion Baptist Church, the high school, an "eight-holer" outhouse (presumably for the high school), and — much to our delight — the floor plans and specifications for the houses to be built for the Consolidation Coal Company's miners.

The extant drawing depicts a six-room house with a kitchen, dining room, living room, and bedroom on the first floor and two bedrooms on the second floor [30]. The Neal home as described by Dorothy Collier was a five-room company house, as were many houses shown in the historical photographs of Buxton. In those cases, there was no bedroom on the first floor, just a kitchen, dining room, and living room. Dorothy, of course, had never seen the architectural drawings. Yet there were specific correspondences between the architectural plans and her recollection of the number and placement of windows and doors as well as the location of the stairs. Her memory of where the stoves were positioned tallied exactly with placement of the chimney on the architect's floor plans; she remembered correctly the presence of a transom window over the front door.

Selecting Furniture from the Sears, Roebuck Catalogue

As indicated above, Dorothy remembered a good many details about the furniture and household equipment in the Neal's Buxton home. To get a further idea of the styles of furniture owned by the Neals, we asked Dorothy to look at pages from the reprinted

[31] Items from Sears, Roebuck and Co. catalogues (left to right): kitchen cupboard or "safe," 1908 (page 378); kitchen chair, 1908 (367); china cabinet, 1902 (749); carved oak dining room chair, 1908 (367); round oak table, 1902 (749). (Facing page, left to right): davenport, 1908 (445); Morris chair, 1908 (449); square oak table, 1902 (752); brass bed, 1908 (430); sewing machine, 1902 (722); heating stove, 1902 (825).

editions of the 1902 and 1908 Sears, Roebuck catalogues.[23] It is important to note that this was done only *after* her actual verbal descriptions had been recorded. So delighted was Dorothy with our little game that we bought a copy of the 1908 catalogue for her to keep! In leafing through the catalogues, Dorothy found exemplars of many of the pieces of furniture that the Neals had once owned. The steel range pictured in the 1902 catalogue [33], for example, was similar to the Neal's cook stove although Dorothy commented that theirs was not quite so "fancy." Other examples were found for furniture once housed in the Neal family kitchen and dining room: the kitchen chairs and safe, and the dining room china closet, table, and chairs [31].

The Neal's large living room stove with nickel decoration, top ornament, and isinglass doors had a fancier parallel in the 1908 Sears, Roebuck catalogue [32]. Examples of other living room furniture were found in the catalogues. A plush-covered davenport bed was similar to that owned by the Neals, although the one pictured did not have carved lions' heads on the arms [31]. A Morris chair in the same catalogue, however, did have the kind of carving that Dorothy had described. The Neal's Morris chair, however, was a simpler style according to Dorothy. A close parallel was found for the stand table with the claw feet and glass balls, but no catalogue illustrations could be found that resembled the Neal's elaborate Aladdin lamp.

For the upstairs bedrooms, Dorothy found catalogue pictures that resembled the Neal's stove, sewing machine, and the brass bed in which her parents slept [31]. She recalled that the large brass balls at the corners of her parents' bed could be taken off the bedposts. Dorothy reminisced that she and her brother used to

[32] (Above) This nickel-plated coal stove with isinglass doors, found in the 1908 Sears, Roebuck and Co. catalogue (650), was a fancier version of the Neal's living room heat source.

[33] (Left) Steel range from the 1902 Sears, Roebuck and Co. catalogue (814). Dorothy commented that theirs was not quite so "fancy."

remove those ornaments and play with them — much to the consternation of their mother.

Among Dorothy's possessions were some articles that belonged to her mother and grandmother in Buxton: several old kerosene lamps, a vaporizer, some china dishes and serving pieces, a porcelain hat pin holder, and some cut crystal knife rests. The china and ironstone dishes and serving pieces included both domestic and imported wares. Several serving pieces were produced in East Liverpool, Ohio, by the Homer Laughlin Company. They were decorated in a delicate floral transfer (Geneseo?) pattern and, according to Dorothy, were "Mama's best dishes." Another set of china, referred to as "Mama's second best dishes," were gilt-edged cream wares represented by plates, two casseroles or covered serving bowls, several platters, saucers, and a sugar bowl.

Ceramics from three different potteries in Tunstall, Staffordshire, England, were included in Dorothy's collection. Grindley Company's Old Mill pattern, a multi-colored transferware, was represented by some plates, a serving platter, and a gravy boat. Luster band ware with a central flower sprig (or tea leaf) design was manufactured by two different pottery firms in Tunstall: Alfred Meakin Company and Wedgwood and Company. Among these pieces were dinner plates and a handled serving bowl. Finally, there was Dorothy's prized possession: a large soup tureen in a brown transferware (Melton?) pattern manufactured by Wedgwood and Company.

The Sears, Roebuck catalogues for 1897, 1902, and 1908 advertise china from the American potteries in East Liverpool, Ohio, as well as the English firms in Turnstall, Staffordshire. So the Neal family might have obtained their china sets via mail order. On the other hand, these items certainly would have been available at the Monroe Mercantile Company (the company store) in Buxton or possibly privately owned stores in Buxton or neighboring towns.

Conclusions

The above information has been presented in an attempt to elucidate the lifeways that once existed in Buxton. To accomplish this goal, we employed an ethnoarchaeological approach that has essentially been ignored in dealing with the African-American experience in Iowa and adjacent states in the prairies and plains. In particular we have focused in on the Neal family as a case study of one of the many experiences African-Americans had in Iowa

during the early twentieth century. Following the model of Adams in his study of the Silcott, Washington, community, we have simultaneously drawn upon historical, archaeological, and ethnographic data. The emphasis here has been on oral historical and ethnographic information relating to material culture and cross-checked by archival sources.

In considering the physical layout of the Neal's yard lot and the arrangement of rooms and furniture within their house, one must comprehend the general cultural context of Buxton. That milieu can be understood on the bases of archival documents as well as the artifacts and structural evidence collected during our archaeological fieldwork at the townsite. The reliability of data provided by our key informant, Dorothy Neal Collier, can be judged by comparing her own memories recorded by different interviewers and on various occasions. Her information can also be substantiated by archival documents.

Beyond the theoretical aspects of the ethnoarchaeological approach, information on the Neal's home in Buxton could serve as a basis for exploring specific individual and family behavior patterns, as opposed to the general cultural systems of the past normally, and often necessarily, dealt with in archaeology. Within the framework of data provided by Dorothy Collier, it would be theoretically possible to return to the Buxton townsite with a refined research design for archaeological explorations. Artifacts and structural remains from the house lot at 34 East 4th Street could be excavated and presumed to be the material remains of an identifiable African-American household. Hypothetically, these data could be compared, for example, to those obtained from the yard lot of an identified Euro-American household in the East Swedetown neighborhood of Buxton. There are many potential avenues of research that could be pursued in terms of ethnicity, economic status, and social class.

The information obtained from Dorothy Collier is also relevant to museology along the lines so masterfully demonstrated by George W. McDaniel in his book titled *Hearth and Home: Preserving a People's Culture*. This study of African-American farm tenant homes was the basis for house reconstructions as exhibits in the Hall of Everyday Life in the American Past at the Smithsonian Institution in Washington, D.C.[24]

Members of the Buxton, Iowa Club, Inc. have for some time expressed a desire to have an interpretive culture center built at the Buxton townsite and have, in addition, called for Buxton

"I'll try to answer

that the simplest way

I can.

It's very important

not only to black people

but to white people

to see that . . .

people can live

in harmony."

— **William Collier**

exhibits to be installed at the State Historical Museum or elsewhere in Des Moines.

Ethnoarchaeological information such as that assembled in this essay can provide a frame of reference for designing dioramas and/or period rooms in a museum or interpretive center. The purpose of such exhibits extends beyond reminiscing or pure nostalgia. The historical experience in that now-abandoned community continues to shape the lives of former Buxton residents and the lives of their children and grandchildren. That heritage is constantly reinforced at meetings of the Buxton Club, its Labor Day picnics, annual banquets, and various community presentations. Members of the Neal family remember Buxton in warm and affectionate terms. Dorothy's son, William Collier, was asked what he thought the message of the Buxton experience was for us today.[25] He responded "I'll try to answer that the simplest way I can. It's very important not only to black people but to white people to see that . . . people *can* live in harmony. That's authenticated by pictures of black and white people dressed together, enjoying themselves together, in church together, working together, playing together" [1, 13, 34]. The experience and

[34] Dr. Edward A. Carter (second from left) at his office in Buxton. Jim Warren (far left) was Dr. Carter's brother-in-law and handyman. The dog on the right is Duke, the Carter family pet. The second man from the right is Dr. Powell. The man at right and the dog on the left are unknown. Identifications by Marion Carter, Edward Carter's daughter. (SHSI Des Moines)

19

perspective of the Neal family are corroborated to a large degree in interviews with many other Buxton residents. These matters have been discussed more extensively elsewhere, but a few examples will make the point here.

Bessie Lewis remarked, "I'm telling you, Buxton is the place that really give the colored person a chance. Give them a chance to do anything that they wanted to do."[26] Lola Reeves, a former school teacher in Buxton, echoed these sentiments: "You know, Buxton to me was a new experience and I really enjoyed it. . . . Going to Buxton with all the people of my own race was a great experience for me. . . . I could exercise my feelings, my potentials, my talent. . . . I was happy."[27]

In another interview, a sociologist pressed former Buxton resident Elmer Buford on the subjects of integration and harmony in Buxton. Somewhat irritated, Mr. Buford answered: "I told you. There wasn't no discrimination down there. . . . Well, you just keep asking me about the black and white. They worked together. They ate together. And if they wanted to, they slept together. And they did everything together down there."[28]

Finally, in terms of the recollections of former Buxton residents, we offer the words of the late Marion Carter, a long-time librarian in Detroit, who was the daughter of Buxton's famous Dr. Edward A. Carter and Rose Warren Carter. In a letter written in 1963, Miss Carter observed that in Buxton there were "all white affairs, all colored affairs, and all all affairs!"[29]

Independent corroboration of these views can be found in newspaper and other publications in the early twentieth century. We note the words published in 1908 by Richard R. Wright Jr. in the *Southern Workman*: "the relation[s] of the black majority to the white minority are most cordial . . . The Negroes do not fear the whites and the whites do not try to make them fear them; there is mutual respect. Both races go to school together; the principal and most of the teachers are colored; they go to the same soda-water fountains, ice-cream parlors, and restaurants; work in the same mines, clerk in the same stores and live side by side."[30]

Finally, for the purposes here, we can reflect upon the observations of the editor of the *Iowa State Bystander* on October 29, 1909. The editor referred to Buxton as "the Negro Athens of the [N]orth," extolled the social, economic, and political structure of the community, and exclaimed, "the population will number about 5,000, of which 3,000 are colored people, and I

can truthfully say that here live some of the race's most successful business men. Here one can study the race from a viewpoint that no other large community offers to the Negro. Here he has absolute freedom to do everything that any other citizen has. Here you can see well-trained doctors, lawyers. Here you can see the public schools with mixed teachers, mostly colored, with a colored principal. . . . Here you can see colored men officers administering the law, providing the punishment and inflicting the penalty; here you can see colored men building the buildings, operating the electric plant, riding in automobiles and carriages; here you can see them farming; here you can see them owning amusements, parks, baseball parks, and their own bands. Here we have the church bells ringing from the colored churches and the YMCA owned and operated on a business basis by colored men, and many other things too numerous to mention."

Such a declaration, in our opinion as outsiders, is extremely instructive, since it was made by the editor of the region's leading African-American newspaper to the community of black people in Iowa.

By 1925, the Buxton townsite had been largely abandoned. For a variety of economic reasons, the Consolidation Coal Company closed down the town and moved their operations elsewhere. For most African-Americans, the move to other communities in Iowa and throughout the United States was a great shock. The prejudice and discrimination they subsequently faced are recalled in many interviews with former residents.

Dorothy Neal Collier reflected on this matter, saying "there was no prejudice. Everybody lived together [in Buxton]. When we went to Cedar Rapids, and went to school, it was so different. It was just, I don't know, it just seemed like it was another world."[31]

The Buxton phenomenon is perhaps all the more remarkable since the African-American experience in Iowa and the American midlands has too often been mentioned only in passing or else totally ignored in textbooks and general syntheses of the area's culture and history.

Buxton was a well-organized, multi-racial community whose residents understood and tolerated each other to a great degree. In that sense, we can all perhaps learn something from the Buxton experience, as illuminated by the Neal family, and benefit from the heritage of that past.

"The Negroes do not fear the whites and the whites do not try to make them fear them; there is mutual respect. . . . races go to school together; work in the same mines, clerk in the same stores and live side by side."

— *The Southern Workman*, **1908**

Notes

1. In addition to Dorothy Mae Neal Collier, William Collier, Mary Jane Collier Graves and Donald Graves, Kenneth and Sharon Collier, and other members of the Neal-Collier family, we express our appreciation to the Buxton, Iowa Club, Inc. It was with their cooperation and assistance that the original research team from Iowa State University carried out the investigations sponsored by the Heritage Conservation and Recreation Service between 1980 and 1982. Members of the Buxton, Iowa Club, Inc. have helped our general research on Buxton in a number of ways, and these individuals have been specifically acknowledged elsewhere.

2. Marvin Harris, *Cultural Materialism: The Struggle for a Science of Culture* (New York: Vintage, 1980), 32–45; Marvin Harris, *The Rise of Anthropological Theory* (New York: Crowell, 1968), 568–604.

3. Iowa Public Broadcasting Network, *You Can't Go Back to Buxton* (Des Moines: IPBN documentary, 1979).

4. Leola Nelson Bergmann, *The Negro in Iowa* (Iowa City: SHSI, 1948; repr., 1969); Robert Rutland, "The Mining Camps of Iowa," *Iowa Journal of History* 54 (1956): 35–42; Stephen Rye, "Buxton: Black Metropolis of Iowa," *AI* 3rd ser. 41 (1972): 939-57; Beverly Shiffer, "The Story of Buxton," *AI* 3rd ser. 37 (1964): 339–47; Jacob Swisher, "The Rise and Fall of Buxton," *Palimpsest* 26 (1945): 179–92.

5. David M. Gradwohl and Nancy M. Osborn, *Exploring Buried Buxton: Archaeology of an Abandoned Coal Mining Town with a Large Black Population* (Ames: Iowa State Univ. Press, 1984; repr., 1990).

6. David M. Gradwohl and Nancy M. Osborn, *Blacks and Whites in Buxton: A Site Explored, a Town Remembered,* video cassette and slide-tape formats, Iowa State University Media Resources Center, Ames, 1986.

7. Dorothy Schwieder, Joseph Hraba, and Elmer Schwieder, *Buxton: Work and Racial Equality in a Coal Mining Community* (Ames: Iowa State Univ. Press, 1987).

8. In these various situations, we drew upon the techniques of ethnoscience as promulgated by James P. Spradley and David W. McCurdy in their book *The Cultural Experience: Ethnography in Complex Society* (Chicago: Science Research Associates, 1972), although we do not follow their system in its entirety. This method, however, typically allows the informant to categorize, code, and define her experience from *her* point of view rather than from that of the interviewers.

9. Colin Renfrew and Paul Bahn, *Archaeology: Theories, Methods, and Practice* (New York: Thames and Hudson, 1991), 487, 166–69.

10. William H. Adams, *Silcott, Washington: Ethnoarchaeology in a Rural American Community* [Reports of Investigations No. 54] (Pullman WA: Laboratory of Anthropology, Washington State University, 1977). Adams explains that "ethnoarchaeology is defined here as the study of a known group of people (ranging from a family to a community) through the synergistic combination of historical, archaeological, and ethnographic methodologies. Ethnoarchaeology is related to, but distinguished from, ethnohistory, historical archaeology, living archaeology, and ethnographic analogy. Ethnoarchaeology employs a continuous model by utilizing the direct historical approach" (viii).

11. Dorothy Neal Collier interview by Tom Freelove, David Gradwohl, and Nancy Osborn, Dec. 1, 1983.

12. Gradwohl and Osborn, *Exploring Buried Buxton*, 39–40, Fig. 20.

13. Dorothy Neal Collier interview by David Gradwohl and Nancy Osborn, March 19, 1982.

14. Dorothy Neal Collier interview by David Gradwohl and Nancy Osborn, Oct. 23, 1988.

15. Dorothy Collier interview, March 19, 1982.

16. Dorothy Collier interview, Oct. 23, 1988.

17. Ibid.

18. Dorothy Collier interview, Dec. 1, 1983.

19. Dorothy Collier interview, Oct. 23, 1988.

20. Ibid.

21. Ibid.

22. Ibid.

23. In line with this investigative procedure with Dorothy Neal Collier are the words of former President Jimmy Carter at the recent dedication of his boyhood home in Plains, Georgia, as a national historic site: "You can take a 1930 or '32 catalog and figure out everything we owned. As a matter of fact, this house is a Sears Roebuck house" *(DMR*, Nov. 19, 2000). The Carter's house had, in fact, been built in 1922 according to plans ordered from the Sears, Roebuck & Co.

24. George W. McDaniel, *Hearth and Home: Preserving a People's Culture* (Philadelphia: Temple Univ. Press, 1982).

25. William Collier, in Gradwohl and Osborn, *Blacks and Whites in Buxton,* 1986.

26. Bessie Lewis interview by Joseph Hraba, Jan. 17, 1981.

27. Lola Reeves interview by Elmer Schwieder and Joseph Hraba, June 21, 1980.

28. Elmer Buford interview by Joseph Hraba, June 30, 1980.

29. Letter from Marion Carter to H.L. Olin, Jan. 7, 1963.

30. Richard R. Wright Jr., "The Economic Condition of Negroes in the North: Negro Governments in the North," *Southern Workman* 37 (1908): 497.

31. Dorothy Neal Collier interview by Dorothy and Elmer Schwieder, Oct. 17, 1980.

David Mayer Gradwohl, professor emeritus of anthropology at Iowa State University, obtained his B.A. degree from the University of Nebraska and his Ph.D. from Harvard. His research involves the prehistory, historical archaeology, and ethnoarchaeology of North America and Europe, focusing particularly upon relationships between material culture, ethnicity, and intra-group variations.

Nancy Osborn Johnsen, adjunct instructor of anthropology at Iowa State University, received her graduate degree at Iowa State. She has been co-principal investigator on numerous archaeological projects through the ISU Archaeological Laboratory and was a professional archaeologist with the National Park Service. Her primary research involves prehistoric and historic archaeology, as well as historic preservation issues.

Holmes County, Mississippi, migrants traveled to Waterloo via the Illinois Central Railroad. (courtesy Ada Tredwell)

Selected Demographics

Iowa's African–American Residents, 1840–2000

by Willis Goudy

In the 1850 census, which was the first decennial count conducted after Iowa became a state, 333 residents were reported as "free colored," while 191,881 were "white." Those were two of the designations possible in 1840 as well, when residents of the Iowa Territory were counted. At that time, 172 Iowans were identified as free colored and 42,924 as white. A second category of other than white residents was used that year; 16 residents of the 1840 territory were labeled "slaves," all of whom were residing in the Dubuque area.[1]

Dropping the category of slave in 1850 foreshadowed continued changes among Iowa residents today designated as African-Americans. For example, the title reported by the U.S. Bureau of the Census changed from "free colored" to "Negro" in 1890 and from "Negro" to "black" in 1980; meanwhile, whites continued to be labeled as such while other groups—American Indians, Asians, and Hispanics, for example—were included in later censuses. Only whites and blacks have been reported in each of the censuses from 1850 through 1990, however.

A total of 324 free colored residents were located in an examination of the microfilm from the 1850 census for Iowa.[2] Charts on the following four pages list these individuals, although caution is urged when reviewing that list because it was difficult to read the microfilm version of the handwritten pages drafted by census enumerators.

The 1850 population of blacks was relatively young, with 43 percent under the age of 15. This age structure in 1850 foreshadowed the influence of youth in the African-American population many decades later. Another 49 percent were 15–44 years of age in 1850, while only 8 percent were 45 or older. Still, what stories the five oldest — a 66-year-old man, two women aged 70, another aged 71, and a woman who was 88 — must have been able to tell.

These free colored residents lived in 106 dwelling units in Iowa. All members were African-American in 51 of them; a total of 249 people lived in these households, which varied in size from 1 to 12 individuals.

Forty-two individuals were listed as the only free colored member of households in which other members were white. In the remainder of the housing units, at least two African-Americans in Iowa lived with members of other races in each one; some of these were hotels or boarding houses but others consisted of families.

continued on page 28

The 1850 population of African-Americans was relatively young, with 43 percent under the age of 15. This age structure foreshadowed the influence of youth in the African-American population many decades later.

African-American Population of Iowa in 1850 (by county)

A listing developed from the microfilm file for Iowa from the 1850 count conducted by the U.S. Bureau of the Census follows. Inhabitants identified as "black" or "mulatto" are included. Names are spelled to the best of the ability of the author of this chapter and a research assistant, Ma En-hua, who provided excellent help in locating names on the microfilm and making an initial attempt at spelling.

Anything designated with an asterisk (*) indicates that even greater difficulty than usual occurred in deciphering the handwriting of the census enumerators, but others may be in error as well.

For some names, a publication called *Iowa 1850 Census Index* [Ronald Vern Jackson and G. Ronald Teeples, *Iowa 1850 Census Index* (Bountiful UT: Accelerated Indexing Systems, 1976)] was consulted, although it was of marginal utility because it did not contain all names, especially when more

(continued on opposite page)

name	age	sex	place of birth	no. in household	read/write
APPANOOSE COUNTY					
Bestina Collins	16	f	Kentucky	7	
Mary Collins	46	f	Virginia	6	✗
Matilda Collins	20	f	Iowa	6	✗
Reuben Collins	16	m	Iowa	6	
Loyd Collins	14	m	Iowa	6	
Calaska* Collins	12	f	Illinois	6	
Spencer Collins	10	m	Missouri	6	
CEDAR COUNTY					
Nancy Adair	38	f	Virginia	4	✗
Sidney B. Grubbs	6	m	Iowa	4	
CLAYTON COUNTY					
Rebecca Cline*	53	f	Maryland	5	
David Baker	35	m	Ohio	5	
occupation: laborer					
CLINTON COUNTY					
William Watt	66	m	Maryland	5	✗
occupation: farmer					
Atcherson Watt	27	m	Missouri	5	✗
occupation: laborer					
Lexa* Watt	14	m	Iowa	5	
Hanah Watt	8	f	Iowa	5	
Jacie* Watt	5	m	Iowa	5	
William Watt Jr.	29	m	Missouri	7	
occupation: laborer real estate: $100					
Ann Watt	28	f	Missouri	7	✗
Joseph Watt	26	m	Missouri	7	✗
occupation: laborer					
Ester Watt	24	f	Missouri	7	✗
Hanah Watt	25	f	Missouri	7	✗
Mary Watt	4	f	Iowa	7	
Elen Watt	4	f	Iowa	7	
Franklin Crage	27	m	Virginia	7	
occupation: cooper					
Mary Crage	26	f	Virginia	7	
Isaak Crage	12	m	Virginia	7	
John T. Crage	8	m	Virginia	7	
Albert G. Crage	7	m	Virginia	7	
Cece C. Crage	4	f	Missouri	7	
Mary E. Crage	1	f	Missouri	7	
Mary Scott	15	f	Pennsylvania	7	
DAVIS COUNTY					
Abram Kenny	20	m	Kentucky	7	
occupation: laborer					
Fieding Buckner	29	m	Kentucky	6	✗
occupation: farmer					
Susan Buckner	29	m	N. Carolina	6	✗
Martha A. Buckner	9	f	Missouri	6	
Mary Buckner	7	f	Missouri	6	
Amanda Buckner	5	f	Missouri	6	
Catherine Buckner	3	f	Missouri	6	
DECATUR COUNTY					
George Mcdanold	30	m	Virginia	10	
occupation: farmer					
DES MOINES COUNTY					
Marks Bents	5	m	Iowa	5	
Catherine Perkins	16	f	Virginia	4	
Mary J. Jackson	14	f	Virginia	4	
Rebecca Brown	16	f	Pennsylvania	11	
H. Tate	35	m	Virginia	7	✗
Maria Tate	28	f	Kentucky	7	
Rachel Burdey	70	f	Virginia	7	
Cassus Philpot	29	m	Kentucky	7	✗
Margaret Philpot	35	f	Maryland*	7	✗
Robert Philpot	8	m	Iowa	7	
Benjamin Philpot	6	m	Iowa	7	
Lewis Philpot	5	m	Iowa	7	
William Philpot	3	m	Iowa	7	
Denice Philpot	2	m	Iowa	7	
Benjamin Landridg	50	m	Virginia	5	✗
Catherine Landridg	54	f	Virginia	5	✗
Catherine Alexander	18	f	Kentucky	5	✗
Charlotte Alexander	9	f	Iowa	5	
James Mortice*	24	m	Kentucky	5	
Robert Young	30	m	Maryland	16	
Hiram Boyd	30	m	Kentucky	3	
occupation: barber real estate: $300					
Julia Boyd	28	f	Virginia	3	
Roseanna Graham	54	f	Illinois*	5	✗
Stephen Tindale	8	m	Missouri	5	
Arabla Haros*	42	f	Virginia	4	✗
DUBUQUE COUNTY					
Daniel Griffin	28	m	Virginia	9	
occupation: carpenter					
Sherman Hagard	24	m	N. Hampshire	3	
occupation: laborer					
Mary Ann Hagard	21	f	Missouri	3	
Mary Eliz. Hagard	2	f	Iowa	3	
Walter Baker	35	m	Virginia	3	
occupation: miner					
Eliza Baker	30	f	Missouri	3	
Thomas Shuvalla	25	m	Missouri	3	
Aaron Baptist	50	m	Kentucky	6	
occupation: laborer real estate: $600					
Mary Baptist	43	f	Missouri	6	
Margaret Baptist	16	f	Missouri	6	
Ann* Baptist	12	f	Missouri	6	
Eli Baptist	11	m	Missouri	6	
Felix Baptist	7	m	Iowa	6	
George Frame	16	m	Delaware	5	
Thomas C. Brown	25	m	Illinois*	4	
occupation: barber real estate $1,100					
Adel Brown	18	f	Minnesota	4	
William Mills	5	m	Illinois*	4	
William Reed	14	m	Iowa	4	
occupation: barber					
George Davis	30	m	DC	40	
occupation: servant					
Moses Robinson	20	m	Virginia	34	
occupation: servant					
Susan Gibson	16	f	Pennsylvania	6	
Amanda Katuche*	9	f	N. Carolina	10	
Anthony Arthur	47	m	Virginia	5	✗
occupation: laborer real estate:$1,000					
Agnes Arthur	40	f	Kentucky	5	✗
Catherine Arthur	12	f	Iowa	5	
Edward Arthur	13	m	Iowa	5	
John B. Arthur	2	m	Missouri	5	
Mary Carter	38	f	Tennessee	1	

name	age	sex	place of birth	no. in household	read/write

HENRY COUNTY

name	age	sex	place of birth	no. in household	read/write
Kate Ramsey*	15	f	Alabama	6	
Wealthy* Tiffany	25	f	Massachusetts	9	
Bryant Oatland	16	m	Indiana	7	
occupation: laborer					
Mary J. Oatland	14	f	Indiana	7	
Abraham Walls	51	m	Mississippi	7	
occupation: farmer					
Mary Walls	20	f	Missouri	7	
Raymond Lewis	20	m	Missouri	7	
occupation: farmer					
Sarah Lewis	16	f	Missouri	7	
Elizabeth Walls	7	f	Missouri	7	
Sarah Walls	3	f	Missouri	7	
Robert B. Lewis	1	m	Indiana	7	
Lewis Collins	38	m	Kentucky	11	
occupation: miller real estate: $1,200					

IOWA COUNTY

name	age	sex	place of birth	no. in household	read/write
Hetty Green	16	f	Virginia	8	

JACKSON COUNTY

name	age	sex	place of birth	no. in household	read/write
Jane Smith	13	f	Illinois	11	
Nancy Smith	47	f	N. Carolina	8	
Louisa Burke	45	f	Missouri	8	
real estate: $400					
Richard Burke	15	m	Missouri	8	
Sylvester Burke	12	m	Iowa	8	
Mary Burke	7	f	Iowa	8	
Mary Borris	88	f	Missouri	8	
Adeline Pattee	23	f	Missouri	8	
Virginia Pattee	2	f	Iowa	8	

JEFFERSON COUNTY

name	age	sex	place of birth	no. in household	read/write
Daniel Russel	39	m	New York	8	
occupation: wagonmaker real estate: $200					

JOHNSON COUNTY

name	age	sex	place of birth	no. in household	read/write
Richard Ward	28	m	Pennsylvania	10	X
John Mitchael*	13	m	Ohio	21	
Albert Brown	29	m	Virginia	7	
occupation: farmer					
Lucinda Brown	27	f	Ohio	7	X
Francis R. Brown	7	f	Ohio	7	
Martha P. Brown	5	f	Ohio	7	
Phebe J. Brown	3	f	Ohio	7	
Frederic D. Brown	8 mo	m	Iowa	7	
Rosan Walter	70	f	Delaware	7	X
Patty Reno	36	f	Ohio	5	
real estate: $1,500					
Francis Reno	16	m	Ohio	5	
occupation: barber					
Rosan Reno	14	f	Ohio	5	
Robert Reno	12	m	Ohio	5	
Nancy Reno	10	f	Ohio	5	
Samuel Jackson	22	m	Maryland*	7	
Jack Badgett	50	m	Tennessee	7	
occupation: blacksmith					
Eloza* Badgett	28	f	Tennessee	7	
Francis C. Badgett	12	f	Tennessee	7	
Willis R. Badgett	10	m	Tennessee	7	
Henryetta Badgett	6	f	Tennessee	7	
Andrew J. Badgett	5	m	Tennessee	7	
Mary S. Badgett	3	f	Tennessee	7	

JONES COUNTY

name	age	sex	place of birth	no. in household	read/write
Milla A. Hester	20	f	Kentucky	4	X

LEE COUNTY

name	age	sex	place of birth	no. in household	read/write
Lucinda Manning	28	f	Connecticut	9	
Jane Dale	7	f	Illinois	9	
John Hiner	28	m	Maryland	2	
occupation: butcher					
Harriet Hiner	30	f	Louisiana	2	
William Agleson	38	m	Pennsylvania	11	
occupation: barber					
Catharine Agleson	33	f	Missouri	11	
William Agleson	16	m	Missouri	11	
James Agleson	9	m	Missouri	11	
Harry Agleson	7	m	Missouri	11	
Samuel Agleson	5	m	Wisconsin	11	
Emma Agleson	2	f	Iowa	11	
Amanuel Agleson	1	m	Iowa	11	
Ann Vashorn	22	f	Pennsylvania	11	
Albert Robison	20	m	Pennsylvania	11	
Carolina Robison	11	f	Iowa	11	
Amanuel Walker	30	m	Kentucky	2	
occupation: porter					
Caroline Walker	20	f	Iowa	2	
Bazeal Goodair	48	m	Illinois	5	
occupation: porter					
Willia Ann Goodair	38	f	Missouri	5	
James W. Goodair	17	m	Missouri	5	
Elisabeth Goodair	8	f	Illinois	5	
Felix F. Goodair	11 mo	m	Iowa	5	
Augustus Tindle	6	m	Missouri	7	
Elisa Armintrout	23	f	Kentucky	5	
David Armintrout	22	m	Kentucky	5	
occupation: cook					
Joseph Schenck	21	m	New Jersey	33	
Sarah Flour*	30	f	Pennsylvania	7	
Ellen Rollins	40	f	Georgia	1	
real estate: $100					
John Brown	25	m	Kentucky	2	
occupation: cook real estate: $50					
Mary Brown	25	f	Virginia	2	
Ede Brown	36	f	Virginia	3	
Lydia Brown	14	f	Iowa	3	
Emma Brown	6	f	Iowa	3	

African-American Population of Iowa in 1850 (by county)

(continued from opposite page)

than one surname was reported in a household. Names are entered in the order in which they were listed on the census form.

Thus, this list should be used with caution. It is at best an approximation of information gathered in the 1850 census.

Age and sex were relatively clear on the census pages. Place of birth, however, was difficult to determine on some of the lines; again, an asterisk (*) is used to denote those that created concern.

The total number in the household is reported so that an estimate of family composition can be made, with very large numbers usually indicating residence in a hotel or boarding house. Marital status is not clear in the 1850 census, so it is difficult to determine family ties.

Blank lines separate households. Thus, the first person listed in Appanoose County was the only African-American in a

(continued on following page)

African-American Population of Iowa in 1850 (by county)

(continued from previous page)

seven-person household. The second unit consists of six persons — all African-Americans.

Although it may be that the first person listed was related to those in the second set, there is no way of knowing that from the census pages. In fact, the first person lived with six others with the same last name reported for her (and the second set) but who were not classified as African-Americans by the census taker.

Ability to read and write was to be obtained only for those older than 20; a mark was entered for those who could not read and write, which is changed to ✗ in this list.

Occupation was to be reported for males who were at least 15 years of age, although in two cases occupations were noted for females. The value of owned real estate was recorded as well. It is not known how thorough census takers were in obtaining all information; many blanks appear on the census forms.

name	age	sex	place of birth	no. in household	read/write
LEE COUNTY *(continued)*					
Jane Buckner	71	f	Virginia	4	
real estate:$300					
Maria Buckner	26	f	Kentucky	4	
Mary Buckner	24	f	Kentucky	4	
Ann M. Buckner	7	f	Iowa	4	
James Smith	40	m	New York	5	✗
occupation: farmer					
Adaline Smith	26	f	Tennessee	5	✗
Noah Smith	7	m	Illinois	5	
Mary Smith	6	f	Iowa	5	
Charity Smith	4 mo	f	Iowa	5	
Oliver Rudd	30	m	Tennessee	4	✗
occupation: farmer real estate:$200					
Margaret Rudd	26	f	Tennessee	4	✗
Mary Rudd	4	f	Iowa	4	
Abigail Rudd	2	f	Iowa	4	
William Powell	33	m	N. Carolina	6	✗
occupation: farmer real estate:$150					
Citizen Powell	40	f	Tennessee	6	✗
Mary Powell	14	f	Illinois	6	
Rebecca E. Powell	12	f	Illinois	6	
Henry Powell	3	m	Iowa	6	
John Copeland	15	m	Illinois	6	
occupation: laborer					
LINN COUNTY					
Fran R. Johnson	22	m	Penn.	11	
Henrietta Washington	21	f	Virginia	5	
David Wesley	5	m	Iowa	5	
LOUISA COUNTY [1]					
Ann Lockwood*	16	f	Delaware	8	
Mary E. Slaughter	13	f	Virginia	6	
Rosanna A. Slaughter	7	f	Iowa	6	
Harvel E. Banks	40	m	Virginia	6	
occupation: farmer real estate:$500					
Mary A. Banks	36	f	Ohio	6	
Agnes J. Banks	9	f	Ohio	6	
Moses F. Banks	5	m	Ohio	6	
Solomon M. Banks	3	m	Ohio	6	
Nancy A. Banks	4 mo	f	Iowa	6	
MARION COUNTY					
Anderson Jeffers	38	m	Virginia	12	✗
occupation: farmer					
Mary Jeffers	37	f	N. Carolina	12	✗
Polly Jeffers	15	f	Georgia	12	
Nancy Jeffers	13	f	Indiana	12	
Johnney Jeffers	11	m	Indiana	12	
Sarah F. Jeffers	8	f	Indiana	12	
Faraley* Ann Jeffers	7	f	Indiana	12	
Walker Jeffers	5	m	Indiana	12	
Anderson F. Jeffers	4	m	Indiana	12	
Eliza A. Jeffers	3	f	Indiana	12	
Ester A. Jeffers	1	f	Indiana	12	
Crathuss* Jeffers	35	m	N. Carolina	12	
occupation: farmer real estate: $400					
Darrel* Jeffers	37	m	N. Carolina	9	✗
Farmer					
Sarah Jefers	41	f	N. Carolina	9	✗
Dolly R. Jeffers	15	f	Kentucky	9	
Thomas Jeffers	13	m	Indiana	9	
William J. Jeffers	11	m	Indiana	9	
Riss* B. Jeffers	6	m	Indiana	9	
Sally Ann Jeffers	5	f	Indiana	9	
Washington Jeffers	3	m	Indiana	9	
George D. Jeffers	1	m	Iowa	9	
David Griffith	41	m	Virginia	8	✗
occupation: plasterer real estate:$800					
Juliana* Griffith	37	f	N. Carolina	8	
Mary Ann Griffith	13	f	Indiana	8	
Nancy J. Griffith	10	f	Indiana	8	
Sarah M. Griffith	7	f	Indiana	8	
John Griffith	5	m	Indiana	8	
David Griffith	3	m	Indiana	8	
Alexander Griffith	1	m	Iowa	8	
MUSCATINE COUNTY					
Jane D. Motts	28	f	Maryland	2	
occupation: seamstress real estate: $400					
Elizabeth Motts	18	f	Maryland	2	
Dennis Greenway	35	m	N. Carolina	7	
occupation: blacksmith					
Mary Greenway	25	f	N. Carolina	7	
James Greenway	13	m	N. Carolina	7	
William Greenway	11	m	N. Carolina	7	
Lewis Greenway	9	m	N. Carolina	7	
Susan Greenway	5	f	N. Carolina	7	
Margaret Fuller	46	f	Virginia	7	
Joseph Cook	43	m	Virginia	4	
occupation: cook real estate: $600					
Bridget Cook	40	f	Missouri	4	
Eliza Cook	11	f	Missouri	4	
Jo A. M. Motts	6	f	Iowa	4	
Thomas C. Motts	41	m	Maryland	6	
occupation: barber real estate:$6,000					
Mahala* Motts	23	f	Delaware	6	
Job Motts	1	m	Iowa	6	
Willis Lane	24	m	Kentucky	6	
occupation: teamster					
George Hooper	20	m	Pennsylvania	6	
occupation: barber					
Dan Johnson	17	m	Ohio	6	
James Ruff	27	m	Tennessee	2	
occupation: cook					
Hulda* Ruff	19	f	Delaware	2	
Ben J. Mathews	43	m	Maryland	4	
occupation: teamster real estate: $500					
Hannah Mathews	26	f	Vermont	4	
Nathan Mathews	12	m	Maryland	4	
Morris Mathews	8	m	Iowa	4	
George Manly	30	m	Virginia	3	
Julia Manly	20	f	Indiana	3	
Sarah J. Manly	7	f	Kentucky	3	
Joseph Hooper	20	m	Penn.	27	
occupation: barber					
William Hooper	12	m	Penn.	27	

name	age	sex	place of birth	no. in household	read/write

MUSCATINE COUNTY *(continued)*

name	age	sex	place of birth	no. in household	read/write
Jacob Pritchet*	30	m	Pennsylvania	5	
occupation: cook					
Debra Pritchet*	24	f	Pennsylvania	5	
Charles Pritchet*	7	m	Pennsylvania	5	
Roseanna Pritchet*	1	f	Iowa	5	
Sarah Davidson	22	f	Kentucky	5	
occupation: teacher					
Isaac Manning	30	m	Kentucky	3	
Caroline Manning	24	f	Connecticut	3	
Mary Clark	24	f	Ohio	3	
Edmund Mathews	47	m	Maryland	5	
real estate:$200					
Jane Mathews	35	f	Maryland	5	
Ellen Mathews	14	f	Maryland	5	
Joseph Watkins	2	m	Iowa	5	
Arch Clark	39	m	Virginia	5	
Ira* Shorten*	21	m	Penn.	7	
Patricia* Williams	4	f	Penn.	9	
Dan Anderson	55	m	Maryland	2	
occupation: preacher					
Ellen Anderson	50	f	Maryland	2	
Morgan Lowery	25	m	Virginia	2	
real estate: $150					
Roberson Buss*	38	m	Bermuda*	2	
real estate: $375					
Alexander Clark	25	m	Penn.	5	
occupation: barber	*real estate: $1,200*				
Catherine Clark	26	f	Virginia	5	
Rebecca J. Clark	1	f	Iowa	5	
Charles Mathews	10	m	Iowa	5	
Sarah Jackson	18	f	Ohio	5	
William Anderson	38	m	Virginia	4	
Margaret Anderson	35	f	Virginia	4	
Charity Anderson	13	f	Virginia	4	
Robert L.* Anderson	8	m	Iowa	4	

MUSCATINE COUNTY *(continued)*

name	age	sex	place of birth	no. in household	read/write
Eliza Manning	64	f	Connecticut	9	
Sarah A. Stebbins	30	f	Connecticut	9	
Isaac Manning	26	m	Connecticut	9	
occupation: laborer					
Peter Manning	19	m	Connecticut	9	
occupation: laborer					
Mary Stebbins	9	f	Connecticut	9	
Joseph Stebbins	6	m	Connecticut	9	
Isabella F. Stebbins	2	f	Iowa	9	
Angeline Stebbins	10 mo	f	Iowa	9	
Julia A. Raperlu*	8	f	Connecticut	9	
A. O. Warfield*	35	m	Maryland	1	
occupation: merchant					
Hillary Wilson	45	m	Virginia	9	✗

SCOTT COUNTY

name	age	sex	place of birth	no. in household	read/write
David Merryweather	49	m	Kentucky	6	✗
occupation: boatman					
Catharine Merryweather	38	f	Maryland	6	✗
David Merryweather	9	m	Indiana	6	
Ellen Merryweather	3	f	Iowa	6	
Joseph Merryweather	1	m	Illinois	6	
Edward Merryweather	8 mo	m	Iowa	6	
George W. Booth	23	m	Maryland	22	
occupation: steward					
John Miller	28	m	Kentucky	22	
occupation: cook					
Watson Warfield*	19	m	Penn.	22	
occupation: cook					
George Francis	39	m	Penn.	22	
occupation: barber	*real estate: $200*				
Rhoda Sims	41	f	Virginia	4	
real estate: $600					
Berry Warwick	25	f	Missouri	4	
John Warwick	1	m	Missouri	4	
Henry Warwick	7	m	Missouri	4	

VAN BUREN COUNTY [2]

name	age	sex	place of birth	no. in household	read/write
William Baker	42	m	Kentucky	5	✗
occupation: farmer	*real estate: $800*				
Ellen Ewing	21	f	Tennessee	10	
Catharine Ewing	3	f	Tennessee	10	
Kate Manning*	61	f	Virginia	4	✗

WAPELLO COUNTY

name	age	sex	place of birth	no. in household	read/write
Patsey Triplett	50	f	Kentucky	4	
real estate: $100					
S* Triplett	20	m	Wisconsin*	4	
real estate: $100					
Lewis Triplett	15	m	Wisconsin*	4	
Newton* Triplett	13	m	Wisconsin*	4	
Isabella Hendershott*	12	f	Missouri	9	

WAYNE COUNTY

name	age	sex	place of birth	no. in household	read/write
Moses Franklin	18	m	Kentucky	8	
occupation: farmer					

African-American Population of Iowa in 1850 (by county)

1 Examination of the microfilmed census pages suggests that seven people were incorrectly identified as African-Americans in Louisa County in the 1850 census. The enumerator placed information on sex identically in two columns, the second of which was supposed to be for race; the bureau didn't notice this in tabulations reported in that census. Thus, such tables apparently include seven persons who were not African-Americans in 1850; the final chart in this chapter probably should list 9 African-Americans in 1850 in Louisa County rather than the 16 noted.

Similarly, summary tables in the census include one African-American in Mahaska County in 1850. Close inspection of the line on the census page for that person suggests that the enumerator tried to erase that designation. Thus, the final chart in this chapter probably should have a 0 rather than a 1 for African-Americans in 1850 for Mahaska County.

2 Summary tables list five African-Americans in Van Buren County in 1850. Inspection of the microfilmed census pages reveals only four names, however.

African-American Population in Iowa, 1840–1990

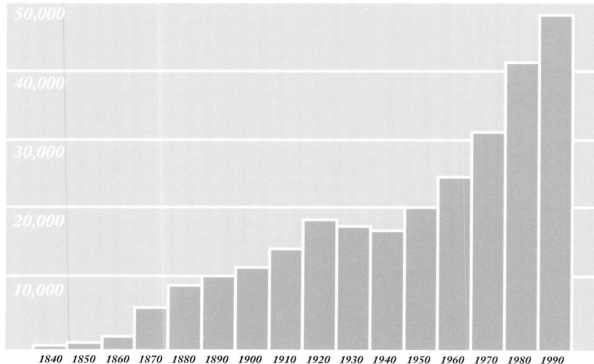

continued from page 23

Fifty-five of the African-Americans living in Iowa in 1850 had been born in this state. Missouri (44) and Virginia (42) were the states of birth of more than a quarter of the others living here that year. Indiana (23), Kentucky (28), and Pennsylvania (20) each accounted for at least 20. An additional 17 states and the District of Columbia were noted as the place of birth for other African-Americans, although more than 10 came only from Illinois (13), Maryland (19), Ohio (18), North Carolina (15), and Tennessee (15).

Similar patterns were noted from 1870 through 1940 by Leola Bergmann in her book, *The Negro in Iowa*.[3] More African-Americans had been born in Iowa than in any other single state from 1880 through 1940, according to her research.

While some of the African-Americans at least 20 years of age could not read or write as of the 1850 census, that was not unusual for members of any race at that time. Occupations were listed for 65 members of this population, 63 of whom were males.

King Calowell, hobo king, Britt, Iowa, on August 10, 1939. Drought and lack of jobs during the Depression forced many Iowans out of the state in search of employment. (SHSI Des Moines)

One of the two women for whom occupations were listed was a teacher, while the other was a seamstress; both lived in Muscatine County. According to census instructions, occupations were to be listed only for males at least 15 years of age; thus, other women no doubt were employed but information on their occupations was not obtained. Fifteen men were farmers, 13 were laborers, 10 were barbers, and 6 were cooks. None of the 15 other occupations listed included more than 2 men (blacksmith, boatman, butcher, carpenter, cooper, merchant, miller, miner, porter, preacher, plasterer, servant, steward, teamster, wagonmaker).

The value of real estate owned by an individual was reported in the 1850 census. This varied from $50 to $6,000 among African-Americans. Most of the 30 who owned real estate noted values closer to the lower figure than to the higher one. For example, 19 listed values of $500 or less while only 6 indicated values of at least $1,000. The median—that point at which half the values were higher and half lower—was about $400.

Population Trends for the State of Iowa

Since 1850, gains occurred in the number of African-American residents of Iowa each decade except from 1920 to 1940. African-Americans first numbered at least 1,000 in the 1860 census and exceeded 10,000 thirty years later in the 1890 census. Numerical growth was similar in the next three decades (1890 to 1920), when another 9,000 were added so that 19,000 were enumerated in the 1920 census. The total declined to less than 17,000 in 1940, although the twenty-year loss was more than overcome by the gain in the 1940s. The largest decennial gains among African-Americans occurred after the 1950 census, with increases of 5,700 in the 1950s; 7,200 in the 1960s; 9,100 in the 1970s; and 6,400 in the 1980s.

As of the 1990 census, African-American residents accounted for 1.7 percent of Iowa's total population. That percentage first surpassed 1.0 in the 1970 census. In the earliest censuses, African-Americans constituted less than one half of one percent of all Iowans. From 1870 through 1960, the percentage grew slowly from 0.5 to 0.9. Thus, although the number of African-Americans in Iowa has increased dramatically across the censuses, fewer than 2 of every 100 residents were African-American in 1990. That's because the population in other racial categories also increased over the decades.

Population Trends for Iowa's Counties

Nine of Iowa's 99 counties reported at least 1,000 African-American residents in 1990. *(See chart, pages 40–41.)* Eight had numbers of that magnitude in 1980, six in 1960 and 1970, and no more than four in any census from 1840 through 1950.

The 1990 census was the first is which every county in the state reported at least one African-American resident. This population was disproportionately represented in a few counties, however. For example, 41 counties had fewer than 10 African-Americans in the most recent census. Two others (Black Hawk, Polk) contained nearly half (48.5 percent) of all African-Americans, and the addition of those living in Scott pushed this to nearly two-thirds (65.1 percent).

The percentage accounted for by the three counties with the highest numbers of black inhabitants peaked in 1970 at 69.7; that is, nearly 7 of every 10 African-Americans lived in Black Hawk, Polk, and Scott counties that year. The least concentration of the top three occurred in 1880, when Lee, Polk, and Pottawattamie had 31.2 percent of all black residents in Iowa. Concentration ranged across percentages in the forties from 1890 through 1930. Then the top three (Black Hawk, Lee, Polk) increased their share of the total African-American population to 56.2 percent in 1940 and 61.6 percent in 1950. It has remained in the sixties since, with Black Hawk, Polk, and Scott including the most black residents at each census from 1960 through 1990.

Polk County has had a greater number of African-American residents than any other county from the census in 1900 to the present. In 1900, about 16 percent of Iowa's African-Americans lived in Polk. This increased steadily to a share of 42 percent in 1950. Since then, however, this measure of concentration has decreased so that Polk had nearly 31 percent of all African-Americans living in Iowa in 1990.

Polk's increase from 1,194 in 1890, the first year in which it had at least 1,000 African-Americans, to 14,799 is dramatic. Lee County was the first to top the 1,000 threshold, however; that occurred in 1870, and Lee has had at least 1,000 African-American residents in every census that followed. But these changes have been much smaller in Lee than in Polk County. Since the 1870 census, the numbers of African-Americans in Lee County have varied from a low of 1,033 in 1970 to a high of 1,679 in 1880.

Other variations are evident, of course. Scott is the only county that had an increase in the number of African-American residents in every census from 1840 to 1990. Polk had only one reversal, which occurred from 1920 to 1930; in Linn, the decrease from 1930 to 1940 was the only contrary trend. Story has increased each census since 1890; so did Black Hawk, with the exception of the change between the two most recent censuses. Johnson also generally has had increases from one census to the next in the number of African-Americans.

Perhaps the most intriguing changes in the African-American population are sudden increases followed by equally rapid declines. The period from 1870 to 1920 in Mahaska is a prime example; so is that from 1890 to 1940 in Monroe. The gain exceeded 1,000 from 1880 to 1890 in Mahaska, but the loss also was of that magnitude from 1900 to 1910. An even greater gain of 1,800 occurred from 1900 to 1910 in Monroe, but the drop of 1,300 from 1920 to 1930 also was extreme. Similar though less dramatic reversals are evident in other counties in south central Iowa that had great increases in African-American residents that were followed by declines that were as large. These trends can be explained by occupational forces at work — especially coal mining — in these and other counties, as will be detailed in other chapters of this volume. Only in the more urban counties of Lee (1860 to

Like these waiters on the riverboat Dubuque, *many African-Americans came to Iowa in the 1850s to find jobs in the thriving river commerce of cities such as Keokuk, Burlington, Ft. Madison, Muscatine, Davenport, Clinton, and Dubuque on the Mississippi River, and Council Bluffs and Sioux City on the Missouri River. (Dubuque County Historical Society)*

Urban / Rural Status of African-American Residents of Iowa, 1900–1990

Population	1990	1980	1970	1960	1950	1940	1930	1920	1910	1900
Total	48,090	41,700	32,596	25,354	19,692	16,694	17,380	19,005	14,973	12,693
Urban	46,679	40,688	31,740	24,419	18,469	15,343	15,185	15,345	9,786	8,097
Rural	1,411	1,012	856	935	1,223	1,351	2,195	3,660	5,187	4,596
Percent urban	97.1	97.6	97.4	96.3	93.8	91.9	87.3	80.7	65.4	63.8
Central cities	36,970	32,471	24,920	19,266						
Urban fringe	1,893	1,809	1,113	845	URBAN CATEGORIES					
Other urban places:										
10,000 +	6,134	5,245	4,501	3,570						
2,500–9,999	1,682	1,163	1,206	738						
1,000–2,499	362	214	178	172						
Other	1,049	798	678	763	RURAL CATEGORIES					

1870), Black Hawk (each census from 1940 through 1980), Polk (1900 to 1910, 1910 to 1920, and each census from 1940 through 1990), and Scott (each census from 1960 through 1990) did gains of at least 1,000 occur in counties other than Mahaska and Monroe. These urban counties sustained increases in their African-American populations through succeeding decades, unlike the more rural counties of Mahaska and Monroe.

Examples of changes on a smaller scale are evident as well. In Louisa County, from 59 to 94 African-American residents were counted from 1860 to 1880. Those numbers fell through the following decades so that in 1960, no African-American was present. One was noted in 1970 and seven in 1980. In 1990, however, 86 black residents lived in Louisa, a number similar to those of more than a century earlier. Again, occupational trends—in this case, meat processing—in that county explain recent change.

Other factors are influential in a few instances. In Jones County, for example, the increase from 1980 to 1990 was exceptionally high. The total African-American population of that county was 299 in 1990; 291 were males. That's a reflection of a penal facility located there; the increase in the decade represents other social factors at work. Thus, caution is urged in reviewing county trends in the number of African-Americans. Many variables affect these counts.

Urban/Rural Trends

One of the difficulties in using the census to portray the African-American population is that much information was reported by white/nonwhite divisions in the censuses before 1970. That makes it impossible to describe trends for separate racial categories. Also, the questions asked varied from one census to the next. In the remainder of this chapter, only items and years for which data were reported for African-Americans alone are reported.

Figures on urban/rural divisions first were reported in the census of 1900. Definitions have been relatively constant since that year, with those living in incorporated places of at least 2,500 inhabitants counted as urban and the remainder as rural residents. African-Americans have been predominantly an urban population in Iowa in every census for which data are reported. The percentage increased from 64 in 1900 to more than 90 in 1940 and following censuses. In contrast, the general population of Iowa did not become at least half urban until 1960 and exceeded 60 percent urban for the first time in 1990.

Actually, the designation of urban fails to capture the concentration of blacks in the state. In the four most recent censuses, which reported more detailed information on urban areas, at least three-quarters of all black residents lived in what are called central cities, which generally means those with at least 50,000 residents. The addition of those living in the urban fringe, which consists of suburbs of central cities, and those residing in incorporated places with at least 10,000 inhabitants takes the percentage to nearly 94 percent. Most African-Americans live in Iowa's largest cities, a factor that has been true for several decades.

Concentration of the African-American population occurs within large cities as well. The U.S. Bureau of the Census divides central cities into census tracts, which usually contain about 2,000 to 5,000 residents in geographic areas bordered by major streets, rivers, or other boundaries. The City of Des Moines was divided into 57 census tracts in 1990; half of all African-Americans living in Des Moines were in 5 tracts; in contrast, it took 21 census tracts to total half of the general population of the city. Although the boundaries of census tracts were different in 1980, half of Des Moines' blacks were in 5 tracts that year as well. Waterloo consisted of 27 census tracts in 1990; more than 50 percent of African-Americans in that city lived in 4 tracts, the same number as reported in 1980. Thus, concentration of African-American residents occurs not only by county but within counties as well.

Job opportunities with the railroads brought ambitious African-Americans, like this young porter, to Ottumwa and other Iowa cities. (Ottumwa Public Library)

The Colored Advance, published in Corning, printed these census statistics in its first issue, dated August 1, 1882. (SHSI Des Moines)

Elsewhere in the state, newcomers established farms. Civil War veteran William Goodlow and his family are pictured on his homestead near Wales. (courtesy Ella R. Stith)

THE COLORED ADVANCE.

Vol. 1. CORNING, IOWA, AUGUST 1, 1882. **No. 1.**

THE ADVANCE,
Published Semi-Monthly by
C. S. BAKER.

TERMS—One year..............$1 00

☞ All bills for advertising will be presented quarterly.

There are about 6,580,793 colored people in the United States, according to census given in 1880.

Missouri has 145,350 colored people, Alabama has 600,1036, Georgia 725,133, Kentucky 271,454, Louisiana 483,655, Iowa 9,516.

In 1850 there was in the United States, 3,204,077 slaves, in 1860 there was 3,952,801, to-day there is not one, and the colored man can be heard say in the language of Patrick Henry, "Give me liberty, or give me death."

Corning has about 115 colored citizens, they have Sabbath-school every Sunday, H. Venerable being Superintendent, G. Lucas assistant Supt., Mrs. Hester Warren has charge of the bible class, Miss Eliza Woods also assists in teaching.

Many of our (white) friends speak of their desire to see the colored people progress, the ADVANCE hopes to receive some subscriptions among them from all parts of the country.

Send in your name and subscription for the ADVANCE before our next issue, Aug. 15th, as the ADVANCE will contain all of the speeches made by the speakers on Emancipation Day in different points, which will be of great interest to our readers.

Death of Mrs. Lincoln.

The ADVANCE is grieved to announce to its readers the death of Mrs. Abraham Lincoln, whom our great creator called from this earth at 8:15 July 16th, but we believe she has gone to a home eternally in the heavens. We clip the following from the Council Bluffs *Nonpariel:*

Springfield, Ill., July 19.—By a suspension of business, public and private, and general attendance at the funeral of Mrs. Lincoln, the citizens to-day testified their respect

Age (in years) by Sex for African-American Residents of Iowa

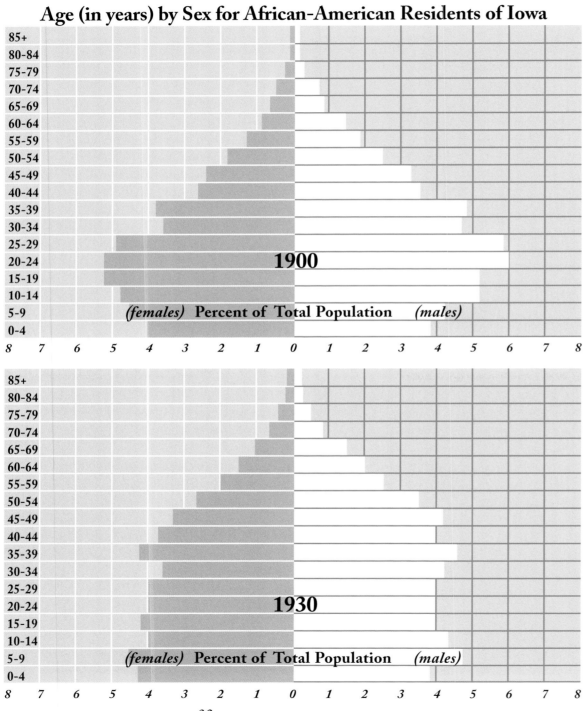

Age and Sex

The population of African-Americans living in Iowa has tended to be relatively young during most decades. *(See chart, pages 38–39.)* In 1900, for example, 27 percent of African-Americans were younger than 15 years old. Another 55 percent were 15 through 44 years of age, during which most families are formed and children are raised. Those 45 years of age and older constituted 18 percent of all African-Americans in Iowa in the census of 1900.

Thirty years later, the respective percentages of younger, middle-aged, and older residents were 25, 48, and 27. The percentage in the two younger age groups were smaller at the beginning of the Great Depression than they had been in 1900. But the addition of another 30 years reveals a different picture. Then, with the baby boom in full bloom, 36 percent of blacks were under the age of 15. Another 39 percent were 15–44, while 25 percent were 45 years of age or older. Although the baby boom definitely had subsided by 1990, still 31 percent of African-American residents were 14 or younger at that census. About 49 percent were in the 15–44 category, while 20 percent were 45 or older. These 1990 figures continued to be influenced by the baby boom; in that year, those born in the baby boom following World War 2 were 25–44 years old, which contributes to the high percentage in the middle-aged category. Blacks were much younger than the general population of Iowa that year and in most others.

That difference is reflected in another manner as well. Iowa's population in 1990 had a higher percentage of older residents than most of the country. More than 15 percent of Iowans were 65 or older that year. Among African-Americans, however, less than 7 percent were that old. The difference also is dramatic among those 85 or older; about 2 percent of all Iowans were of that age in 1990, although about one-half of one percent of African-Americans in this state had reached that age.

African-American males outnumbered females from 1900 through 1950. The difference was more than 1,000 in the censuses from 1900 through 1920. In 1960, however, females were more numerous than males. This trend continued through 1980, although that year there were only 16 more females than males. In 1990, 44 more black males than females lived in Iowa.

Marital Status and Family Type

In 1900, more African-American females and males 15 years of age or older were married than were either single, divorced, or widowed. *(See chart, following page.)* The percentage married was greater for females (57 percent) than males (48 percent) that year, which was true for the 1910–1930 period as well. When data became available again in 1970, however, percentages married fell from the 1930 figures for both sexes. The percentages continued to slide to 1990, when 29 percent of African-American females 15 or older were married; so were 36 percent of African- American males that year. The marital-status category that became the most frequently reported as of 1980 included those who were single.

Widows always were noted more often than widowers, with at least 1,000 African-American females widowed in 1930 and 1970–1990. There were at least 1,000 more widows than widowers in 1980 and 1990. Divorces increased dramatically over the years for which data were available. About 1 percent of both sexes were divorced in 1900; in 1990, 14 percent of females and 11 percent of males were divorced.

Three of four (74.9 percent) families listed in 1960 consisted of a married couple, some of which had children while others did not. *(See chart, following page.)* This dominance of married couples declined steadily through succeeding censuses; by 1990, less than half (49.2 percent) of the families included both spouses. Families of female and of male householders increased throughout this period, with particularly great numerical gains occurring among female householders with no husband present. In 1960, about one in five families were in this category; 30 years later, more than two in five families included a female householder with no husband present.

Among married-couple families, the number with at least one child under the age of 18 remained relatively stable from 1970 to 1990, although those with a child under 6 declined steadily. For female and male householders with no spouse present, however, those with children increased, with particularly large numerical gains occurring among female householders with no husband present.

Selected Socioeconomic Dimensions of the African-American Population

Occupation

Several other dimensions of the population can be noted. On occupation, for example, more males were in a category called "manufacturing and mechanical industries" in 1920 and 1930 than in any other. In second place was "domestic and personal service" both years. Together those two categories accounted for more than half of African-American males employed at those censuses.

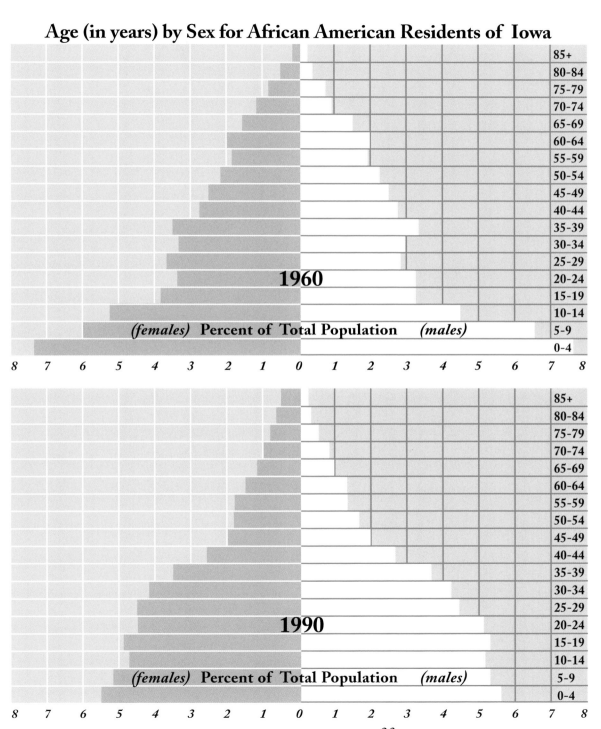

Age (in years) by Sex for African American Residents of Iowa

Marital Status of African-American Residents of Iowa, 1900–1930 and 1970–1990

	Total 15+	Single	Married	Separated	Widowed	Divorced	Unknown
1900							
females	4,148	1,146	2,346		581	48	27
males	5,209	2,258	2,487		338	76	50
1910							
females	4,943	1,112	3,008		677	128	18
males	6,222	2,350	3,221		462	143	46
1920							
females	6,549	1,162	4,279		923	169	16
males	7,861	2,649	4,459		556	160	37
1930							
females	6,188	1,137	3,766		1,009	270	6
males	6,830	2,234	3,841		471	274	10
1970*							
females	11,123	3,192	4,789	731	1,297	1,114	
males	10,253	3,797	5,013	444	419	580	
1980							
females	14,576	5,347	5,025	815	1,486	1,903	
males	14,151	6,169	5,767	502	396	1,317	
1990							
females	16,551	6,856	4,863	886	1,624	2,322	
males	16,496	7,742	5,926	581	385	1,862	

14 years old and over; other censuses used 15 years old and over

Cornett and Pansy Gross Allen and their children, in Ottumwa, early 1900s (courtesy Gwen Sanders)

Family Type for African-American Residents of Iowa, 1960–1990

FAMILY TYPE	1990	1980	1970	1960
All Families	10,551	9,328	6,846	5,593
With own children under 18	6,632	6,147	4,390	
With own children under 6	3,226	3,087	2,404	
Married-Couple Families	5,195	5,327	4,592	4,191
With own children under 18	2,746	3,128	2,739	
With own children under 6	1,300	1,601	1,534	
Familes of Female Householders				
(no husband present)	4,632	3,492	1,980	1,191
With own children under 18	3,451	2,745	1,540	
With own children under 6	1,726	1,363	830	
Families of Male Householders				
(no wife present)	724	509	274	211
With own children under 18	435	274	111	
With own children under 6	200	123	40	

Concentration was even greater among females; more than 8 of every 10 African-American females employed in 1920 were in "domestic and personal service"; this increased to nearly 9 of every 10 in 1930.

Private household work remained an important source of employment for females in 1950 and 1960, although those working in service occupations other than private household situations became the most numerous category. The service category continued to be the leading category for females in 1970, although it was bumped to second place in 1980 and 1990 by "administrative support" occupations. The 1990 census was the first time at least 1,000 African-American females were employed in "professional specialty" occupations.

For males, "service (except private household)," "operative," and "laborer" occupations predominated in 1950, 1960, and 1970.

In 1980, the names of the categories changed but service and operator jobs remained important sources of employment; they were joined by "precision production." Service and precision production jobs continued to be important for African-American males in 1990. *(See chart, following page.)*

Education

In 1940, about 16 percent of females and 14 percent of males 25 years of age of older had completed high school or additional years of education. *(See chart, page 36.)* Those percentages increased to about 40 in 1970, 60 in 1980, and 70 in 1990. In both 1980 and 1990, about 10 percent of females and 15 percent of males in the African-American population had at least completed college.

1920

Total Employed (10 Years of Age or Older)	Females 2,299	Males 7,346
Agriculture	31	382
Extraction of minerals	3	1,120
Manufacturing	195	2,394
Transportation	25	1,113
Trade	54	374
Public service	2	87
Professional service	69	160
Domestic service	1,897	1,636
Clerical occupations	23	80

1930

Total Employed (10 Years of Age or Older)	Females 2,004	Males 5,927
Agriculture	20	253
Forestry and fishing	0	11
Extraction of minerals	0	499
Manufacturing / industry	77	1,896
Transportation / communication	6	976
Trade	20	277
Public service	1	204
Professional service	42	192
Domestic, personal service	1,800	1,565
Clerical occupations	38	54

1950

Total Employed (14 Years of Age or Older)	Females 2,514	Males 5,083
Professional / technical	73	163
Farmers / farm managers	5	57
Managers, proprietors (non-farm)	34	105
Clerical workers	146	167
Sales workers	31	46
Craftsmen / foremen	13	435
Operatives	254	1,313
Private household workers	902	69
Service workers (except private household)	962	1,328
Farm laborers / foremen	5	42
Laborers (non-farm or mine)	62	1,285
Occupation not reported	27	73

1960

Total Employed (14 Years of Age or Older)	Females 3,237	Males 4,853
Professional / technical	199	199
Farmers / farm managers	0	13
Managers / proprietors (except farm)	28	98
Clerical workers	417	263
Sales workers	43	72
Craftsmen / foremen	23	543
Operatives / kindred workers	250	1,310
Private household workers	809	49
Service workers (except private)	1,236	903
Farm laborers / foremen	0	10
Laborers (except farm or mine)	33	1,009
Occupation not reported	199	384

1970

Total Employed (14 Years of Age or Older)	Females 4,771	Males 6,074
Professional / technical	591	492
Managers / administrators (except farm)	82	174
Sales workers	159	83
Clerical workers	1,128	434
Craftsmen	91	923
Operatives (except transport)	472	1,460
Transport equipment operatives	19	373
Laborers (except farm)	57	946
Farmers / farm managers	6	22
Farm laborers / farm foremen	4	20
Service workers (except private)	1,705	1,143
Private household workers	457	4

1980

Total Employed (16 Years of Age or Older)	Females 7,034	Males 8,063
Executive, administrative & managerial	440	671
Professional specialties	811	807
Technicians / related support	155	149
Sales occupations	391	308
Administrative support (including clerical)	1,978	670
Private household occupations	157	9
Protective services occupations	38	165
Service occupations (except protective and household)	1,777	1,125
Farming, forestry, fishing	0	67
Precision production, craft, repair	189	1,272
Machine operators, inspectors	838	1,392
Transportation, material moving	70	698
Handlers, helpers, laborers	190	730

1990

Total Employed (16 Years of Age or Older)	Females 8,229	Males 8,962
Executive / managerial	494	751
Professional specialties	1,023	932
Health & technicians	117	48
Technologists (except health)	109	135
Sales occupations	720	576
Administrative support, clerical	2,203	838
Private household occupations	114	0
Protective services occupations	38	282
Service occupations (except protective and household)	2,084	1,662
Farming, forestry, fishing	0	58
Precision production, craft, repair	311	1,051
Machine operators, inspectors	378	894
Fabricators, assemblers, inspectors	219	351
Transportation	104	403
Material moving equipment operators	9	161
Handlers, helpers, laborers	306	820

General Occupational Categories for African-American Residents of Iowa, 1920–1930 and 1950–1990

Many African-American men and women came to Iowa for the summer to fill domestic jobs at resorts like the Inn on West Lake Okoboji. (Maritime Museum, Arnold's Park)

Education Completed by African-American Residents of Iowa 25 Years of Age or Older, 1940 and 1970–1990

Years of Education	Females	Males
1940 Persons 25 or Older	**4,834**	**5,207**
Grades 1–8 *(or no grades completed)*	2,959	3,559
High school 1–3	946	723
High school 4	571	452
College 1–3	156	168
College 4 or more	63	90
Not reported	139	215
1970 Persons 25 or Older	**7,451**	**6,665**
Grades 1–8 *(or no grades completed)*	2,256	2,325
High school 1–3	2,215	1,714
High school 4	2,206	1,682
College 1–3	517	593
College 4 or more	257	351
1980 Persons 25 or Older	**9,871**	**9,172**
Grades 1–8 *(or no grades completed)*	1,832	1,712
High school 1–3	2,252	1,709
High school 4	3,510	2,906
College 1–3	1,342	1,476
College 4 or more	935	1,369
1990 Persons 25 or Older	**12,030**	**11,270**
Grades 1–8	1,166	1,110
Grades 9–12, no diploma	2,581	2,109
High school diploma	3,684	3,495
Some college, no degree	2,510	2,290
Associate college degree	801	581
Bachelor's degree or more	1,288	1,685

Bill Bibb, a 9th grader at Ottumwa High School, made the news as the "brainiest student," c. 1939.
(Ottumwa Courier)

Housing Tenure Status of African-American Residents of Iowa, 1910–1950 and 1970–1990

	1990	1980	1970	1950	1940	1930	1920	1910
Total housing units	15,486	13,594	8,861	5,155	5,021	4,571	5,108	2,915
Owner occupied	6,010	6,195	4,908	3,143	2,216	1,918	1,698	900
Renter occupied	9,476	7,399	3,953	2,012	2,805	2,528	3,185	1,892
Status unknown						125	225	123

Income and Poverty Status

Income has increased for African-Americans according to the three most recent censuses. More than twice the number of households had incomes greater than $25,000 in 1989 than in 1979. Still, substantial numbers of households reported incomes of less than $10,000 in these censuses. Median household income for African-Americans increased greatly; it was $5,970 in 1969, $12,058 in 1979, and $16,010 in 1989. When inflation is added to the calculations, however, then the median in 1989 had less purchasing power than the medians in 1979 or in 1969. Thus, while the income figures at first suggest improvement in the economic situation of blacks, these trends have not kept pace with inflation.

This is evident when poverty status is examined, because the percentages of blacks in Iowa who are poor increased each census from 1969 to 1989. The number in poverty nearly doubled from 1969 to 1989, while the total number of African-Americans increased by less than half. Increases in the percentages in poverty occurred in various types of families as well. Especially prone to an increase were children, half of whom were poor in 1990. In contrast, the percentage of residents 65 and older who were poor declined, perhaps the only good news in the statistics on poverty for African-Americans. Thus, while many African-Americans have relatively good incomes, a significant proportion does not.

Owner/Renter Status

The decennial census explores housing as well as population. Relatively little information is provided historically by race, however. What is called tenure, which refers to whether the housing unit is owned or rented, has been noted for decades. In 1910, 31 percent of the units were owned by the African-American householders who lived in them. This increased to 1950, when blacks owned 61 percent of the units in which they lived. But that figure has been dropping since; it was 55 percent in 1970, 46 percent in 1980, and 39 percent in 1990, a figure not that different than what was reported in 1910. That trend is in contrast to what has been occurring in the total population, in which 71 percent of the units were owned by those living in them in 1990, while it had been 63 in 1950 or about the same for the total population as for African-Americans that year. These figures on tenure relate to those on income and poverty, of course. With incomes of many African-Americans not keeping pace with inflation, it is understandable that the percentage owning their housing units has been falling.

Concluding Comments

The data noted in this chapter provide a limited portrait of Iowa's African-American population through the decades. Census figures yield an indication of the increasing numbers of the state's residents who were labeled as "colored," "Negro," or "black" in the counts conducted from 1840 through 1990. Changes in definitions of indicators and of how information was reported by race prevent a more detailed review, especially of the period before 1970.[4] The chapters that follow add the detail that is necessary to study African-Americans in this state. What has been provided in this chapter is a base for interpreting comments that are provided in the next chapters.

As this volume was going to press, initial data from the 2000 census were released. Complications arise when data on race from the most recent census are explored, because this was the first census in which respondents could check more than one racial category. In 2000, 61,853 residents indicated that the only racial group in which they should be counted was African-American. *(See chart pages 40–41.)* That represents a gain of nearly 13,800 from the 1990 figure of 48,090, or an increase of 28.7 percent. An additional 10,659 Iowans reported that they were African-Americans but also a member of one or more of the other racial categories. If these individuals are added to those selecting only the African-American category, then the total is 72,512; the gain from 1990 would be more than 24,400, or 50.8 percent.

In 2000, ten counties had at least 1,000 residents who indicated that the only racial category in which they should be included was African-American. Nearly half (45.7 percent) of these residents lived in Polk or Black Hawk counties; this percentage rises to more than two-thirds (69.4 percent) with the addition of Scott and Linn counties. Increases of at least 1,000 occurred in each of these four counties plus Johnson County, led by the gain of more than 3,300 in Polk County. If the more inclusive categorization is used, then residents who were African-American, or African-American and one or more other races, accounted for at least 1,000 residents in 12 counties in 2000. Again, two-thirds (66.9 percent) were located in Black Hawk, Linn, Scott, and Polk counties.

No matter which set of numbers is used, the increase among African-Americans in Iowa was dramatic in the 1990s. Indeed, the numerical change was substantially greater in that decade than ever before. From 2.1 percent to 2.6 percent of Iowa's residents were African-American in 2000. Either end of that range would be the highest percentage ever recorded. Still, fewer than 3 of every 100 Iowans were African-American in the most recent census.

Household Income for African-American Residents of Iowa, 1969–1989

Income Level	1989	1979	1969
< $ 5,000	2,480	2,946	3,820
$ 5,000 – $ 9,999	3,096	2,989	2,944
$ 10,000 – $ 14,999	2,028	1,987	1,517
$ 15,000 – $ 24,999	3,011	3,274	503
$ 25,000 – $ 49,999	3,569	2,292	68
$ 50,000 +	1,648	193	*
Total Households	15,832	13,681	8,852
Median Household Income	$16,010	$12,058	$5,970

*Included in previous category.

Numbers and Percentages of African-American Residents in Iowa Living in Poverty, 1969–1989

Persons, Families, and Unrelated Individuals in Poverty	1989 No.	1989 %	1979 No.	1979 %	1969 No.	1969 %
Persons	16,209	37.1	11,195	28.2	8,189	26.5
Families	3,477	32.7	2,295	24.1	1,517	22.0
Families of female householders with no husband present	2,608	56.2	1,616	45.6	996	50.5
Families of female householders with no husband present with children under the age of 18	2,508	64.7	1,565	49.9	973	58.0
Unrelated individuals	3,136	39.4	2,036	35.1	1,508	50.5
Related children under 18	8,076	50.1	5,625	36.0	4,066	30.1
Persons 65 or older	593	21.3	566	24.2	937	44.3

Notes

1. The information reported in this chapter has been generated from reports published by the U.S. Bureau of the Census for the decennial censuses from 1840 through 1990.

2. The count reported in summary census tables suggests that 333 African-Americans resided in Iowa in 1850. One individual could not be located in a page-by-page check of the census microfilm; the count in Van Buren County was one greater than the number actually listed there. And it appears that seven persons in Louisa County and one in Mahaska County were incorrectly counted as "free colored" by the census bureau. Some others may have been incorrectly classified in one or more counties.

3. Leola Nelson Bergmann, *The Negro in Iowa* (Iowa City: SHSI, 1948; repr. 1969).

4. Those interested in additional census information on blacks in Iowa in 1980 and 1990 could review two publications: Willis Goudy, Sandra Charvat Burke, Liu Dongwang, Jessie Beebe, Rogelio Saenz, and Nak Hoon Lee, *Minority/Majority Groups in Iowa* (Ames: Census Services, Iowa State University [publication number CS95-3], 1995), and Rogelio Saenz, Willis Goudy, and Nak Hoon Lee, *Minority Groups in Iowa* (Ames: Census Services, Iowa State University [publication number Pm-1286], 1987).

Age Groups for African-American Residents of Iowa, 1900–1990

Age	1990 Female	1990 Male	1980 Female	1980 Male	1970 Female	1970 Male	1960 Female	1960 Male	1950 Female	1950 Male
0–4	2,756	2,619	2,196	2,348	1,801	1,961	1,843	1,760	1,045	1,065
5–9	2,466	2,522	2,052	2,167	2,081	2,136	1,496	1,598	955	780
10–14	2,250	2,430	2,034	2,176	2,016	1,974	1,267	1,155	695	725
15–19	2,316	2,558	2,453	2,581	1,876	1,824	951	814	630	635
20–24	2,138	2,440	2,401	2,479	1,478	1,424	831	816	760	880
25–29	2,126	2,067	1,887	2,009	984	924	900	735	790	820
30–34	1,963	2,025	1,438	1,482	938	829	832	749	715	660
35–39	1,626	1,741	1,002	959	870	756	856	803	685	725
40–44	1,248	1,315	883	886	805	758	689	667	625	505
45–49	967	938	854	754	772	714	646	597	485	585
50–54	793	752	809	774	660	601	549	550	645	510
55–59	767	678	711	627	589	544	456	466	400	510
60–64	697	659	575	475	506	450	502	507	345	440
65–69	595	502	527	444	396	374	387	362	375	415
70–74	455	350	396	269	361	312	280	224	235	275
75–79	373	243	268	203	249	191	195	188	150	225
80–84	267	136	200	113	135	110	130	62	*	*
85+	220	92	172	96	121	76	38	40	30	45
Total	**24,023**	**24,067**	**20,858**	**20,842**	**16,638**	**15,958**	**12,848**	**12,093**	**9,565**	**9,800**

*Included with those in a preceding age category

(Far left to right)

Gov. B. F. Carroll (pictured at right) with an inspection team at an Enterprise Coal Company mine east of Ankeny, c. 1908 (SHSI Des Moines)

African-American boatmen on the Lone Star *near Davenport, c. 1870. (Putnam Museum)*

4-H farm camp cooks Clara Farrier and Aunt Eliza Jones, near Clarinda (Nodaway Valley Historical Society)

Age	1940 Female	1940 Male	1930 Female	1930 Male	1920 Female	1920 Male	1910 Female	1910 Male	1900 Female	1900 Male
0–4	599	671	740	651	776	774	624	621	504	479
5–9	675	628	767	796	784	769	662	686	567	554
10–4	726	648	698	710	775	717	624	591	599	633
15–19	718	692	735	679	748	770	670	646	660	641
20–24	675	621	684	679	934	852	714	792	655	749
25–29	635	626	670	682	951	1,081	702	799	610	736
30–34	586	580	649	712	820	894	580	733	437	589
35–39	579	629	751	765	773	1,022	616	785	447	598
40–44	575	611	639	688	617	754	426	607	310	439
45–49	623	632	581	710	508	765	360	576	281	407
50–54	482	571	467	594	396	581	268	398	221	297
55–59	402	475	336	451	237	368	154	283	151	220
60–64	316	382	240	326	192	277	163	204	105	170
65–69	276	303	154	238	118	205	108	140	79	104
70–74	163	204	109	137	93	107	69	97	34	70
75–79	197	194	159	151	67	65	43	53	31	30
80–84	*	*	*	*	33	34	15	29	18	17
85+	*	*	*	*	28	30	20	17	15	18
Unrep.			14	18	34	56	35	63	94	124
Total	**8,227**	**8,467**	**8,393**	**8,987**	**8,884**	**10,121**	**6,853**	**8,120**	**5,818**	**6,875**

Willis Goudy has served Iowa State University as coordinator of census services since 1983. He has released more than 150 applied publications based on census and other secondary data and has given more than 300 presentations throughout Iowa and the world. A professor of sociology, Dr. Goudy has been at ISU for more than 30 years.

African-American Residents of Iowa's Counties, 1840–1990 *Not listed as a county at this census

African-American (one race)	African-American (one race) or African-American and one or more other races	TOTAL county population of all races	County	1990	1980	1970	1960	1950	1940	1930	1920	1910	1900	1890	1880	1870	1860	1850	1840
6	11	8,243	Adair	1	1	4	0	1	5	32	11	21	13	22	8	1	0	*	*
3	5	4,482	Adams	3	1	1	2	2	8	16	9	13	28	45	89	24	0	*	*
21	35	14,675	Allamakee	5	8	6	3	13	13	17	7	19	16	12	38	8	6	0	*
58	74	13,721	Appanoose	79	103	156	124	210	280	341	426	486	368	145	74	35	13	7	*
10	18	6,830	Audubon	1	0	1	2	0	0	0	0	5	3	0	3	1	0	*	*
51	94	25,308	Benton	20	6	4	12	14	7	6	10	9	22	23	20	24	1	0	*
10,179	10,989	128,012	Black Hawk	8,514	8,595	6,644	4,850	2,623	1,528	1,234	856	29	22	12	37	18	18	0	*
95	125	26,224	Boone	62	50	34	29	16	39	49	142	105	235	93	251	11	0	0	*
112	154	23,325	Bremer	70	46	64	21	1	0	3	5	6	6	7	6	17	5	*	*
57	78	21,093	Buchanan	38	25	14	30	26	24	20	21	18	26	20	29	9	2	0	*
72	130	20,411	Buena Vista	56	9	8	3	3	1	0	17	0	3	16	1	0	0	*	*
13	29	15,305	Butler	4	4	0	0	0	8	1	0	1	1	1	1	31	0	1	*
77	95	11,115	Calhoun	30	21	16	11	17	17	21	33	11	3	0	2	0	0	*	*
38	58	21,421	Carroll	7	3	1	3	7	7	17	31	31	32	29	10	0	0	*	*
31	55	14,684	Cass	9	10	5	14	22	7	32	31	22	9	12	21	5	0	*	*
34	56	18,187	Cedar	16	12	3	1	4	1	2	9	21	47	37	53	42	12	2	0
373	537	46,447	Cerro Gordo	303	238	241	213	296	341	322	361	148	58	9	23	4	0	*	*
41	53	13,035	Cherokee	20	7	3	13	3	10	15	24	5	17	5	2	6	0	*	*
7	19	13,095	Chickasaw	4	2	4	2	1	0	0	0	0	3	0	0	3	5	*	*
10	17	9,133	Clarke	3	4	1	4	12	27	37	34	43	69	61	58	26	0	0	*
30	44	17,372	Clay	8	4	3	0	9	6	3	16	0	2	0	2	0	0	*	*
26	44	18,678	Clayton	6	8	6	0	1	6	6	9	26	3	11	1	26	25	2	7
946	1161	50,149	Clinton	732	551	378	334	228	172	233	338	436	182	209	187	129	13	20	10
129	155	16,942	Crawford	59	9	18	5	11	15	11	22	25	15	15	23	1	0	*	*
300	398	40,750	Dallas	63	56	59	112	142	249	409	207	131	23	37	53	25	0	0	*
15	24	8,541	Davis	2	16	9	8	19	22	28	27	43	59	60	60	30	2	7	*
85	101	8,689	Decatur	35	27	13	1	2	1	3	6	34	58	56	129	41	7	1	*
13	22	18,404	Delaware	11	3	6	1	7	19	1	3	2	1	2	2	21	1	0	0
1,511	1,770	42,351	Des Moines	1,327	1,021	798	489	390	265	386	337	429	428	381	425	227	28	25	6
29	57	16,424	Dickinson	16	4	0	2	2	2	2	4	5	4	1	1	0	0	*	*
767	1,007	89,143	Dubuque	354	237	112	83	92	65	89	75	96	118	133	156	167	81	28	72
26	45	11,027	Emmet	19	13	14	1	6	0	8	42	19	7	4	3	3	0	*	*
116	156	22,008	Fayette	48	44	75	39	29	71	104	106	107	89	75	122	70	54	0	*
39	60	16,900	Floyd	8	4	4	1	10	4	9	30	17	15	4	5	3	0	*	*
9	17	10,704	Franklin	6	7	9	3	4	13	11	13	10	5	0	12	5	0	*	*
3	6	8,010	Fremont	4	5	2	3	3	5	17	11	39	64	43	59	29	5	0	*
15	26	10,366	Greene	5	4	6	4	5	5	5	16	1	11	11	16	3	0	*	*
10	18	12,369	Grundy	7	1	4	2	2	1	1	1	11	3	15	0	0	0	*	*
14	25	11,353	Guthrie	7	3	4	6	2	1	1	1	2	7	29	2	5	0	*	*
38	60	16,438	Hamilton	9	10	5	15	4	0	12	4	37	40	19	1	3	0	*	*
11	18	12,100	Hancock	1	6	2	1	5	5	9	9	11	8	2	0	5	0	*	*
116	132	18,812	Hardin	117	60	60	18	24	56	120	72	46	55	80	111	23	0	*	*
13	40	15,666	Harrison	10	8	6	9	7	4	27	23	15	39	26	13	1	1	*	*
302	366	20,336	Henry	211	125	91	100	148	126	135	212	264	367	411	509	465	24	12	16
11	22	9,932	Howard	5	3	2	0	0	0	1	4	12	15	10	19	12	1	*	*
11	17	10,381	Humboldt	9	11	2	0	3	0	1	5	4	2	4	2	0	0	*	*
8	15	7,837	Ida	1	1	4	0	1	0	0	14	2	3	1	0	0	0	*	*
27	36	15,671	Iowa	7	4	3	3	8	3	3	18	5	2	2	15	11	0	1	*
20	50	20,296	Jackson	16	4	6	4	3	0	1	5	0	1	13	9	25	11	9	10
309	367	37,213	Jasper	65	40	55	40	50	54	99	144	182	190	104	121	69	1	0	*

Census 2000

African-American Residents of Iowa's Counties, 1840–1990   *Not listed as a county at this census

African-American (one race)	African-American (one race) or African-American and one or more other races	TOTAL county population of all races	County	1990	1980	1970	1960	1950	1940	1930	1920	1910	1900	1890	1880	1870	1860	1850	1840
104	128	16,181	Jefferson	93	74	122	50	30	59	63	86	79	71	57	72	53	8	1	0
3223	3816	111,006	Johnson	1,979	1,194	552	317	201	89	112	68	65	62	58	105	98	38	22	3
361	415	20,221	Jones	299	102	77	63	51	58	61	67	83	58	34	35	32	7	1	0
8	12	11,400	Keokuk	6	3	3	3	3	2	19	17	17	33	24	15	3	0	0	*
19	35	17,163	Kossuth	8	6	5	9	11	6	5	8	6	3	12	1	0	0	*	*
1066	1293	38,052	Lee	1,112	1,121	1,033	1,039	1,179	1,211	1,353	1,417	1,471	1,632	1,666	1,679	1,563	245	52	11
4919	6250	191,701	Linn	3,334	2,740	1,807	1,183	780	677	765	704	258	258	234	207	48	11	3	1
31	48	12,183	Louisa	86	7	1	0	2	1	19	8	17	8	25	65	59	94	16	17
12	14	9,422	Lucas	4	2	2	10	17	16	45	46	83	194	319	40	31	2	0	*
11	20	11,763	Lyon	2	2	1	1	2	1	1	15	4	0	0	0	0	*	*	*
12	22	14,019	Madison	5	5	3	2	2	2	0	8	5	4	11	10	3	0	0	*
142	177	22,335	Mahaska	42	116	73	52	92	166	211	352	677	1,737	1,592	524	150	16	1	*
134	180	32,052	Marion	104	103	141	88	123	123	146	122	93	44	38	44	36	33	29	*
365	503	39,311	Marshall	279	266	257	253	245	333	351	264	148	167	136	97	37	0	0	*
41	52	14,547	Mills	22	16	11	15	13	23	56	57	47	44	21	24	5	16	*	*
19	21	10,874	Mitchell	2	0	6	0	0	3	2	7	5	15	8	5	1	0	*	*
8	18	10,020	Monona	5	0	0	1	2	3	38	8	0	6	23	88	42	1	*	*
16	33	8,016	Monroe	19	25	23	53	121	202	355	1,652	2,371	553	202	258	49	2	0	*
9	16	11,771	Montgomery	5	8	8	16	17	44	58	54	48	51	38	113	13	0	*	*
294	368	41,722	Muscatine	208	187	132	144	88	81	66	107	137	146	177	179	163	112	69	25
52	66	15,102	O'Brien	8	3	1	3	0	1	4	18	2	0	1	13	6	0	*	*
8	13	7,003	Osceola	3	10	1	0	3	1	0	7	6	1	0	0	*	*	*	*
282	306	16,976	Page	84	37	42	48	106	199	225	250	262	232	234	247	153	1	0	*
9	16	10,147	Palo Alto	8	6	5	2	2	0	0	0	4	0	8	0	0	0	*	*
72	117	24,849	Plymouth	48	46	29	2	4	0	0	0	10	1	9	5	0	0	*	*
21	34	8,662	Pocahontas	4	1	1	1	52	0	0	2	3	0	0	0	0	0	*	*
18,113	20,291	374,601	Polk	14,799	13,700	11,916	10,535	8,323	6,637	5,713	5,837	3,591	2,041	1,194	672	303	13	0	*
671	921	87,704	Pottawattamie	464	443	600	593	638	545	684	612	353	271	327	614	163	9	0	*
103	147	18,815	Poweshiek	87	66	71	26	34	26	26	52	55	51	66	62	79	7	0	*
6	9	5,469	Ringgold	1	0	3	0	2	0	0	0	1	3	0	15	5	1	*	*
30	48	11,529	Sac	4	3	3	1	8	2	13	23	30	6	0	0	1	0	*	*
9,689	11,005	158,668	Scott	7,970	6,620	4,160	1,866	1,150	884	865	745	572	496	274	266	246	39	14	8
13	24	13,173	Shelby	5	6	6	1	1	0	4	7	7	10	1	13	6	1	*	*
64	97	31,589	Sioux	25	35	23	9	3	2	8	14	2	1	0	1	0	0	*	*
1,463	1,701	79,981	Story	1,191	789	303	127	88	66	55	51	8	3	0	9	2	0	*	*
46	81	18,103	Tama	31	13	41	46	18	17	13	25	33	23	45	32	45	0	0	*
2	2	6,958	Taylor	1	1	6	7	7	12	19	34	61	74	96	130	101	0	0	*
28	40	12,309	Union	10	16	17	9	12	22	59	59	70	102	68	90	13	0	*	*
5	15	7,809	Van Buren	10	6	3	6	8	13	44	49	60	102	130	123	211	4	5	2
337	409	36,051	Wapello	270	277	339	468	484	485	447	571	624	793	658	460	193	47	5	*
108	174	40,671	Warren	90	118	30	6	7	6	25	11	47	68	54	63	81	14	0	*
60	99	20,670	Washington	90	29	15	16	18	42	52	108	104	69	75	95	53	13	0	0
4	13	6,730	Wayne	1	0	1	0	7	1	5	6	9	10	20	22	1	11	1	*
1,364	1,556	40,235	Webster	883	797	636	350	301	204	320	399	84	115	43	8	9	4	*	*
21	41	11,723	Winnebago	31	26	18	3	4	2	1	12	2	2	0	1	1	0	*	*
108	132	21,310	Winneshiek	43	93	64	4	5	15	10	3	18	19	10	13	25	0	0	*
2,097	2,763	103,877	Woodbury	1,877	1,126	1,013	1,257	875	875	1,078	1,147	317	292	366	178	44	3	*	*
22	31	7,909	Worth	15	22	25	43	51	51	85	89	16	13	22	9	0	0	*	*
24	49	14,334	Wright	10	0	1	5	6	0	0	5	4	12	2	0	2	0	*	*
61,853	**72,512**	**2,926,324**	**Statewide**	**48,090**	**41,700**	**32,596**	**25,354**	**19,692**	**16,694**	**17,380**	**19,005**	**14,973**	**12,693**	**10,685**	**9,516**	**5,762**	**1,069**	**333**	**188**

Railroad jobs attracted many African-Americans to Iowa in the late 19th and early 20th centuries, despite the discrimination of railroad unions. (courtesy Glenwood and Aileen Tolson)

PART TWO

The rights and responsibilities of citizenship

The William Maxon house was an Underground Railroad station in Springdale. (SHSI Des Moines)

The Underground Railroad in Iowa

by G. Galin Berrier

The Underground Railroad has fascinated Americans for a century and a half, at least since Harriet Beecher Stowe published *Uncle Tom's Cabin* in 1852.

It has all the elements necessary to capture our imaginations: mystery, danger, high adventure, and selfless acts of heroism motivated by devotion to high principle. Unfortunately, there is much less in the way of hard facts to document these legendary achievements than one might wish for. Legends are a combination of both fact and fancy, and in the case of the Underground Railroad it is very difficult to separate the two.[1] This must be kept in mind as we try to reconstruct the story of the Underground Railroad in Iowa.

The term "Underground Railroad" is said to have originated with a Southern planter who, frustrated by the loss of his slave property, said "the Negro escapes to Canada as easily as if they traveled on a railway which ran beneath the ground!"[2]

Visitors to Underground Railroad sites in Iowa can expect to be shown trap doors leading to underground cellars. No doubt these could have been used to conceal fugitives for short periods of time, especially when slave catchers were in close pursuit. But in Iowa, at least, accounts refer with greater frequency to the concealment of fugitives in attics or garrets, haymows, or even out-of-doors in timber or heavy underbrush.[3]

Most Underground Railroad activity in Iowa occurred after the passage of the Fugitive Slave Act of 1850, which provided for a fine of $1,000 and six months in jail for assisting in the escape of fugitives.[4] This would no doubt encourage great secrecy, and few incriminating records were kept. When Wilbur H. Siebert published his pioneering scholarly study of the Underground Railroad a century ago, he attributed the lack of surviving letters, diaries, and scrapbooks to the destruction of any such incriminating evidence even before the beginning of the Civil War.[5] Local Iowa historians agreed that "the trainmasters kept no dispatch books or records of train schedules or of passengers" lest such material be used as evidence against them and knew little of the workings of the organization beyond their immediate neighborhood.[6] Historians have had to depend on the memories of participants and on family stories handed down through succeeding generations.

The Underground Railroad has all the elements necessary to capture our imaginations: mystery, danger, high adventure, and selfless acts of heroism motivated by devotion to high principle.

Josiah B. Grinnell, one of the most ardent and prominent participants in the Iowa routes of the Underground Railroad, welcomed John Brown into his home. (SHSI Des Moines)

Charlotta Gordon McHenry Pyles (from Brown, Unsung Heroines)

Even many years later, in 1928, one descendant of Iowa participants was at pains to point out that his forebears "did not engage in violent, outbreaking, reckless resistance to law" and "took no part [in] any mob for the forcible rescue of fugitives from the hands of law officers." They never spoke of what they did to shelter, feed, or transport fugitive slaves outside of the family. "This is why it is so difficult, so impossible for us to reconstruct in detail the story of what they did. There are no records. They could depend on the absolute secrecy of kin."[7]

But while many Iowans kept their role as secret as possible, others chose to "stand up and be counted." Siebert's list of Iowa agents, while incomplete, contained 116 names, and of a few of these we know a good deal. "It is possible to tell only a part of the story of the Underground Railroad in Iowa" but we do know enough, perhaps, "to show that as an institution the Underground Railroad has played its part in the history of the State."[8]

Never an Organized System

Traditional accounts of the Underground Railroad have tended to suggest a high degree of organization. But in Iowa, despite the involvement of such prominent citizens as Josiah B. Grinnell, Dr. Ira Blanchard of Percival, and Rev. John Todd of Tabor, "the Underground Railroad was never an organized system, and most of the conductors didn't know the whole route."

Abolitionists differed among themselves, and many had only a limited interest in assisting escaped slaves. Few approved of luring slaves away from their masters, and evidence of a well-developed conspiracy simply doesn't exist. Those who did work to free slaves acted largely on their own, without benefit of an elaborate organization.[9] One historian has observed that "much has been written about the Underground Railroad in Iowa in terms so extravagant as to convey the impression that this covert operation of transporting fugitive slaves across Iowa moved with the dispatch, efficiency, and regularity of a time-table that would have been the envy of the Rock Island or Burlington railroad lines," while another cautions that "much that was irregular and unplanned came to be retrospectively systematized under the sinister rubric 'Underground Railroad,' and in Iowa, no less than elsewhere, the metaphor should not be taken too seriously."[10]

There was in fact no large-scale, well-developed organization, but rather a few individuals who were loosely organized, and mostly at the local level. And although their

contribution has often been overlooked, free blacks contributed significantly to whatever organized aid fleeing slaves received.[11]

African-Americans living along the southern boundaries of free states like Iowa would have had frequent opportunities to assist fugitives with little risk to themselves. Perhaps all that was needed was to help ferry runaways across a stream or direct them to the homes of friends.[12] Fugitives depended mostly on their own resources, asking for and receiving minimal help, and that only near the end of their journey after having completed the most dangerous part of it on their own.

Dramatic Stories

One of the most dramatic stories in Iowa is that of Aunt Polka, found hiding in a cornfield near Keosauqua by five elders from local African-American churches who had searched for and found her in the snow. Thinking them at first to be slave catchers, she was said to have leaped on a tree stump, pulled a long knife, and threatened them. She had her baby in her arms and a toddler at her side. She told a remarkable story of having fled from Mississippi with her 14 children. The two oldest boys and two oldest girls had been left with a black family along the way. Eight others had died from lack of food, sickness, or exposure, only the baby girl and toddler having survived.[13] As is usually the case with such accounts, there is no way at this late date to verify it, but it does suggest the extraordinary courage and fortitude such long escapes would have required.

Another Iowa example of a slave making his own way to freedom is John Ross Miller, born a slave in Kentucky and known as "John Graves" in Missouri when he and three others — Alec Nichols, Henderson Hays, and Anderson Hays — "borrowed" two horses and two mules from their masters and headed north. Traveling at night and hiding in the daytime, two days' riding brought them to Winterset in Madison County at about one o'clock on a Saturday afternoon in late October 1861. When some men in town tried to apprehend them, a crowd freed them, gave them something to eat, and sent them off the next morning to Indianola. Miller made his way to Newton, where he worked for a time on a farm before enlisting as "John Sherer" in the 1st Regiment (Colored) Infantry, later known as the 60th Regiment, U.S. Colored Troops. When he returned to Newton after the war, he took the name "John Ross Miller."[14]

Fugitive slaves might thus have entered Iowa at numerous

points along the Missouri border, as the opportunity presented itself. An early student of the Underground Railroad acknowledged that "in fact the great majority of slaves effected their escape alone, and completed the most difficult part of their journey towards freedom unaided."[15]

An advertisement in the *Keokuk Argus* in 1846 offered both a generous reward and expenses for the apprehension of a woman named Lucy, about 36 years of age, who had run away from her master, John T. Dedman, of Waterloo, Clark County, Missouri, on Sunday, May 31, 1846, and was believed headed for a settlement of African-Americans freed earlier in Lewis County, Missouri, and now said to be residing somewhere in the vicinity of Keosauqua.[16]

Such fugitives were sometimes armed and prepared to defend themselves. A man and his wife who concealed themselves for several days in a corn shock on a farm in Jackson Township, Henry County, left behind a dagger ten inches long with a double-edged, six-inch blade. Another fugitive, "stalwart and athletic," was armed both with a heavy club and a knife and would accept food only when it was left at a safe distance. He continued on his way on his own, refusing aid from two local Underground Railroad agents.[17]

The Pyles Family Migration to Iowa

The story of one remarkable family's migration to Iowa with limited assistance from sympathetic whites, that of Harry M. Pyles and Charlotta Pyles and 11 of their 12 children, was told many years later by the daughter of Mary Ellen Pyles, the youngest of the Pyles children. Harry Pyles, fair-skinned and blue-eyed, was a free man. His wife, Charlotta, with high cheek bones, copper complexion, and straight black hair — perhaps resembling her Seminole mother — was a slave on the neighboring plantation of a Mr. Gordon, near Bardstown, Kentucky. Since a child's status in such marriages was determined by that of the mother, all 12 of their children were also slaves, but Harry Pyles was free to visit his family as he wished.[18]

When Mr. Gordon died in 1853, he willed Charlotta and her children to his daughter with the understanding that, consistent with the antislavery principles of their Wesleyan Methodist faith, she would set them free. However, her two brothers, not sharing their sister's religious or antislavery views and jealous of her inheritance, captured son Benjamin Pyles and sold him to a Mississippi slave trader. This treachery convinced Miss Gordon

RUNAWAY on Sunday, the 31st of May, 1846, from the subscriber, living in Waterloo, Clark county, Mo., a Negro woman named LUCY, about 36 years old, very stout and heavy made, very black, very large feet and hands; had on when she left a Blue Calicoe dress and a Sun Bonnet; no other clothing. It is believed she will be conducted to the Territory of Iowa, in the direction of Keosoqua, or beyond that place, to a settlement of free negroes, that was set free by a Mr. Miers, living in Tully, Lewis county, Mo., some years ago. Any person apprehending said slave, and returning her to me, or securing her so that I can get her again, I will pay a liberal reward, and pay all reasonable expenses. Give information to Daniel Hines, Keokuk, or James F. Death, Farmington, I. T.   JOHN DEDMAN.

June 6, 1846.   n21-3w

Advertisement for the return of a slave who escaped Missouri for freedom in Iowa Territory (Keokuk Argus, *June 16, 1846)*

that Charlotta and her children would be safe only if removed from Kentucky to a free state. With the aid of a white minister from Ohio, a Reverend Claycome, they set out in the early fall of 1853 in an old covered wagon drawn by six horses, with four more tied to the back of the wagon as spares to relieve the others.

Besides Miss Gordon and Reverend Claycome, the party consisted of Harry Pyles, his wife Charlotta, their 11 remaining children, a small daughter and son belonging to their eldest daughter Julia, and three small sons of another daughter, Emily.

"In fact the great majority of slaves effected their escape alone, and completed the most difficult part of their journey towards freedom unaided."

— Jacob Van Ek

The husbands of Julia and Emily were slaves on other plantations and so had to be left behind.[19]

Side-Wheel Steamboat

Miss Gordon and her party drove to Louisville, where they boarded a side-wheel steamboat for St. Louis. There a white man named Stone offered to guide them to Minnesota for $100. The terms were agreed to, but the party was no sooner under way than Stone demanded an additional $50, threatening to turn Charlotta and her children over to Missouri slave traders if they refused. Miss Gordon complied, and the party continued north through Missouri. They were stopped frequently but allowed to proceed because of the presence of two white men and a white woman.

By the time the party reached the Des Moines River and crossed into Iowa at Keokuk, the weather had turned cold, so Miss Gordon decided to remain in Keokuk rather than press on north to Minnesota. Harry Pyles, who was a carpenter and stone mason as well as a leather worker, constructed a small brick house for his family and Miss Gordon on Johnson Street in Keokuk. His oldest son, Barney, who had done most of the driving on the journey from Kentucky, found work driving a freight wagon overland from Keokuk to Des Moines.[20]

To ease the financial burden of supporting their large household, Charlotta resolved to obtain the freedom of her two sons-in-law in Kentucky so they could come to Iowa and help. Word came from Kentucky that the price would be $1,500 for each. Somehow, Charlotta's lost son Benjamin learned of this and wrote his mother to say that his freedom, too, could be purchased for $1,500. His mother wrote back to tell him that since he had no wife and children to support, he would have to make his own way to freedom. Benjamin never contacted his family again and was sold to a slaveholder in Fayette County, Missouri, where he was known as "Benjamin Moore."[21]

To raise the funds needed to purchase the freedom of her sons-in-law, Charlotta Pyles went east and made antislavery speeches in Philadelphia. Here she met such prominent antislavery leaders as Frederick Douglass, John P. Gough, Lucretia Mott, and Susan B. Anthony. In six months she had raised enough money and returned to Iowa and then to Kentucky, where she bought her sons-in-law from their owners.

In later years, Charlotta's home became an early stop on the Underground Railroad in Iowa. "Many a slave, coming from Kentucky, Tennessee, and Missouri, found at the gateway into Iowa an enthusiastic member of their own race in the person of Grandma Pyles. She received them into her own home, and . . . helped them to make their escape to Canada." Charlotta died in Keokuk in 1880 at the age of 74.[22]

Charlotta Pyles was not the only free African-American in Iowa who assisted others in search of freedom. In the western part of the state at Council Bluffs, John Williamson, a free mulatto, and his sister and brother-in-law were kidnapped and taken to Missouri, perhaps in part because "Williamson had worked successfully for the Underground Railroad in western Iowa."[23] But Charlotta's story deserves telling in some detail because it challenges many of the traditional assumptions of the Underground Railroad. Although Charlotta and Harry Pyles were helped by sympathetic whites, their vigorous actions on their own behalf were at least as important. This is a useful antidote to the traditional view in which the black fugitive's role is largely passive and the hero of the legendary struggle for freedom is almost invariably the white abolitionist.[24]

Hiding Fugitives

Typical of this traditional view is the story related by a Quaker from Jefferson County, who as "a lad in his teens" was in charge of hiding fugitives in a dilapidated building once used as a slaughterhouse in a woods between a graveyard and a creek north of Fairfield. In his reminiscences many years later, Christian S. Byrkit recalled his mother giving him a half-filled grain sack containing a loaf of home-baked bread, a large piece of cooked meat, and some boiled or baked potatoes to feed a fugitive concealed there.

His last trip, with a runaway on the back of his horse, almost ended in disaster. Startled by two horsemen apparently seeking a fugitive, the horse reared, throwing off both the runaway and a muzzle-loading shotgun slung breech down across the saddle. The gun discharged when it hit the ground. Byrkit finally brought the frightened horse under control a mile or more down the road. The slave hunters brought the shotgun into town the next day, but Byrkit disavowed any knowledge of its ownership. His cap, blown off in his horse's frightened run, was later returned to him by a Quaker farmer. "Son, is this thy cap?" "Yes, Uncle Jonah," young Byrkit replied. "Well, thee should be more careful where thee hangs it up." Presumably the fugitive slave so unceremoniously dismounted

The Pyles' vigorous actions on their own behalf were a useful antidote to the traditional view in which the black fugitive's role is largely passive and the hero of the legendary struggle for freedom is almost invariably the white abolitionist.

got away to the woods in the confusion and darkness.[25]

Among those abolitionists who gave aid and comfort to fugitive slaves, a large place has traditionally been accorded to members of the Society of Friends, or Quakers. In the popular legend, they are portrayed as ever-ready to risk all to help those escaping from slavery. They were among the first to take a principled stand against slavery and to some the Underground Railroad has appeared to be largely a Quaker enterprise. In fact, although some of the best-known abolitionists — including a number in Iowa — were Quakers, others "rejected methods and violent language of the abolition movement."[26]

In Iowa, Congregationalists like Josiah B. Grinnell and John Todd are at least as prominent as Quakers, and one of Siebert's Iowa informants, L.F. Parker of the town of Grinnell, wrote that "in Iowa a number of Methodist ministers were engaged in the work" of the Underground Railroad. Wesleyan Methodists, led by abolitionists Orange Scott and La Roy Sunderland, withdrew from the Methodist Episcopal Church in 1842 in large part over the slavery issue. "Above all, the Wesleyan Methodists were an antislavery movement." They and some other religious groups, such as the Reformed Presbyterians or "Covenanters," were probably just as active in aiding fugitive slaves as the Friends.[27]

A Tradition of Friends

The Quaker tradition of the Underground Railroad is rich in stories of fugitives transported by these plain people in broad daylight under sacks of bran or loads of hay, and of clothing slaves "in the garb of a Quaker woman, with bonnet and veil." Peter Hobson was said to have driven up to D.W. Henderson's hotel in Salem to collect a fugitive disguised in his wife's clothing. "I wish thee would tell Rachel to make haste or we will be too late for the meeting," he allegedly told the innkeeper, and then rode out of town right under the noses of would-be slavecatchers.[28]

Several sources recount an incident said to have occurred at the home of Quaker John Cook near Summit Grove — now Stuart — in Adair County in the winter of 1859–1860. Two young African-American women, sisters from western Missouri, were given shelter after having escaped from a master planning to sell them to the South. Two days later their master appeared and demanded to search the premises. Cook was not inclined to permit this and was about to bar the way when his wife, Anna, appeared and said, "Father, if the man wants to look through the house let

Denmark, in southeast Iowa, was a major center of abolitionist sentiment. Theron Trowbridge's house — still standing — was a station on the Underground Railroad. (SHSI Des Moines)

him do so. Thee ought to know he won't find any slaves here."

"I ask thy forgiveness for speaking so harshly," Cook responded. "Thee can go through the house if mother says so." Finding nothing, the slave owner apologized to Cook and left. At that point, according to one version of the story, Anna Cook went to one of the beds and pulled back the feather mattress, revealing the two frightened girls.[29]

Escape Route to Freedom

Siebert's 1898 book contained a map showing a thick network of escape routes to freedom, resembling very much the railway maps of the time. He was able to document only a few fragments of routes in Iowa. The most detailed attempt to date to map Iowa routes appeared in the *Iowan* magazine in the summer of 1956.[30] It shows a network of routes in southeastern Iowa, at the center of which is the village of Salem in Henry County *(see map, overleaf)*, founded in 1835 by Aaron Street and other Indiana Friends of an antislavery bent. One study has suggested that thanks to the presence of a substantial number of slaves in Scotland and Clark counties in northeast Missouri, in close proximity to abolitionist centers like Salem and the nearby Congregationalist settlement of Denmark, these routes were probably used more extensively than the better-known route made famous by John Brown from Tabor eastward across Iowa.[31]

Salem's Anti-Slavery Friends figure in one of the best-documented episodes on the Underground Railroad because it resulted in a federal court case.[32] It illustrates Salem's leading role during the period prior to the passage of the Fugitive Slave Law

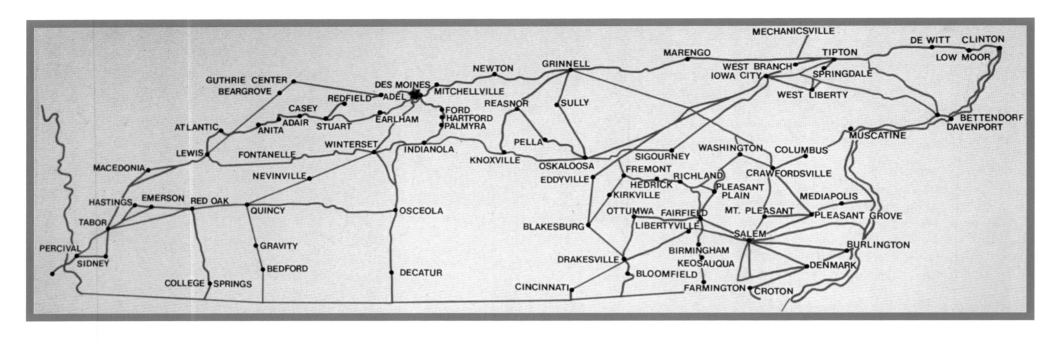

This map of sites on the Underground Railroad in Iowa was created by Curtis Harnack for his article, "The Underground Railroad." (The Iowan, June/July 1956)

of 1850. Slave owner Ruel Daggs came from Virginia to northeast Missouri in the late 1830s and settled with his family and 16 slaves near Luray, west of Kahoka in Clark County. Daggs had a reputation for treating his slaves well but found it difficult to hold onto them with the free soil of Iowa so close at hand, so he decided to sell them farther south.

At the beginning of April 1848, one of Daggs's slaves, probably John Walker, fled from his master and took refuge at Salem. Two months later, encouraged by abolitionist Friends there, he slipped back into Missouri to rescue his wife and any other of Daggs's slaves who might care to chance an escape.[33]

On Thursday evening, June 1, 1848, nine of Daggs's slaves set out for Iowa: Sam Fulcher, 40 to 45 years of age; Sam's wife, Dorcas; John Walker, 22 or 23 years old; John's wife, Mary; Julia, age 18; Martha, age 10; a small boy named William; and two other young children, one an infant, whose names are not known. They headed first to the isolated home of Richard Liggen (or Leggens), where they stayed Friday while a welcome downpour slowed their pursuers. That night Liggen drove them to the Des Moines River, swollen by the rains, which they crossed below Farmington and hid on the Iowa shore Saturday while the rain continued.[34]

Meanwhile, a neighbor of Daggs, James McClure, agreed

to pursue the fugitives. He was joined by a Lee County farmer and former Virginian named Samuel Slaughter, who wanted a share of the reward money Daggs was offering for the return of his property. McClure and Slaughter followed fresh wagon tracks on the rain-soaked ground to the vicinity of Salem. When they overtook the wagon, its only passengers were three young white men who claimed to be returning from a fishing expedition.

Hidden in the Underbrush

Returning to the same spot the next morning, McClure and Slaughter found Fulcher, Walker, and the others hiding in the underbrush. As they prepared to return to Missouri with their captives, they were stopped and surrounded by a dozen men from Salem led by Elihu Frazier, Thomas Clarkson Frazier, and William Johnson. Perhaps realizing that McClure and Slaughter had no arrest warrants and did not know any of the fugitives personally, one of the leaders demanded that the party return to Salem for a hearing before the township justice of the peace, Nelson Gibbs. Another declared that he "would wade in Missouri blood" before he would allow the fugitives to be taken without a hearing.[35]

As the party headed toward Salem, Slaughter lost control of the situation and most of his captives. Walker managed to get away, and Fulcher persuaded Slaughter to let the women and children stop to rest, so that by the time the party, now numbering between 50 and 100, reached the village, only Fulcher and Fulcher's young son were still in custody. Henry Dorland, the village school teacher, mounted a pile of lumber as they passed and exhorted the crowd to remain peaceable. Because Justice Gibbs's office in Henderson Lewelling's house was too small to accommodate the throng, the hearing was reconvened at the Anti-Slavery Friends Meeting House two blocks away.

Aaron Street and Albert Button served as counsel for the fugitives, and when Slaughter and McClure were unable to produce arrest warrants, Gibbs declared in effect that he lacked jurisdiction and dismissed the proceedings. At this point, Paul Way — described by one eyewitness as an old man, in pioneer's work clothes, "with long chin whiskers and a pointed topped lopped down felt hat" and riding an old sorrel mare while leading another horse — came by as if by pre-arrangement. Fulcher mounted the second horse and his child was handed up to him. Way is variously described as having shouted either, "Stop them niggers, don't let them follow me," or "If anybody wants to foller me, let him foller." As Fulcher and his son made their escape with Way on horseback, Slaughter and McClure, vowing vengeance, returned to Missouri.[36]

A few days later, Slaughter and McClure returned with a band of heavily armed Missourians, estimated at anywhere from as few as 60 to as many as 300 men, vowing to search every "nigger-stealing house" in Salem. They set up roadblocks at the exits from town and searched from house to house, beginning with that of Thomas Frazier. But Frazier had been warned, and the fugitives he was hiding had been concealed in the woods. When the search party arrived, they found only Frazier and his family quietly eating dinner.

Other homes were searched, with similar results. Although the crowd of Missourians was unruly, a few of its members were able to restrain the rest, and their abuse of the citizens of Salem was mostly verbal. No homes seem to have been searched where permission was denied. Having come up empty-handed in their search, the Missourians arrested John H. Pickering, Thomas Clarkson Frazier, Isaac C. Frazier, Erick Knudson, John Comer, and three or four others and held them overnight in a hotel. The next morning the Henry County sheriff hurried to Salem from Mount Pleasant and effected a settlement. The Missourians agreed to release their prisoners, who in turn signed a recognizance to

appear at the next term of federal district court to answer charges of robbing Slaughter and McClure of recaptured slaves.[37]

A Needle in a Haymow

There was a saying that it was "as easy to find a needle in a haymow as a Negro among Quakers," and in fact some of Ruel Daggs's slaves did elude capture. Sam Fulcher and his son were hidden east of Salem and then taken to Denmark. John and Mary Walker and their baby also made good their escape. But Dorcas Fulcher, Julia, and two of the children were returned to Daggs, probably for the reward money. Clearly the claim of "not a single slave being retaken" once he or she had reached Salem is not true.

In September 1848, suit was brought for damages under the old Fugitive Slave Law of 1793, and the trial was held in Burlington in the summer of 1850. In the case of *Daggs v. Frazier, et al.,* five Salem Quakers were found guilty of robbing Slaughter and McClure of recaptured slaves and fined $2,900, presumably the value assigned to the five fugitive slaves who escaped to freedom.[38]

Other Quaker settlements in southeast Iowa, like Pleasant Plain and Richland, appear on maps of Underground Railroad routes, and in central Iowa a route from Tabor and Lewis crossed

Henderson Lewelling's house in Salem served as an Underground Railroad station and was the site of a preliminary hearing in the fugitive slave case of Daggs v. Frazier in 1850. (Friends of Lewelling House, Salem)

Adair County to Summit Grove, now Stuart. Here a line went east to the Friends community of Bear Creek, five miles northwest of Earlham. Another Adair County site was Fontanelle, where Azariah Root was said to have harbored fugitive slaves in a grove about two miles west of town. His son Abner wrote of transporting a wagonload of fugitive slaves "to Johnnie Pearson's, who was an old Quaker with a grist mill several miles beyond Stuart in Guthrie County and whose house was another station on the route."[39]

In eastern Iowa, the Cedar County Quaker settlement of Springdale has been described "as a center . . . second to none" on the Underground Railroad. John Brown made his first trip to Cedar County in late October 1856 and received a warm welcome at the Traveler's Rest tavern near West Branch from its proprietor, James Townshend.

At this time he first learned of the strong antislavery sentiment among the Quakers of that area, who were already engaged in assisting fugitive slaves.[40] William Maxson's "gravel" (concrete) house built seven miles northeast of West Branch in 1848 — and demolished 90 years later — had a big basement with a huge fireplace considered ideal for concealing fugitives.[41]

Elsewhere in Cedar County, fugitive slaves were sheltered on the farm of Samuel Yule, northwest of Tipton in Red Oak Township. Yule left this personal record:

Oct. 30, 1853,
Three negroes were at my house that had ran away from Missouri; hid all day in the barn, got supper and James Cousins [father of Congressman Robert Gordon Cousins] took them to Fairview, Jones County.[42]

Fugitive slaves were transported to Posten's Grove in eastern Cedar County and into Clinton County at any of several ferry crossings of the Wapsipinicon River, such as the Buena Vista ferry in Olive Township. At DeWitt, agents included a Captain Burdette, Judge Graham, and Mrs. J. D. Stillman. A station was located a mile south of DeWitt at Rural Home Farm, owned by Robert Lee Smith, who sent at least one party of fugitive slaves to Horace Anthony at Camanche, where another agent may have been "Black Bill" Watts, a former Missouri slave who somehow managed to purchase both his own freedom and that of his wife. In 1923, Robert Smith's son, W. L. Smith, wrote a family history in which he related that "the first black persons I ever saw were two girls whose names were Celia and Eliza and who stayed in

52

our house for weeks waiting for the river to freeze over at Camanche, so it would be safe to cross the ice."

The next party observed by young Smith was a group of seven fugitives, including two small children, who remained at Rural Home Farm for a time before being taken to Horace Anthony at Camanche.

The last to pass through, in the summer just before the Civil War broke out, were two African-American men. Their presence prompted publisher O. C. Bates of the *DeWitt Standard* to write: "Two volumes of the Irrepressible Conflict, one bound in black and the other in brown, passed through our community lately on the way to Canada."[43]

This bears a remarkable similarity to a letter sent May 6th from Low Moor in 1859 by G. W. Weston to C. B. Campbell of Clinton. Low Moor was another Quaker community, and several Friends were active in aiding fugitive slaves.

C. B. Campbell found places to conceal fugitive slaves in Clinton, sometimes in the garret of his own small frame house at the corner of Sixth Avenue South and South Second Street, "within a stone's-throw of the U.S. Marshall's residence." Another hiding place was in a cellar in the gardens of brothers John R. and Andrew Bather, who raised flowers and vegetables on Camanche Avenue, or in the attic of their brick house or the bluffs behind it. On at least one occasion, one of the Bathers used a covered carriage owned by H. P. Stanley to convey an African-American man and his light-skinned wife to Lyons, where Campbell had arranged for a skiff to transport them across the dangerously ice-filled Mississippi River to Fulton, Illinois. From there they were transported by wagon to Union Grove in Whiteside County, Illinois, the wife posing as a free person and the owner of her husband. One version holds that as many as 14 fugitive slaves at one time may have crossed the river here in similar fashion.[45]

One more example of the Quaker role in the Underground Railroad in Iowa is the Friends community of Lynnville in Jasper County, conveniently located between Grinnell and Thomas Mitchell's tavern at Apple Grove, on the old stage road northeast of Des Moines about four miles south of the later town of Mitchellville. Mitchell himself in old age told a story of directing three African-Americans, two males and one female, "on the Grinnell road to a Quaker settlement [Lynnville?] where further guidance would be at hand."

On November 4, 1857, Joseph Arnold and Matthew Sparks

encountered three African-Americans named James F. Miller, Henry May, and John Ross from the Cherokee Nation in Indian Territory . One of them had in his possession a scrap of paper with the names of Arnold and Sparks written on it as sympathetic persons with whom to make contact. They were taken to the house of C. B. White in Lynnville, where one of them is supposed to have made a thank-you speech to the group of antislavery activists assembled there. In another incident, also in 1857, an African-American man, his wife, and year-old child made their way to the home of Joseph Arnold, who kept them overnight before ferrying them across the Skunk River. The next night they were sent on to Grinnell.[46]

Many of the first settlers in southern Iowa came from the South and shared the proslavery views of Missourians south of the state border. But in time more people from northern states with antislavery views relocated to Iowa. One such was J. H. B. Armstrong, who had been involved with aiding fugitive slaves in Fayette County, Ohio. Sometime in 1839 Armstrong moved to Lee County, where he soon began to help fugitives from Missouri reach Salem and Denmark.

In 1852 he removed to Appanoose County near Cincinnati, settling within four miles of the Missouri state line. In one incident in the winter of 1852–53, a 16-year-old African-American boy arrived at Armstrong's home in Pleasant Township with a story of having ridden on horseback by a roundabout route some 200 miles from his master's home in Clark County, Missouri. Claiming to be from a family of 14 or 15 children, all of whom had been sold into slavery when they grew up, he had used the pursuit of a runaway horse owned by his master's son as a pretext for his departure.

After feeding and sheltering the fugitive, Armstrong sent his overnight guest to the home of his brother-in-law, a Mr. Calvert living near Centerville. However, the boy was not allowed to take his master's son's horse with him. Armstrong was a justice of the peace, and after observing that the horse "had either been stolen or had stolen somebody," kept it for a year as a stray and then sold it for charges for its upkeep.[47]

On another occasion, two slaves from central Missouri named John and Archie made their way the 200 miles to Appanoose County and camped in the woods near Armstrong's. A neighbor who disapproved of helping fugitive slaves was being entertained in Armstrong's parlor, so Archie was hustled into a bedroom off the kitchen. After the unsuspecting neighbor departed, Archie was given some food and he and John were then sent on to one John Shephard, where they were given supper. "My God, John!" Archie exclaimed. "Who'd have thought we'd set down to a meal like this?" After staying the night at Shephard's, they were sent on to Drakesville and eventually made it to Canada.

Archie is said to have written saying they were working there for a dollar a day and adding: "I hope the good Lord will bless you for your kindness toward us, and I hope the day will soon come when we will be a people."

At one time, near the end of the Civil War, feeling among Missouri slaveholders against Cincinnati's antislavery activities ran so high that a rumor spread that men were coming from Putnam County to burn the town and exterminate the Armstrong family. A force 50 strong was assembled for their protection, but the "invasion" never materialized. Local sources claim that as many as 40 or 50 fugitive slaves may at one time or another have been sheltered by the people of Appanoose County.[48]

The New England influence affected the Underground Railroad in Adams County, where "the Nevin colony," or Nevinville, founded by New Englanders on 16,000 acres in Colony Township in the northeastern corner of the county, was a station. Others were located at Quincy and possibly Mt. Etna, Brooks, and Nodaway as well. Local people believe the old Wayside Inn near Nodaway, built in 1856 as a stop on the Western Stage Company route between Des Moines and Nebraska City, may have harbored fugitive slaves.

The key figure in Quincy was Rev. Isaac Burns, first minister of the newly constructed Methodist Church, who had been severely beaten by a mob in Missouri and driven out of that state in 1854 or 1855 because of his outspoken antislavery views. Daniel and Martha Ritchey were said to be active in assisting fugitives, and B.F. Allen and David Peterson were known to have conducted fugitive slaves from Quincy to Nevinville. On Sunday, December 20, 1857, Allen and Petersen drove a wagon to the home of Mr. and Mrs. J.L. Ellis at Nevinville and asked "to bring in their load and have it warmed." Concealed under a load of loose hay was a man of middle age who had escaped from his master near the border of Missouri and Kansas. He was hidden for several days at the hotel of B. O. Stephenson before being taken on to Winterset.[49]

The major center of Underground Railroad activity in southwest Iowa was at Civil Bend — now Percival — and Tabor,

"I hope the good Lord will bless you for your kindness toward us, and I hope the day will soon come when we will be a people."

— **Archie, a traveler on the Underground Railroad**

"John Brown respectfully

requests the church at

Tabor to offer public

thanksgiving to

Almighty God in behalf

of himself and company

and of their rescued

captives in particular,

for His gracious

preservation. . . ."

— **John Brown to John Todd, 1859**

The Hitchcock House near Lewis still stands as it did during the 1850s when Rev. George B. Hitchcock was an active stationmaster on the Underground Railroad. (Hitchcock House Society)

The house of Rev. John Todd in Tabor accommodated John Brown and his followers as well as fugitives from slavery in nearby Missouri. (SHSI Des Moines)

settled by antislavery Congregationalists from Oberlin, Ohio, and where nearly everyone in the community was in sympathy with escaped slaves. After 1852 fugitives were brought from Nebraska City across the Missouri River at Old Wyoming by a ferryman named William Bebout, or farther north at Copeland's Ferry. They were then passed on to farmer Lester Platt, Dr. Ira D. Blanchard, Reuben Williams, or Joseph Treat, and taken on to Tabor, where the key agent was Rev. John Todd.[50]

In one notable incident, on July 4, 1854, a Mormon convert from Mississippi by the name of Dennis, his wife, and six slaves bound for Salt Lake City, Utah, camped on Tabor's main street. Five of the slaves — a father and mother, each about 40 years of age, and two children, plus a young man about 21 years old — let it be known that they would welcome a chance to escape from slavery. Their escape was organized by "Deacon" S. H. Adams and blacksmith Jesse West, assisted by John Hallam, James K. Gaston, and Henry Irish, West's apprentice. At about one o'clock in the morning, while the Mormon and his family slept, all his slaves except a 50-year-old servant woman who wished to remain with her master were taken across the Nishnabotna River east of Tabor and hidden there in some bushes, while G. B. Gaston rode to C. W. Tolles on Silver Creek to make further arrangements. A day or two later, Cephas Case and William C. Clark conducted the fugitives northeast to Rev. George B. Hitchcock at Lewis. Later

they were taken to a Quaker settlement near the Des Moines River, which they crossed not far from Oskaloosa. Aided by Quakers and Wesleyan Methodists, they were seen by Reverend Todd's sister at a church in Peoria, Illinois, and were said to have crossed over into Canada at Detroit.[51]

The People of Tabor

John Todd and the people of Tabor played a significant part in John Brown's famous journey across Iowa in the winter of 1858–1859 with slaves forcibly liberated from bondage in northwest Missouri. On December 19, 1858, while Brown and his men were camped in the Osage district of Kansas, George Gill brought into camp an African-American named Jim Daniels, who sought Brown's help to prevent himself, his wife, and children from being sold farther south. The next night Brown and nine others, including Gill, John Kagi, and Jeremiah Anderson, went at midnight to the house of Daniels's master, Harvey Hicklan. Here they seized five slaves by force and looted the house and outbuildings. At another place, five more slaves were taken, as well as horses, a wagon, clothing, bedding, and provisions. Meanwhile, Aaron Stevens and seven others of Brown's men went down the other bank of the Osage River to the home of a well-to-do, popular settler named David Cruise to get a female slave Daniels insisted should be rescued. When Cruise made a sudden movement, Stevens, thinking

The Jordan House in West Des Moines, a station on the Underground Railroad, also hosted John Brown. (Jordan House)

Isaac Brandt welcomed John Brown into his home — another Underground Railroad station — formerly located at East 12th and Grand in Des Moines. (SHSI Des Moines)

James C. Jordan, a native of Virginia, changed from slave catcher to "chief conductor on the Polk County branch of the Underground Railroad." (Jordan House)

he was reaching for a revolver, shot and killed him. Others in Stevens's party also took two yoke of oxen, 11 mules, several horses, and other provisions before rejoining Brown's group on the Kansas side. The property was later described by Brown as "remuneration for the years of unpaid toil," but the authorities took a different view. A false rumor spread that the governor of Missouri had offered a $3,000 reward for Brown's arrest, and Pres. James Buchanan offered one of $250.[52]

Brown and his party of rescued slaves — now numbering 12 with the birth of a child named "John Brown" — came north to Nebraska and crossed the Missouri River above Nebraska City, arriving in Tabor on Saturday, February 5, 1859. The next day was Sunday, and Brown asked the following in a note handed to Reverend Todd:

> *John Brown respectfully requests the church at Tabor to offer public thanksgiving to Almighty God in behalf of himself and company and of their rescued captives in particular, for His gracious preservation of their lives and health, and his signal deliverance of all out of the hand of the wicked hitherto.*

But word of the violence and death on Brown's raid into Missouri had reached Tabor, and the request was refused. Instead, a public meeting was called for Brown to speak in his own defense

to justify his actions. But a Missourian who happened to be staying at the hotel also sought to attend the meeting, and Brown refused to make any statement unless the stranger, who may have had independent information on what had occurred, was excluded. The Missourian held his ground, and "leading persons present strongly insinuated that if no wrong had been done, the actors ought not to be ashamed or afraid to let any and everybody know what they had done." Another account says that Brown was "severely reprimanded as a disturber of the peace and safety of the village." Upset that his Tabor friends would not support him — "I am not yet among friends," he said — Brown left the meeting and went to the house of George B. Gaston to spend the night.[53]

Within a week, on February 11, 1859, Brown and his party left Tabor and, traveling by way of Lewis and Grove City (just east of Atlantic) in Cass County and Dalmanutha in southern Guthrie County, were at the home of James C. Jordan in Walnut Township, west of Des Moines, a week later. Jordan, a Virginia native and one-time slave catcher, had been so repelled by what he had experienced in that line of endeavor that in his new Iowa home he "became chief conductor on the Polk County branch of the Underground Railroad." Brown had no money to pay for ferrying his party across the Des Moines River, so newspaperman James Teesdale, who had known Brown in Ohio in 1857, paid the tolls.[54]

By Sunday, February 20, Brown and his party had reached

Isaac Brandt, a successful businessman on the east side of Des Moines, was also active on the Underground Railroad in central Iowa. (SHSI Des Moines)

Rev. John Todd, the key agent of the Underground Railroad in Tabor, close to the Missouri border (Tabor Historical Society)

John Brown found support throughout Iowa — in Tabor, Lewis, Des Moines, Grinnell, and Springdale — for his anti-slavery efforts in Kansas. (SHSI Des Moines)

the vicinity of Grinnell. Not wishing to travel on Sunday, Brown paid a call on Josiah B. Grinnell: "I am the 'awful Brown' of whom you have heard — Captain John Brown of Kansas." Grinnell responded that he had just been reading about Brown in the *New York Tribune,* including the reward offered for his capture. Arrangements were made to accommodate Brown's party, some in the parlor of Grinnell's house, known in later years as the "Liberty Room." Some of the horses were stabled in Grinnell's barn and the rest at the stable of a hotel in town, where the African-American women were accommodated in an upstairs room in back, barricaded behind boxes and old furniture piled in front of their door.

The African-American men, who were armed, probably stayed at a camp in a grove just south and west of town. That evening Brown spoke at a meeting in a large hall used also as a church, defending his actions and answering questions before an audience of several hundred: "They call me a 'Nigger thief.' Am I? I delivered the poor that cried, and there was none to help."

Later, Brown wrote a letter from Springdale to the people of Tabor contrasting his reception at Grinnell with the one they had accorded him earlier. After listing such tangibles as food, clothing, and two nights' lodging, Brown noted that "Mr. Grinnell spoke at length and has since labored to procure us a free and safe conveyance to Chicago, and effected it," and concluded that "public thanksgiving to Almighty God [was] offered up by Mr. Grinnell in behalf of the whole company."[55]

Brown and his party left Grinnell on or about February 22 and reached the Quaker community near Springdale four days later, February 25. While Brown slipped into Iowa City to confer with William Penn Clarke on how best to transport the fugitive slaves to Chicago, Grinnell himself went to Chicago and persuaded a suspicious John F. Tracy, the general superintendent of the Chicago and Rock Island Railroad, to place a boxcar at his disposal for $50. Tracy reconsidered and withdrew his permission, saying "I would not accept it for $10,000 since we might be held for the value of every one of the niggers." However, by that time the "shipment" had already taken place and the "freight" unloaded at night in Chicago.[56]

It was William Penn Clarke who made the arrangements with the Mississippi and Missouri Railroad's station agent at West Liberty to have a boxcar set out in front of Keith's Steam Mill, where Brown and his party had been hidden after coming the ten

miles south from Springdale. Brown and one of his lieutenants, John Kagi, had dinner at the hotel while waiting for the train to arrive. When it did, a large crowd was present to see them off. Brown apparently rode in the freight car with the fugitives, while Kagi and Clarke rode in a passenger coach.

When the train reached Davenport, where U.S. Marshall Laurel Summers had formed a posse to arrest Brown and capture the fugitives, federal officers walked through the passenger cars but "no Negroes were found, and no suspicion was aroused by the freight car in the rear." When the train reached Chicago, the fugitives were unloaded in secret to avoid embarrassing the railroad, and William Penn Clarke apologized to the railroad company's president for the deception.[57]

Because of this highly publicized trip in 1859 with 12 African-Americans forcibly rescued from slavery in Missouri, John Brown has been credited with "linking the major stations of the Underground Railroad into a cohesive whole. So much of the old abolitionist's labor consisted of relieving slave owners of their human property, and transporting the escapees across Iowa to freedom." Some accounts call the line from Tabor to Springdale "the John Brown line," and it may be the only Underground Railroad route in Iowa of which most people are aware. In fact, the routes in southeast Iowa were probably used longer and may have carried more fugitive slaves to freedom than did John Brown's "Tabor Line." Brown seems to have transported very few slaves across Iowa to freedom, and the line from west to east pre-dated his use of it. Conducting fugitive slaves to freedom was subordinate to Brown's larger goals, as events at Harper's Ferry in Virginia later in 1859 would demonstrate.[58]

Pinkerton Took Charge

According to Grinnell's memoirs, detective Allan Pinkerton took charge of Brown's fugitives in Chicago and sent them to Detroit, which they reached on March 10, 1859. Two days later, they were ferried under Brown's direction to Windsor, Canada, which is usually identified as the ultimate destination of fugitive slaves, especially after 1850.[59] One wonders how many, if any, might have remained in Iowa instead. According to one account, "Negroes who came into Iowa before and during the Civil War often settled on the first suitable piece of land or in the first little village they came to after crossing the border. The town of Amity, Page County, was the first Underground Railroad station north of the Missouri line in the southwestern corner of the State and many fugitives found refuge there and in other villages of the county."[60] If this were indeed the case, enforcement of the Fugitive Slave Law must have been very lax for fugitives to settle openly so close to the border.

More likely, fugitives remaining in Iowa would have been furnished "free papers" by sympathetic whites. Daniel Yockey of Brighton once told of having helped rescue a young African-American boy named Henry Hannah, eight or ten years old, when he was brought to Washington County in 1845 or 1846. Fearing he would be sold into slavery in Missouri, Yockey and George C. Vincent were said to have "captured" Henry from the home of Claudius T. Hendrix and taken him to "old Father Houston" living two or three miles away. Then Henry was passed on to Houston's son-in-law, John C. Ritchey, who lived near Winfield in Henry County. Eventually an Iowa City attorney, James B. Carlton, secured free papers for him.[61]

Two African-Americans living in Davenport, Tom and Jake Bussey, compiled a list of 51 blacks who migrated to Iowa before, during, or just after the Civil War. Five of them are identified as fugitive slaves: William Buckle, from Alabama, living in Iowa City; Auntie Fletcher, from Virginia, living in Des Moines; Eliza Jones, from Kentucky, living in Clarinda; Ralph Montgomery, from Missouri, living in Dubuque; and John Warwick, from Virginia, living in Davenport. However, it is quite possible that these individuals came to Iowa after the Civil War and not by means of the Underground Railroad.[62]

While it is difficult to estimate how many slaves escaped to freedom through Iowa, it was probably not a large number. An account of the route that crossed the Missouri River at Civil Bend (Percival) in southwest Iowa states that while the actual number of slaves transported there is unknown, "several historians estimate the figure in the hundreds and others as more than a thousand.... Dr. Blanchard said it seemed like a million."[63]

But a study of the Underground Railroad routes in southeastern Iowa, which were probably in use longer, suggests that it did not make much of an impact on Missouri's slave population. At most, it may have been a slight deterrent to slavery in border regions like Clark and Scotland counties.[64]

Abolitionists would have been inclined to exaggerate the number of slaves helped to freedom in order to reassure their supporters that their efforts were effective, while slaveholders might exaggerate their losses in their agitation for the passage of more stringent fugitive slave laws. Since statistics are few, many families in southern and central Iowa were free to boast of the hundreds of slaves they were able to help on their way to freedom, "but it is safe to assume that legend has multiplied their numbers many times over. The risks were too great to attract many passengers to this northbound, subterranean line."

What census statistics we have are neither complete nor totally accurate, but they indicate that the entire South lost only about 1,000 slaves each year as runaways. Although Wilbur Siebert argued that the Underground Railroad was "one of the greatest forces that brought on the Civil War," it was rather the very *inability* of the Underground Railroad to seriously undermine the institution of slavery that made the war unavoidable.[65]

There is a great deal that we can never know about the Underground Railroad in Iowa, but we can say that at least some of its romantic legend is in fact supported by credible evidence. We also can say that, while many Iowans took great risks on behalf of fugitive slaves, African-Americans themselves carried out the most difficult part of their escape from slavery, unaided and largely by their own efforts, receiving help from sympathetic whites mainly at the end of their ordeal. Most of the participants, black as well as white, must remain shadowy figures obscured by the mists of time, but they left behind just enough fragments of their stories to cause us to marvel at their courage and devotion to principle.

Barclay Coppock

Barclay Coppoc from Springdale, a lookout in John Brown's 1859 raid on Harper's Ferry, Virginia (now West Virginia), escaped capture. (SHSI Des Moines)

Edwin Coppoc, who was hung with John Brown

Edwin Coppoc enlisted in John Brown's provisional army (left) for the 1859 raid on Harper's Ferry. He was captured, tried, convicted, and hanged with Brown. (SHSI Des Moines)

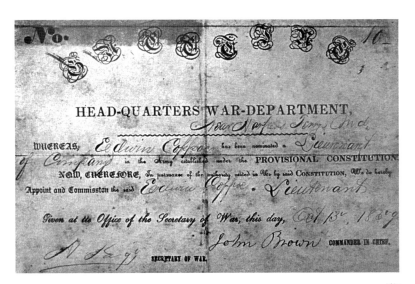

Thomas A. Jenkins made his way via the Underground Railroad to Springdale, where he died in 1902 at age 83. His epitaph reads "called as a slave, died a free man." (SHSI Iowa City)

Notes

1. Larry Gara, *The Liberty Line: The Legend of the Underground Railroad* (Lexington: Univ. of Kentucky Press, 1961), 1–2, 17.

2. George Shane, "Iowa 'Railway' Helped Slaves to Freedom in Canada Century Ago," *DMR*, Dec. 31, 1951, Iowa Clipping File 2, State Historical Society of Iowa (hereafter cited SHSI), Des Moines; Gara, 144 n.1, 162, 173–74. The earliest use of the term is a newspaper story in the *Chicago Western Citizen* of December 23, 1842, recounting an event in upstate New York, but other versions place its origins in Kentucky, Ohio, or Pennsylvania.

3. See Rogers, "Underground Railway, Henry County," July 7, 1938, WPA Project, Iowa Clipping File 2, SHSI, Des Moines, for one of many possible examples.

4. Dorothy Schwieder, *Iowa: The Middle Land* (Ames: Iowa State Univ. Press, 1996), 69; Leland L. Sage, *A History of Iowa* (Ames: Iowa State Univ. Press, 1974), 139–40.

5. Wilbur H. Siebert, *The Underground Railroad from Slavery to Freedom* (New York: Macmillan, 1898; repr. 1968).

6. Ibid., 381; Jacob Van Ek, "Underground Railroad in Iowa," *Palimpsest* 2 (May 1921): 142–43; Ora Williams, "Underground Railroad Signals," *AI* 3d ser. 27 (April 1946): 300; Gara, 6, 9–10.

7. Edward Heizer to L. O. Leonard (January 20, 1928), Underground Railroad Collection, SHSI, Iowa City.

8. Sage, 139; Van Ek, 142. Dr. Steven Faux, director of the honors program at Drake University in Des Moines, has compiled a list of more than 200 known "conductors" and "station agents" in Iowa.

9. Curtis Harnack, "The Underground Railroad," *Iowan* 4 (June/July 1956): 21; Gara, 69.

10. Joseph Frazier Wall, *Iowa: A Bicentennial History* (New York: Norton, 1978), 89; Robert R. Dykstra, *Bright Radical Star: Black Freedom and White Supremacy on the Hawkeye Frontier* (Cambridge: Harvard Univ. Press, 1993), 91.

11. Gara, 91–92.

12. Siebert, 151; Van Ek, 138.

13. Gara, 67–68; "Underground Railway, Van Buren County," 1–2, WPA Project, Iowa Clipping File 2, SHSI, Des Moines.

14. C. C. Stiles, "John Ross Miller," *AI* 3d ser. 19 (July 1934): 385–86.

15. Van Ek, 137.

16. D. A. Garretson, "Traveling on the Underground Railroad in Iowa," *Iowa Journal of History and Politics* 22 (July 1924): 420; Philip E. McPartland, "Way Stations on the Underground Railroad," June 9, 1937, WPA Project, Iowa Clipping File 2, SHSI, Des Moines.

17. Garretson, 426–28.

18. Mrs. Lawrence C. Jones, "The Desire for Freedom," *Palimpsest* 8 (May 1927): 153–54.

19. Ibid., 154–56.

20. Ibid., 157–58.

21. Ibid., 158–59.

22. Ibid., 159–62.

23. John Todd, *Early Settlement and Growth of Western Iowa, or Reminiscences* (Des Moines: Historical Department of Iowa, 1906), 152–53; Hubert H. Wubben, *Civil War Iowa and the Copperhead Movement* (Ames: Iowa State Univ. Press, 1980), 20.

24. Gara, 3.

25. "Underground Railway, Jefferson County," WPA Project, Iowa Clipping File 2, SHSI, Des Moines; Christian S. Byrkit, "A Derailment on the Railway Invisible," *AI* 3d ser. 14 (October 1923): 97–100.

26. Gara, 5–6, 79.

27. Siebert, 95; Frederick A. Norwood, *The Story of American Methodism* (Nashville: Abingdon, 1974), 195–96; Gara, 79–81.

28. Gara, 15–16; Garretson, 420–23, 426, 441.

29. Ruth A. Gallaher, "The Inner Light," *Palimpsest* 9 (July 1928): 236; Garretson, 447–49; "Iowa Yearly Meeting of Friends — Centennial, 1863–1865," 55, and Edith Rule and William J. Petersen, *True Tales of Iowa* (Mason City: Privately published, 1932), 290, both Iowa Clipping File 2, SHSI, Des Moines. See particularly the account by Harmon Cook in Darius B. Cook, *History of Quaker Divide* (Dexter IA: Dexter Sentinel, 1914), 202–5.

30. Siebert, 113, 135–36, 141; Harnack, 20–21. Steven Faux and his honors program students at Drake University plan to document and map Underground Railroad routes in Iowa.

31. Louis T. Jones, *The Quakers of Iowa* (Iowa City: SHSI, 1914), 38–47; Charles E. Smith, "The Underground Railroad in Iowa," M.A. thesis, Northeast Missouri State College, Kirksville, 1971, 86, 117–18.

32. George Frazee, "An Iowa Fugitive Slave Case, 1850," *AI* 3d ser. 6 (April 1903): 9–45.

33. Garretson, 430–31; Dykstra, 91.

34. Frazee, 9–10; Garretson, 430–32, 437; Dykstra, 91–92.

35. Louis Jones, 189–90; Garretson, 432; Dykstra, 92–93.

36. Dykstra, 93–95; Garretson, 432–34; Van Ek, 140–41; Louis Jones, 190–91.

37. Louis Jones, 191; Van Ek, 141–42; *The History of Clinton County, Iowa* (Chicago: Western Historical Co., 1879), 542–43; Garretson, 434–36; Dykstra, 96–97.

38. Dykstra, 97; Louis Jones, 188–89; Leola N. Bergmann, *The Negro in Iowa* (Iowa City: SHSI, 1948; repr. 1969), 23–24; Frazee, 44–45.

39. Garretson, 447; "Underground Railroad, Adair County and Guthrie County," WPA Project, Iowa Clipping File 2, SHSI, Des Moines; Lucien M. Kilburn, ed., *History of Adair County, Iowa and Its People*, vol. 1 (Chicago: Pioneer Publishing, 1915), 206.

40. Louis Jones, 191–92; Frederick Lloyd, "John Brown among the Pedee Quakers," *AI* lst ser. 4 (July 1866): 669–70.

41. Bradford, "House Torn Down," from *West Branch [Iowa] Times,* Sept. 1, 1938, WPA Project, Iowa Clipping File 2, SHSI, Des Moines; Gordon Smith, *John Brown in Cedar County* (Tipton IA: Cedar County Historical Society, 1965), 10–11.

42. Mildred Yule Phelps, "John Brown in Springdale," *Cedar County Historical Review* (August 1958): 1–5.

43. *Clinton County History* (Chicago: Western Historical Co., 1879), 415; *History of Clinton County, Iowa* (Clinton: Clinton County Historical Society, 1978), 55; "Underground Railway, Clinton County," WPA Project, Iowa Clipping File 2, SHSI, Des Moines.

44. *Clinton County History* (1879), 415; Van Ek, 135; Bergmann, 25.

45. *Clinton County History* (1879), 415–16; Van Ek, 136–37; *History of Clinton County* (1978), 55; Estelle LePrevost Yule, *History of Clinton County, Iowa* (Privately printed, 1946), 52.

46. Lois Craig, *Village on the Prairie: A Centennial History of Mitchellville, Iowa* (Des Moines: York Printing, 1956), 31–32; James B. Weaver, ed., *Past and Present of Jasper County, Iowa* (Indianapolis: B. F. Bowen, 1912), 373–74.

47. *The History of Appanoose County, Iowa* (Chicago: Western Historical Co., 1878), 371–72; *Biographical and Historical Record of Wayne and Appanoose Counties, Iowa* (Chicago: Interstate, 1886), 679–80.

48. *Appanoose County History*, 373–75; *Wayne and Appanoose Counties*, 681–82.

49. *Des Moines Register*, June 22, 1998; *History of Adams County, Iowa* (Dallas TX: Taylor, 1984), 14, 19, 40–41, 48; J. Loran Ellis, *The Story of Nevin, An Historical Narrative of the Early Days of the New England Colony in Iowa* (Privately published, 1901), 54–55.

50. Siebert, 33, 38; *Nebraska City News Press*, July 29, 1934, reprinted in *Hamburg [Iowa] Reporter,* Oct. 24, 1946, Iowa Clipping File 2, SHSI, Des Moines; Robert W. Handy and Gertrude Handy, "The Remarkable Masters of a First Station on the Underground Railroad," *Iowan* 22 (Summer 1974): 47–48.

51. Siebert, 6–7; Todd, 134–37; S.H. Adams, "'Tabor and Northern' Excursion," *AI* 3d ser. 33 (October 1955): 128–31; *DMR,* February 27, 1927, Iowa Clipping File 2, SHSI, Des Moines; David C. Mott, "Charles Wesley Tolles," *AI* 3d ser. 14 (April 1925): 629.

52. *DMR,* Feb. 20, 1927; Todd, 158–59. Governor Stewart was not authorized to offer so large a reward, the Missouri legislature passed no such legislation, and no state reward was offered. F.C. Shoemaker, "John Browns Missouri Raid," *Missouri Historical Review* 26 (October 1931): 80–83.

53. Todd, 158–61; Irving B. Richman, *John Brown among the Quakers and Other Sketches* (Des Moines: Historical Department of Iowa, 1894), 46–48, quoted in Siebert, 164; "Underground Railroad, John Brown," WPA Project, Iowa Clipping File 2, SHSI.

54. Lloyd, 715; James Connor, "The Antislavery Movement in Iowa," *AI* 3rd ser. 40 (Summer 1970): 352; *DMR,* Mar. 6, 1927. John Teesdale purchased the *Iowa Citizen* in 1860 and renamed it the *Iowa State Register.*

55. Lloyd, 716; Josiah B. Grinnell, *Men and Events of Forty Years* (Boston: D. Lothrop, 1891), 210–12, 218; *DMR,* March 13, 1927; Siebert, 8–9.

56. Grinnell, 216; *DMR,* March 13, 1927; Lloyd, 717. Grinnell had considerable contact with the promoters of the Mississippi and Missouri Railroad, as the Chicago and Rock Island's Iowa subsidiary was known until 1866 when the two railroads were merged to become the Chicago, Rock Island and Pacific Railroad. Grinnell located his town on the divide between the Iowa and Skunk rivers at the suggestion of one of the railroad's surveyors. "From the beginning of the settlement [in 1854], Grinnell had loyally supported the railroad project. He had assisted the company officials in securing the right of way through Iowa and Poweshiek counties." Dwight L. Agnew, "The Mississippi and Missouri Railroad, 1856–1860," *Iowa Journal of History* 11 (July 1953): 225. Tracy was no doubt reluctant to refuse the request of so influential a citizen and friend of the railroad as Grinnell.

57. *History of Johnson County, Iowa* (Iowa City: Privately published, 1883), 468–69; Lloyd, 717–19; Phelps, 10-11; Benjamin F. Gue, *History of Iowa,* vol. 1 (New York: Century, 1903), 382–83.

58. James Connor, "The Antislavery Movement in Iowa," *AI* 3d ser. 40 (Fall 1970): 467; Charles Smith, 117.

59. Grinnell, 216.

60. *Page County History* (Works Progress Administration, 1942), 928, quoted in Bergmann, 35.

61. Kathy Fischer, *In the Beginning There Was Land: A History of Washington County, Iowa* (Washington IA: Washington County Historical Society, 1978), 238; Edna L. Jones, ed., *Nathan Littler's History of Washington County, Iowa, 1835–1875* (Washington IA: Privately published, 1977), 82.

62. August Richter Papers, SHSI, Iowa City, quoted in James L. Hill, "Migration of Blacks to Iowa, 1820–1960," *Journal of Negro History* 66 (1981–82): 296–98.

63. Handy and Handy, 47–48, 50.

64. Scotland County had 157 slaves in 1850 but only 131 in 1860. Slaves in Clark County numbered 405 in 1860, with a value of $171,300. By 1861, that value had fallen to $135,700. Charles Smith, 112–13, 118–19.

65. Wall, 89; Gara, 36, 38, 192–93; Siebert, 358.

Galin Berrier, adjunct instructor in history at Des Moines Area Community College, taught high school advanced placement and community college courses for many years in the northwest suburbs of Chicago. In 1996, as part of his volunteer work at the State Historical Society of Iowa, he prepared an annotated bibliography on the Underground Railroad in Iowa for students participating in History Day. In writing this chapter, Mr. Berrier is grateful to the staff at the Kirkendall Public Library, Ankeny; to Leslie Czechowski at the Burling Library, Grinnell College; to the staff of the State Historical Society of Iowa libraries, especially archivist Ellen Westhafer; and to Floyd Pearce, Beverly Boileau, and Herbert Standing. The staff of Jordan House, West Des Moines, made available the archive of Underground Railroad materials compiled by Dr. Philip Webber of Central College, Pella. At Simpson College, Callie Slater's undergraduate paper on the Underground Railroad pointed the way to additional sources.

Flag and motto of the State of Iowa — "Our Liberties We Prize and Our Rights We Will Maintain"

A Legal History of African-Americans

From the Iowa Territory to the State Sesquicentennial, 1838–1996

by Richard, Lord Acton and Patricia Nassif Acton

African-Americans in Iowa have a rich legal history. From the 1839 Territorial Supreme Court decision about a former slave to the enactment of the Hate Crimes Act in the 1990s, Iowa law has represented at times the best sentiments and at times the worst prejudices of Iowans but ultimately has secured for African-Americans greater freedom, security, and opportunity. This chapter is a selective re-telling of this history, highlighting those constitutional provisions, court cases, and statutes that — for better and worse — have touched the lives of black and white Iowans.

Racial Laws of the Territory of Iowa

From its inception on July 4, 1838, the Territory of Iowa was governed by racially restrictive laws. The act of Congress that established the territory — known as the Organic Act — provided that only "free white male citizen[s]" were entitled to vote at the first election of the Legislative Assembly or to hold office within the territory.[1] In addition, the act extended existing territorial law — including some racially discriminatory provisions — into the new territory, until such time as the legislature were to change or repeal these laws.[2]

The Iowa Territory had been a part of the Territory of Michigan from 1834 to 1836 and the Territory of Wisconsin from 1836 to 1838. Under the Organic Act, Iowa inherited from the Territory of Michigan "An Act to Regulate Blacks and Mulattoes, and to Punish the Kidnapping of Such Persons."[3] Two key provisions of the act inhibited immigration. A black or mulatto could not settle in the territory without filing with the county clerk a court-attested certificate of freedom. Moreover, he or she had to enter into a $500 bond with surety within 20 days of immigrating into the territory.[4]

The first Iowa territorial Legislative Assembly met at Burlington from November 1838 to January 1839 and replaced the Michigan statute with its own "Act to Regulate Blacks and Mulattoes."[5] The law required would-be residents to produce a certificate of freedom and a bond of $500 before being permitted to settle in the territory.

Moreover, the county commissioners were required "to hire out [persons failing to comply] for six months, for the best price in cash that can be had."[6] The act allowed temporary visitors to bring their slaves with them into the Iowa territory.[7]

The act of Congress that established the territory . . . provided that only "free white male citizen[s]" were entitled to vote at the first election . . . or to hold office within the territory.

Charles Mason, Chief Justice of the Supreme Court of the Iowa Territory, who ruled against slavery in Iowa in the 1839 case of Rachel, a Negro Woman v. James Cameron, Sheriff *(SHSI Iowa City)*

News item from the Iowa Territorial Gazette and Burlington Advertiser, May 18, 1839.

Furthermore, if a claimant proved ownership of a runaway slave, the court was required to order the sheriff to arrest the slave and deliver him or her to the claimant.[8]

In addition to the Blacks and Mulattoes Act, Iowa's first legislature passed a quiverful of racial laws. Blacks could not vote[9] or serve in the militia.[10] Common schools were for whites only.[11] A black person could not be a witness in any court against a white person[12] or serve as a juror.[13]

In January 1840, the territorial legislature passed a law declaring marriages between whites and blacks illegal and void.[14] Two years later, a Relief of the Poor Act forbade blacks from gaining a legal settlement in Iowa, thereby denying them entitlement to public assistance.[15]

Thus, the new Territory of Iowa first inherited and then enacted a number of laws that enforced discriminatory treatment against African-Americans. It would be left to the Iowa courts to mitigate the lot of certain individuals who, in the early period of Iowa's history, petitioned for their freedom.

Iowa's First Test of Slavery — The Case of Rachel

The first known case testing the legality of slavery in the Iowa Territory was heard in 1839. The case was *Rachel, a Negro Woman v. James Cameron, Sheriff.*[16] Chief Justice Charles Mason of the Iowa Territorial Supreme Court — who also sat as a district court judge in Des Moines County — presided over the case in Burlington.

The legal proceedings began on May 2, 1839, with the filing of a petition for a writ of habeas corpus by Thomas S. Easton of Burlington. Easton claimed that he was "the owner of a certain negro woman named Rachel aged about 45 years and a slave for life to your said Petitioner."[17] He had purchased Rachel — "a plain Cook, Washer, and Ironer" — at a slave auction in New Orleans on June 27, 1835, for the sum of $385.[18] Subsequently, Easton had moved with Rachel to Burlington, where he became the city engineer and later the coroner.[19] Easton's petition alleged that Rachel was "wrongfully, illegally and fraudulently held in custody and detained" by Burlington's mayor, David Hendershott.[20]

Judge Mason issued the writ of habeas corpus, and on May 6, Hendershott appeared in court and swore that he was not illegally detaining Rachel. He asserted that Rachel "voluntarily remains with me of her own free will and accord as she of right lawfully may according to the constitution and the laws of the land." Rachel herself appeared in court to confirm Hendershott's testimony.[21]

Undeterred, Thomas Easton on May 7 filed another legal action — this time for "replevin" — claiming that Rachel was his "proper goods & chattel" and demanding her return from Hendershott.[22] The same day the sheriff, James Cameron, took Rachel from Hendershott pursuant to a writ issued by the court clerk. But before the sheriff could deliver Rachel back to Easton, Rachel petitioned Judge Mason to issue a writ of habeas corpus, alleging that she was not Easton's property, and that the sheriff was unlawfully detaining her. She signed the petition with her mark.[23]

Judge Mason ordered that Rachel be brought before him "forthwith."[24] All of the parties appeared in open court to present their arguments, following which Judge Mason adjourned court until the next morning. When the court reconvened at 9:00 a.m. on Wednesday, May 8, 1839, Easton had agreed to dismiss his writ of replevin. Judge Mason thereupon ordered "that the said negro woman named Rachel be discharged from custody." Easton was ordered to pay court costs of $2.43.[25]

While the record is silent on the reason for Easton's change of position, Judge Mason at the hearing evidently made known his legal opposition to slavery and his intention to rule against Easton, who then agreed "voluntarily" to dismiss his case. Certainly this was the essence of the case as reported by the local newspaper: "It has been decided by Chief Justice Mason, at the present term of court, *that Slavery cannot exist in Iowa*. This decision settles the question at least for the present."[26]

SLAVERY IN IOWA.—It has been decided by Chief Justice Mason, at the present term of court, *that Slavery cannot exist in Iowa.* This decision settles the question at least for the present.

The Territorial Supreme Court Rules in the Case of Ralph

Two months after his decision in Rachel's habeas corpus action, Chief Justice Mason sat as part of the Iowa Territorial Supreme Court to hear *In the matter of Ralph (a colored man) on Habeas Corpus.*[27] His decision in this case would become the first published opinion of the Iowa Supreme Court and would permanently settle the question of slavery in the Iowa Territory.

Ralph was born a slave in Virginia. In 1830, at about 35 years of age, he was sold as a field hand to Jordan J. Montgomery and later moved with Montgomery to Marion County in northeast Missouri. During 1834, Ralph and Montgomery made a written contract whereby Ralph was permitted to leave Missouri and reside in the future Iowa Territory. In exchange for his freedom, Ralph agreed to pay Montgomery $500, $50 for his hire, and interest.

Ralph went to Dubuque to mine lead but never paid Montgomery on the contract. So in May 1839, Montgomery (who was in financial distress) sent agents to Dubuque to take Ralph and presumably to sell him. The agents swore an affidavit before a justice of the peace that Ralph was the property of Jordan Montgomery and that they were his representatives. Acting under a provision of the recently enacted Blacks and Mulattoes Act,[28] the justice of the peace ordered the sheriff to arrest Ralph and deliver him to the agents. Ralph was handcuffed, taken to Bellevue, and placed on a boat bound for Missouri.

A fellow lead miner from Dubuque named Alexander Butterworth sought a writ of habeas corpus on Ralph's behalf from Judge Thomas S. Wilson, a member of the Iowa Territorial Supreme Court who sat as a district court judge in Dubuque. Armed with the writ, the sheriff got Ralph off the boat, and the parties went before Judge Wilson, who transferred the case to the Supreme Court.

Sitting on Thursday morning, July 4, 1839 — the first birthday of the Territory of Iowa — the Supreme Court heard arguments from attorneys representing Jordan Montgomery and Ralph. The Court ruled the same day, ordering that "Ralph a man of color is free by operation of Law."[29]

1830 bill of sale between William Montgomery (seller) and Jordan J. Montgomery (buyer) of Ralph, whose Iowa Territorial Supreme Court case—In the matter of Ralph (a colored man) on Habeas Corpus — decided he was a free man in the territory of Iowa. (Records of the Marion County, Missouri, Circuit Court)

"William Montgomery for and in consideration of the sum of eight hundred and twenty dollars . . . has granted bargained and sold to the said Jordan J. Montgomery one negro man by the name of Ralph aged about 35 years [and four other slaves]. . . ."

The order of the Iowa Territorial Supreme Court stating that "Ralph a man of color is free by operation of law . . . [and] that he be dicharged from further duress and restraint," signed on July 4, 1839, by Charles Mason, Chief Justice. (SHSI Des Moines)

In his written opinion, Chief Justice Mason rejected Montgomery's argument that Ralph should be regarded as a fugitive slave. Ralph had come into the territory with Montgomery's permission and had remained there for several years; his failure to pay the contract price for his freedom made him liable for the debt, but did not make him a fugitive slave. The 1820 Missouri Compromise[30] had provided that slavery was "forever prohibited" in a swath of the Louisiana Purchase that included the Iowa Territory. While not expressly forfeiting slave property, this law had the effect of declaring that such property did not exist within the territory. Hence, a master who permitted his slave to become a resident of the territory could not thereafter exercise acts of ownership over him.[31]

The opinion concluded with words of high principle: "When, in seeking to accomplish his object [the claimant] illegally restrains a human being of his liberty, it is proper that the laws, which should extend equal protection to men of all colors and conditions, should exert their remedial interposition. We think,

therefore, that the petitioner should be discharged from all custody and constraint, and be permitted to go free."[32]

The case of *In the matter of Ralph* furnished the precedent in 1848 for the freeing of another former slave, Jim Merry (also known as Jim White). An agent from St. Louis named Horace Freeman came to Bloomington (now Muscatine) and, claiming that Merry was a fugitive slave, sought to drag him from the hotel kitchen where he worked. A justice of the peace — citing the case of *Ralph* — found that Merry had come to Iowa with the implied consent of his owner. He ordered that Merry was a free man and fined Freeman $20 plus costs for assault and battery.[33]

Other Early Iowa Cases

Chief Justice Mason's resounding words in the *Ralph* case did not alleviate the unequal treatment that the laws of the Iowa Territory (and, after 1846, the State of Iowa) meted out, as shown in the case of Rose Ann McGregor. Rose Ann, who was black, came from Illinois with her white husband, John G. McGregor, and by 1845 the couple had settled in the future Marion County, Iowa. They were arrested under the law declaring that all marriages between whites and blacks were "illegal and void."[34] After appearing before two different justices of the peace, the case was referred to a Mahaska County grand jury, which failed to return a "true bill" against the McGregors.[35]

Next the board of county commissioners ordered that the provisions of the Blacks and Mulattoes Act requiring the posting of a $500 bond should be enforced. Rose Ann did not comply. The commissioners then ordered that unless she posted the bond by January 29, 1846, the sheriff would "proceed to sell the said Rose Ann McGregor to the highest bidder for the term of six months for the best price in cash to be had."

When January 29 arrived, the sheriff with a deputy battered down the McGregors' door, seized Rose Ann's gun (she was reputed to be a "good marksman"), and placed the prisoner on a horse to escort her to the county seat. However, Rose Ann soon escaped and galloped home; the following day, she appeared before the commissioners to give the required bond.

Rose Ann's case represented the potential problems faced by African-Americans who were in Iowa as free residents. Moreover, despite the decision in *In the matter of Ralph*, instances of slavery continued to be reported in Iowa for a number of years. In 1840, 11 Dubuque families enumerated 16 slaves among their households in the federal census. As late as 1852, a man called L. P. (Tune) Allen from North Carolina brought two young slaves into Iowa for a year and then sold them to a buyer in Missouri.[36] And when slaves escaped into Iowa from slaveholding states, the courts of Iowa were bound to apply the provisions of the federal fugitive slave law.

Such a case, *Daggs v. Frazier*, came before Judge John J. Dyer in the federal court in Burlington in 1850. A Missouri slave owner sought damages against a number of Henry County residents for interfering with the recovery of fugitive slaves, contrary to the Fugitive Slave Law of 1793.[37] The men — Quakers from Salem — were alleged to have helped nine Missouri slaves, including women and children, to escape in 1848. The jury found six of the defendants guilty on four counts and assessed damages at $2,900.[38]

The attorney for the slave owner argued that the law that governed Iowa upon its admission to the union in 1846 permitted a slave owner to recover fugitive slaves in any state — including Iowa and other free states. "Above all, the law should be vindicated — its supremacy confirmed. The idea that any man or society of men, may be permitted to trample upon the plain letter of the law and Constitution, should be severely rebuked."[39]

Exclusion, Discrimination, and the Constitutions of 1844 and 1846

In anticipation of achieving statehood, Iowans voted in 1844 to call a constitutional convention. Delegates convened in Iowa City in October and drafted the Constitution of 1844, which was sent with a petition for statehood to the United States Congress. Because Congress narrowed the proposed boundaries of the future Iowa, Iowans rejected the constitution. A second constitutional convention was called for May 1846, and the delegates drafted the Constitution of 1846. Iowans approved this constitution in August, and President Polk signed the bill admitting Iowa as the twenty-ninth state on December 28, 1846.

At the 1844 convention, the delegates had nearly enacted a constitutional provision barring African-American immigration into the proposed state. The issue arose as delegates considered a petition to give black men the vote. The convention referred the matter to a committee, and one of the delegates offered a resolution "instructing the committee to inquire in the expediency of excluding from the State all persons of color, or admitting them under severe restrictions."[40] Former territorial governor Robert Lucas, now a delegate, argued that such a measure would be unconstitutional, and that "Missouri was nearly kept out of the Union by inserting such a provision in her Constitution."[41]

Despite Lucas's objections, the convention voted to refer the question to the committee. A few days later, the committee recommended against both the suffrage and the exclusionary proposals. The body of the report strongly supported exclusion, arguing "that the two races could not exist in the same government upon an equality without discord and violence." The report nonetheless concluded that a constitutional article prohibiting settlement would not be "expedient."[42]

The issue, however, was not dead. Edward Langworthy, a leading Dubuque miner, sought to insert a provision in the article on the legislative department that "[t]he Legislature shall, at as early a day as practicable, pass laws to prevent the settlement of blacks and mulattoes in this State." He argued that an exclusionary law was necessary to prevent Iowa from being overrun by blacks from its southern neighbor, Missouri.[43] Some delegates urged that

"It is proper that the laws ... should extend equal protection to men of all colors and conditions.... The petitioner should be discharged from all custody and constraint, and be permitted to go free."

— Chief Justice Charles Mason, 1839

Congress would not accept such a clause in the Iowa constitution, and that "it would endanger our admission into the Union." By the slimmest of margins, the delegates rejected the exclusionary provision.[44]

This controversial debate was not repeated when the second constitutional convention met in 1846, but the Constitution of 1846 — which Iowans approved by 9,492 votes to 9,036 on August 3, 1846 — did include discriminatory provisions modeled after those in the proposed Constitution of 1844. Blacks could not vote[45] or be members of the new General Assembly of the State of Iowa.[46] They were excluded from future census taking and from legislative apportionment[47] and could not serve in the militia.[48]

Moreover, all the existing territorial laws — including racially discriminatory laws — continued until such time as they should be displaced by new legislation.[49] It would be five years before the Iowa legislature compiled a new code of laws, thus giving itself the opportunity to reconsider the statutes affecting African-Americans.

Racial Discrimination under the 1851 Code of Iowa

In 1848, a commission of three men chaired by former Chief Justice Mason was appointed to prepare a code of laws for the State of Iowa. In December 1850, the commissioners submitted their draft code to the legislature.[50] The draft contained a mixture of the discriminatory and the non-discriminatory. A new provision inserted by the commissioners was that only a "white male citizen" could practice as a lawyer.[51]

The draft code also contained provisions carried over from prior law. Jurors continued to be limited to "qualified electors,"[52] a standard that excluded blacks, who under the Iowa Constitution did not have the vote.[53] Public school doors were still closed to black children, and the secretary of the district was directed to "take and place on record a list of the names of all white persons in the district between the ages of five and twenty-one years."[54] The property of blacks and mulattoes continued to be exempt from taxation for school purposes.[55]

The draft code contained no racial distinction for membership in the militia[56]— an omission without legal importance, as the Iowa Constitution provided that only white male citizens should comprise the militia.[57] More significantly, the draft code made no mention of race in respect of legal settlements (and hence entitlement to public assistance), the giving of evidence, or marriage.[58] Nor did it reproduce the provisions of

the Blacks and Mulattoes Act.[59]

In enacting the Code of 1851, the legislature endorsed the code commissioners' discriminatory recommendations on legal practice, juries, and schools.[60] The legislature also added some racial provisions that the code drafters had omitted — the word "white" was inserted in the militia section[61] and the section on legal settlements.[62] One newspaper commented that the effect of the latter was "that a negro can never gain a settlement, or become, *legally*, a county pauper."[63]

The legislature passed a newly worded discriminatory section on evidence: "[A]n indian, a negro, a mulatto or black person shall not be allowed to give testimony in any cause wherein a white person is a party."[64] However, the legislature did not reinstate the territorial prohibition on marriage between whites and blacks that the draft code had omitted.[65] A contemporary account of the House of Representatives debate on the marriage chapter in a newspaper that highlighted racial matters during the 1850–51 session made no mention of interracial marriage.[66] Representative Haun of Clinton (who during that same session would sponsor Iowa's most extreme racial law — the Act to Prohibit the Immigration of Free Negroes Into This State), speaking two weeks after the marriage debate, referred to "revolting marital amalgamation."[67] The overwhelming probability is that Haun and other legislators did not realize they were permitting marriage between the races in enacting the Code of 1851. Similarly, the legislators' speeches suggest they were unaware that they were repealing the Blacks and Mulattoes Act by enacting section 28 of the Code of 1851, which had the effect of repealing all prior statutes not included in the Code.[68]

Indeed, the strong racial bias of the legislators is shown by their enactment of one of the few general laws passed in the 1850–51 session apart from the Code of 1851 itself. This law — which excluded all black immigration into the state — represented the nadir of discriminatory legislation in Iowa.

The 1851 Exclusionary Law

During January 1851, while the Iowa legislature was still grappling with the code, Rep. William G. Haun, a flour miller and whisky distiller from Clinton County,[69] introduced a bill in the House of Representatives "to prohibit the immigration of free negroes into this state."[70] At second reading,[71] Haun, referring to the Blacks and Mulattoes Act, said: "I contend that if we have the

"[F]rom and after the passage of this act, no free negro or mulatto, shall be permitted to settle in this state."

—The Exclusionary Act, approved February 5, 1851

right to restrict, we also have the right to prohibit altogether."[72] He expressed his scorn for the idea of equality between the races: "Wherever the experiment has been tried, or wherever it may be tried it will fail. One or the other must and will have the ascendancy even at the risk of extermination of the weaker party."[73]

Haun argued that other states had passed exclusionary measures,[74] and that most slave states had forbidden manumission unless former slaves were taken immediately out of the state. He estimated that 40,000 slaves would be freed annually and that many would move to Iowa if an exclusionary law was not passed. "Shall we allow our beautiful prairies to be over-run . . . or shall we not rather say to the southern States, take care of your own property [and] if you wish to rid yourselves of your slaves, take means to send them to their native Africa."[75]

Three days later, the bill came up for further debate in the House of Representatives,[76] and several members spoke in opposition. Representative Gamble of Louisa County declared that the existing Blacks and Mulattoes Act "was all sufficient to guard the interests of the State."[77] Representative Folsom of Johnson and Iowa counties said that Iowa had no constitutional power to exclude blacks who had been made citizens of New York and Connecticut. Representative Preston of Linn County argued that the proposed law violated the Northwest Ordinance of 1787, and Representative Wilson of Henry County declared that "the bill could not pass without a violation of the bill of rights, prefixed to the Constitution of the State."[78]

Despite these opposing voices, Haun's bill passed the House of Representatives by a margin of 20 votes to 15.[79] The Senate amended the measure to provide: "This act to take effect, and be in force, by publication in the *Iowa True Democrat,* a weekly newspaper published in Mount Pleasant" — ironically the most racially progressive newspaper in the state.[80] The amended bill passed the Senate by nine votes to seven,[81] and the House concurred in the Senate amendment.[82]

The exclusionary act, approved on February 5, 1851, provided: "[F]rom and after the passage of this act, no free negro or mulatto, shall be permitted to settle in this state."[83] County officials were required to notify offenders to leave the state within three days and, failing such, to arrest and bring them before a justice of the peace or county judge. A fine of $2 per day would be imposed for each day that offenders remained in the state, and they would be imprisoned in the county jail until fines and costs

Petition to the Iowa legislature signed by 33 black men and women from Muscatine, led by Alexander Clark Sr., to repeal "An Act to Prohibit the Immigration of free Negroes into this State" (SHSI Iowa City)

were paid.[84] However, "all free negroes now living in this state, who have complied with the laws now in force, shall be permitted to remain here, and enjoy such property as they may now possess, or may hereafter acquire."[85]

The depth of feeling about the exclusionary law in Iowa's African-American community can be gauged from an 1855 petition to the legislature signed by 33 black men and women from Muscatine County.[86] The petitioners — headed by Alexander Clark, Iowa's most prominent black leader of the nineteenth century — demanded the repeal of the exclusionary law: "We your petitioners deem it unnecessary to say anything about the injustice of the Law, or its oppressive influences upon us as free Colored Citizens of the United States of America but we will submit to the honest consideration of your Honorable body ever hoping that the god of heaven may guide and direct your acts in favor of Justice and oppressed humanity."[87]

The editor of the *Iowa True Democrat* — in whose pages notice of the exclusionary law was supposed to be published — reacted with predictable outrage: "[W]e think our legislature serves the Devil."[88] But despite the Senate amendment, the newspaper never published the law,[89] thus raising the question of whether the law had indeed taken effect. Moreover, the law did not appear with the Code of 1851 itself, but in the separate, slim volume of other laws passed during the 1850–51 session.[90] This added to the confusion over the law's validity, and during the 1850s it is known to have been invoked only once.

The episode occurred in June 1857, when the city marshal of Keokuk served notices on certain black residents directing them to leave town within three days pursuant to the exclusionary law.[91] A newspaper hostile to the marshal reported that "a half score or so of our colored population" were involved,[92] but that the marshal in fact had contemplated "a wholesale business which he has abandoned on 'sober second thought.' "[93]

It is unclear whether anyone was actually expelled from Keokuk. However, during the decade following the enactment of the exclusionary law, the increasing number of black residents in Iowa proves that the law in general lay dormant on the statute books. Indeed, the black population in Iowa rose from 333 in 1850 to 1,069 in 1860.[94]

The Pre–Civil War Period

The years preceding the Civil War saw dramatic political change in Iowa. Congress's passage in 1854 of the Kansas-Nebraska Act — which permitted the people of Kansas and Nebraska to decide whether their territories would be slave or free — solidified anti-slavery sentiment in Iowa. The anti-slavery Whig candidate, James W. Grimes, was narrowly elected governor of Iowa in 1854, thus breaking the Democrats' continuous hold on power since the founding of the territory. Grimes would soon become the preeminent member of the newly formed Republican Party.

An extraordinary case in Burlington in 1855, brought under the Fugitive Slave Law of 1850,[95] riveted Governor Grimes and other Iowans. The case began one day in June, when Dr. Edwin

James, a "station-master" on Burlington's Underground Railroad, crossed the Mississippi River to Illinois accompanied by a black man aged about 50. They were set upon by two agents for a Missourian named Thomas Rutherford, who claimed that the man was a fugitive slave called Dick. All parties appeared before George Frazee, the commissioner for the United States Court for the District of Iowa in Burlington.[96]

"Dick" was remanded in custody for a few days while Rutherford's son was brought from Missouri to identify him. Governor Grimes wrote to his wife (who was visiting relatives in Maine): "I shall certainly furnish no aid to the man-stealers, and it has been determined that the negro shall have able counsel, and a resort to all legal means for release, before any other is resorted to."[97] Grimes sent for a state court judge from Keokuk, and a writ of habeas corpus was prepared and ready to be served, if intervention became necessary.[98]

The hearing commenced on June 26, 1855, and the courtroom was "filled to suffocation by excited people." But to the amazement of them all, the claimant's son, when asked to identify "Dick," said "that he did not know him, and that he had never seen him before." Commissioner Frazee ordered that "Dick" be released, and the spectators in the courtroom and those outside erupted in cheers. "Dick" was "conducted triumphantly from the room" and was soon on his way to freedom in Canada.[99]

Although Iowans' sentiments were decidedly against the Fugitive Slave Law, the state's many discriminatory statutes still were in force. One was the provision whereby "an Indian, a negro, a mulatto or black person shall not be allowed to give testimony in any cause wherein a white person is a party."[100] This provision was upheld in a case decided the year after "Dick's" victory.

A black businessman named Thomas C. Motts sued two white defendants in the Muscatine County district court, seeking payment for some cords of wood.[101] The judge found for Motts in the sum of $304.[102] The defendants appealed to the Iowa Supreme Court on the ground that the district court had erroneously excluded a black witness called by the defendants to testify on their behalf. The Supreme Court, in the 1856 case of *Motts v. Usher & Thayer*,[103] upheld the judgment. The Court reasoned that it was irrelevant that the testimony was offered by the white party. "This language is explicit, and most clearly renders the witness incompetent."[104]

A few months later, the Iowa legislature repealed the

"I shall certainly furnish no aid to the man-stealers, and it has been determined that the negro shall have able counsel, and a resort to all legal means for release, before any other is resorted to."

— Gov. James W. Grimes, June 24, 1855

statutory exclusion of black testimony,[105] because — according to Governor Grimes — "several criminals have 'gone unwhipped of justice' on account of this disability of witnesses."[106] Henceforth, under the new statute, the testimony of "[e]very human being of sufficient capacity to understand the obligation of an oath" would be permitted in legal proceedings.[107]

The Constitution of 1857

In January 1857, another constitutional convention met in Iowa City, but its political composition was very different from the conventions of 1844 and 1846. Those conventions — and indeed all of Iowa politics from 1838 to 1854 — had been dominated by the Democrats. On the heels of the formation of Iowa's Republican Party in 1856, 21 of the 36 delegates at the 1857 constitutional convention were Republican.[108]

The convention was summoned to amend the Constitution of 1846 largely in relation to banking, but racial issues occupied much of its time.[109] The previous month, the now Republican legislature had repealed the code provision that prevented blacks from being witnesses in court. The delegates enshrined this change in the new constitution, approving language in the bill of rights that "any party to any judicial proceeding shall have the right to use as a witness, or take the testimony of, any other person. . . who may be cognizant of any fact material to the case."[110]

There was much wrangling over the education of black youths. Finally the convention agreed on language that left open the question of segregated or integrated schools or, as one scholar has put it, "would make possible the separate education of negroes and whites."[111] Article 9, "Education and School Lands," provided in part: "The Board of Education shall provide for the education of all the youths of the State, through a system of common schools."[112]

The convention refused to enshrine black exclusion in the new constitution, tabling by a vote of 25 to 8 a clause that would have prohibited black immigration into the state.[113] Furthermore, the delegates rejected an amendment to remove from the bill of rights the guarantee of jury trial "in cases involving the life, or liberty of an individual,"[114] thereby ensuring the availability of jury trials for fugitive slaves.[115]

The convention voted to retain the word "white" in the militia clause.[116] Similarly, the word "white" was retained in the clauses on the census, electoral apportionment, and qualifications for membership of the General Assembly.[117] The delegates decided to put the question of whether to delete the word "white" from the article on suffrage to a separate popular vote, at the same election that voters would be asked to approve the new constitution.[118]

In August 1857, Iowa voters narrowly approved the new constitution, but they rejected black male suffrage by the huge majority of 49,267 votes to 8,479.[119] Not until after the Civil War would public opinion change sufficiently to remove this and other discriminatory provisions enshrined in the Constitution of 1857.

The Exclusionary Law Struck Down and Repealed

In February 1863, the constitutionality of the 1851 Act to Prohibit the Immigration of Free Negroes Into This State[120] was tested in the Polk County district court. The plaintiff was Archie P. Webb, a Mississippi-born slave. During the Civil War, Webb was living in Arkansas. When his master left to join the Confederate forces, Webb absconded to the Union camp at Helena, Arkansas, where he was "received into service" in the Dubuque Battery (3rd Iowa Light Artillery). He was permitted to accompany an officer on a recruitment trip to Iowa, and there he remained. Webb worked for Dr. James Wright in Delaware County, and later, when Wright came to Des Moines as the Iowa secretary of state, Webb found employment with a farmer in Delaware Township, Polk County.[121]

Webb moved to Polk County in late November or early December 1862. On January 8, 1863, he was served with a notice, signed by a township trustee, that he must leave Iowa within three days "or we will commence proceedings against you to compel your removal" under the exclusionary act.[122] Webb refused to leave and resisted efforts to seize him, so on January 20, the local sheriff arrested Webb and took him before a justice of the peace.[123] The latter — seeking to avoid the use of the exclusionary law — wanted Webb to admit he was a slave, and not a "free negro" to whom the law applied. Webb "proudly answered that he was a Free Man, and entitled to immediate release!" He was sent to the county jail.[124]

Contemporary accounts give three interlocking reasons for the action against Webb: an attempt to obstruct President Lincoln's Emancipation Proclamation, which had just taken effect;[125] fear of thousands of free blacks coming into the state;[126] and resentment

Gov. James W. Grimes, the anti-slavery Whig Party candidate elected governor of Iowa in 1854 (SHSI Des Moines)

Notice served on Archie P. Webb to leave Polk County in accordance with the Exclusionary Act of 1851, later ruled unconstitutional by Judge John H. Gray in Archie P. Webb v. I. W. Griffith, *1863 (SHSI Iowa City)*

"a native-born free man of color, whether born free or a slave and manumitted, is a citizen within the meaning of the National Constitution."[132]

Judge Gray further ruled that the exclusionary law violated the Iowa Constitution's guarantee that "[a]ll *men* are by nature free and independent, and have certain unalienable rights," since the term *all men* meant "nothing less than all the human race . . . as may be within the bounds of the State of Iowa."[133] The law also violated state constitutional guarantees against unreasonable searches and seizures[134] and the right of jury trials in criminal prosecutions.[135] Therefore, "the judgment of the Court is that the law under which the plaintiff was arrested is inoperative and void [and] that the plaintiff herein is entitled to his liberty."[136] Notice of appeal was filed with the Iowa Supreme Court, but no appeal was ever heard.[137]

A year after Judge Gray's historic decision, the Iowa legislature repealed the exclusionary law.[138] The preamble to the repealing act expressed doubt whether the law was actually in effect, and stated that attempts to enforce the law had been "contrary to the wishes and intentions of a large majority of the people of this State."[139] The *Daily State Register,* after referring to the case of Archie Webb, "who had committed no other crime than that of possessing a black skin," rejoiced that the legislature had now "put it out of the power of other scoundrels to imitate the example of the Polk County Butternuts in the arrest of loyal blacks."[140]

In addition to repealing the exclusionary law, the 1864 legislature removed the word "white" from the section on legal settlement, thus permitting black residents to qualify for public assistance.[141] It also passed a joint resolution that endorsed paying black soldiers the same pay as white soldiers.[142] Influenced by national events, the white iceberg of discrimination was beginning to crack.

Black Male Suffrage and Other Constitutional Amendments, 1865–1880

In June 1865, the Republican State Convention met at Des Moines and adopted as an amendment to a resolution: "Therefore we are in favor of amending the Constitution of our State by striking out the word WHITE in the article on Suffrage."[143] The opponents of the amendment urged that it was premature to put this question to the voters. However, three speakers in favor of the amendment swayed the convention.

Henry O'Connor, a leading lawyer from Muscatine, spoke

by white laborers at the employment of black ex-slaves (known as "contraband") labor.[127]

On January 20 — the day of his arrest — Webb filed a petition for a writ of habeas corpus in the district court, alleging that he had been unlawfully arrested and restrained, and challenging the constitutionality of the exclusionary act.[128] The case was tried before the 31-year-old Judge John H. Gray, who recently had chaired Des Moines's public meeting in support of the Emancipation Proclamation.[129]

On February 2, 1863, Judge Gray — in a lengthy and impassioned opinion — ruled the exclusionary law unconstitutional and ordered that Archie Webb be released. The judge dismissed as "too technical" the argument that the law had never taken effect because it had not been published in the *Iowa True Democrat.*[130] However, the exclusionary law contravened the clause of the U.S. Constitution that provided: "The Citizens of each State shall be entitled to all Privileges and Immunities of Citizens in the several States."[131] He rejected the argument that blacks were not "citizens" within the meaning of this provision, reasoning that eloquently of "the long oppressed but ever loyal and ever faithful negroes, to whose devotion so many of our brave soldiers owe their escape from rebel dungeons and fearful death. . . ."[144] Congressman Hiram Price, in a very powerful speech, "pressed upon the Convention the duty of meeting the question now presented, squarely and fairly and giv[ing] to it a just and noble decision."[145] Finally, Lt. Gov. Enoch Eastman demanded of the delegates: "How can you... insist that loyal negroes shall vote in South Carolina when you refuse to allow the colored soldiers of your own Iowa colored regiment to vote here?"[146]

When the votes were cast, the convention decided by 513 1/2 to 242 1/2 to adopt the amendment. Gov. William M. Stone, in his speech accepting renomination, received the loudest cheers when he said: "[T]he Convention would have been disgraced by the rejection of the amendment added."[147]

The Democrats joined with anti-suffrage Republicans to form a "Soldiers Ticket," which nominated Thomas H. Benton for governor. The Soldiers Ticket adopted a resolution opposing a constitutional amendment to strike the word "white" from the suffrage article. Black male suffrage was the main issue of the campaign, with Governor Stone advocating it in every speech. He triumphed in the election against Benton by 16,375 votes.[148]

However, Stone's majority in 1863 had been much larger — 38,174 votes.[149] One Republican newspaper said of this decline: "[W]e cannot be blind to the fact that the question of Negro Suffrage in the State had a great influence in the matter."[150] Nonetheless, Stone had won handsomely, and although three more years would pass before the constitutional amendment was ratified, Stone's 1865 victory was the key moment. A leading scholar has written: "[W]hen Governor Stone withstood the demagogic assault of Thomas Hart Benton Jr. . . . there was no turning back. . . . Thus 1868's outcome may be seen as mainly a ratification of 1865's result."[151]

Under the Iowa Constitution of 1857, a constitutional amendment had to be approved by two successive General Assemblies and then ratified in a popular referendum.[152] In his second inaugural speech in January 1866, Governor Stone urged the legislature to adopt a constitutional amendment permitting black suffrage, thus submitting directly to the people "this much agitated question."[153] He stressed the part played by 700 black Iowa troops in the Civil War. They had sent a memorial to the legislature asking for the vote,[154] and Governor Stone urged that "the prayer of this memorial should be heard and granted."[155]

The House of Representatives voted on a series of propositions to strike the word "white" from all the relevant sections of the Constitution. In the most important of these, the House approved a proposal for a constitutional amendment to the suffrage clause[156] by 69 votes to 18.[157] It voted heavily in favor of deleting the word "white" from the constitutional provisions on census, Senate apportionment, House apportionment, and the militia.[158] However, the House voted against an amendment to remove the word "white" from the constitutional provision on qualifications to serve in the legislature.[159] Then the Senate proceeded to approve the House's five resolutions to amend the Constitution by 36 votes to 9.[160]

In the summer of 1867, the Republicans nominated Col. Samuel Merrill for governor and adopted a platform that called for constitutional amendments "as will secure the rights of the ballot, the protection of the law, and equal rights to all men irrespective of color, race, or religion."[161] The Democrats nominated former territorial Chief Justice Charles Mason as their candidate for governor, and adopted a platform plank reiterating their opposition to the proposed suffrage amendment.[162] Merrill won the election by the impressive margin of 89,144 votes to 62,657.[163]

In his inaugural address in January 1868, Governor Merrill urged the legislature to maintain its progressive course: "Let us not fail at this session to advance the work inaugurated by our predecessors, of giving to our colored population the enjoyment of those political privileges which have hitherto been denied to them."[164]

The following month, a convention of African-American delegates from various Iowa cities met in Des Moines to support the cause of black male suffrage. Alexander Clark wrote and delivered a stirring address to the convention, which was published in several leading Iowa newspapers. He declared: "We ask only that privilege which is now given to every white, native-born or adopted, male citizen of our State — the privilege of the ballot-box . . . and in this we simply ask that the 'two streams of loyal blood which it took to conquer one, mad with treason,' shall not be separated at the ballot box; that he who can be trusted with an army musket, which makes victory and protects the nation, shall also be intrusted with that boon of American liberty, the ballot."[165]

During the second successive Iowa General Assembly to consider the issue, which convened in January 1868, the House passed by 65 votes to 18 a joint resolution on the proposed five

*Judge Gray ruled that the exclusionary law violated the Iowa Constitution's guarantee that "all men are by nature free and independent . . ." since the term **all men** meant "nothing less than all the human race . . . as may be within the bounds of the State of Iowa."*

"We ask only

that privilege which

is now given

to every white,

native-born or adopted,

male citizen

of our State

— the privilege of

the ballot-box."

— Alexander Clark Sr.,
Speech to the African-American
Convention in Des Moines,
February, 1868

amendments striking out the word "white" from the constitutional provisions on suffrage, census, Senate apportionment, House apportionment, and the militia.[166] The Senate in turn passed the joint resolution by 40 votes to 7.[167]

The year 1868 was a presidential election year, and Ulysses S. Grant was the Repub-lican nominee. The Republicans triumphed in November. Grant duly won Iowa, while the suffrage amendment to the Constitution was passed in a referendum by an official vote of 105,384 to 81,119. The other four constitutional amendments passed by slightly larger margins.[168] Thirty years after the founding of the Territory of Iowa, black men now had the vote. As qualified electors, they automatically became eligible to be jurors.[169]

At the end of December 1868, delegates from seven Iowa cities met in a "Colored State Convention" at Muscatine. They endorsed a resolution proposed by Alexander Clark: *"Resolved,* That this Convention, in behalf of the colored citizens of Iowa, tender their sincere thanks to the Republican party for their noble and manly effort in behalf of manhood suffrage at the November election, by which our enfranchisement was achieved by 25,000 majority."[170]

The one remaining discriminatory provision in Iowa's Constitution retained the words "free white" in the qualifications for election to the legislature.[171] A proposal to delete this from the Iowa Constitution passed the General Assembly in 1878 and 1880; in November 1880, Iowa voters approved the constitutional amendment by 90,237 votes to 51,943.[172] Constitutional discrimination against African-Americans in Iowa had finally ended.

The Iowa Supreme Court Rules on Equal Access to Schools and Common Carriers

Alexander Clark was a man of many parts — a political leader, an orator, a barber, an investor in Muscatine real estate, a conductor on the Underground Railroad, and a recruiter for the Union

army.[173] Clark was also a father of three children and cared passionately about their education. In 1867 he wrote in a letter to the *Muscatine Journal:* "[M]y personal object is that my children attend where they can receive the largest and best advantages of learning."[174]

Clark noted the contrasts between Muscatine's segregated schools. The white schools were conveniently located in the city, while the black school was "nearly a mile from many of the small colored children, keeping more than a third of them from school." The white schools had "globes and charts and competent teachers," whose salaries ranged from $700 to $900 a year. The black school had none of these advantages, and its teacher was paid a yearly salary of from $150 to $200. The white schools "have prepared and qualified pupils by the hundred for the high school; the colored school has never prepared or qualified one that could pass an examination for any class in the high school."[175]

On September 10, 1867, Alexander Clark's 12-year-old daughter, Susan, presented herself at Muscatine's white "Grammar School No. 2" and was refused entry. That same day, the principal of the school wrote to Alexander Clark: "I am authorized by the School Board of this city to refuse your children admittance into Grammar School No. 2."[176]

Clark, as "next friend" of his daughter, filed a lawsuit in the Muscatine County District Court, asking for a writ of mandamus to compel the school board to admit Susan into Grammar School No. 2.[177] The district court ordered the writ, and the board of directors appealed, claiming that it had the right to maintain a separate school for black children. In *Clark v. The Board of Directors, etc.,*[178] the Iowa Supreme Court affirmed the district court's decision, holding that children of color could not be refused admission to Iowa's district schools.

In its opinion, the Court reviewed the history of Iowa's discriminatory school statutes, but noted that the Constitution of 1857 had created a statewide board of education, which was required to "provide for the education of *all the youths of the State,* through a system of common schools."[179] The Court reasoned that this constitutional provision and subsequent legislation[180] removed from the board of directors all discretion to decide "what *youths* shall be admitted."[181]

The Court rejected the board's argument that because it maintained several schools within the district, it could decide which of the several schools a student could attend and, pursuant to this

Alexander Clark Jr. — standing top row fifth from left — the first African-American student enrolled in the University of Iowa College of Law, shown with his 1879 graduating class (University of Iowa College of Law)

discretion, could require Susan Clark to attend the black school. If the board could require African-American children to attend separate schools, it equally could require German, Irish, French, English, and children of other nationalities to attend separate schools. The Court concluded: "[T]he board cannot, in their discretion . . . deny a youth admission to any particular school because of his or her nationality, religion, color, clothing or the like."[182]

In 1870, the Iowa legislature struck out the words "white male" from the statute concerning the qualifications to practice law.[183] Now Alexander Clark could realize an even higher ambition for his children, and his son, Alexander Clark Jr., became the first African-American student to enroll in the university's law department in Iowa City, receiving his law degree in 1879. Clark Sr. himself attended the law school in 1883 and graduated the following year.[184]

Despite Susan Clark's resounding victory against the Muscatine school board, school discrimination was not eliminated altogether. In 1875, two lawsuits were brought against the Keokuk school district, alleging that black children were denied admission to Keokuk's grammar and high schools. In both cases the Iowa Supreme Court, relying on its decision in *Clark v. The Board of Directors, etc.*, ruled in favor of the children.[185]

Another leading case was the Iowa Supreme Court's 1873 decision in *Coger v. The North West Union Packet Co.*[186] The plaintiff, 20-year-old Emma Coger, was a school teacher in Quincy, Illinois. While in Keokuk, she purchased a ticket to return to Quincy by steamboat. Through a fellow passenger, she obtained a dinner ticket to eat in the whites-only section of the boat. When she sat down at the ladies' table, an officer asked her to leave. She refused, and the captain of the boat was called for. Coger testified in court about what happened next:

"The captain came and said, 'Get up from here.' I said I would not, and he caught hold of the chair. . . . As he jerked the chair out I

caught hold of the table, and when he jerked me off, the table cloth came off as I did. I still held to the table. He said, 'Go out on the guards.' I said I would not. I was both hungry and angry. He caught hold of me, and as he did so I caught hold of his sleeve at the wrist. He could not get loose, but endeavored to get his hand free. He struck me over the knuckles with his hands. Failing in this, he struck me twice with his fist on the head. He then took me out through the ladies' and gentlemen's cabin. I did not get any dinner or my money back, nor did I get my ticket back."[187]

Coger brought an action for damages for assault and battery against the steamboat company, and the jury returned a verdict in her favor for damages of $250.[188] The company appealed, and the Iowa Supreme Court affirmed the judgment. "In our opinion," the Court declared, "the plaintiff was entitled to the same rights and privileges while upon defendant's boat, notwithstanding the negro blood, be it more or less, admitted to flow in her veins, which were possessed and exercised by white passengers." Relying on doctrines of natural law, its prior decision in *Clark*, and state and federal constitutional guarantees, the Iowa Supreme Court concluded that "equal rights and equal protection shall be secured to all regardless of color or nationality."[189]

The persistent problem of discrimination in accommodations was illustrated by the 1885 case of *Bowlin v. Lyon*,[190] which was decided upon facts that took place before the enactment of the 1884 Iowa Civil Rights Act. In *Bowlin*, the plaintiff was refused entry to a Cedar Rapids roller skating rink because of his color and brought an action for damages against the rink operators. The district court sustained the defendants' demurrer to the petition, and the plaintiff appealed.

The Iowa Supreme Court affirmed a judgment for the rink operators, distinguishing their business from those — like innkeepers or the carrier in *Coger* — in which "the general public has such interest as that they are properly the subject of regulation by law."[191] A skating rink, by contrast, was "essentially a private business," and the defendants were entitled to limit their invitations to certain classes of individuals.[192] The Court concluded: "The legal rights of the parties would not have been different from what they are if defendants had excluded plaintiff on account of the cut of his coat or the color of his hair, instead of the color of his skin."[193]

Iowa Civil Rights Act of 1884 and Ensuing Case Law

In 1883, to general astonishment, the United States Supreme Court declared unconstitutional an 1875 federal act that had guaranteed equal accommodations in inns, public conveyances, theaters, and other places of amusement.[194] There was deep concern among Iowa's black community.

A hundred people met at the African Methodist Episcopal Church in Cedar Rapids to protest the Supreme Court's decision. They passed a resolution that read: "[A]s a race we will fight unceasing warfare on this line; . . . we will agitate and agitate until there is not left one clause or legal statute in our broad land that a stranger could tell there are two races living here under one flag."[195] In Des Moines, black residents held a public meeting "to give vent to their indignation."[196]

Speakers at a crowded meeting at the federal courthouse in Keokuk called for the state legislature to pass its own civil rights bill during the next legislative session.[197] Some Republican newspapers promised that the legislature would forthwith pass a civil rights law, while Democrat newspapers wrote that representatives of their party would not oppose such a law.[198]

In his inaugural address in January 1884, Republican Gov. Buren R. Sherman declared: "I am in favor of such legislation in our own State, as will secure [civil] rights to every class of our citizens."[199] Before the end of March 1884, the Iowa General Assembly had passed a civil rights bill. The vote in the Senate was 32 votes to 0;[200] and in the House of Representatives, 81 votes to 0.[201] Three states already had civil rights legislation prior to

1884, but Iowa was one of the first to legislate in response to the decision of the U.S. Supreme Court.[202]

Section 1 of the Iowa Civil Rights Act provided: "[A]ll persons within this state shall be entitled to the full and equal enjoyment of the accommodations, advantages, facilities and privileges of inns, public conveyances, barber shops, theaters and other places of amusement; subject only to the conditions and limitations established by law, and applicable alike to every person."[203]

Section 2 made violation of the act a misdemeanor, which under Iowa law was punishable by imprisonment in the county jail for not more than a year and/or a fine of not more than $500.[204] The Iowa Constitution limited the jurisdiction of justices of the peace to non-felony cases in which the punishment did not exceed 30-days' imprisonment or a fine of $100.[205] Thus, a charge under the Iowa Civil Rights Act would have to be tried in the district court following indictment by a grand jury, rather than summarily before a justice of the peace.

The first conviction under the Iowa Civil Rights Act occurred two years later. An Oskaloosa barber named Ben Hall was indicted for refusing to shave a man named C.R. Bennett. Official reports indicate that both men were black.[206] Hall was convicted in the Mahaska County District Court and fined $5.[207] He appealed, and the Iowa Supreme Court in the 1887 case of *State v. Hall*[208] reversed the conviction. The indictment had stated that Hall gave no reason for his refusal to shave Bennett, and this was insufficient to sustain a charge under the Iowa Civil Rights Act. The Court observed that there could be many reasons why Hall refused to shave this customer which would not violate the act. "In such case the defendant would perhaps be lacking in politeness in not giving the reason for his refusal, but this would be no crime."[209]

In 1892, the Iowa legislature amended the Iowa Civil Rights Act by adding to the list of public places covered by the act. The new categories were "restaurants, chop houses, eating houses, lunch counters, and all other places where refreshments are served" and "bath houses."[210] The amending bill passed the House by 61 votes to 7, with 32 absent or not voting.[211] In the Senate, two of the most conservative Democrat senators spoke in support of the amending bill "as in keeping with the general feeling of the times and as a matter of justice to the colored race."[212] The bill passed the Senate by 45 votes to 2.[213] The Young Men's Colored Republican Club, at an enthusiastic meeting in Des Moines, passed

"[A]s a race we will fight unceasing warfare on this line; . . . we will agitate and agitate until there is not left one clause or legal statute in our broad land that a stranger could tell there are two races living here under one flag."

— **Protest resolution in Cedar Rapids, 1883**

a resolution endorsing the action of the General Assembly.[214]

Thirteen years after the legislature amended the Iowa Civil Rights Act, the meaning of the term "eating house" was tested in the 1905 case of *Humburd v. Crawford*.[215] A black juror named W.M. Humburd was not allowed to sit at a dinner prepared by the defendants in their home for jurors deliberating a civil case in the Polk County District Court. Humburd brought suit and was awarded $50 in damages.[216] The Iowa Supreme Court affirmed the judgment in Humburd's favor, finding that the defendants had maintained a public "eating house," rather than a private boarding house, as claimed. Because the evidence indicated that "meals were served by defendants to whomsoever came, at a uniform price . . . this was a sufficient holding out to the world to constitute it a public eating house."[217]

However, the next case to come before the Iowa Supreme Court under the Iowa Civil Rights Act resulted in a more restrictive reading of the statute. The plaintiff was Sue M. Brown of Des Moines, one of Iowa's outstanding black women. Mrs. Brown had founded the Intellectual Improvement Club for Negroes in Des Moines in 1906 and went on to head numerous other organizations.[218]

Sue Brown and her husband, the eminent lawyer and black leader, S. Joe Brown (who had successfully represented W.M. Humburd in his appeal), had attended the Des Moines Pure Food Show sponsored by the Des Moines Retail Grocers' Association. One of the booths was leased by the defendant J.H. Bell Company, which was offering cups of its coffee to ticket holders. White patrons were served coffee, but the person in charge of the booth refused to serve the Browns. Mrs. Brown brought suit, claiming $1,000 in damages for "humiliation, discrimination, and chagrin."

In the 1910 decision, *Brown v. The J.H. Bell Company*,[219] the Iowa Supreme Court affirmed a judgment against Mrs. Brown. Noting that the Iowa Civil Rights Act must be "strictly construed,"[220] the Court reasoned that the defendant was a lessee of the Retail Grocers' Association, which had paid rent to occupy a space for advertising purposes rather than to conduct a "place of amusement" within the statute.[221] Nor was the booth encompassed within the general phrase "all other places where refreshments were served." The coffee being a donation for advertising purposes, the defendant "could refuse to serve any person, no matter what his color, for any reason, or for no reason."[222]

Chief Justice Evans entered a strong dissent. The Pure Food

Des Moines attorney S. Joe Brown and his wife, Sue M. Brown, who both confronted racial discrimination throughout their lives (SHSI Des Moines)

Show, he wrote, was a quasi-public event which, in its entirety, was of the type covered by the civil rights statute. "The statute is simple and direct. . . . Its manifest purpose was and is to protect this burdened race against the further burden of public discrimination and humiliation."[223]

The 1923 Amendment to the Iowa Civil Rights Act

A review of case law in the decades after the enactment of the Iowa Civil Rights Act of 1884 indicates that it was rarely used to redress civil rights violations. The *Humburd* and *Brown* cases had been actions for money damages (although such damages were not specifically provided for in the act); the plaintiff in *Humburd* was successful, while the plaintiff in *Brown* was not. Attempts to bring criminal convictions under the act drew equally mixed results.

According to one scholar, only three criminal convictions under the Iowa Civil Rights Act were obtained between the years 1884 and 1923.[224] The first was the Mahaska County District Court conviction that was reversed by the Iowa Supreme Court in the 1887 case of *State v. Hall*. The second was a conviction in Clayton County District Court in 1905, resulting in a $10 fine.[225] The third was a 1917 conviction in Monroe County, resulting in a $5 fine.[226]

The reason for the lack of convictions under the Iowa Civil

James B. Morris Sr., attorney and publisher of the Iowa Bystander *from 1922 to1974 (SHSI Des Moines)*

understood."[232]

In November 1923, a young black woman named Dottie Blagburn sat in a section reserved for whites only in a Des Moines theater. She refused to leave, and the manager had her removed. With the backing of the NAACP, the theater owner was charged under the Iowa Civil Rights Act in the Des Moines municipal court. An all-white jury convicted the theater owner.[233]

Two more convictions are known to have been obtained in the next five years. Sue Brown — now president of the Des Moines branch of the NAACP — reported in 1928 that since the amendment to the civil rights statute, "three persons have been convicted in the criminal courts for the infringement of the civil rights of Negro citizens."[234]

The following decade was a bleak one for civil rights cases. One scholar has written of the years prior to 1939: "Considerable research in various periodicals revealed no reports of civil rights cases earlier than that time, and the memories of individual informants furnished no clues of any aid."[235] The same scholar surveyed the *Iowa Bystander*, the *Des Moines Register*, and the *Daily Iowan* for the years 1939–50. He found 22 civil rights prosecutions — nearly all in Des Moines, and 10 against a single Des Moines drugstore — of which only 4 resulted in convictions and imposition of fines. There were acquittals in 6 cases, 4 more were dismissed by the court, and the remaining 8 were settled.[236] In this same period, 14 civil suits for damages were brought, 8 of which were companion cases to criminal prosecutions. The civil suits had an even lower success rate than the criminal prosecutions.[237]

Thus, despite progress in amending the Iowa Civil Rights Act to encourage more frequent prosecutions, the enforcement mechanism remained ineffectual for African-Americans seeking equal accommodations. The mood was best summed up by Des Moines lawyer S. Joe Brown in a 1950 interview: "I know that there are many places in Des Moines in which I would not be welcome. I simply don't go to them."[238]

The Katz Drug Store Cases and Their Aftermath

No set of cases more vividly represents the efforts of black Iowans to enforce their statutory rights of equal accommodations under the Iowa Civil Rights Act than those involving the Katz drug store in Des Moines. The statistics highlight an intense campaign against the store by Des Moines's black citizens. In the period 1939–50, 10 of the 22 criminal prosecutions and 9 of the

Rights Act was explained by James B. Morris, a lawyer and editor of the *Iowa Bystander*. In a 1923 letter written as president of the Des Moines branch of the National Association for the Advancement of Colored People (NAACP), Morris wrote that the penalty for violating the Iowa Civil Rights Act "was so great that it was not worth anything, in that it required the grand jury to indict the defendant before he could be tried, and in every case the information has died behind the closed doors of the grand jury."[227]

The local branch of the NAACP discussed the need to "put teeth in the law" with a young Des Moines lawyer named Volney Diltz, who was running for the Iowa House of Representatives."[228] Following his election, Diltz introduced a bill to reduce the penalty for violation of the Iowa Civil Rights Act to a fine of not more than $100 or imprisonment in the county jail of not more than 30 days — thus avoiding the need for indictment by a grand jury. The bill — approved March 28, 1923[229] — passed the House by 79 votes to 1,[230] and the Senate by 34 votes to 0.[231] Morris wrote: "Few people know the effect of this bill and we did not advertise it for the reason that we feared opposition if the thing was

14 civil actions had involved the drug store.[239] Criminal prosecutions against the drug store's manager in 1943, 1944, and 1947 had resulted either in acquittal or dismissal of the charge.[240]

On July 7, 1948, John Bibbs, Edna Griffin, and Leonard Hudson went to the soda fountain at the Katz drug store. They were refused service, and the general manager, Maurice Katz, told them: "I cater to a large volume of white trade and don't have the proper equipment to serve you."[241]

The three customers were all members of the Progressive Party of Iowa, and the party picketed the drug store every Saturday for two months following this incident. Then, in November 1948, a criminal charge against Maurice Katz arising out of the July incident was tried in the Des Moines municipal court. A jury found Katz guilty of violating the civil rights law, and the judge fined him $50.[242]

The case was appealed to the Iowa Supreme Court, which handed down its decision in *State of Iowa v. Katz*[243] on December 13, 1949. The Court — noting that this likely was a "test case" prearranged by the complaints — rejected a number of technical grounds for appeal and unanimously affirmed the judgment of the trial court.[244] While the criminal appeal was in progress, Edna Griffin — the wife of a Des Moines physician and a member of the Women's Army Corps during World War 2 — brought a civil suit in the Polk County District Court for $10,000 damages arising out of the July 1948 incident. After a four-day trial in October 1949, an all-white jury awarded her damages of $1, which her attorney nonetheless deemed a "moral victory."[245] Bibbs and Hudson also brought civil suits.

Protest activities and lawsuits mounted up against the Katz drug store and its manager. During the latter part of 1949, a "Committee to End Jim Crow at Katz" was formed. Its members passed out handbills and staged "sit-downs" at the Katz lunch counter, waiting in vain for hours to be served.[246] After they were refused service on November 12, 1949, Edna Griffin and four others increased the pressure by bringing new civil suits against Katz.[247] Finally, on December 2, 1949 — 11 days before the Iowa Supreme Court decision in *State of Iowa v. Katz* — the besieged Katz drug store capitulated. Eight civil suits and six pending criminal charges were dismissed in the district and municipal courts; a cash settlement of $1,000 was paid among the civil litigants. The next day, members of the "Committee to End Jim Crow at Katz" were given "courteous service — with rapidity" at

the drugstore.[248]

In January 1950, a special committee of the Des Moines branch of the NAACP composed of its president, Luther T. Glanton Jr. (who later would become Iowa's first black judge[249]), attorney S. Joe Brown, and others, called on Iowa Attorney General Robert L. Larson. The committee read a letter urging Larson to enforce the Iowa Civil Rights Act more rigorously: "The violation of this criminal statute has been practiced with impunity for so long a time that there are eating houses, restaurants, and even beer taverns in various cities of Iowa that have displayed in them glaring posters stating that they will not serve Negroes or colored persons and many others who do not so advertise, openly state to any Negro who applies that they will not serve him."[250]

However, enforcement of the act remained unsatisfactory, and three years later, the legislative committee of the Des Moines branch of the NAACP called on Attorney General Leo A. Hoegh "to carry out our requests for the enforcement of the Iowa civil rights laws." As a result, the attorney general wrote to hotel, motel, and restaurant associations, directing compliance with the law.[251]

The Katz drug store located at 7th and Locust in downtown Des Moines, refused to serve Edna Griffin and others in July, 1948, leading to civil and criminal cases against the store. (SHSI Des Moines)

Edna Griffin of Des Moines led the protest against the Katz drug store in July 1948.
(courtesy Stanley Griffin Jr.)

Progressive Party members picketing the Katz drug store in 1948
(courtesy Stanley Griffin Jr.)

In 1954, the United States District Court for the Northern District of Iowa decided the case of *Amos v. Prom, Inc.*[252] The case stemmed from an incident in December 1951, when the plaintiff, her husband, and six friends were refused admission to the Surf Ballroom in Clear Lake. The manager explained that it was company policy not to admit black patrons.

The plaintiff brought a complaint under the Iowa Civil Rights Act, asking for compensatory and exemplary damages. The "pivotal question" considered by the federal court was whether the ballroom came within the act's coverage, an issue that the Iowa Supreme Court had not ruled on.[253] In denying the defendant's motion for a directed verdict, the court construed the act broadly: "The Iowa Act includes within its scope . . . 'all other places of amusement.' [D]ance halls of the type and kind operated by the defendant are within the provisions of the Act."[254]

Despite successes like *Katz* and *Amos*, the Iowa Civil Rights Act continued largely to be unenforced. In 1960, the Governor's Commission on Human Relations reported that "there were many peace officers who were unfamiliar with the Iowa Civil Rights Law."[255] In 1961, a report to the United States Commission on Civil Rights from the Iowa State Advisory Committee was critical of statewide enforcement efforts: "Almost invariably, when it comes to enforcing the civil rights laws of Iowa, the county attorneys . . . simply disregard violations until pressure is brought to bear either by a State organization or by a higher government official. This is the case even when violators openly admit their failure to abide by the law."[256]

The Fair Employment Practices Act of 1963

At the same time as pressure mounted for more effective enforcement of the equal accommodations provisions of the Iowa Civil Rights Act, a battle was being fought on another legal front — this one involving equal opportunities in employment.

After World War 2, a number of attempts were made in the Iowa legislature to provide for nondiscriminatory employment practices. In 1947, a bill was introduced in the House of Representatives to prevent and eliminate "practices of discrimination in employment and otherwise against persons because of race, creed, color or national origin, creating in the executive department a state commission against discrimination."[257] The bill did not make it out of committee, and seven similar bills failed to reach the floor of the House or Senate in the period 1949–55.[258]

In 1955, the legislature passed a concurrent resolution upholding the policy "that no person . . . shall be deprived of the right to work . . . because of race, creed, color, national origin or ancestry," and requesting the governor to appoint a commission to study employment discrimination.[259] Gov. Leo A. Hoegh appointed a Commission to Study Discrimination in Employment, which held hearings in seven Iowa cities.[260]

The study commission reported to the General Assembly in January 1957: "Negroes in Iowa are generally excluded from or given only limited opportunities for employment in . . . professions, office and clerical work, retail trade, transportation, teaching, municipal employment, skilled crafts and trades, and in restaurants."[261] The majority of the commission members supported a law prohibiting employment discrimination by unions and employers on account of race and creating a five-member commission to administer the law, but bills implementing this recommendation never got out of legislative committees.[262]

The election of Iowa's first Democratic governor in 20 years, Herschel C. Loveless, gave new impetus to the movement for an equal employment law. In 1958, Loveless created the Governor's Commission on Human Relations, whose purpose was to study and make recommendations on employment and other areas of racial discrimination.[263] Bills to create a state commission on human rights and to prohibit employment discrimination were introduced by Democratic legislators in 1959[264] and 1961,[265] but again failed to reach the floor of the legislature.

The effort for equal employment legislation continued during the term of Republican Gov. Norman Erbe, who in 1961 appointed a Governor's Commission on Civil Rights. The commission announced as its "most important project" the passage of the Fair Employment Practices bill. A committee appointed to plan legislative strategy decided to focus its efforts on legislators and political candidates rather than on a "mass public campaign."[266]

In November 1962, Democrat Harold Hughes was elected governor, and he encouraged the Erbe commission to continue its work. The commission's efforts were a partial success. Its own bill was blocked in a Senate committee, but Republicans (who had majorities in both Houses) were prepared to accept a bill proposed by the Iowa Manufacturers Association that would make employment discrimination a punishable offense. The bill did not include a provision for a state commission on human rights.

An editorial in the *Des Moines Register* observed that this proposal was "similar in approach" to the Iowa Civil Rights Act of 1884, under which enforcement actions were rare. Still, "a law outlawing discrimination in employment would represent a considerable gain."[267] The compromise bill passed the House by 95 votes to 9,[268] and the Senate by 32 votes to 12.[269]

The Fair Employment Practices Act, approved May 7, 1963, provided: "Every person in this state is entitled to the opportunity for employment on equal terms with every other person. It shall be unlawful for any person or employer to discriminate in the employment of individuals because of race, religion, color, national origin or ancestry."[270] The act also made it unlawful for any labor union or organization to discriminate in membership.[271] Violators would be punished by a fine of not more than $100 or imprisonment in the county jail for not more than 30 days.[272]

Gov. Harold Hughes applauded the new law, but also pointed to its shortcomings: "I think it is unfortunate that the only recourse this law provides for the victim of discriminatory hiring practices is the filing of a charge in court." Hughes promised to appoint a human rights commission "that will look into charges of discriminatory hiring practices, seek to end such practices where they exist by means of education and file charges only if necessary."[273] In July 1963, Hughes duly appointed his own 35-member bipartisan Commission on Civil Rights.[274]

Thus, 80 years after the enactment of its first Civil Rights Act, Iowa added a statutory prohibition against employment discrimination. However, the new statute's method of enforcement — like that of the civil rights law before it — left much to be desired.

The Iowa Civil Rights Act of 1965

The Iowa Civil Rights Act of 1965 was born during the great civil rights movement across the nation. Iowa experienced demonstrations of its own. In August 1963, more than 2,000 people held a rally in Davenport. An NAACP spokesman from Rock Island gave a powerful speech castigating job discrimination in the Davenport police department, the Scott County sheriff's office, and elsewhere in the Quad Cities. The demonstrators adopted resolutions sponsored by civil rights, church, and union groups.[275]

In November, the NAACP held a freedom march in the business district of Fort Madison. Some of the 300 marchers carried a coffin marked, "Here Lies Jim Crow." The following day, 900 people attended a rally at a Fort Madison school. The president of the local NAACP branch urged the crowd to write to their national legislators about the problem of discrimination.[276]

In May 1964, 120 people in Des Moines — led by a young black girl and a young white girl walking hand-in-hand — marched around city hall and the statehouse. They carried signs saying "Enough Double-Talk Pass Civil Rights Bill," and "Fair Housing For Iowa."[277] The next month in Waterloo, 450 people took part in a silent march for freedom organized by the local branch of the NAACP. At city hall, they presented the mayor with a list of grievances about discrimination in jobs, housing, and law enforcement.[278]

On May 14, 1964, Gov. Harold Hughes signed an executive order proclaiming a Code of Fair Practices and prohibiting discrimination on the basis of "race, color, religion, national origin, or ancestry" in state appointments and promotions.[279] In July of that year, President Lyndon Johnson signed the federal Civil Rights Act of 1964,[280] thereby bolstering the cause of those who sought fresh civil rights legislation in Iowa.

A powerful article advocating such legislation was published in the summer 1964 edition of the *Iowa Law Review* by Arthur E. Bonfield, a University of Iowa law professor. Bonfield stressed the narrow scope of the Iowa Civil Rights Act of 1884 and the failure of criminal prosecutions to provide a remedy for anti-discrimination statutes. He recommended the establishment of a civil rights commission and an administrative, rather than a penal, method of enforcement.[281] Bonfield drafted a civil rights bill based on his proposals, which was sent to Dr. Donald Boles, chairman of the Governor's Commission on Human Rights. The bill dealt with discrimination in public accommodations and employment but did not include the sale or rental of housing, which most legislators seemed unready to endorse.[282]

In November 1964, Gov. Harold Hughes won re-election by a huge margin, and the Democrats won majorities in the Iowa House of Representatives and Senate for the first time in three decades. Hughes's own popularity, the national triumph of President Johnson, and the recent reapportionment of the Iowa legislature were important factors in the Democrats' statewide landslide.[283] In his inaugural message to the legislature, Hughes recommended the passage of legislation to create a state Human Rights Commission.[284]

In early February 1965, the Governor's Commission on Human Rights held a major civil rights conference in Des

"Every person

in this state is entitled

to the opportunity

for employment on

equal terms with every

other person.

It shall be unlawful for

any person or employer

to discriminate

in the employment

of individuals. . . ."

— Fair Employment Practices Act of 1963

complaints of unfair or discriminatory practices in public accommodations and employment because of race, creed, color, national origin, or religion. Commissioners or their staffs were authorized to investigate and to attempt to resolve complaints through conciliation. Failing settlement, the complaint would be heard by the commission, which upon the finding of any discriminatory or unfair practice could order remedial action.[291] A complainant or respondent dissatisfied with the commission's order could seek judicial review in the district court.[292] Existing provisions of the Iowa Civil Rights Act of 1884 — which for 80 years had been the bulwark of equal protection in Iowa — were repealed.[293]

Governor Hughes, when signing the Iowa Civil Rights Act of 1965 into law, summed up the hopes of the many Iowans who had brought about its passage. The new law, he declared confidently, was "a big step toward equal opportunity and equal rights."[294]

Major Amendments to the Iowa Civil Rights Act from 1967 to 1991

In 1967, the political climate was ripe for a fair housing amendment to the Iowa Civil Rights Act. Sen. John Ely and ten other senators introduced a bill in April. The Senate passed the fair housing bill by 49 votes to 11; however, it inserted a requirement that a person filing a complaint with the Iowa Civil Rights Commission post a $500 bond.[295]

In the House of Representatives, the two black members gave powerful speeches in support of the bill. Democrat June Franklin of Polk County described Iowa as a leader in civil rights and called for passage of the bill "to let my people go free." Republican Cecil A. Reed of Linn County spoke about his own experience with segregation and said the time had come to allow African-Americans to live wherever they wanted and could afford. "My country tis of thee," he recited. "Sweet land of liberty, of thee I sing. . . . Let freedom ring in Iowa with the passage of this bill." Members of the House burst into applause.[296] Reed then moved the passage of the bill, and the House approved it by 121 votes to 0.[297]

The Discrimination in Housing Act amended the Iowa Civil Rights Act of 1965 to add discrimination in the sale or lease of housing or real property as an unfair or discriminatory practice. The act applied to owners and their representatives,

An NAACP march down Keo Way in Des Moines supporting passage of the Civil Rights Act of 1964 (Tom Patrick photo, Des Moines Register, July 28, 1963)

Moines.[285] At this conference, Hughes expanded on his inaugural statement: "I have . . . recommended to the Iowa General Assembly that it create by statute a state civil rights commission with authority to resolve complaints in the field of public accommodations and fair employment practices, through civil rather than criminal action. . . . [I]f the proposed bill . . . is adopted by the General Assembly, Iowa will have one of the model civil rights acts and agencies in the nation."[286]

Later that month, Rep. Roy Gillette of Story County and 53 other representatives sponsored the introduction of House File 263, a bill to establish a civil rights commission and to prohibit unfair and discriminatory practices in public accommodations, employment, and related programs. It passed with some amendment by a unanimous vote.[287] On the centenary anniversary of Abraham Lincoln's death, upon the motion of Sen. John Ely of Linn County, the Iowa Senate also passed the bill unanimously.[288]

The Iowa Civil Rights Act of 1965,[289] approved April 29, 1965, created the Iowa Civil Rights Commission, whose seven members would be appointed by the governor.[290] The commission was empowered to hold hearings and to rule on including real estate brokers and attorneys, with certain exemptions applied to religious institutions and the rental of owner-occupied units.[298]

The Iowa legislature made numerous amendments to the Iowa Civil Rights Act in subsequent sessions. In 1969, it repealed the requirement of a $500 bond to accompany complaints of unfair or discriminatory practices filed with the Iowa Civil Rights Commission.[299] The following year, sex discrimination was added to the list of prohibited practices.[300] In 1972, civil rights protection was given to persons with physical and mental disabilities,[301] and age discrimination in employment was declared unlawful.[302]

Two years later, the scope of the Civil Rights Act was broadened to include certain unfair credit practices.[303] In 1978, the legislature passed a bill to improve and make more efficient the enforcement of the Act.[304] In 1986, the Act was again amended to bar discrimination in educational institutions.[305] Then, in 1991, additional measures were added concerning discriminatory practices in housing.[306] Thus, by the 1990s, the Iowa Civil Rights Act of 1965 had been extended to protect new classes of individuals and to prohibit additional types of discrimination.

The Iowa Supreme Court
Interprets the Iowa Civil Rights Act of 1965

The Iowa Supreme Court's first decision interpreting the new Civil Rights Act was the 1971 case of *Iron Workers Local No. 67 v. Hart*.[307] The manager of a construction company filed a complaint with the Iowa Civil Rights Commission, alleging that a Des Moines union engaged in unfair and discriminatory practices against black workers the company was attempting to hire. The commission found discrimination by the union, enjoined the union from harassment of any person seeking union membership or giving employment to minority workers, and assessed damages for overhead losses suffered by the company because of the dispute. Following review by the Polk County district court, the case was appealed to the Iowa Supreme Court.

Noting that the Iowa Civil Rights Act of 1965 was "another manifestation of a massive national drive to right wrongs prevailing in our social and economic structures for more than a century," the Court declared that the law should be "construed broadly to effectuate its purposes."[308] The Court

WARRANTY DEED

Louis P. Brown, and
Abbie C. Brown,
  his wife,

  to

Samuel E. Berry, and
Ada Berry.

Dated April 30, 1930.
Filed May   10, 1930.

Grantors hereby convey and warrant unto Samuel E. Berry and Ada Berry the following described premises situated in Polk County, Iowa, to-wit:

Lot 13 in L. P. Brown's Official Plat of Lot One (1) Westwood, in Polk County, Iowa.

The property shall not be sold to, leased to nor occupied by persons of African race or descent.

It shall be used for residential purposes only and no dwelling costing less than $8000.00 shall be erected thereon.

The house shall set back at least 40 feet from the street.

disallowed the award of common law damages as exceeding the commission's statutory authority,[309] but sustained the finding of discrimination. Significantly, the Court rejected the union's claim that provisions of the Iowa Civil Rights Act were unconstitutional because of vagueness or as an improper delegation of legislative powers.[310]

Another example of the Iowa Supreme Court's review of a racial complaint was the 1986 case of *Chauffeurs, Teamsters and Helpers, Local Union No. 238 v. Iowa Civil Rights Commission*.[311] A black complainant alleged that a labor union had discriminated against him on the basis of race because of numerous derogatory and racially motivated incidents. The Civil Rights Commission found discrimination and ordered the payment of emotional distress and punitive damages, and its award was affirmed by the district court.

On appeal, the Iowa Supreme Court held that the union had discriminated against the claimant on the basis of his race, and that the Iowa Civil Rights Commission under an amended statutory provision had authority to award damages for emotional distress.[312] However, the Court disallowed the award

Restrictive real estate covenant for west-side Des Moines residential property, 1930 (courtesy Andrew H. Kahn)

Gov. Harold Hughes shakes hands with Ike Smalls, Des Moines businessman and NAACP national board member, after passage of the Iowa Civil Rights Act of 1965. Robert A. Wright Sr. (right) looks on. (courtesy Robert A. Wright Sr.)

of punitive damages, stating that an administrative agency could not award such damages without express statutory authority.[313]

The application of the Iowa Civil Rights Act to an allegation of "reverse discrimination" was considered in the 1996 case of *Davis v. City of Waterloo.*[314] A white city employee was passed over for a promotion to the job of street department foreman in favor of a black employee. The white employee brought an action claiming employment discrimination on the basis of race under both federal civil rights law and a provision of the Iowa Civil Rights Act. The Iowa Supreme Court affirmed a judgment for the white employee.

The Court declared that race had played a "controlling role" in the promotion decision.[315] It rejected the city's contention that its promotion decision was not discriminatory because it was consistent with the city's affirmative action plan. Such a plan, the Court stated, "is not a license to make race-based employment decisions favoring employees of a minority race over white

employees."[316] The Court upheld the district court's order that the white employee be appointed to a street department foreman's position (without removing the black employee from the position to which he had been promoted), and damages for back pay and emotional distress.[317]

The Work of the Iowa Civil Rights Commission

The drafters of the Iowa Civil Rights Act of 1965 were convinced that racial discrimination was still a serious problem in the state and that an administrative means of enforcement would be more effective than criminal proceedings in challenging racial discrimination. Based on the sheer number of complaints filed with the Iowa Civil Rights Commission since its inception, compared to criminal enforcement under the 1884 act, the drafters appear to have been right on both points.

During the first few years of its existence, the Iowa Civil Rights Commission saw a dramatic increase in its case load, which it attributed to "the Commission's affirmative action posture in ferreting out discriminatory practices on its own."[318] In its fourth annual report, the commission noted that its total caseload (consisting of formal complaints and informal "file matters") had grown from 10 in the period July 1965–November 1965, to 177 in the period December 1968–November 1969.[319] Although the commission reports did not break these numbers down by category, the Iowa Civil Rights Act in this period covered only complaints of unfair or discriminatory practices based on race, creed, color, national origin, or religion.

The number increased again in reporting year 1970 to 169 complaints and 77 file matters, but by now the commission was also hearing complaints of sex discrimination. The 1970 report showed that of the 169 formal complaints, 107 were by color or race.[320]

Because of varying methods of reporting statistical data in years subsequent to 1970, it is difficult to make direct comparisons of the numbers of race-based complaints. (These later reports included not only race categories, but also catchall categories such as "combination" or "other" that included additional race-based complaints, thereby making year-to-year comparison unreliable.) However, from 1986 onward the commission's reports give comparable figures under the category of "race." The peak year in the late 1980s was reporting year 1987, when the commission received 467 race complaints.[321]

The complaints then declined annually, reaching a trough of 269 in 1990.[322] Thereafter, complaints by race grew annually until 1995, when they reached a record of 673.[323]

In the sesquicentennial year of 1996, there were 554 complaints by race, whereas the overall total of complaints to the commission was 2,172.[324] Both the total number of complaints and the number of complaints by race had dropped somewhat from 1995. The commission's comments on the decline in the overall total of complaints can probably be applied as well to the decline in race complaints. The commission reported: "What accounts for this drop in complaint filings? Maybe it's because more people have become aware of their rights and are resolving matters before they get to the point of a formal complaint. Maybe employers and landlords have become more knowledgeable of non-discriminatory ways of doing business. Maybe the number of complaints to be filed has reached a peak. Who knows? Maybe all of these things are factors."[325]

The Iowa Legislature Creates a Commission on the Status of African-Americans and Passes the Iowa Hate Crimes Act

One hundred and fifty years after the Iowa Territory came into being with its plethora of race-based statutes, the legislature passed a law of symbolic importance to black Iowans. In 1988, the General Assembly established a separate division within the Department of Human Rights — now known as the Division on the Status of African-Americans. The legislation created a nine-member commission to "study the changing needs and problems of blacks in this state, and recommend new programs, policies, and constructive action to the governor and the general assembly."[326]

In the debate on the bill, one senator outlined its purpose: "[The creation of the new division] will give [African-Americans] a special identity in the state of Iowa, particularly within the Statehouse complex. It does give them a pipeline to the governor's office [and] a pipeline to whatever may be available in terms of money or opportunities or jobs."[327]

During the same period, legislation was being considered to address the problem of "hate crimes." In 1987, the Iowa Civil Rights Commission drew attention to some racial incidents that had occurred in Albia, Burlington, and Des Moines. In an "Open Letter to All Iowans," the commission emphasized the need "to educate and challenge those who participate in racially motivated

hate/violence incidents."[328] The following year, the legislature passed an act providing that anyone who committed a felony or misdemeanor "because of the victim's race, color, religion, nationality, country of origin, political affiliation, or sex" would have that fact considered as "a circumstance in aggravation" in imposing a sentence.[329] The act was amended in 1990 to expand the classes of protected persons and to provide civil remedies.[330]

The year 1992 saw a major renovation and strengthening of the Hate Crimes Act, spurred by some widely reported racial incidents. The *[Dubuque] Telegraph-Herald* observed that at least 13 cross burnings had been investigated in Dubuque in the previous 3 years.[331] In his January 1992 Condition of the State Address, Gov. Terry Branstad said: "1991 was a year when Iowa's reputation was tarnished by cross burnings and senseless acts of hatred. I know the over-whelming majority of Iowans share my belief that there is no place in Iowa for prejudice and racism. . . . We need to strengthen the hate crimes law to prevent bias-motivated acts."[332]

The new act defined "hate crime" as meaning an assault, arson, criminal mischief, or trespass in violation of individual rights when committed against a person or a person's property because of "race, color, religion, ancestry, national origin, political affiliation, sex, sexual orientation, age or disability" or because of association with such a person.[333] Criminal penalties were increased for certain offenses where the elements of a hate crime were proved.[334]

The Iowa Supreme Court upheld the constitutionality of the Hate Crimes Act in the 1994 case of *State of Iowa v. McKnight*.[335] The case involved an assault on an African-American man in Council Bluffs, in which the assailant used racially abusive language. The defendant was convicted of infringing individual rights under a then-current provision of the hate crimes statute. He appealed, contending his First Amendment rights of free speech had been violated.

The Iowa Supreme Court affirmed the conviction, finding that the statute did not violate free speech rights, nor was it unconstitutionally overbroad. The Court stated: "Had [the defendant] limited his attack . . . to mere words, the First Amendment would have protected his right to do so. He lost that protection when his racial bias toward blacks drove him to couple those words with assaultive conduct toward [the victim]. . . . In these circumstances, the words and the assault are inextricably intertwined for First Amendment purposes."[336]

The Iowa Civil Rights Act of 1965 was "another manifestation of a massive national drive to right wrongs prevailing in our social and economic structures for more than a century."

— Iowa Supreme Court, 1971

Conclusion

The legal history of African-Americans in Iowa falls into four broad historic periods. In the first period, from the founding of the territory until the Civil War, Iowa adopted a series of constitutional and statutory provisions that discriminated against blacks. This discrimination reached its peak in 1851 with the Act to Prohibit the Immigration of Free Negroes Into This State. Despite this institutional discrimination, individuals like Rachel in 1839 and Ralph later the same year successfully petitioned for their liberty in the Iowa courts.

The second period, from the Civil War until 1880, saw the dismantling of discriminatory provisions in Iowa's constitution and statute books. This phase also saw the high-water mark of anti-discrimination judicial activism by the Iowa Supreme Court in the 1868 school case of *Clark v. The Board of Directors, etc.* and the 1873 common-carrier case of *Coger v. The North West Union Packet Co.*

The third period, from 1884 until the mid-1960s, was the era of the Iowa Civil Rights Act of 1884. Although one of the first of its kind in the United States and a great advance over prior law, this statute was limited in its scope and proved ineffective as a remedy for such discrimination as it did seek to cover. A few individuals were successful in criminal prosecutions or civil damage suits, but the great bulk of discriminatory acts had no practical remedy.

The fourth and final period began with the passage of the Iowa Civil Rights Act of 1965. That act and subsequent amendments created the Iowa Civil Rights Commission as an administrative mechanism for enforcing anti-discrimination law in public accommodations, employment, housing, credit practices, and educational institutions. The high volume of race-based complaints lodged with the commission since its inception points both to the need for and the effectiveness of this administrative remedy in combating racial discrimination.

From its 1839 opinion declaring a former slave a free man on Iowa soil to its 1994 decision upholding the constitutionality of the Iowa Hate Crimes Act, the Iowa Supreme Court has often been a progressive influence in the law governing African-Americans. The Court's words 125 years ago in the *Coger* case continue to represent Iowans' highest principles today:

[E]qual rights and equal protection shall be secured to all regardless of color or nationality.[337]

84

The Court's words 125 years ago in the Coger case continue to represent Iowans' highest principles today: "[E]qual rights and equal protection shall be secured to all regardless of color or nationality."

— **Iowa Supreme Court, 1873**

Notes

1. An Act to Divide the Territory of Wisconsin and to Establish the Territorial Government of Iowa, sec. 5, *U.S. Statutes at Large*, vol. 5, 235, 237. The Act was approved on June 12, 1838.

2. Sec. 12, ibid., 239; cf. An Act Establishing the Territorial Government of Wisconsin, sec. 12, ibid., 10, 15.

3. *Laws of the Territory of Michigan* (Detroit: Sheldon and Wells, 1827), 484–86. The Act had been approved on April 13, 1827.

4. Secs. 1, 4, 6, ibid., 484, 485.

5. *The Statute Laws of the Territory of Iowa* (Du Buque: Russell and Reeves, 1839; repr., Historical Department of Iowa, 1900), 69–70.

6. Secs. 1, 2, ibid., 69.

7. Sec. 5, ibid., 70.

8. Sec. 6, ibid., 70.

9. An Act Providing for and Regulating General Elections in the Territory, sec. 12, ibid., 196, 199.

10. An Act to Organize, Discipline and Govern the Militia of This Territory, sec. 6, ibid., 351, 352.

11. An Act Providing for the Establishment of Common Schools, sec. 1, ibid., 191.

12. An Act Regulating Practice in the District Courts of the Territory of Iowa, sec. 38, ibid., 395, 404.

13. An Act Concerning Grand and Petit Jurors, sec. 1, ibid., 295.

14. An Act Regulating Marriages, sec. 13, *Laws of the Territory of Iowa* (Burlington: J.H. M'Kenny, 1840), 39, 42.

15. An Act for the Relief of the Poor, sec. 2, *Laws of the Territory of Iowa* (Iowa City: Van Antwerp and Hughes, 1841–42), 58.

16. The court orders in this case are found in Record A, 206–7, Clerk of Des Moines County District Court, Burlington, Iowa. Supporting documents, including court papers relating to Thomas Easton's habeas corpus and replevin actions, are in File Drawer A-40, Clerk of Des Moines County District Court, Burlington, Iowa.

17. Petition of Thomas Stanley Easton to the Honorable Charles Mason, Chief Justice of the Territory of Iowa, May 2, 1839, File Drawer A-40, op. cit.

18. Copy of Sale from W.H. Martin to Thos. S. Easton, June 27, 1835, File Drawer A-40, op. cit.

19. Philip D. Jordan, *Catfish Bend—River Town and County Seat* (Burlington: Craftsman Press, 1975), 51; John Ely Briggs, "A Commonplace Calendar," *Palimpsest* 19 (1938): 36, 291.

20. Jordan, 36; Briggs, 522.

21. Statement of David Hendershott in open court, May 6, 1839, in *Thomas Stanley Easton v. David Hendershott* (an action for habeas corpus), File Drawer A-40, op. cit.

22. Affidavit of Thos. S. Easton May 6, 1839, *Thomas S. Easton v. David Hendershott* (an action for replevin), filed May 7, 1839, File Drawer A-40, op. cit.

23. Petition of Rachel for a writ of habeas corpus, May 7, 1839, File Drawer A-40, op. cit.

24. Writ of habeas corpus directed to Sheriff James Cameron, signed by Honorable Charles Mason in open court, May 7, 1839, File Drawer A-40, op. cit.

25. Order of Judge Charles Mason, May 8, 1839, in *Rachel, a Negro Woman v. James Cameron, Sheriff*, Habeas Corpus, Record A, 207, Clerk of Des Moines County District Court, Burlington, Iowa.

26. *Iowa Territorial Gazette and Burlington Advertiser,* May 18, 1839 [emphasis in original].

27. 1 Morris 1, 1 Bradford 3 (Iowa 1839). For a more detailed account of the case, see Richard, Lord Acton and Patricia Nassif Acton, *To Go Free: A Treasury of Iowa's Legal Heritage* (Ames: Iowa State Univ. Press, 1995), 40–48; Richard Acton, "To Go Free," *Palimpsest* 70 (1989): 51.

28. An Act to Regulate Blacks and Mulattoes, *The Statute Laws of the Territory of Iowa* (Dubuque: Russell and Reeves, 1839), 69–70. Section 6 provided: "[I]n case any person . . . claiming any black or mulatto person that now is or hereafter may be in this Territory, shall apply to any judge of the district court, or justice of the peace, and shall make satisfactory proof that such black or mulatto person or persons is or are the property of him or her who applies . . . the said judge or justice is hereby empowered and required, by his precept, to direct the sheriff or constable to arrest such black or mulatto person or persons, and deliver the same to the claimant."

29. Supreme Court Order Book, vol. A (1838–53), 6 (SHSI, Manuscript Division, Des Moines).

30. An Act to Authorize the People of the Missouri Territory to Form a Constitution and State Government, and for the Admission of Such State into the Union on an Equal Footing with the Original States, and to prohibit Slavery in Certain Territories, sec. 8, *U.S. Statutes at Large,* vol. 3, 548.

31. 1 Morris 1, 8–9 (Iowa 1839).

32. Ibid., 9–10.

33. D.C. Cloud, "A Fugitive Slave Case: *In re Jim or Jim Merry,*" (typed manuscript), CL 6245, B17, Folder 5 (SHSI, Manuscript Division, Des Moines, Iowa); see also J.P. Walton, "Unwritten History of Bloomington (now Muscatine) in Early Days," *AI* 2d ser. 1 (1882–84): 44, 47–49.

34. An Act Regulating Marriages, sec. 13, *Laws of the Territory of Iowa* (Burlington: J.H. M'Kenny, 1840), 39, 42.

35. The details of this case are taken from John W. Wright, ed., *History of Marion County Iowa and Its People,* vol. 1 (Chicago: S.J. Clarke, 1915), 328–31; Wm. M. Donnel, "Pioneers of Marion County," *AI* 1st ser. 8 (1870): 220, 225–29

36. Homer L. Calkin, "A Slaveowner in Iowa," *Palimpsest* 22 (1941): 344, 345.

37. An Act Respecting Fugitives from Justice, and Persons Escaping from the Service of their Masters, *U.S. Statutes at Large* 1: 302.

38. Details of this case may be found in George Frazee (reporter), "An Iowa Fugitive Slave Case—1850," *Daggs v. Frazier,* D. Iowa, Southern Div., 1850; repr., *AI* 3rd ser. 6 (1903): 9–45.

39. Ibid., 31, 37.

40. Benjamin F. Shambaugh, ed., *Fragments of the Debates of the Iowa Constitutional Conventions of 1844 and 1846* (Iowa City: SHSI, 1900), 26, 29, 33.

41. Ibid., 33.

42. *Journal of the Convention for the Formation of a Constitution for the State of Iowa* (Iowa City: Jessee Williams, 1845), 54.

43. Shambaugh, *Fragments of the Debates,* 66, 155.

44. Ibid., 156.

45. Iowa Constitution of 1846, art. 3, sec. 1, repr. in Benjamin F. Shambaugh, ed., *Documentary Material Relating to the History of Iowa,* vol. 1 (Iowa City: SHSI, 1897), 194.

46. Ibid. art. 4, secs. 4, 5, repr. in Shambaugh, *Documentary Material,* vol. 1, 195.

47. Ibid., art. 4, sec. 31, repr. in Shambaugh, *Documentary Material,* vol. 1, 199.

48. Ibid., art. 7, sec. 1, repr. in Shambaugh, *Documentary Material,* vol. 1, 204.

49. Ibid., art. 13, sec. 2, repr. in Shambaugh, *Documentary Material,* vol. 1, 208.

50. *A Portion of the Report of the Commissioners Appointed to Draft, Revise and Arrange a Code of Laws for the State of Iowa* (Iowa City: Palmer and Paul, 1850). The only known copy of this report is Charles Mason's own copy, located in the Rare Book Room of the University of Iowa Law Library, Iowa City.

51. Ibid., Part Third, title 1, ch. 6, sec. 2, 214.

52. Ibid., Part Third, title 1, ch. 7, sec. 1, 217.

53. See Iowa Constitution of 1846, art. 3, sec. 1, repr. in Shambaugh, *Documentary Material,* vol. 1, 194.

54. *Report of the Commissioners,* op. cit., Part One, title 7, ch. 4, sec. 27, 478; cf. An Act to Establish a System of Common Schools, ch. 80, sec. 51, *Acts, Resolutions and Memorials Passed at the Regular Session of the Second General Assembly, of the State of Iowa* (Iowa City: Palmer and Paul, 1849), 102.

55. See *Report of the Commissioners,* op. cit., Part One, title 7, ch. 5, sec. 2, 480; cf. An Act to Establish a System of Common Schools (1849), sec. 88, 107.

56. *Report of the Commissioners,* op. cit., Part One, title 9, ch. 2, sec. 1, 80.

57. See Iowa Constitution of 1846, art. 7, sec. 1, repr. in Shambaugh, *Documentary Material,* vol. 1, 204.

58. See *Report of the Commissioners,* op. cit., Part One, title 13, ch. 1, art. 2, sec. 22 (First), 109; title 5, ch. 1, sec. 1, 302; Part Second, title 2, ch. 2, sec. 2, 196.

59. See *Statute Laws of the Territory of Iowa* repr, 69–70.

60. *Code of 1851,* secs. 1610, 1630, 1127, 1160.

61. Ibid., sect. 621. The addition was proposed by the House of Representatives. *Iowa House Journal 1850,* 118.

62. *Code of 1851,* sec. 808. See *Iowa House Journal 1850,* 124.

63. *[Dubuque] Miners' Express,* Jan. 8, 1851.

64. *Code of 1851,* sec. 2388. See *Iowa House Journal 1850,* 219; *Iowa Senate Journal 1850,* 215–16. See also *[Fort Des Moines] Iowa Star,* Feb. 6, 1851.

65. The section on the validity of marriage did not mention race. See *Code of 1851,* sec. 1464; cf. An Act Regulating Marriages, sec. 13, *Laws of the Territory of Iowa* (Burlington: J.H. M'Kenny, 1840), 39, 42.

66. See *[Dubuque] Miners' Express,* Jan. 22, 1851.

67. *[Dubuque] Miners' Express,* Feb. 26, 1851 (speech of Representative Haun, Jan. 25, 1851).

68. See ibid; *Iowa House Journal 1850,* 275; *[Dubuque] Miners' Express,* Feb. 12, 1851 (speech of Representative Gamble, Jan. 28, 1851); *Iowa House Journal 1850,* 298.

69. *The History of Clinton County, Iowa* (Chicago: Western Historical Co., 1879), 619–20.

70. *Iowa House Journal 1850,* 145.

71. Ibid., 275.

72. *[Dubuque] Miners' Express,* Feb. 26, 1851 (reporting Haun's remarks on Jan. 25, 1851).

73. Ibid.

74. Ibid. In 1848, the voters of Illinois had approved a constitutional amendment directing the legislature to pass laws to "prohibit free persons of color, from immigrating to and settling in this state." Shortly before the 1851 Iowa debate, a convention called to amend the constitution of Indiana had also added an exclusion measure. JoAnn Manfra, "Northern Exclusionary Measures and the Privileges and Immunities of Free Blacks, 1778–1857: An Unexamined Theme in Antislavery Constitutionalism," LL.M. thesis, Harvard University Law School, 1979, 52, 60, 63.

75. *[Dubuque] Miners' Express,* Feb. 26, 1851.

76. *Iowa House Journal 1850,* 297–300.

77. *[Dubuque] Miners' Express,* Feb. 12, 1851 (report of debate of Jan. 28, 1851).

78. Ibid.

79. *Iowa House Journal 1850,* 299.

80. An Act to Prohibit the Immigration of Free Negroes into this State, ch. 72, sec. 5, *Acts, Resolutions and Memorials Passed at the Regular Session of the Third General Assembly of the State of Iowa* (Iowa City: Palmer and Paul, 1851), 172, 173; see *Iowa Senate Journal 1850,* 267.

81. Ibid., 295.

82. *Iowa House Journal 1850,* 367–68. The House approved the amended bill by a margin of 28 votes to 7.

83. An Act to Prohibit the Immigration of Free Negroes Into This State, sec. 1, 172.

84. Ibid., sec. 2, 172–73.

85. Ibid., sec. 3, 173.

86. *Iowa House Journal 1855,* 319.

87. The petition may be found in "Secretary of State, Negroes, Certain Rights of Petitions," 10–11. Fragment, Box 7, N50/02/06 (SHSI, State Records, Des Moines).

88. *[Centerville] Indiana True Democrat,* March 27, 1851 (quoting the *Iowa True Democrat*).

89. See Nathan E. Coffin, "The Case of Archie P. Webb, A Free Negro," *AI* 3rd ser. 11 (1913–15): 203–4, 213.

90. *Acts, Resolutions and Memorials Passed at the Regular Session of the Third General Assembly of the State of Iowa* (Iowa City: Palmer and Paul, 1851).

91. *[Keokuk] Gate City,* June 6, 1857.

92. Ibid., June 4, 1857.

93. Ibid., June 6, 1857.

94. Leola Nelson Bergmann, *The Negro in Iowa* (Iowa City: SHSI, 1948; repr. 1969), 15 n. 24.

95. An Act to Amend, and Supplementary to, the Act Entitled "An Act Respecting Fugitives from Justice, and Persons Escaping from the Service of their Masters," approved February Twelfth, One Thousand Seven Hundred and Ninety-three, *U.S. Statutes at Large* 9, 462.

96. Details of this case are found in George Frazee, "The Iowa Fugitive Slave Case," *AI* 3rd ser. 4 (1899): 118, 125–34.

97. William Salter, *The Life of James W. Grimes* (New York: D. Appleton and Co., 1876), 72.

98. Ibid., 73.

99. Frazee, 131–33.

100. *Code of 1851,* sec. 2388.

101. Brief of Appellee, *Usher and Thayer v. Thomas C. Motts,* Iowa Supreme Court, File 2454, N36/09/06 (SHSI, State Records, Des Moines, Iowa).

102. *Thomas C. Motts v. Usher and Thayer,* Minute Book F, 225–26, Clerk of Muscatine County District Court, Muscatine, Iowa (judgment for attachment dated Oct. 23, 1855).

103. 2 Cole 84 (Iowa 1856).

104. Ibid., 85.

105. An Act Relating to Evidence (approved Dec. 22, 1856), ch. 19, sec. 1, *Acts, Resolutions and Memorials Passed at the Regular Session of the Sixth General Assembly of the State of Iowa* (Iowa City: State Printer, 1857), 15.

106. Salter, 99.

107. *Code of 1851,* sec. 2388.

108. Benjamin F. Shambaugh, *The Constitutions of Iowa* (Iowa City: SHSI, 1934), 218.

109. See generally "A Lawyers' Convention: The Making of the Iowa Constitution of 1857," in Acton and Acton, 84–92.

110. Iowa Constitution of 1857, art. 1, sec. 4.

111. Shambaugh, *Constitutions of Iowa,* 248.

112. Iowa Constitution of 1857, art. 9, sec. 12.

113. W. Blair Lord, ed., *The Debates of the Constitutional Convention of the State of Iowa, Assembled at Iowa City, Monday, January 19, 1857,* vol. 2 (Davenport: Luse, Lane and Co., 1857), 913.

114. Iowa Constitution of 1857, art. 1, sec. 10.

115. Lord, 736–41.

116. Iowa Constitution of 1857, art. 6, sec. 1.

117. Ibid., art. 3, sec. 33; art. 3, secs. 34–35; art. 3, secs. 4–5; art. 2, sec. 1.

118. Ibid., art. 12, sec. 14.

119. Robert R. Dykstra, *Bright Radical Star: Black Freedom and White Supremacy on the Hawkeye Frontier* (Cambridge: Harvard Univ. Press, 1993), 178.

120. *Acts, Resolutions and Memorials Passed at the Regular Session of the Third General Assembly of the State of Iowa* (Iowa City: Palmer and Paul, 1851), ch. 72, 172–73; see supra notes 83–85 and accompanying text.

121. *Daily State Register,* Jan. 18, 1863.

122. Notice to Arch[ie] Webb Jan. 8, 1863; Affidavit of Service of James L. West, Township Trustee, Jan. 17, 1863, Polk County, Delaware Twp. Justice of Peace Documents relating to removal of Free Negro, Jan. 1863, BL316 f.7 (SHSI, Manuscript Division, Iowa City).

123. Order for arrest, Jan. 19, 1863, signed by Stephen Harvey, Justice of the Peace; Return of Service, Jan. 20, 1863 of Sheriff I.W. Griffith, ibid.

124. *Daily State Register,* Jan. 21, 1863.

125. *Chicago Tribune,* Feb. 3, 1863; *Daily State Register,* Feb. 3, 1864. The proclamation, issued Sept. 1862, declared that on Jan. 1, 1863, slaves held in actively rebellious states would be free.

126. *Council Bluffs Bugle,* Jan. 28, 1863.

127. *Daily State Register,* Jan. 6, 1863.

128. For details about the case of *Archie P. Webb v. I.W. Griffith* and a full text of the opinion, see generally Nathan E. Coffin, "The Case of Archie P. Webb, A Free Negro," *AI* 3rd ser. 11 (1913–15): 200–14.

129. *Daily State Register,* Jan. 6, 1863.

130. Coffin, 213.

131. U.S. Constitution, art. 4, sec. 2.

132. Coffin, 210.

133. Ibid., 211 [emphasis added]. See Iowa Constitution of 1846, art. 2, sec. 1, repr. in Shambaugh, *Documentary Material,* vol. 1, 191 (the state constitution that was in effect when the exclusionary law was passed in 1851).

134. Iowa Constitution of 1846, art. 2, sec. 8., repr. in Shambaugh, *Documentary Material,* vol. 1, 192.

135. Ibid., art. 2, sec. 10., repr. in Shambaugh, *Documentary Material,* vol. 1, 192. See Coffin, 211–12.

136. Coffin, 213.

137. Ibid., 204. There is no record of the case in the reported opinions, and Coffin concludes that the appeal "was evidently never docketed."

138. An Act to Repeal Chapter Seventy-Two of the Acts of the Third Gen. Assembly, Entitled "An Act to Prohibit the Immigration of Free Negroes Into This State," ch. 7 (approved Feb. 5, 1864), *Acts and Resolutions Passed at the Regular Session of the Tenth General Assembly of the State of Iowa* (Des Moines: State Printer, 1864), 6–7.

139. Ibid., preamble, 6.; see also *Anamosa Eureka,* Feb. 19, 1864.

140. *Daily State Register,* Feb. 3, 1864.

141. An Act to Amend Chapter 57 of the Revision of 1860, ch. 40 (approved March 10, 1864), *Acts and Resolutions Passed at the Regular Session of the Tenth General Assembly of the State of Iowa* (Des Moines: State Printer, 1864), 41.

142. Joint Resolution No. 10 (approved Feb. 27, 1864), ibid., 178–79.

143. Benjamin F. Gue, *History of Iowa From the Earliest Times to the Beginning of the Twentieth Century,* vol. 3 (New York: The Century History Co., 1903), 1.

144. *Davenport Daily Gazette,* June 16, 1865 (written by convention delegate Edward Russell, who moved the amendment).

145. Ibid.

146. *Davenport Daily Gazette,* April 16, 1867 (written by convention delegate Edward Russell).

147. *Davenport Daily Gazette,* June 16, 1865.

148. Gue, vol. 3, 2–4.

149. Herbert S. Fairall, ed., *The Iowa City Republican Manual of Politics* (Iowa City: Republican Steam Printing, 1881), 67.

150. *Cedar Valley Times,* Oct. 19, 1865.

151. Dykstra, 240.

152. Iowa Constitution of 1857, art. 10, sec. 1.

153. Benjamin F. Shambaugh, ed., *The Messages and Proclamations of the Governors of Iowa,* vol. 3 (Iowa City: SHSI, 1903), 86.

154. The memorial was from the non-commissioned officers and privates of the 60th U.S. Colored Infantry, "asking that steps be taken for the amendment of the Constitution of the State, and for the repeal of all laws making distinctions on account of color." Alexander Clark and 60 other African-American residents of Muscatine County submitted a similar memorial. *Iowa Senate Journal 1866*, 67.

155. Shambaugh, *Messages and Proclamations*, vol. 3, 85.

156. Iowa Constitution of 1857, art. 2, sec. 1. This section gave voting rights to "[e]very white male citizen."

157. *Iowa House Journal 1866*, 643–45.

158. *Iowa House Journal 1866*, 643, 646–47. The sections the House voted to amend were Iowa Constitution of 1857, art. 3, sec. 33 (census); art. 3, sec. 34 (Senate apportionment); art. 3, sec. 35 (House apportionment), and art. 6, sec. 1 (militia).

159. Ibid., art. 3, sec. 4; see *Iowa House Journal 1866*, 643, 645–46. The vote was 41 in favor of the proposition, 46 opposed, and 10 absent or not voting.

160. *Iowa Senate Journal 1866*, 562–63, 634–36.

161. Fairall, 77.

162. Ibid., 77–78.

163. Gue, vol. 3, 18.

164. Shambaugh, *Messages and Proclamations*, vol. 3, 258.

165. Proceedings of the Colored Convention Held in the City of Des Moines Wednesday and Thursday February 12 and 13, 1868 (Muscatine: Daily Journal Book and Job Printing House 1868), 11.

166. *Iowa House Journal 1868*, 382, 401–2.

167. *Iowa Senate Journal 1868*, 384–85.

168. Shambaugh, *Messages and Proclamations*, vol. 3, 450–52.

169. See *Revision of 1860*, sec. 2720.

170. *Muscatine Weekly Journal*, Jan. 8, 1869.

171. See Iowa Constitution of 1857, art. 3, secs. 4, 5.

172. *Iowa State Register*, Dec. 4, 1880.

173. See generally Marilyn Jackson, "Alexander Clark: A Rediscovered Black Leader," *Iowan* 23 (1975): 43.

174. *Muscatine Journal*, Oct. 31, 1867.

175. Ibid.

176. Ibid., Sept. 14, 1867.

177. The original court papers in the case of *Susan Clark by her next friend Alexander Clark v. The Board of Directors of the Independent District Township of the City of Muscatine* are located in Alexander Clark, Muscatine File, Musser Public Library, Muscatine, Iowa. The district court order of Oct. 26, 1867, is found in Minute Book K, 6, Clerk of the Muscatine County District Court, Muscatine, Iowa.

178. 24 Iowa 266 (1868).

179. Ibid., 271 (citing Iowa Constitution of 1857, art. 9, sec. 12) [emphasis added by court].

180. An act approved April 8, 1862, provided that "in each sub-district there shall be taught one or more schools for the instruction of youth between the ages of five and twenty-one years." An Act to Amend and Consolidate an Act Passed by the Board of Education, Dec. 24, 1859, Entitled "An Act to Amend an Act to Provide a System of Common Schools," and the Amendments Thereto, ch. 172, sec. 12, *Acts and Resolutions Passed at the Regular Session of the Ninth General Assembly of the State of Iowa* (Des Moines: State Printer, 1862) [emphasis added], 206.

181. 24 Iowa at 274 [emphasis added by court].

182. Ibid., 277.

183. An Act to Amend Sec. 2700, of Ch. 114, of the Revision of 1860, *Acts and Resolutions Passed at the Regular Session of the Thirteenth General Assembly of the State of Iowa* (Des Moines: State Printer, 1870), 21.

184. See Acton and Acton, 154–55.

185. See *Smith v. The Directors of The Independent School District of Keokuk*, 40 Iowa 518 (1875); *Dove v. The Independent School District of Keokuk*, 41 Iowa 689 (1875).

186. 37 Iowa 145 (1873).

187. *Emma Coger v. Northwestern Union Packet Company*, Evidence in Chief, Testimony of Emma Coger, 20–21, *Abstracts and Arguments*, 33 June Term 1873 Des Moines (University of Iowa Law Library, Iowa City, Iowa).

188. Ibid., 66.

189. 37 Iowa at 158.

190. 67 Iowa 536 (1885).

191. Ibid., 538.

192. Ibid., 539–40.

193. Ibid., 540.

194. An Act to Protect All Citizens in Their Civil and Legal Rights, ch. 114, *U.S. Statutes at Large*, vol. 18, part 3, 335–37 (approved March 1, 1875); see Civil Rights Cases, 109 U.S. 3 (1883).

195. *Cedar Rapids Gazette*, Oct. 23, 1883.

196. Ibid., Oct. 24, 1883.

197. *[Keokuk] Gate City*, Nov. 1, 1883.

198. *Davenport Daily Gazette*, Oct. 26, 1883.

199. Shambaugh, *Messages and Proclamations*, vol. 5, 321.

200. *Iowa Senate Journal 1884*, 443.

201. *Iowa House Journal 1884*, 514.

202. Milton R. Konvitz, *A Century of Civil Rights* (New York: Columbia Univ. Press, 1961), 155–57. Connecticut, New Jersey, and Ohio also passed civil rights laws in 1884. Ibid., 157.

203. An Act to Protect All Citizens in Their Civil and Legal Rights, ch. 105, *Acts and Resolutions Passed at the Regular Session of the Twentieth General Assembly of the State of Iowa* (Des Moines: State Printer, 1884), 107–8.

204. *Code of 1873*, sec. 3967.

205. Iowa Constitution of 1857, art. 1, sec. 11.

206. *Report of the Secretary of State in Relation to the Criminal Returns of the State of Iowa for the Years 1886 and 1887* (Des Moines: State Printer, 1887), 109, reprinted in *Legislative Documents Submitted to the Twenty-Second General Assembly of the State of Iowa*, vol. 3 (Des Moines: State Printer, 1888), for report of Mahaska County Criminal Convictions stating that the person charged with the offense of "refusing to shave another" and fined $5 was "colored." The race of the customer Bennett is given in *State v. Hall, Abstracts and Arguments*, 72 Iowa, 10, SL-State RI (University of Iowa Law Library, Iowa City, Iowa), 503(a).

207. Ibid.

208. 72 Iowa 525 (1887).

209. Ibid., 527.

210. An Act to Amend Sec. 1 of ch. 105, Acts of the Twentieth General Assembly of Iowa, Relating to Civil Rights, ch. 43 (approved March 26, 1892), *Acts and Resolutions Passed at the Regular Session of the Twenty-fourth General Assembly of the State of Iowa* (Des Moines: State Printer, 1892), 68.

211. *Iowa House Journal 1892*, 493.

212. *Iowa State Register*, March 19, 1892; see also *Cedar Rapids Daily Republican*, March 19, 1892.

213. *Iowa Senate Journal 1892*, 489.

214. *Iowa State Register*, March 22, 1892.

215. 128 Iowa 743 (1905).

216. *[Des Moines] Register and Leader*, May 7, 1904.

217. 128 Iowa at 745–46.

218. Bergmann, 83–84.

219. 146 Iowa 89 (1910).

220. Ibid., 95.

221. Ibid., 98.

222. Ibid., 104.

223. Ibid., 107 (C.J. Evans dissenting).

224. Robert Edward Goostree, "Civil Rights in Iowa: The Statute and Its Enforcement," Ph.D. diss., University of Iowa, 1950, 24.

225. *Report of the Secretary of State Relating to Criminal Convictions of the State of Iowa for the Year Ending September 30, 1904, and the Year Ending September 30, 1905* (Des Moines: State Printer, 1905), 98, repr. in *Legislative Documents Submitted to the Thirty-first General Assembly of the State of Iowa* (Des Moines: State Printer, 1906).

226. *Report of the Board of Parole for the Biennial Period Ending June 13, 1918* (Des Moines: State of Iowa, 1918), 43, repr. in *Legislative Documents Submitted to the Thirty-eighth General Assembly* (Des Moines: State Printer, 1919).

227. Letter from James B. Morris to Robert W. Bagnall, Director of Branches, National Office, NAACP, May 11, 1923, Records of the NAACP, Des Moines, Iowa, Box G68, Folder 1, Library of Congress, Microfilm (SHSI, Manuscript Division, Des Moines, Iowa).

228. Ibid.

229. An Act to Amend Section Five Thousand Eight (5008) Chapter Eleven (11) Title Twenty-four (24) of the Code (C.C. 8888, 8889) Relating to Infringment of Civil Rights, Providing For a Specific Penalty For Violation Thereof, ch. 216 (approved March 28, 1923), *Acts and Joint Resolutions Passed at the Regular Session of the Fortieth General Assembly of the State of Iowa* (Des Moines: State of Iowa, 1923), 198.

230. *Iowa House Journal 1923,* 580–81.

231. *Iowa Senate Journal 1923,* 1036.

232. Letter of James Morris, op. cit.

233. Letter from William E. Taylor, Secretary, Des Moines Branch NAACP to James Weldon Johnson, Secretary, National Office, NAACP, Dec. 15, 1923, Records of the NAACP, op. cit.

234. Letter of Mrs. S. Joe Brown to the president and delegates of the 19th Annual Conference of the NAACP, Los Angeles, California, June 26,1928, Records of the NAACP, op. cit.

235. Goostree, 57.

236. Ibid., 64.

237. Ibid., 66–69.

238. Ibid., 114 (remarks of S. Joe Brown to Robert Edward Goostree, March 18, 1950).

239. Ibid., 64, 68.

240. *Iowa Bystander,* July 15, 1941 and Dec. 7, 1944; Goostree, 61.

241. *State v. Katz,* 241 Iowa 115, 116 (1949).

242. *Iowa Bystander,* Nov. 25, 1948.

243. 241 Iowa 115 (1949).

244. Ibid., 116, 121.

245. *Iowa Bystander,* Oct. 20, 1949; see also ibid., Oct. 13, 1949.

246. *Iowa Bystander,* Dec. 8, 1949.

247. *Iowa Bystander,* Nov. 24, 1949.

248. *Iowa Bystander,* Dec. 8, 1949.

249. *DMR,* July 6, 1991.

250. *Iowa Bystander,* Jan. 5, 1950.

251. *Iowa Bystander,* Oct. 15, 1953.

252. 117 F. Supp. 615 (N.D., Iowa, 1954).

253. Ibid., 616–17, 622.

254. Ibid., 630.

255. *1960 Report of the Governor's Commission on Human Relations,* 10.

256. *1961 Report to the Commission on Civil Rights from the State Advisory Committee,* 152, Gov. Norman Erbe Papers (SHSI, Manuscript Division, Des Moines, Iowa).

257. *Iowa House Journal 1947,* 461 (House File 329).

258. Robert Benjamin Stone, "The Legislative Struggle for Civil Rights in Iowa 1947–1965," M.A. thesis, Iowa State University, 1990, 32–33.

259. *Iowa Senate Journal 1955,* 1062; *Iowa House Journal 1955,* 1492 (Senate Concurrent Resolution 15); see *Iowa Bystander,* May 12, 1955.

260. Stone, 41–42.

261. *Commission to Study Discrimination in Employment in Iowa, Report to the Members of the 57th General Assembly of Iowa* (Dec. 1956), 3, quoted in Stone, 47.

262. Stone, 47–48, 52–55.

263. Letter from Donald Boles, chairman of the Commission on Human Relations, to Gov. Herschel C. Loveless, July 1, 1959, repr. in *Report of the Governor's Commission on Human Relations* (State of Iowa: Des Moines, 1959), "Foreword."

264. *Iowa House Journal 1959,* 272–73, 605; *Iowa Senate Journal 1959,* 145, 409.

265. *Iowa House Journal 1961,* 442, 842; *Iowa Senate Journal 1961,* 88.

266. Minutes of Executive Committee Meeting, Governor's Commission on Civil Rights, July 17, 1962, and Aug. 21, 1962; File, Governor's Commission on Human Rights, Minutes 1961–65, M.S.C. 385, Harold E. Hughes Papers, Box G-17 (University of Iowa Libraries, Special Collections, Iowa City).

267. *DMR,* April 18, 1963.

268. *Iowa House Journal 1963,* 1323–24.

269. *Iowa Senate Journal 1963,* 1124.

270. An Act Making It Unlawful for Any Person or Employer to Discriminate in Employment Against Any Individual, and for a Labor Organization to Discriminate in Membership Against Any Individual, Because of Race, Color, Religion, National Origin or Ancestry, *Acts of the Sixtieth General Assembly,* 1963, ch. 330, sec. 1.

271. Ibid., sec. 2

272. Ibid., sec. 3.

273. *Waterloo Courier,* May 7, 1963.

274. See *DMR,* July 24, 1963.

275. *[Davenport] Times-Democrat,* Aug. 24, 1963.

276. *Fort Madison Evening Democrat,* Nov. 4, 1963.

277. *Iowa Bystander,* May 7, 1964.

278. *Waterloo Courier,* June 28, 1964.

279. Executive Order Number One, Gov. Harold E. Hughes, May 14, 1964; see *Iowa Bystander,* May 21, 1964.

280. Civil Rights Act of 1964, Public Law 88-352, 78 Stat. 241 (1964).

281. Arthur Earl Bonfield, "State Civil Rights Statutes: Some Proposals," 49 *Iowa Law Review* (1964): 1067.

282. Arthur Earl Bonfield, "The Origin and Rationale of the Iowa Civil Rights Act, A Speech on the Occasion of the Iowa Civil Rights Commission Celebration of the Twenty-Fifth Anniversary of the Iowa Civil Rights Act (July 21, 1990)", in "Legislative History of The Iowa Civil Rights Act of 1965, The Iowa Civil Rights Act of 1967, and The Iowa Civil Rights Act of 1978" (Arthur Earl Bonfield private collection, Iowa City, Iowa).

283. Frank T. Nye, "The 61st General Assembly of Iowa," *Palimpsest* 46 (1965): 425–28.

284. "Inaugural Message to the Sixty-first General Assembly by Hon. Harold E. Hughes, Governor of Iowa" (Jan. 14, 1965), *Iowa Senate Journal 1965,* 61.

285. *Iowa Bystander,* Feb. 11, 1965.

286. "Remarks by Gov. Harold E. Hughes to the Iowa Conference on Civil Rights, Des Moines (Feb. 6, 1965)," 10, Box G28, Iowa Conference on Civil Rights Speeches, Jan. 12, 1965, to Feb. 6, 1965, MSC 385, Papers of Harold E. Hughes (University of Iowa Libraries, Special Collections, Iowa City, Iowa).

287. *Iowa House Journal 1965,* 322, 712–13.

288. *Iowa Senate Journal 1965,* 923. The Senate made one amendment to the bill, which the House accepted. *Iowa House Journal 1965,* 1131–32.

289. An Act to Establish a Civil Rights Commission to Eliminate Unfair and Discriminatory Practices in Public Accommodations, Employment, Apprenticeship Programs, On-the-Job Training Programs, and Vocational Schools and to Permit the Study of Discrimination, *Acts of the Sixty-first General Assembly,* 1965, ch. 121.

290. Ibid., sec. 3.

291. Ibid., secs. 5–9.

292. Ibid., sec. 10.

293. Ibid., sec. 14.

294. *[Davenport] Times-Democrat,* April 30, 1965.

295. *Iowa Senate Journal 1967,* 617, 944–49.

296. *Cedar Rapids Gazette,* April 20, 1967.

297. *Iowa House Journal 1967,* 1030–31.

298. An Act Relating to Discrimination in Housing, *Acts of the Sixty-second General Assembly,* 1967, ch. 122, sec. 2.

299. Ibid., sec. 3; see An Act Relating to the Bond Provision in the Fair Housing Law, *Acts of the Sixty-third General Assembly,* 1969, ch. 113.

300. An Act Relating to Sex Discrimination in Employment, Housing and Public Accommodations, *Acts of the Sixty-third General Assembly,* 1970, ch. 1058.

301. An Act Relating to the Civil Rights of Physically and Mentally Handicapped Persons, *Acts of the Sixty-fourth General Assembly,* 1972, ch. 1031.

302. An Act Relating to Age Discrimination in Employment, ibid., ch. 1032.

303. An Act Relating to the Membership, Powers, and Duties of the Civil Rights Commission, *Acts of the Sixty-fifth General Assembly,* 1974, ch. 1254, sec. 4.

304. An Act Amending the Iowa Civil Rights Law, *Acts of the Sixty-seventh General Assembly,* 1978, ch. 1179.

305. An Act Relating to the Organization and Structure of State Government, *Acts of the Seventy-first General Assembly,* 1986, ch. 1245, sec. 1496.

306. An Act Relating to Unfair or Discriminatory Practices in Housing and Real Estate, Providing Civil Remedies, and a Criminal Penalty, *Acts of the Seventy-fourth General Assembly,* 1991, ch. 184. For current provisions of the Iowa Civil Rights Act of 1965 as amended, see *Iowa Code,* ch. 216 (1997).

307. 191 N.W. 2d 758, 761 (Iowa 1971).

308. Ibid., 765–66.

309. Ibid., 767–68. The Court, citing *Amos v. Prom* and *Humburd v. Crawford,* stated that the injured person could continue to seek damages in a civil court action. For current provisions concerning remedial powers of the Iowa Civil Rights Commission, including damage awards, see *Iowa Code* sec. 216.15(8) (1997).

310. 191 N.W. 2d at 771–73.

311. 394 N.W. 2d 375 (Iowa 1986).

312. A 1978 amendment had given the Commission authority to award "actual damages," a term that included emotional distress damages. Ibid., 382–83.

313. Ibid., 384.

314. 551 N.W. 2d 876 (Iowa 1996).

315. Ibid., 881–82.

316. Ibid., 883.

317. Ibid., 885–86.

318. *Fourth Annual Report of the Iowa Civil Rights Commission, January 1970,* 3.

319. Ibid.

320. *Fifth Annual Report of the Iowa Civil Rights Commission, January 1971,* 4, 8–9.

321. *Iowa Civil Rights Commission Annual Report 1987,* 9.

322. *Iowa Civil Rights Commission Annual Report 1990,* 11.

323. *Iowa Civil Rights Commission Annual Report, Fiscal Year 1995,* 5. (Race complaints were 29.6% of 2,274 total complaints filed).

324. *Iowa Civil Rights Commission Annual Report 1996,* 4–5.

325. Ibid., 4.

326. An Act Relating to the Establishment of a Division on the Status of Blacks within the Department of Human Rights, *Acts of the Seventy-second General Assembly,* 1988, ch. 1201, sec. 4. For current provisions of the act, see *Iowa Code,* sec. 216A.141–49 (1997).

327. *DMR,* March 25, 1988 (remarks of Sen. Robert Carr).

328. *Iowa Civil Rights Communicator* 6 (March 1987), 1.

329. An Act Relating to Violations of A Person's Civil Rights and Providing Penalties, *Acts of the Seventy-second General Assembly,* 1988, ch. 1163, sec. 1(3).

330. An Act Relating to Violations of an Individual's Rights, By Prohibiting Acts of Assault and Criminal Mischief, Providing Victims Actionable Civil Relief Against Offenders, Establishing a Program to Monitor Rights Violations, and Providing a Penalty, *Acts of the Seventy-third General Assembly,* 1990, ch. 1139.

331. *[Dubuque] Telegraph-Herald,* April 16, 1992.

332. *Iowa Senate Journal 1992,* vol. 1, 33, 38.

333. An Act Relating to Violations of an Individual's Rights, and Establishing Additional Criminal Offenses, *Acts of the Seventy-fourth General Assembly,* 1992, ch. 1157, sec. 9.

334. See ibid., secs. 4–5; see also ibid., secs. 3, 6. Current provisions of the Hate Crimes Act are found at *Iowa Code,* ch. 729A (1997); see also ibid., ch. 729.

335. 511 N.W. 2d 389 (Iowa 1994).

336. Ibid., 395.

337. *Coger v. The North West. Union Packet Co.,* 37 Iowa 145, 158 (Iowa 1873).

Richard, Lord Acton has degrees in modern history from Oxford University, England. Since marrying an Iowan, he has written extensively on Iowa history and is co-author of To Go Free: A Treasury of Iowa's Legal Heritage *(Benjamin F. Shambaugh Award, 1996). Acton was a British trial lawyer and currently sits in Britain's House of Lords.*

Patricia Nassif Acton received her law degree from the University of Iowa College of Law, where she is Clinical Professor of Law. She has written numerous legal books and articles and is co-author of To Go Free: A Treasury of Iowa's Legal Heritage.

(Above)World War 1 black captains commissioned at Fort Des Moines (SHSI Des Moines)

(Right) Black WAC trainees, Fort Des Moines, World War 2 (SHSI Des Moines)

Black Iowans in Defense of the Nation

1863–1990

by William S. Morris

Gov. William M. Stone, first resisted then accepted black suffrage in Iowa. (SHSI Des Moines)

Military service and sacrifice have been the keys to political, economic, and social progress for black Americans from the Revolutionary War to the Persian Gulf War. For more than two centuries, African-Americans have contributed mightily to the cause of liberty, from Crispus Attucks — the first American to die in the fight for independence from England — to Gen. Colin L. Powell, commander of Allied forces in the victory over Iraq in 1990. This chapter traces the extensive and distinguished contributions to American military efforts by African- Americans from Iowa.

The Civil War

The Black Codes adopted at Iowa's second constitutional convention in May 1846 outlawed chattel slavery, but asserted that only a "white male citizen" could vote, serve as a member of the General Assembly, be included in the state census of population, or be required to serve in the state militia.[2] While Iowa politicians battled over the issue of racial exclusion and the legal status of blacks well into the Civil War, it was unquestionably the service of the men of the 1st Iowa Volunteers of African Descent — later re-designated the 60th Regiment of Infantry, United States Colored Troops (U.S.C.T.) — that compelled the Iowa legislature to officially recognize black male suffrage in 1868 and to repeal the Black Codes from state law in 1884.

William M. Stone, Iowa's governor during the Civil War, for many years resisted black suffrage in Iowa but came to recognize, grudgingly, that voting rights could not possibly be lawfully denied Iowans who spilled blood for the Union.[3] Equality before the law was a principle laid down by the Founding Fathers in 1787, and even moderate Republicans like Governor Stone could not resist the tide of change. In a speech after the war, Stone referred casually to the contributions of Iowa's 60th Regiment, stating how those black volunteers credited to Iowa's wartime manpower quota had exempted over 2,000 white Iowans from the 1864 draft.[4] Missouri was allotted 200 members of the regiment to its own manpower quota, but Iowa received credit for the remaining three-year enlistments.

The United States military already had ample historical evidence of black bravery under fire when the

continued on page 96

> "Once let the black man get upon his person the brass letters 'U.S.,' let him get an eagle on his button and a musket on his shoulder and bullets in his pockets, and there is no power on earth which can deny that he has earned the right to citizenship."
>
> —Frederick Douglass[1]

EBONY HEROES

Selected biographies of black Iowans who served during the Civil War taken from local newspaper obituaries

Who were these ebony heroes, who voluntarily risked life and limb in defense of liberty and union? Black men from across the state were represented in the ranks of the 1st Iowa Volunteers of African Descent, 60th Regiment, as were numbers of escaped slaves from Missouri, according to the 1863 *Report of the Adjutant General and Acting Quartermaster General of the State of Iowa*. A third of the 60th Regiment's Iowans gave their place of residence as Keokuk and nearby towns. Others hailed from Davenport, Des Moines, Newton, Iowa City, and Keosauqua. Approximately half of these men had previously lived in Missouri.

While Iowa's entire black population numbered only 1,500 in 1863, fully 700 black Hawkeyes volunteered for service at Keokuk — a number nearly equal the number of black males of military age in the state. Although some were eventually rejected for medical reasons, the turnout was incredible. Missouri volunteers swelled the 60th Regiment's ranks to 1,153 men.

Biographical information on the enlisted men of the 60th Regiment is sparse, coming largely from hometown newspaper obituaries. Genealogists in Newton have collected a number of obituaries over the years, giving us an insight into the lives of these black soldiers. For example, the *Newton Daily News* noted on December 9, 1919, the passing of Alexander E. Fine, *"one of the best known Negroes of the city."* The *News* reported that Fine originally came to reside in Newton, "in 1862, at the outbreak of the Civil War. He and several other Negroes, [including] Lou Mayes, Walker Waldon, Alex Nichols, Tom Watson, Clem and John Miller, and Will Moore all came here from Savannah, Missouri — being runaway slaves. All have passed away but John Miller who resides in Des Moines. Every one of them enlisted in the Union army and did good service for their country."

The *News* noted that Fine was born in "Andrew County, Missouri in 1841, and lived there as slave property of Clinton Howell until he escaped to Iowa. At the time Alex ran away, he was overseer for several other slaves on the Howell farms.

After the war he returned to his old home in Missouri and was married to Mrs. Sylvia Johnson. They came to Newton and have made their home there ever since." The obituary concluded, "[Fine] had a reputation of being an honorable man and he had many, many friends and acquaintances throughout the city who will be sorry to learn of his death."

On June 21, 1899, the *Newton Journal* reported the passing of Jason Green. "Green was born in Madison County, Kentucky, December 24, 1844. His parents, Nathan and Charity Green, were slaves. . . . [At] the age of nineteen he came to Iowa from Missouri, where the family had moved to enlist for the war... in company with Lewis Mayes and his own brother, Taylor, having determined to be free . . . a second attempt at escape which was successful, and they came to Keokuk, Iowa. While there the men, with three [of Green's] brothers, Taylor, John, and Jason, enlisted for the war. Of the four brothers who were in service, Jason is the last to be called home. Mr. Green has been a sufferer for years, having contracted several diseases while in the war; yet, amid it all, he was patient, and trusting, and had a smile for everyone. As a businessman, Mr. Green was always prompt in the mornings. He was one of the oldest business men in the city, having engaged in the barber business for over twenty-eight years. ... One of his characteristics was independence, which he inherited from his father, who so desired his own and his wife's freedom during slavery that he worked and purchased their independence."

An interesting note on Green appeared in the *Newton Record* on June 22, 1899: "[During their first winter in Newton] Jason Green and Lewis Mayes worked with the families of Robt. Hill and David Matchett and attended the country school, which was very distasteful to some Kentuckians in the neighborhood who objected to sending their children to school with 'niggers.' But the prejudice soon died out, as Jason and Lewis proved apt pupils and worthy of respect."

The death of Anderson Hayes was recorded in the *Newton Daily News* on October 6, 1923. "WELL KNOWN NEGRO IS DEAD: Anderson Hayes Passes Away At The

Old Soldiers Home at Marshalltown Yesterday," said the headline. "At the ripe old age of 87, Anderson Hayes, pioneer resident of Newton, died at the Old Soldiers Home at Marshalltown yesterday afternoon.

He was born a slave in 1836 in the state of Missouri. Running away he came to Newton at the age of 27 and [on] September 11, 1863, enlisted in Company E, 1st Colored Infantry of the Civil War. He was mustered in October 11th of the same year, and was mustered out October 15, 1865 at Devall's Bluff, Arkansas. He returned to Newton, and remained here excluding a few years until he was placed in the Soldier's Home at Marshalltown about two years ago... . He was a member of the G.A.R.'s [Grand Army of the Republic] having attended their reunion in Des Moines last year. He was very active for his age, and made many new friends while there."

Henry (Big Jim) James's obituary in the *Newton Journal* on April 9, 1884, focused almost entirely on his wartime experience. "A colored man named Henry James ... died very suddenly of heart disease in our city on Tuesday morning.... He has quite a history. When Co. B 13th [18th?] Iowa was at Summerville, Alabama in May, 1864, he came and attached himself to it, and followed it home to Newton. He was a model of faithfulness and trustworthiness while in the army, always ready to carry the burdens, do the cooking and other drudgery of the camp, and has frequently been known to crawl to the pickets, when under fire, and carry them their meals. The boys of Co. B will mourn his sudden taking off. He was six feet, eight inches tall."

Lewis Mayes, who had come to Newton in the 1860s with Alexander Fine and several other young men fleeing slavery in Savannah, Missouri, died December 3, 1911. The *Newton Journal* reported the cause of his death as heart trouble. "Mr. May[e]s was a slave in Missouri before the war and came to Newton with others of the Negro race about the time the war ended. He has always resided in Newton or vicinity and never in all these years has he been out of the state but once, when he went to Chicago."

Clem Miller, who died February 10, 1914, had come to Newton even earlier than Mayes, arriving in 1855. "When the civil war broke out," wrote the *Newton Daily News*, "[Clem Miller] enlisted in Company E, 60th U.S. Colored Infantry. After serving the entire war he returned to Newton where he has lived ever since."

John Ross Miller was born into slavery in 1841 and died in Newton in 1923. In 1934, the *Annals of Iowa* gave this account of Miller's flight to freedom: "Among the runaways [slaves relocated from Kentucky to Missouri] were four colored boys by the names of John Graves, Alec Nichols, Henderson Hays and Anderson Hays. John Graves gave me the story of their flight from Missouri. He said, 'They were making preparations to send us all down to Texas, so us boys just borrowed two horses and two mules from our masters and lit out for Canada.

"We thought that it was just a little ways up there. We traveled after night and hid in the brush in the daytime. The second day we traveled during the day and landed in Winterset, Madison County, Iowa, about one o'clock. It was on Saturday in the latter part of October, 1861. I wanted to get some shoes put on my horse, but the blacksmith told me I would have to wait about two hours.

"There was a great crowd in, and a company of militia was drilling, so we done got scared and left. We had gone about two or three miles and was in a long lane when a crowd of men on horseback come on the run down the lane after us. They had shotguns and rifles and was raising an awful dust and making a lot of noise. We was [sure] some scared and thought that our time had come to go to Texas, but it wouldn't do us any good to run, on account of them mules, they couldn't run as fast as horses. One of the men riding after us was riding a big white horse and had a gun on the saddle in front of him. He run past us and then turned and headed us off. They surrounded us and took us back to town, but they couldn't find any officers to put us in jail and while they was lookin' for the officers they formed a ring around us boys to keep the crowd back. They got to talking pretty loud and someone dared anyone to try to come inside that ring, and they hadn't more than said it than the coats began to fly and there wasn't any ring at all. The men that took us out of the ring gave us something to eat and told us which way to go, and we wasn't long in getting out of there. We started east and at the top of a long hill we hid in the brush till night. Then we traveled by the north star and landed in Indianola the next morning.

"We went from there to Newton in Jasper County. I worked on a farm near Newton the following summer for a man by the name of Sherer. I took his name for you know that us colored boys had no names only the names of our masters. I enlisted under the name of John Sherer in the First Regiment (Colored) Infantry, which was afterwards the 60th Regiment U.S. Colored Troops. I served through the war and then come back to Newton."

Sherer later learned his father had taken up the name Miller and still lived in the South, and thereafter changed his name from Sherer to Miller.

On October 11, 1913, the *Newton Daily News* reported the death of Walker Waldon. "Walker Waldon, colored, who for almost fifty years has been a resident of Newton, died at his home in Northeast Newton at 3:30 o'clock this morning at the age of seventy four years. Walker Waldon was born a slave in the state of Virginia in the year 1839. Here with his two brothers, David and Austin, he lived in bondage until the year 1861 [1863?] when President Lincoln issued his Emancipation Proclamation freeing all the slaves in the United States. Mr. Waldon then came north and enlisted in Company E, U.S. Colored Infantry, and went immediately to the front to fight for the liberty of his race. He served through the entire war and receiving his discharge in 1865 came north and settled at Newton. Since that time he has lived in the city and in the same neighborhood. For forty years Mr. Waldon was an influential member of the A.M.E. Church and was a thorough Christian man and a good citizen."

Newspapers in other parts of the state also honored the passing of black Civil War veterans. For example, the *Iowa Bystander* reported the death of John Walker, last black member of the Grand Army of the Republic living in Des Moines, in July 1937. Walker was born into slavery on March 14, 1840, in Albany, Missouri. He escaped to Kansas, where he enlisted at Wyandotte in the 1st Kansas Infantry (Colored) in 1863, later re-designated the 79th Infantry, United States Colored Troops. The 1st Kansas was the first black regiment to engage in combat during the Civil War, fighting at Island Mound, Missouri, October 29, 1862, where several casualties were incurred. Walker went on to fight in the Ozark Mountains and the Tennessee Valley under the overall command of Gen. William Tecumseh Sherman. Mr. Walker's wife served as deputy Polk County recorder after the war, and the couple raised four sons. Walker was member of St. Paul A.M.E. Church, led the six o'clock prayer band, and was vice commander of the Crocker Street post of the Grand Army of the Republic.

The *Des Moines Register and Leader* on December 27, 1915, noted the passing of Jack Howe at the age of 90. The *Register* obituary reads: "His skin was black but he possessed a soul as white and as big a heart as ever inhabited a tonement of clay; not only the best-known character in southwestern Iowa, respected and loved by all." Howe was born a slave in Missouri, escaping at age 35, "and came across into Iowa where he enlisted in the Union Army and served faithfully until the end of the war. After receiving his discharge he came to Bedford, where he resided for the next fifty years. Howe was married, leaving two sons and one daughter, all born after he became a free man.

One son was a soldier in the regular Army for years and was a member of the famous colored regiment which saved the slaughter of Colonel Roosevelt's Roughriders by their timely arrival at the battle of El Caney in Cuba, during the Spanish American War. He afterwards went with his Regiment to the Philippines and died there following a long illness." Howe's obituary, written in the language of the day, ended poetically: "Life's sun is descending low and night is coming on the American slave, and Jack Howe's death is being reenacted almost daily in every state of the Union. It is the passing of the slave and is the last sad chapter in the one great blot on

American history, wiped out by the blood of the volunteer soldier in the great war of the rebellion."

Another fascinating story is that of Lee Moore, which appeared in the *Sioux City Journal* on February 18, 1945. Moore is described as "a 104-year old Negro who recalls, among other things, that he tended saddle horses for General Ulysses S. Grant in the American Civil War, and was an eyewitness to several battles." In 1945, Moore was employed on the Frank Montgomery farm in the 1600 block of 11th Street as a horse trainer and livestock tender. "He lives simply in a small shack on the premises. His daily stint begins early — sometimes before dawn. And he works until late at night. Never married, he does his own cooking and cleaning.

"Mr. Moore claimed to have been born July 12, 1840, in Buenos Aires, Argentina, and enjoyed going down to the dock area as a young man. 'We were down admiring the ships one day and were invited aboard to try out for jobs. Before we got off again, the ship was underway and we were put to work as deck hands. That's the way they recruited sailors in those days. We left the ship when we got to America and I've been here ever since.'

"Moore arrived during the Civil War, and while he never served in uniform, was attached to the union service by a Colonel Moore who hired Lee as a groomsman. 'I was used as bait for rebel marksmen a time or two,' Lee recalled. 'The Colonel's black horse was well known and rebel marksmen used to try to pick him out. The colonel put me on the horse a few times to draw their fire so we could find out where the snipers were hidden. The horse and I always came through without harm.' Moore indicated he tended horses for General U.S. Grant for nearly two years, concluding employment at the battle for Cumberland Gap. He characterized Confederate General Robert E. Lee's style of fighting: 'He would make a surprise attack, grab what food and equipment he could, and then retreat, leading union forces in pursuit.' Moore reported being captured during one of these raids. 'We were noncombatants, and were allowed to continue our usual line of

work behind the Confederate lines.' After the war, Lee became a horse trainer and tended livestock all over the country. At 104 years of age, he claimed to be very well satisfied with life. 'But there's this much about it,' he adds, 'I don't expect to have as much fun during the next 100 years.'"

In March 1928, Milton Howard, a black native of Muscatine who was kidnapped into slavery in the South, escaped, and later joined the Union Army, died in Davenport. Born in 1852, Howard left Alabama and came to Iowa in 1864, entering the 60th U.S. Colored Troops as a drummer boy due to his young age. He was mustered out of service at Devall's Bluff, Arkansas, in October 1865.

Howard went to work at Rock Island Arsenal in 1886. During his service there, he saved the life of the arsenal commandant, Gen. D. W. Flagler, who was walking on ice near a dam adjacent to the arsenal when the frozen underfooting gave way. "The commandant went through the spongy ice and was floundering about in the cold water when Howard came to his rescue and saved his life," noted a report of the incident. "In the summer of 1921, in company with three other men who had served the arsenal for half a century, Howard was sent to Aberdeen, Maryland, by Col. D. M. King in special recognition of his long and satisfactory service. In the history of the arsenal there are only four men who received gold medals for their service, and Howard was one of them."

Howard was living in Davenport when he collapsed while attending Sunday services at the Apostolic Faith Church. He was a member of the August Wentz Post No. 1, Grand Army of the Republic, and left four sons and a daughter behind. It is noteworthy that unlike later veterans' organizations, Grand Army of the Republic posts were not racially segregated.

Doubtless there are scores of other heroic stories still to be uncovered in the archives of Iowa newspapers. Until they are, the foregoing biographies from Newton and elsewhere in the state suggest the degree of commitment to liberty and the Union cause exhibited by the men of the 60th Regiment and other black soldiers from Iowa.

continued from page 91

Civil War began in 1861. Thousands of free black men fought for George Washington during the Revolution; hundreds supported Andrew Jackson during the War of 1812, particularly at the Battle of New Orleans. Black men were among the first non-native explorers of the New World, accompanying Spanish and French expeditions all across the Southwest and west-central North America. A slave named York, a member of the Lewis and Clark expedition of 1804, was likely the first African-American to set foot in what later became the state of Iowa. And Jacob Dodson, an African-American who later fought in the Mexican War, accompanied John C. Fremont on the explorer's brave 1843 expeditions to the Far West.

In 1861, this same Jacob Dodson wrote to U.S. Secretary of War Edwin M. Stanton offering to raise a regiment of 300 free Negroes for the defense of Washington, D.C.[5] "In reply to your letter of 23rd instant," Stanton countered curtly, "I have to say that this Department has no intention to call into the service of the Government any colored soldiers."[6] Stanton's resistance to the idea notwithstanding, following the Confederate shelling of Fort Sumter, commencing April 12, 1861, thousands of free blacks in cities and towns all across the North and South immediately offered their services to both Union and Confederate armies.

Official unwillingness to entertain the idea of Negro enlistments was seated in the belief widely held by most whites that the war would be of short duration. "Jeff Davis & Co. will be swinging from the battlements of Washington at least by the 4th of July. We spit upon a later and longer deferred justice," screamed Horace Greeley's *New York Daily Tribune*. The *Chicago Tribune* boldly roared, "Illinois can whip the South. We insist on the matter being turned over to us."[7] Behind all the editorial and official bravado on the war's abbreviated duration lay a deep-seated hesitation to label the war's goal as the destruction of chattel slavery. Attitudes on the slavery issue were ambivalent. Basically, northern whites would not, in 1861 or 1862, fight a war to destroy slavery, which would mean economic competition with large numbers of freed slaves. Yet neither would these same whites permit expansion of slavery westward, as poor whites could similarly find themselves incapable of "underbidding" black slave labor.

The reality of mass warfare finally struck home in both Washington and Richmond at the Battle of Shiloh in early April 1862. In two days of fighting, 3,500 soldiers were killed and 16,500 were wounded. Thousands more were missing or captured. Seven

thousand Iowans fought at Shiloh. Some 2,600 were killed, wounded, missing, or taken prisoner, and no community in the state was spared losses. Overall, Iowa contributed 58 infantry and cavalry regiments and 4 batteries of artillery to the Union war effort between 1861 and 1865. In the western department of operations, 76,000 Iowans fought. These troops amounted to nearly half the state's prewar white military age population. Iowa units suffered 13,000 casualties, 19 percent of total Union losses. The men and boys from Iowa died from disease in greater proportion than troops from any other northern state. Overall, sickness took more Union lives than Confederate shot and shell throughout the war, and this stark fact is reflected in the losses of the Iowa regiment of color. Of the 1,153 black Iowans and Missourians who served in the 60th Regiment, 11 were killed in action, 2 wounded (one later died), and 332 died of disease.[8]

The Second Confiscation Act and the Militia Act of 1862 authorized President Lincoln for the first time to "receive into the service of the United States, for the purpose of constructing entrenchments or performing camp duty, or any labor, or any military or naval service for which they were found to be competent, persons of African descent, and provided that such persons should be enrolled and organized, under such regulations nor inconsistent with the Constitutions and laws as the President might prescribe."[9]

Double Standard in Pay

The Militia Act provided a double standard in pay for black troops that was not corrected until March 1865: "Persons of African descent who under the law shall be employed, shall receive $10 a month, one ration, $3 of such monthly pay may be in clothes." Outrage over this overt discrimination was exhibited in black regiments all across the North, including the 60th Regiment in Iowa. Apparently a sergeant named Phillips and some other troops in the regiment "agitated the propriety of refusing to accept the seven dollars per month offered by the Government, and refusing to do duty because of it." Fortunately, "Sergeant Barton was able to avoid mutiny by calling on his fellow soldiers' racial pride, saying it was better to serve without pay than to refuse duty, as enforcement of the President's Emancipation Proclamation was essential to the freedom of the Negro race."[10]

However, Lincoln was still hesitant to accept black Americans as combat soldiers in the Grand Army of the Republic and to free all blacks held in bondage in the South. The

"In reply to your letter of 23rd instant, I have to say that this Department has no intention to call into the service of the Government any colored soldiers."

—U.S. Secretary of War Edwin M. Stanton, 1861

Emancipation Proclamation of September 22, 1862, freed slaves held in bondage only in those states in rebellion against the Union as of January 1, 1863. The president was determined to keep the slaveholding border states of Missouri, Tennessee, Kentucky, Maryland, and (later) West Virginia loyal to the Union. Only those slaves in the secessionist states were freed; those residing in border states remained legally chattel slaves until 1865.[11]

Bureau of Colored Troops

On May 22, 1863, the U.S. Department of War issued General Order No. 143, which established the Bureau of Colored Troops. Maj. Charles W. Foster was appointed assistant adjutant general of this office. Fifteen states, including Iowa, raised volunteer regiments under the Corps d'Afrique designation. By 1865, some 178,975 black soldiers served in the Grand Army of the Republic; a further 9,695 served in the U.S. Navy. The black soldiers comprised 135 infantry regiments, 6 cavalry regiments, 12 heavy artillery regiments, and 10 batteries of light artillery. They fought in 39 major battles and 410 minor actions. Of the men of color wearing Union blue, 2,751 were killed in action, and 65,427 died of disease or wounds, or were listed as missing in action.[12] Many historians concur with Lincoln's conclusion that the Union victory could not have been obtained without the service of black soldiers and sailors.

Prominent Iowa businessman and future lawyer Alexander Clark Sr. was unequivocal in his belief that Iowa's black population, augmented by escaped slaves from Missouri, should fully participate in the war — which by 1863 was clearly, of military necessity, being fought to free the slaves. Clark had written Iowa Gov. Samuel Kirkwood as early as 1862, offering to raise black military companies for service with white Iowa units, only to be rebuffed by the governor's secretary, who stated that white troops would not tolerate a racially integrated army.[13]

Organizing Regiments of Ex-Slaves

However, Governor Kirkwood would soon thereafter write to the War Department with a change of heart. "When this war is over and we have summed up the entire loss of life it has imposed on the country, I shall not have any regrets if it is found that a part of the dead are Niggers and that all are not white men."[14] On May 25, 1863, Secretary of War Stanton instructed Brig. Gen. Lorenzo Thomas to start organizing regiments of ex-slaves in the

Mississippi Valley. By November 1863, General Thomas had organized 4 regiments of cavalry, 6 regiments of heavy artillery, 4 companies of light artillery, and 40 regiments of infantry — totaling 56,320 men from Iowa, Arkansas, Tennessee, Mississippi, Louisiana, Alabama, Florida, and Kentucky.[15] An antislavery colonel, William A. Pile, was authorized to enlist black Missourians at St. Louis, and his jurisdiction was extended, with Governor Kirkwood's permission, to include southern Iowa, where numerous former slaves had taken up residence. An Iowa recruiting station was established at Keokuk. Enlistment parties proceeded to "raid" towns and villages in southern Iowa and northern Missouri in order to fill their recruitment quotas.

"There was an ardent desire," amongst Iowa's black population of approximately 1,500, "to assist in accomplishing the defeat of those who were engaged in an attempt which, if successful, meant the perpetuation of human slavery in the Southern states. They therefore gladly embraced the opportunity to enlist as soldiers in the Union Army."[16]

Despite public outcry at their tactics, particularly from pro-Union slave owners in Missouri, white Union officers mustered into service ten companies, six from Iowa — the 1st Iowa Volunteers of African Descent — and four from Missouri, with a total of 911 enlisted men. Alexander Clark Sr. of Muscatine was initially appointed the new regiment's sergeant major, its highest enlisted rank, but he failed the physical examination due to an old leg injury.[17] Nevertheless, Clark was on hand to present the 60th Regiment with its national banner, sewn by the black women of Keokuk and Muscatine, when the regiment was officially organized under the War Department's special orders dated July 27, 1863.

One Major Engagement

The 60th Regiment fought in one major engagement, a bloody battle near Helena, Arkansas, during its first excursion from base camp in July 1864. Eighty Iowans left camp with their Missouri cousins in a 360-man reconnaissance force, all armed with .577 caliber Enfield rifled muskets and accompanied by one battery (two guns) of a black artillery battalion. Confederate Gen. Jo Shelby's rebels surrounded the 60th at Wallace's Ferry near Big Creek. Over 800 Confederates poured heavy fire into the ranks of the black soldiers, who were at the time of the attack preparing breakfast after a long night's forced march.[18]

Iowa Gov. Samuel Kirkwood initially rejected African-American offers to raise a black regiment from Iowa, but changed his mind after seeing first-hand examples of black bravery under fire. (SHSI)

The band of an Iowa Civil War unit (SHSI Iowa City)

a dreadful moment." Just before the final Confederate charge, a detachment of the 15th Illinois Cavalry broke through the rebel encirclement and allowed the black infantrymen to exit the battlefield, bearing their artillery, weapons, and 11 wounded. "Gathering up their dead and wounded, the federal force now began a retreat, stubbornly yielding, inch by inch, each foot of ground, until night threw her mantle of darkness over the scene and the Confederates ceased their firing."[20]

"Colored men stood up to their duty like veterans"

The white commander of the black artillery battery filed the following after-action report: "During the whole fight the colored men stood up to their duty like veterans, and it was owing to their strong arms and cool heads, backed by fearless daring, alone that I was able to get away with either of my guns. They marched eighteen miles [without a break], fought five hours, against three to one, and were as eager at the end as at the beginning for the fight. Never did men, under such circumstances, show greater pluck or daring."[21] District headquarters later stated in a dispatch, "Will they fight? Ask the enemy. The colored troops fought like veterans, none flinched."[22]

The 60th Regiment encountered minor enemy resistance two days after their baptism of fire at Wallace's Ferry. On July 26, the troops traveled down the Mississippi and up the White River, where they clashed with dug-in rebel units. The black Iowans routed the southerners and captured two Texas Rangers in the process. Not long after this, the 60th Regiment returned to Helena, Arkansas, to resume the role assigned to most black soldiers during the Civil War — fatigue duty.[23]

In his *Compendium of the War of Rebellion* (1908), historian Frederick Dyer characterizes the role of the 1st Iowa Volunteers of African Descent in the Civil War as follows: "The records of the First Regiment of Iowa African Infantry constitute a portion of the military archives of this State, and it is therefore given its distinctive place in this work as the only regiment of the Negro race which the State of Iowa sent into the field. It may truly be said of these men that, when the call to arms was extended to them, they responded as freely — in proportion to their numbers — as had the men of other races, and it may also be as truly said that they, of all men, were offered the greatest inducement to enlist, for the time had then come when the success of the Union arms meant the freedom of their race. The opportunity to enroll

Historian Robert Dykstra renders a stirring account of the battle: "Taking cover behind a railroad embankment, they fought desperately amid the suffocating heat and smoke, and ear-splitting crash of musketry. After a severe four-hour fire fight that killed the commander [Adj. Theodore W. Pratt of Keokuk] and three other officers [and three enlisted men], the detachment was on the brink of being overrun." Repeated Confederate charges were repulsed, even though the ebony warriors were outnumbered two to one. "Still grossly outnumbered, the troops executed an orderly withdrawal, alternately marching and skirmishing, carrying the wounded with them, back to Helena."[19]

Another account presents the dicey tactical position of the 60th at Wallace's Ferry: "Their ammunition was nearly exhausted; a few more rounds and their bayonets would be their only protection against a massacre. There was no time for the Phalanx [black] soldiers to maneuver; they were in the jaws of death; it was indeed themselves among the Nation's defenders was long delayed, but when it came, they were found ready and eager to take part in the struggle which ended in the emancipation of four million of their race from the degradation of human slavery. They proved themselves such capable and worthy soldiers, in time of war, that several regiments of Negro soldiers have since constituted a part of the Regular Army of the United States."[24]

Black soldiers in the Civil War faced greater danger in the field than white troops upon capture or surrender, for southern state laws called for the immediate execution of any black troops engaging in incitement of "servile insurrection." Neither were white officers in command of Negro regiments spared such a terrible fate; they too would be executed "as an example" to others fomenting slave revolt. Three black soldiers from the 60th Regiment too severely wounded to be moved during the Battle of Wallace's Ferry were left in the field to the mercy of Jo Johnson's forces. All were murdered. Indeed, Iowa Gov. Samuel Kirkwood's desire to push the issue of black participation in the war resulted in part from his tour of the battlefield where he saw firsthand examples of Negro bravery under fire, and murdered black prisoners of war, shortly after hostilities ceased at Milliken's Bend. In response to a written rebuke from Gen. Grenville Dodge that Kirkwood had backed away from his commitment to black suffrage, the governor responded, "I argued the question of Negro suffrage incidentally in connection with the question of reconstruction [in the South]." Kirkwood conceded, "I am, and have been for some years, decidedly in favor of striking that word [restricting voting and other rights to white men] out of our state constitution and when that question shall be before our people [in 1868] I shall, if my health and strength will permit, use whatever power of argument I may have to persuade them to do that thing."[25]

General Dodge in his youth had been far from an advocate of black military service or suffrage, much less abolition of slavery. His wartime service as commander of Union forces in Mississippi changed these views. "I have some very fine Negro troops, well drilled and doing the same [combat] duty as the white troops." After the war, Dodge would remember the valuable intelligence role played by escaped slaves in his department. "Negroes were also of great aid to us as messengers and coming into our lines with valuable information and I never heard of a Negro giving up a Union soldier, spy, or scout who trusted him."[26]

On November 6, 1865, the *Muscatine Journal* reported that state legislators had received three petitions asking for "the repeal of all laws making distinctions on account of color." The first was submitted by 237 white citizens of Muscatine, the second from Alexander Clark Sr. and 60 other "colored people of Muscatine County," and the third was the petition of the non-commissioned officers (NCOs) and men of the 60th Regiment. Gov. William Stone, once uncomfortable with the idea of arming black Americans, later came to an understanding of wartime necessity. Paraphrasing Stone's evolving views, a *Journal* reporter wrote that the former governor now "believed if they would take out of the war what the black man had done, in various ways, as guides, teamsters, mechanics, laborers, and soldiers, the war would still be raging." Without the black military service, Governor Stone "seriously doubted whether we ever could have conquered the South."[27]

While there were no Medal of Honor recipients in the Iowa regiment of color, the Hawkeye State was home to one black winner of the nation's highest award for combat bravery. James Daniel Gardner was born September 16, 1839, near Yorktown, Virginia. He later enlisted in the 2nd North Carolina Colored Infantry, which was in 1864 re-designated the 36th Infantry Regiment, U.S. Colored Troops. Deployed as part of Union Brig. Gen. Charles J. Paine's 3rd Division, 18th Corps, the 36th was one of nine black infantry brigades stationed near Deep Bottom, southeast of Richmond, Virginia, in late September 1864. Marching overnight to New Market Heights, the 36th easily pushed the Confederate pickets before them.

Their objective was defended by dug-in Texas infantry, and the attacking black regiments suffered heavy casualties, particularly among the ranks of their white officers and black NCOs. The 36th Regiment's commander, Colonel Duncan, suffered four gunshot wounds and went down in a hail of rebel fire. Dozens of wounded black soldiers were executed on the spot by enraged southern troops.

Bodies Carpeted the Bloody Ground

Under the command of the 5th Brigade's Col. John Draper, Gardner and the remains of Company I crossed the field where Colonel Duncan and the lead units of the 36th had been cut down. Dead bodies carpeted the bloody ground, and the horrendous screams of the wounded rattled the souls of the advancing Union soldiers. Under heavy rebel artillery fire, Company I became bogged down in a marsh after their initial

Gen. Grenville Dodge, whose Civil War experience with African-American troops changed him from a reluctant abolitionist and opponent of black suffrage to an ardent supporter of both (SHSI Des Moines)

Virginian James Daniel Gardner earned a Medal of Honor for his heroism at the Civil War battle of New Market Heights near Richmond. After the war he moved to Ottumwa. (Calvary Cemetary, Ottumwa)

Col. Edward Hatch of Muscatine commanded the 9th Cavalry, one of the two units of the legendary "Buffalo Soldiers" who served for 30 years after the Civil War. (SHSI Des Moines)

charge. Despite repeated attempts, Colonel Draper could not rally his inexperienced troops to resume the advance. At last, Private Gardner rose from his position to lead the assault with loud yelling and a fixed bayonet, and his comrades followed him into the jaws of death, inspiring the rest of the brigade to boldly storm the Confederate positions.

The black phalanx could not be stopped, and the 36th forced the rebels off New Market Heights and pursued them to the summit, which was also seized by the 36th troopers. On April 6, 1865, Pvt. (later Sgt.) James Daniel Gardner was among 12 black soldiers awarded the Medal of Honor for bravery at the Second Battle for New Market Heights and nearby Chaffin's Farm. Mustered out of his beloved unit at Brazos, Texas, Gardner soon thereafter moved to Ottumwa, Iowa, purchased a home five miles from the local post office, married, and became a Catholic missionary. He passed away in Pennsylvania while doing missionary work on September 29, 1905, at age 66, exactly 41 years to the day of the Second Battle for New Market Heights. Gardner was buried in an unmarked grave in Cavalry Cemetery in Ottumwa, but on July 4, 1994, a monument was erected in his honor by the Medal of Honor Historical Society, in cooperation with the Wapello County Historical Society, the Ottumwa Civil War Roundtable, and the Ottumwa Cemetery Trustees. The program concluded, "Poor is the nation that has no heroes; shameful is the nation that has them and forgets."[28]

The Indian Wars

The returning veterans of the 60th Iowa would form the backbone of black political, cultural, religious, business, and educational advancement in Iowa from 1865 well into the twentieth century. Their service and sacrifice were directly responsible for the change of heart on the part of a majority of white Iowans toward black suffrage and abolition of the Black Codes from state statutes.

Fittingly, a war-weary Congress on July 28, 1866, approved the formation of six black regiments — the 9th and 10th cavalries and the 38th, 39th, 40th, and 41st infantries. The infantries were consolidated into the 24th and 25th regiments in 1867.[29] As in the War of the Rebellion and the Civil War, black soldiers in the post–Civil War years would distinguish themselves in a variety of roles on the American frontier.

While there had been a number of black officers commissioned during the Civil War, the two highest ranking officers, Lt. Col. (Bvt.) Alexander T. Augusta and Maj. Martin R. Delaney, served respectively as regimental surgeon of the 7th U.S.C.T. and staff recruiter for the 104th and 105th U.S.C.T. Neither man possessed combat experience.[30] A small number of line officers were serving as first and second lieutenants and captains in the U.S.C.T., but Congress decided that utilization of black troops in peacetime would require the use of white officers.[31] While promises of faster promotion and higher rank were used as inducements for recruitment, a large number of distinguished Civil War officers refused to serve with black troops. Two such individuals who declined invitations to lead the 9th and 10th Cavalry regiments were George Armstrong Custer of Michigan and Frederick William Benteen of Missouri (by way of Virginia). "I have no interest in that race of men," Benteen wrote to his wife at the time, noting that he had found his previous service with the black 38th Infantry "personally distasteful." Custer and Benteen would later come together in infamy on June 25, 1876, at the Little Big Horn River in Montana.[32]

Instead, another pair of Civil War heroes would be selected to lead the 9th and 10th — Benjamin Grierson of Illinois and Col. Edward Hatch of Iowa. Hatch had been involved in establishing various departments of the Freedmen's Bureau in the Reconstruction South before being given command of the 9th cavalry. Grierson took command of the 10th.

Officer procurement was initially slow, although two outstanding young officers who would go on to great fame on the western plains — Wesley Merritt and Albert P. Morrow — elected to join the black units. By contrast with officer recruitment, enlisted men joined so rapidly that the ranks were filled almost immediately, often by men unsuited for military service but desperate for work in post-war America. "Thirteen dollars a month was meager pay, but it was more than most could expect to earn as civilians when food, clothing, and shelter were added."[33]

Despite initial difficulties with discipline, camp followers, and officer recruitment, Colonel Hatch was able to organize all 12 companies of the 9th by February 1867. A mutiny en route to San Antonio, Texas, and almost daily clashes with local police clouded expectations of the 9th — particularly the killing of Lt. Seth Griffin of Company A during a mutiny and the shooting of two troopers by Lt. Fred Smith of Company K.[34]

These preliminary difficulties aside, the four black regiments would go on to distinguished service on the western frontier from 1866 to 1891. While primarily utilized in escort, fatigue, and garrison roles, the 24th and 25th infantries would also compile solid service records, going on to serve in the Philippines and in Cuba. The 9th and 10th cavalries would engage hostile Indians, white and Mexican outlaws (including William Bonney), and cattle thieves from Kansas to Texas and New Mexico — becoming two of the finest mounted units in the Army. The black regiments had high re-enlistment rates (ensuring a large number of experienced veterans), low desertion rates, and low rates of courts martial for drunkenness, the scourge of the plains army.

"The experiment with Negro troopers launched in 1866," military historian William Leckie concludes, "proved a success by any standard other than that of racial prejudice. By 1891, the combat record spoke for itself. They had fought on the plains of Kansas and in Indian Territory, in the vast expanse of West Texas and along hundreds of miles of the Rio Grande and in Mexico, in the deserts and mountains of New Mexico and Arizona, in Colorado, and finally in the rugged grandeur of the Dakotas. Few regiments could match the length and sweep of these activities."

The black soldiers were instrumental in defeating the toughest and most rebellious Indian nations west of the Mississippi River, including the Kiowa, Comanche, Ute, Lakota (Sioux), Arapaho, Apache, and northern and southern Cheyenne. Each was eventually persuaded to adopt reservation living, or — like Apache Chief Victorio — was driven from the United States by the 10th Cavalry into the waiting arms of Mexican troops. The efforts of the black regiments, Leckie notes, "were not limited to the battlefield. They built or renovated dozens of posts, strung thousand of miles of wire, and escorted stages, trains, cattle herds, railroad crews, and surveying parties. Civil officials, particularly in Texas and New Mexico, could not have performed their duties without them. Their scouts and patrols opened new roads, mapped vast areas of uncharted country, and pinpointed for oncoming settlers the location of life-giving water."[35] A considerable number of black civilians served the Army as scouts, interpreters, muleskinners, teamsters, and laborers.

The first black West Point graduate, 1st Lt. Henry Ossian Flipper, was assigned duty with Grierson's 10th Cavalry in 1878. The second black graduate of the U.S. Military Academy, 1st Lt. John H. Alexander, was assigned to Hatch's 9th Cavalry in 1887.

Contemporary white advocates of the black regiments ran the gamut from most of their own officers to the famous western artist Frederick Remington, who painted many of his well-known works while campaigning with the troops. Remington spent time in Arizona with a company of buffalo soldiers. He recalled, "the Negro troopers sat about, their black skins shining with perspiration, and took no interest in the matter at hand. They occupied such time in joking and in merriment. . . . They may be tired and they may be hungry, but they do not see fit to augment their misery by finding fault with everybody and everything. In this particular they are charming men with whom to serve. Officers have often confessed to me that when they are on long and monotonous field service and are troubled with a depression of the spirits, they have only to go about the campfires of the Negro soldier in order to be amused and cheered by the clever absurdities of the men."

Remington had no doubt as to their bravery. "Will they fight? That is easily answered. They have fought many, many times. The old sergeant sitting near me, as calm of feature as a bronzed statue, once deliberately walked over a Cheyenne rifle pit and killed his man. One little fellow near him once took charge of a lot of stampeded cavalry horses when Apache bullets were flying loose and no one knew from what point to expect them next."[36]

In all, 18 black soldiers won the Medal of Honor between 1866 and 1898; during this time 7 black sailors received the nation's highest award for bravery. In addition, 4 white officers were awarded the Medal of Honor in command of black troops on the frontier.[37]

Continuity of command enhanced the performance of the black regiments as much as the high reenlistment rates. Colonel Hatch commanded the 9th Cavalry from 1866 until his death in service in 1889; Colonel Grierson led the 10th Cavalry from 1866 to 1890; Col. Joseph H. Potter commanded the 24th Infantry for 13 years; and Col. George Andrews headed the 25th Infantry for 21 years. Historian Robert Utley notes that "unit pride and esprit de corps ran high in the black regiments, the product in part, of the personnel continuity, but also of increasing professionalism, superior performance, a solidarity born of prejudice, and a determination to demonstrate the potential of the black race."[38] Discriminatory issue of inferior horses, rations, equipment, arms, and supplies, made their considerable accomplishments all the more notable.

"Will they fight? That is easily answered. They have fought many, many times. The old sergeant sitting near me, as calm of feature as a bronzed statue, once deliberately walked over a Cheyenne rifle pit and killed his man."

— Frederick Remington

After serving as a buffalo soldier in Troop K, 9th Cavalry, during the Indian Wars, John W. Heath of Virginia settled in Des Moines and raised a family. (courtesy Opie Heath-Knox)

George H. Woodson, originally from Virginia, served in Company I, 25th Infantry, on the plains and later became a prominent attorney in Iowa. (courtesy Morris family)

A handful of black Iowans served in the 9th and 10th cavalries and 24th and 25th infantries regiments during the Indian wars, but record of their achievements is largely restricted to newspaper obituaries and family histories. J. H. McDowell, who died at age 79 in Des Moines in 1937, served in the 24th Infantry Regiment during the plains wars. McDowell had been a classmate of Booker T. Washington while both were enrolled at Hampton Institute. Born in Stanton, Virginia, McDowell became a musician and was made a bugler upon his enlistment in the 24th in 1875. Honorably discharged in 1880, he settled in Iowa, living in Muchakinook in Mahaska County for several years before buying a house at 1211 Center Street in Des Moines. George Woodson served in the 25th Infantry on the plains from 1884 to 1889. Woodson would go on to become a prominent lawyer in Oskaloosa and co-founder of the National (Negro) Bar Association. Another veteran, Mack McGhee Garfield, served in the 9th and 10th cavalries during the Philippine campaign, and later attended the Camp Dodge training ground for black officers and NCO candidates in 1917.[39]

Pvt. John W. Heath, born in Virginia in 1859, enlisted in Company K, 9th United States Cavalry, on December 15, 1879, under the command of Colonel Hatch. Heath was assigned to the Southwest to fight against the legendary Apache war leaders Nana, Victorio, and Geronimo. Under the leadership of Capt. H. K. Parker, Hatch's Company K would distinguish itself in several engagements.

Pursuing Chief Victorio, Colonel Hatch led several companies of the 9th into Arizona in April 1880, but the wily Mimbreno leader doubled back on his trail into New Mexico and headed in the direction of Old Fort Tularosa. "On the evening of May 13," writes William Leckie, "a lone rider on a lathered horse galloped into the Barlow and Sanders Stage Station with the news that Victorio, at that moment, was probably wiping out the small settlement adjacent to Old Fort Tularosa. Fortunately, Sgt. George Jordan and a detachment of 25 buffalo soldiers of K Company were at the station and preparing to turn in for the night.

"Jordan saddled his detachment [which included Private Heath] at once and marched throughout the night, arriving at the old fort on the morning of May 14. Victorio had not attacked, but Jordan set his troopers to work at once building a stockade. Once this task was completed, Jordan carefully stationed his troopers, sent out vedettes, and moved the frightened citizens into the stockade. Courage and fast work saved a slaughter. At dusk the Apaches

struck but were met with a curtain of fire that drove them back. They again attacked and were fought off with equal vigor. This was enough for Victorio. He turned southwest toward the Mexican border, leaving Sergeant Jordan in full control of the stockade. Hatch rode in the following morning, paused only long enough to learn the details, and then pushed on after the fleeing Apaches. For gallantry and courage at Old Fort Tularosa, Sergeant Jordan was awarded the Congressional Medal of Honor."[40]

Private Heath was again in action with Captain Parker and Company K against the Apache war leader Nana in July and August 1881. "Captain Parker and 19 troopers of K Company pursued him about 25 miles west of Sabinal. The Indians entrenched themselves in near impregnable positions, but Parker, outnumbered two to one, attacked at once. In a bitter fight of an hour and a half the gallant buffalo soldiers were beaten off and Nana escaped. Privates Charles Perry and Guy Temple were dead, three other troopers were wounded, and nine horses were killed. Parker cited Sergeant Thomas Shaw for extraordinary courage in action.

"Nana and most of his warriors returned to the Sierra Madres after the fight in Gavilan Canyon, but some of them lingered on — too long as it turned out. On the morning of October 4, Apachewise Captains [Henry] Carroll and H.K. Parker, with F and K companies, hit the trail of these renegades on the eastern slopes of the Dragoon Mountains and followed it until late afternoon when the Apache rearguard was sighted. A 15-mile running fight brought the Indians to bay among the rocks and a sharp engagement of an hour was required to drive them out. The hostiles then scattered like a covey of quail and made for the Mexican border. F and K had three men and a horse wounded, while Indian losses, though believed heavy, were uncertain."[41]

Pvt. John Heath survived the hazards of frontier duty for nearly five years, before he was permanently injured when his horse went down under him while on mounted patrol at Fort Supply in Indian Territory on December 23, 1884. The bone in his left leg was badly fractured below the knee, and Heath was given an honorable discharge for medical reasons on April 12, 1885. Heath thereafter moved to Des Moines, where in 1905 he married Miss Opie Scott and purchased a home at 900 Maury Street. Twelve children were born of their marriage. Heath, who was compelled to retain the services of noted Des Moines lawyer Samuel Joseph Brown in order to apply for an increase in his military pension, died in 1929 and was buried at Laurel Hill

Cemetery in Des Moines.[42]

The close of westward expansion and the Wounded Knee massacre in December 1890 brought finality to the Indian campaign. The buffalo soldiers, both the 9th and the 10th, played decisive roles in the last two engagements of the wars. The 9th rode 108 miles in under 24 hours during a blizzard (and without any winter clothing) to rescue Col. George Forsyth's 7th Cavalry under heavy hostile fire at Drexel Mission during the Wounded Knee incident.

The 10th performed yeoman service in the Southwest against the last Apache fighters, Victorio and Geronimo, resulting in the death of the former and the surrender of the latter with 34 men, women, and children on September 11, 1886. But the dawning of the "American Century" and U.S. economic expansion overseas ushered in a new military challenge for American armed forces, one met head-on by the 9th and 10th cavalries and 24th and 25th infantry regiments.

The Spanish-American War

On February 15, 1898, the battleship U.S.S. Maine exploded in the harbor at Havana, Cuba. Killed were 250 American servicemen, including 22 black sailors. Though it was later determined that one of the ship's boilers caused the blast, at the time the American casualties were thought to be victims of Spanish sabotage.[44] On April 25 Congress issued a declaration of war. With some embarrassment, the War Department was able to immediately muster only 28,000 troops, scattered over myriad posts, primarily in the western states. Pres. William McKinley called for volunteers.[45]

Responding to the call, formations of white soldiers, such as the 71st New York and former Secretary of the Navy Theodore Roosevelt's Roughriders, garnered the lion's share of publicity. But in fact the four black frontier regiments — infantry and cavalry — were indispensable in carrying the Stars and Stripes to victory in Cuba.

Black soldiers earned five Medals of Honor in the battles of El Caney, San Juan Hill, Las Guasimas, and Santiago de Cuba. Sgt. George Berry of the 10th Cavalry carried the colors and led black troops up San Juan Hill to defeat Spanish artillery, machine guns, and infantry. Berry ran the first American flag up the flagpole at the infamous blockhouse — in a hail of Spanish fire.[46] When Roosevelt's Roughriders finally made their historic charge up San

"'If these black fellows get at the Spaniards we will have revenge for the Maine,' said an admiring spectator who wore a Grand Army [of the Republic] button. 'The Dons will know what Sherman meant when he said war was hell. These black boys have been fighting Indians ever since the Civil War. When they showed up on the frontier the Indians called them buffaloes, in derision, because their hair was curly. Before they got through with the Indians, the most desperate band of redskins that ever went on the warpath would break and run at the sight of them. And I want to say here and now that any troops who can beat the American Indian at his own game are fighters from the ground up. The American Indian is the toughest proposition in the fighting line that lives. And these black fighters can outmaneuver, outride, outshoot, and outdevil even the red devil of the plains. They charge with reins between their teeth and a revolver in each hand. They ride like cowboys. They shoot fast as machine guns with each hand. With the saber they are fiends incarnate. When they drive in the spurs and charge home, God help anything in front of them.'

"The veteran spoke no more than the truth. The Ninth Cavalry, U.S.A., command the respect and admiration of the whole army, and are in many respects the most remarkable troops in the service of Uncle Sam. Every trooper is coal black, the tradition of the regiment being against any mixture of white blood. Every one of these black fellows is a giant in size. They are born fighters. They have fought all the way from the Mexican borders to the Canadian line. Climate has no terrors for them. That shows the mettle of the regiment. Still, the popular idea that the regiment goes south because the Negro can stand the heat better than the white man is a great mistake. The regiment has fought well in the north as in the south. . . . The Negro is not so susceptible to either great heat or severe cold as is the white man. This is why the government is now ordering the colored soldiers south for service against Spain. They ought to be a revelation to the world if they are called into action, for few people outside the west know what fighting these men have done against the Indians. Why, they ride like centaurs. . . .

"Col. Edward Hatch was the original commander of the Ninth. He never faltered in his opinion of his black soldiers, and was with them in all their hottest work. . . . When they go into action, they will resort to all the tactics taught them in Indian fighting to conceal their bodies, and the Spanish fighting soldiers will get a lesson in rough and tumble fighting if they ever meet the fighting Ninth."

—Unidentified Civil War veteran[43]

Juan Hill, their black saviors greeted them at the top, having defeated the remnant of the Spanish resistance. A grateful future U.S. president was heard to proclaim, "A bond exists between us, black and white, officers and soldiers, a tie, I trust, that will never be broken." As a result, many black Americans would come to view Theodore Roosevelt as a "second Abraham Lincoln" after his election.[47]

Serving in the black regular army units was Charles Mitchell. Mitchell served in Company B, 9th U.S. Cavalry in Cuba. Born in Grey Creek, Illinois, Mitchell lived in Des Moines for 25 years before his death in June 1939. He enlisted in the Army at Fort Leavenworth, Kansas, and trained in South Dakota and California. Mitchell did not see combat in Cuba but was honorably discharged, later returning to Iowa to work as a coal miner in Buxton.[48] One of Jack Howe's sons, from Bedford, Iowa, served with Pershing's 10th Cavalry that rescued Roosevelt's Roughriders at San Juan Hill. Mack McGhee Garfield rode with the 9th and 10th cavalries, serving in the Philippines after training at Fort Riley, Kansas. Garfield's son-in-law Robert Parkey would become a bomber pilot in the 477th bomb group during World War 2.

Numerous veterans of the four black frontier regiments would later find themselves selected for the U.S. Army's first Officers Candidate School for blacks at Fort Des Moines — the 17th Provisional Training Regiment, commanded by Col. Charles C. Ballou, who had previously commanded the 24th Infantry Regiment in the Philippines and the 10th Cavalry in Mexico.

Black Lieutenants and Non-Commissioned Officers

Little known is the participation in the Spanish-American War of several all-black volunteer regiments from the various states, officered in their entirety by black men. Iowa raised one such company of black soldiers for service in Cuba — Company M, 7th U.S. Volunteer Infantry Immunes, which included all black lieutenants and non-commissioned officers. The company was moved to Macon, Georgia, and prepared to ship to Cuba with other black units, but the war ended before it could be deployed. The unit was mustered out of service February 28, 1899.[49]

Many Iowans associate Fort Des Moines with the 17th Provisional Training Regiment for black officer candidates in 1917, or with the WAAC Training Center during World War 2. Yet the modern Fort Des Moines (the others were constructed in 1835 and 1843) hosted a black infantry regiment shortly after its dedication in November 1901. As the *Des Moines Register and*

Leader explained, "The opening of an army post in Iowa is an event that calls for more than a local celebration. The first fort of regular soldiers within the confines of Iowa is to be dedicated and opened this week."[50] The newspaper declared that the fort "means almost as much as the location here of the state capitol; its dedication is one of the most important events in Des Moines for half a century."[51]

The New Fort Des Moines

Large crowds at the dedication, estimated at 25,000 people, overloaded the city's trolley car system. Troop E of the 8th U.S. Cavalry was the first to occupy the new Fort Des Moines but stayed less than a month, returning to their regiment at Jefferson Barracks in St. Louis.[52]

The replacements for Troop E arrived three weeks later. Much to the surprise of local residents, this unit was neither a cavalry troop nor was it composed of Caucasians. Rather, these were 127 soldiers of Companies C and I of the all-black 25th Infantry Regiment. The *Register* reported the black troopers "tumbled off the train" on the morning of December 3, 1903, and "the advent of troops created a sensation and large crowds gathered to watch the sturdy colored veterans as they swung along with the regulation marching step."[53]

The two black infantry companies were, "in the charge of five white officers," commanded by Capts. J. D. Leitch and R. L. Bush. The 25th troopers' sole responsibility at Fort Des Moines was to guard 40 military convicts sent from overcrowded cells at Jefferson Barracks in St. Louis. General Bates, who had been so impressed with the fort's "magnitude . . . and the excellence of the site," told city officials the black troops would remain until the (white) cavalry returned from Manila the following spring.[54]

Wrong Idea

There was considerable vocal opposition to the arrival of the black infantry in Des Moines. *Bystander* editor John Lay Thompson responded with an article entitled "Wrong Idea," wherein he defended both the troops and Congressman John A.T. Hull, chair of the U.S. House Committee on Military Affairs. "Because a garrison of Afro-American troops has been sent to the new $1,000,000 army post in Des Moines the voters are enraged and threaten to defeat Captain Hull for renomination," Thompson wrote. "It has been proven to be a fact that the Afro-American soldiers are the best in the United States so far as sobriety and good behavior are concerned, as well as in many other essentials in the makeup of good soldiers, and it is a shame that they receive such outrageous treatment by the people they serve so faithfully and well. . . . No real man or set of gentlemen to our knowledge are enraged at our Congressman on this account."[55]

Local organized labor feared the military convicts at the fort would be used as a labor battalion for the remaining construction work at the fort, thereby depriving civilian workers of income. Captain Hull responded, "it is not the intention of the war department to utilize these prisoners in the work of construction at Fort Des Moines in any way that would interfere with the employment of laborers."[56]

Black residents of Des Moines enjoyed amicable relations with the 25th soldiers. Company C hosted a social reception on December 23, 1903, which included a mandolin club and a fine supper, "all cooked and served by members of the Company." Company L hosted an elaborate reception at the fort on March 18, 1904. Sixty guests were treated to an elegant five-course meal in a dining hall decorated with flags and Japanese lanterns.[57]

Close Monitoring of Troops

There are no records of any socializing between soldiers and civilians off post. This was in keeping with army practice at the time, which required close monitoring of the black troops by their officers and the granting of fewer passes than those issued to white troops. Particularly in the South, fears of armed clashes with white citizens often resulted in the establishment of a state of quarantine to prevent any contact between soldiers and civilians. A farewell reception for the 25th infantry soldiers was held April 22, 1904, and they departed Iowa for the regiment's headquarters at Fort Niobrara, Nebraska.[58]

In early May, white troopers from the 11th Cavalry arrived at Fort Des Moines to replace the 25th Infantry. Ironically, the unfounded local fears of rowdy conduct that hampered the 25th were justly earned by the raucous behavior of the 11th. Its commander, Colonel Thomas, ordered early lights out at 8 p.m. due to "the results of criticism on the part of certain individuals regarding the behavior of the soldiers." Thompson could not resist an editorial jab in the *Bystander.* "The [11th Cavalry] privates are a bit sore at the parties who brought about the condition of affairs. They argue that they have just returned from the Philippines

where they seldom saw white people and ought to be allowed a free rein for a little while until they get back in touch with humanity." Thompson concluded, "and they are white soldiers. Company L and C of the 25th Infantry were here for several months, and their commanding officers never had to issue any such orders, and just to think, the white boys have not been here two weeks yet and have made themselves very obnoxious."[59]

Death or Retirement

The years following American involvement in Cuba, Mexico, and the Philippines saw the death or retirement of many veterans in the four black regiments. Stationed at remote outposts in the west, or outside cities in the South, fears of conflict with local white residents meant confinement to post for most black soldiers. An incident involving shots fired into the town of Brownsville, Texas, on August 13, 1906, brought unfounded charges that black soldiers of Company D, 1st Battalion, 25th Infantry Regiment had been the culprits.

A veritable firestorm of southern editorial and political outrage was directed at Pres. Teddy Roosevelt. The president was already under heavy criticism for hosting a formal White House dinner where Booker T. Washington was an official guest. Washington was the first black American to be so honored in the nation's history.

Seeking to mollify southern outrage and shore up badly needed re-election support — and forgetting his black saviors at San Juan Hill and El Caney — Roosevelt summarily discharged every black soldier in the unit, for a "conspiracy of silence." Despite written reports from every white officer on post that all personnel, weapons, and ammunition were present and accounted for, Roosevelt dishonorably discharged every enlisted man in Company D.

Regret for Errors and Injustice

Decades later, the government publicly admitted its error. In 1973, the *Waterloo Defender* reported that Dorsie W. Willis of Waterloo, formerly of Company D, 1st Battalion, 25th Infantry Regiment during the "Brownsville Affray," had received a letter of apology and an honorable discharge from the U.S. Army. Mr. Willis read the last paragraph of the apology, presented to him by Maj. Gen. DeWitt C. Smith. "Trying to make amends," the Army declared, "[we] regret the errors of injustice by [the] previous generation."[60]

"The advent of troops created a sensation and large crowds gathered to watch the sturdy colored veterans as they swung along with the regulation marching step."

—*The Des Moines Register,* **December 1903**

"Iowa is proud that her State Capital was designated as the place where the First Training Camp for Colored Officers was located. . . .

It is a tribute to the colored race . . . that their very best trained men responded to the opportunity thus afforded. The Stars and Stripes is the flag of every race of any country whose people are loyal to the principles for which it stands and obedient to its laws. . . . The history of the advancement of the colored race in this country since emancipation is wonderful. When a race can come out of slavery and in so short a time . . . [be] recognized as they have been in the establishment of this Officers Training Camp, it is a tribute to the race as well as to the great principles of representative government. It is a source of gratitude that the federal government is so loyally supported in this contest by the colored race. It furnishes opportunity for the race to show to the country and the world their gratitude for what has been done for them. . . . They have acquitted themselves like soldiers.

I know I speak the heart-beat of every true American when I say it is their wish that this Training Camp mark a day of better understanding of the race question in this country."

— Iowa Gov. W. L. Harding, 1917 [61]

World War 1

The "Great Experiment" in establishing a training camp for commissioning black officers candidates in 1917 came as the result of a laborious process of local and national politics. Overcoming fears by conservative whites of "armed coloreds" lead by black officers was an enormous obstacle, particularly in the South. While there had been a number of black line officers — first and second lieutenants and captains — in black regiments as early as 1862, only recently had a small number of blacks been promoted to ranks above that of captain. Lt. Col. Charles E. Young, for example, was a West Point graduate who served with the 10th Cavalry. Maj. A. W. Ford, who would become the highest-ranking black officer at the Fort Des Moines Training Camp, was another soldier who had already attained an unusually high rank. [63]

As it happened, no other state in the Union would accept the camp, save for the Hawkeye State. A second training camp, for black officers and non-commissioned officer candidates, was established at Camp Dodge, Iowa. Army concerns of training large numbers of black recruits — 700,000 volunteers — in the South near whites compelled a system whereby southern states were paired with northern states for training of black recruits.

Fort Des Moines during the Black Officers Training Camp, June to October, 1917 (SHSI Des Moines)

Iowa was paired with Alabama.[64]

Interestingly, Camp Dodge trained not only black Americans but also numbers of men of Chinese, Filipino, Mexican, Arab, Jewish, and Native American descent.[65]

Segregation would not be tolerated from any establishment doing business with the Army, but the local press regularly featured articles and cartoons reinforcing the racial stereotypes of the day. One in the *Des Moines Capital* newspaper said, "Pie Eating 'Cullud' Lad At Soldier City Sho-Nuff in Love With Birmingham, Agnes and Camp."[66] For the most part, local media treatment of the Fort Des Moines camp was not nearly as racially derogatory.

Iowa's selection for both posts was due at least in part to the remarkable evolution of racial attitudes among the majority of its white citizens. Historically, Iowans were viewed as more sympathetic and tolerant to the plight of blacks in America. Antebellum Iowa had had an Underground Railroad network transporting escaped slaves to freedom. Iowa had recognized black suffrage in 1868 and had eliminated the "white only" language in its state constitution in 1884. Compared to race relations in most of the South, Iowa was seen by the majority of southern blacks as a mecca of comparative freedom and opportunity. When in May 1917 Iowans read the headline "1,200 Negro Officers To Train

Alabama draftees entering Camp Dodge to train for World War 1 (Iowa's Gold Star Museum, Camp Dodge)

"The call [came] in May 1917 for 1,200 colored men to come thereto and try to accomplish in three months what the rest of this country has had free and full opportunity to do in from one to three years, last past in the preparedness movement. With less than 30 days' notice the superb youth, the very best brain, vigor, manhood of the Race gave up comfort, position, future promise and outlook, in their various civil locations and from the North, South, East and West, started on their voluntary march to Fort Des Moines in answer to the call, and joined the splendid, seasoned, veteran fighters of our Race from the 9th and 10th U. S. Cavalry and the 24th and 25th U.S. Infantry, where all appeared on time and promptly proceeded to their lofty, patriotic work. . . . With the firm belief that all these things must come from the granting of equal rights for every race and people beneath the sun and the spirit of justice and fair play for all, we sacredly and confidently place the glory of the country and the honor of its flag in the keeping of the first Colored men trained at Fort Des Moines and commissioned to fight in the Black Phalanx with the armies of America for the glory of our God, the honor of our country, and the liberty and peace of the world."

— **Iowa attorney George H. Woodson, former member of Company I, 25th U.S. Infantry, 1917** [62]

African-American men registering for military service during World War 1 at Fort Des Moines (National Archives)

Col. Charles Ballou, commander of the Fort Des Moines Black Officers Training Camp established during World War 1 (National Archives)

Ballou to command the post. Ballou had previously led the 24th Infantry Regiment in combat in the Philippines. Champ Clark, speaker of the U.S. House of Representatives, called the camp's establishment "an epoch in American history and a new day for the Negro." Local opposition to the camp was reflected in segregationist views such as those of A. J. Kennedy of the town of Fort Des Moines. Kennedy threatened to protest to Iowa congressmen due to fears that both white and colored persons would have to use the one trolley car line between Des Moines and the post.[69]

These sentiments were outweighed by the majority of public opinion, as expressed by R. B. Patin, executive secretary of the War Camp Community Service of Des Moines. "The Negroes regard the event of this training camp as the greatest in the life of the race since the Emancipation Proclamation, and as such the people of Des Moines were glad to give it recognition," Patin wrote.[70]

Colonel Ballou, commanding officer of the camp, organized an event known as the "White Sparrow" patriotic service, which was held July 22, 1917, at Drake University's football stadium. A singing quartet from the black officers' training camp sang several spiritual songs, followed by an impressive demonstration of

Iowa men who trained at the Black Officers Training Camp (from Thompson, History and Views of the Colored Officers Training Camp, 1917)

Here" in the *Des Moines Capital,* few realized the rocky road the "Great Experiment" had traveled before becoming a reality.[67] Opposition could be expected from conservative whites in the military and in civilian circles, but there was also a surprising amount of hostility from certain segments of the black community. Some accused camp supporters of attempting to set up a "Jim Crow" camp. Despite such opposition, Howard University, the National Association for the Advancement of Colored People (NAACP), the Central Committee of Negro College Men, and much — though not all — of the black press combined to put pressure on Congress, the War Department, and Pres. Woodrow Wilson for establishment of the 17th Provisional Training Regiment.[68]

Finally, after much controversy about the camp's location, the U.S. War Department consented in May 1917 to establish the camp at Fort Des Moines and appointed Col. Charles C.

Fred Anderson and fellow soldiers at Archangel, Russia, in support of the White Russians during the Bolshevik Revolution, 1919 (courtesy Dorothy Garrett Pryor)

Charles P. Howard Sr. (above) and James B. Morris Sr. (below) both earned commissions at the Fort Des Moines Black Officers' Training Camp, then returned to Des Moines after World War 1 for careers in law and journalism. (courtesy Morris family)

formation marching and manual of arms by 1,200 soldiers. Three hundred black officer candidates then stepped forward and sang several familiar spirituals.[71]

Grand ceremonies marked the finish of the training course for the black officer candidates on October 15, 1917. Of the initial 1,250 candidates, 16 had been Iowans. Among the 639 successful candidates who received commissions were 9 Iowans, including Charles P. Howard and James B. Morris. Other Iowa graduates included Hal Short and Harry Short of Iowa City; William M.

Brooks, Vivian L. Jones, Maceo A. Richmond, and Harry E. Wilson of Des Moines; and James O. Redmon of Newton.[72]

Other Iowans participating in the training program included Walter Hutchinson, S. Joe Brown, H. S. Wilson, A. Richmond, and A. J. Booker, all of Des Moines, and E. H. Colbert and a Mr. Campbell of Iowa City. Of the initial 1,250 candidates, many graduates who qualified for commissions did not receive them. After waiting for months to receive their commissions, many became discouraged and left Fort Des Moines and returned to

Black officers and instructors at Camp Dodge during World War 1 (Iowa's Gold Star Museum, Camp Dodge)

assigned to their post in October 1917, the first black draftees, including 127 Iowans, were ordered to report to Camp Dodge. The majority of the black Hawkeyes hailed from Buxton, Keokuk, and Des Moines. Thousands of black men from Alabama, Tennessee, and Mississippi appeared for duty, along with smaller numbers from Minnesota, South Dakota, and Illinois. A total of 5,981 black draftees came to Iowa for training; of these, only 929 were inducted for service during the war.[75]

While the Army did not permit racial discrimination on the part of businesses contracting with the government, there was little if any racial mixing at Camp Dodge.

Black soldiers were given some facilities for social activities — including a black YMCA and the club established for the 366th Infantry, which contained a cafeteria, soft drink stand, game room, music room, reading room, barber shop, and an auditorium with a movie projector. The Red Cross set up Christmas trees during the season and distributed gifts to the soldiers. An open-air movie house was erected in the spring of 1918, and a hostess house was built to accommodate black women visiting the soldiers.

The Knights of Columbus donated one of its halls in Des Moines for use by black troops at Camp Dodge; the dedication

their homes. Most of those commissioned — including 106 captains, 329 first lieutenants, and 204 second lieutenants — would go on to serve with the 92nd Division in France during World War 1. Barred by law from serving alongside white American infantry units, most Negro regiments were attached to the French IV Armée, and thus earned the distinction of logging more combat time than any other infantry regiments in the American Expeditionary Force (AEF).[73]

The 4th Officers' Training School, 92nd Division, opened at Camp Dodge on May 25, 1918, and was, according to the *Camp Dodger* newspaper, "now full steam ahead with 305 enrolled candidates with another 200 expected. The students of this officers training school are for the most part non-commissioned officers of the regular army, and come from many states," Ohio in particular. Lt. Col. Charles F. Bates, formerly in command of the all-black 366th Infantry Regiment, was the school commandant.[74]

A few days after the first black officer candidates were

World War 1 military inductees from Ottumwa in front of the local public library (Ottumwa Public Library)

ceremony was "attended by several prominent white and colored people from Des Moines."[76] The *Camp Dodger* on January 18, 1918, noted "the high class of Negro soldiers" arriving at the camp, including several medical doctors, lawyers, dentists, businessmen, and college students. "There are only a few who cannot read and write," the newspaper reported.[77]

Units organized at Camp Dodge included the 163rd Depot Brigade, 804th Pioneer Infantry Regiment (Colored), 366th Infantry Regiment, and 414th Pioneer Infantry Regiment. A number of black nurses were also trained at Camp Dodge to treat "only men of their own race." A black officers' club was opened at Ninth and Mulberry streets in Des Moines, the largest of its type in the nation. Former Pres. Theodore Roosevelt and Emmet J. Scott, special assistant to the U.S. secretary of war and a black man, addressed the soldiers of the 366th at the Knights of Columbus Hall.[78]

Expertise with Rifle and Bayonet

Graduates of both Fort Des Moines and Camp Dodge were noted by the French for their expertise with the rifle and bayonet. One London newspaper stated that black soldiers in France had "piled up a score in killing Germans which breaks all previous records," and "in the use of the . . . bayonet they excel all others."[79] Both the French and German armies had cause to be impressed with the fighting abilities of black American soldiers. Called "Schwartztodt" (Black Death) or "Hellfighters," the black units attached to the French built a distinguished combat record in World War 1, including heavy fighting around the St. Die sector in France in the final great German offensive near Metz in November 1918.[80]

Overshadowing for a time the accomplishments of black American troops in France during the war was an incident at Camp Dodge on May 14, 1918. Three black soldiers — all from Alabama — were charged with sexually assaulting a white female. The three men "forcibly and feloniously against her will have carnal knowledge of Jessie Barnes," according to the charges leveled against Pvt. Stanley Tramble, Pvt. Robert Johnson, and Pvt. Fred Allen. Two other black soldiers implicated in an alleged plan to assault white soldier Pvt. John Gustafson and his fiancé Jessie Barnes were released due to insufficient evidence.[81]

Gustafson and Barnes identified the suspects the next day, although the alleged assault had taken place about 8:40 p.m. in a

Reception for African-American men and guests at Knights of Columbus Hall at Camp Dodge (courtesy Barbara Smith Kaiser)

This Camp Dodge training unit included Louis Carter Sr. of Sioux City (courtesy Laura Carter Harrison)

Special increment to Camp Dodge, August 23, 1918: Walter S. Warn (left) and David Williams (courtesy Helen Johnson)

dark wooded area. The three men held for court martial identified each other only by sight and did not even know the others' names. A court martial was convened May 31, 1918, at Camp Dodge. Each of the three defendants was tried separately. While the testimony of Pvt. Gustafson, Ms. Barnes, and the three defendants was sometimes contradictory and inconsistent, the three black soldiers all testified that they indeed intended to have sex with Ms. Barnes and that they had paid money to Gustafson to do so. Gustafson claimed he was attacked and knocked unconscious by the assailants and did not actually see the rape. Medical testimony by 1st Lt. Elmer P. Blankenship indicated bruises on the victim's thighs, leg, knees, arm, elbow, and wrist.

Private Tramble was permitted to incriminate himself upon direct examination by the Court after cross-examination by the prosecutor, who elicited the damning response to his question, "Think you had done anything wrong?" Tramble stated, "Yes sir, I knowed we had done wrong." The trial record closes with the statement: "The court was closed, and sentenced the accused Private Stanley Tramble, Company K, 3rd Battalion, 163rd Depot Brigade, to [handwritten] be hanged by the neck until dead, two-thirds of the court concurring therein."[82]

The verdicts were sent to Washington, D.C., for final approval by President Wilson, who confirmed the death sentences. Construction of a scaffold for the executions interrupted civilian celebrations at Hyperion Golf Club on July 4, 1918. A pouring rain did not delay the erection of the platform. The following morning was sunny, hot, and humid, baking hundreds of civilians trying to catch a glimpse of the triple execution by hanging of the three black soldiers. Forty thousand white troops of the 88th Division were in attendance and carried rifles; the 3,000 black troops of the 92nd Division were unarmed.[83]

Long March to the Gallows

Des Moines Tribune reporter Leslie Brooke recorded the events unfolding at Camp Dodge on the day of execution when the soldiers assembled and the death march began. "As the scaffold was approached, 'God save my soul' rent the death-like silence. 'Have mercy' and 'Oh Lord, save me.' The cries of the condemned men echoed and re-echoed. Soon the shrieks of Negro soldiers, unwilling and terrified spectators, driven into an hysterical state, added to the sickening scene. It was terrible. There was no commotion. Fainting and frantic Negroes were promptly carried to the rear. One who lost mental control ran straight for the gallows."[84]

"The Negroes sang continually during their long march to the gallows," a *Des Moines Capital* reporter wrote. "The chant was a weird, minor melody. At times the voices of the doomed men sank almost to a whimper, then rose to a shriek. This incantation was reminiscent of camp meeting days."[85]

The impact of the executions on the white troops in attendance was recalled many years later by Lt. Russell B. Rathbun. "It was a very hot day with no wind; thus, the voices of the condemned men really reached thousands of soldiers surrounding the scaffold. It was a horrible event. Most of us were not experienced soldiers, just ordinary guys. . . . I was concerned that my recruits facing the scaffold might . . . panic . . . I saw some of them weaving in ranks trying to stay at attention."[86]

The *Register* concluded its coverage of the hangings with a mealy-mouthed editorial contrasting the executions with lynchings. "Nothing could be farther apart emotionally than the awed and trembling throng of soldiers which watched the legal hanging of three criminals and the maddened or cynical crowd which makes up a lynch party," the *Register* declared. "There will be no repetition at Camp Dodge of the crime committed by the men upon the gallows, and the race hatred which might have been engendered and persisted under the circumstances is likewise dissolved by the tremendous emotional effect which was produced at the camp yesterday."[87]

Contrary to the *Register* editorial, passions were aroused by the executions, reinforcing claims by some black leaders that the war in Europe was a white man's concern. Germany, some said, had done nothing to black Americans — certainly not on a par with violent oppression from white Americans, particularly in the South. Virulent isolationism advocated by many northern whites combined with the "stay home" sentiment on the part of many blacks, prompted fears by federal officials regarding disloyalty and subversion among the black population.[88]

The executions in Iowa had been preceded in December 1917 by the executions of 19 black soldiers convicted of mutiny and killing civilians in an incident in Houston, Texas, triggered by virulent segregation and police brutality. In January 1918, the Federal Bureau of Investigation intercepted and sent to military intelligence a "letter re Houston Lillian Smith. negress. Disloyalty matter." Ms. Smith lived in Des Moines. In reaction to the executions of the first 13 black soldiers convicted in the Houston incident, she had written a letter in which she declared there was "not a Negro in America that the sun shines on but what their patriotism since the execution of our glorious 13 heroes of the 24th [Infantry] has been dampened to a hundred percent."[89]

No Question of the Black Man's Loyalty

There is some evidence that the NAACP's Joel Spingarn assisted military intelligence agents in identifying disloyal and subversive elements in the black community during World War 1. How serious these sentiments actually were is open to speculation, although the government took them seriously during both world wars. Of interest here are the remarks made in 1919 by Des Moines attorney George H. Woodson concerning the issue of loyalty to the war effort by black Americans. "I made the promise at Council Bluffs that from 50,000 to 100,000 black men would join with the white men in this country for maintaining the honor of the country and the glory of its flag," said Woodson. "I am here to say that in the last world war the Government estimate is that 400,000 Negroes gave their service in this war.

"For 50 years or more there have been suspicions that if ever the solid rock upon which our institutions were based were disturbed it would come from some act and connection with the black man. I am pleased to state that . . . not the slightest intimation has been made to question the black man's loyalty to the country and the honor of his flag. I shall always feel proud for the state of my adoption, that in it a [black officers' training] camp should be carried out to success.

"Long before the campaign of 1916, on November 23, 1915, in my little home, two by four, in Buxton, a man came about half past eight o'clock in the evening . . . and offered me $1000 a month and expenses if I could afford to give up my practice and seek employment to work in the Rock Island Arsenal and become situated so that I could place or have an explosive so placed that it would blow up any part of the arsenal within a year. Having served for five years in Company I, 25th U.S. Infantry, and knowing what to do, having remembered the instructions as to such an emergency, that I should report first to the highest military federal and civil authority, and then to the highest military state authority, and then to the highest civil state authority . . . . Judge Wade entrusted to me the matter of preparing that report so that it could reach the Commander at Rock Island and the War Department. I went over to the Citizens National Bank Building,

prepared that report and took it to the federal building by the time Judge Wade convened court and he signed it in duplicate and it was sent to the Rock Island Arsenal. A few days after that Judge Wade called me in chambers and informed me that the guard had been increased and the Arsenal was well guarded. I am absolutely glad that this task fell to me, even before the great danger threatened us."[90]

Intelligence File Labeled "Negro Subversion"

Perhaps the tension between black loyalty to the war effort and racially discriminatory treatment in America is best reflected in a letter from "A Negro Soldier" to the editor of the *Camp Dodger* in April 1918. If the war is to "make the world safe for Democracy," the soldier wrote, "is that Democracy to include just certain races and peoples, or 'every race under the sun'? If it is to include only a chosen few, it is as great an evil as 'The Divine Right of Kings.' The Negro's motive in fighting is to make America, and the world, a better place for *him*." More than 80,000 black soldiers have been mobilized, "yet while the Negro goes forth to vindicate Belgium, his own is *lynched* here in America. While he goes forth to fight for the womanhood of France, the women of his own race are outraged here in America. In parts of the U.S. black Americans "are not allowed to vote," concluded the soldier's letter, and they are generally "segregated, Jim Crowed, and commanded by those in authority to remain silent." Never published, the soldier's letter turned up years later in a military intelligence file labeled "Negro Subversion."[91]

Black regiments fighting in France, segregated from white troops by law, were deployed with French divisions, often black colonial Senegalese or Moroccan troops. Many a German soldier would come to respect the fighting qualities of black American soldiers, who doubtless exacted some considerable measure of vengeance against white repression and Jim Crow on the hides of the Kaiser's finest.

French commanders were warned by white American officers not to commend black soldiers too strongly for bravery under fire, and to discourage socializing between French women and black soldiers, who "had a penchant for raping white women," according to a document entitled "Secret Information Concerning Black Troops."[92] This report, widely circulated by white Americans in French military circles, emphasized "scientific" evidence of black men's uncontrolled sexual urges and desire for white women.

"If the war is to make the world safe for Democracy, is that Democracy to include just certain races and peoples, or 'every race under the sun?'"

— Letter to the editor of the *Camp Dodger*, April 1918

Marshalltown veterans of World War 1 (courtesy Helen I. Johnson)

Dubuque's Guy Greene earned a commission at Fort Des Moines. (courtesy Barbara Smith Kaiser)

wounded in the leg during heavy fighting in the last great German offensive of the war near Metz in October and November 1918. After long convalescence in European and American hospitals, Morris came home in 1919 to his wife, Georgine, and a new son whom he had never seen, opened his law practice, and in 1922 purchased the *Bystander* newspaper.

Charles P. Howard, a first lieutenant in the 366th Regiment, later became an ardent civil rights lawyer. James W. Mitchell, originally from Atlanta, and Joseph E. Wiley, from Arkansas, would take up residence in Des Moines after the war and establish businesses. Earl W. Mann of Clinton, Iowa, had been an electrician, steam and gas engineer, and automobile mechanic before the war, and returned to these varied pursuits after the Armistice. William McKinley Brooks of Keokuk was a student at the time of his selection for the Fort Des Moines training camp. S. Joe Brown of Keosauqua became a distinguished appellate lawyer. Jesse A. Graves of Moulton would serve as deputy treasurer of Polk County for many years.[94]

Armistice Day Anniversary Commemoration

In 1937, for an article commemorating the nineteenth anniversary of Armistice Day, the *Bystander* interviewed several Iowa veterans who gathered at the Lincoln American Legion Post in Des Moines to recall their whereabouts on November 11, 1918. The gathering included Vivian Jones, Sam Phoane, Leroy Bird, and Spencer Elliston, all veterans of the Great War. First Lt. William T. Johnson, who lived at 1507 Lyon Street in Des Moines, and after the war was employed as a shipping clerk for the Utica Department Store, reported serving in the Marbach Sector with Company A, 366th Infantry Regiment, 92nd Division, from October to November 11, 1918.

Johnson's unit was sent to relieve the French 69th division at 11 o'clock that evening. Companies A, C, E, F, and G advanced under German fire near Champey La Cote, with the goal of capturing Bouxieres. Company H of the 366th Infantry Regiment, commanded by 1st Lt. Charles P. Howard of Des Moines, teamed with Company A, which included Iowans Guy Greene, Irving Turpin, and Pat Kaiser.

The infantrymen attacked and seized Bois Voivrotte, which had been occupied by two platoons of Company F. Though the Americans had been driven out of the town by counterattacking German soldiers, the black Hawkeyes and their comrades charged

Venereal diseases were supposedly rampant among black soldiers and many were reported to have tails.

Racial segregation was therefore required at all times. White Americans cringed in horror at interracial dating between French females and black soldiers. J. B. Morris and James Wardlaw Mitchell would reminisce a half-century later about their romances with French women, called "gluies." The women wouldn't leave the Negro soldiers alone and stuck closely to them — "like glue."[93]

Back Home after the War

Many black Iowans who engaged in combat operations against the Germans during World War 1 became prominent civic leaders back home after the war. For example, J. B. Morris of Des Moines served as a scout and sniper in the army's intelligence corps, deployed with the 366th Infantry Regiment of the 92nd Division. Morris was gassed in one German attack and was later badly

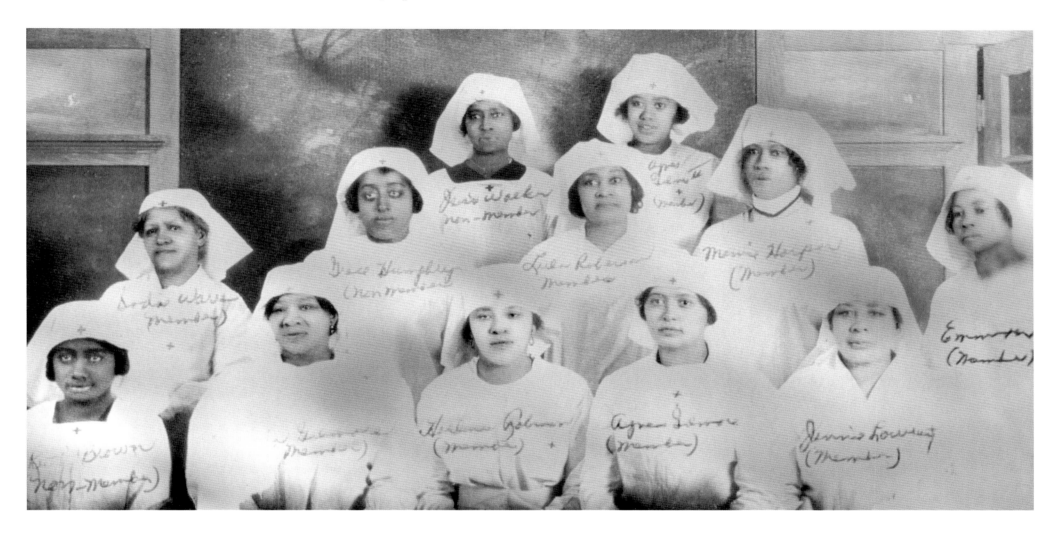

again and again. They finally routed the Germans and reoccupied Bois Voivrotte at 3 a.m. on November 11, 1918.

Black women in Iowa were heavily involved in the war on the home front, supplying pajamas and other clothing items to the Fort Des Moines officer candidates. Several mothers of soldiers sent overseas formed prayer groups in Des Moines, including Mrs. Zella Robinson of 1627 Walker Street, who had two sons in the Army — Cecil B. and Festess T. Stone. Mrs. Smith, Hattie Carey, Josephine Berry, Mrs. Hunt, and Mrs. Bush remembered in 1937 how they "thanked God for the signing of the Armistice, and that their sons were returned to them."

The *Bystander's* question of whether black Americans had benefited from their collective experience received a mixed response from the veterans interviewed in 1937. The "Great Migration" of thousands of southern blacks seeking employment in northern factories opened up new opportunities previously unavailable to the Negro for career, educational, and social and political advancement.[95] But the "Red Scare" of the 1920s and the rise of the Ku Klux Klan in both the North and the South limited political and economic progress for black Americans — despite their war service. It would take another world war to propel black America closer to the goal of equality of treatment and opportunity.

Volunteer nurses in Marshalltown during World War 1 included Helen Johnson's mother, second row, far left. (courtesy Helen I. Johnson)

World War 2

The period between the world wars saw a general decline in the government's treatment and promotion of black soldiers. The forced retirement of Army Col. Charles A. Young, the third black graduate of the U.S. Military Academy at West Point, scandalized the officer corps in 1917. Young, labeled "physically unfit" for further military service, rode a horse from his home in Columbus, Ohio, to Washington, D.C. — and back — to prove his stamina, but to no avail.[96]

However, there were a few signs of change in the years of Franklin Roosevelt's New Deal. For example, Benjamin O. Davis Sr. became the Army's first black general. Davis received his brigadier's stars in 1939. Merrill Anderson of Burlington, who would later attain the rank of master sergeant in the U.S. Air Force, joined the 10th Cavalry in 1933. While conducting mounted maneuvers in Louisiana, Anderson's unit came under gunfire from white townspeople. "They thought we were coming to take over . . . and called us every name in the book," he recalled. "But they didn't know we had live ammunition, too."[97]

The Army was also scandalized during the 1930s by the sad deterioration of the once elite 9th and 10th cavalry regiments and the 24th and 25th infantry regiments. In 1938, the National Colored War Veterans of America requested the War Department to re-officer the four black regular army regiments by 1943.

Uniformed Bootblacks and Stable Hands

A shocking story by LaZetta LiDrazzah for the Associated Negro Press reported that the once-proud units of the Plains Wars had been "reduced to uniformed chamber maids, bootblacks, stable hands, and flunkies for white officers and units. White officers and NCOs carefully selected and cultivated a mob of semi-illiterate colored NCOs who thrived and got special privileges by depriving other Negro soldiers of the few favorable advantages granted the race by the War Department."

The Iowa Democratic League, meeting at Billiken Hall in June 1940, asked the party to push for legislation that would restore the four black regiments to combat status. The GOP pledged its own "Square Deal" platform to end racial discrimination in the armed forces and the civil service. The NAACP weighed in on the Burke-Wadsworth conscription bill, which would guarantee the Negro's right to enlist in all service branches without discriminatory treatment.[98]

Yet astonishingly, even after the Japanese attack at Pearl Harbor, December 7, 1941, the U.S. military was not accepting black volunteers. There were "No Army Vacancies for Negroes," who were told to "Sign Up and Wait."[99] While plans were underway as early as 1939 to allow blacks to enter civilian pilot training, the Army Air Corps and the U.S. Marine Corps refused to admit black volunteers in any capacity.

Sons of Officers Enjoyed Some Advantage

Due to the numbers of black officers commissioned at Fort Des Moines during World War 1, a handful of young men who were sons of these officers enjoyed some advantage in gaining admission to the U.S. Army as early as 1939. James B. Morris Jr., a graduate of the University of Iowa, had obtained his B.A. degree under an Army college scholarship program open only to the sons of commissioned officers. Refused admission to the Air Corps in 1938, Morris entered Army basic training at Fort Leonard Wood, Missouri, where he earned staff sergeant's stripes. Morris noted at the time the advantages of the education he received in the Des Moines public schools and at the University of Iowa; "nearly all [black Iowans] received non-commissioned officers rank."[100]

Sergeant Morris would be assigned to undergo training as an intelligence officer at Camp Brisbane, Australia, where he would graduate first in his class of 700 officer candidates, over white men (and 7 other black candidates) from the finest colleges and universities in America. Upon receiving his commission as a first lieutenant, Morris was assigned to Gen. Walter Krueger's 6th Army, 1st Corps "Alamo Force," which was engaged in bloody fighting in New Guinea and later in the Philippines. Promoted to the rank of captain, Morris would become the first black American army officer to command white troops in combat in U.S. military history. He would lead a group of commandos specializing in guerrilla warfare behind Japanese lines, engaging in reconnaissance, infiltration, and prisoner snatches of enemy officers for interrogation by intelligence officers.[101]

Captain Morris's unit included whites, blacks, Jews, Indonesians, Nisei, Filipinos, and Australians. Despite this field combat integration, racial segregation was still the American rule in base camp. Captain Morris was compelled to pitch his tent away from white soldiers and later admitted the isolation "would have driven [him] stir crazy" but for the regular visits of some white Quakers. Morris surprised a group of black enlisted men one day

Captain Morris's unit included whites, blacks, Jews, Indonesians, Nisei, Filipinos, and Australians. Despite this field combat integration, racial segregation was still the American rule in base camp.

near a bridge under construction, who were astonished to see a black commissioned officer. Even the Australians had been told by white Americans that there were no "colored officers" in the Army.[102]

Captain Morris not only compiled a distinguished record as a combat intelligence officer in the field, but also operated stateside for several months in an undercover role for U.S. Army intelligence against the Japanese "Black Dragon Society" in the Detroit, Michigan, area. Morris was assigned to identify and investigate alleged subversive activities among black factory workers employed in the war industry and to obtain as much information as possible on Japanese operatives. Little is known of the success or failure of this operation nor of such pro-Japanese factions in the United States.[103] A close childhood friend of Morris's, Guy W. Smith of Des Moines, became the first black officer in U.S. Army Counter Intelligence, volunteering for service in 1941 and honorably discharged in 1945.[104] Smith's brothers — Luther and Thomas — would join the famous 332nd Fighter Group, as a fighter pilot and master flight mechanic respectively, both serving overseas in Africa, Italy, and southern Europe.

Black Iowans distinguished themselves in a wide variety of capacities during World War 2. Maj. Robert Hyde of Des Moines served in the Pacific Theater and attained the highest rank of any black Iowan. Joseph Howard, son of Fort Des Moines

graduate Charles Howard, attained the rank of captain and commanded an integrated military police battalion in the Pacific. His unit had black and white officers and NCOs, and Filipino enlisted men guarding Japanese POWs.[105]

First African-Americans Accepted into the Marines

In 1942, Harold Morrow of Des Moines and noted amateur athlete Earl Carr of Cedar Rapids were among the first 100 African-Americans accepted into the Marine Corps. Initially stationed in racially segregated facilities at Montfort Point, a part of Camp LeJeune, North Carolina, both men served overseas in the Pacific Theater. Virgil Dixon, also of Des Moines, served as a forward communications officer in the all-black 758th and 761st tank battalions, the latter known as "The Black Panthers." Dixon served in Italy and France during the Battle of the Bulge in December 1944.

Dixon, a first lieutenant, later recalled an incident during the Italian campaign, a rearguard action against German Field Marshall Albert Kesselring's elite paratroops. The light M-5 Stuart and M-4 medium tanks of the 758th were advancing across an open field at dusk, when three Stuart tanks and one Sherman virtually disintegrated in a barrage of fire from a hilltop two miles away. Field glasses and forward spotters finally located a battery

(Above)James B. Morris Jr., who fought in the South Pacific during World War 2, became the first black officer to command white troops in combat. (courtesy Morris family)

(Far left) Guy W. Smith (second from right, third row) with his class of intelligence officers in Paris, c. August 1944 (courtesy Barbara Smith Kaiser)

First Lt. Virgil Dixon (left) of Des Moines served in Italy in 1944 with the all-black 758th and 761st tank battalions (courtesy Nathaline Dixon)

First Lt. Virgil Dixon with his tank battalion in Italy 1944 (courtesy Nathaline Dixon)

First Lt. Vernon Baker — originally from Clarinda — is the only living African-American World War 2 veteran of the six awarded the Medal of Honor in January 1997.
(U.S. News & World Report)

of heavy German anti-tank guns concealed in a copse of trees. The great range and weight of shell of the high-velocity 88mm guns were capable of destroying any American armor at long ranges. Compounding the risk was the propensity of the M-4 Sherman to catch fire like a "Ronson burner" — the tank's nickname — due to its thin riveted frontal armor and easily ruptured fuel tanks.

Despite Repeated Warnings

The ranking white area commander ordered several of the black tankers forward to recover the bodies of their dead comrades two hours after the Americans had withdrawn from the field. Black officers and NCOs repeatedly warned the white officer that with the delay of almost two hours the German engineers undoubtedly had ample opportunity to enter the destroyed tanks and booby-trap the dead bodies. After a heated exchange, seven black soldiers were ordered forward to collect the corpses. None returned.[106]

Dixon served with the 761st during the Nazi's failed Ardennes offensive in December 1944, where the unit was instrumental in breaking the German ring around Bastogne, freeing the troops of the 101st Airborne Division and destroying a number of German tanks and assault guns. A Presidential Unit Citation was finally awarded the 761st by Pres. Jimmy Carter in 1977, and one tanker from the 761st would receive a posthumous Medal of Honor in 1997 for bravery during battles in Moyenvic and Vic-sur-Seille, France. Sgt. Ruben Rivers' citation read, "with utter disregard for his personal safety," courageously climbed out of his

disabled tank under direct enemy fire, attached a cable to a roadblock that was obstructing his unit's advance, and removed it. His prompt action was instrumental in the success of the attack.[107]

Six other medals of honor awarded to black soldiers during the World War 2 came 52 years after the war ended. The only living recipient, Vernon Baker, is a native of Clarinda, Iowa, currently residing in Spokane, Washington. Baker served as a first lieutenant with the all-black 92nd Division, fighting along the heavily fortified Gothic Line in northern Italy. On April 5, 1945, his platoon of 25 men was ordered to lead the 5th Army attack on Castle Aghinolfi, a reinforced Axis stronghold. Lieutenant Baker knocked out three German machine gun nests with hand grenades and satchel charges, a bunker, and an artillery observation post, killing a number of German soldiers in the process.

Baker's white commander, Capt. John Runyon, fell back with the platoon radioman to summon reinforcements, leaving Lieutenant Baker and 23 soldiers to fend for themselves. Suffering heavy casualties, with no sign of help coming, Lieutenant Baker ordered the 7 surviving soldiers to retreat, destroying 2 more enemy machine gun positions with hand grenades. Baker, a 1938 graduate of Clarinda High School, was awarded the Distinguished Service Cross, the nation's second-highest award for bravery, for his actions at Castle Aghinolfi.[108]

Perhaps the greatest contribution by black Iowans, in sheer numbers, to the war effort came through service with the Tuskegee Airmen, the 99th Pursuit Squadron, and the 332nd Fighter Group. Thirteen black Iowans served in the black air units, both stateside and overseas, a rate higher per capita than blacks from any other state in the nation.[109] The U.S. Congress helped pave the way for creation of the black fighter squadrons in 1939 by passing the Civilian Pilot Training Act Program (CPTP), administered by the Civil Aeronautics Authority, and Public Law 18, facilitating the government's use of civilian schools for training and monitoring of standards.[110]

Black schools were among those institutions receiving federal funds to initiate training programs, but the second school specifically established to train black pilots at Glenview, Illinois, failed to admit any black candidates. The War Department responded to the ensuing criticism by declaring "we are having difficulty in finding 20 qualified students needed to begin instruction and now the War Department is funding and financing the program, and it is the policy not to mix colored and white men in the same tactical organization, and since no provision has been made for any colored Air Corps units in the Army, colored persons are not eligible for enlistment in the Air Corps, so there is no need for additional facilities."[111]

Godfather of the Black Airforce

Between 1932 and 1941, 9 black aviators had earned commercial pilots certificates from the CAA; in addition, there were 102 licensed private pilots and 160 licensed solo pilots.[112] Through the efforts of Judge William H. Hastie — a civilian aide to the Secretary of War and a man known as the "godfather of the black air force" — as well as Sen. Everett M. Dirksen of Illinois and Sen. Harry S. Truman of Missouri, several congressmen, and First Lady Eleanor Roosevelt, pressure was placed on Pres. Franklin Roosevelt to urge the passing of the Selective Service Act of 1940. This bill required all branches of the armed service to enlist Negroes, with no discrimination regarding race, color, or creed. Once the bill was passed in January 1941, the government announced plans to establish a training camp for black pilots at Tuskegee Airfield in Alabama. This announcement was condemned shortly afterward by the National Airmen's Association, but by April 1941 the Tuskegee project was in full swing.

Des Moines's Alexander Is Airfield Architect

The training program for the 99th Pursuit Squadron would commence October 1, 1941. Pay was set at $75 per month, plus $1 per day ration allowance for all pilot trainees. Selected for the 30-week program were 276 men. Nationally known architect Archie A. Alexander of Des Moines was awarded the contract for the construction of the airfield, hangers, repair shops, classroom, dining hall, dormitories, and related structures.[113]

The 66th Army Air Force Training Detachment opened December 1, 1941, under the command of Lt. William T. Smith. Capt. Noel F. Parrish was appointed director of training. All primary school mechanics, instructors, and auxiliary staff were civilians at Tuskegee Airfield, including Ms. Marjorie Cheatham, a black woman who was a licensed and certified aviation mechanic.[114]

The selection process for ground crew and mechanics had been administered through the same black colleges that had processed pilot officer candidates — at Fisk, Morehouse, Tuskegee

Institute, Hampton, and North Carolina A&T.[115] Mechanic McGary Edwards of Elkins, Indiana, was a Tuskegee student in mechanical engineering when he was selected in 1941. First Lady Eleanor Roosevelt had come to his campus to encourage 30 students to apply. Edwards later recalled, "it was quite amazing for me to see the caliber of men being selected for induction. It must be remembered that none of these men were being selected for pilot training, yet their educational level, achievement exam scores, and general qualifications should have rendered them all as officer candidates. Many had already been refused pilot training, and had hoped this avenue would later open the door to their real dream. This was not to be, however, and some of the men had a very difficult time adjusting to their white supervisors, instructors, and officers, most of whom weren't nearly as qualified to teach, nor direct, as were the students."[116]

Despite the obstacles of stateside racism and official indifference, the pilots and ground crews of the 99th and 332nd would go on to establish outstanding service records overseas. In North Africa, Italy, Rumania, France, and Germany, they damaged or destroyed a total of 409 enemy aircraft in the air and on the ground, 40 barges and boats, 1 German naval destroyer, 619 boxcars and rolling stock, 3 heavy gun emplacements, 126 locomotives, 7

Tuskegee Airmen in P40 War Hawk fighter in Tuskegee, Alabama. Left to right: Maurice Esters, Webster City (killed in action over Yugoslavia 1944); Joseph Gomer, Iowa Falls; John Briggs in cockpit, St. Louis, Missouri; and Luther Smith Jr., Des Moines, who is also pictured above. (courtesy Luther Smith Jr.)

James E. Bowman of Des Moines trained as a Tuskegee Airman, but the war ended before he was deployed. (courtesy James E. Bowman)

Robert M. Parkey, left, and his brother, Kenneth L. Parkey, who served in the 477th Bomb Group (courtesy Ronnene Parkey Harris)

radar installations, and 23 buildings and factories. They flew a total of 1,578 missions and 15,533 sorties. Of the 992 pilots graduating from the Tuskegee program, 450 served overseas, with 66 brave men killed in action.

The first Tuskegee airman killed in action was reportedly an Iowan, Maurice (Smokey) Esters of Webster City. In all, 150 Tuskegee airmen were awarded the Distinguished Flying Cross. Several Iowans had distinguished combat careers in the 332nd, including — besides Smokey Esters — George R. Miller, Thurman E. Spriggs, and Luther H. Smith of Des Moines; William V. Bibb and Robert W. Williams of Ottumwa; Clarence Oliphant of Council Bluffs; Joseph P. Gomer of Iowa Falls; Clifford C. Smith of Waterloo; Robert Martin of Dubuque. James Bowman and James and Edward Harris of Des Moines were also trained at Tuskegee but were not deployed overseas. Robert Parkey of Des Moines served with the first black tactical bomber unit, the 477th Bomb Group, which was equipped with B-25 Mitchell bombers. The 477th included Daniel (Chappie) James, later a general in the Air Force. Mose Clinton of Des Moines was another Tuskegee pilot trainee.[117]

Lt. Robert Williams of Ottumwa was credited with shooting down two German Focke-Wulf 190 fighter aircraft on March 31, 1945. He recalled the day in detail some years later. "I dived into a group of enemy aircraft. After getting on the tail of one of the enemy planes I gave him a few short bursts. My fire hit the mark and the enemy plane fell off and tumbled to the ground. On pulling away from my victim I found another enemy plane on my tail. To evade his guns I made a steep turn. Just as I had turned, another enemy plane shot across the nose of my plane. Immediately, I began firing on him. The [enemy] plane went into a steep dive and later crashed."[118]

Bob Williams was a big fan of the Mustang. "It was the finest conventional airplane ever made, and I can whip anyone who says it isn't."[119] Williams was instrumental in bringing the story of the Tuskegee Airmen to cable television in 1995.

The 332nd — which consisted of the 99th, 100th, 301st, and 302nd fighter squadrons — was attached to the 15th Air Force. Lt. Col. Benjamin O. Davis Jr. was given command of the 332nd on October 7, 1943. The black pilots were equipped with Republic P-40s, Bell P-39 Airacobras, Republic P-47 Thunderbolts, and ultimately North American P-51C and D Mustangs. The older P-40s, P-39s, and P-47s did not have sufficient horsepower or rate of climb to take on German Messerschmitt 109G and K and Focke-Wulf 190 fighters, but the P-51s gave the "Spookwaffe" an aircraft capable of tackling the best of the Luftwaffe.[120] Lieutenant Williams nicknamed his Mustang the "Dutchess Arlene" after his girlfriend, Arlene J. Roberts of Moline, Illinois, then a student at the University of Iowa.

Fat Man and Little Boy

Ms. Roberts would go on to type the top-secret plans (on aluminum paper) for the atomic bombs named "Fat Man" and "Little Boy" for the Manhattan Project at the University of Chicago in 1945. In Chicago, she worked alongside noted black physicist Ernest Wilkins Jr. Of her wartime experience, she remarked years later that "no one on the staff at the University of Chicago knew of the nature and magnitude of the project until it was completed. When we were informed that we had helped split the atom for a bomb that could destroy an entire country, many scientists and support staff openly wept."[121] Ms. Roberts later married Capt. James B. Morris Jr. of Des Moines.

Young Luther Smith first flew an airplane, a Ford Trimotor transport, at the age of 13 — sitting on the pilot's lap. Those early flights in the Ford and later in a Stinson Trimotor, recalled Smith, "started me on a lifelong love of flying that has lasted to the [present]."[122] A graduate of Des Moines's Roosevelt High, Luther Smith entered the U.S. Army Air Corps as a cadet in August 1942. Commissioned at Tuskegee in May 1943, Lieutenant Smith went on to escort B-24 Liberator and B-17 Flying Fortress bombers over Italy and Germany, flying 133 missions and destroying 12 enemy aircraft (2 air kills and 10 in ground strafing). From the 15th's Air Force bases in southern Italy, the 332nd flew escort missions over portions of Yugoslavia, Hungary, Austria, Czechoslovakia, Poland, and southwest Germany. On Friday, October 13, 1944, Smith was on search and destroy after escorting bombers to Hungary. Selecting an airfield at Budapest, Smith strafed two German Heinkel He-111 medium bombers. Spotting a railroad yard, Smith's element leader elected to attack the loaded, stationary targets.

The railroad cars were oil tankers, which exploded when hit by machine-gun fire. The massive fireball erupted in front of Smith's low-flying plane, forcing him to fly through the flames, severely damaging his Mustang, and setting the engine on fire. Forced to bail out of the doomed fighter, Lieutenant Smith became tangled in his damaged parachute, and landed heavily in a forest.

John Burrell with tommy gun in World War 2 (courtesy Janice Burrell Cochran)

Frankie Williams's U.S. Navy buddies on liberty in New York City, c. 1944 (courtesy Frankie Williams)

David Bagby, serving in the U.S Coast Guard during World War 2 (courtesy of David Bagby)

Coming to rest on a large tree limb, his hip fractured, Smith was captured by German soldiers. He was taken to a small military hospital near Zagreb, Yugoslavia, where his broken hip was improperly treated, and then moved to a Luftstalag in Austria.[123]

Recounting his experiences in Austria years later, Smith stated he was repeatedly interrogated by Luftwaffe officers early on in his confinement. His interrogators produced a large bound dossier on the 332nd Fighter Group. Reichsmarschall Goering had been keeping a close eye on the black pilots for several years. Fluent in German, Smith never let his captors know he could understand their conversations. Though Smith was never physically mistreated, he would later joke that prisoner rations and quarters were "not comparable to the Ritz."[124] His broken hip never properly healed, and other medical complications required 18 operations and 3 years of hospitalization in German hospitals and later in Allied and U.S. medical facilities. Smith, who retired from active military service in 1947 with a physical disability and the rank of captain, was awarded the Distinguished Flying Cross and Air Medal with six Oak Leaf clusters, as well as the Purple Heart.

Sacrifices Meant a Better Life

Asked 40 years later why he fought for a country that had oppressed black Americans for over 200 years, Smith immediately responded, "we all knew that, despite its many faults, America offered the best deal for Negroes, and was the greatest country in the world. Our sacrifices would mean a better life for our children and grandchildren." Luther Smith would go on to a distinguished career as an engineer with General Electric, where he began working in 1951.[125]

Distinguished mathematician Phillip Hubbard, originally from Des Moines, played an interesting non-combat role in World War 2. As a sophomore at the University of Iowa, Hubbard had tutored seniors in trigonometry and calculus. In 1942 he made a perfect score on the Army's entrance exams. Accused of cheating by test examiners, Hubbard volunteered to retake the exams under close supervision. Again making a perfect score, the Army quietly allowed him to remain an instructor at the University of Iowa.[126]

Fort Des Moines was already well established as the home of the Army's 17th Provisional Training Regiment for black officers during World War 1. During World War 2, the fort hosted the Women's Auxiliary Army Corps (WAAC; later shortened to WAC). Initially restricted to white females, political pressure by the NAACP compelled the federal government to organize a training facility for black women at Fort Des Moines. Col. Louis Erbstein (ret.), later post historian at the Fort, recalled that training officers felt compelled to unofficially ask the white female trainees "whether it was all right with them" if black women were stationed at the camp, albeit in separate facilities.[127]

Lt. Robert Williams of Ottumwa was one of the famed Tuskegee Airmen. (courtesy Morris family)

While Puerto Rican, Chinese, Japanese, and Native-American females were integrated directly into white units, entirely separate units were formed for black females. (Language difficulties later compelled the WAC leadership to assign Puerto Rican women to a single unit.)[128] Following Army policy, two of the first eight WAC companies sent to the field would be entirely composed of Negro women, and 40 of the first 440 officer candidate positions were reserved for black females.[129]

As with the regular Army, nearly 11 percent of all WAC recruits would be black, and it was recommended that black WAC units be stationed in areas where there were already black male troops stationed or near cities with sizable black populations. Equality of treatment was the Army rule, with no discrimination permitted. "On posts where these companies are stationed, it should be fundamental that their reception and treatment should be an exemplification of the rights and privileges accorded officers and soldiers of the United States Army. . . . There will be no discrimination in the type of duties to which Negro women in the WAC may be assigned. . . . Every effort will be made through intensive recruiting to obtain the class of colored women desired, in order that there may be no lowering of the standard in order to meet ratio requirements."[130]

No Evidence of Racial Discrimination

At the insistence of Dr. Mary McLeod Bethune of the Federal Security Agency, Des Moines attorney Charles P. Howard was selected to question black officer candidates at Fort Des Moines about incidents of racial discrimination at the post. Howard found none.[131] A reporter from the *Pittsburgh Courier* newspaper, a black publication, also investigated the situation and found no evidence of racial discrimination. No jokes, or crude remarks, or discrimination in class or training assignments could be uncovered. The black WACs themselves testified likewise. Still, the black WACs were required to use segregated barracks, mess hall tables, and different swimming pool hours, in accordance with official Army policy. And there were reports of disparaging treatment in the city of Des Moines itself.[132]

This state of affairs drew scathing criticism from numerous organizations, including the NAACP, the National Board of the YWCA, the Boston Chapter of the National Urban League, and the Julius Rosenwald Fund. The NAACP's Walter White asked "when is Des Moines in general going to become as democratic as

(Above) WACs stationed at Fort Des Moines during World War 2 (Army Women's Museum)

(Right) Dr. Mary McLeod Bethune, seated on the left, at the WAC Training Camp, Fort Des Moines (SHSI Des Moines)

the white WAACs from the South?" The white WAACs had not objected to the partial integration of Fort Des Moines.[133] Finally, in November 1942, officers' housing and mess facilities were merged, as were service club facilities.

Partial Integration

Officers Candidate School (OCS) companies were also desegregated, there being some precedent for this in male Army units. U.S. Rep. George H. Mahon objected to the partial integration of the women's facilities at Fort Des Moines. Refering to one of his constituents, Mahon complained in April 1943 that "this fine girl along with others is now forced to share the same living quarters, bathroom facilities, restrooms, and reception rooms with Negroes."[134]

WAC recruiting, particularly in the South, was affected by these moves to integrate military facilities.[135] One Army officer reported "hearing constant rumors as to a relaxing of segregation of Negroes at Fort Des Moines. Such rumors are horrifying to people in this section and I know are interfering seriously with recruiting."[136] In response, most Negro organizations stated that the policy of segregation would deter the best-qualified Negro women from enlisting. The War Department concurred with this sentiment, and issued the following policy on Negro WACs: "There is a definite reluctance on the part of the best qualified colored women to volunteer in the WAAC. This is brought about by an impression on their part that they will not be well treated on posts where they may be stationed. This could be overcome by an intensive recruiting campaign with the idea in view of interesting the desired class of colored women in this project and arriving at a thorough understanding of their rights and privileges while in the service." The Army's statement also noted that "an eminently qualified person, preferably a Negro recruiter, will be sent out to colored colleges in order to secure the proper class of applicants."[137]

Early recruits from the first classes of black women graduates at Fort Des Moines were disappointing, both in the quality and quantity of recruits. A preliminary check by the Recruiting Service found that while numbers were plentiful, up to 85 per cent in some localities failed the various tests. The entire Service Command reported that in several months, it had been able to secure only one qualified typist and one clerk against its quota.[138] The lone comparison of available test scores

— a May 1943 sample — indicated 66 percent of the Negro recruits were in the two lowest AGCT groups (IV and V), as opposed to 15 percent of whites. Conversely, only 6 percent of blacks were in the two upper brackets (I and II), compared to 43 percent of white recruits.[139]

This situation was a real embarrassment to the War Department, as many black organizations viewed race, not competence, as the basis for Army job assignments for Negro women. Even elimination of aptitude tests for the motor transport pool produced few qualified drivers. And sending the least-qualified recruits to cooks' and bakers' schools produced a storm of protest from the NAACP, who charged black women were denied technical training, such as radio school slots, which went almost entirely to white women. In July 1943, black WAC officers were withdrawn from field recruiting duty to bolster training, in order to get qualified Negro recruits into the field as quickly as possible.[140]

But the protracted inability by the Army to assign unskilled Negro recruits reflected the fact that the Army in 1943 had few jobs for unskilled and untrainable women of any race. Those black WACs who met the intelligence requirements were successfully trained in specialties including medical and surgical technicians, laboratory, dental, and x-ray technicians, and stenographers and typists. Black women assumed leadership and supervisory roles in a variety of technical capacities at forts Jackson, Bragg, McClellan, Riley, and Sheridan, and Camp Knight, California. The Army Air Corps was particularly pleased with the performance of black WACs, who were assigned to aircraft maintenance, flight line, and laboratory work, as well as photography, post public relations, and map and editorial work in the war room.[141]

A total of 65,000 women were trained at Fort Des Moines during World War 2. The curriculum included military sanitation, first aid, military customs and courtesy, map reading, defense against air attack and chemical attack, company administration, supply, and mess management.[142] Black Iowans at Fort Des Moines included Anna Mae Cropp and Harriette White, both of Des Moines.[143] Not unlike their fathers in World War 1, the black WAAC officers had little or no social life on post and were socially estranged from black civilian residents. The officer's club was off limits to black officers, who were allowed to use the swimming pool for one hour per week, on Friday evenings. After the black swimmers left, the pool was "cleansed and purified."[144]

Ward One army nurses in World War 2 WAC Training Camp, Fort Des Moines station hospital (SHSI Des Moines)

Pvt. Luvinia C. Miller, a civilian free-lance photographer from North Carolina, was assigned to post public relations at World War 2 WAC Training Camp, Fort Des Moines. (SHSI Des Moines)

War Changed the Roles of All Women

The war indelibly changed the role of all women in America forever, both as civilian defense workers and in the military service branches. Many of the obstacles and stereotypes confronting black WACs obstructed their white sisters as well. The Women's Army Corps was an overall success in coming to the aid of the nation in time of war in a conflict that demanded hard sacrifices from all Americans, male and female, black and white.

Sarah Murphy Palmore of Atlanta, Georgia, graduated from the Fort Des Moines facility in September 1942 with 35 other black women. She remembered that the black populace of Des Moines was "very welcoming" to the black WACs. While there was racial segregation, overt discrimination was minimal, and on the whole her impression of military service during World War 2 was "very favorable." Lieutenant Palmore recalled several social events off the post, including being invited to dinner at one home along with sister WAC Natalie Donaldson.[145]

Executive Order 9981 — Desegregation

Despite overt racism and discrimination in training and assignments during the war, black Iowans compiled an exemplary record of service in all theaters of combat and on the home front. Returning black servicemen and women would contribute to an economic expansion unrivaled in American history. They would also form the backbone of the postwar black civil rights movement. Presaging the new post-war era, Pres. Harry Truman officially desegregated the United States military by Executive Order Number 9981 on July 28, 1948, bringing to a close 86 years of official U.S. military policy separating the races. Military efficiency and national security demanded no less, for on June 25, 1950, communist North Korean forces poured across the 38th parallel into South Korea, initiating the Korean War.

The Korean War

"At one point we were the furthest north of any allied military unit during the war," recounts George W. Johnson, originally from Marshalltown, Iowa, who served as a combat medic with a heavy weapons company ("Mike") of the 3rd Battalion, 21st Regiment, 24th Infantry Division, for 21 months during the Korean War. Johnson was drafted into the Army and assigned to a machine gun platoon (the other platoons were equipped with 75mm recoilless rifles and 60mm and 81mm mortars). He served from

October 1950 to May 1952, landing at Inchon "in full pack in deep water." He participated in heavy fighting around Hill So-So, Poor Back, and Hill 76.

Johnson completed his basic training at Fort Knox, Kentucky, and Fort Lee, Virginia, where the barracks and most facilities were racially segregated. All his training officers and NCOs were black, including his company commander — who had been in the Reserves before the war — and "many of these officers were not happy about being recalled to duty after the Second World War." On the front lines in Korea, all the officers and most of the NCOs in Johnson's integrated unit were white, including one officer who "bugged out" under the stresses of combat.

Johnson stated that between 40 and 45 percent of the troops on front-line combat duty in his unit were black. "Despite what most people have seen in Hollywood movies, combat medics in Korea almost never wore red crosses on their helmets or on armbands, and were always armed," he said. He always carried at least a Colt .45 pistol and often either an M-1 carbine or a full-size Garand rifle. The enemy shot at everyone, "particularly medics, because they could often wound or kill several soldiers trying to rescue downed comrades, and the medic was the first to attempt rescue.

"The one thing that made me really angry in Korea was the habit of some idiot soldiers to stand up while under enemy fire, despite having been told time and again to stay down. Of course, when one of these hard heads got hit, the first words out of his mouth were 'Medic! I've been hit!' and off I'd go." Johnson's goal was to get the wounded soldier to the 3rd Battalion aid station within 30 minutes or less. "Then they would usually have a pretty good chance of survival."

Johnson was voted the "soldier most likely to serve for 20 years" by his fellow troopers. While there was racism and racial discrimination in the Army at that time, he said, "it was selective, and I never felt really constrained or hamstrung by it." Enrolled at an art academy in Cincinnati at the time of the North Korean invasion of the South in June 1950, Johnson was proud of the fact that he could have obtained a deferment but wanted to do his duty. "I tried to be a model soldier, and did everything according to regulations. I didn't want anyone accusing me of being a coward." A graduate of Marshalltown Senior High School, Johnson later obtained his master's degree from the University of Denver and taught in the Omaha public schools for 34 years before retiring in 1989.[146]

Al Downey Sr. and friend Harris were stationed in Anchorage, 1951–52. (courtesy Al Downey Sr.)

George W. Johnson of Marshalltown served as a combat medic with a heavy weapons company in Korea. (courtesy Helen I. Johnson)

George Johnson's cousin, Richard D. Warren, also from Marshalltown, served in the Marine Corps in Korea. Another black Iowan serving in Korea was John B. Holway, a graduate of the University of Iowa who was wounded while in the infantry. Holway was later employed by the U.S. Information Agency and authored a book on the Tuskegee Airmen entitled *Red Tails, Black Wings: The Men of America's Black Air Force.*[147] Holway describes the bravery of the many Tuskegee airmen killed in action in Korea and of Charles Bussey, a fighter pilot in World War 2 who commanded a black combat engineer company in Korea that later became integrated.

Neither Bravery nor Cowardice Knew Any Color

Bussey contends that the U.S. Army, looking for scapegoats for the Army's humiliating rout by North Korean troops during the summer and fall of 1950, tried to blame black soldiers for the military's early failures. The former fighter pilot recalled years later that neither bravery nor cowardice knew any color in Korea, but promotions and decorations were not equally awarded. Even though he killed an estimated 258 North Korean soldiers while manning a .50 caliber and a .30 caliber machine gun during an intense firefight at Yechon, the Army would only recognize Bussey's feat with a Silver Star, rather than the coveted Medal of Honor. "Months went by," Bussey writes in his memoir of the war, "and finally the last [battalion] commander, John Corley, a white man, told me, 'Well, I thought I should downgrade this thing' to a Silver Star, the Army's third highest medal. He changed '258' enemy killed to 'numerous' enemy. He was a drinking 'friend' of mine, so I asked him why.

"He said, 'I belong to a group who believe it's our responsibility to keep Negroes in their place, and the most effective way is to deny them leadership. Then there's never any threat to anyone. If the medal was posthumous, no problem. Or if you were an inarticulate enlisted man, I would have no objection. But being who you are, you'd be out encouraging Negroes to do the things you do. Without leadership, Negroes were harmless,' he said, 'but with leaders they could be a threat of some kind. Our country can't afford this, and that's my considered opinion.'

"We were at the Yalu River in the process of fighting the Chinese," Bussey recalls. "That's when I found that whites can run as fast as blacks. Winter came on viciously, and I didn't have time to worry about medals. I never did anything about it."[148]

Two enlisted men in the 24th Infantry Division — Pvt. 1st Class William Thompson and Corp. Cornelius Charlton — did win medals of honor for bravery in Korea, but no black officer received the nation's highest award until Capt. Wiley Pitts was posthumously honored during the Vietnam War.

Black soldiers serving in Korea took a keen interest in Pres. Harry Truman's controversial dismissal of Gen. Douglas MacArthur from command of U.S. and Allied forces in Korea in 1951. According to a story published by James L. Hicks, a New York correspondent for several African-American newspapers, "there won't be any sad songs for General MacArthur from the tan yanks on the front lines in Korea." To explain why, Hicks described a speech given a week earlier by Thurgood Marshall, NAACP special counsel who had returned recently from a tour of Japan and Korea. MacArthur, declared Mashall, was responsible for "maintaining the color line" in America's Far East Command. Moreover, "the rule of segregation is most glaringly apparent in Far East Command headquarters where no colored persons are assigned." Hicks's story, which appeared in the *Iowa Bystander* newspaper, also quoted attorney James B. Morris Jr., who had served in the South Pacific during World War 2. "I shed no tears about MacArthur's summary dismissal," commented Morris."It may have been a rather unusual way to accomplish the result and perhaps unfair to him, but there wouldn't appear to be any legal or constitutional questions as to the President's power to dismiss the general."

Morris spoke candidly of the impact of MacArthur's leadership on African-Americans under his command. "My aversion to him stems mainly from the rotten manner in which he treated Negro troops in the southwest Pacific area. He not only allowed flagrant discrimination and segregation — in many instances he actually encouraged and engendered it by his refusal and/or failure to do anything about terrible situations brought to his attention. My duties as an intelligence officer gave me an excellent opportunity to observe many of these practices in operation. . . . This is neither the time nor the place to give facts and call names, but it can be done. We can quote chapter and verse, and 'Mac' is involved in many of them."

Hicks noted also that another Pacific Theater veteran of World War 2, Carl Kaiser, was "shedding no tears for MacArthur." Kaiser recalled that "many soldiers were having a tough time, and most of the fellows just didn't like the fact that MacArthur and his family were living too good." During World War 2, Kaiser had gone so far as to send a letter to the *Bystander* complaining about the poor quality of rations the troops were compelled to eat in his unit. "We know there is a war going on and that good food is hard to get," Kaiser had written, "but a farmer wouldn't feed our daily meal to his hogs."[149]

"I belong to a group who believe it's our responsibility to keep Negroes in their place, and the most effective way is to deny them leadership. . . . Without leadership, Negroes were harmless, but with leaders they could be a threat of some kind."

— John Corley, Korea

The Vietnam War

*Advanced Individual Training was predominantly black.
That was why they had all those black drill sergeants,
probably. Nothing but black guys in the whole fucking
company. That was particularly alarming to Bob and me.
In fact, word was going around, and it wasn't a quiet word,
that blacks were being drafted for genocidal purposes.
Just to get rid of us — to eliminate the black male.
And we believed it. There was a general consensus in 1968
that there must be a conspiracy against black youth.
We didn't see any black officers coming out of training;
we didn't see any black NCO trainees coming out.
We saw lots of black drill sergeants, and they were all
infantry, and they all had their Combat Infantry Badges.
They had earned their stripes the hard way in Vietnam.*

— *Pvt. 1ˢᵗ Class Stanley C. Goff,
winner of the Distinguished Service Cross* [150]

The U.S. fought an undeclared war in Southeast Asia from 1959, when the first military advisors were sent to assist South Vietnamese forces, until 1973, when the last American combat ground units were finally withdrawn. During this time, over 58,000 American servicemen gave their lives in an ultimately unsuccessful effort to prop up the corrupt and unpopular government of the Republic of [South] Vietnam. The final act in this tragedy was the ignominious departure of the U.S. ambassador, his staff, and Marine security forces from the roof of the American embassy in Saigon on April 29, 1975, as North Vietnamese Army tanks rumbled into the South's capitol. Vitriolic attacks from certain members of the left-wing press and the anti-war movement contended American leaders wasted the lives of its soldiers in a futile attempt to support a badly flawed regime. But history has, over the past two decades, come to view the Vietnam War in a less harsh light.

Official government estimates place the percentage of black soldiers serving in Vietnam at anywhere between 8 and 13 percent of the overall total.[151] The small numbers of black officers and the overwhelming concentration of black enlisted men in front-line combat units in both the Army and the Marine Corps inflated the numbers of black soldiers seeing action and appearing in casualty figures. The Vietnam experience was nevertheless quite varied for each veteran, depending upon his or her assignment, area of the country, service branch, and dates of service.

The first black Iowan to die in combat in Vietnam was Pvt. 1ˢᵗ Class James Flagg of Des Moines. Mortally wounded in a firefight near an unidentified hamlet in South Vietnam on December 16, 1965, the 19-year-old Flagg was a paratrooper with the U.S. Army's 101ˢᵗ Airborne Division. In a letter written a few days earlier to his mother, Mrs. Wilma Canada of Des Moines, on December 10, 1965, Flagg told of his "return to base camp after three weeks of duty in a swamp." Born in 1946, Private Flagg had attended Technical High School in Des Moines and later graduated from North High. He was buried at Glendale Cemetery, and his mother received a posthumous Purple Heart for her son from Maj. Robert D. Henke, Army Deputy Section Commander for Iowa at Fort Des Moines.[152]

A surprisingly large number of black men from Des Moines, who graduated from North, East, and Technical High Schools in Des Moines between 1967 and 1970, were either drafted or enlisted in the armed services for duty in Vietnam. Tony Spears of Des Moines enlisted in the Marine Corps after graduating from Tech High School in June 1967, spending 13 months overseas as a communications expert with the Marine Area Tactical Control Unit (MATCU). Spears served at An Hoa, Marble Mountain, Hill 55, and at LZ Ross and LZ Baldy. His unit coordinated Marine field movements and called in air strikes, and Spears achieved the rank of lance corporal, assigned to string communications (commo) wire and 30-foot radio antennas, "often under harassing sniper fire from Viet Cong guerrillas." Deployed as part of the 3ʳᵈ Marine Division, Spears indicated his unit was "about 10 percent black," but he rotated to various posts in country, and near Marble Mountain, he "was the only black Marine" for several weeks. Race relations were poor in that area, and Spears lamented various clashes between black and white servicemen, including several armed confrontations. "Any time you have large numbers of physically fit young men who have access to firearms, alcohol, and drugs, conflicts which would normally end in a heated argument or fist fights, can quickly turn into deadly encounters."[153]

One of Corporal Spears's best friends, a black man, was severely beaten by whites. In most of his deployments, all Spears's officers and NCOs were white, and it was rare that a black Marine above the rank of lance corporal was encountered. Most black Vietnam veterans agree that black soldiers and Marines were discriminated against in promotions and award of medals. Stateside

"I have an intuitive feeling that the Negro servicemen have a better understanding than whites of what the war is about."

— *Gen. William C. Westmoreland* [154]

Vincent Lewis of Des Moines, shown next to his 155mm howitzer. "The Judge" served in Vietnam as an artilleryman. (courtesy Vincent Lewis)

sanctuary for rest and training, as well as moving weapons and supplies down the Ho Chi Minh Trail complex." Spears credits his faith in God for helping him successfully adjust to civilian life, and today he remains an active member of his church and community.[155]

Vincent Lewis graduated from East High School in Des Moines in June 1969 and was drafted into the U.S. Army in July 1969. He was assigned as an artilleryman with the 23rd Artillery Regiment. Lewis served near the Cambodian fishhook, and his artillery unit was one of the first American units in Cambodia — even as Pres. Richard M. Nixon denied their presence there. Lewis's battery was equipped with 155mm howitzers, and while his unit was "maybe 5 percent black with all white officers and NCOs, black soldiers were heavily deployed on the front lines." He reported little interaction with South Vietnamese peasants or soldiers, "preferring to stay in the field, away from the major LZs."

Echoing the sentiments of most veterans, Lewis entered the Army believing it was important to do his duty and that America was right in standing up to communism in Southeast Asia. He left the Army feeling disillusioned and, like Tony Spears, felt American troops were prevented from winning the war militarily by seizing most objectives only to abandon them to the enemy after a short time. Lewis feels America's leaders let its people down in Vietnam by engaging in a "major deception." He is convinced that the South Vietnamese government was so thoroughly corrupt and unpopular with its own people that "even a total military victory over the North would not have prevented the eventual collapse of the South Vietnamese regime."

Processed in at Fort Des Moines after receiving his draft notice, Lewis felt the captains in his unit were very well trained and capable, but the younger lieutenants were not, on average. Experiencing racial discrimination in rear areas, Lewis agreed that black soldiers were unfairly treated in the award of medals and commendations, but not in promotions, at least not in the Army. He claims many combat veterans refused medals for which they were eligible because of the late war habit of handing medals out "wholesale" to rear-echelon personnel.

Attaining the rank of E-5, Lewis reported that drug abuse, particularly marijuana, was widespread among both blacks and whites because of the drugs' availability and low price. Mood-altering pills and "uppers" were popular with white officers and NCOs who had recently traveled stateside, but these drugs usually made soldiers incapable of functioning in a combat environment. Alcohol, particularly beer and whiskey, were popular with white enlisted men

anti-war protests had little effect on troops in the field, said Spears, but the assassination of Martin Luther King Jr. in April 1968 and the ensuing riots placed great strains on race relations in the military. While on leave stateside, Spears reported being recalled for potential riot control duty.

Tony Spears admitted to experiencing some post traumatic stress disorder (PTSD) after the war and felt his experiences in the Marine Corps were not positive, concluding he "would not do it again, if given the chance." But Spears strongly asserted his position that despite the conclusions by American political leaders that the Vietnam War was unwinnable, "we could have won the Vietnam war in a matter of weeks had our troops been properly trained and utilized. We were not allowed to fight the war in a tactically sound manner in many cases; American and ARVN [South Vietnamese] units would seize and clear an enemy position only to abandon it a few days later, allowing the enemy to reoccupy it without resistance. We were not officially permitted to engage in ground operations in Laos and Cambodia for any length of time, allowing Viet Cong and NVA regulars a nearby and officers, and Lewis maintained these problems contributed to a high rate of "fraggings," which usually involved NCOs recently in-country and combat-experienced enlisted men. "These sergeants recently flown in from the states often had to be educated, and a series of warnings were always given before the actual incident. The victim would be wounded, but not killed, to remove them from the field," said Lewis. "These fraggings were not done without cause, always for unnecessarily endangering men's lives in the field."

Lewis faced enemy snipers on a regular basis and was wounded by shrapnel from counter-battery fire. He has never experienced any PTSD symptoms, and feels Vietnam veterans are unfairly stereotyped as mentally unstable and prone to violence. Lewis feels America does a very poor job educating its young people on the lessons of Vietnam, and every year he lectures students at Valley High School in West Des Moines on the war. He remains firmly convinced that his military experience in Vietnam was positive overall, and gave him "tremendous personal growth and maturity." He concludes, "if given the chance [I] would still do it all over again."

Returning home to an America riven by racial and political divisions, Lewis quipped he immediately reentered school and worked two full-time jobs to make ends meet and "make a better life for my children and my children's children." Lewis obtained his B.A. and M.A. degrees from Drake University and recently recieved his Ph.D. in administration and counseling. He is currently principal at Brody Middle School in Des Moines.[156]

Des Moines attorney Herbert Rogers Sr., originally from Chicago, is a Drake University law school graduate currently in private practice. He volunteered for the Marine Corps in June 1967 and served overseas with Echo Company, 21st Regiment, 3rd Marine Division. He was deployed around Phu Bai, attaining the rank of E-3. Rogers claimed that by 1969 and 1970, much younger boys were coming into the Marine Corps, including high school dropouts that the Marine Corps previously would not accept. Manpower needs throughout the military necessitated relaxing acceptance standards, which had an impact in the field. Race relations in his unit were "actually pretty good, although in my unit blacks did not receive promotions due to discrimination at the battalion level."

A rifleman, Rogers engaged in numerous firefights with the enemy, who often "went unseen" in the bush. One interesting fact was the leadership in the field of 19 and 20-year-old privates and corporals who possessed the combat experience to lead platoons

Herbert Rogers (above) near Danang in 1968 with Echo Company, 21st Regiment, 3rd Marine Division. Rogers was a Chicago native who settled in Des Moines after graduating from Drake Law School. (courtesy Herbert Rogers)

Sherman Burrell (left) of Des Moines, shown here on Fire Base Hill 88, was later disabled by the headwound he received from a land mine in Vietnam. (courtesy Janice Cochran Burrell)

over higher-ranking NCOs. "These brothers had their shit together, and were highly effective against the enemy and respected by their men," Rogers remembered. Front-line stress made many of these young men "appear 40 or 50 years old," said Rogers, and "after they rotated stateside, I became senior platoon leader."

One day, after repeated racial discrimination in promotion and medals, a large number of black Marines walked out of the area of operations toward the battalion rear, fully armed, to protest unfair treatment. "We were walking straight down Highway 1 into Da Nang when a black first sergeant from Golf Company drove up to them near Monkey Mountain. He convinced us to return to our positions, but many of the more militant brothers refused to go. The Marine Corps finally sent some representatives to talk to us and calm things down. The blacks who did not protest received promotions; the militants did not."

Regarding black representation in front line units, Rogers said, "the 1/1 had a large number of brothers, between 30 and 40 percent; my unit, the 2/1 had 10 to 15 percent blacks. Rogers joined the Marine Corps in June 1967, but was not sent to Vietnam until July 1968, returning stateside in August 1969. He was stationed at Camp Pendleton in April 1968 and was assigned to riot control duty following the assassination of Martin Luther King Jr., "which was very distasteful for me," recalled Rogers. Anti-war protesters had little impact upon the front-line troops, but marijuana abuse was widespread among blacks and whites. Acid, heroin, and pills were very uncommon, even in the rear, said Rogers, "and virtually nonexistent in my unit."

Rogers felt his service benefited him personally in many ways. "Were it not for the United States Marine Corps, there is no telling what may have happened to me. As it was, I would later obtain my G.E.D., an undergraduate degree, and graduate from law school in 1982."

Rogers is proud to this day of his Vietnam service but feels American military sacrifices only "prolonged the life of an inherently corrupt regime" in South Vietnam. He lamented that U.S. politicians and civilian society prevented the proper use of the military. "Had we been turned loose, we could have successfully ended the war militarily in a comparatively short period of time." No matter how successful America was militarily in Vietnam, concludes Rogers, "our victories were always undercut by a hopelessly corrupt South Vietnamese government."[157]

Former U.S. Secretary of Defense Robert S. McNamara

agrees. "External military force cannot substitute for the political order and stability that must be forged by a people for themselves. . . . In the end, we must confront the fate of those Americans who served in Vietnam and never returned. Does the unwisdom of our intervention nullify their effort and their loss? I think not. They did not make the decisions. They answered their nation's call to service. They went in harm's way on its behalf. And they gave their lives for their country and its ideals. That our effort in Vietnam proved unwise does not make their sacrifice less noble. It endures for all to see. Let us learn from their sacrifice and, by doing so, validate and honor it."[158]

The Persian Gulf War

The invasion of Kuwait by the armed forces of Iraq in 1990 prompted a massive military response from the United States and its Gulf Coalition partners, led by U.S. Pres. George Bush. Supplementing regular forces with National Guard and Reserve troops from all across America, the world was given a demonstration of U.S. deployment capabilities and military technology.

Despite race and gender integration of the regular armed forces, problems remained in Guard and Reserve units. For example, many of the white soldiers from Iowa carried rural and small-town prejudices overseas with them to the desert, and these attitudes hampered military efficiency and troop morale. Michael Galbreath, a Des Moines native, served in the 1034th Supply and Support Company of the Iowa National Guard during the Gulf War from February through May 1990. Galbreath recalls that the racial antagonism affected not only blacks and other minorities, but also several white female soldiers who had dated or had married black men. "One white woman who was married to a black soldier broke down and cried in front of me one night, because of the harassment by white soldiers who found out she was married to a 'nigger.'" Another soldier "proudly read a letter from his aunt in rural, northern Iowa, which began, "how are the niggers over there?' So you can understand the constant tension that simmered under the surface."[159]

Galbreath had previously served three years in the regular army, stationed at Fort Benning, Georgia, and Fort Bragg, North Carolina, attaining the rank of E-4. He entered the Iowa Guard in 1989. There were very few blacks in his unit, said Galbreath, and the white officers and NCOs in his company simply "ignored the problem" of racial prejudice. Nor did the officers and NCOs

"In the end we must confront the fate of those Americans who served in Vietnam. . . . They answered their nation's call to service. They went in harm's way on its behalf. And they gave their lives for their country and its ideals."

— Robert S. McNamara

view the off-color racial humor as a problem.

Assigned to the transport and handling of fuel and water supplies, both crucial commodities in a mechanized war in the desert, Galbraith has mixed emotions about his military service overseas. Like many Vietnam-era combat veterans, he viewed America's war effort as "strictly economic." In the Gulf, he said, "we were fighting to preserve our foreign oil supplies, and prop up a corrupt regime in Kuwait, period." Michael originally resisted the call to duty overseas, but finally determined to "saddle up and move out."

There were large numbers of blacks in the Guard units from the southern states, said Galbreath, and the regular army "had probably 30 to 40 percent black troops, with an even higher percentage of black NCOs." Indeed, according to several private sources, fully 50 percent of all female U.S. military personnel serving in the Gulf were African-American, and this high percentage was reflected in Guard units from states with large urban areas. (Of historical note is the fact that a black man, Arthur W. Branham, was a charter member of the Iowa National Guard, joining in Algona. Branham later served as a Polk County district court deputy under Judge Ray Fountain. The first African-American district court judge in Iowa, Luther T. Glanton Jr., was also an officer in the Iowa Army National Guard.)

In Michael Galbreath's view, despite the quick and seemingly decisive victory over Iraq by Allied coalition forces, "we only roughly restored the status quo before the war and punished Iraq with sanctions and inspections that were never very effective." Concluding on the U.S. role in Operation Desert Storm/Shield, Galbreath lamented, "Saddam Hussein is still in power, thumbing his nose at us. President Bush lost the 1992 election, and the Persian Gulf continues to tie down large American naval and air forces, at great expense to the United States. I don't call that much of a victory."

The Persian Gulf War nevertheless displayed the awesome firepower of American and Allied forces, and demonstrated the fighting ability of the U.S. volunteer army — integrated with respect to race and gender. The Gulf War also launched the civilian careers of generals Norman Schwartzkopf and Colin L. Powell, the latter becoming the first black chairman of the Joint Chiefs of Staff and commander of Allied forces in the Gulf War, and later U.S. Secretary of State. Both men were junior army officers during the Vietnam War and directly stated time and again that their experience in southeast Asia affected their actions in Operation Desert Storm. Much of the luster lost by the U.S. armed forces after Vietnam, particularly public support of the military, was restored by the performance of American troops in defense of Kuwait. Their senior officers were determined not to repeat the mistakes of Vietnam.

Epilogue

Efforts to eradicate racism and sexism in the modern military are far from complete. But programs to establish equality of opportunity in the armed services have influenced the private sector likewise to break down many of the barriers to advancement by an increasingly diverse American work force. Iowa has played a historically important role in establishing racial and gender equality in the U.S. military. Particularly in the creation of the 17th Provisional Training Regiment at Fort Des Moines and Camp Dodge in World War 1 and the Women's Auxiliary Army Corps (WAAC) during World War 2, Iowa has established a tradition of leadership by example surpassed by no other state in the nation.

"But lest there be among you someone who, like the other members of my race whom I have met in other communities, who contend that this is not our country and that there is no reason why we Negroes should defend its flag, permit me to recall to your mind a few facts from the history of the Negro in America, which to my mind should be sufficient to satisfy even the most skeptical individual that this America is indeed our country and its most beautiful emblem our flag.

"And you should thank him [the Negro soldier] that you are to have so large a part in the bringing to a successful termination this, the greatest wars the world has yet known; for, as your fathers went into the Civil War slaves and emerged free American citizens, so you, though you go into this war in some respects proscribed and Jim Crowed, you shall emerge from it with your civil and political privileges enlarged in the same proportion that you shall have shared in the sacrifices that shall be necessary to prosecute this war to a successful termination.

"In conclusion then, young selected men of my race, accept this glorious opportunity to defend a flag, which speaks of earlier struggles, of patriots and heroes, both black and white, but whose voice has ever been for the freedom and equality of all men regardless of their race or color."

— Samuel Joe Brown, addressing the Negro draft contingent in Fort Dodge, Iowa, July 21, 1918[160]

Lt. Gen. Russell C. Davis, Drake University graduate, former American Republic Insurance executive, and National Guard officer, was promoted to commander of all National Guard career units in 1999. (courtesy Russell C. Davis)

Notes

1. Frederick Douglass, *Selected Speeches and Writings*, ed. Philip S. Foner (Chicago: Lawrence Hill, 1999).

2. Robert R. Dykstra, *Bright Radical Star: Black Freedom and White Supremacy on the Hawkeye Frontier* (Cambridge: Harvard Univ. Press, 1993), 61.

3. Ibid., 212.

4. Ibid., 212; *Report of the Adjutant General and Acting Quartermaster General of the State of Iowa* (Des Moines: Iowa General Assembly, 1866), iv–v.

5. Benjamin Quarles, *The Negro in the Civil War* (Boston: Little, Brown, 1969), 28–29.

6. Ibid.

7. Ibid., 30.

8. *DMR,* Sept. 7, 1994; Dykstra, 196.

9. William A. Gladstone, *Men of Color* (Gettysburg PA: Thomas, 1993), 1.

10. Joseph Wilson, *The Black Phalanx* (New York: Arno, 1968).

11. Gladstone, 22.

12. Ibid., 3-4; Dudley Taylor Cornish, *(The Sable Arm: Black Troops in the Union Army, 1861-1865* (Lawrence: Univ. Press of Kansas, 1987), 228.

13. Dykstra, 196.

14. Ibid.

15. Gladstone, 26.

16. Frederick H. Dyer, *Compendium of the War of the Rebellion* (Washington: U.S. Department of War, 1908), 1733.

17. Dykstra, 196–97.

18. Gladstone, 216; Dykstra, 197–98.

19. Wilson, op. cit.

20. Dykstra, 197–98.

21. Ibid.

22. Charles G. Williams, "The Action at Wallace's Ferry, Big Creek, Arkansas, July 26, 1864," *Phillips County Historical Quarterly* 25 (1987).

23. Dykstra, 198; Dyer, 1734.

24. Gladstone, 145–49.

25. Ibid., 117; Wilson, op. cit.; Hubert H. Wubben, *Uncertain Trumpet: Iowa Republicans and Black Suffrage, 1860–1868* (Ames: Iowa State Univ. Press, 1984), 413; Dykstra, 330–31.

26. Ibid., 331.

27. *Muscatine Journal,* Nov. 6, 1865; Dykstra, 213.

28. Program of the Medal of Honor Dedication Ceremony, July 4, 1994; letter to Prof. Hal Chase, Des Moines Area Community College, from Sue Parrish, Museum Associate, Wapello County Historical Society, Dec. 4, 1996.

29. William H. Leckie, *The Buffalo Soldiers: A Narrative of the Negro Cavalry in the West* (Norman: Univ. of Oklahoma Press, 1967).

30. Gladstone, 49–55. Maj. Francis E. Dumas led the 1st Louisiana Native Guard in the Battle of Port Hudson in March 1863 but resigned his commission later that year.

31. Leckie, 6–7.

32. W.A. Graham, *The Custer Myth* (New York: Crown, 1953), 157–61.

33. Leckie, 9.

34. Ibid., 11.

35. Ibid., 258–59.

36. Robert M. Utley, *Frontier Regulars: The United States Army and the Indian, 1866–1891* (Lincoln: Univ. of Nebraska Press, 1973), 26.

37. Leckie, 10, 38, 91n, 95, 178, 208, 221, 233, 244, 258.

38. Utley, 26–27.

39. *Iowa Bystander,* Aug. 1, 1937; courtesy Mrs. Martha Parkey.

40. Leckie, 220–21.

41. Ibid., 232–34.

42. Information supplied by Ms. Opie Heath-Knox.

43. *Iowa Bystander,* April 29, 1898.

44. Ivan Musicant, *The Banana Wars* (New York: Macmillan, 1990), 6–7.

45. William Loren Katz, *The Black West* (New York: Simon and Schuster, 1996), 265–66.

46. Ibid., 280.

47. Philip T. Drotning, *Black Heroes in Our Nation's History* (New York: Cowles, 1969), 144.

48. *Iowa Bystander,* June 6, 1939.

49. Courtesy Jerome Thompson, SHSI.

50. *Des Moines Register and Leader,* Nov. 1, 1901.

51. Douglas Katchel, "Fort Des Moines and Its African-American Troops in 1903–04," *Palimpsest* 74 (1993): 45, 54, passim; *Iowa Bystander,* July 1, 1901.

52. Katchel, 45.

53. Ibid.

54. Ibid.

55. *Iowa Bystander,* Dec. 17, 1903.

56. *Des Moines Register and Leader,* cited in Katchel, 46.

57. Katchel, 46.

58. Ibid.

59. Ibid., 47–48.

60. *Waterloo Defender,* April 23, 1973.

61. J.L. Thompson, *History and Views of the Colored Officers' Training Camp* (Des Moines: Iowa Bystander, 1917), 6.

62. Ibid., 7–9.

63. Thompson, 16, 119.

64. John Hope Franklin and Alfred A. Moss Jr., *From Slavery to Freedom* (New York: McGraw Hill, 1994), 326.

65. *Des Moines Capital,* March 7, 1918.

66. Ibid.

67. *Des Moines Capital,* May 20, 1917; Leola Bergmann, *The Negro in Iowa* (Iowa City: SHSI, 1948; repr. 1969), 56–57.

68. Thompson, 35, 72.

69. Bergmann, 56–57, citing Emmitt J. Scott, *Official History of the American Negro in the World War* (1919), 82–91.

70. *Des Moines Capital,* May 22, 1917.

71. *Camp Dodger,* Oct. 5, 1917.

72. Scott, 471-81.

73. Ibid.; "Regiment's Pride," *Great Battles* (October 1991), 35-41.

Tuskegee Airmen in training (courtesy Russell Collins)

74. *Camp Dodger,* May 25, 1918; June 7, 1918.

75. *Camp Dodger,* Oct. 19, 1917; Nov. 2, 1917; Bergmann, 58.

76. *Camp Dodger,* Dec. 7, 1917; Dec. 21, 1917; Dec. 28, 1917; May 10, 1917; May 17, 1917; Sept. 6, 1917.

77. *Camp Dodger,* Aug. 2, 1918.

78. *Camp Dodger,* Dec. 28, 1917.

79. *Camp Dodger,* Aug. 9, 1918.

80. "Regiment's Pride," 35–41.

81. *Camp Dodger,* May 31, 1918; Record of Trial by Court Martial of Private Stanley Tramble, Company K, 3rd Battalion, 163rd Depot Brigade, held at Camp Dodge, Iowa, May 31, 1918, at 3:45 p.m.

82. Ibid.

83. *DMR,* July 5, 1918.

84. *Des Moines Evening Tribune,* July 5, 1918.

85. *Des Moines Capital,* July 6, 1918.

86. *DMR,* July 5, 1918.

87. *Des Moines Evening Tribune,* July 6, 1918.

88. Report of A. P. Sherwood, Jan. 16, 1918, Federal Bureau of Investigation, Des Moines Office, Dept. of Justice, RG 163, National Archives, Washington DC.

89. Ibid.

90. Record of the Proceedings of the 25th Annual Session of the Iowa State Bar Association, June 26 and 27, 1919.

91. *Camp Dodger,* April 4, 1918.

92. Scott, op. cit.

93. Author's recollection.

94. Thompson, 32–97.

95. *Iowa Bystander,* Nov. 11, 1937.

96. Thompson, 10, 15.

97. *Cedar Rapids Gazette,* March 17, 1996.

98. *Iowa Bystander,* July 26, 1938; June 13, 1940; Jan. 8, 1941.

99. *Iowa Bystander,* Dec. 11, 1941.

100. "Tradition and Valor," Iowa Public Television documentary, produced by R. V. Morris, 1996.

101. Ibid.

102. Ibid.

103. Letter to author from Sterling H. Dover, Seattle WA, Feb. 13, 1997.

104. Obituary of Guy W. Smith, Inglewood CA, undated newspaper clipping; Nathaline Dixon interview, *May 1999.*

105. Charles Howard Jr. interview, conducted by R.V. Morris, 1989.

106. Ibid.

107. Joseph E. Wilson, "Black Panthers, 761st Tank Battalion," *World War Two* (Jan. 1998).

108. *DMR,* Jan. 12, 1997.

109. Courtesy Dr. James Bowman, member of the Tuskegee Airmen's Association.

110. Robert A. Rose, *Lonely Eagles* (Los Angeles: Los Angeles Chapter, Tuskegee Airmen, 1982), 11–12.

111. Ibid.

112. Ibid., 10–11.

113. *Iowa Bystander,* Jan. 18, 1941; Rose, 23.

114. Rose, 14.

115. Ibid., 11.

116. Rose, 16.

117. Ibid., 156.

118. Stanley Sandler, *Segregated Skies: All-Black Combat Squadrons of WWII* (Washington: Smithsonian Institution, 1992), 136.

119. Rose, 72.

120. Ibid., 62.

121. Arlene Roberts Morris interview, Nov. 1998.

122. "The Legend of Luther Smith," *GE Aerospace Reporter* 26 (Feb. 1988).

123. Ibid.

124. Luther Smith interview, conducted by the author for Multi-Cultural Television, 1988.

125. "Legend of Luther Smith."

126. Rose, 72.

127. Col. Louis Erbstein, AUS (retd.) interview, 1998.

128. Mattie E. Treadwell, *Women's Army Corps* (Washington: U.S. Army Center of Military History, 1954), 589 ["The Employment of Personnel: Minority Groups"].

129. Ibid., 590.

130. Ibid.

131. Ibid.

132. Ibid.

133. Ibid.

134. Ibid.

135. Treadwell, 591.

136. Ibid., 592.

137. Ibid.

138. Ibid., 593.

139. Ibid.

140. Ibid., 594.

141. Ibid., 595.

142. Ibid., 599; Sarah Murphy Palmore interview, Sept. 1998.

143. Courtesy Lynda Walker-Webster.

144. Ibid.

145. Palmore interview.

146. George W. Johnson interview, Oct. 29, 1998.

147. John B. Holway, *Red Tails, Black Wings* (Yucca Tree Press, 1997).

148. Charles M. Bussey, *Firefight at Yechon* (Washington: Brasseys, 1991).

149. *Iowa Bystander,* n.d.

150. Stanley Goff and Robert Sanders, with Clark Smith, *Brothers: Black Soldiers in the Nam* (Presidio Press, 1984), 11.

151. Ibid.

152. *Iowa Bystander,* Dec. 23, 1965.

153. Tony Spears interview, Oct. 29, 1998.

154. Wallace Terry, *Bloods: An Oral History of the Vietnam War by Black Veterans* (New York: Ballantine, 1984).

155. Spears interview.

156. Vincent Lewis interview, Oct. 29, 1998.

157. Herbert Rogers Sr. interview, Oct. 29, 1998.

158. Robert S. McNamara, *In Retrospect: The Tragedy and Lessons of Vietnam* (New York: Random House, 1996), 333.

159. Michael Galbreath interview, Sept. 7, 1999.

160. *Des Moines Register and Tribune,* July 22, 1918.

William S. Morris is a Des Moines attorney whose passion for African-American history was kindled at age 7 by his grandfather, James B. Morris Sr., and by his own curiosity about the absence of black heroes in movie and television westerns and World War 2 movies.

A 1979 cum laude graduate of the University of Iowa, he earned his B.A. in political science, with a minor in U.S. history. In 1983 Morris received his law degree, also at the University of Iowa. Today he is a partner in the law firm of Morris and Morris, which celebrated its 80th anniversary in 1999.

An avid hunter, target shooter, fisherman, and reader, William Morris has previously published a variety of articles, papers, and editorials. He is married to Amelia Hamilton-Morris of Houston, Texas, and has two sons, Omar, age 15, and Stephen, age 8.

Mrs. Houghton's first grade class, Abbott School, Marshalltown, c. 1914 (courtesy Helen I. Johnson)

"You Live What You Learn"

The African-American Presence in Iowa Education, 1839–2000

by Hal S. Chase

African-Americans have influenced every aspect of Iowa culture, and education is no exception.[1] As Thomas L. Webber stated in his book, *Deep Like the Rivers: Education in the Slave Community, 1831–1865,* "tension between the world of whites and the world of the quarter played a crucial role in shaping how slaves thought and acted."[2]

And vice versa.

For example, the general school law passed by the territorial legislature on January 1, 1839, established "common schools" in each county, "which shall be opened and free for every class of white citizens between the ages of five and twenty-one years."[3] This "whites only" policy set the stage for the continuing drama in Iowa education that has run 160 years.

A Play in Three Acts

Through three acts and many scenes, blacks and whites have struggled to move from exclusion to equality. Mutual acceptance, appreciation, and unity have been rare. Rejection, denigration, and conflict have been everywhere.[4]

The first act, "Exclusion," ran from 1839 to 1868, when the Iowa Supreme Court rejected the "separate but equal" doctrine.

The second act, "Tokenism" — whites' practice of admitting only a few blacks to a school, college, or university — had a longer run, from 1868 to 1945. Segregation, disenfranchisement, and lynching also characterized this era, as did organized African-American resistance in the form of the Afro-American League and Council, the Niagara Movement, the National Association for the Advancement of Colored People (NAACP), the National Urban League, the Universal Negro Improvement Association (UNIA) of Marcus Garvey, the New Negro Movement, the Brotherhood of Sleeping Car Porters, and the Congress of Racial Equality (CORE).

All of these and the great migrations of blacks out of the South during World Wars 1 and 2 contributed to the third act. "Integration" — defined here as equal access to public places and transportation, equal voting rights, and equal opportunity — began during World War 2 and continues to the present day.

Through three acts and many scenes, blacks and whites have struggled to move from exclusion to equality. Mutual acceptance, appreciation, and unity have been rare. Rejection, denigration, and conflict have been everywhere.

William Penn Clarke, Quaker abolitionist and equal rights advocate (SHSI Des Moines)

Iowa Supreme Court Justice Chester C. Cole wrote the Clark v. City of Muscatine *decision that ruled against separate schools. (SHSI Des Moines)*

Black and white Iowans have been developing a new relationship in this era, one in which the level of African-American presence in education and other areas of culture has increased dramatically.

Perhaps the greatest change in this contemporary era, and one resulting from World War 2, occurred in the thinking of the white majority. The idea of white superiority was undermined by the horrors of the Holocaust, the Double V campaign by the black press to defeat white racism at home as well as abroad, the March on WashingtonMovement in 1941 to eliminate racial discrimination in the armed forces, government offices, and companies receiving government contracts, and the 1944 publication of Gunnar Myrdal's *American Dilemma*.

The white majority's Eurocentric belief in "western civilization" was also contradicted by Nazi genocide of Jews, gypsies, and homosexuals. From this cultural crisis, the civil rights movement emerged in the late 1940s, 1950s, and 1960s as part of the effort to redefine American civilization in a way that would restore integrity to the ideals tarnished by a long history of white supremacy.[5]

Rev. Martin Luther King Jr. was the spokesman of this movement, which did overcome *de facto* and *de jure* segregation and disfranchisement. King's fusion of Christianity, Ghandi's satyagraha, and Thoreau's civil disobedience — with his unique voice and cadence — created an unprecedented coalition of corporate, foundation, university, and union leaders, religiously committed blacks and whites of all faiths, and the rank and file of the NAACP, CORE, the Southern Christian Leadership Council (SCLC), the Student Nonviolent Coordinating Committee (SNCC), and the National Urban League. When King was assassinated in 1968, his rainbow coalition vanished into the air, which was filled with the sound and fury of "black power," "white backlash," "affirmative action," "reverse discrimination," and "busing."

Amid this dissonance, African-Americans increased their presence in the classrooms, administrative offices, and curricula of schools, colleges, and universities of the state and nation. Yet white racism persisted and shocked the nation when it was revealed so blatantly by the 1991 videotaped beating of Rodney King by Los Angeles police officers and in the opposing reactions of blacks and whites to the acquittal of O. J. Simpson in 1995. This eruption of the racial volcano revived long-standing efforts to go beyond seeing ourselves and others in terms of race — the "outside" — to seeing the essence of each other on the "inside."

The first part of this chapter focuses on how black and white Iowans protested the exclusion of blacks from public schools and succeeded in opening education to all. In the second part, attention is shifted to an era of tokenism in the state's colleges and universities. The third part looks at the integration initiated by civil rights legislation and its impact on the presence of African-Americans in Iowa's classrooms, administrative offices, curricula, and textbooks in public schools. The fourth and final part looks at the beginning of the end of the myth of race. It is more prologue than epilogue. Connecting these acts together is the concept of African-American history as the story of a dynamic, evolving relationship between so-called blacks and whites, which has moved beyond chattel slavery and *de jure/de facto* segregation to integration but not yet into the freedom land beyond race and racism.

For Whites Only (1839–1868)

A majority of Iowa's first legislators apparently believed that Americans of African descent were inherently inferior beings unworthy of public education. As noted above, their first educational bill explicitly excluded blacks. So did subsequent bills passed in 1840, 1847, and 1849. This exclusion of blacks from education was consistent with other "whites only" legislation and clauses in Iowa's constitution, under which the state gained admission to the Union on December 28, 1846.[6]

The exclusion of blacks from education was challenged as early as 1848 by Willet Dorland, a white man, at the first meeting of the State Educational Society when he moved, "Whereas this convention believes that education is the common boon of all men, that taxation and representation should go together, and that the munificent 16th section grant was confirmed by Congress for the perpetual encouragement of popular education; therefore, Resolved, That the word WHITE should be stricken out of our school law wherever found." This resolution produced an "animated and lengthy" discussion resulting in a motion by William Penn Clarke, "Resolved, That the colored population of this State is justly entitled to their school fund, and that some provision ought to be made by law for their education."[7]

Clarke's substitute motion was rejected, and Dorland's original motion was tabled. Undaunted, Dorland successfully offered another motion that correctly predicted the long-term impact of the State Education Society's failure to strike the word "white" from the state's educational law.

"Resolved, That we believe the intellectual, moral, and

political education of our youth depends in great measure upon . . . good and efficient teachers who . . . shall deeply feel the awful responsibility which they assume in giving a bias to the youthful mind, which shall remain with it not only through time but through the endless ages of eternity."[8]

This victory of white racism in the North was not unique to Iowa. In Massachusetts in 1849, Chief Justice Lemuel Shaw established the legal precedent for the doctrine of "separate but equal" in *Roberts v. City of Boston* when he denied the suit of Benjamin Roberts to gain admission of his five-year-old daughter, Sarah, to the primary school in her neighborhood.[9]

In 1858 the Michigan Supreme Court went further and undermined the principle of equality in the "separate but equal" doctrine by upholding the segregationist policy of a steamship company that barred black passengers from cabins, leaving them exposed to the elements on the deck.[10]

In 1867 the Pennsylvania Supreme Court overturned the verdict of a jury which had awarded damages to Mrs. Vera E. Miles, "a person of color," who had sued the West Chester and Philadelphia Railroad Co. for ejecting her from a car when she refused to move to its rear.[11]

The successful attack against the anti-black bias in the North began with the rise of free soil and abolitionist politicians in the 1850s. It gained strength from the northern victory in the Civil War in 1865, and dominated the political scene in the Reconstruction decade that followed. Most notable in this regard was the establishment of the Republican Party in 1854.[12] That same year in Iowa, James W. Grimes, a Whig who later became a Republican, won the election for governor. In his inaugural address he set as his goal that "the elements of education" would be "above, around, and beneath all."

But the legislature failed to act, so in 1856 Grimes appointed a three-man commission headed by Horace Mann, the "father" of the 1837 Massachusetts public education law and in 1856 the president of Antioch College.

Every Youth in Iowa

The first of four fundamental principals in the Mann Report was that "every youth in Iowa was entitled to receive an education in the elements of knowledge." When legislator A. H. Marvin, a Republican from Jones County, tried to implement this in January 1857 with a motion to make Iowa schools "free of charge and equally open to all," George Gillaspy, a Wapello County Republican, declared that blacks "were not by nature equal to the whites, and their children cannot be equal to my children."

William Penn Clarke, now a Republican legislator from Johnson County and still seeking a compatible compromise between exclusion and inclusion, called for "some provision by which [blacks] shall have [a] common share of education." The heated debate ended in February with the passage of a proposal providing education for "all the youth of the state," which allowed for the existence of separate schools for blacks.[13]

One such school had been operating in Muscatine since at least 1850. In that year, the census taker recorded the occupation of Sarah Davidson, age 22, as "teacher."[14] Keokuk had a separate school for blacks in the 1860s, and in 1866 it was located between 8th and 9th on Main Street.[15] A segregated school may have existed in Keosauqua as late as the 1870s.[16] Thus it is not surprising that the school law of 1858 provided for the education of blacks in separate schools, "except in cases where by the unanimous consent of the persons sending to the school in the sub-district, [blacks] may be permitted to attend with the white youth."[17]

Iowa entered the Civil War with legislation that endorsed segregated schools, but the war temporarily changed the black-white relationship in Iowa and in 1868 the Hawkeye State was the first to change its Constitution and guarantee black men the right to vote.

Clark v. The Board of Directors, City of Muscatine

The same year and almost 20 years after the *Roberts* decision, the all-white Iowa Supreme Court joined Alexander Clark Sr. of Muscatine in striking a blow for equality and justice. On September 10, 1867, 12-year-old Susan B. Clark went to Grammar School No. 2, located in her neighborhood, to begin the school year. When Susan was refused admission because she belonged to the "colored race" and was directed to present herself to the separate school for black children, her father sued.

Susan's father, Alexander Clark Sr., was a successful businessman, politician, journalist, and fraternal leader who owned and paid taxes on considerable real estate in Muscatine. Speaking for the Iowa Supreme Court, Justice Chester C. Cole declared: "In view of the principle of equal rights to all, upon which our government is founded, it would seem necessary, in order to justify a denial of such equality of right to any one, that some express sovereign authority of such denial should be shown."

"We believe the intellectual, moral, and political education of our youth depends upon good and efficient teachers who shall deeply feel the responsibility which they assume in giving bias to the youthful mind . . . through eternity."

— **Willet Dorland**

Mrs. Minnie London, principal of a Buxton elementary school (from London, As I Remember)

When he looked, Cole found no such authority. Instead he found its opposite. Article 9, Section 12 of the 1857 Iowa Constitution created a board of education to "provide for the education of all the youths of the State," and therefore, he declared, "if the board of directors are clothed with a discretion to exclude African children . . . they would have the same power and right to exclude German children . . . and so Irish, French, English and other nationalities. . . . For the courts to sustain a board of school directors . . . in limiting the rights and privileges of persons by reason of their nationality, would be to sanction a plain violation of the spirit of our laws . . . [and] would tend to perpetuate the national differences of our people and stimulate a constant strife, if not a war of races." To minimize either of these possibilities he ordered the board to do its "clear legal duty" and "admit the plaintiff to said school, and to equal privileges with the other pupils therein."[18]

The principle of equal access was reinforced five years later in the case of *Coger v. The North West Union Packet Co.* Miss Emma Coger, the plaintiff, was a quadroon schoolteacher in Quincy, Illinois, who had refused to leave the dinner table of a steamboat she had taken from Keokuk when she was asked to do so because she was black. Moreover, she "resisted so that considerable violence was necessary to drag her out of the cabin, and, in the struggle, the covering of the table was torn off and dishes broken, and the officer received a slight injury."

The Doctrines of Natural Law

The all-white male court supported Mrs. Coger, ruling that "in our opinion the plaintiff was entitled to the same rights and privileges . . . which were possessed and exercised by white passengers. . . . The doctrines of natural law and of Christianity forbid that rights be denied on the ground of race or color; and this principle has become incorporated into the paramount law of the Union."

The court followed this principle two years later when it ruled against the separate schools of Keokuk in *Smith v. The Directors of the Independent School District of Keokuk* and in *Dove v. The Independent School District of Keokuk.*[19]

In 1896 the U.S. Supreme Court followed the precedent of *Roberts* rather than those of *Clark, Coger, Smith,* and *Dove* in its infamous *Plessy v. Ferguson* decision, which upheld the implementation of the doctrine of "separate but equal" in a case against segregated railroad cars. Consequently, seventeen states

passed laws legally separating blacks from whites, especially in schools. This segregation lasted until 1954, when Chief Justice Earl Warren, speaking for a unanimous Court in *Brown et al. v. State Board of Education, Topeka,* overturned *Plessy* with the immortal words, "And we conclude that in the field of public education, the doctrine of 'separate but equal' has no place."

Why the U.S. Supreme Court did not follow the *Clark, Coger, Smith,* and *Dove* precedents until the *Brown* case is a question outside the scope of this chapter. What is relevant to African-American history in Iowa education is its omission in Irving H. Hart's history of the Iowa State Education Association. Writing in the same year as the *Brown* decision, Hart hailed only Dorland, Clarke, and other white members of the state teachers association as "pioneers of educational idealism in Iowa" for their egalitarian vision on racial integration. His own vision did not include *Clark, Coger, Smith,* or *Dove* whose legal suits successfully attacked segregation, or the role of the white justices who ruled in Clark's and Coger's favor.

Hart also failed to mention the existence of integration in the schools of Buxton, the coal-mining community in southeast Iowa that had a slight black majority during its existence from 1900 to 1922. Minnie London was the principal at one of the three elementary schools.[20] Moreover, Hart did not note from the facts of the *Smith* and *Dove* cases that the *Clark* decision had not eliminated separate schools in Iowa.[21]

However, exclusion did give way to inclusion, but it was limited, and thus the second act in Iowa's black-white drama in education was tokenism, the practice of whites admitting only a very few African-Americans to a school, college, or university.

Tokenism (1868–1954)

The history of opening the doors of higher education in Iowa parallels that of its public schools. Apparently, the doors to Iowa's colleges and universities were initially closed, and it took the combined efforts of blacks and whites to open them. Moreover, when the doors did open it was only to allow through a token few — until 100 years later.

In one of the earliest known cases, a black male was excluded from Cornell College in Mt. Vernon. In either 1853 or 1854, college trustee Allison Willits met a young black man of "remarkable ability" in Muscatine.[22] Willits invited him to Mt. Vernon to get a college education on a scholarship. When the young man arrived, "objections were raised and the board met to consider the matter." Although "no members expressed personal objection," some were concerned that the black student's presence "might be detrimental to the reputation of the College." Therefore, the board voted on the question: "Should the boy be refused admittance to the College on account of his race?" The majority voted yes, but it was not until trustees Jesse Holman and Elisha Waln, who had also consistently voted no, were absent, that the board decided that the young man would not be admitted. If Willits, Holman, and Waln protested the decision, no record of it has been found, and admission of blacks to Cornell College did not occur until 1870.

One reason for this timing may have been the admission of African-Americans to Iowa Wesleyan in 1869.[23] Grinnell admitted its first black student in 1863. In November, Prof. L. F. Parker, the acting principal of Iowa College, as Grinnell was then known, wrote the trustees asking for their approval or disapproval of an application for admission from "the daughter of Alexander, a colored resident of Muscatine."[24] With one exception, the all-male group supported her admission.

They based their stance on their religious and moral beliefs. For example, Rev. Asa Turner, a zealous abolitionist who was instrumental in the founding of Denmark Academy in 1845, declared: "I hope for the honor of Grinnell and the honor of Iowa, the honor of the United States, and our common humanity, no colored person be refused whose character and qualifications would make the instructions of the college useful to them." A passionate commitment to religious teachings was also a major factor in the founding of Tabor College in 1857. In the early 1870s Tabor's preparatory department was headed by Prof. A. S. McPherron, who had a brother teaching school in Montgomery, Alabama. McPherron's brother convinced him to grant admission to Edward L. Blackshear, an African-American from Montgomery, who went on to have a fine academic career at Tabor. Years later, Blackshear praised the McPherron brothers and his other mentors as "pilgrims of the prairie" who personified the Tabor College mission:

Noble men with holy purpose,
Inspired by the love of God,
On Iowa's swelling prairie,
Laid deep and broad the great foundations,
To rear a temple to their God,
The cornerstone was Christ's salvation,
Offered freely unto all.[25]

The Civil War was a large factor in the change from exclusion to inclusion, but when Amity, Cornell, Grinnell, Tabor, and other colleges and universities opened their doors to blacks it was only for one, two, or three students.[26] For instance, when Samuel H. Johnson of Keokuk entered the junior section of the preparatory department at Cornell, the *Collegian* reported, "the first colored man ever admitted to our college is attending Cornell this year. He is an intelligent man and has been taken into [Amphictryon], one of the literary societies of the institution. His name is Johnson. He was a slave six years ago."

Johnson's experience in slavery probably explains why he was selected the following January as one of the featured speakers at an "Emancipation Proclamation Celebration" held in nearby Cedar Rapids.[27]

One of Grinnell's first black students, James Jenkins, who graduated from the preparatory division in 1871, may also have been enslaved. Dr. Ephraim Harris brought Jenkins back to Grinnell from New Orleans after serving there as an army physician in the Civil War.[28]

Far more notable was Whitefield McKinlay, who attended Grinnell intermittently from 1872 to 1882. He went on to a successful career in real estate and banking in Washington, D.C., and served as one of Booker T. Washington's most loyal lieutenants, which contributed to his appointment to political office by presidents Theodore Roosevelt and William Howard Taft.[29]

An early notable black student at Cornell was Charles Sumner Ruff, who went on to found the *Iowa Bystander* in Des Moines in 1894. Apparently named for Charles Sumner, the famous white abolitionist and Republican senator from Massachusetts who had pleaded Sarah Roberts' case, Ruff resided in Mt. Vernon where his father, Jimmy, owned and operated an ice cream parlor very popular with Cornell students. Consequently, he probably did not experience the housing discrimination that black men and women generally encountered on Iowa campuses before World War 2.[30]

However, he did experience racial discrimination and won admiration for his courage in confronting it. One day Ruff was advised not to attend chapel because a student was going to deliver a speech that included a reference to the colored race that might embarrass him. After consulting his father, Charles attended and "his demeanor on that occasion won him many friends." Also in

Although Tabor College was an abolitionist stronghold, very few blacks were admitted during its existance from 1857 to 1945. (Mills County Historical Society)

Susan Mosely, one of the first African-American women to graduate from an Iowa college (Iowa Wesleyan University)

chapel that day was the famous Methodist Bishop Matthew Simpson, ardent abolitionist and close friend of Abraham Lincoln. Following the student's oration, he rose and reflected on his own college days. "There sat beside me in chapel and during recitation one of the brightest and most thorough students I ever knew, who is now a missionary in Africa, and I am proud to call him my friend, although his face is black."[31] The students cheered, but they did not engage in any direct action to pressure the administration to admit more black students as their counterparts would do a century later.

Moreover, the white students probably perceived the few black students who were admitted to Iowa's colleges as exceptions to the widely held stereotype among them that African-Americans were intellectually inferior. But the achievements of the few African-Americans admitted to Iowa's colleges and universities chipped away at the myth of white superiority that was erected by WASPs at the turn of the century.[32]

One of the first to do this was Alexander Clark Jr., who broke the color barrier at the University of Iowa by earning a law degree in 1879, one of the earliest African-Americans in the United States to do so.[33] Despite this notable achievement, Clark Jr. did not make half the mark that his father did when he went through the one-year program in 1883–84. "Immensely popular," Alexander Clark Sr. was elected class treasurer, "and his speeches, writings, and activities . . . were a subject for comment throughout his law school career." For example, the campus newspaper reported that his presentation in a moot court case "captivated the members of the court by storm."[34]

Susan Mosely, Iowa Wesleyan, B.A. 1885, M.A. 1888, may have been the first African-American female to graduate from an Iowa college or university. She was born in Missouri and moved to Mt. Pleasant, Iowa, with her family in time to graduate from its high school. She entered Iowa Wesleyan in 1881 and belonged to the Ruthean Society, which she served as president in her senior year. After graduation she pursued a career in education that included positions at Clark University in Atlanta, Bennett College for women in Greensboro, North Carolina, and Wiley College in Marshall, Texas.[35]

About a decade later, Keosauqua's S. Joe Brown confounded believers in black intellectual inferiority by graduating Phi Beta Kappa from the University of Iowa in 1898, perhaps the first African-American to achieve this distinction from a college or

university west of the Mississippi River. He further contradicted the idea of white supremacy when he earned his L.L.B. at Iowa in 1901, and he continued contradicting it throughout his distinguished career as an attorney and NAACP leader in Des Moines.[36]

Brown's academic achievements were certainly outstanding, but George Washington Carver, a student at both Simpson College and Iowa State University (then Iowa State College), did even more to undermine the white stereotype of black intellectual inferiority with his widely heralded achievements in botany and chemistry. Carver began his higher education at Simpson College in the fall of 1890, enrolling as "a select preparatory student."

A year later, Carver's art teacher, Miss Etta Budd, who recognized his love for and extraordinary talent with plants, persuaded him to pursue a degree in botany or agriculture at Iowa State where her father, Dr. Joseph L. Budd, was professor of horticulture.[37] When Carver arrived in Ames in May 1891, he was banned from living in the dormitory, so some of his professors arranged for him to live in the vacant former office of Prof. Louis H. Pammel in North Hall and to work there as a janitor. Pammel, an authority on poisonous plants, was Carver's major mentor, but Carver also studied under and assisted Prof. James G. Wilson. Wilson later served presidents McKinley, Theodore Roosevelt, and Taft as U.S. secretary of agriculture.

Carver was also close to Henry C. Wallace, who later served Presidents Harding and Coolidge as secretary of agriculture. His son, Henry A. Wallace — who would become U.S. secretary of agriculture, U.S. vice president, and founder of Pioneer Hi-Bred — credited his love and success in botany to Carver's teachings on their long walks through the fields around Iowa State.

Carver's classmates revered him, calling him "Doctor," which was short for plant doctor. He also gained kudos for his contribution to the campus chapter of the YMCA and praise from Iowa State athletes for his massages. Similarly, Carver rose from private to captain in the campus cadet corps of the National Guard. He was also honored for his art. Judges of the Iowa Artists Exhibition of 1892, sponsored by the Iowa State Teachers Association, selected four of his paintings to be shown at the World's Columbian Exposition in Chicago the following year, and his classmates chose him to be their poet laureate.[38]

Carver had an equally significant impact on Iowa State professors. When the only job offer Carver received after earning his Bachelor of Science degree in 1894 was one from a local florist,

Professor Pammel offered him a two-year assistantship. As such, Iowa State perceives him to be its first African-American faculty member. A more striking example of Carver's influence on the ISU faculty occurred in 1896 when Booker T. Washington offered him a position at Tuskegee Institute as head of the Agricultural Department.

Dr. Wilson, not known for sentimentality, wrote to Washington on Carver's behalf, "I assure you I would not hesitate to have him teach our classes here," Wilson began. "With regard to plants . . . we have nobody who is his equal. . . . It will be difficult for me to find another student who will quietly do the religious work that Mr. Carver has been doing, who will bring the same gracious influence to bear on the boys coming here from the Iowa farms. . . . These are warm words, such as I have never before spoken in favor of any young man leaving our institution, but they are all deserved. If you should conclude to take him from us I will recognize the finger of Providence and submit."[39]

Few African-Americans have had as much impact on their Iowa classmates and teachers as Carver. But others clearly carried that tradition forward. One of these was Frank Jeremiah Armstrong of Marion, Iowa. Armstrong entered Cornell College in 1895, apparently withdrew the following year, returned in 1897, and remained until his graduation in 1900. He was one of the most popular and acclaimed students on campus, playing a major role in the Adelphian Literary Society and starring on the baseball team. When Booker T. Washington came to speak at Cornell in January 1900, Armstrong introduced him. The Wizard of Tuskegee was so impressed that he hired Armstrong when he graduated to assist his personal secretary, Emmett J. Scott. At his commencement, Armstrong delivered a speech entitled, "The Future of the American Negro," and four years later he was invited back to speak at the college's fiftieth anniversary celebration.[40]

Henry Freeman Coleman from Boone was another African-American who had a significant impact on students and faculty as both an undergraduate and later as a teacher and administrator. A far greater orator than Armstrong, Coleman was not influenced by Washington or his public philosophy of accommodation. Coleman entered Cornell in 1905 on the Mary Ambrose Elwell Memorial Scholarship, established by Elwell's husband to provide deserving graduates of Boone High School the opportunity for higher education. Although he lettered in football and belonged to the "C" Club, Coleman earned far greater fame as a speaker.

George Washington Carver attended Simpson College and earned B.S. and M.S. degrees from Iowa State College. He went on to teach at Tuskegee Institute in Alabama. (SHSI Des Moines)

Frank J. Armstrong, Marion native and Cornell College graduate, excelled in speech and baseball. (Cornell College)

*Henry Freeman Coleman,
Boone High School graduate,
went on to become a star in debate
and athletics at Cornell College.
(Cornell College)*

This talent was recognized as soon as he arrived in Mt. Vernon. In September 1905 he was elected to the Miltonian Literary Society, and consequently he participated in speech contests around the state.

In his senior year he won first place in the statewide meet in Cedar Rapids with a speech entitled "The Philosophy of the Race Problem." Unlike Booker T. Washington, who Mr. Elwell admired, Coleman was neither apologetic nor accommodationist.[41] He began his speech with an engaging parody of the plea which Henry Grady, the editor of the *Atlanta Constitution,* made famous as the spokesman for the "New South."

Like Grady, Coleman vividly portrayed poor southern whites and then challenged his audience to "picture, if you can, the newly liberated slave. He, too, is ragged, half-starved, and heavy-hearted." But instead of appealing for the assistance of southern whites, as Washington had done in his famous Atlanta Address of 1895, Coleman emphatically blamed the existing "race" problem on "a people solicitous, not for congress, but for its own injured pride and prestige, a South of hostility and vengeful jealousy."

Next, he pointed out that "justice and opportunity," not accommodation, "are the prime requisites in the solution of this problem." Then he launched a series of attacks on southern white racists, targeting Rev. Thomas Dixon, author of *The Klansman* (1905) by quoting his dire prediction about the fate of educated Negroes: "The educated negro cannot live and labor in the same land on equal terms with the whites. . . . Sooner or later he will feel upon his throat the clutch of the white man's unwritten laws. . . . Laws which deny to him the possibility of a career, and drive him to a choice between a suicide's grave and a prison cell."

Then Coleman scorned the contradiction between Dixon's professed Christianity and his violent metaphor, "Are we to believe that the white race of America . . . will establish the principles of civil and religious liberty by clutching the negro's throat, and forcing him to a prison cell or a suicide's grave?"[42]

Coleman's second target was the "prominent Senator from South Carolina," Benjamin (Pitchfork Ben) Tillman. Tillman's utterances were "more dynamic in hate." To Tillman's favorite question, "What would you do if your daughter were ruined by a black wretch?" Coleman instantly rejoined, "But what would you do if you were a negro, possessed of education and Christian training, and your wife, your daughters were never safe from those who assume all black women are unchaste?"

Finally, he directly confronted his audience, "Will you accept,

then, these pernicious doctrines of foul injustice and base intimidation masked behind the fair-sounding terms, white supremacy and Anglo-Saxon domination?" Or, like Lincoln, "strive for peace and harmony between the races . . . brothers in industry, brothers in freedom, [and] brothers in the love of eternal justice."

When the judges declared Coleman the runaway winner, bedlam broke out, confirming the intense spirit of rivalry reported by the *Des Moines Register and Leader.* Coleman recalled "someone seizing and shoving me, football fashion, into a howling mob, some of whom were standing on the seats and waving their arms in a frenzy . . . [and] being boosted repeatedly into the air."[43]

Despite his earning graduate credit at Atlanta University and the University of Chicago, Coleman was not offered a position by any college or university in his native state. Instead he began a long and successful career in segregated colleges in the South, most notably Wiley College in Texas, where he served as professor of English, debate team coach, and ultimately dean of the college.[44]

Piney Woods Country Life School

Another Iowan whose outstanding achievements in education both within and without the state confounded the white racism prevalent at the turn of the twentieth century was Laurence C. Jones. Born in Springfield, Missouri, Jones migrated north when he was 16 and settled with an aunt and uncle in Marshalltown,

Aerial view of Piney Woods Country Life School, Piney Woods, Mississippi (courtesy Janice Burrell Cochran)

Iowa, where he became the first African-American to graduate from the high school in 1903. With the financial assistance of some local whites, he enrolled in the University of Iowa that fall. For the next four years he pursued a bachelor's degree in philosophy in order to fulfill his ambition to found a school in the South. After graduating in 1907 he took a position under William Holtzclaw, the founder of the Utica Institute in Utica, Mississippi. Two years later he began efforts that led to the founding of the Piney Woods Country Life School in neighboring Rankin County. From 40 acres, a cabin, and $50 donated by a successful black landowner in November 1909, Jones built a school with assets of 2,000 acres, 42 teachers, 250 students, and a national reputation when he died in 1975.[45]

Jones's success, like that of Booker T. Washington at Tuskegee and William Holtzclaw at Utica Institute, was indebted to his talent for winning the support of wealthy whites. One of the most significant of these was Capt. Asa Turner of Des Moines, who had spoken so eloquently for the admission of black students to Grinnell in 1863. He served as the first chairman of Piney Woods's board. Iowa lumber magnate William O. Finkbine of Des Moines was another major supporter. So was Mrs. Dena Maytag, wife of the founder of the washing machine company based in Newton, Iowa.

Harvey Ingham, editor of the *Des Moines Register and Leader*

provided publicity as well as cash.[46] Jones knew how to win the support of ordinary white Iowans as well and did so by regularly touring the state during the summer with the Cotton Blossom Singers in a homemade bus.[47] He also reached ordinary black Iowans. Dan Young, "a noted colored character of Tipton," left "between $4,000 and $5,000" to Piney Woods when he passed away in 1923.[48]

African-American presence in Iowa education went beyond the student body but, excepting Carver, it did not exist within the faculty until 1945. It came from the outside in the form of nationally known black speakers. Frederick Douglass, the greatest antebellum abolitionist speaker, was one of the first when he spoke at Cornell College sometime soon after the Dred Scott decision. Following Douglass's speech about his life and escape from slavery, President Fellows asked him what he would do if he met his former master on the street. "What would I do? I would kill him on the spot."[49]

Former U.S. Sen. Blanche K. Bruce (R–Mississippi), the leading Reconstruction Era black politician, also spoke at Cornell after the Civil War and — like Booker T. Washington who spoke there later — Bruce emphasized the progress that blacks had made in agriculture, business, politics, and education. Yet "the common school system is of slow growth. It is the duty of the North to assist in driving ignorance from the South by affording facilities for acquiring the rudiments of education."[50]

In the joy of spraying a human orchard,

Laurence C. Jones

Asa Turner of Denmark and Des Moines was the first chairman of the board of Piney Woods School. Turner is pictured with Laurence C. Jones, founder of the school. (from Jones, Piney Woods and Its Story)

Missouri native Laurence C. Jones graduated from Marshalltown High School and the University of Iowa. He went on to found the Piney Woods Country Life School. (from Jones, The Bottom Rail)

Piney Woods supporters and financial backers during a visit to the school (left to right): William O. Finkbine and Charlotte Fleming of Iowa; Beulah Peck, New Jersey; Dorothy Finkbine, Mrs. William Finkbine, and Helen Knotts of Iowa; and J. B. Sutherland, Minnesota. (from Jones, Piney Woods and Its Story)

The Cotton Blossom Singers from Piney Woods Country Life School traveled in this homemade bus when they made fund-raising appearances in Iowa and other states during the summer months. (courtesy Wilma Merfield)

Frederick D. Patterson, a Texas native and Iowa State University M.A. graduate, became president of Tuskegee Institute and founded the United Negro College Fund. (from Patterson, Chronicle of Faith)

As noted, Booker T. Washington spoke at Grinnell in 1900 and at the University of Iowa commencement in 1902. His ideological adversary, Dr. W. E. B. DuBois, also spoke at Grinnell.[51] However infrequent, their appearances on Iowa campuses reinforced the fact that African-Americans were capable of higher education and of overcoming the segregation, disfranchisement, and lynching that was prevalent at the time. This progressive message was the essence of the J. N. (Ding) Darling front-page cartoon tribute to Washington in the *Des Moines Register* on the occasion of his death in 1915.[52]

This progress is reflected in the increase of black students at Iowa colleges and universities in the early years of the twentieth century, excepting Cornell, which had no black students from Coleman's graduation in 1910 until 1949, and Palmer College of Chiropractic, which refused to admit blacks as late as 1951.[53] But the numbers remained low and the pattern of tokenism continued as it did in the nation. Before World War 2, African-American presence in northern colleges and universities was "miniscule," estimated at slightly more than 5,000. By 1947 this increased to more than 60,000.[54]

Among the students who had an extraordinary impact on and off their campuses from World War 1 to World War 2 were Solomon Butler at the University of Dubuque; Archie Alexander and Fredrick (Duke) Slater at the University of Iowa; and Jack Trice, Frederick D. Patterson, and Rufus B. Atwood at Iowa State University. Their high profiles on campus and their subsequent achievements paralleled that of their contemporary Paul Robeson, the Rutgers Phi Beta Kappa who was the first black named by Walter Camp to his All-American football team. Alexander and Slater were also selected as All-Americans, and Trice might have been had he not died of a football injury in 1923.[55]

All were household names on their campuses, but Butler, who is much less known currently, had a national reputation that probably eclipsed that of even Slater in their own time. From 1915 to 1919, Butler was the star of the University of Dubuque. He led the football team at quarterback, the basketball team at guard, the glee club with his bass voice, and the prestigious Philophronia and Van Vliet societies as an elected officer. But it was his achievements in track that caused all that saw them to marvel. Butler set records in the 100 and 200 meters, and his broad jumping took him to the Penn Relays. His victories there won him an invitation to the Olympic trials, where his performance earned

him passage to the 1920 games in Antwerp. Had he not pulled a muscle there and been unable to compete, he may have duplicated Jesse Owens's multiple-medal performance in Berlin 16 years later. Nonetheless, Butler was Dubuque's campus and town hero, and he was invited back as late as 1950 to give the keynote speech at the annual "D" Club banquet.[56]

Frederick D. Patterson and Rufus B. Atwood were not star athletes or campus heroes during their years at Iowa State, but their subsequent careers in education brought them national recognition.

Frederick D. Patterson first linked his fate with Iowa when he encountered Dr. Edward B. Evans as a professor at Prairie View College in Texas. Resolving to follow in his footsteps and become a veterinarian, Patterson moved to Des Moines after graduating from Prairie View to establish residency, which would mean considerable savings in tuition. After working a summer at the Fort Des Moines Hotel, he enrolled at Iowa State. Following graduation in 1923, he accepted a position at Tuskegee Institute. Twelve years later he became its third president, a position he held until becoming head of the Phelps Stokes Fund, a leader in black educational research, in 1953. While still president of Tuskegee, he founded the United Negro College Fund in 1943, which currently provides significant funding for 39 historically black schools.[57]

Rufus B. Atwood, a native of Kentucky, enrolled in Iowa State in 1920 for a second bachelor's degree following his graduation from Fisk University. After earning that in 1923, he accepted an offer from Prairie View, perhaps resulting from the influence of his Iowa State roommate and Prairie View alumnus, Frederick D. Patterson. After six years there, he accepted the presidency of Kentucky State Industrial College for Colored Persons (now Kentucky State University), which he filled successfully until retiring in 1962.[58]

Despite the increase in African-American presence in the World War 1 era and the high profile of a few students, *de facto* segregation contaminated Iowa higher education until the end of World War 2.

Edith Comley of Webster City graduated from Drake in 1910 and in 1912 Leta Cary and Ada F. Hyde were the first black women to graduate from the University of Iowa. But like Carver, Trice, Patterson, and Atwood at ISU, and Brown, Alexander, and Slater at the University of Iowa, Cary and Hyde could not live in the dormitories. Therefore, in September 1919, Sue Brown led an effort by the Iowa Federation of Colored Women's Clubs to purchase a house, later named in her honor, at 942 Iowa Avenue in Iowa City to house black female undergraduates. This remained the main residence of African-American women at the university until 1946, when Esther Walls, Virginia Harper, Leanna Howard, and Gwen Davis integrated Currier Hall .[59]

Black men were also barred from the dormitories until after World War 2, including Richard (Bud) Culberson, the Iowa City native whose parents boarded male students and who, as the first black basketball player in the Big 10, helped the Hawkeyes win their first Big 10 championship in 1945.[60]

Several boarding houses for black men became beloved centers of African-American life. Tate Arms, owned and operated by Bettye and Junious Tate, was one of these. For 35 years the Tates offered room, board, laundry, and psychological support to some 20 young men in their 20-room home at 914 South Dubuque Street.

The house of Estella Louise Ferguson also served as headquarters for the local chapter of Kappa Alpha Psi. From about 1928 to 1958, Mother Ferg (also known as Stella) provided much more than room and board. Her influence may have reached into the white student body as well. "Stella" is still the cheer the University of Iowa Rugby Club gives in its huddle, with hands stacked one upon the other, before the kick-off of every half.

Another notable boarding house was operated by Allyn and Helen Lemme. Mrs. Lemme organized the Negro Forum in her home, and she influenced white citizens in Iowa City to the extent that the local school board named a new elementary school for her in 1970.[61]

At Iowa State "The Interstate Club" at 202½ East Main filled a similar need even though it was not a family home. Students organized and operated it, and among their leaders in its early years were Frederick D. Patterson and Rufus B. Atwood, mentioned above.[62]

African-Americans made strenuous efforts to gain greater equality in higher education in Iowa from World War 1 through World War 2. These efforts were reinforced by the existence of the black officers training camp at Fort Des Moines from May to October 1917, which included about 1,000 black male college graduates, among them S. Joe Brown. These efforts were also encouraged by the nationwide "New Negro Movement" and by the Harlem Renaissance in the 1920s.

All of this local and national support was needed given the rise of the Ku Klux Klan in Iowa and the nation at the same time.[63] Support included protests and demonstrations by students at historically black colleges in the South for an end to white leadership, particularly that of white presidents. Apparently no similar protests took place at Iowa's colleges or universities, but a group of African-Americans and whites in Des Moines did campaign for black teachers in the public schools in the early 1920s.[64]

This joint effort began in May 1924, the peak year of Klan activity in Iowa. The rise of the Klan may have motivated George W. Webber, general secretary of the Central Des Moines YMCA, to suggest a joint meeting of the religious work committees of the Central Y (white) and Crocker Y (black) to discuss the establishment of an interracial commission.

The Red Summer of 1919

Webber was definitely motivated by the success of the Commission on Interracial Cooperation (CIC) initiated by Dr. Will W. Alexander. Alarmed by the wave of post-war race riots known as the Red Summer of 1919, Alexander founded the CIC that fall with money from the YMCA, the Rosenwald Fund, and the Phelps-Stokes Fund. He believed that "the solution of interracial problems . . . rests directly upon the hearts and consciences of the Christian forces of our land."[65]

Leta Carey (left) and Ada F. Hyde (right) were the first African-American women to graduate from the University of Iowa. (from The Hawkeye, *1912)*

Sue M. Brown Hall, located at 942 Iowa Avenue, was purchased by the Iowa Association of Colored Women's Clubs to house African-American women students, because they were excluded from the University of Iowa dormitories until 1946. (courtesy John Jackson)

These young women integrated the Currier Hall dormitory at the University of Iowa in 1946. (from The Hawkeye, *1947)*

Agnes Samuelson, a Shenandoah native, was the first woman to serve as state superintendent of schools, 1927–39.
(from Smith, Development of Iowa Department of Public Instruction, 1900–1965)

To rally these forces in Des Moines, Webber arranged a weekend retreat for black and white leaders at the Y camp near Boone. From this came a steering committee of 30 men, 15 black and 15 white. Prof. H. T. Steeper, the white principal of West High School, chaired the group. Attorney and NAACP leader S. Joe Brown was vice chair. Webber served as secretary-treasurer. Other black members included Archie Alexander of the engineering firm of Alexander and Repas, James B. Morris Sr. of the *Iowa Bystander,* Rev. George W. Robinson of Corinthian Baptist Church, and attorneys Charles P. Howard Sr. and W. Lawrence Oliver. Harvey Ingham, editor of the *Des Moines Register and Tribune,* stood out among the other white members. Ten women, five black and five white, joined the group a year later.[66]

Desiderata of the Des Moines Negroes

Black members were asked to submit "some of the practical objectives that they felt the Negroes of Des Moines would like to have attained."[67] Like Woodrow Wilson's plan for world peace following World War 1, they agreed on 14, which they called "The Desiderata of the Des Moines Negroes." Among these were several pertaining to education:

- A Negro in the attendance department
- At least one Negro teacher in Franklin and Logan schools, which had black enrollments approaching 50 percent
- A course in Negro history
- A Negro member of the school board

By 1927 S. Joe Brown was quoted saying that "the prospects for the hiring of a Negro teacher were 'good.'" This statement was made on the basis of meetings that Brown and Morris had had with school administrators, who apparently agreed to hire at least one black teacher. If so, the administrators reneged and Brown, Morris, and the others had to wait almost 20 years for the hiring of the first black teacher by the Des Moines schools.

Nevertheless, the two men pointed out in their pamphlet *20 Years of Interracial Work in Des Moines* that "while few of these objectives have been fully realized, we are pleased . . . to report that some progress has been made toward the majority of them."[68] The school board did not hire any African-Americans as teachers in its classrooms or as truant officers in its attendance department, but it did place several black Drake University education majors in the city's elementary and high schools as practice teachers. It also

hired several black women as secretaries in the attendance and adult education departments.[69]

These efforts in Des Moines lagged behind those of the state and school districts where African-Americans held greater political clout. In 1918 the state's Department of Public Instruction hired Sarah Jett as a secretary, and she served there with extraordinary distinction for 40 years.[70] In addition, in January 1927 Anthony Burrell succeeded in appointing an African-American woman to teach at the Oralabor School after he was elected to its school board. Apparently this added to his political standing, because he and his daughter, Mrs. Cal Rice, were re-elected to the board in March of the same year.[71]

The Des Moines Interracial Commission's work also lagged behind Iowa State Teachers Association (ISTA) efforts to reduce racial discrimination.

For example, in 1931 Agnes Samuelson, Shenandoah native and state superintendent from 1927 to 1939, invited Lulu Merle Johnson — a native of Gravity, Iowa; a 1928 University of Iowa graduate; and in 1941 the first black woman to earn a Ph.D. from the University of Iowa — to be a guest of the ISTA for a breakfast meeting during its annual convention. Johnson's presence indicates that the ISTA held a progressive position on racial equality. But

Beginning in 1918, Sarah Jett served the Iowa Department of Education as a secretary for 40 years. (SHSI Des Moines)

Gravity native Lulu M. Johnson earned three degrees from the University of Iowa — including the first Ph.D. awarded to an African-American woman. (courtesy John Jackson)

the inclusion of "Dixie" as one of four songs that entertained the group reveals the continuing presence of white racism, however unconscious or unintended.[72]

ISTA's opposition to white racism is also questioned in light of the remarks of one of its keynote speakers that year. Florence Hale, a specialist in rural education and president of the Maine NEA, told the delegate assembly that while she was in a southern state to speak on rural education, she was greeted by several Negro supervisors. "Very soon a big Negro woman that looked as though she could carry even me right out of the room, said of Mr. Lambert [her rural supervisor], 'He is the best supervisor, just as they told you. Why ma'am, you know it don't make a bit of difference that his skin is white, his heart is just as black as any man's.'"[73]

However, the following year, Agnes Samuelson eliminated any doubt about ISTA's position on racial equality by making "equal educational opportunity for all children of the state" the first point in her famous 12-point program announced in 1932. Yet her unequivocal stand against racial discrimination was contradicted the following year by the content of the keynote speaker. W. A. Sutton, ex-president of the NEA and superintendent of the Atlanta schools, began by pointing out that he had been "reared on a plantation with a thousand other

Anthony Burrell was a miner at Oralabor who successfully ran for the school board in 1910 and got an African-American teacher hired in 1927, the year his daughter Mrs. Cal Rice (right) was also elected to the board. Both photos are from the Des Moines Register, *March 9, 1927. (courtesy Janice Burrell Cochran)*

negroes, and we all had a big time together." Then he lapsed into an extended anecdote replete with denigrating racial stereotypes that he apparently intended to be humorous. "As I was riding down in south Georgia not so very long ago, I came to an old well . . . . Seated by the side of the old well was an old negro mammy . . . and I said, 'Aunty, may I have a drink of water?' She said that I could. There was nothing there but the bucket and I said, 'Aunty, if you don't mind would you get me a glass?' She said, 'Yes sir, I get you one if you want it, but so far as we is concerned you can just drink out of the bucket. We don't care.'"[74]

Deep into the Pit of Racist Stereotypes

Sutton's subsequent remarks dug deeper into the pit of deplorable racist stereotypes by focusing on the large number of children the woman had and their Biblical names that extended from Adam for her firstborn to Judas for her last. When Sutton asked why she would name her last child Judas, the punch line was, "It's better that he never been born."[75]

There is no record of the delegates' immediate reaction to the genocidal implications of Sutton's statement. But the following year a majority of the Delegate Assembly obviously rejected such thinking by passing a resolution mandating that "nominations will be made from the floor of the delegate assembly with no limitation on either the number or the race, color, or previous condition of servitude of the nominees."[76]

Moreover, 1935 marked the beginning of a clear trend of keynote speakers to explicitly denounce racism. Rabbi Abba Silver of Cleveland, Ohio, declared, "We ought to expose the falsity, the villainy, the menace of national chauvinism, race snobbery, and religious intolerance."[77] Dr. Rufus von Kleinsmid, president of the University of Southern California, put the same message in a Christian context a year later, concluding "Friends, you and I belong to a profession whose privilege, whose duty, whose challenge, whose loving service is . . . to split the sky in two, and for all people, for all races, for all tongues, for all nations, let the light of God shine through."[78]

The same year, Agnes Samuelson reinforced this theme by declaring unequivocally, "Many lessons learned from others, As we learn to call them brothers."[79] The one notable exception to this trend appeared in a speech to the assembly by Lord Marley, chief opposition whip in England's House of Lords. Marley assured

"Many lessons learned from others, As we learn to call them brothers."

— Agnes M. Samuelson

147

Des Moines native and Drake graduate Harriette Curley (left) became the first black teacher in the Des Moines public schools. (courtesy Harriet Curley Bruce)

Ottumwa's Marie Moore (right), was hired by the Ottumwa public schools as a special eduaction teacher in 1958 after receiving a degree in occcupational therapy from the University of Iowa. (Des Moines Register clipping courtesy Frances Hawthorne)

In 1952, Lily Williams Furgerson (left) became the first black teacher in the Waterloo schools. (Grout Mueum)

Alverra Orr (right), a Florida native and Fisk University graduate, in 1962 became the first black teacher in the West Des Moines schools. (Des Moines Register)

the delegates "that we have looked at Ethiopia from all sides and it is quite worthless [and] . . . the victory of Italy over the Ethiopians was a magnificent victory over not an army but mainly naked savages."[80] Overall, ISTA was in the forefront of the movement against white racism before World War 2, and remained there by ratifying the following as the third most important plank in its 1946 platform, "Adequate educational opportunity for every child and adult irrespective of race, creed, color, or residence."[81]

We Shall Overcome: The Integration Era

The movement against segregation accelerated during World War 2. For the first time African-Americans were admitted to the Marine Corps, the Army Air Corps, and the officer ranks of the U.S. Navy.[82] In Iowa this trend appeared in the partial integration of the WAAC Training Camp at Fort Des Moines where the women trained together but roomed in separate barracks. These changes in the armed forces contributed to similar changes on the campuses of Iowa's colleges and universities.

For example, at Drake University in March 1946, Perry Harris — a World War 2 veteran who had earned the rank of master sergeant — entered Drake on the G.I. Bill and starred at halfback on the football team. Nevertheless, he was excluded from the "D" Club. Believing it was because of his race, Harris took his case to Drake president Henry G. Harmon, who

Evelyn Walker Freeman and her third grade class at Lincoln School, Sioux City, 1960 (courtesy Evelyn Walker Freeman)

referred the matter back to the "D" Club, which voted to end its *constitutional* ban against blacks.[83]

As noted, Betty Estes, Esther Walls, Virginia Harper, and others integrated Currier Hall at the University of Iowa that fall.[84] Three years later, Elaine Graham Estes and others integrated Drake's dormitory for women.[85] This change at Drake must have been gratifying to Luther T. Glanton Jr., who became Iowa's first black district judge in 1965, because he had been excluded from the dormitories, restrooms, and even the restaurants located near Drake when he attended its law school from 1939 to 1942.[86]

The breakdown of segregation also occurred in the Des Moines schools. The board hired its first full-time African-American teacher in 1946. Harriette Curley was a Des Moines native and East High School graduate who earned her education degree at Drake and had done her practice teaching in Des Moines. She was hired to teach kindergarten at Perkins Elementary School.

While most welcomed her, a few did not. Neil Adamson, a realtor, spoke for a group of 20 who protested her hiring "purely on economic grounds," saying that a black teacher would lower property values. Prospective homebuyers would shun the Perkins School area because they would not want their children to be taught by a Negro.[87] The Des Moines school board rejected this racist reasoning and upheld the hiring of Curley.[88]

But it was six more years before the board hired the first black male teacher, Nevin Bruce, a Des Moines native and Harriette Curley's husband.[89] The year after the *Brown* decision, Supt. C. O. Hoyt, known as "Dad," hired four black teachers: two men, Lacey Spriggs and LeRoy Mitchell; and two women, Betty Jean (Evans) Hyde and Gertha Jones.[90]

First Black Teachers Hired throughout Iowa

Other Iowa cities with significant African-American populations hired their first black teachers in the 1950s. Waterloo hired Lily Williams Furgerson, the wife of Dr. Lee Furgerson in 1952.[91] Sioux City hired Evelyn Walker Freeman in 1955 after her graduation from Morningside College, and Ottumwa hired Marie Moore, the daughter of Dr. Gage Moore, in 1958 after her graduation from the University of Iowa.[92]

The suburbs moved with even more deliberate speed than the cities. In 1962 West Des Moines's school board hired Alverra Orr to teach the fourth grade at Phoenix Elementary School.

Unlike others mentioned, Mrs. Orr was a native of Florida and a Fisk University graduate who accompanied her husband to Des Moines for his medical training at the osteopathic college.[93]

The hiring of black school administrators occurred a good deal later than the hiring of teachers. It was 1966, 20 years after the hiring of Curley, that Des Moines's school board promoted native son Lacey D. Spriggs, East High and Drake graduate, to principal of Irving Junior High. Ten years later the Waterloo school board became Iowa's first to name a black high school principal by promoting Walter Cunningham, East High and UNI graduate, to principal of his alma mater.[94]

Deliberate Speed of Integrating Administrators

One reason for the "deliberate speed" of integration at the administrative level may have been the underlying racial prejudice of administrators revealed in the following experience of Dr. James E. Bowman. In 1954, Bowman, a Des Moines native and a graduate of North High School and Drake University, applied for a position in the Des Moines Public Schools because of his mother's failing health. At the time he was teaching at Wiley College in Texas under Dean Henry F. Coleman (Cornell College class of 1910). At the end of his interview, Cress O. Hoyt, personnel director for the Des Moines Public Schools, asked Bowman where his home was. Thrown off guard by the obvious answer, Bowman still replied, "Des Moines." Hoyt then declared in unforgotten words, "A man's home is where his job is, and you don't have a job here."

Fortunately for Des Moines and Iowa, Dr. J. Edgar Stonecipher intervened. Bowman was hired and worked his way up the administrative ladder. After ten years of teaching, he became director of federal programs for the Des Moines Public Schools in 1965. In 1971, Superintendent Dwight Davis appointed him director of elementary education. In 1980 he became Des Moines's first black assistant superintendent and served in this capacity until his retirement in 1989.[95] At that time Bowman was succeeded by another African-American, Dr. Raymond Armstrong, who served until 1996, when he took a superintendent's position near St. Louis.

Other evidence of the decline of racism resulting from World War 2 in Iowa, as well as the rest of the United States, includes the three-day statewide "Conference on Racial Minorities" held November 15–17, 1945, at Cornell College, and the admission in 1946 of black students to Scattergood School, a Quaker secondary boarding school near Iowa City.[96] The need for such a conference was clear from the exclusion of African-Americans from the dormitories at the University of Iowa and Iowa State, cited above. Even where they were admitted to the dormitories, as at William Penn College, there was an administrative effort to segregate socially. As Julius Winston vividly remembered, Dean Stranahan told freshman at an orientation meeting in August, "Now the student body at William Penn welcomes these boys . . . and the faculty embraces the colored boys with love and affection. But, of course, they don't date the white girls."[97]

The need for such a conference was also revealed by the publication of Gunnar Myrdal's *American Dilemma*, released the previous year. Myrdal's book was a two-volume tome on the racial discrimination against African-Americans, funded by the Carnegie Foundation.[98] The same year, the need was made clear when the *Cornellian* polled four students in every class on race relations with these questions: "Would you favor admitting Negro students to Cornell?" Ten answered yes and two answered no. "Would you live in the same dormitory as Negro students?" Seven said yes and five said no. "Would you be willing to have a Negro as a roommate?" Only two answered yes, ten said no.[99]

Whatever the motivations of the conference organizers were, there is no doubt that they wanted a high-profile event. As keynote speaker they chose Richard Wright, nationally known author of

Above left and right: Des Moines school leaders James E. Bowman (courtesy Bill Paxson, Des Moines Public Schools) and Dwight M. Davis (courtesy Gwendolene Harris)

Below left and right: Principals Lacey Spriggs, Des Moines (courtesy Lacy Spriggs) and Walter Cunningham, Waterloo (Grout Museum)

William Penn College students and faculty, 1945. Black students included Julius Winston (third from left) and Don Howard (fifth from right) in the top row. African-American biology professor Madeline Clarke Foreman is seated above the sign. (William Penn College Archives)

Director Lenore Goodenow with students in front of the old schoolhouse at Scattergood School in 1946 (SHSI Des Moines)

the best-selling *Native Son* (1940). Wright's novel was a powerful statement on the impact of racism on American society. It vividly depicted the short, violent life of Bigger Thomas, a young Mississippi migrant to Chicago whose accidental murder of his employer's daughter gave him a great sense of liberation. Wright's Cornell speech, "The American Negro Discovers Himself," claimed that the initiative for this new era of integration came from within the black community, but clearly there were whites who also wanted an end to segregation, disfranchisement, and lynching.[100]

The Rosenwald Fund

One of these was Julius Rosenwald, a major shareholder of Sears, Roebuck and Company, who established a fund at the turn of the century to improve Negro education. The majority of his money went for the construction of schools for blacks in southern states, where the facilities were separate but grossly unequal. However, between 1917 and 1939 the Rosenwald Fund provided scholarships for 4 black students at the University of Iowa, 5 at

Grinnell, and 19 at Iowa State University. Grinnell College received a grant from the Rosenwald Fund for a student exchange program with Tougaloo College in Mississippi.[101]

The student exchange program lasted until 1947, the year that Branch Rickey broke the ban against black players in major league baseball by signing Jackie Robinson to play for the Brooklyn Dodgers and the year that Pres. Harry S. Truman established a commission to study civil rights in the United States. Following the release of the commission's report, *To Secure These Rights* (1948), Truman endorsed a federal civil rights bill and ended segregation in the armed services with Executive Order 9981. These two actions caused the Dixiecrats — a "whites only" southern wing of the Democratic Party — to defect. This solidified Truman's support among civil rights supporters in northern cities, which contributed to his legendary upset victory in November 1948.

The *Des Moines Register* clearly had this in mind the following January. Its article about the election of Fred Martin as the first black president of the Ames High School student body carried the headline "Ames H.S. Students Stage Own 'Greatest Political Upset.'"[102] Labor unions — especially the UAW, whose membership contained a significant percentage of blacks — provided crucial financial support to the civil rights movement of the 1950s and 1960s that began with the Montgomery bus boycott in 1955. Foundations also provided key funds such as those of the Field Foundation to the Voter Education Project (VEP) led by SNCC from 1961 to 1965. At the same time, the NAACP continued its successful campaign against the exclusion of blacks from Southern graduate schools by winning decisions in the *Sipuel* (1949) and *Sweatt* (1950) cases.[103]

In Iowa this new era was ushered in by the outstanding play of athletes rather than that of attorneys. Like their turn-of-the-century counterparts Archie Alexander and Fredrick (Duke) Slater, athletes named Culberson, Tunnell, Wheeler, and Roberts became household words to Hawkeye fans.

Richard (Bud) Culberson was an Iowa City native who first attended historically black Virginia Union University due to the influence of Clifton R. Jones, a doctoral student at Iowa and friend of Culberson's aunt Lulu M. Johnson. Culberson transferred home to the University of Iowa in 1944, not only breaking the racial barrier in Big Ten basketball, but also helping the Hawkeyes win their first Big Ten championship in 1945.[104] A few years later,

Emlen L. Tunnell led the Iowa football team with powerful gains from his fullback position and went on to an illustrious career in the National Football League.

In the 1950s, the Hawkeyes benefited from the talents of Ted Wheeler, who won a place on the U.S. Olympic track team, and Simon Roberts, who became the first black All-American wrestler and the captain of the Iowa team. Drake's star black athlete in these years was Johnny Bright, a dazzling quarterback from Ft. Wayne, Indiana, whose passing and running led the nation in total yards in 1949 and earned his selection as an All-American the following year.[105]

Achievements of Black Athletes

In the 1960s outstanding achievements by black athletes became commonplace, especially in basketball. Since 1946, at the University of Iowa alone, African-Americans have been named the most valuable Hawkeye player 29 times, All Big Ten 10 times, and drafted into the National Basketball Association 23 times. These extraordinary achievements have been recognized since 1976 by inductions into the Iowa Black Alumni Association Hall of Honor. At Drake, black stars like Willie McCarter and Dolph Pulliam led the Bulldogs to the Final Four of the NCAA tournament in 1969.[106]

In addition to the significant impact of outstanding black athletes on Iowa campuses in the 1940s, '50s, and '60s was the impact on students, faculty, and administrators of historically black schools where an extraordinary number of Ph.D.s and M.A.s from the University of Iowa and Iowa State went after receiving their graduate degrees. This network of Iowa and Iowa State professors created a pipeline of black graduate students to each institution, especially during the segregation era.[107] Dr. Philip G. Hubbard cites 220 from the University of Iowa who taught at 68 institutions in 32 different fields.

Among the most notable of these is Margaret Walker Alexander, the author of *Jubilee*, who taught at Jackson State in Mississippi for years; Dr. Vivian Henderson, president of Clark College and board chair of the Ford Foundation; and Eddie Robinson, outstanding football coach at Grambling State University.[108] Notables from Iowa State were the previously mentioned Frederick D. Patterson, president of Tuskegee and founder of the United Negro College Fund, and Rufus B. Atwood, president of Kentucky State.

These accomplishments not only indicate the talent and character of the individuals, but they also reveal the state of race relations in the country. Especially in the '40s, '50s, and early '60s, almost all the positions open to black Ph.D.s were in black schools, but a few Iowa colleges and universities were among the first in the nation to integrate their faculties.

The first known full-time African-American professor in Iowa was Madeline Clarke Foreman, a widow, who was hired by William Penn College in 1945 to teach biology. She was a native of Virginia who earned her bachelor's degree at Howard University and her M.A. at Ohio State. Before coming to William Penn, she had taught at Hampton Institute.[109]

The first African-American to teach at the University of Iowa was the outstanding theologian Howard Thurman. Reverend Thurman came to Iowa City from Howard University's School of Theology as a visiting professor in the summer of 1946 and returned for a year in 1947-48.[110]

Dr. Philip G. Hubbard stayed much longer. A Des Moines native, North High graduate, and University of Iowa B.A., M.A., and Ph.D., Hubbard was appointed to Iowa's College of Engineering faculty in 1954. Twelve years later, when he was promoted to dean of academic affairs, he became the first black administrator in a state university. Hubbard later scored another first when he became vice president for student services. Another major African-American presence at the University of Iowa was Dr. Darwin Turner, who headed the Afro-American Studies program for over a decade.[111]

(Above left) The University of Iowa's first black professor, Dr. Howard Thurman, a Howard University–educated theologian. (courtesy Philip G. Hubbard)

Darwin Turner (above right), director of the University of Iowa's African-American studies program in the years 1971–1991 (courtesy Jean Turner)

Madeline Clarke Foreman, the first full-time black professor in Iowa, came to William Penn College to teach biology in 1945. (William Penn College)

Dr. Phillip G. Hubbard grew up in Des Moines and graduated from the University of Iowa. He rose through the ranks at his alma mater, from assistant professor of engineering to dean and vice president. (from Hubbard, My Iowa Journey)

Prof. Ruth Bluford Anderson, who grew up in Sioux City, led the University of Northern Iowa's Department of Social Work and influenced many students and faculty there during her 21-year tenure. (courtesy Ruth B. Anderson)

Iowa State broke the barrier in 1894, if one perceives George Washington Carver's assistantship as a faculty appointment. Professor Wilson's statement to Booker T. Washington that "I would not hesitate to have him teach our classes here," suggests that Carver was not responsible for any classes.[112]

Fred Graham, who was appointed to the Department of Engineering, and Russell Tounds, who was appointed to the Department of Agriculture in the 1960s, did have their own classes, as did Andrew Hunter, who began teaching multicultural education in the 1970s.

The first black administrator was Charles Samuels, who served as Iowa State's first affirmative-action officer from 1973 until his retirement in 1992.[113] Dr. George A. Jackson has been another major African-American presence at Iowa State in recent decades. Since he was hired as director of minority affairs in 1978, Jackson has taught courses, advised minority students, presided over the Black Cultural Center, presented sensitivity training to Iowa State faculty on teaching minority students, and acted as a liaison between African-American students and the administration during protests, such as the successful one to rename the football

stadium for Jack Trice and the unsuccessful one to rename Carrie Chapman Catt Hall. (Students objected to the university honoring Catt because of the racist implications of some of her remarks.)

Jackson was promoted to vice president for student affairs and then to assistant dean of the Graduate College. During his tenure, the number of African-American students increased from about 175 to about 10 times that number due to such special efforts as Project 400 — initiated in 1973 — and the George Washington Carver Scholarships that started about a decade later.[114]

Drake hired its first black professor, Dr. S. J. Williamson, in 1952, but he was a psychologist at the nearby Veterans Hospital and hence only a part-time instructor teaching one course one night a week.[115] Drake hired its first full-time black professor in 1957. Dr. Eddie V. Easley was a native of Virginia and graduate of Virginia State who earned his Ph.D. in Economics at Iowa State University. The same year he joined Drake's marketing department, and excepting a one-year leave of absence to teach elsewhere, Easley remained at Drake until 1984, serving as marketing department chair from 1966 to 1984 and as assistant dean in the school of

Dr. George A. Jackson has served Iowa State as director of minority affairs, vice president of student affairs, and assistant dean of the Graduate College. (courtesy George A. Jackson)

Dr. Eddie V. Easley, Drake's first full-time black professor (courtesy Dr. Eddie V. Easley)

Mary Frances Everhart, who was raised in Red Oak, influenced thousands of high school and junior college students during her 40-year career in the Oakland, California schools. (courtesy Mary F. Everhart)

Roger Maxwell influenced hundreds of secondary students who took his band classes at Brooklyn-Guernsey-Malcom High School and thousands more across the state whose teachers used his jazz band books. (courtesy Roger Maxwell)

Business. Easley was a very popular professor. He won Drake's Teacher of the Year award in 1968, a time when some Iowa colleges and universities were just hiring their first black faculty members.[116]

The University of Northern Iowa hired its first black professor, Dr. Henry F. Parker, who taught Latin and Greek, a few years prior to this, but Ruth B. Anderson was not hired until 1969. It was she and not Parker who had the greater impact. For 21 years she influenced thousands of students and more than a few instructors as a teacher of social work. Professor Anderson's impact was heightened when she led her program to departmental status, and it spread far beyond the bounds of the campus due to her participation in an extraordinary number of community projects in Waterloo and service on several state boards.[117]

James (Sam) Randall of Coe College is another example of a long-standing African-American presence and influence on an Iowa campus. Hired initially for just one year in 1969, he returned in 1971 and has taught African-American literature every semester since.[118] Cornell, Grinnell, and the University of Dubuque also hired their first black faculty members in the mid and late 1960s, but none stayed as long or had the impact of Hubbard and Turner at Iowa, Jackson at Iowa State, Anderson at UNI, or Randall at Coe.[119]

Two at the community college level whose long tenure added to their impact were Zack Hamlett and Fred Gilbert at Des Moines Area Community College (DMACC). Hamlett became head of the DMACC's Urban Campus when it was created in 1969 and served as its dean until his retirement in 1987. Fred Gilbert, New Orleans native and Xavier University graduate, earned his education doctorate at Iowa State. Gilbert succeeded Hamlett as DMACC's Urban Campus dean. When he was promoted to vice president in 1990, Mary Chapman succeeded him as dean.[120]

In addition to the increased presence of African-American faculty and administrators in Iowa colleges and universities after World War 2 was the increase of African-American presence in the curriculum. Generally, African-American courses started to appear in catalogs in the late 1940s, usually in sociology departments under a heading that included such terms as "race," "racism," or "race and ethnic relations."[121]

However, it usually took the demands of black students before African-American history and literature courses became part of the curriculum. At the University of Northern Iowa and the University of Dubuque, Afro-American history was not offered until 1969 and 1970 respectively, when white professors began offering it at both.[122]

These examples represent the difficulty that universities and especially colleges had in hiring black faculty. Retaining black faculty members proved equally challenging. For example, Cornell was able to hire graduate students like Fred Woodard, who had been an Iowa Wesleyan undergraduate, from the Afro-American Studies department at nearby University of Iowa on a part-time basis, but it did not succeed in hiring him for a full-time position.[123]

The scant number of black professors, administrators, and African-American courses — and overt incidents of white racism — led to numerous student protests in the late 1960s and early 1970s. At Iowa State in the spring of 1964, track star Morgan Langston, from Washington, D.C., charged that track coach Ron Lawson advised him to stop dating a white co-ed or "it might be impossible to renew his scholarship." The case went to the Iowa State University Human Rights Commission, which declared, "[the university] unequivocally opposes pressures by any university representative to prevent interracial dating."[124] It is notable that this incident did not spark a student demonstration as similar incidents would do on a number of Iowa campuses in the late 1960s and early 1970s.

One of the earliest of these took place at the University of Dubuque. On December 5, 1968, the members of a student organization named the Black Presidium prepared an open letter to the university charging that the university was racist because:

- Blacks were treated as aliens
- Blacks' cultural uniqueness was not considered
- The curriculum was detrimental to the emotional, psychological, and educational well-being of blacks
- The university supported and condoned racist institutions such as fraternities, admissions, and room assignments

These premises were followed by a list of eight demands, including recognition of the Black Presidium, along with a $500 annual budget for its activities, plus live black entertainment, black speakers, counselors, admissions officers, administrators, and professors to teach "black-oriented" courses. The students also called for an increase in black enrollment to 100 students. These demands were largely met.

The following year a separate house, called the Black Presidium, was established. In February 1973 the first annual "Black

DMACC's Dr. Fred Gilbert, the first black vice president of an Iowa community college, is current dean of the Urban Campus. (courtesy Fred Gilbert)

Dr. Mary Chapman (right) succeeded Dr. Fred Gilbert as dean of DMACC's Urban Campus in 1990 and served for ten years. Here she presents Larry Carter Scholarships to DMACC students. (courtesy Mary Chapman)

Week-end" was held, featuring speakers Muhammad Ali and Dick Gregory. Divisions between blacks and whites widened shortly thereafter when A. J. Stovall was fired from his position as head resident of Smith Hall for verbally assaulting his supervisor, Dean of Students William Donahue. There were sit-in demonstrations in Steffens Hall, negotiations, and ultimately some sort of settlement with Stovall, who left the university. Two years later, the name of the Black Presidium was changed to Sol Butler Memorial Center in honor of the university's most famous black alumnus.[125]

The circumstances surrounding the protest at the University of Northern Iowa in 1970 were very different. In the fall of 1967 a black graduate student gave Dr. Charles E. Quick an article about the Center for Inner City Studies that had been established in Chicago by Northeast Illinois State College (now Northern Illinois University). Quick led a group there in December and on the basis of its findings the group submitted a six-point proposal to UNI Pres. James W. (Bill) Maucker. The points included recruitment of minority students and faculty, courses on minorities, in-service programs on minorities for prospective teachers, and a center in East Waterloo.

COURIMGE was established at the University of Northern Iowa in March 1968. Left to right: Thomas Ryan, Ronald James, and chairman Daryl Pendergraft
(from Lang and Pendergraft, A Century of Leadership and Service: A Centennial History of the University of Northern Iowa)

This proposal led to the creation of COURIMGE (Committee on University Responsibility in Minority Group Education) chaired by Daryl Pendergraft, executive dean and vice president for student affairs and field service.

Weekly meetings began in March 1968 and led to the hiring of a director of educational opportunity programs and special community services. When he resigned three days before he was scheduled to begin, history professor Thomas Ryan accepted the position on a part-time basis. Robert K. Murphy was hired a year later. Meanwhile, Dr. Ross A. Nielsen and Dr. James Albrecht successfully recruited black students from Waterloo to attend Price Laboratory School.

Commitment to Improve Black-White Relations

In the fall of 1969 UNI-CUE (the university's Center for Urban Education) was established in East Waterloo, and Ruth B. Anderson was hired to teach social work. All this seemed to realize President Maucker's commitment to improve black-white relations at UNI, in Waterloo, and in Iowa's schools, which he declared in his address to the faculty in September 1968. "This is the most crucial and biggest project . . . facing the university. There must be recognition of the centrality, pervasiveness, and depth of the racial issue."[126]

On November 6, 1969, 35 members of the Afro-American Society went to Vice President Lang's office and presented him with their "New Demands." When Lang asked if they would like to discuss them, he was told, "there's nothing to discuss." As in the University of Dubuque demonstration of a year earlier, UNI was denounced as a racist institution. In addition to a black cultural house, more black faculty, courses, and financial aid were demanded. In March 1970 black students occupied President Maucker's residence, coincidentally while his wife was seriously ill. The students left about 36 hours later before the campus police arrived to remove them, but Maucker's actions were seen as lenient, and he left UNI that summer. That fall the Ethnic Cultural Minorities House was established in the large Victorian residence on the campus that it still occupies.[127]

The movement to increase African-American presence in Iowa's public schools, as shown above, dates to the first meeting of the Iowa Educational Society in 1848 and Alexander Clark Sr.'s victory over the "separate but equal" doctrine 20 years later. The efforts of S. Joe Brown and other blacks in Des Moines in the

> "This is the most crucial and biggest project . . . facing the university. There must be recognition of the centrality, pervasiveness and depth of the racial issue."
>
> — James W. Maucker, President, University of Northern Iowa, 1968

1920s to get an African-American hired as a teacher should also be remembered. So should Agnes M. Samuelson's clarion call for equal educational opportunity in the 1930s. Yet it was the Civil Rights Act of 1964, the Voting Rights Act of 1965, and the Open Housing Act of 1968 that initiated the integration era in Iowa's schools. Among the most important of the matching Iowa laws for public education were:

- Chapter 280.3, which mandates uniform school requirements, explicitly prohibiting discrimination on the basis of race, color, creed, sex, marital status, or national origin in the public schools of Iowa. This covers "all the components of the educational program." The Iowa Civil Rights Commission and the Iowa Department of Education are charged with monitoring and enforcement.[128]

- Chapter 256.11, Iowa School Standards, requires that all school programs be taught from a multicultural, nonsexist perspective. Standards for this were set by Section 6704.5(8) of the Department of Education Administrative Rules, and the department was designated as the monitoring and compliance agency.[129]

- Chapter 601 A.9 adds admission and recruiting, intramural and interscholastic athletics to the types of discrimination prohibited and places enforcement with the Iowa Civil Rights Commission.[130]

- Chapter 280.4 requires that bilingual or English as a Second Language programs be provided for students whose primary language is one other than English.[131]

- Chapter 19B.11 requires all school districts and area education agencies to file an annual report to the director of the Department of Education showing the results of the affirmative action plans that this legislation mandated.[132]

In 1994 the Bureau of School Administration and Accreditation of the Iowa Department of Education distributed "A Model Multicultural, Nonsexist Education Plan." In addition to providing a rationale, the plan gave specific goals and objectives for 17 different program areas. It also presented "Provisions for Infusion into Curriculum," suggestions for inservice activities and their documentation, examples of

University of Northern Iowa African-American students protesting policies with a sit-in at President Maucker's residence in March 1970. (from Lang and Pendergraft, A Century of Leadership and Service: A Centennial History of the University of Northern Iowa)

Mary Lynne Jones, director of multicultural affairs for the Des Moines Public Schools (courtesy Bill Paxson, Des Moines Public Schools)

"systematic input by women, minority groups, and persons with disabilities in developing and implementing the plan," and suggestions for an "ongoing system for monitoring and evaluating the plan."[133]

The following year the department distributed "Scope of the Educational Equity On-Site Review," which outlined the areas, people, materials, and programs that departmental personnel would investigate to determine if the district was in compliance with the multicultural, nonsexist mandate of Chapter 256.11.[134] Departmental reviewers included African-Americans committed to the mandate, such as Judge Brown, who had been one of the first black teachers in Fort Dodge.[135]

The laws and their implementation and enforcement contributed to the creation of positions devoted exclusively to the administration of multicultural programs like the one in the Des Moines system currently held by Mary Lynne Jones. They also contributed to the creation of special schools to enhance integration like King Elementary in Des Moines and Casady Alternative. Such schools attracted talented and extraordinarily committed teachers and administrators like Thomas Simmons at King and Dr. Kittie Weston-Knauer at

Dr. Kittie Weston-Knauer, a Drake graduate from North Carolina, has served the Des Moines Public Schools since 1973 as teacher, vice principal, and — since 1999 — principal of Scavo Campus. (courtesy Bill Paxson, Des Moines Public Schools)

Ruth Ann Gaines
1998

Ruth Ann Gaines, has taught drama at Des Moines East High for years and was selected as Iowa's Teacher of the Year in 1998. (Iowa Arts Council)

Casady and raised the number and percentage of African-American teachers and administrators in Iowa's public schools.[136]

Hues of Humanity

The movement also motivated Iowa's teachers' union, the Iowa State Education Association (ISEA). The ISEA established a Minority Affairs Committee in 1984 and its Human Relations Award in 1990. Five of the first eight recipients were African-Americans.[137]

In 1994, the ISEA began sending the presidents and minority members of its locals a copy of its Minority Involvement Plan, and in 1997 the ISEA sponsored a summer teacher workshop entitled "Hues of Humanity: Sensitivity, Diversity, and Leadership."[138] That year Ruth Ann Gaines became the second African-American to be named Iowa's Teacher of the Year. The first was Betty Jean Hyde in 1965.[139]

All this contributed to the presence of 306 African-American teachers and administrators in Iowa public schools, 15 employed by Area Education Agencies, and 18 in community colleges by the end of 1997.[140] This trend of increasing numbers of black teachers should continue, given the corresponding rise in the number of minority students in the classroom. Both the Holmes Group report, "Tomorrow's Teachers," and the Carnegie Forum's report, "A Nation Prepared: Teachers for the 21st Century," presented proposals to accelerate the training of more African-American teachers.[141]

Development of Curricula

The civil rights movement of the 1970s and 1980s also contributed to the development of curriculum materials by teachers, administrators, and UNI professors. In 1970 and 1971 a group spearheaded by Dr. James E. Bowman and Wes Chapman developed materials, units and courses as well as a desegregation plan to increase the African-American presence in the Des Moines schools.[142]

At the same time, Jane Elliot, who taught in Riceland, Iowa, received national media attention for her "Brown Eyes-Blue Eyes"

The 1998 recipient of the Milken Award was Tim Tutt, third grade teacher at Hanawalt Elementary School in Des Moines, shown here with student Jordan Robertson. (courtesy Marilee Robertson)

In 1965, Betty Jean Hyde was named Iowa's Teacher of the Year, the first African-American to be selected for the honor. (courtesy Bill Paxson, Des Moines Public Schools)

In 1970 and 1971, Wes Chapman helped develop curriculum materials and a desegregation plan to increase African-American presence in the Des Moines Public Schools. (courtesy Mary Chapman)

Perry native Maude White returned to Des Moines in 1964 to earn B.A. and M.A. degrees at Drake. In 1980 she founded the Des Moines Tutoring Center "because schools put up barriers." (courtesy Maude White)

activity, in which elementary students experienced discrimination first-hand based on their eye color.[143]

In 1985 Lynn Nielsen, Janet McClain, Joan Duea, and Betty Strub — all education professors at UNI — developed several units about black history. A decade later they developed black history units in their "Explorations in Iowa History Project," which for nominal sums offered material for 38 different lessons.[144]

Another outgrowth of the civil rights era, and one that developed outside the public school system, was the rise of non-profit day care and tutoring centers. In 1966 Evelyn Davis established Tiny Tots, paralleling the efforts of the federally funded Head Start Program, with the philanthropy of local residents, most notably that of real estate magnate Bill Knapp.[145] Tiny Tots still operates as an independent entity.

About the same time, Dr. Henry F. Parker established Parker Academy in Waterloo, which had an Afrocentric perspective in its curriculum.[146] Tutoring centers that focused on the needs of African-American students were also established. Maude White,

A teacher with her students at the Tiny Tots Day Care Center in its early years (courtesy Evelyn Davis)

Dr. Henry F. Parker developed and taught "Culture of the Ghetto" and founded the Afrocentric Parker Academy in Waterloo while he was teaching Latin at the University of Northern Iowa. (University of Iowa Alumni Association)

Evelyn Davis, founder and leader of Tiny Tots preschool program since 1966 (Gary Fandel photo / Des Moines Register)

Nolden Gentry, second from right, served on the Iowa Board of Regents and later was elected to the Des Moines School Board. (courtesy Harold Goldman)

Gregory D. McClain of Cedar Falls, a member of the State Board of Education (Iowa State Board of Education)

a native of Perry who had a varied career before returning to Des Moines in 1964 and earning her B.A. and M.A. at Drake, founded a tutoring center in 1980 because "schools put up barriers." Unlike Tiny Tots, her tutoring center became a United Way agency after 1993, but it is still separate from the Des Moines school system.[147]

The civil rights legislation also contributed to the election of blacks to local school boards and the State Board of Regents. For example, Nolden A. Gentry — a Rockford, Illinois, native who was recruited to the University of Iowa by Chicago Judge Frederick (Duke) Slater to play basketball and settled in Des Moines after earning his undergraduate and law degrees — in 1968 became the first African-American appointed to the Iowa Board of Regents.

This exposure contributed to Gentry's election two years later to the Des Moines school board. Gentry, the school board's first black member, served until 1980.[148]

Other African-Americans who have served on the Iowa Board of Regents include Virginia Harper of Fort Madison, Dr. Percy Harris of Cedar Rapids, and Betty Jean Furgerson of Waterloo.[149] The civil rights laws opened the doors of national offices as well. In 1973 James A. Harris, a Des Moines native and

art teacher at Callanan Middle School, became the first black man to be elected to the presidency of the National Educational Association due to a successful campaign managed by his colleague, Pat Ferrone, a long-time ISEA activist.[150]

The civil rights era also brought the beginning of another era of white backlash. This was sparked by affirmative action initiatives and fueled by the *Bakke* decision of the U.S. Supreme Court in 1978, which overturned the use of numerical quotas in admissions by the University of California, Davis.

The "benign neglect" and "southern strategy" policies of the Nixon Administration and the "ethnic purity of neighborhoods" thinking of the Carter Administration widened the gap. The policies of the Reagan Administration divided black and white even further.[151] Nevertherless, African-American presence has continued to increase in Iowa education in the 1970s, '80s, and '90s.

Given the changing demographics of public education in Iowa and the nation, "minorities" will become a majority in the early years of the twenty-first century. This will bring home the question Harold Hodgkinson posed: What "we" (the majority) will call "them" (the minority) once "we" realize "they" aren't.[152] One answer is "us." Another is "Americans," the most heterogeneous

James A. Harris, whose career in education included teaching art at Callanan Middle School, was the first African-American elected president of the National Education Association. (courtesy James A. Harris)

Iowa Board of Regents, 1989. Dr. Percy Harris of Cedar Rapids is standing second from right. (Iowa Board of Regents)

Iowa Board of Regents, 1990. Betty Jean Furgerson is seated second from right (Iowa Board of Regents)

Iowa Board of Regents, 1999. Seated, left to right: Lisa Ahrens; Deborah Turner, Mason City; Owen Newlin; Bev Smith, Waterloo. Standing left to right: David Fisher, Ellen Kennedy, Roger Landa, David Neil, Clarkson Kelly (Iowa Board of Regents)

people on earth, who have been developing a new culture for some 500 years from the best of Africa, the best of Europe, and the best of the Americas. Racism has impeded this process, and because it has been handed down and carefully taught, however unintentionally, by parents, teachers, and schoolmates, it has left its mark on us and others "not only through time but through the endless ages of eternity," as Willet Dorland pointed out 150 years ago.[153]

The truth of the saying "you live what you learn" is a two-edged sword. One edge defends the *status quo* by undercutting new ideas for change. The other edge clears a new path for those who would cut loose from the lessons of their beloved parents and teachers and fare forth side by side with fellow men and women even though they may be of different "races."

All will labor in vain to defend or cut the cord of prejudice who do not seek to "unriddle this riddle of outside in, of white men's children in black men's skins," and learn that "there is nothing outside a person that by going in can defile, but the things that come out are what defile. For it is from within, from the human heart, that evil intentions come: fornication, theft, murder, adultery, avarice, wickedness, deceit, licentiousness, envy, slander, pride, and folly."[154]

The question:

What "we"

(the majority)

will call "them"

(the minority)

once "we" realize

"they" aren't.

One answer is "us."

Another is "Americans,"

the most heterogeneous

people on earth. . . .

Notes

1. The author is indebted to Mrs. Ruby Sutton of "Sweet Dubuque" for the title of this chapter and its many levels of meaning — in this chapter and in my life. Ruby Sutton interview, July 30, 1997.

2. Thomas L. Webber, *Deep Like the Rivers: Education in the Slave Quarter Community, 1831–1865* (New York: Norton, 1978), 152.

3. Arnie Cooper, "A Stony Road: Black Education in Iowa, 1838–1860," *AI* 3rd ser. 48 (1986): 114.

4. The standard works on Iowa education give little attention to African-Americans or the impact of their presence. See Clarence R. Aurner, *History of Education in Iowa,* 2 vols. (Iowa City: SHSI, 1914), esp. 17, 414; Richard N. Smith, *Development of the Iowa Department of Public Instruction, 1900–1965* (Des Moines: Iowa Department of Public Instruction, 1969); Irving H. Hart, *Milestones: A History of the Iowa State Teachers Association 1854–1945 and Iowa State Education Association 1945–1954* (Des Moines: Iowa State Education Association, 1954), and Fred R. Comer, *Coming of Age: Teachers in Iowa, 1954 to 1993* (Des Moines: Iowa State Education Association, 1993); John Ely Briggs, *Iowa: Old and New* (Lincoln NE: University Publishing Co., 1939), 389–407. For state records, see *Biennial Reports of the Superintendent of Public Instruction,* Iowa Department of Education Library, Des Moines. The author thanks Mary Jo Bruett for her help with sources in the Iowa Department of Education Library.

5. Richard Dalfiume, "The 'Forgotten Years' of the Negro Revolution," *Journal of American History* 55 (1968): 90–106.

6. Cooper, 115–23.

7. Hart, 4–5.

8. Ibid., 5.

9. Leon F. Litwack, *North of Slavery: The Negro in the Free States 1790–1860* (Chicago: Univ. of Chicago Press, 1961), 147–48.

10. Charles A. Lofgren, *The Plessy Case* (New York: Oxford Univ. Press, 1987), 120–21.

11. Ibid., 118–20.

12. Robert R. Dykstra, *Bright Radical Star: Black Freedom and White Supremacy on the Hawkeye Frontier* (Cambridge: Harvard Univ. Press, 1993). See also Robert J. Cook, *Baptism of Fire: The Republican Party in Iowa, 1838–1878* (Ames: Iowa State Univ. Press, 1994).

13. Cooper, 123–29.

14. See appendix to chapter 2 titled "African-American Residents of Iowa in the 1850 Census."

15. Essie M. Britton, "The Negro in Iowa: History of the Colored Race of People Residing in Keokuk and Vicinity," undated typescript at the Keokuk Public Library. See the facts of the *Coger* case later in the text for additional evidence of a segregated school in Keokuk.

16. Hearne Bros., "Afro-Americans' Contributions to Iowa" (map), in folder marked "Negroes in Iowa," State Historical Society Library, Des Moines.

17. Cooper, 129.

18. Richard, Lord Acton and Patricia Nassif Acton, *To Go Free: A Treasury of Iowa's Legal Heritage* (Ames: Iowa State Univ. Press, 1995), 130–32.

19. Richard, Lord Acton and Patricia Nassif Acton, "A Legal History of African-Americans from the Iowa Territory to the State Sesquicentennial, 1838–1996," Chapter 3, supra, 73, 87 and footnotes 185 and 187.

20. Minnie London, "As I Remember" [Typescript Dr. Hubert L. Olin papers, SHSI Des Moines]; Lynn Nielsen and Lynn Dykstra, "Interview Summaries of Mrs. Valetta Fields [daughter of Minnie London] and Mrs. Marjorie Brown," in *The Great Depression in Waterloo: The Black Experience* in "Explorations in Iowa History Project," Malcolm Price Laboratory School, University of Northern Iowa, Cedar Falls.

21. Hart, 4–5.

22. The young black man *might* have been Alexander Clark Sr., who would have been about 26 at this time and a successful barber and real estate investor. Ada Sherwood, *At Old Cornell*, undated pamphlet cited in memorandum to the author, dated Aug. 6, 1997, from Dr. C. W. Heywood, Cornell College, titled "Black Students at Cornell." Copy in Cornell College Archives. Dr. Heywood provided a good deal of the information cited below about the African-American presence at Cornell College.

23. Ibid.; Louis A. Haselmayer, *A Sesquicentennial History of Iowa Wesleyan College, 1842–1992* (Mt. Pleasant: Iowa Wesleyan, 1992), 28.

24. Stuart A. Yeager, "The Black Experience at Grinnell College through Collected Oral Interviews and Documents, 1863–1954," Senior thesis, Grinnell College, 1984, 2.

25. Ibid., 8. For Turner, see John Ely Briggs, "Schools," in *Iowa, Old and New* (Lincoln NE: University Publishing Co., 1939), 399–401; [Tabor College] *Cardinal*, 1900, 62–64; idem., 1905, 66–69; *Forget-Me-Nots of an Alumnus* (n.p., 1907).

26. *Amity College Catalogue, 1879–80* (Blanchard IA: Blanchard Record, 1880), 5; *Amity College Catalogue, 1911–12*, 56. For statistics on "tokenism," see W. E. B. DuBois, *The College Bred Negro* (Atlanta: University Press, 1902), 12, and Paul S. Pierce, "Negro Alumni of the College of Iowa," in W. E. B. DuBois and Augustus G. Dill, eds., *The College-bred Negro American,* Atlanta University Publication No. 15 (Atlanta: Atlanta Univ. Press, 1911), 26–27. The author thanks Richard Breaux for the lead to this data.

27. *Cornell Collegian*, Nov. 1, 1870.

28. Yeager, 2.

29. Shereen Ali, "Multicultural Review of Grinnell College" (Grinnell: Grinnell College, 1996), 6–7. For McKinlay's close relationship with Booker T. Washington, see Louis R. Harlan, *Booker T. Washington: The Wizard of Tuskegee, 1901–1915* (New York: Oxford Univ. Press, 1994), 351.

30. Cornell College catalogs for 1873–75 and 1876–77; *Collegian,* May 1, 1871. Grinnell was an exception to the general rule of Iowa colleges and universities excluding blacks from their dormitories before World War 2. Yeager, 46–47.

31. Sherwood, 33–34.

32. For treatments of the link between white supremacy and Darwinian thought, see Richard Hofstadter, *Social Darwinism in American Thought,* rev. ed. (Boston: Beacon, 1955), 170–200, and Allen Chase, *The Legacy of Malthus: The Social Costs of the New Scientific Racism* (Urbana: Univ. of Illinois Press, 1980).

33. Philip G. Hubbard, *New Dawns: A 150-Year Look at Human Rights at The University of Iowa* (Iowa City: University of Iowa Sesquicentennial Committee, 1996), 12; Acton and Acton, 154–55. Richard Breaux's review of Hubbard's *New Dawns* in *AI* 58 (Spring 1999): 228, states that George L. Ruffin, Harvard 1869, was the first African-American law graduate in the U.S.

34. Acton and Acton, 155–57.

35. Bulletin of Iowa Wesleyan University, No. 6 (Mt. Pleasant: Iowa Wesleyan, 1905), 150. See also the folders marked "Susan Mosely (Grandison)" and "Black Graduates of Iowa Wesleyan University — 1st in Iowa Other Colleges," compiled by Louis A. Haselmayer, in the Iowa Wesleyan College archives, Mt. Pleasant, Iowa. The author thanks archivist Lynne Ellsworth for her assistance.

36. Lynda Walker-Webster, ed., *Iowa Days* [National Iowa Club Reunion Homecoming booklet] (Des Moines: Harvest Printers, 1996), 81.

37. Joseph W. Walt, *Beneath the Whispering Maples: The History of Simpson College* (Indianola: Simpson College Press, 1995), 145–50.

38. Rackham Holt, *George Washington Carver,* rev. ed. (New York: Abingdon Press, 1963), 82–108. For Wallace's credit to Carver, see page 92.

39. Holt, 96–97.

40. *Cornell College Catalogs,* 1895–96, 1897–1900; *Cornellian,* Oct. 14, 1899; Jan. 20, 1900; Cornell 50th Anniversary Book, 217–18.

41. For an interpretation of Booker T. Washington's thought as apologetic and accommodationist, see August Meier, *Negro Thought in America 1880–1915: Racial Ideologies in the Age of Booker T. Washington* (Ann Arbor: Univ. of Michigan Press, 1963).

42. *Cornellian,* March 14, 1910.

43. *Des Moines Register and Leader,* March 5, 1910; March 6, 1910 (Coleman's entire speech).

44. *The Wiley Reporter,* Feb. 1957, clipping in the Cornell College Archives. Collis H. Davis, who graduated from Grinnell in 1922, was another who had a distinguished teaching career, all of it at Hampton, which he attended prior to Grinnell. At Hampton, Davis served as head of the chemistry department, dean of students, registrar, and administrative assistant to the president. Yeager, 57, 76, 95, 102.

45. Arnold Cooper, *Between Struggle and Hope: Four Black Educators in the South, 1894–1915* (Ames: Iowa State Univ. Press, 1989), 51–54. For Jones at the University of Iowa, see Hubbard, *New Dawns,* 12–13.

46. Laurence C. Jones, *Piney Woods and Its Story* (New York, 1933). See photo of Jones and Turner opposite the title page and the photo of W. O. Finkbine and party between pages 124 and 125. For Mrs. Maytag, see the Piney Woods website at *www.pineywoods.org/ history.htm.* For Ingham, see the inscription in the Cowles Library at Drake University, quoting Laurence C. Jones, *The Bottom Rail* (New York: Fleming H. Revell Co., 1935): "'To Harvey Ingham, In appreciation of your interest and help in strengthing the bottom rail.' [Signed] Laurence C. Jones."

47. Photograph showing the Cotton Blossom Singers' bus provided by Wilma Merfield of Monticello, Iowa; see also "Sweet Memories of Dixie," by Lawrence C. Jones, sheet music, SHSI Des Moines.

48. *DMR,* Nov. 15, 1923.

49. Sherwood, 33.

50. *Cornellian,* Dec. 1887.

51. For Booker T. Washington and DuBois at Grinnell, see Yeager. For Booker T. Washington at the University of Iowa, see *Iowa State Register,* June 12, 1902. S. Joe Brown's graduation from the law school was the focal point of this article, which included Brown's photo.

52. *DMR,* Nov. 16, 1915. The author is indebted to John Zeller for copies of the newspaper articles on Booker T. Washington.

53. Heywood, "Black Students at Cornell." Exclusion seemed to remain the policy of some colleges well into the twentieth century. Memorandum to the author from Natalie Vander Broek, "African-American History at Central College," Oct. 23, 1997; George W. McDaniel, "Catholic Action in Davenport: St. Ambrose College and the League for Social Justice," *AI* 3rd ser. 55 (Summer 1996): 259; "Black Graduates of Iowa Wesleyan University — 1st in Iowa Other Colleges"; DuBois and Dill, eds., section 6. "Negro Alumni of the Colleges of Iowa," by Prof. Paul S. Pierce, cites only 34 graduates: 11 from the University of Iowa, 6 from Drake, 5 from Iowa Wesleyan, 3 from Tabor, 2 each from Iowa State and Coe, and 1 each from Grinnell, Cornell, William Penn, and Highland Park. The author is indebted to Richard Breaux for sharing this source.

54. James R. Mingle, "The Opening of White Colleges and Universities to Black Students," in *Black Students in Higher Education,* ed. Gail E. Thomas (Westport: Greenwood, 1981), 18–21.

55. Hubbard, *New Dawns,* 16, 26.

56. *The Key* [University of Dubuque yearbook], *1915,* 88, 92; *1916,* 74; *1917,* 55, 103, 105, 108, 114; *1918* not paginated but see pages for football, basketball, track, Glee Club, and Philophronia Society; *1919,* 35, 36, 82, 93, 102, 109, 116; *1920,* 46, 72, 90, 111, 119–20, 128 for his school records; *1921,* 64, 110, 116 (an account of his being knighted by the king of Montenegro); *1922,* 46; *1950,* 70, University of Dubuque Archives, Dubuque.

57. Martia Graham Goode, ed. *Chronicles of Faith: The Autobiography of Frederick D. Patterson.* (Tuscaloosa: Univ. of Alabama Press, 1991), 10–12, 18, 26, 187–89.

58. Gerald L. Smith, *A Black Educator in the Segregated South: Kentucky's Rufus B. Atwood* (Lexington: Univ. of Kentucky Press, 1994), 6–29, esp. 26–29.

59. *Des Moines Register and Leader,* July 28, 1912; *Iowa Bystander,* Sept. 12, 1919; Hubbard, *New Dawns,* 13, 199. A fifth student, Nancy Henry, joined the original four in Currier Hall at mid-term. Esther Walls interview, June 29, 1999. Richard Breaux generously provided assistance for the photographs of Cary and Hyde.

60. Hubbard, *New Dawns,* 27; Richard T. (Bud) Culberson interview, June 29, 1999.

61. Jean C. Florman, "Traces: Personal Accounts of a History Nearly Lost," *Iowa City Magazine,* Jan. 1995; Michael Kelley interview, Sept. 28, 1998.

62. Smith, 26–28.

63. Rallies called "Klanklaves" were held from Davenport to Sioux City in 1924. A larger Klanklave was held in 1926 in Des Moines, where the Klan enjoyed the support at the highest level of the police department. See Ginalie Swaim, "Images of the Ku Klux Klan in Iowa," *Palimpsest* 76 (1995): 64–75; John Zeller, "Ku Klux Clan in Iowa: Articles from the *Des Moines Register* and *Des Moines Tribune,* 1921–1927," compiled for the Des Moines Police History project, 1997. The cover of the spiral-bound compilation is a copy of a June 12, 1926, photo from the *Des Moines Tribune* showing police superintendent John W. Jenny on his horse in full Klan regalia.

64. Alain Locke, ed., *The New Negro* (New York: Albert and Charles Boni, 1925); Nathan I. Huggins, *Harlem Renaissance* (New York: Oxford Univ. Press, 1971); Raymond Wolters, *The New Negro on Campus* (Princeton: Princeton Univ. Press, 1975).

65. S. Joe Brown, S. E. Thompson, and James B. Morris, comp., *20 Years of Interracial Work in Des Moines: A Brief History of Des Moines Interracial Commission* (n.p., 1944), 2. For "Red Summer," see Arthur I. Waskow, *From Race Riot to Sit-In: 1919 and the 1960s* (New York: Doubleday and Co., 1966), 1–224. One of the members of the Chicago Commission on Race Relations, established to study the Chicago riot of July 1919, was Des Moines native and University of Iowa graduate Harry Eugene Kelly. See also Herbert Shapiro, *White Violence and Black Response from Reconstruction to Montgomery* (Amherst: Univ. of Massachusetts Press, 1988). For the CIC, see Morton Sosna, *In Search of the Silent South: Southern Liberals and the Race Issue* (New York: Columbia Univ. Press, 1977), 20–41. For Will W. Alexander, see Wilma Dykeman and James Stokely, *Seeds of Change: The Life of Will Alexander* (New York: Norton, 1962).

Dr. Hal S. Chase discovered African-American history after moving to Frankfort, Kentucky, from Des Moines at age eight in 1951. There he learned that whites from the North were "damn Yankees" and identified with blacks in the segregated minds of his white schoolmates. Blacks identified him as white, except for his friend, John Sykes, who saw beyond the outside.

Seeking the inside led to degrees in American civilization at Washington and Lee (B. A.), Stanford (M.A.), and the University of Pennsylvania (Ph.D.) — with specialization and publication in African-American history.

Dr. Chase teaches at Des Moines Area Community College. Since 1984 he has also served Farmers and Merchants State Bank as its majority shareholder. He and his wife, Avril, have four adult children — Heather, Parker (married to Celia), Spencer, and Ashley — and two grandchildren, Colin and Kelsey.

66. Brown, op. cit.

67. Ibid., 2–3, 16.

68. *Des Moines Tribune,* June 16, 1954.

69. Brown, 6.

70. *Des Moines Tribune,* March 1, 1958.

71. *Iowa Bystander,* March 19, 1927. The author thanks Mrs. Janice Burrell Cochran of Des Moines for sharing this and other family history.

72. Iowa State Teachers' Association (ISTA), *Proceedings* (1931), 6. The author is indebted to Bill Sherman, former public relations director of ISEA, for his generous assistance in making the records of the ISTA/ISEA available.

73. Ibid., 29; *Des Moines Tribune,* July 24, 1941.

74. ISTA, *Proceedings* (1933), 67–68.

75. Ibid.

76. ISTA, *Proceedings* (1934), 53.

77. ISTA, *Proceedings* (1935), 22.

78. ISTA, *Proceedings* (1936), 52.

79. Ibid., 110.

80. ISTA, *Proceedings* (1937), 92, 101.

81. Hart, 183.

82. Richard M. Dalfiume, *Desegregation of the U.S. Armed Forces: Fighting on Two Fronts, 1939–1953* (Columbia: Univ. of Missouri Press, 1969); Phillip McGuire, ed., *Taps for a Jim Crow Army: Letters from Black Soldiers in World War 2* (Lexington: Univ. of Kentucky Press, 1983).

83. *DMR,* March 1, 1946.

84. Betty Estes Williams interview, Jan. 15, 1997.

85. Elaine Estes interview, Jan. 7, 1997.

86. *DMR,* Jan. 1, 1977.

87. *DMR,* Sept. 4, 1946.

88. *DMR,* Sept. 4 and 17, 1946; Harriette Curley interview, Aug. 1, 1998.

89. *Des Moines Tribune,* June 14 and 16, 1954; *Iowa Bystander,* March 20, 1958.

90. Bob and Betty Hyde interview, June 28, 1999.

91. Betty Jean Furgerson interview, June 14, 1998.

92. Telephone interviews with Evelyn Walker Freeman, July 25 and August 5, 2000; *Iowa Bystander,* May 29, 1958.

93. *Iowa Bystander,* Sept. 6, 1962.

94. *Iowa Bystander,* April 7, 1966. Also hired in 1955 were Betty Hyde and Leroy Mitchell.

95. James E. Bowman interview, July 11, 1997.

96. *Cornellian,* Oct. 27, 1944, and Nov. 23, 1945.

97. Julian Winston, "A Minority at Penn," *William Penn College Bulletin,* Reunion Extra, No. 115, 14.

98. For white opposition to racism in the 1930s and '40s, see James Agee and Walker Evans, *Let Us Now Praise Famous Men* (New York: Ballantine, 1960); Myrdal, op. cit.; Sosna, op. cit.; John Glen, *No Ordinary School: Highlander School* (Lexington: Univ. of Kentucky Press, 1985); Myles Horton, with Judith and Herbert Kohl, *The Long Haul: An Autobiography* (New York: Teachers College Press, 1990), chapters 8 and 9. Horton was Highlander's founder.

99. *Cornellian,* Oct. 27, 1944.

100. *Cornellian,* Nov. 23, 1945.

101. Yeager, 56–57.

102. *DMR,* Jan. 30, 1949. Fred Martin, the son of John Martin, the night janitor and bellhop at the Ames Sheldon-Munn Hotel, was elected after he was "spontaneously" nominated by Betty Lou Jones, a white student.

103. The history of the civil rights movement of the 1950s and 1960s is voluminously documented. Two of the best surveys are Harvard Sitkoff, *Struggle for Equality* (New York: Hill and Wang, 1981), and Juan Williams, *Eyes on the Prize* (New York: Penguin Books, 1987), which accompanies an eight-part video series.

104. Richard T. (Bud) Culberson interview, June 29, 1999.

105. Hubbard, *New Dawns,* 26–27; *The Quax* [Drake University yearbook], 1950.

106. Hubbard, *New Dawns,* 26–27; Dolph Pulliam interview, Sept. 3, 1997. The Black Alumni Association's Hall of Honor at the Iowa Memorial Union in Iowa City indicates that the only inductees for athletics are Slater, Tunnell, and Eddie Robinson, the Grambling football coach who earned his M.A. at the University of Iowa.

107. Margaret T. Dungey, "African-American Graduate School Experiences at the University of Iowa, 1937–1959, An Oral History," Ph.D. diss., University of Iowa, 1997, 97–103.

108. Hubbard, *New Dawns,* 127–40.

109. Folder: "Negroes," William Penn College Archives, Oskaloosa. See also Quaker yearbooks for 1946 and 1947 and the William Penn College catalogs, 1945–48, and *DMR,* April 14, 1946. The author thanks Bill Douglas for this last item, which helped in his search for information about Madeline Clarke Foreman.

110. Hubbard, *New Dawns,* xvi–xvii, 26–27.

111. Philip G. Hubbard, *My Iowa Journey: The Life Story of the University of Iowa's First African-American Professor* (Iowa City: Univ. of Iowa Press, 1999).

112. Holt, *Carver,* 105.

113. Memorandum to the author from Jill Osweiler, Iowa State University Archivist, July 2, 1999.

114. Dr. George A. Jackson interview, Sept. 24, 1997.

115. Dr. S. J. Williamson interview, Sept. 28, 1998.

116. Dr. Eddie V. Easley interview, Sept. 28, 1998; *Iowa Bystander,* June 26, 1968.

117. Ruth B. Anderson interview, May 24, 1999; Ruth Bluford Anderson, *From Mother's Aid Child to University Professor: The Autobiography of an American Black Woman.* (Iowa City: University of Iowa School of Social Work, 1995); William C. Lang and Daryl Pendergraft, *A Century of Leadership and Service: A Centennial History of the University of Northern Iowa,* vol. 2 (Cedar Falls: UNI Alumni Association, 1995), 255–80. Mrs. Noreen Hermansen (Director of Alumni Affairs), Dr. John Baskerville (History), and Dr. Janet McClain (Education) generously assisted the author's research at the University of Northern Iowa.

118. James (Sam) Randall interview, June 30, 1999.

119. The first black faculty members at both Cornell and Grinnell were music professors: William Jones at Cornell and Denis de Coteau at Grinnell, *Cornellian,* 1967. E-mail to author from Grinnell archivist Leslie Czechowski, July 2, 1999. At the University of Dubuque, Dr. Robert Murungi, from Kenya, taught philosophy. *The Key* [Univ. of Dubuque yearbook], 1967.

120. Fred C. Gilbert interview, Sept. 11, 1997.

121. The notable exception to this trend occurred at William Penn College, which offered "General Sociology IIb: Study of Special Social Problems Such as the Negro Problem" in 1917. See *William Penn College Catalog,* 1917, 51. In 1936 this course became "Sociology 308: The Race Problem." Grinnell offered a course titled "Race Relations" in the Sociology Department in 1944–45; Czechowski to Chase, July 2, 1999. Central College offered a course titled "Race Problems," also in Sociology, the following year; *Central College Catalog, 1945.* The author is indebted to Megan DeSmidt for her research on Central College. The University of Dubuque followed this pattern by a decade; see University of Dubuque catalogs, 1957–1970.

122. Dr. Ralph Scharnau provided the author a copy of his syllabus for History 122 (Afro-American History), offered in Spring 1971 at the University of Dubuque. Interview with Dr. Tom Ryan, University of Northern Iowa, May 24, 1999. Iowa Wesleyan also introduced a black studies program in 1969. Louis Haselmayer, *A Sesquicentennial History of Iowa Wesleyan College, 1842–1992* (Mt. Pleasant Iowa: Iowa Wesleyan College, 1992), 58.

123. Heywood, op. cit. Woodard stayed at the University of Iowa, where he is now vice president.

124. *DMR*, May 6, 1964.

125. "Black Students, Their Problems, 1969-1970," undated clipping from a University of Dubuque student newspaper, University of Dubuque Archives, Dubuque.

126. Lang and Pendergraft, 255–60.

127. Ibid., 265–77. A demonstration by black students at Central College in May 1970 met a different response: their demands were rejected, and Central's Pres. Kenneth J. Waller was quoted as saying, "I think the atmosphere here is basically good for blacks. Nobody's shooting at them here." *DMR*, June 4, 1970.

128. "Major Educational Equity Legislation Affecting Iowa Schools," unpublished document issued by the Iowa Department of Education, given to the author by Judge Brown, an equity coordinator for the Iowa Department of Education at the time. Judge Brown interview, July 22, 1997.

129. Ibid.

130. Ibid.

131. Ibid.

132. Ibid.

133. "A Model Multicultural, Nonsexist Education Plan," Iowa Department of Education, 1994.

134. "Scope of the Educational Equity On-Site Review," Iowa Department of Education, 1995.

135. Judge Brown interview, July 22, 1997.

136. Thomas Simmons interview, Feb. 11, 1998; Dr. Kittie Weston-Knauer interview, Feb. 24, 1999. For statistics, see "Minority Enrollment in Iowa Public Elementary and Secondary Schools," in *Annual Condition of Education Report, 1996* (Des Moines: State of Iowa, 1996), 4–5, 18–19, 21, 74, 91, and staff file labeled "All Minority Staff, Public Schools, 1996–97," Iowa Department of Education, Des Moines, provided to the author by Judge Brown.

137. Minority Affairs files, Box 1, ISEA Archives, Des Moines.

138. These are four-page bulk-mailed brochures with a form letter addressed to "Local President and Minority Members" on the front page, signed by ISEA Pres. Robert J. Gilchrist, and dated Feb. 4, 1994; Feb. 3, 1995; Feb. 1996; and Feb. 1997.

139. Ruth Ann Gaines interview, Feb. 27, 1998; Betty Jean Hyde interview, June 28, 1999.

140. "All Minority Staff, Public Schools, 1996–1997."

141. Holmes Group, "Tomorrow's Teachers"; Carnegie Forum, "A Nation Prepared: Teachers for the 21st Century."

142. James E. Bowman interview, July 11, 1997; Dr. Mary Chapman interview, July 14, 1997.

143. Jane Elliot interview, June 23, 1997.

144. Nielsen, et al., *Black History* [Unit III Products], rev. ed. (Cedar Falls: Malcolm Price Laboratory School, University of Northern Iowa, 1987).

145. Evelyn Davis interview, Oct. 6, 1999.

146. Lang and Pendergraft, 262.

147. Maude White interview, April 14, 1997.

148. Nolden Gentry interview, Feb. 3, 1998.

149. Photographs from the offices of the State Board of Regents, Des Moines.

150. Rev. James A. Harris interview, Aug. 28, 1998.

151. For a provocative historical analysis tracing this "backlash" to Lyndon B. Johnson and "liberal" Democrats rather than "conservatives" and Ronald Reagan, see Stephen Steinberg, "The Liberal Retreat from Race during the Post-Civil Rights Era," in *The House that Race Built*, ed. Wahneema Lubiano (New York: Pantheon, 1997), 13–47.

152. For an analysis of U.S. educational demographics, as well as the quotation, see Harold L. Hodgkinson, "A True Nation of the World," *Education Week*, Jan. 18, 1995 , p. 32

153. For the concept of the emergence of a trans-Atlantic culture resulting from the fusion of European, African, and Native-American cultures, see Paul Gilroy, *The Black Atlantic* (Cambridge: Harvard Univ. Press, 1993).

154. Mark 7:1–8, 14–15, 21–23.

Al Downey in his high school band uniform, 1950s (courtesy Al Downey Sr.)

Johnny Long, shown here with Henry Putney in the early 70s, became the first black supervisor at Marquette/Monarch Cement Co. of Des Moines in 1974 after twenty years with the company and serving as an officer of the local United Cement, Lime, and Gypsum Workers / A.F.L.-C.I.O. (courtesy Johnny Long)

PART THREE

Economic opportunity and achievement

Henry G. Matthews and friends pose on tractor at his farm between Beebeetown and Logan, Iowa. (courtesy Henry G. Matthews)

African-Americans in Iowa Agriculture

A Portrait, 1830–2000

by Valerie Grim

Although the majority of African-American farm families arrived in rural Iowa between 1870 and 1910, some migrated to Iowa during the territorial period and the period of early statehood. These often risked their lives trying to settle in Iowa, a place they believed was more friendly toward African-Americans. Some were free blacks who wanted to own land and to have access to greater economic and social opportunity. For example, Rev. Davis Watrous, a United Brethren minister who moved to Fayette County from Kankakee, Illinois, in 1851, apparently enticed six families from his previous church to settle in Westfield Township the following year. The Bass, Epps, Graham, Lewis, Tann, and Wilson households were listed in the 1856 census. Tann was a tanner and Bass was a blacksmith, but the others were farmers.[1] Others were fugitive slaves who moved to Iowa to escape slavery. And there were those who believed that Iowa was tolerant enough to help blacks avoid being re-enslaved after the Civil War.[2]

Iowa's nineteenth-century history was ambivalent as far as African-Americans were concerned. Even though some believed Iowa was tolerant of racial diversity, the state's record revealed mixed attitudes toward race. This was most evident in the way white citizens handled racial issues dating back to the days of early statehood — when slavery, though limited, nonetheless existed in Iowa. For example, Lydia Applewhite, born a slave in Missouri in 1845, was sold to an Iowan family in Keokuk in 1855. She worked on their farm estate as both a house servant and a field hand.[3] Like Lydia, black slaves in Iowa performed the traditional agricultural roles of working the fields, raising livestock, and planting large gardens for consumption and commercial purposes, just as they did in the rural South.[4]

But slavery was not firmly implanted in Iowa nor was it extensive. Thus, free blacks and fugitive slaves saw fewer risks in migrating to Iowa in comparison with many other states. Blacks who escaped to Iowa believed that it was a kinder and gentler state, a place where blacks could purchase land, farm, build communities, and construct cultural and social institutions without the intimidation they experienced in the rural South.[5]

The experience of the Stevens family is one of the best examples of many black families who worked as slaves in the South but after emancipation sought out Iowa as the land of the free.

Blacks who escaped to Iowa believed that it was a kinder and gentler state, a place where blacks could purchase land, farm, build communities, and construct cultural and social institutions.

Richard Payne (above) and Linous Rowden Payne (below) (courtesy Lola E. Jones)

George Stevens was born a slave in 1820 in the South. Jane Motley Stevens, his wife, was born in Tennessee. She was an illegitimate child and was disowned by her grandfather, a slave master, because he did not approve of her mother's relationship with a northern overseer. Consequently, Jane was placed in the slave quarters and raised as a slave. After emancipation, the Stevens family came to Keokuk and settled on the Dandridge farm, which eventually became their home.[6] Similarly, Richard Payne and his wife, Linous Rowden Payne, were taken to Hamburg from Louisiana by their owners, the Paynes, and emancipated.[7]

Free African-American families who migrated to Iowa between 1830 and 1850 were farm people. Most came from Illinois, Missouri, Ohio, and Indiana.[8] In Iowa, rural migrants made their living from the land growing crops, livestock, and vegetable and fruit products for self-sufficiency and for sale. Some engaged in the lumber business, cutting trees from their land and selling it to the mills.[9]

James Carr Heizer came to Iowa in 1842 at age 14 from Ohio and settled at Kossuth in Des Moines County near Burlington. Another migrant, Charles Adams, was encouraged to migrate from Virginia to Oskaloosa in 1845 by the availability of land and the promise of more cordial race relations. Samuel Hall, born in South Carolina in 1812, was a slave in Tennessee for 37 years. After emancipation, he moved to Washington, Iowa, where he farmed more than 40 years.[10]

Westfield Township, Fayette County, Iowa

In the 1850s a small colony of free African-Americans migrated from Kankakee, Illinois, and settled in Westfield Township, Fayette County. As free families, they established farms that have been operating for more than 140 years. Richard Colwell, born a slave in Kentucky in 1848, moved to Shenandoah in 1872 to farm. William Owen Van Vaxen Goodlow, who had joined Union troops in his native Mississippi and returned with them to Missouri, later moved from Missouri to a farm he purchased near Wales in Montgomery County in the 1880s.[11]

Martha Templeton, a slave born in North Carolina in 1841, came to Perry in 1913 to work as a plow girl. John Sweat moved to Allamakee County in 1866 from Tennessee. In rural Iowa, Sweat became owner of a Jefferson Township farm where he and his white wife reared a large family of children. From Mississippi came Turner W. Bell, born in 1862. Bell was a self-made lawyer who

William Owen Van Vaxon Goodlow (courtesy Ella Goodlow Stith)

dedicated his life to ensuring that rural African-Americans in Iowa were not intimidated, as blacks were in the rural South. Bell used the black church as a public forum to inform rural African-Americans of their rights under the Constitution.[12] The Winstons farmed from the late nineteenth century to the middle of the twentieth century south of Ottumwa, and the Westerns farmed during the same period south of Oskaloosa. Gwendolene Harris's grandfather built a substantial home on his Dallas County farm.[13]

When Adam and Martha Johnson left the cotton fields of Tennessee, they farmed for several years in Illinois. In the 1880s they moved into Iowa, going across the southern counties to the western part of the state. In Taylor County, near Gravity, Adam Johnson bought 160 acres of land. When the Chicago, Burlington and Quincy Railroad came through, he sold some of his land to the company, but still kept enough for himself to leave a well-developed farm to his sons. From this farm Lulu M. Johnson, granddaughter of Adam and Martha, went to the University of Iowa, where she earned B.A., M.A., and Ph.D. degrees in history.[14]

Thus rural migrants settled on farms located in the interior of the state. But they also established residence in Iowa's river towns, where they combined various vocations and occupations with farming. Examples of how river towns provided opportunities for rural migrants to Iowa can be seen in the experiences of some

Gwendolene Harris's grandparents' home in Dallas County (courtesy Gwendolene Harris)

Dubuque residents. In the 1840s, approximately 30 African-Americans, of which more than half came from rural backgrounds, lived in Dubuque. While it is difficult to discuss these few persons as a rural transplanted African-American community, it is possible to demonstrate how they began to transplant their agrarian ideas of freedom and their sense of responsibility to themselves and members of their race.

Of the rural migrants who resided in this river town during the 1840s, according to Robert R. Dykstra, one-fourth lived in white people's homes. The family structure was primarily nuclear, and as a collective group the families represented eight different occupations: carpentry, mining, barbering, domestic service, and wage work. Some combined their vocation with farming: Thomas C. Brown, the African-American barber, owned land worth $1,100; Anthony Arthur, a wage worker, possessed $1,000 worth of land; and Aaron Baptiste claimed $600 in land.[15] William Matthews came to Missouri Valley as a dining car waiter on the railroad but left it when he established the Sunnyside Dairy on property he had purchased.[16] Anthony Burrell, who migrated to Oralabor at the turn of the twentieth century, supplemented his miner's pay by farming.[17]

African-Americans who helped to diversify Iowa's rural population from the Civil War through the 1940s were typically members of nuclear families. Extended kinship also existed. In

William Matthews in front of his Sunnyside Dairy milking barn in Missouri Valley (courtesy Henry G. Matthews)

Iowa's Negro Farm Families Have Pioneer History

By Ed Heins
(Register Staff Writer)

FAYETTE, IA.—This northeast Iowa area is one of the few in the state with a number of Negroes involved in farming.

In Fayette County, Negro farm families have figured in the life of the area from pioneer days. Many of the families came into the area in the mid-1800's in covered wagons.

The Dixon family is one of the most prominent. Mrs. Sara Dixon, 88, and three sons and a daughter live on a 160-acre farm southeast of Fayette.

The late Bill Dixon, husband of Sara, was a director of the Arlington Co-operative Creamery at Arlington. The Dixons have a neat farm in the rolling hills of Fayette County.

Ralph Dixon, one of the brothers and the family spokesman, said they have 12 milk cows, 21 registered Shorthorns which produce calves for sale, a market hog herd and two Belgian mares which also produce offspring for sale.

Ralph farms with two brothers, Irving and Everette. Another brother Ivan, farms near Arlington.

Melvin C. Wangsness, Fayette County extension director, describes the Dixons as "highly skilled livestock farmers."

"They were breeding purebred draft horses when I first came to Fayette County in the 1940's."

Ralph Dixon said there is still a demand for draft horses.

"But, if you don't have a good one, it isn't worth anything," he added. He said he has traveled 50 miles to have the two mares bred to a good-quality stud.

ANOTHER Negro with an outstanding—and unusual—farming operation is Atrus Stepp, 66, who farms northwest of Fayette.

Stepp has 357 acres of land in two farms, which are used for corn, soybean and hay crops. But, he is best known in Fayette County for his melon farming.

A life-long resident of the county, Stepp grew melons in Fayette County until 1946. Then, because of a lack of suitable sandy soil in the area, he moved his melon operation to Illinois, across the river from Muscatine.

Last year, he returned to Fayette County to plant 80 acres of melons in the lands along the Volga River.

His son, Wayne, 34, said continuous melon farming in one field causes a melon disease problem, forcing the farmers to rotate their fields. After an absence of 18 years, the elder Stepp is now back using the fields he used in the 1940's.

The melon raising is helped along by using top-quality seed, some costing as much as $85 a pound.

Atrus Stepp's mother, the late Mrs. Julia Stepp, was honored in 1957 by the city of Fayette with a Julia Stepp Day on the occasion of her 100th birthday. She was born in Fayette County in 1857.

R. E. Cousins, of Fayette, the city mayor who proclaimed the day for Mrs.

Stepp, recalled that he had gone to school in his childhood with members of the Negro families in the county.

Cousins recalled walking home with Irving Dixon one day when Dixon found a dynamite cap and put it in his pocket. The cap exploded, blowing one of Irving's hands off. Although handicapped by the loss of his hand, he drove a milk route for the Arlington creamery for 30 years.

EUGENE GARBEE, president of Upper Iowa University, said "No one ever thinks about the distinction of Negroes and whites in the area because the Negro farm families are so much a part of the whole community."

Ralph Dixon was one of the members of the First Methodist Church of Fayette who greeted Bishop James Thomas when he came recently to help with dedication of the new church building. Bishop Thomas is the first Negro to ever lead the 300,000 Iowa Methodists.

Delbert Dean, a neighbor of Atrus Stepp, is another of the Negro farmers who has a well-run operation. He received help from the county extension officials in setting up his cattle-feeding facilities.

Other Negro farmers in Fayette County include Lester Moore of Hawkeye and Don Dean of Fayette (Delbert Dean's father).

Wangsness said, "They'd all qualify as good farmers in any community."

Ralph Dixon with some of the Shorthorn cattle.

The Dixon and Stepp families were farming pioneers in Fayette County (Des Moines Register, Feb. 7, 1965)

Anthony Burrell with his horse on the farm near Oralabor (courtesy Janice Burrell Cochran)

fact, upon arrival, newcomers tried diligently to settle next to kin, and some stayed a few months with family members until they could establish themselves. But to a large extent, two-parent families dominated the household structure. The average number of children was five. The majority of the migrant families who moved from the southern plantations to mining and river towns were illiterate, semi-skilled, very religious, and quite sociable.[18]

Small Productive Farms

Like black farmers in the South, Iowa's rural African-Americans wanted to establish small, productive farms on the kind of land that produced high yields. Most were looking to establish homesteads ranging between 40 and 100 acres. Some owned less than 40 acres, while many others were able to acquire much more than 100 acres.[19]

The size of farm families, farm ownership, and acres in production varied among African-Americans. In the 1880s, there were at least 300 farm families. By 1900, this number had increased to 325. Although the Great Depression in the 1930s caused some decline in the number of African-Americans involved in Iowa's agricultural and rural life, 280 families continued to live on the land. By the 1960s even further declines had occurred as a result of migration, foreclosure, and the sale of land. The increasing cost of farming due to technological adoption and the cost of fertilizer, insecticides, and chemicals added to the decline of African-American families involved in farming. By 1970 there were approximately 170 black farm families, fewer than 1,000 individuals. African-American participation in Iowa's agricultural and rural life continued to decline, with only 92 families in 1974, 54 in 1984, and 33 in the 1990s.[20]

The sizes of farms have varied, with one family farming as many as 1,000 acres during the first decade of the twentieth century and another as few as 17 acres during the 1940s. The average size appears to have been 120 acres. The average number of individuals involved in farm production also fluctuated, with an average of five per household. Style of farming and management of farms differed as well, with some renting and share-renting farms. Unlike the rural South, the origin of the majority of the migrants between 1850 and 1880, the African-American families that migrated to Iowa adopted the family-farm mode of production. They used family members as their primary labor force. One of the most rewarding experiences in organizing and managing their Iowa farms was the opportunity to make decisions for themselves and to market their own crops. These opportunities had never before existed for the majority of the rural migrants because white landlords in the South controlled every aspect of production and marketing of the crops.[21]

Most farmers were diversified producers, growing various crops and livestock as well as engaging in truck farming. A few farmers tended to be more commercial, growing primarily staple crops and some consumer items. The Baldwins of Clarinda produced crops and livestock on 80 acres they owned and on an additional 417 acres they managed. They grew 120 acres of corn, 90 acres of oats, 22 head of horses, 65 head of cattle, and 95 head of hogs. This style of management was typical of at least 100 other African-American farm families in Iowa during the first half of the twentieth century.[22]

In keeping with the changing structure of agricultural production already taken place in the North and East, a few of Iowa's African-American farmers began to modernize their farm operation over a period of 20 years. Some black farm families began to use more advanced farming and livestock implements. They also began to practice scientific farming, applying the latest techniques to increase yields, prevent erosion, and replenish the soil. The operation of Mr. Sellers, who lived in North Everly in northwestern Iowa, illustrated this development. Using the most advanced planting and cultivation implements, as well as the most

William Matthews tending cows and calves at the Sunnyside Dairy. (courtesy Henry G. Matthews)

Stepp's melon stand was located on the family's farm north of West Union. (from Heritage of Fayette County, Iowa)

The Boldridge family outside their farmhouse near Irvington in Kossuth County (courtesy Bob Boldridge)

improved cream separator and chicken incubator, Sellers grew oats, corn, vegetables, and fruits. He also used his 200-acre farm to raise hundreds of chickens, 40 head of cattle, 11 horses, and a large number of Chester White hogs, which were considered the best hogs in the business. Sellers, the only black farmer within a 60 miles radius of Everly, was highly respected by his white neighbors. Several times he was elected director of the rural school.[23]

Between 1900 and 1930, a few African-American farmers were included in Iowa's elite group of agricultural producers. In 1906, the *Iowa State Bystander* reported that black farming had been established throughout Iowa. The reporter listed the location of several of Iowa's leading African-American producers, including the Montgomerys in Coin, the Stewarts near Hollyville, and the Cooks near Clarinda. For many years, these families operated farms comprising hundreds of acres. Also in Clarinda lived Thomas Jones, a blacksmith and one of the oldest and most highly esteemed farmers of the community. He raised 35 thoroughbred Poland-China pigs, which took first and second prizes at state fairs.[24]

Iowa's black farmers understood not only farm diversification but also the early concepts of agribusiness. Some knew that it was important for African-American farmers to be involved in agriculture beyond the production and marketing of their individual crops. Some understood the need to be connected to input and output industries. In Muscatine, for example, truck farmer J. P. Johnson was a man of astute business skills. He also was a gardener and had one acre of cucumbers contracted with the Heinz Cannery

Micky Matthews regularly helped her husband with chores on their farm. (courtesy Henry G. Matthews)

Factory for 50 cents a bushel. He had one acre of sweet corn and two acres of tomatoes under contract with another cannery, at 20 cents per bushel.[25] William H. Matthews's Sunny Side Dairy in Missouri Valley, already noted, was another example of connecting input and output.[26]

Johnson was not alone in his agribusiness pursuits. Nelson Lee, also of Muscatine, established a lucrative business growing watermelons and sweet potatoes. Among rural black Iowans, Nelson was considered the most successful of all fruit and vegetable contractors. Lee sold his produce to large wholesale houses in Chicago and New York. To improve the efficiency of his operation, Lee built a track from his farm to a local railroad line so his products could be shipped to the main railroad line in Des Moines in a timely manner.[27] Artus Stepp's success growing and marketing melons was also widely known, at least around Fayette County. Stepp's Melons was a popular destination point, and Fayette County's Watermelon Days are a tribute to his acceptance and influence in the community.[28]

Horse Trading Is a Lucrative Business

Horse trading was another business in which blacks engaged. Among the many trading horses were the Baldwin and Stevens families. George Stevens traded horses every day and he rarely returned home with the same horses. Often Stevens was able to secure some form of compensation for the trade in addition to the exchange of horses. The Baldwins kept horses for trade and purchase. They kept a steady stream of horses ready for sale or trade. It was horses that brought Bill Boldridge Sr. to Hancock County from Missouri in 1902. He had established a reputation as an excellent horse breaker and sought the better opportunity of a rented farm near Woden, where he managed a diversified operation that included corn, soybeans, oats, cattle, and hogs. He also raised chickens and a large vegetable garden with the help of his wife, Fanny Rose, who canned the produce. He used horse teams into the 1940s for both work and transportation. It was not clear how many families engaged in this activity or how much money was earned, but it appears to have been a lucrative business that became an alternative means for some blacks on the land to earn a living.[29]

Agriculture and rural life offered great opportunities for African-American women on the farm to create public and private places for themselves. Iowa's black farm women actively engaged

The sizes of farms have varied, with one family farming as many as 1,000 acres during the first decade of the twentieth century and another as few as 17 acres during the 1940s.

Grace Jeffers Western cans produce with her children on their farm south of Oskaloosa. (courtesy Charlene Western Montgomery)

Betty Lou Western helps her father milk, c. 1944. (courtesy Charlene Western Montgomery)

William Henry Jr. (courtesy Henry G. Matthews)

in the production of crops, the trading of horses, and other agricultural pursuits. African-American farm women were also expected to help feed, clothe, and house their families. In Everly, for instance, Mrs. Sellers grew a large apple orchard and sold fruit. Her daughter, Pauline Sellers, raised and sold onions as well as honey from her beehives. Together mother and daughter raised dairy cows and chickens and sold milk, butter, and eggs. Mrs. Thomas Johnson and Mrs. Sellers's mother helped to care for the other fowl on the Sellers farm.[30]

Gender-specific Labor

African-American women's work on farms in Iowa tended to be more gender specific. Unlike southern black farm women, who worked in the fields planting, cultivating, and harvesting cotton, Iowa farm women worked primarily around the home, doing garden work and overseeing fruit and poultry production. The work of Mrs. Thomas Jones in Clarinda is an example of how black farm women contributed to the economic survival of the farm and family. During the spring of 1910, Mrs. Jones sold 157 goose eggs at 5 cents a dozen, 170 guinea eggs at 25 cents a dozen, and from 5 to 23 dozen hen eggs per week. She owned more than 500 young chickens and purchased an incubator to properly care for them. At one time she owned 42 setting hens for continuous egg production.[31] In Creston, Mrs. Henry Martin produced beautiful fruit orchards, while in Gravity Mrs. Robert Johnson raised more than 300 young chickens, 32 hens, 14 turkeys, and

Mrs. Russell Downey of Ottumwa earned additional income by raising chickens and selling their eggs. (courtesy Al Downey Sr.)

many ducks, goslings, and guineas. She and her husband milked 12 cows and owned their own cream separator.[32] Each of these women sold their goods and produce.

In addition to raising produce and livestock to supplement the family's budget, some of the black farm women in Iowa also started hair-dressing, catering, laundry, and dressmaking businesses. They had customers in rural and urban communities. Clarinda's Mrs. Lydia Barlett was a dressmaker, while Mrs. N. C. Black was a hairdresser. Mrs. Gilbert catered meals from her chop house. Some women owned tonsorial shops. Because of such women's commitments to their families, one *Bystander* reporter wrote, "Oh if more of us people would go on the farm, our race would be better respected."[33]

Black farm women also performed work that was consistent with their roles as household managers. Many served as family bookkeeper, a responsibility that often involved balancing the checking account, managing the payroll, and keeping the time cards or number of hours hired hands worked. Mrs. C. A. Marshall of Anthon performed these tasks for her family. By accepting responsibilities of this sort, African-American farm women played a role in helping to make farming a business and in keeping themselves at the center of family and work activities.[34]

Rural African-American women in Iowa did not depend on farming, economic production, and participation in the market economy for their total social network. Other activities provided the opportunities to socialize. Canning, sewing, and quilting parties were organized. Women's clubs, such as the Friendly Society of Kossuth County, were formed. Through these organizations, women helped shape community ideology concerning care for the sick and elderly, the orphaned, and the poor and illiterate.[35]

The production of food for consumption and commercial purposes, however, often created an overlap in the work roles of men and women on the farm. The experiences of African-Americans in rural Iowa showed that men and women jointly raised orchards, livestock, and vegetable gardens. Both sexes marketed produce and participated in delivering products to their customers. These shared responsibilities gave women a strong sense of importance within the home and placed them at the center of household management and production. In this instance, the sharing of responsibilities also reinforced patriarchy, because food production created the opportunity for men to act as breadwinners of the family, an important concept for a community of people who struggled against popular perceptions that black men were lazy and did not provide for their families.[36]

On the farm, children were actively involved with work. Because farming was a family affair, children helped produced the crops and other goods to help the family survive. Thus during the farm season they plowed, pulled and chopped weeds, and helped harvest the crop. In addition, they cared for livestock and chickens. Children also milked the cows and helped to sell the milk; they made and sold butter. They sold eggs, vegetables, and fruits from their gardens and orchards. Children were instrumental in helping parents transport goods to the market and to individual customers throughout rural Iowa. While boys hunted and fished in large numbers to help provide additional food for the family, girls canned, sewed, and quilted to help ensure that family nutritional, clothing, and bedding needs were met.[37]

Although farm life was busy, African-Americans found time to celebrate life. Leisure time was important to family bonding. On the farm in Iowa, fathers and sons fished and hunted together and participated jointly in the care of the lawn. Sporting activities, such as baseball and croquet, provided the opportunity on Saturday afternoon for fathers and sons to develop affectionate relationships.[38]

Women spent considerable time grooming their daughters. Mothers and daughters attended teas and quilting parties. Women also took charge of planting flowers and trees around the home, church, and school. Much of women's leisure time was spent teaching their daughters to cook, sew, and clean. In addition, dressmaking and hairdressing provided the opportunity for women and girls on the farm to interact and to engage in activities that taught girls how to be ladies. Through women's clubs, girls were taught proper etiquette. Lectures on spirituality and morality were given to encourage girls to remain chaste.[39]

Leisure time also provided the opportunity for men, women, and children to develop community institutions. In this instance, blacks on the farm joined whites and other groups in constructing community facilities. In Algona, African-Americans participated equally in the building of schools, churches, farm-houses, barns, and roads. Algona's Frank Siemen recalled situations where the few black families in his community were helped with the building of their barn as well as the harvesting of their crops. Likewise, he could remember the help African-American families gave to whites

throughout the community as they helped with building barns, schools, and the planting and harvesting of white farmers' crops. In addition, blacks and whites who lived in the same rural community worked together to cut wood for buildings, and every member of the community spent time carrying logs, nailing boards, and painting the facilities. The men typically dug roads so community members could have access to the schools and churches.[40]

Most African-American rural families spent their leisure time at church and school functions. Rural blacks in Iowa tended to be members of the African Methodist-Episcopal faith. There were some Baptists and Presbyterians whose religious practices were typical of southern rural blacks. Rural African-Americans built their churches primarily in town, often combining their resources with urban blacks to erect churches they could manage and control. The black church provided the opportunity for families to share fellowship and feelings of love, peace, and power. Those who traveled to town to worship packed lunches, so that Sunday would not only be a complete day of worship but a chance for

Russell Downey (top left) and his friends, Rice Lintz (top right) and Hank Williams, hunting near Ottumwa (courtesy Al Downey Sr.)

Gwendolene Harris's grandmother entertains the minister and friends at her home in Dallas County. (courtesy Gwendolene Harris)

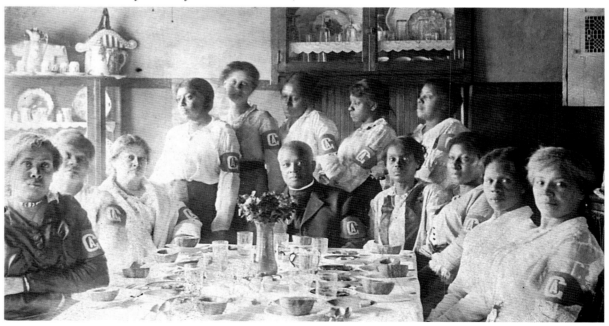

families to spend time together discussing farming, child rearing, finances, and other issues pertinent to rural social and economic development. In rural churches as in urban churches, Easter, Thanksgiving, and Christmas programs created the opportunity for parents and children to work together to spread joy and laughter and to help each other get through sorrow.[41]

Education about Life and Survival on the Farm

The rural school also served multiple purposes for Iowa's black families who made their living from the land and who believed that some of their leisure time should be spent educating their children. The school was the place where children were educated about life, how to survive on the farm, and how to use the land to be self-sufficient. Because education had to be practical and immediately useful, girls were taught domestic skills, while boys were given lessons in agricultural production. The rural school was more than an incubator for learning. It was another place of interaction where teachers, parents, and children came together to create a rural society that emphasized moral living, hard work, honesty, and community development through property ownership. To avoid conflicting with the farm season, school terms were divided into two sessions, winter and late fall. Like the rural church, the rural school was also a place of leisure where families came to

Sandra and Ray Matthews attended Mrs. Plumb's one-room school near their family farm outside of Logan. (courtesy Henry G. Matthews)

enjoy plays, cantatas, and Thanksgiving and Christmas programs. To a large extent, children in all-black settlements in the late nineteenth century received the greatest opportunity to display their talents. Those in all-white communities tended to be less visible, although they were permitted to participate in all school activities.[42]

African-Americans who owned farms and other properties in Iowa understood the need to provide for those less fortunate than themselves. Property holders understood also that they had to take the lead in bringing services and jobs to the community. Thus black landowners were eager to rent acreage to young farmers and to provide jobs for day laborers. Mr. and Mrs. Robert Johnson in Gravity gave employment to several young African-American men, while C. A. Marshall in Anthon hired more than a dozen boys and girls to work on the Sutton ranch he managed. In Iowa's rural communities, black businessmen and landowners provided opportunities to black children because they wanted to keep young people on the farm and to enhance community survival through cooperation and a mutual exchange of respect and resources.[43]

Blacks who owned land took the lead in securing medical services for rural black people. They went to town and identified a doctor, usually a European-American, who generally agreed to provide medical service. Because Iowa's rural communities were seldom predominantly African-American or places where a large number of blacks settled at one time, white doctors generally felt comfortable serving blacks because most knew that there was no other place for blacks living in small towns to get assistance. Medical treatment was provided by both house calls and office visits, but childbirthing brought the doctor to the countryside most often. African-American women in rural Iowa, like those throughout the United States, had their babies at home during the late nineteenth and early twentieth centuries. A few midwives practiced medicine, but many families sought a doctor's advice to ensure proper care.[44]

While families during the nineteenth century spent considerable time laying horse and wagon routes across the prairie, black and white landowners and business people launched a successful campaign at the turn of the twentieth century to have dirt roads covered with gravel. Rural road improvements enhanced service to rural communities in many ways. In harvest and planting seasons, farm families were able to avoid wasting time getting back and forth between their fields and the market. In addition,

Because education had to be practical and immediately useful, girls were taught domestic skills, while boys were given lessons in agricultural production.

improved roads made possible faster mail service and encouraged the development of rural mail delivery.[45]

For African-American farmers in Iowa, the greatest providers of information were the state's black newspapers, published in large numbers before the massive adoption of radio and television. The *Iowa State Bystander* illuminated the life, history, and cultural experiences of blacks in America, especially of those in rural Iowa.[46] Created primarily to report the activities of the black middle class, the *Bystander* nevertheless dedicated some space to discussing rural black family life. Typically stories described people and their lifestyles: Mr. Henry Martin and his wife have a fruit orchard. Mr. Baldwin's folks are still on their 400-acre farm. William Headley is working in the poultry house. In Clarinda the colored people are doing well; most of them own their own homes and work on farms adjacent to the city. Mr. G. W. Hollingsworth owns a small truck farm on the city limits; he works his farm and also works in the mine. Henry Fairbrother of Oskaloosa raised 2,180 bushels of sugar beets, worth $260, on one acre. Mr. P. Towmley is a corn doctor.[47] Short reports of this kind kept Iowa's black farm families abreast of developments that related to agriculture and rural living, and they informed farm families about who to contact when specific farm problems arose.

More importantly, the *Iowa State Bystander* provided a voice for rural blacks to be heard. In this newspaper black farmers discussed their successes and failures, what they believed was critical for black rural survival, and the necessary steps rural African-Americans had to take to advance economically and politically. The *Bystander* also gave families on the land the opportunity to read about how most rural families lived, especially in Iowa. "It was spiritually uplifting for African-American farm families to read of the success of others throughout the state," Ruby Ewing recalled, "because it helped us feel connected."[48]

The *Iowa State Bystander* also kept rural blacks abreast of political and economic developments. The *Bystander* announced local and national political meetings and discussed issues raised in the meetings. For example, on November 13, 1896, in an advertisement reading "Farmers Congress Called," the newspaper reported, "the organization is non-partisan in its nature and its purpose is to discuss and recommend to Congress and the legislatures of the various states legislation meant to benefit agricultural interests."[49] Announcements of this sort not only connected Iowans to a larger political constituency, but informed black farmers about public issues and the need for them to participate in political activities.

The *Bystander* especially encouraged black farmers to vote and to run for political positions. The paper also called for legislation supporting the education of their children and giving farmers control over marketing and shipping their crops, defining tax rates, and determining the value of land. In addition, the paper called for the creation of black businesses and urged African-Americans to patronize all-black enterprises. The *Bystander* took the lead in promoting the establishment of institutions to serve the intellectual, spiritual, and physical needs of black people.[50]

Importance of Material Culture

The emphasis the *Bystander* placed on housing and other properties owned by Iowa's African-American community was an indication of the importance of the development of material culture for Iowa's black population. Mr. Sellers bought single and double buggies to transport his family. Mr. Thomas G. Jones owned a nice farmhouse, only two miles from town, where he entertained guests from out of town. Mr. Henry Martin and his wife owned several lots and rented their houses to family members and migrant families. Robert Johnson rented his farm for cash and spent his time operating a barber shop. In addition, Johnson owned the brick building that housed his shop. Johnson had a nice home in town where he also entertained guests.[51] Many of these homes possessed the latest in household technologies, such as ice boxes and radios, custom-made furniture, sewing and washing

William H. Matthews built a showcase home (left) on his farmstead outside Missouri Valley. (courtesy Henry G. Matthews)

The parlor of Gwendolene Harris's grandparents' home was decorated with prized possessions and family portraits. (courtesy Gwendolene Harris)

machines, wood stoves, and the latest china and silverware.

The best homes also possessed state-of-the-art cisterns, indoor plumbing, running water, and nice grounds.[52] The growth in rural African-Americans' material culture was an indication that black farm people understood how to increase and improve property as well as how to make decisions about their resources, an opportunity that many had not had in the rural South. The *Bystander* reporter's emphasis on quality of life was also in keeping with the progressive movement sweeping throughout the country during the late nineteenth and early twentieth centuries. For African-Americans it was essential that reports describing positive developments among blacks be released since rural life in Iowa and other predominantly agricultural states was being criticized for being too isolated and too destitute during the first three decades of the twentieth century.[53]

Articles in the *Bystander* demonstrated how closely linked rural African-Americans' material culture was to propertied business and labor culture. One *Bystander* writer reported in 1903 that "an eight mile overland drive brought us to Gravity where there lives only two colored families, Henry and Robert Johnson, who appeared to have been the most prosperous team of brothers in the area. They both own beautiful farms with houses within one-half mile of the post office."[54] A *Bystander* reporter traveling in 1906, noted "we next went down the Mississippi River to Muscatine, Iowa where dwells about five hundred colored representatives of which some are doing well."[55] He continued: "Several owning small farms or truck gardens of ten to one hundred acres of the valuable Muscatine land. Mr. Fairfax and Mr. Nelson Carr are two more reliable and successful farmers. They are doing something to help build up this race of mine."[56]

The culture shared by African-Americans in Iowa also included the values and ideas that families adopted to survive. To combat any thinking that rural blacks in Iowa were lazy and going to be dominated like southern African-Americans, some blacks dedicated themselves to living as model citizens. This was evident not only in the kind and amount of property they owned, but also in the management schemes they used to produced their crops. Some African-American farm families chose to employ white hands to promote the black race and to show that African-Americans were people who could function in both worlds. "Mr. Bly owns a nice fruit farm; he has about two acres in strawberries and the day that we were there he had about fifteen pickers, mostly

white. He delivers his own berries to the market; he lives one and one-half miles from town. Mr. Bly is solving the race problem."[57] In addition, "Mr. Milligan, a successful farmer and gardener living only one and one-half miles from town, . . . has four acres of strawberries, two acres of cherries and a lot of other fruit and garden vegetables. They had nine other pickers hired, only one was black."[58]

Black and white families in rural Iowa, like those in the South, understood that economic needs and agricultural demands would at times put both races in the same place. Yet it was generally understood that in social and cultural activities the races were to be as separate as the fingers on the hand. Not every one adhered to societal norms, however. Interracial marriages took place, and rural black children sometimes attended school with white children when only a few African-Americans lived in the area.

For some blacks on Iowa farms, life could be filled with tragic moments. Farmer Robert Shelton was hunting along the banks of the Grand River when he shot and killed a squirrel. He drowned while trying to rescue the game from the river. George W. Bark, a farmer who lived two miles north of Maynard, set fire to his house and attempted suicide by shooting himself. Children were sometimes injured on the farm. Some were killed, others maimed, while still others were bruised by machinery and affected by over-exposure to heat, cold, and long work hours.[59]

Blacks Enjoyed a Decent Living on the Farm in Iowa

While it appeared that blacks enjoyed a decent living on the farm in Iowa, they were expected to stay in their place. Blacks and whites lived segregated lives, a lifestyle that was quite familiar to African-Americans who migrated from the rural South. With the exception of the few times that whites attended black fund-raisers, discrimination against African-Americans was practiced throughout the state. It was most evident in theaters, restaurants, and hotels. Intermarriage between blacks and whites was largely unacceptable to both races, and violations of this sacred code were dealt with harshly. Despite the codes of racial segregation, some black farmers, however, did take white women for wives and some white families refused to discriminate against African-Americans because of the color of their skin. Robert Boldridge, one of five children born to William and Dorothy Boldridge, was raised on a 210-acre farm seven miles south of Algona in the 1940s and 1950s. "The thing most people would find to be quite astonishing and

Mrs. William Goodlow's elaborate satin dress indicates her husband's success in farming — and how she followed urban fashion trends. (courtesy Ella Goodlow Stith)

some downright unbelievable," he wrote, "is just how insignificant the racial aspects of it were. . . . The stark reality of it all is that we weren't much different from any other families who farmed in the area during that period. We knew them as our neighbors, they knew us as the Boldridges."[60] Boldridge continued: "One of our neighbors was an older farmer who would always come around and sometimes tell these off-color racial jokes. The guy was really harmless. He was just trying to be cute. My mother thought he was a jerk but my dad overlooked his personality flaws because this neighbor was the person who combined our oats and soybeans and his wife was our babysitter."[61]

Despite the Boldridges' experience, the historical record shows that Iowa had racial problems even though black children usually attended school with white students, like the Boldridges, the Matthews, and Ruby Marshall Ewing, who lived on a farm in Anthon during the first two decades of the twentieth century. But while poor whites angrily attacked the black southerners who came to work as strikebreakers, it is not evident in Iowa's history that white landowners conspired to prevent African-Americans from buying land as white farmers had in the South. Neither did they oppose school integration as vehemently as southerners.[62]

Rural Families Did More than Farm

But in Iowa's agricultural and rural life, families did more than farm. Agricultural and rural life involved not only the production of goods but also the study of agriculture and rural trends so that families would have knowledge available to help them improve farming and their standard of living. In keeping with this way of thinking, African-Americans reached beyond the immediately practical matters of farming and rural life to become involved with agricultural study and research. A few African-Americans attended Iowa State University, Iowa's land grant institution, to study agriculture and help improve the quality of life among black Iowans on farms and in rural areas.[63]

Among the many African-Americans with rural backgrounds who attended Iowa's institutions of higher learning, George Washington Carver's experiences indicate why Iowa State University is considered one of the preeminent places for rural and agricultural training. George Washington Carver was born in Missouri during the Civil War and orphaned in infancy. Homeless as a child, Carver migrated to Winterset in his late twenties and entered Simpson College in 1890. Later he enrolled at Iowa State, where he earned a B.S. degree in 1894.

The Goodlow's extended family (left to right): Aunt Delia Goodlow Thornton, Uncle Sige, Ella, Mary Frances Everhart, Ernestine Thornton, Rosie Robinson, Claude Everhart (baby), Mary Jane Goodlow Everhart, and Richard Black (courtesy Ella Goodlow Stith)

(Above left) Dorothy and William Boldridge with their children (from left): Bob, Mary, Billy, Ruth Ann, and Nathalie — at home on the family farm near Algona (courtesy Bob Boldridge)

This unidentified young man was one of the Piney Woods School summer interns in Iowa. (courtesy Wilma Merfield)

Carver was given a position on the faculty as assistant botanist in the Experiment Station, a position he held for two years. In 1896, Iowa State granted him a master's degree, and during that same year he left Iowa to become the head of a newly organized agricultural department at Tuskegee Institute. Carver received numerous honors for his research concerning peanuts and sweet potatoes.[64]

Understanding the need of black farmers for information to help improve production, Carver began to publish his research in black newspapers and magazines in 1914. He wrote primarily for Tuskegee's *Negro Farmer* newspaper, which was read by African-American farmers in Iowa.

In the words of the *Iowa State Bystander*, "*The Negro Farmer* is the name of a new farm journal just started in Tuskegee, Alabama by some of the citizens of Tuskegee. It is published in the interest of the Negro farmers throughout the United States and will meet a long felt want. We welcome it and shall encourage it, for our agriculturalists should be encouraged. Then again the Negro farmer, like the white farmer, is going to be a mighty power in the making of our race problem. We have a few colored farmers that are farming and owning farms from 160 to 1,000 acres of valuable Iowa land and there is no race prejudice out on these farms. These white farmers buy and sell their corn, wheat, oats, hogs, cattle, chickens from the colored farmers, so let us thoughtful and leading men encourage the Negro Farmer and urge him to stay on the farm and buy more farms. So we welcome this new journal, *The Negro Farmer*, to our office and hope for it a large and useful influence in this country."[65]

Laurence C. Jones and Piney Woods School

Some 20 years after Carver's birth, Laurence C. Jones was born in Missouri. He moved to Marshalltown in 1904, and after graduating from high school he graduated from the University of Iowa in 1907. Jones became interested in what Booker T. Washington was doing for blacks in the rural South and left Iowa to teach at Utica Institute in Mississippi. His migration to rural Mississippi proved to be a great move because it was there that Jones started a rural boarding school for African-American children in Piney Woods in 1909. Jones's affectionate relationship with people in Iowa helped to secure needed funds for Piney Woods. Because Iowans gave their time and money, a building called Iowa Hall was erected in their honor.[66]

The connection between Jones and Iowa proved valuable for the students in this rural Mississippi school. Understanding that midwestern farmers practiced a different system of farm production and management and that they applied the latest agricultural research to their operation, Jones sent many of his students to Iowa to work and study with white farmers. This apprenticeship provided not only the opportunity for rural black children to gain additional knowledge about agriculture, but it kept alive that North-South connection that was rapidly developing in Iowa. The presence of these students also meant that the state of Iowa would have to invest resources in black rural and agricultural life because these students from rural Mississippi were critically observing the differences in rural life among blacks in both places.[67]

As Jones established connections in Iowa to acquaint African-American students from rural Mississippi with midwestern farming, a few black farmers in Iowa were establishing a relationship with researchers from the Iowa Agricultural Experiment Station. African-American farmers developed working relationships with researchers at the station to help them not only become better farm managers but also to learn how they could increase their profits through improved yields. Like their white counterparts, black agricultural producers were concerned with preservation and conservation.[68]

During the years 1910 through 1920, Iowa's African-American farm families participated in two important rural activities: the Country Life Movement and the Extension Service. Both were organized to help improve the living conditions of Iowa's rural people. In addition, Iowa's African-American land-owners took the lead in developing social-welfare programs within the black church to meet the needs of the black communities. In Iowa, black landowners advocated progressivism. They supported the establishment of schools and fought hard to have their children educated. They pushed for improved roads and called for rural blacks to become involved in the campaign for rural mail delivery.[69]

To improve life for their children, African-American farmers connected their children to programs organized by the Extension Service. Black boys and girls, like white children of similar age, participated in livestock and vegetable production programs. Typically called 4-H programs, girls took advantage of the domestic programs offered by Extension. The skills children obtained as a result of participating in this program contributed to the survival of the rural black community in that they prepared young boys and girls to be responsible citizens, persons able to provide for their households.[70]

Iowa's Extension programs also benefited African-American women. Rural women participated in activities that emphasized family and community survival skills. Sewing, food and nutrition, and other domestic programs were available, including home demonstration activities in which women learned more about modern household management and technology.

During the Great Depression, black women and men left farms and moved to towns such as Sioux City, Waterloo, and Ottumwa, where they found employment in the slaughtering and meat packaging plants. Railroads also hired former farm hands as porters and waiters.[71] During this time, John Deere, a major manufacturer of farm implements, continued to recruit blacks from the rural South to work in its Des Moines factory. Filling this particular need for laborers and southern rural migrants' need for work, John Deere played a major role in transplanting African-American blues music culture to Iowa and the Middle West. Many of John Deere employees were former plantation workers from the South, including several blues musicians who had learned their craft in Mississippi, Alabama, and Georgia.

Reluctance to Accept Government Handouts

Surviving the Depression was especially difficult for African-American farmers. Like most American families, many black households were reluctant to accept government handouts. Many waited until the last possible moment to ask for help, preferring either to ask family members for assistance as they attempted repeatedly to find work with a private employer rather than work on a relief project. Black people in Iowa "always believed that they had to provide for themselves and not depend on the government or anyone else for food, shelter, clothes, or money."[72] To maintain a sense of pride and feelings of self-sufficiency, most families continued to plant large gardens that produced a substantial part of their food supply, which during hard times could be sold to earn an extra income.[73]

Black farm women held the family together during the lean years, especially when their husbands, brothers, fathers, and sons could not find work. During the 1930s, African-American women throughout Iowa labored increasingly to produce their family food supply and to raise extra farm products either to be sold for income or bartered to reduce expenditures. Those who lived on the farms attempted to increase their sale of poultry and dairy products, and they sometimes offered such services as cooking, mending, sewing, and babysitting to middle-class white families when their own families were experiencing economic hardship.[74]

Numerous examples exist throughout Iowa's history of how African-Americans contributed to agriculture and agriculturally related activities. For example, black farm families contributed to the war effort. During World Wars 1 and 2, they raised produce and livestock. Rural women gave their surplus vegetables, eggs, and dairy products to families who struggled to survive with the meager rations given by the government. Even young black boys and girls supported the war by offering to raise vegetables and livestock to help feed the hungry and by working in agriculturally related industries.[75]

Henry Sr. and Arthur Bagby tended their family garden as children during the Great Depression at their home on the east side of Des Moines. (courtesy David Bagby)

Theodore (Tubby) Matthews (above) with the mules used on the farm, before his brother Henry (below) got his first tractor, c. 1951 (courtesy Henry G. Matthews)

Following World War 2, the adoption of farm and household technologies by African-American farmers was slow. Many were not given the opportunity to participate in federal farm programs. Limited income and production on smaller acreage made it nearly impossible for the majority of black farm families in Iowa to forge ahead with the purchase of improved tractors, plows, and other farm implements like white farmers who were supported by the government. Unless farm subsidies could be secured from the government, even the purchase of improved commercial fertilizers, seeds, insecticides, and pesticides would be difficult. Because of the cost of modernizing farming in the 1950s and 1960s, an overwhelming majority of blacks in agricultural production in Iowa continued to employ labor intensive strategies to produce their crops, and many never participated in federal farm programs that would have helped them finance their operations.[76]

Although they could not buy into the technological revolution at the same pace as white farmers, many black farmers during the 1940s did make some significant household purchases. Modern conveniences such as electricity, running water, and other labor-saving devices, like washing and sewing machines, gas stoves and heaters made it possible for black women to leave the farm to search for greater economic opportunity. Believing it essential to help their families survive, some African-American farm women worked in factories in nearby towns, and others continued to work as cooks, cleaning women, laundresses, seamstresses, and hair-dressers. They also remained actively engaged in farm production as laborers and managers of the child labor force as they searched for better economic opportunities in rural Iowa.[77]

Cry for Greater Inclusion

For Iowa's rural black population, the cry for greater inclusion had been sounded for many decades, dating back to the late nineteenth century. In 1884 the last enactment of major nineteenth-century legislation took place regarding African-Americans when the General Assembly passed the Civil Rights Act, patterned after the federal Civil Rights Act of 1875. The law declared that "all persons within this state shall be entitled to the full and equal enjoyment of the accommodations, advantages, facilities and privileges of inns, public conveyances, barber shops, theaters and other places of amusement."[78] Eight years later the General Assembly added more categories to the law, including restaurants, lunch counters, bath houses, and other places where refreshments are served. With this legislation Iowans within 16 years had decided to extend full legal rights to black males, provide public education to African-American children, and guarantee access to many public facilities. Whatever legislative hostility the state legislature had earlier shown toward African-Americans, by the late nineteenth century Iowa was one of the most progressive states in the nation in terms of legal equality for blacks.[79]

More than a half century later, across America the civil rights movement ushered in many changes for the poor, the oppressed, the downtrodden, and people of color. In 1965 the General Assembly created a state-funded Iowa Civil Rights Commission. Legislative reapportionment had increased the representation of urban areas in the General Assembly, a crucial prerequisite to the establishment of the commission. The struggle to create such an organization reached back to the days following World War 2 and included many hearings that clearly documented widespread economic discrimination against African-Americans on and off the farm.[80] Because long-term systematic discrimination could be documented, Iowa political leaders during the civil rights movement encouraged the state's citizens and local governments to support federal legislation designed to improve race relations as well as the overall quality of life for blacks and the poor.

In Iowa, the greatest evidence of the impact of the Civil Rights Act of 1964, the Voting Rights Act of 1965, and local and state anti-discriminatory laws can been seen in the number of black families who continued to farm and who were now participating in federal farm programs. During the civil rights era, at least 15 black Iowa farmers became involved in farm programs; only 2 or 3 blacks had ever had been active before.[81]

Change was also evident in the number of blacks who moved into non-producing agriculture-related positions. Between 1965 and 1980, a few blacks began to hold state positions involving agriculture and rural life. In 1965 at age 18, Viola Winston became president of the Wapello County Girls' 4-H organization in Ottumwa, Iowa. Winston was the first black to hold this position, which involved serving more than 300 girls in county 4-H club work. Her mother, Mrs. Booker Pearl Winston, was chosen to serve as a local leader of the Merry Maids 4-H club, to which Viola and her younger sister Linda belonged. The Winstons owned 40 acres on Route 6, five miles southeast of Ottumwa, where they raised beef cattle and Poland China pigs. Although John Winston, Viola's father, was an employee of the Morrell packing plant, he spent his evenings and days off working on their farm. The children, including Viola, had baby bees for projects, and Timothy Allen Winston, the son, competed in a livestock show where his Poland China pig won the grand championship.[82]

Keeping African-American children involved in these kinds of activities was the goal of Sheilah Marie Manley. In the 1980s, she was the only black 4-H youth leader in Iowa. Her main task involved connecting urban-based 4-H youth groups to rural life in the state. Her objective was to use the 4-H as a vehicle to train rural and urban blacks to live above the level of survival, while at the same time obtaining leadership skills in their community as they reached maturity.[83]

Throughout the 1970s and 1980s, Iowans involved in agriculture worked to ensure that African-American representation in agriculture and related fields remain an aggressive part of the state's commitment to equal opportunity. Consequently, those involved with state and federal programs began to establish connections with southern land-grant institutions and regional and state agencies in search of blacks trained in a variety of agricultural pursuits. This relationship produced other kinds of African-American migrants, those who were now moving to Iowa for an opportunity to apply their technological and scientific training in non-farm production areas.[84]

Blacks Who Could Offer Expert Advice

Black soil scientists and those who worked for distributors and companies that produced agricultural chemicals and sold farm implements, for instance, were a part of the transition of African-Americans into mainstream American agriculture. Now among the population were blacks who could offer expert advice about plant breeding, conservation, farm implements, and marketing.[85]

Four African-Americans currently residing in Iowa represent the diverse interest that blacks have always had in this state's agricultural history. Hal Cosby, a native of Mississippi and a graduate of Alcorn State University, is a soil conservationist with the U.S. Department of Agriculture (USDA). Cosby has worked

Viola Winston made news with her election as Wapello County Girls 4-H president in 1965. (Ottumwa Courier)

Winstons Reap Happiness From Farm

John Winston (right) and one of his sons tending cattle on their farm near Ottumwa (Ottumwa Courier)

Gary Cornelious with organic vegetables on his farm near Boone (courtesy Gary Cornelious)

his way up from field agent with the federal government to managing an entire agricultural district. Like Cosby, other blacks are involved with the implementation of federal programs in Iowa. Wendell Jones, for example, is a district conservationist for the USDA Natural Resource Conservation Service in Iowa City. He offers expert advice to farmers concerning the use of natural resources and encourages farmers to adopt conservation practices. Together, Jones's and Cosby's professional stature represents the validation of black expertise in fields of agriculture traditionally occupied by whites. The dissemination of knowledge is one of the ways Cosby and Jones reach out to black farmers within the state and keep them abreast of technical developments, not only in federal farm programs but in producing and marketing their goods as well. These soil conservationists represent the transition of some blacks from the field to the office, a place where knowledge and expertise are highly respected.[86]

Outstanding Examples

An outstanding example of this trend is Dr. Michael J. Martin. Born and raised on a farm near Orrville, Alabama, he was the fifth of eight children who grew up helping his father farm their 240 acres. In his senior year at Alabama A&M, he was recruited to Iowa State University, where he earned his master's (1980) and doctorate (1982). He immediately went to work for Garst Seed, where he rose rapidly. By 1989 he was research director for all breeding of corn, soybeans, sorghum, canola, and sunflowers. From 1995 until his retirement in 2000, he was head of all corn research, breeding, and marketing for Advanta, which had acquired Garst and its ICI parent corporation. Currently, Dr. Martin continues to conduct research on a contract basis and operates a hunting preserve on 1,300 acres near Luther.[87]

Gary Cornelious's involvement in agriculture builds on and extends African-Americans' role in Iowa's agricultural and rural life. Since the 1980s, Cornelious has been involved with various forms of agricultural production in the state. One of 33 black agricultural producers remaining in Iowa, Cornelious's diverse farming operation bridges the past and the present. Farming a little less than 50 acres of land in Boone County, Cornelious grows soybeans and corn. He has diversified his operations by producing organic food products, which he sells to individual wholesalers and grocery stores throughout Iowa. Added to his truck farming is a livestock business that specializes in the production of hogs, goats, chicken, turkeys, and sheep. Cornelious is recognized as a competitive farmer and has won many local and state contests for quality produce and livestock.[88]

Within the last three years, Cornelious has received two appointments that give him the opportunity to help fight for equity in the implementation of federal farm programs. At the state level, he has been appointed to the local agricultural service committee, a position given to him to help safeguard against discrimination in the implementation of farm programs to people of color. At state Farm Service Committee meetings, Cornelious and others review applications and approve loans for Iowa farmers seeking support. In addition to assisting African-American and other minority farmers at the state and local levels, Cornelious has also been involved in the Black Farmers' Agriculturalist Association, a nationwide organization that has brought suit against the USDA for long-term systematic discrimination against black farmers, especially in the southern states. His efforts have helped create awareness of farm discrimination throughout Iowa and the Midwest. Cornelious has been appointed the association's media specialist and public-relations liaison, positions that allow him to combine his farming activities with his academic training in videography and photography.

Cornelious's involvement with the black farmers' movement led to his being among 20 minority farmers invited to the White House to discuss pending lawsuits and discrimination with President Clinton in December 1997. Because of his work, Cornelious's alma mater, Luther College, has awarded him its Distinguished Service Award.

Cosby, Jones, and Cornelious represent a major change from the years when African-Americans in Iowa primarily involved themselves in the production and marketing of agricultural goods and crops. While Iowa's black farm population is currently quite small, its presence symbolizes the African-American role in Iowa's history. That role will continue. Today black men and women come to Iowa State University to study agricultural economics, agricultural education, agricultural engineering, agricultural journalism, rural history, and rural sociology. They will carry on the African-American rural tradition, which has involved farming, establishing communities, erecting institutions, and building networks that have helped black Iowans survive the transition from southern to midwestern living. From territorial days, through statehood, and into the present, this tradition has supported a people whose understanding of democratic principles, possession of property, and development of family has strongly contributed to Iowa's diverse rural and agricultural heritage.

Dr. Michael Martin (third from right) retired from research, production, and marketing for Garst Seed to develop and market his own line of wild animal feeds. (courtesy Dr. Michael Martin)

Notes

1. *Past and Present of Fayette County, Iowa* (Indianapolis: B.F. Bowen, 1910), 131–32; Thomas Draper Peterman (West Union: West Union Argo, 1902); Census of Westfield Township, Fayette County, Iowa, 1856 and 1880. The author is indebted to Mrs. Frances R. Graham for this data.

2. According to Robert R. Dykstra, the arrival of former slaves into Iowa can be categorized in three general ways: (1) those who came in the 1840s and 1850s by way of the Mississippi River; (2) those who came in the same period but traveled up the Missouri River; and (3) those who came in the post–Civil War era, mainly as coal miners. Robert R. Dykstra, *Bright Radical Star: Black Freedom and White Supremacy on the Hawkeye Frontier* (Cambridge: Harvard Univ. Press, 1993; repr. Iowa State Univ. Press, 1996). See also Leola Bergmann, *The Negro in Iowa* (Iowa City: SHSI, 1948; repr. 1969); Dorothy Schwieder, *Iowa: The Middle Land* (Ames: Iowa State Univ. Press, 1996), 83–109; *DMR*, Jan. 21, 1863; John Carl Parish, *George Wallace Jones* (Iowa City: SHSI, 1912), 127; *United States Census, 1840*, 59, 79, 87–101; Joel H. Silbey, "Proslavery Sentiment in Iowa, 1838–1861," *IJH* 55 (1957): 289; and Randall Bennett Woods, *A Black Odyssey: John Lewis Waller and the Promise of American Life, 1878–1900* (Lawrence: Regents Press of Kansas, 1981); Homer L. Calkin, "A Slave-owner in Iowa," *Palimpsest* 22 (1941): 344; Philip Dillon Jordan, *William Slater and the Slavery Controversy* (Iowa City: Univ. of Iowa Press, 1935).

3. For a discussion of Iowa as a place of escape for slaves and free blacks, see James Connor, "The Anti-slavery Movement in Iowa," *AI* 40 (1970): 343–50; "Albright Farm Was Site for Old Stage Line for Smuggling Negroes Out of the South," *Madrid Register News*, June 29, 1950; "Negro Slavery Given Death Blow at Burlington, Iowa in 1839," *DMR*, July 21, 1935; "Traded Slaves for Grundy County Land," *Lineville Tribune*, Jan. 15, 1942; and Curt Harnack, "The Iowa Underground Railroad," *Iowan* 4 (1956): 20.

4. For a comparison of black and white migratory experiences, see Hope Wallace, *Millar Scrogin, Maria Annettee Northrup, March 25, 1844–July 1, 1915* (Geyserville CA, 1979); "Woman, Born in Slavery and Later Freed by A. Lincoln, Celebrates 100th Birthday," *Davenport Democrat*, March 13, 1945; "Was Former Slave and One of the Founders of 3rd Baptist Church," *Davenport Times*, July 28, 1945. For a discussion of Ralph White, see "An Iowa Fugitive Slave Case," *AI* 2 (1896): 531; John C. Parish, "An Early Fugitive Slave Case West of the Mississippi River," *IJH* 6 (1908): 88; Henry K. Peterson, "The First Decision Rendered by the Supreme Court of Iowa," *AI* 34 (1957–1959): 304; Jacob A. Swisher, "The Case of Ralph," *Palimpsest* 7 (1976): 33; "The Case of Ralph," *Clear Lake Republican*, Dec. 13, 1938; "Court of 1838 Is Re-enacted," *DMR*, Sept. 13, 1938.

5. For a discussion of rural southern black migration to Iowa, see Schwieder, *Iowa: The Middle Land*, 83-109; Bergmann, 1–35; Dykstra, *Bright Radical Star*, 3–171. For a comparison of black and white migration into Iowa, see Hoyt Sherman, "From Oskaloosa in a Wagon," *AI* 33 (1956): 281–88; Martha E. Shivvars, "A Quaker Woman's Life," *IoWoman* 3 (Summer 1982): 14–16.

6. Robert R. Dykstra, "Dr. Emerson's Sam," *Palimpsest* 63 (1982); Margaret A. Bonney, "Iowa's Black Heritage," *Iowa History Teacher* (Fall 1989): 1–4; William L. Hewitt, "So Few Undesirables: Race, Residence, and Occupation in Sioux City: 1890–1925," *AI* 50 (1989): 158–79.

7. Lola E. Jones interview, July 1998. Jones is the Paynes' granddaughter.

8. Dykstra, *Bright Radical Star*, 85–86; See also Bergmann, 38–39; *[Keokuk] Weekly Gate City*, April 22, 1874; *Lee County History* (WPA, 1942), 15; Ruth S. Beitz, "Going Up to Glory Very Slow," *Iowan* 16 (Spring 1968): 42–45, 49–50, 54; Bonney, 1–4.

9. Dykstra, *Bright Radical Star*, 80–90; Schwieder, *Iowa: The Middle Land*, 83–108; Bergmann, 1–35; Otha D. Wearin, *I Remember Yesteryear* (Des Moines: Wallace-Homestead, 1974); Granville Stuart, *Forty Years on the Frontier As Seen in the Journals and Reminiscences of Granville Stuart*, ed. Paul C. Phillips (Glendale CA: Arthur H. Clark, 1957).

10. For discussions of Charles Adams, see "Former Slave," *Oskaloosa Herald*, Jan. 17, 1948, and "Charles Adams, Former Slave Dies at 102," *Oskaloosa Herald*, Sept. 10, 1947. For a discussion of Samuel Hall, see Orville Elder, *Samuel Hall, 47 Years of a Slave: A Brief Story of His Life Before and After Freedom Came to Him* (Washington IA: Journal Print, 1912) and "Slaves 94 Years Old Visiting in Town," *Davenport Democrat*, June 30, 1912. See also "Kato Johnson, Once a Slave, Is 88 Today," *Ottumwa Courier*, March 25, 1943; "Georgia Kennedy, Once a Slave, Dies at 102," *Ottumwa Courier*, Dec. 27, 1943; "Aunt Betty Lewis, A Memory of Days Gone By, Tells of Antebellum Times," *Davenport Democrat*, Feb. 11, 1912; and "Rev. P.M. Lewis, Born a Slave in Virginia, Passes His 85th Birthday," *Waterloo Courier*, March 8, 1934.

11. Unpublished manuscript biography of William Owen Van Vaxen Goodlow by Luther Givehand, his great grandson; Ella R. Stith interview, July 1999.

12. For a discussion of Turner Bell, see "Born a Slave, He Fights for Rights of Minority Groups," *DMR*, Nov. 2, 1947. On Richard Colwell, see "Dick Colwell Ex-Slave, Dies," *Shenandoah Sentinel*, March 25, 1933. On John Sweat, see "Pioneer Negro Resident Dead," *Waukon Republican and Standard*, Sept. 17, 1930. On Martha Templeton, see "Pleased with 107-Year Gifts," *Perry Chief*, Dec. 22, 1948, and "Party for Perry Woman Near 108 Years of Age," *Des Moines Tribune*, Dec. 22, 1948.

13. Gwendolene Harris interview, February 2000.

14. Schwieder, *Iowa: The Middle Land*, 83–91. See also Dykstra, "Dr. Emerson's Sam," 80–81; Bergmann, 35–40; Mollie Wright, "Former Slave Had Long, Happy Life Since Emancipation," *Burlington Hawkeye-Gazette*, Oct. 14, 1947; Hennie Weaver, "Born a Slave, Aunt Hennie Weaver Is Now Landowner," *Burlington Gazette*, Nov. 6, 1922; and John Walker, "Pair in Des Moines Recall Slave Days," *Des Moines Tribune*, Feb. 12, 1930.

15. Dykstra, *Bright Radical Star*, 13–14. For a discussion of these migrants' early experiences, see also Ver Planck Antwerp, "Source Material of Iowa History: Reminiscences of Early Iowa," *IJH* 52 (1954): 343–64; Alvin C. Leighton, "Source Material of Iowa History: Pioneer Reminiscences of Wapello County," *IJH* 57 (1959): 331–54; *United States Census, 1840, Dubuque County* [Families 59–61, 63, 65, 67, 71, 73, 79, 87, 89, 91, 101]; and *United States Census, 1850, Dubuque County* [Families 3, 1424, 1634, 1654, 1664, 1732, 1733, 1743, 1765, 1827, 1911, 1953].

16. Henry G. Matthews interview, Dec. 28, 1999.

17. Janice Burrell Cochran interview, March 17, 2000.

18. For a comparative discussion of who Iowa's migrants were and what social, economic, cultural, religious, and political skills they brought with them, see Dorothy Schwieder, et al., *Buxton: Work and Racial Equality in a Coal Mining Community* (Ames: Iowa State Univ. Press, 1982), 1–175; Marvin Bergman, *The Iowa History Reader* (Ames: Iowa State Univ. Press, 1982), 37–342; Dykstra, *Bright Radical Star*, 3–195; Leland Sage, *A History of Iowa* (Ames: Iowa State Univ. Press, 1996), 52–216; Bergmann, op. cit.; David M. Gradwohl and Nancy M. Osborn, *Exploring Buried Buxton: Archaeology of an Abandoned Iowa Coal Mining Town with a Large Black Population* (Ames: Iowa State Univ. Press, 1984), 57–186; Schwieder, *Black Diamonds: Life and Work in Iowa's Coal Mining Communities, 1895–1925* (Ames: Iowa State Univ. Press, 1983), 27–126; Dorothy Schwieder, *Patterns and Perspectives in Iowa History* (Ames: Iowa State Univ. Press, 1973), 41–403; and *The WPA Guide to the 1930s* (Iowa City: SHSI, 1938), 1–169.

19. United States Censuses, Iowa, 1840 through 1950. See also *Iowa State Bystander*, Des Moines, Iowa, 1894–1930; *History of Johnson County, Iowa* (Iowa City: SHSI, 1883); *History of Van Buren County, Iowa* (Chicago: Macmillan, 1883); *United States Census, 1840*; *Census of the United States, 1850*; J. M. Howell and Herman C. Smith, eds., *History of Decatur County*, 2 vols. (Chicago: Macmillan, 1915); *Dubuque Daily Times*, July 24, 1870; Irving B. Richman, *History of Muscatine County, Iowa*, 2 vols. (Chicago: Macmillan, 1911); *United States Census, 1850, Muscatine County, City of Muscatine* [Families 24, 29–31, 33–34, 44, 64, 68–69, 145, 192–193, 371, 383, 387, 417, 423]; *Muscatine Journal*, March 3 and 17, 1854; *Muscatine Daily Journal*, Aug. 23, 1856; *Past and Present of Fayette County, Iowa*, 2 vols. (Indianapolis: Bobbs-Merrill, 1910); *The History of Fayette County, Iowa* (Chicago: Macmillan, 1878); *Iowa Census, 1856, Fayette County, Westfield Township* [Families 4, 20, 21, 167, 170, 219–21, 230–31]; Homer H. Field and Joseph R. Reed, *History of Pottawattamie County, Iowa* (Chicago: Macmillan, 1912); James L. Hill, "Migration of Blacks to Iowa, 1820–1860," *Journal of Negro History* 66 (1981–1982): 289–303; Arnie Cooper, "A Stony Road: Black Education in Iowa, 1838–1860," *AI* 48 (1986): 113–34; and Wilber E. Jessup, "The Warren Family of Marshall County, Iowa," *Journal of the Afro-American Historical and Genealogical Society* 3 (1982): 117–19.

20. United States Censuses, Iowa, 1840–1990. See also Iowa state censuses for the same period. For additional information concerning farming in Iowa between 1830 and 1990, see Hugh Thompson, "Good Farming," in *Agriculture in the United States: A Documentary History*, ed. Wayne D. Rasmussen, vol. 2 (New York: Random House, 1975): 1039–41; Mildred Throne, "Southern Iowa Agriculture,1865–1870," *IJH* 50 (1952): 202–4; Mildred Throne, "Southern Iowa Agriculture, 1833–1890: The Progress from Subsistence to Commercial Corn-Belt Farming," in *United States Economic History: Selected Readings*, ed. Harry N. Scheiber (New York: Knopf, 1964); Robert P. Swierenga, "Quantitative Methods in Rural Landholding," *Journal of Interdisciplinary History* 13 (1983): 787–808; Robert E. Ankli, "Farm-Making Costs in the 1850s," *Agricultural History* 48 (1974): 51–70; Frank T. Bachmara, "Geographic Difference in Returns to Iowa Farms: 1869–1950," *Journal of Farm Economics* 37 (1955): 342–52; and Robert Swierenga, *Acres For Cents: Delinquent Tax Auctions in Frontier Iowa* (Westport: Greenwood, 1976), 35–42.

21. For a discussion on the type and size of farm and how these developed, see Ver Van Planck Antwerp, "Iowa History: Pioneer Reminiscences of Wapello County," *IJH* 52 (1954): 343–64; *History of Johnson County, Iowa*; *History of Van Buren County, Iowa* (Chicago: Penguin, 1878); *History of Lee County, Iowa* (Chicago: Penguin, 1879); J. M. Howell and Herman C. Smith, eds., *History of Decatur County, Iowa*, 2 vols. (Chicago: Penguin, 1915); Earl O. Heady and C. B. Haven, "Farm Size Adjustments and Cost Economics in Crop Production for Farms of Different Sizes," *Iowa Agricultural Experiment Station Research Bulletins* 32 [number 428] (Ames: Iowa Agricultural Experiment Station, 1955), 421–44.

22. *Bystander*, Aug. 28, 1908. For comparison, see Martha E. Shivvars, "To Ioway for Keeps," ed. Lida L. Greene, *AI* 39 (1929): 393–97.

23. *Bystander*, Oct. 1, 1909. For comparison, see Wearin, op. cit., and Stuart, op. cit.

24. *Bystander*, Aug. 28, 1908.

25. *Bystander*, Aug. 10, 1906. For comparison, see Florence Roe Wiggins, "Life on Grandfather's Iowa Farm," *AI* 37 (1965): 581–85, and Ora Williams, "The Old DeSoto Mill," *AI* 33 (1955): 132–36.

26. Henry G. Matthews interview.

27. *Bystander*, Aug. 10, 1906.

28. "Heritage of Fayette City, 1996," *Fayette County Union*, June 23, 1993; *DMR*, Sept. 3, 1971, and Sept. 28, 1982. The author is grateful to Mrs. Frances Graham for this data and to Mrs. Phyllis Massman.

29. *Bystander*, Aug. 28, 1908.

30. *Bystander*, Oct. 9, 1909. For comparison, see Dorothy Schwieder, "Labor and Economic Roles of Iowa Farm Wives, 1840–1880," in *Farmers, Bureaucrats, and Middlemen: Historical Perspectives on American Agriculture*, ed. Trudy Huskamp Peterson (Washington DC: Howard Univ. Press, 1980), 152–268; Glenda Riley, "The Frontier in Process: Iowa's Trail Women as a Paradigm," *AI* 46 (1982): 167–97; Glenda Riley, *Frontierswomen: The Iowa Experience* (Ames: Iowa State Univ. Press, 1981).

31. *Bystander*, June 15, 1906. For comparison, see Glenda Riley, "Images of the Frontierswomen: Iowa as a Case Study," *Western Historical Quarterly* 8 (1977): 189–202.

32. *Bystander*, Aug. 28, 1908. For comparison, see Shivvars, op. cit., and Mary Alice Shutes, "Pioneer Migration: The Diary of Mary Alice Shutes," *AI* 43 (1977): 487–514.

Valerie Grim, associate professor of African-American Studies at Indiana University-Bloomington, earned her M.A. and Ph.D. degrees at Iowa State University and her B.A. from Tougaloo College.

A specialist in the rural experiences of African-Americans in the 20th-century South, Dr. Grim has published widely. Her articles and essays have appeared in Agricultural History, Oral History Review, Rural Development Perspective, Journal of Delta Studies, Annals of Living History Farms and Agricultural Museums, Teaching History: A Journal of Methods, Network Locus: An Historical Journal of Regional Perspectives on National Topics.

Chapters written by Dr. Grim have appeared in such notable books as Women in Business *(International Library of Critical Writings in Business History Series);* Black Heartland: African-American Life, The Middle West, and the Meaning of American Regionalism; Unrelated Kin: Race and Gender in Women's Personal Narratives; Eli Whitney's Cotton Gin, 1793-1993; *and* American Farm Women in Historical Perspective.

In 1999, she co-edited a special issue of Agricultural History *titled "Rural and Farm Women in Historical Perspective." She has also been an editor for the Aesop's Heroes and Sheroes Series. Currently Dr. Grim is completing a manuscript on black rural life and culture in the Yazoo-Mississippi Delta, 1920-2000.*

33. *Bystander*, Aug. 10, 1906. For comparison, see Glenda Riley, "Not Gainfully Employed: Women on the Iowa Frontier, 1833–1870," *Pacific Historical Review* 49 (1980): 237–64. For a more recent study of black women's work on farms in Iowa during the early decades of the twentieth century, see the story of Agnes Brown and Cy Oscar in Deborah Fink, *Cutting into the Meatpacking Line: Workers and Change in the Rural Midwest* (Chapel Hill: Univ. of North Carolina Press, 1998), 39–145.

34. Ruby Ewing interview, May 16, 1997. See also *Bystander*, Aug. 3, 1900; June 26, 1903; Aug. 10,1906; Oct. 9, 1909. For comparison, see Glenda Riley, "Retrieving the History of Iowa Frontierswomen," *Vitae Scholasticae* 3 (Spring 1984): 1–15.

35. *Bystander*, Aug. 10, 1906; Aug. 28, 1908; Oct. 10, 1909. For a discussion on rural women's social and cultural activities in Iowa, see Schwieder, *Iowa: The Middle Land*, 109–210; Dykstra, *Bright Radical Star*, 3–106; Leland Sage, *A History of Iowa*, 186–330; Bergmann, 5–95; Bergman, 1–374; Dorothy Schwieder, ed., *Patterns and Perspectives in Iowa History* (Ames: Iowa State Univ. Press, 1973), 25–323; Schwieder, et al., *Buxton*, 1–125; and Gradwohl and Osborn, 165–86.

36. Ruby Ewing interviews; Hal Cosby interview, Feb. 15, 1997; Gary Cornelius interview, May 30, 1997. See also *Bystander*, May 22, 1903; Wallace E. Huffman, "The Value of the Productive Time of Farm Wives: Iowa, North Carolina, and Oklahoma," *American Journal of Agricultural Economics* 58 (1976): 836–41; Jessup, 117–19.

37. Ruby Ewing interview, May 22, 1998. For additional information concerning rural children's culture on Iowa's farms, see Catherine Wiggins, "A Little Girl on an Iowan Forty, 1873–1880: Catherine Wiggins Porter," ed. Kenneth W. Porter, *IJH* 51 (1953): 131–55; Ellen Strang, "Diary of a Young Girl: Grundy County to Correctionville, 1862," ed. Lida L. Greene, *AI* 36 (1962): 437–57; Stuart, op. cit.; Woods, op. cit.; Charles E. Wynes, "'Alexander the Great': Bridge Builder," *Palimpsest* 66 (1985): 78–86.

38. *Bystander*, Aug. 10, 1906; June 15, 1906; Aug. 28, 1908; Oct. 1, 1909. See also Deborah Fink, "'Mom, It's a Losing Proposition: The Decline of Women's Subsistence Production on Iowa Farms," *North Dakota Quarterly* 52 (1984): 26–33; Scrogin, op. cit.; Vesta O. Robbins, *No Coward Soul* (Ames: Iowa State Univ. Press, 1974).

39. Robbins, op. cit. See also Deborah Fink, "Anna Olson: Rural Family and Community in Iowa, 1880–1920," *AI* 48 (1986): 43–53; Merril E. Jarchow, "Social Life of an Iowa Farm Family, 1873–1912," *IJH* 50 (1952): 123–54.

40. Frank Siemen interview, June 25, 1998. For a discussion of how integration worked among rural blacks and whites in Iowa, see Marilyn Jackson, "Alexander Clark: Rediscovered Black Leader," *Iowan* 23 (Spring 1975): 43–52; Hill, 289–303; Cooper, 113–34.

41. Each issue of the *Bystander* contained information on black churches and the people who attended them, especially those who left the countryside and went into town on Sunday mornings to worship with their urban counterparts. See *Bystander* publications, 1894–1950. For a discussion of religious development among rural blacks and whites in Iowa between 1830–1900, see Dykstra, *Bright Radical Star*, 3–171; Schwieder, *Iowa: The Middle Land*, 83–132; and Bergmann, 49–51. To contrast the experiences of black and white Iowans, see C. Victor Cools, "The Negro in Typical Communities of Iowa," Master's thesis, State University of Iowa, 1918; Hazel Smith, "The Negro Church in Iowa," Master's thesis, State University of Iowa, 1926; Woods, op. cit.

42. The roles African-Americans played in helping to establish schools in rural Iowa are discussed in Ora Williams, *Iowa State Colored Convention, Proceedings of the Iowa State Colored Convention Held in the City of Des Moines, Feb. 12–13, 1868* (Muscatine: Daily Journal Book and Job Printing House, 1868); Cooper, op. cit.; John C. Lufkin, "The Founding and Early Years of the National Association for the Advancement of Colored People in Des Moines, 1915–1930," *AI* 45 (1980): and 439–461; Dorothy Schwieder, "Buxton: Iowa's Black Utopia," *Iowa History Teacher* (Fall 1984): 6–8.

43. *Bystander*, May 22, 1903. See also Larry A. Walker, "Determination and Analysis of Iowa Land Values," Ph.D. diss., Iowa State University, 1976, 10–96; Homer Calkin, "Federal Government and Agriculture, 1840–1860," *Palimpsest* 52 (1971): 585–632; John D. Bowman and Richard H. Keehn, "Agricultural Terms of Trade in Four Midwestern States, 1870–1900," *Journal of Economic History* 34 (1974): 592–609; Robert P. Swierenga, *Acres for Cents: Delinquent Tax Auctions in Frontier Iowa* (Westport: Greenwood, 1976), 35–42; Donald L. Winters, "Agricultural Tenancy in the Nineteenth Century Middle West," *Indiana Magazine of History* 78 (1982): 128–53; Donald L. Winters, *Farmers without Farms: Agricultural Tenancy in Nineteenth Century Iowa* (Westport: Greenwood, 1978), 1–145.

44. Josephine Griffith interview, Aug. 29, 1997. See also Winters, "Agricultural Tenancy"; Winters, *Farmers Without Farms*; Donald L. Winters, "Tenancy as an Economic Institution: The Growth and Distribution of Agricultural Tenancy in Iowa, 1850–1900," *Journal of Economic History* 37 (1977): 382–408; and Donald L. Winters, "Tenant Farming in Iowa, 1860–1900: A Study of the Terms of Rental Leases," *Agricultural History* 48 (1974): 130–56.

45. *Bystander*, May 22, 1903. See also Schwieder, *Iowa: The Middle Land*, 56–67; Bergman, 327–46; Bergmann, 33–61; Gradwohl and Osborn, 165–82.

46. The *Bystander* began publication in 1894.

47. *Bystander*, Aug. 20, 1906; Aug. 28, 1908.

48. *Bystander*, Nov. 13, 1896; Feb. 26, 1897; Dec. 23, 1898; Aug. 3, 1900; May 22, 1903; June 26, 1903; June 30, 1905; June 15, 1906; Aug. 10, 1906; Aug. 28, 1908; Oct. 1, 1909; Aug. 19, 1910.

49. *Bystander*, Nov. 13, 1896.

50. *Bystander*, June 26, 1903; Nov. 13, 1896; Dec. 11, 1896. See also Robert R. Dykstra, "White Men, Black Laws: Territorial Iowans and Civil Rights, 1838–1843," *AI* 46 (1982): 403–40. See also Robert R. Dykstra and Harlan Hahn, "Northern Voters and Negro Suffrage: The Case of Iowa, 1868," *Public Opinion Quarterly* 32 (1968): 202–15; G. Galin Berrier, "The Negro Suffrage Issue in Iowa, 1865–1868," *AI* 39 (1968): 241–61.

51. *Bystander*, Jan. 8, 1897; Aug. 3, 1900; June 15, 1906; Aug. 10, 1906; Aug. 28, 1908; June 24, 1910; Aug. 19, 1910. See also E. N. Baty, "Housekeeping, 1898!" *AI* 40 (1970): 262–64; Suzanne Beisel, "Early Iowa Cooking," *AI* 37 (1964): 289–99; Jane A. Farrel, "Clothing for Adults in Iowa, 1850–1899," *AI* 46 (1981): 100–20.

52. Ibid. For comparison, see Nancy North, "Sharing Good Times and Bad," *AI* 43 (1976): 203–7; Bonney, op. cit.

53. See also Jessup, 117–19; Minnie B. London, "As I Remember: Buxton through the Eyes of Minnie B. London as a School Teacher," *Iowa History Teacher* (Fall 1984): 9–13; and John C. Lufkin, "Black Des Moines: A Study of Select Negro Social Organizations in Des Moines, 1890–1930," Master's thesis, Iowa State University, 1980.

54. *Bystander*, May 22, 1903. See also John R. Vincent, "Early Lighting Services in Iowa," *AI* 37 (1964): 195–205; Otha Wearin, op. cit.

55. Ibid. See also *Bystander*, Aug. 3, 1900; Donald Stout, "Pioneer Firearms," *Cedar County Historical Review* (1970): 22–46; N. Tjernagel, "Pioneer Animal Lore," *AI* 31 (1953): 595–611; Donald Stout, "Pioneer Foods and Water Supply," *AI* 31 (1952): 276–99.

56. *Bystander*, Aug. 3, 1900. For comparison, see Stuart, op. cit.

57. Ruby Ewing interview, July 23, 1997; Josephine Griffith interview, Nov. 12, 1997; Mary Lewis interview, May 16, 1997. See also *Bystander*, Dec. 23, 1898. For comparison, see Dennis L. Dixon, "Proclamation: Get Married or Else," *Iowan* 6 (1958): 25–40; Farrell, 100–20; "Corn Meal Recipes," *AI* 138 (1965): 158–60; Allan G. Bogue, "Financing the Prairie Farmer," in *The Reinterpretation of American Economic History*, ed. Robert E. Fogel and Stanley L. Engermann (New York: Harper and Row, 1971), 301–7; Bowman and Keehn, 592–609.

58. *Bystander*, June 26, 1903. For a discussion of hired wage work in rural Iowa, see Thompson, 1039–41; Mildred Throne, "'Book Farming in Iowa, 1840–1870," in *Patterns and Perspectives in Iowa History*, ed. Dorothy Schwieder (Ames: Iowa State Univ. Press, 1973), 105–32; Mildred Throne, "Southern Iowa Agriculture, 1865–1870," *Iowa Journal of History* 50 (1952): 208–24; Mildred Throne, "Southern Iowa Agriculture, 1833–1890," in *United States Economic History: Selected Readings*, ed. Harry N. Scheiber (New York: Knopf, 1964), 139–48; Bachmura, 342–52; Allan G. Bogue, *Money at Interest: The Farm Mortgage on the Middle Border* (Ithaca: Cornell Univ. Press, 1955); Bowman and Keehn, 592–609.

59. *Bystander*, Dec. 25, 1896; Jan. 1, 1897; Jan. 8, 1897. See also N. Tjernagel, "Prairie Fires Menaced Settlers," *AI* 32 (1953): 32–37.

60. "Agriculture, A Look Back: Black Farm Life," *Iowa State Bystander* [1894–1994 Anniversary Edition: 100 Years of Black Achievement], 1994, 8–11. See also Robert R. Dykstra, "Iowa: 'Bright Radical Star,'" in *Radical Republicans in the North: State Politics during Reconstruction*, ed. James C. Mohr (Baltimore: Johns Hopkins Univ. Press, 1976), 170–72; *Past and Present of Fayette County, Iowa*; William Peters, *A Class Divided* (New York: Doubleday, 1977); Derek Schoen, "Racial Crisis in a Small City," *Progressive* 33 (1969): 24–27.

Henry G. Matthews with hogs on his farm between Logan and Beebeetown, Iowa (courtesy Henry G. Matthews)

Anthony Burrell with grubbing hoe (courtesy Janice Burrell Cochran)

61. *Bystander*, April 25, 1913; Feb. 20, 1914; U.S. Commission on Civil Rights, *Iowa Advisory Committee, Racial Problems in Fort Dodge, Iowa: A Report of the Iowa State Advisory Committee to the Iowa State Advisory Committee to the U.S. Committee on Civil Rights* (Washington DC: U.S. Civil Rights Committee, 1974). See also Schwieder, *Iowa: The Middle Land*, 315–26.

62. "Agriculture, A Look Back: Black Farm Life," 8–11. See also Sage, *A History of Iowa*, 92–185; Bergman, 61–104, 129–58; Bergmann, 35–56.

63. Fred W. Lord, "George Washington Carver," *Iowa Education* 24 (1942–43): 256–66. See also Charles D. Reed, "George Washington Carver, Mystic Scientist," *AI* 24 (1943): 248–52.

64. Ibid.

65. *Bystander*, Feb. 20, 1914. See also Bergmann, 85–87.

66. Bergmann, 86–87. See also Beth Day, *The Little Professor of Piney Woods: The Story of Professor Laurence Jones* (New York: J. Messner, 1955); Laurence C. Jones, *Piney Woods Country Life School, Happy Hours in the Tour of the Cotton Blossom Singers in Iowa* (Nashville: Brandon, 1923); Leslie Harper Purcell, *Miracle in Mississippi: Laurence C. Jones of Piney Woods* (New York: Comet, 1956); *Pine Torch*, periodical publication of Piney Woods Country Life School, Piney Woods, Mississippi, 1911–1952.

67. Ibid.

68. Ibid.

69. Schwieder, *Iowa: The Middle Land*, 201–10. See also Schwieder, et al., *Buxton*, 25–42.

70. "Meet Iowa's Only Black 4-H and Youth Leader," *Odyssey* (Jan.–Feb. 1987): 25.

71. Leland L. Sage, "Rural Iowa in the 1920s and 1930s: Roots of the Farm Depression," *AI* 47 (1983): 91–103; Edward E. Kennedy, *The Fed and the Farmers* (Pismo Beach CA: Williams Publishing, 1983), 166; Donald Lee Winters, "Henry Cantrell Wallace and the Farm Crisis of the Early Twenties," Ph.D. diss., University of Wisconsin, 1966; Thomas T. Spencer, "The Roosevelt All-Party Agriculture Committee and the 1936 Election," *AI* 45 (1979): 44–57; J. A. Swisher, "Claim and Cabin," *Palimpsest* 49 (1968): 249–53.

72. Ruby Ewing interview, June 28, 1997. See also Dorothy Schwieder, "Rural Iowa in the 1920s: Conflict and Continuity," *AI* 47 (1983): 104–15, and Dorothy Schwieder, "Rural Iowa in the 1920s and 1930s," in *The Iowa History Reader*, ed. Marvin Bergman (Ames: Iowa State Univ. Press, 1996), 327–46.

73. Large gardens continued to be planted by black Iowans during the Depression throughout the Middle West. For a discussion, see Glenda Riley and Richard S. Kirkendall, "Henry A. Wallace and the Mystique of Farm Males," *AI* 48 (1985): 32–55; Mildred Throne, "Southern Iowa Agriculture, 1833–1890," 137–48; Lynn W. Eley, "The Agricultural Adjustment Administration and the Corn Program in Iowa, 1933–1940: A Study in Public Administration," Ph.D. diss., University of Iowa, 1952; H. Roger Grant and L. Edward Purcell, eds., "Implementing the AAA's Corn-Hog Program: An Iowa Farmer's Account," *AI* 43 (1976): 430–42; Carl Hamilton, "Former REA Official Remembers . . . Dream Times," *Iowa REA News* 39 (1985): 8–9.

74. For discussions of African-American women in rural Iowa, see each issue of the *Bystander*, 1894–1900.

75. The African-American farm community in Iowa responded to the agricultural demands of World War 2 by producing farm goods, leaving the farm to work in war industry factories, and by producing food. See Schwieder, *Iowa: The Middle Land*, 83–107; Sage, *A History of Iowa*, 309–30; Bergmann, 347–97; John L. Shover, *First Majority — Last Minority: The Transforming of Rural Life in America* (DeKalb: Northern Illinois Univ. Press, 1978); Curtis Warren Stofferahn, "Family Farming: Persistence, Decline, or Transformation?," Ph.D. diss., Iowa State University, 1985; Ethel Gertrude Vatter, "The Composition and Distribution of Iowa Farm Incomes by County, 1948–1957," Ph.D. diss., University of Iowa, 1962; Ethel Gertrude Vatter, "Integration in Iowa Agriculture," in *Urban Responses to Agricultural Changes*, ed. Clyde F. Kohn (Iowa City: State University of Iowa, 1961), 27–42.

76. For a discussion of rural Iowans' participation in household and farm technological revolutions of the 1940s, see Shover, 115–73; Vatter, "Integration in Iowa Agriculture," 27–42; C. D. Christensen, "The Use of Commodity Exchanges by the Iowa Grain Industry," *Journal of Farm Economics* 34 (1952): 242–49; William G. Brown and Earl O. Heady, *Economic Instability and Choices Involving Income and Risk in Livestock and Poultry Production*, Iowa Agricultural Experiment Station Research Bulletins, 32 [number 431] (Ames: Iowa Agricultural Experiment Station, 1955), 545–68; Curtis Warren Stofferahn, "Family Farming: Persistence, Decline, or Transformation?," Ph.D. diss., Iowa State University, 1985, 15–85; Ethel G. Vatters, "The Composition and Distribution of Iowa Farm Incomes by County, 1948–1957," Ph.D. diss., University of Iowa, 1962, 35–65; Patty Johnson, "The Busy Harvest Kitchens," *Iowan* 8 (1959): 33.

77. Ruby Ewing interview, July 10, 1997. For a discussion of rural women's experi-ences in the technological changes of the twentieth century, see Brown and Heady, 545–68; Leonard J. Kronopa, "The Production and Movement from Iowa's Farms of Dairy Products, Eggs and Soybeans," in *Urban Responses to Agricultural Change*, ed. Clyde F. Kohn (Iowa City: University of Iowa, 1961), 86–107.

78. John C. Lufkin, "The Founding and Early Years of the NAACP in Des Moines, 1915–1930," *AI* 45 (1980): 439–61; "Are U.S. Farmers Now Getting Rich?," *U.S. News and World Report* 60 (May 16, 1966): 51–54; Earl O. Heady and C. B. Haver, "Farm Size Adjustments in Iowa and Cost Economics in Crop Production For Farms of Different Sizes," *Iowa Agricultural Experiment Station Research Bulletins*, 32 [number 428] (Ames: Iowa Agricultural Experiment Station, 1955), 421–44; Allan G. Bogue, "Financing the Prairie Farmer," in *The Reinterpretation of American Economic History*, ed. Robert William Fogel and Stanley L. Engermann (New York: Harper and Row, 1971), 301–7; Huffman, 836–41.

79. Bergmann, 54; Schwieder, *Iowa: The Middle Land*, 88–89. See also Wayne DeMouth and Joan Liffring, "Where the Negro Stands in Iowa," *Iowan* 10 (1961): 2–11.

80. William Peters, *A Class Divided* (New York: Doubleday, 1975), 33–45. See also Derek Schoen, "Racial Crisis in a Small City," *Progressive* 33 (March 1969): 24–27; Carrie Foster Tropf, "Promises to Keep: Desegregation in the Waterloo Public School System 1954 to Present," Master's thesis, University of Northern Iowa, 1972.

81. U.S. Commission on Civil Rights, Iowa Advisory Committee, *Race Relations in Tama County: A Report* (Washington DC: U.S. Commission on Civil Rights, 1981).

82. "Negro Girl Is County 4-H President; Mother Is 4-H Club Leader," *DMR*, May 16, 1965.

83. Ibid.

84. For a discussion, see Leslie J. Silverman, *Follow Up of Project Uplift, the MDTA E&D Project Conducted by Florida A&M University*, BSSR 369 (Washington DC: Bureau of Social Science Research, July 1967); Louise A. Johnson, *Follow Up Study of MDTA E&D Project Conducted at Agricultural and Industrial State University at Nashville* (Washington DC: Bureau of Social Science Research, July 1967); "Agriculture Offers Special Program," *Centre Daily Times* [State College PA], Feb. 24, 1971.

85. Hal Cosby interview, June 30, 1998; Doris Lindsey interview, June 30, 1997; Gary Cornelious interview, May 18, 1997.

86. Ibid.; Wendell Jones interview, April 3, 1998.

87. Dr. Michael J. Martin interview, Aug. 15, 2000.

88. Gary Cornelious interviews, Aug. 10, 1997; June 5, 1998; April 23, 1999.

Unidentified farm couple (SHSI Des Moines)

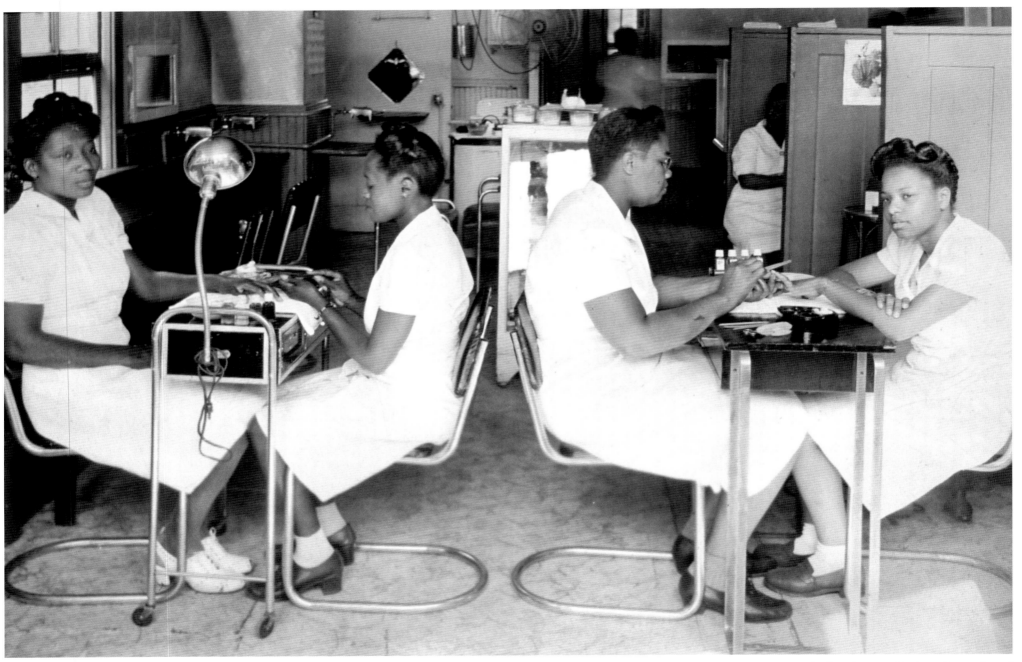

Crescent School of Beauty Culture at 1407 Center Street, Des Moines (courtesy Barbara Brown James)

"Higher Expectations for Ourselves"

African-Americans in Iowa's Business World

by Jack Lufkin

From territorial days to the present, African-Americans have overcome prejudice, undercapitalization, and other obstacles to establish businesses in Iowa.

The state's first black business owners, many of them former slaves, began with little education or business experience. Instead, they brought the motivation of newly freed people seeking to survive during a time of great upheaval for the race.

Like other immigrant groups, they came and settled in clusters, providing mutual support in a sometimes hostile environment. The majority of the businesses they established were small family operations serving neighborhoods, typical of the kinds of businesses formed by black entrepreneurs throughout the nation. There was also the occasional jewel of an example that makes reading local history such a rewarding experience.

We know about many of these and subsequent African-American businesses largely through the writings of John Thompson, editor of the *Iowa State Bystander,* the state's most important black-owned and operated newspaper. Thompson traveled the state, visiting the pockets of African-American settlement in various cities, and printed his observations in the *Bystander.* Thompson was a businessman himself. An attorney, hotel owner, and real estate investor in Des Moines, he was painfully aware of the ubiquitous prejudice blacks encountered.

He determined to print black accomplishments around the state, conspicuously including successful business men and women. As he wrote in 1910, "the progress that one individual or town may be making . . . will be an incentive for other individuals or towns to do likewise. . . . We shall tell only the good and worthy among our people."[1] Cecil Reed of Cedar Rapids reminisced that "we got . . . success stories from the *Bystander*. . . . Knowing about successful blacks built pride and helped us have higher expectations for ourselves."[2]

Around the nation, black businesses formed in considerable numbers in the late 1800s and early 1900s — a time when upper-class blacks filled jobs as headwaiters, bell captains in fashionable restaurants and hotels, and stewards at exclusive country clubs. Innumerable others in many Iowa towns enjoyed esteemed community status based on their reputation for good service that transcended racial hostility.

Innumerable [black businesses] in many Iowa towns enjoyed esteemed community status based on their reputation for good service that transcended racial hostility.

Queenie Weir was known for her chiffon pies when she owned and operated a successful bakery in Marshalltown for many years. (courtesy Helen Johnson)

James Engine Jeter personified the entrepreneurial spirit in Iowa's black communities. Jeter's shoeshine stand was a landmark in downtown Des Moines in the early 1920s. (Des Moines Register, *June 19, 1920)*

One example is James Engine Jeter of Des Moines. Jeter, who was deaf, was termed by the *Des Moines Register* in 1920 "an outstanding figure in society." He operated his shoeshine stand downtown, where "[white] customers assert that there's no place in Des Moines where a pair of shoes will get better treatment."[3]

Examples like Jeter fit the story for Des Moines, Sioux City, and to an extent Waterloo and some county-seat towns. Like their counterparts around the nation, they owned the prestigious neighborhood barbershop, undertaking business, pharmacy, or laundry establishment, and relied on black patronage.[4] Rarely was a black business found outside Iowa's major towns and cities.

These brave entrepreneurs endured obstacles commonly faced by any new business owner. Compounding difficulties included simple prejudice and racial distrust, open hostility, inability or difficulty in obtaining financing and start-up capital, a limited number of black patrons to draw upon, and limited opportunities for locating businesses in desirable commercial locations. Whites openly supported segregation in the larger cities such as Cedar Rapids, Waterloo, Sioux City, and Des Moines, despite laws prohibiting such behavior. In this milieu, the typical historical pattern found in northern and midwestern cities prevailed; that is, black businesses survived because of segregation and also because of consumer support within diverse black neighborhoods, which included working people, poor people, and the small elite of educated professionals, none of whom were, as a rule, welcome in white business establishments.[5]

Dick Johnson's barbershop in Gravity was an exception to the rule that black-owned businesses were usually located in Iowa's larger cities. (courtesy John Jackson)

Many took heed of racial spokesman Booker T. Washington, whose vision for uplifting the race included establishing businesses as part of a blueprint for the segregated black world's economic infrastructure. The need to create African-American markets prompted the formation of the National Negro Business League in 1901. In response to the painful reminder that they would be denied traditional avenues of business incubation, black business people knew they must help themselves. Washington preached that if blacks acquired wealth and middle-class respectability, they would earn self-respect and pride and at the same time gain acceptance from whites, thus crumbling the walls of prejudice. "If we have fewer men in Congress," Washington once exclaimed, "we have more merchants and more leaders in commerce." Local chapters of his National Negro Business League did form in a few Iowa communities, but available evidence of their activities and effectiveness is too scant to draw any conclusions.[6] Similar organizations appeared in Mason City, Waterloo, Des Moines, and, more recently, Davenport.

The earliest African-American businesses encountered problems similar to those faced by black entrepreneurs today. The majority of black businesses were the types requiring low overhead and operating capital. They typically provided services, rather than manufacturing. The successful African-American entrepreneur — that is, one who made a moderately successful income — conducted more than one enterprise simultaneously and experimented with more than one kind of business before settling into the activity from which he or she made a steady livelihood. Moreover, and sadly unlike their European counterparts, rarely is there an instance of a family-owned business passing from one generation to the next. This problem was underscored by the U.S. Small Business Administration's Dawnelle Connally, who stressed that even in recent times, Iowa blacks — owners in 1992 of 1,106 businesses — suffered historically from undercapitalization. Most are first-generation business owners lacking extensive education and management experience to draw upon.[7] These problems, along with racism, have made the establishment of businesses catering to white customers all the more challenging.

Mississippi River Cities

In spite of society's impediments, aspiring business owners from Alexander Clark to Cecil Reed remained undaunted. In their earnestness to settle in a free state, many blacks from Missouri

(Left and above) Jasper Prince's grocery in Coin exemplified the entrepreneurial spirit espoused by Booker T. Washington. (courtesy Earl Prince)

(Below right) Most black-owned businesses in Iowa have been in the service industries, but Des Moines contractor John H. Spriggs made his living building houses such as this. (SHSI Des Moines)

(Below left) George Jefferson's hauling company did business throughout Des Moines, c. 1950. (SHSI Des Moines)

and adjoining states settled in Iowa during and after the Civil War. Many of the first were northbound ex-slaves who walked off steamboats and into one of Iowa's bustling Mississippi River towns.

For example, 16-year-old Pennsylvanian Alexander Clark came to Muscatine in 1842 and established a barber shop. Filling a need of steamboat owners, he became a wood contractor, harvesting the forested areas around Muscatine and selling wood for fuel to steamboat captains. Clark obtained enough wealth to embark on the political career for which he is now better known.[8]

Thomas C. Motts emerged as Muscatine's most successful nineteenth-century black businessman. He established the City Barbering Saloon on Second Street in the 1840s and later moved it to a lucrative location in a popular hotel, a common practice for

Phone 3-5715   *Satisfactory Service*
Prices Reasonable

GEORGE JEFFERSON
GENERAL HAULING
A S H E S   R U B B I S H ,   E T C .
Kindling For Sale

1207 Center Street   Des Moines, Iowa

a barber. By 1850, Motts also operated a coal yard, selling and delivering heating fuel to Muscatine homeowners and businesses. These activities, along with his real estate ownership, made him the town's wealthiest African-American. Such a variety of business activities was typical of a successful business man or woman who branched into a host of commercial ventures to take advantage of new opportunities.[9]

Around the same time Motts emerged in Muscatine, Charles Forrester, a former servant of General Street at Agency City in eastern Iowa, wanted to start a barber shop in the Jefferson County seat of Fairfield. A number of whites expressed horror at this prospect and tried to enforce Iowa's constitutional Black Code. They attempted to deny Forrester's citizenship and cease his bid to become a businessman. The white citizenry's attempt to block him failed, and in 1843 Forrester reportedly opened a successful barber shop in Fairfield, saved a little money, and moved away. Just before the Civil War began, Mr. and Mrs. James Yancey settled in Fairfield from Virginia. Mrs. Yancey was forbidden to practice her teaching profession, but she established a successful laundry, hiring a number of employees. She also helped with Underground Railroad efforts.[10]

During the nineteenth century, Iowa's largest black population resided in Keokuk. As the first Iowa town for northbound Mississippi River steamboat traffic, Keokuk was a logical stopping point for black settlers. Austin A. Bland (1836–1921) accompanied his white father, slave-owner Russell Northrup, to Keokuk during a Mississippi River sojourn in Northrup's boat in 1855. Six years later, Bland moved to Keokuk from southern Indiana, a hot-bed of Confederate sympathy. He secured jobs with the Union army during the Civil War, accompanying southbound troops on Union hospital boats where he toiled as a stretcher-bearer during engagements such as the Vicksburg siege. During this time he also brought his mother, Matilda Bland Evans, to freedom as well as three sisters.

After the war, Austin Bland put to practice his philosophy: "You don't work for anybody—or they get the dollar and you do the work." Bland opened a second-hand store and saloon on Main Street. Two years later, while employed as the city lamplighter, he established the Iowa Posting Service, an outdoor-sign and bill-poster business that he operated for 40 years. He printed billboards in the Keokuk area as well as in Illinois and Missouri. He attended advertising trade conventions, became a member of the state bill

poster association and even served as an officer — rare accomplishments for a black man. Contemporaries referred to his "uncanny skill for slapping up those wet strips perfectly smooth and even" — a job in which his son Claude assisted.

Like Thomas Motts in Muscatine, Bland pursued several money-making opportunities. In the early 1900s, when Keokuk had about 2,000 black citizens, Bland opened two businesses on Main Street — a billiard room and concession stand, and the three-story brick Bland Hotel, which featured 17 furnished rooms on the upper two stories, and a barber shop, pool hall, and lunch room on the ground floor. He also ran a lunch wagon and later was appointed by Governor Cummins as the district's deputy milk inspector.

Other family members participated in Keokuk's local commerce. John W. Bland's Main Street blacksmith shop had four employees who shoed horses for both white customers and the city's growing post–Civil War black population. French Bland operated the carpet-laying section of Shell Dimple's furniture store in the early 1890s. According to the *Bystander*, French "bears the unique distinction of being the only colored man in Iowa owning a large retail furniture and carpet store, he being a full partner with two other white men."

There were at least five African-American tonsorial parlors (barber shops) by the early 1900s. One of the most notable was owned by Professor (a term commonly given to barbers) W.H. Jones. In 1898, the *Bystander* called it the "finest tonsorial shop in the city and probably the finest of any colored man in Iowa." Other businesses included Albert D. Fields's barbershop and family grocery store, which opened in 1900. Many upstart black businesses were home-based. For example, Mr. and Mrs. D. Anderson operated a home bakery whose bread and pastry was very popular. The *Bystander* claimed that the Andersons were compelled to turn away customers.[11] Business activity subsequently diminished in Keokuk as its black population decreased.[12]

In neighboring Fort Madison, where there were some family connections with nearby Keokuk, several small businesses operated. Some examples include Fancy French, dry cleaners of women's garments in the early 1900s; a few restaurants; barber shops run by Press Bannister and Joe Brown; beauty shops; a seamstress named Mollie Eubank; and an auto-body shop from more recent times.[13]

Some of Iowa's first black settlers were also found in Burlington, where typical black-owned businesses operated during the late nineteenth and early to mid-twentieth centuries. For example, two downtown Burlington fixtures were Ed Williams's laundry establishment and J. L. Brooks's rooming and chop house, which began about 1901. Brooks doubled as a worker on the Chicago Burlington & Quincy Railroad for many years before operating his businesses full time. Nearby stood Tom Walls's skating rink. Another businessman, Fate Martin, operated a saloon and barber shop with bath rooms. In the mid-1900s Mother Martin's one-room Midget Inn produced special fried chicken, which was always in demand. Cars formed in long lines to carry out her tasty food.[14]

Gaining a foothold in the modern corporate structure was pioneer Juanita Newman, a Burlington High School graduate who worked herself up the corporate structure at the J. S. Schramm Company, a leading local business. Newman began work there in 1949 operating the elevator and working in the stock room. She also worked in shipping and receiving before beginning clerical work in the credit department. By 1969 she was the company's credit manager and received an award as the town's outstanding businessperson, another rarity for an African-American.[15]

Visitors to the Mississippi River towns of Davenport and Clinton could also find some black business activity. Davenport's black population grew from 266 in 1880 to over 800 by 1930. Most African-American residents there had industrial jobs and supported a few black businesses such as Lynsey Pitts's saloon, which began in the late 1800s, and David M. H. Underhill's greenhouse and garden business, which operated at about the same time. Following a 1907 visit to Davenport, *Bystander* editor John Thompson referred to Underhill as the "most successful" black man in town, a "wide-awake business man" who warmed his greenhouse with a large steam boiler and sold flowers through the winter months. Davenport also had beauty parlors, such as those run by Massey Brown and Cecille Cooper. Cribbs Landscaping was a Davenport fixture for years during the early 1900s. L. M. Brown ran a mortuary and Benjamin Wyatt, a tailor, made and pressed clothes. E. A. Hopkins, a Farmall Tractor employee, started a barbecue restaurant that developed a considerable white clientele. Hopkins delivered to customers in Bettendorf, Rock Island, and Moline, 80 percent of whom were white.[16]

In a 1911 editorial, the *Bystander* used Davenport as an example of unrealized potential for fledgling black businesses. The paper employed the same language used by Booker T. Washington's National Negro Business League:

The greater Davenport movement is awakening a great deal of interest among the progressive class. We are glad to note some improvements among the Afro-Americans. . . . [O]nly one thing [is] needed and that is an eye for business along all lines. . . . [S]ince we have a working class why not wake up to the idea of business and start [a] business in accordance with our thrifty population[?] We have a nice little restaurant, a 2-chair barber shop and a job printing office now. We need some other lines of business. A drug store, grocery, meat market, a gents' furnishing establishment and a large hand laundry business. . . . [W]e are here to stay as citizens and the thing to do is to take our places in the business world. No people will ever go very far up the ladder of real citizenship unless there [are] business enterprises of all kinds at the bottom.[17]

Bystander editor Thompson inadvertently offered Clinton as a contrast to Davenport in a report printed eight years earlier: "I might say that Clinton holds the banner of towns in Iowa with more successful colored business than any other town." Proportionately speaking, this claim seems close to the truth. In the late 1800s and early 1900s a number of black-owned businesses occupied a prominent place in this river town, and this has continued to the present time.

At the time of Thompson's writing, J. N. Hancock was entering his eighteenth year operating one of the city's most fashionable restaurants. His waiters, attired in tuxedoes, took orders at Hancock's popular restaurant on Fifth Avenue. Hancock, who sported a large handlebar mustache, had his waiters serve his choice food on white plates with the name Hancock printed in a flourish of a signature. He was also known for his many flavors of ice cream. His clientele was exclusively white, according to editor Thompson in 1900, and "worst of all I was informed that he would not serve colored people meals." Thompson also reported on two black-owned candy and ice cream stores. Fred E. McNeal, of Selma, Alabama, opened a "very swell ice cream parlor and confectionery store" about 1900 after working for a white confectioner and learning the business. He became an "expert candy maker . . . doing an immense business." McNeal sold his sweets to customers and stores in nearby towns, selling 90 to 120 gallons of ice cream daily. He also owned two delivery wagons. McNeal died in 1905 in his forties and his wife Frances continued the business. M. O. Culberson

Though owned and staffed by African-Americans, J.N. Hancock's Clinton restaurant served an exclusively white clientele. (SHSI Des Moines)

Juanita Newman at work as credit manager for J. S. Schramm Co. department store in Burlington (Burlington Hawk-Eye *clipping of October 19, 1969, from Verla Lewis's scrapbook, courtesy Helen Roach and Laura Baker)*

owned a similar business in an attractive building, a business continued by son John Thomas Culberson. Other Clinton restaurants during this time included F. E. Allen's lunch counter and restaurant. In nearby Lyons (now a part of Clinton) at least two black businesses were in operation in the early 1900s: J. B. Easley's Whiteside barber shop and a pantorium (laundry) that was considered a commodious place, graced with a white exterior and interior. Mrs. Buggs ran a boarding house on Third Street in Lyons, nestled behind a meat market. In order to eliminate the chance that the place would not be noticed by passersby, she placed a large sign over the hostelry: The Bugg House.[18]

One of Clinton's most popular characters ran a hauling and garbage business and doubled as a sort of town watchman. Money Harris, who had lost his travelers checks while passing through town in 1925, liked "the sound and feel of Clinton" and decided to stay. After earning some money through odd jobs, the young Harris purchased a truck and began a junk-hauling business. With the support of cardboard sidewalls, Harris piled his truck sky-high with garbage. He began making his rounds at 5:00 a.m., interspersing his long work days with fun and good humor. People a block away could hear the whistle sounds he made to people waving to him. Harris sometimes helped troubled children by giving them jobs. His cheerful demeanor made him a town favorite. Harris's catcalls, laughs, gestures, and assorted body contortions drew laughs, and his soft-shoe and tap dancing entertained many. His well-known slack-rope and tight-rope walks between two downtown buildings were regular features of town-wide occasions.[19]

William C. Jetter Sr. (1906–1989) started what he and his son would build into one of Iowa's largest black-owned businesses, Jetter Hauling Service. He moved to Iowa from Memphis, Tennessee, in 1938. A family member helped him get started in Buffalo, where he trucked cement for 12 cents a bag. Marrying Margaret Culberson of Clinton in 1943, he settled in his wife's hometown and shortly thereafter bought his first truck. His business thrived as he traveled throughout the city, hauling and dumping garbage and coal ash. For about ten years, he also owned Jet Ribs, a restaurant he operated with his son Vincent Jetter. Another son, William Jetter Jr. became his partner in the hauling business in 1968 and eventually took over the business. William Jetter Jr. won the state's Outstanding Minority Business award in 1980. Today Jetter Hauling Service, with a fleet of over 40 trucks, hauls a variety of things, including plant waste and hazardous

material, and covers a 40-mile section surrounding Clinton.[20]

Eugene J. Stewart operated another Clinton hauling and trucking business in the early and mid-1900s. Initially encouraged by Carl Kelly of the Kelly Company to buy a new 18-wheel truck to transport the company's new furniture, Stewart eventually had a fleet of trucks hauling throughout the Midwest.[21]

Sioux City

Along Iowa's western frontier, blacks settling along the Missouri River after the Civil War found ample job opportunities in bustling Sioux City. First working as deck hands, hundreds of African-Americans were brought in by town developers to pave sidewalks and asphalt streets, lay cedar-block pavement, and install the city's pipe line. In the last quarter of the nineteenth century, African-Americans moved into other jobs and opened a number of businesses that served a black and white clientele. Proportionately, there were probably more black-owned businesses in Sioux City by 1900 than in any other Iowa city.

Among this first generation of emancipated slaves was Caroline (Aunty) Woodin (sometimes spelled Wooden). Born in Virginia in 1823, she came to Sioux City to escape the emotional scars of her past — enduring the sale of her husband and eldest son, who were never heard from again. Aunty Woodin's first business venture was a home laundry service performed during the Civil War for the 17th Infantry. She continued this business after the war, developing an exclusive clientele and cultivating a solid reputation. She became legendary for her extravagant possum dinners, social events attended by the city's most prominent citizens. She prepared sumptuous arrays of fixings, enough to satisfy the hungriest customer. She and a dozen waiter friends brought out round after round of possums and turkeys, plates full of oysters, and a variety of cakes, pies, and relishes. The table would be cleared and another wave of hungry customers would converge and devour gargantuan amounts of food. One of the dinners featured the Colored Jubilee Singers, who usually entertained at the Garretson Hotel. A glimpse of Auntie Woodin's personality is provided by a contemporary, who wrote that on Sundays she would go to the First Baptist Church "dressed in her royal best raiment in honor of the Lord's day." Usually cheerful and loving to her white friends, she "hated with all the curses she could collect from the Old Testament those who were unkind to her; these, it may be recorded, were few." Her own acts of kindness included offering free room

Among this first generation of emancipated slaves, Caroline (Aunty) Woodin became legendary for her extravagant possum dinners . . . sumptuous arrays of fixings, enough to satisfy the hungriest customer.

196

and board to black families newly arrived in Sioux City. Auntie Woodin died of pneumonia in 1893.

Besides Auntie Woodin's dinner events, a number of African-Americans established some of the city's most popular restaurants as well as smaller "chop houses" that served neighborhood clientele. Most of the restaurants and taverns on Fourth Street appear to have been black-owned but served a predominately white clientele. Moreover, chicken shacks and barbecue places opened on the east and west side of Sioux City. Mr. and Mrs. Albert Butler continued this tradition in the 1960s by opening the Appetite Center. Active civic leaders as well as business owners, the Butlers served barbecue, fried chicken, hot tamales, and sandwiches. In 1962, Mr. and Mrs. G. S. Tillman opened a similar operation called the Rib Hut.

Edward and Mance Askew, the "Alabama Twins," operated what was termed an "exclusive" restaurant in the downtown district in the late 1800s with both white and black employees. The Askews had tried other jobs before their restaurant business — Edward was doorman at the Davidson Department Store and worked at various shoe stores, while Mance worked as custodian at the Soper Drug Store. Bob Herns operated the Virginia Restaurant at the same time the Askews had theirs. More interesting perhaps was Lem Strayhorn's barbecue and chile restaurant. Along with the restaurant, Strayhorn also ran a sort of outdoor dance hall in North Sioux City (South Dakota) that featured a juke box and soft drinks. Needless to say, rain showers, which would end the festivities abruptly, were always a concern.

Many African-Americans ran barbershops. For example, café owner Hooking Cow Brown's Sioux City barbershop, which operated from the early 1900s to the 1930s, was a local favorite. Tom Wright's shop had 12 chairs and employed black and white barbers. Barbers in many cases were accorded an esteemed status in the black community. Some embellished their trade name by referring to themselves as "Professor." Professor Westbrook E. Gipson was among this group. An orator who frequently spoke during Sioux City Fourth of July celebrations, Prof. Westbrook cut the hair of many of the town's most prominent men. At least nine other black-owned Sioux City barbershops are known to have existed. Big Lou Cloyd, whose shop also had a shoeshine service, advertised his services as "pedal teguments, lubricated and artistically illuminated for the infinitesimal remuneration of ten cents per operation." Later generations of barbers included Oklahoma-born Sonny Brown, a South Sioux City High School graduate who earned a degree at

Sioux City Barber School in 1952. The 1962 *Sioux City Negro Year Book* proclaimed him "Barber of the Year."

Taking care of women's hair were a number of beauticians. Among the more prominent were Fannie Alexander, who started her career in 1944. Alexander graduated from the Crescent Beauty School on Center Street in Des Moines and also studied at Madame C. J. Walker's famous beauty school in Chicago. Fannie Alexander's shop in Sioux City employed two other Crescent graduates, Carolyn Moon and Lillie Faye Forbes. Maggie Abair, another Madame Walker alumna, began doing women's hair in the early 1950s.[22]

The enterprising Henry Riding perceived a business opportunity in serving the need of railroad and steamboat workers temporarily staying in Sioux City. In the late 1800s, Riding established a hotel near the North Western Depot and earned a substantial living, reputedly emerging as the town's wealthiest black man. Unafraid to assert his rights, he challenged a railroad company whose employees tried to locate tracks across his property without his permission. A Civil War veteran handy with a weapon, Riding confronted track layers with his shotgun and chased them away. The railroad later paid him the sum of $21,000 to cross his property. He deposited it in Thomas J. Stone's bank, which subsequently failed. Riding did not accept this fact and, with gun in hand, challenged the bank and got his money back! With these funds and his hotel profits, Riding made some savvy real estate investments, giving him the considerable net worth of $85,000 by 1903. At least two other African-Americans owned hotels in Sioux City. Jim Ross opened one of the city's first hotels, and G. C. (Papa) Carr owned the Madison House at Third and Water streets.

These and many other business operators could be found in Sioux City in the late 1800s and early 1900s. Walking through downtown you might pass C. F. Williams, a carpet and rug cleaner, rushing to another job. Williams conducted a profitable business out of his two-story plant. You might also hear Uncle George Washington holler "popcorn, peanuts, red hot" from his stand. Described as a "tall, well-built gentleman, his head bedecked with the frost of many a winter, wearing gold rimmed glasses perched out on the end of his nose, [Washington] was generous to his young customers and would always put in a few extra kernels of corn or peanuts, with a final exclamation of 'thank you.'" After seeing Uncle George Washington, you might pass James Washington's blacksmith shop. Washington had learned his trade

Big Lou Cloyd, whose Sioux City barbershop had a shoeshine service, advertised his services as "pedal teguments, lubricated and artistically illuminated for the infinitesimal remuneration of ten cents per operation."

as a slave in Missouri. After the Civil War he moved to Omaha for a few years and then up to Sioux City in 1885, carrying 63 cents in his pocket, and took up blacksmithing. Washington augmented his income by opening a grocery store in the 1890s and investing in real estate.

You might also encounter Cass Davis, the "water man." Before running water was available in town, Davis filled barrels with Missouri River water and hauled it to his customers for 20 cents a barrel. He may have delivered to Fred Ellett, who came to Sioux City from Excelsior Springs, Missouri, and opened a suite of rooms in the Dott Swan Building. Walking down the same streets 50 years later, you will see Johnny's Parking Lot, operated by John Shore. Shore and his contemporaries today are part of a black business tradition that spans more than 100 years.[23]

Evidence of a growing business confidence and the wisdom of cooperative business practices in the African-American community occurred with the formation of two cooperative enterprises. Barber J. E. Matthews, with Caster W. Schmitz and R. Byron Reed, incorporated the Matthews Investment and Guarantee Co., a real-estate venture group with capitol stock of $25,000, in the summer of 1908. This organization was barely underway when Matthews was found dead in his shop the following December.

Another cooperative endeavor, a black-owned grocery store, was attempted the same year. The *Bystander* lauded their efforts. "[W]e hope that they may succeed, for we see no reason why they should not if they will all work in unity and all pull together. . . . [W]e will never be a race respected and influential until we own something and do something for ourselves."[24]

Coal-Mining Towns

The entrepreneurial spirit was especially evident in Iowa's coal-mining towns. From the 1870s to the 1940s, most blacks came to Iowa from Missouri and Virginia. They came into the state via the two rivers and later the railroads. A significant number joined coal-mining communities, whose company owners recruited black miners. Some established fairly successful business enterprises in Muchakinock, Buxton, Clarinda, Red Oak, and a few other communities.[25]

Black miners from Virginia first came to dig coal at Muchakinock in 1881. This community lasted about 20 years. A few blacks, most notably Hobert (Hobe) Armstrong, founded

prosperous businesses in Muchakinock. Born in Knoxville, Tennessee, in 1850, Armstrong moved to southern Iowa in the mid-1870s. He married a local German farmer and developed close business ties with the Iowa Central Coal Company.[26] He recruited black miners from the South, purchased company mules, established coal-hauling contracts, and owned the town's meat market. He also bought about 18 farm properties in the area, raised thoroughbred horses, and later rented houses to residents in nearby Buxton. The *Bystander* reported Armstrong was "probably making more money than any colored man in Iowa." Another leading business owner was B. F. (Frank) Cooper, a Clinton druggist who opened a drugstore in the 1890s. His means were substantial enough to sponsor and support the local baseball team, the Muchakinock Unions. Other black-owned businesses in Muchakinock included three restaurants, two barber shops, two saloons, and a shoe repair shop.[27] Black and white customers alike patronized these businesses in the racially mixed coal-mining community.

Buxton holds special memories for Iowa's African-American citizens, and for good reason. The *Bystander* captured the enthusiasm this short-lived town generated when it thrived in 1909:

> Here one can study the race from a viewpoint that no other large community offers the Negro. Here he has absolute freedom to everything that any other citizen has. Here you can see well trained doctors, lawyers. Here you can see the public schools with mixed teachers, mostly colored, with a colored principal . . . . Here you can see colored men officers administering the law. . . . Here you can see colored men building the buildings, operating the electric plant, riding in automobiles and carriages; here you can see them farming, here you can see them owning amusements, parks, baseball parks . . . and many other things too numerous to mention.[28]

In this exuberant atmosphere, black-owned businesses fared well. Despite competition from a large department store owned by the coal company, other businesses progressed and even flourished. Some just moved over from Muchakinock, such as B. F. Cooper, whose new drug store was built in the summer of 1901 on the northern edge of Buxton, a section known as Coopertown. Described by the *Bystander* in 1904 as "single (ladies of D. M. look out)[,] he is a nice man to meet and is well liked by all. He is making and saving his money." A year later the *Bystander* commented on Cooper's "land office business. His income is perhaps more than any one colored man in the town, except one other," no doubt a reference to Armstrong. Cooper also operated a grocery store that adjoined his two-story drugstore. The upper story of this building housed clubrooms for lodges and secret societies for meeting, socializing, and drinking. A baseball enthusiast, Cooper organized the Buxton Wonders team, which played all over Iowa. Sadly, in 1916 a fire raged through Coopertown, engulfing the drugstore and other shops, and Cooper never recovered.[29]

Rivaling, if not exceeding, Cooper's business interests were those of real-estate investor Reuben Gaines Sr., a light-skinned man who sported a thick handle-bar mustache. Formerly a resident of Muchakinock, Gaines founded a suburban community of Buxton called Gainesville. He bought land adjacent to the Consolidation Coal Company site and helped develop it by opening a barber shop and a hotel. Five other businesses came into being in Gainesville, along with a handful of homes. The *Bystander* claimed Gaines earned over $200 per month, a handsome sum for the time. His lifestyle, the newspaper claimed, certainly was more princely than that of the average Buxton coal miner. On his 40 acres in Mahaska County, Gaines built a 10-room house with a large barn and "many other new improvements," including a hot-water furnace. His land, located along the county road, contained a shoe store run by his son, Reuben Jr., a drug store, a restaurant, a livery and feed barn, two saloons, a millinery store, and a tailor shop — all presumably part of Gainesville. Gaines also built the "fireproof" Buxton Hotel at a cost of $10,000, a two-story cement structure equipped with modern steam heat. "Mr. Gaines is a very pleasant, unassuming man to meet. He has an industrious and lovable wife and three children," the kind of man, the *Bystander* insinuated, that fellow blacks should emulate. He even bought a two-seat automobile for his son in 1909, "the first colored man to buy a machine to our knowledge in Iowa," according to the *Bystander.*

And his son inherited his father's business sense, moving buildings to the new — and short-lived — coal town of Haydock, and assuming a similar business role as that of his father in Buxton.[30]

Other black-owned businesses in Buxton were typical of black America at the time. Some not as typical included Diana Harrison's millinery shop, which enjoyed a fine local reputation for stocking the latest styles, and James Roberts's cigar factory, one of the few of its kind in Iowa. Roberts hand-rolled brands

Buxton tailor George L. Neal (right) did a thriving business in the coal-mining town's glory days. (courtesy Mary Collier Graves)

Daddy Montgomery (above), born into slavery in 1852, became a successful businessman in Clarinda, where he operated a taxi and hauling service (right). (courtesy Pat Cassatt)

such as "The Roberts," "The Buxton Wonder," "The Gem of Iowa," and "La Rosa De Buxton." William London, who worked at the company store at both Muchakinock and Buxton, opened his own businesses in these communities, selling insurance (a rarity for a black man), stoves, and pianos, and a millinery store as well.[31]

Buxton's black barbers flourished. The *Bystander* describes what a customer could expect at the shop of Arthur Fletcher:

> *The entire space in the front of the three very pretty chairs is heavy plate mirror, so that one can see the shine on his shoes and the top of his head as well. In the center of the room is the stand for shampooing and massaging to which special attention will be given. A beautiful bath tub is also installed, the only one in the city. In front is an electric revolving barber pole which is very beautiful. The [3] gentlemen who will give the best attention in this elegant new shop . . . is a tonsorial artist for all that word means. "Skinny" the porter will see to it that you have clean towels for your bath and will also give you a nice shine. . . . [T]he only thing that bars the colored man from these luxuries is the price. He is just as welcome as the flowers in May.[32]*

Obviously, when African-Americans were given the chance, they could succeed in the business world in spite of the racist obstacles placed in their path.

Southern Iowa

Buxton offered an opportunity unique to Iowa's history — and rare anywhere in America for that time period. More typical

in southern Iowa, usually in the county seats, were small pockets of black business owners.

Page County, for example, had slightly over 200 African-American residents. Most of them, with the exception of a few black farmers, lived in Clarinda. There several individuals made a mark on the local economy. During one of *Bystander* editor John Thompson's first visits, he met an enterprising veterinarian named William Gibson. In addition to his medical practice, Dr. Gibson owned a livery and a feed and coal office. Thompson was intrigued by Gibson's office display of "peculiar interesting specimens" taken from the animals he treated. Dr. Gibson's Clarinda neighbor Thomas Jones owned a blacksmith shop in partnership with a white man in the late 1890s. Jones's son Allen also worked there, did blacksmith work at Buxton for a few years, and returned in 1910. Other black businesses in Clarinda in the early 1900s included Mrs. R. E. Wilkinson's boarding house and restaurant and E. B. Cook's carpet-cleaning business and the refreshment stands he operated during county fairs and chautauquas. H. H. Cook, possibly a relative of E. B. Cook, owned a barber shop and a grocery store with Thomas Dunn. Though they strongly encouraged black patronage, they told Thompson that only about 2 percent of their trade was with blacks.

Yet another Clarinda business favorably impressed Thompson. Thompson was staying at the home of Mr. and Mrs. J. W. Williams, and he spent a day observing their grocery and restaurant. The Williams's served three meals from 5 a.m. to 10 p.m. The day Thompson was there about 30 dinners were served. At supper, they served 8 white men and 1 black man, and many bought one of about 50 pies baked daily by Mrs. Williams. Thompson whimsically wished that white southerners could have joined him to watch a successful black-run business operation.

Another black-owned Clarinda restaurant was operated by R. T. Lain. Lain's Busy Bee, on Ninth Street, opened in the early 1900s, burned to the ground in October 1916, and was rebuilt the following spring. Lain kept boarders on the second floor, including a "ladies waiting room." On the first floor, he stocked groceries, served lunches and short orders at the counter, and had tables set in the rear area for his regular boarders.

Clarinda's answer to Clinton's Money Harris was a beloved town character named Lewis Franklin (Daddy) Montgomery. Born in slavery in Springfield, Missouri, in 1852, he drove a stagecoach in Missouri after the Civil War. In 1899, he came to Clarinda, where citizens hired his hack for rides to Clarinda's huge chautauquas and Fourth of July celebrations. He also served as a drayman, garbage collector, and hauler. Montgomery had a soft spot for children and rode them around town in his garbage wagon, which later stirred fond recollections for many. His grandson, Lewis Montgomery, would later establish a trucking business.[33]

Neighboring Red Oak, 30 miles north of Clarinda, had a black population barely exceeding 100 people in 1880, and that number declined to only about 50 by 1950. Like most county seats, Red Oak had a fairly successful black barber, Oscar Conner, and a newsstand and shoeshine operated by Buster Carson. But Red Oak's most notable black business was the music store owned by Pearl S. Everhart. Born in Chariton, Iowa, in 1869, Everhart's father, Benjamin, was a stagecoach driver. Everhart graduated from Red Oak High School and began working as a newspaper carrier. During the early 1890s he sold pianos and organs in southwestern Iowa and eventually opened his music store on Red Oak's town square with the help of a local Jewish businessman named Jimmy Thomas. Everhart also had a music shop in Villisca, 22 miles from Red Oak. In 1916, he married Rose Goodlow of Wales, and she assisted in the store as he made sales calls and deliveries. Contemporaries describe Everhart as short and stout, always well-dressed, cheerful, and whistling. A self-taught musician, he played classical music on the piano and sold sheet music, phonographs, and a variety of musical instruments — including pianos, violins, banjos and mandolins — in addition to original paintings by Picasso, Van Gogh, and Tanner. It is alleged that he sold Glenn Miller his first instruments. A white woman who worked in the store, Blanche Smith, played the piano at the local Beardsley Theatre during silent movies.

Everhart's stature in the music business rose to the point that the Schaff Brothers Piano Company of Chicago began manufacturing pianos bearing his name. According to the *Bystander*, several Everhart pianos were shipped to him from Chicago. He sold all but one, which he kept for a sample. Initially unaware that Everhart was black, Schaff Brothers decided not to ship additional pianos. Everhart sued and won and got the pianos delivered.

The economic downturn in Iowa following World War 1 destroyed Everhart's business, and he sold out in 1928 after a bitter legal battle with his former friend, Jimmy Thomas. Pearl Everhart

(Above and left) Pearl Everhart's Red Oak music store, home of the Everhart piano, c.1917 (courtesy Mary Frances Everhart)

Kitten and Buck Johnson at Darden's Cafe on East Main in Ottumwa (courtesy Gwen Sanders)

You are cordially invited to attend a Tea, announcing the opening of the Modernistic Beauty Salon Located at 211½ East Main Street Ottumwa, Iowa Sunday, August 1, 1948, 2 to 6 pm.

Announcing the grand opening of the Modernistic Beauty Salon in Ottumwa, 1948 (SHSI Des Moines)

Mt. Pleasant barber Sam McCrackin (courtesy Don Young)

died in 1938 a broken and bitter man. *The Red Oak Express's* obituary said "while he was of the Negro race, he mingled with the business interests, and at one time was quite successful." Thus even though he "was one of the best known business men in Red Oak," he was constantly reminded of his race. Everhart's daughter, Mary Frances Everhart, recalled him taking her to a Red Oak Ku Klux Klan rally in the 1920s so she would not forget the tenuous position of blacks in American society.[34]

Visitors to other southern Iowa towns in the early 1900s could occasionally encounter a black businessperson. In Ottumwa, where most blacks worked at the meatpacking plants, African-Americans owned two delivery businesses, two barber shops, and a lunch room.[35] In Centerville, most blacks engaged in coal mining, but a few operated businesses. Mrs. Scott Richmond, considered a leading dressmaker in town, had both black and white clients, and Lulu Pullen was the town's only hairdresser in the early 1900s. Ottumwa laundry owner Cutter

Robinson also managed the Jolly Entertainers Show, a racially mixed troupe that performed in the area.[36]

In Mt. Pleasant, east of Ottumwa, at least three black barbers did well, including Samuel Gunnel, whose barber shop opened for business in the 1860s. African-Americans also owned a shoe shop and a feed stable in Mt. Pleasant.[37]

Iowa City's sparse black population gave rise to few businesses. Most visible for the community was Hayward Douglas Short's shoe-repair business. Short designed the shoe-shine chairs for his shiners, who numbered as many as 18 at one time. It was a nickel-and-dime operation, but shined shoes were a fashion must. Short's business branched into delivery and pick-up as well as contracts with the military during World War 2. The shop, which stayed in the family after Short's death in 1946, closed in 1970.[38]

Segregation at the state university prompted the formation of an Iowa City business fostering community cohesiveness among African-Americans. Although the State University of Iowa had long admitted black students, blacks were banned from living in university dormitories until shortly after World War 2. Bettye and Junious Tate, who moved to Iowa City in 1927, responded to this situation by converting their home into a boarding house for black male students, calling it Tate Arms. Bettye instituted strict rules and made all the men earn their keep. They had to be gentlemen; they could not bring in girls or alcohol; and they were forbidden to use profanity. Bettye in turn treated them like family. The Tate Arms was home to generations of students until it closed in 1965.[39]

Cedar Rapids

In nearby Cedar Rapids, the local black population could boast a few businesses integral to the community's life. Among the most notable from the earliest times was Marshall Perkins's restaurant, which operated from the late 1800s until the 1950s. Located near the downtown area, the Perkins's restaurant was part of the "Black Block," where several hundred of the town's black citizens lived in the early 1900s. Located nearby were J. A. (Dad) Baker's restaurant, pool hall, and barber shop. In other black residential areas were Fine's Laundry Cleaner and a small grocery store. When University of Iowa student Gabriel Victor Cools visited Cedar Rapids around 1917, he reported the "economic possibilities of the colored people were as good as any one could desire." But he also observed a need for greater patronage of black-owned stores. In his view, older residents did not believe in patronizing any black businesses. Only the newcomers from the South were accustomed to "buying black."

Despite Cools's claim, other black businesses existed in Cedar Rapids, some of them at least moderately successful. Several cleaning businesses ran at various times in the early 1900s. One was operated by Cecil Reed, who came to Cedar Rapids in 1923. Reed held a variety of jobs — newsboy, handyman, chef, dancer and singer, jukebox repairer, landlord, and motel owner — before his election to the Iowa House of Representatives in 1967, which launched his public-service career. Reed's Floor Care Store, his main business, opened in the 1940s. In 1954, with his sister Edith Atkinson and his wife Evelyn, Reed opened the Motel Sepia on his acreage along Highway 30 outside of Cedar Rapids. At that time, few places would accommodate black travelers, including nationally prominent musicians stopping for a performance.

Reed later became the first black member of the Cedar Rapids Chamber of Commerce. Among his colleagues in the city's black business community was Earl Toombs, whose laundry dated from the early 1900s. Toombs sold the business to Tom Mason in 1935, and it stayed under Mason's name until 1990 even though it changed hands to brothers Elmer and Louis Smith in 1946.[40]

In communities with small black populations, it was imperative for black businessmen and women to cater to white customers and cultivate trust. Examples are scattered throughout the state, including two in Colfax, the mineral-springs tourist town about 20 miles east of Des Moines. Walter H. Humburd, who opened the Elite Tonsorial Parlor about 1884, was among the handful of blacks who settled in Colfax and Jasper County following the Civil War. According to the *Colfax Clipper*, he was reported to be "inaugurating a reform by keeping his barber shop closed on Sunday." Humburd moved his barber shop first to a corner drug store and eventually to a hotel basement — two businesses with predominantly white customers. Evidence indicates Humburd was not totally welcomed in town. Following the presidential election of 1884, the victorious Democrats disfigured the town by painting red those business establishments owned by Republicans. To add insult to injury, Humburd's doorstep was "befouled in the most disgraceful manner." Another black businessman in Colfax, C. R. Bennett, who operated the European Brick Restaurant, had his business disfigured at the same time.[41]

Marshall Perkins's restaurant staff, Cedar Rapids, c. 1900 (courtesy Connie Hillsman)

Horace Spencer, one of three brothers who owned a cement contracting business with branches in Iowa and Illinois (courtesy Meredith Saunders)

James Herman Banning attended Iowa State, then barnstormed all over Iowa in his plane Miss Ames. *(Hardesty and Pisano,* Black Wings: The American Black in Aviation*)*

Clara Romey Comley (above)and Charles Comley (right) were caterers in Webster City. (courtesy Robert Boldridge)

Northern Iowa

Small black communities, with accompanying businesses, could be found in Fort Dodge and Mason City. As in most county seats, citizens there could find black barbers along the town squares. One of Mason City's first black settlers in the 1880s was barber Charles Watson, who sponsored a popular baseball team called Watson's Colts. His shop had four chairs, a shoeshine stand, huge mirrors and towel stands, several baths, and a pool hall. Lou Taylor had a barber shop in the downtown Cerro Gordo Hotel at the same time. J. D. Reeler provided service as a chiropodist as well as a barber. Also in Mason City in the early 1900s was W. L. Jones, a barber who also made money from a hand laundry and a poultry business.

The Spencer Brothers, who established a cement contracting company when they arrived in Mason City from Chicago in 1917, attempted a multi-city operation. Brother Harvey ran the Jacksonville, Illinois, operation; John had Grinnell, Iowa; and Horace located in Mason City, where they were headquartered. The Spencers had apparently tried to open a business in Washington, Iowa, in 1909, but it was short-lived.[42]

A few black-owned businesses have made their mark on Fort Dodge's economy. Community leader Harry Merriwether and his wife ran Harry's Chicken Shack. La Salle Altman owned the Farmer's Exchange, a bar with the only R&B jukebox in town. Contemporary black-owned businesses include Warren Gamble's Ford auto dealership and Dorothy Bodaddy's Motivation Beauty Salon. Fort Dodge was also home to the notorious Creole Inn bordello, run by madam Emma Jacobs and her "fancy man," Lee Lewis, for three decades. Known throughout Iowa, the Creole Inn reputedly lasted longer than other establishments of its kind because of Jacobs's influential clients.[43]

Des Moines

By World War 1 Des Moines had become the center for black life in Iowa. As might be expected, the state's capital city boasted the most diverse and the largest number of black-owned businesses in Iowa. Many fit historical patterns of black-owned enterprises, such as beauty shops, barbers, restaurants, and nightclubs. A few exceptions stand out. First there is the business of Robert N. Hyde, an employee turned inventor turned entrepreneur. Hyde came to Des Moines from Virginia in about 1876 and got his first Des Moines job as a janitor at the

Kirkwood Hotel. While working at the hotel, he concocted and patented an effective cleaning compound, which he and his partner T. W. Henry began marketing. The success of H. and H. Soap, along with other cleaning products, kept their family business going into the 1960s. Hyde also invented an electric cleaning machine, and members of his family eventually branched into real estate.[44]

The career of Archie Alexander (1888–1958) offers a unique story of a successful black-owned business in Iowa. Born in Ottumwa, Alexander was one of the early black graduates of the University of Iowa, receiving his engineering degree in 1912. Then he formed a construction firm in Des Moines and received contracts for major projects across America. In Iowa he built the State University of Iowa's heating plant and powerhouse, in addition to bridges and other structures. Alexander was appointed territorial governor of the U.S. Virgin Islands in 1954.[45]

The Center Street neighborhood north of downtown Des Moines embodied the spirit of the city's black residents. Consolidating into a black residential and business area beginning in the late 1800s and early 1900s, the neighborhood's demise occurred during urban renewal in the late 1960s. In the interim, a long list of businesses came into being. Several became primary places in the memories of past residents and gave rise to key figures in the history of African-Americans in Iowa.

The fascinating career of job printer and hustling entrepreneur Robert E. Patten is a case in point. Patten's Center Street neighborhood business was vital to the local black community, even though he was not necessarily as wealthy as other African-American business leaders. Born in rural Georgia in 1883, Patten secured his first job working as a farm hand. An opinionated man, given to expressing his views in writing, Patten was motivated to work for himself. He learned that in order to avoid editorial interference or censorship, he needed to publish his own opinions. These twin desires spurred him toward a printing career. Traveling the country by rail in search of opportunity, Patten through unknown circumstances eventually settled in Buxton and established a photography and printing business in about 1900. Around 1910, he moved to Des Moines, which remained his home until his death in 1968.

As the black community's only job printer, Patten produced business cards, flyers announcing a sale of the week, wedding invitations, and broadsides for dances and parties at local dance

halls. He also printed leaflets promoting the Unity Coal Supply Company in the early 1900s, one of several community cooperatives he worked to create. His Cooperative Buying Club, another such effort, urged lodges, church groups, and other black organizations to purchase in bulk. This enterprise, which existed primarily on paper, embodied the spirit of W. E. B. DuBois and Booker T. Washington's dreams of self-sufficient capital augmenting black business operations. Gwendolyn Fowler, a long-time Des Moines resident and a friend of Patten's, indicated that the failure of the cooperative buying and selling club deeply embittered him.

Patten sold other products as well. He was a sales agent for Lucky Heart cosmetic and household products in the 1930s. Lucky Heart, a Memphis, Tennessee, company, employed an Amway-like selling approach of products targeted primarily at African-Americans. These included perfumes bearing names such as "Hot Love," "Gardenia," and "Lucky Lovin," among others. Patten also helped fellow black entrepreneur Lawrence J. Chapman of Des Moines market his Uneedor Chemical Company products, which included cosmetics, cleaning formulas, and hair treatments. Patten was known to deliver his wares and his stacks of job-print materials in the handle-bar basket of his bicycle.

Patten's ambitions spurred him to sell books throughout the Midwest. Calling on all-black schools, Patten sold books that "all colored Men — White as well — should read," including such titles as *The United Negro, The Negro Revealed, The New Negro,* and W.E.B. DuBois's classic *The Souls of Black Folk.* Patten also sold posters depicting black heroes such as Booker T. Washington, boxer

Inventor Robert N. Hyde made his fortune developing soaps and other cleaning products.
(Iowa Bystander)

*Below left and right:
The signs posted outside his office indicate the range of Robert Patten's professional interests.*
(SHSI Des Moines)

Like his father, E. Hobart De Patten was a tireless entrepeneur. The Novelty Nook Gift Wagon was one of his many successful business ventures. (SHSI Des Moines)

Robert Patten's print products included this business directory, issued in 1939. (SHSI Des Moines)

Improvements in hair-care methods, the invention of the permanent wave and effective curling irons, and the rise of Madame C. J. Walker's beauty school and products empire made beautified hair available to the average black woman. With a steady clientele and relatively low overhead, including the ability to begin the business in one's own home, beauty parlors emerged as important places of community interaction for women. Owners of the more successful beauty parlors were important community leaders. They were often privy to customers' secrets and became dispensers of a wide range of personal advice as well as gossip.

Perhaps the most prominent black Des Moines beautician was Pauline Brown Humphrey (1906–1993), founder of the Crescent School of Beauty Culture located on Center Street. Humphrey enrolled in Madame Walker's prestigious beauty school in Chicago in 1935. Four years later, she was a licensed cosmetologist and opened Iowa's first beauty school. But before opening the school she had to become certified to teach in Iowa. After some searching, she found a school in Fort Dodge open to African-Americans. Humphrey endured a grueling daily commute, 70 miles each way, to Fort Dodge to achieve certification.

Once opened in Des Moines, the Crescent School had about 30 students per semester. The school's motto reflected Humphrey's persistence against strong odds: "Aim High and Hold Your Aim." A formal commencement ceremony, sometimes held at the Corinthian Baptist Church, marked graduation. In addition to the Crescent School, Brown operated the segregated beauty shop for black women enlistees when the Women's Army Corps established its first base at Fort Des Moines during World War 2. She also developed her own cosmetic preparations, a product line she named Myrise Paule. She and other Des Moines beauty shops sponsored the "Copper Colored Review" and the "Bronze Spotlight," where students could perform procedures typically found in black beauty parlors: marceling, straightening, bleaching and tinting, permanents, pressing and styling, facials, manicures and pedicures, and cutting and conditioning.[48] She had scholarship contests for students and helped place her students all over the country.

Des Moines's black barbershops, the men's domain, flourished along Center Street and a few places in the nearby downtown. In the 1920s, one of the most noteworthy was the Tonsorial Deluxe Shop of Spencer Curry, who specialized in "bobbing."

In 1928, the best-known barbershop, Hardaway's Tonsorial Parlor, opened its doors to business. Rozenting Hardaway came

Jack Johnson, and Frederick Douglass and inspirational images of black angels and a black Jesus figure. He marketed calendars and printed books and pamphlets espousing his own social philosophy. Patten created a "School of Co-Operative Philosophy" — evidence that he combined hustle with strong socialistic-utopian leanings.[46]

Like his father, E. Hobart De Patten had a number of businesses. He printed with his father and also sold novelty items. From his Novelty Nook Gift Wagon — a panel truck — he sold toys, games, cards, stationery, and ice cream. Proceeds from this business went into land investments. In the 1950s, the younger Patten operated a launderette, a restaurant, and a shine parlor. Like many others, De Patten saw his businesses decline greatly as urban development — the construction of Interstate 235 and the expansion of Iowa Methodist Hospital — essentially destroyed the once-cohesive Center Street community.[47]

Robert Patten printed innumerable items for black-owned beauty parlors that came into fashion in Des Moines at the turn of the century as they did in black communities all over the country.

to Des Moines from Texas in 1924, worked for some Des Moines barbers for a few years, moved to Chicago for a year, and then came back and took over Spencer Curry's shop. Hardaway carried a full line of services found in the best shops, including shoe shines and hair preparations and cosmetics such as hair pomades, base creams, and talcum powders. By his twenty-fifth year in business, Hardaway's shop had served 300,000 customers. He had trained a number of barbers who went on to start their own shops, and Hardaway himself had become a prominent community leader. In addition to Hardaway, the Gray brothers — Seymour and Howard — operated a barber shop in Des Moines.[49]

Since blacks were welcome at few white eating establishments, restaurants thrived in the segregated Center Street neighborhood. Over the years a procession of eateries opened and closed, a few

remaining until Center Street's demise. When Gabriel Cools visited Des Moines in 1918, he indicated that there were 12 restaurants, but only two "are in any true sense restaurants. The others are more or less unpretentious places which cater to the less discriminating classes," he wrote. Cools went on to offer a physical description of a typical restaurant.

The café was in the basement. There were half a dozen tables over which were thrown pieces of brown paper which functioned as table cloths and these were not . . . clean. The concrete floor was unclean . . . with no sign of having been washed in a decade. And to add to the grotesqueness of the place a new Victrola was being displayed in a conspicuous position.[50]

Lena's Beauty Salon was one of many serving the African-American community in 20th-century Des Moines. (SHSI Des Moines)

Men gathered at Marco Chiese's cigar store, as well as at neighborhood barbershops. (SHSI Des Moines)

Sampson's popular Chicken Shack on Des Moines's east side featured dining and dancing. (SHSI Des Moines)

Two other establishments that he did consider typical got a little better review.

> One sees . . . an attempt at conforming to some kind of hygienic standards. They were kept fairly clean and the service at least, was not repulsive. . . . The proprietor of the smaller place was more attentive to the conduct of the business. Everything was new, from the soda water fountain to the chairs, and the tables were covered with clean white cloths — a decided improvement over the brown paper covers.[51]

Another restaurant, Cools said, "had the preposterous name of 'Cafeteria.'" None of these establishments were identified precisely, but Cools's descriptions suggest the range of dining facilities available in the neighborhood.[52]

One of the most popular Center Street restaurants was the 18-seat Community Luncheonette, which opened in 1935. Arthur P. and Goletha Trotter, husband and wife, opened early for breakfast and stayed open until late at night. During World War 2, when the black population of Des Moines grew significantly, the Trotters served 300 meals daily. They also cooked for visiting black celebrities. The Trotters retired in 1956, and their restaurant became known as the Burke Café, operated by R. J. Burke.[53]

Black customers could also dine at any number of Des Moines night spots. One of the most popular was the Sepia Supper Club, which featured Saturday night shrimp dinners. Opened by the barbering Gray brothers in 1940, the Grays' sister Gladys Bates (Carter) ran the restaurant. Carter and her business partner Corrine Adams were also locally known for the tantalizing chicken dinners prepared at their east-side restaurant. Other Des Moines night spots serving meals included the Shelburn Garden, a very popular place on Center Street in the early and mid-1900s.[54]

The city's east-side African-American neighborhood was home to a restaurant and night spot called Sampson's Chicken Shack. Elizabeth and George Sampson's place was located in a house that had been converted into a restaurant, with a dance area in an annex. The Sampsons served chicken and barbecued rib dinners. Advertising cards printed by Robert Patten told prospective customers: "If you are in the dog house at home, you're always welcome at Sampson's Chicken Shack."[55]

Throughout much of Iowa's history, white-owned funeral parlors customarily did not serve African-Americans. Hence blacks had to open their own. The first opened around World War 1. For

example, Vivian Jones came to Des Moines from Buxton and began his funeral business in 1918, partly in response to the unusually high death rate caused by the postwar flu epidemic. Jones later sold his business to Tug Wilson, and when Wilson died in 1937, John Estes purchased the business. John Estes Jr. later sold the business to Frederick and Linda Nichols, and it now operates as the Estes-Nichols Funeral Home. Lafayette (Lafe) Fowler started L. Fowler and Son Funeral Home within a year of Vivian Jones. He came to Des Moines from Kansas City in 1912 and became involved in renting hearses to area funeral homes. He gained experience working for Harbach and Lilly's funeral homes in Des Moines and was encouraged to begin his own business for black patrons.[56]

Traditionally, pharmacies have served as informal community centers where customers could obtain their medicines, buy a delicious malt, and chat. On the east side of Des Moines, the Walker Street Pharmacy and, earlier, the Blagburn and Shelton Pharmacy were owned by African-Americans. From the start of their retail trade in 1917, Blagburn and Shelton regularly held special sales promoting products such as baby cough syrup (17 cents), Unguentine skin ointment (26 cents), Ever-Ready Safety Razors (89 cents), Dr. Palmer's Skin Whitener preparations (price unknown), and Simmon's Liver Preparation (87 cents).

Future pharmacist Jimmy Mitchell first came to Des Moines as a candidate at the Fort Des Moines Colored Officers Training Camp during World War 1. After serving as an officer in the war, he returned to Des Moines and opened his popular Community

John Estes Jr. and John Estes Sr., Des Moines funeral directors (courtesy John Estes Jr.)

Tracy Blagburn and later his son E. Tracy Blagburn operated the Blagburn and Shelton Pharmacy on Des Moines's east side. (courtesy Norma Jean McKelvy)

Lewis Fulton included a moving company among his successful business ventures. (courtesy Gwen Kee)

Pharmacy on Center Street. With his wife Azalia, also a pharmacist, Mitchell dispensed medicines, prescriptions, and malts at their drug store. The Mitchells were prominent community leaders. Jimmy Mitchell worked in the state post office — a prestigious position for blacks at that time — and drove for Iowa Gov. William S. Beardsley. Mitchell also owned the Billiken nightclub on Center Street. In addition to the Mitchell pharmacy, closed in the 1960s for urban-renewal razing, pharmacies owned by blacks included Marion Williams's pharmacy, which opened in 1951; the Bell and Holberts pharmacy; and the Gaines pharmacy.[57]

A small number of black-owned service businesses dotted other areas of Des Moines during the early 1900s. Lewis Fulton's glass repair shop on the city's east side is a testimony to dedicated professionalism. A 1937 East High School graduate, Fulton struggled with low-paying menial jobs and suffered a host of racial indignities during his youth, which motivated him to become successfully self-employed. After taking a number of jobs, he got work as a welder at John Deere and operated a moving company and furniture company during his off hours. He also began the Fulton Glass Company, which has been in business since 1963.[58]

Urban renewal in the 1960s destroyed Center Street's spirit and displaced many of its businesses. Some reopened along University Avenue and in other areas of town. Though the destruction of Center Street damaged the sense of community,

the spirit of entrepreneurship remained undeterred and black-owned businesses have been a continuing presence in Des Moines. Ada and Emery Jackson exemplify this spirit. Emery, a trained commercial artist from the Cummins Art School in Des Moines, began his career free-lancing, designing and making book covers and working as a sign painter. During the 1960s, a friend suggested starting a business preparing bulk mailings for advertising purposes. The Jacksons received a Small Business Administration loan, put their house up for collateral, and began Pameco (an acronym formed by the initials of family members) in January 1970. The Jacksons were among the first pre-sort mail companies in Iowa, handling millions of items. Their business, which they turned over to their son in 1991, eventually employed 125 persons, doing mailings for Meredith Corporation, Ethan Allen, local insurance companies, and many others.[59]

At about the time the Jacksons were beginning their careers, young Melvin Harper of California joined his brother Eugene in Des Moines and in 1956 started a trailer-manufacturing business for a new company called U-Haul. When this concern moved off to Chicago, Mel became involved in a number of other Des Moines businesses. These included the Vets Club, the Harper House bar and restaurant, Robert's Lounge, and the West Des Moines-based construction company he currently owns.[60] Of this same generation is Silas Ewing, whose employment company began operations the same day as Emery and Ada Jackson's mailing company.

Waterloo

One of the last cities in Iowa to experience a growth spurt in its black population was Waterloo. Just before the World War 1 years, lured by the demand for workers in its railroad yards and its burgeoning factory and meatpacking plants, a few hundred African-Americans arrived in Waterloo in a short period of time. Some of the newcomers opened businesses. Community activist J. D. Hopkins, for example, was a proprietor of a small restaurant and pool hall across from the Illinois Central Railroad yards. Hopkins was followed by a host of other black-owned businesses, including boarding houses and restaurants. Some failed, but among those that emerged as community fixtures was John Spates's restaurant, which started in the 1940s. Spates owned the Masonic Building, housing a grocery store, barber shop, dance hall, pool hall, ice cream parlor, and beauty shop. The B & M (Bryant and Moss) grocery store, another long-standing business, began in the 1930s. The White Rose Laundry, begun by Joe Williams in the 1940s, specialized in suede and leather repairs and alterations. The White Rose closed in 1970.

Denman Phillips (1921–1989) came to Waterloo from Mississippi in the late 1940s and enjoyed a successful career in the construction trade. Advertising his specialty in 1966 as sidewalks, curbs, gutters, street widening, floors, and driveway work, Phillips did asphalt and concrete work, remodeled post-office buildings in

Waterloo businessman Cuba E. Tredwell Jr., 1973
(Waterloo Defender)

(Right) Deep Rock Service Station, Waterloo, 1966
(Waterloo Defender)

(Far right) Waterloo's Denman Phillips Garage, 1952
(Waterloo Post)

Lloyd Ward, former CEO of Maytag Corporation (Des Moines Register)

Monroe Colston, Chamber of Commerce and Greater Des Moines Foundation (Iowa Bystander)

Franklin Greene, co-owner, Quality Ford, West Des Moines (courtesy Franklin Greene)

Richard White, retired general manager of John Deere Des Moines (Iowa Bystander)

Iowa and Minnesota, and finished streets. He also built the Social Security Building in Waterloo. Eventually Small Business Administration contracts netted him a million-dollar job building a highway in Ankeny.[61]

A number of the neighborhood businesses that appeared in black Waterloo from 1930 through the 1950s banded together to form the Black Business Men and Women and Professional Association. The association publishes a directory and engages in cooperative efforts to promote minority businesses in the area. Among the original members of the association were the owners of the Deep Rock Service Station, the grocery owned by D. C. Stokes, and B. P. Steptoe's Mobil Gas Station.

Cuba E. Tredwell Jr. was among those attempting to break the color barrier in the field of real estate. He became involved through his own frustrating attempt to purchase a home in the late 1960s. Tredwell, who at the time worked for the Illinois Central Railroad, enrolled in real-estate courses in 1970, obtained his license, and began his own agency, partly to assure that all listings are available to him.

Other modest-sized African-American owned businesses continue to hold their own in Waterloo's economy.[62]

Participation in the American Dream

Thus have Iowa's black entrepreneurs occupied traditional businesses as well as a few unusual enterprises. But whatever their trade, throughout Iowa history black businessmen and women have remained fully aware of the dual need to sell their service or product as well as themselves to often-suspicious white customers. Their forbearance stands as an inspiration from John Thompson's day to the present. If he were alive today, Thompson would smile to learn that Lloyd Ward recently headed one of Iowa's best-known companies, the Maytag Corporation in Newton, and that blacks like Frederick Buie own new economy businesses like Keystone Electrical Manufacturing Company. Yet no doubt Ward and his colleagues, despite such lofty symbols of progress today, recognize that many blacks still stand "outside in" the business world.

Black executives at prestigious Iowa companies, along with black business owners such as Franklin Greene of Quality Ford, formed Partners in Economic Progress (PEP), whose goals resemble those articulated by Booker T. Washington's National Negro Business League nearly a century ago. PEP's mission is more succinct and contemporary in flavor: "To provide the rocket fuel for full participation of African-Americans in the American dream."

"To provide the rocket fuel for full participation of African-Americans in the American dream."

—PEP Mission Statement (Partners in Economic Progress)

Born in Memphis, Tennessee, Jack Lufkin received his B.A. degree from Memphis State University (University of Memphis) and his M.A. in history from Iowa State University. He has been with the State Historical Society of Iowa since 1980 and became museum curator in 1986. Lufkin has published a number of Iowa history articles and curated many exhibits at the new Iowa Historical Building.

For help in the preparation of his chapter, the author extends special thanks to E. Hobart De Patten for breathing life back into history. (Mr. De Patten, your dad's print shop collection is an important reminder that history occurs everyday, all around us.) He is indebted also to many colleagues at the State Historical Society of Iowa for support in countless ways. Lastly, thanks to Brad Ver Ploeg, a diligent volunteer researcher from Newton, for finding so many items in the Bystander *— and to Hal Chase, whose persistence has made this book publication possible.*

Notes

1. *Iowa State Bystander*, June 24, 1910.

2. Cecil Reed, *Fly in the Buttermilk* (Iowa City: Univ. of Iowa Press, 1993), 31.

3. "Deaf Mute, Minus an Arm and a Leg, Is Des Moines' Bootblack Extraordinary; James Engine Jeter Comes Up Smiling," *DMR*, June 19, 1920.

4. August Meier and Elliott Rudwick, *From Plantation to Ghetto* (New York: Hill and Wang, 1976), 212–18; Juliet E.K. Walker, *The History of Black Business in America: Capitalism, Race, Entrepreneurship* (New York: Macmillan, 1998).

5. For general descriptions of the condition of black communities in the North and Midwest, see August Meier and Elliott Rudwick, *From Plantation to Ghetto*; John Hope Franklin, *From Slavery to Freedom: A History of Negro Americans* (New York: Knopf, 1967); Allan Spear, *Black Chicago: The Making of a Negro Ghetto, 1890–1920* (Chicago: Univ. of Chicago Press, 1967); Kenneth Kusmer, *A Ghetto Takes Shape: Black Cleveland, 1870–1930* (Urbana: Univ. of Illinois Press, 1976).

6. David Lewis, *W.E.B. DuBois: Biography of a Race* (New York: Holt, 1993), 220, 239; Louis Harlan, *Booker T. Washington: The Making of a Black Leader* (New York: Oxford Univ. Press, 1972), 266-71; Meier and Rudwick, *From Plantation to Ghetto*, 213-18.

7. Dawnelle Connally interview, July 28, 1997.

8. Robert R. Dykstra, *Bright Radical Star: Black Freedom and White Supremacy on the Hawkeye Frontier* (Cambridge: Harvard Univ. Press, 1993; repr. 1997, Iowa State Univ. Press), 14.

9. Dykstra, 14.

10. "The Negro In Iowa," unpublished manuscript, Iowa WPA Project, 1935, SHSI; Susan Fulton Welty, *A Fair Field* (Detroit: Harlo Press, 1968), 103–04, 133.

11. Marie Grigsby, "Austin Algernon Bland," unpublished manuscript, 1997, in author's possession; "A Brief History of the Bland-Toomes Family and The Mission of the Church of St. Mary the Virgin Where They Worshipped," undated pamphlet; *Bystander*, March 13, 1896; July 2, 1897; Aug. 19, 1898; June 27, 1902; Aug. 21, 1903; Sept. 9, 1904; Sept. 6, 1907; Aug. 26, 1910.

12. According to Deloris Bradley of Keokuk, the following black-owned businesses, for which little or no additional evidence is available, operated in Keokuk during the 1900s: Roddy's Ice Cream Parlor; Brown and Chaney's haircuts, shaves, and taxicabs; Fred Holmes Dance Pavillion; Bill and Bessie's house of ill repute; Obie's Restaurant; Montrose Beckley's Pool Hall; Mr. Jones's Barbershop; Bundy's Knife and Scissors sharpening service and kindling wood sales; Ketterer's & Singleton's Meat Market; Blessed Martin Restaurant; Depression Inn; Israel and Bland's Catering and String Music; Morris Bar; Collins Bar; Mason's Funeral Home; Fred Holmes's Ice Wagon; Phil Holt's Rags and Junk; Raymond Bradley's Hauling; Bill Bradley's Bakery; Robert Bradley's Restaurant; Joe Scott's recycling; Jay Scott's construction and home improve ment; Rev. J.T. Brown recycling.

13. Specific information is limited. Virginia Harper and Marjorie Marsh interview, May 21, 1997; Frances E. Hawthorne, *African-Americans in Iowa A Chronicle of Contributions* (Iowa City: Iowa Humanities Board, 1992), 29.

14. Specific information about Burlington is frustratingly scant. The best resource was an interview with Geraldine Brown, Burlington, May 22, 1997. Other businesses mentioned in the interview included barbers Spain Herderson, John Ivey, J. H. Purry, S. Gunnell; silversmith W. North; F. Martin's saloon and billiard parlor; Harvey Jones's restaurant; John Rooks's restaurant; Oliver Alexander's boarding-house. See also *Bystander*, June 20, 1902; Aug. 7, 1903; Sept. 9, 1904.

15. Jeanette Quinn, "Salute Local Woman on National Business Women Week," *Burlington Hawkeye,* Oct. 19, 1969.

16. Transcripts of interviews with Davenport blacks, conducted in 1979 by students at Palmer Junior College, available at the Davenport Public Library; *Bystander*, Aug. 3, 1900; Aug. 23, 1901; Aug. 3, 1906; July 5, 1907; July 10, 1903.

17. *Bystander*, June 2, 1911.

18. "History of Clinton County, Iowa," (Clinton: Clinton County American Revolution Bicentennial Commission, 1976), 288; Vincent Jetter interview, July 17, 1997; Bob Soesby interview, June 12, 1997; *Bystander*, July 27, 1900; June 26, 1903; Feb. 17, 1905; July 28, 1905; May 10, 1912.

19. Everett A. Streit, "Once Upon a Time," *Clinton Herald,* June 2, 1992; "History of Clinton County," 271; Vincent Jetter interview, July 17, 1997.

20. William Jetter Jr. and Vincent Jetter interviews, July 17, 1997; *Clinton Herald,* Feb. 24, 1987; Oct. 19, 1988. Other Clinton businesses from this time period included Al's on Main, owned by Allen Stubblefield, and PaPa Pete's restaurant, owned by Huston Peters.

21. News clippings and photographs in the personal collection of Vincent Jetter; Vincent Jetter interview.

22. Doubtless other beauticians preceded these women, but the record is not readily available.

23. Information concerning businesses in Sioux City was gleaned from the following sources: "The Negro in Sioux City," Sioux City Public Library, newspaper clippings and files; S.E. Gilbert, "The History of the Negro in Sioux City from 1855 to 1900," unpublished manuscript in "The Negro in Iowa," WPA files, SHSI, Des Moines; George Boykin, Sanford Center, scrapbooks and manuscript collections; William L. Hewitt, "Blackface in the White Mind: Racial Stereotypes in Sioux City, Iowa 1874–1910," *Palimpsest* 71 (Summer 1990): 68–79; William L. Hewitt, "So Few Undesirables: Race, Residence, and Occupation in Sioux City, 1890–1925," *AI* 50 (1989/1990): 158–79; *The Sioux City Negro Year Book* (1962 and 1978), published by James Ruffin; Lani Pettit, "Black Persons from Sioux City's Early History" and "Auntie Woodin," *The Wahkaw* [Woodbury County Genealogical Society Newsletter] 6 (1987); "Sioux City's Negro Citizens Own $200,000 Worth of Property," *Sioux City Tribune*, Aug. 14, 1903; Sue Marks, "Early Blacks Brought Rich Culture to City," *Sioux City Sunday Journal*, Feb. 11, 1979; Lani Pettit interview, March 22, 1997; *Bystander*, Aug. 24, 1894; Dec. 23, 1898; June 22, 1906; Sept. 4, 1908.

24. *Bystander*, July 24, 1908; Dec. 11, 1908; Jan. 10, 1908.

25. W. Sherman Savage, *Blacks in the West* (Westport CT: Greenwood, 1976), 4–7.

26. John Thompson took umbrage with his view of racial uplift, which was to marry a white woman and encourage his many children to do the same.

27. Dorothy Schwieder, Joseph Hraba, Elmer Schwieder, *Buxton: Work and Racial Equality in a Coal Mining Community* (Ames: Iowa State Univ. Press, 1987), 13–39; *Bystander*, Sept. 9, 1898.

28. *Bystander*, Oct. 29, 1909.

29. Schwieder et al., *Buxton*, 48, 60, 109, 154, 190, 191; *Bystander,* Aug. 19, 1904; Oct. 20, 1905; Nov. 23, 1906; Nov. 4, 1910; Oct. 29, 1909; Dec. 27, 1912.

30. Schwieder et al., *Buxton*, 48–49, 60, 109, 193, 195–97, 200–1, 209, 217; *Bystander*, Aug. 19, 1904; Nov. 4, 1910; Oct. 29, 1909; Dec. 27, 1912.

31. *Bystander*, Nov. 25, 1904; Nov. 23, 1906; Oct. 29, 1909; Dec. 27, 1912; Schwieder et al., *Buxton*, 202–3.

32. *Bystander*, Aug. 23, 1912.

33. Information about blacks in Clarinda obtained from oral histories conducted by the Page County Historical Society; Pat Cassat interviews, Page County Historical Society, Clarinda; press clippings provided by Pat Cassat; *Bystander*, Sept. 2, 1898; May 29, 1901; June 6, 1919; Nov. 30, 1917; July 19, 1901; July 30, 1909; June 24, 1910; March 30, 1917; Dec. 27, 1918. According to Cassat, other black business people in Clarinda included Lewis (Shorty) Arnett, who had a floor sanding and ice business in Clarinda and Shenandoah. He also raised foxhounds and coon dogs in the 1950s. Others include barbers Henry Webb, George Norris, and Joseph Griggs; hairdresser and manicurist Caddie Farrier; weaver Merrill Griggs; garage owner Henry Farrier; Joe Howes and Robert Franklin, owners of race horses; and oil station owner Eugene Griggs.

Pauline Brown Humphrey, founder of the Crescent School of Beauty Culture, Des Moines, c. 1949 (courtesy Barbara Brown James)

Coalie Davis, proprietor of an Ottumwa ice cream parlor (Ottumwa Public Library)

Cecil Reed and his son Richard operated Reed's Floor Surfacing in Cedar Rapids. (Cecil Reed, Fly in the Buttermilk)

34. Mary Frances Everhart interviews, July 1, 1997, and Aug. 22, 1997; Ruth Ann Draper interview, June 20, 1997; *Red Oak Express*, Jan. 10, 1938; *Red Oak Independent*, Christmas 1894 magazine; *Bystander*, Sept. 13, 1907; Aug. 28, 1908; April 23, 1909; July 30, 1909.

35. *Bystander*, July 21, 1899; July 6, 1900; June 20, 1902; July 16, 1909.

36. *Bystander*, Oct. 18, 1912; Bill Heusinkveld and Marjorie Ousley interview, May 15, 1997. According to these individuals, Cutter or Cutler Robinson also had a shoeshine business, Chuck Morris owned a car wash, Paul Davis was a contractor, Fred and May Ridding had a cleaning business, and Viola Everson was a caterer.

37. Donald Young interview, June 1, 1997; Glenwood Tolson interview, June 3, 1997; *Official Directory and Financial Report of Henry County, 1914* (n.p., n.d.); *Bystander*, July 21, 1899; July 6, 1900; June 20, 1902; Aug. 7, 1903; July 16, 1909. The same *Bystander* references report similar businesses in Knoxville and Fairfield with the exception of one: Fairfield's J. Richmond, who in 1909 was mentioned as the only black auctioneer in Iowa.

38. Jean C. Florman, "Personal Accounts of a History Nearly Lost," *Traces* (January 1995): 14, 16, 18.

39. Brendan Brown, "Tate's Open House Offered Shelter to Black Students," *Daily Iowan*, Feb. 26, 1997.

40. Information on Cedar Rapids was gathered from interviews with Vernon Smith and Pamela Nosek of Cedar Rapids and Shirley Cutchlow of the African-American Heritage Foundation in Cedar Rapids; oral history interviews of Edith Atkinson and Virgil Powell housed at the History Center, Linn County Historical Society; Cecil Reed, *Fly in the Buttermilk* (Iowa City: Univ. of Iowa Press, 1993), 30, 32, 73-77, 95-97; *Bystander*, Aug. 16, 1901; July 1, 1904; July 6, 1906; June 28, 1907. Other businesses for which cryptic references appeared during the course of research include: Earl Meriwether, tailor; Charles Pew, ice cream parlor; Aaron Gates, pantorium; Susan Clark, dress shop; Jack Byrd, restaurant; I.D. Marshall, carpet cleaning; Elmer and Vesta Smith's restaurant; F. Perkins, carpet cleaning; O.B. Claire, newsstand; Thomas Jackson, barber, J. Baker, pool hall and barber; Mrs. Scott Richmond, dressmaker; Lulu Pulllen, beauty parlor; William Price, second hand store; George Rice funeral home; and Montrose Johnson, embalmer.

41. Larry Ray Hurto interviews, June 1996 and November 1996. See also *Colfax Clipper*, Nov. 15, 1884; Jan. 3, 1885; March 28, 1885; Aug., 1891; Aug. 1893; and Lee Schmitt, *The History of Barber Shops and Beauty Parlors in the Town of Colfax, Iowa before the Year of 1940*, unpublished manuscript, 1994, 2, 4, 5, 7. The notebooks of Alice B. S. Turner (1859-1915), housed in the Colfax Public Library, consist primarily of clippings from newspapers of Jasper County, mainly Colfax. The notebooks contain an obituary of black barber Jason Green, who practiced in Newton.

42. *Bystander*, Aug. 13, 1909; July 22, 1910; Feb. 16, 1917; Terry Harrison interview, Mason City Public Library, and Arthur Fischbeck, Mason City historian; Thomas C. B. Tyler, "1890: Early Negroes in City," *Mason City Globe-Gazette*, Centennial Edition, June 1, 1953.

43. William Sayles Doan interview, May 27, 1997; William Sayles Doan, *A Book of Days Fort Dodge* (Fort Dodge: Messenger Press, 1991), 161; Jane Burleson, "Black Fort Dodge," *Iowa State Bystander* [1894–1994 Anniversary Edition: 100 Years of Black Achievement], 1994, 66–67.

44. Barbara Beving Long, *Des Moines and Polk County: Flag on the Prairie* (Northridge CA: Windsor Publications, 1988), 63; Lillian McLaughlin, "D.M.'s Phenomenal Businessman Hyde," *Des Moines Tribune*, Feb. 17, 1968.

45. *The Communicator*, Feb. 1995.

46. Information about Robert Patten taken from items found in the Robert E. Patten collection, SHSI Des Moines; interviews with collection donor and son, E. Hobart De Patten; and Jack Lufkin, "Patten's Neighborhood," *Iowa Heritage Illustrated* 77 (1996): 122-44. Other invaluable sources of information were interviews with Gwendolyn Fowler of Des Moines and Patten's granddaughter, Barbara Oliver Hall.

47. Gaynelle Narcisse, *They Took Our Piece of the Pie: Center Street Revisited* (Des Moines: The Bystander Company, 1996), 11; interviews with E. Hobart De Patten.

48. Narcisse, 13; materials found in Robert E. Patten collection. General information about black beauty culture business in Des Moines obtained in interview with Gwendolyn Fowler, May 1995. Another beauty school in Des Moines was Morrow Beauty School. There were also numerous other beauty parlors in Des Moines during the 1900s such as: Berline Beauty Shop owned by Bernice Lanier, Midge's Beauty Saloon, Petite Beauty Salon owned by Blanche E. Lee, Eldora Chapman's Beauty Lounge, Nettie Bell Cox's Polly's Beauty Shop, Helen Bolden's Evalon Beauty Salon, Lena's [King] Beauty Salon, Catherine Mease-Elmore's shop, Agnes Eppright's Miniature Shop, Pearl Jerrers, Victoria Hendricks, and Ruth's Beauty Shop, owned by Ruth Carolyn Moore.

49. *Bystander,* Jan. 28, 1928; Nov. 5, 1953; materials found in Robert E. Patten collection.

50. Gabriel Victor Cools, "The Negro in Typical Communities of Iowa," M.A. thesis, State University of Iowa, 1918, 26.

51. Ibid.

52. Ibid.

53. *Bystander,* Aug. 1, 1946; items in Robert E. Patten collection.

54. Some of the other night spots included Bryson's Entertainment Center, Watkins Hotel, the Blue Circle Hall, the 1113 Club, the Nip, and the Hole. Most of the information about the night spots is taken from the Robert E. Patten collection, plus interviews with E. Hobart De Patten, Donald Lee, Gwendolyn Fowler, and Gaynelle Narcisse.

55. Print collection of Robert E. Patten; interview with Gaynelle Narcisse, Des Moines, Nov. 1995.

56. Gwendolyn Fowler interview, Sept. 20, 1995; Elaine Estes interview, Oct. 1995; *Bystander,* Dec. 26, 1930.

57. Robert V. Morris interview, Aug. 20, 1996; Donald Lee, Gwendolyn Fowler, and E. Hobart De Patten interviews; Robert E. Patten collection.

58. Gwendolyn Kee, "Lewis Henry Fulton: A Mini Portrait," unpublished paper, 1998, in author's possession.

59. Ada and Emery Jackson interview, July 23, 1997; *DMR,* May 9, 1988.

60. Melvin Harper interview, July 3, 1997.

61. Microfilm copies of two short-lived black newspapers of Waterloo during the 1950s and early 1970s, the *Waterloo Defender* and the *Waterloo Post,* are housed at the University of Wisconsin; Robert Neymeyer, "May Harmony Prevail: The Early History of Black Waterloo," *Palimpsest* 61 (1980): 80–91; information gleaned from interview meeting with Waterloo residents Rose Middleton, Venilla Byrd, Ruth Anderson, Denman Phillips Jr., Ada Tredwell, Ernst VanArsdale, Melvina Scott, and Roosevelt Taylor, July 7, 1997; "Minority Business and Professional Directory," (n.p., ca. 1970), which contains a number of businesses.

62. Like other cities, a rich amount of data on business and other aspects of black Waterloo awaits discovery and compilation. Other businesses for which there were brief references include: Shelton's Beer Tap, B & R Sandwich shop, businesses of Scott Mardis and Vivaret Norman, and Mack Butler's rug cleaning business, Ellie's Restaurant, Plantation Bar B.Q., a house of prostitution, Jimmy's Lounge, Stevenson's [Standard] Service Station, Wes Lee's hot tamale stand, Black Loan Company, Taylor's Lounge, and the Blue Shadow.

Fowler and Son Funeral Home, (left to right) Lafayette H. Fowler Sr., L. H. Fowler Jr., and Ella Sipes Fowler, October 28, 1934 (courtesy Larry G. Fowler)

Sioux City horse-drawn omnibus conductor (Sioux City Public Museum)

African-American Wage Earners in Iowa

1850–1950

by Ralph Scharnau

Iowa may seem an unlikely place to chronicle the experiences of black wage earners. In a state where most people claimed German, Irish, English, and Scandinavian ancestry, African-Americans never accounted for even 1 percent of the total population until 1970.[1]

Yet the work as well as the community experiences of these Iowans paralleled those of other black Americans. "The story of the Negro in Iowa is more than the story of a handful of black people thrown across the face of a huge farming state," begins a Depression-era history of African-Americans in Iowa. "[I]t is the drama of twelve million black souls everywhere."[2]

In the years encompassing the Civil War and World War 2, Iowa's black labor force held a wide variety of jobs. Traditional employment in domestic and personal service coexisted with transportation, mining, and manufacturing work. While some African-Americans took jobs as farm hands and a few even owned farms, most worked in Iowa's urban areas. Black enclaves developed and expanded as Southerners migrated to the state after the Civil War and again during the labor shortages created by World Wars 1 and 2.

> *"The story of the Negro in Iowa is more than the story of a handful of black people thrown across the face of a huge farming state. . . . [I]t is the drama of twelve million black souls everywhere."*
>
> — *Jack Smith, WPA, 1940*

Unidentified black coal miner in Iowa with co-workers and mule-drawn equipment (SHSI Iowa City)

Unidentified trackman (courtesy David Bagby)

Sioux City packinghouse workers at Silberman Packing Company, c. 1880 (Sioux City Public Museum)

Unidentified pullman car porter (SHSI Des Moines)

(Below, left to far right)

When a group of black women reported for work at the Liddie and Carver overall factory in Cedar Rapids, the white female employees staged a unanimous walkout. (Cedar Rapids Evening Courier, *September 2, 1897)*

A Muscatine street paving crew, c. 1920 (Muscatine Public Library)

Unidentified African-American worker in the Hotel Blackhawk barbershop, c. 1910 (Putnam Museum)

Unidentified East Des Moines postal carriers in 1896 (SHSI Des Moines)

Many of these Iowans held jobs as domestics or service workers, but of particular interest to us here is the growing black work force holding positions as laborers in the steamboating, mining, railroading, meatpacking, military weaponry, and farm equipment industries.

Patterns of Black Employment, 1850–1900

The towns, especially those located on the Mississippi and Missouri rivers, offer revealing glimpses of nineteenth-century work among the state's African-Americans. Everywhere black women earned money by performing household chores such as cleaning, cooking, and caring for children in private residences. Black women also served as chambermaids and cooks on steamboats. Sioux City's Pearl Street was said to be named after an admired black woman who cooked for one of the boats that navigated the Missouri River. Women also found jobs as laundresses and chambermaids in river city hotels.[3]

Some black women could be classified as self-employed operators of home-based enterprises. In the late 1850s, Dubuque's Agnes Arthur ran a boarding house. Sioux City's Caroline (Auntie) Wooden operated a home laundry in the early 1870s. The *Dubuque City Directory* for 1899–1900 lists dressmaking as the occupation of Mrs. Amanda Blanks.[4]

Considered fit only for home-related domestic chores, black women were generally excluded from factory work. The hiring of black women for industrial jobs could arouse the anger of the white female work force. When a group of seven young black women reported for work at a Cedar Rapids overall factory on September 2, 1897, the white women employees staged a unanimous protest. They threatened to quit if the black women were hired. The company foreman told the black women that "under the circumstances he would be compelled to draw the color line."[5]

African-American men also worked at low-paid domestic and personal-service occupations. The most common male occupations included porters, janitors, cooks, and waiters, working in hotels and restaurants and on steamboats and railroads. A few black men found industrial jobs. As early as 1840, a Muscatine sawmill owner employed several black males.[6] In 1870, the southwest Iowa town of Clarinda had a population of 1,022, including 153 African-Americans who had migrated from Missouri, Kentucky, Virginia, and Tennessee. Many of the town's black males worked for the Clarinda Butter, Poultry and Egg Company or the Berry Company's farm seed and baby chicks operations.[7] In 1894, Fort Dodge had a "small, young and lively" black population. Black men there worked in local mines, mills, and railyards.[8]

The early transportation system of Sioux City owes much to the labor of black males. The city brought in "nearly 500 Negro laborers" to construct boardwalks and asphalt streets and to lay pipelines.[9] Another important construction project involved the laying of railroad tracks. Black laborers performed similar construction tasks in other river towns, such as Council Bluffs, Muscatine, Keokuk, Davenport, and Burlington. Black Iowans also worked on the erection of "round houses, private residences, and industrial plants."[10]

With just over 2,000 black residents, Polk County had Iowa's largest black population in 1900. Over 80 percent of these people resided in Des Moines, the state capital. The city's African-American class structure in the mid-1890s can be divided into three occupational categories. The tiny elite included professional men — a physician, a lawyer, and four ministers — along with small businessmen, a restaurant owner, a rug-cleaning establishment manager, and 41 barbers. Another group included those identified as miners, plasterers, dressmakers, teamsters, and printers, as well as a handful with such city jobs as fireman, policeman, and mail carrier. About two-thirds of the employed African-American community worked in traditional jobs as laborers, porters, waiters, cooks, janitors, domestics, bootblacks, and laundresses.[11]

Steamboat Jobs

While Des Moines displayed the greatest employment diversity, steamboat jobs on the Mississippi and Missouri rivers attracted large numbers of black men. The rivers stimulated economic growth through regional trade in furs, lead, lumber, and grain; through distribution of manufactured goods; and through transportation of passengers traveling between towns, arriving as new settlers, and migrating further west. River traffic moved largely in keelboats until the 1840s, when steamboats began to dominate the waterways. The state's river towns received an early influx of free black riverboat workers in the 1840s and 1850s, a period that coincided with rapid east to west settlement. Some came looking for new work opportunities, others were recruited by steamboat lines, and still others deserted from abusive working conditions on southern packets.[12]

The first black migrants served as ratters and lighters, loading and unloading keelboats at two rapids areas along the Mississippi River, one at Keokuk and the other at Davenport. With increased settlement and river traffic, more and more blacks took jobs on steamboats. The earliest free black settlers at Burlington escaped from southern freight packets. The founding of Sioux City and the arrival of African-Americans occurred at nearly the same time in the mid-1850s. James A. Jackson recruited the city's first blacks

Cook Sam Broaddus relaxing with co-workers in Denison (SHSI Iowa City)

(Below) African-American officers on the Des Moines police force, c. 1910 (courtesy John Zeller)

Many African-American men found seasonal employment in Iowa's steamboat traffic. Pictured here is the packet steamer Andrew S. Bennett *of Sioux City, c. 1880. (Sioux City Public Museum)*

Roustabouts on the Sydney
(SHSI Des Moines)

Waiters on the passenger steamer Quincy *of Dubuque*
(Dubuque County Historical Society)

220

to work as deck hands on his ferryboats.[13] Following the Civil War, blacks supplanted Irish boatmen and, noted one commentator, "in a few years practically monopolized steamboat labor."[14]

Labor on steamboats paralleled that of industrial workers elsewhere. The elite white staff consisted of the captain, clerk, pilot, engineer, and mate. Wage earners included those identified as cabin crew or deck crew. Cooks, waiters, stewards, cabin boys, and chambermaids comprised the cabin crew, a mixture of black and white men, boys, and some women. The main body of workers, the deck crew, served as firemen, cargo handlers, and capstan and pump operators. These tasks carried the risk of injury or death from broken machinery, explosions, fires, or simply falling overboard. Disciplinary measures carried risks too, as crew members might be clubbed, beaten, or knocked down. There were even reports of deck hands being stabbed, shot, or thrown overboard. Wage rates and work fluctuated according to seasonal factors and market conditions. Most steamboat men averaged eight to nine months of employment. During the busy season they worked seven days a week. Occasionally, deck hands resorted to strikes to force wage increases or retaliate for brutal treatment. The typical steamboat worker was a young, strong, and itinerant male who worked irregularly.[15]

Besides the uncertain wages, long hours, and physically demanding and dangerous toil, black crew members also faced instances of overt discrimination that resulted in violence. In June 1857, the white mate of the *Saracen* received "a saucy answer" from a black cabin hand. The affair escalated into an armed melee, with citizens of Fort Madison intervening to rescue the severely beaten black man. Before the pitched battle ended, several aboard the boat suffered wounds and one on shore was killed.[16]

Another incident occurred aboard the *Pembina* in 1864. While docked at Dubuque a group of rough "levee loungers" who "objected to the colored hands" boarded the boat and attacked them with "clubs, etc." The ship's officers drove off the invaders with iron bars, had five arrested, and three went to jail.[17] A race riot erupted shortly after the steamer *Dubuque*, with a mostly black deck crew of 30, left the wharf at Davenport on July 29, 1869. An African-American deck hand assisting with the collection of fares was assaulted by a drunken raftsman.

Soon a mob of about 25 raftsmen began attacking all of the black employees on the boat. Using chunks of coal, stones, knives, and clubs, the rioters beat, slashed, and threw their victims overboard. Only after no more blacks could be found did the slaughter end. Fueled by race hatred and aggravated by alcohol, five African-Americans lost their lives during the bloody spree. The eight rioters convicted of manslaughter received penitentiary sentences that ranged from one to ten years.[18]

Despite the rough work, black steamboat men experienced a sense of adventure, a degree of autonomy, and a level of compensation not found in other jobs.

Coal Miners

While steamboat labor provided employment for black Iowans, the post–Civil War era brought a new job category. The development of Iowa's largest nineteenth-century industry — coal mining — became the leading occupation among African-American males. In 1870, railroad tracks reached the Missouri River, and mining began a dramatic surge that peaked in 1917. Coal camps sprang up in rural areas away from population centers. A majority of the coal-mining communities that dotted the Iowa landscape by 1895 included some black residents. In 1900, they accounted for nearly 10 percent of the state's miners.[19]

Coal mining became a way of life for male miners and their families. Work in coal mines was highly dangerous and dirty, and it was also isolated and independent. Seasonal fluctuations in demand and mobility occasioned by exhausted coal veins characterized the industry. Most miners lived in company towns where the operators owned the housing, stores, and other community enterprises. Rents, consumer goods prices, wages and hours issues, and workplace conditions constituted the major areas of contention between the miners and the companies.

Initially black men entered the state's coal fields as strikebreakers during the early 1880s. They came from Missouri, West Virginia, Virginia, and Tennessee. Often the striking white miners greeted the strikebreakers with violence, and militia companies or sheriff's officers were summoned to restore order. Some coal operators also began to hire southern blacks as regular mine workers.[20]

The Cuzzens family — Alice, Will, Martha, and William — outside their company home in Buxton, c. 1910 (SHSI Des Moines)

Miners outside the Scandia Coal Company mines near Madrid, 1940 (courtesy Evelyn Davis)

Essentially, the operators viewed African-Americans as cheap labor for a rapidly expanding coal industry in a sparsely settled region. Whether they arrived as unsuspecting strikebreakers or regular wage earners, black laborers understood their own economic self-interest. Mining jobs paid substantially better than the farm and service jobs they had held in the South. Although many of the blacks lacked mining experience, they knew the hard work and discipline connected with cotton fields, artisans' shops, or mills. Besides, the coal operators placed the novices with skilled miners until they could function independently. Furthermore, some of the black strikebreakers had previously worked in coal mining and experienced industrial conflicts. Fortified with cultural pride and motivated by self-help, black miners saw themselves not as pawns of capitalists but as workers eager to improve their standard of living by taking jobs previously closed to them.[21]

Whether regular miners or strikebreakers, blacks found that some mining communities accepted them, while others barred their entry. Although African-Americans usually accounted for a small minority in coal-mining communities, Muchakinock emerged as a predominantly black town. The camp's population varied in the 1880s and 1890s, but African-Americans accounted for up to two-thirds of the residents. There, black community life developed, complete with a brass band, an annual fair, two churches, lodges, two schools, a meat shop, a drug store, a law practice, two newspapers, a YMCA, a mutual protection society, and Republican political activities. In September 1898, the *Iowa State Bystander*, a Des Moines-based black weekly newspaper, referred to Muchakinock as "the colored Athens of Iowa" and estimated its population at "about 1500 of which fully 1000 are colored." Although socially distanced from one another, the African and European heritaged people living in Muchakinock apparently experienced relatively harmonious race relations.[22]

Unions, Occupations, and Communities

Whether they worked in the coal fields, on the steamboats, or in the river towns, black men and women learned that most trade unions excluded them. White workers, both unionists and their unorganized brethren, usually depicted African-Americans as a servile, cheap labor force that threatened their wages and standard of living. Considered capable of only menial work and denied access to apprenticeship programs and union protection,

black laborers nonetheless found new work opportunities when some employers sought to protect or increase their profit margins by hiring more workers, by driving down wage scales, by replacing striking employees, or by thwarting militant labor unity. Traditionally confined to low wage jobs, blacks readily accepted any employment promising increased pay. While many were offered only unskilled domestic and personal service jobs, some took jobs as semiskilled assistants, and a few managed to hurdle the color bar and become artisans. Yet most black carpenters, blacksmiths, stone masons, and other skilled workers could only survive by becoming handymen.[23]

Three unions managed to overcome racial antipathy among their members and organize African-American workers. The miners' local founded in 1881 at Ottumwa was the first known all-black affiliate of the Knights of Labor. The Knights subsequently organized black laborers locals at Des Moines in 1886 and Burlington in 1888. Some other black workers joined with white workers in mixed Knights locals representing a variety of job classifications.[24]

While adopting a policy of welcoming black miners to its ranks in 1891, United Mine Workers district officials found implementation of the policy thwarted by the continued use of black strikebreakers in the 1890s and tensions among regular miners in integrated work forces. Finally, the African-American men at Muchakinock joined the United Mine Workers in 1900. The mine superintendent there capitulated to the union threat of a recognition strike that he feared would result in bloodshed.[25] Among skilled black workers, printers joined the Typographical Union No. 118 in Des Moines. Thaddeus Ruff, a black printer, held elected office in the union.[26]

During the last half of the nineteenth century, the work and community experiences of black Iowans differed from those of the state's other residents. At this time, large throngs of newcomers surged into Iowa, most of them representing European ethnic groups. The press and government officials cordially greeted them, touting the advantages of the state's fertile land and expanding railway network. African-Americans received no such welcome. Rather, they confronted the realities of race prejudice. Although no longer subjected to antebellum black codes restricting their migration and civic equality, Iowa's black population still faced unofficial discrimination and segregation. They endured racial slurs, bigoted behavior, and sporadic violence.

Fortified with cultural pride and motivated by self-help, black miners saw themselves not as pawns of capitalists but as workers eager to improve their standard of living by taking jobs previously closed to them.

Unlike a majority of Iowa's population, most African-Americans lived in urban enclaves. When the number of black settlers reached a certain level, a community ethos developed. Places with only 50 black residents and those with 500 or more displayed varying degrees of cultural cohesiveness. Black urbanites collected money to build churches and schools, started businesses and social groups, celebrated their newly won freedom, and saved money to purchase homes.

In spite of Iowa's status as a premier farm state, the black labor force held mostly non-agricultural jobs. Many African-American men and women labored as porters, cooks, day laborers, housekeepers, janitors, and waiters. These jobs entailed long hours, poor pay, low status, and deference to the employer. Riverboat and mine work, both dangerous and physically demanding occupations, accounted for the largest concentration of black males. Yet the seasonal nature of steamboating and coal mining often forced them to seek other employment. In search of work opportunities during slack times, coal miners and deck hands could only find traditional unskilled jobs as domestics and service workers.

Employers often proved unwilling to hire black workers for anything but the most menial occupations. They saw African-Americans as a profitable supply of cheap labor, unskilled and unorganized. Besides the employers, blacks encountered workplace discrimination from fellow workers, supervisors, and the general public. Away from the supportive influence of home, family, and fellowship groups, the workplace brought them into contact with those who harbored racial animosity.

While examples of racial hostility abound, African-Americans occasionally experienced instances of equality. During a strike at the Coalville mine in 1881, the operator imported 75 black strikebreakers from Tennessee. Upon the arrival of the strikebreakers, the white miners offered them a deal. In return for refusing to work, the strikers would furnish them with living expenses. The blacks accepted the offer, and an interracial coalition emerged. The onset of warm weather decreased the demand for coal, and the miners, both white and black, were forced by economic necessity to return to the mines. Violence was averted and black and white unity was achieved, even though the three-month strike for higher wages was lost.[27]

A less dramatic example of nondiscrimination occurred at Dubuque in the fall of 1872. A black railroad porter went to a local restaurant for breakfast. A white waitress refused to take his order, and seven others defiantly backed her. The restaurant manager fired all eight of the waitresses. (A few asked to be reinstated the next day.)[28]

In their daily lives and on the job, black Iowans struggled against poverty and injustice. By 1900, African-American wage earners had worked hard, preparing and serving food, carrying baggage and cleaning rooms, loading and unloading steamboats, laying tracks, and mining coal. They labored in jobs where racial hostility could create oppressive conditions. Yet the black labor force displayed a work ethic that produced both economic growth for the state and civic pride in the black community.

Emergence of a Black Industrial Work Force, 1900–1950

The opening of the twentieth century found African-Americans eager to take jobs that promised economic betterment. This quest for an improved standard of living proved to be a long one, requiring tenacity and courage. A survey of the years 1900 to 1950 reveals black Iowans with both traditional and new employment.

Many of these wage earners held low-pay and menial domestic and personal-service jobs. Women still worked as maids, cooks, and seamstresses. Men still held jobs as porters, janitors, and unskilled laborers. By the 1920s, however, railroading and meatpacking largely superseded steamboating and coal mining as leading jobs for African-American males. By the 1940s, farm equipment jobs assumed added importance for black men. Two world wars expanded employment among both men and women. Some regular factory production jobs finally began opening for black women at mid-century.

Railroad Laborers

Between the 1850s and the 1910s, the state and the nation experienced urban growth and industrial expansion caused by railroad development. Supplanting steamboats, trains conquered the Iowa landscape, opening the bounty of the land, connecting countryside and city, stimulating commercial activity, spawning ancillary industries, moving people and goods swiftly, reliably, and cheaply. Rail travel triumphed over all other forms of land and river transit, the steamboats' final demise coming with the development of the modern freight-hauling towboat and barge after 1910.[29]

Railroads played a role in the decline of another transient and seasonal business, coal mining. Railroads were a major

The seasonal nature of steamboating and coal mining often forced African-Americans to seek other employment. In search of work during slack times, they could only find traditional unskilled jobs as domestics and service workers.

purchaser of Iowa coal in the 1870s. By the 1920s and 1930s, however, the same railroads turned to coal suppliers outside of Iowa. Rising oil and gas usage exacerbated the crisis and contributed to plummeting coal sales.[30]

The closing of coal mines and the decline of steamboat transit coupled with the explosion of railroad operations brought significant increases in black employment on Iowa's railways. The first trunk lines reached the state in the mid-1850s. Fifty years later, Iowa's trackage totaled nearly 10,000 miles, "one of the most dense rail networks of any state."[31] By 1895, 24 urban places in Iowa serviced railroads as division headquarters with both operating and shop functions. These communities had from 100 to nearly 700 railroad employees.[32]

Iowa's rapidly expanding railway system absorbed a number of displaced black miners and steamboat men. The railroads also recruited southern blacks. Division towns with a sizable contingent of black railway workers included Dubuque, Burlington, Des Moines, Waterloo, Council Bluffs, Davenport, Cedar Rapids, Clinton, Ottumwa, and Sioux City. In the small town of Manly, black railroad workers lived in boxcars and shanties built by the Rock Island Railroad. Similar living conditions prevailed for a community of 21 black families on the south side of Des Moines near the Great Western Railroad roundhouse.[33]

Railway work required a large and dispersed labor force that performed a variety of tasks. The division of labor reflected different skill levels between and sometimes within occupational classifications. When railroads hired workers, they traditionally turned to males. In Iowa and other northern states, African-American men often found employment as porters or waiters, the lowest paid and most servile jobs. Others held unskilled jobs as laborers in railyards, car shops, and roundhouses, as section hands laying, repairing, and maintaining track, or as helpers for firemen, brakemen, mechanics, switchmen, and flagmen.[34]

Only a few black males held skilled railroad jobs. These included machinist H. G. Williams of Clinton, brakemen M. Pease of Mason City, and steamfitter W. C. Buice of Des Moines. Railroading posed dangerous working conditions, and black laborers filled jobs with high rates of injuries and deaths. Although subjected to unsafe work sites, they received good wages compared to other blacks employed as farm hands, day laborers, and domestic servants.[35]

During the labor shortages created by World War 1, the number of unskilled African-Americans working as laborers and helpers dramatically increased in such towns as Cedar Rapids, Perry, Council Bluffs, and Des Moines. In wartime Perry, the 200 African-American workers included a dozen black women, clad in overalls, who worked in the roundhouse. A black foreman supervised African-American section hands in Des Moines during the summer of 1919.[36]

Most black railroad workers faced racial discrimination in terms of employment, promotion, and unionization. Railroad employers often considered them fit for only the lowest paid, unskilled, dangerous, and dirty jobs. To railway managers, blacks represented cheap labor and a bulwark against white militancy and unionism. Blacks also usually found themselves excluded from advancement to better-paid skilled positions. White workers often viewed African-Americans as a threat to their wages, working conditions, and standard of living.

The railway unions, composed of white, skilled workers, barred blacks in their rituals and constitutions. By drawing a sharp color line, whites maintained a monopoly on such skilled jobs as engineers, conductors, firemen, and brakemen as well as expressman and telegraphers. The railroad carriers adopted employment schemes that rewarded only white males.[37]

By the late nineteenth century, railroad managers and railroad brotherhoods quietly collaborated to keep African-Americans in low level and menial occupations. "When the federal government assumed control of the nation's rail network [during World War 1]," writes labor historian Philip S. Foner, "it simply sanctioned the informal agreements between railroad management and the unions by prohibiting the hiring or advancing of Negroes to positions they had not occupied in the past."[38] After World War 1, the collusion between the railroad unions, the railway managers, and the federal government continued to make subordination and exclusion the hallmarks of black railroad labor. These

Unidentified workers of the Iowa Railway & Light Company of Marshalltown (courtesy Helen I. Johnson)

Most black railroad workers faced racial discrimination in terms of employment, promotion, and unionization. Railroad employers often considered them fit for only the lowest paid, unskilled, dangerous, and dirty jobs.

discriminatory practices frustrated and angered African-American railway employees like West Des Moines resident Dalton Lloyd. Despite 50 years of service as a yard worker for the Rock Island Railroad, Lloyd complained of triple jeopardy as management, unions, and government blocked his promotion to a more responsible and better paying position. Besides registering complaints about discriminatory practices, black employees requested job transfers, sought seniority-based promotions, and a group in Des Moines joined a short-lived brotherhood of black railroad men during World War 1.[39]

Two nationwide railway shopmen's strikes in 1911 and 1922 brought a number of African-Americans to Iowa. The Illinois Central Railroad operated a large maintenance and repair shop in Waterloo, the railroad's main division point between Chicago and Omaha. In the fall of 1911, skilled white shopmen — machinists,

molders, and blacksmiths — walked off their Waterloo jobs in a dispute over wages and union recognition. Many of the shopmen's unskilled assistants — mostly immigrant Italians and Bulgarians — joined the strikers. Illinois Central officials sought replacement workers. Unable to recruit enough strikebreakers locally, the company turned to recently arrived immigrants and southern blacks.[40]

Attracted by advertising that promised good paying jobs and free travel passes, black workers from the Deep South made the journey to Waterloo. A significant number of these strikebreakers came from Mississippi. Some had worked for the Illinois Central and lost their jobs because of "the violence of white strikers or the curtailment of work due to the strike."[41] Others came from rural areas of Mississippi and adjoining states with no knowledge of the walkout. Illinois Central boxcars

Illinois Central Railroad workers in Waterloo, c. 1915 (SHSI Des Moines)

provided not only a typical means of transit to Waterloo but also temporary residences in the railroad yards. During the course of the strike, which lasted nationwide almost four years, the Illinois Central closed its shops in Watervalley, Mississippi, and announced the expansion of its Waterloo facilities. The Illinois Central tracks that ran from Watervalley to Waterloo became a main line of black migration.[42]

The strikers suffered defeat after a long and bitter struggle. The walkout intensified racial prejudice as well. Since the shopcraft unions limited membership to white workmen, black replacement workers severely undermined the strike. Strikers angrily denounced the company's decision to import black scabs. The presence of African-American strikebreakers also generated hostile feelings in the community. Many sympathetic townsfolk sided with the strikers' demands for union recognition and improved wages. The African-American newcomers also experienced segregated housing in the "smoky row" district near the Illinois Central tracks. Public accommodations restricted black patrons. Race-baiting journalists fanned the flames of intolerance by asserting that more black residents meant increased crime and lawlessness.[43]

Animosity toward black railroad workers also flared during a 1922 strike in Manly. The Rock Island Railroad built a roundhouse there in 1913. The railroad actively recruited workers for its new facility. The roundhouse work force also expanded because of the labor demands created by World War 1. The newcomers included 90 blacks. Suddenly one-tenth of the town's population claimed an African-American heritage. According to William J. Maddix's account, "they came primarily from small towns in Oklahoma and Arkansas, attracted by the railroad's promise of jobs and free housing."[44]

The "free housing" consisted of boxcars and shanties provided by the railroad and located a mile north of town. Blacks could not buy or build homes where whites lived. The local newspaper depicted the "dusky" section as one with rampant crime, alcoholism, gambling, and prostitution. At the work site, African-Americans predictably were hired as laborers and helpers at the Manly roundhouse. They usually worked on maintenance crews. These crews moved and serviced the locomotives and fired stationary boilers to provide heat and mechanical power. Blacks held jobs classified as hostler helpers, fire builders, and engine wipers. The work was usually heavy and hot as well as dangerous and dirty.[45]

Racial tensions reached a climax in the summer of 1922 during a railway strike. Local Rock Island shopmen joined in a nationwide walkout precipitated by a second round of wage cuts and opposition to contracting out and piecework.[46] White workers in the unionized crafts — machinists, boilermakers, sheet metal workers, electricians, car men, and blacksmiths — urged their fellow black employees to participate in the work stoppage. The African-American workers refused and remained on their roundhouse jobs. They argued that the unions' all-white policy barred them from membership. The incensed white strikers retaliated with a boisterous demonstration. The incessant blaring of their car horns finally forced the black workers to evacuate the roundhouse. The Ku Klux Klan responded by burning a cross near the facility. Fearful wives of African-American workers convinced Rock Island officials to grant their husbands a leave of absence until the strike was settled in the fall of 1922.[47]

William Barnett celebrates his 1958 retirement from the Rock Island Railroad in Manly. Pearl Barnett is beside her husband. Henry Johnson is third from left, front row; A. D. Tate, sixth from right; Prophet Dunn, fifth from right; and John Page, far right. (MacNider Art Museum)

Railroad workers on a diesel locomotive, presumably in the Quad Cities (Putnam Museum)

down workplace barriers in hiring, assignment, promotion, and wages. The case of Benjamin Tredwell illustrates that real progress came in a painfully slow manner. Tredwell began working for the railroad in Mississippi as a teenager on July 4, 1916. Two years later, during World War 1, he migrated to Waterloo. Hired by the Illinois Central, he worked as a mechanic for over 50 years. Even though he possessed a master mechanic's knowledge of locomotives, the company and the union connived to classify his job as mechanic's helper for 25 years.

Tredwell used the federal Fair Employment Practices Committee that operated during World War 2 as a lever to finally receive the recognition and pay associated with the mechanic title. Although he joined an affiliate of the American Federation of Labor, Benjamin Tredwell resented how the company and the union applied the color line in job catagories.[50] During the first half of the twentieth century, the carriers and the unions showed little interest in ending railway job discrimination.

Packinghouse Workers

In addition to railroading, the meatpacking industry in Iowa offered job opportunities for black workers.[51] Led by slaughtering and meatpacking, food products consistently ranked first according to value of products among Iowa's manufactured goods from 1860 to 1925. Rapid expansion occurred during World War 1 and during the industry's decentralization, away from large cities, beginning in the 1920s. Meatpacking became the most important industrial employer in cities like Ottumwa, Sioux City, Waterloo, and Cedar Rapids. Iowa soon led the nation in meat-products employment.[52]

As early as 1900, African-Americans accounted for about 13 percent of the work force at the John Morrell and Company meatpacking plant in Ottumwa.[53] However, Sioux City soon became the premier locale for black packinghouse workers. The first significant introduction of black meat industry workers there came during the strike in 1904, when several hundred unionized white workers at the Cudahy and Armour packing plants walked off their jobs in a nationwide action to demand wage increases. The packers responded with a strategy that involved obtaining black strikebreakers, an injunction, and the militia, tactics that broke the strike after two months of bitter conflict. Frustrated and angry strikers vented their rage on the black strikebreakers with both verbal and physical assaults. After

Employment in the railway industry peaked in the 1920s. Although the number of African-Americans working on Iowa railroads increased during the decade, trouble lay ahead. During the 1930s, black railway wage earners in Manly and other cities across the nation faced both economic and technological threats to their job security. The Great Depression caused railroad companies to thin their work forces. The introduction of diesel locomotives brought added unemployment as they required smaller track and repair shop maintenance crews than the old steam-powered ones. Given their unskilled status and lack of seniority, African-American railroad workers usually found themselves in the first-fired group.[48]

The traffic boom created by World War 2 served as only a temporary catalyst for black railroad employment. Beginning slowly in the 1920s, the railway industry declined as automobile and truck production soared. In Iowa, railway abandonment reached several hundred miles in each of the decades between 1920 and 1960. Shrinking rail lines brought sharp work force reductions. The job losses hit blacks first and hardest as the carriers eliminated unskilled laborers, helpers, and passenger service positions.[49]

From the years of the railroad industry's expansion to those of its retrenchment, African-American workers sought to break the strike ended, whites refused to work with the black strikebreakers, who, with the acquiescence of the mayor and company officials, left the city.[54]

Black strikebreakers played a role during another failed nationwide strike in the winter of 1921–22. A wage-and-hour dispute precipitated a walkout by locals of the Amalgamated Meat Cutters and Butcher Workmen (AMCBW), a craft union affiliated with the American Federation of Labor (AFL), at the Morrell plant in Ottumwa and the Cudahy, Armour, and Swift plants in Sioux City.

While some black packinghouse workers supported the union, most remained on the job during the walkout. Sensing an opportunity for economic advancement, other blacks entered the plants as strikebreakers. Violent clashes occurred between strikers and strikebreakers at both locations. Faced with "several hundred deputy sheriffs" in Sioux City and "250 [Iowa National Guard] troops" in Ottumwa, the strikers ended their work stoppage. The confrontation destroyed the local unions in both cities. In the

aftermath of the strike, the anti-union packers at Sioux City and Ottumwa adopted representation schemes and welfare policies designed to encourage company loyalty and restrain union sentiment. With these management initiatives and the AMCBW's continuing reluctance to organize African-American workers, the Iowa meatpacking industry remained an open shop citadel until the labor unrest of the 1930s.[55]

Arrival as strikebreakers constituted one way black employment in Iowa's packinghouses grew. Former miners and southerners also migrated in search of new jobs. During the World War 1 era and after, Iowa packers in Cedar Rapids, Sioux City, and Waterloo expanded their labor forces and hired black workers.[56] Using city directories, William Hewitt calculated that the percentage of Sioux City's black workers employed in the meat industry rose dramatically from less than 1 percent in 1916 to about 18 percent in 1920 and reached nearly 44 percent in 1925.[57]

Traditionally the meatpacking industry operated with male-only production workers. Packers might hire a few African-

(Above) Edward King earned a good living by working in Waterloo packinghouses. (SHSI Iowa City)

(Left) Rath packinghouse worker, presumably a member of UPWA Local 46 in Waterloo after World War 2 (SHSI Iowa City)

American women for domestic-type jobs, but the low skilled, exhausting, and hazardous jobs went to African-American men. They usually worked on the kill floor, a place where noise, stench, and heat filled the air. The jobs carried titles like hog shackler, beef lugger, and hide shaker. Small cuts and bruises as well as respiratory illnesses and back injuries accompanied the work routines. Despite these nauseating working conditions, the employment offered an important benefit — good pay. Wages of black meat workers sometimes doubled that of their fellow laborers with domestic and personal service jobs. The killing floor workers actually occupied an important place in the plant. They started the production process, and the tasks they performed created a potential for advancement to more skilled positions. Packinghouse work also offered reasonable job security.[58]

The Depression of the 1930s brought an end to job expansion and security as Iowa packinghouses began laying off employees. Packers reduced hours, wages, and jobs while increasing production pressures. The hard times fell heavily on black workers. Usually the first fired, they survived by taking odd jobs, finding federal work relief, relying on black women's domestic work, and tapping mutual help activities within the black community.[59]

Ironically, a new packing plant opened at Fort Dodge in December 1934. Building of the Tobin packinghouse had started in the previous year. Marshall Wells, a local black worker, recalled his experience at the work site: "Me and another fellow went down and applied for a job to get work on the construction of the place, but they said they didn't want any blacks down there." Yet when the plant began operating in December 1934, a small crew of experienced black and white butchers from Chicago arrived to train the workers. The Tobin labor force included no new black employees until World War 2 when Wells himself was hired.[60]

The 1930s Depression also marked renewed unionization efforts in Iowa packing plants. Waves of worker unrest reached packinghouses in Waterloo, Sioux City, Cedar Rapids, Ottumwa, Fort Dodge, Mason City, and Des Moines. The flurry of organizational campaigns received added momentum with the passage of national legislation for the first time giving workers the right to organize unions of their own choosing and to bargain collectively with their employers over wages, hours, and working conditions. To combat worker militancy, the vehemently anti-union packers adopted a series of tactics: dismissing union activists; exploiting work force racial, ethnic, gender, and skill divisions;

establishing company unions; insisting that employees sign yellow dog contracts that prohibit union membership; defying the right to organize law; and labeling organizers as outsiders and Communists.

Initially holding secret meetings, union activists soon began openly confronting management with demands for recognition and with a variety of job actions that included traditional walkouts, sit-down strikes, slowdowns, and other forms of resistance. With concerted and persistent direct action on the shop floor by the workers themselves in the late 1930s and early 1940s, Iowa's meat-industry wage earners finally won union recognition and their first contracts.[61]

When locals first organized, they affiliated with the revived AMCBW or with two more recently founded industrial unions, the Midwest Union of Packinghouse Workers (MUPW), based in Cedar Rapids, and the Independent Union of All Workers (IUAW), based in Austin, Minnesota. These fledgling groups provided some of the leadership and organizational structures for the formation of the Packinghouse Workers Organizing Committee (PWOC). Founded by the Congress of Industrial Organizations (CIO) in 1937, the PWOC superseded the MUPW and IUAW and emerged as the dynamic center of the packinghouse union movement. In 1943, the PWOC became the United Packinghouse Workers of America (UPWA).[62]

The formation of the MUPW, IUAW, and the PWOC — industrial unions dedicated to inclusive organizing — brought a new dimension to the movement for worker solidarity. The craft-oriented AMCBW had made only feeble attempts to organize African-Americans. Those blacks who joined the Amalgamated preferred the protection it provided to the "sham" of company unions. But even if they joined the AMCBW, blacks frequently had no voice in union affairs and continued to face job discrimination in terms of wages, promotions, and working conditions. This began to change in the 1930s as MUPW, IUAW, and PWOC appeals to labor unity engaged black activists in the struggle to unionize Iowa's packing plants and advance racial equality. Some went on to hold leadership positions, particularly as union stewards.[63]

One of the earliest black local-union presidents was Arthell Shelton. In 1930, Shelton began working on the beef-kill floor at Sioux City's Swift plant. Known as "Sweet Potato," Shelton's tough-guy reputation, left-wing sympathies, organizational skills, and

The hard times of the

Great Depression

fell heavily on

black workers.

Usually the first fired,

they survived by

taking odd jobs,

finding federal work

relief . . . and tapping

mutual help activities

within the black

community.

Charles Hayes, vice president of AMCBW, speaking at a retirement party for Ralph Helstein at the Hotel Roosevelt in Cedar Rapids (SHSI Iowa City)

Meeting of a meatcutters' union, probably late 1930s (SHSI Iowa City)

leadership position put him at the center of PWOC efforts to unionize at Swift in the late 1930s. Shelton coordinated the 1937–38 organizing drive that brought 65 percent of the production workers into the union ranks. The company rejected union efforts to secure recognition and negotiate grievances. Frustrated unionists finally voted to strike.

The walkout lasted from September 29, 1938, through January 1939. The turning point in the strike came in mid-October when a riot ensued as strikebreakers were escorted across union picket lines by armed deputies. With the appearance of National Guard troops, the jailing of 40 union leaders, and Swift's refusal to consider any settlement offers including arbitration, the strike ended. Shelton and other key leaders were not rehired, but the union regrouped and finally won a certification election in 1942.[64]

The 1940s and 1950s — World War 2 and the post-war years — marked the critical period of advance toward racial equality in Iowa packing plants. As the plants added new employees, the unions expanded their membership base and grew more assertive. The influx of significant numbers of black men and, for the first time, black women, forced both management and labor to confront their racial and gender biases. Black packinghouse workers took a leading role in the struggle to end discrimination. Some of the new African-American employees joined a cadre of veteran blacks to demand equal workplace rights for themselves. Slowly the discriminatory barriers began to crumble.

Progressive black and white union members launched a campaign to seek job equity not only for blacks but also for Hispanics and women. They forged their anti-discrimination

Armour workers attending a grievance settlement meeting in Omaha, 1948 (SHSI Iowa City)

Percy Burt and Merle Thompson at a meeting of UPWA Local 46 in Waterloo (SHSI Iowa City)

program under the banner of the UPWA. The UPWA's commitment to interracial unionism required struggle when faced with resistance from employers and fellow unionists. Packers would only consider black women for janitorial jobs while African-American men were traditionally confined to working in the cut and kill sections of the plant. Promotions were virtually nonexistent. Black women were ignored by unions. Black male unionists' needs and interests went unaddressed, and they were absent from the union's leadership ranks.[65]

To address these issues, the UPWA insisted upon contract language that included fair employment practices by the company and the union. The union launched organizing drives, recruiting members among female and black workers and encouraging them to run for elected union offices. The UPWA sought to end the classification of jobs as male/female or white/black with different pay scales, to institute job bidding by qualifications, and to initiate seniority and equal pay for equal work. As packers responded to these pressures from union activists, jobs opened for blacks in previously all-white and all-male departments. Women made their production work debut in the sliced-bacon department. They also eventually took jobs in other departments and even on the kill floor. Men finally began working in the better paid "knife jobs." A few became electricians, plumbers, or performed other skilled work in the mechanical and boiler shops.[66]

None of these gains came without encountering resistance. Some of the white workers, both men and women, resented the black newcomers. Their responses varied from verbal insults to quit threats or work stoppages. When Ada Tredwell entered the frozen-food department at the Rath Packing Company in Waterloo, a white woman told the boss that she "didn't want to work with that nigger." Until the 1960s, male UPWA officials seemed reluctant to address gender-based issues of job and pay inequities. Union men with racial and gender animosities found it difficult to welcome black men and women as fellow unionists and as union officers. Then, too, black leaders did not always agree with one another on shop floor tactics. Concerned about profit margins and fearing racial turmoil, companies moved slowly to implement new policies that prohibited discrimination. Some employers ignored job equity agreements or refused to enforce them. Often it took union grievances, legal challenges, or government orders to force compliance.[67]

Waterloo's Rath Packing Company, one of the largest meatpackers in the nation, provided the most important Iowa setting for UPWA Local 46's extraordinary experiment in racial solidarity. The African-American work force at Rath increased with the migration of blacks from the South during and immediately following World War 2. By the late 1940s, about 20 percent of Rath's 5,000 employees were African-American.

Two radical white unionists, Punchy Ackerson and Lowell Hollenbeck, constantly prodded workers to adopt interracial unionism and to support anti-discrimination initiatives. Ackerson and Hollenbeck collaborated with a group of talented and energetic black leaders, which included Russell Lasley, Percy Burt, Robert Burt, Charles Pearson, Jimmy Porter, Ada Tredwell, and Anna Mae Weems. These leaders agitated for equality and unity in a variety of ways: recruiting new union members; building coalitions with white workers; filing grievances in response to job, pay, advancement, and seniority inequities; winning elections to union offices and policy-making committee positions; taking job actions to protest company discrimination; helping workers in other locals build interracial unionism; organizing union anti-discrimination committees; promoting civil rights through active involvement with community groups like the NAACP; and running anti-racist candidates for city council. The most stunning example of nondiscrimination policy at Rath occurred when both the company and the union agreed that white workers who walked out rather than work in an integrated department would lose their jobs. Unlike the largely rhetorical support for nondiscrimination among most other unions, the UPWA showed its commitment to social equality and industrial democracy.[68]

Local 46's support for racial equality and its shop floor power were tested in the strike of 1948, when a wage dispute sent UPWA workers to the picket lines across the country. In Waterloo, angry confrontations occurred between pickets and strikebreakers. When pickets forcibly prevented an African-American scab worker, Fred Lee Roberts, from entering the plant, he shot and killed white union founder Chuck Farrell, and a riot ensued. The tragic incident failed to break the interracial unity and determination of the strikers. After a little more than two months of bitter confrontation and the presence of National Guard troops, however, the international called off the strike.

Upon returning to the plant, the discouraged union members discovered that the company gave super-seniority to those, including one African-American, who worked during the strike.

The company also instituted an incentive system that workers characterized as "inequitable" and a "speedup." While over 20 of the striking white and black men and women stood trial on conspiracy and inciting-to-riot charges, a jury acquitted Fred Lee Roberts of murder. Two Local 46 leaders received prison sentences.[69]

The UPWA had suffered a humiliating defeat. "In the strike's aftermath," notes historian Bruce Fehn, "union leaders feared and suspected that the packing companies would again use race to divide workers and open UPWA-organized plants to raids by rival unions — either company unions or the AFL's Amalgamated Meat Cutters and Butcher Workmen."[70] Local 46 struggled to rebuild union strength and reinforce racial solidarity. Union members who crossed the picket lines were fined and pressured to rejoin the union. The local also mounted a campaign to sign up new members. When the company imposed the higher job standards and refused to abandon super-seniority, unionists retaliated with short work stoppages. By the mid-1950s, the company finally agreed to eliminate the super-seniority clause, and the union regained some of its shop-floor power as membership among Rath employees climbed from a post-strike low of 50 percent to 85 percent.[71]

Besides helping with the reorganization of the Rath union, black activists took new leadership positions in the crusade to end racial discrimination. Russell Lasley, a Local 46 leader and international union vice-president, became director of the UPWA's Anti-Discrimination Department, established in 1950. While Lasley carried the banner at the national level, Percy Burt, who held a number of Local 46 offices, served as president of the union's human relations committee. His community involvement included terms as president of the NAACP and membership on the Waterloo Human Rights Committee. Percy's brother, Robert Burt, was a union steward and chaired the local's human rights committee for 12 years.

Ada Tredwell, one of the earliest female unionists, fought job bias at Rath, and she promoted improved race relations through the NAACP and YWCA. Charles Pearson, a young militant who held posts as steward and vice-president of the local, headed the local's anti-discrimination committee. Pearson worked closely with two other dynamic young leaders, Jimmy Porter and Anna Mae Weems. Elected union trustee, Porter became active in the local's human-rights committee and in Waterloo's civil rights movement. Anna Mae Weems joined the union, integrated several departments with previously all-white women, served as steward, chaired the local's human-rights committee, and attended conventions of district and international anti-discrimination committees. She also became a leading civil-rights figure in Waterloo, picketing, boycotting, and cajoling local businesses to open their employment and services to African-Americans. She served as president of the NAACP and brought rank-and-file workers into the profession-dominated ranks of the organization.

Despite the reservations of some black conservatives and the resistance of some white racists, Local 46 compiled a remarkable record of building interracial unity in the Rath plant and in the Waterloo community.[72]

Arsenal Employees

In addition to a sizable presence in the food and transportation industries of meatpacking and railroading, blacks also took jobs in factories producing durable goods. One such manufacturing enterprise hiring black workers was the Rock Island Arsenal. Constructed in 1862, the arsenal sits on a 946-acre island in the Quad Cities area of the Mississippi River. Milton Howard, a black Muscatine native who became a legend at the facility, retired in the early 1920s after some 50 years of service as a custodian.[73]

Employment at the arsenal followed a cyclical pattern, with soaring wartime growth followed by dramatic declines in peacetime. Stimulated by the production demands of the world wars, large numbers of men and women from the Rock Island area and from the South, blacks and whites, took jobs at the facility. World War 1 employment peaked at 13,263 in November 1918. In August 1918, the *Bystander* estimated that 1,000 arsenal workers were black. By 1924, the arsenal's work force had plummeted to 618. On July 7, 1943, during World War 2, employment peaked again, at 18,675. The onset of the Cold War mitigated somewhat the arsenal's usual labor-force decline associated with peacetime.[74]

Like long-time arsenal employee Milton Howard, African-American men usually worked as janitors.[75] However, with the labor scarcities created by both wars, a number of the arsenal's black male employees held other unskilled jobs as helpers in the shops, foundry, and warehouses, and as laborers loading and unloading trucks and boxcars.[76] When white and black males entered military service, the arsenal also turned to women. In 1944, during World War 2, women comprised 32 percent of the arsenal's labor force.[77] Women replaced men in the shops, offices, and

Anna Mae Weems became a leading civil-rights figure in Waterloo, picketing, boycotting, and cajoling local businesses to open their employment and services to African-Americans.

Daisy Lowney and Rachel Carey operating their machines at the Rock Island Arsenal in April 1943 (Rock Island Arsenal)

warehouses. Like their male counterparts, black women usually had unskilled jobs. Yet World War 2 marked a turning point for both black men and black women. Because of an urgent need for skilled workers, the arsenal provided in-service training and opened its own apprenticeship school. As a result, hundreds of workers, including some African-American men and women, qualified as machine operators and took other skilled positions.[78]

African-American arsenal employees enjoyed higher wages than most of their fellow Davenport workers. Working conditions at the arsenal also seemed less racist than those at other local workplaces. Perhaps the unity inspired by the war production effort muted racial tension. Still some white employees from the South disliked working with blacks. Black access to production jobs came only when no additional white workers could be found to fill war

orders. Aside from becoming a "janitor boss," promotion opportunities for blacks appeared nonexistent. Despite these racial limitations in the workplace, the Rock Island Arsenal provided one of the earliest examples of significant numbers of blacks working in a factory setting. In wartime emergencies, moreover, some even worked at skilled jobs.[79]

John Deere Wage Earners

While employment at the arsenal fluctuated wildly, an Iowa agricultural equipment producer provided steadier work on its way to becoming the state's largest manufacturing employer. In 1837, John Deere, a journeyman blacksmith, developed a self-scouring steel plow that he parlayed into a prominent national enterprise with a reputation as a high-wage employer. Headquartered in

Dorothy Claytor ran a lathe in the 1940s at John Deere, Waterloo. (Grout Museum)

Melvin Moss working in the engine room at John Deere's Dubuque Works in the late 1970s (courtesy Melvin Moss)

Moline, Illinois, John Deere and Company expanded into Iowa, purchasing production facilities in Ottumwa (1900), Waterloo (1918), and Ankeny (1947), and building new plants at Dubuque (1947) and Davenport (1974). In 1955, employment in Deere plants reached approximately 9,500.[80]

Waterloo was the only Deere plant in Iowa that employed a significant number of African-Americans in production jobs. The Deere presence in Waterloo began in March 1918 with the purchase of the Waterloo Gasoline Engine Company for $2.3 million. Here Deere added the popular "Waterloo Boy" tractors to its successful line of farm implements.[81] With high farmer demand and worker shortages resulting from World War 1, the first blacks were hired. By 1920, the Waterloo plant had a contingent of 47 black wage earners.[82]

Males dominated production work at the John Deere plant. The company hired black women as custodians. The "black jobs" for males were the hazardous and fatiguing ones in the foundry and mill room. Most African-Americans started working in the foundry. There they shook the castings out of the molds. The "shake-out" jobs subjected the workers to high heat and noise levels; to air filled with dirt, dust, and sand particles; to poor lighting; and to the intense pace of piecework.

Despite the protective gear provided by the company, foundry work still took a terrible toll on the workers' health. Edwin Hollins recalled "spitting up black" for two years after leaving the foundry and taking a trucking job with another local company in the 1950s. Anna Mae Weems remarked that foundry work eventually killed her father.

After gaining experience in the foundry, the company usually transferred African-Americans to the mill room. Here they cleaned the castings. Mill room men still faced dirty, unhealthy, and dangerous working conditions.[83]

Following work force expansion in the 1920s, the Great Depression cut employment at the company from 2,000 to 300.[84] The massive layoffs nearly wiped out Deere's small group of black wage earners. Those still working faced reduced hours and wage cuts.[85]

With recovery underway in the late 1930s and conversion to wartime production in the 1940s, employment levels for both men and women rose rapidly at the Deere plant. Waterloo experienced another influx of black job seekers from the South. With the company's new hires, the number of black employees reached about 50 or 60 in the mid-1940s and climbed to several hundred in 1955. Black male employees still worked on the dirty jobs in the foundry and in the mill room, with a few in the core room. Similarly, black females still held janitorial jobs.[86]

When the unions finally opened their ranks to black workers, the company began addressing its job segregation practices. Organized under the banner of the AFL, early unionization efforts at John Deere came from white skilled workers, leaving the black workers without representation. The company broke a fledgling white machinists union following a strike in 1919. Deere's policy of requiring employees to sign yellow-dog contracts and to join a company union finally ended in the mid-1930s with the passage of national legislation granting private-sector workers the right to join unions and bargain collectively, free of employer coercion and company unions.

The formation of the CIO, which broke away from the craft-oriented AFL, set the stage for a spirited rivalry among several AFL and CIO unions at the Waterloo plant. After a long struggle, the CIO-affiliated United Auto Workers (UAW) became the official bargaining agent for Deere workers in 1942. Chartered as Local 838 in Waterloo, the UAW union aggressively built its membership by crossing skill, gender, and race lines. For the first time, a significant number of Deere's African-American wage earners joined the union ranks.[87]

For black workers at Deere the struggle against racism and sexism had just begun. They faced discrimination from both the company and the union. The company continued its practice of placing black men and women in the worst jobs and refusing to

promote them. Defying the sacred union tenet of seniority, experienced black workers were expected to train newly hired white workers who received preferential job treatment and rapid advancement to supervisory positions. Some African-Americans responded by refusing to show the white newcomers how to do the job. Black unionists complained that Local 838 seemed reluctant to fight racial bias in the plant, including race- and sex-based pay differentials. Union leadership positions remained exclusively white.[88]

After taking a machinist course, Cuba Tredwell, a union member who worked in the mill room, bid on a shop job in 1946. Some of the plant foremen told him that "a black man could never run a machine for John Deere." Backed by his local, the case went to arbitration. The arbitrator ruled that Tredwell was qualified, and he became, in his own words, "the first black that ever run a machine at John Deere." In the 1950s, union members elected Cuba Tredwell to the office of steward.[89]

Cuba Tredwell's wife, Ada, entered the Rath work force as a janitor in 1941. Five years later Ada Tredwell joined her husband at Deere, lured there by the prospect of better wages. Perhaps because of Cuba Tredwell's arbitration victory, the company gave Ada Tredwell a job as a machine operator. She disliked the work, and after two months she returned to Rath in early 1947. Comparing the two workplaces, Ada Tredwell noted that black women at Deere had wider employment options than those at Rath. Besides custodial work, she found black women holding a variety of production jobs at Deere.[90]

In seeking job equity, black wage earners also turned to Local 46 at Rath. With assistance from that local's task force, the Deere workers filed racial discrimination grievances and established an anti-discrimination committee modeled after the one at Rath. With pressure from black unionists, Local 838 became a vehicle to combat job and wage injustices. The union won equal pay for women in 1944. In the 1945 contract, the company agreed to a clause outlawing racial discrimination in employment, and the 1949 contract added sex to the nondiscrimination clause.[91]

Further progress on workplace equity issues was interrupted by a 1950 strike. Worker outrage over piecework and incentive rates provided the impetus for the four-month walkout. With both union and nonunion scabs entering the plant and charges of corruption circulating about union officials, Local 838 ended the walkout and returned to work. During the strike, most African-

Although justifiably suspicious of organized labor, many blacks adopted the philosophy that even a bad union was better than none. Without the union, said Rath employee Robert Burt, "you . . . have nobody to protect you."

Americans remained loyal to the union, refused to cross picket lines, and some assisted with union-sponsored food and money distribution. As Local 838 began the difficult task of rebuilding union solidarity, black union members insisted that true unity demanded a renewed commitment to racial fairness. By the mid-1950s, a group of black UAW activists joined their UPWA counterparts from Rath in agitating for civil rights at the community level too.[92]

Struggle for Workplace Equality

The civil-rights activism of black unionists originated in their protracted struggle for workplace equality. Iowa's African-Americans had experienced a profound transformation in employment during the first half of the twentieth century. While still mostly employed in service jobs, new horizons beckoned with better paying industrial occupations. The decline of the steamboat and mining industries added job seekers in the state's urban centers. Labor scarcity created by World Wars 1 and 2 accelerated the influx of migrants. The newcomers, many of them from the South, formed concentrated black workforces in the railroad, meatpacking, military weaponry, and farm-equipment industries. The wages earned by these workers provided a foundation for African-American communities in cities like Waterloo, Davenport, Cedar Rapids, Des Moines, and Sioux City.

At their work sites, African-Americans confronted racism and sexism. Viewing their capabilities as limited to menial labor, employers confined male and female black workers to race and gender stereotyped jobs that required low skill and received low wages. Often expected to work harder than white toilers, African-Americans seldom qualified for overtime pay. Black workers also confronted minimal or non-existent wage increases and white-only promotion policies. Such discriminatory practices increased profit margins for employers and maintained preferred job and pay advantages for white male employees. Unions displayed their complicity by generally excluding blacks from membership. During walkouts by white workers, moreover, some employers retaliated by tapping a ready reserve of black strikebreakers, inflaming racial divisions. Under these circumstances and in the absence of any governmental fair-employment initiatives, black wage earners experimented with various forms of work site protest and launched mutual-support projects in the black community.

By their perseverance and militancy, African-American workers provided the impetus for the long, difficult, and ongoing process of overcoming racial inequities in employment. The anti-union attitudes of black wage earners resulted from their experiences with an anti-black labor movement. However, newly organized industrial unions like the UPWA and UAW began opening their ranks to African-Americans with passage of a national collective-bargaining law in the mid-1930s, with support from churches and community groups like the NAACP, and with pressure from black and white activists. The unionization of black men and women signaled at least a contingent commitment to racial unity and to racial equality.

Although justifiably suspicious of organized labor, many blacks adopted the philosophy that even a bad union was better than no union. Robert Burt, a union steward at Rath, stated that without the union, "you . . . have nobody to protect you."[93] Some African-Americans eagerly embraced the union's egalitarian principles and fought to implement them. Rath union activist Ada Tredwell respected the "real push among black union members to equalize" black women's job opportunities.[94] The UPWA started to uphold the rights of black workers and became a vehicle for combating discrimination in the plant, in the union, and in the community.

By 1950, the first signs of change become apparent. A few black men held skilled jobs while a few black women made their entrance in production work. A few African-Americans also held union leadership positions. These modest advances coincided with a two-decades-long effort — led by black labor and civil rights leaders — to insert fair-employment practices codes into the National Labor Relations Act, into state law, and into city ordinances.[95]

African-American wage earners in Iowa and across the nation share a common legacy. Derryn E. Moten characterized the African-American experience in Iowa as one of "reluctant accommodation."[96] In Iowa and across the nation, race played a role in creating workplace tensions, eliciting discriminatory practices, and thwarting inclusive unionization. Segregation stalked public accommodations, housing sites, and recreation facilities in Iowa's towns and cities as well as those elsewhere. The racial divide, however, could not obliterate the reality of the shared labor experiences among working-class Iowans with native white and black as well as immigrant backgrounds. Even in a largely white state like Iowa, certain interracial workplaces served as centers of

Modest advances coincided with a two-decades-long effort — led by black labor and civil rights leaders — to insert fair-employment practices codes into the National Labor Relations Act, into state law, and into city ordinances.

CIO convention in Cedar Rapids, August 20–22, 1942 (SHSI Iowa City)

daily contact. Beginning in the 1930s, union organizers made common interests the basis for collective action. The UPWA proved that class solidarity and community cohesion could mitigate the divisive effects of racial antagonism.

From the middle of the nineteenth century to the middle of the twentieth century, the wage-earning black men and women in Iowa displayed a powerful work ethic. Income from their industrial jobs helped build and sustain a range of community institutions, groups, and services. They challenged workplace racial barriers erected by employers, unions, and the government. When admitted to union membership, African-American workers used these class-based organizations, along with community-based groups, to seek employment equity and justice. Their struggle remains an unfinished task.

Ralph Scharnau teaches U.S. history at Northeast Iowa Community College, Peosta. His publications include articles on labor history in Iowa and Dubuque. A native of Illinois, Scharnau is a member of the American Federation of Teachers (AFT) and the NAACP. He and his wife, Ruth, live in Dubuque; they have three children and two grandchildren.

In writing this chapter, the author received assistance from staff members at the following libraries and archives: Waterloo Public Library; Linn County Historical Society; State Historical Society of Iowa, Iowa City and Des Moines; State Historical Society of Wisconsin; Rock Island Arsenal Museum; Nodaway Valley Historical Society; University of Northern Iowa Library; and Davenport Public Library. For encouragement and insight, I extend special thanks to Mary Bennett at the State Historical Society of Iowa, Merle Davis and Shel Stromquist at the University of Iowa, and Harry Miller at the State Historical Society of Wisconsin.

Notes

Portions of this chapter were presented at Missouri Valley History Conferences held in Omaha, Nebraska on March 7, 1997, March 14, 1998, and March 11, 1999; and at the Northern Great Plains History Conference held in Sioux Falls, South Dakota on October 1, 1998.

1. Willis Goudy et al., *Minority/Majority Groups in Iowa* (Ames: Census Services, Department of Sociology, Iowa State University, 1995), 67.

2. Jack Smith, "The Negro in Iowa," typescript, Works Progress Administration, 1940, 1, SHSI, Des Moines [hereafter cited as Blacks in Iowa Collection]. A Des Moines weekly black newspaper, the *Iowa State Bystander*, chronicled the African-American experience in Iowa for nearly a century, beginning in the 1890s. Republican in politics and independent in religion, the *Bystander* promoted employment and castigated prejudice. For an early overview of African-Americans in Iowa, consult Leola Nelson Bergmann, *The Negro in Iowa* (Iowa City: SHSI, 1948; repr. 1969), 3–90.

3. Blacks in Iowa Collection, 307; S. E. Gilbert, "The History of the Negro in Sioux City from 1855 to 1900," typescript, 1940, 1–2, Blacks in Iowa Collection.

4. Blacks in Iowa Collection, 13; W. A. Adams, comp., *Directory of the City of Dubuque, 1857–1858* (Dubuque: W.A. Adams, 1858), 77, 191; W. H. McCoy, comp., *Dubuque City Directory, 1899–1900* (Dubuque: Telegraph Company Publishers, 1900), 120.

5. *Cedar Rapids Gazette*, Sept. 2, 1897.

6. Robert R. Dykstra, "Dr. Emerson's Sam: Black Iowans before the Civil War," *Palimpsest* 63 (1982): 76. Dykstra's article became chapter 1 of his book, *Bright Radical Star: Black Freedom and White Supremacy on the Hawkeye Frontier* (Cambridge: Harvard Univ. Press, 1993).

7. Pat Cassat, Project Director, Iowa Humanities Board grant, "'We Ask No Special Favors': The Black Heritage of Clarinda, Iowa," typescript, 1992, 1, 3, Nodaway Valley Historical Society.

8. Jane Burleson, "Black Fort Dodge," *Iowa State Bystander* [1894–1994 Anniversary Edition: 100 Years of Black Achievement], 1994, 66.

9. Gilbert, 2.

10. Iowa Writers' Program, Works Progress Administration, *Woodbury County History, Iowa* (Sioux City: n.p., 1942), 110–13; Blacks in Iowa Collection, 278–79, 307; William L. Hewitt, "So Few Undesirables: Race, Residence, and Occupation in Sioux City, 1890–1925," *AI* 50 (1989–90): 161–62; Bergmann, 38–40.

11. Blacks in Iowa Collection, 339–42; *Twelfth Census of the United States, 1900: Population*, part 1, 538, 616; Bergmann, 35, 46–48. See also John Charles Lufkin, "Black Des Moines: A Study of Select Negro Social Organizations in Des Moines, 1890–1930," Master's thesis, Iowa State University, 1980.

12. Edwin B. Espenshade Jr., "Urban Development at the Upper Rapids of the Mississippi," Ph.D. diss., University of Chicago, 1944, 58–59, 114–15; Timothy R. Mahoney, *River Towns in the Great West: The Structure of Provincial Urbanization in the American Midwest, 1820–1870* (New York: Cambridge Univ. Press, 1990), 36, 49–51; James L. Hill, "Migration of Blacks to Iowa, 1820–1960," *Journal of Negro History* 66 (1981–82): 292.

13. Ben Hur Wilson, "Over the Rapids," *Palimpsest* 4 (1923): 361–62, 373–74; Louis C. Hunter, *Steamboats on the Western Rivers: An Economic and Technological History* (Cambridge: Harvard Univ. Press, 1949), 451; Blacks in Iowa Collection, 278–79; Gilbert, 1–2; Hill, 293; *Woodbury County History*, 109–10.

14. Wilson, 376.

15. Hunter, chapter 11.

16. William J. Petersen, *Steamboating on the Upper Mississippi* (Iowa City: SHSI, 1968), 359; *Dubuque Herald*, June 5, 1857.

17. Franklin T. Oldt, *History of Dubuque County Iowa* (Chicago: Goodspeed Historical Association, c. 1911), 227.

18. *Dubuque Herald*, Aug. 1, 1869; Ruth A. Gallaher, "A Race Riot on the Mississippi," *Palimpsest* 2 (1921): 369–78.

19. Ronald L. Lewis, *Black Coal Miners in America: Race, Class, and Community Conflict, 1780–1980* (Lexington: Univ. Press of Kentucky, 1987), 191; Dorothy Schwieder, *Black Diamonds: Life and Work in Iowa's Coal Mining Communities, 1895–1925* (Iowa State Univ. Press, 1983), ix–xi, 118; Dorothy Schwieder, Joseph Hraba, and Elmer Schwieder, *Buxton: Work and Racial Equality in a Coal Mining Community* (Ames: Iowa State Univ. Press, 1987), 20; Hubert L. Olin, *Coal Mining in Iowa* (Des Moines: State of Iowa, 1965), 27, 31; Jacob A. Swisher, "Mining in Iowa," *Iowa Journal of History and Politics* 43 (1945): 312–14.

20. Schwieder, *Black Diamonds*, 151; Schwieder, et al., *Buxton*, 16–18; Olin, 35, 37, 55.

21. Schwieder, *Black Diamonds*, 151–52; Schwieder, et al., *Buxton*, 16; Olin, 49; Mark Stern, "Black Strikebreakers in the Coal Fields: King County, Washington — 1891," *Journal of Ethnic Studies* 5 (1977): 60–70.

22. Blacks in Iowa Collection, 287–94; *Iowa State Bystander* [hereafter cited as *Bystander*], Sept. 9, 1898; Schwieder, *Black Diamonds*, 122–23; Schwieder, et al., *Buxton*, 16–17, 20–39.

23. E. Hobart De Patten Sr. interview, Aug. 7, 1996. De Patten offers insightful comments about employment among black men and women as well as the exclusionary policies of trade unions.

24. Ralph Scharnau, "The Knights of Labor in Iowa," *AI* 50 (1991): 869–70; *Portrait and Biographical Album of Des Moines County, Iowa* (Chicago: Acme, 1888), 751; *Journal of United Labor*, April 15, 1881, 109; June 10, 1886, 2096; *Cedar Rapids Standard*, June 10, 1886; Jonathan Garlock, comp., *Guide to the Local Assemblies of the Knights of Labor* (Westport: Greenwood, 1982), 125, 127; Sidney H. Kessler, "The Organization of Negroes in the Knights of Labor," *Journal of Negro History* 37 (1952): 257.

25. Schwieder, *Black Diamonds*, 152–53; *Oskaloosa Daily Herald*, Sept. 12, 1900; Bill R. Douglas, "'Fighting Against Hope': Iowa Coal Miners and the 1891 Strike for the Eight-Hour Day," typescript, April 1977, Labor Collection, SHSI, Iowa City.

26. *Bystander*, Jan. 25 and Aug. 2, 1895.

27. Schwieder, *Black Diamonds*, 151.

28. *Dubuque Daily Times*, Sept. 24, 1872.

29. William Nelson Whitehill, *Ups and Downs of Iowa's Railroads* (Marshalltown: Marshall Printing Co., 1977), 24–25; John F. Stover, *American Railroads* (Chicago: Univ. of Chicago Press, 1961), 170–79; Hunter, 604–5, 637–40.

30. Schwieder, *Black Diamonds*, 157–58, 168.

31. John Schmidt, "Where Have All the Railroads Gone?," *DMR*, April 10, 1988.

32. Shelton Stromquist, *A Generation of Boomers: The Pattern of Railroad Labor Conflict in Nineteenth-Century America* (Urbana and Chicago: Univ. of Illinois Press, 1987), 159–61.

33. Blacks in Iowa Collection, 278, 307, 329–30; *Bystander*, May 14, 1915; June 6 and 13, July 18, Oct. 24, 1919; Dec. 7, 1978; Bergmann, 32–35, 38–40; Hill, 295; Gilbert, 2–3; William J. Maddix, "Blacks and Whites in Manly: An Iowa Town Overcomes Racism," *Palimpsest* 63 (1982): 132; Louis Bultena and Harold Reasby, "Negro-White Relations in the Waterloo Metropolitan Area," typescript, 1955, Iowa State Teachers College, Cedar Falls, Iowa, 3. Folder 13, Box 347, United Packinghouse Workers of America Papers, State Historical Society of Wisconsin, Madison, WI.

34. Arthur (Duke) Moore interview, Nov. 18, 1981; Percy Burt interview, March 31, 1978; Cuba E. Tredwell and Benjamin Tredwell interview, March 15, 1978; Marshall Wells interview, July 30, 1981, Iowa Labor History Oral Project [hereafter cited as ILHOP], SHSI, Iowa City, Iowa; Thomas C. B. Tyler, "1890: Early Negroes in City," *Mason City Globe-Gazette* [Centennial Edition, Section 4], June 1, 1953, 10; Bergmann, 38–40. See also the *Bystander*, Oct. 6, 1900; Dec. 27, 1901; June 27, 1913; May 14, 1915; Oct. 4, 1918; June 6, June 13, July 18, 1919; Gabriel Victor Cools, "The Negro in Typical Communities of Iowa," Master's thesis, University of Iowa, 1918, 18, 19, 99, 100; James Sutton interview, April 10, 1997; Philip S. Foner, *Organized Labor and the Black Worker, 1619–1973* (New York: International Publishers, 1974), 121; Farwell T. Brown, *Ames: The Early Years in Word and Picture, From Marsh to Modern City* (Ames: Heuss Printing Co., 1993), 63–64; Simon O. Roberts, "Davenport," Jane Burleson, "Black Fort Dodge," and Virginia Harper and Lois Eichacker, "Fort Madison," appearing in the *Bystander* [Anniversary Edition, 1894–1994: 100 Years of Black Achievement], 1994, 62, 66, 69–70; Eric Arneson, "'Like Banquo's Ghost, It Will Not Down': The Race Question and the American Railroad Brotherhoods, 1880–1920," *American Historical Review* 99 (1994): 1607–8; Sterling D. Spero and Abram L. Harris, *The Black Worker: The Negro and the Labor Movement* (New York: Atheneum, 1969), 285.

35. *Bystander*, July 26, 1912; Sept. 8, 1916; Feb. 10, 1966; E. H. Downey, *History of Labor Legislation in Iowa* (Iowa City: SHSI, 1910), 90–91. For a vivid description of black railway jobs, see Arthur Moore's ILHOP interview.

36. *Bystander*, Oct. 4, 1918; June 6 and 13, July 18, 1919; Percy Burt, Cuba and Benjamin Tredwell, and Marshall Wells interviews, ILHOP.

37. *Bystander*, Sept. 8, 1916; Feb. 24, 1933; May 24, 1956; Foner, 45, 71, 103, 121, 154–55; Arthur (Duke) Moore, Percy Burt, and Cuba and Benjamin Tredwell interviews, ILHOP; Arneson, 1602, 1604, 1608–9, 1614, 1622, 1628; W.L.F. of Missouri Valley, Iowa, "Current Comment," *Locomotive Firemen's Magazine*, Nov. 1899, 594; Howard W. Risher, *The Negro in the Railroad Industry* (Philadelphia: Univ. of Pennsylvania Press, 1971), 35–37, 57; Spero and Harris, 57–58; William H. Harris, *The Harder We Run: Black Workers Since the Civil War* (New York: Oxford Univ. Press, 1982), 40–41, 45.

38. Foner, 133. See also Spero and Harris, 299–300; Risher, 39.

39. *Bystander*, June 6, 1919, Jan. 6, 1972; See also Arneson, 1611–12, 1632.

40. Bob Neymeyer, "The Negro Community in Waterloo, Iowa: The Early Years, 1912–19," typescript, 1978, University of Northern Iowa Library, Cedar Falls, Iowa, 6–7; Robert Neymeyer, "May Harmony Prevail: The Early History of Black Waterloo," *Palimpsest* 61 (1980): 84–85; Barbara Beving Long, *Waterloo, Factory City of Iowa: A Survey of Architecture and History* (Waterloo: n.p., 1986), 19–20, 72, 130; Bultena and Reasby, 2–3. For an insider's view of the strike, see Carl E. Person, *The Lizard's Tail: A Story from the Illinois Central and Harriman Lines Strike of 1911 to 1915 Inclusive* (Chicago: Lake Publishing, 1918). Also consult Colin J. Davis, *Power at Odds: The 1922 National Railroad Shopmen's Strike* (Urbana and Chicago: Univ. of Chicago Press, 1997), 27–30.

41. Neymeyer, "The Negro Community," 6.

42. Neymeyer, "The Negro Community," 6, 9–10, 12; Neymeyer, "May Harmony Prevail," 85, 86; Long, 72, 130; Bultena and Reasby, 2–3; Person, 5; Davis, 26.

43. Neymeyer, "The Negro Community," 11–14, 23–31; Neymeyer, "May Harmony Prevail," 85–89; Davis, 29.

44. Maddix, 132. A student at the University of Iowa and a native of Manly, William J. Maddix conducted the research for his undergraduate thesis and subsequent *Palimpsest* article in the late 1970s. Steve Savage, a University of Iowa journalism student, interviewed Maddix about his research and wrote an article that appeared in the Dec. 7, 1978, issue of the *Bystander*.

45. Maddix, 132–33, 135, 136; *Bystander*, Dec. 7, 1978.

46. Davis, chapter 3.

47. Maddix, 133; Davis, 15–25, 66, 68–69, 92, 156.

48. Maddix, 134–35; Risher, 3, 10, 17, 24; Stover, 231; Cuba and Benjamin Tredwell and Arthur (Duke) Moore interviews, ILHOP; Whitehill, 70; Foner, 189.

49. *DMR*, April 10, 1988; Whitehill, 78–83; Risher, 9–10, 17, 20, 21.

50. Cuba and Benjamin Tredwell interview, ILHOP.

51. Incisive overviews of black packinghouse workers can be found in Rick Halpern and Roger Horowitz, *Meatpackers: An Oral History of Black Packinghouse Workers and Their Struggle for Racial and Economic Equality* (New York: Twayne, 1996); Roger Horowitz, *"Negro and White, Unite and Fight!" A Social History of Industrial Unionism in Meatpacking, 1930–1990* (Urbana and Chicago: Univ. of Illinois Press, 1997).

52. Ruth L. Hoadley, *Industrial Growth of Iowa* (Iowa City: State University of Iowa, 1928), 12, 16–19; H. H. McCarty and C. W. Thompson, *Meat Packing in Iowa* (Iowa City: State University of Iowa, 1933), 7; Walter A. Fogel, *The Negro in the Meat Industry* (Philadelphia: Univ. of Pennnsylvania Press, 1970), 8, 27–28, 47, 59; Wilson J. Warren, "The Limits of New Deal Social Democracy: Working-Class Structural Pluralism in Midwestern Meatpacking, 1900–1955," Ph.D. diss., University of Pittsburgh, 1992, 94.

53. Wilson J. Warren, "Evangelical Paternalism and Divided Workers: The Nonunion Era at John Morrell and Company in Ottumwa, 1877–1917," *AI* 56 (1997): 336–37. See also *Bystander*, July 6, 1900, Sept. 20, 1918.

54. Thomas P. Christensen, "An Industrial History of Woodbury County," *Unionist and Public Forum* [Sioux City], Aug. 3, 1939, Feb. 8, Aug. 1, 1940; McCarty and Thompson, 64; Fogel, 24; Hewitt, 173–74; Ralph Scharnau, "The Labor Movement in Iowa, 1900–1910," *Journal of the West* 35 (1996): 25; Warren, "The Nonunion Era at Morrell-Ottumwa," 334.

55. Warren, "The Limits of New Deal Social Democracy," 305–10; Kenneth Ellis interview, Oct. 20, 1978, and Harry (Buster) Hunter interview, Jan. 16, 1980, ILHOP; Hewitt, "So Few Undesirables," 174–75; Christensen, Aug. 15 and 22, 1940; Wilson J. Warren, "The Welfare Capitalism of John Morrell and Company, 1922–1937," *AI* 47 (1984): 497–517.

56. *Bystander*, Sept. 20, 1918, June 20, 1919; Fogel, 27–28; Earl Carr interview, April 18, 1986, and Sam Davis interview, July 1, 1986, United Packinghouse Workers of America Oral History Project [hereafter cited as UPWAOHP], State Historical Society of Wisconsin, Madison, Wisconsin; Neymeyer, "The Negro Community in Waterloo," 16; Warren, "The Limits of New Deal Social Democracy," 127.

57. Hewitt, 175.

58. See the interviews with African-Americans in the ILHOP and UPWAOHP collections, as well as Halperin and Horowitz, *Meatpackers*, 6–11, and Horowitz, *"Negro and White, Unite and Fight!"* 17–24.

59. Henry Simmons interview, Sept. 7, 1978, ILHOP; Marshall Wells and Percy Burt interviews, ILHOP; Ada Tredwell interview, July 29, 1986, UPWAOHP.

60. Henry Simmons and Marshall Wells interviews, ILHOP.

61. Shelton Stromquist, *Solidarity and Survival: An Oral History of Iowa Labor in the Twentieth Century* (Iowa City: Univ. of Iowa Press, 1993), chapter 3; Sr. John Marie Daly, "History of Unionization in Waterloo, Iowa," manuscript, Creighton University, n.d., UPWA Local 46 Records, Box 1, Folder 17, SHSI, Iowa City, 21–22, 26–27, 31–33; Peter Rachleff, "Organizing 'Wall-to-Wall': The Independent Union of All Workers, 1933–1937," in *Unionizing the Jungles: Labor and Community in the Twentieth-Century Meatpacking Industry*, ed. Shelton Stromquist and Marvin Bergman (Iowa City: Univ. of Iowa Press, 1997), 52–53; Warren, "The Limits of New Deal Social Democracy," 320–35; Eddie L. Simmons interview, Jan. 12, 1980, Tom Cohagen interview, Oct. 18, 1978, Harry (Buster) Hunter and Percy Burt interviews, ILHOP; Earl Carr and Sam Davis interviews, UPWAOHP; Roger Horowitz, "'It Wasn't a Time to Compromise': The Unionization of Sioux City's Packinghouses, 1937–1942," *AI* (1989/1990): 241–68; Horowitz, *"Negro and White, Unite and Fight!"* 50, 53, 104–23, 167, 189, 216, 222–25, 236, 237; "1938: Packinghouse Workers Union Certified," *Mason City Globe-Gazette* [Centennial Edition, Section 6], June 1, 1953, 8.

62. Ibid.

63. Percy Burt, Harry (Buster) Hunter, Eddie Simmons, and Henry Simmons interviews, ILHOP; Earl Carr and Sam Davis interviews; Charles Pearson interview, July 17, 1986; Robert Burt interview, May 7, 1986; Jimmie Porter interview, May 8, 1986; Everett Dietz interview, May 6, 1986; Don Blumenshine interview, April 16, 1986, UPWAOHP.

64. Harry (Buster) Hunter interview, ILHOP; Horowitz, "'It Wasn't a Time to Compromise'," 241–68; Horowitz, *"Negro and White, Unite and Fight!"* chapter 5.

65. See interviews with African-American packinghouse workers in the ILHOP and UPWAOHP collections.

66. Percy Burt and Marshall Wells interviews; Ed Nixon interview, April 7, 1980; Donovan Tompson interview, July 28, 1978; Jeannette Haymond interview, Nov. 9, 1977; John Jordan interview, April 7, 19, 1978; Jesse Frazier interview, April 19, 1980; Jane Burleson interview, Aug. 5, 1981, Julia Naylor interview, Aug. 7, 1981, ILHOP; Earl Carr, Sam Davis, Robert Burt, Charles Pearson, Jimmy Porter, and Ada Tredwell interviews; Magnolia Fields interview, April 19, 1986, Anna Mae Weems interview, May 9, 1986, UPWAOHP; Bultena and Reasby, 9–12.

67. Ibid. For post–World War 2 era gender issues in the UPWA, consult the following: Dennis A. Deslippe, "'We Had an Awful Time with Our Women': Iowa's United Packinghouse Workers of America, 1945–75," *Journal of Women's History* (1993): 10–32; Bruce Fehn, "'Chickens Come Home to Roost': Industrial Reorganization, Seniority, and Gender Conflict in the United Packinghouse Workers of America, 1955–1966," *Labor History* (1993): 324–41; and Deborah Fink, *Cutting into the Meatpacking Line: Workers and Change in the Rural Midwest* (Chapel Hill: Univ. of North Carolina Press, 1998).

68. Percy Burt interview, ILHOP; Robert Burt, Charles Pearson, Jimmy Porter, Ada Tredwell, and Anna Mae Weems interviews, UPWAOHP. See Bruce Fehn, "'The Only Hope We Had': United Packinghouse Workers Local 46 and the Struggle for Racial Equality in Waterloo, Iowa, 1948–1960," *AI* 54 (1995): 185–216.

69. Percy Burt interview, ILHOP; Robert Burt, Charles Pearson, and Ada Tredwell interviews, UPWAOHP; Daly, 43–51; Fehn, "'The Only Hope We Had,'" 194–96; Stromquist, *Solidarity and Survival*, 178–83. For a recently published account of the strike, consult Bruce Fehn, "Ruin or Renewal: The United Packinghouse Workers of America and the 1948 Meatpacking Strike in Iowa," *AI* 56 (1997): 349–78.

70. Fehn, "'The Only Hope We Had,'" 196.

71. Robert Burt and Charles Pearson interviews, UPWAOHP; Percy Burt interview, ILHOP; Daly, 51–54.

72. Percy Burt interview, ILHOP; Robert Burt, Charles Pearson, Jimmy Porter, Ada Tredwell, and Anna Mae Weems interviews, UPWAOHP; Fehn, "'The Only Hope We Had,'" 198, 200–1, 208–13.

73. Thomas J. Slattery, *Rock Island Arsenal: An Arsenal for Democracy* [World War 2 50th Anniversary Commemorative Edition] (Rock Island: Historical Office, U.S. Army Armament, Munitions, and Chemical Command, 1992), 1, 3. For additional information on Milton Howard, consult the clippings and photographs housed at the Rock Island Arsenal Museum.

74. Slattery, 3, 15; *Bystander*, Aug. 9, 1918; Thomas P. Christensen, "An Industrial History of Scott County: The Twentieth Century, 1900–1936," *AI* 22 (1940): 389–90.

75. "The War Years: A Historical Look at Rock Island Arsenal during 1942–1945," *Rock Island Arsenal Record* [Special 50th Anniversary Commemorative Edition], Aug. 12, 1995, 69; Vincent Gooding, Ernest Harris, and Betty Ann Davis interviews, "An Oral History of the Black Population of Davenport, Iowa" [hereafter cited as OHBPD], Hope D. Williams, director, Davenport Public Library, 1979.

76. E. A. Hopkins, Lucille Clark Taylor, and Vincent Gooding interviews, OHBPD; "The War Years," *Rock Island Arsenal Record*, 86.

77. Slattery, 14.

78. Slattery, 14, 15, 17; "The War Years," *Rock Island Arsenal Record*, 76; Lucille Clark Taylor interview, OHBPD.

79. Ernest Harris, Lucille Clark Taylor, Vincent Gooding, and Betty Ann Davis interviews, OHBPD.

80. Wayne G. Broehl Jr., *John Deere's Company: A History of Deere & Company and Its Times* (New York: Doubleday, 1984); Dorothy Schwieder, *Iowa: The Middle Land* (Ames: Iowa State Univ. Press, 1996), 237–38, 299.

81. Broehl, 403–7.

82. Neymeyer, "The Negro Community," 7, 15.

83. Stromquist, *Solidarity and Survival*, 244–48; Daly, 13; Cuba Tredwell interview; Roosevelt Taylor interview, July 8, 1981; Edwin Hollins interview, July 9, 1981, ILHOP; Robert Burt, Jimmie Porter, and Anna Mae Weems interviews, UPWAOHP.

84. Daly, 16, 17.

85. Cuba Tredwell interview, ILHOP; Broehl, 513–14.

86. Cuba Tredwell and Eddie Simmons interviews, ILHOP; Charles Pearson interview, UPWAOHP; Bultena and Reasby, 12.

87. Broehl, 428–35, 528–31, 555–56; Daly, 8–13, 21, 23–26, 29–31, 33, 35–36; Cuba Tredwell, Roosevelt Taylor, and Edwin Hollins interviews, ILHOP.

88. Cuba Tredwell interview, ILHOP; Jimmie Porter interview, UPWAOHP.

89. Cuba Tredwell interview, ILHOP.

90. Ada Tredwell interview, UPWAOHP.

91. Robert Burt, Charles Pearson, Jimmie Porter, and Anna Mae Weems interviews, UPWAOHP; Percy Burt and Cuba Tredwell interviews, ILHOP; Mel Valentine, comp., *UAW Local 838: Our History* (Waterloo: n.p., 1977), 13–15, 25, 26.

92. Robert Burt, Charles Pearson, Jimmie Porter, and Anna Mae Weems interviews, UPWAOHP; Percy Burt, Cuba Tredwell, Roosevelt Taylor, and Edwin Hollins interviews, ILHOP; Valentine, 30–36; Daly, 57–61; Broehl, 578–81; Stromquist, *Solidarity and Survival*, 208–13.

93. Robert Burt interview, UPWAOHP.

94. Ada Tredwell interview, ILHOP.

95. A litany of demands for work site equality appear in the pages of the *Bystander*.

96. Derryn E. Moten, "Iowa," in *Encyclopedia of African-American Culture and History*, ed. Jack Salzman, David Lionel Smith, and Cornell West, vol. 3 (New York: Macmillan, 1996), 1395. A recent study of the racial parameters of work can be found in Jacqueline Jones, *American Work: Four Centuries of Black and White Labor* (New York: Norton, 1998).

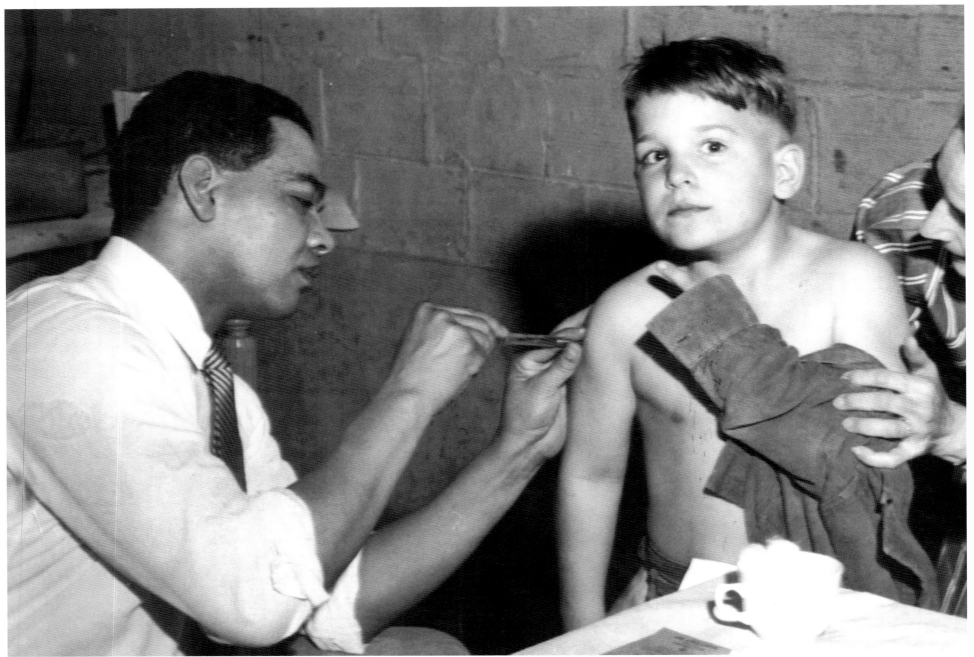

Dr. William H. Harper Jr. giving a polio shot at the Keokuk Clinic, 1962 (courtesy Phyllis Harper-Bardach)

Healing Hands, Questing Hearts

African-American Physicians in Iowa

by Steven Berry, M.D., and Erin Herndon, M.D.

The year was 1965, and Julius Connor was a man on a mission, the quintessential American mission, as he recalls it.

The 31-year-old physician, along with his wife and three young children, had long outgrown their rented bungalow. The family of five was in need of more space: it was time to go house-hunting.

A trip to a local bank's loan officer proved an easy exercise. A young professional man with a healthy income, Dr. Connor easily exceeded the bank's minimal requirements. The realty agent he subsequently contacted by phone was no less enthusiastic. The man sounded excited at the prospect of meeting the Connors.

But then, what real estate agent wouldn't be pleased to encounter a house-hunting doctor with a pre-approved bank loan? Julius could practically hear hands rubbing together in glee through the static on the line.

Was he new to Des Moines? the agent wondered, sounding friendly — but curious.

New to Des Moines? "I explained that I wasn't," Dr. Connor remembers. "I'd come to Iowa right after graduating from medical school at the University of Nebraska. I interned at Mercy Hospital in Des Moines, then completed a pediatric residency at Blank Memorial Hospital. After finishing residency, my family and I moved to Washington, D.C., where I was in private practice for a year." Dr. Connor shakes his head, remembering that year. "We weren't prepared for the sheer size of D.C. Quite frankly, we didn't like living in a place that big. I grew up in Omaha, and the midwestern sensibility, the pace of life I was used to, was very different from the pace of life in D.C., of course. As a teacher, my wife was also concerned with the quality of education available to our children, one of whom was of school age. The public schools in Washington weren't great."

Serendipitously, the young midwesterners were soon able to take advantage of another career opportunity.

"I'd long had an interest in public health and was accepted into a master's program in public health at Harvard University, graduating in 1964," Dr. Connor explains. "Coming out of Boston, I had several career options, in various places. But Selena and I had never forgotten Des Moines, the affinity we both had felt for the town. In the end, we decided to move back to Iowa.

Dr. Julius Connor served Polk County as director of public health from 1965 until his retirement in 2000. (courtesy Dr. Julius Connor)

Dr. Julius Connor and fellow interns at Mercy Hospital in Des Moines (from Greiner and McMahon, Those Who Come to Bless: Mercy Hospital 1893–1993, 100 Years of Healing)

"In 1965, I was appointed director of public health for Polk County. Our third child had been born by that time. So we needed a house. A good-sized home. . . ."

Hence the long-ago call to a realtor. The call that Julius Connor has never really forgotten.

The agent was quite surprised, he recalls. Surprised that he hadn't run across Julius before. He'd sold homes to quite a few young doctors, and knew, or at least had heard of, most of the new doctors in town, but — no matter.

He was, as it turned out, available that weekend. If Dr. and Mrs. Connor wanted to look at a few properties. . . .

They were free, in fact. And they wanted to buy a house.

Two days later, they met the agent on the sidewalk in front of a property they'd decided to view. Julius Connor's features tighten as he relates what happened next.

"It was comical, in a way, how he — the agent — looked past us. *Through* us. It was as if we were suddenly invisible."

They were the Connors? the agent asked, incredulous.

Yes. They were.

He was . . . *Doctor* Connor? That nice-sounding fellow on the phone?

One and the same.

Comprehension dawned. The agent regarded the well-dressed young couple with narrowed eyes, before pursing his lips.

"He told us he was sorry to have wasted his time and ours. The bottom line was this: he couldn't sell that house, or any house in that neighborhood. At least, not to us."[1]

Flash-forward to 1997.

We are interviewing Dr. Connor, Steve Berry and I.

Steve is a pulmonologist, a critical-care specialist, one of only a handful of young black subspecialty physicians in the Midwest. I am an internist, a generalist. My name is Erin Herndon.

As members of the fifth generation of African-American physicians to practice medicine in Iowa, we have endured fewer hardships, fewer struggles for acceptance, than our long-ago predecessors. Daily, we benefit from those who made the rough places plane.

And their stories are fascinating, full of the richness of black Iowa's history.

Some of the personal chronicles we unearthed are heart-rendingly sad. Others fill us with pride, pride in the stories of black Iowans overcoming the insurmountable in the unflinching pursuit of their dreams.

In the course of our research, Steve Berry and I grew to better appreciate the racial and cultural bonds we share with these early physicians. We also came to understand that we, and all present-day black Iowa physicians, owe those who came before us a debt of such enormous proportion that we freely acknowledge we can never repay it.

Co-authoring *Outside In's* chapter on medicine will, we hope, in some ways, suffice as payment. We owe the men — and women — who paved our way *something*. Some sort of acknowledgment.

A heartfelt thank-you.

Partial payment, true.

But for Dr. Connor, the simple fact that we are here, that we are practicing the art, seems payment enough.

Julius Connor speaks slowly, matter-of-factly, into the microphone, no trace of anger in the eyes behind the wire-rimmed glasses. Thirty-two years have gone by since he encountered institutional racism in the form of discriminatory real-estate practices designed to keep blacks both literally and figuratively "in their place." In those 32 years, he has seen tremendous changes in Iowa's population landscape.

"Diversity in Iowa's medical community is a reality. There has been an enormous increase in the number of black physicians, both in the subspecialty fields and in primary care, over the years. Black physicians have also assumed a teaching role in local and university residency programs, something that gratifies me."

Has he any regrets? This soft-spoken man, widely regarded as one of the deans of African-American physicians in Iowa, pauses to carefully ponder his response.

We wait for his answer, watching the tape in the recorder spin. The question occurs to both of us simultaneously: do we have regrets? Would our widely disparate professional lives have taken a different spin altogether had we not lived in Iowa?

Steve and I have, in many ways, trailed this man's footsteps, following a path he and others have blazed. But compared to iron men like Julius Connor and his stalwart cohorts — Dr. E. A. Carter and Dr. Arthur J. Booker; Dr. E. T. Scales and Dr. Clyde Bradford; Dr. Gage C. Moore and Dr. Lee Burton Furgerson; Dr. Harry Harper Sr. and Dr. Robert Carney; Dr. Meredith Saunders and Dr. Walter J. Riley — next to such men, we are raw recruits.

These men paid dues we cannot begin to imagine. By dint of incredible perseverance, they wedged open a door previously marked "whites only," allowing us to walk through.

While we were cutting our teeth on chemistry and physics, Julius Connor was becoming what he is today — a highly regarded member of the state medical community and a force to be reckoned with, all without raising his voice, or losing his imperturbable, legendary calm.

Does he have regrets? His professional life. . . ?

"No, of course not! In one year as a practicing physician, I gave 100 shots for measles. But in my first year as a public health administrator, I saw to it that 1,000 shots were given."

It's a fair-enough answer. Steve hesitates only a moment before addressing the obvious. The challenges Julius Connor has faced in his professional life, the methods by which he overcame them, have been unique, and uniquely fulfilling. Has his personal life been equally so?

Personally speaking, Dr. Connor has one regret. Only one.

Thirty-two years later, he remembers it vividly. "We finally built a house, Selena and I. Like with so many other things in our lives, neither of us was going to accept 'no' for an answer."

He smiles at that, at his own youthful fervor, a half-smile that doesn't quite reach his eyes.

It's a smile that reveals the truth of the matter. And the truth is that even after 30-some years, after so many accomplishments, kudos, and acclaim, what happened to Dr. and Mrs. Julius Connor on that suburban sidewalk in 1965 is every bit as clear in the doctor's mind as if it had happened yesterday. It's also clear that the passage of time has not rendered the memory any less painful.

"We'd 'adopted' Iowa, you see. We wanted to live and work here, raise our family here. In a way, becoming part of this community was a dream for us. We weren't going to give up. We weren't going to leave here."

This time, his smile is the genuine article. He pauses again, reflecting on a turbulent past. Then he says something that Steve and I have both had occasion to think, but never actually voiced.

"After all, you don't give up on your dream."[2]

Like Dr. Connor, scores of African-American physicians have sought — and sometimes found — their dreams in Iowa. Undeterred by its rural character and their own overwhelmingly minority status, these men and women settled in communities ranging from barely-there hamlets to bustling river towns, beginning in the mid-1830s. By the time the Iowa Territory attained statehood in 1847, census records indicate that about 300 African-Americans, reported as "free colored persons," counted themselves among Iowa's first citizens.[3]

More followed. The end of the Civil War brought thousands of newly freed slaves to the rural midwestern United States. Iowa, with its fertile farmland, wide-open vistas, and relatively liberal, well-educated populace, attracted thousands of freemen and their families.

A lucky few farmed their own land. Most labored for others. The coal-mining community of Buxton, south of Des Moines, was established as a "company" town, largely peopled by the descendants of slaves, with its own school, stores, hospital, and physicians.

The sleepy little town of Valley Junction (now West Des Moines) began life in 1890 as a Rock Island train stop, to which young African-American men from the Deep South were lured to work with the promise of honest wages for hard work.

More freemen came to the river towns of Muscatine, Moline, Rock Island, Davenport, and Dubuque, where river barges and steamboats made work plentiful and wages high. Waterloo, in the northeastern corner of the state and centrally located Des Moines,

Dr. Clyde Bradford personified the profile of over-worked physician, community servant, and spokesman for over two decades in Des Moines. (courtesy Sunny Bradford)

After fighting alongside Union forces as a fugitive slave during the Civil War, Dr. Jacob Dulin eventually settled in Des Moines in 1878 and divided his time between medicine and the ministery.
(Bystander, *April 19, 1918*)

both blessed with lucrative manufacturing bases, were magnets of opportunity for many African-Americans who migrated north between the world wars.

Some worked the railroad yards. Many toiled as laborers, porters, domestics, and janitors. Later, African-Americans worked in factories and mines or on the killing floors of meat-packing plants, doing the dirtiest, most dangerous, least desirable jobs, but at least, and at last, collecting a wage for their trouble.

Some were physicians.

By 1890, the number of African-Americans residing in Iowa had risen to roughly 10,000. Although the largest number of black Iowans were concentrated in Lee, Mahaska, Monroe, and Polk counties, smaller groups were scattered across the state. The official state census of 1890 indicates that among these 10,000 souls were those employed as laborers, farmers, cooks and seamstresses, barbers, blacksmiths — and at least three were labeled "physician and surgeon." Polk County, with an African-American population numbering approximately 1,200, boasted nine high school graduates, seven farmers, four lawyers, one pharmacist — and one physician.[4]

Both Medical and Pastoral Training

The first African-American to practice medicine in Iowa was probably Dr. Jacob Dulin.[5] Born into slavery in Littleton, Virginia, in about 1830, Dr. Dulin joined a band of fugitive slaves, and fought alongside Union forces during the Civil War. Sometime after attaining his freedom, he journeyed to St. Louis, where he completed both medical and pastoral training. He divided his time there between an active ministry and medicine, becoming a major force in that most venerated of African-American institutions — the church.

Dr. Dulin relocated to Iowa in 1878, making his way to Des Moines. Initially, he made his living as a Baptist minister, organizing the Olive Baptist Church in Des Moines. By the turn of the century, however, he had begun to devote more and more of his time to medicine, developing so large a practice that he reluctantly withdrew from his pastoral duties.

A thumbnail sketch of the doctor's personal history can be found in the pages of the *Iowa Bystander*, the state's first newspaper "for the race."[6] Dated May 24, 1907, the double-column entry is a compelling glimpse of a multi-faceted man, even allowing for the journalistic excesses of the period.

Given the times in which they lived, the self-congratulatory tone of Dr. Dulin's unknown biographer is understandable, perhaps even laudable.

This man, the reader is almost immediately informed, was born a slave. The mixed-race offspring of a slave woman and her owner, Jacob Dulin had the same lowly status as his mother. That is to say, he had no status. He was born of a slave, therefore *he* was a slave. He came from nothing, the child of a people of no means or consequence.

Yet this former slave, not a free man until after the age of 35, had, incredibly, "accumulated property . . . including a lovely residence and sanitarium."

A man who had once been the property of another had, quite astonishingly, become "a member of the Benevolent Order of Masons."

He had also acquired "a carriage and a driver, and is a credit to our race, for he is full of work for the race."

If Jacob Dulin could find in himself the strength to succeed so spectacularly, so brilliantly, against all odds, against the ravages of civil war and the desperate straits of his birthright. . . . The unspoken message was crystal-clear: *If Jacob Dulin could succeed, by no hand than his own, then, by God, so will I! So will we all.*

Black Iowans were in need of encouragement in those early years. Factual slavery had ended a generation ago, but *de facto* slavery was still very much alive in the form of economic, social, and cultural repression, triple horns on the monstrous head of racism.

A People in Need of Heroes

A people so often shunted aside was in need of heroes. And Iowa's early black physicians, whether they desired the role or not, often filled it. They were "race men," as contemporary newspaper accounts complimentarily termed them, black men who, by dint of their role as healers, assumed the more relevant mantle of leadership.

Physicians also became leaders as a secondary function of being members of a tiny elite, often the best educated individuals in their communities. Higher education was revered by the average black Iowan at the turn of the century, all the more so because such an education was unattainable for all but the most fortunate — or the most driven.

To some extent, black physicians also moved between black and white Iowa, the only African-Americans truly allowed to do so.

At the turn of the century, white doctors commonly treated black patients. In many instances, black doctors treated white patients too. Many white Iowans were either ignorant (or maliciously aware) of the African-Americans living in their midst. And while many viewed blacks as a people beneath contempt, black physicians were often seen as somehow being separate, apart from the larger group.

Unofficial Goodwill Ambassadors

The mystique of the physician is well-established in American culture. Not so mysteriously, African-American physicians in Iowa found themselves benefiting from that same cachet, a cachet that often catapulted them into the governing hierarchies of their communities. At the same time, the respect with which all doctors were held allowed African-American physicians to serve in the capacity of unofficial goodwill ambassadors.

In 1895, around the same time that the American Association of Colored Physicians and Surgeons (the name was changed to the National Medical Association in 1903) was forming in Atlanta, Georgia, Dr. Jacob Dulin was joined by Dr. Edward F. Johnson, the second African-American physician in Des Moines.

Dr. Johnson received his medical degree from the then well-known Drake University Medical College. Like Dr. Dulin, he was active in church and had also "gained some prominence in politics, having been a delegate to county and state conventions."

Unlike Dr. Dulin, he did not make Iowa his permanent home. In June 1898, the newly married Illinois native departed Des Moines for Indianapolis, Indiana.

In April of that same year, Dr. Robert S. Brown, a native of Staunton, Virginia, graduated from medical school in Chicago, and relocated to Oskaloosa, Iowa. On June 1, 1895, Dr. Brown was appointed as physician and surgeon for the Colon mines, near Oskaloosa.

This was an appointment of some note. No African-American physician had ever before received such an honor, despite the large number of black men laboring in the coal mines of southern Iowa.

The precedent was soon broken. Dr. F. H. Lawther arrived in Iowa from Chicago in 1896 and was appointed company doctor at the Keb mining camp, deep in Mahaska County. Early in June 1897 the *Bystander* came forward, duly wishing him "all success."[7]

Despite their apparent good fortune, it soon became obvious to Dr. and Mrs. Lawther that a rough-and-tumble mining camp was not the best place to raise their large brood. Besides, F. H. Lawther was not made of the same stern stuff as, say, a Jacob Dulin. Dr. Lawther was a "sufferer from many diseases, prominent among them . . . the asthma," according to newspaper reports.

Although born and raised on a farm in Missouri, he had lived in Chicago for many years. In fact, he had graduated from medical school in Chicago, from the College of Physicians and Surgeons, in 1891. Dr. Lawther had labored long and hard to leave his rural upbringing behind.

And he'd succeeded — until he landed in the dusty coal-mining camp that was to be his home.

Keb was the name. Keb was the camp, a place surely as ugly as its name. Like most coal-mining communities, Keb consisted of a few rude dwellings and was situated far from any city. The blighted little settlement's only link to civilization was a single, rutted, near-impassable dirt road.

Upon his arrival, the dapper, city-dwelling Lawther must surely have thought he'd died and gone to hell.

Less than four months later, the Lawthers had moved to Des Moines, where the ubiquitous *Bystander* interviewed Mrs. Lawther and found her "quite intelligent, and a very interesting lady to meet."

Where Dr. Lawther could cough deep, bringing up the last of the coal dust. Where people were civilized — for the most part.

Three years later, he was dead at 60, never having regained his shattered health.

Sturdier men took his place.

Men like Dr. A. G. Edwards, who arrived in Des Moines in August 1901 with his wife and two children in tow. A graduate of Meharry Medical College, Dr. Edwards had practiced medicine in Knoxville, Tennessee, and had been a professor of anatomy in the medical department of Knoxville College, the first "person of color to be selected to the faculty of that college."

By all accounts, Dr. Edwards was a "fine gentleman . . . and will succeed."[8]

Succeed he did. But it was rumored that Edwards was not happy in Iowa. A true academician, he may have been dismayed to find himself adrift in what he would have considered a midwestern backwater. It soon became obvious that there were no medical faculty appointments to be had in Des Moines.

To some extent,

black physicians . . .

moved between

black and white Iowa,

the only

African-Americans

truly allowed

to do so.

Dr. John H. Williams, Meharry Medical School graduate, began practicing in Des Moines in 1908. (Bystander, May 1908*)*

Dr. E. A. Carter, one of three doctors hired by the Consolidation Coal Company to practice in Buxton (SHSI Des Moines)

But there was work, surely, and plenty of it. Work enough that he was able to "purchase a new rubber-tired buggy and a beautiful black horse" by May 1902.[9]

There is no mention of Dr. Edwards in Des Moines city directories between 1902 and 1905. A cryptic newspaper notice appears on August 15, 1905, indicating "that our physician, Dr. A. G. Edwards, has returned to our city and will reopen his offices. His family returns tonight. . . . We predict for him abundant success and better business than ever. We need him here, and let's keep him."

The notice of April 24, 1908, is almost anticlimactic: "Dr. A. G. Edwards, who has been our only colored physician for several years, has decided to locate in Omaha. He has closed his office here and is now in Omaha. His family will remain here for awhile. It is too bad to lose the doctor. Our city is certainly large enough to support a colored doctor, yet Dr. Edwards wanted a larger field."

Fervent wishes for the doctor's continued success are, for once, conspicuously absent. Was Des Moines's small African-American community irritated at being left in the lurch by the brilliant Dr. Edwards? Perhaps. Or perhaps Dr. Edwards and Iowa had simply tired of each other at the same time.

Into the void stepped young Dr. John H. Williams. Also a Meharry Medical School graduate, he began practicing in Des Moines in May 1908.

Dr. Cornelius M. Wilson quietly took up practice a few years later, arriving in Des Moines in 1913, having relocated from the tiny hamlet of Hennessey, Oklahoma. Racism and worry took their toll on Dr. Wilson. He died 3 years later, at the age of 42.

Around the same time, in Buxton, Iowa, the Consolidation Coal Company, a forward-thinking conglomerate, hired three physicians as company doctors. One of them, Dr. E. A. Carter, a University of Iowa Medical School graduate, was African-American.

Consolidation proved to be ahead of its time in hiring and labor-management practices, with an unspoken but closely observed tradition of racial parity. Not only were black and white miners paid equal wages, but they lived side by side in company housing. The local affiliate of the United Mineworkers Union, aided by Consolidation, offered health insurance to the miners, a then unheard-of benefit, at a cost of 25 cents a month. Within a short time, the plan was extended to cover miners' families as well,

Dr. E.A. Carter (third from left) with classmates and cadaver in his anatomy class at the University of Iowa, c. 1900 (SHSI Des Moines)

for the additional sum of 50 cents per month. Routine medical care was provided on-site at offices in Buxton with emergency and surgical services available at the Albia Miners' Hospital, the most up-to-date facility in the region.

Doctors employed by Consolidation Coal Company still delivered babies at home for an additional fee (about five dollars), but other medical treatment, including prescriptions, was included in the monthly fee the miners paid.

Carter, Williams, and Wilson were all M.D.'s, as it happens, all graduates of accredited medical schools. Of the three, Dr. Carter had the strongest ties to the racial and social utopia that was Buxton.

Paradise Lost

But paradise was soon to be lost. Around 1919, the Buxton mines began shutting down, having exhausted the coal supply within easy reach of the surface.[10]

One by one, the townspeople of Buxton abandoned their homes, in search of new mines or other employment. Shortly after the close of World War 1, Dr. Carter left Iowa for good. He thrived in Detroit, where he was soon the principal of a large private practice.

Dr. Williams remained active in the Des Moines area for an unknown period of time, assuming an active role in the community, a "race man" who was among the best the city had to offer.

Des Moines's black citizenry enjoyed exceptional medical services in the first decade of the twentieth century. Drs. Williams and Wilson were decent men and competent physicians.

But they were soon overshadowed by a stellar presence.

Arthur J. Booker shot into town, as if fired from a cannon, in the summer of 1910. Topping off his years of medical study at Northwestern University in Chicago with an additional year of study in London and Paris, he set the local medical establishment on its ear.

As reticent and soft-spoken as A. G. Edwards had been flamboyant, Dr. Booker was still a man to be reckoned with. Amazingly, he applied for and was appointed to the position of department chair in human anatomy at Drake University's Medical College, where he taught for two years before resigning to tend a growing private practice.

No less an accomplished diagnostician, he was welcomed by his white colleagues as their acknowledged equal, if not their professional superior. He was the first African-American physician in the state to be accorded such respect.

Booker bore the praise lightly, wisely realizing that self-aggrandizement was not in his best interest. Rather than seek wider acclaim, he wove his own life into the larger life of the African-American community that sustained and supported him, becoming an integral part of that community over the course of the next 15 years.

Bystander records for the years between 1921 and 1927 no longer exist. It was during that time, in about 1925, that Arthur Booker relocated to Los Angeles, California. The reasons for his departure remain unknown, but it is known that he continued to practice medicine for at least a decade after the move.

Taking Dr. Booker's place — but hardly filling his shoes — was Dr. Charles A. Adams, a transplanted Texan who arrived in Des Moines in about 1921. By all accounts, he acquitted himself well and built a thriving practice. Tragically, he died of unknown causes in 1926, at the age of 49. A brief note appeared in the *Bystander*, dated October 22, 1927, indicating that his widow and daughter were leaving the area for Savannah, Georgia, where Mrs. Adams, an accomplished and university-trained musician, had accepted a post as head of the department of music at a small black college.

Although he was no Arthur Booker, Dr. C. A. Adams was a skilled physician, trained in the treatment of human disease at a then well-regarded college of medicine.

But many of the "doctors" who arrived in Iowa at the opening of the twentieth century were neither.

Outright Quackery

Modern medicine was in its infancy. Lack of decent facilities, lack of medical knowledge, and outright quackery was the established norm, not the exception. African-American doctors, like their white counterparts, were often possessed of meaningless diplomas from non-accredited schools.

No less a personage than the esteemed Dr. J. Dulin worked his cures through the vagaries of "magnetism," a long-defunct, pseudo-scientific technique of treatment, wherein the body's ills were mended by "correcting acquired defects in the patient's electro-magnetic field." A popular mode of treatment in Europe in the mid-nineteenth century, magnetism soon had its proponents in this country as well.

Dr. A. J. Booker
Physician and Surgeon

Has Moved to

413 Sixth Avenue
Up Stairs.

Announcements for the practices of Dr. A. J. Booker and Dr. C. A. Adams appeared in the Bystander, *October 1913 (above) and May 1921 (below).*

DR. C. A. ADAMS
Physician and Surgeon
Office Suite 22 Shops Building
Corner East Fifth and Locust
Office Hours—10-12 A. M. 2-4 P. M.
7-8 P. M. Sundays 1-3.
Des Moines, Iowa

Prof. J. M. Wilson, The Eminent Healer,

Is far ahead of the average healer. He called upon a lady over four months ago who lives at 1520 West Walnut street. Her case was a very critical one. She was badly swollen; her limbs were perfectly stiff and she was in so much pain that she had not been able to sleep but very little for seven days and nights. She sent for Dr. Wilson, the magnetic healer. He had been in the room but ten minutes when the patient was perfectly easy and the swelling began to disappear and she got a good night's sleep. On the third day she was able to be up, and on the fifth day after receiving the first treatment she was able to walk where she pleased. She has been healthy ever since, and has sent many friends to Dr. Wilson for treatment. He has cured 95 per cent of all cases he has treated, and many of his cures have surprised the medical profession. He uses no drugs or instruments, but cures where all others have failed to give relief. Dr. Wilson also has the power to cure patients at distance at their own home and afflicted persons would do well to write or call on him and be cured.

Wilson's Institute of Healing
Fifth and Walnut street. Seebergea Block. Iowa 'Phone 263.

Dr. J. M. Wilson, who practiced in Des Moines, promised miraculous "magnetic cures" — even from a distance. (Bystander, December 1899)

"Vapor therapy" was also embraced as a legitimate means of treating everything from "the dropsy" to gout and was enthusiastically practiced by Dr. T. H. Phillips in the river town of Keokuk. He had cultivated a large, bi-racial following by 1900, touting himself as the local "massage and vapor-bath" specialist. The good doctor had become something of a local institution, receiving both the keys to the city and enthusiastic praise in 1915, on the occasion of his eighty-sixth birthday celebration.

Upon his death five years later, local newspaper accounts characterized him as a well-respected, semi-retired "practitioner of the medical arts."[11]

Similarly, Prof. J. Wilbur Norris, self-described as a "masseur, chiropathist, and physical trainer" opened his doors to a burgeoning practice in Sioux City, Iowa, in 1902. Promising a wide range of "absolute cures," his combination "bath-chambers and massage parlor" did a land-office business for 17 years before closing abruptly in 1919.[12]

Herbalist William Lovell was chronicled in the December 26, 1926, edition of the *Des Moines Sunday Register Magazine*. Lovell, the son of a slave mother and an Indian father, was touted as "one of the last of the once-famous Indian medicine men," having learned the secrets of "herb healing" from his father as a boy. Originating in Missouri, Lovell relocated to the southern Iowa town of Hayesville, near Sigourney, in August 1926. There he was soon concocting "strange potions of herbs" in "boiling kettles" with which he treated hundreds of the local citizenry — with resounding success!

The white physicians of Keokuk County were not amused. As Lovell's reputation grew, eclipsing their own, they decided to fight back, charging the "Hayesville Medicine Man" with practicing medicine without a license. Lovell could scarcely deny the charges.

By all accounts, he faced his accusers with equanimity. Hundreds of southern Iowans "were treating with the old Indian . . . most of them . . . willing to tell of miraculous healings." According to the *Register*, at least 200 people were willing to testify in court — in the herb doctor's defense.[13]

But none of these early herbalists and hucksters could hold a candle to the widely advertised claims of Dr. J. M. Wilson.

To wit, Dr. Wilson promised to "positively cure" where all others had failed. An early *Bystander* advertisement, dated November 3, 1899, asserted that the "marvelous healer" had received his medical training at the (non-existent) National College

of Lima, Ohio, in a program of electrophysics and therapeutics. Not only could he heal, the lurid prose promised, Dr. Wilson was capable of healing *at a distance*. Those interested in receiving the benefits of his restorative powers were invited to send a 2-cent stamped envelope, along with a complete description of their illness. A cure, it seemed, would be delivered by return post.[14]

As incredibly fanciful as these claims seem today, they were part and parcel of medical practice at the turn of the century. In defense of its practitioners, modern medicine was only just coming into being. Biology, long considered the slower child of the sciences, had lagged far behind the advances made in both chemistry and physics, the so-called "hard sciences."

The inevitable result? Until the early 1900s, men of medicine (there were few women) knew more about the celestial bodies than they did their own. But that was about to change. The discoveries of Pasteur and Lister, the birth of bacteriology, and the revolutionary concepts of infectious disease were making their way into American medicine, politics, and public policy. Scientific advances were transforming medicine.

Along with an understanding of infectious disease — the number one cause of death at the turn of the century — came, for the first time, the means to treat it. But specific remedies came at a price.

Part of the expense of improved health-care for Americans was the hidden expense of training new physicians, of equipping new state-of-the-art laboratories and hospitals, and establishing pharmacies capable of compounding and dispensing the new medicines.

What was to be the defining moment of modern medicine proved a near-fatal blow to African-American medical education and practice.

Disaster Arrived in Two Distinct Parts

The first was financial. Money — lots of it — was necessary to bring medical training institutions, first established in the era of the horse-and-buggy, into the automobile age. Only a generous endowment allowed a medical-training institution to provide its students with a crucial component of their education — training hospitals.

The second part was technological, related to the veritable explosion of information in the biological and medical sciences that occurred at the turn of the century. The advent of drugs that were actually effective, of anesthetic agents that allowed more than the most rudimentary of surgeries, wrought profound changes in the practice of medicine. Increasingly, patients required treatment and prolonged recuperation from illness within the confines of a hospital setting.

Training institutions devoted to the task of educating African-American physicians found themselves failing on both fronts. While white medical schools were often well-funded by way of high enrollment fees, the largesse of affluent alumni, and the endowments of sponsoring religious bodies, African-American institutions often lacked such resources.

The typical African-American medical-school student was impoverished, making any increase in tuition fees an unconscionable burden.

Alumni of predominantly black institutions were often in the unenviable position of struggling to make a living in poverty-stricken rural communities. And black fraternal and religious organizations, locked in a struggle for day-to-day survival, had neither the way nor the means to provide much-needed bequests.

Well into the latter half of the twentieth century, hospital training programs and opportunities remained elusive for African-American graduates. Until the 1920s, most black physicians were grudgingly allowed only "courtesy privileges" to admit and care for black patients and were often categorically denied full staff membership in white hospitals. Most black physicians were also barred from local medical-society membership.

Because only physicians accorded full staff membership were allowed surgical privileges, African-American physicians were often forced to turn surgical patients over to white colleagues. Consequently, black practitioners had only rare opportunities to acquire or retain surgical skills.[15]

The simple fact remained that until the late 1940s, black doctors were fully welcome at only a handful of "colored" hospitals located in major metropolitan centers.

The accreditation tightrope was a tough one to walk. Simply remaining accredited was a high-wire balancing act for most African-American schools. To do so, most found it necessary to improve or create a physical plant, usually by building or adding onto a hospital. Finding the necessary funds to do so was the gust that sent most institutions swaying.

From whom could the schools solicit capital? African-Americans at the turn of the century were sensitive to the need for their own institutions. But asking for millions of dollars from a population only two generations removed from slavery was an exercise in futility. The spirit was willing — but the pocketbook was empty.

Why not, then, solicit funds from private industry, or from charitable, non-discriminatory philanthropic groups?

Why not, indeed?

Enter the Flexner Report

In 1909, Abraham Flexner prepared a report entitled *Medical Education in the United States and Canada*. Hired by the Carnegie Foundation to critique medical schools in North America, Flexner would strongly influence the setting of standards for medical colleges.

His report also led, quite directly, to *the closing of all African-American medical colleges in this country, with the exception of Meharry Medical College and Howard University Medical College* by the year 1923.[16] [Emphasis supplied.]

Flexner's trustees found, quite correctly, that for the preceding 25 years, there had been an "enormous over-production of uneducated and ill trained" medical practitioners in the United States. In addition, the foundation report noted that this overproduction of "ill-trained men . . . is due to the existence of a very large number of commercial schools" with dubious admission criteria, chief among them the prospective physician's ability to pay tuition.

Flexner took American universities to task for failing to "appreciate the great advance in medical education and the increased cost of teaching it along modern lines."

He further asserted that "a hospital . . . is as necessary to a medical school as is a laboratory of chemistry or pathology."

Certainly, Flexner's trustees had the best of stated intentions: "In the preparation of this report the Foundation has kept steadily in view the interests of two classes which in the over-multiplication of medical schools have usually been forgotten — first, the youths who are to study medicine and to become the future practitioners, and secondly, the general public, which is to live and die under their ministrations."[17]

The Flexner report was the starting point in a national initiative to standardize medical education while incorporating the greatly expanded role of the biological sciences in that education.

MEDICAL EDUCATION
IN THE
UNITED STATES AND CANADA

A REPORT TO
THE CARNEGIE FOUNDATION
FOR THE ADVANCEMENT OF TEACHING

BY
ABRAHAM FLEXNER

WITH AN INTRODUCTION BY
HENRY S. PRITCHETT   53 9₀
PRESIDENT OF THE FOUNDATION

BULLETIN NUMBER FOUR

576 FIFTH AVENUE
NEW YORK CITY

The Carnegie Foundation funded Abraham Flexner's report, Medical Education in the United States and Canada, *in 1909. (Carnegie Foundation)*

Feb 20-1947

Dr. Dennis Zachary has followed his grandfather, E. Thomas Scales, into family practice at Mercy Hospital in Des Moines. (Mercy Hospital)

Hundreds of schools, both black and white, closed in the wake of the report. Most of the failed institutions were factually obsolete. One of them, the Knoxville Medical College, a "colored" school established in 1900, advertised itself in a catalog that was briskly dismissed by Flexner et al. as a "tissue of misrepresentations from cover to cover."

Of the 14 African-American medical colleges operating in 1868, only 7 were extant in 1909. Abraham Flexner made painfully clear which 2 of the 7 were deserving of financial support. "The way to help the Negro is to help the two medical schools that have a chance to become efficient — Howard at Washington, Meharry at Nashville."[18]

Winnowing the nation's black medical schools down to the two "fittest" resulted in an acute shortage of black doctors. White institutions remained unwilling to accept more than a few African-American candidates per year.

Even Howard and Meharry encountered great difficulties. Neither would have survived the medical revolution of the early twentieth century without philanthropic assistance from the Rosenwald, Rockefeller, and National Research foundations, as well as major fund-raising efforts on the part of alumni and friends of each institution.

But survive — and thrive — they did.

So did Dr. Emmett Thomas Scales. Born in College Grove, Tennessee, at the turn of the century, Dr. Scales was the rarest of

the rare — a black graduate of a predominantly white medical college, the University of Iowa. A subsequent internship was served at an African-American institution, Chicago's Provident Hospital. The young doctor returned to Iowa, arriving in Des Moines in 1928. Within weeks, he was the toast of the city's black citizenry.

Kind, caring, impeccably trained, Scales personified the ideal family physician. He was also a top-flight clinician. In recognition of that fact, he was granted the aforementioned "courtesy privileges" at Mercy Hospital in Des Moines as early as 1929. Not until 1940, however, did he become a full member of Mercy Hospital's attending staff of physicians.

By the late 1930s Dr. Scales had become a member of the Iowa Lutheran Hospital staff, another private, church-affiliated facility. In the early 1940s, he joined the staff of Broadlawns General, a county-supported hospital serving the indigent of central Iowa.

Dr. Scales plunged into his position with enthusiasm, making changes that vastly improved the departments of endocrinology and metabolism, and establishing diabetic outpatient clinics there in 1946. The following year, Scales witnessed the appointment of Dr. Lawrence Whitfield, a University of Illinois Medical School graduate, as "the first Negro resident physician" at Broadlawns.

In 1950, Scales was elected chief of the department of internal medicine at Broadlawns Hospital, a coup nearly without precedent in Iowa.

But Precedent Did Exist

Dr. Gage C. Moore of Ottumwa enjoyed the distinction of serving as chief of staff at both Ottumwa and St. Joseph hospitals, elected to the posts in 1945. Family physician to thousands of Ottumwans, Dr. Moore first established a practice there in 1936.

The advent of World War 2 interrupted his practice. The doctor served at the front with the Army medical corps for three and a half years before returning home in ill health in 1945. Sadly, he died of a sudden heart attack on July 17, 1949, at the age of 43. His death both stunned and momentarily united Ottumwa. *Bystander* accounts of his funeral indicated an attendance of "more than a thousand persons, white and colored, from [all] over the state."[19]

Despite Moore's accomplishments in Ottumwa, no African-American had ever before been named section chief in a Des

Moines hospital, public *or* private, before E. T. Scales. The doctor's detractors were incensed but found solace in the fact that his appointment was at a county-run and funded institution. No private institution would risk losing its lucrative endowments by allowing a black man to serve as head of a department!

Nonetheless, his supporters were jubilant — recalling the ubiquitous "courtesy privileges" of the 1920s and 1930s. Emmett Scales had just accomplished the impossible.

A scant two years later, he did it again. Elected chief of staff at Mercy Hospital in 1952, Scales silenced the nay-sayers. Mercy was a well-endowed private facility with Catholic affiliations. It was, and is, widely regarded as one of the best private medical hospitals in the state. In one fell swoop, Dr. E. T. Scales had finally been acknowledged as the cream of the crop.

Interestingly, despite broad recognition of his clinical acumen, Dr. Scales was refused privileges at Iowa Methodist Hospital, the only other large facility in the Des Moines area, until after he was elected Mercy Hospital's chief of staff. When the board of directors of Methodist finally offered him privileges, he refused them outright, still angry at the original slight.

Despite his impressive credentials and the tacit approval of most of his peers, Dr. Scales was aware that more than a few of his colleagues at Mercy resented his leadership position. Some were openly contemptuous, refusing to comply with his instructions or directions.

Highly disciplined, he held frustration in, pouring his energies into the care of his patients. In 1958, he was elected chief of staff at Broadlawns General Hospital, the first African-American to be so honored.

What limited free time he had he spent in what would now be called community activism, promoting the new-fangled concept of civil rights. Dr. Scales served on the board of directors of the Des Moines Interracial Commission, the Des Moines branch of the NAACP, and an inter-city YMCA, among numerous others.

The doctor and his wife, Lillian, the sister of Dr. Gage C. Moore, were at the center of black Des Moines's fledgling social life as well. He held office in Kappa Alpha Psi, the national black social fraternity. Mentor to many, Dr. Scales epitomized the best of African-American physicians in the extent to which he involved himself in his community. He gave freely of his time, his money, and himself to the city that welcomed and sustained him for over 30 years.

Gage C. Moore (above) was an outstanding student and athlete at Estherville High School. (Emmet County Historical Society)

Dr. Gage C. Moore (left) in his Ottumwa office (courtesy Jo Moore Stewart)

In many ways, he was among the first African-American physicians in Iowa to break through the invisible color line. Fittingly, his grandson, Dr. Dennis Zachary, a family practice physician, is a member of the medical staff Dr. Scales once headed at Mercy Hospital.

When E. T. Scales died at 58 of a sudden heart attack, his legacy was untouched by the taint of scandal.

Clyde Bradford

worked hard —

too hard to see old age.

He died at 65,

continuing the most

unfortunate of

African–American

physician trends

— that of dying young.

Dr. J. Alvin Jefferson was not so lucky. The unassuming Jefferson became the object of ridicule, as well as front-page news, when he was sued by a young white nurse in May 1936 — for breaking his promise to marry her! The actual charge brought against him was "breach of promise" for breaking off the supposed engagement.

The newly widowed Jefferson saw his impeccable reputation, the reputation he had struggled to build over a 25-year period, destroyed in a single day of sensational testimony.

Was he guilty, or wasn't he? All of Iowa hung onto this question on May 13, 1936.[20] Was the balding, bespectacled baby doctor actually guilty of any wrongdoing? Had he done the unthinkable — and wooed a white woman? The trial mesmerized Depression-weary Iowans as few other entertainments could.

Dr. Jefferson was found not guilty and paid his accuser the sum of $1. Within months, he'd remarried — a suitable, sensible young black woman from Tuskegee with whom he hoped to put disgrace behind him.

The whole sordid episode was soon forgotten, however, in the face of an even more startling development.

Nothing sold newspapers faster than the case of Dr. H. H. London. Hubert Hawthorne London was an anomaly, a black Iowa native who had graduated from the State University of Iowa Medical School in 1920. Born and raised in Buxton, of educated parents, young Hubert seemed to have all the makings of a "local boy makes good" success story.

Relocating to Des Moines after completing medical school, he was practically guaranteed a lucrative practice. Except that success seemed to elude him at every turn. Handsome, bright, and outgoing as a youth, Hubert had married his college sweetheart, only to watch his marriage unravel after the death of an infant son.

Slowly, imperceptibly, he withdrew into madness. His busy practice dwindled, then dissolved.

Twice he ran afoul of the law. Twice his attorney pleaded not guilty by reason of insanity. By 1935, he had been briefly committed to the state insane asylum in Clarinda, where he convalesced.

And brooded.

By 1939, Hubert London was dry as tinder waiting for a match. When a municipal court bailiff came to his door to serve a summons for a moving traffic violation on the morning of Monday, October 2, 1939, the fuse was lit. Hubert flashed into flame.

254

Screaming obscenities, he barricaded himself in the house and fired round after round of buckshot into the quiet street. The police were summoned, and an Old-West style shoot-out ensued. When it was over, Hubert was injured, having sustained gunshot wounds to his leg and thigh.

He died the next day, as miserable and alone in death as he had become in life.[21]

Hubert London was 46 years old.

Dr. J. Alvin Jefferson, his brother in scandal, died one month later, a heart-attack victim, at the ripe old age of 63.

Fortunately for black Iowans, Dr. Clyde Bradford remained. A native of Shreveport, Louisiana, Dr. Bradford had studied medicine at Meharry Medical College, graduating in 1929. After completing an internship and residency in Kansas City, Missouri, he arrived in Des Moines in 1933.

Four years later, he was appointed to the staff of county doctors by the Polk County Board of Supervisors, charged with providing care for all "colored patients of the county." No African-American in the state had ever been appointed to what was then regarded as quite a prestigious position.

Dr. Bradford's practice flourished. Between 1933 and 1965, he provided medical care to thousands of black and white Iowans. He was appointed to the staff of both Veteran's and Broadlawns Polk County hospitals. He was a member of both the AMA and the Polk County Medical Society.

But none of these accomplishments allowed him to escape the shadow of racism.

In September 1954, the doctor confirmed *Bystander* newspaper reports that he had been unable to purchase a house he desired in Des Moines, even though he was able to supply the asking price — in cash.

"My housing problem is difficult," the beleaguered Bradford was quoted. "We've been trying for a number of years to get a home, or a piece of ground, in a desirable neighborhood. It has been pretty rough."

The ugly encounter did not sour Bradford on Des Moines. Along with Dr. E. T. Scales, he was among the first black doctors in the city to welcome a lanky young resident, Dr. Julius Connor, to Des Moines — with entreaties to stay.

Clyde Bradford worked hard — too hard to see old age.

He died at 65, continuing the most unfortunate of African-American physician trends — that of dying young.

Fortunately, Harry Dandridge Harper Sr. refused to follow trends. The groundbreaking physician set precedents instead. Born February 12, 1900, the eighth of nine children of a black working-class Fort Madison family, he eventually returned to the city of his birth to practice medicine — for 45 years! Harry was joined in practice by his younger brother, Dr. George Edward Harper, in 1939. The two remained partners until George's death in 1965.

Harry and George Harper were two scions of a legendary black Iowa family. Although their parents, George and Rhoda Harper, lacked formal education, they made clear to their children that educational achievement was paramount.

Ernst, their eldest, attended dental school at Meharry University, where he met and married Mildred Hawkins of Lexington, Missouri. Mildred was a pharmacist, and their combined pharmacy-dental practice was an instant success in turn-of-the-century black St. Louis.

A second son, William, attended Howard University and eventually went on to complete medical school there as well. He was there, in Washington, D.C., when he received word that his mother had died in Fort Madison.

Half a continent from home, William was destitute. With just enough funds to pay for either his tuition or a train ticket home, he faced a hard decision. Which was he to do?

Dutifully, he queried his family by telegram. Should he stay in Washington? Or come back to Fort Madison for the funeral?

The close-knit Harpers were unanimous in their reply — stay in school, they replied. Rhoda would have wanted him to continue his studies.

William stayed, completing his education with honors. In 1918, he returned to Iowa and settled in Keokuk, where he remained in practice from 1918 until his death in 1958.[22] His son, Dr. William Harper Jr., practiced medicine in Keokuk until *his* death in 1975.

Anna Harper, sister to Harry, George, and William, left home in the 1920s for college in Chicago, followed by a highly successful career as an educator.

He queried his family by telegram. Should he stay in Washington? Or come back for the funeral? The close-knit Harpers were unanimous in their reply — stay in school.

Dr. Harry D. Harper Sr. practiced medicine in his hometown of Fort Madison for 45 years. (courtesy Lois Harper Eichacker)

Dr. George E. Harper II practiced with his brother Harry from 1939 until 1965. (courtesy George E. Harper III and Robert B. Harper)

Dr. William H. Harper Sr. practiced medicine in Keokuk from 1918 until his death in 1958. (courtesy Phyllis Harper-Bardach)

Dr. Lee Burton Furgerson, a Texas native, settled in Waterloo after earning his M.D. at the University of Iowa. (Grout Museum)

Dr. Warren Nash practiced medicine and social activism in Waterloo for 25 years. (Grout Museum)

The youngest sister, Naomi, attended the University of Iowa and became a teacher. She eventually married a minister, and one of their sons, Rev. Charles Wesley Jordan, served as the Methodist bishop of Iowa before his recent retirement.

Born into this milieu, Harry D. Harper could not fail to excel: first completing his premedical studies at the University of Iowa, and then graduating from Howard University Medical School. Some years later, he received the coveted Medical Alumni Award from Howard for "service, dedication and contributions to medicine."

Harry had intended to complete his medical education in Iowa. However, after enrolling in Iowa's College of Medicine, he learned that students "of African descent" could not participate in obstetrics and gynecology training at Iowa. To obtain this part of his education, he was told, he would have to travel to a black institution, a notion utterly unsatisfactory to the practical Harry. What other crucial parts of his medical education, he wondered, might suddenly become unavailable to him?

Concluding it would be futile to stay and find out, he enrolled at Howard University Medical College in Washington, D.C., and flourished in this new and supportive environment.

Upon receipt of his medical degree, Dr. Harper served his internship at Freedman Hospital in Washington, D.C., before returning to Fort Madison in 1926.

Obstacles awaited him at his return, first among them the fact that no one in town would rent him office space. Finally, a daring white citizen offered to fix up his old coal shed, intending that the young doctor could use the space if he desired. The dilapidated structure became Harry's first office.

In 1927, Harper married. By the time the former Lillie Grinage journeyed to Fort Madison to join her new husband, he had moved his practice into a small store-front building.

The practice grew slowly at first. White Fort Madisonians were initially reluctant to allow a black doctor to treat them. Neither was he well received by the local medical community. And despite a growing, multi-ethnic practice, he was not allowed local hospital privileges for many years.

But Harry Harper persevered. Slowly, business picked up. The young doctor built a sterling reputation, caring for African-American, Mexican-American, and eventually Caucasian patients as well. He learned to speak fluent Spanish in order to serve his Hispanic patients better.

Yet Dr. Harper found time to meet needs that were more than medical. Family members still recall the many calls he received from local African-Americans, relating stories of racial discrimination.

Such stories abounded as many businesses in Iowa in the early 1960s openly refused to serve blacks. Signs in public places discouraging blacks from entering were commonplace.

When Dr. Harper was apprised of such a sign, they say, he would get on the phone, call the county attorney, and, according to family members, "most times, things were taken care of quietly." But at times, his active participation was required.

Like the incident at the new municipal swimming pool. A young black man phoned Dr. Harper at his office one afternoon to tell him, "we were told we would not be able to swim in the pool this afternoon."

Harry Harper saw red. As a member of Fort Madison's chamber of commerce, he had canvassed the town raising money for that pool! He had *given* money, his own money, toward its construction, only to hear of blatant discrimination at a municipal facility!

Not true, city fathers were quick to assert. The five Harper children were certainly welcome to use the pool.

Good, Harry responded. Because, as it happened, he was sending his son and several other youngsters over to the pool that very afternoon, and he expected to hear that they were able to enjoy it. The message was received by a chastened city council. And the pool was thereafter open to all.[23]

Open to all. Those words ring true to the indomitable spirit of Dr. Harry D. Harper. Over the course of a long and fruitful professional life, he was elected chief of staff at Sacred Heart Hospital in Fort Madison. He was also a member of numerous professional organizations, including the National and American Medical Associations, the Iowa Medical Society, of which he was a life member, and the Lee County Medical Society.

Despite winning the hard-fought battle for acceptance at home, Dr. Harper was cognizant of the ongoing struggle of all African-Americans. He was a long-time president of the Fort Madison branch of the NAACP and was an honorary life member of the NAACP. He also served on the Governor's Study Commission on Discrimination in Employment in Iowa. In addition, he was a member of the Iowa Civil Rights Commission, serving as chairman of that body in 1969 and 1970. Dr. Harper was repeatedly listed in *Who's Who in the Midwest* between 1954 and 1976.

Dr. Harry Harper Sr. died January 1, 1977, at the age of 76, the honored son of a town that had grown to revere him.[24]

Other Black Iowa Physicians Also Made Their Marks

Dr. Lee Burton Furgerson was among them. Born and reared in Texas, Dr. Furgerson received his medical degree from the University of Iowa in 1925 and began practice in Waterloo in 1927. Continuing a time-honored tradition, Dr. Furgerson wove his life into that of his adopted hometown. He was a member of the Kappa Alpha Psi social fraternity, the American Medical Association, the Boy Scouts of America, the Cedar Lodge, the YMCA, the American Legion — and the National Association for the Advancement of Colored People.

Unfortunately, Dr. Furgerson participated in another time-honored tradition of black doctors. He died at the age of 49, from complications related to a stroke. His brother-in-law, Dr. Warren Nash, a 1953 graduate of Creighton University Medical School, practiced in Waterloo for 25 years and was the major instigator of the modernization of the Allen Hospital emergency department. He too suffered a premature death at age 56.

Why did so many black Iowa doctors die young? The answer to that question is probably buried with the physicians themselves, but nonetheless begs analysis.

Did Overwork Play a Role?

Undoubtedly it did. In the days before household telephones were ubiquitous and house calls were common, overwork was probably regarded as an unavoidable occupational hazard.

Tuberculosis and other infectious ailments were common in African-Americans at the turn of the century, as was the still-common specter of hypertension and its attendant complications. Startling discrepancies in virtually all health indicators between white and African-American citizens — ranging from low-birth-weight infants, to premature death from all causes — were simply acknowledged as the status quo at the turn of the century. African-American physicians, despite a higher socio-economic status, suffered — and died — from the same afflictions as the majority of their patients.[25]

Historians of the period also cite the chronic stresses associated with racism as a contributing cause to early-age death.

Though hard to quantify, the day-to-day struggle for existence in an overtly racist society doubtless played a role.

Against the odds, Dr. Percy Harris of Cedar Rapids has enjoyed a long and distinguished career in medicine. Harris faced unusual adversity as a youth growing up in Mississippi and Memphis in the 1920s and 1930s. His father died in an automobile accident when Percy was two. Eight years later his mother died of tuberculosis, and Percy himself spent two years as an invalid in the same sanatorium. During a visit to his aunt's Waterloo home as a teenager, Harris decided to stay in Iowa. He graduated from East High in Waterloo in 1947. During his high school years, he met Lileah Furgerson, Dr. Lee Furgerson's daughter. The couple married in 1950 while Harris attended Iowa State Teachers College in Cedar Falls. The Harrises subsequently moved to Washington, D.C., where Percy earned a bachelor's degree at Howard University in 1954. After completing medical school at Howard in 1957, Dr. and Mrs. Harris moved to Cedar Rapids. There Dr. Harris opened a practice, helped raise a family of 12 children, and took part in the emerging civil rights movement.[26]

Another African-American physician who has refused to become a statistic is Dr. Robert M. Carney of Grinnell. Recruited to Iowa by Dr. Clarence Douglas, a Meharry classmate, in 1959, Dr. Carney came to eastern Iowa with a wait-and-see attitude. He liked what he saw and has been there ever since.

Born near Steubenville, Ohio, in 1928, he was raised for a time by his paternal grandparents after his mother died of pneumonia when he was five years old. A young sister died shortly thereafter of complications from rickets. Robert Carney remembered those deaths and many others like them, a memory that later hardened into his resolve to study medicine.

He left Ohio for the Army in 1946, ultimately attending college at the University of Hawaii, while still in the service. An Army buddy encouraged him to continue his studies at Fisk University, a historically black college. The young Ohioan heeded this advice, graduating from Fisk in 1952 with a B.A. in zoology. Next he pursued a master's degree in physiology while engaged in cancer research. Meharry Medical College followed. In 1958, armed with an M.D. degree, he came to Cedar Rapids, Iowa, to serve a rotating internship at Mercy Hospital.

A year later, he recalls, he "hit the road" in Iowa, invited by no fewer than 25 small towns to interview for practice opportunities.

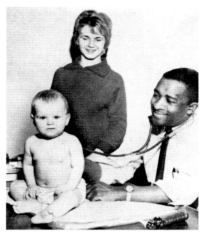

Dr. Percy Harris of Cedar Rapids has served his community's medical and social needs since 1957. (Cedar Rapids League of Women Voters)

Dr. Clarence Douglas, who practiced medicine in Belle Plaine until his retirement in 1991, delivered triplets Dale, Diane, and Denise Slaymaker in 1970. (courtesy Dr. Robert Carney)

Dr. Robert M. Carney has practiced medicine in Grinnell since 1965. (courtesy Dr. Robert Carney)

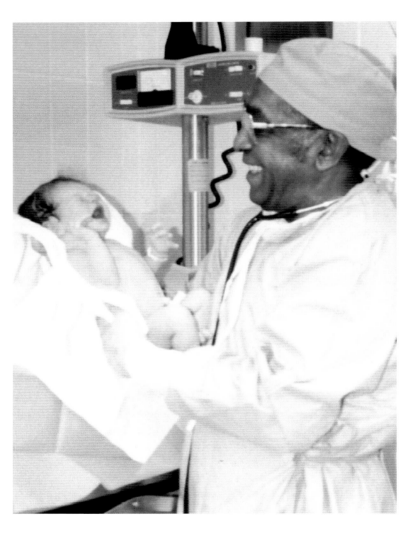

These Places Wanted a Doctor

"They were actively recruiting," Dr. Carney recalled. "It was 1959, and there I was, driving all over rural Iowa, being offered jobs. *Good* jobs. These places wanted a doctor, and believe me, color wasn't a problem. Several places offered me housing, bank financing, whatever I needed to get started. Because my friend Clarence Douglas was in eastern Iowa, in Belle Plaine, I was most interested in [the nearby town of] Brooklyn. Plus, there was — I don't know — a *goodness* about the people in Brooklyn. A wholesomeness," Carney could sense, if not fully express.

"Like the other small towns I had visited, they needed a doctor, and they were willing to give me a good start. They offered me financing, a clinic, an established clientele. Whatever I wanted."

What he wanted most, though, was to return to Ohio. "That was my home. My family was there. Naturally, I wanted to go back."

His reception was frosty. Steubenville, he remembers, was "not ready" for him. "It was a rude awakening," Dr. Carney says. "This was my hometown. I'd been born there, gone to school there as a boy." Throughout his travels, he had always wanted to return to practice medicine in the city of his birth. But — "Steubenville was like Mississippi in the '50s: No bank would loan me money. No one would sell me decent housing, much less an office building. I was not encouraged."

He left, within weeks of what was to have been his triumphant return.

Did Brooklyn, Iowa, still need a doctor? a disheartened Carney inquired of his friend, Clarence Douglas.

A resounding yes was the answer. Was Carney still interested? He was — and returned to Brooklyn, to an enthusiastic welcome. Robert Carney entered private practice in eastern Iowa in 1959, the town of Brooklyn his home base. In 1964, he became medical examiner for Poweshiek County, a position he held until 1998.

In 1965, Dr. Carney moved his practice 15 miles west, to Grinnell, Iowa. But he remained active throughout eastern Iowa, maintaining hospital privileges in Marengo and at Mercy Hospital in Iowa City. Grinnell became his home, his office on Broad Street a local fixture, until 1988. At that time, he assumed responsibility for the Belle Plaine clinic from his old friend Clarence Douglas, after Dr. Douglas's retirement.

In 1992, Robert Carney finally decided to retire — if nearly daily *locum tenens* work can accurately be described as retirement. "Oh, I still work," says the hearty 73-year-old. "But I play a lot of golf, too!"[27]

Did he ever run into prejudice? What happened in Ohio in 1959 — did any of it happen again, here in Iowa?

"Of course I ran into ignorant people, especially at the beginning. There were people who challenged me, who made my life tougher. What they didn't know was that none of that stuff bothered me. Not coming from where I've come. Not having lived through what I've lived through.

"Sure, there was prejudice. There still *is* prejudice. But I stopped letting that bother me a long time ago. The thing is, though, that I had left home because of prejudice. They didn't even give me a chance at home. Here, they gave me a chance, a good chance. So I made up my mind that I wasn't going to leave. In fact, I was *determined* to stay."

Despite his determination, Carney is sure he would not have survived his trial by fire had he come to Iowa "with a chip on my shoulder."

He has done well here, he feels, because he was simply the right man for the job. "I'm the kind of guy who talks to patients, who takes the time to get to know them, to care about them. I understand that, as a physician, I truly *am* my brother's keeper."

His patients trust him, he stresses. Trust him to keep their secrets, safeguard their health, deliver their babies (864 of them, at last count), and care for their old folks.

Carney says now, simply, "They cared about me. And I cared back."[28]

Since Dr. Robert Carney's arrival in the Grinnell area, he has been joined by a host of other African-American physicians.

Among them is Dr. Phillip Brooks, a radiologist born in Ontario, Canada, but reared in the United States. After completing his medical studies at Meharry, Brooks relocated in Michigan for internship and residency. A two-year stint in the Indian Health Service, spent in Browning, Montana, introduced the life-long city dweller to the grandeur of the American West. Brooks's initial reluctance to journey to Montana turned into wonder at the soul-stirring peace and beauty of the wilderness. His love affair with Montana survived a career move to Iowa. Brooks still vacations out West. But he has made his home — and livelihood — in Grinnell since 1989.[29]

Dr. Marvin Henderson and Dr. William Hunter also practice in Grinnell. So does Dr. Ronald Charles, an orthopedic surgeon and a black South African.

All had different reasons for relocating here and for remaining in Iowa. All are outstanding physicians, principals in flourishing practices, and mainstays of the communities that support them.

Dr. Clarence Douglas is only a memory in nearby Belle Plaine. In sports-mad Iowa, a local football stadium has been named after him, an honor that would have given the gentle Douglas pause.

But his legacy lives on in the form of Grinnell's new breed of black doctors and in Robert Carney himself, the pioneering "outsider" from Steubenville, Ohio, whose grit and determination allowed him to flourish in a place and a time where he could have perished.

What Kept Him Going?

"Sheer cussedness," Carney says, accompanied by equal doses of patience and persistence.[30]

None of the state's early black doctors needed the strength to persevere more than Iowa's first black osteopathic physicians. As one of the first African-American graduates of Des Moines's Still College of Osteopathy and Surgery (now Des Moines University — Osteopathic Medical Center), Dr. Stanley Griffin broke new ground in 1949.

At that time, osteopathic practitioners were an embattled group, often forced into uneven turf battles with hostile M.D.'s. Dr. Griffin became both an expert proponent of the osteopathic tradition as well as the tenets of community involvement. (His wife, the former Edna Williams, was a local civil-rights activist, sitting down and demanding service at the then-segregated Katz Drug Store lunch counter in Des Moines in 1948.)

Joining Stanley Griffin in the osteopathic tradition was Dr. Leon Jones. Born in Waterproof, Louisiana, but reared in Boston, Dr. Jones completed undergraduate work at Tougaloo College in Tougaloo, Mississippi, before receiving his medical degree at now-defunct Kansas City Medical College. In 1946, he came to Des Moines to enter Still College of Osteopathy and Surgery for additional training, graduating in 1949. He remained on staff at Still while also engaged in private practice for the next 12 years, only to succumb to a heart attack at his desk in 1962.

Age at death? Forty-nine.

Among his pallbearers was Dr. Eustace J. Ware. Dr. Ware was a pharmacist for a number of years before pursuing his dream of becoming a doctor. He graduated from Still College and was a colleague of Dr. Jones. Dr. Julius Connor remembers studying for the state licensing exam with Dr. Ware, many years ago. "He was a fine man, and a good doctor," Connor recalls.

Black Des Moines agreed with that assessment. Dr. Ware's inner-city office was a busy one — until the doctor's untimely death of renal failure while he was still in his fifties.

Pictured here with his wife, Edna, after his retirement, Dr. Stanley Griffin graduated from Des Moines Still College of Osteopathy and Surgery (now Des Moines University — Osteopathic Medical Center) in 1949 and built a successful practice in the years that followed. (First Unitarian Church of Des Moines)

Dr. Stanley Griffin
OSTEOPATHIC PHYSICIAN
Hours: 10 a.m. to 12:00 (Noon)
Monday Though Saturday
1 p.m. to 5:30 p.m. Tuesday,
Wednesday and Saturday
408½ East Walnut   Phone 2-0301

Following in the wake of Drs. Griffin, Jones, and Ware was Dr. Fred Strickland. This osteopathic physician, active in numerous venues in Des Moines's African-American community, has maintained an active practice in the city since 1980, while tirelessly promoting community activism. Using the forum of the black church, Dr. Strickland has done much to motivate and inspire an entire generation of young black Iowans.[31]

Dr. Erin Herndon was one of those young people. Growing up in West Des Moines, she had no thought of becoming a doctor — until the day she heard Fred Strickland speak.

The occasion was Career Day at a Des Moines high school. Teachers, lawyers, even a local black TV newscaster were present, but only one person representing medicine.

A student at the College of Osteopathic Medicine and Surgery (as it was then called), Fred Strickland spoke to a room full of adolescent idealists with the voice of authority. Study and hard work were only the first part of his take-home message. He also took the time to remind the youngsters to dream — to dream big.

Herndon took him up on it. A bright but previously unfocused student, she completed high school in three years, in a hurry to begin premedical studies at Simpson College in Indianola.

Entering medical school at the University of Iowa in the summer of 1979, Herndon graduated in May 1983, only seven years behind the first African-American female medical graduate at Iowa, Dr. Florence Battle Shafiq.[32] (Dr. Edward A. Carter, the first male African-American medical graduate, received his degree in 1907, going on to achieve the top score on the state licensing exam held the following year.)

Another "First"

Yet another "first" at Iowa was Dr. Deborah Ann Turner. In 1978, the Iowa native became only the second black female physician to earn a medical degree from the College of Medicine. In 1985, she became the first female African-American gynecologic oncologist in the United States.

Another member of the Iowa class of 1983 was Dr. Ronnie Hawkins. The Mississippi native ultimately chose family practice as his clinical milieu and Des Moines as his home.

At the forefront in black civic affairs in his adopted city, Hawkins has managed to conceal a keen intellect — and a razor-sharp wit — behind a soft-spoken facade. But when community involvement or mentoring young black Iowans are the topics at hand, topics that retain contemporary relevance, Dr. Ronnie

Dr. Erin Herndon was inspired to practice medicine by Dr. Frederick Strickland. (courtesy Dr. Erin Herndon)

Dr. Deborah Ann Turner was the first black female gynocologic oncologist in the United States. (courtesy Dr. Deborah Ann Turner)

Hawkins often leads the discussion.

A family man, he has chosen to remain in Iowa for all the obvious reasons. Superior public education. A stable statewide economy. A clean, crime-free environment.[33]

Less obvious, but just as important to the family physician, is the opportunity Iowa affords him to "have an impact. To matter. I wanted to make a difference. In Iowa, I can."

When Dr. Hawkins left Broadlawns in the mid-1980s, his position on the hospital's staff was filled by Chicago native Kevin Moore. Dr. Moore, a University of Iowa medical school graduate, had at that time already completed a three-year family practice residency at Broadlawns. Attracted to Iowa by the state's emphasis on quality public education, Dr. Moore and his family settled permanently in Des Moines. He readily admits that periodically he needs a "big city fix," but Des Moines is his home now. It's been a good choice, he says, for both him and his family.[34]

In contrast, Herndon's reasons for remaining in Iowa after medical school were entirely personal. Still unmarried, she elected to stay close to a support system of family and friends during the

difficult years of internship and residency training. Iowa Methodist Medical Center, a tertiary care center in Des Moines with University of Iowa affiliations, filled the bill nicely.

As it turned out, her decision proved to be a good one. Following the successful completion of an internal medicine residency, she entered practice in Des Moines, becoming only the second black female physician to enter private practice in Iowa.

"The road I chose to walk in 1986 was high, narrow, and, at times, achingly lonely," Herndon recalls. "But it also ran straight and true, through the landscape of my dreams."[35]

Iowa also held Dr. Steve Berry's dream. Born and raised in St. Paul, Minnesota, the 6-foot-5 Berry attended Luther College in Decorah, Iowa, an institution he heard about through a high school classmate. Berry began college as a business and finance major. He credits one of his cousins, an enthusiastic pre-med student, as first interesting him in the biological sciences. Before long, his interest became a fascination, one that led the former prep basketball star to pursue a medical education.

Graduation from the University of Minnesota Medical School in 1978 was followed by an internal medicine residency in Kalamazoo, Michigan. In 1983, Berry completed the pulmonary medicine subspeciality program at the University of Iowa — and took the leap of faith that would lead to the assumption of Emmett Scales's mantle as a leader among African-American physicians in Iowa. "I answered a blind ad," Berry reveals when asked how he decided to settle in Des Moines. "A pulmonary and critical care group in Des Moines had placed an ad for a third partner in the trade journals. I happened to answer it and was hired nearly on the spot."

The group grew phenomenally, both in number and stature, and is now a prestigious nine-member consortium.

Adding immeasurably to that prestige, was Berry's election as chief of staff at Mercy Hospital Medical Center in 1992 — the first African-American to hold the post since Emmett Scales had done so in 1952.

Despite the passage of 40 years, Berry's election to chief of staff at Mercy was nearly as newsworthy as Scales's had once been. Comparisons abounded.

"In fact, I did feel a certain kinship with Dr. Scales," Berry says. Enough so that during his year as Mercy's top physician, he cemented relationships with key Mercy Foundation administrators, relationships that would later allow him to originate the

Pulmonologist Dr. Steve Berry settled in Des Moines after a residency at the University of Iowa. In 1992 Dr. Berry was elected chief of staff at Mercy Hospital. (courtesy Dr. Steve Berry)

Dr. Ronnie Hawkins, originally from Mississippi, and Dr. Kevin Moore from Chicago both began their careers at Broadlawns Hospital and now specialize in family medicine at Mercy Hospital in Des Moines. (Mercy Hospital)

Dr. Onyebuchi Ukabiala practices
pediatric surgery at Mercy Hospital
in Des Moines. (Mercy Hospital)

Dr. Veronica Butler
(courtesy Dr. Veronica Butler)

Emmett T. Scales Endowment Fund. The fund, a scholarship trust created for the express purpose of increasing the number of African-American nurses in central Iowa, was Berry's baby.

"Nursing was a glaring example of the paucity of skilled minority staff working at a facility that sits in the middle of Des Moines's inner city," he explains. "There were other examples, but nursing was the most obvious deficiency. Creating the fund with the active support of the hospital allowed me both to honor one of my predecessors as well as doing something concrete to increase diversity among local nurses."

Other comparisons with Emmett Scales have to do with Berry's well-earned reputation as a meticulous, methodical clinician.

He admits that "the fear of missing something, of overlooking something important in a case, still drives me. Black physicians are still under somewhat of a magnifying glass; as a critical care specialist, caring for some of the sickest patients in the hospital, the stakes are even higher."

Racism, Berry says, has not been overt but is nevertheless something he contends with on a daily basis. "Patients often register surprise," when he walks into an exam room. "Many of them comment on my height," he notes, "although it's perfectly obvious the reason for their astonishment is my skin color." Berry has learned to use these potentially awkward remarks as an ice-breaker.

But how has he compensated for the increased scrutiny, the sure and certain knowledge that his work is held to a higher standard? The only way he can. "I do my best for each patient each day," he offers with the simple conviction of the man who carries Emmett Scales's legacy forward.[36]

For Dr. Steve Berry, as for Emmett Scales, only the best will ever do.

The best. Onyebuchi Ukabiala is among them. An Ibo born in Nigeria, "Buchi," as he prefers to be called, always knew he would be a doctor. Surgery held a particular attraction for him, as the specialty that would allow him "to perform miracles" with his hands.

His formal education, through medical school, was completed in Nigeria, after which he pursued post-graduate training in surgery in Great Britain. Pediatric surgery subspecialty training followed in Pittsburgh. He was then recruited to Des Moines.

"American medical education is very different than that in England," Buchi states, in precise British-accented tones. "Here, there is a much greater emphasis on speaking up, on displaying one's knowledge."

He soon learned, then learned to excel at, the American style.

American racism was yet another obstacle to be overcome. "Quite frankly, I had to be three times as good as a white competitor" to survive residency and build a practice.

Yet survive — and thrive — he has.

Onyebuchi Ukabiala brings a unique perspective to the concept of the black physician in Iowa. That the Nigerian native has found his niche here in the American Midwest is truly a lesson in the value of perseverance, of ultimate triumph over adversity.

Dr. Ukabiala freely admits that upon his arrival in Iowa, he felt like a stranger in a strange land. Over time, he developed a comfort and ease in his new home.[37]

As did Dr. Veronica Butler.

Butler, of Ottumwa, was the first black woman doctor to enter private practice in Iowa. A native of Detroit and a 1976 medical graduate of Howard University, Dr. Butler's first clinical interest was internal medicine. However, a two-year stint in the discipline at Henry Ford Hospital in Detroit disabused her of that notion.

Always Wanted to Care for People

"I had always wanted to care for people, to have contact with them. Turns out, I wasn't interested in high-tech, low-touch medicine. So I went into family practice and found my niche."

After completing her residency, Dr. Butler first worked in inner-city Detroit in 1981.

"It was a modern-day war zone. People were poor in a way that I had never experienced, and I had *grown up* in Detroit, for heaven's sake! I'm a child of the radical '60s — to the point that in college I was a member of the Black Panthers.

"But I had grown up comfortable, in the black middle-class. Nothing — and I mean *nothing* — about my middle-class upbringing prepared me for that practice.

"I was appalled, frankly, at how few of my patients possessed even the most rudimentary essentials of modern life. 'Frills' like medical care were absolutely beyond their reach.

"I'll never forget my very first patient. You know what his chief complaint was? Not 'I'm running a fever,' or 'I have chest pain.' His complaint was, 'I'm hungry.' I never forgot that. In a land of plenty, I had patients who were hungry."

Challenged to find broader solutions for the medico-social problems she encountered but too impatient to implement them, she enrolled in the Masters of Public Health program at the University of Michigan in 1982, but left Michigan a month short of receiving her degree.

For Iowa.

Why Iowa? "That's what my family said," Dr. Butler chuckles. "'Why Iowa?'"

She came to Iowa for largely personal reasons. "I was in burn-out, tired of trying to save the world one patient at a time. I was tired of crime, tired of big-city life. I was also divorced, with a seven-year-old daughter, and I wanted her to grow up in a more nurturing environment. Both of us were ready for a better life."

Fairfield, Iowa, provided that environment. In 1983, Dr. Butler joined a now-retired family doctor in Ottumwa and was soon busy practicing the kind of medicine she had forgotten existed. Life in Iowa soon revived her old interest in political action.

"Three years ago, I ran for governor of Iowa," she says, on the Natural Law party ticket. "The Natural Law party is nationwide. But it originated in Fairfield, and basically supports the de-politization of public policy," she continues. "So many decisions that affect our day-to-day lives are made arbitrarily, for all the wrong reasons, by the people who govern us. The Natural Law Party urges people to support candidates who make decisions on a local basis."

Dr. Butler laughs. "I certainly didn't win, but I enjoyed running! And I accomplished my goal, which was to encourage voters to examine the issues rather than the personalities. I also got to travel the state, which was fun. Iowans are, by and large, a decent people."

Is she glad she came to Iowa?

An emphatic "yes" is the answer. "I have really blossomed here," Veronica Butler says proudly. More quietly, but just as emphatically, she adds, "I'd call Iowa my home."[38]

Professional Ambitions

Iowa has been Dr. Clifford Smith's home nearly his entire life, though local reaction to his professional ambitions was not enthusiastic at first. When Smith was in elementary school in Waterloo, he asked a local architect about pursuing a career in architecture. "Blacks can't make it in architecture," he was told. Later, when he asked his high school principal what classes he

should take to go to college, the principal told him not to waste his time — that he would help Smith get a good job washing cars.

Though still segregated, the military offered more opportunity to African-Americans, so Smith enlisted. He advanced to the air corps training school at Tuskegee but was dismissed from the program just short of graduation when he filed an official complaint regarding a white officer's use of the word "nigra." Undaunted, Smith returned to Iowa and enrolled at the University of Iowa under the GI Bill of Rights. After graduation, he applied to Iowa's medical school. When he was turned down, he accepted a place at the Meharry School of Medicine connected to Fisk University in Nashville.

In 1962 Dr. Smith returned to Iowa, moving with his wife and children to MacGregor and beginning his practice. The initial response to his arrival was cool and even hostile, but Dr. Smith slowly began to win the acceptance of the townspeople. When he applied for a loan at the local bank, he was able to fulfill their unusual requirement of getting 25 patients to co-sign his note. By the late 1970s, his practice had grown to 3,000 patients.

Mahatma Ghandi of Rural Medicine

In the mid-80s Dr. Smith sold his clinic to Gundersen Lutheran of La Crosse with the thought of slowing down, but that didn't happen. Nurses, patients, and colleagues testify to his extraordinary and continuing commitment to his patients. According to Kathy Wessels, his nurse for almost 20 years, none of Dr. Smith's patients ever complained of their long waits in the waiting room, because "they all knew that when they got back in the back, they'd get their fair amount of time." Sally Scarff, a patient for 36 years, remembers how Dr. Smith would "pull up that chair right close to you and look you right in your eyes and make you feel he really cared about you." A medical colleague called him the "Mahatma Ghandi of rural medicine."

These testimonies somehow came to the attention of the National Rural Health Association, which in 1998 named Dr. Clifford Smith the Rural Health Practitioner of the Year, a title deserved as much for his healing hands as his questing heart.[39]

Dr. Meredith Saunders has always called Iowa home. A native of Mason City, Iowa, he attended the public schools there, later earning both his B.S. and medical degrees from the University of Iowa. In 1956, Saunders was the only black graduate from the College of Medicine. He then interned at the Edward W.

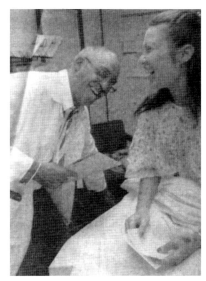

Dr. Clifford Smith, named Rural Health Practitioner of the Year in 1998, served patients around McGregor in northeastern Iowa for 35 years. (Des Moines Register)

Dr. Meredith Saunders, an opthalmologist, has practiced in Des Moines since 1965. (courtesy Dr. Meredith Saunders)

Dr. Walter Riley has practiced surgery in Des Moines since 1970. (Mercy Hospital)

Des Moines surgeon Dr. Willie McClairen Jr. (Mercy Hospital)

Sparrow Hospital in Lansing, Michigan, in 1956 and 1957.

From there, he enlisted in the Army, serving in the medical corps. While overseas, he was moved from the field dispensary to the hospital in Frankfurt, Germany, where he was assigned to orthopedics. It was in Germany that Saunders had his first in-depth experience with surgical practice. The experience was transforming. For the first time, the young African-American physician began to believe that he could pursue his true interest in medicine — ophthalmology.

He interviewed at the Mayo Clinic in 1958, hoping to land a coveted residency position.

Not Interested in Integrating Their Program

"They told me, quite bluntly, that they had never had a Negro resident or fellow — and that they weren't interested in integrating their program."

Chastened, he deferred his dream. After leaving the Army in 1959, Saunders plunged into civilian medicine, soon realizing that employment opportunities for black practitioners were severely limited. Still, there was the small matter of supporting a growing family. He did so by working in emergency rooms in Lansing, Michigan.

Finally, between 1961 and 1964, he was able to pursue further training in disorders of the eye at Homer C. Phillips Hospital in St. Louis, Missouri. In 1965, he entered private practice in ophthalmology in Des Moines, the first African-American physician to do so.

Along with an active private practice, Dr. Saunders was named chief of the ophthalmology section at Broadlawns Polk County Medical Center soon after his return to Iowa. Full privileges at Mercy, Iowa Methodist, and Iowa Lutheran hospitals in Des Moines followed.

Saunders was soon tapped to assume a leadership position in Iowa's capital. In 1966, he was appointed to the City Planning and Zoning Commission by the Des Moines City Council, an appointment regarded by state civil rights leaders as a big step in the right direction. Generous with both his time and talents, he has served on the boards of virtually every local civic and charitable institution, as well as on the board of the Des Moines Chamber of Commerce.

But despite community-wide acceptance, the most poignant moment of his long years in practice happened soon after Saunders returned to Iowa.

He had just entered one of his exam rooms where a patient, an elderly black man, awaited him.

"You the doctor?" the patient asked with surprise. Saunders recalls the man's astonishment. "He didn't think I was. He was actually looking past me, looking for the doctor, who, in his mind, had to be white. When he realized I was, in fact, the doctor, he gave me a look I remember to this day. A look of delight — and such unbelievable pride.

"That patient made me glad I'd come back to Iowa. I'd had other opportunities to go elsewhere. But I chose to come back."

Why? "Oh, a combination of things," Saunders remembers. "But a big part of my decision had to do with a conversation I had with Harry Harper Sr. around the time I was trying to make up my mind. 'Come home, Meredith,' he said. 'We need you right here.'"[40]

Iowa needed surgeon Walter Riley too. The Georgia native earned his M.D. from Meharry in 1964, followed by a year spent in internship in Pottsville, Pennsylvania. Dr. Riley then spent two years in the Air Force, attaining the rank of captain before completing two years of a surgical residency at the Des Moines V.A. Medical Center. A final residency year was completed at the University of Iowa.

In 1970, the young surgeon accepted a four-year position at the Des Moines V.A. In 1974, Walter Riley entered the private practice of general surgery, only the second African-American to do so in Des Moines. (The first, Dr. Robert M. Johnson, entered practice in 1960, but left Iowa for California a few years later.) Riley was one of only a handful of African-American surgeons in private practice in the state.

"Believe me, I had plenty of incentive to go into private practice," Riley says today, with a twist of wry humor. "Five children and a mortgage — I'd call that incentive!"

What the unassuming Riley doesn't say is that his 20-plus years in successful practice owes much to surgical skills that were the stuff of renown, skills that resulted in enviable patient outcomes. In addition to expertise, Riley offered both patients and colleagues the comfort of his easy-going, down-home persona.

Yet he got things done. Riley was a trailblazer, most often cited as the man who paved the way for the minority physicians who followed him, particularly those in surgical and subspeciality fields.[41]

Riley's busy practice doubled when he was joined by his nephew, trauma surgeon Dr. Willie McClairen Jr., in 1990. Born and raised in Philadelphia, McClairen is a 1985 graduate of Hershey Medical School. His medical education was followed by a five-year surgical residency at the Medical Center of Delaware. McClairen has enjoyed a leadership role as a trauma surgeon at Mercy Hospital Medical Center, a position of unusual prominence.[42]

But there was still room in Des Moines for Dr. Cass Franklin. The skilled transplant surgeon relocated to Iowa in 1986, when Mercy Hospital, interested in initiating a community-based renal transplant program in Des Moines, contacted Tufts Medical Center. An acknowledged leader in transplant surgery technology and training, Tufts has produced a number of physicians who have gone on to head transplant programs around the globe.

Were any Tufts graduates interested in community-based (as distinct from university medical center) transplantation? Mercy's search committee asked.

Several were. But Dr. Cass Franklin got the final nod. The self-described army brat, born at Walter Reed Hospital, is the son of a career military man and a nurse. Cass decided on a career in medicine at age eight, while attending schools in France and Germany. Every subsequent educational move he made was designed to support and augment this early choice.

He completed his undergraduate studies at Howard University. After receiving his medical degree from Temple University, Franklin pursued a surgical residency at Presbyterian Hospital in Philadelphia. It was during that time that he developed an interest in transplant surgery. Franklin's grueling five-year surgical residency was followed by a two-year transplant fellowship program, topped off by an additional transitional year spent honing his skills.

When Mercy Called, Cass Franklin Was Ready

Moreover, he was excited by the opportunity to get in on the ground floor of a new concept in surgery, that of community-based transplantation. For the first time in Iowa, patients being considered for transplantation would not have to leave their families behind in order to travel to a university medical center for surgery. Rather, the necessary skilled personnel and facilities would be made available to them — right at home.

Home. Family. Words that resonate with Cass Franklin,

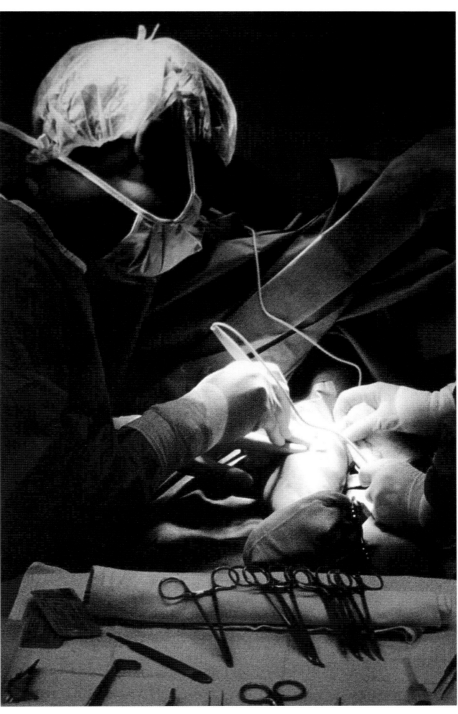

Dr. Cass Franklin performs transplant surgery at Mercy Hospital in Des Moines. (from Greiner and McMahon, Those Who Come to Bless)

Dr. Vera Stewart, Des Moines radiologist (courtesy Dr. Stewart)

and even more so with his wife, Dr. Vera Stewart, a Des Moines-based radiologist. The husband-wife team is one of a handful of African-American physician spouses in the Midwest.

"I met Cass in medical school," Dr. Stewart reveals. "He excelled there, as he has always excelled. I, on the other hand, found medical school a struggle. The only thing that kept me there, apart from my husband, was knowing I didn't have the nerve to face my 'our daughter the doctor' parents if I quit."[43]

The granddaughter of sharecroppers, Stewart was born at home on a South Carolina family farm but reared in the Washington, D.C., area.

Vera loved school and the learning process, graduating at the top of her class. Following high school, the girl whose parents had eleven months of formal education between them was off to Mount Holyoke on a full scholarship. There she was encouraged to expand her horizons by studying the three subjects she found the most interesting, namely biology, political science, and philosophy.

She was encouraged to consider medicine in her senior year by one of her professors. "I would never have considered it, had not someone I respected brought it to my attention as a possible career. I chose Temple," of the five medical schools that accepted her. Serendipitously, so did young Cass Franklin, and the two were married in 1976.

The couple than completed residency training in their respective disciplines. The four years that followed were, Vera says, demanding yet exhilarating.

"Cass was meeting the requirements of the Tufts transplant program. And I had finally become a practicing radiologist at Brigham and Women's Hospital in Boston. For four years, I practiced academic medicine. I taught residents; I lectured. I authored several articles. And, somehow, I found time to have our second child!"

The move to Iowa was a joint decision. "We've always made career decisions as a team. Cass had come with me to Boston. Now it was my turn to go to Des Moines with him," despite worries regarding what life would be like in Iowa.

Metropolitan Life to Smaller Midwestern City

The transition from metropolitan life to life in a smaller midwestern city was easier for the busy professional family than many of their friends and relatives believed it would be.

"A good friend of mine, an African-American psychiatrist, heard about the move and made it a point to ask me why in the world I was moving my black children to the middle of white America — the implication being that I was doing my children irreparable damage by bringing them to a place where they would be the victims of overt racism, Stewart confides.

"My response to that was that my children would be fine, just as I would be fine here. Yes, as a black family, we would be in the minority, but we are a strong family. We brought our core, our beliefs, our faith in God and ourselves, with us.

"Our children have been happy here, just as they would have been had we stayed out east. Besides, racism, both subtle and overt, is everywhere. No matter where we lived, our children were ultimately going to have to learn to deal with it."

Warming to her subject, Stewart adds with quiet certainty, "I've always believed that I am part of a oneness, a wholeness, that is far more important than my color or my sex. And as a result of that belief, I don't feel out of place anywhere I go."

The mother of three admits that her life, both professional and personal, has taken some unexpected turns. "I started working full-time in 1982, through all our moves, through the births of my children, and truthfully I loved most of my work experience. But I made the difficult decision to go part-time this year [1997]."

Stewart ticks off the reasons for the change on her fingers. "First of all, it was time to spend more time taking care of myself and my family. If I have any personal regrets at all, it's that I've often 'poured myself out' at work; there were times when very little was left over emotionally for the very people I loved most, the people waiting for me at home. And like many working moms, I simply grew tired of cheating myself and my family out of the best I had to give.

"Second, I've always been disturbed by women who were directionless. One morning I woke up and realized that my own personal direction had changed. I gave myself permission to stand still and listen to my own new course."

Professionally, Stewart has had few disappointments. Her experience in Iowa has been overwhelmingly positive, partially, she believes, because of her own positive attitude. "Iowa could have been a nightmare for my family. Instead, [moving here] has ultimately proved to be a blessing."

Her observations regarding black physicians in Iowa

medicine are no less cogent. "Black doctors in Iowa have much more of a presence now, certainly more than in 1986 when we first entered practice here. As a group, we've definitely learned the rules of the game. My hope is that, in time, we'll be writing — and re-writing — some of those rules."[44]

Not to mention headlines.

Dr. Paula Mahone has written both. The 43-year-old physician recalls with obvious chagrin her initial reaction to the recruiter who first approached her about coming to Iowa. As a perinatalogist — a specialist in high-risk obstetrics — Mahone was accustomed to recruiters calling.

A 1987 graduate of the Medical College of Ohio, the Youngstown native went on to complete an obstetrics-gynecology residency in Atlanta at Emory University.

Following a three-year fellowship in maternal-fetal medicine at the University of Rochester in New York, the well-credentialed Mahone was a sought-after commodity.

"Recruiters called our home all the time, at all hours of the day and night. But this particular offer was better than most. Both my husband and I had a high degree of interest — until we found out where the position was located."

Des Moines? As in *Iowa?*

"Our initial reaction was 'Thanks, but no thanks.'"

But her husband, who had a doctorate in education, subsequently heard about an opportunity for an educator at Drake University — also in Des Moines. The couple began to reconsider their initial decision. "In the end, we decided there was no harm in flying out here and taking a look around."

Mahone was pleasantly surprised at what she found. "I knew the African-American population was small," but the community was welcoming. "I realized that this could be a great opportunity for me if I was ready to meet the unique challenges" practicing in Iowa would entail.

No stranger to discrimination, Dr. Mahone had experienced overt racism during her fellowship years at Rochester. "There were patients who'd refused to allow me to examine them. Mind you, they'd be sick, their babies in trouble, it'd be two o'clock in the morning — and they'd refuse my care, until the head nurse could assure them that I knew what I was doing."

She shakes her head. "I've experienced racism here too, both subtle and overt. I've met patients, both white and black, who have never had a black physician before. Often, they're surprised when

I walk into the room. They're sometimes unsure just how to approach me. But," Mahone says flatly, matter-of-factly, "they usually get over it."

If she had to make the decision to come to Iowa again, would she decide differently?

"No," she states without hesitation. "I have always been interested in medicine. It is truly a noble profession. And it's a position of respect, especially in the African-American community. But being a physician in Iowa has allowed me to develop interpersonal skills I would not have otherwise."[45]

Being a physician in Iowa also allowed Mahone and her African-American partner, Dr. Karen Drake, to make medical history.

On November 19, 1997, at 12:48 p.m., Mahone and Drake began the cesarean-section delivery of the world's first known living septuplets — a feat without equal in modern medicine.

The world came to Iowa in the weeks following the record-breaking births of four boys and three girls at Iowa Methodist Medical Center in Des Moines.

Perinatologists Dr. Paula Mahone (left) and Dr. Karen Drake attracted world attention when they delivered the McCaughey septuplets in November 1997. (Iowa Methodist Medical Center, Des Moines)

The story of two gifted black women doctors who presided over the history-making pregnancy and delivery proved absolutely riveting.

The World Took Notice

And Drs. Mahone and Drake met the world with aplomb. Whether during one of many national press conferences or while receiving a simple plaque of appreciation from local school children, the young doctors conducted themselves with the remarkable poise of seasoned professionals. Nightly, images of the pair were beamed across the country, around the globe, as a startled world sat up and took notice.

Seven babies, born at once, of one mother, is, of course, interesting. But the story of the two gifted black women doctors who presided over the history-making pregnancy and delivery proved absolutely riveting.

Who, the world wondered, in mid-November 1997, were these two African-American women? They couldn't be *doctors*?! Partners? World-class physicians? But they were. Next question.

Where, exactly, in the world, is *Iowa*?

Without breaking stride, Mahone and Drake reigned in pandemonium, calmly assuming their places in history. Neither yet 40, they became famous overnight.

Nor did either allow fame to overwhelm her.

During the difficult months of their patient's pregnancy, both Mahone and Drake found solace in a shared, unshakable faith. Devoutly religious, Mahone expressed her beliefs succinctly. "I consider this a miracle," she stated at an interview shortly after the births. Later, when asked to comment on how she and Drake had contributed to that miracle, Mahone said simply, "God is in the center of this."[46]

It remained for the world — and proud Iowans of all colors — to add that talent, confidence, patience, and persistence are often found at the center of miracles.

Patience and Persistence

Two qualities Iowa's African-American physicians either possess in abundance or learn to cultivate.

Patience with the process of proving oneself, as many times, and in as many ways, as proves necessary for acceptance.

Persistence in the process of taking personal root in the welcoming richness of fertile black soil.

Iowa soil, arguably the best in the world.

The best soil for letting dreams — big dreams — take root.

Iowa soil,

arguably the best

in the world.

The best soil

for letting dreams

— big dreams —

take root.

In 1951, Idah M. Smith became the first black graduate of Iowa Methodist School of Nursing. (courtesy Barbara Smith Kaiser)

Laura Carter Harrison was the first black L.P.N. to graduate from Iowa Western Community College. (courtesy Laura Carter Harrison)

An artist's rendition of Dr. D. D. Palmer giving his first chiropractic adjustment — to Harvey Lilliard in 1895. Ironically, Palmer College excluded black students until the 1950s. (painting by Jim Dyess / Palmer College)

Notes

1. Dr. Julius Connor interview, April 1997.

2. Ibid.

3. *Seventh Census of the United States, 1850* (Washington: U.S. Census Office, 1853).

4. *Twelfth Census of the United States, 1900* (Washington: U.S. Census Office, 1901).

5. Des Moines city directories, 1886–1902.

6. *Iowa Bystander*, May 24, 1907.

7. Ibid., June 3, 1897.

8. Ibid., May 24, 1907.

9. Ibid., May 2, 1902.

10. Dorothy Schwieder, Joseph Hraba, and Elmer Schwieder, *Buxton: Work and Racial Equality in a Coal Mining Community* (Ames: Iowa State Univ. Press, 1987).

11. *Iowa Bystander*, June 6, 1902; Oct. 21, 1920.

12. *DMR*, Dec. 26, 1926.

13. Ibid.

14. *Iowa Bystander*, Nov. 3, 1899.

15. Herbert Morais, *International Library of Negro Life and History: The History of the Negro in Medicine* (New York: Publishers Company, Inc., 1970).

16. Abraham Flexner, *Medical Education in the United States and Canada* (New York: Carnegie Foundation, 1910).

17. Ibid.

18. Ibid.

19. *Iowa Bystander*, July 20, 1949.

20. *Des Moines Tribune*, May 13, 1936.

21. *DMR*, Oct. 3, 1939.

22. Phylis Harper-Barbach interview, Oct. 1, 2000.

23. *Burlington Hawkeye*, Feb. 14, 1976.

24. *Fort Madison Evening Democrat*, Jan. 3, 1977.

25. C. W. Birnie, "The Influence of Environment and Race on Disease," *Journal of the National Medical Association* (1910): 243–51; Marcus Goldstein, "Longevity and Health Status of Whites and Non-whites in the United States," ibid. (1954): 83–104.

26. The authors are grateful to Jeremy Brigham for providing biographical information about Dr. Percy Harris.

27. Dr. Robert Carney interviews, Sept. 14 and 15, 1997.

28. Ibid.

29. Dr. Phillip Brooks interviews, Oct. 2 and 3, 1997.

30. Carney interviews.

31. Dr. Fred Strickland interview, Aug. 1, 1997.

32. Dr. Erin K. Herndon interview, Aug. 1, 1997.

33. Dr. Ronnie Hawkins interview, Sept. 10, 1997.

34. Dr. Kevin Moore interview, Oct. 3, 2000.

35. Herndon interview.

36. Dr. Steven Berry interview, Aug. 1, 1997.

37. Dr. Onyebuchi Ukabiala interview, Oct. 4, 1997.

38. Dr. Veronica Butler interview, Sept. 28, 1997.

39. *DMR*, Dec. 6, 1998.

40. Dr. Meredith Saunders interview, July 18, 1997.

41. Dr. Walter Riley interview, July 4, 1997.

42. Dr. Willie McClairen interview, July 8, 1997.

43. Dr. Cass Franklin interview, Oct. 18, 1997.

44. Dr. Vera Stewart interview, Oct. 18, 1997.

45. Dr. Paula Mahone interview, Oct. 28, 1997.

46. Ibid.; Dr. Karen Drake interview, Feb. 18, 1998.

Dr. Alice Thompson was a chiropodist in Muscatine for 40 years (courtesy Joan Liffring-Zug)

Dr. Erin K. Herndon, a board-certified internal medicine specialist with the Iowa Clinic in Des Moines, received her M.D. from the University of Iowa College of Medicine in 1983 and entered private practice in 1986. Dr. Herndon enjoys writing fiction, spending time with her 6-year-old daughter, Iris, and serving as medical director for the Mae E. Davis Free Medical Clinic in West Des Moines. She is married to freelance writer and photographer Eric Salmon.

Dr. Steven G. Berry was born in 1952 in St. Paul, Minnesota, where he graduated from high school in 1970. After receiving his bachelor's degree at Luther College, Berry entered medical school at the University of Minnesota. Later he completed internal medicine residency training in Michigan and pulmonary fellowship training in Iowa City. Since 1983, Dr. Berry has resided in Des Moines, where he works with a group of physicians specializing in pulmonary, critical care, and infectious disease medicine. Dr. Berry and his wife, Linda, have four children ranging in age from 7 to 12.

The authors gratefully acknowledge the considerable help and expertise of Des Moines historian John Zeller in researching information for this chapter.

The University of Iowa College of Law, 1899, included Herbert R. Wright of Marshalltown, who would later serve the U.S. as consul to Honduras and Venezuela.
(from the University of Iowa Hawkeye, 1900)

The Legacy of Black Attorneys in Iowa

by Alfredo Parrish

Many years before African-Americans could practice law in Iowa, they understood the vital role education would play in their complete emancipation from the vestiges of slavery. In Iowa, as elsewhere in the United States following the Civil War, blacks recognized the legal system as one of their strongest allies in their quest for true freedom. The rules of law, as codified in statutes and memorialized in cases, represented formidable barriers to opportunity, but they were also vehicles that would enable those who understood them to break down these same barriers.

No one understood this better than Alexander Clark. Not only did he understand the importance, he was willing to take deliberate and decisive steps to insure that his children obtained the quality of education to which they were entitled. Clark's determination served as the catalyst to spark a series of legal confrontations which would prove instrumental to the introduction of African-Americans into the Iowa legal community.

In 1867 Clark's daughter sought admission to Muscatine's all white grammar school but was denied entry.[1] Clark filed a lawsuit on behalf of his daughter in Muscatine County District Court, seeking a writ of mandamus to compel the school board to admit his daughter. The district court ordered the writ, and the school board appealed.[2] The Iowa Supreme Court affirmed the district court's decision and held that African-Americans could not be denied admission to Iowa's district schools.[3]

In 1874, A. H. Watkins became the first African-American admitted to practice law in Iowa. Watkins was admitted on judicial recommendation.[4] In 1878, Alexander Clark Jr. of Muscatine became the first African-American student to enroll at the University of Iowa's College of Law in Iowa City.[5] Five years after his graduation, Clark's father, Alexander Clark Sr., graduated from the same institution.

T. W. Bell was another pioneer attorney. Bell was admitted to the Iowa Bar in 1886 but moved to Kansas soon thereafter.[6] Finally, Marshalltown native Herbert Richard Wright graduated from the University of Iowa's College of Law in 1901 and was appointed to the U.S. Consulate in Honduras until 1908, when he became United States consul in Venezuela.[7]

The rules of law . . . represented formidable barriers to opportunity, but they were also vehicles that would enable those who understood them to break down these same barriers.

Gertrude E. Rush received her degree from Des Moines University in 1914. (Iowa Women's Archives)

After gaining access to Iowa's law schools and obtaining the right to practice, blacks in Iowa used their legal knowledge to gain greater freedoms for minorities.

In the decades following the turn of the century, the influence of black attorneys grew rapidly. They became civic and community leaders, judges, prosecutors, board members, and trial attorneys. Like their predecessors, they continued to fight for racial equality at all levels.

Gertrude E. Durden Rush, probably one of the most important figures in Iowa's history, was born in Navasota, Texas. She graduated from Quincy Business College in Parsons, Texas, in 1906, and moved to Des Moines in 1907. On December 23, 1907, Gertrude E. Durden married prominent Des Moines attorney James B. Rush.

After receiving her degree from Des Moines University in 1914, Gertrude — against tradition and custom — was tutored in law by her husband.[8] After sitting for the Iowa bar exam in 1918, Gertrude Rush became the first African-American woman to gain admittance to the Iowa Bar and to practice law in Iowa.[9] Despite her accomplishments, Gertrude was denied membership in the American Bar Association in 1925. In response to this denial, Gertrude Rush became one of the five co-founders of the National Bar Association, which originated in Des Moines, Iowa.[10] Rush not only helped pave the way for African-American attorneys in Iowa, she advanced the rights of African-American women in the community. Six years after Gertrude Durden Rush's landmark admission to the Iowa Bar, Beulah Wheeler became the first African-American woman to graduate from the Drake University's College of Law in 1924.[11]

Legal and Civic Leader

Not only was Gertrude Rush an activist in the legal community, she was a civic leader. In 1911 she served as president of the Iowa State Federation of Colored Women's Clubs. In 1917, she established the Protection Home for Women and Girls. In addition, she was appointed chairman of the Department of Law and Legislation of the National Association of Colored Women in 1924.

In addition to being an accomplished attorney and civic leader, Rush gained recognition as a playwright and songwriter. Her most notable works — *Uncrowned Heroines*, *Black Girl's Burden*, and *Shadowed Love* — were published and performed in 1912 and 1913.[12] In 1962, she died of a stroke in Des Moines, Iowa.

During the peak of his legal career, around 1915, James B. Rush was the most widely known criminal trial attorney in Iowa. Born in Montgomery County, North Carolina, Rush received his law degree from Howard University's School of Law. On February 14, 1891, he gained admittance to the Marion County Bar in Indiana, where he practiced until 1894. He was then admitted to the Arkansas Bar in Fort Smith, Arkansas, and embarked on a practice in federal courts. Rush arrived in Des Moines in 1897, married Gertrude Durden, and maintained a healthy practice until the time of his death.

Another graduate of Howard University School of Law who was influential in the development of the African-American legal community was George Woodson. Born into slavery on December 15, 1865, in Wytheville, Virginia, Woodson graduated from Petersburg College in Virginia before entering Howard University's

School of Law.[13] Upon receipt of his law degree, Woodson settled in Oskaloosa, Iowa, and later established a legal practice in Buxton, Iowa. As his reputation grew, so did public support for his political aspirations. In 1898 Woodson became the first African-American lawyer nominated as county attorney for the Republican Party.

Woodson's role in the public sector positioned him to play an important role among Iowa's African-Americans and within the larger community as well. In 1915, Woodson led the charge in Davenport, Iowa, against the showing of the racially charged film *The Birth of a Nation* at a local movie theater. Between 1921 and 1933, Woodson served as deputy collector of the United States Customs for the Port of Des Moines. During this time, Woodson was appointed by U.S. Secretary of Labor James J. Davis to the first all-black commission to investigate industrial and economic conditions in the Virgin Islands. In addition, President Coolidge named Woodson chairman of the Virgin Islands in 1924.

Founding of the National Bar Association

During the annual meeting of the Iowa Negro Bar Association in February 1925, at a time when there were approximately 1,200 African-American lawyers in the United States, George Woodson lobbied for a resolution that called for the creation of the National Bar Association. According to its national charter, the purpose of the National Bar Association was to "advance the science of jurisprudence, uphold the honor of the legal profession, promote social intercourse among the members of the American Bar, and protect the civil and political rights of all citizens of the several states and of the United States." On August 1, 1925, African-American lawyers from seven states and the Virgin Islands met in Des Moines to formally establish the National Bar Association. George Woodson, along with Samuel Joe Brown and Charles P. Howard, incorporated the National Bar Association in Des Moines on July 29, 1926.[14]

Charles P. Howard's interest in the law developed from personal experience. Following his father's death in a union fight over the exclusion of blacks from fireman positions, Howard decided to become active in the struggle for equality of opportunity. Born March 19, 1895, in Abbeville, South Carolina, he attended Morris Brown College in Atlanta, Georgia, and subsequently graduated from Drake University Law School in 1922. At the age of 26, Howard became a member of the Iowa Bar. In short time,

he also emerged as a valued member of the legal community and had a prominent role in the public sector. Howard served as legal counsel for the Polk County Insanity Commission in the late 1920s. On April 8, 1932, Des Moines Mayor Dwight Lewis appointed Howard city prosecutor.

Black Exodus from the Republican Party

Following his election in 1948 as a delegate to the GOP national convention, Charles P. Howard led the black exodus from the Republican Party. When he resigned as a member of the Republican Party, he became a member of the Progressive Party, which during the 1948 election supported Henry A. Wallace for president. In 1939, Howard helped his sons launch the *Iowa Observer*, an African-American weekly newspaper that they built into a chain of seven weeklies.

continued on page 276

Charles P. Howard, a Des Moines attorney prominent in the Republican Party until 1948, when he backed the Progressive Party's presidential candidate, Henry A. Wallace of Iowa. Howard is pictured here with his wife and three sons, two of whom became attorneys. (courtesy the Morris family)

The National Bar Association

by Cleota P. Wilbekin, Ph.D.

Dr. Cleota P. Wilbekin served as History Co-chair of the National Bar Association in the years 1975–1995. A native of Des Moines, Dr. Wilbekin received her Ph.D. at Northwestern University. She is currently president of the Bench and Bar Spouses Foundation, an affiliate of the National Bar Association.

In 1924, there were five African-American lawyers practicing in Iowa: George H. Woodson, S. Joe Brown, Gertrude D. Rush, James B. Morris, and Charles P. Howard. (Bystander publisher John Lay Thompson was also a member of the Iowa Bar, but he devoted most of his career to his newspaper.)

The five lawyers had earlier had difficulty gaining membership in the American Bar Association (ABA). The ABA initially rejected their applications, but then reversed itself, making an exception to its whites-only rule and admitting them to membership.

At that point, however, the Iowans were incensed by their treatment at the hands of the ABA and decided to start their own professional organization. They called it the National Negro Bar Association, later renamed the National Bar Association (NBA). Letters of invitation were sent to black lawyers throughout the United States and the Virgin Islands. Sixty responded positively, and the association was brought to life.

The association's first national meeting, held in August 1925, took place in the chambers of District Judge Hubbert V. Herback at the Polk County Court House. Attending the meeting were the five founders, plus charter members Wendel Green, Jesse Baker, and H. Haynes of Chicago; C.H. Calloway, David Henderson, and L.A. Knox of Kansas City; W.J. Farances of St. Paul; W.C. Matthews of Boston; Gustave Aldrich of Tacoma, Washington; and D.

Hamilton Jackson of St. Croix, U.S. Virgin Islands.

Woodson, Brown, and Howard filed the NBA's articles of incorporation in July 1926. The association's objective, they wrote, was to "advance the science of jurisprudence, uphold the honor of the legal profession, promote social intercourse among the members of the bar, and protect the civil and political rights of all citizens of the several states and of the United States."

George Woodson of Des Moines was chosen to be the NBA's first national president.

Arnette Hubbard of Chicago, the first woman to head the NBA, was elected president in 1981.

Over the years the NBA spawned several affiliate groups, such as the Womens' Division, the Judicial Council, the Black Law Students Association, the National Bar Institute, the National Association of Bench and Bar Spouses, Inc., and the Bench and Bar Spouses Foundation.

As of 2001, there were 87 local NBA chapters with a total membership of 18,000

minority lawyers. The NBA is part of a minority coalition that includes the American Indian Legal Society, the Asian Pacific Lawyers of America, the Women Lawyers of America, and the Hispanic Legal Association.

The NBA also formed an international coalition of lawyers and judges with the Society of Black Lawyers of England and Wales and with lawyers in Zaire, South Africa, and the Ivory Coast. The coalition has brought delegations of African lawyers and judges to the United

States, and NBA representatives have visited nations around the globe. NBA members went to South Africa to witness the release of Nelson Mandela and later to assist in post-apartheid voter registration.

At home in the U.S., the NBA currently conducts seminars and workshops throughout the year and maintains cordial relations with the ABA. The NBA sponsors periodic minority summits and in various ways makes its legal assistance available to the African-

American community. NBA efforts have been particularly effective in local legislative action and at congressional hearings. NBA representatives have also participated in the rating of federal judicial nominations.

In recent years the NBA and its founders have been honored — for their courage in challenging social inequities and for their commitment to the rule of law — by Iowa Gov. Terry Branstad, the Iowa General Assembly, and the City of Des Moines.

Through the foresight of Elaine Estes, former director of the Des Moines Public Library, the library now houses a collection of historical documents related to the NBA's founders. Tulane University and the National Bar Association's headquarters in Washington, D.C., have NBA collections as well. Two monuments paying tribute to the NBA can be found in Des Moines: one at St. Paul AME Church at 13th and Day streets, and the other at the Des Moines Public Library downtown.

Founders of the National Bar Association (left to right): Gertrude Durden Rush; Charles P. Howard; S. Joe Brown; James B. Morris Sr.; and George H. Woodson.

continued from page 273

Following World War 2, Howard became deeply involved with the peace movement, and his political ambitions took on international proportions. In 1950, he was one of 12 people elected from the United States to the 101-member presidium of the World Peace Conference that met in Warsaw, Poland. Although at the time his activities were labeled un-American, Howard believed that political independence could lead to a renewed world community of nations. To the displeasure of many, Howard accepted an invitation from Joseph Stalin to visit Russia following a trip to Warsaw. Howard's open sympathy with communist organizations posed problems for him.

Howard's trial practice had spanned nearly 30 years, from 1922 to 1951, when he surrendered his license to practice law amid allegations of unprofessional conduct. Howard had represented 75 men facing the death penalty, never losing one to execution, and his reputation as a criminal trial lawyer had grown legendary. He had also led the legal battle against the Katz Drug Store, effectively ending discrimination in Iowa public accommodations. Following the surrender of his law license, Howard left Des Moines and settled in New York City, where he did public relations work for small African nations at the United Nations. He also wrote a syndicated column focusing on the movement for independence in Africa.

Born in 1922, Joseph C. (Big Joe) Howard followed in the footsteps of his father, Charles P. Howard. Like his father, Joseph C. Howard served in the military. In 1944, towards the end of his sophomore year at the University of Iowa, he enlisted in the Army, where he spent time in the Philippines and Okinawa. Howard returned to the University of Iowa in 1947, following an honorable discharge as a first lieutenant. Three years later, he completed his studies in history and philosophy. He immediately took up the study of law at the University of Washington, but in 1951 he transferred to Drake University Law School. In 1954 Howard received his law degree from Drake, where he became the first African-American admitted to Phi Alpha Delta Legal Fraternity. Howard went on to a distinguished career as a jurist in Maryland, becoming that state's first black federal court judge in 1968.[15]

Archie M. Greenlee received a B.A. from Drake University in 1948.[16] Following graduation, Greenlee served in the Pacific Ocean during World War 2. After the war, Greenlee passed the Iowa Bar exam and set up a private practice with attorney William Parker on East Walnut Street in Des Moines. At the time, Greenlee also made plans to set up additional offices in both Davenport and the Quad Cities, areas of the state he felt needed a minority presence in the legal community.

Iowa's First Interracial Law Firm

At about the time Greenlee graduated from Drake, Oscar Jones received his B.A. from the University of Iowa. Jones subsequently matriculated to Drake's Law School, where he received his law degree in 1952. He went on to become Centerville's first African-American attorney. Soon thereafter, Oscar Jones and his former law school classmate, Ted W. Rockwell, formed Iowa's first interracial law firm.[17] Their partnership spanned 26 years, from 1957 to 1983. In 1961, Jones and Rockwell obtained Iowa's largest verdict for the death of a minor.[18]

Another pioneer in the legal community in Iowa is Willie Glanton. Born in Hot Springs, Arkansas, she received her B.S. degree from Tennessee State University at Nashville and her law degree from Robert H. Terrell Law School in Washington, D.C. She gained admission to the Iowa Bar in 1953 and began her law practice in 1955. Shortly thereafter, Willie Glanton became the first female prosecutor in Des Moines municipal courts.[19] Later she would also become the first female appointed assistant Polk County attorney.[20] In 1962, Willie and her husband, Judge Luther Glanton Jr., traveled to Africa and Southeast Asia as goodwill ambassadors for the United States.[21] Two years later, Willie Glanton

Oscar Jones co-founded Iowa's first interracial law firm. (courtesy Oscar Jones)

Although at the time his activities were labeled un-American, Howard believed that political independence could lead to a renewed world community of nations.

became the first African-American elected to the Iowa legislature, representing Polk County.[22] In the second year of her term, she resigned her position to accept an appointment as counsel for the federal Small Business Association, the first African-American to receive such an appointment.[23] She was able to make all these accomplishments at only 44 years of age. Glanton's career and dedication to public service continued to grow, and following the death of Des Moines Councilman Russell LaVine in 1980, she was appointed to the Des Moines City Council. She was the first minority representative to sit on the City Council.[24] Not surprisingly, in 1996 Willie Glanton was inducted into the Iowa Women's Hall of Fame.

Willie Glanton did not fight for the rights of minorities on her own. To many, her husband, Luther T. Glanton, was a hero in fighting for the disenfranchised. According to former Iowa Gov. Robert Ray, "Luther was a remarkable human being. He was a great leader because he had a fundamental understanding of people and their problems, and was able to overcome prejudice and biases."

Born in Murfreesboro, Tennessee, Luther T. Glanton Jr. graduated from Tennessee State University at Nashville in 1939 and became the first African-American law student at Drake University, where he received his law degree in 1942.[25] His academic credentials also include advanced studies at the Sorbonne, Northwestern University, and the University of Virginia. Following completion of his education, Glanton served his country for almost five years in the Army before entering private practice. Between 1947 and 1949, Luther T. Glanton served as president of the Des Moines branch of the NAACP. He was re-elected to the position in 1950.

Shortly after entering private practice, Luther T. Glanton Jr. entered the public sector of the legal community and became the first African-American assistant Polk County attorney. He served in this capacity from 1951 to 1956. In 1958, Gov. Herschel Loveless chose Glanton's name from among seven candidates to fill a municipal court judge vacancy left by Don L. Tidrick. The following year, Judge Glanton was officially elected to that post. In 1973, during the reorganization of Iowa's judicial system, Glanton was appointed district associate judge. Based on his excellent performance, in 1976 Governor Ray appointed Glanton to the District Court, where he served until his retirement in 1985. Commenting on Glanton's tenure on the bench, one Des Moines attorney said, "a man of Glanton's caliber transcends race, sex, and religion."[26]

Polk County District Court Judge D. J. Stovall, appointed by Gov. Terry Branstad in 1995 (courtesy D. J. Stovall)

William F. Parker of Waterloo became the first African-American municipal court judge in Iowa. (Grout Museum)

Luther T. Glanton paved the way for other African-Americans to enter the judiciary. Gov. Terry Branstad appointed George Stigler to the District Court bench in 1985 and D. J. Stovall as district associate judge in 1995.

Other figures in the Iowa legal community have come to prominence over time. One was John Lay Thompson, who received his law degree from Drake University in 1898 and was immediately elected file clerk for the Iowa State Senate, a term that lasted three years.[27] Between 1903 and 1908, Thompson served as deputy county treasurer for Polk County. During this time, he purchased the *Iowa Bystander* from William Coalson, renaming it the *Iowa State Bystander*. Beginning in 1903, Thompson also held a position in Iowa's Hall of Archives in Des Moines.[28] During the annual meeting of the National Business League in 1912, Thompson was elected treasurer of the National Negro Press Association.[29]

Luther Glanton and Willie Stevenson Glanton both broke barriers for African-Americans in the legal profession in Des Moines and Iowa. (courtesy Willie Stevenson Glanton)

Direct Descendant of Original Jamestown Slaves

Samuel Joe Brown — whose father, Lewis Brown, was a direct descendant of the original 20 slaves brought to Jamestown in 1619 — was born July 6, 1875, in Keosauqua, Iowa. Brown graduated from Ottumwa High School in 1892 and in 1898 became the first African-American to graduate with a liberal arts degree from the University of Iowa. He was also the first African-American at Iowa to become a member of Phi Beta Kappa. In 1899, Brown received his law degree from the University of Iowa and in 1903 became one of the first recipients of the M.A. degree from the University of Iowa.[30]

Following a one-year term as head of the departments of Greek and mathematics at Bishop College in Marshall, Texas, Brown began his legal practice in Buxton, Iowa. There he opened an office with George Woodson.[31] The two men also opened law offices in Muchakinock and Albia. In the course of their practice, the two of them represented 25 men and 5 women charged with first-degree murder. None were executed.[32]

In 1905, Brown took his first case to the Iowa Supreme Court, becoming the first African-American attorney to present an argument to the state's highest court. In 1908, he sat on the commission that drafted the government charter for the city of Des Moines and in 1916 became the first African-American attorney to run for a judicial post in Iowa.[33] That same year, Brown

organized the Iowa Colored Bar Association and served as its first president. Nearly ten years later, in 1925, he co-founded the National Bar Association, which was formally incorporated July 29, 1926, in Des Moines. In 1928, Brown again ran unsuccessfully for a municipal judgeship in Des Moines. During the 1930s, however, he was appointed city solicitor and assigned the duty of codifying city ordinances.

Another individual who rose in the African-American legal community was James B. Morris. Born 1890 in Atlanta, Georgia, James B. Morris Sr. graduated from Virginia's Hampton Institute in 1912, before receiving his law degree from Howard University in 1915.[34] Morris relocated to Des Moines in 1916 and began practicing law a year later, when he was admitted to the Iowa Bar.[35] He specialized in pension and tax issues.[36] Shortly after his practice began, Morris was inducted into the Army in the 17th Provisional Training Regiment at Fort Des Moines. He was subsequently commissioned a lieutenant in the 366th infantry, 92nd Division, at Fort Des Moines. From there, Morris served in France as battalion intelligence officer.[37]

Upon his return from France in 1919, Morris served as Polk County treasurer.[38] Morris believed that communication was the "key to equality," and pursuing this principle in 1922 he purchased the *Iowa Bystander* from John Thompson.[39] James B. Morris Sr. served as the *Bystander's* editor for the next 50 years. He sold the paper in 1972, when he was 82. In 1925 Morris co-founded the National Bar Association and was three times elected president of the Iowa Negro Bar Association.[40] In 1932, he was secretary and publicity director for the Republican State Central Committee. Appearing before the city council on December 10, 1934, Morris attacked the Des Moines Traffic Control Commission for its failure to consider blacks for employment at testing stations.[41]

Father's Footsteps

Following in his father's footsteps, James (Braddie) Morris Jr. had a distinct impact on Iowa's legal community. Born in 1919, he graduated from the University of Iowa in 1941 and served as a U.S. Army captain in the South Pacific during World War 2. After the war, he graduated from the University of Iowa College of Law. Admitted to the bar in 1949, he joined his father's law practice in Des Moines. In 1950, he became the first black assistant Polk County attorney and, in 1951, the first African-American to receive the Jaycees' Young Man of the

University of Iowa graduate S. Joe Brown went on to a distinguished career as an attorney and civil rights leader after receiving his B.A. (1898), LL.B. (1899), and M.A. (1903) degrees. Brown was the university's first black member of Phi Beta Kappa. (SHSI Des Moines)

(Left to right) In 1919 James B. Morris Sr. founded what is today Iowa's oldest black-owned law firm. He was followed into the legal profession by his son, James B. (Braddie) Morris Jr., and his grandsons William Morris and James B. (Brad) Morris III. (courtesy Morris family)

Year Award. A prominent NAACP leader, Brad Morris Jr. had a successful career as a trial lawyer until his death in 1976. Today his attorney sons — James B. Morris III and William Morris — continue to operate Iowa's oldest black-owned law firm, founded by their grandfather in 1919.[42]

The prominence and excellence of the black legal community has not diminished over time. Many more prominent African-Americans have held highly visible positions in recent years.

Black Dolls Depicted as Pickaninnies and Mammies

In July 1994, Inga Bumbary-Langston became the new Civil Rights division chief of the U.S. Attorney's office for the Southern District of Iowa.[43] Earlier in her career, in 1982, Bumbary-Langston had entered private practice and began handling administrative law and employment with the Brown, Winnick, Graves, Donnelly, Baskerville and Shoenbaum law firm.[44] Subsequently, however, she held a series of government posts. She served as assistant attorney general and executive director of the Iowa Civil Rights Commission.[45] In 1987, while still director of the Civil Rights Commission, Bumbary-Langston attacked Iowa stores that sold black dolls depicted as "pickaninnies" and "mammies."[46] When Des Moines Mayor Pat Dorrian sought to dismantle the commission in 1989, Bumbary-Langston fought to maintain the human rights department intact.[47] In 1990, at the age of 33, she received a one-year fellowship at Harvard's John F. Kennedy School of Government. Bumbary-Langston resigned as executive director of the Iowa Civil Rights Commission in 1992, and two years later was appointed to her position with the U.S. Attorney's office in the Southern District. Within a year she advanced to the U.S. Attorney's Civil Rights section.

The career of Don Nickerson is familiar to most Iowans. Born in 1951 near Wilmington, Delaware, Nickerson's experiences in North Carolina during the early years of school integration provided him with the inspiration to pursue a legal career.[48] Like many African-Americans of his generation, Nickerson recognized early on that the law was part of every black person's existence. It could be used as a legitimate tool to create equality.[49] In 1974 Nickerson graduated from Iowa State University with degrees in both journalism and sociology. He worked at WHO as a radio and television reporter until he was persuaded to apply to law school

at Drake University.[50] Graduating from Drake's Law School in 1977, he went to work for defense attorney Alfredo Parrish until he was hired by Roxanne Conlin as an assistant U.S. attorney.[51] In 1990 Nickerson went into private practice briefly, starting the firm Babich and Nickerson, where he specialized in immigration work.[52] Two years after being honored for his representation of Central American and African-American refugees who sought asylum in Iowa, Pres. Bill Clinton nominated Nickerson as U.S. attorney for the South District of Iowa.[53] Nickerson was sworn in on March 5, 1994, becoming Iowa's first African-American U.S. attorney.[54]

Nolden Gentry and Robert Wright Sr. are other members of the African-American community who have played an important role in the advancement toward racial equality.

Gentry was born in Rockford, Illinois, and came to Iowa as a basketball player for the University of Iowa. Following law school, Gentry worked for the FBI and was then appointed an assistant Iowa attorney general. In 1970, he was elected to the Des Moines School Board, eventually serving as its president.[55] During his tenure, the board voted to desegregate the Des Moines schools.[56] Gentry remained on the board for 16 years. In 1981, he joined the firm of Brick, Seckington, Bowers, Swartz and Gentry. In addition

Don Nickerson with well-wishers at the Iowa capitol (courtesy Don Nickerson)

Don Nickerson (courtesy Don Nickerson)

Inga Bumbary-Langston has served in the U.S. Attorney's office in Des Moines since 1991. (courtesy Inga Bumbary-Langston)

Odell McGhee of the Polk County Attorney's office (courtesy Odell McGhee)

to his private practice, Gentry has been prominent in the community as a member of the executive committee of United Way and the boards of directors of Des Moines Utility, Firstar Bank, and Delta Dental Plan. He was also counsel for the Des Moines Chamber of Commerce.[57]

Odell McGhee has first-hand knowledge of the pain of racial discrimination and has worked hard to right injustices. Born in Liberty, Mississippi, in 1952, McGhee learned the price that African-Americans had to pay for their rights. His grandmother's house was burned down after his aunt Irma Lucas helped register black voters in southern Mississippi.[58] McGhee attended Cornell College in Mount Vernon, Iowa, where he became the first in his family to graduate from college.[59] Later, McGhee received his law degree from Drake University.[60] Currently Odell McGhee serves as assistant Polk County attorney.[61] He has also been president of the Iowa chapter of the NAACP.

Robert Wright Sr. has been a leader in the fight for civil rights for more than 50 years. Born in Chicago, Wright came to Des Moines when he was ten and was raised by his grandparents in the Chesterfield area.[62] In 1943 he graduated from East High School, where he was a two-time all-city football player.[63] Robert Wright became a Des Moines police officer to earn money for law

school.[64] Upon completion of his law degree, he gained admission into the Iowa Bar and has spent a great deal of his practice addressing issues such as school busing and the city's desegregation policies.[65] During his 53 years of work for the NAACP, Wright served as president of the Iowa and Nebraska State Conferences, played a key role in establishing the Iowa Civil Rights Commission, and in 1982 was instrumental in the fight to increase the number of minority employees in the Des Moines Fire Department.[66] In 1998, Robert Wright Sr. received the Martin Luther King service award for his commitment to civil rights.[67]

Thomas Mann became the first African-American to be elected to the Iowa Senate. Taking office in 1982, he spent eight years as District 43 senator in the Iowa legislature before making the decision not to seek a third term in 1990.[68]

Born in 1947 in Selma, Alabama, defense attorney Alfredo Parrish was originally set on becoming a doctor. That all changed when he witnessed the fight his own parents waged for their livelihood as teachers. In the midst of the civil rights movement, his father announced a bid for county supervisor and his mother openly criticized the school board. As a result, Parrish's parents were fired from their teaching jobs and remained unemployed for seven years. Although their jobs were later reinstated, this

(Left) Robert Wright Sr., police officer, attorney, and NAACP leader (courtesy Robert A. Wright Sr.)

(Far left) Des Moines attorney Nolden Gentry (courtesy Nolden Gentry)

experience left an indelible mark on Parrish and became a catalyst for his decision to embark on a career in law.[69]

In 1967, Parrish received his B.A. degree from the University of Dubuque and went on to receive a law degree at the University of Iowa in 1970. His first job was with the Polk County Legal Aid Society. In 1984, he borrowed money on his car to start his own law practice.[70]

Today Parrish is one of Iowa's best-known criminal defense attorneys. Representing clients in more than 200 jury trials in state and federal courts, Parrish's high-profile cases have included the first case tried under the federal "three strikes" law; *State v. Welton*, in which the defendant was acquitted of shooting a Des Moines police officer; *U.S. v. Hildebrand*, the federal trial of one of the "We the People" defendants; and the trials of Teri Lass, accused of her infant son's murder; of Warren Wood, accused of cruelty to animals during the farm crisis of the mid-1980s; and of John Franklin, accused of killing his parents. Parrish argued *Posters and Things v. United States of America* before the U.S. Supreme Court, plus more than 100 cases before the Iowa Supreme Court, the U.S. Court of Appeals, and the Iowa Court of Appeals.

In addition to maintaining his extensive private practice, the largest criminal defense practice in Iowa's history, Parrish has recently committed himself to the fight against the practice of racial profiling by law enforcement agencies.

A Tradition of Law

African-American lawyers have made major contributions to Iowa's strong legal heritage since the frontier period. As early as the 1860s, Alexander Clark Sr. introduced Iowans to a concept of civil rights — separate is *not* equal — that would be upheld nearly a hundred years later by the U.S. Supreme Court. Since Clark's early struggle to gain his daughter's admittance to the Muscatine public school, generation after generation of black lawyers have made their mark on Iowa history. Their ranks include Gertrude Rush, George Woodson, Charles P. Howard, Luther Glanton, Willie Glanton, S. Joe Brown, James B. Morris Jr., and Inga Bumbary-Langston. They and dozens more like them have struggled continually to ensure African-Americans claims to full equality before the law. And while in *Outside In* we consider their achievements as part of black history, in truth their achievements must be viewed as victories for every Iowan in a never-ending struggle to protect the rights of all American citizens.

In the midst of the civil rights movement, [Parrish's] father announced a bid for county supervisor and his mother openly criticized the school board. . . . [both] were fired from their teaching jobs and remained un-employed for seven years.

Notes

1. *Muscatine Journal*, Sept. 14, 1867.

2. Alexander Clark, Muscatine File, Musser Public Library, Muscatine, Iowa; District Court order: 10–26–67 Minute Book K, 6, Clerk of the Muscatine County District Court, Muscatine, Iowa.

3. *Clark v. Board of Directors*, 24 Iowa 266 (1868), 267–71, 274–77.

4. Frances E. Hawthorne, *African-Americans in Iowa: A Chronicle of Contributions, 1830–1992* (Iowa City: Iowa Humanities Board, 1992).

5. Alexander Clark Jr. received his law degree in 1879. Alexander Clark Sr. received his law degree from the University of Iowa in 1884.

6. "Atty. Woodson Celebrates 25 years as Lawyer," *Iowa State Bystander*, Jan. 27, 1921.

7. *Who's Who of the Colored Race*, ed. F. L. Mather, vol. 1 (1915), 293.

8. "Rush, 79, Passes," *Iowa Bystander*, Sept. 13, 1962.

9. "Only Colored Woman Now Member of State Bar," *Des Moines Tribune*, Oct. 4, 1918. In fact she remained the only African-American woman to practice law in Iowa until the 1950s. "Pioneering Lives Are Remembered," *DMR*, Aug. 23, 1994.

10. Ibid.

11. "Negroes to Form Bar Association to Cover Nation," *Spartanburg Sun*, Feb. 28, 1925.

12. *Who's Who in Colored America*, ed. Thomas Yenser (1950).

13. "Local Dreams Become a National Reality," *New Iowa Bystander*, May 26, 1983; "George Woodson for Representative," *Iowa Bystander*, May 10, 1912; "Atty. Woodson Celebrates 25 years as Lawyer," *Iowa State Bystander*, Jan. 27, 1921.

14. Ibid.

15. Hon. Kweisi Mfume, "A Black Man First, Then a Judge: A Tribute to Judge Joseph Howard," U.S. House of Representatives, Jan. 28, 1992.

16. "Passes Bar," *Iowa Bystander*, June 6, 1950.

17. *DMR*, Dec. 7, 1990.

18. Hawthorne, *African-Americans in Iowa*.

19. "Woman Attorney Sets New Precedents," *DMR*, July 19, 1964.

20. Ibid.; "Three to Receive Awards at NCCJ Banquet Tonight," *DMR*, May 11, 1990; "Four Inducted into Women's Hall of Fame," *DMR*, Aug. 28, 1996.

21. "Glanton Enjoys Range of Work in Community," *DMR*, March 31, 1989.

22. "Mrs. Glanton Quits House," *DMR*, March 21, 1966.

23. "Small Business Administration Honors Willie Glanton," *Downtowner*, July 28, 1982.

24. "Women of Vision to Be Honored at Banquet," *DMR*, Aug. 23, 1991.

25. Hawthorne, *African-Americans in Iowa*.

26. "Glanton to Retire as Judge; Wants Black Successor," *DMR*, April 10, 1984.

27. *Who's Who of the Colored Race*, ed. F. L. Mather, vol. 1 (1915), 262–63.

28. *Who's Who in Colored America*, ed. J. J. Boris, vol. 1 (1927), 201.

29. *Report of the Thirteenth Annual National Negro Business League*, Chicago, Illinois (Aug. 21–23, 1912), 168–69.

30. "Veteran Lawyer, Scholar, Fraternal Leader, Fighter for Civil Rights, Dies," *Iowa Bystander*, July 27, 1950.

31. Ibid.

32. Ibid.

33. Ibid.

34. "Morris Brothers Pursue Inherited Goal," *DMR,* April 21, 1982. The grandsons of J. B. Morris: all graduates of North High School in Des Moines, Iowa. James B. (Brad) Morris III, graduated from the University of Iowa College of Law and set up practice in the Morris law firm in Des Moines. He became an executive member of the Des Moines Branch of the NAACP, a member of the Citizens Advisory Board, and columnist for the *Iowa Bystander.* William Morris graduated from the University of Iowa College of Law. Robert Morris attended Drake University Law School. "J. B. Morris, Civil Rights Leader, Editor, Publisher — Dead at 87," *New Iowa Bystander,* Jan. 5, 1977.

35. "A Living Legacy of a Des Moines Black," *DMR,* May 20, 1991.

36. "James B. Morris," *Iowa Bystander* advertisement, Feb. 3, 1927.

37. "J. B. Morris, Civil Rights Leader, Editor, Publisher — Dead at 87," *New Iowa Bystander,* Jan. 5, 1977.

38. Ibid.

39. "The Father of Black Communications in Iowa," *New Iowa Bystander,* May 27, 1982.

40. "Morris Heads Barristers for Third Term," *Iowa Bystander,* Jan. 18, 1930.

41. "Morris Attacks Auto Test Board," *Iowa Bystander,* Dec. 14, 1934.

42. The author is grateful for the help of Robert V. Morris in providing biographical information about James (Braddie) Morris Jr.

43. "Bumbary-Langston Taking Federal Post," *DMR,* July 4, 1994.

44. Ibid.

45. Ibid.

46. "Rights Chief Sees Racism in Black Dolls," *DMR,* Feb. 4, 1987.

47. "Official Urges D.M. to Retain Human Rights Department," *DMR,* July 28, 1989.

48. "Nickerson: Prosecutor, Father, Cancer Survivor," *DMR,* Jan. 9, 1998.

49. Ibid.

50. Ibid.

51. "Brush with Death Gave Life New Perspective," *DMR,* Nov. 5, 1993.

52. "Lawyer Nickerson Closer to U.S. Attorney," *DMR,* Sept. 11, 1993.

53. "Human Rights Activists to Be Recognized for Work," *DMR,* Dec. 10, 1991.

54. "Sworn In," *DMR,* April 6, 1994.

55. "Minority Leaders," *DMR,* Jan. 16, 1990.

56. "A Rude Awakening," *DMR,* Sept. 22, 1997.

57. "Whatever Happened to. . . ?," *DMR,* Oct. 28, 1991.

58. "A Commitment to Responsibility," *DMR,* May 5, 1996.

59. Ibid.

60. Ibid.

61. Ibid.

62. "D. M. Lawyer Still Defends Civil Rights," *DMR,* July 2, 1997.

63. Ibid.

64. Ibid.

65. Ibid.

66. "Hall Of Famers to Be Saluted as Black Role Models," *DMR,* n.d.

67. Ibid.

68. "Des Moines Lawyer Was First Black Elected to Senate," *DMR,* Dec. 20, 1989.

69. "Living the Law," *Waterloo Courier,* June 26, 1994.

70. Ibid.

Involved throughout his career in defending and promoting civil rights, Parrish has also worked to make the legal system more understandable to citizens. He has taught community college classes in business and criminal law, worked on task forces to implement quality in the courts and direct use of camera in the courtroom, and written manuals and guides for lawyers and citizens explaining the legal process.

An avid amateur athlete who has competed in marathons and triathlons, Parrish is married to attorney Margaret Stuart. He has four children, two of whom are lawyers.

(Left to right)

Milton Fields practiced law in Waterloo in the 1920s, 30s, and 40s. (Grout Museum)

W. Lawrence Oliver succeeded in law, politics, and business in Des Moines from the 1930s to the 1970s. (courtesy Barbara Oliver–Hall)

George Stiegler, municipal judge in Waterloo (Grout Museum)

Iowa Bystander *delivery boys — brothers Russell, Lewis, Robert, and Kenneth Kemp — 1945 (courtesy Robert V. Morris)*

The Black Media in Iowa

1868–2000

by Robert V. Morris

From human rights and politics to education and everyday life, no institution has had a more profound impact on America's diverse population than the media. The mainstream print and electronic media have historically provided an interpretation of world and national events that most Americans have accepted and supported through political and social action.

Blacks have historically experienced a starkly different relationship with the mainstream media. This bittersweet experience has shaped the way blacks view the white media and white society in general and has provided the backbone for the growth of the black media nationwide.

Since the end of the Civil War, no institution has played a greater part in the survival and prosperity of our country's African-American citizens than the black press and later black radio and television. They have often stood alone against the forces of racism and oppression, often providing an alarming contradiction to the mainstream media's interpretation of justice and truth.

Nowhere in America has the black press played a more critical role of communicating between the widely spread communities of black citizens than in the state of Iowa. From the Mississippi River ports of Davenport and Muscatine to the coal-mining towns of Buxton and Muchakinock to the bustling cities of Des Moines and Waterloo, Iowa's black residents learned of each other through the black press. Though small in number, black Iowans disproportionately contributed to the growth and development of this agricultural state, providing a fascinating history of sacrifice and achievement. If not for the black press, this tremendous Iowa heritage would be lost forever.

A chronological history of Iowa's black media from 1868 through the present day is dominated by the press until the 1970s when black radio came to the state. The black press featured events and profiles of individuals that shaped our state and nation throughout this period. The history of the black media in Iowa indicates a direct correlation between the impact of world events and their resulting national focus on race relations, with periods of great prosperity and sharp decline for the black press. Demographic shifts in Iowa's black population also created and destroyed its newspapers at an unusual rate for such a small population.

Nowhere in America has the black press played a more critical role of communicating between the widely spread communities of black citizens than in the state of Iowa.

Following the Civil War, the stage was set for the rise of the black press in Iowa through several key political events and a growing black population. According to the U.S. Census, Iowa's black population rose from only 1,069 in 1860 to 9,516 in 1880, bolstered by a migration of southern freemen, creating a legitimate need for the dissemination of news to the scattered black citizens. Most of the black migrants worked as coal miners or farm hands in rural Iowa.

The "colored state convention to the people of Iowa in behalf of their enfranchisement," held in Des Moines in 1868 and chaired by Rev. S. T. Wells, provided an early glimpse of growing black political activity that would serve as the backbone of the black press. Energized by slavery's end but saddened by the assassination of emancipation Pres. Abraham Lincoln, the convention launched the fight for black rights in Iowa. "The oppressor is now entirely powerless, and our race [is] on the threshold of the day which shall give us all our rights as men."[1]

The unprecedented convention was keynoted by Muscatine activist Alexander Clark Sr., who appealed to Iowa's white citizens for equality: "To the people of Iowa: To every true, honest and liberty-loving citizen of Iowa do the colored men of your proud commonwealth appeal for sympathy and aid in securing those rights and privileges which belong to us as freemen."[2]

Established some 14 years later, many historians credit the *Colored Advance* (1882) of Corning with being Iowa's first black newspaper, although Keokuk's *Western Baptist Herald* could have preceded it by one year in 1881. Most of Iowa's black newspapers and journals shared certain characteristics during their usually short existence including:

- Direct sponsorship from a church, lodge, or political party
- Dependence on the community status or personality of the publisher
- Dependence on a black economic pocket, such as the coal towns and river ports
- Shaky finances and production capabilities from start to finish, resulting from initial under-capitalization, a limited market, and racial discrimination by advertisers

After publication of the *Iowa State Bystander* newspaper began in Des Moines in 1894, virtually every new black publication in central Iowa used competitive criticism of the *Bystander* as their

reason for existence. To the *Bystander's* credit, it survived all its competitors and often told the story of their demise.

1881: *The [Keokuk] Western Baptist Herald*

The *Western Baptist Herald* was published in Keokuk around 1881 and could have been Iowa's first black-owned publication. Edited by Mrs. Amos Johnson, the weekly Baptist newspaper served that community with local news through 1885.[3]

1882: *The [Corning] Colored Advance*

On August 1, 1882, the *Colored Advance* became Iowa's first documented black-owned semi-monthly newspaper. It was published semi-monthly in Corning by journalist and musician C. S. Baker, who worked days at the white-owned *Adams County Gazette* and led his Olio Concert Band at night while editing the newspaper as a side enterprise. The newspaper's lifespan is undocumented.

A farming community with only 115 black residents, Corning's white community provided critical support as readers and subscribers. "Many of our (white) friends speak of their desire to see the colored people progress; the *Advance* hopes to receive some subscriptions among them from all parts of the country."

Publisher Baker's mission statement pleaded the newspaper's cause and importance. "[The *Advance*] is the only paper in the state under the control of colored writers, and that gives special attention to southern politics, advocating those with liberal principles which must certainly triumph over the proscriptive policy of the bourbon Democracy."

Baker blended reports from national newspapers and statewide sources with humor to create an attractive journalistic style for his readers' enjoyment. "A young colored man named Clayton Grass shot himself in Dubuque, July 10th, the ball passing through his body. He is still living, but with no prospect of recovery. It is reported he was crossed in love, although his friends claim the shooting was accidental. . . . At Ottumwa the other day, a colored man named Hammond took morphine because a saddle-colored girl went back on him, but the doctors pumped him out, and he remains in this world of blighted hopes."

Like Iowa's later black newspapers, the *Advance* called for support from its readers but unlike those papers, actually apologized for its own shortcomings. "Our readers will remember that under the disadvantages that we as a race labor under, it will be impossible

"The colored people should patronize our race enterprises, they should trade with the stores that give the Bystander *their ads. . . . Please remember these things before spending your money elsewhere."*

—*John Lay Thompson*

for us to compete with other journals, but if we expect to rise to be a people in the future, we must make a start."[4]

1883: *The [Des Moines] Rising Son*

Iowa's second, or third, black newspaper was the *Rising Son*, published in Des Moines in 1883 and edited by Harry Graham who founded the Western Negro Press Association in 1896. The four-page Republican weekly newspaper contained local and national news but collapsed financially in 1885.[5]

1890: *The [Oskaloosa] Iowa District News*

Published in Oskaloosa in 1890, the *Iowa District News,* was a four-page monthly edited by Rev. C. S. Jacobs and L. J. Phillips, reported Republican politics and local news but only lasted one year.[6]

1889: *The [Des Moines] Weekly Avalanche*

Founded in Des Moines in September of 1889, the *Des Moines Weekly Avalanche* featured the motto of "Equal Rights to All: Special Privileges to None." Edited by A. S. Barnett and later attorney Albert Lincoln Bell, the Republican political journal served 2,300 subscribers until its demise in 1894.[7]

1893: *The [Oskaloosa] Negro Solicitor*

The *Oskaloosa Negro Solicitor* arrived in Mahaska County in 1893 with editor and Democratic Party activist George Taylor, serving nearly 1,700 subscribers over its six-year life. The newspaper often featured the activities of noted soldier and attorney George Woodson but ceased publication in 1899.[8]

1894: *The Iowa State Bystander*

With a motto of "Fear God, tell the truth and make money," the *Iowa State Bystander* was born on June 8, 1894, in Des Moines. "It was the brainchild of several forward thinking Negroes in Des Moines who realized that the existing daily press left the Negro out in the production of their papers and the news about them generally. Derogatory news always made the headlines."[9]

The ten new owners of the Bystander Publishing Company, led by businessman William Coalson, elected Charles Ruff as editor, Thaddeus Ruff as associate editor, and John Reeler as manager. The Ruff brothers had a financially rough time and were replaced by a fiery young man named John Lay Thompson in 1896.

PATRONIZE THOSE WHO WANT YOUR BUSINESS

IOWA BYSTANDER
NEW MANAGEMENT

PUBLISHED IN THE INTEREST OF THE COLORED PEOPLE

VOL. XLII NO.46   DES MOINES, IOWA FRIDAY, APRIL 24, 1934   PRICE FIVE CENTS

"I remember when the *Bystander* started," said Harry McCraven, who at age 15 sold the *Bystander* for a nickel a copy. "William Coalson was heading it then. I used to sell the *Bystander,* along with a couple of other papers, up and down Locust Street."[10]

John Thompson, who earned a law degree from Drake University in 1898, edited the *Bystander* into the new century and purchased the newspaper outright in 1911. He implemented statewide subscription drives and news coverage and introduced columns such as "Race Echoes" and "Secret Orders."[11]

"[Thompson] made it the *Iowa State Bystander* indeed by securing reporters in Ottumwa, Keokuk, Davenport, Oskaloosa, Waterloo, Iowa City, Clinton, Cedar Rapids, Ft. Madison, and even a few in surrounding states including South Dakota. He traveled throughout the state visiting these reporters and collecting subscriptions."[12]

Long before economic boycotts became a popular tactic of the civil rights movement of the 1950s and 1960s, Thompson called for black boycotts against white businesses who would not advertise in or subscribe to the *Bystander* or hire black workers in 1896. "The colored people should patronize our race enterprises, they should trade with the stores that give the *Bystander* their ads; also trade with the stores that employ colored help. . . . Please remember these things before spending your money elsewhere."[13]

Leaving no stone in the black community unturned, Thompson chided black parents for their parenting deficiencies while pushing for higher morality and the self-improvement of the black race. "Parents, both father and mothers, should be more careful in the rearing of their children; they should be taught while young, nay while a babe upon their mother's knee, the evils of wrongs and its results, the evils of disobedient children, and where it would lead to, the evils of bad company and the troubles that may follow. Show them the right and wrong way."[14]

John Lay Thompson became editor of the Bystander *in 1896. The newspaper's masthead became recognized throughout the state as the chief source of news for and about Iowa's African-American citizens (SHSI Des Moines / Robert V. Morris)*

A community leader, *Bystander* publisher Thompson railed against Negroes who he considered non-participants in his self-improvement campaign, mixing harsh criticism with humor to create a readers' delight: "We [respectable black citizens] are sometimes ashamed and often embarrassed to meet or see some of our people, especially upon the streets and public highways not because they are colored, but because of their action noise, untidiness, and boisterousness. Again we must emphasize that if we will ever make the race we hope for, to be respected and considered like other races, we must respect ourselves, stop this foolishness and fun making, get down to solid business, learn some trade, attend to your own business, stop gossiping, go to work and get wealth and knowledge."[15]

A statewide communications network, "Iowa's Leading Colored Paper" was also endorsed by numerous black organizations, including the Afro-American Protective Association of Iowa.[16]

1896: *The Oskaloosa Gazette*

Mahaska County's *Oskaloosa Gazette* was published in 1896 by deaf mute John Howlett as a four-page Republican weekly and survived less than one year. Failing financially from the beginning, Howlett unsuccessfully attempted to force the local AME church to support his newspaper by threatening to expose the promiscuous behavior of its board members.[17]

1897: *The Iowa Baptist Standard*

Published in Des Moines in 1897, the *Iowa Baptist Standard* was edited by the Rev. F. Lomack under the motto of "The Advancement of People in General and the Afro-American in Particular." The four-page Baptist newspaper received little attention outside the denomination and only survived until 1899.[18]

1897: *The Iowa State Watchman*

This Republican weekly newspaper was also published from Des Moines in 1897 by the Rev. F. Lomack and often featured political news and the activities of noted attorney George Woodson but survived for only two years.[19]

1897: *The Muchakinock State*

"An Independent Journal," published in 1897, the *Muchakinock State* was edited by J. Edward White with political and local news on the coal-mining community, but lasted only one year.[20]

1899: *The Sioux City Searchlight*

The *Sioux City Searchlight* appeared in 1899 and was edited by G. C. Carr, surviving only three years under the Searchlight Publishing Company. The four-page weekly was politically independent and sold for $2 per year.[21]

Bystander publisher Thompson ended the century by calling for the black race to concentrate on development in five key areas:

- The acquisition of wealth
- Increased family training, developing
- The church
- The state
- The schools

"Let us broaden our minds, awaken to the true conceptions of a good citizen, then you will be united."[22]

1903: *The Buxton Gazette*

Founded in 1903, the *Buxton Gazette* reached 950 subscribers by 1908 but died in 1909 under the Buxton Publishing Company. The eight-page Republican journal reported political and local news and was edited by Rev. A. L. DeMond in the unincorporated coal-mining town.[23]

1903: *The Buxton Eagle*

Edited by the controversial John Sharp, the *Buxton Eagle* changed printing locations often during its shaky year of existence in the predominately black coal-mining town and Sharp earned a reputation as unethical.[24]

1907: *Iowa Colored Woman*

Founded in Des Moines by Mrs. Sue Brown, activist and wife of the noted attorney S. Joe Brown, the *Iowa Colored Woman* monthly journal featured news about the Iowa State Federation of Colored Women's Clubs. The four-page paper carried the motto "Sowing Seeds of Kindness" and survived until 1909, when its second editor, Mrs. A. L. DeMond, left the state.[25]

1908: *Sioux City Afro American Advance*

Published by the Rev. Cornelius Reid, pastor of Mt. Zion Baptist Church, the *Sioux City Afro American Advance* weekly newspaper appeared in December of 1908 as a Republican paper for $1.00 per year. In 1910, Norris and Ellett Publishing

---

The Iowa

Baptist Standard

was edited by

the Rev. F. Lomack

under the motto,

"The Advancement

of People in General and

the Afro-American in

Particular."

Company took control under editor J. Wilbur Norris reporting political and local news but ceased publication in 1912.[26]

1912: *The Buxton Leader/Advocate*

Edited by D. F. Whittaker, the *Buxton Leader* and the *Buxton Advocate,* edited by M. Montgomery and D. C. Butler, were the coal town's last black newspapers, neither realizing its second anniversary as the decline of the coal mines signaled their demise. Many of their Buxton readers were relocating to Des Moines, where they took up subscriptions to the *Bystander.*[27]

In 1915, a human rights movement in Iowa was sparked by the formation of the Des Moines Branch of the National Association for the Advancement of Colored People (NAACP). Its first president was the noted black attorney Samuel Joe Brown, who was a respected community leader and an articulate spokesman for black rights. A 1901 graduate of the University of Iowa's College of Law, and its first black Phi Beta Kappa scholar, Brown brought immediate credibility to the NAACP in Des Moines and drew the interest of *Bystander* publisher Thompson.

By 1915, world events were prominently featured on the pages of the *Bystander* such as the German sinking of the cruise ship *Lusitania*. A constant and often cynical critic of Pres. Woodrow Wilson, Thompson responded to Wilson's public outrage: "I dare say that if a hundred or more Americans who were on the Lusitania were colored American citizens, Wilson would not have made even a protest."[28]

Over the following two years, the *Bystander* served as a weekly newsletter for the NAACP, reporting its political and social events. In addition to racial issues concerning his people, *Bystander* publisher Thompson was a student of the war in Europe and the looming possibility of American involvement, which he opposed: "Let us stay home, develop our country, and treat all our American citizens with equality and justice."[29]

By the spring of 1917, President Wilson had led America into the war in Europe and war fever was gripping the nation. North and South, black Americans flocked to Army enlistment stations to participate in Wilson's "War to End All Wars." The thought of Negroes trained in weapons and tactics struck fear in the hearts of white southerners whose reign of terror and Jim Crow segregation had oppressed their Negroes since the Civil War.

Even after War Secretary Newton Baker had agreed to ship black enlisted troops North for training, the NAACP's demand for a training facility for black commissioned officers was too much to take.

Under pressure from the NAACP and fearing nationwide racial conflict that would harm the war effort, President Wilson allowed the creation of a single officers candidate school for Negroes, which he would label his "Great Experiment." To *Bystander* publisher Thompson's delight, the 17th Provisional Training Regiment would be based at Fort Des Moines, Iowa. As Thompson noted in his 1917 book, *History and Views of Fort Des Moines Officers Training Camp*, through the words of prominent attorney George Woodson: "With less than thirty days notice the superb youth, the very best brain, vigor, manhood of the Race gave up comfort, position, future promise and outlook, in their various civil locations and from the North, South, East and West, started on their voluntary march to Fort Des Moines in answer to the call. . . . God grant that their efforts and sacrifices may open a brighter and better day for all the down-trodden people of the earth and especially the oppressed Colored people in these United States."

A period of great prosperity for the *Bystander* began with the Officers Candidate School at Fort Des Moines, and Thompson would take full advantage. The camp would host 1,000 black men who were college graduates and faculty ranging from black institutions including Howard, Morehouse, and Tuskegee to white schools including Harvard and Yale. Another 250 black non-commissioned officers from the famed 9th and 10th Cavalry "Buffalo Soldiers" and 24th and 25th Infantry would attend.

Recognizing the tremendous financial opportunity and no longer a war critic, Thompson devoted headlines, columns, and entire special issues to camp activities and also covered the Alabama Regiment black enlisted troops across town at Camp Dodge. He worked closely with Fort Des Moines commander Col. Charles Ballou on public relations and to head off trouble between black soldiers and the surrounding white community.

On July 22, Thompson devoted an entire section to covering the "White Sparrow Patriotic Ceremony" at Drake Stadium, where 10,000 spectators watched the candidates march and sing. The brain child of camp commander Col. Charles Ballou, the event was planned to ease white community fears of the black candidates by entertaining them. It was a great success.[30]

"God grant that [the black officers'] efforts and sacrifices may open a brighter and better day for all the down-trodden people of the earth and especially the oppressed Colored people in these United States."

—*George Woodson, 1917*

Of the 639 remaining officer candidates who received their commissions on October 15, Thompson had grown close to a young lawyer who had assisted him with the *Bystander* the year before. Second Lt. James B. Morris was a writer and trained printer, a fellow Thompson knew could help him if only he could survive the war. Assigned to the all-black 92nd Division, 366th Infantry in France, future *Bystander* publisher Morris would barely survive a near fatal wound at the Battle of Metz in 1918.

Although the enthusiastic Thompson had published a book on the Fort Des Moines camp, his dream of post–war racial equality turned into a nightmare at war's end. Negroes were lynched and murdered North and South during the bloody "Red Summer" of 1919, and the *Bystander* stepped up its crusade for anti-lynching legislation and ending discrimination.

The rise of racial hatred and polarization triggered an economic downturn for the *Bystander*, requiring more time from the weary Thompson, who was seeking to expand his law practice and other business interests. In 1919, Thompson sold the newspaper to his secretary Mrs. Emerald Marsh, who floundered, and he looked for another owner.

Prof. Laurence Jones had founded a school in Piney Woods, Mississippi, and sought to develop a printing and journalism program there. Well-known in Des Moines for his constant fund-raising visits, Jones envisioned the *Bystander* as a learning tool for his students while overlooking the economic problems such distance would bring. His ownership of the *Bystander* lasted less than two years. "The base of operations was too far removed and [Jones] failed to realize that it took experienced people to run a newspaper."[31]

1922: Morris Purchases *Bystander*

After recovering the *Bystander* from Professor Jones, publisher Thompson searched for yet another owner who was an experienced printer, journalist and, most of all, a fighter. In stepped James B. Morris, a trained printer, who met the criteria. Morris was a war hero, lawyer, and deputy treasurer of Polk County, and possessed a long association with the Republican Party and eastern newspapers.

Morris purchased the *Bystander* in November 1922 for $1,700. He quickly learned the hard lessons of Negro newspaper survival, including the economic, political, and social realities of the business. His editorials immediately took a strong position for

civil rights and equal opportunity in employment, reasoning that unless those people for whose benefit primarily the paper was being operated could make money, the *Bystander* could not continue.[32]

Publisher Morris, aided by his brother Clyde and his NAACP activist wife, Georgine, expanded *Bystander* content and circulation and added columnists including war buddy and attorney Charles Howard, whose editorial column was entitled "The Observer." Howard's increasingly militant editorials often led to disagreement between the two men, but their friendship endured.

Outraged by the racially segregationist policies of the American Bar Association, *Bystander* publisher Morris and columnist Howard blasted the ABA, and, along with three other lawyers — George Woodson, Samuel Joe Brown, and Gertrude Rush — founded the National Negro Bar Association on August 1, 1925. *Bystander* publicity was critical in launching the organization into the Negro press and triggering its rapid national expansion. Woodson, who Howard wrote "has done more to make the Iowa Negro lawyer respected and feared than all other Negro lawyers combined," became the NBA's first national president and later president emeritus.[33]

Howard, who was described by Morris as "a scrapper who was always in the fight," sporadically published his column in the *Bystander* after 1929 and moved around the Midwest, returning as Des Moines city prosecutor in 1932.[34]

Although leading each edition with bold headlines on crime and racial atrocities occurring across the nation, Howard's "Observer" column regularly presented strong editorials on controversial topics. In 1927, Howard wrote what could have been the motto of the black press: "I would rather die and go to hell, than to let my children know that by my silence, by my acquiesce, I permitted to grow stronger the sentiment that they were not entitled to absolutely every thing that everybody else in this country is entitled to."[35]

By 1928, the *Bystander* was fiercely campaigning for attorney S. Joe Brown's candidacy as Des Moines's first black municipal court judge. Although raising support from many white individuals and groups, Brown's 7,612 votes were a distant third to the white incumbent, Judge T. L. Sellers. Howard found hope that "Negroes can and will organize politically under their own leadership,"[36] and disgust in the outcome: "If there is any group that takes pride in itself with nothing to be proud of, it is the Des Moines Negro group."[37]

Morris's editorials immediately took a strong position for civil rights and equal opportunity in employment.

By late 1937, J. B. Morris had tired of the Depression's crunch on his newspaper and sought to sell the newspaper and concentrate on his law practice. Leland Green, a black Sioux City journalist and printer, took control as publisher on December 1, with Morris remaining as editor. Although boastful of his talent upon his arrival, by the end of 1938, Green was begging for help as he wrote in his final issue as publisher: "The status of the *Bystander* has reached its lowest ebb in history.... If the Negroes and their friends want the *Bystander* to continue, it can be done, but only with reasonable cooperation actually put into practice."[38]

Stepping back in as publisher and editor, J. B. Morris launched a frantic effort to revive the newspaper by improving content and ad support. Incredibly, the tide of demise was turned with funds from the historically hostile white community. About *Des Moines Register* and *Tribune* editor Harvey Ingham, who had been a charter member of the local NAACP in 1915 and a long-time friend, Morris wrote: "We missed a couple of issues of the *Bystander*. Harvey Ingham called to see what had happened. I told him we were having a rough time, and he said, 'Here's $100 and here's a list of men for you to call on. They want to see the *Bystander* survive.'"[39]

Bystander publisher Morris bolstered community pride and readership by sponsoring talent contests and cooking schools "for the purpose of training housewives and servants in private homes, and the public in general, advanced methods of homemaking."[40]

Later that year, *Bystander* "Health Talks" columnist and prominent black physician Dr. Hubert London died suspiciously from wounds "not considered serious" two days after a gun battle with 16 policemen at his home.[41] The newspaper voiced the black community's demand for justice, which ended with the public disclosure of Dr. London's history of extreme mental illness.[42]

1928–1938: *The Sioux City Weekly Review,* *Enterprise,* and *Silent Messenger*

A series of black newspapers appeared and failed in Sioux City between 1928 and 1938. The *Weekly Review* (1928–30); the *Enterprise* (1936–38), edited by J. N. Boyd; and the *Silent Messenger* (1937–38), edited by S. Edward Gilbert, all came and went from the Missouri River town.[43]

James B. Morris Sr., publisher of the Iowa Bystander *from 1922 to 1971 (courtesy Joan Liffring Zug)*

1939: *The Iowa Observer*

Spawning from the *Bystander* column, the *Iowa Observer* became an independent publication in Des Moines in 1939 and was published by attorney Charles P. Howard and his son Charles Howard Jr. The *Observer* reached 3,500 subscribers by 1944 and blossomed into the Howard Newspaper Syndicate with papers in several other states. The *Observer* ran controversial local and national editorials and survived until 1949.

THE OBSERVER COVERS IOWA LIKE THE DEW

The Iowa Observer, *spawned from a* Bystander *column, was founded in 1939 by Des Moines attorney Charles P. Howard. (courtesy Robert V. Morris)*

An outspoken activist, Howard Sr.'s political alliances and friendship with the controversial entertainer/activist Paul Robeson drew the wrath of the post–World War 2 anti-communist movement, and his troubles with the bar and his taxes grew. The Cold War attacks on Charles P. Howard Sr. peaked with his keynote address to the Progressive Party National Convention in 1948 and visit to Russia in 1950, after which his publishing career was in decline although he served as a Negro Press correspondent to the United Nations for many years afterward.

By the economic depression's end in 1939, another organization had been created that, along with World War 2, would signal a time of great prosperity for the *Iowa Bystander*. In 1939, Georgine Crowe Morris, wife of J. B., founded and became first president of the Iowa State Conference of NAACP Branches. Her network of NAACP chapters became an instant source of statewide news and subscription gathering for the *Bystander* and the newspaper served as the NAACP's weekly newsletter.

1940–1945: World War 2

The pre-war climate and eventual beginning of World War 2 brought a frantic rise in advertising and subscriptions to the *Bystander*. News of the activities and status of black troops was notoriously missing from the white press, and the *Bystander* rose to the occasion. "World War 2 produced a splurge for the *Bystander* enjoying its largest circulation."[44]

Bystander coverage included news of the black Women's Auxiliary Army Corps (WAAC) at Fort Des Moines, including public facility discrimination and the fighting in Europe and the South Pacific.[45]

On July 8, 1943, publisher Morris was proud to run a wire story on his son, U.S. Army Lt. James (Braddie) Morris Jr., who was "ranking man in his class and is regarded as one of the most promising young officers here," according to *Chicago Defender* war correspondent Enoch Waters at Camp Columbia, Brisbane, Australia. *AFRO* war correspondent Vincent Tubbs reported that "J.B. Morris of Des Moines, Iowa headed the class to the end."[46] Publisher Morris was equally sad to report a story on his son's best friend, U.S. Army Lt. Luther Smith, who, as part of the all-black 332nd airforce, had been shot down over Yugoslavia and was missing in action.[47]

1942: *Davenport Sepia Record*

Published by Charles and Ann Toney, the *Davenport Sepia Record* circulated two annual issues before it died in 1943. Toney described the publication as the "forerunner of *Ebony* Magazine."[48]

1946: *Eyes* **Magazine**

In April 1946, *Eyes* debuted in Iowa City as "The Negroes' Own Picture Magazine" and served a national market. The monthly picture magazine was published by William Ferguson and edited by H. Fontellio-Nanton and sold subscriptions for $2.50 per year. In its initial issue, the editor wrote, "We have no ax to grind, no special interests to boast. Our aims are to give our readers facts, expressed truthfully, as our cameraman sees them."[49] The magazine featured lifestyles of the emerging black middle socioeconomic class and relocated to San Francisco, California, in 1948, seeking a larger market but finding death instead.

1951: *Iowa Sepia News*

Once again using criticism of the *Bystander* as its reason for existence, another publication, the *Iowa Sepia News*, appeared in Des Moines in March 1951. It claimed the "Largest Negro Circulation in Iowa," and was edited by Archie Greenlee and George Daniels. Allegedly serving 3,100 subscribers at its peak, the 16-page weekly folded in 1952.[50]

As the 1950s began, black servicemen were being shipped overseas for a war in Korea and the *Bystander* and the Waterloo papers led the black press coverage. The 1954 *Brown v. Board of Education* court decision brought an end to legalized racial segregation and the *Bystander* carried on the message to the masses.

Also in 1951, Fort Dodge native Herbert Cox launched Iowa's first black-oriented gospel and jazz radio programs on white-owned station KXEL (1540AM) in Waterloo.

Members of the Eyes *magazine staff in 1946 included Arlene Roberts, publisher William Ferguson, and editor H. Fontellio-Nanton. (courtesy Robert V. Morris)*

Herbert Cox at Waterloo radio station KXEL — the first to offer jazz and gospel programming aimed at a black audience (Grout Museum)

1952: *The Waterloo Post*

"Serving the people of Waterloo," the *Post* was launched in March 1952 under publisher B. P. Steptoe as that city's first black weekly newspaper and survived until 1956. Steptoe wrote: "It is a funny thing; . . . running a newspaper dedicated to local Negro news here will be a pleasure rather than just a job."[51]

Abounding with advertising, the *Post* featured columns ranging from Dr. Robert Harvey's "Your Teeth and Your Life" and the sermon or family of the week to city editor Robert Robinson's "Over the Back Fence" gossip feature. Robinson assured readers that "they tell me that the good man will get his reward in heaven. But as for me, I'm not ready for heaven yet. I'd like to get a little appreciation right here on earth."[52]

Like *Bystander* publishers Thompson and Morris, Steptoe took every opportunity to inspire his community with constructive criticism and humor. Reflecting on the scandalous residents of Waterloo's infamous Oneida Street, he scolded: "By wearing dirty-ragged, ill smelling clothing, although soap is both cheap and plentiful, they also advertise their lack of training and their lack of intelligence. Such a condition breeds segregation; discrimination against, not only the loud, uncouth, ignorant representatives, but also mitigates against the neat, well dressed, and intelligent Negro."[53]

1956: *The Waterloo Star*

Rising behind the death of the *Post*, the *Waterloo Star* arrived in September of 1956 with editor Albert Garrison and assistant editor Rev. George Stinson. With former *Post* columnist Robert Robinson's "Over the Back Fence" as a popular feature, the newspaper boasted a bright future and attacked discrimination in Waterloo throughout its short existence of less than a year: "We feel that there is discrimination in public and private employment here in this city and such discrimination, such consequent arbitrary denial of job opportunities to large groups of inhabitants this city, foments strife, creates unrest, disturbance, disorder and group tensions, and subsequently and adversely affects the general welfare and good order of the city."[54]

1966: *The Waterloo Defender*

This eight-page bimonthly tabloid was edited by Harry Caesar with the motto, "We Will Inform the Public . . . Without Fear or Favor!" The *Defender* reached 5,000 subscribers by 1973 but died without fear or favor in October of 1975, returning briefly in 1979.

However, through its initial nine-year run, the *Defender* joined the *Iowa Bystander* as the state's only operational black presses.

The *Defender's* first issue in February 1966 announced: "We are beginning today what we plan will be the start of a long and mutually friendly relationship. . . . We pledge ourselves to be a positive force in the community and heartily subscribe to the concept of being an asset to Waterloo."[55]

Full of advertisements, the *Defender* sought to inspire the black community with enthusiastic portrayals of local activism. "Waterloo is now on the move; things are happening for the Negroes now that many people figured 20 years before the turning of the tide. Violence is not the answer. The answer lies in one category, known as education."[56]

The *Defender* covered the controversial tenure of imported activist Donald Frey, who was sarcastically regarded as "a self-appointed savior of Waterloo,"[57] the city's first race riot in July of 1967,[58] and a long and violent picket at Logan Plaza in 1972. After folding in 1975, the newspaper returned with vigor in 1979 with a new format. "The *Defender* is back, with new life and a new emphasis. The *Defender* is designed to provide a vehicle for communication between members of the community. Communication which cannot take place in the majority owned media of Black Hawk County."[59] The newspaper crashed a short time later.

1963–1971: Black Power and the Vietnam War

The long-running war in Vietnam, the resulting peace movement, and the parallel civil rights and black power movement offered an abundance of volatile issues that made good newspaper copy for the black press. As with World Wars 1 and 2 and the Korean conflict, the *Bystander* featured the exploits of black soldiers overseas and at home and voiced support for the soldiers. Publisher Morris wrote: "A man who refuses to defend his country has no right to expect that country to defend him."[60]

The *Bystander* headlined news of the first death of a Des Moines–born soldier in Vietnam in their Christmas 1965 issue; Army Pvt. James Flagg of the 1st Division was killed in combat on December 16. Sgt. Claude Onley died in early 1966, joining his brother William, who was killed in combat in World War 2.[61] Ironically, Sgt Onley's life that he declared he would "rather be fighting over there than here" was ended by "friendly fire" from American troops two weeks after his arrival. He left a wife and three children.[62]

"The South could not keep Negroes down by mob violence. The Negro cannot win with it either."

The black press was gaining respect from its white counterparts for its ability to access information from black activists often not available to the dailies. The growing white readership of the *Bystander* led to increased advertising from the white business community. Morris wrote: "For years, big advertisers looked upon Negro newspapers as a duplication of circulation. But no more . . . big business is extending more cooperation with Negro business and thus more of its advertising dollar."[63]

The black power movement was expanding and the black media covered it all. The break from the Nation of Islam of its controversial spokesman Malcolm X in 1964 followed by his assassination in February of 1965 was covered in the *Bystander*. Later that year, the Los Angeles, California, Watts section summer riots left 32 dead and 600 injured, and *Bystander* publisher Morris took the journalistic opportunity to reach the white establishment. "Most [white] people can't understand why, in light of great advancement by the Negro, that he would resort to the conduct such as that exhibited in Los Angeles. They have never stopped to think. And yet it's simple: he [the Negro] wants the same thing his white acquaintance has; civil rights; an opportunity to advance to the top, money, good homes, good schools and a chance to win if he makes the grade. And he is not getting it."[64]

The rise and fall of the Oakland, California-based, Black Panther Party was featured in the *Bystander* and *Defender* between 1967 and 1971. With active Panther chapters in Des Moines and Waterloo, the two newspapers were provided ample copy for information-hungry readers — including the alleged police bombing of Panther headquarters in Des Moines in 1968.

Des Moines's first significant racial disturbance occurred at Good Park in July 1966. *Bystander* publisher Morris reasoned that "the South could not keep Negroes down by mob violence. The Negro cannot win with it either."[65]

Perhaps the most spirited period for the *Bystander* during the 1960s was the assassination of Dr. Martin Luther King Jr. and the resulting race riots that swept the nation. The disturbances in Des Moines pushed race relations to a new level of fear and conflict, and the *Bystander* took a perspective of hope in the assassination. "There can be a great awakening in America as a result of Dr. King's untimely assassination and the dream which he so often spoke about can become a reality."[66]

1971: Morris Sells *Bystander*

In November 1971, the aging publisher J.B. Morris sold the *Iowa Bystander* to Raymond Ray, who renamed the newspaper, in its new tabloid format, the *New Iowa Bystander*, and shortly thereafter returned the newspaper to Morris. Morris then sold it to KYNA radio owner Carl Williams, who also failed and sold out to Triple S Publications of West Des Moines, under white publisher Loren Sampson.

During these transition periods the various *Bystander* editors shifted focus from original news stories and editorials to more syndicated columnists and Associated Press wire stories, losing much of its community appeal and reader interest.

The exception was the period 1979–84, when Triple S hired J. B. Morris's grandsons, University of Iowa students Robert and William Morris, as editor and managing editor respectively. Under the Morris brothers, the *Bystander* featured controversial original lead stories and often militant columnists, to once again become the talk of the town. Cover stories ranging from the Black Panther Party and the Black Liberation Army to gang violence and police misconduct shocked and excited readers. Columnists like former Black Panther Kalonji Saadiq and militant CORE activist Edna Griffin led to record *Bystander* street sales and subscriptions.

In May 1983, the *Bystander* published Iowa's first feature article on black gang formation and violence, a topic which was hastily followed by the majority press *Des Moines Register*.[67] Upon opening a television programming company in early 1984, the Morris brothers left the *Bystander*, and Triple S sold the paper to Garrison Communications, owned by Marshall Garrison, the youngest son of original *Waterloo Post* editor Albert Garrison Sr. Garrison failed in 1985. In 1990 Garrison sold the *Bystander* name to Jonathan Narcisse, who began weekly publication in 1995.

1971: Des Moines KYNA– FM Radio

FCC licensed in Des Moines in 1971 by Carl Williams's Contemporadio, Inc., KYNA-FM radio became Iowa's first black commercial radio station. An early success, the station declined and was sold to white businessmen in 1973. In 1971, Williams had expanded his media interests by acquiring the *New Iowa Bystander* newspaper from J. B. Morris and had published it as a weekly tabloid until financial problems forced its sale to white-owned Triple S Publications in 1975.[68]

Jonathan Narcisse, current publisher of the Iowa Bystander *(courtesy Jonathan Narcisse)*

1975: *Roots* on ABC-TV

Alex Haley's award-winning *Roots* mini-series brought the black American experience to network television under the artistic eye of Des Moines native Joseph Wilcots. Hollywood's first black cinematographer, Wilcots served as director of photography on all but the first episode of *Roots*, as well as the sequel, *Roots: The Next Generations.*"

1978: Waterloo KBBG-FM Radio

In 1978, the FCC granted a broadcasting license to Waterloo activist Jimmie Porter's Afro American Community Broadcasting, Inc. KBBG-FM Waterloo (88.1) was Iowa's first black-owned non-profit radio stationk serving under the motto "We Communicate to Educate." The station has grown and opened a new facility to serve a significant broadcast area in Black Hawk County.

1978: *The Sioux City Negro Yearbook*

In 1978, the *Sioux City Negro Yearbook* was published by Ruffin Communications, Inc., mistakenly claiming to be "Sioux City's First Negro Publication." (See discussion, page 288, of the *Sioux City Searchlight*, the *Afro-American Advance*, and others.) The yearly publication featured articles on churches, organizations, sports and individuals, including a "Man of the Year, 1977–78." The Missouri River port has long boasted a significant black community.

1979: Cedar Rapids KOJC-FM Radio

Airing in June 1979, KOJC-FM (89.7 FM) became Cedar Rapids's first black-owned and operated radio station. Sponsored by the Oak Hill Jackson Community as a non-profit organization, founders Robert and Agnus Love, Nelson Evans, and Robert Irwin aired the station to a small broadcast area. Weakened by internal strife, the station left and returned to the air several times before closing in 1992.

1981: *The Des Moines Inner City Challenger*

Published in Des Moines in 1981 by Vance Hawthorne, the *Inner City Challenger* featured the motto, "We wish to plead our own cause. Too long have others spoken for us." Critical of the then white-owned *Bystander*, the 12-page monthly grew into a local news magazine, the *New Challenger*, but failed in 1984.

1982: Des Moines KUCB-FM Radio

FCC licensed in Des Moines in 1982 to Urban Community Broadcasting Company, KUCB-FM became Iowa's second non-profit radio station. The station, founded by community activists and former Black Panthers Charles Knox and Joeanna Cheatom, left the air several times and experienced limited growth during its existence at 89.3FM and was formally closed in 1998. KUCB's license was awarded by the Federal Communications Commission to a gospel group led by artist Rocky Weston and aired as KJMC-FM in 1999.

(Below, left to right)

Joe Wilcots, award-winning cinematographer of Roots *(courtesy Robert V. Morris)*

Jimmy Porter, founder and CEO, and Lou Porter, vice president of KBBG radio in Waterloo (KBBG)

Kalonji Saadiq (born Clive De Patten) was a mainstay of Des Moines radio station KUCB (courtesy Hobart De Patten)

1984: Des Moines MCTV

First cablecast in Des Moines in June of 1984, Multi-Cultural Television (MCTV) was Iowa's first non-white oriented commercial television programming service. A product of Morris Broadcasting Company, Inc., the for-profit business was owned by Robert Morris and attorney William Morris. In addition to Des Moines, MCTV's locally produced and syndicated programs were also cablecast briefly from 1984 to 1985 in Omaha, Nebraska, and Kansas City, Missouri, before the firm closed in 1988.

1986: *The Des Moines Communicator*

Launched as a weekly newspaper with the motto "Help Us to Help You Communicate" in November 1986, the *Des Moines Communicator* was published by Rev. Roderick L. Bradley. The local newspaper was purchased by Jonathan Narcisse of Merit Publishing in 1990 and was incorporated into the *Greater Metropolitan News Central* in 1996. Narcisse also publishes the *Iowa Bystander* along with several suburban newspapers.

1994: *The Iowa State Bystander* Magazine

Published in 1994 as a special "100ᵗʰ Anniversary Issue" by Morris Communications of Des Moines, the *Iowa State Bystander* served as Iowa's first full-color magazine on black history. Edited by Robert Morris and attorney William Morris (grandsons of *Bystander* publisher J. B. Morris), 15,000 free copies of the magazine were distributed to public schools and libraries statewide. The commercial magazine covered a wide range of topics from Iowa's black farmers in Kossuth County and black war heroes to Des Moines native and *Roots* cinematographer Joe Wilcots and Davenport football star Roger Craig who won three Super Bowl rings with the NFL's San Francisco 49ers.

1994: *Tradition and Valor,* the IPTV Documentary

In February of 1994, Iowa Public Television provided the state's first look at black history on screen with the statewide airing of "Tradition and Valor." Co-produced, co-written, and directed by Robert V. Morris, the 55-minute award-winning documentary featured Des Moines's Morris family as soldiers, journalists, lawyers, and civil rights leaders over a 90-year period. Narrated by veteran actor Robert Guillaume, the documentary blended archival photographs and film footage with live interviews to tell the Morris story. A powerful book of the same name, published by Sunflower

Press in 1999, expands the Morris story and features over 60 archival photographs.

1995: *The Tuskegee Airmen* on HBO

In 1995, the Home Box Office (HBO) network cablecast *The Tuskegee Airmen* as a 90-minute feature film. Written by the late U.S. Army Lt. Robert Williams of Ottumwa, the movie told the story of the all-black World War 2 combat flyers known as the 332ⁿᵈ air force and the 99ᵗʰ Pursuit Squadron "Redtales" of which Williams was a member. Williams's character was played by noted actor Laurence Fishburne.

Due to their superior schooling compared to the southern recruits, 13 Iowans successfully flew with the distinguished combat unit and were featured extensively in the national Negro press.

Interestingly, Lieutenant Williams's P-51D Mustang fighter plane was named "Dutchess Arlene" after his wartime sweetheart, University of Iowa co-ed Arlene Roberts. She would become the first cover girl for *Eyes* magazine in 1946, marry *Bystander* publisher J. B. Morris's son James (Braddie) Morris Jr. in 1948, and give birth to this author in 1958.

1996: Davenport KFQC–AM Radio

Boasting a professional format, KFQC–AM Davenport (1580) became Iowa's first black-owned commercial AM station, serving the Quad Cities until its demise in 1998. The station's owner was Marshall Garrison, son of Albert Garrison Sr., co-founder of the *Waterloo Post* and former publisher of the *Iowa Bystander.*

In 1984, William and Robert Morris — grandsons of James B. Morris — launched Multi-Cultural Television (MCTV) as a regional cable programming service in Des Moines. (courtesy Robert V. Morris)

Tradition and Valor (1999) is the saga of a unique Iowa family. (Sunflower Press)

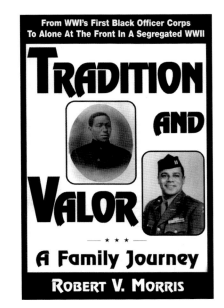

From WWI's First Black Officer Corps To Alone At The Front In A Segregated WWII

TRADITION AND VALOR

★ ★ ★

A Family Journey

ROBERT V. MORRIS

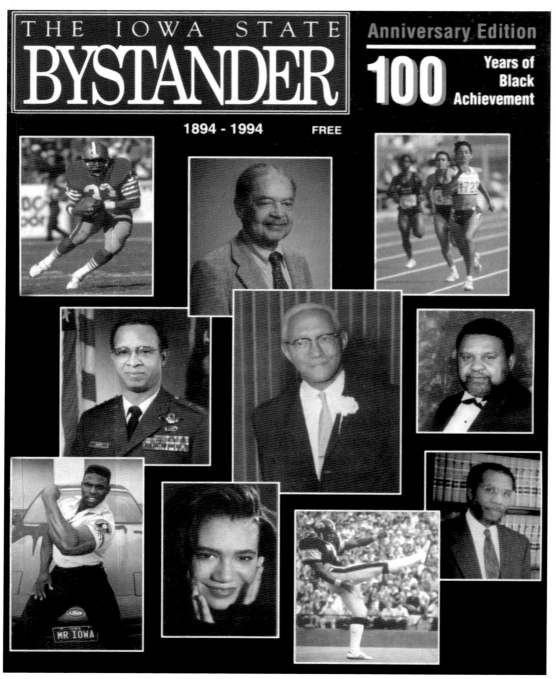

A special 100th anniversary issue of the Iowa State Bystander *was published by Morris Communications of Des Moines in 1994. (courtesy Robert V. Morris)*

1996: *Des Moines Greater Metropolitan News Central*

Published as a multi-cultural combination of several existing newspapers including the *Communicator*, the *Des Moines Greater Metropolitan News Central* was launched by Narcisse Printing and Publishing Company editor Jonathan Narcisse in 1996. Reaching 12,000 subscribers, the newspaper is published on a weekly basis along with the *Iowa Bystander* and several suburban newspapers.

1998: *Waterloo United Communicator*

"Approaching changes from the Past into the Present onto the Future" is the theme of the monthly *Waterloo United Communicator* newspaper. Founded in 1998 by its publisher Floyd Bumpers and associate editor Charline Barnes, Ed.D., the newspaper combines local news items with editorials on religion and health issues.

1999: Des Moines KJMC-FM Radio

Receiving the broadcasting license of the long-troubled KUCB, KJMC-FM launched a varied music format in early 1999 at 89.3 and continues to expand its programming and audience reach throughout central Iowa. Popular gospel musicians Rocky Weston and Larry Nevilles led the station into the new century.

Through a half-dozen wars, an economic depression, and an ongoing human and civil rights movement, the black media has served and survived in Iowa. Although most of its newspapers have vanished and its electronic media have struggled for stability, Iowans have been treated to a feast of journalistic creativity that has recorded black history for posterity and influenced the white media to become more considerate and fair in their portrayals of black people.

Racism remains firmly entrenched in American society and in much of the white media, but the torch of hope carried so gallantly by the black media still burns as bright as ever — a symbol that somehow, and someday, the dream of racial equality will be realized all across this great land.

Bystander publisher J.B. Morris said it best for Iowa's black media in his June 17, 1971, farewell editorial: "Many of the objectives in mind at [the *Bystander's*] beginning are being achieved. The daily press is seeing the light and have discontinued many of the objectionable features which existed in 1894. Certainly a business that has operated for 77 years has some merit, has earned a place in the hearts of people, and produced some satisfaction to those who have, in any way, had a part in its niche in the community."

Notes

1. Iowa State Colored Convention, resolution, Feb. 12, 1868.

2. Alexander Clark, Keynote address, Iowa State Colored Convention, Feb. 13, 1868.

3. *A Bibliography of Iowa Newspapers, 1836–1976* (Iowa City: SHSI, 1979).

4. *Corning Colored Advance*, Aug. 1, 1882.

5. *Bibliography of Iowa Newspapers*

6. *Ayer's Newspaper Annual, 1891,* 219.

7. *Weekly Avalanche*, Jan. 20, 1983.

8. *Ayer's Newspaper Annual, 1891,* 219.

9. *Bystander,* June 10, 1971.

10. Ibid, June 6, 1969.

11. Ibid., Nov. 13, 1896.

12. Ibid., June 10, 1971.

13. Ibid., Nov. 13, 1896.

14. Ibid., Dec. 25, 1896.

15. Ibid., Dec. 22, 1899.

16. Ibid., Dec. 18, 1896.

17. *Ayer's Newspaper Annual, 1897,* 255.

18. *Iowa Baptist Standard,* May 21, 1897.

19. *Ayer's Newspaper Annual, 1901,* 276.

20. *Ayer's Newspaper Annual, 1902,* 280.

21. *Ayer's Newspaper Annual, 1901,* 276, *Ayer's Newspaper Annual, 1902,* 276.

22. *Bystander,* Dec. 22, 1899.

23. *Ayer's Newspaper Annual, 1908,* 243.

24. *Buxton Eagle,* Oct. 10, 1903.

25. *Ayer's Newspaper Annual, 1909,* 250; *Ayer's Newspaper Annual, 1910,* 248; *Bystander,* Jan. 3, 1908; Jan. 8, 1909.

26. Ibid., Dec. 18, 1908; April 2, 1909; *Ayer's Newspaper Annual, 1910,* 280; 1911, 298.

27. *Buxton Advocate,* June 23, 1911.

28. *Bystander,* April 15, 1915.

29. Ibid., Dec. 10, 1916.

30. Ibid., July 25, 1917.

31. Ibid., June 10, 1971.

32. Ibid., June 10, 1971.

33. Ibid., Feb. 19, 1927.

34. Ibid., April 8, 1932.

35. Ibid., April 16, 1927.

36. Ibid., March 31, 1928.

37. Ibid., Sept. 22, 1928.

38. Ibid., Dec. 9, 1937.

39. *Des Moines Tribune,* March 13, 1972.

40. Ibid., April 13, 1939.

41. *DMR,* Oct. 5, 1939.

42. *Bystander,* Oct. 5, 1939.

43. *Ayer's Newspaper Annual, 1912,* 294; Monroe Work, *Year Book and Annual Encyclopedia of the Negro,* (Tuskegee: Negro Yearbook Publishing, 1937-38).

44. *Bystander,* June 10, 1971.

45. Ibid., Oct. 22, 1942.

46. Ibid., July 8, 1943.

47. Ibid., Nov. 2, 1944.

48. Charles and Ann Toney interview with Hal Chase, May 4, 2001.

49. *Eyes,* April, 1946.

50. *Iowa Sepia News,* April 11, 1951.

51. *Waterloo Post,* March 22, 1952.

52. Ibid., April 12, 1952.

53. Ibid., July 24, 1952.

54. *Waterloo Star,* Oct. 25, 1956.

55. Ibid., Feb. **11,** 1966.

56. Ibid., June 17, 1966.

57. Ibid., Nov. 18, 1966.

58. Ibid., July 21, 1967.

59. Ibid., Sept. 20, 1979.

60. *Bystander,* Aug. 5, 1965.

61. Ibid., Dec. 23, 1965.

62. Ibid., Jan. 15, 1966.

63. Ibid., June 17, 1971.

64. Ibid., Aug. 19, 1965.

65. Ibid., July 7, 1966.

66. Ibid., April 11, 1968.

67. Ibid., May 1, 1983.

68. Ibid., June 17, 1971.

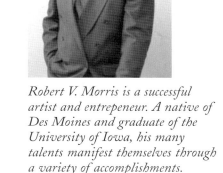

Robert V. Morris is a successful artist and entrepeneur. A native of Des Moines and graduate of the University of Iowa, his many talents manifest themselves through a variety of accomplishments.

Morris's first solo book, Tradition and Valor *(Sunflower Press, 1999),* highlights a list of publications that includes Family Reunion: Essays on Iowa *(ISU Press, 1995),* and the Iowa State Bystander *100th anniversay* magazine *(Morris Communications, 1994).* Morris is also an award-winning television producer, director, and writer. The television documentary, Tradition and Valor *(Iowa Public Television, 1994),* is among the 150 video and film projects he has produced for government and major corporate clients.

Morris is founder and executive director of the Fort Des Moines Memorial Park and Education Center, which is scheduled to open in 2003. The 4-acre, $12 million dollar center will be the nation's largest memorial to black and female officers and soldiers.

Robert is husband to Vivian and father of Jessica, Robert Jr., and Brandon.

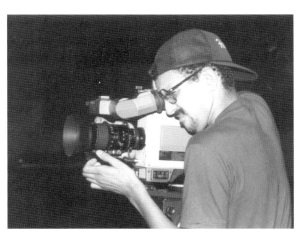

Howard University film professor and Des Moines native Steven Torriano Berry has produced numerous independent films and published several books. (courtesy Robert V. Morris)

Vance Hawthorne, born and raised in Des Moines, has risen through the ranks of the Des Moines Register *to his current position as editor for the newspaper's "Work and Money" section. (courtesy Vance Hawthorne)*

Churches constitute the heart and soul of Iowa's African-American community. Pictured here is the Mt. Pleasant Second Baptist Church, c. 1947.
(courtesy Glenwood and Aileen Tolson)

PART FOUR

Strengthening Iowa's black communities

When a Russian delegation visited an Iowa farm in 1964, University of Iowa student Vernon W. Wilkerson staged a peaceful protest against racial discrimination in the U.S. (SHSI Des Moines)

(Opposite)The founding members of the Niagara Movement included George H. Woodson, a prominent Iowa attorney who practiced in Buxton and later in Des Moines. (SHSI Des Moines)

Civil Rights Organizations in Iowa

by Jeremy J. Brigham and Robert Wright Sr.

The African-American struggle for civil rights and equal opportunity occurred in Iowa, the agricultural heartland of the country, as it did everywhere else in the United States. Its form was shaped by local circumstances and leadership.

The following account traces the emergence and development of organizations to address racism in Iowa from the World War 1 period through 1955 and in some cases into the 1990s. Chief among these organizations is the National Association for the Advancement of Colored People (NAACP). Others active in some Iowa cities after World War 2 include the Congress of Racial Equality (CORE) in Davenport and Des Moines, the Black Panthers in Des Moines, and the Catholic Interracial Council in Davenport and Waterloo.

The NAACP came into existence in New York City on February 12, 1909.

The Niagara Movement, formed in 1905 by W. E. B. DuBois and other black leaders in response to the widespread practice of lynching in the South and to race riots in several cities across the country, provided an important organizational cornerstone for the NAACP.

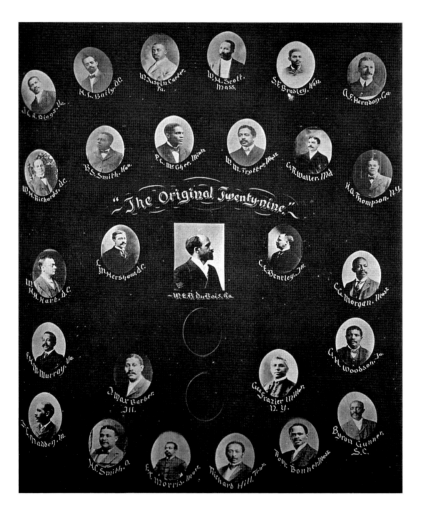

The African-American struggle for civil rights and equal opportunity in Iowa, the agricultural heartland of the country, was shaped by local circumstances and leadership.

The 1908 riots in Springfield, Illinois, a place strongly associated with the memory of Abraham Lincoln, provided the spur to both black and white to organize for the purpose of appropriate legal response.[1] The coalition of white and black leaders accomplished more than either could alone, partly for financial reasons but also for access to decision-making communities and legitimacy in the larger community.

Early in its history the NAACP was particularly dedicated to establishing legal protections against lynching. As key issues changed in the course of its first century, the NAACP remained at its core a steadfast ally of all people in lower income groups and a staunch advocate of their interests. Throughout its history, the NAACP has involved itself with struggles:

- To end residential segregation
- To secure every citizen's right to vote
- To gain justice in the courts
- To end discrimination in the armed forces
- To ensure equal job and educational opportunities
- To abolish Jim Crow in interstate travel
- To oppose imperialism

Incorporated in 1911, the NAACP in its first dozen years made significant legal strides against racial housing segregation and exclusion of blacks from juries, but local practices in many places across the country, both south and north, continued to be discriminatory.[2] By 1917 the NAACP required a minimum of 50 dues-paying members before authorizing a branch. These branches served their local communities, calling on state or federal officials and lawmakers to intervene when necessary. They could bring cases to the attention of the national NAACP, which might take them up if they broke new ground.

The national needed the local branches for financial support. The locals experienced a sense of pride in being a branch, but to keep a branch alive required more than pride in membership. It required action. For action to occur, it needed issues. For issues, it needed a community large enough to generate them as well as a sufficient number of leaders to articulate them. The branches provided crucial opportunities for African-Americans to develop leadership and other organizational skills. The branches also offered a source of status otherwise unavailable to many in the social climate of the early twentieth century.

In Iowa 23 communities between 1914 and 1939 corresponded with the national NAACP about starting, restarting, and operating branches.[3] The state capital, Des Moines, was a major center of activity. Branches in Mississippi River cities, such as Keokuk and Davenport, and Missouri River cities, such as Sioux City and Council Bluffs, were particularly significant. Waterloo, where there was a major repair shop for the Illinois Central Railroad, was also an important city for the NAACP. Fort Madison, the site of the state prison, became an important location for an NAACP branch by the mid-1920s. People in several interior towns, often railroad or coal-mining towns, organized branches. Centerville, Ottumwa, Manly, Mason City, Perry, Fort Dodge, and Marshalltown were among them. Cedar Rapids, the home of several agriculture-related industries, developed a branch in 1918 and again in 1942. In addition there were branches or authorized committees (membership less than 50) at various times in college or university towns — Ames, Grinnell, and Iowa City. In several smaller Iowa towns, the rise and fall of a local branch can be linked to the rise and fall of the black population, which was often greater in 1920 than in 1940. Mines were closing down by the early 1920s and many other forms of employment dried up during the Depression of the 1930s, which forced people into larger cities either in Iowa or in other states.[4]

Des Moines

Iowa's first NAACP branch, and the twenty-fifth nationally, was established in Des Moines in 1915.[5] Spurred first by a request of Mary Child McNerney, NAACP national secretary, to attorney S. Joe Brown, the Des Moines branch organized with 35 members and grew to 200 within the first year. Its first task was to fight a "Jim Crow" marriage bill in the Iowa legislature. The following year, 1916, saw the release of "The Birth of a Nation." This film depicted blacks as violent and prone to rape white women, which incited white fear and reaction. Despite many efforts to prevent showing the film, ultimately a court ruling allowed it.[6]

In the next few years in Des Moines as in other cities across the country, African-Americans were sought to ease labor shortages caused by World War 1. When whites returned to communities where African-Americans had settled, social conflict increased. Partly a labor conflict, this was also a neighborhood conflict involving tight-knit ethnic Catholic parishes in several Great Lakes and other northern cities.[7] The Iowa manifestations of the national

The coalition of white and black leaders accomplished more than either could alone, partly for financial reasons but also for [their] access to decision-making communities and legitimacy in the larger community.

conflict spurred the organization of several Iowa branches of the NAACP in the years following World War 1.

In Des Moines, two segments of the black population had arrived in the World War 1 era with a sense of autonomy and leadership that contributed to the movement for equal opportunity. One group was from Buxton, the largely African-American coal-mining town in nearby Monroe County that flourished from 1900 to 1920.[8] Many people from this town moved to Des Moines as the coal-mining industry waned.

The other group consisted of the black soldiers who had taken leadership training during World War 1 at Fort Des Moines and Camp Dodge, both in Des Moines. These training camps had found a home in Iowa partly due to the efforts of national NAACP president Joel Spingarn and the faculty at Howard University. After serving in the war, many black soldiers returned to the Des Moines area to work and raise a family.

Five African-American attorneys — S. Joe Brown, Gertrude Rush, Charles P. Howard, J. B. Morris, and George Woodson, all of whom would achieve national prominence — provided leadership in Des Moines and throughout Iowa in the 1920s and after. Brown graduated Phi Beta Kappa from the University of Iowa in 1898 and received an LL.B. in 1901.[9] His wife, Sue, was also a powerful leader statewide during the 1920s, especially in developing a junior branch of the NAACP in Des Moines and promoting the idea in other communities.[10] S. Joe Brown became the first president of the Des Moines branch of the NAACP and later provided leadership at both state and national levels.

In the early 1920s the Des Moines branch fought a residential segregation case brought by Dorothy Quail and gained passage of a city council resolution against segregated bathing beaches. The branch also blocked an effort by the Des Moines school system to put all 800 black children in one school.

In addition to the NAACP, people in Des Moines organized a Commission on Interracial Cooperation (CIC) in 1924. In February 1925 Des Moines sent representatives to the National Conference of Interracial Commissions that had been called jointly by the Commission on Race Relations of the Federal Council of Churches and the CIC.[11] After a series of informal luncheon meetings between whites and blacks, the black members were asked to submit a list of their objectives. They called the list "The Desiderata of the Des Moines Negroes." ["Negroes" was the politically correct term of the time. Generally, in this chapter I

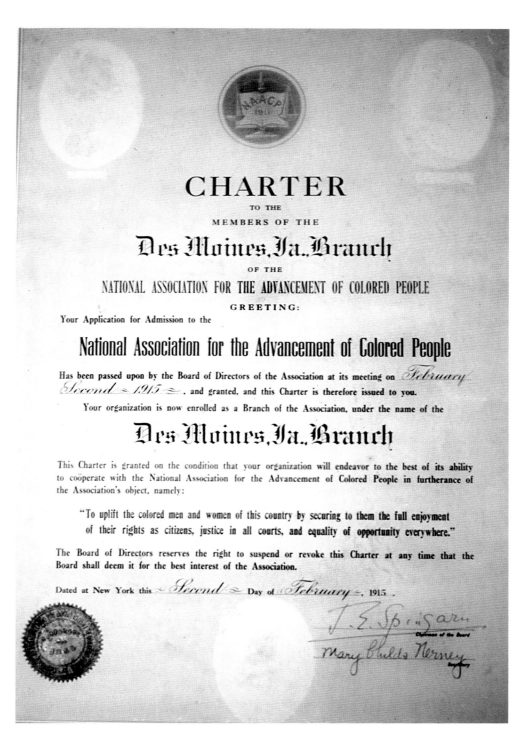

The charter of Des Moines branch of the NAACP, dated February 2, 1915 (SHSI Des Moines)

Ike Smalls (above) was elected president of the Des Moines branch of the NAACP in 1941. (SHSI Des Moines)

The Des Moines branch of the NAACP mounted this patriotic display during World War 2. At left is S. Joe Brown, president of the Des Moines branch. (SHSI Des Moines)

will use "black" or "African-American" in its place.] The African-American representatives called for:

- Abolition of separate bathing beaches and any other discriminatory practice supported by public taxes
- Abolition of discrimination in the buying and renting of property
- Ending segregation in places of public accommodation
- Ending the exclusion of blacks from grand jury lists
- Better employment in city and county government
- Better representation by (and in) labor unions
- More mail carriers and a clerk in the post office
- Black employees in the attendance office in the schools where more than half the population was black
- Better attendance of whites at black-sponsored meetings when the general public was invited
- More opportunities for black speakers to address white audiences, especially children
- Black history course in the public schools
- 200 white men and women to become members of the NAACP
- Fully equipped YMCA and YWCA in black neighborhoods
- Black member on the Des Moines Board of Education

Twenty years later the commission considered its objectives to see how many had been achieved.[12] Separate bathing beaches had ended. Of the three public pools, two frequented

predominantly by whites were open to blacks, and the third, predominantly black, had black lifeguards. An African-American served on the Polk County Grand Jury. Black employees worked for the county, the city, and the state in more than just menial positions. The post office employed several black clerks and carriers. While there were still no black teachers, there had been black teacher's aides and helpers in the attendance department. Black speakers had addressed white audiences on several occasions and served as instructors in the Sunday School Association.

There were more than 200 white members of the 650-member NAACP. Though still not fully equipped, the black YWCA and YMCA had made improvements in their facilities. The YMCA was expected to be more serviceable after the end of World War 2, when space for USO activities would be unnecessary.

Historian Jack Lufkin has argued that despite the interracial organization in both the NAACP and the CIC, actual gains were minimal and often transitory.[13] The black community was too divided and competitive, and too small, he says, to wield real power. Not enough white support was available for a black candidate for office to win.

But good will and cooperation did exist, and black elites continued to watch out for the lower classes. Certainly the commission worked with other groups to achieve its goals. For example, in 1930 it federated with the Ministerial Association and the Polk County Council of Religious Education to form the Des Moines Council of Churches. When the Council of Churches ceased to function in 1940, the Interracial Commission continued to function independently.

In Des Moines during these 20 years, from 1920 to 1940, the commission received from, and provided support for, the NAACP, worked with the churches, challenged the major public institutions, and achieved some quantifiable results, even if falling short of its ultimate goals. Over the years the commission served to bring blacks and whites together, both in fellowship and in audiences to hear speakers, often speakers of national renown. Among them were Booker T. Washington, Mrs. Booker T. Washington, and Dr. George Washington Carver, a graduate of Iowa State University at Ames.

In 1940, Georgine Morris founded the Iowa State Conference of Branches, which drew together the state's five most active NAACP branches — Des Moines, Keokuk, Council Bluffs, Davenport, and Marshalltown — as well as leaders from smaller or less active branches in Mason City, Ottumwa, and Waterloo. Des Moines members on the Iowa Conference's board were Georgine Morris, the first president; Gladys Carr, secretary; S. Joe Brown, executive board; attorney Caspar Schenk, chair of legal redress committee; and Mrs. Robert Root, chair of press and publicity. In 1942 Ike Smalls joined the executive board and took on the chairmanship of the press and publicity committee. Robert Wright was president of the Des Moines youth group. In 1943 Mrs. F. O. Morrow Jr. became the assistant secretary, and Clara Webb became director of the youth councils. Several other Des Moines members took leadership of committees: Helen Beshears, education committee; Mrs. William Neal, press and publicity; and Rev. Allen O. Birchenough, speakers bureau.

Ike Smalls became president of the Des Moines branch in 1943. In 1945 he became first vice-president of the state conference. Other Des Moines members on the state board were Clara Webb, assistant secretary; James B. Morris, board member and chair of legal redress; Judge Thomas Guthrie, board; S. Joe Brown, education and historian; and Georgine Morris, finance. Des Moines branch membership in 1945 was 1,262. Keokuk, the next largest branch, had 433 members.

Des Moines branch officers in 1946 were A. P. Trotter, president, and Mrs. Neal, secretary. Ike Smalls was elected president of the Iowa Conference at its annual meeting in 1945. One of Smalls's first activities as president was to thank U.S. Sen. B. B. Hickenlooper of Iowa for his investigation of Sen. Theodore Bilbo of Mississippi.[14] By the end of 1946 other Des Moines members were active on the state conference board. They were Clara Bayles, education; Dr. C. R. Bradford, health; A. A. Alexander, speakers bureau; E. C. Harris, veterans; and Sarah E. Jett, chairman, credentials.

After the annual meeting in 1947, S. Joe Brown remained historian; Smalls, Trotter, and James and Georgine Morris chaired committees; and Judge Guthrie also served on the board. James Morris was chair of legal redress; attorney Charles Howard, speakers bureau; Smalls, press and publicity; attorney Luther T. Glanton, veterans affairs; Georgine Morris, organization; Bayles, program; and Trotter, credentials. Trotter was at the time president of the Des Moines branch, whose membership stood at 2,007. The Des Moines leaders were much in evidence in the state conference, though the most prominent positions were taken by people from other parts of the state.

A Des Moines demonstration against "Dog Government" in Birmingham, Alabama, May 29, 1963 (Jervas Baldwin photo / Des Moines Register clipping courtesy Linda Frazier Carter)

Gloster Current, NAACP director of branches, spoke at the ninth annual session of the Iowa state conference of branches in 1948 in Des Moines.[15] Current criticized the U.S. Congress's failure to enact civil rights legislation and pass an anti-lynching bill, which was too weak anyway since it only denounced lynching. He also pointed out a lack of action on the poll tax and on the Fair Employment Practices Commission (FEPC).

The Republican Party in general had not supported the FEPC because employers wanted to be free to choose their employees, that is, to discriminate. Other legislative efforts — such

The successful lawsuit against the Katz Drug Store in the late 1940s was a major milestone in the civil rights movement in Iowa. Pictured here is the Katz Drug Store, located in the heart of downtown Des Moines, surrounded by protesters. (SHSI Des Moines)

as measures to outlaw segregation in the assignment of Negro units, to bar racial discrimination in interstate travel of troops, to guarantee that no inducted or enlisted person would be required to train or serve in any state which segregated, or to require manufacturers who sold to the military not to practice discrimination in employment, or to protect troops against lynching — had all been defeated in Washington. Even motions to guarantee civil rights in the nation's capital had failed. Current ridiculed the hypocrisy of protecting democracy abroad while not taking steps to defend it at home.

The NAACP had won some victories, however. The U.S. Supreme Court had determined that restrictive covenants could not be enforced by the states. Although African-Americans had been denied the right to register in many places in the South, more black students had been admitted to graduate schools. Still, Current said, the Democrats' statements of support for equality and an end to discrimination in their platform were not accompanied by legislative action. He also said there were some black "bandannas" south and north that thought equality wasn't needed.

Current reminded his listeners that the NAACP was not a southern organization. Even though 65 percent of its branches were in the South, only 28 percent of its members were there. Overall, in 1948 the NAACP counted 1,629 city and county branches in 44 states, the District of Columbia, and the Territory of Hawaii. In his speech, Current also praised both S. Joe Brown, who led Iowa into the NAACP and had been involved in many ways for half a century, and Ike Smalls, who had worked to bring Jews and all Iowans into the civil rights movement.

At the 1948 state NAACP conference meeting Glanton was elected first vice-president; Delores Beard, youth advisor; attorney Newton Margulies, speakers bureau; and S. Joe Brown, historian.

In 1950 Glanton became state conference president and Arthur Bryant became youth regional director. Brown continued as historian; Georgine Morris, state director of branches; James Morris Sr., legislation; Margulies, speakers bureau; James B. Morris Jr., veterans affairs; and Ike Smalls, Sarah Jett, and Clara Bayles, board members. The membership of the Des Moines branch in 1950 was 1,163, but declined in 1951 to 997 and further in 1952 to 953. S. Joe Brown, who founded the branch in 1915, died in 1950. That year, Ike Smalls, who had been active in the Iowa organization since 1930, became a vice-president on the national NAACP board.[16]

Again in 1952 the board's officers represented branches from around the state. Delores Strange, the youth director, was from Des Moines, as was Guy Greene, the publicity chair. Other members of the board from Des Moines included William Bell, James Morris Jr., and Georgine Morris. Membership was back up to 1,011 by 1954.

In the fall of 1955, several members of the Des Moines branch took on various positions in the state conference. Archie Greenlee, president of the Des Moines branch, became first vice-president, and Bessye Greene, the branch's secretary, became second vice-president. Des Moines's Leola Hubbard was the conference's recording secretary.

During the 1950s many people came to Des Moines to speak on behalf of the NAACP. Most prominent was Martin Luther King Jr., who spoke to 2,300 people in 1959 to commemorate the NAACP's fiftieth anniversary. Appearing at the Fighting Fund for Freedom (FFF or Four-F) banquets to raise money for the NAACP included Count Basie in 1962, Roy Wilkins in 1963, and Langston Hughes in 1967.

In 1961 Robert Wright Sr., who had been president of the youth group in 1942, became president of the Des Moines branch.

continued on page 311

(Opposite page, upper left)
Martin Luther King Jr. at Cornell College in 1962 (Cornell College)

(Opposite page, upper right)
Martin Luther King Jr., with his press secretary Tom Offenburger (courtesy Chuck Offenburger)

(Opposite page, lower left)
The program of an NAACP Freedom Spectacular in the 1960s (SHSI Des Moines)

(Opposite page, lower right)
A Freedom Fund banquet in the 1960s (courtesy Robert Wright Sr.)

(Below, left) A march to the Iowa State Capitol in observance of the death of Martin Luther King Jr., April 1968. (Des Moines Tribune clipping courtesy Rose Burrell)

(Below, right) "We Mourn King" reads a sign at the April 8 march on Iowa's capitol following the murder of Martin Luther King Jr. (courtesy Rose Burrell)

The Des Moines Commission on Human Rights, founded in 1951, played a key role in the civil rights movement in Iowa. (courtesy Robert Wright Sr.)

Robert Wright, long-time leader of the NAACP's Des Moines branch, pictured in 1999 (courtesy Robert V. Morris)

The Des Moines Commission on Human Rights

As a result of a 1951 League of Women Voters survey on discrimination in Des Moines, a mayor's Commission on Human Rights was established.[17] Its plan was to use persuasion and education to implement three objectives: to handle complaints of discrimination, to promote fair employment practices with regard to racial, religious, and nationality groups, and to determine the extent of discrimination. The Commission was to report its findings to the Des Moines City Council.

By 1953 the Commission felt that permanent status was necessary if it were to make progress in dealing with discrimination. A coalition organized to persuade the City Council to pass the ordinance creating the 1954 Commission included the League of Women Voters, the United Packinghouse Workers, the NAACP, the National Conference of Christians and Jews, the American Friends Service Committee, and the Council of Churches.

The next year, when the Des Moines Commission on Human Rights was established by ordinance, its name became the Des Moines Commission on Human Rights.

On April 9, 1956, the City Council created the Des Moines Commission on Fair Employment Practices, which outlawed discrimination in employment on the basis of race, color, religion, or national origin.[18] On February 11, 1957, the Employment Practices Commission became part of the Des Moines Commission on Human Rights and Job Discrimination.[19]

Housing discrimination had become a more acute problem in Des Moines in the years after World War 2. On December 18, 1961, the City Council passed a resolution declaring that discrimination in "selling, renting or financing residential property solely by reason of racial intolerance . . . is morally wrong." This resolution followed by less than a week a widely reported vote in a major Cedar Rapids church (St. Paul's Methodist) to approve the sale of property for a house

to Percy Harris, a black doctor. On June 1, 1964, fair-housing practices were added to the purview of the Des Moines Commission on Human Rights, which was given the right to investigate complaints of discrimination in the renting, selling, or financing of housing throughout the city. In 1966 the ordinance was amended to exempt only owner-occupied duplexes, thus widening the powers and increasing the caseload of the Commission. In September 1968 the ordinance was again broadened to include public accommodations and injunctive relief. Originally seven members served on the Commission; the number was increased to ten in January 1969. In the 1970s their authority was expanded yet again to include matters of sex, age, and disability.[20]

Wright held the post until 1968, longer than any person up to that time. He was also president of the Iowa Conference of Branches for the same period. He led the fight for the desegregation of the Des Moines schools and tackled discrimination in labor unions.

Several busloads of people from Des Moines traveled to Washington, D. C., for the March on Washington in August 1963. For that event, Larry Carter was bus captain and Robert Wright head of the delegation. Ike Smalls, who was elected to his thirteenth term as national NAACP vice-president, died in 1964.

In 1965 the state board of the NAACP met to plan for the state conference's twenty-fifth anniversary and the fiftieth anniversary of the Des Moines branch. Representatives came from Burlington, Des Moines, Fort Madison, Keokuk, Manly, Mason City, Ottumwa, Omaha, Sioux City, and Waterloo. Cedar Rapids and Davenport were not represented. Robert Wright, national vice-president from 1965 to 1967, became a member of the board of directors of the national NAACP in 1968. In 1974 the Des Moines branch began an "Employer of the Year" program to reward corporations that promoted blacks within their ranks.

Wright again served as president of the state branch in 1975, 1977–79, and then from 1990 to the present (2001). Larry Carter succeeded Vincent Chapman as president of the Des Moines branch in 1981.

In 1982 the branch brought litigation against the City of Des Moines to require the city to hire African-Americans as firefighters. The city agreed to a consent decree to hire one black for every non-black firefighter hired. In 1984 the consent decree was modified to provide for a one-one hire of blacks and whites until black representation was 6.8 percent of the work force.

The 1980s saw ongoing negotiations with CEOs in Des Moines to promote hiring of African-Americans at middle and upper-level management positions. By 1987 there were 19 black firefighters in the Des Moines fire department. By 1990 there were 36, 12.3 percent of the department, which was a great achievement.

In 1989 Larry Carter was elected to the NAACP National Board of Directors. During the year he spoke at breakfasts and banquets in Minnesota, Kansas, and Missouri.

In the 1990s the Des Moines branch continued to monitor incidents of racism, including cross-burnings, unjustified arrests, and discrimination in places of business. The branch also continued to recognize businesses with exemplary records of racial justice.

continued on page 314

Russell Lovell, Drake University law professor and NAACP attorney, led the successful suit to open the ranks of the Des Moines Fire Department for Dennis Moore and Greg Perry in 1985. (courtesy Russell Lovell)

The Desegregation of the Des Moines Fire Department
1981-1994

by Russ Lovell

> "One of [Larry Carter's] greatest achievements was integrating the Des Moines Fire Department."
>
> —**Iowa Gov. Tom Vilsack and Lt. Gov. Sally Pederson**[21]

Larry Carter, the second African-American from Iowa elected to the NAACP's national board (courtesy Larry Carter)

The Des Moines Fire Department (DMFD) was founded in 1882 and for 82 years not a single African-American was hired as a firefighter. The first black firefighter was hired in 1968 — after enactment of both the Civil Rights Act of 1964, at the federal level, and the Iowa Civil Rights Act. An enforcement action brought by the Iowa Civil Rights Commission resulted in the hiring of three African-American firefighters,[22] but progress proved fleeting. The black firefighters immediately faced pervasive racial discrimination within the department in their everyday treatment, leading two to resign and leave Des Moines.

The re-segregation of the DMFD did not go unnoticed by Des Moines's black community, and the department's discriminatory reputation deterred African-Americans from applying. By 1981 there was only 1 black firefighter (out of 311) in the DMFD. There had been only 4 black firefighters in the department's 100-year history.

Two of the black firefighter candidates rejected by the Des Moines Civil Service Commission (CSC) in the 1980 selection process — Dennis Moore and Greg Perry — came to the NAACP for help. Drake Law School professor Russell Lovell, who had been active on the Des Moines NAACP Legal Redress Committee since he came to Drake in 1976,[23] led the NAACP litigation effort to desegregate the fire department. Lovell filed the NAACP's class action case in U.S. District Court in Des Moines in August 1982.[24] Within 30 days, the NAACP litigation led to the hiring of 5 black firefighters.[25] However, the full measure of relief required a joint, sustained effort by Lovell, co-counsel Robert Wright Sr., and Des Moines branch president Larry Carter over the next 13 years.

The City of Des Moines soon backed out of the negotiations due to objections concerning affirmative-action hiring relief by some City Council members, requiring NAACP attorneys to prepare for a complex and lengthy trial. Lovell and co-counsel Greg Biehler took a dozen depositions and engaged in

extensive factual investigation, document research, and witness preparation. On the eve of trial, Lovell secured a detailed consent decree that the City Council approved, on a 4–3 vote.

Class-action cases necessarily involve large numbers of persons, who may have varied and different interests. It is not uncommon for disagreements to arise in the settlement of a class action. Such a disagreement first arose within the City Council, and then within the Des Moines NAACP, as to whether the proposed decree should be approved. At this point the NAACP's national general counsel, Tom Atkins of New York City, was asked to join the litigation team. Atkins came to Des Moines and — following a meticulous review of the consent decree and meetings with Des Moines NAACP leaders — embraced the consent decree as negotiated. Atkins and Wright played key roles in unifying the NAACP around the consent decree.

In January 1985 U.S. District Judge Harold Vietor approved the consent decree: "[The consent decree] is a very professional work product reflecting a high level of skill in the field of complex civil rights litigation."[26] The decree required a restructuring of the firefighter recruitment and selection processes, including revision of tests and selection criteria. It mandated that the City hire one black firefighter for every non-black firefighter hired until African-Americans comprised 6.8 percent of the DMFD's permanent firefighter workforce.[27] This affirmative action relief sought to achieve the black representation on the fire department that would have resulted had there not been a century of segregation. It also sought to break down the walls of segregation by encouraging African-Americans to apply for future openings. Finally, the decree required the federal court to retain jurisdiction of the case and monitor the City's progress in complying with the decree.

The consent decree of 1985 was truly a watershed achievement, but it took ten more years and the combined efforts of attorneys Lovell and Wright, working closely with Larry Carter (and later attorney Max Schott), to effectuate the decree's promise. Full implementation of the consent decree presented significant challenges — because judicial and political support for affirmative action remedies was eroding.[28] But by 1994, a transformation had been worked. African-Americans held 36 of the non-probationary 288 uniformed positions in the DMFD (12.5 percent), and the DMFD's pervasive discriminatory culture had been largely eradicated.

In July 1998, Larry Carter, Robert Wright Sr., and Rev. Keith Ratliff, president of the Des Moines branch of the NAACP, had occasion to reflect on the case: "No case litigated in Des Moines has had a greater impact for the black community.[The firefighter case] broke down the barriers formed by 100 years of exclusion and segregation. It was a precedent of great symbolism and bottom-line impact. The firefighter case established important legal precedent, but, most importantly, it immediately helped people and opened wide the doors of opportunity.

"The successful integration of the fire department is found not just in the numbers — 36 black firefighters — but in their quiet demonstration of competent job performance and their public service. Those 36 black firefighters reflect the diversity of our community and the very best of affirmative action. They hold jobs on which they can support a family. Jobs once denied citizens of Des Moines'[s] black community now mean salaries and benefits far in excess of a million dollars annually."[29]

Sometimes systemic change is so long in coming that the individuals who stuck their necks out to be plaintiffs reap no rewards. That was not the experience in this case. Dennis Moore and Greg Perry both became Des Moines firefighters and have had rewarding careers with the DMFD. A photograph of them, posing in front of a DMFD fire truck with Prof. Russell Lovell, is symbolic that in this civil rights case it all came together — individual relief and systemic change. Des Moines is a better community as a result of the NAACP's efforts.

"Of all the battles Carter fought — and there were many — the most pronounced was his effort to integrate the Des Moines Fire Department."

—Des Moines Register[30]

Davenport

The NAACP Branch in Davenport was the second branch formally established in Iowa. The Davenport branch organized on November 26, 1915, and was approved by the national NAACP Board of Directors on December 11, 1916. As different language and rules were adopted in 1917, the Davenport branch received its executive authorization on October 18, 1918.

Finally in 1918 — under the leadership of Rev. T. W. Lewis; Lewis Henry; Robert Taylor, a physician; and L. M. Brown, a funeral director — the branch was recognized by the national NAACP office. In 1915 Lewis had written the national office asking for information, and in 1916 Brown wrote to the NAACP about the formation of a "Negro Protective" to fight the performance of "Birth of a Nation." Buxton attorney George S. Woodson had spent several weeks in Davenport leading the battle against the play.[31]

In 1921, L. M. Brown wrote to James Weldon Johnson, secretary of the national NAACP, describing the difficulties facing the Davenport branch: a president difficult to work with and a local preacher who refused to provide any support or encouragement to the cause. On the other end, the national office was embarrassed when a check from the Davenport branch bounced.[32] The historical record contains no information about the outcome of this correspondence.

Nonetheless, the Davenport branch continued its work. In 1937, branch president Newton Taggert wrote to Fourth District Rep. Fred Bierman and Eighth District Rep. Fred Gilchrist about an anti-lynching bill in Congress. Bierman and Gilchrist responded that while they personally held lynching to be wicked, neither was sure what basis the Constitution provided to make a law against it. Mrs. Rosabel Sample, branch secretary, sent copies of these letters to Walter White, national secretary, so that he would know of their attitudes.

Charles Toney emerged as a leader of the Davenport branch in the 1940s. Toney was born in Eau Claire, Wisconsin, in 1913, lived in Clinton during his childhood, and moved to Davenport in the 1930s, where he became an employee of John Deere in 1938. Key issues facing the local chapter during the 1940s included a restaurant lawsuit and access to Davenport's municipal pool. Toney, who took on the municipal pool issue when his son was denied entry, had experienced this issue earlier in Clinton in the 1930s when a new pool was built there. At Deere, Toney was a welder with many years of service to the company. He also had a college degree in chemistry. He challenged Deere's management with a request to compete for an executive position, which he won, going on to become a company executive.[33] When in 1951 the Iowa Conference held its annual meeting in Davenport, Toney and Michael Laurence, also of Davenport, were panel discussants in a session on labor and industry.

Before the national civil rights movement took form in the 1960s, Catholic leadership on civil rights issues was a significant force in Davenport. Father Bill O'Connor at St. Ambrose College was especially strong on civil rights issues. Working with him were Father Ed, also at St. Ambrose, Penny Rule, and Father Griffin. They formed a study group, the League for Social Justice, which was officially interdenominational but was supported largely by individual Catholics. In the early 1950s the League surveyed the community to see what problems African-Americans experienced in regard to public accommodations. The survey found that most doctors, dentists, and real estate agents would not serve black or Mexican-American patients or customers. Only one restaurant, the one Toney and the Davenport branch had brought suit against, served blacks.[34]

Davenport attorney Tom Kelly, a key NAACP leader in the 1960s (courtesy Tom Kelly)

A Ku Klux Klan "Klankave" in Davenport, 1926 (SHSI Des Moines)

Growing out of the League's work came the Catholic Interracial Council (CIC), a group that worked with the NAACP through the civil rights period. The CIC was active in many large cities in the Northeast, often challenging the closed ethnic communities Catholics had laboriously and systematically established there.[35] It brought to Davenport speakers and activists such as Father Groppi from Milwaukee, Sargent Shriver, Martin Luther King Jr., and Julian Bond. Charles Toney was for a time president of the CIC in Davenport.

The CIC also took the initiative to file cases with the Iowa Civil Rights Commission regarding perceived housing discrimination. One case involved Marc Jarrett, rejected by Slavens Manor in 1967 because he was a bachelor. It was known that bachelors lived in the apartment complex and vacancies were available. The Iowa Civil Rights Commission reported the case to Gov. Robert Ray in 1969, in order to make observations about the Manor's conduct rather than to seek specific action, since Jarrett had found suitable housing for himself.

Another Davenport leader was Bill Cribbs, a graduate of the University of Northern Iowa in the 1950s and later an employee of John Deere. In 1969, following his term as president of the

local NAACP branch, Cribbs became the first director of the Human Rights Commission in Davenport, a position he held until 1972. During this time, both Tom Kelly and Charles Toney also served on the commission. Cribbs subsequently became a legislative aide for First District Rep. Ed Mezvinski until the latter's defeat in 1976 by Republican Jim Leach. Cribbs then worked for John Deere's Waterloo plant in personnel and human relations from the late 1970s until 1990, when he returned to Davenport.

Tom Kelly, a third significant figure in the Davenport NAACP in the turbulent 1960s, grew up in Des Moines where he knew the Morris family, publishers of the *Bystander*. Kelly received his law degree in 1954 and was persuaded by Des Moines lawyers to move to Davenport. There he set up a practice in 1958, becoming the first black lawyer in town. Jack Schroeder, a state senator, provided him with considerable material support to become established in his profession. Kelly then worked with Bill Cribbs, Jack Schneider, and Charles Toney to transform the leadership of the local NAACP branch. During the 1960s, Kelly worked with Loras College in Dubuque when there were difficulties with black youth from Chicago. In 1964 and 1965 he hosted a high school student, Leon Clark, from Holmes County, Mississippi, in a

When they wrote Iowa's congressional representatives about an anti-lynching bill, the congressmen responded that while they personally held lynching to be wicked, neither was sure what basis the Constitution provided against it.

Dr. Harry D. Harper, a member of the Iowa Civil Rights Commission, 1965 (63*rd* General Assembly, Iowa State Register, 1967–68)

James A. Thomas, executive director of the Iowa Civil Rights Commission, 1965 (63*rd* General Assembly, Iowa State Register, 1967–68)

Lafayette J. Twyner, D.D.S., a member of the Iowa Civil Rights Commission, 1965 (63*rd* General Assembly, Iowa State Register, 1967-68)

Alvin Hayes Jr., executive director of the Iowa Civil Rights Commission, 1969–1973 (65*th* General Assembly, Iowa Official Register, 1971–72)

Officers of the Ottumwa branch of the NAACP in the 1950s (from left): Roy Winston, vice-president; Clyde Robinson, treasurer; Mrs. Leona Davis, secretary; George Jackson Jr., president (Ottumwa Courier clipping / Ottumwa Public Library)

This itself was evidence of discrimination. Adding the burden of $500 to claim discrimination would add insult to injury. In the late 1960s the Davenport branch was strengthened by a fairly substantial black population estimated at about 5,000 in the Quad Cities, including Davenport and Bettendorf in Iowa and Rock Island and Moline in Illinois. The Davenport branch struggled with the fact of four cities in two states. This was in some ways an advantage but in other ways a disadvantage. It certainly meant a more complex system of governance and a greater metropolitan area than any other in Iowa other than Des Moines and Omaha-Council Bluffs.

Ottumwa

Ottumwa's branch of the NAACP organized in 1918 with 25 members. Six of the original members were housekeepers, four were porters, three were janitors, three were laborers, two were ministers, and seven worked in other occupations. William Page, one of the ministers, was president; laborer Edgar Lee was vice-president; housekeeper Katherine Moss was secretary; and barber Samuel Mitchell was treasurer. Three years later the national office urged the branch's vice-president, Mr. Gooch, to call a meeting to determine whether the president was willing to fulfill his office. If not, the national office advised, the branch should call for his resignation. Subsequently, in a letter to new branch president Byron H. Williams, the national office advised that the treasurer be bonded for at least $100 to guard against embezzlement in the future.

The Ottumwa branch showed signs of life only sporadically for the next 15 years. By 1925 the branch had become dormant, but charter member Frances Hicks was ready to reorganize it. J.O. Winston wrote from Ottumwa to the national office in 1926 regarding the anti-lynching bill, receiving in response encouragement to keep up the pressure back home on U.S. Senator Cummins of Iowa.

In 1928 the national office was pleased to hear that a Reverend Tutt had worked with Selby Johnson of Keokuk to revive the Ottumwa branch. But nothing further happened until 1939, when the branch was reorganized with 49 members. Roy Winston was president; John Crayton, vice-president; George Jackson Jr., secretary; and Paul Junkins of Bloomfield, treasurer.[37]

In 1946 Ottumwa reported 84 members, which grew to 103 in 1947, its peak year. Ottumwa's Dr. Gage C. Moore served on the Health Committee of the Iowa Conference, and Roy Winston,

program designed to provide African-Americans from the South a chance to experience a different cultural situation.[36]

The Davenport NAACP entered into the fray of civil rights activity quite directly, at times violating the national protocol in order to do so. As an example of its activist, confrontational period, the youth group of the Davenport NAACP called itself the Black Power Youth Council and wore black shirts as their uniform. One of the issues that the NAACP branch addressed was the requirement of a $500 bond to be paid by those claiming discrimination in a program designed to enforce housing codes and eliminate substandard housing. They estimated that enforcing codes would displace 15 to 20 percent of the non-white community.

A Ku Klux Klan procession in downtown Ottumwa, 1924 (Ottumwa Public Library)

an original board member of the Conference, continued in that capacity. In the early 1950s the branch was inactive, but a revival of interest spurred membership, which rose to 51 in 1954. Ottumwa hosted the state conference that year.[38]

The closing of Ottumwa's meatpacking plants in recent decades has reduced the city's African-American population, and the NAACP branch there has been inactive in the 1990s.[39]

Cedar Rapids

The Cedar Rapids branch of the NAACP was granted executive authorization on January 13, 1919, following an organizational meeting with S. Joe Brown from Des Moines on December 6, 1918. Brown's trip had been delayed due to the quarantines associated with the flu epidemic.[40] However, the flu provided only a minor delay compared to the three and a half year gap between the initial May 1915 letter of interest from Mrs. E. W. Gresham to Brown, in which she mentioned the impression Joel Spingarn had made on her during his visit to Des Moines, and just over two years after Roy Nash from the national office had written to L. D. Lowery regarding starting a branch in Cedar Rapids.[41] The specific concern expressed in these letters is support in Cedar Rapids for a bill regarding the "lynching evil" as reported in *The Crisis*, the magazine of the NAACP.

In 1926 the national NAACP office sought to revive dormant branches. Cedar Rapids was one of these. Mrs. S. J. (Sue) Brown of Des Moines had been in touch with the national office, which wrote to Elnora Gresham. In response, someone impersonating Gresham's husband wrote back to the national office suggesting that Mrs. Gresham should be paid.[42] The letter writer maintained that Mrs. Brown was paid. Distraught about the letter sent over her husband's name, Elnora Gresham insisted it was not her husband who wrote it. She expected no payment, she said, for she worked only "for the good of the Race.[43]

No revival of the Cedar Rapids branch occurred in 1926, or in May 1927, when a letter went out from the national office to Rev. S.H. Gibson. In June 1928, at Keokuk activist Selby Johnson's request, another letter was mailed to Cedar Rapids, this time to Dr. W.H. Beshears, the branch president.[44] Still nothing happened to resuscitate the branch.

NAACP field secretary William Pickens wrote again in January 1933 to Beshears, with a copy to George W. Ashby, pleading for financial support and announcing a planned visit in

April. Ashby said he would do what he could. In March Pickens wrote again, asking for specific information about the black community in Cedar Rapids, but on April 11, Ashby sent a wire canceling the meeting, claiming he could not make suitable arrangements.[45]

Pickens wrote once more to Beshears, in April 1938, offering help to reorganize the branch, but nothing happened in Cedar Rapids until a cause and a leader emerged in the 1940s. In 1942, Coe College student protests against segregation at the city's first public swimming pool stimulated reorganization of the local branch of the NAACP. Viola Gibson, who had arrived in Cedar Rapids in 1909 as a young girl from Tennessee, became the students' adult advisor and confidant. Gibson had been nurtured by Jane Boyd, founder of a local settlement house that provided services to European and African-American immigrants in Cedar Rapids. Gibson participated in neither Bethel AME or Zion Missionary Baptist, the main black churches, but organized her own preaching station, the Christ Sanctified Holiness Church. Boyd's settlement house became the source of leadership for civil rights efforts in the 1960s. The revived Cedar Rapids NAACP branch also received support from the clergy and members of Bethel African Methodist Episcopal Church, which had been established in 1871.[46]

The Cedar Rapids branch was especially active in the 1960s. The branch's housing committee in 1961 focused on local realtors' refusal to show African-Americans suitable houses in all neighborhoods of the city. Many realtors believed that African-Americans would be happiest "with their own kind." Homeowners often wished to limit the sale of their house to those of whom they approved. In response, members of the NAACP and the Council of Churches formed a Council on Human Relations to address the issue of fair housing. The council was an independent organization, which allowed those who were members of neither the NAACP nor the Council of Churches (a Protestant group) to be actively involved also. This included Catholics, Muslims, Unitarians, Jews, and people not affiliated with a particular denomination.

In 1961 a black physician, Dr. Percy Harris, was unable to find a suitable home for himself and his family in Cedar Rapids. Robert Armstrong, owner of a local downtown department store and a board member of St. Luke's Hospital, which had recruited Harris, became determined to find him a home. Dr. Harris and Armstrong went together to look at many properties but all were

Viola Gibson, organizer of the Cedar Rapids NAACP branch in 1942, is pictured here in 1964. (courtesy Harambee House)

Sue M. Brown, a key figure in the African-American quest for equality in Iowa (SHSI Des Moines)

too small, too large, or too expensive. Finally Armstrong donated an acre of his own 22-acre estate to his church, St. Paul's Methodist, as part of a fundraising effort for an education wing. Armstrong instructed Dr. Harris to make an offer on part of the land, which Dr. Harris did. Several of Armstrong's neighbors in this upscale neighborhood, some of them members of his own church, organized to protest the sale. But on December 13, 1961, the 3,000-member church voted 461–290 to proceed with the sale of the acre to Dr. Harris.[47]

The work of the Council on Human Relations proceeded apace after this much-publicized scandal in a prominent mainline protestant church. Blacks and whites of several faiths went together to inquire about buying property in a variety of neighborhoods all over the city. Catholics, Jews, Friends, and Unitarians joined the Council of Churches.

The council also sought to establish a city commission to carry out fair housing. Such a commission had been an early goal of the council, but in 1960 and 1961 the city was apparently not ready. In October 1963 the Cedar Rapids City Council established the Mayor's Advisory Commission on Human Rights. The commission was given no legal basis on which to threaten or bring action against anyone who might deny blacks the opportunity to buy a home. Nevertheless, these local activities were significant in raising public awareness at a time when the United States was in the midst of heated debates over the Civil Rights Bill, which passed on July 6, 1964.

From August to October 1964 the NAACP carried out a survey of black opinion regarding civil rights problems in Cedar Rapids. The intention was to challenge a survey conducted the previous spring by the City Council that had shown that 75 percent of the citizens of Cedar Rapids felt there were no civil rights problems.[48] The Bethel AME Church, the Mt. Zion Baptist Church, the Jane Boyd Community House, the Negro Civic Organization, the Negro Elks, and Dr. Percy Harris together compiled a list of 323 families. Pairs of interviewers — one black, one white — called on each family at home and asked the adults a set of questions. The final list included the names of 346 families and unattached individuals; 63 were never contacted because no one was at home when the interviewers came to call. Eighty-three percent of the families contacted thought there were problems with fair housing; 59 percent, with public accommodations at places of business; 57 percent, with fair employment practices; 28 percent,

joining groups of their preference; and 19 percent, placing children in schools. Chief among the problematic businesses were barbershops, with 79 people complaining. Businesses falling in the midrange of complaints were restaurants (30), lunch counters (19), hotels (25), and motels (16). Fewer complaints were leveled at beauty parlors (12), taverns (10), gas stations (5), and department stores (3). Eighteen complaints were registered against unions and 13 against social clubs.

The interviewers learned that most of the African-Americans interviewed generally avoided situations where they would be refused, thus reducing the likelihood of experiencing problems with the various services. They also learned that some black citizens moved away from Cedar Rapids because suitable housing could not be found. Meanwhile, in a survey of Cedar Rapids landlords to see how many rented without discrimination, the Commission on Human Rights discovered that owners of multiple unit buildings were more likely to rent without discrimination, while owners of single units were more likely to discriminate.[49]

In 1965, Iowa passed its own Civil Rights Bill. A Fair Housing Bill followed in 1967. With the passage of these bills by the Iowa General Assembly, pressure grew in Cedar Rapids to have a local human rights commission with legally binding authority. Hugh (Hooty) Gibson, son of Viola Gibson, was among the more outspoken advocates of a commission to address the rights of the common man. Intense public debate about this in the spring of 1969 resulted in submission of a proposed ordinance to the city council in late June. In October the city council, led by Interim Mayor Steve Shank, passed the ordinance, which established an autonomous human rights commission. Bill Cotton, a Methodist minister, was hired as executive director in January 1970, as was commission secretary Mary Evans. The commission began right away to look carefully at the city's and the school system's hiring practices.[50]

Keokuk

The first communication from Keokuk regarding the establishment of an NAACP branch came in March 1919 from Solomon Williams, secretary of the organizing committee. The Rev. J. Sterling Moore wrote a follow-up to Williams, and by July Williams, Moore, and their colleagues in Keokuk had the necessary forms, signatures, and contributions to begin an NAACP branch.

Their application was authorized in August. The application's signers included a wide representation of occupations and professions: several ministers, a schoolteacher, a chauffeur, plus teamsters, railroad men, a paper hanger, a butler, the manager of a rock quarry, barbers, an elevator man and lady, poultry dressers, hair dressers, domestics, laborers, an ice man, a fireman, a physician, and mail carriers. Keokuk in 1919 was a community of 14,000 people. One in ten was African-American.

Lynching topped the concerns of the Keokuk branch organizers. Father Giglinger of Keokuk's St. Mary's Catholic Church declared "lynching is a crime against God and Man and like slavery should be abolished forever." Father Giglinger revealed his partisan attitude when he went on to say that "lynching has never occurred in an exclusive Catholic locality and its occurrence has caused the darkest spot in American History."[51] The national office urged Iowa branches to keep up pressure on Iowa's Senator Cummins to support anti-lynching legislation.

Mrs. Selby Johnson, a schoolteacher, began in 1926 to build a junior division in the Keokuk branch, as mentioned in the section on Ottumwa. She also worked to start a new branch in Fort Madison in 1926, and in 1927 expanded her efforts in a campaign to revive Iowa's dormant NAACP branches and to start new ones. She had prospects for a new branch in La Grange, Missouri. At the same time she worked to revive branches in Quincy, Illinois, 40 miles south of Keokuk, as well as in Ottumwa, Burlington, and Cedar Rapids in Iowa.

In May, Mrs. Johnson traveled to both Ottumwa and Cedar Rapids to stir up those branches. Succeeding in reorganizing the Ottumwa branch with 25 members, and feeling encouraged about the Cedar Rapids branch, she planned to go on to reorganize the Davenport branch and to start a branch at Marshalltown. In time, however, Mrs. Johnson fretted that organizational work in Keokuk lagged while she sought to organize and reorganize branches elsewhere. In 1929 she turned her attention to business pursuits and the Keokuk branch languished.

Eight years later, in March 1937, local ministers called for a mass meeting to reorganize the branch. Forty-four names appeared on the membership list sent to the national office on March 16, 1937. Mrs. Selby Johnson, the first name on the list, had resumed her organizational efforts. On March 29, another list was submitted. This one had 53 names, including W. W. Gross, president; Lewis A. McGee, vice-president; and Selby Johnson,

Attending the 1945 NAACP State Conference of Branches sixth annual meeting in Cedar Rapids were (left to right) Rev. D. D. Bell of Mt. Zion Missionary Baptist Church; Rev. Andrew Parks of Bethel African Methodist Episcopal Church; Julia Reed; S. Joe Brown; Viola Gibson; Edith Reed Atkinson; unidentified woman; unidentified man; and Georgine Morris. (courtesy Edith Reed Atkinson)

secretary. Pickens, once national field coordinator and now director of branches, visited Keokuk on February 22, 1938. The branch's membership worked hard to prepare for his visit.

In 1939 the Keokuk branch established a youth council, and in 1940 the branch participated in organizing the Iowa Conference of Branches. In 1945 Keokuk won the state conference trophy for best work done by a senior (adult) group. With 301 memberships, Keokuk had the third largest membership in the state, following Des Moines and Waterloo. Despite the large membership, however, Keokuk's membership was unable to generate the required "tax" of five cents per member to fund the state conference. Within six years, by 1951, the branch had expired. Reasons for its collapse are not apparent, though a number of factors might be responsible: inflated or unrealistic membership reports; deceased or departed leaders; economic hardships; and internal conflicts.

Centerville

Centerville's Schuyler Jones wrote to the national office on August 6, 1919, with 26 names of people who had paid their dues to join the NAACP. Jones recognized that his list did not include the required 50 names, but he wanted to go on record with hope that 24 more could be found. By June 1920 a total of 52 were signed up, and the board gave executive approval for Centerville's

TWELVE KLAN POINTS

1. The immigration bars must be kept up.
2. The moral standard and the American home must be maintained.
3. The Protestant churches must be kept Christian and militant.
4. The public school must be fortified, strengthened and kept in the hands of Americans.
5. The Constitution must be respected.
6. The flag must be honored.
7. The laws must be obeyed and enforced.
8. Good men must not shirk jury service.
9. The courts must not be influenced or controlled.
10. The ballot must be cast as a sacred duty.
11. Big and good men must be selected for office.
12. Our Anglo-Saxon Protestant Christian civilization must be preserved.

The "twelve points" of the Ku Klux Klan, whose message of hate was addressed to Jews and Catholics as well as blacks (SHSI Des Moines)

A Ku Klux Klan gathering in Cherokee, Iowa, September 11, 1924 (SHSI Des Moines)

Robert Bagnall, the director of branches, responded forcefully. "The most prejudiced southern white, almost without exception, has some pet Negro to whom he will give much consideration, but he may eagerly join in a lynching and burning of other Negroes, and the denial to them of all their rights," Bagnall wrote to Emma Hicks. "In this particular instance, the Centerville Klan regards the Jew as its more dangerous enemy, and so seeks to play off one group against the other, in order to effectively divide them. An old trait of warfare is divide and conquer. If the Klan can get the Jew and the Negro to stand against each other, its program can be more easily carried out. The National Association for the Advancement of Colored People has made a thorough examination of the Klan. It is fundamentally hostile to the Negro as is manifested in its history and in the first and principal clause of its creed — WHITE SUPREMACY," Bagnall continued. "In the North, the Klan has as its program in reference to the Negro the enforcement of segregation; the bringing about of separate schools, which are always inferior schools; the shutting out of the Negro from white institutions of higher learning; the nullifying of the Negro vote; the shutting out of Negroes from what they term "white men's jobs," by which they mean any decent jobs; the limiting of Negroes to menial positions; the passage of 'Jim Crow' laws of various sorts."[52]

Hicks wrote the national office again in 1931 to encourage William Pickens to visit, saying that a miners' strike had been going on for three years. She said that they needed a branch, particularly because incidents of lynching had gotten as close as Maryville, Missouri. Hicks read Pickens's response in church and had it read at the lodge. Pickens was apparently ready to visit, but Hicks thought that Schuyler Jones should make the arrangements. There is no indication that the visit actually took place.

Following World War 2, the Centerville branch reorganized and hosted the State Conference annual meeting in 1946, with Ella Baker, director of branches, as guest speaker. A Jewish woman, Ruby Malawsky, was Centerville branch president and served on the executive board of the state conference, and Louise Bolden was the branch's secretary. Centerville's mayor, Mr. Hood, served on the branch's executive board. Membership was strong in these immediate post-war years: 144 members in 1945, 148 in 1946, and 117 in 1947. By 1949 the Centerville branch was down to only 5 members and by 1951 it was inactive. Reasons for the branch's sudden demise are uncertain. The contentiousness of the

branch charter on July 12. Of the occupations listed by the branch's charter members, 2 were professionals — a lawyer and a pastor — and 8 were miners. In addition, 18 were listed as "do" (presumably domestics), an equal number listed no category, and 6 other occupations were noted as well.

Four years later, the branch was dormant. Despite the fact that denial of accommodations was common in Centerville, according to Emma Hicks there was a lack of attendance at meetings. African-Americans were refused service at soda fountains and the "best" cafes, and were required to sit upstairs at the opera houses and in restricted seating at the movies. Yet local NAACP meetings were sparsely attended, and the work of the NAACP was left to five or six individuals. Many people refused to see problems or act on them, wrote Hicks in a March 1924 letter to the national NAACP office. Writing again in July, Hicks asked about the Ku Klux Klan. Apparently the Klan had given $100 to the black church in town, which made many blacks think the Klan was their "best friend." Mrs. Hicks believed the truth was otherwise, but needed a statement from the national office to convince people.

1948 national elections and the revelation that the NAACP's traditional allies, the Republicans, wouldn't take definite stands for civil rights may have been contributing factors to the dramatic collapse of the branch.

Council Bluffs

Council Bluffs, across the Missouri River from Omaha, received its charter from the national office in late 1920. The branch began with 68 members, out of 500 or 600 described in its application as "our people" in the city at that time. Of the original members, 23 listed themselves as artisans, 19 as domestics, 6 as laborers, 3 as ministers or pastors, 3 railroad employees, and 12 in other categories. The first branch president was railroad man W.C. Carter. Artisan L.L. Williams was vice-president; machinist A.W. Fitz, secretary; and domestic D.M. Mixon, treasurer.

In 1924 the Council Bluffs group wrote the national office about an anti-marriage bill pending in the Iowa legislature. The national office encouraged the branch to stay in touch with attorney James B. Morris, president of the Des Moines branch, in regard to the bill. Though the bill did not pass in 1924, its return was anticipated for the next year.

The Council Bluffs branch was effectively dormant during 1925, due to "lack of efficient officers."[53] In 1926, the branch took part in the NAACP's campaign to win passage of a federal anti-lynching bill, and people in Council Bluffs received urgent pleas to contact Senator Cummins regarding the bill.

In 1928 Mabel Fletcher wrote to the national office regarding starting a women's branch, but was told that there were no provisions for such a branch. The women could, if they wished, form an auxiliary, but it would be part of the regular Council Bluffs branch.

William Teal, president of the branch in 1929, undertook to reorganize it. The national office encouraged him to invite Dr. John Singleton, president of the Omaha branch, to speak. However, the Council Bluffs branch remained inactive through 1930, despite the claim that there were 3,000 African-Americans in town.[54] In 1931 Winonah Teal succeeded in gathering some people together to form a group and receive a new charter. Issues addressed by the group included the refusal of a local business college to admit black students, the barring of African-Americans from city-owned bathing beach, and the racial coding of voters on the registration books of Iowa.[55] The national office responded that civil rights

law did not likely provide a cause for action in regard to the business college, but did so in regard to the city-owned bathing beach. The NAACP encouraged first the use of public opinion, especially with the force of influential persons both white and colored. If that were to fail, then an attorney might be engaged.[56]

The Council Bluffs branch co-sponsored a musical contest on February 9, 1932 to honor the birth of the NAACP. The Beck School of Music was a major co-sponsor, with Prof. Milo Smith, music director of the local public schools assisting. The event took place at the Tabernacle Baptist Church at 14th Street and A Avenue.[57]

The next year was a difficult one for the national office, which was forced to lay off Bagnall — for 12 years director of branches — plus two clerks. Salaries of other workers were cut three times that year. Along with one of the salary notices came a plea to work hard on a membership drive.[58]

The branch's 1933 report estimated the black population of Council Bluffs at about 600. Black employment was largely in railroad work, with only one city employee, a custodian, and a few street workers employed by the local unemployment relief

(Top) A Ku Klux Klan parade in Des Moines, 1926, and a handbill announcing the Klan's parade (Des Moines Register / SHSI Des Moines)

Russell Nash of Cedar Rapids served as president of the Iowa Conference of NAACP Branches in 1963 and 1964. (Cedar Rapids Gazette)

M. F. Fields, Waterloo attorney, was among the founders of the NAACP branch in his community. (Grout Museum)

committee. There were no state or school employees. The report thought the chances of African-Americans working on public works meager.

The branch reported it had fought discrimination of colored girls in swimming classes in public and high school programs and had protested signs in restaurants saying "No Colored Trade Solicited." The report also noted that sports teams from prejudiced states only play local teams if colored players were removed.[59]

Because of "petty and insignificant reasons for discord," the branch was in difficulty at the end of 1933. Fitz reported that he had borne half of the expenses of the branch himself. He asked William Pickens, NAACP field secretary, to write the treasurer and others to stir their sense of responsibility.[60] Fitz also reported to the national NAACP Legal Department an incident in Fremont, Nebraska, while he was there on sales business in 1937. He had developed ignition trouble with his car, such that he was forced to abandon the car in the middle of the street. Walking toward a garage, he remembered he needed cash, which he kept in a secret place in his car for such emergencies. When he returned to his car, five police officers rushed up in a car, arrested him roughly, called him "Rastus" and "Sambo," and put him in jail overnight without allowing him phone calls to friends in Fremont or family in Council Bluffs. He was charged with vagrancy and lack of visible means of support after being held incommunicado for 15 hours. Fitz pleaded not guilty. He was then also charged with loitering. A white woman was brought in claiming he had accosted her. However, Fitz knew many people in Fremont and he was able to bring in several character witnesses. His case was dismissed with the advice not to return to Fremont.

Fitz did return, and in his letter to the national office he inquired about suing the city. Charles Houston, special counsel for the NAACP, advised Fitz that Nebraska law should be examined to determine if such a suit were possible. Certainly the officers could be sued. Houston urged Fitz to find a lawyer in Omaha on a contingency fee basis, particularly if any of the officers owned property.[61] Unfortunately, the records of the NAACP branch do not indicate the outcome of this case.

When the Iowa Conference organized in 1940 in Des Moines, Council Bluffs was one of six branches listed in a *Des Moines Register* news release. The others were Keokuk, Davenport, Marshalltown, and Mason City (which contributed board members but had been inactive for some years). Board members also

represented Ottumwa and Waterloo.[62] In a list of branch presidents for 1943, none was named for Council Bluffs, but the branch was apparently still active. The next year's Council Bluffs contribution of $1.85 to the Iowa Conference indicates that at least 37 members had contributed their nickel dues. The branch reported 78 members in 1945, and in 1946 George Cooper served as president and Inez Willis as secretary. Mrs. C.H. Copeland from Council Bluffs was secretary of the Iowa Conference and a member of its program committee. Mrs. Copeland's husband, a minister, had previously worked to reorganize the Fort Madison branch.

In 1960, 165 of the 593 African-Americans living in Council Bluffs were members of the local NAACP branch, which eventually merged with the Omaha branch.

Waterloo

The NAACP branch in Waterloo began in 1921, with an original 13-member executive committee that included 10 men and 3 women. Of the 13, 4 were white. Two of the white men were clergy and 1 was a judge. Among the 9 African-Americans, 2 were clergy: W. W. Ewing of the Antioch Baptist Church and H. C. Boyd of the African Methodist Episcopal (AME) Church. Black attorney M. F. Fields was also a member. R. A. Broyles was the branch's first president. Robert Garland was treasurer, and Gussie Mardis was secretary.

The Waterloo NAACP's early challenges had to do with establishing churches and building homes for the city's nearly 900 African-Americans, 400 of whom had come to Waterloo to work on the Illinois Central Railroad in the years 1912-15, which were years of strike. The rest arrived during World War 1. This sudden migration from very rural areas of the South, particularly in central Mississippi, to a small city on the agricultural edge of the industrial North put tremendous stress on the internal structures of the African-American community as well as on the city of Waterloo as a whole.[63]

During the 1920s the branch received appeals from various people who believed they had been treated unfairly by law-enforcement officials, sometimes involving very difficult circumstances for families. Due to compromising circumstances — such as breaking of bond or repeat offenses — the national office could not take these cases on for litigation, but the local branch sought to provide families what support and relief it could.

In 1928 R. A. Broyles wrote the national office explaining

that many of the 1,400 African-Americans in Waterloo, a town of 40,000, did not want to be in an organization with whites. Many had had very negative experiences with whites before fleeing Mississippi for Waterloo. Broyles said he hoped in time they could overcome that strong prejudice. However, for now he wished the national office, which required some participation by whites, would understand the branch's difficulty with that requirement.

In 1930 the branch, claiming to represent 2,200 people, worked to secure a position on the police force for a black person.[64] Frustrated in its efforts, the branch sought help from the national office. The branch also became involved in a case in Dubuque, 90 miles to the east, in which a white woman sought the arrest of a young black teenager who allegedly bumped into her while running. At about the same time a 12-year-old white boy was killed in Dubuque, arousing fears that a black person had done it. In this charged atmosphere, the black teen was sentenced to seven years in Eldora, a state training school. After some months, during which attorney M. F. Fields and many people in Dubuque worked on the case, the boy was released, demonstrating the effectiveness of an organized response even in a heated social climate.

Iowans working on the Dubuque case felt the national office demonstrated a certain obtuseness in requesting a local lawyer's statement regarding the affair. The boy charged in the bumping incident was one of seven children, whose father was unemployed. The family had sought legal help because they couldn't afford a lawyer themselves. Particularly at the beginning of the Depression years, there were limits to what the national office could do to respond to local issues around the country.

In 1933 the Communist Party sought to discredit the national NAACP in the case of the Scottsboro boys, who had been accused of raping a white woman in Alabama. Local NAACP leaders found themselves having to defend the NAACP against charges in the Communist Party *Daily Worker* that the boys' mothers were being ejected from NAACP meetings. The fact was that the women were not the boys' mothers, but had been set up by the Communist Party to present themselves as such. This conflict between the NAACP and the Communist Party in the hard-pressed industrial city of Waterloo is just a local instance of the unusual challenges faced by the NAACP during its early years.

In 1941 Dr. Lee Furgerson, a black physician who had been an NAACP member at least since 1931, wrote Roy Wilkins of the Urban League in 1940 about establishing an Urban League center

in Waterloo. The Urban League might be entitled to receive Community Chest funds, Furgerson reasoned, and it would help the NAACP greatly to have community support for programs addressing issues of racial justice. There is no indication that an Urban League office was established, but that same year Furgerson was elected vice-president of the new Iowa State Conference of NAACP branches. M. F. Fields, an original member of the branch, served as a member of the conference executive committee. In 1943 Fields was president of the conference and of the Waterloo branch as well. In 1944 Waterloo paid $13.05 to the state conference, second largest after Des Moines's contribution of $46.00.[65] At 5 cents per member, this would indicate at least 261 members. In 1945 Waterloo's membership for the year was 208, fourth largest branch in the state after Des Moines, with 1,262 members; Keokuk with 433; and Davenport with 241.[66]

In 1946 several Waterloo people served on the state conference board and committees: Lyda Page was assistant secretary; M. F. Fields was on the board, serving as finance and program chair; Mrs. Fields was education committee chair; Lee Furgerson was health committee chair; and V. Norman was labor committee chair. By 1947 Waterloo reported the second highest membership in the state, 292 members, its largest enrollment ever. Des Moines recorded 2,007.[67] In 1950 the State Conference annual meeting was held on a Sunday afternoon at the Waterloo YWCA, with Thurgood Marshall, special counsel in the national office, the theme speaker.

Waterloo maintained its second ranking position for many years but in the early 1950s was overtaken by the newly organized Sioux City branch. Conference officers from Waterloo in 1952 included only Vaeletta Fields, vice-president. Her husband, attorney M. F. Fields, had died, leaving a significant void in local and state leadership ranks.

In the years following World War 2 both the John Deere Company tractor works and the Rath packing houses grew rapidly in Waterloo, again attracting increased numbers of African-Americans, particularly from central Mississippi along the Illinois Central Railroad lines. Many people came to the city from Holmes County and neighboring areas to join their relatives who had moved north earlier.

With the Supreme Court's *Brown v. Board of Education* decision there was a general sense of relief that the tide had turned and that the basis of segregation was demolished. The NAACP

The migration from very rural areas of the South to a small city on the agricultural edge of the industrial North put tremendous stress on the internal structures of the African-American community as well as on the city of Waterloo as a whole.

regained strength in the 1960s — dealing with issues of public accommodations, fair housing, and employment — and continued to be an active organization in the late 1990s. But during the 1960s the NAACP, which was focused on national legal action, was not ready to mobilize people for more immediate community needs. For local issues, people in Waterloo formed the East Side Community Group, which drew together friendship networks established through the city's churches and the NAACP.

Serious conflict developed following an event at Waterloo's Midtown Center on September 8, 1968. A cultural program featuring poetry and black literature readings was accompanied by skits that claimed to accurately depict the American political system. Apparently in response to the program, over the next few days students called for courses on black history at Waterloo's East High School. On Friday, September 13, a fight at a football game led to the burning of Shepherd's lumber yard. For the first time in Waterloo since the Rath meatpacking strike in 1948, the National Guard was called out to restore order.

U.S. Rep. H.R. Gross maintained that the troubles were instigated by Black Panthers, but others denied this. Many local people called for a citizen's committee to investigate the causes of the civil disorders, including events at East High School, plus "alleged outside agitators, alleged police harassment and the role of the news media."[68] At the same time ten local businessmen called for a "Committee for Equal Law Enforcement" to ensure that "habitual criminal violators" would not be released on the streets.

On Monday, September 16, at a meeting attended by 300 people, the Board of Education heard a list of grievances from the black community. The community demanded a black student union at East High and the hiring of more black teachers. Waterloo Mayor Lloyd Turner asked the National Guard to remain in town through the Dairy Cattle Congress, a major exposition attracting thousands of people to the city in late September.

Two years later tension remained a problem at football games in Waterloo. An alliance between the schools and law-enforcement agencies raised concerns among black residents, and an NAACP committee was formed to look into the nature of the alliance. Ruth Anderson, head of the committee, asked that the NAACP be included in future meetings between the schools and law enforcement.[69]

Burlington

In February 1921, Thetha Graham of Burlington requested information from John Shillady at the national office about beginning a Burlington branch, and three months later, on May 24, executive authorization was granted. There were 44 members listed on Burlington's application. Of those identified by occupation, there were two clergy, a beauty culturist, a contractor, a laborer, and a poultry dresser. Judging from national records, the Burlington chapter was not very active in its first few years. In 1927 Selby Johnson of Keokuk sought to revitalize the branch, as did Cecil Rideout in 1936. Johnson's efforts were apparently futile, but Rideout's work resulted in a reorganized branch that included a few of the original members of 1921.[70]

A committee formed in 1948 conducted an intensive survey of Burlington's black population focusing on education, housing, and employment. Completed in 1951, the survey reported that 300 of Burlington's 30,000 residents were black. Of 56 black heads of household surveyed, a disproportionate number of those 25 and older had less than a high school education. A high percentage (89 percent) of black heads of household were employed. Compared with Burlington's white population, more black heads of household were employed in unskilled jobs and fewer in manufacturing industries. African-Americans were dispersed in small clusters throughout the city. While their rate of home ownership was higher than average for the city, their homes were older and in greater need of repair than the city average. Many real estate firms (8 of 13) and all rental agencies either would not serve blacks or practiced restrictions in their service. The survey also found that many Burlington businesses (55 percent), especially restaurants and taverns, would not serve blacks. Another 25 percent had qualifications regarding service, such as limiting service to carry-outs, serving only after normal hours, or segregated seating.[71]

The Burlington NAACP reorganized at this time and reported 71 paid memberships in 1950. The Burlington branch hosted the state conference in 1952 and provided the conference with its president, Betty Holsteen, a white public school music teacher.[72]

Iowa City

In November 1921, William Edwin Taylor, writing on behalf of the 50 "colored students" at the University of Iowa, contacted NAACP secretary James Weldon Johnson regarding the students' problems finding housing. While the university faculty and staff

---

On June 29 R. A. Dobson, who had written the national office seven years earlier, sent the NAACP a check for an impressive $125, representing membership fees collected at an organizational meeting. On July 10, 1922, the Sioux City branch was officially in business.

treated the students equally with others, townspeople behaved otherwise. The African-American students banded together to buy a house on contract, but forces gathered to deny them possession once their identity was learned. Attorney S. Joe Brown from Des Moines had taken on their case. William Taylor, a law student in his sixth year at the university, was acting as plaintiff. Taylor asked whether the NAACP could advance money for the mortgage. Johnson responded that it was impossible for the NAACP to do such a thing, but encouraged Taylor to seek support from the various branches in Iowa. There was no further reference to this case in the records of the branches.[73]

More than four decades later, on September 9, 1963, an Iowa City Human Relations Commission established by ordinance began meeting. Its primary concern was housing, an issue that had earlier brought together an ad hoc fair-housing committee that represented many organizations, including the clergy and religious leaders of Iowa City, the League of Women Voters, and "social concerns" groups of various local churches. The League of Women Voters seems to have been the strongest non-religious group working on these problems. No NAACP or other group specifically representing black people in Iowa City was involved in local housing issues at the time the committee's efforts produced the ordinance creating the commission.

Early on, the commission learned that the worst housing discrimination occurred in accommodations recommended by the University of Iowa hospital. Several of the renters listed by the hospital discriminated on the basis of race. The commission also discovered the questionable practice of asking for "color" on the local voting registration form and suggested that it be removed or blocked out.

One of the main accomplishments of Iowa City's Human Rights Commission was the City Council's approval of a much-debated Fair Housing Ordinance. Passed on August 18, 1964, the ordinance came just two and a half months after Des Moines established a Fair Housing Practices statement. Both preceded the state ordinance by three years. In August 1965, at the advice of the Human Rights Commission, the Iowa City Council's attorney began including a non-discrimination clause in city contracts.

Without a paid staff, the commission struggled some in its first few years. Nonetheless during 1972 the commission took several steps to further civil rights. Promoting an Affirmative Action and Equal Employment policy that the city adopted in

May, the commission also sought to eliminate restrictions on minority memberships in private clubs. When the Iowa Attorney General advised against pursuing this matter, the commission looked at possible grounds for action based on age or physical or mental disability.

Not until 1979 was an NAACP branch formed in Iowa City, with Robert V. Morris as president. The branch pushed for an affirmative action policy rather than just a plan,[74] tackled race discrimination at a local disco,[75] raised a cry when the Ku Klux Klan threatened Washington, D. C. Representative Walter Fauntroy,[76] and criticized the state's police academy for having all-white classes. However, the basic nature of the NAACP was reactive, which made sustained action difficult. By 1990, with no one willing to take on leadership of the Iowa City branch, what momentum remained passed to the African-American Council at the University of Iowa. There were more issues being addressed on campus than in the surrounding Iowa City community at that time.

Sioux City

In the fall of 1914 Mary Child McNerney of the national office wrote to three people in Sioux City — George Austin, L. Maxwell, and L. F. Sadler — regarding Dr. Joel Spingarn's organizing trip to Iowa scheduled for late November. None of them apparently responded. But in February 1915 Sioux City's Dr. R.A. Dobson wrote W. E. B. DuBois regarding material to organize a branch. McNerney sent two copies of a branch constitution and the requirement for "fifteen representative colored people, including some white people if possible."[77] But again nothing happened.

Years later, in 1922, in response to a letter from J. N. Boyd in Sioux City, the director of branches sent some literature and a request for the names of 50 people with a list of their occupations. D. W. Short, writing on stationery of the Cedar Hill Lodge No. 80, F.A.A.Y. Masons, wrote the NAACP for the same material, as did Robert M. Williams, pastor of Haddock Memorial M. E. Mission. The director of branches sent the same form letters to all of them. Only Williams responded, announcing an open meeting to be held July 9, 1922. Inexplicably, on June 29 R. A. Dobson, who had written the national office seven years earlier, sent the NAACP a check for an impressive $125, representing membership fees collected at an organizational meeting. Executive authorization was swift. On July 10, 1922, the Sioux City branch was officially in business.

Robert V. Morris, founder and president of the NAACP branch in Iowa City, 1979–81 (courtesy Robert V. Morris)

Rev. John Brigham, president of the NAACP branch in Sioux City, 1950–51 (courtesy John Brigham)

SANFORD CENTER
GIVEN TO THE PEOPLE OF
SIOUX CITY BY STELLA AND
ARTHUR SANFORD TO FURTHER
INTERRACIAL UNDERSTANDING
AND BETTER COMMUNITY LIVING

Plaque dedicating Sioux City's
Sanford Center, which was built
in 1951. Standing in front of the
building are George Boykin, Arthur
Sanford, and Jack Robinson.
(Sanford Center)

Of the 117 people who signed the branch's application and contributed to its start, there were 18 butchers, 17 housewives, 11 custodians, 9 ministers, 8 packing house employees, 5 porters, 5 proprietors (pool hall, cafe, carpet cleaners, brothel, and shoe-shining parlor) and 24 people in other occupations. Among them were the editor of the *Sioux City Tribune*, the president of Methodist Morningside College, and a lawyer.

Two years later the branch sought assistance for a young man who had spent ten years in prison at Fort Madison. The local branch believed he had been a scapegoat in the death of a white man. Walter F. White responded with the guidelines by which the national NAACP measured cases. White wrote that "first, the NAACP enters those cases only where it is clearly evident that injustice has been done or is about to be done because of color and, second, where such activity by the Association will result in a decision affecting the rights of colored people generally."[78]

Two months later, J. N. Boyd, publisher of the black *Enterprise* newspaper in Sioux City, wrote for guidance in dealing with a plan by some white officials to set aside a tract of land in a local cemetery "for our people."[79] Robert Bagnall, director of branches, urged action by "the colored citizens and the better whites of the city" against this proposal, adding "it is bad enough for attempts to be made to [J]im [C]row the living, but is certainly the limit when they attempt to [J]im [C]row the dead."[80] A few days later, Bagnall sent Boyd a letter for use in the *Enterprise* newspaper. "I am astonished to learn that the local authorities most

likely actuated by the propaganda of the Ku Klux Klan have submitted to the colored people the humiliating proposition that they agree to a separate tract of ground as a municipal [Jim Crow cemetery]," wrote Bagnall.

"It is reprehensible to attempt to segregate the living because of color or race; but it is a shameless act to attempt to segregate the dead on the theory that even the corpses of white and colored people should not be lodged in the same ground. This propaganda smacks of the rankest Southern sentiment, and indicates that there is an attempt to turn Iowa into a place just as prejudiced as Texas. Every self-respecting colored person should bitterly protest against this unfair and uncalled-for attempt and to make it his business to use whatever influence he has to defeat for re-election any city official who countenances such attempts.

"This attempt is an insult to the colored citizens of Sioux City. It is an effort to create a caste condition and to impress a brand of inferiority on Negroes. Liberal minded whites who believe in democracy in America should be just as much against such efforts as colored people."[81]

The Sioux City branch was inactive from 1925 to 1928. J. N. Boyd sought to revitalize it in 1928 and in 1930. In late 1930 or early 1931 a community forum was organized to address issues such as the case of the Scottsboro boys.

A. J. Hicks, expressing an interest in supporting the defense fund, wrote to William Andrews, the NAACP's special legal assistant, asking for information about *The Liberator*, a magazine covering the case. Bagnall responded that *The Liberator* was a Communist organ. The Communist Party through the International Labor Defense (ILD), he said, had attempted to take over the case completely while discrediting the NAACP.

Henry R. Kendricks, secretary of Sioux City's community forum, wrote in 1932 that the forum would like to be the nucleus of a reorganized NAACP branch. Bagnall encouraged Kendricks to contact Boyd, who was sent the branch's charter from 1922. C. C. Bush, a dentist, responded that due to previous bad experiences and the propaganda of the ILD, many people were unwilling to become NAACP members. Only 28 had been recruited at that point, too few to form a branch. Bush also wondered if ministers were automatically members. Director of Branches Robert Bagnall answered there were no automatic memberships of any kind. In other correspondence between Bush and the national office, William Pickens also reiterated that ministers were not automatically members, unless an individual chapter made that rule for themselves.

In November 1932, Boyd wrote Walter White that he had found the original charter, but that of the 38 members who gathered to consider the direction of the NAACP, perspectives and opinions were so divergent that nothing could be decided. Still, Boyd offered to head up the chapter if no one else could pull it together. Bagnall authorized Boyd to call a meeting to elect officers. Boyd's efforts were apparently frustrated, then and in the years ahead. In 1939, he wrote to E. Frederic Morrow, branch coordinator, about efforts to revive the Sioux City branch, hoping again that its charter would not be revoked. Again in 1945 Boyd offered to organize the branch, which had now been dormant since 1926.

In July 1946, Rev. H.R. Boston wrote inquiring about starting a branch. In September Gloster Current, the NAACP's director of branches, at the recommendation of Iowa State Conference President Ike Smalls, wrote Oscar Nevings about starting up the branch. The national office became aware that they were working with two people and wanted to be sure the two were working together. Again Boston wrote, asking that someone from the national office come explain the NAACP to local people. Ike Smalls arranged for S. Joe Brown to address a mass meeting on Sunday, February 9, 1947. Three months later, on May 24, 1947, Morningside College professor John Magee announced the organization of the NAACP's Sioux City branch with 92 members.[82] Chartered on July 9, 1947, the reorganized branch's first president was Mrs. Earl Roadman, wife of Morningside College's president.

According to Miss Kendricks, daughter of the community forum's secretary, Sioux City's NAACP branch was reorganized with "massive support." Charles Howard, past president of the Des Moines branch, spoke at a December 1 meeting, linking the urgency of the NAACP to the fact that "a million Negroes served in the armed forces during world war." Howard noted that "representatives of the [NAACP] organization appeared before the United Nations to present an analysis of discrimination in America."[83] Clearly the involvement of African-Americans in the war and the creation of the United Nations stimulated support for the NAACP in the late 1940s.

In 1949 the Sioux City branch hosted the Iowa Conference. A major theme for panel discussions was community coordination, especially for the purpose of abolishing discrimination in employment. Thurgood Marshall, special counsel for the national association, conducted a workshop and gave the address at a public meeting Sunday afternoon. The Rev. John Brigham, minister of the First Unitarian Church, wrote Marshall that summer, announcing the branch's decision to take legal action against discrimination at Sioux City's municipal pools. Brigham also asked if the Iowa Conference could afford a secretary to work with the branches across the state. Leroy Carter responded that only three states, each with more than 15,000 African-Americans, had such secretaries and even then it was difficult to raise enough money to support them.[84]

In 1950 three members of the Sioux City branch held state offices. Brigham was on the board; David Singer, a Jewish attorney, was second vice-president; and Mary Cabell was secretary. In 1951 Singer became president. In 1952 Helen Calloway was secretary, and Singer served on the conference board.[85]

In the early 1950s, the branch focused its attention on communications and continued recruiting. Marjory Bovis contacted the national office about starting youth chapters, and John Brigham inquired about radio scripts. The NAACP sent Brigham a question-and-answer script and a copy of "The Ordeal of Sergeant Dunbar," a half-hour dramatization broadcast over NBC on February 10, 1951, and encouraged him to contact radio station WMCA in New York for other scripts.[86]

The branch enrolled 124 members in 1951 but had had no renewals by October 1952. Brigham, who was president in 1950-51, was succeeded by Rabbi Albert Gordon. The membership was 178 in 1953 and 154 in 1954. The first black president, Mrs. Helen Crosswhite, who had served previously as branch secretary, was installed December 16, 1954.

One of the NAACP's national projects in the early 1950s was for blacks and whites together to test racial discrimination at restaurants and hotels. A black person seeking a hotel room might be denied. Then a white person would seek a room. If one were made available to the white person, then they would return together to confront the management. Discrimination in accommodations touched the famous as well. Boxer Joe Louis was refused service in a Sioux City hotel coffee shop, and opera singer Marian Anderson was refused lodging in a local hotel.[87]

On February 16, 1951, Jewish, Unitarian, and black NAACP leaders succeeded in persuading the city to pass a human rights ordinance to prohibit discriminatory practices based on race, color,

"It is reprehensible . . . to segregate the living because of color or race; but it is a shameless act . . . to segregate the dead on the theory that even the corpses of white and colored people should not be lodged in the same ground."

religion, creed, or ancestry. At first the ordinance addressed only the employment of municipal employees, but in 1958 the ordinance was amended to be applicable to all employers of ten or more employees.

Employment of black teachers was another struggle. The first black teacher in Sioux City, Evelyn Freeman, was hired in April 1955 after a yearlong effort.[88] Freeman had been a substitute teacher for two years, but her application for full-time work was put off because she allegedly had difficulty maintaining discipline and then because she had gone "over the superintendent's head" in going to the school board. The next year she resumed substitute teaching, and the NAACP made plans to meet with the Board of Education in March 1955. But the NAACP was told to wait until two new people were elected to the Board of Education. In response, the NAACP urged questioning of the candidates' position on hiring black teachers. In the meantime, there were new reports of Freeman having a discipline problem at a local junior high school. The next school year, Freeman was finally given a contract, and she began teaching at Lincoln Elementary school on September 1, 1955. The following year Curtis Hayes was hired to teach at Woodrow Wilson Junior High. He left in June 1960 for California, and Freeman followed suit the next June. After a year passed, another black teacher was hired and a few years later a fourth. Still, in 1968 there were but two black teachers in the Sioux City public schools.

African-American job applicants faced discrimination in other fields as well. In 1955, James Daniels and Eddie Simms applied for positions on the Sioux City police force. One was considered to be too old, the other was told he had applied too late.[89] As late as 1968 there were still no blacks on the Sioux City police force. Although Sioux City had a civil rights commission in these years, there was no paid staff until January 13, 1964, which made its impact negligible.

The history of the Sioux City branch shows strong support at times mixed with times of conflict and distrust. Clearly the immediate post-war periods were times of high organization. By contrast, organization was difficult from the late 1920s into the early 1940s.

The collaboration of white Methodist (especially at Morningside College), Unitarian, Jewish, and African-American leaders in Sioux City in the late 1940s was somewhat unique among

the chapters. Jewish leadership was a factor in Centerville and Des Moines as well, particularly around World War 2, and multi-religious support coalesced in Cedar Rapids in the 1960s. Many people recognized that anti-Semitism and American racism were linked, as the NAACP had recognized in the 1920s regarding the agenda of the Ku Klux Klan. Thus in many communities Jewish and black people joined with others for the pursuit of justice and dignity for all people.

Ames

W. G. Madison, a plumbing engineer in Ames, wrote the NAACP on February 8, 1927, that although there were few local cases of discrimination, they seemed intractable. Things seemed to be getting worse, wrote Madison, and African-Americans had formed an "Ames Protective League," which its members saw as a potential NAACP branch. But to reach the required 50 members they would have to enlist every local African-American plus a few white people. Robert Bagnall, the director of branches, responded that the national office would authorize an Ames branch with fewer than 50 members. Over the next few years the branch continued to maintain memberships in the 25–30 range.

H. C. Huling, responding to a letter from William Pickens in 1932, reported that the Ames branch was down to 14 or 15 members. A visit by Pickens was ill-advised, wrote Huling, since the branch was too small to host him. In fact, they had to give up their meeting place, since the cost of $24 per year was beyond their means. Pickens did, however, visit the small branch on April 13, 1933, receiving $10 toward his travel costs. That September the national office requested funds to help find discriminatory passages in various industrial codes. The branch sent in the $2 requested.

In 1935 Mrs. C. A. Anthony wrote Iowa's U.S. senator, L. J. Dickinson, regarding the anti-lynching bill. Dickinson promised to "keep her view in mind."[90] Timothy T. Lewis, branch secretary, forwarded this letter to Walter White at the national office, as the only response the branch had received from their Iowa legislators. The NAACP secretary responded by encouraging Lewis to write Dickinson back asking him to submit an anti-lynching bill as part of a goal to have 100 such bills on the floor. Twenty-three had already been submitted.[91]

In February 1938, the branch announced its termination. Its leaders had died and most members had moved away from

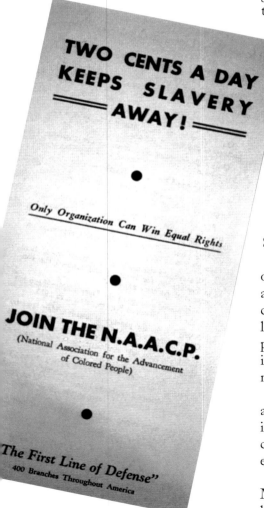

An NAACP membership appeal during World War 2 (SHSI Des Moines)

Ames. Despite this, Pickens in New York again offered to visit the branch in 1939. M. D. Lawrie sought to make clear to him that they were too few in number to carry on or host a meeting with him. This response only strengthened Pickens's resolve, which he made clear in a letter full of flexibility and recommendations for the Ames branch.[92] Lawrie responded, adding that not only had members moved away but so had the favorably inclined clergy. An attempt at a meeting would produce only three or four people. Pickens persisted, announcing that he would be in Ames on March 22.[93] Finally in September, Lawrie wrote saying the only people interested besides himself were his wife and one other person. As it turned out Pickens visited Marshalltown that week with great success, helping the branch there secure its existence.

After World War 2 the situation in Ames, home of Iowa State University, was similar to that in Cedar Falls and Iowa City. A Human Relations Commission, established by ordinance in 1977, sponsored seminars on fair housing and cultural diversity. Since 1991 it has also addressed questions of housing and employment for people of alternative sexual orientations.

An NAACP branch was established in Ames in 1995. There had been a student branch since the early 1980s, but with a changing student body, its leadership and membership ebbed and flowed. Over the years the student branch had raised issues of racial balance on the faculty and in the curriculum, but issues in Ames itself had not been addressed. Since its formation, the community branch has focused on employment and curriculum in the city schools, service at restaurants, and employment at the Iowa Department of Transportation, which is located in Ames. The biggest issue at Iowa State University recently has concerned the naming of a campus building for Iowa suffrage leader Carrie Chapman Catt, some of whose remarks in the early 1900s have been interpreted as racist.

Fort Madison

The Fort Madison branch had three beginnings — the 1920s, the late 1940s, and the 1960s. On February 9, 1927, the NAACP granted executive authorization for a local chapter upon receipt of a dollar each from 55 people — 20 house workers, 20 laborers on the Santa Fe railroad, 3 pastors, and 8 others. The first president was Lucy King, a house worker.

In 1931, 1933, and again in 1939, the national office, desperately in need of funds, tried to revive the local branch.

Iowa NAACP leaders (left to right) Bessie Blake, Estherville; Dr. Harry Harper, Fort Madison; Norma Ashby, Fort Madison; and Robert Wright Sr., Des Moines, pictured here in the 1960s (courtesy Robert Wright Sr.)

Rev. C. H. Copeland of Bethel AME Church wrote of his efforts to resuscitate the branch in 1939.[94] That year also, the president of the Fort Madison branch sought legal advice when her son was harassed by local police. Harassment was a weapon used against the black community, causing great worry and demoralization, particularly in a community without African-American lawyers.

Fort Madison's Dr. Harry D. Harper Sr. earned an undergraduate degree at the University of Iowa. He went on to Howard University because the University of Iowa obstetrics program denied him entry based on his color. Returning to Iowa to practice medicine in Fort Madison, Dr. Harper contributed to the reinvigoration of the branch in the 1950s and 1960s and became chair of the Iowa Human Rights Commission.[95] In the 1940s Harper's daughter, Virginia, participated in the integration of Currier Hall at the University of Iowa.[96] Ms. Harper continued to provide leadership in Fort Madison until her death in early September 1997.[97]

Two issues the Fort Madison branch worked on vigorously over the years were, first, the situation of African-Americans in the Iowa State Prison and, second, the preservation of communities in neighborhoods threatened by highway construction. A major issue at the prison was the hiring of guards. African-American inmates advocated hiring guards of the same background. In the 1970s a branch of the NAACP was established within the prison.[98]

Georgine Morris, founder of the Iowa State Conference of Branches, which drew together leaders of NAACP branches in Des Moines, Keokuk, Council Bluffs, Davenport, and Marshalltown, as well as representatives of other Iowa communities. (courtesy Robert V. Morris)

Lionel Foster of Mason City (Mason City Globe Gazette)

Mason City

Eugene Bell wrote to Robert Bagnall on May 25, 1927, regarding establishment of an authorized NAACP committee in Mason City.[99] A group in Mason City hoped eventually to become a branch but at that point had only 11 members. In November, Bell wrote the NAACP Executive Committee that the Mason City group had an executive committee and also a set of officers — two different groups of people. John Taylor was chair of the executive committee and Horace Spencer was president. On December 2, the Mason City branch received executive authorization by the national office. Among the 50 original members were 19 housewives, 7 laborers, 3 cooks, 2 ministers, and 19 other people listing 15 different occupations. Cement contractor Horace Spencer was president; railroad employee Paul Scott, vice-president; clergyman A. L. Woolfolk, secretary; and housewife Emma Stratton, treasurer.

Bell wrote Bagnall at the end of the next year that branch meetings had ceased. The branch had been meeting alternately in the two churches served by the pastors in their membership, but one of the pastors was dismissed and the other church held too many meetings to allow the NAACP space. During the first year the branch had made three investigations of incidents but "found nothing contrary to good judgment."[100] The branch also raised $104.75 to care for the widow and two children of one of the pastors who had signed on as a founding member of the branch.

Apparently the Mason City branch secretary had not kept good records. As a result, many of those who signed up as members did not receive certificates of membership. This handicapped efforts to get renewals. Mason City branch vice-president Paul Scott during this year sought to organize a group in Fort Dodge as well as to work in Mason City.

In 1931 Eugene Bell wrote the national office saying that things were going poorly again. He had been injured, he explained, and had been out of commission for a year and a half. Paul Scott, the branch's president, was unable to hold regular meetings since he was out of town frequently in his work as a cook on the railroad. Bell complained that Scott also attempted to handle many issues on his own rather than consulting with the board.[101]

Bell wrote again in 1934 to say that people were unwilling to "start up" again because of a bad feeling remaining from the inability of Scott, the president, to prove that he had submitted money to the national as he claimed he did. In 1939 Scott himself

wrote the national office, saying that he intended to start the branch up again. Apparently he was successful. Officers of the revived branch were Scott, chairman; Marie Maddox, secretary; and Mrs. A. A. McGinty, treasurer. In 1940 Scott was treasurer, and Mrs. McGinty served on the executive board of the newly formed Iowa Conference of Branches.[102]

In 1942 Scott was vice-president of the conference, but by 1945 there were no members of the Iowa Conference of Branches' executive board from Mason City. In 1946 Mrs. P. L. Scott was second vice-president of the conference. For the next two years, Reverend Scott was on the state conference executive committee, but after 1949 there was no representation from Mason City at the state conference.[103]

Mason City reported 73 members in 1945 and 66 in 1946 but by 1947 the branch had become dormant with only 9 members, according to its president, Rev. Jordan Ray. The branch reorganized again in the 1960s and 1970s but then again lapsed.

In 1964 Mason City formed a Human Rights Advisory Commission, led by Willie Haddix and others. This was a "blue-stocking committee" that sought to keep things quiet.[104] The commission did not become pro-active until a part-time secretary was hired in 1972. (The position became full-time in 1973.) In 1978 the commission ordinance was rewritten to provide for a full-time director, who was hired in 1979. The current commission, which conducts its own investigations, has been directed since 1973 by Lionel Foster, who is also the president of the State Association of Human Rights Commissioners.[105]

Marshalltown

At the recommendation of Keokuk's Selby Johnson, the national office wrote D. N. Crosthwaite on May 20, 1927, inviting Crosthwaite to organize an NAACP branch in Marshalltown. There was no recorded response to this invitation. However, in September 1932, I. L. Brown wrote Robert Bagnall requesting information about starting a branch. As only 15 people could be found by March 1933, the national office granted Marshalltown status as an authorized committee. The president was Brown; vice-president, J. P. Burton; secretary, James Wilder; and treasurer, Mrs. I. L. Brown. Another 10 names were submitted the next month, 7 more in May 1934, and an additional few in succeeding months.

In 1935 William Pickens, NAACP field secretary, offered to visit Marshalltown, but Brown responded saying that they could not host as "we have been pretty hard hit here this winter."[106] When Pickens persisted, saying that the money was not so important, Brown accepted the offer, setting March 24 as the date. Pickens requested a change to March 22 and then to March 27 or 29. Finally the date was lost altogether because of "the slowness with which Marshalltown and Des Moines acted in answering our letters."[107]

In February 1936 only five people renewed their memberships. "Everyone is out of work here and a [it is a] hard winter on top of that," Brown explained. "[I]t is hard to get money as it is badly need at home." Brown noted also that there was a local coal shortage, and he apologized to Pickens that the situation there advised against a visit until the spring.[108]

On March 15, branch secretary Rose Bannon wrote to the national office of her desire to stimulate new interest in the NAACP. On March 26, Bannon, having been chosen membership campaign director, wrote Juanita Jackson asking for pamphlets and membership cards. A few days later Brown sent Walter White a dollar for membership from Marshalltown Mayor G. W. Darling. Bannon arranged for a 95-day campaign from May 1 to August 4, with a goal of $100 (100 members). The results of this campaign are not clear from the historical record.

In 1938 Bannon wrote Jackson again regarding their annual membership drive, which began with a "wonderful program with a large attendance."[109] Fred O. Morrow, president of the Des Moines branch, delivered the main address.[110] In May the Marshalltown branch sponsored a Republican rally, which was well attended. This is an indication of the strength and political relevance, as well as the party affiliation, of the local branch, which was characteristic of the late 1930s.

In September Bannon wrote the NAACP of the achievement of 45 paid members and of close connections with people from the Des Moines branch, particularly Georgine Morris and Fred Morrow. Morris's report on the annual meeting of the national NAACP resulted in an effort in Marshalltown to organize a youth council. Willa Brown was elected youth advisor but lacked materials to start the council. Within the branch itself, Bannon was convinced that the goal of 50 members was within reach, even though there were only 300 Negroes in the city.[111] By the end of October they had achieved the 50 members, after "eight long years working for it."[112]

Executive authorization was granted on November 4, and election of officers was held on November 11, 1938. I. wL. Brown

was elected president; F. W. Wilder, vice-president; Bannon, secretary; and Samuel Brown, treasurer. Of the 50 members, 20 were laborers and 7 were housewives. An unusual number of public officials were members, starting with Mayor Darling and including the city clerk, the county recorder, and a state representative. There were two ministers and a social worker as well.

In January 1939 Bannon invited William Pickens, director of branches, to visit Marshalltown if he was in or near Des Moines in March. Plans for the visit developed somewhat slowly, though Bannon assured the national office on March 14 that "at this late date the women are going to work hard, for a big meeting."[113]

When Pickens finally visited Marshalltown he spoke on "The Fight for Democracy" to a capacity crowd at the Second Baptist Church. Bannon wrote to the NAACP saying that "he is the most outstanding, inspiring personality of our Race ever to visit the city and taught us much about the early American Negro."[114]

In 1940 Bannon became the first education committee chair in the new state conference. Miss Jesse Walker of Marshalltown became chair of the speakers bureau. In 1942 Marshalltown's Rev. A. Nelson was second vice-president of the conference; Ealy Morrow, treasurer; and Bannon, education chair. In 1943, when the state conference chose Marshalltown for its first annual meeting outside Des Moines, Rose Bannon Johnson became secretary as well as chair of the conference's education committee, and Ealy Morrow remained treasurer. Reverend Nelson was president of the local Marshalltown branch at that time.

In January 1945, Rose Johnson remained secretary, Irma Morrow was youth council advisor, Nelson was speakers bureau committee chair, and Margaret Dobbin was youth council president. By February Artis Maxwell was on the executive board and Mildred Spencer was president of the youth council, making 5 of the 19 officers of the state conference members of the Marshalltown branch, second only to Des Moines, which provided 9. Membership in the Marshalltown branch in 1945 was 105.

In 1946 Wilmer Johnson, Rose Bannon Johnson's husband, was president and Maggie Clark secretary of the Marshalltown branch. In 1947, the Marshalltown branch membership reached its all-time high of 121. That same year Rose Johnson became the first non-Des Moines president of the state conference, a position she held for two years. Mrs. Johnson's increasing influence was remarkable. Her commitment to the NAACP was evident over

Rose Bannon Johnson of Marshalltown (courtesy Rose Bannon Johnson)

Lulu Wallace, founder of the Clinton branch in 1944 (courtesy Deborah Greene)

Clemmie Hightower (left), first secretary of the Clinton branch; Vinson Jetter (right), also of Clinton (courtesy Clemmie Hightower / Vinson Jetter)

the previous decade, beginning with her willingness to reverse decisions of a weary Marshalltown committee president back in 1936, to lead a successful membership drive in 1938, and then to see through a visit by Pickens in 1939, even when the branch's president had not encouraged him to come.

By 1950 Rose Johnson had completed her terms as president, but she continued to serve on the executive committee and to chair the education committee of the state conference. Artis Maxwell was chair of the program committee. Marshalltown branch membership was 112.

From 1952 to 1954 Wilmer Johnson, who had been the Marshalltown branch president, served as the state conference president. Rose Johnson was on the board. In March she wrote Gloster Current, director of branches, inviting him to visit the Marshalltown chapter during the spring membership drive. She also spoke for Waterloo, where M. F. Fields had just died, and for Cedar Rapids, Ottumwa, Davenport, Council Bluffs, and Mason City. She expressed disappointment in David Singer of Sioux City, who had done nothing as state conference president despite the high hopes everyone had had for him. She appealed to Current to "scour" Iowa to "revive us again."[115] Marshalltown branch membership had dropped to 92 in 1951 and 70 in 1952.

At the conference's annual meeting in 1953 at Cedar Rapids, Irma Morrow and Rose Johnson both participated in panel discussions, Morrow on community coordination and Johnson on teaching race relations in Iowa schools. In 1955, Johnson took on yet another role, chair of the Four-F program. That year Morrow was the Marshalltown branch president and Maggie Clark was secretary. Memberships in the branch continued to decline: 52 members in 1953 and 46 in 1954. A slight rebound, to 51, occurred in 1955.

The Morrow family had provided leadership for the black community from the early years of the century. Irma Morrow's father, a foreman on the Chicago Northwestern railroad, brought 300 people from Alabama. Irma, three years old when her family arrived in Marshalltown in 1914, became a prominent leader in the years following World War 2. The local NAACP branch — created to deal with housing, employment, and accommodations issues common across the country — had the support of the Marshalltown mayor, who maintained publicly that America was a country for all people and that discrimination was not to be tolerated.

By the 1980s the branch had ceased activity, but in 1990 the Rev. Emanuel Yeboah from Ghana became acquainted with Mary Robinson, the state president, who encouraged him to start a branch. The 1990s branch has drawn primarily on white membership. One of its cases involved an Asian Indian's effort to find suitable housing, suggesting possible future directions for NAACP activity, as Iowa communities become increasingly diverse.

Clinton

Clinton, a small city on the Mississippi River, developed its NAACP branch in 1944, due to the leadership of Lula (Katie) Wallace.[116] Wallace brought the idea and materials to start an NAACP branch back with her from a trip to Kansas City, Missouri, where she had met Roy Wilkins touring the country to promote the NAACP. Wallace became the Clinton branch's first president, and Clemmie Hightower was its first secretary. Their goal at the beginning was primarily educational: to inform the black community of the history and goals of the NAACP, and thus draw them into the larger regional and national discussion.

That they were overlooked at the state conference meeting in Cedar Rapids the next year suggests the extent to which they operated on their own, while others in the state were in touch with one another. Thereafter they were included. Wallace and Hightower were succeeded by Fred Judson and Roy Dabner, respectively. Later, in the mid-1950s, Judson and Hightower were still active. In 1955, Judson was president and Hightower was secretary. Soon after, however, the branch subsided for lack of leadership and issues. The feeling in the late 1950s was that the work had been done.

Another civil rights group, Interfaith Interracial, emerged in Clinton in the early 1960s. Led by a Presbyterian minister and two Catholic laymen, together with members of the black community including Clemmie Hightower and Vinson Jetter, this group focused on cross-cultural understanding.[117] Coming together at the same time as the national Catholic Interracial Commission was gaining strength and as the National Council of Churches was promoting its Commission on Race and Religion, groups like Interfaith Interracial established a basis for white Protestant and Catholic cooperation with the black community on race issues.

One of Interfaith Interracial's projects tested open housing, especially for rental property. A black couple would respond to an advertisement, and upon being rejected or told that "it had just been rented, or was no longer available," a white couple would inquire at the same place. If the white couple found that the property was still available, then the owner was confronted. The process was similar to techniques used in Sioux City in the early 1950s and Cedar Rapids in the early 1960s. Gradually Interfaith Interracial made some progress in achieving a more open housing situation. However, the Presbyterian minister who led the group found his own church reacting negatively to his involvement, and he was pressured to move to another congregation.

Encouraged by people from Davenport, the Clinton NAACP branch reorganized in the 1970s. Roy and Nadine Dabner led the effort. In 1980 the branch reported a membership of 80. The Rev. Lionel Davis Sr. served as president of the local chapter in 1986 and became the second vice-president of the Iowa-Nebraska Division, serving on the membership committee.

In 1993 Vinson Jetter reorganized the branch once more.[118] Since then the branch has developed youth programs to serve an influx of black families moving to Clinton from Chicago, Louisiana, and Mississippi. A major project for the branch has been Youth for a Safe Non-Violent Summer, a summer fair sponsored by the NAACP and funded by the Drug Free Community Schools Committee. Begun in 1995, the fair is held each summer. The branch also helped with a summer program for troubled youth, housed at the Bethel AME Church.[119] Thus Clinton presents a good example of a branch rising, falling, and rising again as a result of changing leadership and changing issues.

Grinnell College and Grinnell

In 1920 Hosea Campbell, a black Grinnell College student, wrote to W.E.B. DuBois. The national office's response came from Catherine Lealtad, who asked whether Campbell wanted to start an NAACP branch. Having discussed the matter with other students — both the four blacks on campus and some whites — Campbell decided against it. Most of the white students knew so little of the organization, he reasoned, that it would be hard to explain it to them.[120]

In 1947 Professor John H. Burma wrote to Charles P. Howard of Des Moines about a possible Grinnell College branch. Apparently Burma had had some contact with Howard's son regarding an exchange program, part of which had already taken place involving some white female students going to Hampton Institute in Virginia.[121] Howard contacted national membership

secretary Lucille Black about this, and then wrote Gloster Current. He was a bit amazed that an all-white group would want to join the NAACP, he said, but he recognized that the exchange with Hampton had stirred interest and that such a move was in keeping with the abolitionist and liberal traditions of the college. Howard also noted interest in the NAACP on the part of white faculty and students from the South, both at Grinnell and at Drake University in Des Moines.

A month later, in early January 1948, Current wrote an encouraging letter to Burma, who responded in February asking for information. Phyllis Hook, secretary-treasurer of the Grinnell group sent in memberships for 61 people in April.[122]

New officers elected in May 1950 included Andrew Billingsley, president; Don McInnes, vice-president; Ruth Sears, secretary-treasurer; Louisella Kurth, publicity; and Alan Lee, membership. In February 1951, Sears respectfully declined the request to contribute to the national Defense Fund, begging poverty as college students. The next week she wondered if they could become an official college chapter. This was met with support and approval by the national office. At the end of the school year in June 1952, the chapter disbanded, turning over its entire budget of $5.17 to the national office. Thus ended a four-year experiment on a primarily white college campus.[123]

Seventeen years later, representatives of the Grinnell Ministerial Association and the League of Women Voters approached Grinnell's City Council in 1969 to request the formation of Commission on Human Rights to deal with fair housing issues, based on the 1965 Iowa Civil Rights Law. Grinnell College had talked about diversity issues and local leaders felt they should have a local entity to respond to situations. There was no real opposition, and the local human rights ordinance, based on the state ordinance, was passed in 1969 and took effect in January 1970. The ordinance at first had no subpoena power, but later amendments provided this. Between 1970 and 1997, 40 claims were addressed, but not all had probable cause. One complaint about racial discrimination at a local restaurant resulted in a determination that the establishment was just badly managed.[124]

Cedar Falls

An indication of how the social climate had changed in Iowa by the early 1970s is the organization of the Cedar Falls Human Rights Commission in 1974. The Cedar Falls group was trained

Sociology professor John Burma, organizer of the Grinnell College branch, 1948 (Grinnell College Archives)

Ruby Sutton, president of the Dubuque NAACP, presenting awards to winners of the Martin Luther King Jr. essay contest (courtesy Ruby Sutton)

A Des Moines march urging passage of the Civil Rights Act, July 1963 (Tom Patrick photo / Des Moines Register)

by the Education Director of the Iowa Civil Rights Commission. The processes of investigation and conciliation had already been established. Complaints on the basis of race during 1975 were filed by both blacks and whites.[125] Home of the University of Northern Iowa, Cedar Falls traditionally experiences more problems in the university community than in the town at large. As in Iowa City, many complaints were thus made within the university system, which is not under the jurisdiction of the city's civil rights commission.

Dubuque

In 1840 more than half the African-Americans in the Iowa Territory lived in Dubuque.[126] However, Dubuque quickly became a hostile environment. Working-class Catholic Germans and Irish came to settle Dubuque during the middle and late nineteenth century, drastically changing the ethnic balance of the city in a short time. With no core of African-Americans to establish churches or social organizations, others bypassed the city. While there was communication between individuals in Dubuque and the national NAACP offices before World War 2, no branch was organized until much later in the century.

A 1980s attempt to attract more minority people to Dubuque resulted in a wave of fear and defensiveness in the community. In 1989 black and white community leaders established a branch of the NAACP. Issues addressed included: discrimination in the schools, including name-calling among the students and a lack of multicultural or non-sexist curriculum; housing issues; jobs; and treatment by the police before and after arrest.

All these issues were being addressed to one extent or another when a series of cross-burning incidents scandalized the city's name in the early 1990s. Since then, many steps, some quite innovative, have taken place. An investigation of discriminatory attitudes among teachers has resulted in the development of teacher sensitivity programs. Many groups in the community have been supportive of the NAACP — the Dubuque Christian Alliance, the Catholic Diocese, Loras and Clark Colleges, the University of Dubuque, and Emmaus Bible School — but none of them actually stood beside the NAACP. Still, there were many supportive individuals, and the branch's first membership drive in 1991 netted 400 people, many of them white. By 1997, however, the membership had dropped to about 100.[127]

Other Branches

Over the years, people in several other communities communicated with the national NAACP office: Fort Dodge, Manly, Montrose, Muscatine, and Perry, but ultimately were unable to form branches.[128]

Conclusion

While the NAACP reached into Iowa early in its history, successfully establishing a branch in Des Moines and sponsoring the establishment of many more branches by the early 1920s, it was a struggle to keep the branches going during the 1920s and 1930s. The Depression took a toll on these branches, forcing many to suspend operations. The effect of the Depression was two-fold. It reduced black employment, and thus reduced the resources of the black community as a whole. The creation of the state conference of branches in 1940 gave the stronger branches reason to reach out to others, and gave people in the smaller ones opportunities for leadership at the state level. While branch membership varied from year to year — and some branches failed while others came into being — overall there was stability for several years after World War 2.

Renewal of civil rights efforts in Des Moines, Sioux City, Burlington, Fort Madison, Clinton, Davenport, and Waterloo followed the war and continued into the early 1950s. With the *Brown v. Board of Education* decision in 1954, a major goal appeared achieved. A counter-movement, signified by the creation of the southern white citizens' councils following this decision, indicated the work that remained to be done in gaining civil rights for African-Americans. A new movement, to fulfill the promise of justice, was mounted.

The civil rights movement, beginning in the South in the mid-1950s, reached Iowa in the early 1960s, providing a new burst of energy into the NAACP's ongoing effort to address civil rights concerns. The Harris housing case in Cedar Rapids was one of the first signs of this resurgence in Iowa. Each Iowa community had its own issues, and activity around these local issues often led to cooperative efforts between the NAACP and groups with largely white memberships. This cooperation led to the establishment within city governments of human rights (or relations) councils (or commissions) in communities throughout Iowa, thereby legitimizing and institutionalizing the movement to preserve and extend equality for all Americans.

NOBODY'S BORN A BIGOT.

There is no mind more open or heart more willing to love than that of a young child. But teach a child hatred and prejudice and the mind begins to close, the heart to harden. Until finally, a bigot is born. Sometimes what we don't teach our children is more important than what we do.

National Conference Of Christians And Jews
Learning To Live Together: The Unfinished Task.

Janice McCulloch and Rudy Simms have led the National Conference for Community and Justice (formerly the National Conference of Christians and Jews) in Des Moines for the past 20 years. (Des Moines branch NCCJ)

Notes

1. Mary Ovington, *How the National Association for the Advancement of Colored People Began* (Baltimore: NAACP, 1914), 1.

2. For a brief overview of NAACP history, see the organization's website at <http://www.naacp.org/about>.

3. Alphabetically, first year of contact in parentheses, these are: Ames (1927), Burlington (1921), Cedar Rapids (1915), Centerville (1919), Clinton (1915), Council Bluffs (1921), Davenport (1916), Des Moines (1916), Dubuque (1930), Fort Dodge (1927), Fort Madison (1926), Grinnell College (1920), Iowa City (1924), Keokuk (1919), Manly (1931), Marshalltown (1927), Mason City (1927), Montrose (1915), Muscatine (1935), Ottumwa (1915), Perry (1926), Sioux City (1914), and Waterloo (1921). Iowa box, NAACP Files, Manuscript Division, Library of Congress [hereafter LC].

4. County (and town) with peak black population before 1980: Appanoose (Centerville), 486 (1910); Cerro Gordo (Mason City), 361 (1920); Clinton (Clinton) 436 (1910); Dallas (Perry), 409 (1930); Dubuque (Dubuque), 167 (1870); Henry (Mt. Pleasant) 509 (1880); Marshall (Marshalltown), 351 (1930); Muscatine (Muscatine), 179 (1880); Pottawattamie (Council Bluffs), 684 (1930); Wapello (Ottumwa), 793 (1900); Worth (Manly), 89 (1920). See also Chapter 2 of this book.

5. The order of executive authorization for branches is as follows: Des Moines (1915) Davenport (1918), Cedar Rapids (1919), Keokuk (1919), Centerville (1920), Council Bluffs (1920), Waterloo (1921), Burlington (1921), Sioux City (1922), Fort Madison (1926), and Mason City (1927). Fort Madison also became a branch during the 1920s. People in Ames and Manly sought to form branches, but lacked the necessary 50 signatures and $1 contributions. Groups under 50 were considered committees rather than branches. Iowa NAACP Files, 1913–1939, LC.

6. John Charles Lufkin, "Black Des Moines: A Study of Select Negro Social Organizations in Des Moines, 1890-1930," M.A. thesis, Iowa State University, 1980, 126–29.

7. John T. McGreevy, *Parish Boundaries: The Catholic Encounter with Race in the Twentieth-Century Urban North* (Chicago: Univ. of Chicago Press, 1996).

8. Dorothy Schwieder, Joseph Hraba, and Elmer Schwieder, *Buxton: Work and Racial Equality in a Coal Mining Community* (Ames: Iowa State Univ. Press, 1987).

9. Brown was a native of Keosauqua, a small town in southeast Iowa, graduated from high school in Ottumwa, served as principal in the public school at Muchakinock, the mining town predecessor to Buxton, and for a year was a professor of Greek and Latin at Bishop College, Marshall, Texas. Lufkin, 105.

10. Ibid., 62.

11. For the history of the CIC, see Marshall Ducey, ed., *The Commission on Interracial Cooperation, Papers, 1919–1944* (Ann Arbor: University Microfilms International, 1984) and *The Association of Southern Women for the Prevention of Lynching, Papers, 1930–42: A Guide to the Microfilm Editions* (Ann Arbor: University Microfilms International, 1984).

12. S. Joe Brown, S.E. Thompson, and James B. Morris, *Twenty Years of Interracial Work in Des Moines, Iowa, A Brief History of Des Moines Interracial Commission* (Des Moines: Des Moines Interracial Commission, 1944).

13. Lufkin, 149.

14. Ike Smalls to Sen. Bourke Hickenlooper, Jan. 9, 1946, Iowa NAACP Files, 1940–1955, LC.

15. Gloster Current speech, 1948, Iowa NAACP Files, 1940–1955, LC.

16. Smalls was one of several honorary vice-presidents. Robert Wright, personal communication with author, June 10, 1999.

17. The members of the 1951 Commission were Mrs. Edith Webber, C.L. Sampson, Rev. Ben C. Bobbitt, Marvin W. Schmidt, Rabbi Eugene Mannheimer, James McDonnall, and James B. Morris Sr. *History of the Des Moines Human Rights Commission* (n.p., 1969, mimeograph in author's possession received from Leola Davis, Aug. 19, 1997).

18. Ibid.

19. This commission was established by Ordinance 5775. Ibid.

20. These members were Silas S. Ewing, chairman; Richard L. Sirfus, vice-chairman; Nathaniel R. Craddock; Mareo Dellaca; Rabbi J.B. Goldburg; Robert B. Huston; Mrs. Brenda LaBlanc; Monsignor Edward B. Pfeffer; and Lynn K. Vorbich. Ibid.

21. "A Message from Governor Tom Vilsack and Lt. Governor Sally Pederson," Des Moines, November 2000.

22. Melford Fonza, Gordon Nash, and Walt Williams were hired through a negotiated settlement. Although each completed his probationary year and achieved permanent firefighter status, Nash and Fonza left Des Moines principally as a result of on-the-job racial harassment they experienced. Those in command at the DMFD did nothing to stop the harassment. Both resigned their hard-earned DMFD positions without any employment in hand. Eventually, Nash and Fonza were hired by the fire departments of Atlanta, Georgia, and Pasadena, California, where each achieved notable success. Nash rose to the rank of lieutenant. Fonza rose through the ranks to battalion commander and, eventually, was selected to be Pasadena's fire chief.

23. Lovell had served as a law clerk to U.S. Court of Appeals Judge Floyd Gibson and as director of litigation for both the Legal Services Organization of Indianapolis and the Indiana Center on Law and Poverty before coming to Drake. He had served as lead counsel for the Indiana NAACP Conference in *Bailey v. DeBard*, the class-action suit that successfully desegregated the Indiana State Police Department in the mid-1970s.

24. The NAACP's principal claims were based upon the anti-discrimination provisions of Title VII of the 1964 Civil Rights Act (federal) and the equal protection clause of the 14th Amendment. While an affirmative-action hiring remedy was a central goal of the litigation, the Reagan Administration was an outspoken opponent of affirmative action. Its Justice Department refused to assist the plaintiffs in the suit, and there was concern it might enter the suit as an opponent. The complex suit sought individual hiring relief for plaintiffs Moore and Perry and class-wide relief that would work major changes in the recruitment-hiring-retention system. Relief was sought that would encourage African-Americans to apply for future firefighter openings, require fair consideration of black applicants for employment with tests and criteria that were job-related, and require creation of a work environment in which black firefighters felt welcome and could succeed. It also required the federal court to monitor implementation, as one of Larry Carter's fears was the empty "revolving door," whereby the City might purposefully select "weak" black candidates with the intention of flunking them out in the drill school.

25. Aware that the City was in the late stages of completing its 1982 selection process for firefighter, plaintiffs' counsel immediately sought an injunction barring the City from hiring any new firefighters until the lawsuit was decided. Lovell negotiated an order in which the CSC "consented" to certification of one black for one non-black.

26. *Moore v. City of Des Moines*, 766 F.2d 343 (8th Cir. 1985), cert. denied, 474 U.S. 1060 (1986).

27. The long-term hiring goal was based on the black percentage of the city's overall population. The hiring goal built in important safeguards to ensure that court-ordered remedies would actually be attained. The most important safeguard was a provision that counted only those who achieved non-probationary firefighter status as "hires." This provision built in a significant disincentive to any who might seek to subvert the decree through a "revolving door" of hiring "weak" black candidates and promptly firing them for poor performance, thus addressing the longtime concern of Larry Carter.

28. The Reagan Justice Department opposed affirmative action, and in 1989 the U.S. Supreme Court dealt affirmative action a serious setback with its decision in *Croson v. City of Richmond*. Lovell, Wright, and Schott were successful in persuading Judge Vietor that the consent decree's affirmative-action relief constituted goals "with teeth" but were not impermissible "rigid quotas." The consent decree's detailed and intricate provisions provided both constitutional and legal bases for the affirmative-action hiring relief at the core of the remedy.

29. Letter to Drake University, nominating Russell Lovell for the Madelyn M. Levitt Distinguished Community Service Award, July 15, 1998. Professor Lovell was selected for the 1998 Levitt Award, recognizing outstanding community service by a member of Drake University's faculty or staff.

30. "He Won the Good Fight" [editorial], *DMR*, November 2000: "The next time there's a fire engine barreling down the street, take a good look who's on the truck. If there's an African-American on board, give credit to Larry W. Carter. Carter, 63, died Sunday afternoon at Mercy Medical Center following complications of diabetes.
     "Carter was president of the local branch of the National Association for the Advancement of Colored People for 12 years until 1993. He served as a member of the NAACP national board and was a force in local politics.
     "Of all the battles Carter fought — and there were many — the most pronounced was his effort to integrate the Des Moines Fire Department. That may not seem such a big deal today, but the fact it happened within recent memory points to a community that was slow, if not reluctant, to embrace change. Fire departments nationwide, often bastions for families passing down jobs from one generation to the next, were never receptive to diversity in the work force. Carter's taking the issues on — and winning — demonstrates his tenacity for waging the good fight when he knew right was on his side."

31. S. Joe Brown to Roy Nash, Nov. 17, 1918, Davenport, Iowa, NAACP Files, 1913–1939, LC.

32. Robert W. Bagnall to L.M. Brown, July 23, 1921, Davenport, Iowa, NAACP Files, 1913–1939, LC.

33. Jack Schneiders interview, Des Moines, Aug. 20, 1997.

34. Toney and his wife had experienced discrimination personally in Davenport in 1941, when they were refused service at a hamburger shop downtown. Toney brought suit against the restaurant, winning the case in a court ruled over by a blind judge. Charles Toney interview, Aug. 30, 1998.

35. See McGreevy, op. cit.

36. Tom Kelly interview, Aug. 30, 1998.

37. Ottumwa, Iowa, NAACP Files, 1913–1939, LC.

38. Ottumwa, Iowa, NAACP Files, 1940–1955, LC.

39. Robert Wright Sr., personal recollections, January 25, 2000.

40. S. Joe Brown to Walter F. White, Dec. 7, 1918, Cedar Rapids, Iowa, NAACP Files, 1913-1939, LC.

41. Roy Nash to L.D. Lowery, Oct. 5, 1916, Cedar Rapids, Iowa, NAACP Files, 1913–1939, LC.

42. Fred Gresham (signed) to NAACP, May 25, 1926, Cedar Rapids, Iowa, NAACP Files, 1913–1939, LC.

43. Elnora Gresham to NAACP, June 10, 1926, Cedar Rapids, Iowa, NAACP Files, 1913–1939, LC.

44. Robert Bagnall to W.H. Beshears, June 11, 1928, Cedar Rapids, Iowa, NAACP Files, 1913–1939, LC.

45. George W. Ashby to William Pickens, April 11, 1933, Cedar Rapids, Iowa, NAACP Files, 1913–1939, LC.

46. The church had received its property from Mary Weare Ely, whose first husband had been a physician in the Union Army along the Mississippi River and whose family owned much of the property of the southeast section of Cedar Rapids at that time. Jeremy Brigham, "Transforming Places," Ph.D. diss., University of Iowa, 1997, 115.

47. Ibid., 119–23.

48. The members of the Community Coordinating Committee of the NAACP were Mary Alice Ericson, Chairman; Myra Ervin, Past Chairman; Adel Beck; William Brown; Earl Carr; Emmett Collins; Russell Collins; Wardell Diggs; Doris Hamilton; Percy Harris; Russell Nash; Ruth Nash; and Cecil Reed. Interviewers were Linda Abodeely, Mrs. Lawrence Baker, Jan Baldridge, Fred Barnett, Mrs. John Berger, Mrs. Karl Blaise, Mrs. Amity Blakey, David Breed, Robert Brown, William Brown, Mrs. Francis Camizzi, Emmett Collins, John Wesley Collins, Russell Collins, Mrs. Russell Collins, Juan Cortez, Bill Davis, Lewis Davis, Wardell Diggs, Polly Ely, Mary Alice Ericson, Myra Ervin, Helen Gallagher, Mack Gibson, Ruth Griffith, Doris Hamilton, Lorene Harrington, Dr. Percy Harris, Susan Jess, Katherine Kollman, Bernice Lapp, Arthur Lewis, Wilbert Mitchell, Grace Pilkington, Anne Rapp, Betty Rhatigan, Clarence Scott, Mrs. Edward Smith, Elmer Smith, Mrs. Vernon Smith, Frank Snider, Eva Stanley, Rev. J.K. Trembath, Emma Turner, Carolyn Wellso. "The Negroes' View of Civil Rights Problems," prepared by the Cedar Rapids branch of the NAACP and submitted to the Cedar Rapids Commission on Human Rights, 1964.

49. Ab Igram and Ralph Coty, *Toward Equality* (Cedar Rapids: Commission on Human Rights, 1973).

50. Ibid.

51. Mrs. Selby Johnson to the Secretary of the NAACP, Oct. 24, 1919, Keokuk, Iowa, NAACP Files, 1913–1939, LC.

52. Robert W. Bagnall to Emma Hicks, July 19, 1924, Centerville, Iowa, NAACP Files, 1913-1939, LC.

53. Charles Davis to NAACP, Dec. 10, 1925, Council Bluffs, Iowa, NAACP Files, 1913-1939, LC.

Jeremy Brigham is a minister and an educator. For 21 years, he served Unitarian Universalist churches in Arizona, Ohio, and Iowa. Since earning a Ph.D. in social and political geography at the University of Iowa in 1998, Dr. Brigham has taught geography at the University of Northern Iowa and Coe College and sociology at Mt. Mercy College. He and his wife of 34 years, Selma, have three daughters and five granddaughters.

Dr. Brigham acknowledges the help he received in preparing this chapter from Hal Chase, who provided leadership and inspiration; the University of Northern Iowa, which provided travel funds to conduct research at the Library of Congress; the State Historical Society of Iowa, which funded copying of archival material; the many people who consented to be interviewed for this chapter; and my family, which supported me throughout the process of research and writing.

Robert A. Wright was born in Chicago in 1926, but raised in Des Moines's southeast "bottoms" by his grandparents, Fred and Gertrude McCann. He graduated from East High in 1943 with academic and athletic honors and joined the army. He served as a non-commissioned officer in Europe and later earned a commission in the ROTC at the University of Iowa, where he graduated in 1949. He joined the Des Moines police force in 1952 and earned his law degree from Drake University two years later. In addition to private law practice, Wright has served the NAACP as State Conference president since 1965, earning the sobriquet, "Iowa's Mr. Civil Rights." He has been married to Berniece Kelley since 1946 and they have two children and seven grandchildren.

54. This must have included both Omaha and Council Bluffs.

55. William Teal to Robert W. Bagnall, June 16, 1931, Council Bluffs, Iowa, NAACP Files, 1913–1939, LC.

56. "WTA:ED" [name not specified], Special Legal Assistant to William Teal, June 23, 1931, Council Bluffs, Iowa, NAACP Files, 1913–1939, LC.

57. Musical contest program, Feb. 9, 1932, Council Bluffs, Iowa, NAACP Files, 1913–1939, LC.

58. Walter White to A.W. Fitz, Jan. 19, 1933, Council Bluffs, Iowa, NAACP Files, 1913–1939, LC.

59. A.W. Fitz and Ezra Capleton William Pickens, March 14, 1933, Council Bluffs, Iowa, NAACP Files, 1913–1939, LC.

60. A.W. Fitz to William Pickens, Nov. 30, 1933, Council Bluffs, Iowa, NAACP Files, 1913–1939, LC.

61. A.W. Fitz to NAACP Legal Department, Oct. 31, 1937, Council Bluffs, Iowa, NAACP Files, 1913–1939, LC.

62. DMR, Jan. 19, 1940. An Iowa Bystander article appearing July 5, 1945, refers to four active branches in 1940. My guess is that the four present at the first meeting would have been Des Moines, Waterloo, Keokuk, and Marshalltown, but that additional chapters were recently or nearly organized in the other communities.

63. Robert Neymeyer, "May Harmony Prevail: The Early History of Black Waterloo," Palimpsest 61 (1980): 80–91.

64. Lincoln Club to NAACP, Aug. 25, 1930, LC. The Census Bureau reported 1,234 African-Americans in the city in 1930, so the claimed number was 1,000 too many.

65. Of the other four branches contributing, Marshalltown paid $4.65; Cedar Rapids, $3.45; Ottumwa, $2.60; and Council Bluffs, $1.85. Iowa Division, NAACP Files, 1940–1955, LC.

66. Other branches reporting were Centerville, 144; Cedar Rapids, 127; Marshalltown, 105; Ottumwa, 84; Council Bluffs, 76; Mason City, 73; and Clinton, 32. Iowa Division, NAACP Files, 1940–1955, LC.

67. A new branch, reporting 117 members, had formed in Sioux City by 1947. Sioux City, Iowa, NAACP Files, 1940-1955, LC.

68. Waterloo Courier, Sept. 15, 1968.

69. For an autobiographical account, see Ruth Bluford Anderson, From Mother's Aid Child to University Professor (Iowa City: University of Iowa School of Social Work, 1985).

70. Ida Baker and James Brooks are two. Burlington, Iowa, NAACP Files, 1913–1939, LC.

71. Burlington Self-Survey of Human Relations [Complete Report] (Burlington: Burlington Self-Survey Committee, 1951), Grimes-Salter Room, Burlington Public Library.

72. Iowa Conference, NAACP Files, 1940–1955, LC.

73. William Edwin Taylor to James Weldon Johnson, Nov. 2, 1921; Johnson to Taylor, Nov. 10, 1921, Iowa City, Iowa, NAACP Files, 1913–1939, LC.

74. "Progress: We Can Make It Happen," president's address, Feb. 1981, personal collection of Jeremy Brigham.

75. First Annual Freedom Fund Banquet program, Sept. 20, 1980.

76. William Morris, personal communication with author, Dec. 7, 1997.

77. Mary Childs McNerney to Dr. R.A. Dobson, March 15, 1915, Sioux City, Iowa, NAACP Files, 1913–1939, LC.

78. Walter F. White to M.E. Whitlock, Jan. 5, 1925, Sioux City, Iowa, NAACP Files, 1913–1939, LC.

79. Boyd wrote on stationery of the Enterprise, a weekly newspaper published "primarily in the interests of colored Americans." According to the masthead, Boyd was publisher, Rev. Williams and attorney A. J. Hicks were contributing editors. Sioux City, Iowa, NAACP Files, 1913–1939, LC.

80. Robert W. Bagnall to J.N. Boyd, Feb. 28, 1925, Sioux City, Iowa, NAACP Files, 1913–1939, LC.

81. Robert W. Bagnall to J.N. Boyd, March 4, 1925, Sioux City, Iowa, NAACP Files, 1913–1939, LC.

82. The president was Mrs. Earl A. Roadman; Rev. H.R. Boston, first vice-president; Father Francis. J. Friedel, second vice-president; Helen Crosswhite, secretary; and Dorothy Kay, treasurer. Board members were Rabbi A.A. Gordon, Mrs. C.S. Berkstresser, Mrs. R.A. Dobson, Rev. Nelson Baxter, Miss Martha Kendricks, and Mrs. Mary Cobbell. Sioux City, Iowa, NAACP Files, 1940–1955, LC.

83. Sioux City Journal, Dec. 2, 1947.

84. John W. Brigham to Thurgood Marshall, July 20, 1949; Leroy Carter to John W. Brigham, July 28, 1949, Sioux City, Iowa, NAACP Files, 1913-1939, LC.

85. Singer committed suicide between June 1952 and June 1953. J.W. Brigham interview, Sioux City, Nov. 24, 1998. He was listed as deceased in the 1953 annual program folder, Sioux City, Iowa, NAACP Files, 1940–1955, LC.

86. Edna F. Freeman, NAACP Department of Public Relations, to Brigham, Feb. 4, 1952, Sioux City, Iowa, NAACP Files, 1940–1955, LC.Royce W. Barnum, "The NAACP in Sioux Royce W. Barnum, "The NAACP in Sioux City," undergraduate research paper, Morningside College, Sioux City, Summer 1968, in author's possession.

87. Personal communication with John W. Brigham, Nov. 24, 1998; Royce W. Barnum, "The NAACP in Sioux City," undergraduate research paper, Morningside College, Sioux City, Summer 1968, in author's possession.

88. Freeman, op. cit.

89. Ibid.

90. L.J. Dickinson to Mrs. C.A. Anthony, Feb. 20, 1935, Ames, Iowa, NAACP Files, 1913–1939, LC.

91. Walter White to Timothy T. Lewis, March 14, 1935, NAACP files, 1913–1939, LC.

92. William Pickens to M.D. Lawrie, Feb. 23, 1939, LC.

93. As it turned out, William Pickens was greeted in Marshalltown by a capacity crowd at the Second Baptist Church. See the Marshalltown report. April 1, 1939, Marshalltown, Iowa, NAACP Files, 1913–1939, LC.

94. Copeland moved to Council Bluffs, where his wife was active in the 1940s. Fort Madison and Council Bluffs, Iowa, NAACP Files, 1913–1939 and 1940–1955, LC.

95. Philip G. Hubbard, New Dawns: A 150-Year Look at Human Rights at the University of Iowa (Iowa City: University of Iowa Sesquicentennial Committee, 1996), 13.

96. Ibid., 199.

97. Virginia Harper interview, Aug. 17, 1998.

98. Ibid.

99. Eugene Bell to Robert Bagnall, n.d., Mason City, Iowa, NAACP Files, 1913–1939, LC.

100. "Statement of Activities of the Branch," NAACP standard form, signed by Eugene Bell, secretary, 1928. Mason City, Iowa, NAACP Files, 1913–1939, LC.

Sioux City native George E. Hayes has led his city's civil rights movement as director of the Human Rights Commission and the NAACP. (courtesy George E. Hayes)

Chapter Thirteen

101. Eugene Bell to Robert Bagnall, Jan. 15, 1931, Mason City, Iowa, NAACP Files, 1913–1939, LC.

102. The Iowa Conference referred to P.L. Scott as "Reverend," but this title was never used in the Mason City correspondence of Paul L. Scott. Mason City, Iowa, NAACP Files, 1913-1939 and 1940-1955, LC; Iowa Conference, Iowa NAACP Files, 1940–1955, LC.

103. Ibid.

104. Lionel Foster interview, Mason City, May 19, 1997.

105. Of the 22 human rights commissions around the state, only 11 are staffed. The smaller towns and those with unstaffed Commissions refer problems to the Iowa Civil Rights Commission. Lionel Foster interview, Mason City, May 19, 1997.

106. I.L. Brown to William Pickens, Feb. 12, 1935, Marshalltown, Iowa, NAACP Files, 1913–1939, LC.

107. William Pickens to I.L. Brown, March 22, 1935, Marshalltown, Iowa, NAACP Files, 1913–1939, LC.

108. I.L. Brown to NAACP, Feb. 25, 1936, Marshalltown, Iowa, NAACP Files, 1913–1939, LC.

109. Rose Bannon to Juanita Jackson, Jan. 24, 1938, Marshalltown, Iowa, NAACP Files, 1913–1939, LC.

110. Newspaper clipping, n.p., n.d., Marshalltown, Iowa, NAACP Files, 1913–1939, LC.

111. Rose Bannon to NAACP, Sept. 10, 1938, Marshalltown, Iowa, NAACP Files, 1913–1939, LC.

112. Rose Bannon to NAACP, Oct. 30, 1938, Marshalltown, Iowa, NAACP Files, 1913–1939, LC.

113. Rose Bannon to William Pickens, March 14, 1939, Marshalltown, Iowa, NAACP Files, 1913–1939, LC.

114. Rose Bannon to NAACP, April 8, 1939, Marshalltown, Iowa, NAACP Files, 1913–1939, LC.

115. Rose B. Johnson to Gloster Current, March 11, 1952, Marshalltown, Iowa, NAACP Files, 1913–1939, LC.

116. James D. (Bounce) and Lula K. (Katie) Wallace came to Clinton in 1910, where Mr. Wallace worked on the Northwest Railroad and Katie cleaned houses. At first they lived in a boxcar. Vincent Jetter, Clemmie Hightower, and Deb Green interviews, Aug. 18, 1998; undated newspaper clippings in possession of Vincent Jetter; *History of Clinton County, Iowa* (Clinton: Clinton County American Revolution Bicentennial Commission, 1976).

117. The Presbyterian was Dr. Dempsey; the Catholics were Dr. Lyon, a dentist, and Ed Michl. Ibid.

118. Jetter, raised in Clinton, served as a page at the state legislature in 1963. Ibid.

119. Vincent Jetter interview, Aug. 17, 1998.

120. Grinnell, Iowa, NAACP Files, 1913–1939, LC.

121. Hampton Institute in Virginia was Booker T. Washington's alma mater. Sylvia Reedy Gist, "Educating a Southern Rural Community: The Case of Blacks in Holmes County, Mississippi, 1870 to the Present," Ph.D. diss., University of Chicago, 1994.

122. Grinnell, Iowa, NAACP Files, 1940–1955, LC.

123. Ibid.

124. Don Shields interview, May 19, 1997.

125. Cedar Falls Human Rights Commission, *First Annual Report*, Feb. 16, 1976.

126. Robert R. Dykstra, *Bright Radical Star: Black Freedom and White Supremacy on the Hawkeye Frontier* (Cambridge: Harvard Univ. Press, 1993).

127. Evelyn Jackson, personal communication with author, Aug. 18, 1997.

128. Iowa NAACP Files, 1913–1939, LC.

Members celebrate the 30th anniversary of the Des Moines Branch of the NAACP. (courtesy Willetta Bibbs Carter)

Iowa Gov. Leo Elthan with Archie A. Alexander to announce President Eisenhower's appointment of Alexander as governor general of the Virgin Islands in 1954 (SHSI Des Moines)

The African-American Legacy in Iowa Politics

by Ronald N. Langston

The story of African-Americans in Iowa politics combines bravery, daring, genius, and guts. African-Americans forged ahead — despite Herculean obstacles — in their struggle for freedom and full participation in local, regional, and national culture. Several towering figures made great contributions in this rite of political, social, and economic passage, and many had small or bit parts. All belong to the continuing movement from "outside in," from political marginalization to the centers of political power in Iowa.

The Prairie Pioneer Progressive Legacy

The political framework that gave Iowa its early character was a mixture of national and local issues that were held fiercely by factions throughout the territory. "The prairie and territorial legacy of Iowa towards African-Americans," wrote Iowa historian Leland L. Sage, "opposed the institution of slavery and its extension but [remained] anti-Negro with regard to issues of equality."[1] At one end of the spectrum were residents who abhorred slavery and were openly radical about opposing slavery as an institution. At the other end were those whose motives were purely economic, seeing the extension of slavery as a threat to the value of their labor. In between were labor reformers, representatives of various immigrant groups, and many other political factions. By the late 1850s, these factions were beginning to coalesce. The social, political, and economic glue that held them together, wrote Sage, combined "humanism with piety, morality, and economic progress."

The themes that emerged in the pre-war years were precursors of Lincoln's commitment to saving the Union. Lincoln hated slavery but would not end slavery if it put the union at risk. Such were the compromise sentiments of the new Republican Party. "We oppose slavery, but will limit our opposition to the question of extension into the new territories." Iowa's state constitutional conventions had a slightly different slant. The Negro was not welcome, not accepted as an equal, and fiercely resented as a competing laborer.[2]

The Struggle for Civil Rights and Civil Liberties

Early African-American leaders were engaged in continuous battles that ranged from opposition to slavery to safeguarding the establishment of statehood.

Several towering figures contributed to this rite of political, social, and economic passage, and many had small or bit parts. All belong to the continuing movement from "outside in," from political marginalization to the centers of political power in Iowa.

Abolitionist Gov. James A. Grimes supported constitutional amendments to extend rights to blacks in 1857. (SHSI Des Moines)

Political activist Alexander Clark Sr. was a guiding force in legislation for Negro suffrage in Iowa. (University of Iowa College of Law)

Where African-Americans stepped forward to challenge the status quo, there was usually help from Quakers, Abolitionists, Free Soilers, and anti-slavery sympathizers. Opposition to slavery — and later the struggle for civil rights — would be the major issues around which Iowa's African-American political leaders emerged.

In 1857, Iowa was in the midst of revising its original Constitution of 1846.[3] "Iowa's third constitutional convention was called primarily to repeal the state's Jacksonian prohibition on banking."[4] However, it was "the race issue that so nearly proved the document's undoing."[5] Governor Grimes — a known and active abolitionist — was supported in the legislature by "the presence of seasoned anti-slavery men in the Republican camp."[6] Political pressure from anti-slavery white constituencies would move the anti-slavery wing of the Republican Party toward the first legislative steps of equality for blacks in Iowa.[7] Although the Iowa public did not support by vote to amend the Constitution to include blacks, two provisions did pass the legislature. The first was a personal liberty clause of the bill of rights; the second was the legalization of black testimony in court.[8]

Early Iowa Models of African-American Political Leadership

In the midst of the great debate on banking and black suffrage emerged Iowa's first African-American political leader, Alexander Clark Sr. Clark was born in Pennsylvania in 1826. His father, a manumitted slave, was half-Irish; his mother was the daughter of black parents.[9] At the age of 13, he moved to Cincinnati, where an uncle taught him the barbering trade.[10] At 15, in 1842, he was living in Muscatine, where over the next dozen years he worked in several business pursuits. By 1854, Clark had established himself as one of the city's prosperous entrepreneurs. His fortune was the product of "investing the profits from his tonsorial enterprise in timber land and then contracting to supply local steamboat companies with wood."[11]

Active in local and state politics, Clark was a Republican. He fought for the right to vote, equal educational opportunity, and public accommodations. His early activities focused on the repeal of the Iowa Exclusion Act, which prohibited blacks from immigrating to Iowa. He was the lead signatory of "free colored persons" on a petition presented by Dr. Reasin Pritchard calling for the repeal of the exclusionary law.[12] Clark and other free blacks

"petitioned hard for an improvement in their legal status."[13]

In Iowa in 1868, "the local matter of greatest importance was the question [of] ratification of the Negro suffrage amendment . . . the first to be added to the Constitution of 1857, carried by a vote of 105,384 to 81,119, a two-to-one split of the 186,503 votes on the proposition."[14] Nationally, the federal government was debating the ratification of the 15th Amendment to the U.S. Constitution. "When the amendment to enfranchise the Negroes was up for decision in Iowa, [Clark] was one of the guiding spirits in the colored convention that was called in Des Moines in 1868 to promote their cause."[15]

Clark continued to distinguish himself as an energetic fighter for Negro rights. He spoke and toured throughout Iowa and the South, and according to historian Leola Bergmann he was popularly known as the "colored orator of the West."[16] In December 1869, in his hometown of Muscatine, an African-American convention was held. Delegates from around the state were present and Clark was appointed to attend a national African-American convention.[17] As a national delegate he represented black Iowans in a meeting to congratulate President Grant and Vice President Colfax on their election. He also served as a state delegate to the state Republican convention. In 1872, he served as a delegate at large to the Republican Party's national convention, and in 1876 as an alternate delegate.[18]

Alexander Clark Sr. again distinguished himself when he received a presidential appointment to the Republic of Liberia by Pres. Benjamin Harrison. He took his post in November 1890.[19] In June 1891, Clark died in office.[20]

Republicans remained in power throughout the late nineteenth century, but the party's commitment to black rights weakened steadily. White southerners reasserted institutionalized racism through de jure segregation. In northern states discrimination was de facto. Both combined to undermine Reconstruction. In 1896, the U.S. Supreme Court in *Plessy v. Ferguson* held that state-sanctioned segregation was constitutional.[21] For the record, the state of Iowa participated and sanctioned the spirit of *Plessy*. Segregation was practiced in Iowa until 1954, and many would argue through 1968.

However, there is evidence that the frontier-era political culture of Iowa continued to shape Iowa's post–Civil War history. Particularly in organizational politics at the local or precinct level, Lincoln's legacy regarding individual liberty and freedom had apparently taken root. It was here that Iowa's political culture developed a sense of fairness and openness to ideals and principles. This grassroots political culture would nurture generations of Iowa civic and community leaders, including many African-American leaders who refused to let the doctrine of "separate but equal" go unchallenged.

In 1892, George E. Taylor of Oskaloosa established himself as a defender of the Negro's civil, political, and social rights when he published "An Appeal to the Negro" and organized a national convention of the National Colored Men's Protective Association of America in Indianapolis.

Taylor had been a leader in both the Republican and Democratic parties. He began his youth as a Lincoln Republican and believed in the GOP's moral commitment to abolish slavery. He was a patriot, an American nationalist devoted to saving the Union. He was politically devoted to Lincoln. Central to preserving the Union was the defeat of efforts to extend slavery into the West, the end to slavery in the South, and the elimination of violence against the Negro people.

Taylor was three when the Civil War started, and eight years old when Lincoln was assassinated. Reared and educated in LaCrosse, Wisconsin, Taylor felt the strong influence of Republican prairie politics on his personal political development — which served as the foundation for his later disappointment and disaffection with the GOP. Much of Taylor's career was spent in Wisconsin, where he published several newspapers — the *LaCrosse Wisconsin Evening Star*, the *Wisconsin Evening Star*, and the *Wisconsin Labor Advocate* — but in 1891, he settled in Oskaloosa.[22] In Iowa he published the *Negro Solicitor* and for a time served as superintendent of the coal mines at Coalfield. In 1904, he moved to Ottumwa, where he practiced law.[23]

Sometime during this period he became involved in the Colored Peoples National Protective Association, and by 1892 he was listed as its president. Chronologically this places the Colored People's National Protective Association before the establishment of the National Association for the Advancement of Colored People (NAACP), on February 12, 1909.[24]

Taylor may have been influenced to call the national colored convention from a similar National Convention of Colored Men held in October 1864 in Syracuse, New York.[25] In his open letter to the national Negro community, Taylor had come to the conclusion that the Republican Party had been

Standard Bearer
of
National Liberty Party
For President, U. S. A.
1904

Notice:- The only Negro who ever made the race for President.

Very Truly,
Geo. E. Taylor.

Iowa's George E. Taylor, candidate for president, National Liberty Party, 1904 (SHSI Des Moines)

unfaithful to its origins — the abolition of slavery and the full enjoyment of freedom and equality under the law for African-Americans.

> *Republican Party Untrue.* What has been our experience? Twenty seven years have come and gone since we were clothed with the rights of citizenship, by law, and endowed with all the privileges incident thereto, and yet during this period, 10,091 Negroes have been shot down like dogs; skinned alive; hung to trees or burned to stakes, without the interference of the federal government only in once instance. But we are told to be patient, wait! Yes wait! Wait until the majority of our race are murdered, and possibly by the time public sentiment will be awakened sufficiently to force us to waft our way Bishop-Turnerward, across the sea, or more likely into the middle of some *black sea.*[26]

The reference to Bishop Henry McNeal Turner, leader of the African Methodist Church (AME), is of particular interest. Bishop Turner in the early 1890s was at the height of his powers as an orator and African-American leader.[27] Elected bishop in 1880, Turner "turned his attention to what he believed was God's plan for African-Americans — to return to the land of their ancestors in order to Christianize it."[28] It is surprising that Taylor, who prided himself on the rights of Negroes, would make such a frontal attack on the "Voice of African Pride," and someone who W. E. B. DuBois eulogized in 1915 "as the last of the 'spiritual progeny of African chieftains.'"[29]

Four years later, in 1896, Taylor again published "A National Appeal to the American Negro, Why We Should Favor the Chicago Platform."[30] Denouncing the Republican Party, Taylor appealed to the national African-American community to support the Democratic Party:

> For the first time in the history of our citizenship, fellow Negroes, are we confronted in a National campaign with issues that cannot [be addressed] as purely, strictly, partisan.
>
> For the first time in the history of our citizenship, do we find the Democratic Party platform declaring for measures which point more directly in the line of advantage to our race, than does that of the Republican Party.[31]

Now speaking as a Democrat, Taylor urged his fellow Negroes to turn away from the GOP. He became a delegate to the Democratic National Convention in Chicago. He was moved by the single issue of the "silver question" and entered the great debate between the two major political parties whether to enact a national gold standard or silver, which later becomes commonly referred to as the "coinage" issue.

Taylor presents a precise analysis of the Republican platforms since 1868. In doing so he finds a deliberate if not strategic absence of any reference relating to the Negro.[32] The abandonment of the Negro, he asserts, was linked to the GOP's renewed interest in the South — both financially among southern planters and politically among key sections of the electoral South.[33]

There were other issues of great concern to Taylor, such as the lynching and murder of Negroes and the disenfranchisement of the black voters by state action, which reversed the outcome of the Civil War on behalf of Negroes. By 1896, these elements had transfixed Taylor into pursuing direct redress at the national level of participatory democracy, the political party convention. He would spend his time, resources, and political skill understanding the national, sectional, and local consequences of American public policy on the national Negro community.

Gold Only Standard Threatens the Negro

Taylor viewed the 1896 Republican platform and the McKinley acceptance speech in support of the "gold only standard of finance as a threat to laborer, farmer and especially, the Negro." He wanted free coinage because he believed (as did the Democrats in 1896) that gold of itself was unable to supply the money demands of the country. Gold as the core instrument of finance disadvantaged all but the wealthy. Taylor demonstrated great understanding of the national and international intricacies of finance:[34] "History proves that in all of the gold standard countries wages reached the highest notch under bi-metalism, long before the single gold standard policy was inaugurated. To prove this point the reader need not go further than the history of this country."[35]

Taylor's second major statement of 1896 foreshadowed his eventual move to the National Liberty Party. He had come to the conclusion that the political assets the Negro offered nationally were not appreciated or respected. His observations and conclusions

---

Bishop Henry McNeal Turner, leader of the African Methodist Church (AME) . . . "turned his attention to what he believed was God's plan for African-Americans — to return to the land of their ancestors in order to Christianize it."

are worth noting, for this was just four years prior to his standing for the presidency of the United States as the National Liberty Party candidate:

> Like an untried massive engine, neither the Negroes of the United States or the Republican or Democratic parties know or appreciate the political strength of the race. The reason is obvious. We have generally voted and trained with the Republican Party, which has generally been successful.

> In 1892 we vowed our enmity towards Harrison as a rebuke for the unkindness he had shown us. In Illinois, Indiana, Iowa, New York, Michigan, and a few other states our influence or political strength was in a measure felt. Now, just compute a little: There are nearly 10,000,00 Negroes in the United States (according to the best authority), which gives us a right to claim about 2,000,000 votes.

> We are scattered through the doubtful states in large enough proportions to turn such states whichever way we may cast our vote. If such doubtful states go Republican then the cry is "Oh, it's just as I supposed. I know the darkies were all right, etc."

> But if our vote turns such doubtful states silverwards the GOP will begin to look around and inquire "What's the matter with John that he went back on us?" And the victorious silverite will exclaim: "Well, we made a good fight and those Negroes came to our rescue nobly, and we must reward them!"

> The future result will be that we shall then not only share with others in the beneficence of suitable finance laws, but that we will be more properly noticed and rewarded by the silverites for our loyalty to them and also by the Republicans as a bait to coax us back into the old fold.

> When as a race we have placed ourselves in such a position we shall share, as other races do, the honors of political victories and we never can hope to until we do this.

> There is power in the Negro vote, great power, Shall we exercise this power to our own advantage or shall we continue to serve the political god with golden yoke because Abraham Lincoln was a Republican and through the providence of events he proclaimed that "human slavery must cease."

> The body of John Brown lies molding in the clay, and in company with that good "old Abe," his soul goes marching on.[36]

The most striking aspect of Taylor's comments is the high level of national political sophistication he commanded on the value of strategically maximizing the Negro vote. Without question, the ability to fully understand the intricacies of grassroots party politics and to integrate a vision and strategic plan places Taylor among the preeminent African-American political leaders of his day.

By 1904, as the National Liberty Party candidate for president, Taylor was in full rhetorical style. His national appeal as president of the National Colored Protection Association had become the voice of the National Liberty Party.[37]

> Every Negro who is loyal to his race and the powers that made him a free man must join with us in heart, if not in action, in this effort to emphasize the fact that the Constitution of the United States is no respecter of person. But that all American citizens are entitled to the exercise of all the rights of citizenship, regardless of race or color.[38]

G. H. Woodson: Best of the Best

There often comes along an individual who by the sheer embodiment of individual persona, intellect, and skill represents the best of the best. Such is the case of George H. Woodson. His place in Iowa history is not well known, but his accomplishments nationally are highly revered. Woodson was a graduate of Howard Law School, Washington, D.C. In 1896, he moved to Iowa, and according to historical records lived "first in the black mining communities of Muchakinock and Buxton, and later moving to Des Moines in 1918."[39] Woodson was elected vice president of the Mahaska County Bar Association and nominated by the Republican Party as county attorney.[40] He may have been the first

Attorney George H. Woodson (SHSI Des Moines)

The Negro Republican Voters League justly worried that black voters would switch their political allegiance from Republican to Democrat in 1934. (SHSI Des Moines)

James W. Ford was the Communist Party candidate for vice president in 1932 and 1936. (SHSI Des Moines)

African-American in Iowa nominated to the Iowa House of Representatives or county attorney.[41]

Along with Gertrude Rush and Charles Howard, Woodson founded the Iowa National Bar Association and became its first president.[42] He later founded the National Negro Bar Association and became its first president as well. In Iowa he was an active member of the Iowa Bar Association, and in 1919 he formally addressed the bar at its annual meeting on the subject of black soldiers in the American war effort.[43]

Disaffection from National Republican Party

It began as George Taylor predicted in 1892. The GOP had become untrue to the vision of Lincoln and had abandoned the mantle of securing full and equal rights for the Negro.[44] Between 1896 and 1912, the national GOP preoccupation with a southern strategy and presidential politics further eroded Negro confidence in the national GOP platforms and mandates.[45] The 1932 election of Franklin D. Roosevelt completed the shift of the black vote to the Democratic Party, though several astute

African-American political leaders had been sounding the alarm for decades.[46] George Taylor was probably the first black Iowa political leader to do so.

Archie Alexander (Alexander the Great)

Another little-known political pioneer is Archie Alphonso Alexander. Alexander's activism at the local, state, and national levels in the 1940s and 1950s would eventually win him a diplomatic post.

Alexander follows in the tradition of Alexander G. Clark, George E. Taylor, and George Woodson, men who went into politics after successful business careers. Alexander also shared their commitment to the continuing struggle for civil rights and equal opportunity.

Born in 1888 in Ottumwa, Alexander was raised in a solidly working-class household. The Alexanders moved to Des Moines when Archie was young. He was an excellent scholar and athlete, and after finishing high school he enrolled in the engineering program at the University of Iowa. There he joined Kappa Alpha Psi, a premier African-American social fraternity, and years later served as its national president. Degree in hand, Alexander went on to a brilliant engineering career that spanned 45 years. He was a world-class designer and civil engineer, and he built bridges, freeways, million-dollar apartment buildings, power plants, and railroad trestles all over the country.[47]

It is said that as a youth Alexander was not encouraged in his career aspirations, and in the beginning he was not exactly welcomed by the engineering profession. Alexander had trouble finding work when he moved back to Des Moines after completing his degree. When he finally found a job, at March Engineering, it was not as an engineer but as a day laborer at 20 cents an hour. But Alexander rose quickly at March Engineering and soon took charge of the firm's bridge construction in Iowa and Minnesota, earning $70 a week.

Two years after joining March Engineering, Alexander left to form his own company with fellow engineer George F. Higbee. Their firm would become one of the most successful in the country.[48]

Business success afforded Alexander the opportunity to engage in politics, and Iowa Republican politics would become his launching pad to national prominence. A life-long Republican, Alexander worked closely with local Iowa Negro Republican Voter Leagues throughout the state. A contemporary of Benjamin Lucas,

S. Joe Brown and Sue Brown, and the *Bystander's* J. B. Morris, Alexander dedicated himself to building grassroots organizations to support local, regional, and national Republican candidates.[49]

Alexander proved to be an effective organizer, and because of his wealth and status as a businessman he moved easily between the black and white worlds of politics and race. Twice, in 1932 and 1940, he served as assistant to the chairman of the Iowa Republican Central Committee. In 1952 he joined the Eisenhower for President Club. He made many friends among Iowa's Republican leadership in Des Moines and in Washington, D.C., and in 1954 President Eisenhower named Alexander governor of the Virgin Islands.

Alexander's success as a national political figure was short-lived. He found frustration in his efforts to build relationships with the Virgin Islanders and grew impatient with the slow pace of the governor's office. He resigned his post in 1956 and returned to Des Moines. Two years later, suffering from ill health, Archie Alexander died at his home on Chatauqua Parkway.[50]

Blacks Elected to the Iowa General Assembly, 1965–1998

Willie Stevenson Glanton of Polk County was elected to the Iowa House of Representatives in November 1964. In January 1965, she and James Jackson of Blackhawk County were the first blacks to be sworn and seated in the Iowa legislature. One of 11 new Polk County Democrats elected to office in 1964, Glanton was no novice to politics, especially to organizational politics.

Willie Stevenson was born in Hot Springs, Arkansas, to a close-knit family in an equally close-knit African-American community. She was raised in Hot Springs, Arkansas. "Hot Springs was a resort town, known for international travelers and national visitors," she said. "The police were not prone to harass blacks. It was segregated, but not like traditional southern towns such as Little Rock. Little Rock was [racially] mean; Hot Springs [in comparison] was laid back, almost comfortable."[51]

Her parents were the primary source of her political drive and development. Her father, "very much the activist," organized the Negro Civic League in Hot Springs Arkansas.[52] Her mother was equally active in civic organizations and taught the elementary grades at the local private Presbyterian Church school.[53] Both parents were active Democrats.[54] Willie's first recollection of participating in a political campaign was a family effort that involved defeating the local poll-tax referendum.[55] Her father was a "traditional southern family man; in other words, he [was] the

Ottumwa native Archie Alexander's activism at the local, state, and national levels in the 1940s and 1950s would eventually win him a diplomatic post. (SHSI Des Moines)

In 1964, Willie Stevenson Glanton became the first African-American woman elected to the Iowa General Assembly. (Iowa State Register)

strong patriarch."[56] She attended the private school where her mother taught and later went on to the segregated public schools in Hot Springs. Her father wanted her to be a teacher like her mother,[57] but by age 11 she knew she wanted to be a lawyer and to "free up people."[58]

Early influences on Willie were her eighth and ninth grade teachers. Her eighth grade teacher was instrumental in developing the young girl's vision of who she wanted to be and what she wanted to achieve. Willie visualized her objectives by cutting out pictures representing what she wanted to be, how she saw herself, and the kind of life she wanted to live. "Snapshots of [my] future life in pictures."[59] Her ninth grade teacher was instrumental in developing Willie's interest in English and the discipline of speaking and writing well.

These early parental and mentor relationships, coupled with life in the Hot Springs community, nurtured her girlhood dream of becoming a lawyer. After high school graduation she studied for a year at Arkansas State and then went on to Tennessee A and I State University at Nashville, where she graduated with a bachelor's degree in business education. Her advisor at Tennessee State was the wife of the college president.

This student-advisor relationship was a milestone in Willie's development. Her advisor had a "strict no-nonsense" pedagogic style. "She was very demanding and insisted on excellence from her students."[60] It was through this relationship that Willie, along with other female students, prepared to take a national government exam that led her to Washington, D.C.

Willie moved to the nation's capitol to attend the Robert H. Terrell Law School. Washington provided the perfect environment for Glanton to work and study. She was employed in the Ordinance Ward of the War Department. Immediately identified as someone who helped others, she was promoted within the department.[61]

Though she did not intend to stay so long, Willie spent seven years having a "great time getting to know Washington." She met national leaders such as Mary Church Terrell and Mary McCleod Bethune, both of whom she admired as being gracious and dignified.[62] Terrell and Bethune would serve as models of personal and public conduct for Willie as she matured into womanhood. These national leaders also mirrored the character of her earlier childhood role models.

In Washington Willie Stevenson also met her future

James Jackson of Waterloo served one term in the state legislature in the 1960s. (Iowa State Register)

husband, Luther T. Glanton Jr. Luther Glanton had already distinguished himself during World War 2 as an army intelligence officer. Service in war was followed by an assignment as a staff attorney at the Nuremberg trials in Germany. At the time of their meeting, Luther Glanton was assistant Polk County attorney in Des Moines. He would later achieve further prominence as one of Iowa's first African-American judges — first appointed and later elected — and as an outstanding jurist. Married in Hot Springs in 1951, the Glantons moved to Des Moines immediately after the wedding.

Willie Glanton's political life began in earnest when she arrived in Des Moines. Her first priority was to begin her career as an attorney. This meant preparing for the Iowa Bar, setting up a law office, and building a legal practice. As a result of segregation and discrimination, it was difficult to find office space downtown, but by 1955 she had established a law office on Ninth Street. In 1956, she became the first African-American woman to become an assistant county attorney in Polk County.

Shortly after establishing herself in Des Moines, Willie Glanton joined the League of Women Voters.[63] The League proved to be one of the pivotal centers of influence socially, politically, and organizationally in the community. She also became active in the Democratic Club, the Democratic Women's Club, the John F. Kennedy Club, and the Roosevelt Club.[64] These clubs served as the organizational foundation for political and social activities and became the arena in which Glanton legitimized herself as an organizational activist and party insider. She quickly gained a reputation as a hard worker, going door to door on election day on behalf of the Democratic Party. She was a contributor to campaigns and was regularly seen at Democratic organization meetings. She worked on the telephone banks and performed critical precinct tasks — including yard-sign efforts, mailings, and the nuts and bolts activities that make campaign winners or losers.[65] The social and particularly political club relationships would serve her well in the future.

Persistent grassroots organizational work over the years brought Glanton to the attention of Gordon Gammack. A respected journalist, Gammack visited Glanton at her home and asked her to consider running for office.[66] Glanton said she "did not aspire to run for office," but she was close to the Democratic Party and considered by many a true insider.[67] As an insider Glanton benefited from her activist role and her cross-cultural skills. She was viewed as a team player. Equally significant, Glanton did not doubt her party's support for her candidacy on the basis of race or gender."[68]

In June 1964, Willie Glanton was one of 11 Democrats elected to represent the party against the Republicans in November. The Polk County Democratic Party ticket also included William J. Reichardt, Clark R. Rasmussen, William Palmer, Bernard J. O'Malley, Walter F. Maley, Lee H. Gaudineer, James P. Denato, James T. Caffrey, William Wheatcraft, and Mattie B. Bogenrief.[69] Glanton and Bogenreif were among a handful of women who would enter the Iowa legislature in January 1965. The total number of votes cast among the 11 newly elected legislators placed Glanton only second behind Reichardt. Reichardt, during the 1950s an All-American fullback at the University of Iowa, was clearly the popular figure of the day. But Glanton trailed Reichardt by only 20 votes on election day.[70] This was an amazing accomplishment. It was Glanton's first attempt, and the first attempt by an African-American woman, to be elected to the Iowa General Assembly.

While serving in the Iowa House, Glanton continued her commitment to "freeing up" people. Fair housing was a key issue for Glanton. She had clashed with Arthur Kirk, a leader in the Iowa Association of Realtors, over this issue in the late 50s. After Glanton's resignation in March 1966, Cecil Reed of Linn and June Franklin of Polk counties carried the campaign forward with the editorial support of the *Des Moines Register and Tribune*.[71] In the spring of 1967 the association sent a letter to all legislators opposing the fair-housing bill. But after an Iowa Poll showing 61 percent favored its passage and an impassioned speech by Cecil Reed on its behalf, the legislature passed the Iowa Fair-Housing Act in April 1967, a year before the federal law.[72]

In 1966 Glanton resigned her seat in the Iowa legislature to take a staff position as a lawyer with the Small Business Administration (SBA). This was another historic first for Glanton and Iowa. Glanton continued her commitment to civil and human rights and focused renewed energy on the subject of women's rights. She remained at the SBA until her retirement. Today, Willie Stevenson Glanton resides in Des Moines and remains active in various civic and religious organizations.

James Jackson joined Willie Stevenson Glanton in Iowa political history by being one of the first two African-Americans elected to an Iowa legislature. Like Glanton, Jackson entered the political arena well-grounded in local organizational politics and strong community roots. He was a product of the Waterloo public school system, graduating from Waterloo East High School. Later he was an outstanding collegiate basketball star at the University of Northern Iowa.

Jackson's initial political environment included his church — the prestigious and historic Antioch Baptist Church of Waterloo — the NAACP, the Family Services League, and the labor movement through the Iowa State Education Association (ISEA). Jackson also was a leader and Grand Lecturer of the Knights of Pythias (Iowa Chapter Black Masons), following in the steps of George E. Taylor.

During the 1960s, Jackson was prominent in the public-policy discourse concerning civil rights and equality of opportunity. Historically a racial hotspot dating back to the immigration of African-Americans from the Deep South to break the railroad strikes in the 1910s, Waterloo is a blue collar, working-class Democratic town divided by a train track into eastern and western halves. The division drawn by the railroad was more than a community boundary line. It was a social, economic, and political divide.

Jackson served one term in the Iowa House of Representatives, where he distinguished himself as a leader in the areas of civil rights, housing, and education. School board member Nolden Gentry of Des Moines, who lived in the same apartment complex as Jackson, within walking distance of the capitol, said "Jackson was a highly skilled and articulate professional. He was always well prepared and had great communication skills that were not limited to the issues of the Waterloo black community."[73] After his service in the Iowa House of Representatives, Jackson went on to a successful business career.

June Franklin was elected to the Iowa House of Representatives in 1966, succeeding Willie Stevenson Glanton in the heavily Democratic Polk County house district seat that in November 1966 included the core of the African-American community.[74] She was 36 years old when she was sworn into office.[75] The former June A. Griggs, Representative Franklin was born in Clarinda and graduated from Clarinda High School. Later she attended Drake University.[76] Professionally, she was a trained legal secretary and a licensed insurance and real estate agent. Her place in Iowa political history follows the path of engagement in civil rights and specifically fair-housing opportunity. In this sense she succeeded Willie Glanton, James Jackson, and later Cecil Reed

June Franklin, elected to the Iowa General Assembly from Des Moines in 1966, helped win passage of Iowa's fair-housing bill.
(Iowa State Register)

Republican Cecil Reed of Waterloo sponsored Iowa's fair housing bill and other key legislation during his term in the Iowa House of Representatives. (SHSI Des Moines)

in challenging the status quo on fair and equal housing laws — in Iowa and throughout the U.S.

Franklin's entrance into politics began at the grassroots. Active in several Democratic social clubs and party efforts, she was also very active in several community organizations. This combination of the politician and the community activist linked her with key organizations in which she often served a leadership role. Her affiliations included the Polk County Community Action Council, Greater Opportunities Inc., the Des Moines Chapter of the NAACP, Americans for Democratic Action, the John F. Kennedy Democratic Club, the Polk County Democratic Women's Club, and a special blue-ribbon committee to revise the rules of the Democratic Party.[77]

While serving in the legislature, Franklin demonstrated an ability to work well with members of her political caucus. She served on the Appropriations, Schools, Cities, Towns, and Tax Revision committees in her first session.[78] In recognition of her demonstrated leadership skills, she was elected during the 63rd General Assembly to the position of Assistant Minority Leader of the Democratic House. This alerted the political establishment that Franklin was not just a member of the Democratic caucus but one of its primary leaders who would assist in the daily management of the legislative agenda. Franklin is the first African-American to hold such a leadership position in either major political party in Iowa.

Franklin is unique as an African-American in Iowa because she is a Roman Catholic, but she easily crosses many social, economic, political, and cultural lines. Known to be very active in the NAACP and a frequent visitor and participant in Baptist and African Methodist Episcopal circles in Des Moines's central inner city community, she is equally comfortable in establishment circles within area neighborhoods.

As a legislator, Franklin was also active in communicating and coordinating the activities of state elected officials nationally. She consistently expressed concern about the state of the nation with regard to the impact of the racial riots, poverty, and the treatment of African-American elected officials.[79] She served three terms in the Iowa House of Representatives.[80]

Cecil Reed was elected to the Iowa House of Representatives in 1966. He has the distinction of being the first Republican of African-American descent elected to the Iowa legislature. Reed follows in the progressive Republican legacy of George Woodson.

Reed and Woodson were similar in the respect and admiration they earned in their communities. They dedicated their personal and public careers to the uplift of African-Americans locally and nationally. Civil rights was the top priority for both, especially with regard to jobs and housing. And both men were active in their local Republican precinct and district organizations.

Born in Collinsville, Illinois, in 1913, Reed traces his family roots back to Robert E. Lee on his mother's side. Reed's grandmother married Henry Lee, the half-brother of General Lee.[81] (Unlike many African-Americans, Reed was fortunate in his ability to capture intact his family tree on both sides of his family.[82])

The Reed family developed a reputation for being hard working and self-reliant. Cecil Reed carried on this tradition. He was particularly skilled at building relationships. One of his key relationships was with the Catholic church and specifically with several nuns in raising money for nursing homes.[83]

At the outset of his political career, Reed had no campaign experience or finances, but he did have a strong network of friends who encouraged and helped him launch his campaign for the Iowa legislature. Motivated by a belief he could help solve many of the problems concerning race, economics, housing, and civil rights, Reed defeated his Democratic opponent and began his career in the Iowa legislature.[84]

In entering the Iowa legislature, Reed followed the path of Willie Glanton and James Jackson. These African-American legislators shared a passion for civil rights, focused especially on ending discrimination in housing. However, Reed was "determined not to be a one issue legislator."[85] He made a strategic decision to broaden the scope of his legislative interest to include vocational education, highway safety, and housing.[86] Reed served on four committees: Conservation, Industrial and Human Relations, Roads and Highways, and State Planning and Development. The ranking Republican on the Conservation Committee, he spoke with authority on behalf of the Republican Party on conservation matters.

Reed proved to be an imaginative and energetic legislator, pursuing several innovative legislative projects. The first involved improving the dangerous stretch of highway between Cedar Rapids and Iowa City. The second involved building a four-lane highway between Iowa and Illinois. The third involved "a plan that would divide Iowa into six quadrants, each with at least one hospital."

The goal of the hospital legislation was to use medical helicopters to reach accident patients faster at the scene of an accident. Although his bill was not voted out of committee, the idea of using helicopters to better serve accident victims was adopted by other states.[87]

Reed joined others in the legislature who supported the concept of vocational technical schools. In addition, Reed was one of the first legislators to actively promote teaching African-American history in Iowa schools. He used a legislative procedure called a "concurrent resolution" to make his point and was supported by school administrators.[88]

The legislation that meant the most to Reed was the fair-housing bill.[89] "To me, not being able to rent a place or own property is one of the cruelest problems anyone can suffer."[90] With the encouragement of Gov. Harold Hughes and the help of the only other African-American in the Iowa legislature — Rep. June Franklin — Reed engaged in a lengthy battle to enact fair housing legislation in Iowa. Here he learned the art of compromise. This often meant being at odds with June Franklin, whom he respected as a persuasive and committed speaker on civil rights. "This experience taught me a valuable lesson: I'll take half a loaf, a slice, or a crumb and it will later develop into something better than you expected."[91] With the assistance of bipartisan support from two fellow legislators from Cedar Rapids, the fair-housing bill passed the Senate and moved to the House for final deliberation as amended. Reed recalls the event as a standing-room-only affair of high drama that went on for three hours. On the call for final passage, there were no dissenting votes. It was a unanimous victory for Reed as the bill's sponsor and floor manager.[92]

Reed occasionally presided over the House of Representatives when Speaker Maurice Berringer could not be there. These occasions marked the first time an African-American served in this esteemed position in the Iowa legislature.[93] Reed went on to other honors after his legislative career ended. Gov. Harold Hughes appointed him to head the Iowa Employment Security Commission, which made Reed one of the highest-ranking state officials in Iowa.[94] Later, Gov. Robert D. Ray appointed Reed to the Governor's Educational Advisory Committee.[95] Thus, in a variety of ways, Reed had greater political impact in less time than most of his contemporaries. He was much respected and earned the admiration of his colleagues throughout the political establishment. In his autobiography, Reed also acknowledges the

contributions young people made to his campaigns. He notes how they kept him energized with their fresh ideas and youthful courage. During legislative sessions in Des Moines, Reed lived among the pages at the local YMCA and befriended many of them. Young people were vital to Reed's campaigns in Cedar Rapids as well.[96]

William Hargrave was born in 1939 in Mississippi. He served in the military for 20 years and retired in 1968.[97] Hargrave is representative of the thousands of African-Americans from the Deep South who for various reasons, but most notably employment and education, found their way north up the Mississippi River to Iowa. In Hargrave's case, Johnson County and the University of Iowa would serve as the staging ground for his eventual election as deputy county sheriff and as a member of the Iowa General Assembly. Law enforcement and issues relating to county government would serve as his legislative mantle during his public career.

In November 1972, Hargrave was elected to the Iowa House of Representatives, where he served until 1978. He was the fifth African-American to be elected to the Iowa legislature. Taking up the torch for civil rights and equality of opportunity, Hargrave was a savvy, street-smart politician with a rough exterior. But he could laugh and charm his political friends and adversaries, and he brought to the legislature a workingman's passion on the public-policy issues. Hargrave often worked late in the evenings, visiting with legislative colleagues and working out differences with various interest groups.

Peter Middleton, who graduated from the University of Iowa College of Law in 1974, was the sixth African-American elected to the Iowa General Assembly. He arrived in January 1975. Middleton was a popular figure in Waterloo. He graduated from East High School, attended Rochester Junior College, and earned his undergraduate degree from Morningside College in 1968.

Middleton was elected to the Iowa General Assembly from Waterloo and distinguished himself at the Statehouse in the areas of labor law, education, and civil rights. At the age of 29 he was one of the youngest members in the legislature. A tall man with a large frame, he made a commanding presence when he entered the rotunda or either legislative chamber. Middleton was bright, and he pursued his legislative objectives in a cerebral, lawyer-like manner. He could be equally passionate and stubborn on matters such as labor and civil rights. He served two terms in the Iowa House.

In the 1970s William J. Hargrave Jr. represented Iowa City in the Iowa General Assembly, where he became an influential legislative leader. (Iowa State Register)

Rep. M. Peter Middleton, elected at age 29 to the Iowa General Assembly from Waterloo, became an authority on labor law, education, and civil rights. (Iowa State Register)

Albert L. Garrison served one term in the Iowa House representing Waterloo.
(Iowa State Register)

Sen. Thomas Mann Jr., the first African-American elected to the Iowa Senate
(Iowa State Register)

In 1977 Albert L. Garrison, a native of Waterloo, entered the Iowa House of Representatives, where he served for one term. Upon his arrival, he quickly recognized the historic significance that he was one of three African-Americans sitting all at once in the Iowa General Assembly. Representatives Hargrave, Middleton, and Garrison would often huddle in the corners of the rotunda or in the back of the House chamber to discuss legislative strategy or issues of common interest. Their voices gave special significance to issues of housing, civil rights, labor law, and county government.

Garrison was in the first group of African-Americans to serve at the managerial level of the federal Internal Revenue Service. He also served in the U.S Department of Defense and the U.S. Navy, and as a reserve officer in the U.S. Air Force. He retired from the reserves with the rank of major. His private-sector experience included employment with Massey Ferguson, Sperry Rand, and Waterloo Industries, Inc. His professional associations included memberships in the American Society of Engineers, the American Welders Society, the American Society of Quality Control, and the Society of Automotive Engineers. Added to his public and private sector associations were memberships in various community and civic organizations. He served on the Waterloo Planning and Programming Commission and chaired the Waterloo Low Rent Housing Commission. Garrison was also active in the Knights of Pythias. A graduate of Waterloo East High School and Drake University with a B.S., Garrison also holds a B.A. degree from Upper Iowa University.

Garrison brought to the Iowa legislature a broad level of expertise and experience that extended beyond areas — such as civil rights, housing, and education — traditionally associated with African-Americans in public service. His knowledge of law and especially tax law served him well in areas of finance and budgeting. He understood county government and the issues relating to strategic planning and programming, and he showed great depth at integrating all his knowledge and experience within the legislative process.

Thomas Mann was elected to the Iowa Senate in November 1982. Mann's path to the General Assembly was the result of a short but brilliant career in public service, coupled with active participation in the greater Des Moines area, and a commitment to community service. His persistence in pursuing a state senate seat resulted in his becoming the first African-American elected to the Iowa Senate. Elected twice to the Iowa Senate — once

in 1982, then again in 1988 — Mann did not serve out his full second term.

Mann was born in Tennessee.[98] A product of the 1960s, Mann made an early commitment to civil rights through the politics of community action. In the next evolution of civil rights enforcement — protecting the gains hard fought during the 1960s — Mann chose law and the political arena as his battlegrounds.

Mann's Iowa journey began as a student at the University of Iowa College of Law. He was popular, articulate, and demonstrated the intellectual skills in academics that would serve him well later in the public policy and legislative arenas. Upon graduation from law school in 1977, Mann secured an appointment as an assistant Iowa attorney general.

In 1976 Gov. Robert D. Ray — with the advice of his administrative assistant Cora Douglas, and also with the support of the local and state NAACP — appointed Mann director of the Iowa Civil Rights Commission. Mann's energy, legal skills, and political savvy increased the state agency's visibility. As a result of his strong community and fraternal affiliations, he was able to unite the efforts of the NAACP and those of labor and community leaders in Des Moines and other key urban areas — Waterloo, Davenport, Sioux City, Mason City, and Cedar Rapids.

The struggle for fair housing that had been so important to Willie Glanton, June Franklin, and particularly Cecil Reed found new voice and substance with Tom Mann. Mann benefited from a positive climate of change with regard to equal justice in Iowa. This is not to infer that change came easily or that there were not challenges to civil rights, such as "affirmative action policy." The casework and backlog of new cases regarding discrimination based on race were equaled in number by new cases of gender and age.

The creative tension between the Iowa Manufacturers' Association (an association of business and industrial representatives) and the Iowa Civil Rights Commission had a long history dating back to the late 1960s and throughout the 1970s. Key issues such as the "right to sue" and 180-day administrative release to enter court on the plaintiff's own behalf were hotly contested. Mann proved to be undaunted by the criticism from the Iowa Manufacturer's Association.

Over time Mann had his detractors and supporters, who usually lined up along business and labor lines. In an attempt to bring equality to girls basketball in Iowa's schools, Mann sought to change Iowa's traditional "3-on-3" girls basketball because it placed Iowa girls at a disadvantage with players from other states. Along with other interested parties, Mann wanted to usher in the same "5-on-5" full-court basketball game played in other states. Though well intentioned, this effort triggered fierce reaction statewide and may explain why Governor Ray shortly thereafter replaced Mann as director of the civil rights commission.

With quiet skill and tenacity, Mann reappeared in the public policy arena with a re-appointment to the Office of the State Attorney General in 1980. He became active in the Iowa Democratic Party, joining its board, and he became an advisor to the local and state chapters of the NAACP. He was also associated with the American Red Cross. Within two years — by 1982 — Mann had positioned himself for a run to the Iowa Senate in a newly reapportioned district.[99]

In November 1982, Mann was elected to the Iowa Senate, where he served until 1990. As a state senator he had a collegial presence and was highly respected for his intellect, calm demeanor, and attention to detail. Formerly a trial attorney, he found allies within the ranks of the Iowa Trial Lawyers Association, organized labor, the Iowa State Education Association, and the civil and human rights communities. Mann was often sought after to address technical legal questions by both Democrats and Republicans.

During the 1990 legislative session, apparently for health reasons, Senator Mann informed colleagues and friends that he would not seek another term. The informal announcement generated much surprise from both sides of the political aisle. Senator Mann had been a very quiet, positive figure in the Iowa Senate. Although historically he was the first African-American elected to the Iowa Senate, the issue of his race was never a focal point. This is in large measure due to his professionalism as a lawyer and his proven commitment to public and community service.

Tom Baker's roots in the Des Moines African-American community run deep. These roots have defined him socially and economically throughout his life. They are also the foundation of his impressive rise to political power — locally, statewide, and nationally. Streetwise and politically perceptive, Baker has attained membership and leadership positions within the public, private, civic, and community sectors of Des Moines. His bases of support, although wide, have essentially centered on the north-central and northeast sides of Des Moines.

Baker graduated from North High School in 1959. During

the 1960s, he served in the U.S. Army and attended Howard University in Washington, D. C., Baker — who defines himself as a "working man" and "small business entrepreneur" — was a factory worker for 15 years at Delevan Manufacturing in Des Moines. He was active in the UAW Local 552 bargaining committee, where he championed workers' rights and the hiring of minority and female workers. In 1979, he began a career in self-employment through several entrepreneurial ventures. He became the owner of TMT Janitorial Service. As a small business owner, he learned first-hand how difficult it is for minority-owned businesses to get started. He founded the Targeted Small Business Program for Minorities and Women and became an activist speaking out on minority concerns. In 1986, he received the Iowa Small Business Advocate of the Year Award and the Iowa NAACP President's Award for Outstanding Community Services. The Iowa Minority Advocate Award followed in 1987. Baker has been a member of the Polk County Charter Commission, the Iowa White House Conference on Small Business Steering Committee, the Des Moines Civil Rights Commission, and Des Moines Public Housing, and he has chaired the Des Moines Private Industry Council.

Tom Baker served three terms in the Iowa General Assembly as a member of the House of Representatives. The district that elected him has historically elected Democrats to the legislature; his predecessors were Willie Glanton and June Franklin. Thus Baker's place in Iowa political history begins in the "grassroots" community, but it includes as well a broad foundation of support from all sectors of the community. The road to political success and power for Baker has not been easy within the Democratic Party. On several occasions he has had to fight off primary challenges and Central Committee back-room attempts to defeat him.[100] He has proven himself a master of political survival, baffling and intriguing the experts with his ability to win.

While in the legislature during a period of Democratic majority, Baker served as chair of the Subcommittee on Economic Development. Through his street smarts and charm, Baker developed alliances with Governor Branstad and Allen Thoms, director of the Iowa Department of Economic Development. Baker often noted he received more cooperation from the Republican governor — and the governor's staff and appointees — than from his own Democratic caucus. For example, it was not uncommon to see Baker socializing and conducting political

Tom Baker of Des Moines, a powerful political force first as a state legislator and later as chair of Polk County's Board of Supervisors (courtesy Tom Baker)

Nathan Brooks won election to the Polk County Board of Supervisors in November 2000. (courtesy Nathan Brooks)

George Boykin, executive director of the Sanford Center in Sioux City since the 1970s, won election to the Woodbury County Board of Supervisors and is currently its chair.
(Sioux City Tribune)

business and informal conversation with Thoms at Mel's Bar and Grill in West Des Moines over chicken gizzards, Tabasco, and cold beers.

Baker was adept at political infighting and equally skilled at developing and mastering political relationships. He was also capable of politically attacking and socially challenging his political adversaries. His political style is known to be a mixture of rough and grumpy — and charming — with razor-sharp street smarts. His close political allies included then-president of the NAACP Larry Carter; Evelyn Davis, founder of Tiny Tot Day Care Center; and Robert Wright Sr., the Iowa-Nebraska Chair of the NAACP. Baker is also a long-time member of the historic and powerful Corinthian Baptist Church. Corinthian Baptist has served as a social, political, and often economic center of influence throughout Baker's career.

Baker remains today one of the last examples of the older "up from the grassroots" political success story. He is a product of the post–World War 2 years and *Brown v. Board of Education* and the civil rights era of the 1960s. Certainly the politics of protest have shaped his public policy development. However, Baker has also moved beyond the politics of protest to a view of economic power through business ownership as an important and legitimate step to success.

Baker believes in the government's power to make changes in the social, political, and economic lives of the disadvantaged. He witnessed the government's role in changing the military and the court's role in desegregating the schools and pursuing civil rights. It is within this context that Baker places confidence in the government's ability to assist minority-owned businesses to compete in the marketplace.

In 1996, Baker was elected to the Polk County Board of Supervisors after a hotly contested Democratic primary and subsequent general election. In 1999, he was elected the board's chairman. However, in the Democratic primary of 2000, Baker faced black opponent Nathan Brooks, a relatively unknown neighborhood activist. Originally from Cedar Rapids, Brooks was a Drake University graduate who had no experience in city politics other than a term on the Des Moines Housing Board. Brooks portrayed Baker as an unethical, incompetent, and ineffective leader who openly opposed neighborhood association priorities. A mean-spirited campaign ended in Baker's defeat and possibly the end of his career in elective office.

Brooks's victory was the result of several factors. He and political strategist Cornell Fowler devised an effective media campaign highlighting Baker's deficiencies. The Brooks campaign also benefited from several timely *Des Moines Register* articles that were critical of Baker. Finally, Nathan Brooks had close personal ties to Des Moines Mayor Preston Daniels. This combination of assets was sufficient to bring down the powerful Tom Baker, at least for the present.

George Boykin grew up in South Sioux City, Nebraska, near the stockyards and packing houses where his father worked. Originally from rural Mississippi, the Boykins moved to South Sioux City around the time of George's birth in 1940.[101] Like Ruth Anderson in Waterloo, Jane Burleson in Fort Dodge, and William Hargrave in Iowa City, Boykin can be seen as a transplanted southerner. A quiet, down-to-earth outdoorsman, Boykin acquired a love for fishing and hunting from his father and uncles. As a child he learned the value of living off the land and a respect for nature. In 1971, he graduated from Morningside College, where he majored in sociology and minored in music.[102]

Boykin's professional career has been in social services, with an emphasis on children and family services. In 1968, he began a career in social work at the Sanford Center, where today he serves as executive director.

Entry into Politics Was Prompted by Frustration

Boykin's entry into politics was prompted by his frustration with the local schools' disciplinary policies toward at-risk youngsters like the ones he counseled at the Sanford Center. Dissatisfied with the Sioux City School Board, Boykin decided to make changes from the inside. In 1971, he was elected to a school board seat he would hold for four terms, until 1983. By then, Boykin had his sights set on Woodbury County's Board of Supervisors. His 1983 election as supervisor made him the first African-American elected to the board in the county's history. Known for his calm demeanor and steadiness behind the scenes, Boykin is a hard worker and has been consistently re-elected to the Woodbury Board of Supervisors since 1983. He was elected again in 2000.[103]

Wayne Ford's place in Iowa political history is still evolving. He succeeded Tom Baker from the legislative district that earlier elected Willie Glanton and June Franklin. All were Democrats, and each demonstrated the ability to win by attracting crossover voters representing diverse demographic perspectives.

Like Baker, Ford represents the grassroots model of political participation. They share a background in the politics of protest and social action through governmental intervention. Executive director of Urban Dreams, Ford has worked in the social services arena for years, beginning with the Model City community program. He was active in the programming of KUCB radio, a local community-based radio station. Ford also was an active voice on WHO-AM radio, where he had a weekly talk show.

Over the years, Ford became skilled in developing strategic alliances with the private sector. In so doing he has been able to blend social activism with entrepreneurial and business approaches targeted to assisting disadvantaged, low income, and unemployed individuals find jobs in the public and private sectors.

In the spirit of Glanton and Franklin, Ford has become an active insider within the Democratic Party and especially the Polk County political organization. He has assisted many fellow Democratic candidates from all over the state to run for elective office. He has become one of the "go to" Democratic elected officials who are sought after for political advice by state and national Democratic Party leaders and activists, especially in urban areas. Ford has expressed interest in higher office.

In the 1970s, in collaboration with local Hispanic leaders, Ford initiated the Brown and Black Coalition presidential forums. Starting in 1976 with Jimmy Carter, through Ford's enterprise, the Coalition has been visited by at least one of the candidates in every presidential campaign. Ford says the forum is the first of its kind in America, the only forum where presidential candidates are requested to focus on "brown and black issues." The forum has also attracted national leaders, authors, and speakers such as Harvard philosopher Cornell West, Rev. Jesse Jackson, vice presidents Walter Mondale and Al Gore, and former U.S. Sen. Bill Bradley. Designed to be non-partisan, the forum has faced reluctance on the part of Republicans. Neither their presidential candidates nor the leaders of the local Republican political organization have accepted the Coalition's invitations to speak.

The Gubernatorial Campaign of 1998

In June 1998, former U.S. Congressman Jim Ross Lightfoot, the Republican candidate for governor, shocked an enthusiastic Republican convention in Cedar Rapids with the selection of an black woman as his choice for lieutenant governor.[104] The months leading up to the historic moment had been filled with much

Rep. Wayne Ford of Des Moines, who blends social activism with an entrepreneurial approach to urban development, gained national prominence when he addressed the Democratic National Convention in August 2000. (courtesy Wayne Ford)

speculation as to who would join Lightfoot in facing the Democrats in the fall. Democratic nominee Tom Vilsack had selected Sally Pedersen of Des Moines, a political unknown.[105]

The Lightfoot campaign was concerned about Iowa urban areas and in particular urban and suburban women, who tended to be moderate and focused on education, pocket book issues, and personal privacy.[106] Approaches to Mayor Lee Clancy of Cedar Rapids, Mayor Ann Hutchinson of Bettendorf, and Des Moines businesswoman Barbara Lukusky, owner of Merle Norman Products, yielded no running mate for Lightfoot.

Almo Hawkins, Republican candidate for lieutenant governor in 1998 (courtesy Almo Hawkins)

Leon Mosley (right), the popular conservative from Waterloo, co-chaired the Iowa Republican Party in the late 1990s. (courtesy Leon Mosley)

Lightfoot, a conservative from southwest Iowa, was heavily supported by the Christian Right of the GOP. He needed a candidate acceptable to the pro-life and social conservative factions of the convention. Years earlier, Gov. Terry Branstad selected Joy Corning of Black Hawk County, a pro-choice moderate, which caused a stir at the convention. Lightfoot — and particularly his wife, Nancy, who served as de facto campaign manger — did not want to revisit the issue of a pro-choice candidate on the ticket.

In late May or early June, the Lightfoot campaign began entertaining the idea of having a minority representative on the ticket. It would be historic and would put to rest the criticism that Lightfoot was a closet racist and that the Iowa GOP was insensitive to minorities, especially Hispanics and blacks. The Lightfoot campaign considered Leon Mosley of Waterloo. Mosley was a local political icon. A black conservative, Mosley was pro-life, a no-nonsense law-and-order man who thrilled Iowa audiences everywhere he appeared. A county supervisor, Mosley was a confident vote-getter in local elections. He was also a member of the Republican Iowa State Central Committee. But Mosley declined Lightfoot's offer, preferring to fight his political battles at the local level. (It should be noted that late in 1997 and early 1998, Mosley had entertained the idea of running for governor.[107])

In the moments before Lightfoot was introduced to the party's June 1998 convention, whispers were quickly spreading that Lightfoot had chosen an African-American woman as his running mate. Lightfoot came up to the platform accompanied by a striking black woman — Almo Hawkins — who immediately lit up the stage. Everyone held their breath at first and then gave voice to their excitement. Marlys Popma, an activist with the Iowa Christian Coalition and the pro-life movements and a resident of Jasper County, made the formal nomination of Hawkins as lieutenant governor.

The selection of Popma as Hawkins's nominator was no accident. It was strategically designed to send the right message to any doubtful Christian or social conservatives at the convention. Popma would later note that Hawkins "complete dedication to the Lord is what makes her tick."[108] With great joy in her voice and electricity in her eyes, Popma's nomination and speech put Hawkins into the convention record and the Iowa history books. It was a truly great moment.[109] Hawkins, then 61, had accomplished what no other African-American in Iowa political history had before her — a place at the top of a major party's political ticket.

To place Hawkins politically, prior to her nomination in 1998, she had a long-time association with Terry Branstad. In many respects one of his protégés, she had worked for the governor in several capacities and was then serving as his director of the Department of Human Rights. She also served as the governor's administrative assistant. Although an active Branstad supporter, Hawkins was not known as an activist Republican or loyal GOP partisan.[110] She had a history of registering as a Democratic. In 1996 she voted in the Democratic primary but changed her affiliation back to the GOP for its June 2 primary.[111] According to Tom Baker, Hawkins may have voted in the 1996 Democratic primary election to help him in a tight campaign for his party's nomination as supervisor.[112] She did not have a history of grassroots campaigning, caucus activity, or precinct party participation.

Hawkins was known as a very articulate and poised public speaker with years of professional experience as a TV reporter. She had also proven herself to be an able public administrator, though she had her detractors. Al Sturgeon, a former Democratic state senator, led a successful legislative effort to eliminate the Department of Human Rights. Under Hawkins's leadership, Sturgeon said, the agency had become "useless," with Hawkins only concerned with "shielding Governor Branstad from politically embarrassing advocacy initiatives by the commission."[113] Hawkins response was that "[Sturgeon's] very out of touch."[114] In an interview with the *Register*, Hawkins described herself as someone who "never forgets who she is or where she came from" and someone who understands what it means to come from a humble background, and to have lived through family tragedy and loss.[115]

Political loss came in November, when the Lightfoot-Hawkins ticket was soundly defeated by the Democratic ticket headed by Tom Vilsack. It would be the first time in 30 years that a Democrat had captured the governor's office. In a statement described by some as odd, Hawkins noted that although she never "encountered racism during her campaign to be Iowa's first African-

American lieutenant governor," she suspected her race could be one reason why she and Lightfoot were defeated. She further wondered if all Iowans were ready to elect a black woman to a high state office.[116]

Local Leadership Models

In November 1991 Al Saunders was elected mayor of Marble Rock, Iowa, thus becoming the first African-American elected mayor of an Iowa town or city.[117]

Marble Rock is approximately 26 miles southeast of Mason City, Saunders's childhood home. Saunders grew up in a family with deep roots in Iowa and the Midwest. His grandfather owned a home in Mason City, and his mother and father still live there. Saunders and his siblings were thus third-generation Iowans. The Saunderses trace their family back to Alabama, Kentucky, and Illinois.[118] (For $200, Al Saunders's great-uncle served in the Civil War in the place of a white man.)

Saunders is a quiet and unassuming man in his early seventies. He has led what he describes as a maverick lifestyle, challenging racial barriers and the status quo since his youth. He attended various colleges and universities, beginning at Mason City Junior College, then going on to the University of Iowa. He left the university after a year and enlisted in the U.S. Navy in July 1951. His tour of duty completed, Saunders returned to the University of Iowa.

The experience of military service strengthened Saunders's resolve to be treated equally. In an act of protest, Saunders walked into a local Iowa City barbershop to have his hair cut. After being refused service, Saunders and the Congress of Racial Equality (CORE) successfully brought suit. (The owner of the barbershop eventually went out of business.) Saunders was asked to leave the University of Iowa on at least two additional occasions involving, in his words, the "fight for justice and what was right."[119]

Approaching age 30, Saunders found himself on the campus of Parsons College in Fairfield, Iowa. He walked into the office of President Roberts, told his life story, and asked for another chance at getting a degree. The president was impressed and gave Saunders a note for the registrar. Later Roberts helped Saunders get a job in a local iron-casting company to supplement his $160 monthly income from the military. Saunders graduated from Parsons College in 1960.

During the next 30 years, Saunders lived all over the world,

Mason City native Al Saunders was elected mayor of Marble Rock after retiring and settling there in the 1980s. (courtesy Al Saunders)

Jane Burleson went from union activist to Fort Dodge city councilwoman.
(Messenger *clipping courtesy Jane*

primarily in the Far East. Working for the U.S. Department of Defense as a security specialist, he developed expertise in anti-terrorist activity.

Saunders resettled in the Midwest after leaving the military, first in Missouri, then in Mason City, and finally in Marble Rock. There he purchased a large home to accommodate the furniture and other treasures he had collected over the years. Within a year of his arrival in Marble Rock, Saunders had become part of the 300-person community. Approached by the former mayor and other community leaders about pursuing public office, Saunders ran a straightforward campaign and defeated the incumbent mayor by a margin of 2 to1.

Saunders had not been active in politics previously, and he did not become a party man after his election. But he held strong convictions about justice and equality, and he was self-confident and culturally rooted in Iowa. When political opportunity presented itself, Saunders was ready for the challenge. The choice was a natural one, for he believes that "people, especially young people, should participate in government service. It is an important factor in our lives. [Participation] is a way to get things done."[120]

Jane Burleson of Webster County

Jane Burleson's political career was inspired by Mississippi grassroots activist Fannie Lou Hamer, who rose to national prominence at the 1964 Democratic National Convention. Like Hamer, Burleson is high-spirited, fun-loving, and hard-driving. She is also a superb public speaker. Hers are the politics of protest, coupled with grassroots community organization. An active union worker and organizer, she enjoys a solid base of political support in Fort Dodge's working class and minority communities.

Like Willie Glanton and June Franklin, Burleson has worked her way up the ranks of Webster County's Democratic Party organization. In 1996, after serving on the Fort Dodge School Board and the City Council, she ran for a seat in the Iowa State Senate. Though she lost the Democratic primary, she remains a strong voice for working-class families and the disadvantaged.[121]

Des Moines's First Black Mayor

In 1991 Preston Daniels became the first African-American elected to the Des Moines City Council. Six years later, in 1997, he was elected mayor of Des Moines. Originally from Chicago, Daniels was raised in the Chesterfield section of southeast Des

Moines, commonly called the "southeast bottoms."[122] Journalist Denise Edington has noted that "Preston Daniels came from the poor side of town. He scratched his way out, earning respect and prestige along the way."[123] Entering public life as a community activist, Daniels's 1991 run for the Des Moines City Council was motivated by a concern for what was happening to the city's neighborhoods.[124] In that election, Daniels challenged incumbent Connie Cook, herself a well-known community activist and elementary school principal who was also active in the local Chamber of Commerce. Daniels's victory was very narrow, but not enough to warrant a recount by Cook.[125] In defeating Cook, Daniels captured an at-large Council seat.

According to former Drake Neighborhood Association president Marty Schmitt, Daniels was instrumental in changing the council's approach to allocating resources and implementing decisions affecting the neighborhoods.[126] Daniels asserted that during the 1960s and 1970s city government had ignored the needs of Des Moines's residential neighborhoods. Here Daniels echoed the sentiment of residents near downtown who watched development occur in the center of the city without benefiting the neighborhoods. But Daniels, who often referred to himself as a "process person," had little desire to polarize the issue and focused instead on finding solutions.[127]

In his years on the Council, Daniels enjoyed a strong working relationship with then-mayor Arthur Davis. One of their collaborations focused on attracting new employers to Des Moines. Equally important to Daniels and Davis was keeping a strong business core in the downtown area. Davis, one of Des Moines's top business leaders, counseled Daniels closely on the importance of city government partnering with the business community.

In 1997, shortly after Davis's death, Daniels emerged as a possible candidate to succeed his friend. Although ready to take the helm of the council, Daniels refused to compete against Councilwoman Christine Hensley, also a good friend of his. When Hensley decided not to run, Daniels stepped up, saying "This is something I was supposed to do."[128]

Daniels's strongest opponent in the October primary was Jim Cownie. A successful businessman and community leader with deep roots in Des Moines, Cownie raised $156,000 for his campaign. Daniels raised less than $30,000. Nevertheless, Daniels proved to be more effective with voters. Daniels stung Cownie in the primary, winning the vast majority of precincts.

Cownie fared well in the wealthy "South of Grand" area, in the southwest precincts, and in several northwest precincts — that is, in the city's affluent neighborhoods. He won but one precinct on the city's more modest east side.[129] By contrast, Daniels found strong support in all but the wealthiest areas of the city.

Daniels's campaign strategy for the November election emphasized the demographics revealed by the October primary, characterizing the race as a contest between a traditional Democrat and a high-profile Republican contributor. Daniels was aided by the intervention of U.S. Sen. Tom Harkin. Democratic contributor William Knapp apparently became annoyed by reports that Harkin directed part of Knapp's contribution to the Daniels campaign. But Harkin's help was pivotal to Daniels, both in terms of money and campaign machinery. Daniels also benefited from a split within the Polk County Democratic organization. Cownie had several high-level Democratic Central Committee members working on his campaign. Other Democratic activists, such as former state representative Jack Hatch, objected to Democrats assisting Cownie, who was well known as a Republican contributor. During recent elections at the city and county levels in Polk County, organized political efforts by southside Italian and eastside Irish political leaders have begun to surface against black candidates. Most notably, the mayoral contest between Preston Daniels and James Cownie found activist Democrats (elected Democrats and Central Committee members) supporting a registered Republican candidate (Cownie) instead of the Democratic candidate (Daniels).

Daniels skillfully characterized Cownie as a white "South of Grand" millionaire without credentials to lead — other than his ownership of a successful cable business. Compared to Daniels's image as a grassroots neighborhood activist, Cownie was portrayed as a member of the Des Moines elite. While the Des Moines mayoral election is historically non-partisan, Daniels's campaign defined the race as Republicans versus Democrats — that is, between the haves and the have-nots. Daniels also proved to be very effective at sustaining the support of organized labor. In a lengthy interview with the *Cornerstone*, published by the Central Iowa Building and Construction Trades Council, Daniels demonstrated deep understanding of labor issues. Although Cownie was certainly not an enemy of labor, he was not as effective as Daniels in responding to questions. Daniels noted in the interview that having "grown up in a union family and having been a member of union locals at both John Deere and UPS, I understand the

Mayor Preston Daniels, whose rise in Des Moines politics was marked by his continuing effort to bring new employers to the city (from Greater Des Moines: Iowa's Commercial Center)

*Clinton Mayor LaMetta Wynn took
office in 1996, following many years
of distinguished community service.
(Harry Baumert photo/
Des Moines Register)*

importance of unions, their values and work ethic. They are important . . . because they helped me achieve a livable working wage."[130] Daniels further noted that Cownie's "past performance with labor as the head of Heritage Cablevision did not demonstrate either a sympathetic or supportive view of labor issues."[131] Daniels's efforts in working the neighborhood associations — and his characterization of Cownie as a businessman concerned only about downtown — proved to be the winning formula in the November election, which Daniels won handily.

LaMetta Wynn Makes History

Once describing herself as ordinary, as someone who did not make history, Clinton's LaMetta Wynne was quick to add that she does want to make a difference.[132] Despite her self-effacing remarks, beginning in the 1980s LaMetta Wynne has became one of the most prominent public officials in Clinton political history. She represented one of the best examples of the organizational model of political leadership, serving in the Clinton Chamber of Commerce, the DuPont Citizens Advisory Committee, and the Mount St. Claire College Board of Trustees.[133] In 1983 Wynne was elected to the Clinton Board of Education.[134] In 1992 she sought a fourth term, stating her desire to serve a year for each of her ten children.[135] Known for her conservative style of dress and calm demeanor, Wynne used the art of persuasion and education to make her point and to champion issues. She carefully created a straightforward public-service image as someone who could be trusted. In one of her re-election bids, she said "you should vote for me because although you may not agree with me 100 percent on all issues, you can trust me to give careful thought and consideration to all issues and make decisions based on what is best for the kids and the district."[136] Wynne was re-elected by a landslide.[137]

In January 1996, Wynne made Iowa history as the first African-American woman to hold the office of mayor in Iowa.[138] Again she proved she was a strong voter favorite, capturing 53 percent of the vote in a city less than 45 percent African-American.[139] Thus reports of her victory noted that although the day had historic significance, race was not an issue in the election.

Conclusion

Iowa's African-American political heritage has three benchmark personalities, three individuals who loom especially large on the state's historical landscape. The first is Alexander G. Clark Sr., who established the African-American vision of equality and justice in the early years of statehood. A skilled politician, Clark allied with sympathetic white political leaders to enact repeal of Iowa's racist Black Codes. He also battled the discriminatory Negro Suffrage Laws in the Iowa Constitution.

Clark was known well beyond Muscatine, where he lived most of his adult life. He convened what was probably Iowa's first statewide African-American convention. In 1886 he was a key figure at the State Colored Convention in Des Moines, and he later represented Iowa at the National Colored Convention in Washington, D.C. Active in Republican Party politics, Clark was a delegate to state and national political conventions. His leadership skills and his dedication to Republican principles were brought to national attention in 1890, when Pres. Benjamin Harrison appointed Clark minister resident and consul general to the Republic of Liberia.[140]

However, Clark's most significant contribution to Iowa's African-American political heritage had been made more than 20 years earlier. In 1867, when his daughter was barred entry into the Muscatine public school, Clark brought suit against school officials. In the case of *Clark v. The Board of Directors, 1868,* the Iowa Supreme Court ruled that children of color could not be refused admission to public schools. The Court's landmark decision prohibits discrimination based on race, national origin, or creed in Iowa public schools.[141]

The second benchmark personality in Iowa's African-American political heritage is George E. Taylor. Like Clark, Taylor showed tenacity and courage in his lifelong struggle to advance the political rights of blacks in Iowa and across the nation.

Taylor devoted much of his time and money to the remote possibility of his becoming president of the United States. But putting aside his own political aspirations, Taylor believed that a unified black voting bloc at state political conventions, particularly in key battleground states, could pressure both major political parties to address issues important to African-Americans. Perhaps his ambitions were beyond reach, but Taylor had a keen political intellect. He spent his life trying to make the rhetoric of equality a reality for black Americans through legislative means. Long overlooked by scholars, Oskaloosa's George E. Taylor may have been the first African-American to see the potential of bloc voting to influence government policy on racial issues.

The third benchmark personality in Iowa's black political heritage is Almo Hawkins, Republican candidate for lieutenant governor in 1998. Hawkins's selection as Jim Ross Lightfoot's running mate surprised and pleased many Iowans, who saw it as a major milestone in the state's political evolution. Probably Alexander Clark Sr. and George W. Taylor would view 1998 that way too. Both men had a firm faith in the political process. They would cheer the Hawkins candidacy as a major victory in the long fight to secure for all Iowans rights and liberties guaranteed by state and national constitutions.

This victory was not diminished in any way when the Lightfoot-Hawkins ticket lost to the Democrats in November, for the fact had been established that an African-American could be a major-party candidate in Iowa. The question now has to do with who will be next to build on what was accomplished by Alexander Clark Sr., George E. Taylor, and Almo Hawkins. The political heritage they have started remains an unfinished agenda of hope and opportunity.

Taylor believed that a unified black voting bloc at state political conventions, particularly in key battleground states, could pressure both major political parties to address issues important to African-Americans.

Ronald N. Langston has over 25 years experience in the public, private, and non-profit sectors: in legislative research, governmental affairs, administrative management, corporate marketing, micro-enterprise business development, sales, real estate, and public policy. He has served as sales representative with Crowley Mandelbaum Real Estate Services; economic development director, Institute for Social and Economic Development (ISED), Iowa City; assistant director for national markets and corporate officer for the Principal Financial Group; vice president, Des Moines Chamber of Commerce Federation; legislative assistant, U.S. Senate; presidential appointee to the U.S. Department of Health and Human Services, Washington, D.C.; and research analyst, Iowa Legislative Service Bureau.

In the elections of 1996 and 2000, he was the Republican candidate from Iowa Senate District 36, Polk County. In 1997, Mr. Langston was appointed to the Iowa Department of Transportation (IDOT) Commission by Gov. Terry E. Branstad.

On March 19, 2001, Langston was sworn in as the 14th director of the Minority Business Agency (MBDA). As director, he serves at the pleasure of the President of the United States and reports directly to the U.S. Secretary of Commerce.

Mr. Langston holds degrees from the University of Iowa, City University of New York (CUNY), and Harvard University.

Notes

1. Leland Sage, *A History of Iowa* (Ames: Iowa State Univ. Press, 1974), 118. For a comprehensive review of white perceptions of blacks, see Winthrop D. Jordan, *White Over Black; American Attitudes towards the Negro, 1550–1812* (Chapel Hill: Univ. of North Carolina Press, 1968). See also G. Galin Berrier, "The Negro Suffrage Issue in Iowa, 1865–1868," *AI* 3rd ser. 39 (1968): 241–61. Anti-abolitionist sentiment in Iowa is noted in Thomas A. Lucas, "Men Were Too Fiery for Much Talk: The Grinnell Anti-Abolitionist Riot of 1860," *Palimpsest* 69 (1987): 12–21.

2. Leola Bergmann, *The Negro in Iowa* (Iowa City: SHSI, 1948; repr. 1969), 6–8.

3. Robert Cook, *Baptism of Fire: The Republican Party of Iowa, 1838–1878* (Ames: Iowa State Univ. Press, 1993), 75.

4. Ibid., 80.

5. Ibid., 76.

6. Ibid., 80.

7. Ibid., 94.

8. Ibid.

9. Bergmann, 51.

10. Ibid.

11. Ibid.

12. Cook, 77.

13. Ibid., 94.

14. Sage, 180.

15. Bergmann, 52.

16. Ibid.

17. Ibid.

18. Ibid.

19. Ibid., 53. Richard Lord Acton and Patricia Nassif Acton, *To Go Free: A Treasury of Iowa's Legal History* Ames: Iowa State Univ. Press, 1995), 155–56.

20. Bergmann, 53; Acton and Acton, 156.

21. *Plessy v. Ferguson,* 163 U.S. 537 (1896).

22. *DMR,* Dec. 15, 1912.

23. Ibid.

24. Alton Hornsby Jr., *The Black Almanac: From Involuntary Servitude, 1619–1860, to the Age of Disillusionment, 1964–1972* (New York: Barrons, 1972), 48.

25. John Hope Franklin, *From Slavery to Freedom: A History of Negro Americans,* 3rd ed. (New York: Vintage Books, 1967), 284. The convention "discussed questions of employment, enfranchisement, and the extension of freedom."

26. George Taylor, "A National Appeal," July 14, 1892.

27. *African-American Voices of Triumph, Leadership* (Alexandria: Time-Life Books, 1993), 150.

28. Ibid., 151.

29. Ibid.

30. Taylor, "National Appeal to the American Negro, Why We Should Favor the Chicago Platform," [Document 1] Aug. 8, 1896; [Document 2] Sept. 21, 1896.

31. Ibid. [Document 1], 1.

32. Ibid. [Document 2], 3. "Upon all of the above issues," wrote Taylor, "Mr. McKinley argues at great length and offers not the slightest suggestion as to what should, or might, or could be done to harmonize matters between the Negro and the whites in those sections where naught but discord and turbulence are said to prevail."

33. Ibid.

34. Ibid., 9. Taylor: "For more than twenty years the prices of commodities and labor in this country have been on the decline and history discloses the fact that when the prices of staple commodities and labor decline 'confidence' also declines, as if from sympathy. When prices are advancing and wages are going up 'confidence' is restored and money goes in search of opportunities for investment."

35. Ibid., 8.

36. Ibid. [Document 2], 13–14.

37. George Edwin Taylor, "The National Liberty Party's Appeal," *The Independent,* Oct. 13, 1904, 844–66. This is the full text of Taylor's national platform.

38. Ibid., 846.

39. Acton and Acton, 233. Woodson came to Mahaska County in 1896 and moved to Buxton in 1900. See Bergmann, 43.

40. Bergmann, 43.

41. Ibid.

42. Gertrude Rush was the first black woman to practice law in Iowa and to become a member of the Iowa Bar Association. She later became the president of the Iowa National Bar Association. See Acton and Acton, 233.

43. Ibid.

44. Taylor, "A National Appeal," 2.

45. Paul D. Casdorph, *Republicans, Negroes, and Progressives in the South, 1912–1916* (University AL: Univ. of Alabama Press, 1981), viii. Casdorph details the schism of the Old Confederacy and the struggle for the presidency between Theodore Roosevelt and Howard Taft. He writes, "an important outcome of the titanic confrontation between the Roosevelt and Taft loyalists . . . is that both camps made it nearly impossible for the Negro to continue his association with the GOP after 1912."

46. Ibid.

47. Charles E. Wynes, "'Alexander the Great,' Bridge Builder," *Palimpsest* 66 (May/June 1985): 78.

48. Ibid., 78–90.

49. *DMR,* Oct. 6, 1932.

50. Ibid., 78–80.

51. Willie Stevenson Glanton interviews, Jan. 25, 1999, and Feb. 1, 1999.

52. Ibid.

53. Ibid.

54. Ibid.

55. Ibid. The poll tax was a "practice of requiring voters to pay a tax to vote. In the past the practice was used in the South to prohibit blacks from voting." It was made unconstitutional by ratification of the 24th amendment in 1964. *Random House Encyclopedia* (New York: Random House, 1977), 2496.

56. Willie Glanton interviews.

57. Ibid.

58. Ibid.

59. Ibid.

60. Ibid.

61. Ibid.

62. Ibid.

63. Ibid.

64. Ibid. The Roosevelt Club was the blackw Democratic club and was chaired by James Rhodes of Des Moines. The Roosevelt Club also served as a de facto social organization for the city's black elite.

65. Willie Glanton interviews.

66. Ibid.

67. Ibid.

68. Ibid.

69. *Iowa Official Register, 1965–66* (Des Moines: State of Iowa, 1965), 415.

70. Ibid., 396.

71. Willie Glanton interviews; *DMR,* Mar. 2, 1966; Aug. 4, 6, and 24, 1966; April 9, 15, 21, and 23, 1967. Author thanks John Zeller for these citations.

72. Cecil A. Reed, with Priscilla Donovan, *A Fly in the Buttermilk: The Life Story of Cecil Reed* (Iowa City: Univ. of Iowa Press, 1993), 128.

73. Nolden Gentry interview, Fall 1998.

74. *Iowa Bystander,* July 21, 1966.

75. *Iowa Official Register, 1967–68* (Des Moines: State of Iowa, 1967), 81.

76. Ibid.

77. *Iowa Bystander,* Dec. 3, 1964.

78. *Iowa Bystander,* May 30, 1968.

79. *Iowa Bystander,* Aug. 17, 1967.

80. *Iowa Official Register, 1967–68, 1969–70,* and *1971–72* (Des Moines: State of Iowa, 1967, 1969, 1971).

81. Reed, 2–3.

82. Ibid., 5–6.

83. Ibid., 110

84. Ibid.

85. Ibid., 122.

86. Ibid.

87. Ibid., 123–24.

88. Ibid., 126–27.

89. Ibid., 128–32.

90. Ibid., 128–29.

91. Ibid., 130.

92. Ibid., 131.

93. Ibid., 135.

94. Ibid., 133. The Iowa Employment Security Commission was later renamed the Iowa Job Service Department and today is called the Workforce Development Department.

95. Ibid., 135.

96. Ibid., 139.

97. *Iowa Official Register, 1974–75* (Des Moines: State of Iowa, 1974), 68.

98. *Iowa Official Register, 1983–84* (Des Moines: State of Iowa, 1983), 36.

99. *Iowa Official Register, 1982–83* (Des Moines: State of Iowa, 1982).

100. Baker, Sullivan, and Shulte were the challengers in the 1996 contest for Polk County supervisor.

101. George W. Boykin interview by Hal Chase, Summer 2000.

102. Nick Hytrek, "Outdoor Life Beckons Boykin after Community Service," *Sioux City Journal,* Feb. 18, 2001.

103. Ibid.

104. *DMR,* June 14, 1998.

105. *DMR,* June 16, 1998.

106. *DMR,* June 14, 1998.

107. Ibid. Leon Mosley interview, June 13, 1998.

108. *DMR,* June 14, 1998.

109. Ibid.

110. *DMR,* June 17, 1998.

111. Ibid.

112. Ibid.

113. Ibid.

114. Ibid.

115. Ibid.

116. *DMR,* Dec. 20, 1998.

117. Al Saunders interview, Summer 1999.

118. *DMR,* Jan. 26, 1992.

119. Saunders interview.

120. Ibid.

121. *DMR,* June 14, 1998. *Fort Dodge Messenger,* April 25, 1981; Nov. 9, 1983; April 26, 1990.

122. *Business Record,* July 28, 1997, 10–11.

123. Ibid.

124. Ibid.

125. *DMR,* Nov. 6, 1991.

126. Ibid.

127. Ibid.

128. Ibid.

129. *DMR,* Oct. 9, 1997.

130. *The Cornerstone,* Aug. 18, 1997.

131. Ibid., 4.

132. *DMR,* Feb. 15, 1999.

133. *Clinton Herald,* Aug. 27, 1992.

134. Ibid.

135. Ibid.

136. Ibid.

137. *Clinton Herald,* Jan. 3, 1996.

138. Ibid.

139. Ibid.

140. Acton and Acton, 155–56.

141. Ibid., 130–32. *Clark v. Board of Directors* 24 Iowa 266 (1868).

(Left to right)

Perry native Art Johnson has won two terms as Dallas County sheriff. (courtesy Art Johnson)

Fred Morris Brown's long career of public service in Des Moines County included serving as a deputy sheriff from 1969 to 1979, then as elected Commissioner of Parks and Public Property for the city of Burlington. (courtesy MarSeine Brown)

Sioux City friends, c. 1950 (Sioux City, Iowa Club of Los Angeles / Sioux City Public Museum)

Unsung Heroines

African-American Women in Iowa

by Kathryn M. Neal

Three questions are relevant to an exploration of the history of African-American women in Iowa: How have black women survived — and in some cases, thrived — in a state in which African-Americans have never exceeded two percent of the general population and in a larger society that has often viewed their race and gender as liabilities? How did they settle in Iowa? And what did they do once they arrived?[1]

This chapter provides a broad sweep of black women's presence in Iowa. By no means is it a comprehensive study. An examination of nearly 170 years of African-American women's history in Iowa could compose a book in itself. African-American women have lived in Iowa during every decade since the 1830s, in rural as well as in urban environments.

They also have been involved in virtually every aspect of the state's social and economic history, contributing to areas that include but are not limited to the arts, business, education, journalism, the legal profession, literature, medicine, the military, and religion. Of the thousands of stories that could be told, this chapter will feature stories of the lives of women whose roles fall into two categories:

women who were or are pioneers and women who have served as builders of their communities. The term "pioneers" refers to women who helped pave the way in a profession or broke ground in a particular set of circumstances — for example, those who were early settlers in a particular area or early civil rights activists. "Builders of community" refers to women such as club organizers and volunteers who played significant roles in establishing and sustaining community ties. Of course, some women fit both categories.

Despite efforts made by white officials to prevent their settlement, a small number of African-Americans made Iowa their home in the decade prior to the state entering the Union on December 28, 1846. Attracted to the prospect of greater economic opportunities, they traveled from the South along the Mississippi and Missouri rivers and settled in the area's southern border communities.[2]

While some of these women and men arrived in the territory as free people, others were brought in as slaves or domestic servants. Still others fled southern states as fugitive slaves.

Of the thousands of stories that could be told, this chapter will feature stories of the lives of women whose roles fall into two categories: women who were or are pioneers and women who have served as builders of their communities.

While it is difficult to determine who was the first African-American woman in the territory, what she and the other early female settlers did occupationally once they arrived is much more clear. Throughout most of the nineteenth century, African-American women (and men) could typically secure only low-paying, low-skill jobs. Commonly, those black women who worked outside the home became cooks, domestics, housekeepers, and laundresses.[3] Even well into the twentieth century, domestic work would be one of the primary occupational venues open to black women, not only in Iowa but also throughout the country.

The eastern Iowa town of Dubuque can lay claim to some of the earliest African-American settlers. As one of these residents, Charlotte Morgan can certainly be called a pioneer. Morgan's story, although sketchy, illustrates the threats faced by and the endurance required of African-American women living in Iowa during the early years of settlement. She and her husband, Nathaniel (also known as Nat) Morgan, moved to Iowa from nearby Galena, Illinois, a mining town from which many other Dubuque settlers hailed. The couple obtained jobs in a boarding house in town in 1833. By the following year, Charlotte Morgan was noted as one of seven charter members of Dubuque's and the territory's first place of worship, a Methodist church. She went on to become a laundress in one of the town's hotels.

Despite the fact that her husband was accused of theft and lynched by an angry mob in 1840, Charlotte Morgan continued to reside in Dubuque. In 1850, she was serving as a live-in housekeeper for two miners who had immigrated from Britain and Scotland. Whereas there had been ten free black households in Dubuque in 1840, apparently only two remained in 1850. Charlotte Morgan headed one of these.[4] Unfortunately, we do not know what became of Charlotte Morgan. Her story has been pieced together from census records, references in newspapers, and local histories. Most African-American women in Iowa from this period remain unknown or anonymous.

During the 1850s, the largest number of African-Americans resided in Muscatine, a lumber-milling center.[5] While black women in nineteenth-century Dubuque and other Iowa towns continued to fill low-paying occupational roles, historian Dorothy Schwieder notes that "[b]ecause census takers did not typically single out women who took boarders into their homes, it is possible that women earned money from that practice, thus serving as unacknowledged but independent wage earners."[6]

During the antebellum years, African-American women also entered Iowa via the Underground Railroad, the escape routes and centers of which dotted the state's landscape. The precise number of women who traveled this route cannot be easily determined because of the clandestine nature of the network and shortage of documentation. While Quakers played a significant role in helping these fugitive slaves flee to safety, some black Iowans took action as well.[7] A noteworthy pioneer in this vein was Charlotta Pyles, whose antislavery efforts not only helped to sustain her own family unit but also might have increased the state's African-American population to some extent.

Charlotta Pyles was not born in Iowa. Rather, she and her twelve children were enslaved and living on the Kentucky plantation of a family named Gordon in the early 1850s. Harry Pyles, Charlotta's husband, was a free black who operated a nearby harness and shoe-mending shop.[8] When the plantation master died, he bequeathed Charlotta Pyles and her children to his daughter, Miss Gordon, who promised to give the family its freedom. In fall 1853, Charlotta, her husband, eleven of their children, and Miss Gordon headed west en route to Minnesota. However, the threat of the coming winter caused the group to settle in Keokuk, Iowa.[9]

Once in free territory, Charlotta Pyles set about to purchase the freedom of her two sons-in-law, who remained enslaved in Kentucky — in part to ease the financial burden that caring for her daughters' families was placing on her own. To earn the $3,000 that would enable her to free these men, Pyles obtained letters of recommendation from prominent whites and traveled throughout the East, appealing to antislavery proponents on behalf of her sons-in-law. Along the way, she became acquainted with such notable figures as Frederick Douglass, Lucretia Mott, and Susan B. Anthony. Charlotta Pyles, who had never received an education, moved audiences with her pleas, and in the course of six months she raised the funds necessary to secure the men's freedom. Yet these efforts proved to be only the beginning of her activities. "Many a slave, coming from Kentucky, Tennessee, and Missouri, found at the gateway into Iowa an enthusiastic member of their own race in the person of Grandma Pyles," her granddaughter recounted. "She received them into her own home, and, with the aid of many white friends she had made on her trip, helped them make their escape to Canada." Charlotta Pyles died in 1880 at age 74.[10]

Even well into the twentieth century, domestic work would be one of the primary occupational venues open to black women, not only in Iowa but also throughout the country.

With the onset of the Civil War, federal initiatives brought additional African-American women to the state. In 1863, the Union Army implemented a relocation program, which resulted in at least 4,000 freed slaves—most of them women and children—being sent to Iowa and other Midwestern states.[11] While it is not known exactly how many African-American women were sent to Iowa, the towns where these individuals were relocated included Keokuk and Mount Pleasant.[12] In Keokuk, at least, the women found themselves subjected to jobs for which they were paid less than unskilled white workers, thanks to the efforts of the local provost marshal. White Iowans in other areas openly opposed the entrance of former slaves into the state through organized efforts.[13]

The enlistment of black men into the military also affected African-American Iowa women during the Civil War years. Enlistment into Iowa's black regiment, the 60th U.S. Colored Infantry, began in the late summer of 1863. As historian Leslie A. Schwalm points out, "In Iowa, the enlistment of black men meant that for the remainder of the war, black women and their children negotiated white racism and the erosion of black freedom largely on their own and at precisely the moment when white midwesterners reacted loudly and violently to the perceived threat of black migration out of the South to the Midwest." Some black women in Muscatine and Keokuk responded to this situation by organizing to support the state's black regiment, while others decided to risk the dangers of the battlefront by accompanying their men to the camps.[14] No matter what their experiences, African-American women in Iowa managed to weather the war years. However, there would be a variety of other battles to come.

The End of Slavery Intensified Fears

The Civil War and the end of slavery intensified the fears of many white Iowans. Even those individuals who had harbored abolitionist or antislavery sentiments questioned how the newfound freedom of African-Americans throughout the nation might affect their families, towns, and the state as a whole. They wondered if the end of slavery might bring an influx of African-Americans into Iowa, if cheap black labor would pose economic risks to white workers, and whether social threats — such as integrated schools and interracial marriage — would intensify. Prejudice and discrimination resulted, laying the groundwork for the largely separate existences that black and white residents would lead in most Iowa cities even into the 1900s.[15]

To be sure, school integration did come to Iowa. Following the war, the struggle for educational rights for African-Americans was waged in Muscatine. During the 1850s, the majority of the state's African-Americans resided in Muscatine, a lumber-milling center.[16] More significantly, Muscatine had a strong tradition of education in the African-American community. A young African-American schoolteacher was a part of this population — a Kentucky native named Sarah Davidson.[17] So, too, was the prominent black family of Alexander and Catherine Griffin Clark.

In 1855, a baby girl, Susan V. Clark, was born to Alexander and Catherine.[18] Growing up, Susan and her older sister Rebecca were educated primarily in their Muscatine home, yet they apparently also attended classes in other homes and in a de facto school that was operated out of the town's African Methodist Episcopal Church.[19] In 1867, Susan was denied admission to Muscatine Public School No. 2. Her father was prompted to file a lawsuit, which was tried at the district-court level. It is not entirely clear how active a role Susan — or, for that matter, her mother — played in Alexander Clark's decision to take the matter to court, but it is noteworthy that when the case was appealed to the Iowa Supreme Court in 1868, it was registered in the name of "Susan V. Clark by her next best friend Alexander Clark vs. the Muscatine Board of Education."[20] In July 1868, the Iowa Supreme Court rendered public-school discrimination illegal, deciding that no student could be excluded from a common school because of race, nationality, religion, dress, and so on.[21] The Clarks emerged victorious, but racial discrimination would continue to plague various aspects of African-American Iowans' lives into the next century.

From the Civil War's end through the early decades of the twentieth century, African-Americans continued to migrate into Iowa. They settled primarily in the state's agricultural counties on the southern border, Mississippi River counties to the east, Missouri River counties to the west, and "a parallelogram of counties running in a southeasterly direction from Polk County," which included Marion, Mahaska, Monroe, and Wapello counties.[22] Work in the coal mines attracted many of the male migrants.[23] Although some African-Americans therefore lived in coal-mining camps, a growing number of others settled in urban areas from the outset or began to move from rural to urban environments starting in the 1880s.[24] An overwhelming majority of black girls and women during this period held domestic or personal-service positions.

"In Iowa, the enlistment of black men meant that for the remainder of [the Civil War], black women and their children negotiated white racism and the erosion of black freedom largely on their own. . . ."

— Leslie A. Schwalm

According to the 1920 census, 1,897 of the 2,299, or 82 percent of respondents selected this category. The category "manufacturing and mechanical industries" came in a distant second, with 195 of the 2,299 (or roughly 8 percent) black females choosing it.[25] However, economic survival was not the sole concern of black women at this time. At the turn of the century, groups of African-American women in Iowa would also devote their attention to moral and social issues.

Educational and Social Uplift and Racial Pride

Paralleling a national trend that some historians have argued was a natural outgrowth of the Progressive movement, African-American women in Iowa formed many clubs during the early decades of the twentieth century.[26] The establishment of the National Association of Colored Women (NACW) in 1896 served as an impetus for the creation of these clubs, most of which shared missions based on educational and social uplift and racial pride.[27] Besides offering opportunities for social interaction, they also provided vehicles for combating the racial and sexual stereotypes attributed to black women by many white Americans. If members of black women's clubs in Iowa resembled those in the NACW, they were primarily middle-class, educated, and proponents of the Protestant work ethic.[28]

With Mrs. Helena Downey at the helm as president, the Iowa State Federation of Afro-American Women's Clubs was organized in Ottumwa in June 1902.[29] The name would be changed to the Iowa Federation of Colored Women's Clubs (IFCWC) sometime within the first few years of its existence. Early IFCWC members developed their mission in the spirit of the motto of their parent organization, the NACW, "Lifting as We Climb." The motto of the state federation would become "Sowing Seeds of Kindness." The preamble of the club's 1903 constitution states, "Whereas Experience has shown that knowledge may be more readily acquired by a combination of efforts rather than by single ones, and feeling the need of an organized and united effort for the betterment of the home and social life of the Afro-American people, we thereby do unite into a State Federation."[30] First on the list of objectives in the constitution was the charge "to secure harmony in action and co-operation among women in raising their home, moral and civil life to the highest standard."[31] Besides Ottumwa, clubs in such towns as Davenport, Dubuque, Oskaloosa, Keokuk, Cedar Rapids, and Des Moines, and the coal-mining

Unidentified Iowa women in late Victorian dress, c. 1900 (photo above courtesy Robert Boldridge; below, Aldeen Davis)

camp of Muchakinock would become part of the state federation.[32] In 1910, the IFCWC would unite with the NACW and become incorporated three years later. The name of the organization was changed to the Iowa Association of Colored Women's Clubs in 1938 (hereafter referred to as the IACWC).[33] During the early 1960s, it would change again, albeit briefly, to the Iowa Association of Club Women.[34] The desire to eliminate "Colored," which was becoming an outmoded term, from the organization's name no doubt reflects a gradual shift in racial identity of its members. Interestingly, the members chose to remove all reference to race. However, by the time of the organization's 1969 convention in Des Moines, "Colored" had returned.[35]

Improvement of black women's home and social lives has remained a focus for the IACWC, yet concern for the welfare of children and for civil rights have also merited attention over the years. The organization's statement of purpose listed in the program for the 1969 convention reflects such changes. According to this statement, the IACWC exists

- To promote the education of women and girls through local, state and regional activities and the sponsorship of institutes at each biennial convention

- To raise the standard of the home and to advance the moral, economic, social and religious welfare of the family

- To protect the rights of women and children who work; to encourage the use of our influence for the enforcement of civil rights for all citizens; and to obtain equal opportunity for qualified women in all areas of employment

- To promote interracial understanding, justice and peace among all people[36]

Nearing its centennial, the association continues to function both as a social outlet and as an agent for community service.

Two particularly noteworthy pioneers and community builders in Des Moines, whose activities spanned much of the first half of the twentieth century, also happened to serve as presidents of the IFCWC. Gertrude Rush and Sue M. Wilson Brown (1877–1941) contributed to the civic, economic, political, religious, and social arenas of the state's African-American communities. Born in Staunton, Virginia, but reared in Oskaloosa, Sue M. Wilson married attorney S. Joe Brown in 1902.[37] The couple settled in Des Moines, where each strove to enhance the lives of African-Americans locally and nationally. Sue Brown established a number of clubs, including the Intellectual Improvement Club in 1906 and the Des Moines League of Colored Women Voters. She founded the *Iowa Colored Woman,* the journal of the IFCWC, in 1907 and served as its editor until 1909.[38] From 1915 to 1917, she presided over the IFCWC.

In 1925, Brown broke ground as the first female president of the Des Moines branch of the NAACP, a chapter which her husband had helped to create a decade earlier. She would serve a six-year term.[39] Brown was also quite active in religious organizations — as a member of the Des Moines branch of the Church Women's Interracial Commission, for example — and in Republican politics. In addition, she was a published author. She wrote, among other books, the *History of the O.E.S. (Order of the Eastern Star) among Colored People,* yet another organization to which she belonged.[40]

As her social and political activities illustrate, the effects of Brown's leadership extended well beyond the city limits of Des Moines. For example, in 1917, as she prepared to retire from her presidency of the IFCWC, Brown appointed a committee to aid African-American female students at the State University of Iowa (now the University of Iowa) in Iowa City. Black students at that time (and well into the 1940s) were not welcome to live in university dormitories. Most women had to find housing with faculty members, for whom they would work as domestics and thereby earn their keep. The committee selected a two-story home at 942 Iowa Avenue, which was purchased by the club, and in 1919 established it as the Iowa Federation Home, a dormitory for black coeds that would operate at the university throughout the 1940s.[41]

While the activities of Gertrude Durden Rush (1880–1962) were as varied as Sue Brown's, Rush's primary accomplishment lay in the legal profession. The Texas-born Rush moved to Iowa from Kansas in 1907. In 1914, after receiving her bachelor's degree from the former Des Moines University, she married local attorney James B. Rush and later began to study law at Drake University Law School. In 1918, Gertrude Rush passed the Iowa State Bar Examination, becoming the first — and, until the 1950s, the only — African-American woman to practice law in the state of Iowa. Despite this achievement, she and four black male colleagues found themselves denied admission into the American Bar Association in 1924. The following year, the quintet founded their own organization based in Des Moines, the National Bar Association.

Federated Women's Club, Des Moines (courtesy Lynda Walker-Webster)

In 1912, Rush herself established the Charity League, a welfare organization for African-Americans; its establishment helped lead to the hiring of an African-American probation officer in Des Moines's juvenile court. Gertrude Rush was also involved in the IFCWC on the local and state levels, serving as state president from 1911 to 1915, and was an active member of several other clubs and organizations as well as her church.[42]

During the period when Brown and Rush were embarking on their pioneering initiatives, a plethora of women's clubs flourished in the predominantly African-American coal-mining camp of Buxton, which existed in Monroe County from approximately 1900 to 1920. Women residents established a chapter of the Federated Colored Women's Clubs early in the camp's history. Between the years 1903 and 1911, these women would go on to form several other clubs and organizations, including the Ladies Industrial Club; the True Reformers, a secret society; the Sweet Magnolia Club; the Silver Leaf Club, reportedly one of the camp's most elite; the Fannie Barrier Williams Club; the Self Culture Club; and the Progressive Women's Club. Lodges — such as the Order of the Eastern Star, the Court of Calanthia, the Household of Ruth, the Virginia Queen's Court, and the Knights and Daughters of the Tabernacle — also attracted the membership of many Buxton women.[43]

To the east, in Keokuk, another group would spring to life during the early years of the new century. In 1913, ten women

Sue M. Wilson Brown (1877–1941), whose commitment to women's advancement through professional associations and service organizations may be unrivaled in Iowa history (Iowa Bystander)

Maude Burkett's ice cream social, Buxton, c. 1910 (SHSI Des Moines)

created the Self-Culture Club. Their mission included discussion of current events and news, as well as the study of black history. Although initially organized for African-American women only, some white women have been accepted as members over the course of the club's history.[44] As of 1998, the Self-Culture Club still exists, making it one of the oldest groups in Iowa.

Another product of the club movement, African-American panhellenic organizations, would also arrive in Iowa during the early twentieth century. Local chapters of the four national black sororities — Alpha Kappa Alpha, Delta Sigma Theta, Zeta Phi Beta, and Sigma Gamma Rho — have been established in Iowa throughout most of this century. The first to come were chapters of Delta Sigma Theta. In 1919, the Delta chapter was formed at the State University of Iowa (now the University of Iowa) in Iowa City.[45] The Phi chapter was established at Drake University in Des Moines four years later.[46] Drake was also home to Beta Gamma, the premier chapter of Alpha Kappa Alpha, which was founded in 1932.[47] The formation of black sororities on Iowa campuses, though few, was no doubt linked to the relative increase in African-American women attending college at that time. Pioneering college graduates from that era include Adah Hyde Johnson, class of 1912, one of the first black women to graduate from the University of Iowa.[48] At Iowa State Teachers' College (now the University of Northern Iowa), Vivian B. Smith earned that distinction when she graduated in 1916.[49]

Nineteenth Amendment Is a Victory for All Iowa Women

While a number of black Iowa women were primarily concerned with improving their collective images during the mid–1910s, there is evidence that some joined their white female counterparts in seeking the passage of an amendment to the U.S. Constitution that would grant women voting rights. Vivian Smith illustrates this phenomenon, having been a member of the Waterloo Suffragette Council.[50] The women of Buxton provide another example; they spoke out publicly in favor of granting women the right to vote by participating in a June 1916 family parade on suffrage.[51] When the nineteenth amendment was finally ratified nationwide in 1920, it was a victory for all Iowa women.

United States involvement in World War 1 (1917–1918) opened new avenues of volunteer work for African-American women. Some, for example, became involved in the efforts of the Red Cross. Members of a Sioux City organization promised to donate 50 pairs of pajamas to the Red Cross each week that the war continued.[52] During the Christmas holidays in 1918, the Red Cross in Des Moines played a role in brightening the holiday season for African-American soldiers who remained at Camp Dodge. The Red Cross undertook several measures to ensure that all of the soldiers stationed at the camp enjoyed the season. One such endeavor called for officers in the camp to identify the soldiers who had neither friends nor family nearby. Many of these so-called "friendless" soldiers were African-American, so "[a] big Christmas tree was set up by the Red Cross for their special benefit at the colored hostess house."[53] The hostess house had been established in the camp during the summer of 1918 for the African-American women who visited the stationed soldiers.[54] In Marshalltown, women from the predominately black Second Baptist Church were among the more than 21 groups of women from that area who offered their assistance to the Red Cross.[55] The war effort also presented an opportunity for some women to apply their occupational skills to helping the cause. Caterer Marie Bell, for instance, taught classes on the cold-pack canning method to black Des Moines women.[56]

Georgine Crowe Morris (1890–1977) provided assistance during the war in a rather different way. In 1919, she learned to speak French and then taught the language to African-

Delta Sigma Theta group in front of the old St. Paul's AME church in Des Moines, c. 1917 (Grout Museum)

*Georgine Morris and her family
(courtesy Morris family)*

American wives who were awaiting the return of their military husbands who had been shipped off to France. A year earlier, Georgine Crowe had married James B. (J. B.) Morris, a lawyer and U.S. Army second lieutenant. J. B. Morris himself had been stationed in France.

Georgine Morris's efforts to aid black women during World War 1 represent but one example of her attempts to unify African-American communities in and out of Iowa.[57] Born in Madison County, Virginia, Georgine Crowe moved with her family to Baltimore in 1899 to escape the Jim Crow segregation that prevailed in Virginia. After graduating from the Maryland Institute of Technology with a major in textiles and designing, she enrolled at Howard University in Washington, D.C., where she continued her studies in those areas. While attending Howard, she met J. B. Morris, her future husband. In 1918, the couple married and settled in Des Moines, shortly before J. B. Morris was sent to fight in the war. Four years later, following his return, Georgine Morris assisted him in purchasing, and then publishing, the *Iowa Bystander*. A weekly newspaper, the *Bystander* served as an organ for communicating news of black Iowans throughout the state. At the same time, Georgine Morris put her training to work as a professional seamstress and designer.

The 1920s would also mark the beginning of Georgine

Morris's long-time involvement with the NAACP. During that decade, as a member of the Des Moines branch of that organization, she joined its struggle to stem the growth of the Ku Klux Klan within Iowa.[58] In 1939, she strove to promote unity among the state's NAACP chapters by organizing the Iowa State Conference of NAACP Branches and became its first president. The following year, she was elected president of the Des Moines NAACP. During the 1940s, Morris assisted the NAACP on the national level by participating in a dangerous initiative. She became the Des Moines branch organizer for the national office, under the executive direction of Walter White, with whom she had been acquainted while living in Baltimore. White assigned Morris to travel between NAACP branches in the Deep South because she could "pass" for white due to her light complexion. However, one of these missions nearly became fatal when Morris's true identity as a black person was discovered, and she was attacked by a mob of whites in Houston, Texas.

Georgine Morris continued to strive for the rights of African-Americans and the creation of better communities throughout the rest of her life. In the 1950s, she founded the Des Moines chapter of the Links, Inc., a national organization for black women that is dedicated to promoting civic, cultural, and educational activities among disadvantaged African-Americans.[59]

By 1930, the majority of African-American women in the state (1,800 of 2,004) would identify themselves as engaged in "domestic or personal service," according to that year's census. Of that group, 1,333 classified themselves as servants, 149 as laundresses, and 66 as housekeepers. The census category with the next highest number (77) was "manufacturing and mechanical industries," which accounted for almost 4 percent of total respondents.[60] Forty-two African-American women selected the heading "professional service." Within this category, 10 women identified themselves as teachers and 8 as musicians or teachers of music. Thirty-eight women placed themselves under the heading of "clerical occupations," store clerks excepted.[61]

Black Women Remained Trapped in Domestic Jobs

As the decade wore on, most Iowans felt the blow of the Great Depression. Not surprisingly, African-Americans, who numbered less than 1 percent of the state's total population, had the greatest difficulty securing work during this period. The jobs they managed to obtain continued to be unskilled and semiskilled positions.[62] Most African-American women remained trapped in domestic jobs, but many also experienced layoffs as the adverse economic conditions rendered such work less necessary.[63]

World War 2 (1941–45) changed the face of the American worker. Single and married women entered the work force en masse, fulfilling their patriotic duty by filling vacancies left by men sent off to fight. However, not all women benefited from this phenomenon. "The image of a smiling Rosie Riveter was etched into the consciousness," historian Paula Giddings writes. "But the great employment wave withered to a trickle when it came to [b]lack workers in general and [b]lack women in particular."[64] Dorothy Schwieder speculates that African-American women in Iowa moved beyond the occupational categories they had been forced to accept, as did their counterparts in a few other cities.[65] Relegated primarily to unskilled and servile positions, even those who managed to obtain jobs in industrial factories and defense plants tended to find their employment to be tenuous at best.[66]

A different role awaited a small group of African-American women who would have an effect on the Iowa home front. More than 20 years after black male soldiers were trained at Fort Des Moines, 39 black women from the U.S. Women's Auxiliary Army Corps (WAACs) would be trained there. While these members of the all-black 3rd Platoon of the 1st Company of the 1st Training Regiment shared the camp with white WAACs, their facilities remained segregated, as did the rest of the military.[67] In her military memoir, black officer Charity Adams Earley recounts her surprise that the WAAC barracks would be segregated by race.

The enlistees, black and white, had traveled to Fort Des Moines together. Yet shortly after their arrival, a white second lieutenant said, "Will all the colored girls move over on this side."[68] The white WAACs were then called by name to be taken to their barracks. The "colored girls" were collectively directed to theirs. Nonetheless, Earley recalls that "[e]ven though segregated, our quarters were like the others, as we later found out. There were two floors of large rooms that accommodated about ten to eighteen

A young woman's smile belies the mood of the times. The year is 1936, a period of economic hardship in Iowa, when there were fewer factory jobs than there were men and women to fill them. (SHSI Des Moines)

women. We each had a tall locker behind the head of the bed and footlocker at the foot. We would soon learn that all of our possessions had to be stored in those two containers and had to be arranged in precise military order. The showers, toilets, basins, and laundry equipment were in the basement. These were adequate if no one lingered too long over her activities. The adjustment that was most difficult to handle was the lack of privacy. Individual shower stalls and wash basin cubicles were things of the past."[69]

The African-American WAACs, particularly those like Earley who had arrived at the training center when it opened, explored the city of Des Moines. Physically, she found the city easy to navigate. Social navigation was not quite so simple. "My impression," she writes, "was that the citizens of Des Moines were tolerant, at best, of the members of the WAAC, but more understanding about the benefits of the Training Center presence. There was no apparent segregation, although there were separate 'everythings,' except perhaps schools. However, discrimination was present even though frequently underground. It seemed to me that before the WAAC [training center] was established, there had not been enough Negroes to cause concern. They were not just a minority, but a less-than-1-percent minority." Earley and some of the other WAACs found themselves able to dine without incident at some of the nicer restaurants in the city. But when they informed their fellow officers that they had done so, those officers would

7th Co., 3rd Regiment, 1st WAAC Training Center, Fort Des Moines, Iowa, May 8, 1943 (courtesy Dorothy Oliver Carr)

Pauline Brown Humphrey (1906–93) operated the Crescent School of Beauty Culture at three successive locations in Des Moines from 1943 to the early 1980s. (courtesy Barbara Brown James)

374

apparently not believe them. Those officers "would enter the restaurant and ask if they served Negroes," she said. "The same place others of us had eaten the day before would now have a hostess or cashier who would reply, 'No, we do not.' The very next day the original group would go to that restaurant and have no problem."[70]

Crescent School of Beauty Culture

Linked to the arrival of the female enlistees was a pioneering entrepreneurial effort. Pauline Brown Humphrey (1906–93), possibly the first African-American woman certified to teach cosmetology in the state, broke further ground by opening the first beauty salon for black WAACs at Fort Des Moines. The government had requested that she do so, an obvious attempt on its part to maintain practices of segregation. Yet it was an idea that proved fortuitous for Humphrey.[71] This shop, which Humphrey established in 1943, was not her first business venture. Four years earlier, she had launched the Crescent School of Beauty Culture in Des Moines at a time when few financial lenders and product suppliers were willing to do business with an African-American woman. Humphrey went on to open a chain of cosmetology shops.[72] According to her daughter, Barbara James, beyond opening a salon for the WAACs, Humphrey "recognized a need for beauty services in the smaller Iowa community and elected to do something about it. She met this challenge first by sending her graduates out to [serve] the cities at specified times and later by establishing shops in strategic areas that could serve several towns. Still later she put on a big campaign to entice students from those communities to enter school and return to provide the service for their own community."[73] For several decades, Pauline Humphrey's beauty school and salons provided black women throughout the state of Iowa with a means by which to gain economic independence. She is still another example of an African-American woman in Iowa who was both a pioneer and a builder of her community.

During the World War 2 years, segregation still reigned at many of Iowa's colleges and universities, as well as in other American institutions. Attempts at inclusiveness would begin slowly once the war ended. Although the University of Iowa admitted African-American students in the nineteenth century, they would not be allowed to live in the dormitories until the 1940s. In 1946, five young women — Gwen Davis, Virginia Harper, Nancy Henry, Leanna Howard, and Esther J. Walls — officially integrated the Currier Hall dormitory on that campus.[74] Prior to the full integration of the residence halls, many African-American female students had found housing in the Iowa Federation Home. Male students, however, lived in private homes with African-American families in Iowa City. The women in these host families — Frances Culberson, Estella Ferguson, Wilda Hester, Helen Lemme, and Elizabeth (Bettye) Tate — helped to sustain the African-American community by housing these students.[75]

One of these women in particular illustrates the pioneering efforts of black Iowa women. Helen Lemme (1905–68), born in Grinnell, Iowa, graduated from the University of Iowa. She and her husband Allyn settled in Iowa City during the late 1920s. Besides serving as a research technician at the university's Department of Internal Medicine, Lemme also participated in several church and political organizations. Her accomplishments included serving as a member of the Democratic Party's Black Caucus and as president of the Johnson County League of Women Voters. In 1955, she became the first person to receive the Iowa City Woman of the Year Award. She continued to work toward building and sustaining the Iowa City community with her active involvement in its Human Rights Commission for three years, from its inception in 1963. Lemme died as a result of a fire in her home. Following her death, an Iowa City elementary school was named in her honor, the first in town to bear a woman's name.[76]

Post-War Integration

Early efforts toward integration in post-war Iowa encouraged additional black women pioneers. The field of nursing, for example, saw the hiring of Dollie (Dee) Wilder Haughton (1919–98) as the first black registered nurse at the University of Iowa Hospitals in 1947.[77] That same year, Barbara McDonald Calderon (b.1915) settled in Des Moines and became the state's first African-American visiting nurse. Calderon had served as an Army nurse during World War 2, stationed in Arizona and California. Her duties in Des Moines included daily visits to patients with acute illnesses as well as to expectant and post-partum mothers. She attended to both black and white families, which provides a small indication of a slight improvement in race relations.[78]

Another pioneer used the written word to help build community throughout the state of Iowa. Journalist Marie Ross made history by becoming the first black woman to join the Iowa Press Women in December 1948, a designation she also held in

Patricia Ray on an automobile excursion, 1940s. The World War 2 years saw improved employment opportunities for women throughout the U.S. In Iowa, business careers and military service attracted significant numbers of black women. (SHSI Des Moines)

The Sources of Black Women's History in Iowa

Ideally, an historical overview of the experience of African-American women should be told in their own words. Diaries and journals, letters, reminiscences, club and organizational records, photographs, memorabilia, oral histories — these are the sources of black women's history. The story of Iowa's black women told in this chapter relies as much as possible on this type of material.

However, it must be noted that despite recent collecting efforts, Iowa's historical societies, archives, and libraries contain relatively little manuscript material documenting the lives of African-American women. And most of the documents collected thus far date from the twentieth century; primary sources from the nineteenth century remain scant. Historian Darlene Clark Hine has written that "there is an urgent need to discover and collect more primary source materials pertaining to the lives and experiences of ordinary middle western black women in both urban and rural communities."

Iowans in particular must heed Hines's call. We must build up our archival collections at the State Historical Society of Iowa and at the state's colleges and universities. We must gather together and protect whatever we can find — documents, journals, and photographs — that will help historians write biographies of Iowa's black women and histories of their clubs, local sorority chapters, and other organizations.

— KMN

the National Federation of Press Women.[79] From 1947 into the early 1950s, Ross, who was society editor for the *Iowa Bystander,* wrote a column titled "The Personal Touch" for that newspaper. She covered local and national affairs that she deemed important to her African-American readership; issues and events ranging from church life to education to the Korean War to holiday preparations were topics in her column. Ross's writing, notes historian Gladys Talcott Rife, "often called attention to problems in Iowa by quoting the remarks of visitors, thus removing the onus from herself." Occasionally, however, Ross described her experiences with racism.[80] In the mid-1950s, Ross left the *Bystander* to write for the *Kansas City Call.*[81]

Despite the entrance of Ross and other women into new professional arenas within the state, their successes were the exception rather than the rule. The 1950 census reflects relatively little significant change in the occupational concentration of black women in Iowa. Due to a reconfiguration of categories within this census, there appears to be no strong majority of African-American women under any one heading. Yet most African-American women remained in service-oriented positions. Most respondents (962 of 2,514, or 38 percent) identified themselves as "service workers, except private household." Coming in a close second was the category "private household workers," which yielded 902 responses or approximately 36 percent of the population of respondents.[82]

The years following World War 2 found some black Iowa women immersed in struggles for economic and civil rights. Labor union activity became the vehicle through which a number of African-American women sought to fight job discrimination. In Iowa's meatpacking plants at this time, women of all racial backgrounds were paid less on average and often confined to certain positions, such as those in the bacon slicing and sausage processing departments. Frequently, they were dismissed from these jobs before men with less seniority in other departments. During World War 2, women were allowed to hold what were considered to be "men's jobs," but as historian Dennis A. Deslippe points out, "[a]t the war's close, packinghouse owners, in collusion with male unionists, followed the common practice of helping oversee a massive layoff of females and a continuation of unequal wage rates, sex-based occupation classifications, and separate seniority lists."[83] Black women tended to receive the most undesirable tasks in the state's packinghouses, such as flushing out hog casings.

Employment Barriers Begin to Crumble

In the case of Waterloo's Rath Packing Company, known for its discriminatory practices towards African-Americans, black women were not employed in any other departments besides the janitorial service until the early 1950s. When Ada Burt Tredwell became one of the first African-American women to join the Rath staff in 1941, for example, she was assigned to scrubbing and waxing floors.[84] The United Packinghouse Workers of America (UPWA) Local 46 — the plant's union, which was composed of an interracial group of members — and its Anti-Discrimination Committee conducted investigations and exposed unfair practices at Rath and other Iowa packinghouses. Due to the efforts of Local 46, member Anna Mae Weems became the one of the first black women to work in Rath's sliced bacon department in 1954. Although Weems, Tredwell, and other black women placed in formerly all-white departments encountered hostility from their white female co-workers, some employment barriers had begun to crumble.[85]

In the decades since, black women have continued to be involved in union activities. Fort Dodge native Jane Burleson (b.1928), for example, transformed her involvement into a political career. She began employment at George A. Hormel and Company in 1948 as a member of that packing plant's sliced bacon department. Such jobs apparently were not reserved for white women only at Hormel, as they were at the Rath Company in the late 1940s. Burleson was reassigned to the sausage production line until it was discontinued and then transferred to the cut floor, where she remained until 1981. During the 1970s, she became active in UPWA Local 31, which she served as recording secretary. She founded and presided over a local chapter of the A. Philip Randolph Institute, a labor group named after the black leader who organized the Pullman porters, and served on executive boards. In 1984, she became the first woman and first black elected to the Fort Dodge City Council. Still a councilor in 1998, Burleson decided to run for a seat in the Iowa House of Representatives.[86]

Struggle for Civil Rights at Home and in the South

Members of Iowa's black communities participated in the struggle for civil rights at home and in the South from the late 1940s into the 1960s. In 1948, Edna Griffin (1909–2000), John Bibbs, and Leonard Hudson filed suit against the Katz Drugstore in Des Moines to end the store's well-known policy of refusing to serve African-Americans. They won the initial case but staged

Nathaline Dixon, one of the first African-Americans to work at Bankers Life (now Principal), serving workers coffee in 1940 (courtesy Nathaline Dixon)

outdoor protests and sit-ins when the drugstore continued to violate the state's civil rights law. Although Katz filed an appeal, the Iowa Supreme Court upheld the original decision in 1949, thereby rendering discrimination in public accommodations to be a criminal act throughout the state. Griffin remained a strong activist. In the 1960s, she started the Des Moines chapter of the Congress on Racial Equality (CORE) and participated in the 1963 March on Washington.[87] In 1998, a half-century after Griffin's historic stand, the Flynn Building, which once housed the Katz drug store in downtown Des Moines, was renamed in honor of Edna Griffin. A plaque bearing the names of Griffin, Bibbs, and Hudson was placed on the building by the state of Iowa and the Iowa Civil Rights Commission earlier that year.[88]

Like Griffin, Cecile Cooper (1900–97) strove to enhance her community through organized action. Born in Missouri, Cooper was a beautician by trade. She attended Walker's Beauty Academy in Chicago but later settled in Davenport. From the 1950s to the 1970s, Cooper participated in more than 30 volunteer organizations, both religious and secular, in the Quad Cities area. Among her many community-building accomplishments, she founded the Quad Cities Negro Heritage Society and the Semper Fidelis Federated Women's Club. In 1960, at considerable risk to their safety given the volatile climate of the time, Cooper and other volunteers traveled to the Mississippi Delta to deliver food and clothing to its residents. During the mid–1960s, she assisted the Council of Churches of Scott and Rock Island counties in their support of the Delta Ministries by hosting a series of ice cream socials.[89]

As the era of civil rights activity emerged in Iowa, the occupational status of black women changed very little. According to the 1960 census, the largest percentage of women (1,236 of 3,237, or 38 percent, a slightly lower percentage than in the previous decade) reported that they were service workers. Domestic work in private homes continued to claim the second highest number of women, 809, or roughly 25 percent, but the percentage of women who placed themselves within that category had decreased by approximately 11 percent from the previous census. The percentage of women who described themselves as clerical workers was nearly 13 percent (417 of 3,237), an increase of 7 percent from one census to the next. Slightly fewer women described themselves as operatives (machine operators) — 250, or almost 8 percent. One hundred ninety-nine women, 6 percent of the total number of black women reporting, classified themselves as professional, technical, or kindred workers, the fifth-highest category.[90]

The 1970 census indicated significant changes for African-American women during the 1960s. Service work remained the top category reported, accounting for 1,705 of the 4,771 respondents (almost 36 percent). Yet the percentage of women in clerical positions increased considerably from the 1960 census. Nearly 24 percent of the respondents placed themselves in this category (1,128 of 4,771). The occupational category with the next-

highest percentage of women respondents was that of professional, technical, and kindred workers, more than 12 percent or 591 of total respondents. The percentage of women in this category was double that of the 1960 census. Machine operators and those in similar trades described nearly 10 percent of the respondents, while just slightly fewer, still more than 9 percent, fell into the category of private household workers.[91] It is particularly noteworthy to consider that as the twentieth century progressed, domestic work became simply one occupational path that black women could take, rather than the primary avenue they were forced to accept. Still, as evidence from the census indicates, African-American women in Iowa were not hired in executive or managerial positions in great number during the 1950s and 1960s.

Occupational status notwithstanding, political advancement came to African-American women during the civil rights movement. In 1964, attorney Willie Stevenson Glanton of Des Moines became the first black woman to be elected to the Iowa General Assembly. Glanton, who represented Polk County as a Democrat in the 61st General Assembly for the 1965–1966 term, was not the only member of her family in the legal profession. Her husband was Judge Luther T. Glanton Jr. Besides her involvement in politics, Willie Glanton has been active in organizations that serve the African-American community, such

Jane Burleson, Fort Dodge city councilwoman (Fort Dodge Messenger)

Cecile Cooper, Davenport activist (Iowa Women's Archives)

Edna Griffin, civil rights activist (Sher Stoneman photo / Des Moines Register)

Helen I. Johnson, center, of Marshalltown receives a Volunteer of the Year award from Gov. Terry Branstad. (courtesy Helen I. Johnson)

Know Your Neighbor panel (courtesy Helen Stein)

Sister Mary Denis   Mrs. Arthur Stein, Jr.   Mrs. J. B. Morris, Jr.   Mrs. David Kruidenier, Jr.

The late Martha Furgerson Nash, Waterloo activist (Waterloo Courier)

as the Des Moines chapters of the Links, Inc., and Jack and Jill of America, Inc.[92] During the mid-1960s, she also participated on the Des Moines Know Your Neighbor panel, a group of women from various racial and religious backgrounds who traveled across the state and the country, promoting tolerance.[93]

Willie Glanton served only one term in the Iowa General Assembly, yet she paved the way for another black woman to win a seat during the 1967–68 term. A. June Griggs Franklin (b. 1930), at that time a legal secretary, was elected to represent Polk County. Franklin's political involvement in the Democratic Party began when she participated in party activities surrounding the 1960 presidential election. Several years later, she was asked to run for the state legislature by some of her fellow party members. While Franklin lived near Willie Glanton, she said that her decision to vie for a seat in the Iowa General Assembly was not influenced by Glanton's having served. "I just sort of did my own thing," she said. "I've always been independent, and I don't do something

Attorney and state representative Willie Stevenson Glanton (courtesy Willie S. Glanton)

because somebody else does it or because they did it or anything."[94] The Clarinda native would serve three terms as a Democratic representative. As of 2000 she and Glanton remain the only African-American women to have served in the General Assembly. Like Glanton, Franklin was involved in several other organizations, such as the Des Moines NAACP and the Polk County Community Action Council.[95]

Groundbreakers

The period following the civil rights era in Iowa has been marked by several groundbreaking events, the ramifications of which are still developing. Since the establishment of the Iowa Civil Rights Commission in 1965, greater but by no means complete integration has begun to make its way into the workplace and many social, civic, and political clubs. Since the 1960s and 1970s, educational and professional gates have increasingly opened to black women in Iowa, but only part way. Figures from the 1980 and 1990 censuses bear out this claim. The 1980 census, which introduced still another revision of occupational categories, reported the largest percentage of black women in Iowa — 1,978 of 7,034, or 28 percent — in jobs in the category "administrative support occupations, including clerical." Following at a close second was the category "service occupations, except protective and

household" (1,777 responses, or 25 percent of the total). Categories with the third- and fourth-highest responses were "machine operators, assemblers, and inspectors," and "professional specialty occupations," each with nearly 12 percent. Only a little more than 6 percent of African-American women reported employment in "executive, administrative, and managerial occupations."

Relatively little had changed by the 1990 census, when approximately half of the 8,229 respondents held either administrative support or service-oriented positions. There was a slight gain in the category of "professional specialty," with 1,023, or slightly more than 12 percent. "Sales occupations" was the fourth-highest category, with nearly 9 percent, while "executive, administrative, and managerial occupations" remained fifth with 6 percent, or 494 of 8,229 responses. Fifty-four more women chose the latter category in the 1990 census than in 1980, but since the overall population of respondents increased from one compilation to the next, the percentage of women in that category dropped slightly.[96]

Thus, even into the 1990s, the phenomenon of "firsts" continues among African-American women in the workforce — individual stories that provide role models for more extensive social and economic change that has yet to occur. The career of Billie Davis Lloyd (1940–91) provides another example of an African-

Evelyn Davis, Democratic Party loyalist and Tiny Tots founder (courtesy Evelyn Davis)

Terry Caldwell Johnson, Polk County Manager (courtesy Terry Caldwell Johnson)

Elaine Estes, retired director of the Des Moines Public Library (Chuck Anderson photo / Des Moines Register)

Marguerite Cothorn, Des Moines social worker and political activist (Iowa Women's Archives)

Maude White, founder of the Des Moines Tutoring Center (Iowa Women's Archives)

American woman who overcame the odds to became both a pioneer and an organizer of her community. Born in Centerville, Lloyd grew up in Muscatine. While building a career in social work, Lloyd became a divorced mother of five and became a recipient of ADC (Aid for Dependent Children). She worked her way off public aid, obtaining a position as a social worker for the Scott County Social Services.[97] In 1979, Lloyd established the Quad Cities Conference on Black Families "to enhance communications and improve interpersonal relationships between white human services providers and Black consumers."[98] Lloyd directed this annual conference until 1985. In 1988, Lloyd paved the way once more when she was appointed district supervisor of the Waterloo branch of the Department of Employment Services (Job Services of Iowa), the first African-American woman to hold such a post.[99]

Another contemporary pioneer made her mark in municipal politics. In November 1995, LaMetta Wynn became the state's first African-American female mayor when she was elected in Clinton. Wynn, who had made an unsuccessful bid for the post two years earlier, won in a city where just 4 percent of the population of 29,000 is African-American. In some respects, Wynn was a pioneer long before her political election. She was born LaMetta Johnson in 1933, the youngest of nine children and a member of the only black family in Galena, Illinois. In 1955, she graduated from the nursing school of St. Luke's Hospital in Cedar Rapids. That year she also married Thomas Wynn, who worked for the Rock Island Arsenal. They settled in Clinton and eventually reared ten children. LaMetta Wynn built a career as a nurse and supervisor in Clinton hospitals and in recent years has served as a home health-care coordinator. As has been the case with other Iowa women, Wynn participated extensively in volunteer activities. For instance, she spent a dozen years as a member of the Clinton School Board, three as board president.[100]

Where Wynn secured a top political seat on the local level, Almo Hawkins sought one on the state level. Hawkins, director of Iowa's Department of Human Rights and a former newscaster, was selected by Republican gubernatorial candidate Jim Ross Lightfoot to be his running mate in 1998. No African-American has yet served as the state's lieutenant governor.[101]

African-American women in the state have continued to work toward sustaining the communities in which they live. For example, Mary Dickens (b.1925) has devoted much of her time to others. As a board member of Iowa Citizens for Community Improvement, Dickens helped organize the first National Night Out in Waterloo. The event features block parties throughout the city and is intended to discourage crime and to send positive

Black women in the state have continued to work toward sustaining the communities in which they live.

Elzona Trosper of Sioux City, former Sanford Center director (Sanford Center)

Aldeen Davis, columnist and Muscatine NAACP leader (courtesy Diana Davis Lloyd)

Ida Johnson, founder of Davenport United Neighbors (Quad-City Times)

Ruth B. Anderson, Univerity of Northern Iowa (courtesy Ruth B. Anderson)

messages to children. In addition, Dickens bakes pies and other sweets for shut-ins, children, and the Salvation Army, sometimes baking as many as 81 pies during the week before Mother's Day. Dickens has also volunteered at four Waterloo nursing homes and has been an active member of several service organizations, such as Habitat for Humanity, the Waterloo Women's Civic Club, and the United Methodist Church.[102]

That black women continue to make such inroads in Iowa indicates progress, but exactly how much progress has been made when those successes come so late in the twentieth century? Nearly a century ago, in her 1905 presidential address, "Needs of Race Organization," Mrs. Belle Graves told the members of the Iowa Federated Colored Women's Clubs, "No race climbs faster than its women."[103] And only with the preserving and telling of women's stories can Iowa's black history rise to the occasion. The stories of these women and their organizations represent but a few of the countless others that enrich the history of African-Americans and women in Iowa.

In 1905, Belle Graves said, "No race climbs faster than its women." And only with the preserving and telling of women's stories can Iowa's black history rise to the occasion.

Four generations, clockwise from top of photo: young Billie Nathaline Wilkinson; her mother, Nathaline Bragg Dixon; great-grandmother Maggie Proctor Abner; grandmother Bertie Bell Proctor Bragg; and aunt Marguerite Bragg Morton (courtesy Nathaline Bragg Dixon)

Notes

1. In her monograph, *Black Women in the Middle West Project: The Michigan Experience* (Ann Arbor: Historical Society of Michigan, 1990), historian Darlene Clark Hine poses similar questions. Hine has contributed to the literature on midwestern black women via the project she has directed to collect manuscript material from women in Illinois, Indiana, and Michigan. See the aforementioned work and *The Black Women in the Middle West Project: A Comprehensive Resource Guide, Illinois and Indiana: Historical Essays, Oral Histories, Biographical Profiles, and Document Collections* (Indianapolis: Indiana Historical Bureau, 1986).

2. Dorothy Schwieder, *Iowa: The Middle Land* (Ames: Iowa State Univ. Press, 1996), 83.

3. Ibid., 84–85.

4. Robert R. Dykstra, "Dr. Emerson's Sam: Black Iowans before the Civil War," *Palimpsest* 63 (1982): 71, 73, 75.

5. Ibid., 76.

6. Schweider, 86.

7. Leola Nelson Bergmann, *The Negro in Iowa* (Iowa City: SHSI, 1948; repr. 1969), 22.

8. Mrs. Laurence C. Jones, "The Desire for Freedom," *Palimpsest* 8 (1927): 153. The author of this article, also known as Grace Morris Allen Jones, was the granddaughter of Charlotta Pyles. Jones was quite accomplished in her own right; a native of Burlington, Iowa, she became an educator both in Iowa and at the Piney Woods Country Life School in Piney Woods, Mississippi, which her husband founded.

9. Ibid., 154, 158.

10. Ibid., 158–60, 160–61, 163.

11. Leslie A. Schwalm, "Slavery and Freedom in the Midwest: African American Women in the Civil War Era" (paper presented at the "Women of the Midwest: History and Sources" conference, June 14, 1997, Madison, WI), 6.

12. Ibid., 7.

13. Ibid., 7–8. See also Robert R. Dykstra, *Bright Radical Star: Black Freedom and White Supremacy on the Hawkeye Frontier* (Cambridge: Harvard Univ. Press, 1993), 199–200.

14. Schwalm, 8–9.

15. Glenda Riley, *Frontierswomen: The Iowa Experience* (Ames: Iowa State Univ. Press, 1981), 99.

16. Dykstra, "Dr. Emerson's Sam," 76.

17. Ibid., 78.

18. Marilyn Jackson, "Alexander Clark: A Rediscovered Black Leader," *Iowan* 23 (Spring 1975): 45.

19. Ibid., 46. Separate schools for black students also had been established in Keokuk and Dubuque: Bergmann, 50; Schwieder, *Iowa,* 194. See also Arnie Cooper, "A Stony Road: Black Education in Iowa, 1838–1860," *AI* 3ʳᵈ ser. 48 (1986): 129.

20. Jackson, 46.

21. Ibid., 46. See also Schwieder, *Iowa,* 88.

22. Bergmann, 33–34.

23. Schwieder, *Iowa,* 84.

24. Ibid., 194.

25. This and subsequent census information was taken from data compiled by Willis Goudy for "Selected Demographics: Iowa's African-American Residents: 1840–1990," chapter 2 in this book.

26. Robert H. Wiebe, *The Search for Order, 1877–1920* (New York: Hill and Wang, 1967), 165, 173–74.

27. Paula Giddings, *When and Where I Enter: The Impact of Black Women on Race and Sex in America* (New York: William Morrow, 1984; repr. Bantam Books, 1985), 95; Darlene Clark Hine, "Lifting the Veil, Shattering the Silence: Black Women's History in Slavery and Freedom," in *Hine Sight: Black Women and the Re- Construction of American History* (Brooklyn: Carlson Publishing, 1994), 15; and Gerda Lerner, "Early Community Work of Black Club Women," *Journal of Negro History* 59 (1974): 167. See also Earline Rae Ferguson, "A Community Affair: African-American Women's Club Work in Indianapolis, 1879–1917," Ph.D. diss., Indiana University, 1997, and Ferguson's essay, "Sisterhood and Community: The Sisters of Charity and African-American Women's Health Care in Indianapolis, 1876–1920" in *Midwestern Women: Work, Community and Leadership at the Crossroads,* ed. Lucy Eldersveld Murphy and Wendy Hamand Venet (Indianapolis: Indiana Univ. Press, 1997).

28. Giddings, 95.

Kathryn M. Neal served as assistant archivist at the Iowa Women's Archives, University of Iowa Libraries, and director of its African-American Women in Iowa project from 1995 to 1999. She is currently curator of the Givens Collection of African-American Literature in Special Collections and Rare Books at the University of Minnesota Libraries.
She holds a B.A. in English from Carleton College in Northfield, Minnesota, an M.A. in journalism from the University of Minnesota, and a master's degree in Information and Library Studies with a concentration in archival administration from the University of Michigan.

The author would like to thank Mark A. Greene for his insightful suggestions for revision in the chapter's early stages. She also would like to thank Karen Mason and other former colleagues in the Iowa Women's Archives and Matthew Schaefer and Mary Bennett of the State Historical Society of Iowa in Iowa City for their research assistance. Finally, but not least, the author expresses gratitude to the many largely unsung heroines whom she met while directing the African-American Women in Iowa project. They have left an inspiring and indelible mark on the author's life and spirit.

29. Iowa Association of Colored Women's Clubs [IACWC], *Proceedings of the Fiftieth Annual Convention* (June 8–11, 1952), 1, Box 1, IACWC Records, Manuscript Collection, SHSI, Des Moines. IFCWC members might appear to have been ahead of their time in their use of the adjective *Afro-American*. Actually, the term enjoyed considerable popularity (as adjective and as noun) during the late nineteenth century and a few decades of the early twentieth century. The history of the Baltimore newspaper *The Afro-American* dates back to 1892, for example. [See Bruce Kellner, ed., *The Harlem Renaissance: A Historical Dictionary for the Era* (Westport: Greenwood, 1984; New York: Methuen, 1987), 5.] Yet the origin of *Afro-American* dates back even further: A magazine bearing such a title was published in New York as early as 1859 [Jannette L. Dates, "Print News," in *Split Image: African-Americans in the Mass Media*, ed. Jannette L. Dates and William Barlow (Washington: Howard Univ. Press, 1990), 372.]

Cheryl Brown, Miss Iowa 1970–71, was the first African-American to compete in the Miss America Pageant.
(Miss America Pageant)

30. Iowa State Federation of Afro-American Women's Clubs, *Proceedings of the Second Annual Meeting* (May 1903), 2, Box 1, IACWC Records.

31. Idem.

32. Ibid., 6–7, 14–15.

33. IACWC, *Proceedings of the Fiftieth Annual Convention*.

34. The programs for the 1963, 1964, and 1966 conventions each bear this name change or simply the initials, IACW. Box 2, IACWC Records.

35. Iowa Women's Association of Colored Women's Clubs, Inc., *Proceedings of the 67th Annual State Convention* (June 6–7, 1969), Box 2, IACWC Records.

36. Ibid., 5.

37. *Who's Who in Colored America: A Biographical Dictionary of Notable Living Persons of African Descent in America, 1941–1944*, 6th ed., (Brooklyn: Thomas Yenser, 1941–1944), 86.

38. Idem; Allen W. Jones, "Equal Rights to All, Special Privileges to None, The Black Press in Iowa, 1882–1985," in *Black Press in the Middle West, 1865–1985*, ed. Henry Lee Suggs (Westport: Greenwood, 1996), 84.

39. Jack Lufkin, "The Founding and Early Years of the National Association for the Advancement of Colored People in Des Moines, 1915–1930," *AI* 3rd ser. 45 (1980): 449; *Who's Who in Colored America*, 86.

40. "Four Women Receive High Honor," *IoWoman* 25 (Sept./Oct. 1995): 1. *IoWoman* is the newsletter of the Friends of the Iowa Commission on the Status of Women. *Who's Who in Colored America*, 86; Bergmann, 83–84.

41. "Iowa Federation Home Operated by Iowa Federation of Colored Women's Clubs," promotional booklet, 1929, Iowa Federation Home vertical file, Iowa Women's Archives, University of Iowa Libraries, Iowa City.

42. Biographical sketch in program for the National Bar Association Annual Gertrude E. Rush Award Dinner (May 22, 1982), Folder: Church, civic groups and clubs, Box 1, Mary E. Wood Papers, Iowa Women's Archives; *Iowa Bystander*, May 7, 1981; *Iowa Women's Hall of Fame* [booklet] (Des Moines: Iowa Commission on the Status of Women, 1994), 45; Bergmann, 74.

43. Dorothy Schwieder, Joseph Hraba, and Elmer Schwieder, *Buxton: Work and Racial Equality in a Coal Mining Community* (Ames: Iowa State Univ. Press, 1987), 156–57. See also Judith Powers, "The Buxton Heritage: An Iowa Mining Community Provides Hope for Racial Justice and Harmony," *Iowa Woman* (Spring 1984), 3, 9.

44. Karen Ball, "Club's Purpose: Self Culture," unidentified and undated publication in *We Shall Overcome: Black History K–3*, comp. Jacqueline Scott (Keokuk: Iowa Department of Education, 1988). Scott's work, an educational packet, was developed as part of an Iowa Department of Education Phase 3 Education Grant project. A photocopy of the packet may be found in the Jacqueline Scott Papers, Box 1, Folder: Educational material; *We Shall Overcome*, 1988, Iowa Women's Archives.

45. Earl M. Rogers to Paula Giddings, Feb. 17, 1987, Delta Sigma Theta vertical file, University Archives, University of Iowa Libraries, Iowa City.

46. "Presenting Our Founder," in the program for Des Moines Alumnae Chapter of Delta Sigma Theta Sorority, Inc. (March 1, 1987), Folder: Delta Sigma Theta, Phi chapter, 1951–1987, Box 2, Catherine Gayle Williams Papers, Iowa Women's Archives.

47. Marjorie H. Parker, *Alpha Kappa Alpha in the Eye of the Beholder*, 3rd ed. (Washington: Alpha Kappa Alpha Sorority, 1978, c.1979), 181.

48. *YWCA of Greater Des Moines: A 1982 Calendar.*

49. Robert Neymeyer, "May Harmony Prevail: The Early History of Black Waterloo," *Palimpsest* 61 (1980): 90.

50. Idem.

51. Schwieder, et al., *Buxton*, 158. See also *Iowa Bystander*, June 9, 1916. Darlene Clark Hine contends that "[n]either the Great Migration to southern and northern cities nor the ratification of the Nineteenth Amendment . . . altered the political status and material conditions of the majority of black women." Black women's involvement in the Iowa suffrage movement and the effects of the vote on their lives bear further study. Darlene Clark Hine, "Lifting the Veil," 18.

52. Bergmann, 59.

53. Earl S. Fullbrook, *The Red Cross in Iowa*, vol. 2 [*Iowa Chronicles of the World War*, ed. Benjamin F. Shambaugh] (Iowa City: SHSI, 1922), 139–40. See also *DMR*, Dec. 25, 1918.

54. Bergmann, 58–59.

55. Dorothy Apgar, *Marshall Memories* (Marshalltown: Marshalltown Historical Society, 1992), 89.

56. Bergmann, 59.

57. Biographical time line submitted to the author by Georgine Morris's grandson, Robert V. Morris, Dec. 30, 1997. This and subsequent information about Georgine Morris came from this source.

58. See Robert J. Neymeyer, "In the Full Light of Day: The Ku Klux Klan in 1920s Iowa," *Palimpsest* 76 (1995): 56–63. Neymeyer illustrates that as membership in the Ku Klux Klan increased in the West, Midwest, and South during the 1920s, so did it in the state of Iowa, specifically. He contends that nearly every county, most cities, and several small towns in Iowa had local Klan units called "klaverns."

59. Darlene Clark Hine, Elsa Barkley Brown, and Rosalyn Terborg-Penn, eds., *Black Women in America: An Historical Encyclopedia*, vol. 1, *A–L* (Bloomington and Indianapolis: Indiana Univ. Press, 1993), 723.

60. Bergmann, 71–72. Bergmann drew these figures from the *Fifteenth United States Census, 1930*. See the table "General Occupational Categories by Sex for African-American Residents of Iowa, 1920–1930 and 1950–1990," by Willis Goudy, in chapter 2 of this book. While Bergmann asserts that the second largest number of respondents (42) fell under the category "professional service," Goudy's data reveals that the category "manufacturing and mechanical industries" yielded 77 respondents.

61. Bergmann, 71–72.

62. Schwieder, *Iowa*, 267.

63. Ibid., 268.

64. Giddings, *When and Where I Enter*, 235. See also Hine, "Lifting the Veil," 19.

65. Schwieder, *Iowa*, 283.

66. Hine, "Lifting the Veil," 19.

67. Schwieder, *Iowa*, 281.

68. Charity Adams Earley, *One Woman's Army: A Black Officer Remembers the WAC* (College Station: Texas A&M Univ. Press, 1989), 19–20.

69. Ibid., 21.

70. Ibid., 86–87.

71. Barbara James, "Pauline B. Humphrey (Feb. 4, 1906–March 1, 1993), page 1 of undated biographical essay, Folder: Pauline Humphrey, Small Collections Vertical File; Pauline Humphrey Papers, Iowa Women's Archives.

72. Idem. See also Amy Ruth, "Pauline Humphrey: Of Dreams and Beauty Shops," *Goldfinch* 15 (1993): 18–20.

73. Ibid., 2.

74. Photograph caption, 1946, Folder: Photographs; Student life, 1946–1951, Box 3, Esther J. Walls Papers, Iowa Women's Archives. Virginia Harper (1929–1997) and Esther Walls (b.1926) furthered their roles as pioneers. Harper, of Fort Madison, Iowa, became the first black woman appointed to the Iowa Board of Public Instruction and the Iowa Board of Parole. Biographical sketch, March 22, 1984, Folder: Biographical information; Personal, 1948–1998 (scattered), Box 1, Virginia Harper Papers, Iowa Women's Archives. In 1948, the Mason City, Iowa-born Walls, who later built an extensive career in librarianship in New York, became the first black female student elected to the Alpha of Iowa Chapter of the Phi Beta Kappa Honor Society. Resume (page 1), Folder: Biographical material; Awards, appointments, and resumes, 1958–96 (scattered) and undated; and S. Joe Brown to Esther Walls, April 1, 1949, Folder: Correspondence; General, 1949, Box 1, Esther J. Walls Papers, Iowa Women's Archives.

75. Philip G. Hubbard, *New Dawns: A 150-Year Look at Human Rights at The University of Iowa* (Iowa City: University of Iowa Sesquicentennial Committee, 1996), 17.

76. "Native Iowan Honored at Dedication," *Everybody Magazine* 12 (Nov./Dec. 1970); Folder: Lemme Family, Small Collections Vertical File; Lemme Family Papers, Iowa Women's Archives.

77. Obituary notice for Dee Wilder Haughton, *Iowa City Press-Citizen,* July 30, 1998.

78. *DMR,* March 1948 ("Barbara M. Calderon"), Folder: Barbara M. Calderon, Small Collections Vertical File, Barbara Calderon Papers, Iowa Women's Archives.

79. Photograph caption, late 1940s, Folder: Photographs; National Federation of Press Women, 1940s–1950s and undated, Box 1, Wilma Belden Collins Papers, Iowa Women's Archives; Membership roster, Folder: Membership records; Membership lists, 1938–1950, Box 3, Iowa Press Association, Inc., Records, Iowa Women's Archives.

80. Gladys Talcott Rife, "Iowa's Rural Women Columnists, Especially of the Fifties: Their Cultural and Historical Import in a Comparative Context," Ph.D. diss., University of Iowa, 1988, 156–69. The quotation appears on page 157.

81. Elaine G. Estes, "The Iowa Bystander and J.B. Morris," *Iowa State Bystander* [1894–1994 Anniversary Edition: 100 Years of Black Achievement], 1994, 45.

82. See the table "General Occupational Categories by Sex for African-American Residents of Iowa, 1920–1930 and 1950–1990," by Willis Goudy in chapter 2 of this book.

83. Dennis A. Deslippe, "'We Had an Awful Time with Our Women': Iowa's United Packinghouse Workers of America, 1945–1975," *Journal of Women's History* 5 (1993): 12. See also Ruth Milkman, *Gender at Work: The Dynamics of Job Segregation by Sex during World War II* (Urbana: Univ. of Illinois Press, 1987), 99–127.

84. Bruce Fehn, "'The Only Hope We Had': United Packinghouse Workers Local 46 and the Struggle for Racial Equality in Waterloo, Iowa, 1948–1960," *AI* 3rd ser. 54 (1995): 202–3, 185–86. Fehn consulted the oral testimony of Ada Burt Tredwell, interviewed in Waterloo on July 29, 1986, as part of the United Packinghouse Workers of America Oral History Project (UPWAOHP), State Historical Society of Wisconsin, Madison.

85. Fehn, 185–86; Anna Mae Weems interview, May 9, 1986, UPWAOHP, State Historical Society of Wisconsin, Madison.

86. *Fort Dodge Messenger,* April 25, 1981; *DMR,* June 14, 1998; revision form for *Who's Who among African Americans,* Folder: Biographical material, 1956–1998, Jane Burleson Papers, Iowa Women's Archives.

87. Amy Ruth, "Edna Williams Griffin: Civil Rights Activist," *Goldfinch* 15 (1993): 11–13.

88. *DMR,* Jan. 26, 1998; *Cedar Rapids Gazette,* June 18, 1998; *DMR,* June 21, 1998; *Iowa City Press-Citizen,* July 7, 1998; *DMR,* July 8, 1998, July 19, 1998, Aug. 23, 1998.

89. Unidentified newspaper clipping, July 9, 1964, Folder: Newspaper clippings, 1964–1978, Box 1, Cecile Cooper Papers, Iowa Women's Archives; *Quad-City Times,* Jan. 29, 1978. Other biographical information within this passage was taken from the following sources: Father Duncan commentary for tribute to Cecile Cooper, Nov. 1, 1970, and Aldeen Davis for tribute to Cecile Cooper, Nov. 1, 1970, Folder: Correspondence, 1966–1979, including letters from Fred Schwengel, Box 1, Cecile Cooper Papers, Iowa Women's Archives.

90. See the table relating to occupational categories in chapter 2.

91. Ibid.

92. *Iowa Official Register, Fifty-first Number, 1965–1966* (Des Moines: State of Iowa), 73. Founded in 1938, Jack and Jill of America, Inc., was established by African-American mothers and wives of professional men in Philadelphia as a play group for their children, to introduce them to cultural, educational, and social activities. In the years since, it has become a national organization with branch clubs in various cities. Information cited from: Darlene Clark Hine, Elsa Barkley Brown, and Rosalyn Terborg-Penn, eds., *Black Women in America: An Historical Encyclopedia,* vol. 1 *[A–L]* (Bloomington and Indianapolis: Indiana Univ. Press,1993), 619–20.

93. *Iowa Official Register, Fifty-first Number, 1965–1966* (Des Moines: State of Iowa), 73. For more information about the Des Moines Know Your Neighbor Panel, see the June Parker Goldman Papers and the Arlene Roberts Morris Papers, Iowa Women's Archives.

94. A. June Franklin, interview transcript, Des Moines, 1991, 9, 14, Folder: Transcripts, Franklin, June, Box 2, "A Political Dialogue: Iowa's Women Legislators," Iowa Women's Archives.

95. *Iowa Official Register, Fifty-second Number, 1967–1968* (Des Moines: State of Iowa), 81; *Iowa Official Register, Fifty-third Number, 1969–70* (Des Moines: State of Iowa), 83.

96. See the aforementioned table pertaining to occupational categories by Willis Goudy in chapter 2.

97. Billie Davis Lloyd biography, 1, Folder: Personal activities, Biographical information, 1960 and undated, Box 1, Billie Lloyd Papers, Iowa Women's Archives.

98. Quad Cities Conference on Black Families (Nov. 8–9, 1979), program, Folder: Professional activities, Quad Cities Conference on Black Families, 1979, Box 1, Billie Lloyd Papers, Iowa Women's Archives.

99. Billie Davis Lloyd biography, 2.

100. *Des Moines Sunday Register,* Jan. 7, 1996.

101. Hawkins's nomination garnered considerable media attention. See, for example, stories appearing in *DMR,* June 14, 1998; *Cedar Rapids Gazette,* June 14, 1998; *DMR,* July 17, 1998; *Cedar Rapids Gazette,* Aug. 23, 1998, Aug. 30, 1998.

102. *Waterloo Courier,* Aug. 4, 1992. See also Amy Gades, "Pie Maker Gives Shut-in Moms a Treat," *Waterloo Courier,* c.1991, Folder: Mary Dickens, Small Collections Vertical File; Mary Dickens Papers, Iowa Women's Archives. Additional information came from a personal interview with Mary Dickens,Waterloo, May 15, 1997.

103. Iowa State Federation of Afro-American Women's Clubs, *Proceedings of the Fourth Annual Meeting* (May 22–24, 1905), 8, Box 1, IACWC Records.

Jennifer Caudle of Davenport reigned as Miss Iowa 1999–2000. (Miss Iowa Pageant)

Deacons and deaconesses of Corinthian Baptist Church, Des Moines, 1920s (Corinthian Baptist Church)

The Church

by Frances E. Hawthorne

The story of African-American churches in Iowa is a chronology of moral and social leadership. From the frontier era to the present, the churches have been the spiritual heart of Iowa's African-American communities. They have been the hubs of community and family activity, secular and sacred. They have channeled their communities' energy and supported black Iowans' continuing quest for equal rights and treatment under the law. Predominantly Methodist and Baptist, African-American churches have been by choice separate and apart. Today, more than 150 years after the formation of the first black church in Iowa, their history stands as a fitting symbol of the physical and spiritual fortitude of African-Americans in Iowa.

Frontier Churches

African-Americans came to Iowa years before it officially gained statehood in 1846. Some came as fugitive slaves. Others had purchased their freedom from their owners. Still others had never been slaves. Though Iowa was a northern state, free from slavery by legal mandate, in practice Iowa in the early 1830s sought to exclude African-Americans and mulattos with "black codes," laws that provided civil rights for "free whites" only. Undaunted by exclusion from public accommodations in early Iowa, blacks built their own churches or refurbished structures that had once housed corner groceries and one-room schoolhouses. In one case even an old tavern was converted into a place of worship. Some congregations were able to build new structures from the start. Others moved to new edifices after a few years of tough beginnings.

From the first, these places of worship were beacons of spiritual affirmation and secular life in African-American communities around the state, in both rural and urban areas.

Some church members walked or drove miles in buggies or wagons to spend the entire Sunday in worship at the closest church. There they participated in annual reunion Sundays, basket dinners, church anniversaries, children's programs and plays, holiday celebrations, heritage activities, bridal showers or weddings, wakes or funerals, choir days, church business meetings, baby contests, and programs by various church auxiliaries, trustees, missionaries, usher boards, or deacon boards.

From the first, these places of worship were beacons of spiritual affirmation and secular life in African-American communities around the state, in both rural and urban areas.

A Methodist Episcopal church (Dubuque) ledger page showing pledges of African-American members (St. Luke's Methodist Church)

During weekdays a variety of secular activities for individuals and families were available to church members and non-members alike. These included Boy Scouts, Girl Scouts, debates, homework and tutoring sessions, clothing rooms, food banks, homeless feeding programs, voting campaigns, counseling centers, refugee harbors, widows and widowers programs, housing programs, job centers, public school classes, adult centers, quilting bees, day cares and nurseries, protest meetings, and business boycotts.

The first African-Americans in Iowa settled in Dubuque. They went there to work in the lead mines. Dubuque's first church, Methodist in denomination, was integrated. Organized in June 1834, the church asked its first members — a half dozen of whom were black — for 25 cents each for organizing fees. Historian Robert R. Dykstra notes that "[at] least six local blacks, some of them said to have been slaves, pledged modest sums to the Methodist building fund and had their names dutifully inscribed on a circulating subscription paper: 'Uncle Tom' (50¢), Caroline Brady (12½¢), Walton Baker (25¢), Sam Welsh (25¢), Nathaniel Morgan (50¢), and Tilda (25¢). A black woman, Charlotte Morgan, wife to Nathaniel, was one of the seven charter members of the interracial congregation."[1]

Many African-American churches have claimed to be the first or oldest in Iowa. Some ceased to function years ago due to declining membership. A few persist, strengthened by stable membership and healthy operating funds. Establishing church buildings as early as the 1860s were a half dozen congregations in various parts of the state. St. John Methodist Church in Mt. Pleasant, organized in 1863, is regarded by many as being the first actual building erected. It was organized in 1863, held services for years, but has since become defunct.

Another source indicates that years before the Mt. Pleasant church formed, a congregation was organized in Muscatine. Apparently the first meeting of the Bethel African Methodist Episcopal Church was held on Muscatine's Front Street in Muscatine in 1847. Property was purchased in 1849, and Bethel AME Church was established. The Muscatine congregation paid only $40 for the property. One of Iowa's renowned citizens, Alexander Clark Sr., was superintendent and the Rev. G. C. Booth was pastor. (During the Civil War, Rev. R. H. Cain served in Muscatine. He moved to Charleston, S.C., after the war and served two terms in Congress during the Reconstruction Era. He later became the fourteenth bishop of the African Methodist churches.)

As African-Americans continued to arrive from points east and south, and continued to build churches, antislavery sentiment spread westward across the northern United States. In Iowa abolitionism found many of its strongest proponents among the ministers of the state's white congregations, particularly the Quakers (Friends) and the Congregationalists in southeastern Iowa. These abolitionists declared war on Iowa's Black Codes as well as on the institution of slavery in the South.

Ministers in Iowa towns such as Denmark and Salem delivered sermons denouncing slavery and urging their members to join them. Their efforts resulted in the first abolition association in Iowa, organized in 1840 in Denmark. White pastors of Virginia Friends (Quakers) located in Salem and Denmark also opened one of the first stations on the Underground Railroad, the escape route for fugitive slaves headed for freedom. Many church members followed the lead of their pastors and offered their homes as safe havens. Antislavery sentiment was strong in southern Iowa. Across the state line in Missouri, 115,000 African-Americans were enslaved.

Though Iowa's Black Codes attempted to limit the influx of African-Americans, free men of color and former slaves who had purchased their freedom or escaped on the Underground Railroad were a continuing presence in the Iowa Territory. When they came to Iowa, they brought their churches with them, since they were not always welcomed into the congregations of churches established for the general population. For example, in 1852 a few black families left Illinois for northeast Iowa. Traveling by wagon train, the group settled in Westfield Township in Fayette County. When one of their members was killed in a ditch cave-in, he had to be buried on his farm because the law did not allow blacks to be buried in the town cemetery. The group later established its own cemetery, originally called Stonehouse Cemetery and renamed Pleasant Hill Cemetery. They also built their own Stonehouse School, which was used as a place of religious worship.

These African-American pioneers in Fayette County included T. R. Bass, Seymour Wilson, Judge Brown, Frank A. Dean, Abel Valentine, Lemuel Epps, Joel Epps, John H. Epps, Thomas Graham, Charles Graham, James Howard, William Lewis, Albert Lewis, Samuel Maxfield, George Moore, John Swan, John Tann, Thomas Valentine, Isaac Collins, and William Dean. Tombstones in Pleasant Hill Cemetery today refer to early families buried there.

Many African-Americans who fled slavery in antebellum Missouri settled in river towns just north of the Iowa border. Burlington, which was a thriving river port for 20 years before the Civil War, was home to St. John's AME Church. St. John's was founded by three freed slaves: Father William Emanuel, Ross Mudd Cauden, and Mrs. A. Carter. Mary Palmer was the church's first organist. Geraldine Brown, a longtime resident of Burlington and a prominent local historian, has documented the vitality of the frontier community served by St. John's. In those early years, African-Americans lived throughout the city, held a variety of well-paying jobs, and owned property there.

In 1864 Keokuk Methodists organized Bethel AME Church, located for a short time at 12th and Des Moines streets but moved four times thereafter. The other locations included space over a department store and drugstore. Eventually the congregation settled at 14th and Blondeau streets. Historian

Muscatine's Bethel AME Church, established in 1849, included in its congregation Alexander Clark Sr. (SHSI Des Moines)

"Old Negro Church," Tipton, one of several African-American churches organized in Iowa prior to the Civil War (SHSI Iowa City)

Keokuk's Bethel AME Church choir, 1913 (courtesy Marie Grigsby)

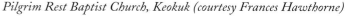

Pilgrim Rest Baptist Church, Keokuk (courtesy Frances Hawthorne)

Rev. Baker Brown, pastor of Burlington's AME church, one of Iowa's oldest (courtesy Helen Johnson)

Essie M. Britton reported that in April 1871 the church building, then under construction, was destroyed in a storm and had to be rebuilt.

Three other churches were erected in Keokuk in the early years. Trinity Methodist Episcopal's congregation built its church in 1857 with materials shipped by boat from Tennessee. The church was hailed as one of the largest edifices in Iowa at that time. The congregants of Pilgrim Rest Baptist Church, organized in 1871, met in a wood-frame stucco church with frosted windows. Pilgrim Rest Baptist Church's congregation had originally been part of Seventh Street Baptist Church, organized in 1864. Seven years later 40 members of the congregation left the church with their minister, Rev. O. M. Jones. A church council was called but was unable to settle the dispute that had arisen within Seventh Street Baptist's congregation. So Pilgrim Rest Baptist Church was organized. The Seventh Street Baptists went on to build another church at 7th and Concert streets in 1873. The 1873 structure was demolished many years ago.

Rev. William Brown, a former slave turned preacher, pastored at Pilgrim Rest from 1871 until 1879. Reverend Brown compared his experiences in Iowa with the discrimination practiced during his days in white churches shortly after slavery ended. "They would let us join their churches, but we had no voice," he recalled. "Sometimes they held special meetings for colored people; at such meetings we could sit in any seat that we wished to; other times we had reserved seats away by the back door."[2]

After the Civil War

The first African-American church organized in Des Moines was the Burns African Methodist Episcopal Church, which was founded in 1868, the year the Civil War ended. Some time earlier, a segregated school had been started on the east side of Des Moines to serve African-American students. When Burns AME was founded, the school was moved to the church's basement. Three years later, the Iowa Supreme Court ruled that all children regardless of race must be admitted to public schools. This ruling resulted from a court case initiated by Muscatine's Alexander Clark Sr. on behalf of his daughter, Susan. She became the first African-American to attend an integrated school in Iowa. After graduating from high school, Susan Clark married a Methodist minister and moved to Cedar Rapids.

Iowa City supported a black Methodist congregation, which was formed in 1868 — the same year as the repeal of Iowa's Black Codes, when the term "free whites" was eliminated from the state's Constitution. Nearby, in Washington, Iowa, an AME congregation had been founded in 1862. Original members included Thomas Jefferson Armstrong, Samuel G. Carter, A. C. Carter, Caleb White, George W. Black, Mary Jefferson, Sarah Carter, Sarah G. Black, and Fannie Palm. Their first church was a small frame building northeast of the Washington town square. A new church, the Shorter Chapel, was built on South Avenue C in the mid-1870s and remained there for a century. It was torn down several years after the church closed in 1972.

In the decades following the Civil War these and many more African-American churches would flourish in Iowa communities. In Cedar Rapids in 1870 Bethel AME organized under Rev. J. W. Lewis. The congregation erected a new building in 1874, which would become not only the oldest but the largest African-American church in Cedar Rapids. Mt. Zion Baptist Church was organized in Cedar Rapids in 1871. Growing as their city grew, both churches filled their communities' desire for "strong gospel preaching."

The late nineteenth century saw a surge of enthusiasm within the Methodist faith across Iowa. St. Paul's AME Church was organized in Des Moines in 1872 with 17 charter members. The church was formed in a small cottage at 1215 Park Street under the pioneering leadership of the Rev. John W. Malone of the Illinois Conference. Reverend Malone sent Rev. George W. Benson to serve as the church's first pastor. Initially located at the southeast corner of 2nd and Center, the congregation's first church building was completed in April 1882. Thirty miles away, in Jasper County, another black Methodist congregation met in an old frame schoolhouse. Located in the northeast part of Newton, the schoolhouse was purchased in 1877 and "rebuilt into a respectable church edifice which still serves the congregation," wrote historian James B. Weaver in 1912. Weaver noted that the church "includes many of the colored people of the place, there being only the one African church in Newton."[3]

Members of the Burns United Methodist Church in the 1920s (courtesy Barbara Kaiser)

Burns United Methodist Church was the first African-American church organized in Des Moines. Pictured here is the Women's Society of Christian Service, c. 1925. (courtesy Barbara Kaiser)

Founded in 1872, St. Paul's AME Church (lower left) in Des Moines was first located at the southeast corner of 2nd and Center. (courtesy Gwendoline Harris)

The Richard Allen Chorus of St. Paul's AME Church, Des Moines (courtesy Lynda Walker-Webster)

Second Baptist Church, Marshalltown (courtesy Helen Johnson)

Second Baptist Church mission, Marshalltown, 1942: Rose Johnson, Helen Johnson, Betty Jones, Toni Scott, and Emma Rutherford (courtesy Helen Johnson)

Abe and Sadie Bryant, Anna Myrtle, Elzy Jones, Louis and Alice Johnson, Manual and Rosa Jackson, William and Mary Johnson, Carrie Suter, Mary Sellers, Eliza Cottoms, and Mrs. Fitchu Carter.

In 1898 in Des Moines, Corinthian Baptist Church was organized by Rev. Samuel Johnson, state missionary, and 21 other persons in a house on West 12th Street. The congregation was led originally by Reverend Bates. Rev. George Robinson, the church's longest serving pastor, served the congregation from 1917 until 1948. Reverend Robinson was followed by Rev. Norman Olphin (1951–1967) and Rev. Frederick W. Strickland (1968–1990).

One by one, African-American churches came into being, with African Methodist Episcopal churches dominating the rolls in Iowa. These included: AME in Clinton, 1874; Baptist in Ottumwa, 1875; AME in Washington, 1879; AME in Council Bluffs, 1880; Baptist in Fort Madison, 1881; Baptist in Clinton, 1887; Bethel Baptist Church in Colfax, 1896; Maple Street Baptist, Des Moines, 1899. By 1906, more than 70 African-American churches existed in Iowa. Most were Baptist or African Methodist Episcopal, but whatever their denomination the churches functioned in similar ways to provide for the spiritual life of their congregants and to improve the quality of life in their communities.

A number of African-American churches that formed in Iowa left little or no record of their organizational year. Among them is an AME church established in Colfax. Another such congregation is the AME church in Iowa City, a long-standing

Baptist congregations also flourished in Iowa's African-American communities. In 1896 the Second Baptist Church was organized in Marshalltown. After meeting for a number of years in various homes, the small congregation bought a modest building formerly housing a paint shop at 516 Bromley Street. The church began with 18 members, including C. P. and Martha Gilmore, George R. and Sadie Warn (later changed to Warren),

Bethel AME Church, Clinton (courtesy Hal Chase)

Rev. James L. Wharton, minister at St. Jacob's AME in Clarinda, c. 1906 (Nodaway Historical Society)

Rev. William Shaw, pastor (courtesy Gwen Sanders); Second Baptist Church, Ottumwa (Ottumwa Public Library)

institution that has left behind a scant legacy of historical documents or photographs. Jean C. Florman notes that "[despite] a history spanning 126 years, the African Methodist Church at 411 South Governor [in Iowa City] remains a religious and social center little-known outside of its membership."[4] According to Dianna Penny, church organist and daughter of the late Fred L. Penny, former AME minister, "the Iowa City AME church was founded as a mission church. It has always been a small congregation, initially because there were not many Blacks in Iowa City and later because it catered to a transient student population."[5] The church's small clapboard structure, built in 1868, was located outside of Iowa City because, at the time, blacks were not allowed to own property inside the city limits. In later years Dianna's brother, Fred Nicholas Penny, became pastor of an AME church in Clinton.

In addition to Baptist and Methodist congregations, African-Americans in Iowa joined Episcopal churches. The first of these to appear was St. Mary the Virgin, a mission of the Holy Cross Episcopal Church, organized in 1887 in Keokuk at 13th and High streets. St. Mary's was housed in an old schoolhouse that had been completely overhauled and refurbished. A news article in Keokuk's *Constitution-Democrat* newspaper reported "[the] membership of this mission is composed of some of the most prominent colored people in the city." An active mission until 1959, Saint Mary the Virgin "retained its High Church traditions over the years and had some notable Black priests. One of the first was the Rev. Henry A. S. Hartley, M.D., from Port of Spain, Trinidad, who served for

Not all African-American congregations were established in Iowa's larger cities. Pictured here is Keosauqua's Colored Methodist Church, c.1900, looking from Main Street toward the school house. (Van Buren County Historical Society)

(Far left) Education was a key component of the churches' contribution to the community. This is an AME district Sunday school annual meeting, held in Waterloo during the 1910s. (SHSI Iowa City)

An AME Sunday school convention held in Clarinda in about 1906 included Sue M. Brown and S. Joe Brown, who are pictured fourth and fifth from left in the front row. Rev. James L. Wheaton (holding child) is at the center of the photo. (Nodaway Valley Historical Society)

nine months in 1894."[6] Other priests followed Rev. Hartley, until the bishop of Iowa eventually placed the mission under the care of the rector of St. John's.

Buxton: Iowa's Black Utopia

At the turn of the twentieth century, many African-Americans were recruited from the South to work in Iowa's coal-mining camps. At first, the most important of the camps was located at Muchakinock, near Oskaloosa in Monroe County. However, in 1900 the Consolidation Coal Company established Buxton, which would soon eclipse the older camp.

Buxton was an extraordinary experience in the history of

St. Mary the Virgin congregation, sanctuary, and choir, 1920s, Keokuk (courtesy Marie Grigsby)

African-Americans in Iowa. According to historian Dorothy Schwieder, "Buxton attracted national attention because of its hospitable environment for blacks. Heralded as one of the great mining camps in the country, Buxton was widely known as a model mining community where blacks and whites lived side by side in racial harmony."

Against a racist national backdrop of Jim Crow legislation and *Plessy v. Ferguson*, economic upheavals, and massive migrations of southern black sharecroppers to northern cities, Buxton grew and flourished. African-Americans ran the Buxton company store, its restaurants, and its YMCA. Here were Iowa's first black school principals and teachers teaching in integrated school. Here African-Americans owned and operated hotels and other businesses. They held professional jobs, owned shops, and managed businesses. Community activities were shared by all races.

Based on her interviews with former Buxton citizens and their descendants, Dr. Schwieder wrote that "[the] black churches played an important spiritual and social role in the lives of Buxton's black residents." Buxton boasted no fewer than eight black churches: three Baptist churches, three African Methodist Episcopal churches, a Church of God, and a Congregational church. Former residents say African-American churches succeeded in Buxton because black residents wanted them, not because they had been shut out of white congregations.[7]

On February 6, 1914, the *Iowa Bystander* reported that 538 persons had attended the Mt. Zion Baptist Church and 375 had attended St. John's AME Church in Buxton that week.[8] African-American churches were the center of all Buxton's community activities. They sponsored service clubs, garden clubs, booster clubs, children's study clubs, social clubs, debates, night school, plays, elite women's groups, lodges and fraternal organizations, suffrage groups, and music groups — including a nine-piece African-American orchestra to accompany the choir at St. John's.

Buxton's population grew to nearly 8,000 residents. Over 6,000 were African-Americans. Only 50 years removed from slavery, Buxton was a utopia for African-Americans. The community thrived for two decades before the mines played out. Afterwards Buxton families migrated to Iowa's growing cities, including Davenport, Dubuque, Sioux City, Waterloo, and Des Moines, and to some smaller communities as well, establishing congregations wherever they settled.

St. John's Baptist Church, Mason City and New Bethel Baptist Church, Manly, July 25, 1946 (courtesy Everet Jeffries)

Mt. Zion Baptist Church, Sioux City (courtesy Laura Harrison)

Mt. Zion Baptist Sunday school, Oralabor (courtesy Joann Jones)

The Great Migration and World War

The period from about 1915 through the World War 2 era saw a great migration of African-Americans from the South to urban centers in the North. A similar migration to Iowa paralleled the national exodus from the South. "Thousands of African-Americans migrated to Iowa during the period 1915 to 1940," reports the State Historical Society of Iowa brochure, "African-Americans in Iowa's Past."[9] They came hoping to find a good education, higher wages, and a better way of life. Typically they turned to churches and social organizations after they arrived to get help adjusting to their new surroundings. Their social and spiritual needs varied, and the churches responded accordingly. Most of all, churches and social organizations gave the uprooted southerners a sense of community, common goals, and the will to begin their lives anew in a new land.

Such was the case with Mt. Zion Baptist Church, founded in Cedar Rapids in 1914. Organized as part of the Iowa Baptist Convention, the church's two charter members were Anna Joyce and W. L. Warren. In Fort Dodge at around the same time, a group of Methodists originally from Missouri organized Coppin Chapel AME in a small frame building at 1st Avenue and 4th Street. Coppin Chapel's first minister, named in 1917, was the Rev. Matthew R. Rhonene, a native of Trinidad, British West Indies. Reverend Rhonene had become a member of the AME Church in Canada before he came to Fort Dodge to take a government job.

Many other new congregations appeared, especially in Des Moines, in the World War 1 era, including First Colored Methodist Church in Des Moines, 1909; Bethel AME, originally called Lee's Mission, in Des Moines, 1909; Union Baptist in Des Moines, 1915; Kyles AME Zion in Des Moines, 1915; Shiloh Missionary Baptist in Des Moines, 1917; and Payne AME Church in Waterloo, 1919. Mt. Hebron Baptist began in a boxcar south of the railroad tracks in West Des Moines in 1920. In the same year in Des Moines, Mt. Olive Baptist started in a small building on South Union Street. In Fort Madison an AME church was organized in 1924.

Mt. Zion Baptist Church, Cedar Rapids (courtesy Connie Hillsman)

*Malone AME Sunday School,
Sioux City, c. 1915
(courtesy Laura Harrison)*

These congregations appear to have had strong support in their respective communities. According to an article in the *Iowa Journal of History and Politics,* "approximately two thirds of the 5,000 African-Americans in Des Moines in 1918 were church members, the majority affiliated with the Baptist and Methodist denominations."[10] Adding to the impact of the Great Migration was the arrival of African-American military personnel in central Iowa. During World War 1 military training camps at Fort Des Moines and later Camp Dodge drew families of African-American soldiers to Des Moines. The membership rolls of local black churches grew even further.

Affiliated or cooperating with the churches were a variety of social organizations that emerged to serve the African-American community. The Des Moines Homemakers League, for example, was organized to help African-Americans find good housing. There were also adult education classes. Most of these met in church basements, where space was provided free and was centrally located for most residents. In addition, African-Americans organized their own chapters of fraternal orders, such as the Masons and Elks. By and large, African-American social organizations focused on improving the quality of life for families and provided a much-needed support system in the African-American community. If individuals or families needed assistance they knew that help was available to them in the church.

Among the more outspoken African-American religious leaders in Iowa at this time was Christian socialist George Slater. Reverend Slater was pastor of Bethel AME church in Clinton from 1912 to 1919. He came to Iowa from Chicago, where he had been prominent in the socialist movement of that era. Iowans knew of him already, since before his Clinton appointment he had spoken on socialism at a meeting in Ottumwa. Reverend Slater's presence in Iowa may have been one of the reasons the national Christian Socialist newspaper was launched in Webster City, Iowa.

During the decade following World War 1, African-American churches remained the hub of community activities, serving as meeting places for both worship and secular activities. Several events in the early 1900s are particularly noteworthy. St. Paul AME Church had the honor of banqueting a number of noted African-Americans, including Booker T. Washington and his wife during their visit to Des Moines. Mrs. Washington, then president of the National Council of Colored Women, was also a guest speaker at St. Paul AME.

Another event involved Iowa Gov. Nate Kendall. The Des Moines NAACP was founded in 1915. In 1921 the Des Moines Chamber of Commerce responded positively to a request for support by the NAACP. A local ministerial association had also endorsed the NAACP's efforts. Governor Kendall, in an exceptional show of leadership, addressed a convocation of city ministers and other clergymen at Maple Street Baptist urging his listeners "to support the NAACP beyond a verbal endorsement. In a written proclamation the governor encouraged the clergy to become active members of the organization," reported the *Iowa Bystander* of May 19, 1921.[11]

In 1926 Des Moines had a dozen African-American churches. Statewide membership in black churches totaled 8,577, which did not include black members of predominantly white congregations. Ten years later, at the height of the Great Depression, this number decreased to 6,134 members in a total of 83 churches. There were 20 Baptist churches, with a total of 4,000 members and 6 AME churches with more than 1,000 members in each. Another denomination, the Church of God in Christ, had about 300 members in 8 churches in 1936. Included

in a 1937 listing of African-American churches were two new denominations. One was the Christ Sanctified Holy Church in Cedar Rapids. The other was the First African-American Presbyterian Church located at 504 East Boone in Marshalltown.

During the years of economic depression, African-American churches continued to be sources of support and assistance to Iowa's black families. With the coming of war in 1941, Fort Des Moines brought new people to Des Moines and new worshippers to the churches. They came from all over the United States, and they included candidates for regular officer training schools, for the Tuskegee Airmen, and for the Women's Auxiliary Army Corps.

Since World War 2

The end of World War 2 initiated a period of great change in the lives of African-Americans nationwide. Migration from the South to the North continued. In 1948 Pres. Harry Truman signed Executive Order 9981 integrating the armed forces. And in 1954 the U.S. Supreme Court's decision in *Brown v. Board of Education* overturned the "separate but equal" doctrine of *Plessy v. Ferguson* that had prevailed since the 1890s. Through these

Jesse Garrison, charter member of Rosehill Church of God in Christ, Waterloo (courtesy Mary Reasby Hodge)

Congregation of Malone AME in Sioux City (Sioux City Public Museum)

St. Paul's AME congregation, 1926, Bishop A. L. Gaines, pastor (SHSI Des Moines)

Rev. Allen Simpson, Iowa's first African-American Catholic priest, Ottumwa, 1949 (SHSI Des Moines)

James S. Thomas, Methodist Bishop for Iowa (Simpson College Archives)

years of change, African-American churches stayed in the forefront, hosting meetings on civil rights and voting rights and helping school children survive the transition to busing and integrated schools. The churches also supported sit-ins and protest marches around the nation, including the famed Katz Drugstore sit-ins in Des Moines when African-Americans were refused service at a local lunch counter.

Sociologist Andrew Billingsley has remarked that "[from] the beginning community service has been an element of Black religious expression."[12] A variety of services typically offered by African-American churches are social in nature, designed to help families and communities. This was certainly true in Iowa, and the black churches' community service tradition became even more pronounced in the second half of the twentieth century. Along with affirmative action and classroom integration, the church's various social service programs represented a shift — or an expansion — from a traditional emphasis on personal salvation to an emphasis on social salvation for the community as a whole.

In these years, African-American churches were moving into a new era of social service programs and community concerns. The African-American churches had long been in the forefront of efforts to sustain families. Now they were also responding to new challenges: substance abuse, AIDS, single-parent families (male and female), homelessness, teenage pregnancy, and gang violence. A surge in social service programs began in the 1960s, influenced by the Black Panther Party's breakfast programs to feed school children. In Des Moines one such program began at Trinity Methodist Church at 8th and College, across the street from Moulton Elementary School. The breakfast program continues today. Several other churches were approached by the Panthers to help them serve breakfast to other inner-city school students.

Older established churches with sufficient resources expanded their community outreach efforts, recruiting volunteers from members and non-members alike. Serving the whole family — children, youth, adults, and senior citizens — was the goal of these congregations and their leaders. Representing a cross section of social classes, typically these African-American churches are stable fixtures in the urban neighborhoods where they were originally established. Some of their members who have, over the years, moved from the central city to new homes in the suburbs return on Sundays to worship in African-American congregations

in the inner city. Others, however, have become members of predominantly white congregations. Integration of congregations into inter-church alliances also took place. Black churches of Methodist denominations were being offered inclusion into the predominantly white United Methodist alliances. These congregations continued their strong community outreach activities.

Though fewer new churches were launched in the post–World War 2 period than in previous years, there was increased black participation in several denominations, including the Church of God in Christ and the Roman Catholic Church. African-American Catholic ministries grew nationally, numbering two million in 1989. In Iowa there were only 212 Catholics in the entire diocese that includes Cedar Rapids, Dubuque, Waterloo, Mason City, and Ames. Thirteen of them had been recorded in Cedar Rapids. A Catholic ministry established in Des Moines met at one of the Catholic cathedrals, but it had no separate building for worship.

Blacks in Iowa also joined the Muslim faith. The American Muslim Mission (then called Nation of Islam) was organized in the 1930s nationwide, but a mosque was not established in Iowa until 1975. This was the American Muslim Mission Center, located at 307 College Avenue in Des Moines.

Several African-American ministers in Iowa have made distinguished contributions to the religious life of the state. One of these was Bishop James S. Thomas Jr. Reverend Thomas was appointed resident bishop of the Iowa United Methodist Church from 1964 to 1976, the first African-American to hold the position in the state. Also serving as resident bishop was Rev. Charles Wesley Jordan, who was elected to the position in 1992. Prior to his appointment, Bishop Jordan had served as a district superintendent, and as a conference councilperson in the Northern Illinois Conference. He had also been a member of the boards of directors of several prominent agencies and institutions in Iowa. Bishop Jordan's mother is Mrs. Naomi Harper Jordan, a native of Fort Madison. Appointed to a second four-year term in July 1996, Bishop Jordan oversees a United Methodist Church with 202,000 members in 900 churches. Three months after his second appointment, Bishop Jordan was also elected president of the 63-member General Board of Church and Society for the United Methodist Church.

Due to their effectiveness in responding to the social and spiritual needs of their churches and their communities, several of Iowa's African-American ministers have retained the support of their congregations for many years. Among those ministers who led their congregation for long periods of time were Rev. H. R. Fields, who was at Mt. Olive Baptist Church in Des Moines for 34 years; Rev. James Harris of Mt. Hebron Baptist Church of West Des Moines (now Des Moines) for 43 years; and Rev. Norman R. Olphin and later Rev. Frederick Strickland Sr., who served Corinthian Baptist for lengthy terms. Rev. Henry I. Thomas has served Union Baptist Church in Des Moines since 1968. Many other ministers have also served their flocks for 10 years or more in Iowa.

Though not a minister, attorney S. Joe Brown of Des Moines made key contributions to the religious lives of blacks in Iowa. In 1898 Brown became the first African-American to receive a liberal arts degree from the University of Iowa and the first black student west of the Mississippi to be elected to Phi Beta Kappa. Throughout his life he was active in the affairs of the African Methodist Episcopal Church. For ten years, from 1920 to 1930, he was the sole black member on the executive committee of the Polk County Council of Religious Education. When the Des Moines Area Council of Churches was organized in 1930, Mr. Brown was elected one of the five directors at large, the only African-American serving in that capacity.

The first ordained female minister to serve in an Iowa African-American church was Christina McDonald, a member of the Bethel AME Church of Cedar Rapids. Beverly (Gladys) Taylor learned about Reverend McDonald from official church papers that Mrs. Taylor's mother, Nina Bragg, had in her possession. Mrs. Taylor wrote, "Bethel is very proud to have had a lady member of our church serve in the ministry field. The records in the minutes of 1950–51 annual conference show that Sister Evangelist Christina McDonald was ordained a minister. She is said to be the first woman minister of Iowa in the AME church. She served in Iowa City and Washington, Iowa. The family tells me of her being sent to Muscatine where the people were not ready to accept a lady minister. She didn't fight the rejection and returned to Cedar Rapids for a while, then moved on to California."[13]

Another group of influential church leaders in Iowa is the Black Ministerial Alliance of Des Moines, composed of local church ministers. This organization coordinates activities among the city's black churches and also works within the larger religious community and other related social service organizations in the metropolitan area. For example, Rev. Keith Ratliff, pastor of Maple Street Baptist Church, served the Alliance as president during the 1990s and still serves as president of the Des Moines Chapter of the National Association for the Advancement of Colored People.

Islamic Center of Des Moines (left) and Muhammad Mosque, Des Moines (courtesy Hal Chase)

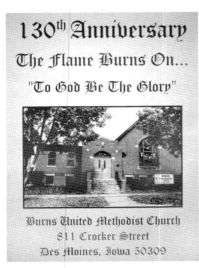

Burns United Methodist Church celebrates another milestone (courtesy Frances Hawthorne)

A Tradition of Service and Self-Help

African-American churches have had a profound influence on the lives of their members and on Iowa's black communities in general. From camp meeting days in early Iowa to today's modern air-conditioned edifices with family life centers and education wings, probably no other social institution matches the church's impact. Churches are community focal points, and church leaders are nearly always perceived as community leaders as well. Black clergy provide spiritual guidance, but they have also been mighty advocates in the continuing quest to achieve the full rights of citizenship for all African-Americans.

Day to day, black churches also offer social services of all kinds. As Erica E. Smith wrote in the *Iowa State Bystander*'s one-hundredth anniversary issue: "The Black church has a strong history of looking out for its people. The 'looking out' has become more vital than ever before in the history of Black Americans. Black churches are reaching out by setting up afternoon school programs, summer programs, and other forms of networking."[14]

Rev. H. I. Thomas, longtime pastor of Union Baptist Church, concurs. Union Baptist is a hub of local life, supporting 15 community programs and providing leadership in times of crisis, such as the flood emergency of 1993. "We have what we call job opportunities on Sundays," said Reverend Thomas. "We work very closely with all the business people in town. Employers contact us weekly with city jobs, government jobs and these jobs are read off on Sunday mornings."[15] In Waterloo, Rev. Michael Coleman's Antioch Baptist Church performs a comparable function in its community. "The Black church helps more than any social agency. We help keep families together and spend more money on benevolence. When you think about the church, it is the only institution fully controlled by Blacks. It stands above any other institutions," said Reverend Coleman.[16]

These and other African-American church leaders are committed to sustaining their proud traditions of service and self-help. Rev. Charles A. Woolery, recent pastor of Burns United Methodist Church, the state's oldest continuous congregation, has faith they will. "We are the first church of the African-American community in Iowa and with that title we have a responsibility. We have a proud past, but I believe we have an even more promising future and it depends on the pastoral and lay leadership. Pastor and people are in parish ministry together. If we are serious and sincere about what our mission is, I believe we can remain viable because we serve a God who can supply us with the power to become an eternal flame."[17]

The Baptists are the largest denomination in Iowa and the United States — as suggested by this photo of the 1925 State Baptist Convention at the original Corinthian Baptist Church in Des Moines . (courtesy Laura Carter Harrison)

Mt. Zion AME, Ottumwa (Mt. Zion AME)

Notes

1. Robert R. Dykstra, *Bright Radical Star: Black Freedom and White Supremacy on the Hawkeye Frontier* (Cambridge: Harvard Univ. Press, 1993), 7.

2. *Keokuk Constitution-Democrat*, n.d.

3. James B. Weaver, *Past and Present of Jasper County, Iowa* (Indianapolis: B. F. Brown, 1912), 189.

4. Jean C. Florman, "Traces: Personal Accounts of a History Nearly Lost," *Iowa City Magazine*, January 1995, 19.

5. Ibid.

6. *Keokuk Constitution-Democrat*, Feb. 3, 1890.

7. Dorothy Schwieder, Joseph Hraba, and Elmer Schwieder, *Buxton: Work and Racial Equality in a Coal Mining Community* (Ames: Iowa State Univ. Press, 1987), 210.

8. *Iowa Bystander*, Feb. 6, 1914.

9. *African-Americans in Iowa's Past*, State Historical Society of Iowa brochure, n.d.

10. *The Negro in Iowa* (Iowa City: SHSI, 1948; repr. 1969), 66.

11. *Iowa Bystander*, May 19, 1921.

12. Andrew Billingsley, *Climbing Jacob's Ladder: The Enduring Legacy of African-American Families* (New York: Simon and Schuster, 1992), 352.

13. Beverly (Gladys) Taylor, correspondence with the author, n.d.

14. Erica E. Smith, "Let the Church Say Amen," *Iowa State Bystander* [Anniversary Edition, 1894–1994: 100 Years of Black Achievement], 1994, 53.

15. Ibid.

16. Ibid.

17. Rev. Charles A. Woolery, correspondence with author, n.d.

Frances Hawthorne is the author of African Americans in Iowa: A Chronicle of Contributions, 1830–1992. *A retired school administrator, she has been a veteran volunteer with the American Association of Retired Persons (AARP) at the local and national levels since 1992. Ms. Hawthorne graduated from Lincoln University (Missouri) with a bachelor's degree in journalism in 1951 and received a master's degree in teaching from Drake University in 1972. Her honors include the YWCA Woman of Achievement Award and Drake University's Outstanding Alumni Award. She has also been inducted into the Iowa African-American Hall of Fame.*

An old clock still calls members to worship at the Faith Temple Church in Waterloo, where Belinda Smith (right) is pastor and Isabella Johnson is a deacon. (Doug Wells photos / Des Moines Register)

YWCA youth group in front of the Blue Triangle YWCA in Des Moines (courtesy Nathaline Dixon)

Chapter Seventeen

Social, Fraternal, Cultural, and Civic Organizations

by Lynda C. Walker-Webster

This chapter may capture only a portion of Iowa's African-American social, fraternal, cultural, and civic organizations, but it will nonetheless provide a sense of the numerous activities that have occupied the leisure and volunteer time of black Iowans from the late nineteenth century to the present.

It is still difficult for many Americans, both black and white, to perceive that African-Americans reside in Iowa. The time and distance of travel between the social and familial village of origins, the slave pens of Africa's western shores, the slave ports of North America, and the boundaries of the state of Iowa — when compared to the history of North America and the United States — can be measured only by the depth and perception of an individual's own conceived moment of our time in history.

Most of Iowa's pioneer African-Americans settled in clusters. Some came to work in the lead mines of antebellum Dubuque or in the busy commercial towns along the Mississippi River. Another group settled along the Volga River in Fayette County in northeastern Iowa.[2] Other black settlements appeared along the western border of Iowa, on the Missouri River's steamboat routes.[3]

Later, after the Civil War, African-Americans would settle in the mining areas of south-central Iowa and in manufacturing and trade centers such as Waterloo and Des Moines.[4]

These early black settlers in Iowa initially took part in social organizations related to their churches. In *The Souls of Black Folk*, written in 1903, W. E. B. DuBois pointed to the church as the social center of Negro life in the United States.[5] Using a black Baptist church in Virginia as an example, DuBois noted that in addition to its religious and Sunday school functions, the Virginia church was home to two or three insurance societies, women's societies, secret societies, and mass meetings of various kinds. The church was also a place of entertainment, holding suppers and lectures in addition to the five or six religious meetings on its weekly schedule.

Iowa churches were no different, though perhaps in the frontier era their activities were on a smaller scale. DuBois wrote that in the South "practically everyone" was a church member. By this he meant that whether or not they were enrolled officially or attended Sunday services regularly, all felt the church was the center of their social life.[6] It gave them a sense of belonging.

"The African slave was immediately Americanized! He was separated from his family, tribal, religious, and language relationships at once! He had no visitors or letters from home. Of no other group was this true."

— *Anna Arnold Hedgeman,*

1922 Annual Convention of Iowa Masons in Riverside Park, Sioux City (courtesy Laura Carter Harrison)

In a sense, the church was an extended family for these people whose cultural and social roots were all but destroyed by slavery in the South and other forms of institutionalized racism throughout the United States.

The decades following the Civil War were a time of starting anew for African-Americans in Iowa and throughout the nation. Many black Americans put down new roots and built for themselves new cultural and social environments. The church was probably the key to their success in this endeavor, in Iowa and throughout the nation. Certainly in Iowa the first African-American clubs and social organizations were formed in and around the church. Thus the church was not only a spiritual beacon and an "Amen Corner," but it was a community gathering place and in some cases an educational facility as well. For example, the black community that formed in Fayette County in the early 1850s was not looked upon favorably by white people in the area. Black settlers were required to initiate their own cemetery, which they named Pleasant Hill. With stones they built their own school, Westfield Township School No. 4, which they called Stone House. The building not only functioned as a school for the settlers' children, but also as their church and the center of their social life as well.[7]

This pattern is evident years later too. Iowa's small-town newspapers in the past often read like diaries of their communities. Such was the case in Oskaloosa, where the *Oskaloosa Herald* shortly before 1900 began featuring a column titled "Our Colored Society: The Ins and Outs of the Local Colony." For years the column was written by Alexander Clark Jr., a prominent local barber who in 1879 became the first black graduate of the University of Iowa.[8] In addition to the usual social chitchat, Clark always listed the activities of each church, including those not related to the congregations but using church facilities.

In Iowa, the African Methodist Episcopal Church (AME) and the Baptist Church showed continued growth across the state from the late nineteenth and well into the twentieth centuries. Even in the smallest of towns where black Iowans resided could usually be found one of each. Both denominations supported a number of specialized religious auxiliaries. One was the Missionary Society, which functioned to help those in need, inside and outside the church. Iowa's black churches also sponsored literary societies, whose mixed membership of men and women sought to improve themselves intellectually. There were quilting bees and sewing circles, where the women of the congregation not only made needed household items while "in the company of their sisters," but also counseled, gave advice, and shared community news. These church get-togethers were perhaps the earliest social gatherings among African-Americans in Iowa.

The church spawned many social organizations with religious purposes, and it encouraged the development of others of a more general character. Many key community organizations, while not religious in nature, were formed by individuals who were considered the "movers and shakers" of their denominations. The mere involvement of these individuals gave these activities great credibility in the community. Moreover, fraternal lodges such as the Masons, the Knights of Pythias, the Odd Fellows, and the Elks also included religious references in their doctrines. In addition, many lodge meetings and "turn outs" were held at the churches following Sunday services.

The Formation of Iowa's Fraternal Orders: The Front Runners

During the late nineteenth century a burst of recruiting activity took place among fraternal organizations across the nation, and before long the enthusiasm reached Iowa's borders. National offices encouraged the formation of local chapters or affiliates, and a bevy of organizational efforts could be found in virtually every city with a sizable black community in Iowa in the late 1800s.

While many African-American social organizations were founded in the decades following the Civil War, perhaps the most prominent among the national fraternal orders to formally organize chapters in Iowa were the Prince Hall Masonic Order (1872),[9] the Odd Fellows (1881),[10] and the Knights of Pythias (1891).[11]

While some of the fraternal orders were primarily social in nature, many addressed serious contemporary political and educational issues as well. Regardless of their specific purposes, the fraternal orders were critically important in the development of self-esteem and leadership in Iowa's black community as a whole.

Ironically, most black fraternal orders were offshoots of their white counterparts, which of course rejected them for membership, but they offered great opportunities for the social and intellectual development of their members.[12] This strengthened their societies and garnered much-deserved respect from their communities. Within these organizations — especially among the officers, both male and female — were to be found the leaders of the local black community.

The Masons

The venerable Prince Hall Masons, originally called the Grand Lodge of Masons #1, is the oldest continuous fraternal group among black Americans. Fraternal and mutual-benefit societies had existed among blacks since the earliest establishment of free and segregated communities in the late 1700s. One respected early group was the Free African Society, founded by Richard Allen, Absolom Jones, and their associates. The Free African Society encouraged its members to live orderly and sober lives, to support one another in sickness, and to provide for the benefit of widows and fatherless children.[13] Similar in their pledge to one another, the Prince Hall Masons were founded in Boston in 1775 by Prince Hall, an immigrant from Barbados, and 14 other men.[14]

In his organizational quest, Prince Hall felt a separate lodge was needed to provide camaraderie for African-Americans.[15] Hall in particular encouraged the establishment of mutual-benefit organizations throughout the post-revolutionary period.[16] Two centuries later, in 1965, there were estimated to be 312,000 Prince Hall Masons located in 38 states, Canada, and Nassau. The auxiliary to the men of the order, the Daughters of Isis, listed about 6,500 women in 117 courts.[17]

Some Masonic chapters and affiliates in Iowa were considered secret societies. Others formed to address specific interests or to alleviate undesirable conditions. In all of them, high office meant great respect in the community. The elegant regalia — the decorated fez and tassel, the fringed and decorated sashes, the pins and aprons — were worn with pride and esteem. When the entire lodge turned out for special celebrations, often held during or after church services on Sunday, lodge members always seemed to stand especially erect, proud to represent the order and proud to be Masons.

The Masonic family within Iowa has been exceptionally active from its inception. At one time chapters existed virtually everywhere African-Americans resided in Iowa. If a chapter did not exist in a town, it can be certain there was one not too far away. Today the Masons have lodges in Des Moines, Sioux City, Davenport, Fort Madison, Clinton, Waterloo, Cedar Rapids, Marshalltown, and Burlington. The current Most Worshipful Grand Master is Kenneth Collier of Des Moines.[18]

The first organized Masonic Lodge in Iowa was North Star #3, which gained prominence throughout the state. The first Worshipful Master was J. S. Carter. Other officers were Archie Brown, Jeff Logan, J. L. Lewis, and J. T. Allen. In 1876 there were

Masonic Order group at Old Corinthian Baptist Church, Des Moines, includes Albert Saunders and his father-in-law, Ray McAlister. (courtesy Meredith Saunders)

40 members, with J. Page serving as the Worshipful Master.[19] In March 1895, E. T. Banks and G. H. Cleggett of Des Moines were present in Sioux City to install the Commandery and Royal Arch Masons that had been formed there.[20] In 1903 Harrison Gould was serving as the Most Worshipful Master of North Star Lodge #3. That year's souvenir booklet of the Northwest AME Conference noted that Mr. Gould, who was just 26 years old, was one of the most influential men in the social life of Des Moines and of his church (St. Paul's).[21]

On August 1, 1912, the *Des Moines Register and Leader* carried a news article headlined "Negroes Purchase Hall for Lodges."[22] Subtitled "Undertake Project of Public Character," the column pointed out that the North Star Lodge had inaugurated a

new era in its history. The newspaper reported that while lodge members had built many churches, and that many owned their own homes, they had now undertaken a "project of the pretentious public character contemplated by this organization."

What the lodge had done was simply purchase a half block of land on Center Street between 10th and 11th. The purchase price was $8,100 for the building, with an additional $1,200 for improvements for the property. The organization had capital of $20,000, so there were ample funds to furnish the new hall and maintain it in the future. The plan was to make this hall the social center for the black people of the city. The men directing this enterprise were E. Tracy Blagburn (a local pharmacist), president; Harrison Gould, vice president; Gus Watkins, treasurer; and Vivian

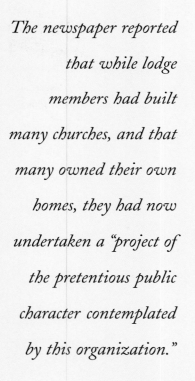

The newspaper reported that while lodge members had built many churches, and that many owned their own homes, they had now undertaken a "project of the pretentious public character contemplated by this organization."

Order of the Eastern Star (courtesy Helen I. Johnson)

Jones (a local undertaker), secretary. Other lodge members involved in the project were John L. Thompson (of the *Iowa Bystander),* Branham Hyde (the inventor), H. E. Jacobs, James H. Woods, and Effie Watkins.[23]

Other Masonic chapters active in Des Moines over the years have included Doric Lodge #30, North Star Lodge #2, Olive Branch #32, Zeid Court #90, and William Frank Powell Consistory #46.

The Ladies of the Auxiliary

The Daughters of Isis of Des Moines, Zeid Court #50, was organized in 1921, originally being called Iada Court. The first officers were Illustrious Commandress Sally Gater; First Lt. Commandress Rilla Seymour; and Second Lt. Commandress Mable Johnson. These officers were authorized on August 4, 1921, when a charter was granted them to serve in these respected offices by Imperial Commandress Excell H. Moore.[24] After 25 years as Iada Court, the chapter became the Fiftieth Court of the Daughters of Isis. Reorganizer Victoria Hendricks was appointed to the office of Illustrious Commandress. The chapter's new charter was presented on August 4, 1946.[25] Since then, Zeid Court #50 has produced over 42 Illustrious Commandresses and 6 Imperial Deputies of the Desert, including Ellaree Taylor, past deputy; Hiawatha Potter (deceased); Wilmetta Jones, past deputy; Ella Mae Burks (deceased); Bertie Hogan, past deputy; and Dorothy Garrett, now serving. Zeid Court #50 has also produced two Deputies of the Oasis: Mildred Graves, past deputy, and Barbara Robinson, now serving.[26]

Sue Brown, an honored member of Zeid Court #50, wrote *The History of the Order of the Eastern Star among Colored People.* Only two Daughters of Zeid Court #50 have ever been awarded the highest honor of Past Imperial Commandress: the late Jessie Newsome, who was awarded the honor on August 4, 1987, and Bertie M. Hogan, who received the award on August 20, 1990.[27]

Electra Grand Chapter, Order of the Eastern Star, was organized in May 1907 by W. H. Milligan, the first Grand Master of Iowa from Cedar Rapids. The first Grand Matron was Ida B. Palmer of Burlington, who was inducted at the first Annual Grand Session in Cedar Rapids in 1907. Five chapters were inducted into the Grand Chapter at that time. The officers' degrees were confirmed by J. H. Sims, Worthy Grand Patron, Missouri Jurisdiction.[28] Electra Chapter #17, O.E.S., was organized in Keokuk in June 1881.

While the local chapters have usually met monthly, the state Grand Chapter meets yearly in the various towns in Iowa. Two chapters of O.E.S exist in Des Moines, Princess Oziel #9 and Princess Zorah #10. There are 14 subordinate chapters that report to the Electra Grand Chapter. In 2000, the group held its ninety-first annual meeting. Presiding Grand Matron was Sheila Bullock of Waterloo. Grand Patron was Edward Bell of Ottumwa. Betty Taylor of Davenport was Associate Grand Matron, and Ferrell Turner of Clinton was Grand Associate Patron.[29]

Clemmie Hightower, an octogenarian from Clinton who has been a very loyal O.E.S. member, feels that while Des Moines has the oldest chapter, Waterloo's chapter has been the most active. Mrs. Hightower recalled grand officers from the years 1957 to the present who are still living: Gladys Taylor (Cedar Rapids), Marjorie Marsh (Fort Madison), Mildred Graves (Des Moines), Willetta Fluelin (Des Moines), Iver Jeane Bailey (Marshalltown), Haley Houston (Des Moines), Charlotte Weldon (Burlington), Alberta Crump (Des Moines), Aretha White (Waterloo), and Meredith Burke (Clinton). Mrs. Hightower also named the Royal Grand Matrons Ruby Jewett (Des Moines), Betty Garr (Ottumwa), and Janice Riddley (Des Moines).[30]

The Masonic family has two important "turn out" days. One is Easter Day, one of their star points, when they ask for the people to be free. The other is St. John's Day. St. John is felt to have been the most representative of men of his day.[31]

Their Youth: The Isiserettes

For the last nearly 20 years, the Daughters of Isis (Des Moines) have been proud to have as their youth ambassadors the renowned Isiserettes. This outstanding drill-and-drum unit has traveled throughout Iowa and the Midwest and into some of the nation's larger cities.[32] The Isiserettes (of Zied Temple #90 and Zied Court #50) are in great demand for parades, half-time performances, and many other special occasions. The primary drill-and-drum unit is composed of middle school and high school boys and girls, with many other elementary youth participating in the younger unit. The Daughters of Isis have been applauded for their work with this youth group, which builds character and self-esteem and instills a sense of pride and dedication among African-American youth. The Isiserettes have received many awards. Those in charge of the group are Barbara Robinson (organizer), Joan Hill

The Isiserettes drill and drum squad is sponsored by the Des Moines Daughters of Isis (courtesy Joan Hill)

Iowa District Grand Lodge No. 30
and the Iowa District Grand Household of Ruth No. 21

Grand United Order of Odd Fellows

40ᵗʰ Annual Session of the Odd Fellows, Des Moines, September 1922 (SHSI)

(directress), and Bertie Hogan (treasurer). Instructors include Kevin Bell, Johnetta Douglas, Marie Fisher, Simmone Hill, Cory Williams, Larry Young, and Pam Williams.[33]

The Odd Fellows

The Odd Fellows established lodges in early Iowa but African-American lodges of the order have not been active in Iowa for some time. Peter Ogden, a black ship steward from England, founded Philomethean Lodge #646 for Negroes in New York City in 1843. Founded on principles of friendship, love, and truth, the Odd Fellows were determined to be a power for good through the length and breadth of the land. Their doctrine states that the hand of brotherly love and friendship is all-inspiring to its members and extends freely and cordially to all who knock at their door and affiliate themselves with the order.[34] (The African-American branch of the Odd Fellows, founded by Mr. Ogden, was allowed because he had held membership in the majority lodge in England but was denied membership in America.[35])

Charity Lodge #2192 was organized in Des Moines in 1881, and a state Grand Lodge was organized in 1882. By 1894, when the Grand Lodge of Iowa convened in Fort Madison, there were several additional lodges in Iowa: Reliance Lodge (Burlington), Muchakinock Lodge (Muchakinock), Virginia Lodge (Cleveland), T. A. Cheek Lodge (Mount Pleasant), Upper Light Lodge (Oskaloosa), and Albia Lodge (Albia).[36] Documentation of when the Odd Fellows became inactive in Iowa has not been located.

The Knights of Pythias and the Courts of Calanthe

The Knights of Pythias and their auxiliaries have been active in Iowa since the late nineteenth century. Founded in 1864 in Washington, D.C., the Knights of Pythias held its first Supreme Lodge meeting in 1880.[37] Its purposes, proclaimed at that time, were "to uplift the fallen, to soften the asperities of life, to subdue party spirit, to lessen the suffering of a brother, to care for the widows and orphans, to bury the dead, administer to the wants of the sick, elevate man from his degraded position to a higher plane of intelligence and morality and place man upon a platform of social equality."[38]

The first Knights of Pythias lodge in Iowa was established in Ottumwa in July 1891, followed by the organization of the Grand Lodge of Iowa at an 1894 meeting in Oskaloosa officiated by R. M. Mitchell of Chicago. Sir A. G. Clark of Oskaloosa was the first Grand Chancellor and Sir C. R. Foster of Muchakinock was the first Grand Keeper of Records and Seals.[39] Unfortunately, the order died quickly; there was no visible effort on the part of the officials to save it.[40] But on November 1, 1895, national Supreme Chancellor James C. Ross appointed Sir George Taylor of Oskaloosa as Acting Grand Chancellor to revive the order. Taylor held this appointed position until August 20, 1896, when he was elected to the position by the Grand Lodge Session at Burlington. The officers were encouraged by Taylor's report, and although he was not able to hold a Grand Lodge session the following year, he was successful in organizing new lodges and building up some of the older ones. In fact, Taylor was so successful in this endeavor that when the Grand Lodge met in Ottumwa in August 1899, there were more Knights and more lodges in good standing than had ever existed before in the state of Iowa.[41]

As with many of the early organizations, Knights of Pythias lodges have become inactive in some of the towns where they once thrived. In the early 1900s, Cedar Rapids, Clinton, Sioux City,

Buxton, Mount Pleasant, Ottumwa, Burlington, Oskaloosa, Muchakinock, and Marshalltown all had lodges and/or courts. Today, there are five lodges and nine courts in Iowa.[42] Among these are G. G. Stokes Lodge #8 (Davenport), Independent Lodge #4 (Des Moines), Perseverance Lodge #14 (Mason City), and Furgerson Lodge #5 (Waterloo).[43] Current Grand Chancellor for Iowa is Lloyd Green of Waterloo.

The Grand Worthy Counselor for Iowa is Olabelle Williams Black, also of Des Moines. The Honorable Benjamin Hooks is the National Supreme Chancellor for the Knights of Pythias.[44] Donald Austin of Des Moines is Supreme Worthy Counselor.

The Order of Calanthe is the women's auxiliary of the Knights of Pythias. Founded in 1883 in Vicksburg, Mississippi, on principles of fidelity, harmony, and love, the goals of the women's order are to (1) unite fraternally all mothers, wives, widows, daughters, and sisters of sound health and good moral character who are socially acceptable; (2) to give moral and mental aid to its members and those who depend on them; (3) to educate its members socially, morally, and intellectually; (4) to establish a fund for the relief of sick and distressed members; and (5) to establish a widow's and orphan's fund.[45]

The first Grand Court of the Order of Calanthe in Iowa took place on November 8, 1915, in Des Moines, with Sir Joseph L. Jones, Supreme Worthy Counselor officiating. Eva Owens of Buxton was made the Grand Worthy Counselor and Agnes Bolden of Buxton was made Grand Register of Deeds.[46]

Barbara Sue Williams of Des Moines is a trustee and Imperial Treasurer for Imperial Council, Princess of Omar. Ms. Williams speaks with pride of her involvement in the activities of

Imperial Council certificate for Ray McAlister (courtesy Meredith Saunders)

Mt. Pleasant barber Sam McCracken in his lodge uniform (courtesy Don Young)

Far left: Perfect Asher Lodge #34, Mason City, dinner or other lodge function (courtesy Meredith Saunders)

Mary Ruth Simmons, P.G.D.R., Iowa District Deputy, and Past Grand Club member (courtesy Lynda Walker-Webster)

the Knights of Pythias. It is a pride of belonging but also of doing, being part of an organization that annually donates to underprivileged families, non-profit organizations, and scholarship funds, and sends cards to the sick and the bereaved.[47]

Local courts of Calanthe that remain active in Iowa are Rebecca Court #3 (Des Moines), Alberta King Court #12 (Davenport), Harriet Ross Tubman Court #14 (Davenport), Esterlight Court #9 (Des Moines), Tyre Court #11 (Des Moines) and Samari Court #9 (Des Moines), B. F. Parker Court #8 (Mason City), Arria Court #5 (Waterloo), and Sojourner Truth Court #10 (Waterloo).[48] Youth departments include Winters Court and Junior Knights (Davenport), Angel Court and Junior Knights (Des Moines), Tyre Court Guiding Lights – Junior Knights (Des Moines), G. G. Stokes Junior Knights (Davenport), and Estelle Young Court and Junior Knights (Waterloo).[49]

Other Knights of Pythias auxiliaries active in Iowa are S. B. Boyers Nurses Unit (Des Moines); Colors Unit, Police Unit, Screaming Eagles Uniform Rank (all in Davenport); Iowa Doves Uniform Rank and Iowa Hawks Uniform Rank (Waterloo); and the statewide Grand Court Nurses Unit. In addition,

Hawkeye Elks Walking Club, outside former Rest at 12th and Center streets, Des Moines (courtesy Mary Ruth Simmons)

chapters of the Dramatic Order of Omar are active in Des Moines (Razel Tent #1 and Hazfia Temple #2) and in Waterloo (Kareem Tent #1).[50]

The Elks

The Elks have had a very strong presence in Iowa's African-American communities over the years.[51] The national organization — the African-American Elks Grand Lodge, also known as the Improved Benevolent Protective Order of Elks of the World — was organized in 1899 in Cincinnati by Benjamin Franklin Howard and dedicated itself to

- Education, supporting educational achievement by granting scholarships
- Civil liberties, striving for full citizenship for all people
- Athletics, developing competition by team work in all sports
- Economics, advocating the study of earning and buying power in communities
- Health, encouraging alertness in individual and group healing programs
- Junior Elks, sponsoring activities for young people to eliminate delinquency
- The National Shrine, building a place for the aged members of the order to spend their golden years
- The Antler Guard, organizing marching clubs, drill teams, and drum and bugle corps.[52]

On December 7, 1908, the Elks' Hawkeye Lodge #160 was organized in Des Moines by some of the city's early black leaders. Charter members were Al Smith, Robert N. Hyde, J. Smith, W. L. Jones, C. W. Smith, L. J. Shelton, Branham Hyde, Jeff Logan, C. W. Williams, L. Miller, J. Simms, William Fletcher, and R. Smith. T. Gilles Nutter was the Grand Exalted Ruler at that time.[53]

Rose Temple #33, the auxiliary to the Des Moines Elks lodge, was organized in June 1921. Charter members were Sally Gater, Nina Hamilton, Mary McDowell, Lena Wilkinson, Nora Dixon, Mary Wilkinson, Melissa Hamilton, Henrietta Henderson, Samentha Smith, and Lillian Burrell. At the time of Rose Temple #33's organization, Mamie E. Hodges was serving as the Grand Daughter Ruler and George W. F. McMeahen as the Grand Exalted Ruler.[54]

The African-American Order of Elks has always taken pride in its support of youth and education. Annual Elks-sponsored oratorical contests have attracted young high school students of all races and from all walks of life to compete for scholarship money. In 1925 Arnastatia Scott of Des Moines won the regional and national championships. Later Ms. Scott graduated from Howard University in dental surgery and gave distinguished service for her country overseas.[55] The Elks are always proud to announce that the late Dr. Martin Luther King Jr. himself was an Elks oratorical contest winner.

In addition to its fraternal business, the Des Moines lodge has often spent time raising funds while providing a good time for the community as a whole. On September 3, 1937, Hawkeye Lodge #160 sponsored a dance at the Shrine Temple Ballroom featuring Earl (Fatha) Hines. Admission was 75 cents, plus 8 cents tax.[56]

By 1943, Hawkeye Lodge #160 had grown to include 103 members, with 91 members in the ladies auxiliary. Led by Exalted Ruler Norville E. Tillman, the lodge that year bought property at 783 12th Street in Des Moines, spending more than $13,000 to improve the property for lodge activities. The debt was liquidated within five years, and on Sunday, December 5, 1948, the lodge held a mortgage-burning ceremony at the Billikin Ballroom.[57] Present at the ceremony were Iowa Gov. Robert D. Blue, Des Moines Mayor Heck Ross, and Grand Exalted Ruler Dr. J. Finley Wilson, who was the featured speaker.[58] A life membership was presented at this event to Elk Brother A. J. Claybrook, who was honored as the mainstay of the lodge and a major factor in its upward progress and many successes.[59]

Several years earlier, in May 1940, the Daughter Elks had honored their new members at a colorful tea held at the Blue Triangle YWCA. Attired in exquisite floor-length gowns, the ladies were addressed by guest speaker Sue Brown, one of the great African-American leaders of Iowa in the twentieth century. In addition, a history of the organization was presented by Gertrude Hyde North, who was a charter member of the temple.[60]

In addition to the Daughter Elks, the Des Moines Lodge and Temple generated several other clubs and units within their order, some of which have received regional and national acclaim. For example, the Elks' Antlers Walking Club was a group of Elk brothers whose dapper attire rivaled the gentlemen on the pages of *GQ* magazine. Sharply attired in matching suits, ties, hats and walking sticks, the Elks' Antlers were show stoppers at parades and conventions. In their heyday, the group numbered between 25 and 30 members.[61]

Elk lodges also sponsored educational units, nursing units, charity units, and youth groups. The celebrated Rose Temple Drill Patrol of Des Moines was an example. This group became so accomplished — and unbeatable in competition — that units from other temples around the state and region refused to compete against it. The Past Grand Club was another elite group within the lodge and temple. Members were admitted into this club only by individually raising $1,000 for the Educational Department. Thus they earned the right to purchase and wear their beautifully jeweled collars.[62]

Helen Williams, P.G.D.R. and Past Daughter Ruler, Rose Temple #33 (courtesy Lynda Walker-Webster)

Elks' Club Popularity Contest, 1950s (left) and exterior of the Elks Club (below) at 12th and Center streets, Des Moines (courtesy Janice Burrell Cochran)

Many buildings owned by local fraternal organizations would eventually fall victim to urban renewal. The original Elks lodge was located in the heart of Des Moines's black metropolis, just a few steps off Center Street in the hub of black business and social life. Now the Elks "Rest" is located on East 14th at Walker Street. The purple and gold building, one of only a few local properties owned by a fraternal order, remains a popular village gathering spot. It is often referred to as "the Old Folks Home." Current Exalted Ruler Ron McClain, once a member of the Elks' Junior Herd, later served as a young adult assistant over the Drum and Bugle Corps. The lodge continues to host an annual golf tournament drawing participants from around the nation and a large Easter egg hunt for children. Mariruth Wheels is the current Daughter Ruler of Rose Temple.[63]

Elks Club Dance, Padmore Temple #729, Cedar Rapids, 1960s (courtesy Connie Hillsman)

Their Youth

Hazel Jewell #212, active from the 1940s through the mid-1960s, drew many young African-American women into its activities.[64] Jessie Mae Rogers of Rose Temple #33 was one of the last known Guardian Mothers of this group. In the years of its peak activity, all of the girls in the temple were members of the majorette section of the Elks' Junior Herd. The Junior Herd was a competitive majorette and drum and bugle corps whose energy was electrifying. Wherever they performed, they drew large crowds of onlookers. In parades, swarms of mostly young people would follow them on the sides for miles, as the majorettes hit every step to the rhythm of the beating drums. Even in their silent drills, they moved together strategically and the effect was breathtaking.

When they think of this pulsating group, local folks recall such dynamic leaders as Marian Solomon Irvin, Wanda Ashby McClain, and later Wanda's sister Gayle Ashby Watkins. Other outstanding leaders were Veronica White and Pam Singleton Williams, who now serves as one of the directors of the popular Isiserettes marching team. The late Col. Frieda M. Garland is given much credit for the early training of the Junior Herd, whose military-style precision coupled with the latest dance movements made the group a sensation in Iowa and beyond. In the 1950s and 1960s, the Herd won trophy after trophy at the Middlewestern State Association Convention's competitions. In some years, however, they faced threatening competition from the Waterloo drill team, not to mention strong competitors from Omaha and Minneapolis.[65]

Youth groups like the Junior Herd and Hazel Jewel #212 provided great socialization opportunities, for when the competitive drills were over and the awards presented, friendships had been established within the state and throughout the Midwest. At the Willkie House Community Center, the Junior Herd, like other local youth groups, held teen dances and fundraisers to support their travel to midwestern competitions.[66]

Other Elk Lodges and Temples in Iowa

Until the last 20 or 30 years, there was a rich camaraderie among Iowan Elks' lodges and temples. Most of the lodges were established around the turn of the century and involved prominent men and women who might be termed the founding generation of African-American society in Iowa. As in many organizations, after the initial generation passed away, the newer and younger members did not always possess the dedication and commitment of their predecessors.

As membership dwindled, lodges became inactive, especially during the late 1960s and 1970s. Waterloo's Scott Mardis Lodge #1581 and its sister temple, Melrose #277, were among the first in the state to fade out. In Fort Dodge, Highland Lodge #327 and sister temple Emma V. Kelley #726, which had been strongly influenced by the membership of Marshall and Frances Wells, became inactive not long after the demise of the Waterloo group. Fidelity Lodge #1058 and Padmore Temple #729 in Cedar Rapids would also soon fade. However, there were individual members who remained loyal to the order and continued to attend both Middlewestern States Association and Grand Lodge activities.[67]

In more recent years, Quad City Lodge #1485 and Imperial Temple #1105, which drew members from Davenport, Rock Island, Moline and East Moline, also became inactive. The Lodge folded first, and the Temple attempted to hold on. However, without a strong and active lodge, survival proved impossible. Currently the social and fraternal fellowships that remain intact within Iowa are the Des Moines order and the order in Sioux City. Savoy Lodge #373 and Eureka Temple #314 of Sioux City, while they struggle with their small membership, continue to run their own club as a business endeavor and a place of leisure for the community.[68]

The Middlewestern States Association and Grand Lodge Affiliations

The Middlewestern States Association is the governing body that covers the Elks lodges and temples in Iowa, Nebraska, Colorado, Oklahoma, Kansas, Minnesota, Wyoming, and Manitoba, Canada.[69] Normally the association convenes its annual convention in June, holding a smaller mid-winter meeting months prior to the convention. There have been many Iowans, both men and women, who have held prominent elected and appointed positions within the order.

Among the men who will long be remembered in Elkdom in Iowa and the Midwest are Norville Tillman (Past Exalted Ruler), John Williams (Past Exalted Ruler), A. J. Claybrook (Past Exalted Ruler), Ronald Carter (Past Exalted Ruler and former State Director of Education), Mr. G. Browne (State Deputy and Commissioner of Education), all of Des Moines. Also, Mr. George W. Turner (State Director of Education) of Cedar Rapids, Marshall Wells (Past Exalted Ruler) of Fort Dodge, and Albert Butler (Past Exalted Ruler and District Deputy) of Sioux City.

The late attorney Charles P. Howard of Des Moines served as the Grand Commissioner of Public Relations of the National Shrine as well as Assistant Legal Advisor for the Grand Lodge. J. G. Browne was the first Commissioner of Education for the State of Iowa.

(Left to right)

Elks Club Dance, Fidelity Lodge #1058, Cedar Rapids, 1960s (courtesy Connie Hillsman)

Elks Club Cedar Rapids Fidelity Lodge #1058, 1940s (Grout Museum)

Among the women, the late Mrs. Victoria Hendricks of Des Moines once served in the prestigious position as president of the Middle Western States Association Auxiliary. She would then be followed by a woman of great magnitude and organization, Mrs. Arretta M. Butler of Sioux City, who would serve as president of this body of women for more than 30 years. Mrs. Bernice Carter, formerly of Des Moines, would also serve in the position as first vice president of the auxiliary for a short period, as well as serving as a very dedicated local Directress of Education.

The late Mrs. Gertrude Hyde North of Des Moines served the state of Iowa for a number of years as the State Deputy. Mrs. Mary Ruth Simmons of Des Moines served for nearly a decade as Loyal Daughter Ruler of Rose Council of Iowa and as District Deputy for Des Moines and Sioux City, only recently relinquishing both positions. She was succeeded by Mrs. Gloria Lane as Loyal Daughter Ruler of Rose Council, and by Mrs. Roberta Robinson as District Deputy.

Arretta Butler (above), P.D.G.R. and former Middle Western States Auxiliary President(courtesy Lynda Walker-Webster); (below) Brotherhood and Sisterhood Drum and Bugle, Des Moines (courtesy Patricia Graves Miller)

Other Fraternal Orders

Research in the files of the *Iowa Bystander* and the *Des Moines Register* produced news items related to other fraternal and secret societies, but without reference to the time of their founding. One such item, from a 1922 article in the *Register*, reads as follows:

> *"The United Brothers of Friendship and the Sisters of the Mysterious Tent gathered in Des Moines on August 15, 1922. Approximately 1,000 African-American members of this order came to the city by train to attend a four-day national convention. Drill teams and bands were a great part of the festivities.*
>
> *"An opening joint meeting of the men and women was held with Des Moines Mayor Carl Garver and Iowa Governor Nathan E. Kendall giving the welcome and speaking to the convention delegates. One of the leaders for this event was C. G. Williams of Kansas City, Missouri, who had been appointed Superintendent of Education for the 'colored' people of that state.*
>
> *"The main events to be held by the society were to be held at the Shrine Auditorium. A memorial and some of the meetings were held at Maple Street Baptist Church, followed by a 50-voice choir presenting a musical at the auditorium, which was free to the public.*
>
> *"At the close of his talk, Mayor Garver turned the keys of the city over to the visitors and declared that he would extend every courtesy to them."*[70]

No other data on the United Brothers of Friendship and the Sisters of the Mysterious Tent has been located, but a 1931 NAACP pamphlet titled *A Few Facts about Iowa Negroes* lists the following fraternal organizations, which may have been affiliated with this or another of the aforementioned orders:

- King David's Temple #444 K. T.: H. J. Rodgers, C. M.
- Arctic Tabernacle #472, Knights and Daughters of Tabor: Mrs. Mattie B. Scott, H. P.
- King Solomon Commandery, K. T.: A. D. Green, E. C.
- Fraternal Temple Association, William Walker, President[71]

The Brotherhood and Sisterhood, Inc., functioned in Des Moines for several years in the 1950s and 1960s. The organization had a beautiful building on the corner of 13th and Center, which was not only used for their meetings but also rented out to organizations and individuals for dances, style shows, weddings, receptions, and many other social events. At one time the Brotherhood and Sisterhood sponsored a group of majorettes and a drum corps that were very popular within the community.[72]

Greek Letter Organizations: The Fraternities

Most, but not all, of the black Greek letter organizations were founded in the early twentieth century at what are now referred to as Historically Black Colleges and Universities (HBCU). The HBCU were educational institutions established by passionate and philanthropic northerners for the needs of newly freed slaves following the Civil War. These educational institutions not only served as an affordable source of higher education, but also instilled ethnic pride and self-esteem into a people whose ethnic identity had been all but demolished. The HBCU also came to serve as avenues for cultural development and social leadership among black people.

Thus while segregation was an institution within itself, out of it came the establishment of many positive organizations that facilitated camaraderie and scholastic achievement among black students. Black fraternities and sororities now exist on campuses in every part of the nation. Within them there has been a sense of belonging to something quite special. This feeling has carried over into the graduate chapters, where a sincere cohesiveness exists.

Sigma Pi Phi (The Boulé)

Sigma Pi Phi, one of the most prestigious non-collegiate, professional fraternities, was organized in 1912 in Philadelphia. The purpose of Sigma Pi Phi is to bind men of like qualities into a close, sacred, and fraternal union. The constitution of this fraternity states that "[it] is wise and good that men of ambition, refinement and self-respect should seek the society of each other, both for the mutual benefit and to be an example of the higher type of manhood."[73]

Sigma Pi Phi's Iowa chapter, Gamma Eta Boulé, was organized in Des Moines in 1984 at the exclusive Embassy Club in the Financial Center Building. Judge Luther T. Glanton, one of the local founders, served as the first Sire Archon. Charter

Sigma Pi Phi, Gamma Eta Boulé, Des Moines (courtesy Paul W. Danforth)

members initiated in 1984 were Timothy Barker, Udell Cason, Wesley Chapman, Moses S. Clinton, Paul W. Danforth, Francis T. Fair, Luther T. Glanton Jr., Frederick M. Graham, Zack Hamlett, Edward C. Harris, Robert N. Hyde, Oscar E. Jones, John F. Mapp Jr., S. Walter Riley, Meredith R. Saunders, Gilbert Spears, Fred Strickland Jr., Edward Tate, Walter E. Thompson, Robert Wright Sr., and Robert Wright Jr.[74]

Under the leadership of Sire Archon Paul W. Danforth, Gamma Eta Boulé celebrated its tenth anniversary in June 1994 at Hoyt Sherman Place with a social hour and dinner. Grand Sire Archon Dr. Huel D. Perkins presented the closing remarks at the ceremony.[75] Currently, the chapter has 30 members. Most are from within the Des Moines metropolitan area, with one from Fort Madison and one from out of state. The current Sire Archon is Francis Fair.[76]

Alpha Phi Alpha Fraternity

Of the college-organized fraternities, Alpha Phi Alpha was the first to be established nationally. Founded in 1906 on the campus of Cornell University, Alpha Phi Alpha was followed several years later by Kappa Alpha Psi, founded at Indiana

(Right) Alpha Phi Alpha fraternity dance, Des Moines, c.1970 (courtesy Paul W. Danforth)

(Below) Kappa Alpha Psi, Omega Chapter of Des Moines (courtesy Bertharina Cropp)

University in 1911, and Omega Psi Phi, founded at Howard University also in 1911.[77]

Alpha Phi Alpha's current national membership is estimated in excess of 50,000, with 467 active undergraduate chapters and 243 alumni chapters. The fraternity's Alpha Nu Chapter was founded at Drake University in 1922. From the outset, the Alpha Nu Chapter included Iowa State University students as well. Declared inactive in 1949, the chapter was later revived as an active campus fraternity in 1976.[78]

Alpha men take pride in their brotherhood and hold its values and rituals in the highest esteem, for which they have received great respect in the community. Many have gone on to distinguished careers. Lawrence W. Howard, 1948's "Alpha Man of the Year," noted that two of the chapter's members from Drake went on to become college presidents. Rufus B. Atwood headed Kentucky State University and F. D. Patterson headed Tuskegee Institute.[79] The local graduate chapter of Alpha Phi Alpha, Zeta Kappa Lambda, has an approximate membership of 25. Julian Collins is the current Basileus.[80]

Kappa Alpha Psi

Kappa Alpha Psi, currently with more than 74,000 members in 167 undergraduate chapters and 186 alumni chapters, was organized at Indiana University in 1911. The fraternity's Twenty-fourth Omega Chapter was established at Drake University in 1925.[81]

The Des Moines chapter of Kappa Alpha Psi is no doubt the largest active fraternity in Iowa. The chapter has formed an independent fundraising organization, the Kapsi Foundation. An annual fall picnic and a chartered bus trip to see a Minnesota Vikings or Kansas City Chiefs football game is hosted each November. In February the men hold a special sweetheart affair for Valentine's Day. The chapter has also sponsored cultural events, such as a Des Moines Civic Center concert featuring Billy Taylor and Ramsey Lewis several years ago.[82]

This level of activity has been typical of the chapter throughout its history. In a 1940 article about a Kappa social event following the Drake Relays, the *Iowa Bystander* commented that "[the] Omega chapter of Kappa Alpha Psi entertained their friends at the home of Dr. and Mrs. William Ritchey. The party was to honor the visiting Kappa men and their guests to Des Moines and to the Drake Relays. The guests were from Minnesota, Missouri,

1919 Kappa Alpha Psi, Gamma Chapter, University of Iowa (courtesy John Jackson)

Members of the Silhouette Club (the wives of Kappas), Des Moines (courtesy Bertharina Cropp)

Illinois, and Nebraska [and] also from Sioux City, Waterloo, Fort Madison, and Iowa City. Omega Chapter members and their wives who were present included Mr. and Mrs. Archie Alexander, Mr. and Mrs. C. Adams, Mr. and Mrs. Matthew Johnson, Atty. and Mrs. Lawrence Oliver, Dr. and Mrs. E. T. Scales and Dr. and Mrs. L. D. Furgerson and all pledges. Also present were some of the parents of Gamma Chapter at the University of Iowa."[83]

By 1950, perhaps the highest national Kappa position that had been reached by an Iowan was that of Grand Polemarc, held by Archie A. Alexander. Mr. Alexander, who had been a successful football player at the University of Iowa, earned the nickname "Alexander The Great."[84] Curtis Jenkins is the current Polemarc.

Omega Psi Phi

Omega Psi Phi was founded on the campus of Howard University in 1911, but the Iowa chapter of this fraternity was not established until many years later. The cardinal principles of the fraternity are uplift, perseverance, scholarship, and manhood. In the summer of 1947, a group of Omega Psi Phi men — often referred to as the "Q's" — entertained Howard University president Dr. Mordecai Johnson at the Grace Ransom Tea Room in Des Moines. Dr. Johnson was in Des Moines to speak to the 8,000 people attending the International Sunday School Convention.[85] The local Omega men in attendance included Aurelius Whaley,

Delta Sigma Theta, Founders' Day, 2000, Phi Chapter and Delta Patroness Club (courtesy Venita Wells)

Luther T. Glanton, Dr. James M. Powell, Marsh Houston, Dr. Stanley Griffin, S. Joe Brown, and Rev. G. W. Robinson. They were on hand not only to welcome Dr. Johnson to Iowa, but also to establish plans for organizing a chapter of the fraternity in Iowa. A month later, in August 1947, the Mu Omicron Chapter of Omega Psi Phi was organized in Des Moines by William Pinkett, the district representative of the fraternity.[86]

Temporary officers of the newly established chapter were Luther T. Glanton, Basileus; Marsh Houston, Keeper of Records and Seals; Dr. J. Murphy Powell, Keeper of Finance; Dr. Stanley Griffith, Neophyte Commander; and Lee G. Thompson, Keeper of Peace. Permanent officers were to be elected on September 7, 1947. Others initiated into the fraternity following the organizational ceremony were Rev. Jesse Hawkins, William L. Ware, Dr.

Eustace Ware, Arthur Bryant, Dr. Leon Jones, and Robert Parkey.[87]

At the time the Iowa chapter was established, there were 135 chapters of Omegas throughout the country.[88] The fraternity now has a membership of more than 42,000, with 433 active chapters and 232 alumni chapters.[89]

While many Omega alumni men reside in Iowa, most are not active members. The local alumni chapter has at this time approximately 12 active members. Ron Mels is the current Basileus. The only current active undergraduate chapter of the fraternity is at Iowa State University.

The fraternity continues to play an active role in the community and in national fraternity affairs. During election years, the fraternity holds massive voter registration campaigns. At Christmas time it takes part in the "Toys for Tots" collection drive.

In 1998, the chapter held a youth recognition dinner at the Des Moines Botanical Center for approximately 50 elementary and middle-school youth. The local Mu Omicron Chapter entertained the regional conclave of the Omegas in 1996 at the Hotel Marriott in Des Moines.[90]

Greek Letter Organizations: The Sororities

Most African-American sororities were established in the first two decades of the twentieth century. Alpha Kappa Alpha, the oldest, was founded in 1908, followed by Delta Sigma Theta in 1913 and Zeta Phi Beta in 1920, all on the campus of Howard University in Washington, D.C. Sigma Gamma Rho was founded in 1922 at Butler University in Indianapolis.[91]

Delta Sigma Theta

The first sorority to found a chapter in Iowa was Delta Sigma Theta. The Phi graduate chapter was established in Des Moines in 1923, with Adah Hyde Johnson, Lillian Jacobs, Mary E. Wood, Enola V. Thompson, Viola Jones, Ethel Bowman, and Lillian Edmunds as charter members. Gertrude E. Rush was chosen by the Grand Chapter to be a national honorary member and was thus included as a part of the founding group. In 1919 at the University of Iowa, Adah Hyde Johnson had been initiated into the sorority's Delta Chapter, which was considered the first Negro sorority west of the Mississippi River. Edna Johnson Morris — who had been attending Wilberforce University in Ohio and was serving as the Grand Recording Secretary — helped set up Phi Chapter in Des Moines through the services of Adah Hyde Johnson.[92]

Because all Delta chapters at the time were to be designated as undergraduate or alumni groups, Phi Chapter was called a "mixed group." Its membership included graduate and undergraduate women. And because the University of Iowa's Delta chapter had become inactive over the years, for a long time Phi Chapter was the only chapter to accept students into the sisterhood, until the Iowa City chapter was revived in the 1970s. The Phi Chapter's alumni women were very particular about character and exercised a strong influence in this regard.[93]

The Deltas were well-known for their annual Jabberwock programs that raised money for scholarships. First held in Boston in 1925, a Jabberwock was a talent show that drew participants from throughout the community. The *Iowa Bystander* reported on April 11, 1940, that:

"Phi Chapter of Delta Sigma Theta is going to be holding their sixth annual program at the Jewish Community Center on April 18. There were eight pledge clubs to entertain with humorous and 'fantastical' skits. The 'Jabberwock' was said to be an imaginary creature because of the different parts of other animals that are needed to make him sufficiently fascinating. With those facts in mind, the Deltas originated the idea of having a stunt night composed of various stunts and skits presented by many different organizations. Thus, it became an annual event by Delta's everywhere."

The sorority used this program as a fundraiser for many years.[94]

For more than 20 years the Deltas have used the proceeds from the Ebony Fashion Fair to award scholarships. In 1998, Phi Chapter awarded seven scholarships to local graduating seniors: Eboneice Cason and Justin Griffis (Hoover High School); Shawntae Smith and Jerri White (Roosevelt High School); and Tiffany Berger, Cynthia Clark, and Philip Hales (North High School).[95]

Other projects that Phi Chapter has participated in have been "Story Hour" at Willkie House, which was usually followed by a craft project period. The Deltas also initiated an African-American library, with the chapter donating books, at Willkie House. At one time they also assisted young children by helping to finance their dancing, music, or some other developmental activity. In the 1960s the local chapter received the Delta's National Award for its reading project. In the late 1970s and early 1980s the sorority held five scholarship and financial aid workshops, which were held at the YWCA of Greater Des Moines.[96]

Founders' Day is always felt to be a very special occasion when sorority members active and inactive gather together in sisterhood. Often a national Delta officer or a recognized individual will serve as the speaker for the occasion, which usually involves a luncheon and discussion groups. "Patterns of Sisterhood" has served as a theme involving the Delta principles. "Delta Days" is a national special occasion that is celebrated at the nation's capitol. The local chapter celebrated the event in Des Moines with activities at the state capitol.[97]

The Des Moines Deltas have also partnered with Tiny Tot Family Outreach Center. Not only have they donated mittens and given Christmas baskets, but money from 1992 pledges paid for renovation of a room in the building, turning it into a children's library, complete with books. A more recent local activity has been

The Deltas initiated an African-American library at Willkie House. . . . they also assisted young children by helping to finance their dancing, music, or some other developmental activity.

Alpha Kappa Alpha, Iota Zeta Omega Chapter, Des Moines, 1998 (courtesy Laverne Jones)

(Right) AKA Debutante Scholarship Cotillion, Iota Zeta Omega Chapter, Des Moines, 1998 (courtesy Lynda Walker-Webster)

Habitat for Humanity, the house-construction program initiated by former Pres. Jimmy Carter. Habitat for Humanity is a nationwide Delta project.[98]

According to Renee Hardman, past Basileus of Phi Chapter of Delta Sigma Theta Sorority, the Phi Chapter is the largest of the women's sororities in the state. Their membership, both active and inactive members, is nearly 100. Two are life members. There has been an active Delta auxiliary support group known as the Delta Patroness Club.[99] Nationally, the Deltas have a membership of 195,000. Undergraduate chapters are active on the campuses of Drake University and the University of Iowa. Graduate chapters are located in Ames, Iowa City, Waterloo, Davenport, and Des Moines.[100] Des Moines hosted the Regional Conclave in 1999. The current Basileus is Valerie Griffis.

Alpha Kappa Alpha

Alpha Kappa Alpha is the oldest Greek-letter organization for African-American women in the United States. Established by Ethel Hedgeman-Lyle at Washington's Howard University in 1908, the sorority was conceived as an instrument for enriching the social and intellectual aspects of college life.[101] Over the years, the sorority has become more of a service organization, encouraging high scholastics and ethical standards, promoting

unity and friendship among college women, maintaining a progressive interest in college life, and serving mankind. The sorority became incorporated in 1913, branching out and becoming a channel through which selected college-trained women worked to improve the social and economic conditions in their city, state, and nation.[102]

Twenty-four years following the founding of the national sorority, a chapter was formed in Des Moines.

On Friday, November 12, 1932, Miss Theresa Barker, Midwestern Regional Director of Alpha Kappa Alpha Sorority, and Miss Antoinette Westmoreland of Kansas City, Missouri, drove to Des Moines to organize Beta Gamma Chapter, the first chapter in the state of Iowa of Alpha Kappa Alpha. The young women who were to become the charter members of the chapter were: Mrs. Azalia Mitchell, Misses Lucille Baker, Anna Mae Manuel, Ruth Marie Brown, Gwendolyn Wilson (Fowler), Wilda Mullins, Marie Johnson, Willie Lee Campbell, and Kathryn Glass. On the following afternoon, a sightseeing tour was taken [and] a dinner arranged by the candidates preceded the initiation on Saturday evening. On Sunday morning, Mrs. A. P. Trotter was hostess at a squab breakfast. A tea was given by the chapter on Sunday afternoon at the home of Mrs. J. B. Morris Sr.[103]

Beta Gamma Chapter

A few months later, on February 23, 1933, Beta Gamma sponsored a "big time" floor show, featured as the "Ballyhoo Dance," held at the Billikin Ballroom. Entertainment was provided by Jerry Hayes and his Joy Generators and by Cab Black, Vincent Wilson, Dorothy Tolson, Peanuts Lee, and Marie Knowling and Her Rhumba Dancers.[104]

In 1942, the Beta Gamma sorors entertained world-renowned singer Marian Anderson at the home of Dr. and Mrs. William Ritchey following her Thanksgiving night concert at the Shrine Auditorium.[105] Guests of the evening were visiting AKAs, members of the Ivy Leaf pledge club, and members of the AKA Patroness Club and their escorts. The Beta Gamma sorors present that evening were Margaret M. Patten, Basileus; Madames Gwendolyn Fowler, Alice McCraney, Maxine Banning, Marie Roberts, Maurice Evans, Marian Bartlett, and Geneva Morrow. Other guests included Miss Anderson's accompanist, Mr. Frank Rupp, and her traveling manager, J. Jofe.

Like the Des Moines Deltas, Beta Gamma had been a "mixed" chapter, with both graduate and undergraduate women. Eventually the graduate chapter became known as Iota Zeta Omega and the undergraduate chapter as Eta Tau, with pledges from Drake University and Iowa State University in Ames. Epsilon Theta is the undergraduate chapter at the University of Iowa.[106] The Iota Zeta Omega Chapter of Alpha Kappa Alpha has a current membership of 22 active sorors and about 50 inactive sorors in the area. All sorors come together in February, attired in elegant black, to commemorate their annual Founders' Day. They gather in ceremony and rededicate themselves to sisterhood in fellowship and in unity.[107] Nationally, the AKAs have approximately 140,000 members with 179 active undergraduate chapters and 243 alumni chapters.

Each year the community looks forward to the sorority's spring Debutante Scholarship Cotillion, held at the Polk County Convention Center complex. For the 1998 Cotillion, the sorority presented 11 area high school girls, who made their bow to society. Elegantly attired in beautiful white flowing gowns, they waltzed first with their fathers or a male family member and then with their selected escort for the evening, dancing to the choreography of Sorors Alice Boyd and Charlotte Duncan-Wagner. Each debutante was presented with a beautiful necklace and a book scholarship. Special awards and scholarships were presented to:

- Eboneice Cason (Hoover High School),
  Essay Award Winner and Billie Jean Morrow Scholarship
- Angela Steward (Hoover), Wilda B. Hester Scholarship
- Amandalynn Webster (Roosevelt), Miss Incentive Award
  (raising the most money for scholarships)
- LaTonya Allen (North), Miss Congeniality Award
  (most all-around and helpful deb)

Other 1998 debutantes were Maya Coleman, Tianna Morrow, and Ayana Hobson (Roosevelt); Stephanie Hill and Neysa Greer (Hoover); Jamie Ziegler (Urbandale); and Rawshanda Gardner (East).[108]

Recently, the sorority has become very concerned with improving mathematical and science literacy. On a national level, the sorority is attempting to build a senior residency in Winston-Salem, North Carolina, to increase a presence in the nation's capital for lobbying purposes, to uplift the black family and to build and strengthen a partnership with Red Cross. (Iota Zeta Omega had a table at a recent Juneteenth celebration.)[109] Local sorors who serve in a national capacity are LaVerne Jones (Building and Properties Committee); Betty Gause (Educational Advancement Foundation); and Dr. Mary S. Chapman (Members Standards Committee).[110] Iota Zeta Omega has conducted workshops with the Omaha chapter of AKAs and each autumn holds cluster workshops to review the national programs and initiatives. The regional director is Alberta Jones of Tulsa, Oklahoma.

University of Iowa students, c.1920
(courtesy John Jackson)

Zeta Phi Beta, Nu Mu Zeta chapter, Des Moines (courtesy Frances Hawthorne)

are undergraduate chapters at Iowa State University and the University of Iowa. Drake's undergraduate chapter became inactive within the past five years when the last two active pledges graduated.

For years as a fundraiser and high-profile cultural event the local chapter held a massive African-American musical and dramatic production, "Rhomania," at Hoyt Sherman Place. This event was replaced ten years ago by the "Black College Fair," which has attracted nearly 200 students annually. Local HBCU graduates play a major role in this event, encouraging and informing students about the colleges they themselves attended. Peggy Whitaker — a library media specialist with the Des Moines Public Schools and one of the charter members of the local Sigma Gamma Rho chapter — sees education as the main focus of the sorority. The goal is to teach more African-American youth about the importance of getting into the college track. The key to achieving that goal, Whitaker feels, is to reach young people.[113]

Zeta Phi Beta

Zeta Phi Beta, founded at Howard University in 1920, now has a national membership of 100,000. It is the first sorority to have a chapter in Africa, established in 1948.[114] Activities at the sorority's 1994 conclave in Orlando suggested Zeta Phi Beta's range of interests: leadership development, service programs, and youth development opportunities. The group also took a pilgrimage to Eatonville, Florida, to honor the late novelist Zora Neale Hurston.[115]

Zeta Phi Beta was the last sorority to organize a chapter in Iowa: Nu Mu Zeta Chapter was formed in Des Moines in 1985. Charter members were Frances Hawthorne, Mary Ann Spicer, Gloria Jackson, Veola Perry, Grayphenia Bayles, and Heidi Lue. The chapter currently has an active membership of 15. Soror Joyce Bruce, dean of students at Meredith Middle School, is the current Basileus.[116] Nu Mu Zeta Chapter has two life members: Joyce Bruce and Frances Hawthorne. Soror Bruce is also the State Director of the Zetas in Iowa.[117]

In past years the sorority sponsored an academic competitive event entitled "Zeta Blue Review," which involved youth from fourth through sixth grade. The sorority now hosts the "Zeta Blues Festival," which features local jazz and blues musicians who donate their time and talent to raise money for Zeta's scholarship fund.

Frances Cuie, a senior member of the local chapter, has 48 years of dedicated membership with the sorority.[111] "Beyond the Ivy," an acknowledgment of sorors who have passed away in the not too distant past, now numbers five: Wilda B. Hester, Billie Jean Morrow, Marian Morrison, Gwendolyn Wilson Fowler (a charter member who passed away in 1997 at the age of 92 and was known as the mother of the local Alpha Kappa Alpha sorority), and most recently Leahgreta Spears, a driving force behind the local chapter. LaVerne Jones is the immediate past Basileus, and Deborah Gordon is the new Basileus of the sorority.[112]

Sigma Gamma Rho

Sigma Gamma Rho sorority, the third African-American sorority established in Iowa, was founded in 1922 at Butler University in Indianapolis. Currently Sigma Gamma Rho has 72,000 members nationwide. The Iowa chapter — Epsilon Theta Sigma — was organized in Des Moines by six women: Peggy Whitaker, Diane Walls, Carrie Thomas, Billie Jean Stone, Linda Nwoke, and Diana Scott. The first three women pledged as undergraduates, and the others joined the graduate chapter. Currently Sigma Gamma Rho has 12 Iowa members. There

One participant in this annual event was the late popular singer and pianist, Irene Myles Terry. In 1996 the sorority named their scholarship in her memory.

Zeta's graduate chapter contributes to many other local non-profit causes, including "Adopt-A-Family," Willkie House Community Center, and the Tiny Tot Day Care and Outreach Center's library. At Martin Luther King Elementary School, where soror Marlene Doby is principal, the Zeta sisterhood has supported the "parent university" and given scholarships for music lessons. In addition, the local Zeta chapter has sponsored the Martin Luther King Reading and Library Group, donating money for books.[118] The sorority also sponsors a group of auxiliary women known as Amicae.

Iota Phi Lambda

In addition to the sororities already described, Iowa has also been home to a businesswomen's sorority, the Alpha Delta Chapter of Iota Phi Lambda. Information about the founding dates of the national and local organizations could not be located, and it is uncertain if a national group exists today. But evidence of local activity in past decades appears in the files of the *Bystander*. For example, in August 1937 a garden party was held at the home of Mrs. Hattie McGruder at 1628 Carpenter Street in Des Moines to raise money for the sorority's scholarship fund. A dance platform was erected and music was provided by a string orchestra. Bingo and cards provided other diversions. Officers of the sorority at the time of the garden party were Susie L. Hart, president; Clara Johnson, vice president, Evelyn Brooks, recording secretary; Beatrice Robinson, financial secretary; Lena Wilson, treasurer; and Dorothy Wheels, journalist.[119]

Ten years later, in 1947, the *Bystander* covered another of the sorority's scholarship fundraisers, this one a style and floor show held at the former Sepia Club on Center Street. Taking its theme from the music of Gershwin, the show featured Alberta Bates singing "Summertime" and Speck Redd, known as the "Wizard of the Piano," playing other selections from "Porgy and Bess." Also featured was the singing of the Martin Sisters and the dancing of the Saunders Sisters. Other performers included Esther Saunders, Irene Myles, the Gray Brothers' Orchestra, and Eddie Eugene, who brought down the house according to those present. The style show focused on business attire for the working woman. Modeling in the style show were Inez McQuerry (Morrow), Shirley

Herndon, Velma Jones, Evelyn Brooks, Maxine Watkins, Alberta Bates, Barbara Barker, and Helen Warn.[120] In her remarks, mistress of ceremony Annabelle Payne stressed the ambition of every businesswoman and noted that one of their sorors, Fannie Mae McGregory, had received a $50 scholarship from Drake University, where she was a junior majoring in accounting.[121]

The Sororities: A Summary

A recent article in *Ebony* magazine regarding the boom among black sororities noted a popular perception that sorority women were primarily concerned with fashions and social events.[122] The foregoing review of Iowa's four African-American sororities reveals the gross inaccuracy of these perceptions. In their genuine commitment to philanthropic missions, exercised through the strong bonds of sisterhood, sorority members have for many decades demonstrated that they have the condition and progress of black America at heart. In their unity of purpose, they also possess enormous economic and political power. In Iowa, and throughout the United States, African-American sororities reach out into their communities to deal with such issues as teen pregnancy, drug abuse, health care, the elderly, economic development, and preparing a new generation of young people to be competitive academically, psychologically, and technologically for the next century.[123]

The Omega: A Conclusion

Criteria for invitation and selection of individuals into the membership of specific fraternities and sororities has varied from chapter to chapter and campus to campus across the nation. Each has its own explanation as to what type of personal profile it is looking for. The criteria may be less explicit today than it was back in the formative years. Thus many young viewers have laughed along with Spike Lee's movie "School Days," which spoofs the competition among Greek organizations on campus. But rigorous selection criteria persist in some African-American social organizations to the same degree it has for generations.

The Private Social Clubs: An Introit

Men's and women's private social clubs have had their own criteria for membership. Their by-laws and charters often defined their choices of who to accept into their fold and who to exclude. Membership into some clubs had been by invitation only. Others

In their unity of purpose, [black sororities] also possess enormous economic and political power. In Iowa, and throughout the United States, African–American sororities reach out into their communities.

were "just tell someone that you were interested in joining." There have been some where entrance into the club was often bought by favor, finance, or some other deed for someone who was already a member.

African-Americans have not differed from other groups in ranking people socially according to occupations, economic status, church or religious affiliation, the car they drive or house they live in, and perhaps a few other measures. According to anthropologist Ashley Montague, usually individuals move from one social stratum to another only by means of the economic process. By acquiring economic power, one rises in the social hierarchy; by the loss of economic power, one falls.[124] In *Wouldn't Take Nothing for My Journey Now*, Maya Angelou says that "any person who has charm and some confidence can move in and through societies ranging from the most privileged to the most needy. Style allows the person to appear neither inferior in one location nor superior in the other."[125]

With African-Americans, however, there is another factor. And while this is not really a secret, it remains a delicate subject — the issue of skin color. Many would like to keep the subject suppressed, but it will somehow manage to come up in one area or another in various aspects of black society. African-American skin color ranges from the palest of ivory to the darkest of ebony. Where one fell on the color chart weighed heavy at one time. Since the black pride explosion in the late 1960s, however, the issue has not

had such a profound effect on our views of one another. Yet in the past, sometimes we allowed our secrets to become our enemies. E'nuff said!

The Private Men's Clubs

Iowa's African-American community gave rise to several private men's clubs; four of the largest were the Dark Horses of Cedar Rapids, and in Des Moines the Roosevelt Club, the Monarch Club, and the Royal Dukes.

The Roosevelt Club

The Roosevelt Club is perhaps the oldest African-American men's social club still in existence in Iowa. Organized in Des Moines more than 75 years ago, the Roosevelt Club is one of the most respected social organizations in central Iowa. The club was organized by business and professional men, and these origins have been reflected in the character of the membership throughout most of the club's history. Some of the charter members were Gad B. Tucker, J. B. Morris Sr., Bonnie Herndon, A. P. Trotter, and James Mitchell. Over the years, the makeup of the club has changed somewhat, but obtaining membership in this organization has never been an easy task.[126]

Like many of the prominent social clubs nationwide, the Roosevelt Club took pride in their annual formal dances with live music. Each member was allowed to invite a certain number of guests to the dance, which was normally held at one of the local hotels. The men were attired in fine tuxedos and the women in elegant ball gowns. (Attire among many men's groups has now been scaled down to suits of a semiformal nature.) The Roosevelt Club was also popular for its wild game dinners and its summer picnics. Today the club hosts a family night with good food, games, and fellowship. Virgil Miller is currently president of the club, whose membership averages between 25 and 30 men.[127]

The Monarch Club

The Monarch, the next private men's club to be established in the Des Moines area, was organized in 1923 in the kitchen of Charles Winn. The club had about 15 charter members, including Clarence Adams, C. Hendricks, Morris DeSleet, Ezra Ewing, T. L. Howard, Rozenting Hardaway, and Adam Johnson.[128] These were very respectable men, well-known in the black community.

"Any person who has charm and some confidence can move in and through societies ranging from the most privileged to the most needy. Style allows the person to appear neither inferior in one location nor superior in the other."

— **Maya Angelou**

Roosevelt Picnic

Like some of the men who joined the Royal Dukes Men's Club, the men who formed the Monarch Club had initially been denied membership into the popular Roosevelt Club. Thus they formed their own clubs.[129] At the organizational meeting, the Monarch men expressed their mission, motives, and interests. They established their by-laws and operating principles, and they set a limit on a membership of 50 men.[130]

The Monarch Club is famous for its beautiful holiday formal ball, featuring live music, which is still held on the Saturday following Christmas Day. This affair has always been the center of the holiday entertainment in Des Moines. With out-of-town guests and family members coming to the city to visit, the ball became a reunion of sorts. Some Monarch Club members would host pre-dance cocktail hours at their homes, while others might prepare elaborate or soulful hors d'oeuvres for their private tables at the dance. Over the years, the gala ball had been held at such places as the Billikin Ballroom, Club 100, the Val Air Ballroom, and the Jewish Center on Polk Boulevard. The 1998 ball was held at the Airport Holiday Inn.[131] Over the years, the Monarchs have also held an annual Fourth of July picnic at various parks around the city. The presidency of the Monarch Club is currently held by William Brewton.[132] Monarch Club membership is now under 50 members, and the auxiliary L.T. Club (for "Lion Tamers"), organized many years ago by wives of club members, has become inactive.

The Royal Dukes

The Royal Dukes, Inc., social club was another of the early pioneering private men's groups organized in the Des Moines area. Several of the club's founders had been members of an earlier men's social club called the Dashing Eagles. When that organization disbanded, some of its members sought to join another organization of that era, referred to as the mature and "classy" Beaux Esprit Club.[133] They were denied membership. In protest, a few of these men decided to establish their own club for social and civic purposes.

On a Sunday afternoon in October 1927, nine young "men about town" gathered at the home of Don Parker for the purpose of organizing the new club. Those charter members were William Brown, Chuck Dixon, Lafayette (Gink) Fowler, Howard Hart, Marion Mann, Hunter Matthews, Don Parker, Bert Parker, and Wesley Reed. Chuck Dixon was elected first president. The club name was selected and the blue-and-white club colors chosen. Like many other black private social clubs, the Royal Dukes held their meetings in one another's homes, because other meeting places were not available to them.[134]

The Royal Dukes Club, which was officially incorporated in 1977, has always included prominent and well-respected men from the local African-American community. It has been in continuous operation since its formation. Gink Fowler was the last surviving charter member, and James Bethel now holds senior

(Far left to right)

Roosevelt Club picnic, Des Moines (courtesy Nathaline Dixon)

Monarch Social Club, Des Moines (courtesy Edward Reeves)

Royal Dukes Social Club, Des Moines (courtesy Gordon Wolder)

Knoxville Men's Gun Club, c.1900
(SHSI Iowa City)

Olympian Club, that thrived for many years. Sponsor of various athletic events, the Olympians hosted an annual summer swim meet at Good Park. Linda (Frazier) Carter, whose father, Jesse Frazier, was a member of the club, fondly remembers helping her father run the refreshment stand during competitions. The stand, a two-by-four shed, sold candy, gum, pop, and popsicles. Linda Carter also remembers several of her father's fellow club members, including Ozzie and Harold Morrow, Willie Wells, John Estes Sr., Frank Robinson, Everett Mays, Brad Morris, and William Clinton.[139]

In Cedar Rapids, a private men's social club called the Dark Horses flourished for some time. Mention of the organization's name in Cedar Rapids provokes warm memories. Eyes light up — especially when people recall the club's annual formal dance. Though the dates of organization and dissolution are elusive, a photo of the members and their guests has survived. The Dark Horses are likely to have been comparable in structure and activity to the men's clubs in Des Moines.[140]

The Women's Clubs with a National Connection
Iowa Association of Colored Women

A club women's presence in early Iowa that thrived was the Association of Colored Women. There were many women's organizations at local levels that existed among black women in the latter portion of the nineteenth century. Mostly in the 1890s there were many outstanding women who were moving to the front on behalf of black women.

On July 21, 1896, the National Federation of Afro-American Women and the National League of Colored Women united in Washington, D.C., and organized the National Association of Colored Women (NACW). Mary Church Terrell was the first elected president and served in that position from 1896 until 1901. Great and notable women taking part in this organization were Ida B. Wells Barnett, Mrs. Booker T. (Margaret) Washington, Hallie Q. Brown, Josephine St. Pierre Rufin, Mary McLeod Bethune, Daisy Lampkin, Mrs. Lawrence C. Jones, and Dr. Mary B. Talbert.[141]

Hundreds of local clubs formed across the nation in the wake of the Washington meeting, including many in Iowa. While many African-American women's clubs had formed in Iowa prior to the NACW, none had the intense mission of black womanhood at heart as much as this organization. The Iowa State Federation of Colored Women's Clubs was organized in Ottumwa in June 1902

status with 49 years of membership in the Royal Dukes. In 1957, Mr. Bethel created the Royal Dukes crest and established a 25-year service award. The plaques given to members until 1957 were crafted by the late Des Moines artist and teacher Leroy Mitchell.[135]

The club held its fiftieth anniversary celebration at the Adventureland Palace Theater in Altoona, Iowa, on October 22, 1977. The formal dancing party was entertained by the Fabulous Kings and Traditions En Cameo. At that celebration, 25-year service awards were presented to James Bethel, Robert (Bob) Calderon, and Lawrence Graves. Mr. Calderon was club president at the time.[136]

For many years the club held an annual formal affair; however, now they host their invitational formal approximately every five years. Each Valentine's Day they plan a special occasion to entertain their wives.[137] A somber yet impressive sight is to view the group — en masse in their crest blazers — at the funeral of one of their members.

Other Men's Clubs

While it is certain other private men's clubs existed in Iowa, research has produced only spotty information about their membership or activities. References to meetings or an occasional event appear in the pages of the *Iowa Bystander*. For example, on August 26, 1937, the El Producto Men's Club held a large dance at the Shrine Auditorium Ballroom in Des Moines, where they were entertained by Nat Towles and his Gallant Fourteen Southern Gentlemen.[138] Also in Des Moines was a men's athletic club, the with Helena Downey as the first president. This group would unite with the National Association in 1910 and would become incorporated in 1913. In keeping with the National Association, in 1938 the Iowa Federation of Colored Women officially changed its name to the Iowa Association of Colored Women (IACW).[142]

In 1952, the Des Moines Federation hosted the IACW's annual convention at St. Paul AME Church, then located at 12th and Crocker. State president Maude Spencer of Mason City presided at this convention, which marked the group's fiftieth anniversary. NACW president Ella Stewart was among the many convention speakers.[143]

During those first 50 years, the IACW had overcome many problems in working for the advancement for women and girls in Iowa. One of the IACW's major projects was the purchase in 1919 of a house in Iowa City for young black women attending the University of Iowa.[144] The effects of institutional racism made

Iowa Association of Colored Women's Clubs, Sioux City conference, May 27, 1928 (SHSI Des Moines)

Iowa Association of Colored Women's Clubs, Davenport, May 1903 (SHSI Des Moines)

Iowa Association of Colored Women's Clubs, 45th annual convention, Sioux City, June 1948 (SHSI Des Moines)

The house at 942 Iowa Avenue, Iowa City, purchased by IACW for University of Iowa coeds who were barred from the dormitories (Iowa Women's Archives, University of Iowa)

the home was sold in 1950 and the income converted into war bonds. Over the years more than 1,000 women who had been refused campus housing had lived in this home while they obtained their education at the University of Iowa. Five years after the sale of the home, the IACW donated $5,000 to Simpson College for the George Washington Carver Science Hall. An engraved bronze plate with the association's name is located inside the building.[147]

The IACW met annually around the state in cities and towns where there were clubs. In the years 1902–1952, the clubs held their annual conventions in Buxton (1908); Burlington (1922); Cedar Rapids (1904, 1911, 1915, 1921, 1946); Council Bluffs (1926, 1933, 1937, 1945, 1951); Davenport (1903, 1913, 1920); Des Moines (1906, 1910, 1914, 1916, 1918, 1923, 1932, 1938, 1943, 1944, 1947, 1952); Iowa City (1924, 1930, 1934); Keokuk (1907, 1927); Marshalltown (1919, 1941, 1950); Mason City (1929, 1939, 1942); Muscatine (1905); Ottumwa (1902, 1909, 1917); Sioux City (1912, 1927, 1931, 1936, 1940,1948); and Waterloo (1928, 1935, 1949).[148]

The association held its sixty-fifth annual convention in 1967 at the Savery Hotel in Des Moines. National vice president Juanita Brown welcomed the delegates to the convention, whose theme was "The Club Women's Responsibility in the Great Society." It is noteworthy that the delegates at this convention — as earlier, at the 1952 convention — were also addressed by prominent leaders of the Des Moines Women's Club.[149] In 1967, the IACW reported 185 members belonging to at least 15 clubs. Emma Turner of Cedar Rapids was the newly elected president; Etta Grider of Sioux City, first vice president; Jeanne Morris of Des Moines, second vice-president; Pauline Humphrey of Des Moines, treasurer; and Erma Carr of Des Moines, secretary.[150] At the time of the 1967 convention, 12 of the association's 35 presidents were still living.

Without question the IACW and the clubs it represented promoted the leadership of many African-American women in Iowa. Because so many women rose to the occasion, it may be unfair to mention names for fear of omitting some important individuals. However, it would be a greater injustice not to highlight a few of those key individuals recorded in the histories of the association and of the local black women's clubs in Iowa.

Cedar Rapids: Emma Turner

Council Bluffs: Inez Willis Ware

Des Moines: Sarah Jett, Audra Alexander, Jessie Walker, Lillian Edmunds, Pauline Humphrey, Helen Wimberly,

this project necessary, for black women were not allowed in university housing. Earlier in the university's history, when there were only a few black women on campus, the students were often able to find housing in private homes or as working domestics. However, when their numbers kept growing, the need for housing became paramount. One of the driving forces behind this project was Sue Brown, and she made certain it became a reality. Mrs. Brown chaired the home's board of trustees for a number of years. In 1938, the IACW added a scholarship and loan fund to its programs in Iowa City. Loans were available to students, and scholarships ranging from $25 to $50 were granted to worthy students.[145]

On May 23, 1940, the *Iowa Bystander* reported that the black club women and girls of Des Moines had endured a steady downpour to participate in a citywide Tag Day to raise money for the IACW home in Iowa City. A total of $409.68 was raised by the group, which included Sue Brown, Sophie Nichols, Audra Alexander, Sara Jett, J. W. Tutt, Mabel Mason, Rose Lovelady, Jessie Bell Davis, Meredith Carl, Mrs. Cecil Taylor, and Gertrude North. Local clubs participating included the Women's Christian Temperance Union, Modernistic Senior, Modernistic Junior, MYVJ, Mary Church Terrell, and 20th Century. The Scholarship Committee also took part in the fundraising effort.[146]

University housing became available to black women students in the years after World War 2. Having served its purpose,

Roberta Frazier, Gertrude North, Jeanne Morris, Lora Warden, Sophie Nichols, Sue Brown, Fannie Danforth, Goletha Trotter
Indianola: Martha White
Marshalltown: Addie Howard, Rose Johnson
Mason City: Maude Spencer
Sioux City: Elzona Trosper, Buelah Webb, Daisy Smith, Luberta Bentley
Waterloo: Vaeletta Fields[151]

The Iowa club woman who will best be remembered is Sue Brown. Mrs. Brown, the wife of prominent Des Moines attorney S. Joe Brown, was a dynamic club, civic, cultural and church woman. She was active at the local, state, and national levels. Positions Mrs. Brown held in connection with the association were president of IACW, life member of the Frederick Douglass Memorial and Historical Association, parliamentarian of the National Association, member of the Administrative Board of the NACW, president of the Central Association of Colored Women, chair of the board of the Iowa Association Home, and author of *The History of the Central Association of Colored Women*.[152] Renowned African-American artist Bessie Viola Johnson, a resident of Burlington and a club woman herself, painted an oil portrait of Mrs. Brown that hung in the Iowa City university women students' home for many years.[153]

Some of the local women's clubs represented in the IACW after it was organized in 1902 were:

Burlington: Progressive Club
Cedar Rapids: Criterion Club, George Washington Carver Club, Silver Leaf Club
Council Bluffs: 20th Century Civic and Art Club
Davenport: Lend-A-Hand Club, Semper Fidelis Club
Des Moines: Mary Church Terrell #1 Club, Mary Church Terrell #2 Club, Mary B. Talbert Club; Modernistic Club, WCTU Club, Rosa L. Gregg Club, Des Moines City Federation, Parliamentary Law and Culture Club, Tawasi Club
Marshalltown: Paul Lawrence Dunbar Club, Jessie E. Walker Federated Club
Muscatine: Muscatine Federated Club
Oskaloosa: Mother's Club
Ottumwa: Ida B. Wells Club
Sioux City and Sioux Falls: Hour of Pleasure Club, Young Matron's Art Club
Waterloo: Mary McLeod Bethune Club[154]

Specific club names could not be identified for organizations in the following places, though it is presumed that each had at least one active club: Buxton, Indianola, Iowa City, and Keokuk.[155] In addition, it is likely that other clubs belonging to the state

(Left to right)

Mrs. S. Joe (Sue) Brown, Des Moines (SHSI Des Moines)

Mrs. Archie (Audra) Alexander, Des Moines (courtesy Lynda Walker-Webster)

Mrs. Maude M. Spencer, Mason City (courtesy Lynda Walker-Webster)

Mrs. Rose Johnson, Marshalltown/Des Moines (courtesy Rose Johnson)

(Above) *Hour of Pleasure Club,*
Sioux City, c. 1950
(courtesy Laura Carter Harrison)

(Top right) Parliamentary Law and
Culture Club, Des Moines, c.1950
(courtesy Lynda Walker-Webster)

(Bottom right)Rosa L. Gregg
Federated Women's Club, Des Moines
(courtesy Mary Ruth Simmons)

association existed, but research has not yet produced conclusive evidence.

Clubs still part of the state association today are the Criterion Club of Cedar Rapids, the Semper Fidelis Club of Davenport, and the Tawasi and Parlimentary Law and Culture Clubs of Des Moines. Approximately 100 Iowa women are presently active in IACW clubs. Delores Morgan of Cedar Rapids heads the state association. The association's most recent past-president, Dr. Lenola Allen-Sommerville of Des Moines, represented Iowa well at a recent national convention in Albuquerque, where she was crowned "queen" for raising more than $2,000 for the organization.[156]

The Tawasi Club of Des Moines was founded in 1962 by Lora Warden, Leoma Ward, and Helen Duke, each of whom recruited ten other women. The Tawasi Club periodically holds fundraisers, including an annual banquet, to augment their scholarship fund. Depending on the monies raised, four or five

scholarships may be presented to young women during the state association convention.[157] Geraldine Daniels, daughter-in-law of founder Lora Warden, has been referred to affectionately as the "Tawasi Queen" by citizens of Des Moines. She has been a loyal and hard working member, giving countless hours to raising money for the organization.

The Federated Girls' Clubs

Over the life of the state association, girls' clubs have been active in conjunction with the women's clubs. While none are in existence today, one of the last very active girl's clubs was the La Cremedelles (Cream of the Crop). Directed by Gertrude Hyde North, this club was active in the early 1960s. Some of its members were Ginger Miller, Ronene Parkey, Paula Heariold, Arthurlene Propes, Elsa Cawthorne, Lois Walden, Billie Wade, and Robbie Lynn Hawkins.

Another local federated girls' group must have existed, as indicated by the participation of other "Association Girls" in a 1964 debutante cotillion sponsored by the Iowa Association of Colored Girls. An *Iowa Bystander* headline from June 1964 reads "Eight High School Graduates Bow to Des Moines in Debutante Cotillion Ball Given by IACG." This event, sponsored by the IACW, was held at the Brotherhood and Sisterhood Hall. A "queen" contest held as a fund-raiser led Janice Carter, a 1964 North High graduate, to be crowned "Miss Association of 1964." Jennifer (Ginger) Miller, a Grandview College freshman, was the runner-up and was named "Princess." Other debutantes presented at the cotillion were GaVerna LaMar, Mary Lynne Jones, Jaquita Robinson, June Robinson, Ronene Parkey, Connie Evans, and Juanita Whitney. Iowa Association of Colored Girls participating in the affair were Arthurlene Propes, Billie Wade, Ginger Miller, Robby Lynn Hawkins, Joyce Jackson, and Bobbie Patterson. The event planning committee included the State Supervisor of Girls of the Iowa Association, Gertrude North, as well as the Association's Helen Wimberly, Audra Alexander, Alta Herndon, and Goletha Trotter.[158]

The Links, Inc.

The Links organization was founded in Philadelphia in 1946 by the late Margaret Roselle Hawkins and Sarah Strickland Scott. Considered one of the most prestigious women's organizations in

Paul Lawrence Dunbar Club, IACW, Marshalltown (courtesy Lynda Walker-Webster)

(Left to right, all courtesy Lynda Walker-Webster)

Mrs. Inez Willis, past president, Iowa Association of Colored Women

Mrs. Ella P. Stewart, Iowa Association of Colored Women's Clubs

Miss Jessie E. Walker, past president, Iowa Association of Colored Women

Mrs. Roberta Frazier, president, Des Moines District, Iowa Association of Colored Women

Founders of Links, Inc., Des Moines
(Links, Inc.)

the nation, the Links has a membership of nearly 10,000 women in 266 chapters located in 40 states, the District of Columbia, Nassau, Bahamas, and Frankfurt, Germany. The organization continually redefines its purposes, sharpens its focus, and expands its program dimensions in order to make the name "Links" not only a chain of friendship but also a chain of purposeful service. Headquartered in its own building in Washington, D.C., the Links renders services individually and collectively for educational, civic, and intercultural pursuits in the following program areas: National Trends and Services, International Trends and Services, and Services to Youth and the Arts. Through its chapters and its foundation, the Links has granted more than $15 million to charitable organizations and institutions, with $2 million going to the United Negro College Fund. The organization fosters economic development, educates and informs the general public about issues central to the well being of African-Americans, and encourages public policy that is responsive to their needs. Finding

talent to assist has been no problem for this organization. Throughout its history, the Links has attracted many distinguished and dedicated women. Many have made a significant difference in their communities as role models, mentors, activists, and volunteers.

In November 1957, a group of African-American women gathered in Des Moines to organize a Links chapter. These charter members were Audra Alexander, Hulette Barnett Belle, Gloria Bowman, Mabel Brooks, Harriet Bruce, Elaine Estes, Erma Estes Gayden, Willie Glanton, Lillie Harper, Alta Herndon, Girtha Jones Mitchell, Azailia Mitchell, Georgine Morris, and Mary Ritchey. Willie Glanton and Elaine Estes are the only charter members still living, except for Erma Estes Gayden, who moved away from the area. Linda Carter is the current president of the chapter, which has 34 members.[159]

Over their more than 40 years of service, the Des Moines Links chapter has sponsored a variety of positive activities in the

MYOB Club, Sioux City, organized by Mrs. Beulah Webb, 1928 (courtesy Laura Carter Harrison)

(Below) Deluxe Club dance, Des Moines, c.1950 (courtesy Lynda Walker-Webster)

community, including the popular "I Am Somebody" program. In collaboration with the Des Moines Art Center staff, Links members also worked with middle-school girls to experience the art of African mask-making in conjunction with a Des Moines Art Center exhibit titled "Secrecy: African Art that Conceals and Reveals." In February 1998, the Des Moines Links chapter sponsored a three-week long exhibit at the Polk County Heritage Gallery titled "Black Dolls: A Link to Cultural Identity and Bridge to International Understanding." In February 2000, the chapter co-sponsored a month-long black film festival at the Des Moines Art Center. Many events with speakers were held in conjunction with this exhibit. In September 1999, the chapter sponsored "A Roomful of Sisters" reception at the Des Moines Botanical Center, which also honored several local women. For several years the Des Moines Links chapter has also partnered with the Iowa Council of International Understanding in hosting Caribbean and African delegations visiting Des Moines. In 1995, the Links chapter worked

with the Iowa Commission on the Status of African-Americans and the Iowa Council of International Understanding in sponsoring and hosting a community luncheon and dialog on Africa with female leaders from 12 African countries.[160]

Private Women's Clubs

When Leola Nelson Bergmann published *The Negro in Iowa* in 1948, she counted 20 or more clubs with educational and social purposes for Negro women in Iowa. Among them she listed chapters or local affiliates of the National Association of Colored Women's Clubs and a University Women's Club with a membership of 15 college women. She also identified 14 secret Negro societies, 6 of them women's branches of men's organizations, such as the Masonics, Odd Fellows, Knights Templar, Knights of Pythias, United Brothers of Friendship, and the Elks.[161] Schwieder,

Hraba, and Schwieder's 1987 book on Buxton states that while some African-American women took part in clubs, lodges, and church organizations, not all of them did. The authors noted that family size undoubtedly determined the amount of time that married women spent away from home. Likewise, family income affected the extent to which black women participated in activities outside of the home.[162]

The Mary Church Terrell Clubs

The Mary Church Terrell Club, formed in Des Moines in 1906, would later come to be known as Mary Church Terrell #1 when a younger group formed and called itself Mary Church Terrell #2. The clubs were named after African-American educator, author, lecturer, and civil rights activist Dr. Mary Church Terrell. First president of the National Association of Colored Women's Clubs, Dr. Terrell was re-elected three times in succession from 1896 through 1901.[163]

Among those organizing the earlier Mary Church Terrell Club were Gertrude E. Rush, the first African-American female lawyer in Des Moines and one of the founders of the National Bar Association; Maude Thompson, wife of John L. Thompson, editor of the *Iowa Bystander;* and Jessye Bell Davis and others. Soon to join their ranks were the daughters of local inventor Robert N. Hyde, Gertrude Hyde North and Adah Hyde Johnson.[164] This club became affiliated with the Federated Colored Women's Club

Mary Church Terrell #2, Des Moines, (above) in the 1940s and (right) in the 1990s (courtesy Leola Davis)

in 1906 and with the National Association in 1910. However, in the 1970s it became a private women's club. At the Iowa association's annual convention in June 1952 the club had a membership of 14.[165]

In 1931 Gertrude Hyde North, a member of the Mary Church Terrell #1 Club, brought together two high-school girls, sisters Dorothy and Jesserean Sharon, to form the first membership of a younger club. Jesserean served as the first president. Charter members included Ola McCraney, Dora Elva Mackey, Doris Jones, Cornelia Leonard, Doris Bailey, and Irene Glass.[166] Today's Mary Church Terrell Club #2 is an active social club working on civic concerns and charitable programs. In the 1950s, the club was instrumental in organizing, along with other local clubs, a fundraising drive for the Willkie House Building Fund. The club is a life member of the NAACP and makes contributions to scholarship funds. A 1976 Recognition Ball honored the memory of the club's namesake, and a portrait of Mary Church Terrell was donated to hang in the Willkie House library.[167]

In 1978 the club celebrated with a Jubilee Tea whose theme was "Roots of Mary Church Terrell #2," tracing the roots of the club and its membership up to that point. Two years later, in 1980, the club celebrated its fiftieth anniversary. Still a very vibrant group of about 13 women, now mostly in their seventies and eighties, the club's members remain very involved in community, church, civic, and cultural activities. The club hosts an annual invitational

Halloween outing for themselves and their guests, as well as a Christmas luncheon at a local hotel. Ms. Dora Elva Mackey is the current president.[168]

Concerns about the advancing age of the members of the Mary Church Terrell #2 Club led in 1974 to the formation of a Mary Church Terrell Club for the baby boomer generation. Darlene Johnson served as the first president of Club #3, which is not only carrying on the legacy of its namesake and the clubs that came before it but has its own strong mission to encourage the growth of women and children. Mary Church Terrell #3 takes great pride in creating open forums to share its goals and to network with one another and with the community. The activities of the younger group have ranged from sponsoring bus trips for recreation to sponsoring teen dances, granting stipends for music lessons for youth, and supporting school board candidates. Elsa Conner is

Mary Church Terrell Club #2, Des Moines, 1950s (courtesy Leola Davis)

(Left) Mary Church Terrell Club #3, Des Moines (courtesy Elsa Conner)

*Three Purpose Club
(courtesy Josephine Pickett)*

*(Below right) The Puella LeGatoes
at Willkie House benefit
(courtesy Bertharina Cropp)*

*(Below) The Puella LeGatoes teen
group and Mrs. Lillian Snyder, Des
Moines (courtesy Bertharina Cropp)*

the current president. The club hosts an annual Christmas party and family outings in the summer, such as picnics and cookouts. Many members have pursued busy professional careers, and in recent years demanding schedules have limited many activities. Still, club members do their best to make time for volunteer activities within their communities.[169]

The Three Purpose Club

The Three Purpose Club was organized in Des Moines nearly 70 years ago. Julia Proctor, now residing in Cincinnati, and Edith Webb are two charter members still active in the club, along with the club's dozen other members. The club meets twice a month, with each member rotating as hostess, and focuses its activities on social services, intellectual improvement, and fellowship. The Three Purpose Club makes monetary contributions to the homeless and to the food pantry as well as to the battered and abused women's shelters. At Christmas time the club conducts a canned-goods drive.[170]

The Winthrop Club

In October 1947, 12 women met to organize the Winthrop Club in Des Moines. Many had been members of the Junior Modernistics Club, which was part of the state association and had lasted until several of the members graduated from high school and married. Thus they reorganized as the Winthrop Club, an adult civic and social organization. Among the charter members were Ellen Robinson, Idella Cushionberry, Venita Wells, Louise Ware, Launa Quincy, Nadine Ware, and Gwen Turner. Still active, the Winthrop Club currently has nine members who meet monthly at the home of a member or at a restaurant. The club celebrated its fiftieth anniversary in 1997.

The Winthrops have hosted many formal dances. The first was held at the Billikin Ballroom, which had been decorated to perfection for the event. Another, titled the "Black and White Ball," was held at the Hyperion Country Club. Other club activities have included an annual family picnic, taking members' mothers to dinner, and involvement with Willkie House activities, such as training teen girls in proper etiquette. The club has raised over $500 for the Willkie House Library. The current president is Mrs. Nadine Ware.[171]

The Puella LeGatoes, Des Moines

The Puella LeGatoes initially organized as a teenage girls' club in the 1940s and continued on as a women's social organization well into the 1960s or early 1970s. The group's original advisor was Lillian Snyder, a white woman who had been a volunteer at the Negro Community Center, where she worked with teen-aged girls. Mrs. Snyder helped organize the group and served as advisor until she moved to Minnesota. Some of the group's original members were Betty June (Hayes) Dixon, Willa Mae (Hayes) DeVan, Shirley (Turner) Harper, Idah Smith, Betty Jane Martin, Nancy Smith, Paula (Smith) Morton, Katherine Strothers, and Bertharina (Strothers) Cropp. As a youth group, the Puella LeGatoes met weekly and took part in community activities. For example, they did a dance routine at a fundraiser for Willkie House sponsored by the Winthrop Club at the Fort Des Moines Hotel.[172]

As the teen group evolved, the faces of the membership changed and became an almost entirely different group of women. The adult group of the Puella LeGatoes held formal dances each year, as well as other social and civic activities. A 1963 *Iowa Bystander* article carried the story of the club's third Parisian Ball, held on May 18 at Killinger Music Hall. The theme was "I Love Paris in the Springtime," and the decorations provided a truly Parisian atmosphere for club members and guests as they danced to the music of the Cletus Williams Combo. There were pastel poodles, quaint lanterns, and an Eiffel Tower, creating an elegant atmosphere for the dancers. Highlighted in the *Bystander* story were Gail Adams, Berniece Wright, Dorothy Bell, Doris Savage, Edith Sharp, Corliss Williams, Betty June Dixon, Delores Brewer, Glenda Russell, and June Franklin.[173] In time, many of the club's members left Des Moines, some moving as far away as California, and the club became inactive. Bertharina Cropp, one of the charter members as a teenager, remained in the club until the very end.[174]

The Booklover's Club

The Booklover's Club is the oldest remaining and continuously active organization associated with the Des Moines YWCA. Organized in 1925 at the old Blue Triangle YWCA in the era of institutionalized racism, the club's ten charter members were interested in literary and intellectual improvement. In 1946, the national YWCA office agreed to integrate its programs. Thus the Des Moines Central YWCA, following the mandate of the National YWCA, closed programs at the Blue Triangle. The Booklover's Club, which had consisted of black women, accepted their first white member in 1958, Mrs. Jack (Bo) Cleveland. Integration was difficult to accept at first, but as membership increased, other white women joined the club also. Today the club has approximately 25 members, who meet monthly except in the winter months. The current president is Lisa Wilson.

Each year at the club's Christmas luncheon for their members and guests, Memorial Textbook Scholarships are granted to two black women attending Des Moines Area Community College Urban Campus based on need. These scholarships are possible through special contributions and memorial gifts. The club has also contributed books to Willkie House and Forest Avenue Library.[175]

The Self-Culture Club of Keokuk

The Self-Culture Club, organized in Keokuk in 1913, included among its 11 charter members Mrs. Ollie Gross, Della Bland, Stella Bland, Mable Bland, Irela Bland, Myrtle Bland, Letha Johnson, Ella Drain, Artisha Fields, and a Mrs. Ashby. Each charter

Booklover's Club, Des Moines (courtesy Josephine Pickett)

(Above, left to far right)

Just Rite Club, Manly, c.1930 (courtesy Meredith Saunders)

Atelier Guild, Ottumwa, c.1950 (courtesy Gwen Saunders)

Highlight Club, Manly, c.1940 (courtesy Meredith Saunders)

Young Matrons Art Club, Sioux City (courtesy Laura Carter Harrison)

member was asked to invite one friend to become a member, and to keep the membership at 20. Their motto was "To Be Rather Than to Seem." Mrs. Gross selected their club name because the focus was to be on the study of literature and on the discussion of current events. At its meetings, in addition to the order of business and current events, the club discussed any pending race issue news, Roberts Rules of Order, United States history, English poets, Negro authors, and state capitols. Programs included debates, papers, vocal and instrumental music, and book or magazine reviews.

The Self-Culture Club has a long and rich history among African-American citizens in this southeastern Iowa river town. The club has sponsored a charity club to help others throughout the community, established a membership in the NAACP, and during the Civil Rights movement sent donations to the South to help with various cases. The local group also hosted many social activities, such as Christmas parties, seasonal teas, formal receptions for visiting dignitaries, and summer picnics.[176]

The Ladies' Afternoon Social Club of Cedar Rapids and the Merry Fourteen Club of Des Moines

Many of the clubs described here conducted their activities with elegance and flair. Judging from accounts in the *Iowa Bystander* files, such characteristics have marked African-American social organizations back to before the turn of the century. For example,

the *Bystander* of January 3, 1896, carried a story describing an event sponsored by the Ladies' Afternoon Social Club of Cedar Rapids. "The first LeapYear party of the season was given by the Ladies' Afternoon Social Club on January 2 at the pleasant home of Mr. and Mrs. Lewis Austin on B Street," wrote the *Bystander*. "The home was neatly arranged for the occasion, and the cheerful fire within made the guests forget about the blustering wind and nipping frost without. There were 40 guests present who enjoyed themselves at games and in conversation. The Renix Brothers Mandolin Club, consisting of five pieces, discoursed sweet and classical music during the serving. The club had just returned from an extended tour, and is an excellent musical and gentlemanly organization." The newspaper reported that "an elegant supper was served at 11:00 p.m. The ladies of the club each served their several guests. It was a rather cold night for the ladies to see the gentlemen home and we believe the order was changed to the usual methods of escort. The guests departed at midnight, and those living a long distance procured hermetically sealed conveyances as a protection against the first really cold weather of the season."[177]

The same issue of the newspaper covered a story about the Merry Fourteen Club of Des Moines. "Mrs. G. W. Denny's cozy cottage was the scene of merriment on New Year's Day," reported the *Bystander*. "The Merry Fourteen closed the Christmas festivities with additions of a few other invited guests, with an elaborate

dinner, served in the hostess' usual grand style. The tables were arrayed in beautiful china, fine linen, exquisite cut glass and the last but not least, an abundance of good things."[178]

The Dilettante Club of Des Moines

The sophisticated and cultured ladies who made up the Dilettante Club came together in 1932 primarily to help finance the Negro Community Center's Annual Art Exhibit. On May 14, 1940, the club sponsored its annual musical tea at Center Street's LaMarguerita Hotel. The program listed solo performances by Calvin Dacus, Roberta Maupin, and Benjamin Dacus. Club president was Mrs. Dalza Hammitt, and Mrs. Charles Howard was vice president.[179] On June 15, 1950, the club held its annual musical at Drake University. The program featured a classical recital by Artie McNair, then a Drake piano student. In 1950, the club had 14 active members and an annual associate membership of 60 others who helped sponsor the scholarship fund. In addition to raising money for the art exhibit and the art-students' scholarship fund, the club promoted art studies among its members.[180]

The Onanas Club

The Onanas Club — no longer in existence — was organized in April 1962 in the home of Mrs. Tempie Harris. The club elected Phyllis Williams its first president and included among its charter

The Onanas Club, Des Moines (courtesy Camille Bradley)

members Sharon Brewton, Rhoba Turner, Beverly Strothers, Marginell Clayburn, Hazel Grant, Celeste Graves, Naomi Jeffers, Viola Moore, Beverly Wallace, and Elaine Williams.[181]

The Onanas were a group of young married women who held their first invitational formal on November 30, 1963, at Killinger Music Hall. The theme for the occasion was "Oriental Splendor," and the ballroom's tables were graced with replicas of Japanese pagodas. A 20-foot dragon hung from the ceiling, surrounded by flying fish and Japanese lanterns, all made by local artist and teacher Leroy Mitchell. Club members were attired in full-length evening gowns, each adorned with a corsage of blue gardenias, and the club supplied blue-covered matchbooks with silver lettering saying "Have a Light on the Onanas." Members and their guests danced to the music of Rufus Spates and his band. Elaine Williams was president of the club at the time.[182]

Mixed-Gender Clubs

The Associated Iowa Clubs

In August 1937, the Minnesota-Iowa Club hosted the first annual convention of the Associated Iowa Clubs in Minneapolis. Talmadge B. Carey, president of the Minnesota-Iowa Club, welcomed the Associated Iowa Clubs to the convention, held in conjunction with the Central States Golf Tournament. "In our effort to provide for you good wholesome recreation and pleasure,"

said Carey, "we have not forgotten that there are many perplexing problems confronting our group today, problems that must be solved if we are interested in our children and our posterity. We believe that you, along with others here assembled, shall resolve that this organization shall develop a constructive program and lend its influence toward the practical solution of some of these problems."

The parent club of the Associated Iowa Clubs was the Original Iowa Club of Chicago. Organized in February 1932, the Original Iowa Club of Chicago was headed by A.J. Brookins. "Realizing the social and economic possibilities of an organization comprising a multiplicity of clubs with a oneness of purpose," Mr. Brookins said, "this club in 1934 began a program of promoting and encouraging the organization of Iowa Clubs in various cities."

The Milwaukee-Iowa Club, led by president Nealie Golden, was organized in 1934 primarily to stimulate interest in a yearly pilgrimage to Buxton. Later, however, club members began to feel African-Americans were weakly organized in civic activities and constructive urban programs and that it was necessary to turn the club's attention toward civic development. Thus at the 1937 convention of Associated Iowa Clubs, they proposed a program of action to deal with the needs of Negroes, particularly their place in their community, their economic problems, and their hopes for better housing. Club members also advocated more job opportunities in industry and apprenticeships for Negro youth.

Another Iowa Club organized in Milwaukee was the Iowa Advancement Club of Milwaukee, formed in March 1937 by Lee A. Meadly. Meadly saw their mission as creating a spirit of friendliness and harmony. The club also supported efforts to better the social and civic life of Iowa Negroes living in the Milwaukee area. The club's main themes were fidelity, honesty, and advancement.

Clubs attending the 1937 Minneapolis convention included the Minnesota-Iowa Club (Talmadge B. Carey, president); the Original Iowa Club of Chicago (A. J. Brookins); the Milwaukee-Iowa Club (Nealie Golden); the Iowa Advancement Club of Milwaukee (Lee A. Meadley); the Iowa Club of Mason City (William L. Werginton); and the Iowa Club of Des Moines (Mattie Brooks Scott).[183]

The entire front page of the *Minneapolis Spokesman* on Friday, August 13, 1937, welcomed the Associated Iowa Clubs convention to be held the coming weekend. "This welcome takes on a warmer tinge," declared the *Spokesman*, "as we remind ourselves that here comes a group, not only assembled from all over the United States,

(Above right) Royal Entertainers Club, Ottumwa, 1935 (courtesy Gwen Saunders)

(Below right) Iowa Club of Des Moines, 1990s (courtesy Lynda Walker-Webster)

(Below) Sojourners Club, Clarinda (Nodaway Valley Historical Society)

through the all too often tenuous hold of a secret society bent solely on a search of pleasure, but here is a group of kindred souls with much of a similar experience and outlook, who come to review in many cases, friendships of past days."[184]

Headquarters for the convention was the Phyllis Wheatley House, where delegates and visitors paid 25 cents to register. On Saturday, August 14, many of them joined a 40-cent sightseeing tour of Minneapolis. That evening a grand ball and reception, costing 45 cents for admission, was held at Happ's Country Club. On Sunday the annual picnic of the Iowa clubs was held at Glenwood Park, with speakers, games, and community singing. The picnic lunch was furnished free to registered delegates and visitors. Music was provided by a glee club and a quartet. Later in the afternoon an athletic program was held for boys and girls and foot races for young men and ladies.

The National Iowa Clubs, Sequel to the Associated Iowa Clubs

The demise of the thriving African-American community in Buxton sent its residents off in many directions to new homes. For years after, the Associated Iowa Clubs kept former Buxtonites in touch with one another. In time the Associated Iowa Clubs

organization itself became inactive, though Buxton reunions took place periodically. Typically the reunions were picnics held on the vacated land where Buxton once stood or in a park in Des Moines.

Beginning in 1969, a group of Iowans living in the area of Oakland, California, gathered to celebrate Memorial Day and to reminisce about life in Iowa. By the early 1970s their annual weekend included a barbecue and a picnic, fun and games, and a dance held at the Helmet Club in Berkeley. This gathering drew people from all over California, especially from the Los Angeles area, and each year more and more people came. They came from California and neighboring states, and some came from as far away as Iowa itself. In time the weekend affair was moved to a hotel, where the weekend's organizers added a hospitality suite and held their dance in the hotel ballroom. The Oakland group became officially chartered and called itself the Ebony Iowa Club.[185] Organization of the Ebony Iowa Club was followed by the formation of the Los Angeles Iowa Club, the Iowa Club of Colorado, the Minnesota Iowa Club, the Iowa Club of Des Moines, and lastly the Iowa Club of D.C., Maryland, and Virginia. There has been interest and speculation that groups of former Iowans want to organize in such places as Atlanta, Phoenix, and Chicago as well.

The six existing Iowa clubs listed are under the umbrella of the National Iowa Club, Inc. (NIC) governing board. This board meets independently of the clubs each March in Las Vegas to discuss the business and policies governing the clubs. The clubs host an "Iowa Days" reunion annually on the first weekend in August. The reunions rotate through the cities where the clubs are located, with that specific club serving as the host. In 1999 the National Iowa Club, Inc., board itself will host the annual reunion in Las Vegas. Marie Calderon of the Iowa Club of Des Moines is the current NIC president.

In 1996, the Iowa Club of Des Moines hosted Iowa Days, which attracted more than 3,000 people. The event always draws more people on home turf than when it is held in other cities. The "home-spun" African-Americans who still reside in Iowa, as well as those who come home for the occasion (especially those from the Des Moines area), ride on a fundamental high for months afterwards. The town is transformed by the homecoming scene. "It's just a village thing," and it becomes amazingly spiritual!

The Iowa Club of Des Moines, which organized in 1987, first hosted Iowa Days in 1990. When the club hosted again in 1996, the homecoming theme was "Remembering Center Street," the former heart of African-American social life in Des Moines. All of the lodges, private clubs, and other businesses owned by African-American proprietors were once located directly on — or "just off" — this key street. The Friday night get-together at the 1996 reunion in the Savery Hotel's Terrace Ballroom had a streetscape of the Center Street clubs. The crowd assembled at the Savery that evening cannot be described as "standing-room only" but rather "breathing room only." Guests spilled out into the foyer and onto the skywalk.

The estimated attendance at the Saturday picnic was more than 3,000 persons. John and Ann Jackson, who then lived adjacent to the park where the picnic was held, said it looked more like 4,000. Chartered buses brought the visitors from the hotel to the park, and the Iowa Club of Des Moines provided free food and beverages. Many individuals brought their own food set-up. Dr. Evelyn K. Davis and her sister Clara Wade, longtime Des Moines residents originally from Hiteman in Monroe County, always prepare a feast, setting up a table to serve friends and folks who drop by their table. For Evelyn this is a time of reuniting old friends and meeting new ones. "If I see someone that I don't know," she said, "it is more than likely that I knew their parents or grandparents. The Iowa Days are a wonderful social occasion!"

On Saturday evening, the folks donned their fine apparel and filled the entire second floor of the Polk County Convention Center. While there was a live band pumping music throughout the hall, most people spent the time talking, hugging, sharing, and catching up on old times. Each year, the host club grants a scholarship to deserving African-American high school students. The National Iowa Club matches the host club's donation. In 1996, the Des Moines host club not only matched the national club, but matched the combined amount, enabling two young women to receive scholarships. A substantial amount was also provided by the Des Moines club and the national club for a community donation. That gift was awarded to the Friends of Forest Avenue Library.

Thus the Iowa clubs, originally formed for the purpose of socializing, have evolved into benevolent organizations, awarding scholarships every year, making donations to many charitable organizations, contributing to senior citizen affairs and housing projects, and giving Thanksgiving and Christmas baskets to needy individuals and families. Based on Iowa friendships and good times

> *"If I see someone that I don't know it is more than likely that I knew their parents or grandparents. The Iowa Days are a wonderful social occasion!"*
>
> *— Evelyn K. Davis*

remembered, each club remains truly social in the fullest sense of the word.[186]

In August 2000, the Ebony Iowa Club, co-hosting with the Iowa Club of Des Moines, held Iowa Days in Des Moines at the Marriott Hotel.

The Iowa Buxton Clubs and the
Buxton Iowa Club, Inc., of Des Moines

Former Buxton residents and their descendants have created a number of social organizations over the years. At one time there was an Iowa Buxton Club #1 and an Iowa Buxton Club #2, both in Des Moines. Membership in the Iowa Buxton Club #1 included many of the generation that left Buxton as young people, but the club became inactive when most of its members passed away in the years after World War 2. The Iowa Buxton Club #2, made up mostly of the descendants of the first group, functioned concurrently with Club #1 during the 1950s and 1960s. More recently, the Iowa Buxton Club #2 was renamed the Iowa Buxton Club, a social club that presently exists.

There is also a Buxton Iowa Club, Inc., that is more of a cultural organization concerned with the preservation of the history of Buxton, Iowa. Incorporated in October 1987, this group's objectives are to fully research and reconstruct the history of Buxton, its people, and its culture, so as to enhance the positive racial and ethnic heritage of the era. The club also endeavors to preserve heirlooms and mementos now possessed by former Buxton families, to establish means by which black students can learn of their Iowa cultural heritage, to acquire a portion of the original town site and to have it placed on the National Federal Register of Historic Places, to develop templates for descendants to trace their family histories, and to encourage the annual reunions.

Many of the club's objectives have been met. Now on the National Register of Historic Places is a two-acre portion of the town site that includes the Buxton cemetery. Club members themselves spent a great deal of time clearing the cemetery of debris. On Saturday, September 3, 1983, the club held a special reunion at the Marriott Hotel with Rev. C. T. Vivian, an associate of the late Dr. Martin Luther King, as the keynote speaker. On the same day, the Iowa Public Broadcasting Network aired a documentary titled "You Can't Go Back to Buxton." On Sunday, a worship service was held at Mount Olive Baptist Church, followed by a picnic at Birdland Park.[187] The late Paul Wilson, a

former Buxton resident and brother of Sue Brown and undertaker Tug Wilson, was considered to be the premier archivist of Buxton memorabilia and history.

The Polk County Old Negro Settlers

An undated *Bystander* clipping from sometime in 1940 notes that the annual reunion and picnic of the Polk County Old Negro Settlers took place near the lagoon in Union Park. The group had been organized in 1885, and at the 1940 reunion two of the club's charter members, Alec Wilburn and Douglas Miller, were still living. Both were in their eighties. The annual Old Settlers event always included afternoon and evening programs, in addition to the picnic dinner normally held at 5 p.m.[188]

The American Legion Auxiliaries in Des Moines and Keokuk

Keokuk's John McCampbell American Legion Post #596 was chartered in January 1936, with Lewis A. McGee as the first commander. In addition to McGee, charter members were Cecil Clark, Harrison R. Young, Jasper C. Cook, James R. South, George Haywood, Walter Warren, Clarence E. Crowson, Joseph Fields, Scott Estelle, Raleigh Myers, John W. Hawkins, Scott Johnson,

*Buxton Club #2, Des Moines
(courtesy Lynda Walker-Webster)*

Benjamin E. Toomes, and Phelps C. Jones. The organization functioned in accordance with the American Legion's national governing body, but it also served as a community service organization aiding brother veterans, doing charity work, and assisting with parties for children at special times of the year. Many of the post's members have received special certificates for faithfulness in the performance of their duties.

The auxiliary to John McCampbell Post #596 was organized by Post Commander Lewis A. McGee and Post Adjutant Raleigh Myers in June 1936 and received its charter in May 1938. The first officers were Mrs. Kenneth South Myers, president; Gertrude Scott, vice-president; Ruth B. Toomes, secretary; Buelah Clark, treasurer; Alma Stewart, chaplain; and Blanche Hawkins, sergeant-at-arms. There were 13 charter members. The auxiliary worked under the direction of the post to aid local veterans and their families, to cooperate when calls were received, to aid veterans at Knoxville and other veteran's hospitals, and to foster Americanism among young people. Auxiliary members also assisted with the parties the post held for children in the community.[189]

In Des Moines, the Roy Leonard Rollen V.F.W. Auxiliary

Post #5487 was organized in July 1946 at the Crocker Branch of the YMCA. The post was named after a Des Moines native, the son of Lillian Rollen, who lost his life in 1942 while serving in the Navy in the Pacific. Charter members of the auxiliary were Helen Allen, Anna Brooks, Gladys Childs, Samanthia Davis, Arlene Graves, Josie Gibson, Rose Johnson, Lessie Manuel, Mabel Mason, Lillian Rollen, Beatrice Smith, Jennie Smith, Thelma Smith, Josephine Stewart, Murlean Taylor, Bernice Williams, and Emma Williamson.

In 1967 the auxiliary celebrated its twenty-first anniversary with a special banquet. Lawrence James, a member of the post for nine years, had been serving as commander the previous year. His senior commander was Don Murray. Other post officers included Frank Moore, vice commander; John Williams, quartermaster; Ted Carr, adjutant; and Wilbur Caswell, chaplain. Post trustees were Dr. Julian Mason, Larry Dorsey, and James Clyce. The auxiliary's president at the time of the anniversary was Henrietta McKee. Evelyn Davis was senior vice president; Vivian Pruitt, junior vice president; Lessie Garrett, secretary; Emma Williamson, treasurer; and Anna Brooks, chaplain.[190]

The Friendship Club, Clinton

The Friendship Club has provided fellowship among African-American men and women in Clinton for more than 50 years. Maude James is the president, Clemmie Hightower is the secretary, and Leatha James is the treasurer. The club is a social and Bible study group that meets monthly, alternating between the local AME church and the Baptist church. The club serves an evening meal or a repast of some type and has a short program.[191]

The Bow Knots Club of Des Moines

The Bow Knots Club was organized in Des Moines during the 1950s. Membership is by couples. Charter members were Rufus and Edythe Ann Spates, Speck and Meta Redd, Aurelia and Gene Rhodes, Virgil and Fay Winters, Marsh and Haley Houston, and Mr. and Mrs. Rhone. Of the charter members, all of the men are now deceased but many of the wives are still living. The club has welcomed other couples and continues to be active. During the club's early years, members would take family vacations together at the Lake Idewild Resort area in Michigan. Attending ball games, horse races, and other family-related activities were also part of the Bow Knots' social agenda.[192]

Bow Knots Club at Idlewild Lake, Michigan, c.1950 (courtesy Aurelia Rhodes)

The Saturday Night Bridge Club, Des Moines

Many Des Moines couples participated in the Saturday Night Bridge Club, which was quite active during the 1930s and 1940s. According to an August 1937 *Iowa Bystander* clipping, on one particular Saturday evening the club met at the Carl Weeks mansion. Hosted by Mr. and Mrs. Alexander Ward, this was a special occasion. Mr. Weeks spoke with the group and gave them a tour of the mansion. The club served refreshments and then played bridge for the evening. Mr. and Mrs. Archie Alexander, Mr. and Mrs. A. P. Trotter, Mr. and Mrs. Charles Winn, Mr. and Mrs. Bert Harris, Mr. and Mrs. Matthew Johnson, and Mr. and Mrs. James Mitchell were all active members in the Saturday Night Bridge Club.[193]

Youth Social and Cultural Clubs

Over the course of African-American social history in Iowa, many youth groups have been sponsored by schools, churches, and community organizations. Several adult clubs established their roots as youth groups, and several fraternal and community organizations have had youth divisions. Some have had national connections, while others functioned as independent local organizations. One such club was the Billikin High School and College Dance Club for teenagers and young adults, which was founded in August 1937 by Des Moines pharmacist and business proprietor Azalia Mitchell. Only high school and college students were eligible for membership. Mrs. Mitchell, who served as sponsor and advisor for the group, was assisted by Dora Elva Mackey and Miss Wheels. Admission to the club's initial event was by invitation only, and private membership cards were given at that time. On the grand opening night, a cabaret dance and floor show were held at the Billikin Night Club. The club also sponsored amateur nights for cash prizes.[194]

The Ebbonettes Club and the LaDemoiselles Club, Des Moines

The Ebbonettes Social Club for teenage girls in Des Moines, founded in 1961 under the umbrella of Willkie House, was organized for cultural and social purposes. Willkie House director Charlene Wharton was advisor to the group. Mary Ruth Simmons served as the club's director and sponsor. The Ebbonettes at the outset were 12 girls aged 15 to 17 from all over the city. Charter

The Ebbonettes, Des Moines mother–daughter social club (courtesy Lynda Walker-Webster)

members were Linda (Hunt) Glover, Phyllis (Sharp) Hall, Leslie (Johnson) Clevert, Lynda (Walker) Webster, Joyce Jackson, Sandra (Merritt) Townes, Sally (Merritt) Burrell, Geraldine (Bruce) Ward, Robbie Lynn Hawkins, Sharon (Brown) Jackson, Martha Canafax, and Linda (Johnson) Hawkins. The club's first president was Lynda Walker.

Some of the Ebbonettes' most popular events were teen dances held at Willkie House and at the Brotherhood and Sisterhood Hall. Their invitational holiday semiformal dances were also very special occasions. The club held many fundraisers to help with their activities, such as fashion shows, raffles, and dinners. Venerable Des Moines printer Robert Patten made their invitations, as he did for many local social organizations.

After graduation, the Ebbonettes went off to college and careers, and their organization ended. A few years later, however, many of the same girls re-organized as a club for college and career women. They named their new group the LaDemoiselles. Delphia Barnett sponsored and advised the LaDamoiselles. Old members who remained were Phyllis Sharp, Leslie Johnson, Linda (Johnson)

Hawkins, and Lynda Walker. Newcomers included Darlene (Jenkins) Greenfield, Gayle (Ashby) Watkins, JoAnn (Henderson) Rose, Georgeann (Tywater) Johnson, Patricia (Johnson) Spriggs, Juanita (Whitney) Johnson, and Jaquita Robinson.

The goals of the LaDemoiselles were purely social and cultural. In the two or three years the club existed, it sponsored a number of successful events. One was a gala Valentine's Day dance at the Hotel Fort Des Moines attended by many Drake, Grandview, Simpson, and Iowa State students. After three or four years, many of the members began graduating from college, getting married, and moving away. The group got together for a final community social event together and then retired to the home of Juanita Whitney for a farewell slumber party.[195]

The Ambassadors, Des Moines

The Ambassadors, a teen boy's club, was formed in the late 1930s or early 1940s at the Negro Community Center. Encouraged by their mothers, the Ambassadors' goal was to help their members develop into gentlemen by providing a positive social, cultural, and athletic environment for them. Some of the Ambassadors were Raymond Monroe, Victor Massey, Harold Spangler, Donald Spangler, John Estes, Leonard Spangler, Ed Morton, Donald Massey, Bill Cropp, Harold Lewis, John Cooley, Sonny Dixon, Buster Boone, Junior Gates, Richard Williams, and "Mufty."[196] It is not certain how long the club lasted, but its membership continued to evolve as the boys grew into men and at one point the Ambassadors became a men's club.

(Below right) Ambassadors as adult group (courtesy Samuel Bradley)

(Below) Ambassadors as youth group (courtesy Bertharina Cropp)

The Philomatheon Debs, Des Moines

The Philomatheon Debs were organized in April 1961 by Donnetta Clayborne, Kimberly Reeves, and Paula Walker, under the direction of the late Mrs. Lee Gurtha Hughes. Other girls who took part in the Philomatheon Debs were Manala Hendred, Deborah Anderson, Joan Robinson, Noretta Fowler, Marsha Fowler, Cecelia Thompson, René Semple, Dorothy May, Pamela Williams, Karen Heath, Judy King, Carla Burse, and JoEllen Spriggs.

The Philomatheon Debs worked hard each year hosting a graduation ball for group members graduating from high school. The first ball, held in 1964 with the theme "Stairway to the Stars," celebrated the graduation of Debs Karen Heath, Judy King, and Marsha and Noretta Fowler. Attorney Robert Wright served as master of ceremonies for the occasion.[197] In 1966, when the Debs celebrated their third annual graduation ball, attorney Willie S. Glanton was their speaker. All three of the club's charter members were honored at the 1966 ball.

A Junior Debs group was also founded to ensure that the club would continue to involve young women in its activities. Charter Junior Debs were Charmayne Wright, Gloria King, Denise White, Deborah Rogers, Bobbretta Elliston, Brenda Bethel, Dee-Dee May, Linda Walker, Garoldine Bryson, and Edith English. The girls of both groups represented high schools from all parts of Des Moines.[198]

Jack and Jill of America, Inc., Des Moines Chapter

Jack and Jill is a nationwide parent and youth organization founded in 1938 in Philadelphia by Marian Stubbs Thomas. The Des Moines chapter of Jack and Jill organized in November 1962. The objectives of this non-profit organization are to provide educational, cultural, civic, recreational, and social programs for children. While youth-based, Jack and Jill is governed by mothers having children aged 2 to 19 and willing to subscribe to the objectives and policies of Jack and Jill of America, Inc.[199]

Mothers who were charter members of the Des Moines chapter were Billie Jean Morrow, Inez Morrow, Dorothy Wallace, Arlene Morris, Frances Hawthorne, Willie Glanton, Venita Wells, Barbara James, Barbara Kaiser, Ellen Robinson, Delores Spriggs, Chrystal Peavy, Dorothy Lewis, Gloria Bowman, Barbara Parkey, Jeanette Bethel, and Berniece Wright. Edith Sharp and Dorothy Garrett joined the group shortly thereafter. The charter members were installed in a candlelight ceremony by the late Margaret E. Simms from the Central Region office in St. Louis. The first

teen president was Herbert (Herbie) Cawthorne. Though the Des Moines chapter was inactive for several years, Jack and Jill has been reactivated locally by Valeska Buie, a newcomer to the Des Moines area. Kim Carr-Irvin is current president. Youth president ia Lanita Williams.

Homes for Social Organizations: Our Community Centers, Settlement Houses, and Ys

Segregation prevented the black community from sharing in the mainstream of social life in the United States throughout much of the twentieth century. As a result, the early social and recreational life in the African-American community owes a lot of its vitality to the community centers, settlement houses, and "colored" YMCAs and YWCAs in black neighborhoods throughout the nation.

Iowa too was a victim of segregation. Community centers and Ys that played a major role in four of Iowa's larger cities were the Negro Community Center (later to become Willkie House) in Des Moines, the Booker T. Washington Center (later to become

The Crocker Street Y's winning basketball team of 1934–35 included (left to right) Eugene Wilson, James Allen, Eugene Brown, Benny Elmore, Morton Graves, Oscar Glass, and coach Allen Ashby. (courtesy Willmetta Carter)

Mary McLeod Bethune at the old Negro Community Center, Des Moines, c.1944 (Willkie House)

the Sanford Center) in Sioux City, the Jesse Cosby Center in Waterloo, and the Jane Boyd Center in Cedar Rapids. In addition, former Buxton residents recall the impact the YMCA played in that community.

Willkie House, Des Moines

The oldest of these institutions still existing is the Negro Community Center, now known as Willkie House, which opened its doors at 907 15th Street sometime shortly after 1919. Herbert Wright served as executive director for the center. However, in July 1922, a petition signed by several hundred citizens of the African-American community was presented to the city's Welfare Bureau, demanding that Mr. Wright be removed and replaced with a "trained worker." The petition stated that "the budget from which the center was supported was raised by taxation and voluntary contributions. In order to give Negro citizens of Des Moines the facilities afforded them in larger cities . . . the Colored center's share of the fund should be sufficient to replace the Executive Secretary with someone who would direct our social and civic activities . . . so that our boys and girls might have greater opportunities to make better and more useful citizens." Among the signers of the petition were members of the Roosevelt Club, the Women's Protective League, the DuBois Association, and the Mary Church Terrell Club. In 1924 Lillian Edmunds, originally from Birmingham, Alabama, became assistant to Negro Community Center director Wilder J. Moore. Mrs. Edmunds, a trained nurse with a pharmacy degree from Des Moines University, would eventually replace Mr. Moore.[200]

The Negro Community Center was for many years a beacon to the black community. A well-used, well-supported, and well-respected facility, the center was especially important to the community in the Depression era. Many notable persons visited the center over the years, including First Lady Eleanor Roosevelt and Dr. Mary McLeod Bethune.[201] A 1935 typed report by Mrs. Edmunds titled "Some General Facts about the Negro Community Center" opens as follows: "The Negro population of Des Moines is about 6,000, and the center is reaching about 70% of this population. It is our aim to provide a higher civic and social life, to promote the proper use of leisure time, and to sponsor and maintain educational and cultural enterprises."[202]

Mrs. Edmunds stressed that there was an activity or a club for every member of the family. For girls there was Camp Fire. For boys there was scouting. For both boys and girls there were many club opportunities, plus orchestra and dramatics. For adults there was an English class taught by an Iowa State graduate student. For the ladies there was also a sewing room, where they could come to make garments and bedding for the needy or participate in a quilting group. The men had a community band, a ball club, and a choral group that gave free concerts during the summer months.[203] Many social clubs met weekly at the center, such as the Royal Dukes and the Monarchs. Two groups that would become well-known and synonymous with Willkie House would be the Atelier Guild, a group of young women who were interested in crafts, and the Dilettante Club noted earlier.[204]

The Negro Community Center also had an art club, a library, an employment system, an emergency service, a Parent's Guidance League, the Golden Agers, and a Community Garden Club to stimulate interest in better homes and gardens, as well as bird lore. In the 1930s, the center offered classes that trained women to be proper in maid work. This class brought in speakers and hosted an elegant tea at graduation time.[205] The center also housed the Well-Baby Clinic, staffed over the years by various local African-American physicians such as Dr. Clyde Bradford, Dr. Robert Johnson, and Dr. J. A. Jefferson.

As the African-American population of Des Moines grew, so did the numbers of people participating in activities at the center. More children were attending the center's youth programs, more social clubs were forming, and still other social clubs were looking for affiliation or for a place to hold their meetings. Mrs. Edmunds's 1935 report had stressed the fact that the Jewish Community Center, the Southside Community House, and the Roadside Settlement House on the city's southeast side, as well as various Protestant and Catholic churches, were serving Des Moines's white citizens. However, all Negro activities in Des Moines, even WPA projects, were housed at the Negro Community Center, which was an old residence without any equipment and just one paid worker. Mrs. Edmunds further added that there were 35 boys and girls in the Junior Mixed Chorus, 40 women in the gym class, 35 in the band — and that 124 organizations were served at the center that year, an increase of 24 organizations from the year before. Overall attendance for the year was 38,115 people for all of the center's activities.[206]

In the years following Mrs. Edmunds's report, the center's board of directors looked for ways to meet the center's growing needs. Appeals were made to the community and to various foundations in the community. In June 1945, the trustees of the Gardner Cowles Foundation agreed with the center's board, then headed by architect Archie Alexander, that a modern building was "badly needed" in Des Moines to serve the Negro community adequately.

The Cowles Foundation first granted $100,000, then another $25,000 toward building a new community center. Answering the foundation's challenge to the Negro community to raise a portion of the funds, donations by 767 Negro citizens and organizations produced another $13,000. For example, the Monarchs talked of furnishing one of the rooms for the anticipated new facility.[207] The Cowles Foundation also requested that the new center be named in memory of the late American statesman and humanitarian Wendell Willkie.[208] On June 14, 1951, the *Bystander* reported that the old building housing the former center had been sold, with the proceeds applied to the cost of the new structure. The new structure was to be located on the site of the old McHenry School at 900 17th Street.[209]

Staff members overseeing the transition from the old Negro Neighborhood Center facility to the new Willkie House were Lillian Edmunds, director; Arthur Edmunds, program assistant; James Bowman, boy's worker; Joyce Smith (Fant), girl's worker; and Mary Craddock (Rollison), secretary. Board members at the time of the transition were Archie Alexander, president; C. W. Harvey, vice president; Mrs. Willis Grant, secretary; Mrs. Thornburg Cowles, treasurer; plus Albert J. Robertson, Arthur Hill, Carl W. Mesmer, J.S. Russell, John Coleman, Mrs. Rudolph Weitz, Henry Wilcots, Mrs. Gregory Ransome, W. Lawrence Oliver, and Dr. E. Thomas Scales. Mr. Oliver chaired the fundraising campaign.[210]

A 1946 fund-raising brochure indicated a high level of activity at the center which would be replaced by the new facility. Clubs listed included Kit Kat, Bright Eyes, Blue Flowers, Young Teens, Brown Cubs, Puella LeGatoes, J.C.C., Mohawks, Rockettes, Voice Staff, Garden Club, Dilettante Club, and six organizations with a national affiliation.[211] Without question Willkie House remains embedded deeply in the minds and hearts of many people, especially those who as youngsters enjoyed the popular dances and weekly roller-skating sessions in the gym.

Willkie House has been remodeled since its opening and continues as a home away from home for many young people.

Lillian Edmunds was director of Willkie House for many years. (courtesy Margaret Garrison)

Willkie House, Des Moines, 1951 (Willkie House)

Across the street to the east today stands a beautiful elementary school named after Lillian Edmunds, who will always be associated with Willkie House and with the old Negro Community Center. Many directors followed Mrs. Edmunds — including Charlene Wharton, Helen Stevens, John Mapp, Marsha Collier, Jerry Jenkins, and presently Paulette Wiley — and with their leadership the center has continued to thrive. Today, though Willkie House struggles to finance its programs, it serves a broader multi-cultural population than ever before. Fred Gilbert currently serves as Willkie House's board president.

The Sanford Center, Sioux City

The Sanford Center on the west side of Sioux City, once known as the Booker T. Washington Center, began serving the city's African-American citizens in 1933. In 1925 Mary Treglia had become director of the Community House on the city's east side, which was home to nearly 20 different nationalities. The Community House provided a social gathering place, where clubs were organized for boys and girls as well as adults. Mrs. Treglia also formed the Women of All Nation's Club for mothers of the neighborhood, which lasted for decades and acknowledged the diverse backgrounds of the citizens of the area.

Sioux City's Community House, like the Negro Community Center in Des Moines, offered adult classes in English, reading, writing, and conversation for immigrants, as well as providing leadership and meeting space for many clubs and other activities.

Elzona Trosper, executive director, Sanford Center, Sioux City (Sanford Center)

But the Community House did not welcome the African-American population of Sioux City. Though Mrs. Treglia was considered a friend to all people, her philosophy seemed to be that separate facilities were necessary for white and black citizens of Sioux City. Although interested in providing educational and recreational programs for the African-Americans, Mrs. Treglia also seemed to accept racial segregation as gospel. For example, she resisted when a group of black women wanted to join the Women of All Nation's Club and suggested that the black women form their own club.

Meetings in the late 1920s with community leaders and representatives of various black men and women's clubs explored ways to provide a gathering place for the city's black residents. Eventually, the group elected officers and asked Mrs. Treglia to serve as executive supervisor of its new Booker T. Washington Center.[212] In time the center's programs expanded to include an educational program and a nursery school. There were also classes in music appreciation, public speaking, shorthand, history, science, and English. In 1936, the center opened a pre-school nursery for children of working mothers. Though established to serve the black people of Sioux City, the center welcomed white people as well, and the center's facilities were heavily used by all, particularly children.

Other visitors to the center included military personnel. Because of racial prejudice and segregation, black servicemen stationed at the Sioux City Air Base were prohibited from using local recreational facilities. In a de facto sense, they were restricted

to the air base. At the request of a concerned local army official, the Washington Center opened a servicemen's center. Staff and volunteers decorated and furnished a room for the men.

Elzona Trosper, an African-American, was executive director responsible for the Washington Center's day-to-day operation, but Mary Treglia helped to develop its programs and assisted with the general administration. Stella Sanford, who was active in the Community House, also played a large role in the Washington Center. In 1951 she and her husband, Arthur Sanford, financed the construction of a new facility under the supervision of Mrs. Treglia. Considered one of the most modern facilities of its kind in the United States, the Washington Center's large new building provided ample space for recreation, education, and social gatherings. Because of their generous support, the center's board of directors renamed the Booker T. Washington Center in the Sanfords' honor.[213] The Community House and the Sanford Center continued to operate with separate boards and budgets.[214] On October 23, 1953, the Sanford Community Center celebrated its twentieth anniversary, honoring Mrs. Treglia at that time.[215] Currently directed by George Boykin, the center continues to thrive with various programs to meet the changing needs of the community.

The Jane Boyd House, Cedar Rapids

The Jane Boyd House, located in the Oak Hill section of Cedar Rapids, was founded in 1921. Named after a first grade teacher turned social worker who came to Cedar Rapids from Tipton, Iowa, the center has served a multi-ethnic, low-income community from the time of its founding to the present. Now in its fourth building, Jane Boyd House offers a panoply of services to Cedar Rapids's black community, as well as to other ethnic groups. The building is used for club and community meetings and for many of the community's social events. It is home to the local neighborhood association, and the Cedar Rapids City Council has met there in its rotation around the Cedar Rapids area.

The center offers many community services, most of them "hands-on," with others being referrals. Areas addressed include tenant/landlord disputes, social security problems, and family issues. Despite the presence of many other professional agencies in the community, residents in this area have made Boyd House their agency of choice. Whatever the need, it usually can be met. There is a food bank at Boyd House, and bread is distributed twice

Young men's group, Sioux City, c.1949 (courtesy Frankie Williams)

weekly. There is also a clothing closet and a furniture connection.

The center has been a haven for children from the beginning. The Boyd House pre-school has operated for 45 years, providing care for three and four-year-olds four days a week, currently for $15 per week. For the minimal cost of membership, young people can participate in such sports as baseball, basketball, and karate. Families with several children and limited resources for outside entertainment and recreation have found this to be a great resource that fits well into their budget. Adults who came to the center as children return to serve as volunteers with their own children. The center has also embraced children that society has labeled "at risk." Parent education is another important part of the center's program, offering classes for single and teen parents.

A satellite center of Jane Boyd House, Harambee House in the Wellington Heights neighborhood focuses on middle school and high school students and gears its program for positive youth development. Harambee House students come to the main center for their athletic activities.

With the Oak Hill Manor senior-citizen complex right next door, Boyd House has provided a convenient congregate meal site. On occasion children from the pre-school have entertained the seniors at lunchtime with singing. Also at the center is an after-school club for latchkey kids from kindergarten through fifth grade. The after-school programs are designed to enhance their education, provide recreational activities, and raise self-esteem. Children in this program have adopted some of the senior citizens living next door and each spring make and deliver May baskets to them.

On Mondays people from all over Cedar Rapids and beyond the city limits come to receive treatment at the free medical clinic. St. Luke's Hospital and Mercy Hospital provide the clinic with rotating volunteer doctors and nurses, and there is one paid clinic administrator. The five-year old clinic, established by Dr. James Bell, has a well-child clinic, a women's clinic, and a men's clinic. Adults and children come for general services, including physicals for sports or for employment. Women may obtain a pap test or breast exam. There is lead screening and testing for HIV and sexually transmitted diseases.

Thus in a variety of ways Jane Boyd House serves a vital role to the African-American community of Cedar Rapids. Elizabeth Bender served as the executive director for 40 years. Currently Linda Winston is executive director, and Dorothy Petersen directs social development and developmental education.[216]

The Jesse Cosby Center, Waterloo

The Jesse Cosby Center in Waterloo was founded in 1966 and named after a community leader well-known for his work with African-American youth, especially a local youth choir. The Cosby Center remains a community gathering place, home to many African-American clubs and organizations. The Masons hold their lodge meetings there, as does the African-American Museum Society, and families use the facility for reunions and special celebrations. The Cosby Center is also a meeting place for a local AA group. In summer the Cosby Center offers recreational activities and a summer meals program. Once a church, the building now has an addition that serves as a congregate meal site, with both eat-in and "meals on wheels" accommodations. The center also provides low-income families with rent assistance, utility assistance, food vouchers, and other needed services.

The Cosby Center recently received a local grant from SPICE to research the barriers to medical assistance for African-Americans and how to overcome them. The staff is also researching the possibility of establishing a performing arts program for young people. Currently, Warren Wortham is executive director, and Willa Mae Wright is president of the board.[217]

Crocker Branch YMCA and Blue Triangle YWCA, Des Moines

Two other Iowa institutions that originated in the era of segregation were the Crocker Branch YMCA and the Blue Triangle YWCA. Located at 14th and Crocker in the heart of the black community on the west side of Des Moines, the Crocker Branch YMCA thrived as a neighborhood institution until the city's main YMCA finally opened its doors to African-Americans. Fond memories of the old Crocker Y still linger in the minds of the "boys," now senior citizens, who gather every spring for the Crocker Y reunions during Drake Relays weekend.

The Crocker Branch YMCA perhaps would not have become a reality without the driving force of local attorney S. Joe Brown. Brown's is a name that turns up repeatedly in the annals of African-American history in Iowa, attached to many causes and organizations, whether fraternal, civic, legal, cultural, religious, or educational.[218] Shortly after being discharged from military service at Fort Des Moines in 1917, Brown became aware of the Army's branch YMCA in downtown Des Moines — for white soldiers. Knowing that between 10 and 20 thousand Negro draftees were soon to be trained at Camp Dodge, he inquired as to what services

Adults who came to the [Jane Boyd House] center as children return to serve as volunteers with their own children.

Quentin Mease, executive director, Crocker Street YMCA (courtesy Jacqueline Harris)

would be open to them. When informed that none were to be available, Brown approached the state's YMCA secretary in charge of Army Y work. Brown was promised that if he could secure a suitable building and organize a committee to oversee the work, services could be made available to Negro soldiers.[219]

Brown very quickly secured the basement of Union Congregational Church, located at 10th and Park streets. His committee consisted of Rev. George W. Robinson (Corinthian Baptist Church), Rev. Samuel L. Birt (St. Paul's AME Church), attorney John L. Thompson, Harrison Gould, A. M. White, C. L. Stewart, and George Smith. Edward Ross of Kansas City was appointed executive director of the new Park Street Army YMCA, which opened on January 1, 1918. This service organization would continue until after the signing of the Armistice in November 1918, when all of the soldiers were discharged.[220]

One of the center's most successful activities had been a boy's Bible class. It was suggested that this effort should be taken over and continued by the local YMCA board. Though receptive to the idea, the board agreed that if the Negro citizens could furnish a meeting place, the Y board would secure funds needed for the salary of an executive secretary.[221] A new management committee formed, chaired by Dr. W. H. Lowrey. A building was erected, named the Crocker Street Branch YMCA, and formally opened on July 1, 1919, with Ernest C. Robinson as its first executive secretary. Rev. A. L. Gaines, bishop of the Northwestern Conference of the AME Church, was guest speaker at the dedication services.[222]

The Crocker Branch had a comprehensive program, with varied activities for boys and young men. Boy's clubs, basketball, softball, baseball, tennis, track, boxing, camping, religious education classes, table tennis, reading, hiking, discussion groups, father and son events, and many other social and recreational pleasures were included in its activities. These activities continued at the original location at 14th and Crocker until 1945, when the Y moved to 1333 Keosauqua. The Y's new home was the former USO building for black soldiers and WAACS. It was much larger than the Y's original building, and it contained a recreational center, a kitchen, and several club rooms. The added space of the new facility allowed the Y to expand its services to include women and girls. A. P. Trotter chaired the Committee of Management from 1939 to 1957.[223]

In the late 1940s the activities of the Crocker Branch YMCA increasingly merged with those of the YMCA programs of Des Moines and the North Central YMCA Council. Mr. Trotter, as chairman of the Committee on Management, was given a seat on the board of directors of the Des Moines YMCA. Many of the lay leaders of the Crocker Branch also sat on committees related to the total YMCA work in the city.[224]

Some of the men serving as executive secretary of the Crocker Branch YMCA over the years were Gordon Kitchen, Arnold Bannister, La Mar Ellis, Paul A. DeVan, James F. Dixon, and Quentin R. Mease.[225] Mease, a former resident of Buxton, became executive secretary of the Crocker Y at age 19. Now in his 90s and residing in Houston, Texas, Mr. Mease is one of the directors revered by many of the "Crocker Branch Reunion Bunch" since their younger days. He served the Crocker Branch for several years before going off to the armed forces. After leaving the service, Mr. Mease obtained his master's degree in social work from George Williams College in Chicago. In 1949, he was sent by the YMCA to Houston on a special three-year assignment as director of the Building Program. In 1950, he became executive director of the Bagby Street Branch YMCA, now the South Central Branch YMCA. He held that position until his retirement in 1975. Mr. Mease's community involvements in Houston have been extremely numerous, including many years' service on the Harrison County Hospital District Board, 25 of them as chair. A Houston hospital has since been named in his honor.[226] The men of Crocker Branch were fortunate to have Quentin Mease come their way.

The Crocker Branch YMCA, a historic institution conceived out of separatism, encouraged generations of African-American boys and girls to fulfill their potential as Christian men and women. Many who have participated in the Y's activities have become outstanding leaders in education, business, and the professions, as well as in social service organizations, throughout the nation. Each year since 1978, during Drake Relays week, a reunion of the Crocker Branch brings together many of these individuals to share precious moments from the past.

There is always talk at the reunions about those special days at summer camp. The men hold those camp experiences dear to their hearts. All summer long as young men, they would look forward to going off to the camp near Boone. The summer camp scheduled its sessions for white campers first, reserving only the very last session of summer for black campers. Yet they still loved it. Just being there was a joy and a privilege for these mostly low-income young men from around the city.[227] An undated *Iowa Bystander* clipping from the period when Quentin Mease was still in charge announced that the number of campers ranged between 130 and 145 boys.[228] Dr. James Bowman, a former camper, recalls that the Y Camp seemed like the land of plenty, especially the food. It was, he said, like "dying and going to Heaven."[229]

When the Crocker Y reunions began, event organizers had a list of 280 names. Now there are fewer than 120 names on the list. Forty men attended the twentieth reunion in 1998. Quentin Mease was present at the affair, which was held at the new John R. Grubb YMCA, the first Y built in the African-American community of Des Moines since the Crocker Branch.[230] Most of the men attending the reunion were in their mid-70s. Out of the harsh reality of its beginnings in segregation came strong bonds of lifelong brotherhood among the men of the Crocker Branch, and their reunions always warm the hearts of onlookers as well as the men themselves.

The Blue Triangle YWCA

The Blue Triangle, a segregated branch of the YWCA of Greater Des Moines, was established in 1919 and existed until 1947. A cultural, educational, and social center for women, the Blue Triangle Y also provided recreational activities.[231] An undated *Bystander* clipping titled "Getting in Trim" announced a body-building class and reducing exercises, complete with a body-building machine. The class met every Friday afternoon for two hours. The article noted humorously that the class was open to all adults . . . of all sizes.[232] The Y building, a large house at the top of the hill at 14th and Center, stood as a beacon to young women. It was a comfortable place with floral chintz drapes, airy wicker furniture, and a piano in the common room.

A legacy of the Blue Triangle that lives on today is the previously mentioned Booklover's Club. On August 7, 1947, the *Iowa Bystander* noted that

> . . . the August temperature, which has been hitting and passing the 100 degree mark this week, was ideal last Friday when members of the Booklover's Club of the Young Women's Association gathered at the home of Mr. and Mrs. William Paris, 1120 17th Street, where Mrs. Paris was hostess at a picnic meeting. Clouds hovered about the sky throughout the afternoon.

> Members dressed in cool frocks came laden with baskets, bowls and bags filled with a variety of foods that made a grand feast when spread on tables that had been extended on the velvety lawn. Under the shade trees, and surrounded by high hedges and flowers growing in attractive plots, the Booklovers found comfor-table seats in lawn chairs and swings which were dressed in colorful handmade coverings. Mrs. John Drew, one of the first-comers, with a guest, Mrs. Mary A. Smith of Minneapolis, got an early start on battling the mosquitoes. Other members, Mesdames Gertrude North, Godfrey Williams, Maude Woods, Cecelia Carl, Mable Mason, J. G. Browne, Lillian Scales, were arriving as Mrs. Jeanne Morris, nearby neighbor came with one of her favorite angel food cakes . . . a surprise for the picnic menu. Another neighbor, Mrs. J. Q. Evans, made several trips with trays of her specialty . . . hot rolls. Mrs. Maude Howard, former member, found a seat in a swing as member Korinne Jackson, sporting a birthday orchid, deposited a large bowl of her favorite dish, Spanish rice.

> There were salads, meats, relishes, and all of the picnic bill of fare brought by other members, which served as topics for discussion of "how did you make it?" and "what's in this?" and "my diet!". . . . But all of the food managed to be devoured. To add to the dessert, the hostess, Mrs. Paris, whipped up one of her favorites, a cherry-rice dish made simply with rice, whipped cream and cherry sauce.

> Mrs. Margaret Lowrey, president of the club, held a brief opening and presented Mrs. Adah Johnson who reviewed the book of the month, Chequer Board by Nevil Shute. Following discussions and comparison with Kingsblood Royal by Sinclair Lewis, officers agreed that the summer meetings were drawing more of the members out to the book reviews, and then set their next meeting for Friday, August 15, at Union Park where they will join the Old Settlers' picnic.[233]

How many other stories of the camaraderie of so many black social, fraternal, cultural, and civic organizations lie untold in the minds of many of Iowa's African-American residents — and in newspaper archives and in clippings in drawers and boxes hidden or forgotten? We fear to think of the history tossed out by someone with the shrug, "what good is this?"

The Crocker Branch YMCA, a historic institution conceived out of separatism, encouraged generations of African-American boys and girls to fulfill their potential as Christian men and women.

(Above) As this invitation indicates, the YMCA buildings in Buxton were used for social and community events. (SHSI Des Moines)

(Above right) Mason City Hi Y group, 1953 (courtesy Meredith Saunders)

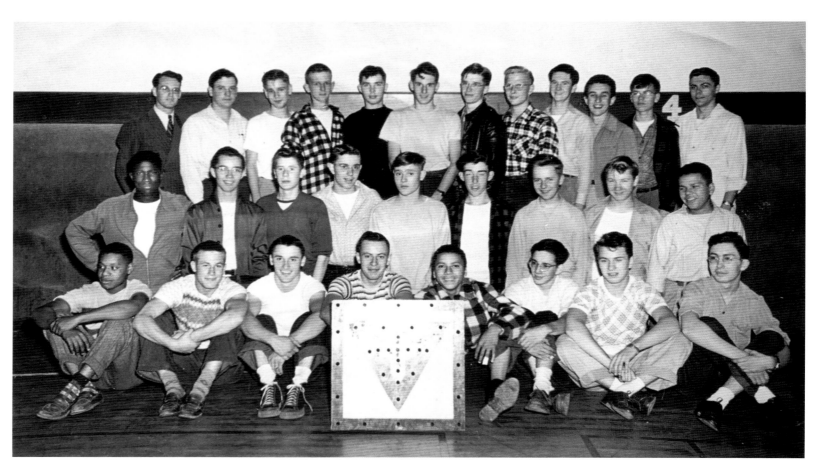

A Multitude of Iowa's African-American Organizations

Through an extensive search of the files of the *Iowa State Bystander*, the *Iowa Bystander*, the *Persinger Times*, and the *Persinger Saturday Review* — and by tapping the memories of a multitude of individuals — the names of many other clubs and organizations have been uncovered. The list on pages 56–57 contains organizations that were in existence for various periods of time between the mid-1880s and the present. In some cases it is uncertain what their origins, purposes, or missions may have been, or whether they may have been church or fraternally connected. Yet whatever its limitations, this listing, like the historical sketches that precede it, reflects the extensive and continuing involvement of Iowa's African-Americans in social organizations.

Conclusion

Throughout their history, Iowa's African-Americans have joined clubs and organizations of their personal choosing — reflecting their specific interests or according to what felt best or fit their own profiles — or those that they have been invited to join. (Lest we forget, there were individuals who declined or chose not to partake in any social organizations.) Whatever the reasons for their joining, whatever their underlying passions, people have involved themselves in the missions of their respective organizations. They have truly aligned themselves with the membership or perhaps in other cases they have been carried by the membership. Some became leaders. Others became reliable and dedicated workers, the backbone of a strong organization. Like individuals, organizations will always be

judged by people in other organizations as well as by their own membership. Throughout history, caste and class have played a major role in shaping social relationships and in the way we perceive one another.

People continually put others in categories, attempting to draw lines between lower, middle, and upper classes of all ethnic groups. In 1957 the late E. Franklin Frazier, former chair of the Sociology Department at Howard University, rocked the middle class of black America with his widely read and controversial book titled *Black Bourgeoisie.* Professor Frazier attempted to determine how people viewed black society, especially the black middle class. Frazier found that African-Americans, like all other people, are judged on manifold levels. They are judged by those of the majority race, by other races, and most certainly by those of their own race.[234]

But we would be wise to remember the words of Booker T. Washington. "Do not judge us by the heights we have attained," Washington said, "but by the depths from which we've come!"[235]

Though our paths to the present have differed, we have all come from the same beginnings. For some, the paths have been smooth; for others, the paths have been rough. Many paid awesome dues for the progress made by a multitude. In many ways, the climb has been prolonged. It has been nearly a century and half since Emancipation and much has happened.

In Iowa as elsewhere in the United States, African-American organizations have sustained our communities. Many individuals have worked hard, given their lives and souls to their fraternal lodges, clubs, sororities and fraternities. But greater yet is what many of these organizations have given back. Brotherhood. Sisterhood. Family. Self-esteem. Fellowship. And an infinite array of other bequests and accolades.

(Above) YWCA campers near Boone (courtesy Nathaline Dixon)

(Left) Y Boys Camp leaders and counselors, 1954 (courtesy Ron McClain)

A Multitude of Iowa's African-American Organizations

Through an extensive search of the files of the *Iowa State Bystander,* the *Iowa Bystander,* the *Persinger Times,* and the *Persinger Saturday Review* — and by tapping the memories of a multitude of individuals — the names of many other clubs and organizations have been uncovered. The following list contains organizations that were in existence for various periods of time between the mid-1880s and the present. In some cases it is uncertain what their origins, purposes, or missions may have been, or whether they may have been church or fraternally connected. Yet whatever its limitations, this listing, like the historical sketches that precede it, reflects the extensive and continuing involvement of Iowa's African-Americans in social organizations.

Albia
- Young People's Social Club
- Charity Lodge #2192

Burlington
- Silver Crescent Club
- Hyacinthia Dramatic Club
- Progressive Club
- Princess Hager #7
- Anna Griggs Signet Club

Buxton
- Knights and Daughters of the Tabernacle
- Virginia Queen's Court
- WCTU
- Odd Fellows
- Masonics
- Elks
- Knights of Pythias
- Gold Palace Gun Club
- Ladies Industrial Club
- Federated Women's Clubs
- Sweet Magnolias Club
- Silver Leaf Club
- Fidelity Club
- Literary Society
- Fannie Barrier Williams Club
- Self-Culture Club
- Progressive Women's Club

Cedar Rapids
- Ladies Afternoon Social Club
- Ladies Industrial Club
- King's Daughters
- Busy Bee Club
- Dark Horses
- Fleur De Lis Club
- Sister's Club
- Just Us Club
- Carnation Club
- Fellowship Club
- Criterion Club
- George Washington Carver Club
- African-American Women's Club

Clinton
- Friendship Club
- Masonites

Council Bluffs
- 20th Century Civic and Art Club

Des Moines
- Ambassadors
- Au Fait Club
- Atelier Guild
- Arctic Tabernacle #472
- Billikin High School and College Dance Club
- Bonne Aimees
- Bee Hive Sewing Circle
- Buxton Club #1
- Buxton Club #2
- Buxton Iowa Club, Inc.
- Bow Knots Club
- Bright Eyes
- Blue Flowers
- Brown Cubs
- Community Center Garden Club
- Donkeys
- Dilettante Club
- DBQ Club
- Deluxe Club
- Dramatic Club
- Daughters of Des Moines Club
- El Producto Club
- El Domingo Club
- Elegant Eight Bridge Club
- Elite Society
- Ebbonettes Club
- Entre Nous Club
- Frederick Douglas Club
- Four L's Club
- Fortnightly Club
- Fraternal Temple Association
- Grand Auction Bridge Club
- G.O.P. Negro Club
- Golden Ager's Club
- Rose L. Gregg Club
- Hands of Love Club
- Lockhart Club
- H.B.S.R.C. Club
- Association of Iowa Clubs, Inc.
- Iowa Buxton Club
- Intellectual Improvement Club
- Jolly 12 Club
- Jolly "S" Club
- Jack and Jill
- King Solomon's Commandery #9
- King Solomon's Commandery #2
- Knights of Pythias
- Knights and Daughters of Tabor
- Knights of the Templar
- Kit-Kat Club
- King David's Temple #444
- Ladies Afternoon Social Club
- LaParisiane Club
- L. T. Club
- LaMercredi Club
- Links, Inc.
- La Mesa Savings Club
- LeCremedelles Club
- LaDemoiselles Club
- Loyal Friends Club
- La Copperettes Club
- Merry Fourteen Club
- Modernistic Club
- Mary Church Terrell Clubs (#1, #2, and #3)

- Mother's Club
- Manhatten Club
- Mary McLeod Bethune Club
- Masonics
- Monarchs
- Mohawks Club
- Mary B. Talbert Club
- Naomi Court #3
- Negro Republican Women's Club
- Odd Fellows
- Onanas
- Old Settlers' Club
- Olympian Club
- Pathfinder's Club
- Pin Club
- Puella LeGatoes Club
- Philomatheon Debs
- Progressive Club
- Royal Senators
- Royal Contract Bridge Club
- Regal Contract Bridge Club
- Royal Dukes
- Roosevelt Club
- Rockets Club
- Rhythm Frolic Club
- Saturday Night Bridge Club
- Sophisticated Does
- Social Arts Club
- Shakespeare Club
- Socialite Queens
- Silhouettes
- Sister's Club
- T-CWANS

- Top Hatters Club
- 20th Century Club
- Ten Keys Club
- T.O.B. Club
- Three Purpose Club
- Triple A's Club
- Treble Leaf Art Club
- Thimble Club
- United Brothers of Friendship Club
- Vogettes Club
- WYLTK Club
- Widow's Industrial Club
- Winthrop Club
- WCTU, Young Men's Social Club
- Young Men's Republican Club

Fort Madison
- Fidelity Lodge #30
- Odd Fellows

Keokuk
- Princess Hagar #7
- Star Lodge #5
- Noble Tent #99
- Rebecca Tent
- Get-Together Club
- Self-Culture Club
- Union Lodge #1
- York Lodge #8
- Colored Girl's Rescuers

Marshalltown
- Paul Lawrence Dunbar Club
- Just-Rite Club

Mason City
- Just- Rite Club

Muchakinock
- Household of Ruth
- Sons and Daughters of Israel

Oskaloosa
- Mother's Club
- Progressive Club
- Knights of Pythias

Ottumwa
- Ottumwa Royal Entertainers
- Knights of Pythias
- Ida B. Wells Club
- Elite Social Club
- Entre Nous Club
- Pleasure Club
- Ladies Antiquarian Club

Sioux City
- Hour of Pleasure Club
- Young Matron's Art Club

Waterloo
- Mary McLeod Bethune Club

Lynda Walker-Webster, whose family settled in Iowa in the 1850s, is a published poet, freelance writer, and inspirational speaker. Former editor of Hawkeye Happenings *and columnist for the* Iowa Bystander, *she is historian for the National Iowa Clubs, Inc., and for St. Paul AME Church in Des Moines. She has served on the boards of many local, regional, and national civic and cultural organizations.*

Ms. Walker-Webster studied at Drake University, New York University, Yale University, and the University of Illinois — Chicago. She has traveled in Europe, Africa, the Caribbean, and South America, studying and documenting behavioral, cultural, and ethnic mores. She has also worked as a scribe for a medical research team. Currently a housing counselor in the Department of Community Development of the City of Des Moines, Lynda Walker-Webster lives in Des Moines with her daughter, Amandalynn.

Author's acknowledgments: A most sincere thanks to all of the organizations and individuals that searched their archives and memories to provide me with historical information and documentation, and mostly for entrusting me with their precious pictures. This assistance has enriched my reflections and broadened my perspective regarding the social, fraternal, cultural, and civic involvements of our African-American brothers and sisters who crossed the borders into Iowa, dating from those early territorial days to the present. I especially thank those to whom I returned for a second interview — after my briefcase, full of interview notes, was taken from the library.

But most of all, I thank my two Amandas. I thank Amanda Walker for planting the seed while I listened to our history at her knees as a child. I thank Amandalynn Webster for being patient while suffering through parental neglect as I struggled through this chapter, twice!

Notes

1. Anna Arnold Hedgeman, *The Trumpet Sounds* (New York: Holt, Rinehart and Winston, 1964). Born in Marshalltown, Iowa, in 1899, Anna Arnold Hedgeman grew up in Anoka, Minnesota. In 1922 she received her B.A. degree from Hamline University in St. Paul, Minnesota, and later did post-graduate work at the University of Minnesota and the New York School of Social Work. From 1922 to 1924 she was professor of English at Rust College in Holly Springs, Mississippi. Subsequently she served as executive director at many YWCA branches in New York City, as that city's first consultant on racial problems, and as the first woman member of the New York mayor's cabinet. In 1946 Anna Arnold Hedgeman was appointed dean of women at Howard University in Washington. She was named one of "50 Extraordinary Women of Achievement in New York City" (1978) and featured in "I Dream a World," a major photographic exhibit about women that toured the nation in the 1990s.

2. Robert R. Dykstra, "Dr. Emerson's Sam: Black Iowans before the Civil War," *Palimpsest* (1982): 81.

3. William L. Hewitt, "So Few Undesirables: Race, Residence, and Occupation in Sioux City, 1890–1925," *AI* 50 (1989/1990): 160, 161, 172.

4. Dorothy Schwieder, Joseph Hraba, and Elmer Schwieder, *Buxton: Work and Racial Equality in a Coal Mining Community* (Ames: Iowa State Univ. Press, 1987).

5. William Edward Burghardt DuBois, *The Souls of Black Folk* (New York: Vintage, 1968), 139.

6. Ibid., 140, 141.

7. Dykstra, 81.

8. The *Oskaloosa Herald* column "Our Colored Society: The Ins and Outs of the Local Colony and Their Friends" was written by A. G. Clark in the years 1903–1915.

9. Augustus Low and Virgil A. Clift, *The Encyclopedia of Black America* (New York: McGraw-Hill, 1981), 395.

10. August Meier and Elliott M. Rudwick, *From Plantation to Ghetto: An Interpretive History of American Negroes* (New York: Hill and Wang, 1966), 83.

11. Barbara Sue Williams interview; "The Knights of Pythias and the Order of Calanthe," privately printed history provided by Ms. Williams.

12. Low and Clift, 395–96.

13. Ibid., 395.

14. Ibid., 395.

15. Ibid., 395.

16. Ibid., 396.

17. Ibid., 396.

18. Bertie Hogan, Mildred Graves, and Clemmie Hightower interviews. All are members of the Masonic family and OES.

19. J. M. Dixon, *Centennial History of Polk County and Early Des Moines* (Des Moines, 1876)

20. *Iowa Bystander*, March 1, 1895.

21. *1903 Northwest Annual AME Conference*, hosted by St. Paul AME Church, Des Moines. Conference booklet in author's possession.

22. "Negroes Purchase Hall for Lodges: Undertake Project of Public Character," *Des Moines Register and Leader*, Aug. 1, 1912.

23. Ibid.

24. "The Daughters of Isis," typescript provided by Bertie Hogan, Des Moines.

25. Ibid.

26. Ibid.

27. Ibid.

28. Ibid.; Bertie Hogan, Mildred Graves, and Clemmie Hightower interviews.

29. Ibid.

30. Ibid.

31. Clemmie Hightower interview.

32. Bertie Hogan, Mildred Graves, and Clemmie Hightower interviews.

33. "The Daughters of Isis."

34. "Oddfellows to Meet," *Iowa Bystander*, July 20, 1894.

35. Low and Clift, 395.

36. Ibid.

37. Barbara Sue Williams interview; unpublished documents on the Knights of Pythias and the Courts of Calanthe, in author's possession.

38. Ibid.

39. Barbara Sue Williams interview; unpublished documents on the Knights of Pythias and the Courts of Calanthe, in author's possession.

40. Ibid.

41. Ibid.

42. Ibid.

43. Ibid.

44. Ibid.

45. Ibid.

46. Ibid.

47. Ibid.

48. Ibid.

49. Ibid.

50. Ibid.

51. "69th Middlewestern States Association Convention," June 17–21, Des Moines, Iowa. Booklet in author's possession.

52. "Hawkeye Lodge #160, Mortgage Burning Ceremony," Dec. 5, 1948. Souvenir booklet in author's possession.

53. Ibid.

54. Ibid.

55. Ibid.

56. Ibid.

57. Ibid.

58. Ibid.

59. Ibid.

60. *Iowa Bystander*, May 23, 1940.

61. Mary Ruth Simmons and Helen Williams interviews. Mary Ruth Simmons, PGDR, is Past Loyal Daughter Ruler, Rose Council, and Past District Deputy. Helen Williams, PGDR, is Past Daughter Ruler, Rose Temple #33.

62. Ibid.

63. Mary Ruth Simmons and Helen Williams interviews.

64. Ibid.; interviews with Gayle Ashby Watkins and JoAnn Henderson Rose, both former members of the Junior Herd Majorettes, and the author's personal remembrances as a former member herself.

65. Ibid.

66. Ibid.

67. Helen Williams, Mary Ruth Simmons, Arretta M. Butler, and Albert Butler interviews. Arretta M. Butler, PGDR, is past president Middlewestern States Association and auxiliary president. Albert Butler, PGER, is district deputy of Iowa.

68. Albert Butler interview.

69. "Hawkeye Lodge #160, Mortgage Burning Ceremony."

70. Ibid.

71. "A Few Facts about Iowa Negroes," 1931. NAACP brochure in author's possession.

72. Patricia (Graves) Miller interview. Ms. Miller is a former member of the Sisterhood Majorette Group.

73. Sigma Pi Phi, Gamma Eta Boulé Chapter, "10th Anniversary Celebration," July 4, 1994. Booklet in author's possession.

74. Ibid.

75. Ibid.

76. Paul W. Danforth interview. Mr. Danforth is Past Sire Archon of Gamma Eta Boulé.

77. Low and Clift, 397.

78. Betty Gause interview. Ms. Gause was director of Student Activities, Drake University.

79. Lawrence C. Howard, "The Des Moines Negro and His Contribution to American Life," *AI* (1950): 215. Mr. Howard, a Des Moines native and Drake University graduate, was a member of Alpha Phi Alpha Fraternity and Phi Beta Kappa.

80. Paul W. Danforth interview. Mr. Danforth is a member of Alpha Phi Alpha.

81. Low and Clift, 397; Betty Gause interview.

82. Clinton Burkhall Jr. interview. Mr. Burkhall is a member of Kappa Alpha Psi.

83. *Iowa Bystander,* April 25, 1940.

84. Howard, "The Des Moines Negro," 216.

85. *Iowa Bystander,* Aug. 7, 1947.

86. *Iowa Bystander,* Sept. 4, 1947.

87. Ibid.

88. Ibid.

89. Low and Clift, 397.

90. Donald Graves Jr. interview. Mr. Graves is former Basileus of Mu Omicron Chapter, Omega Psi Phi.

91. "Black Sorority Boom," *Ebony Magazine,* Oct. 1998, 72; see also Low and Clift, 397.

92. "History of Phi Chapter of Delta Sigma Theta Sorority," typescript provided by Soror Eleanor Archer, in author's possession.

93. Ibid.

94. *Iowa Bystander,* April 11, 1940.

95. "History of Phi Chapter." Soror Sharon Coleman interview.

96. "History of Phi Chapter."

97. Ibid.; *Ebony Magazine,* Oct. 1998, 69; Lynn Morrissey, "Delta Sigma Theta Sorority Marks 85 Years of Community Action," *American Legacy* 4 (1998): 28.

98. Soror Reneé Hardman interview. Ms. Hardman is Basileus, Phi Chapter, Delta Sigma Theta Sorority.

99. Ibid.

100. Low and Clift, 397; Soror Sharon Coleman interview.

101. *Ebony Magazine,* Oct. 1998, 72.

102. Ibid.

103. *Iowa Bystander,* Nov. 18, 1932.

104. *Iowa Bystander,* Feb. 17, 1933.

105. *Iowa Bystander,* Dec. 2, 1942.

106. Soror Dr. Mary S. Chapman interview. Dr. Chapman is Past Basileus, Iota Zeta Omega Chapter, Alpha Kappa Alpha Sorority.

107. Low and Clift, 397; Soror Dr. Mary Chapman interview.

108. Iota Zeta Omega Chapter, Alpha Kappa Alpha Sorority, "The 21st Annual Scholar-ship Cotillion Memory Book and Program," April 11, 1998. Booklet in author's possession.

109. Soror Dr. Mary Chapman interview.

110. Ibid.

111. Soror Frances Cuie interview. Mrs. Cuie, a retired buyer for Younker's department store (unusual for her time), is a proud and dedicated member of AKA.

112. Soror Dr. Mary Chapman interview.

113. Peggy Whitaker interview. Ms. Whitaker is a charter member, Soror and Anti-Basileus, Epsilon Theta Sigma Chapter, Sigma Gamma Rho.

114. *Ebony Magazine,* Oct. 1998, 72.

115. *Communicator,* Aug. 6, 1994.

116. Soror Frances Hawthorne interview. Ms. Hawthorne is a charter member, Nu Mu Zeta Chapter, Zeta Phi Beta Sorority.

117. Soror Joyce Bruce and Soror Paula Duke interviews. Ms. Bruce is basileus and Ms. Duke a member of Nu Mu Zeta Chapter, Zeta Phi Beta Sorority.

118. Soror Frances Hawthorne interview.

119. *Iowa Bystander,* Aug. 19, 1937.

120. *Iowa Bystander,* Sept. 18, 1947.

121. Ibid.

122. *Ebony Magazine,* Oct. 1998, 70.

123. Ibid.

124. Ashley Montague, *Man's Most Dangerous Myth: The Fallacy of Race* (New York: Columbia Univ. Press, 1945), 78.

125. Maya Angelou, *Wouldn't Take Nothing for My Journey Now* (New York: Random House, 1993), 28.

126. Paul W. Danforth and Edward C. Harris interviews. Mr. Danforth and Mr. Harris are long-time members of the Roosevelt Club.

127. Ibid.

128. Harbon Merritt, Chauncey Bailey, and Edward Reeves interviews. Mssrs. Merritt, Bailey, and Reeves are long-time members of the Monarch Club.

129. Chauncey Bailey interview.

130. Ibid.

131. Ibid.; Harbon Merritt interview.

132. Ibid.

133. James Bethel interview. Mr. Bethel is a retired member of the Royal Dukes. See also "Royal Dukes 50th Anniversary Souvenir Program," Oct. 22, 1977. Booklet in author's possession.

134. James Bethel and Virgil Miller interviews. Like Mr. Bethel, Mr. Miller is a Royal Dukes member. See also "Royal Dukes 50th Anniversary Souvenir Program."

135. Ibid.

136. Ibid.

137. Virgil Miller interview. Mr. Miller is a Royal Dukes member.

138. *Iowa Bystander,* Aug. 26, 1937.

139. Linda (Frazier) Carter interview. Ms. Carter is the daughter of Olympian Club member Jesse Frazier.

140. Informal conversations with a group of Cedar Rapids young women at a social event, July 1998.

141. Elizabeth Lindsey Davis, *Lifting As We Climb: The History of the National Association of Colored Women* (n.p., 1933), 5.

142. Iowa Federation of Colored Women's Clubs (IFCWC) files, SHSI Des Moines.

143. Ibid.; see also IFCWC 50th anniversary convention booklet, 1952.

144. Davis, *Lifting As We Climb,* 152.

145. IFCWC files.

146. *Iowa Bystander,* May 23, 1940.

147. See Iowa Association, "65th Annual Convention," June 2–11, 1967, for a historical sketch. Booklet in author's possession.

148. Iowa Association. "50th Anniversary Convention," June 8–11, 1952, booklet.

149. Iowa Association, "65th Annual Convention Booklet"; see also "50th Anniversary Convention."

150. Iowa Association, "65th Annual Convention Booklet."

151. Ibid.; IFCWC files.

152. Davis, *Lifting As We Climb,* 198; St. Paul AME Church, *125th Anniversary Book,* Oct. 1998.

153. *Burlington Hawkeye,* Oct. 20, l969.

154. Iowa Association, "50th Anniversary Convention Booklet."

155. IFCWC files.

156. Geraldine Daniels interview. Ms. Daniels is a member of the Tawasi Club and the IACW.

Hiram Lodge #19 F. & A.M. Davenport, 1962 (courtesy Melvin Grimes)

157. Ibid.

158. *Iowa Bystander* clipping, June 1964; Ronene (Parkey) Harris interview.

159. Tereé Caldwell Johnson, "The Links, Inc., Des Moines Chapter: 40th Anniversary Narrative" [for slide presentation], Nov. 1997. Ms. Johnson is a past president of the chapter.

160. Ibid.; Linda Carter interview.

161. Leola Nelson Bergmann, *The Negro in Iowa* (Iowa City: SHSI, 1948; repr. 1969), 62–63.

162. Schwieder, Hraba, and Schwieder, 158.

163. "History of Mary Church Terrell Clubs," typescript in author's possession; Davis, *Lifting As We Climb,* 163.

164. Ibid.

165. Leola Davis interview. Ms. Davis was a member of Mary Church Terrell #3.

166. "History of Mary Church Terrell Clubs."

167. Ibid.; Leola Davis interview. Ms. Davis is a member of Mary Church Terrell #2.

168. Leola Davis interview. Mary Church Terrell #1 and #2 were IACW clubs but have been independent of the federation for approximately 20 years.

169. Elsa Connor interview. Ms. Connor was president of Mary Church Terrell #3. See also unpublished documents regarding Mary Church Terrell #3, in author's possession.

170. Josephine Pickett interview. Ms. Pickett was a member of the Three Purpose Club.

171. Ellen Robinson interview. Ms. Robinson was a member of the Winthrop Club.

172. Bertharina Cropp interview. Ms. Cropp is a former member of the Puella LeGatoes Club.

173. *Iowa Bystander* clipping, May or June 1963, in author's possession.

174. Bertharina Cropp interview.

175. "Booklover's Christmas Luncheon Program," 1997; Leola Davis interview.

176. Essie Britton, " The Negro in Iowa: History of the Colored Race of People Residing in Keokuk and Vicinity," undated typescript in author's possession.

177. *Iowa Bystander,* Jan. 3, 1896.

178. Ibid.

179. *Iowa Bystander,* May 19, 1940.

180. *Iowa Bystander,* June 15, 1950.

181. *Iowa Bystander,* April 26, 1962.

182. D. Camille Bradley interview. See also *Iowa Bystander* clipping, December 1963, in author's possession.

183. "First Annual Convention of Associated Iowa Clubs and Central States Gold Tournament," Minneapolis, Aug. 14–15, 1937, souvenir program booklet.

184. *Minneapolis Spokesman,* Aug. 13, 1937.

185. *San Francisco Examiner,* May 26, 1991.

186. Lynda Walker-Webster, Iowa Club of Des Moines member and editor of *Hawkeye Happenings,* newsletter of the National Iowa Clubs.

187. "Buxton Iowa Club," 1983. Brochure in author's possession.

188. *Iowa Bystander* clipping, 1940, in author's possession.

189. Britton, "The Negro in Iowa."

190. "Roy Leonard Rollen VFW, Auxiliary Post #5487, Twenty-first Anniversary,"1967. Booklet in author's possession.

191. Clemmie Hightower interview.

192. Aurelia Rhodes and Fay R. Winters interviews. Ms. Rhodes and Ms. Winters are charter members of the Bow Knots Club.

193. *Iowa Bystander,* Aug. 19, 1937. It is not clear if the mansion noted in this article is the Salisbury House or a previous mansion in which Mr. Carl Weeks may have resided.

194. *Iowa Bystander,* Aug. 5, 1937.

195. Author's recollections, clippings, and club notes collected as a member of both organizations.

196. Bertharina Cropp interview. Ms. Cropp is the wife of Ambassador member William (Bill) Cropp.

197. Undated Philomatheon Debs brochure; Paula Walker Lane, Marsha Fowler Madison, and Noretta Fowler Wadsworth interviews. Ms. Lane was an organizer and charter member of the Philomatheon Debs.

198. Lane, Madison, and Wadsworth interviews.

199. "History of Jack and Jill, Inc.: National"; "History of Jack and Jill, Inc.: Des Moines"; Veola Perry interview. Ms. Perry is a past parent member of the Des Moines local chapter.

200. *Iowa Bystander* clipping, Spring 1951. See also "Negro Citizens Ask Community Center Head Be Removed," *Des Moines Register and Leader,* July 9, 1922.

201. Photos of the Willkie House and the old Community Center show Eleanor Roosevelt and Mrs. Edmunds escorted into the Center by a local Boy Scout Troop. Other photos show Dr. Mary McLeod Bethune inside the Center with various groups.

202. Lillian Edmunds, "Some General Facts about the Negro Community Center" [Executive Director's Report], 1935.

203. Ibid.

204. Ibid.

205. *Iowa Bystander* clipping, 1930s or 1940s, in author's possession.

206. Edmunds, "Some General Facts."

207. *Iowa Bystander* clipping, Spring 1951, in author's possession.

208. Ibid.

209. *Iowa Bystander,* June 14, 1951.

210. "A Portal to New Opportunity," a Willkie House brochure from the early 1950s.

211. Ibid.

212. Suzanne O'Dea Schenken, "The Immigrant's Advocate: Mary Treglia and the Sioux City Community House, 1921–1959," *AI* 50 (1989/1990): 187, 194.

213. Ibid., 194.

214. Ibid.

215. Ibid., 194–96; Arretta M. Butler interview. Ms. Butler is a former Sanford Center board member.

216. Dorothy Petersen interview. Ms. Peterson is director of Social Development and Developmental Education, Jane Boyd Center, Cedar Rapids, Iowa.

217. Warren Wortham interview. Mr. Worthan is director of Jesse Cosby Center, Waterloo, Iowa.

218. "50th Anniversary Program and History of Crocker Branch YMCA," booklet.

219. Ibid.

220. Ibid.

221. Ibid.

222. Ibid.

223. Ibid.

224. Ibid.

225. Ibid.

226. Jacqueline (Mease) Harris interview. Ms. Harris is the niece of Quentin M. Mease. See also "A Tribute to a Community Builder: Honoring Quentin Mease," a program brochure produced by the Human Enrichment of Life Programs, Inc., in connection with the 1980 Helping Hands Award Program, Houston, Texas, Feb. 12, 1980.

227. *DMR,* June 7, 1998.

228. *Iowa Bystander* clipping, late 1930s, in author's possession.

229. *DMR,* June 7, 1998.

230. Ibid.

231. Conversations in 1997 with local women who used, or whose mothers used, the Blue Triangle facilities.

232. *Iowa Bystander* clipping from the 1940s, in author's possession.

233. *Iowa Bystander,* Aug. 7, 1947.

234. E. Franklin Frazier, *Black Bourgeoisie* (New York: Simon and Schuster, 1957), 1–8. See also Low and Clift, 398.

235. St. Clair Drake and Horace R. Cayton, *Black Metropolis: A Study of Negro Life in a Northern City* (New York: Harcourt, Brace, 1945; repr. 1962), 716.

The old Jewish Community Center at 9ᵗʰ and Forest in Des Moines was used by the African-American community, notably as the early home of the Tiny Tots Day Care Center.

The People's Institute Band of Keokuk, Iowa (courtesy Marie Grigsby)

PART FIVE

Black Iowans in sports, entertainment, and the arts

Sports have a way of bringing people together, here in Keosauqua and everywhere. (courtesy Harold Craig)

"Pride to All"

African-Americans and Sports in Iowa

by David R. McMahon

Charles P. Howard came to Des Moines in 1919 to earn a law degree. He was probably Drake University's first African-American football player. After graduation, Howard stayed in Des Moines for many years, building a reputation as an able if controversial lawyer and a man of decidedly progressive politics. On April 2, 1920, an article by Howard appeared in the *Iowa Bystander* under the title, "Negro Athletes." In his article, Howard shared his views on recent advances for African-Americans in the area of sports. He hoped the article would serve as "a source of knowledge" for the older members of the community, "inspiration to the younger ones, and pride to all, to know of these achievements."[1]

Although Howard advocated greater progress for African-Americans in sports and society, even he could not avoid adopting some of the racial stereotypes of his day. "There is one class of events in which the Negro seems particularly adapted and that is in the sprints," he contended. "There are many reasons for this, chief among which are the facts, that *the Negro is of a nervous and excitable temperament,* requisites which are primarily essential in a sprinter; also *a less rigorous and exacting course of training is necessary* in this class of events than in others [emphasis added]." Howard excused poor progress in other areas, saying "it was in this class of events that Negros [sic] first made a success, and this inspired others to try the same. In fact all the records in running races held by our own people, are confined to races not greater than a quarter mile."[2]

How ironic that a white Iowan, Francis Cretzmeyer, helped disprove the myth that black athletes were unsuited for distance races. The inscription on a marker at a field named in his honor in Iowa City reads in part: "At a time when American track and field coaches thought that black athletes were genetically inferior and emotionally incapable of running long distances, he accepted them with the same warmth and enthusiasm he showed with all his athletes."[3]

In 1956, Cretzmeyer coached four athletes to the Olympic Games in Melbourne, Australia — two of them were African-Americans. One was Charles (Deacon) Jones, perhaps the University of Iowa's best all-time distance runner and a participant in the 1960 Olympics in Rome. Ted Wheeler was the other.

"At a time when American coaches thought that black athletes were genetically inferior and emotionally incapable of running long distances, [Francis Cretzmeyer] accepted them with the same enthusiasm he showed all his athletes."

The University of Iowa's Edward Gordon won a gold medal at the 1932 Olympics in Los Angeles. (SHSI)

(Center) Jesse Owens, who appeared at the 1935 Drake Relays, was later given the title "Athlete of the First Half-century" by meet officials. (from Spiegel, Drake Relays: 75 Years of Excellence)

(Right) Wilma Rudolph, winner of the 100-meter dash in the 1960 Olympics in Rome, helped debut women's competition at the Drake Relays in 1961. (from Spiegel, Drake Relays: 75 Years of Excellence)

University of Iowa track coach Francis Cretzmeyer instructing his runners, 1950s. Ted Wheeler, second from right, participated in the 1956 Olympics and succeeded Cretzmeyer as coach in 1978. (University of Iowa Photo Services)

In 1978, Wheeler became the first black track and field coach at the University of Iowa.

Asked years later why he had chosen Iowa, Wheeler said "it was the only place a black distance runner could go, back then.... As soon as schools found out that I had a real good suntan," he joked, "and that I was real tall [6'5"], they lost interest."[4]

Some of us are apt to think of two sports histories, one white and one black, but our sports history is inseparable and intertwined. Charles Howard might have been black, but his thinking showed the influence of racial stereotypes prevalent in his day. Cretzmeyer was white, and the beneficiary of a society predicated on "whiteness," but he furthered the cause of racial equality when he fielded African-Americans in athletic events normally reserved for whites. Wheeler, an African-American raised in a segregated society, shattered racial barriers as an athlete and a coach while representing a predominately white university from an almost all-white state.[5]

Unfortunately, scholars have ignored sports history in Iowa. Like Howard's article, this chapter attempts to fill the void. While it brings sources together in a way that no writer has attempted before, the account of the black athlete offered here is far from complete. Focusing on African-Americans in baseball and college sports in Iowa, the chapter challenges others to join the collaborative effort of reconstructing Iowa's sports history.[6]

Baseball

Iowa and the national pastime were linked long before Hollywood came to Dyersville to film *Field of Dreams* in the late 1980s. The impact of Iowans on the game was most pronounced in the period beginning in the late nineteenth century and ending with the desegregation of baseball in 1947. Baseball has been one of the most widely studied sports in Iowa, but few who have studied this history have focused on region *and race*. Iowans, both black and white, contributed to the history of the game in substantial ways. Some of the best black baseball and softball players who ever played competed in Iowa. The following examines a few of the major players and stories of Iowa baseball history.[7]

Bud Fowler

Iowa's first African-American professional baseball player, Bud Fowler, was born John W. Jackson near Cooperstown, New York, on March 16, 1858. He picked up the name "Bud" because he liked calling people by that name. He later adopted Fowler as his surname. Baseball researchers once considered Fowler the first black major leaguer, but that honor now goes to Moses Fleetwood Walker, who played for Toledo of the American Association. Later researchers pointed out that Fowler spent his entire career in the minor leagues. But Fowler was the first black to play extensively in professional baseball. His ten seasons in organized baseball stood as a record until Jackie Robinson broke it in his last season with the Brooklyn Dodgers in 1956. In his early days in baseball, Fowler moved around the country fairly easily, often playing on white teams until racial lines hardened at the end of the nineteenth century. By the mid-1890s, organized baseball excluded African-Americans. In later years, Fowler stayed with the game as a player, manager, and owner of all-black teams.[8]

Fowler made Iowa sports history by playing on a team from Keokuk in 1885. *Des Moines Register* sportswriter Maury White debunked the myth that Keokuk was the first major league team to sign Fowler. A team from New Castle, Pennsylvania held Fowler's first contract in 1872, making him the first black player to earn a salary. In subsequent years a committee of baseball researchers downgraded Keokuk's club from major to minor league status, thus ending Keokuk's claim as the first team to sign a black major leaguer. What had not changed, said White, was Fowler's status as "Iowa's first black professional baseball player."[9]

Baseball historians had long known about Fowler's season

Journeyman Bud Fowler joined Keokuk's roster in 1885, thus becoming Iowa's first black professional baseball player. (from Peterson, Only the Ball Was White)

with Keokuk, but little was known about what he did there. Historian Ralph Christian filled in some of the missing details, focusing on approximately six months, from late January to late July 1885, when Bud Fowler called Keokuk home.[10]

Fowler made his way to the Midwest, and ultimately Keokuk, hoping for better opportunity after experiencing prejudice in the East. The driving force behind Keokuk's effort to field a team in the Western League in 1885 was R.W. (Nick) Curtis, who signed Fowler to the team. A story handed down for generations stressed the egalitarianism of the owner and his sense of fair play. Curtis had apparently hired Fowler sight unseen and only found out that he was black when he picked him up at the train depot. By honoring the contract, Curtis showed he harbored no racist beliefs.[11]

Christian argued it was unlikely that Curtis was unaware of the color of Fowler's skin when he hired him. An enthusiastic promoter of baseball, and an expert evaluator of baseball talent, Curtis might have signed Fowler in part to attract Keokuk's African-American residents to his baseball games. Of Keokuk's 10,693 residents, 1,166 (nearly 11 percent) were black.[12]

Not only was Fowler the first black professional baseball player in Iowa in 1885, he also became Iowa's champion pedestrian that year. Fowler kept himself in top physical condition with walking matches. He demonstrated quite a flare for self-promotion in arranging and winning many pedestrian contests. But Fowler's main accomplishments came on the baseball diamond. According to Christian, Fowler played superbly even while Curtis struggled to keep the team afloat and get Keokuk admitted into the Western League. A favorite of fans and teammates, Fowler was the last player to leave town when the team and league folded later that season.[13]

As a ballplayer, Fowler possessed wit and charisma in addition to talent. But not all Iowans were as progressive on the race question as Nick Curtis, the man who hired Fowler. Another Iowan, Cap Anson, was one of the most influential men in baseball — and a racist.[14]

Cap Anson

In 1852 Adrian (Cap) Anson was the first white baby born in Marshall County. Before becoming a major league star and manager, Anson proved his worth on the diamonds of Marshalltown, Iowa. In the big leagues, he had a lifetime batting average of .334, was the oldest major leaguer to hit a grand slam at 42, and the second-oldest player to hit a home run — he hit two on his last day in baseball in 1897. He was also the first player to reach 3,000 hits. Although his talents as a player were considerable, he was even more skilled as a manager and promoter. Among other things, he invented the hit-and-run play, spring training, and use of a pitching rotation. In 1939 he was inducted into the Baseball Hall of Fame.[15]

But Anson also helped establish the precedent for no African-Americans in the major leagues. The barring of African-Americans lasted from about the mid-1890s to 1947, the year Jackie Robinson broke the color barrier as a player for the Brooklyn Dodgers. In 1883, Anson insisted he would not play if officials allowed Moses Fleetwood Walker of Toledo to take the field. He relented only after his share of gate receipts was threatened. On July 19, 1887, he famously yelled, "Get that Nigger off the field!," referring to George Stovey of the Newark Eagles. Later, he persuaded the New York Giants not to promote Stovey from the minors to the majors. That is how Anson helped establish the color line in baseball. Sol White, a former baseball player and the game's first black historian, was the first to single out Anson in this regard.[16]

Anson displayed his racism for all to see in his autobiography, *A Ball Player's Career.* In his book, Anson tells a story about the

team mascot, Clarence Duval, who earned his living as a clown, representing the White Stockings on a world tour in 1888–1889. Using the stereotypes of the day, Anson variously referred to Duval as a "little darkey," a "little coon," and a "no account nigger."[17]

When Anson's team arrived in Omaha, Nebraska, on October 25, 1888, they were greeted by a large crowd and one familiar face — Clarence Duval. "Here Clarence Duval turned up and thereby hangs a story," Anson wrote. "Clarence was a little darkey that I had met sometime before while in Philadelphia." He went on to describe Duval as "a singer and dancer of no mean ability, and a little coon whose skill in handling a baton would have put the blush [to] many a bandmaster of national reputation."[18]

Calling Duval an "ungrateful rascal" for running out on him (with a woman, allegedly), Anson nonetheless enlisted him to help promote his team. "Tom Burns smuggled him into the carriage that day, tatterdemalion that he was, and when we reached the grounds [Duval] ordered us to dress ranks with all the assurance in the world, and, taking his place in front of the players as the band struck up a march, he gave such an exhibition as made the real drum major turn green with envy, while the crowd burst into a roar of laughter and cheered him to the echo."[19]

Despite Duval's crowd-pleasing performance, Anson was angry, wanting to punish him for his earlier desertion. His players talked him out of it and convinced Anson to bring Duval along with them to San Francisco. Duval's performance at a subsequent game so impressed the club owner, A. G. Spaulding, that Duval remained with the team on a trip to Australia. But wary of Duval running out on him, Anson made him sign an ironclad contract — "one that carried such horrible penalties with it in case of desertion that it was enough to scare the little darkey almost to death," Anson admitted. "To my astonishment, he kept his word, remaining with us through the trip and returning with us to Chicago." But his loyalty earned little praise or affection from Anson. "Outside of his dancing and his power of mimicry he was however, a 'no account nigger,' and more than once did I wish that he had been left behind."[20]

Historian David L. Porter has concluded that "for all his contributions to the game, Anson also established an unwritten rule banning black players from organized baseball. His rigid belief in the segregation of black and white players and his enormous popularity discouraged other owners from recruiting blacks."

"Anson also established an unwritten rule banning black players from organized baseball. His rigid belief in segregation and his enormous popularity discouraged other owners from recruiting blacks."

— **David Porter**

Writer Ocania Chalk, describing Anson's racism, focused on the story of Duval. Black mascots were common in those days, Chalk said; white audiences expected black mascots to be clowns or act like buffoons. Chalk estimated that Anson's mascot could not have been more than 15 years old. Chalk judged Anson guilty of racism, but he did not find him totally responsible for barring African-Americans from baseball. "Despite his conservative views and influence, Anson could not have been powerful enough single-handedly to keep known black players out of the major leagues," Chalk argued. "Even as strong-willed an individual as he was . . . could not determine the racial mores of an entire nation."[21]

Other writers stressed Anson's personal responsibility for barring African-Americans from baseball, even if they did not know the source of his racism. William C. McDonald noted, "No one has adequately explained why Anson, born and reared in an all-white town in Iowa, harbored such hatred for African-Americans. But his influence on baseball and on black-white relations was enormous for by the 1890s the color line had been drawn in major league baseball." Art Rust echoed McDonald's sentiments: "Anson hated blacks with an unnatural vehemence. The reason for that is unknown, but the effect of it was to close the door of organized baseball to the black man for six decades."[22]

Black Baseball

But banning African-Americans from the major leagues did not stop them from playing baseball. Eager to prove their worth on the diamonds of Iowa, black baseball flourished in the state during the era of segregated baseball. It was a phenomenon of the

Midwest that black players continued to play with and against white players. Despite the ban on blacks in organized baseball, total segregation did not exist in many small towns and medium-sized cities where the game was played. At times even Cap Anson himself swallowed his racism and umpired all-black and integrated contests in Iowa. The exceptional performances of early black teams like the Algona Brownies and players like John Donaldson with the All Nations foretold a day when blacks would be welcomed as the equal of whites on playing fields across the country.

No one really knows when the first black team played in Iowa but an article in the *Iowa Bystander* announced the formation of the Des Moines Capitals in 1898. Earlier, the paper announced the appearance of the world-famous Page Fence Giants from Michigan, advertised as being "the best colored team in the United

Adrian (Cap) Anson of Marshalltown, pictured with his Chicago team, agitated — successfully — for the exclusion of African-Americans in the major leagues. Team mascot Clarence Duval is seated near the center of the picture, baton in hand.
(from Anson, A Ball Player's Career)

*The Algona Brownies,
1903 "Colored Champions of the
West" (Algona Publishing Company)*

States." The Giants were scheduled to appear in Des Moines, Cedar Rapids, and Burlington. The *Bystander* reported: "This will be the first opportunity that many will have of seeing a professional colored team play ball."[23]

In later years the *Bystander* chronicled other black teams and black players. In 1900, a player was killed when two black teams assaulted each other during a baseball game in Albia, Iowa. "It is not known who fired the fatal shot," the paper reported, "but bad blood had existed between the ball teams for some time past." In 1902, the paper reported stories about the Des Moines Giants and the Ottumwa Browns, two black baseball teams that had formed in the area. Nearly twenty years later, in 1920, the *Bystander* printed an advertisement from a local team. The "original" Capital City Giants had re-organized, billing themselves as "the fastest Colored Ball Club in the State of Iowa." The ad also noted: "We fill engagements for Home Comings, Carnivals or any kind of Attraction with a Clean Exhibition." M. J. Bradford signed the ad as the team's manager.[24]

Many other teams played in central Iowa during the era of segregated baseball. Teams rose and fell as money and interest dictated. Some of the teams that played in central Iowa were the Des Moines Brownies, Gould's Invincibles, Enterprise Browns, Boone Brownies, and Scott's Little Giants.[25]

There were others too, including the Buxton Wonders, one of Iowa's best black baseball teams. Located in Monroe County not far from Des Moines, Buxton was an attractive place to live for African-Americans, while it lasted. Black workers in Buxton made a living wage — most worked for the Consolidation Coal Company — and participated in the social and civic life of the community like almost nowhere else. Historian Janice Beran, who has studied sports and recreation within the black community, concluded "the relative absence of a color line in sports within the town of Buxton was a reflection of both the Consolidation Coal Company and the community's readiness to provide equally for all its members." While wary of welfare capitalism, she labeled it "a successful experiment" that demonstrated "that achieving a democratic society which had eluded other mixed race communities was possible."[26]

The Buxton Wonders represented their unique community in baseball games played throughout the region. They played black teams at home and often took to the road to find other competition. Baseball was by far the most popular sporting activity in Buxton itself. For members of the community, playing baseball was a welcome respite from toiling in the mines. Ball games became tremendous social events, times when residents relaxed and had fun. None of the Buxton Wonders ever played on other black teams in the region. They were definitely a team made up of local players.

While almost half of all Buxton residents were black, the almost all-white town of Algona was home to one of black base-

ball's greatest teams, the Algona Brownies. The Brownies earned fame as the "Colored Champions of the West" in 1903.[27]

Maury White asked the following question in his article on the Algona Brownies: "How did a pristine northern Iowa town of 5,000 come to field one of the best black baseball teams in the nation almost a century ago?" White's answer was E. J. Murtagh, a local banker and the man behind the Brownies. White noted how the team took on more African-Americans each year, until becoming an all-black team in 1903. Scott Snyder, a white man and a former player-manager, remembered his experience with the Brownies. "It was interesting," he said, "because it convinced me that the color of a man's skin made no difference in his baseballing ability."[28]

The Brownies meteoric rise to fame was over almost as soon as it began. In 1901, the Brownies lost the state tournament to a team from Waseca, Minnesota, in a game umpired by Cap Anson, the chief architect of the color line in baseball. In 1902 the team won the Iowa State Amateur Championship, a championship "amateur" in name only. The purse was $2,500. The Brownies reached the pinnacle of success in 1903 as "Colored Champions of the West." That year they defeated a perennial black baseball power, the Chicago Union Giants, in 11 out of 15 games. Inexplicably, the team disbanded in 1904, and the former players moved away to catch on with teams elsewhere.[29]

White's article is important for alerting *Register* readers to the forgotten history of black baseball in Iowa. Kenneth Pins did the same with an article on the Cedar Rapids Colored Giants.

Pins wrote about the day when a black team from Cedar Rapids faced a white team from Worthington, a small German-Catholic community in eastern Iowa. On a hot Fourth of July in the mid-1920s, Pins's great-uncle, Les Ament, "integrated" the Giants when car trouble left some of the team members stranded on the road and unable to reach the game. As it turned out, the newly recruited Ament — the white boy from Worthington — scored the winning run for the Giants. In appreciation, Ament's black teammates treated him to ice cream and cherry pie at a local cafe after the game.[30]

Though neither man could remember the other's name, Les Ament, Pins's uncle, and Lloyd Capes, a former Colored Giant, told remarkably similar stories about a time long since past, when African-American teams from big cities traveled to small Iowa towns to play baseball. Despite his uplifting story about his uncle and the Colored Giants, Pins offered a sober conclusion. "It would be tempting to think of this and other games in small towns with the Colored Giants in the 1920s and 1930s as something other than what they were, a heartening oddity in a nation otherwise divided by race."[31]

The Cedar Rapids Giants, c. 1920, a popular barnstorming team of the early 1900s (courtesy Mary Collier Graves)

(Below, far left to right)

Keosauqua High School's baseball team, c. 1921, was integrated before the major leagues were. (Van Buren County Historical Society)

In 1910, the all-white University of Iowa baseball team had an African-American boy as its mascot. (University of Iowa Hawkeye, *1911)*

Company baseball teams were common in the early years of baseball. The Iowa Railroad and Light Corporation sponsored this all-black team in Marshalltown. (courtesy Helen Johnson)

The Des Moines Police Department's integrated baseball team (from Zeller, Behind the Badge)

The Buxton Wonders were a source of pride for their community. (courtesy Mary Collier Graves)

471

J. L. Wilkinson and the Negro Leagues

If Cap Anson is the Iowan most responsible for slamming the door on African-Americans in major league baseball, Wilkinson is the Iowan most responsible for opening it back up again. "Even if J. L. Wilkinson had not owned one of the first two professional teams to play under the lights regularly," wrote historian John Holway, "he would have earned a high place in baseball history and in the Hall of Fame as a man who gave Satchel Paige his second chance — and Jackie Robinson his first." Holway argued that "without Wilkinson, it is just possible that Robinson might have never been ready for his date with history in 1947, and big league integration might either have failed or most likely been postponed several years longer."[32]

Born in 1874 near Algona, Iowa, Wilkinson played baseball before succumbing to injuries that ended his career on the field. Yet he stayed with the game, becoming a legendary team owner and promoter of baseball. The All Nations, based in Des Moines,

was an early Wilkinson invention around the turn of the century, featuring players from different nationalities and races, including Cuban, Asian, black, and white players. Wilkinson billed a female on the team as "Carrie Nation." The All Nations entertained audiences and played competitive baseball, especially when legendary black pitcher John Wesley Donaldson was on the mound. Donaldson averaged almost 20 strikeouts a game and once pitched 3 consecutive no-hitters. The draft during World War 1 stole many of the team's best black players for the war effort.[33] But the All Nations continued to play into the 1920s. John Donaldson was the team's manager and star player.

Wilkinson's greatest adventure came next. He founded and owned the Kansas City Monarchs, the "Yankees of the Negro Leagues." When Rube Foster organized the Negro National League in 1920, he had intended to limit it to black teams and black owners. Wilkinson was the exception to the rule because of his progressive stance on race and because he held the lease to the

J.L. Wilkinson and Satchel Paige
(from Ribowsky, Don't Look Back*)*

(Above and right)
John Wesley Donaldson, star pitcher
for J. L. Wilkinson's All Nations team,
pictured far right
(Sioux Falls Daily Press clipping
courtesy David Kemp)

Local Boy Will Hurl Against Dragons

When the Kansas City Monarchs, famous Negro baseball team from the National Colored league, play the Des Moines Western League club Monday night, Chet Brewer (right), former Des Moines boy, who since the departure of John Donaldson, has become known as the greatest of the Negro pitchers, will hurl for the invaders. In 19 games this season Brewer has lost only two. Ted Young (left) has been catching for the Monarchs for nine years, and is a veteran of the National league.

Chet Brewer of Des Moines, an outstanding pitcher (courtesy Clark Yeager)

American Association park in Kansas City. As a white man, Wilkinson had certain advantages over other league owners. He brokered deals that were probably unavailable to black owners. But the Monarchs' owner was good for black baseball and good for black players. Former Monarch Newt Allen recalled "he was one white man who was a prince of a fellow. He loved baseball, and he loved his players. And he traveled right along with us every day, stayed at the same hotels we stayed at. One of the greatest owners I've ever known."[34]

For his first Monarch club, Wilkinson gathered together some former players from the All Nations and ex-soldiers from the 25th Infantry. An old yarn suggests that Casey Stengel, a star player for the Kansas City Blues, recommended the player-soldiers to Wilkinson. Phil Dixon has pretty much dispelled this myth. The 25th Cavalry team had received considerable attention in the Kansas City newspapers. Bullet Rogan was starring for the Monarchs a couple of years before Stengel ever saw the military

teams play. But what is important is that such a legendary figure as Stengel recognized the talent of the All Nations, 25th Cavalry, and Monarch players.

Arguably the best franchise in the Negro Leagues, the Monarchs earned ten Negro League pennants from 1920 to 1948, and won two out of their four Negro World Series appearances. During the dark days of the Depression, Monarch baseball brightened the night sky. Wilkinson developed a portable lighting system that kept his team, and black baseball, afloat. No team contributed more major leaguers than the Monarchs when integration finally came in 1947. A short list includes such stars as Jackie Robinson, Satchel Paige, Ernie Banks, and Iowa's own Gene Baker.[35]

Despite his achievements and humanitarianism, J.L. Wilkinson had been forgotten by Iowans until recently. Even Maury White, the dean of Iowa sportswriters, had never heard of him — until a Japanese sportswriter contacted White seeking information about the first Japanese professional baseball player. The sportswriter, Kazuo Sayama, had been researching the career of Jap Mikado when he wrote White for help. Mikado, whose real name is Goro Mikami, played on Wilkinson's All Nations team. Although very little was learned about Mikado, White reacquainted Iowans with Wilkinson through a series of articles published in the *Des Moines Register*. Wilkinson was once again part of Iowa's sports memory.[36]

Wilkinson and the Monarchs also laid claim to the best black baseball players from Iowa, Chet Brewer and Gene Baker. Brewer dominated the Negro Leagues as an outstanding pitcher. He was born in Leavenworth, Kansas, in 1907 but his family moved to Des Moines when he was just a boy. In an interview years later, Brewer described his thoughts regarding his family's move to Des Moines. "Des Moines was like a breath of fresh air for us," he said. "We got rid of racial prejudice we found in Kansas. Everything there was either all-white or all-black." In Des Moines, Brewer lived in an integrated neighborhood and attended an integrated school. Brewer noted with some humor that "we blacks could go to movies in Des Moines and not have to sit with the projector."[37]

In high school, Brewer excelled in sports and played baseball for semi-pro teams during the summer. In 1925, he joined the Kansas City Monarchs, playing with the team on and off for many years. Brewer became the first African-American to play in the Mexican League, and in 1966 he was

"[J. L. Wilkinson] loved baseball, and he loved his players. And he traveled right along with us every day, stayed at the same hotels we stayed at. One of the greatest owners I've ever known."

— Former Monarch Newt Allen

Drawing of Gene Baker by black artist George Lee
(*from* Lee, Interesting Athletes)

*Bob Feller and Satchel Paige became teammates in 1948,
when Paige signed with the Cleveland Indians. (Bob Feller Museum)*

*Gene Baker of Davenport, Iowa's first
and only black major leaguer when
the Chicago Cubs called him up in
1953, also played for the Pittsburgh
Pirates. (from Baraks,* Quad-City
Sports Greats)

inducted into the Mexican Hall of Fame. Unfortunately, integration came too late for Brewer to make it to the big leagues. But Brewer had a productive career as a scout and an instructor for the Pittsburgh Pirates' farm system from 1954 to 1974. He also ran a youth baseball league in Los Angeles, where a park was named in his honor. He was inducted into the *Des Moines Register's* Iowa Sports Hall of Fame in 1984. He died March 26, 1990, in Los Angeles.[38]

The first African-American and native Iowan to make it to the major leagues was Gene Baker, a native of Davenport who played for the Chicago Cubs and Pittsburgh Pirates in the years 1953–1961. Before joining the Cubs, Baker played on the Monarchs with another future Cub, Ernie Banks. Baker also played for a Cubs farm team in Des Moines. Although Baker was called up to the majors first, Banks was the first black to start on the Cubs in 1953. Banks also took over Baker's preferred position of shortstop. Once Baker adapted to his new position, second base, Banks and Baker became a sensation in Chicago as the first black double-play combination in the major leagues. Banks and Baker were also best friends. In Chicago, they had their own fan club and newspaper, *The Keystone Capers.*[39]

In addition to being an all-state athlete in Iowa and a major leaguer, Gene Baker's list of accomplishments includes being one of the first black managers in organized baseball. In 1961, Baker managed the Pittsburgh Pirates' farm team in Batavia, New York, and later scouted the Midwest for the Pirates for over 20 years. He died in Davenport in December 1999 at the age of 74.[40]

Bob Feller, Satchel Paige, and Jackie Robinson

No account of baseball in Iowa would be complete without mentioning the Iowa connections of the most flamboyant and celebrated Negro League player of all time, Leroy (Satchel) Paige. Paige made many memorable visits to Iowa. His biographer, Mark Ribowsky, described the first meeting between Paige and Iowa's Bob Feller as a "flame-throwing contest." Ribowsky wrote that "over the first three burning innings, Feller struck out eight and Satch seven; each gave up one hit. The black team pulled out a late win, but what endured was the memory of Paige and Feller and the high heat they made in the cornfield that day. In time, the two of them would enter into a business relationship that, unlike the Paige-Dizzy Dean duels, would make racial trammels move like ten-pins."[41]

Jackie Robinson and Bob Feller both entered the Hall of Fame in 1962. (Bob Feller Museum)

Writer Hal Leibovitz captured Paige's version of that day, supposedly in the pitcher's own vernacular. "First time I seen [Feller] was in 1936," said Paige. "I throwed against him in an exhibition game in Des Moines, Iowa after he finished his first season with Cleveland. The lights was bad and we both was strikin' out everybody. I winned that game by one run. But man that boy was fast."[42]

Satchel Paige and Bob Feller shared a talent for making money and phenomenal pitching ability — but the media constructed images of the two players in very different ways. Feller became the all-American boy, while Paige acted the part of a black huckster. Much has been made of the careers of Paige and Feller, but few people have fully realized how they worked together to end segregation in baseball.

The Paige and Feller duels paved the way for integration. In 1946, Feller and Paige toured the country in twin Tiger aircraft left over from World War 2. More than 46,000 fans packed into Yankee Stadium to see the Paige and Feller all-stars square off, and more than 400,000 fans saw the tour in 32 games over 26 nights. The barnstorming tour rocked organized baseball to its foundations. Nothing demonstrated the absurdity of banning

African-Americans from baseball more than these games. Fans of both races flocked to the black-white clashes. Barnstorming had so unnerved baseball commissioner Kennesaw Mountain Landis that he banned white players from playing until after the World Series was over. But when he died, he was replaced by A. E. (Happy) Chandler, who was more amenable to barnstorming.

Owners were still annoyed because the barnstormers earned more on the short tour than participants made in the World Series. Some players collected more in a few weeks than they could make in an entire season of major league baseball. The revenue considerations alone made owners rethink their stance on African-Americans and major league baseball. But more importantly, black players had shown they could play with major leaguers. Barnstorming paved the way for the acceptance of black stars in the major leagues.[43]

In his autobiography, Feller claimed he had helped Paige reach the Hall of Fame with those barnstorming tours. In true Feller fashion, he described their relations in a business-like way. "Satch and I were friends, teammates and business associates. We were together in one capacity or another for my whole pitching career. We were a successful partnership, always above-board with each other. We worked hard for each other in our mutual endeavors and at the end of our projects we were still friends." The two men became major league teammates in 1948, when the Cleveland Indians acquired the aging pitcher for their ball club. Cleveland had already become the first American League team to sign a black ballplayer, Larry Doby. Paige's dream of playing in the majors was now fulfilled, although his playing time was limited. Paige became the first black to pitch in a World Series, although he entered late in a game that had already been pretty much decided.[44]

The Paige-Feller relationship highlights the positive contributions one Iowan made to major league baseball. Yet Feller's reputation has suffered due to a few unfortunate remarks he made about Jackie Robinson. Before Robinson had quite caught on in organized baseball, reporters were eager to hear what Feller had to say about the young black player. Reporters asked Feller about Robinson, because no white man in baseball had more contact with black players than he did. On one occasion, Feller responded tersely to reporter's questions by stating that Robinson was too muscle-bound for the majors and better suited for football, a sport Robinson excelled at while a student at UCLA. He also said that a white player of equal talent would not be considered for the

Much has been made of the careers of Paige and Feller, but few people have fully realized how they worked together to end segregation in baseball.

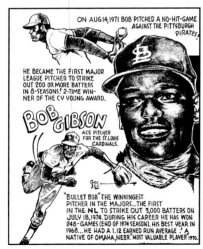

Before he made the majors, Bob Gibson honed his baseball skills playing for the Estherville Red Sox. (from Lee, Interesting Athletes)

majors. Feller's remarks angered Robinson and were a source of friction between the two men years later. Robinson called Feller's remarks archaic and racist. In sport histories and documentaries since, Feller is often used as the whipping boy for America's racism because of his remarks.[45]

But Feller was not the only one to doubt Robinson's abilities. Some black players, like Paige, were hurt when Robinson was picked to be the first African-American in the major leagues, but they kept a united front for the public. According to Mark Ribowsky, Paige's biographer, Robinson was formerly a second-stringer on the Kansas City Monarchs, and the Monarchs' roster alone featured black players with more raw talent and playing experience than Robinson. But Branch Rickey made the right choice. The first African-American to integrate baseball in the modern era possessed talent as a player and the character to withstand racial insults and intimidation. Chet Brewer, one of black baseball's best pitchers, admitted that he could not have taken the abuse Robinson so graciously endured while integrating major league baseball.[46]

Robinson's rookie-of-the-year honor in 1947 was the first step in a career that led eventually to the Hall of Fame. Robinson and Feller were inducted in 1962, and both men understood the irony. Arnold Rampersad, Robinson's biographer, stated that Robinson "held no grudge" against Feller. "He told Feller it was a pleasure to be inducted with him." Feller later recalled it was "extra meaningful" for him too. Maury Allen said the tension between the two men was more about economics than race anyway. When

they played against each other in the late 1940s, barnstorming in the California winter league, "Feller was the drawing card." But Robinson "wanted more integrated seating made available and a larger portion of the gate for black players. . . . Nothing makes a ball player madder than sharing money," wrote Allen. "Feller answered Robinson's demands the only way he knew how: he threw at his head during one game."[47]

While Feller's career is the stuff of legend, a reconsideration of his place in baseball history is needed. His impact on race relations was much more positive than Cap Anson, no matter what his motives. In his autobiography, Feller stated plainly that "playing against black players and having them on my team was nothing new or special to me. Dad recruited black players for our Oakview team back on the farm."[48]

Black Major Leaguers and Baseball in Iowa

Iowa supplied fields of dreams for other black players. Even though Gene Baker was the first African-American from Iowa to play in the major leagues, the state helped develop the careers of other African-American baseball players. Both Bob Gibson and Ozzie Smith played in Iowa before becoming legendary St. Louis Cardinals of the National League. Gibson is already a Hall-of-Famer; Smith probably will be.

Elected to the Hall of Fame in 1981, Gibson was one of the most intimidating players in baseball and perhaps the greatest pitcher to perform in the World Series. His career also coincided with the rise of black athletes in the 1960s. But before he became well known, he played baseball during the summer in Iowa.[49]

In his autobiography, *A Stranger to the Game*, Gibson recalled playing in such Iowa communities as Glenwood, Hamburg, Avoca, Exira, Onawa, Logan, Harlan, Missouri Valley, Shenandoah, Red Oak, Griswold, and Woodbine. When he traveled the backroads of Iowa searching for baseball games, he saw a life much different from the one he knew growing up in the projects in Omaha, Nebraska. "My most serious baseball during those years came during the summers, when I took to the small towns and played semi-pro for $350 a month." Gibson recalled that "to keep things on the up-and-up, I was given a summer job along with a spot on the local team." At Estherville, Gibson "drove a trash truck for the Ford dealership, hauling boxes out to the edge of a cliff and dumping them into a landfill." Meanwhile he hit .381 in the Sac County League.[50]

It is as if his early days playing baseball in Iowa fulfilled the ghostly voice in *Field of Dreams* who said "ease his pain." Gibson's autobiography conjured up pastoral images such as this: "The World Series? For Gibson, it was heaven, Iowa without the knuckles, a day in the park devoted to nothing but the pure pursuit of being the best." Although Iowans sometimes greeted him with suspicion, he was allowed to develop his talents as a baseball player, and his memories of Iowa are for the most part happy memories.[51]

Ozzie Smith's Iowa connection stems from his days as a player in the MINK League. MINK stands for Missouri, Iowa, Nebraska, and Kansas. Since the 1960s small towns like Clarinda have hosted collegians from all over the United States during the summer, freeing them to play baseball and to pursue their dreams. In 1976 and 1977, before his major league career began, Smith played in Clarinda. The two magical summers he played in the MINK League left a lasting impression on Smith and on the community. Drafted by the San Diego Padres in 1977, Smith was traded to St. Louis in 1982, where he became one of the best, and most acrobatic, shortstops the game has known. Now that his major league career is over, he returns to Clarinda occasionally to lend his support for baseball in the community.[52]

Softball

African-Americans have also made important contributions to the history of softball in Iowa. Promoters of softball firmly established the game in Iowa in the twentieth century. According to Irv Kawarsky, a recognized expert on the subject, softball came to the state around 1926 and the first night league was organized in Des Moines in 1933. Although whites have dominated men's softball in Iowa, two black teams captured state titles in the years since tournaments were first organized in the 1930s. The Willkie House Vets took the title in 1947, and the Hot-N-Tots did the same in 1951. Both teams hailed from Des Moines.[53]

A three-run seventh inning helped propel the Willkie House Vets past the Boyt Harness team of Des Moines, 6–4, in 1947. The teams played at Walker Field in Des Moines. The Hot-N-Tots prevailed against Tony's Famous Foods of Fort Dodge, 3–1, in 1951, before more than 2,500 fans in Boone, Iowa. Johnny Bright, Drake's all-American football player, pitched for the victors. The Hot-N-Tots are recognized as being one of the best teams of the 1950s and indeed of all-time in Iowa.[54]

Advertising the Famous Iowa Colored Cowboys (SHSI)

The Hot-N-Tots, winners of the 1951 Iowa men's softball title (courtesy Bruce Smith)

"Pee Wee" Williams
"Mickey" Collins
"Rudy" Lee
"Smiley" Hammond
"Breaky" Breakfield
"Tarzan" Green

"Popeye" Smith
'Babe Compound' Favors
"Cool Papa" Rogers
"Fat" Mitchell
"Flash" Kinzer

VS HINTON MERCHANTS
PLACE HINTON, IOWA
DATE SEPT. 1st TIME 8:30 ADMISSION 50¢

IF YOU HAVE NOT SEEN THE GHOSTS DON'T DIE UNTIL YOU DO
Don't miss this Softball Circus - Harold "Speed" Williams Attraction
OGDEN, UTAH
P. O. BOX 1431

From a display describing the Sioux City Ghosts' unique history, part of the Sioux City Black Homecoming Exhibit, 1998 (courtesy Frankie Williams)

Sioux City Ghosts pitcher Reginald Williams in the 1930s (Sioux City Public Library)

The Sioux City Ghosts thrilled audiences from the 1930s through the 1950s. (courtesy Frankie Williams)

Black players are among the all-time greats in Iowa softball history. Bobby Vandever, a catcher for the [Des Moines] Iowa Pack and the Willkie House Vets, was one of "the best of the very best." Many other African-Americans earned renown on the softball diamonds of Iowa, including Al Carr and Arnie Green of Cedar Rapids; L. J. Favors and Fuji Fulton of Sioux City; Moe Eubanks of Des Moines; Ben Edwards of Des Moines and Cedar Rapids; and Bob White, a manager of black teams for over 50 years.[55]

The Sioux City Ghosts are the most legendary of Iowa's black softball teams. The Iowa Amateur Softball Association inducted these barnstormers into its Hall of Fame in August 1983. The Ghosts, the first team to be so honored, began in Sioux City during the Great Depression of the 1930s and played into the 1950s. Softball's answer to the Harlem Globetrotters of basketball and the Indianapolis Clowns of baseball, the Ghosts entertained fans while winning most of their games. They recorded more than 2,000 victories and fewer than 100 losses during their history. Later, the Smithsonian Institution in Washington, D.C., collected their memorabilia and made it part of a traveling exhibit.[56]

College Sports

African-Americans rank among the all-time great athletes in intercollegiate competition, despite the barriers society placed in their way. In 1895 Carelton (Kinney) Holbrook became the first African-American to represent an Iowa college in varsity competition in 1895. In 1895 and 1896, Holbrook attended the University of Iowa, where he played football and participated in track and field for two seasons. Maury White figured Holbrook was among the first dozen or so African-Americans to compete at the college level in the United States.[57]

In 1889, Henry Lewis Jackson and William Tecumseh Jackson played at Amherst College in Massachusetts, becoming the nation's first African-American athletes to play college sports. That same year, Iowa squared off against Grinnell in the first college football game played west of the Mississippi River.

In addition to having the first black player in Holbrook in 1895, the University of Iowa also became the first college team in the state to play *against* a black player in 1892. From 1892 to 1894, George Flippen played against the Hawkeyes as a member of Nebraska's football team. Iowa faced Flippen again when he played with the Chicago Physicians and Surgeons football team in 1897. Flippen's team won, but he was fined $5 and costs for assaulting a spectator.[58]

Verne C. Green played on William Penn's tennis team in the late 1920s. (William Penn College Archives)

William Penn College's integrated football team, 1923. Like William Penn, many of Iowa's small colleges have largely untold histories of African-American athletes. (William Penn College Quaker, *1923)*

Frank Holbrook, the first African-American to play intercollegiate athletics in Iowa (University of Iowa Hawkeye, *1898)*

Henry F. Coleman played on Cornell's football team in 1906 and 1908. (Cornell College)

Archie Alexander with his University of Iowa football teammates, 1909 (University of Iowa Hawkeye, *1911)*

Many black athletes have followed in Duke Slater's footsteps at the University of Iowa. (University of Iowa Photo Services)

More black athletes came after Holbrook and Flippen. In 1904, Henry Thomas played football at Coe College in Cedar Rapids. Archie Alexander followed in Holbrook's footsteps at the University of Iowa in 1909. In 1913, Eugene Collins ran track and played football at Coe, as did his brother George starting in 1918. In 1915, Sol Butler began his outstanding career as a multi-sport athlete at the University of Dubuque. Fred (Duke) Slater joined the Hawkeye football team in 1918, playing for four glorious seasons. He also lettered in track.[59]

Charles Howard and Howard Porter Drew broke racial barriers at Drake University in football and track respectively. Both men had participated in sports as undergraduates elsewhere before coming to Drake to study law in 1919. Iowa State's first African-American athlete was Jack Trice, who died tragically after sustaining injuries in a game against Minnesota in 1923. (Cyclone Stadium was renamed in his honor in 1997.) Holloway Smith, a tackle, followed Trice at ISU in

Tuberculosis cut short Ledrue Galloway's athletic career at the University of Iowa. (University of Iowa Hawkeye, *1926)*

1926 and 1927, but there were no other black varsity athletes at Iowa State until John Crawford played basketball there in 1956.[60]

Iowa colleges were among the first to allow blacks to participate in college sports, but the legacy is decidedly mixed. During the early period of intercollegiate sports only the best black athletes were wanted and even they faced racial insults and discrimination at times. Even worse, opportunities for African-American women were basically nil until Congress passed Title IX in 1972.[61]

The athletic histories of Iowa's two major universities reveal much about racism and sports during the first half of the twentieth century. Iowa State's long drought of black athletes from 1927 until the 1950s can be explained by its affiliation with the Big Six Conference (later the Big Eight, now the Big Twelve). The conference barred black athletes from competition because games were played at colleges that were located in states that practiced segregation. Harold Robinson, a football player at Kansas State University, was the first African-American to break the color barrier in the conference in 1949. It took ten more years before every college in the conference had fielded a black player, Missouri being the last.[62]

Iowa, meanwhile, played in the Big Ten Conference (formerly the Western Conference). The Hawks competed against basically midwestern competition, while Iowa State faced more southern and western teams. At a time when there were no black athletes at Iowa State, the University of Iowa enjoyed a small but steady stream of black players through the 1920s, 1930s, and 1940s. In the 1950s, Iowa rose to national prominence in football under the leadership of Forest Evashevski. Iowa continued to use home-grown talent, but its success came more and more from the use of out-of-state players, especially African-Americans like the Steubenville, Ohio, trio of Calvin Jones, Frank Gilliam, and Eddie Vincent.[63]

By the 1950s, Iowa had a long and distinguished history of black athletes in football. But not every sport at Iowa was open to black athletes from the very beginning. At one time there was a tradition among Big Ten schools of not allowing African-Americans to participate in wrestling and basketball. Dick Culberson broke the Big Ten's barrier in basketball as a Hawkeye in 1946; Simon Roberts became the first African-American to win an NCAA wrestling championship in 1957 at 147 pounds; and Cal Jones was the first black player to win the Outland Trophy in 1955, an award given to the nation's best lineman. Other black stars like Carl (Casey) Cain in basketball, and Ted Wheeler and Deacon Jones in track and field, added to Iowa's appearance as a racially progressive university in the 1950s.[64]

Above: Dick Culberson integrated the Hawkeyes (and possibly the Big Ten) in the 1945–1946 season. (University of Iowa Hawkeye, *1946)*

(Far left) Davenport's Simon Roberts became the first African-American to win an NCAA wrestling title, taking the 147-pound class as a Hawkeye in 1957. (from Baraks, Quad-City Sports Greats)

(Center) All-American Carl (Casey) Cain, who made up one-fifth of Iowa's Fabulous Five teams of the 1954–1956 era, won a gold medal at the 1956 Olympics. (University of Iowa Photo Services)

Emlen Tunnell had a brief but brilliant career at the University of Iowa following World War 2. (from Rust, Illustrated History of the Black Athlete)

Minnesota Vikings head coach Dennis Green played and coached at Iowa in the late 1960s and early 1970s. (University of Iowa Special Collections)

Ozzie and Don Simmons of Fort Worth, Texas, played for the University of Iowa in the 1930s. (University of Iowa Hawkeye, 1937)

When the University of Iowa hired George Raveling in 1983, he became the first black to head a Big Ten men's basketball program. (University of Iowa Photo Services)

C. Vivian Stringer fulfilled her promise to take the University of Iowa women's basketball program into the big time. On February 3, 1985, more than 22,000 fans packed UI's Carver-Hawkeye Arena to watch Stringer and her team, setting an NCAA attendance record. (University of Iowa Photo Services)

While Iowa might have been more welcoming to blacks than some other colleges, particularly those in the South, the situation was still less than ideal for the black athlete. There were few social opportunities for African-Americans in Iowa City. Iowa City boasted of friendly people and a small black community, but African-Americans faced subtle forms of discrimination almost daily. Black students were routinely steered away from the residence halls and toward off-campus housing. Some black players claimed mistreatment from their coaches, as in the case of Ozzie Simmons, who made headlines in 1936 when his relationship with Coach Ossie Solem soured.

In later years the university recruited athletes whose academic skills were marginal, exacerbating existing problems. Connie Hawkins was a case in point. This talented basketball player left school after just one year, embroiled in a betting scandal that nearly ruined his career. In 1969, black football players expressed their disgust with the current system by boycotting spring practice. One of the boycotters was Dennis Green, the future coach of the Minnesota Vikings.[65]

Much had changed in college sports by the 1970s, and black participation in sports was no longer an issue. However, issues such as academic standards and eligibility, gender equity, and the hiring of black coaches and administrators now grabbed headlines.

In 1983, the University of Iowa took the bold step of hiring two African-American head coaches, George Raveling for men's basketball, and C. Vivian Stringer for the women's basketball program. Stringer was the more successful of the two. From 1983 to 1995, she made Iowa a national power in women's basketball, before leaving for Rutgers with a contract that made her the highest-paid women's coach in the country. Raveling's stint at Iowa ended much sooner. After a few mediocre seasons, he left amid stories that Iowa fans could not accept Raveling because he was black.[66]

The University of Iowa's experience is just one part of a larger history in Iowa with respect to sports and race. More study is needed on the black college athlete in Iowa. In 1920, the same year Charles Howard published his article on the black athlete in the *Iowa Bystander*, the *Des Moines Register* announced its all-Iowa college football team. Already black athletes were a powerful presence. "The outstanding feature of this year's selection is the fact that two Negroes, Slater of Iowa and Collins of Coe, are named on the first selection and Butler of Dubuque College and Seminary, another Negro, is placed on the second eleven."[67]

Four athletes in particular stand out from the early years of the black athlete in Iowa. Sol Butler of the University of Dubuque, Duke Slater of the University of Iowa, Jack Trice of Iowa State University, and Johnny Bright of Drake University all left lasting impressions on those who saw them. More importantly, their achievements earned them a permanent place in Iowa's public memory. Their careers and the stories others have told about them merit a closer look.

Sol Butler

Solomon Butler ranks among the greatest of the early African-American athletes. Sportswriter Ocania Chalk said that Butler might have been deemed "the best of them all" had he played closer to urban centers. As proof of his abilities, Chalk spoke of Butler's "electrifying" performance in a football game in 1917, when his Dubuque team thrashed Buena Vista of Storm Lake, 125–0. In that game, Butler averaged "twenty-five yards per carry with a one-hundred-yard punt return, a fifty-yard run, and a day's total of five touchdowns."[68]

Although Butler excelled in football, his greatest achievements came in track and field. It all began in 1914 when Butler was in high school in Hutchison, Kansas. During a track meet he set the national high school record for the 60-yard dash. Butler later enrolled at the University of Dubuque, where he competed in sports from 1915 to 1919. While a student at Dubuque, Butler was twice named All-American as the nation's best broad jumper. In 1919 he nearly broke the Olympic mark in the broad jump at the Inter-Allied games, an athletic contest held in Europe shortly after the end of World War 1. His showing there lead experts to believe he would win the gold in 1920 at the Olympics in Antwerp.[69]

Unfortunately Butler pulled a muscle during the competition and was unable to finish. Chalk wrote: "Butler tried mightily to force his injured body to perform, but he had to retire. He stood aside, a lonely and dejected figure, with tears streaming down his face." Undoubtedly, the pressures on him must have been enormous. But his failure to win at Antwerp in no way diminished his accomplishments as an athlete.[70]

Butler exhibited stunning athletic gifts in an era of relatively

unsophisticated athletic training. When he left the University of Dubuque in 1919, he owned school records in six events: 220-yard hurdles, shot put, running broad jump, discuss throw, 100-yard dash, and 200-yard dash. He was a one-man track team. (Earlier, in high school, Butler had competed in a meet in Illinois in which he won so many events that officials changed the rules to prevent such an occurrence from ever happening again.) Butler's athletic talents were suited to sports other than track and field as well. He was said to have a build like the great Babe Ruth and could play basketball, football, and baseball with almost equal facility.[71]

Butler might have enrolled at the University of Illinois had it not been for an enterprising pastor from Bettendorf, Iowa. Rev. Benjamin Lindeman, pastor at the First Presbyterian Church in Bettendorf, witnessed one of Butler's athletic performances and was so impressed he embarked on recruiting him for his alma mater, the University of Dubuque. Butler had recently moved to Rock Island to be with his high school coach, who had taken a job there. Lindeman found Butler shining shoes one day and made his sales pitch. Whatever he said worked, because Butler enrolled at

(Above left) Sol Butler with his University of Dubuque teammates (University of Dubuque)

Hopes were high for Sol Butler in the 1920 Olympics at Antwerp until he hurt himself during the competition. (University of Dubuque)

Dubuque as the university's first African-American student. As part of the deal, Sol's brother Benjamin also enrolled. Ben often served as Sol's trainer.[72]

Dogged by allegations that he was a professional, Butler gave up his amateur status before he could try his luck again in the 1924 Olympic Games. In 1921 he played for the Lincoln Athletic Club's basketball team; in 1922 he played basketball for the *Chicago Defender*. Since those teams were known to schedule competition against semi-pro and pro teams, charges of professionalism shadowed Butler during his remaining amateur competitions. He soon turned in his amateur card to the AAU, but not before winning another broad jump championship, this time in Bridgeport, Connecticut.[73]

Until his body wore out, he played professional football and basketball. In football, his teammates included the likes of Jim Thorpe and former Iowa standout Duke Slater. In 1923, his rights were sold to the Hammond (Indiana) Pros for $10,000. In 1932, Butler played for Fritz Pollard's Stars, a semi-pro team that featured black players like Duke Slater and Joe Lillard. In addition to professional sports, Butler tried his hand at acting. Hollywood gave him bit parts as an African native in several Tarzan movies.[74]

A Tragic End

Butler thus spent a good part of his life in athletic competition. But in his spare time he worked hard in the communities where he lived trying to better the lives of youth. Sadly he met a tragic end working in Pappy's Lounge in Chicago in December 1954. Butler had ejected a patron, Jimmy Hill, earlier that evening for "molesting" a waitress. The disgruntled Hill returned two hours later and shot Butler. The manager of the tavern thereupon shot and killed Hill. Butler died that night in the hospital. His sisters accompanied his body back to Wichita — where Sol Butler's story had begun 59 years earlier.[75]

In 1958, the *Des Moines Register* made Butler part of its Iowa Sports Hall of Fame. Bert McGrane stated that Butler "was, without a doubt, one of the greatest of the athletes who have ever represented Iowa schools." McGrane also noted that "he belongs even now with Morgan Taylor and Edward Gordon of Iowa as the greatest ever to hit the take-off board for Iowa schools." The Black Presidium, a cultural center for African-American students on the campus of the University of Dubuque, was renamed the Sol Butler Memorial Center in 1979 to honor his memory.[76]

Duke Slater

Born in Normal, Illinois, in 1898, Duke Slater and his family moved to Clinton, Iowa, when he was just a boy. At Clinton High School, Slater played football despite his father's wishes. But his talents were obvious to anyone who watched him play. Friends and sponsors helped him enroll at Iowa as a member of the wartime Student Army Training Corps in 1918.[77]

Duke Slater's four seasons at the University of Iowa, 1918–1921, earned him All-America status as a tackle for the Hawkeyes. During his tenure, Iowa went 23–6–1. When his playing days were over at Iowa, Slater continued in football as a professional player and coached football at an Oklahoma high school for a time in the 1930s. In 1928 Slater had completed his law degree from Iowa, and would go on to become a judge in Cook County's Superior Court, a position he held until his death in 1966.[78]

Although Walter Camp snubbed Slater when he assembled his All-America teams — Camp listed Slater on the third team in 1919, and on the second team in 1921 — most experts, fans, and players agreed that Slater was one of the best football players in the land. Years later, in 1946, 600 sportswriters agreed that Slater merited a spot on their all-time All-America team.[79]

Slater's last season at Iowa was also Iowa's best ever. In 1921 Iowa finished the season undefeated, arguably the best team in the nation. The Hawkeyes were named national co-champions with Cornell and Lafayette, crowned champs of the Big Ten, and received a Rose Bowl bid (which the university declined). Iowa's biggest victory came in a stunning 10–7 upset over Notre Dame in Iowa City. Led by Knute Rockne, the Irish were undefeated in 20 games and were odds-on favorites to win the national championship that year. Photographer Fred Kent's picture of a helmetless Slater sealing off the entire Irish line as Gordon Locke plunged through the hole to score a touchdown helped cement the legend of Duke Slater.[80]

Slater was the first African-American to be named to the *Des Moines Register's* Iowa Sports Hall of Fame in 1951, its inaugural year.[81] James A. Peterson, a Chicago businessman, honored Slater with one of his famous dinners in 1958. For some time Peterson had been hosting dinners to honor football greats like Red Grange, Jim Thorpe, and George Gip. But this time dinner came with a commemorative book, *Slater of Iowa*. A poem at the back of the book reflected the tone of the evening and the thrust of the book.

Until his body wore out, [Sol Butler] played professional football and basketball. In football, his teammates included the likes of Jim Thorpe and former Iowa standout Duke Slater.

Tall as the corn from his native state

Strong as the best in the Middle West

True to the word his father taught

Loved by the team his struggles wrought

Proud of those who he helped to fame

Grateful to the sport that built his name

Modest son of a great University

Reflecting credit, honor and dignity

Hailed by the students with great affection

Forever now a fond recollection

Humbly to the greatness that is his

Slater of Iowa.[82]

Slater's death in 1966 was big news in Iowa and nationally. During that year's August 16 radio broadcast of *It's Sports Time with Phil Rizzuto,* the host spoke about Slater's death and the example he set during his life. "With all the tensions, racial and otherwise, making the rounds today," Rizzuto said, "Duke Slater must have been a lighthouse in the dark skies of South Chicago!" The *Sports Time* host also noted how Slater's life represented the promise of America: "The son of a Negro clergyman, Slater must have been raised to stand on his own two feet! Proud in his knowledge that in America, as in no other country, a man regardless of creed or color can advance by the sweat of his brow and the muscle of his mind!"[83]

Besides revealing Rizzuto's own particular take on Slater's life, the broadcast showed the extent to which Slater was a national hero. African-Americans all over the United States looked to Slater as a role model. A rare slice of newsreel footage once distributed to black audiences shows Slater accepting an award at an Iowa home football game in the 1930s. Over the years, Slater was a frequent visitor during the football season and made other special trips to Iowa to support causes close to him. In 1972, the university named one of its dormitories Slater Hall. Duke Slater was not the first African-American to attend the University of Iowa, but he shed a positive light on the university and encouraged other African-Americans to go there.[84]

Fred (Duke) Slater, college football icon (University of Iowa Photo Services)

Duke Slater and the Clinton football team, c. 1916 (Putnam Museum of History)

In 1921 Duke Slater led the University of Iowa to a victory over Notre Dame and an undefeated season. (from Lamb and McGrane, 75 Years with the Fighting Hawkeyes)

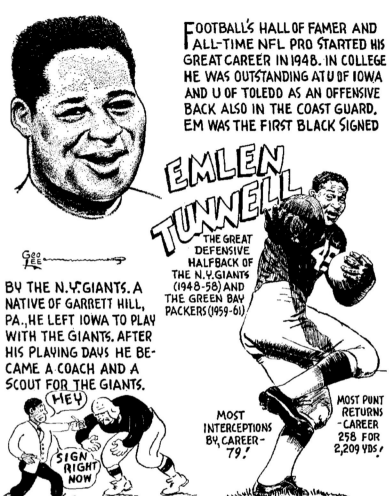

One of the first black athletes to follow Slater at Iowa was Ledrue Galloway, an all-state football player from Omaha, Nebraska. Members of the local black community warned him not to attend Nebraska because, in those days, as a member of the Missouri Valley Conference, Nebraska did not use black players. Galloway lettered in football at Iowa in 1924 before falling ill to tuberculosis. As the Hawkeyes prepared for a game against Illinois the next year, they received a telegram from their former teammate. It said: "There will be twelve Iowa men on the field to beat Illinois. I am with you." Tragically, Galloway died in 1926 at the age of 22.[85]

As the years went by, more African-Americans came to Iowa to play football. Ozzie Simmons, who idolized Duke Slater, arrived in 1933. After World War 2, many black veterans showed up to try out for Dr. Eddie Anderson's football camp. One of them was Emlen Tunnell, a future NFL Hall-of-Famer and the first African-American to play for the New York Giants. In his 1966 autobiography, Tunnell said he had never seen so many black players in his life before he attended Iowa's tryouts in 1946. "Most of them came for the same reason I had," Tunnell wrote. "They knew they would be given a chance to play. Great Negro players were part of the tradition at Iowa, going back to the days around World War 1."[86]

Jack Trice

Jack Trice never got the chance to match Slater's achievements because his career was snuffed out almost before it began. Iowa State's first African-American football player, Trice sustained critical injuries in a game against the Minnesota Gophers in 1923. His playing career was brief, but the example Trice set on the field and off has inspired faculty and students at Iowa State ever since.

In 1997, ISU's Cyclone Stadium was officially renamed "Jack Trice Stadium," ending a lengthy controversy. For years faculty and students had advocated the name change — ever since the new stadium was built in the mid-1970s. Activists lobbied the administration to honor Trice, but success came slowly. First the field was named after Trice, and then in the 1980s a bronze statue of Trice was constructed. But students wanted the statue moved close to the stadium and the name changed. They finally prevailed some 74 years after Trice's death.[87]

The renamed stadium was dedicated shortly before kickoff in a 1997 game that matched the Cyclones against Oklahoma State. Over 44,000 people watched as the covering came down revealing the new name, "Jack Trice Stadium." Meanwhile, the ISU band played "The Battle Hymn of the Republic." An hour earlier the refurbished statue of Trice was also unveiled to the public. Martin Jischke, president of the university, told how Iowa's first African-American player had brought the Iowa State community closer together. "Jack Trice's soul — his life and his death and what he stood for — has brought Iowa State people closer together again and again, and it will continue to do so for future generations." In conclusion, he noted, "now we have a special place to gather, reflect, and celebrate his contributions to this university."[88]

Who was this legendary Jack Trice anyway, the man who had inspired Iowans for more than 75 years? Trice was born the son of Green and Anna Trice in Hiram, Ohio, in 1902. He played football at East Tech High School in Cleveland before following his coach, Sam Williaman, to Ames. Trice played on the freshman squad in 1922 before moving up to the varsity in 1923. He was an excellent student. He dreamed of learning agriculture. Trice's playing time was limited in his first real season because opposing teams objected to his race. While playing against the Gophers in the first half of a ball game in Minneapolis, he injured his shoulder. Leaving the game

In 1997 ISU renamed its football stadium in honor of Jack Trice, who died of injuries sustained in a game against the University of Minnesota in 1923. (Iowa State University)

"Jack Trice's soul —

his life and

his death and what

he stood for —

has brought

Iowa State people

closer together

again and again,

and it will continue

to do so for

future generations."

— ISU President Martin Jischke

momentarily, he returned only to get stomped as he tried to "roll block" the Minnesota line. His injuries forced him out of the game but were not thought serious enough to stop him from traveling home with the team.[89]

By the time the Cyclones returned home it was obvious that Trice's injuries were worse than previously thought. He died on Monday, October 8, 1923.

Iowa State students and faculty turned out in droves for his funeral. Before the funeral, someone discovered a letter Trice had written himself the night before the Minnesota game. It told of

Jack Trice and his teammates, 1922 (Iowa State University)

how he carried the burden of his race as a black football player at ISU. It read, in part: "The honor of my race, family and self is at stake. Everyone is expecting me to do big things. I will." The letter was read at the funeral, and in the years since his death it has continued to inspire those who read it.[90]

Trice's injuries were accidental and not racially motivated, but black players in his day took risks when they stepped onto a football field. They had to be better and stronger than the others and sometimes withstand brutal play.

Ozzie Simmons was punished repeatedly in a game against the Minnesota Gophers in 1934. Simmons, an All-American and one of the most electrifying performers in college football, withstood several late hits until he finally left the game. Iowa fans were so incensed that even the governor of Iowa, Clyde L. Herring, entered the fray. The night before the 1935 Minnesota-Iowa game he predicted an Iowa win and said ominously, "Moreover, if the officials stand for any rough tactics like Minnesota used last year, I'm sure the crowd won't."[91]

Minnesota Gov. Floyd B. Olson responded by betting a prize hog on the game in order to take some of the steam out of the controversy. Now a trophy in the likeness of a pig, "Floyd of Rosedale," is passed on to the winner of the annual Iowa-Minnesota game. It is important to remember its origins and the black player who was at the center of the controversy.[92]

The specter of racial violence often loomed over the playing fields of Iowa. But the potential for violence was higher when Iowa teams crossed state borders, especially when they headed south. Iowa's first African-American football player, Kinney Holbrook, was met rudely by Missouri fans in Columbia in 1896. They chanted "Kill the Negro!" and other obscenities. The game ended in a brawl, as Iowa walked off the field with a 10–6 lead in hand.[93]

The Johnny Bright Incident

Yet nothing in Iowa sports history compares to the Johnny Bright incident. In 1951 Bright was Drake's star football player and the nation's leading rusher. But he garnered worldwide attention when he was knocked out of a ball game against Oklahoma A&M. Bright suffered a broken jaw when Wilbanks Smith hammered him with a forearm as the Drake star was running away from the play. The incident started a national controversy because *Register* photographer Don Ultang had caught the illegal

blow on film. The hit that gave Bright a broken jaw earned the *Register* a Pulitzer Prize.[94]

Drake protested the action to no avail. Once a charter member of the Missouri Valley Conference, Drake dropped out in protest of the Bright incident. They hurled allegations that coach J. B. (Ears) Whitworth had encouraged his players to treat Bright roughly. And yet the Aggies were never sanctioned, nor were there any penalties assessed on the field for the numerous infractions that occurred.[95]

Johnny Bright missed two of his last three games, his jaw wired shut and a tooth extracted so that he could be fed through a straw. He ended his career at Drake as the all-time leading rusher in college football history. Undoubtedly, he is the greatest athlete to wear a uniform at Drake. Drafted by the Philadelphia Eagles, Bright skipped the NFL and spent the rest of his life in Canada playing football in the Canadian Football League. He also taught school. The *Des Moines Register* inducted him into its Iowa Sports Hall of Fame in 1970. Bright died in 1983.[96]

COOK (O) SMITH (O) BRIGHT (O)

Drake's Johnny Bright running for daylight during a 1949 game against ISU (SHSI Des Moines)

Johnny Bright, Drake University's greatest athlete (courtesy Frankie Williams)

Wilbanks Smith of Oklahoma A&M lowers the boom on an unsuspecting Johnny Bright. Don Ultang's photograph won the Des Moines Register *a Pulitzer Prize. (Des Moines Register)*

Conclusion

The stories of Sol Butler, Duke Slater, Jack Trice, and Johnny Bright remind us of the tremendous challenges African-Americans have faced in our history. We are all thankful to them and those who have given their stories wide circulation so we do not forget. But much more can be done to uncover the experience of African-Americans in sports in Iowa. College football in Iowa dominated much of this essay's discussion of college sports. This reflects its central place in our culture and its coverage in the sports media. But more work needs to be done on the hidden histories of basketball, track, wrestling, gymnastics, and other sports. Athletics in our high schools and communities deserve our attention as well. Perhaps the most neglected aspect of black sports history in Iowa is African-American women. In recent years they have gained publicity for their exploits on the playing fields of Iowa. What are their stories? Some of the Iowa women to attract our interest recently include Natasha Kaiser-Brown, C. Vivian Stringer, and Nina Smith.[97]

These are just some of the areas needing our attention. Charles Howard was right to assert that the achievements of African-Americans in sports gave pride to all. Certainly Iowa should be proud of its sports history, and it is right that we should document and interpret African-American contributions to that history. In the future may we be mindful of the positive steps black and white Iowans have taken together in the cause of racial justice through sports. This is why we should not forget J. L. Wilkinson, Jack Trice, Duke Slater, and the other sports heroes of our past.

More work needs to be done on the hidden histories of basketball, track, wrestling, gymnastics, and other sports. . . . More can be done to uncover the experience of African-Americans in Iowa sports .

The Dark Horses basketball team (Ottumwa Public Library)

Louis Dade of Fort Madison broke barriers as a golfer and golf instructor. Dade won the 1939 Iowa Amateur Golf Championship. (courtesy Cecilia Hitch and Louis Dade)

Iowa's boxer Michael Nunn celebrates another victory. (Putnam Museum of History)

Frankie Williams coached Bobby Moore and Frankie Williams Jr. in the 1961 Junior Golden Gloves. (courtesy Frankie Williams)

Allen Ashby, sportswriter for the Iowa Bystander, organized tennis tournaments at Good Park for many years. (courtesy Margaret Garrison)

Selected as Drake Relays' outstanding performer in 1964, Davenport's Gayle Hopkins ran in the 1964 Olympics in Tokyo. (Putnam Museum of History)

Former San Francisco 49ers All-Pro running back Roger Craig, who grew up in Davenport, is one of many Iowa athletes to play professionally. (Iowa Bystander)

A young lady helps her favorite boxer into the ring. (Willkie House)

Drake University's basketball team made it to the Final Four in 1969. (Drake University Sports Information)

Perhaps the most neglected aspect of black sports history in Iowa is African-American women. In recent years black women have gained publicity for their exploits on the playing fields of Iowa. What are their stories?

Thelma Howe played for Bedford High School's integrated girls basketball team of 1923–1924 (courtesy Ruth Parrish)

Notes

1. Charles P. Howard, "Negro Athletes," *Iowa Bystander*, April 2, 1920.

2. Ibid.

3. The plaque is located at Francis X. Cretzmeyer Field in Iowa City, Iowa.

4. Mike Finn and Chad Leistikow, *Hawkeye Legends, Lists, and Lore: The Athletic History of the Iowa Hawkeyes* (Champaign: Sports Publishing, 1998), 103.

5. For more on Ted Wheeler, see the Faculty Vertical Files at the University of Iowa Archives, Iowa City, IA.

6. Two excellent introductions to the field of sports history are S.W. Pope, ed., *The New American Sport History: New Approaches and Perspectives* (Urbana and Chicago: Univ. of Illinois Press, 1996), and Steven A. Riess, ed., *Major Problems in American Sport History* (Boston and New York: Houghton Mifflin, 1997). See also David K. Wiggins, *Glory Bound: Black Athletes in a White America* (Syracuse: Syracuse Univ. Press, 1997).

7. *Field of Dreams* was directed by Phil Alden Robinson and starred Kevin Costner and Ray Liota. Released in 1989 by Universal, the film was based on a story in W.P. Kinsella's *Shoeless Joe Jackson Comes to Iowa* (Boston: Houghton Mifflin, 1980). Baseball has been the subject of an enormous amount of popular and scholarly writing. Geoffrey Ward, *Baseball: An Illustrated History* (New York: Knopf, 1994), is an excellent popular history, while Benjamin G. Rader's *Baseball: A History of America's Game* (Urbana: Univ. of Illinois Press, 1992), is an excellent study written by a sports historian. For biographical essays, see David L. Porter, ed., *Biographical Dictionary of American Sports: Baseball* (Westport: Greenwood, 1987). For a general grasp of Iowa's contribution to the game, see Jerry E. Clark, *Anson to Zuber: Iowa Boys in the Major Leagues* (Omaha: Making History, 1992).

8. See the entries on Fowler in Porter, *Baseball*, 213–14, and in James A. Riley, *Biographical Encyclopedia of the Negro Baseball Leagues* (New York: Carroll and Graf, 1994), 294–95.

9. Maury White, "Believe It or Not: Story of Keokuk's Jackie Robinson," *DMR*, July 29, 1997.

10. Ralph Christian, "A Breakthrough Season: Bud Fowler and the 1885 Keokuks," unpublished essay, courtesy Jack Lufkin, SHSI.

11. Ibid., 1.

12. Ibid.

13. Ibid., 2, 5.

14. For brief assessments of Anson's career, see Donald Dewey and Nicholas Acocella, *The Biographical History of Baseball* (New York: Carroll and Graf, 1995), 13–14, and the entry on Anson in Porter, *Baseball*, 10–12.

15. Porter, *Baseball*, 10–12.

16. See Jerry Mulloy, comp., *Sol White's History of Colored Baseball, with Other Documents of the Early Black Game, 1886–1936* (Lincoln: Univ. of Nebraska Press, 1995), xvi–xxi, 76–77. See also *DMR*, Jan. 9, 2000.

17. Adrian C. Anson, *A Ball Player's Career: Being the Personal Experiences and Reminiscences of Adrian C. Anson, Late Manager and Captain of the Chicago Base Ball Club* (Chicago: Era, 1900).

18. Ibid., 148.

19. Ibid., 148–49.

20. Ibid., 150.

21. See David L. Porter, "Cap Anson of Marshalltown: Baseball's First Superstar," *Palimpsest* 61 (1980): 98–107 (quote from page 102); Ocania Chalk, *Pioneers of Black Sport* (New York: Dodd, Mead, 1975), 17–20, 26–37.

22. William W. McDonald, "The Black Athlete in American Sports," in *Sports in Modern America,* ed. William J. Baker and John M. Carroll (St. Louis: River City, 1981), 95; Edna and Art Rust Jr., *Art Rust's Illustrated History of the Black Athlete* (Garden City: Doubleday, 1985), 3–7.

23. The articles from the *Bystander* are contained in a file compiled by John Zeller. Once a forgotten chapter in baseball history, the Negro Leagues have received scholarly attention in recent years. See Dick Clark and Larry Lester, *The Negro Leagues Book* (Cleveland: Society for American Baseball Research, 1994), and Riley, op. cit. Three classic works that stimulated research on the Negro Leagues are Robert Peterson, *Only the Ball Was White* (Englewood Cliffs: Prentice-Hall, 1970); John Holway, *Voices From the Great Black Baseball Leagues* (New York: Dodd, Mead, 1975); Donn Rogosin, *Invisible Men: Life in Baseball's Negro Leagues* (New York: Atheneum, 1983).

24. Undated *Bystander* clipping, in author's possession.

25. Matthew Sonka, "Negro Baseball in Iowa," undergraduate research paper, Simpson College, Indianola, Iowa, 1997.

26. Janice A. Beran, "Diamonds in Iowa: Blacks, Buxton, and Baseball," *Journal of Negro History* 75 (Summer/Fall 1990): 81–95. The quotation appears on page 93. For more on Buxton, see Dorothy Schwieder, Joseph Hraba, and Elmer Schwieder, *Buxton: Work and Racial Equality in a Coal Mining Community* (Ames: Iowa State Univ. Press, 1987), 94, 153–54.

27. Maury White, "The Story of the Algona Brownies: A Black Team Became 'Best of the West,'" *DMR*, Aug. 28, 1994. See also David Kemp and Roger Wilden, "The Algona Brownies, Champs of the West," *Baseball Research Journal* 17 (1988): 76–79. For complete rosters of the Algona Brownies, see Clark and Lester, 56–57.

28. White, "The Algona Brownies."

29. Ibid.

30. Kenneth Pins, "The Colored Giants: They Made a Bit of Small-town History," *DMR*, Aug. 22, 1993.

31. Ibid.

32. John B. Holway, "J.L. Wilkinson: The Gift of Light," in *Blackball Stars: Negro League Pioneers* (Westport: Meckler, 1988): 327–43. (The quotation appears on page 327.) For a brief summary of the team's history, see Clark and Lester, 29. For brief sketches of Wilkinson's life, see Porter, *Baseball*, 608–9; Riley, 242–43.

33. Ralph Christian corrects major errors and adds significant details to published accounts in "James Leslie Wilkinson: The Iowa Years, 1878–1916," an unpublished essay, courtesy of the author. For more on Donaldson, see Riley, 242–43. Mark Ribowsky, *Don't Look Back: Satchel Paige in the Shadows of Baseball* (New York: Simon and Schuster, 1994), reports that John Donaldson led the Colored House of David team from Sioux City in 1929.

34. Holway, 237.

35. See Janet Bruce, *The Kansas City Monarchs: Champions of Black Baseball* (Lawrence: Univ. Press of Kansas, 1985).

36. Maury White, "A Forgotten Chapter of Baseball History: Remarkable Iowan Pioneered Black Teams, Women Players," *DMR*, Aug. 21, 1994; Maury White, "Mystery of 'Jap' Mikado Is Solved: Japan's First Pro Ball Player Started in Des Moines in 1902," *DMR*, April 7, 1996. For Sayama's earlier article, see "A Black Team in Japan," *Baseball Research Journal* 16 (1987): 85–88. Rosters of the 1916 and 1917 All Nations are listed in Clark and Lester, *The Negro Leagues Book* (1994), 68–69.

37. Ron Maly and John Holway, "Baseball's Great Brewer Joins Register Hall," *DMR*, April 1, 1984. For more on Brewer, see John Holway, "Papa Chet: Chet Brewer," in *Black Diamonds: Life in the Negro Leagues from Men Who Lived It* (Westport: Meckler, 1989): 18–38.

38. Maly and Holway, "Brewer Joins Register Hall." See also Rev. David Polich, "The Color Line in Baseball and Iowans Who Played Large in Its History," unpublished paper in author's possession.

39. Clark, *From Anson to Zuber*, 128–29; Larry Moffi and Jonathan Kronstadt, *Crossing the Line: Black Major Leaguers, 1947–1959* (Iowa City: Univ. of Iowa Press, 1994), 83–84. For more on Baker, see "Most Important Negro in Baseball," *Ebony*, May 1, 1956, 100–4.

40. *Quad-City Times*, Dec. 3, 1999. Researcher David Kemp disputes the claim that Baker was the first black manager in the minor leagues. Sam Bankhead managed Farnham in the Provincial League in 1948.

41. Ribowsky, 148–49. Other works on Paige include Leroy Satchel Paige with Hal Leibovitz, *Pitchin' Man: Satchel Paige's Own Story* (Westport: Meckler, 1948; repr. 1992). See also Leroy Satchel Paige, with David Lipman, *Maybe I'll Pitch Forever* (Lincoln: Univ. of Nebraska Press, 1962; repr. 1993).

42. Paige, *Pitchin' Man*, 69.

43. For more on Paige and barnstorming, see Bruce, op. cit.; Jim Kaplan, "Bittersweet Barnstorming," *Sports Illustrated*, Feb. 16, 1981, 45; Bruce Chadwick, *When the Game Was Black and White: The Illustrated History of Baseball's Negro Leagues* (New York: Abbeville, 1992), 1–14, 60–82, 161.

44. Bob Feller, with Bill Gilbert, *Now Pitching, Bob Feller* (New York: Carol, 1990), 139. For short biographical sketches of his career, see Dewey and Acocella, 138–39, and Porter, *Baseball,* 176–77. See also the Bob Feller Hometown Exhibit in Van Meter, Iowa.

45. For example, see Ken Burns, "The Sixth Inning: The National Pastime," *Baseball,* Public Broadcasting System television documentary, 1994.

46. Ribowsky, 230. The best book on the Feller-Robinson controversy is Arnold Rampersad's definitive biography, *Jackie Robinson: A Biography* (New York: Knopf, 1997). Other useful studies of Robinson include Glen Stout and Dick Johnson, *Jackie Robinson: Between the Baselines* (San Francisco: Woodford, 1997); Jules Tygiel, *Baseball's Great Experiment: Jackie Robinson and His Legacy* (New York: Oxford Univ. Press, 1997); and Maury Allen, *Jackie Robinson: A Life Remembered* (New York: Franklin Watts, 1987). For a brief sketch of Robinson's career, see Porter, 479–81.

47. Rampersad, 361; Feller, 213; Allen, 162.

48. Feller, 213.

49. See the author's entry on Gibson in George B. Kirsch, Othello Harris, and Claire E. Nolte, eds., *Encyclopedia of Ethnicity and Sports in the U.S.* (Westport: Greenwood, 2000).

50. Bob Gibson, with Lonnie Wheeler, *A Stranger to the Game: The Autobiography of Bob Gibson* (New York: Penguin, 1994), 38.

51. Ibid., xiv.

52. Pat Cassete and Merl Eberly of Clarinda, Iowa, provided the author with information on Smith. See also David L. Porter, ed., *Dictionary of American Sports: 1989–1992, Supplement for Baseball, Football, Basketball, and Other Sports* (Westport: Greenwood, 1992), 206-7.

53. Irving Kawarsky, formerly of Des Moines, Iowa, and now of Shawnee, Kansas, shared his knowledge of softball with me in a series of letters. Irv Kawarsky to David McMahon, Aug. 9, 1999, and Aug. 31, 1999, in the author's possession. See also Kawarsky's *The History of Iowa Men's and Women's Fast Pitch Softball, 1924–1991* (Riverside IA: self-published, 1991), and his "The Evolution and History of Softball in the United States," M.A. thesis, Drake University, Des Moines, 1956.

54. Kawarsky, *Fast Pitch Softball,* 138–44, 182–88.

55. See the program produced by the Des Moines Softball Hall of Fame, "25th Annual Men's Fast Pitch Tournament," May 16–17, 1998, 8–9, in the author's possession.

56. "Legendary Ghosts to Be Honored," *Sioux City Journal,* July 28, 1983; clippings file compiled by Mrs. Linda Hopp of Moville, Iowa, in the author's possession.

57. Maury White, "100 Years of Black Athletes in Iowa," *DMR,* Sept. 3, 1995. Holbrook's first name is referred to as "Frank" or "Carelton" by various sources. For the former, see "Holbrook Made History as Tipton and U of I Player," *Cedar Rapids Gazette,* June 30, 1996. For the latter, see Finn and Lestikow, 243.

58. Maury White, "100 Years of Black Athletes in Iowa."

59. Ibid.

60. Ibid.

61. For perspective on this issue, see David K. Wiggins, "Prized Performers but Frequently Overlooked Students: The Involvement of Black Athletes in Intercollegiate Sports at Predominantly White University Campuses, 1890–1972," *Research Quarterly for Exercise and Sport 62* (1991): 164–77.

62. Maury White, "100 Years of Black Athletes in Iowa."

63. For more on this, see David R. McMahon, "The Black and Gold: African Americans and Athletics at the University of Iowa," a paper delivered at the Sport and Cultural Distinctiveness Symposium in May 1999 at Iowa City, Iowa, in the author's possession.

64. See Finn and Lestikow, 101–3.

65. See Philip G. Hubbard, *New Dawns: A 150-Year Look at Human Rights at Iowa* (Iowa City: University of Iowa Sesquicentennial Committee, 1996), 26–27; Greg Johnson, "Diversity," *Sesquicentennial Spectator Special* (Iowa City: University of Iowa, 1996–97), 6–7; Herbert C. Jenkins, "The Negro Student at the University of Iowa: A Sociological Study," M.A. thesis, University of Iowa, 1933; Finn and Lestikow, 64–65; David Wolf, *Foul!: The Connie Hawkins Story* (New York: Holt, Rinehart, and Winston, 1972); Dennis Green, with Gene McGivern, *No Room for Crybabies* (Champaign: Sports Publications, 1997), 4.

66. Faculty Vertical Files, University of Iowa Archives, Iowa City; biographical sketch of C. Vivian Stringer in the Janice Beran Papers, Iowa Women's Archives, University of Iowa Library, Iowa City; *Iowa City Press-Citizen,* March 7, 1986.

67. Ocania Chalk, *Black College Sport* (New York: Dodd, Mead, 1976), 178.

68. Chalk, 184. Chalk gives extensive treatment to Butler in his book. I must also thank Ralph Scharnau and Hal Chase for passing along information to me. The file I have contains correspondence, newspaper clippings, and other material that was copied from a file at the University of Dubuque. Cited hereafter as the Sol Butler File.

Don Graves broke the color barrier in 1958 when he coached the girls and boys basketball teams at Randall High School. (Bob Long photo / Des Moines Register)

(Right) Natasha Kaiser-Brown, one of Iowa's great female athletes, competed for Des Moines Roosevelt High School. (courtesy Barbara Smith-Kaiser)

69. Ibid., 302–4; Roger Crimmins, "Olympic Trials — Sol Butler, UD Olympian," Sol Butler File.

70. Chalk, 350.

71. Ibid., 312.

72. Ibid., 302–4. See letter from Henry J. Reemtsma to Ocania Chalk, Oct. 27, 1975, in Sol Butler File.

73. Chalk, 312–14.

74. Ibid., 315–16. For more on African-Americans in professional football, see Robert W. Peterson, *Pigskin: The Early Years of Pro Football* (New York: Oxford Univ. Press, 1999).

75. Chalk, 317.

76. See clippings in the Sol Butler File. See also *DMR*, March 30, 1958. The Sol Butler Memorial Center no longer exists.

77. David L. Porter, ed., *Biographical Dictionary of American Sports: Football* (Westport: Greenwood, 1987): 530–32. For more on Slater, see the Alumni Vertical File, University of Iowa Archives, Iowa City.

78. Porter, ed., *Biographical Dictionary of American Sports: Football*, 530–32.

79. Ibid.

80. See Dick Lamb and Bert McGrane, *75 Years with the Fighting Hawkeyes* (Dubuque: William C. Brown, 1964), 69–73; Murray Sperber, *Shake Down the Thunder: The Creation of Notre Dame Football* (New York: Henry Holt, 1993), 116.

81. Bert McGrane, "First Football Residents of Iowa's Hall of Fame: Berwanger, Devine, Kinnick, Layden, Slater," *DMR*, March 18, 1951.

82. James A. Peterson, *Slater of Iowa* (Chicago: Hinckley and Schmitt, 1958).

83. "Iowa's Duke Slater Dead at 67," *DMR*, Aug. 16, 1966; "Ex-Grid Star Slater Dies," *Daily Iowan*, Aug. 16, 1966. See transcript of "It's Sports Time with Phil Rizzuto," University of Iowa Alumni Files, University of Iowa Library, Iowa City.

84. "Rare Short Subjects: The Negro in Industry, Sports and Entertainment," Media Services, University of Iowa Library, Iowa City; "In Memory of Duke," a program for Slater Hall Dedication Ceremony, sponsored by the Black Students Union, Oct. 27, 1972, University of Iowa Alumni Files, University of Iowa Library, Iowa City; "UI Slater Hall Dedicated, Family Attend Homecoming," *Daily Iowan*, Oct. 30, 1972. For more on Slater, see Gus Schrader, "Duke Slater: Helmetless Star Tackle Was All American On, Off Field," in Mark Dukes and Gus Schrader (ed. Francis J. Fitzgerald), *Greatest Moments in Iowa Hawkeyes Football History* (Chicago: Triumph, 1998), 18–19; "Hawkeye Hero: Fred "Duke" Slater, a Mountain of a Man," in Finn and Lestikow, 33.

85. *Omaha Monitor*, Sept. 28, 1923, and Sept. 10, 1926; Lamb and McGrane, 93.

86. Emlen Tunnell, with Bill Gleason, *Footsteps of a Giant* (Garden City: Doubleday, 1966), 68–69.

87. Thomas R. O'Donnell, "Students Want Statue Renamed," *DMR*, Oct. 1, 1996; "Trice Stadium to Be Recommended," *DMR*, Nov. 17, 1996; Donald Kaul, "A Long Crusade for Jack Trice," *DMR*, Feb. 4, 1997; "Trice Unveiled at Iowa State," *DMR*, Aug. 15, 1997; "Support Swells for Jack Trice Stadium," *Iowa Stater*, Feb. 1997.

88. "Inspiration on an August Evening," *DMR*, Sept. 3, 1997; Martin Jischke, "Honor Trice's Sacrifice, Inspiration," *DMR*, Sept. 6, 1997. See also Maury White, "The Legend of Jack Trice," *The Iowan* (Fall 1997): 49–52, and Steve Jones, *Football's Fallen Hero: The Jack Trice Story* (Logan IA: Perfection Learning, 1999).

89. In addition to the Jack Trice references previously cited, see also "Who Was Jack Trice?," Iowa State University web site, www.iastate.edu/ 80~athletics_info/fb/jacktrice.html.

90. The letter is in the collection of the Iowa State University Library, Ames.

91. Matt Trowbridge, "The Man behind Floyd of Rosedale," *Iowa City Press-Citizen*, Nov. 25, 1989.

92. Ibid.

93. See Robert Wilson Meinhard, "History of the State University of Iowa: Physical Education and Athletics for Men," M.A. thesis, University of Iowa, 1947, 84–86.

94. Maury White, "Mugging of Bright Made History," *DMR*, June 11, 1990; Jane Burns, "Photos that Made History," *DMR*, July 13, 1999.

95. See Janice Beran, "Racism Rears Its Ugly Head in the Midwest, Football, 1923 and 1951," a paper presented at the North American Society of Sport History, May 1990, in the Janice Beran Papers, Iowa Women's Archives, University of Iowa Library, Iowa City.

96. "Maury White, "Bright Joins Hall," *DMR*, March 29, 1970; Bill Bryson, *The Babe Didn't Point and Other Stories about Iowans and Sports* (Ames: Iowa State Univ. Press, 1989), 46–48. Warrick Lee Barrett, *Johnny Bright, Champion* (Edmonton: Commonwealth, 1996).

97. For more on the silver medalist in the 4 x 400 relay at the 1992 Barcelona Olympics, see Shelly Stork, "Natasha Kaiser-Brown," undergraduate research paper, Simpson College, Indianola IA, 1997. For more on C. Vivian Stringer, see the Faculty Vertical File at the University of Iowa Archives, Iowa City. For more on Nina Smith, the first African-American "Miss Iowa Basketball" and 1999 *Parade* magazine and *USA Today* player of the year, see *DMR*, April 7, 1999.

David R. McMahon is a Ph.D. candidate in history at the University of Iowa. He has published essays and reviews on African-American history, sport history, public history, and immigration/ethnic history. At Iowa he has taught various courses on the history of the twentieth century. Dave lives in Lone Tree with his wife, Shannon, and daughter, Delaney.

The author gratefully acknowledges the assistance given to him by Outside In's *other authors, the staff at the University of Iowa's Main Library, and to the many Iowans and former Iowans, like William Naber and Irving Kawarsky, who gave him invaluable information. David Kemp of Sioux Falls, South Dakota, contributed important details on baseball history.*

This essay is dedicated to the memory of Earl F. (Tony) England.

UNI's Tony Davis rides his opponent. (UNI Sports Information)

Larry Taylor (left) and Jerry "Flakes" Burrell with students at their studio in the Black Theology Center of Des Moines, c. 1970 (courtesy Rose Burrell, photo by Glenn McKinney)

Iowa and the Artist of African Descent

by William S. Doan

This chapter deals with the impact Iowans have had on the history of African-American art, as well as some of the accomplishments of contemporary black artists who have lived and worked in Iowa. The definition of *art* used for this essay includes traditional and non-traditional forms of painting, sculpture, photography, printmaking, graphic arts, and non-commercial performance arts.

It is true that Iowa is better known for agriculture than aesthetics, but America's heartland has supplied major talents who have graced the nation's cultural centers with their creative gifts. Although far from the key urban centers of African-American culture, both black and non-black Iowans played historically important roles in the development of African-American art throughout the twentieth century.

Iowa and the Harlem Renaissance

It seems at least ironic, if not illogical, that Iowa, overwhelming white and rural, should have made significant contributions to black culture in the United States. But the Harlem Renaissance, the first flowering of African-American artistic expression powerful enough to be called a movement, was actively promoted by two non-black Iowa natives, Carl Van Vechten and William E. Harmon.

Carl Van Vechten was born in Cedar Rapids in 1880. He left Iowa to attend the University of Chicago, but after two years in the Windy City, Van Vechten found the Midway campus as boring and constrictive as his native state, so he moved on to New York. There he became a prominent critic, author, and artist. James Smalls, a contemporary black writer, wrote that "of all the key players in New York in the years spanning the 1920s until his death in 1964, Van Vechten was perhaps the most well-known and the most influential — earning a reputation as a connoisseur and chronicler of Harlem and its black inhabitants through his activities as novelist, music and dance critic, patron of the arts, and photographer." Likewise, in his book *Harlem Renaissance* Nathan Irvin Huggins called Van Vechten "a kind of midwife" to a movement that produced painters such as Aaron Douglas, Palmer Hayden, Archibald J. Motley Jr., and Hale A. Woodruff, as well as sculptors Richmond Barthé, Sargent Claude Johnson, and Augusta Savage.[1]

The Harlem Renaissance, the first flowering of African–American artistic expression powerful enough to be called a movement, was actively promoted by two non-black Iowa natives. . . .

Carl Van Vechten, born in Cedar Rapids, became a leading figure in the Harlem Renaissance of the 1920s. (SHSI Des Moines)

However, not all critics are so kind in their assessments of Van Vechten's patronage and that of his wealthy white friends. Sharon F. Patton, author of a history of African-American art, blames these white patrons for "segregating New Negro art from the artistic mainstream."[2] The issue that Patton raises remains a point of sometimes bitter debate among black artists and their supporters: Is there a "black aesthetic," and who may define it?

Earlier in the twentieth century, an exhibition of African art at the Trocadaro Museum in Paris so moved the great Spanish artist Pablo Picasso that he began to make daring experiments that eventually changed the course of European art. Should the artist of African descent follow the lead of African-influenced European artists toward styles that were, at the time, confusing even to those viewers who were highly educated? Or, instead, should the artist render the life of black people in terms that were easily understood by all?

The most famous African-American painter of the generation that preceded the artists of the Harlem Renaissance was Henry Ossawa Tanner (1859–1937). Tanner learned by experience that the art patrons of the eastern United States, and later the elite of Paris, were not interested in his sympathetic portrayal of black subjects. This most gifted of artists, trained by the great Thomas Eakins, hoped that his portraits of real African-Americans would provide a counterbalance for the grotesque, mocking imagery common in the work of white genre painters of the period. When the art world of his day proved indifferent, in order to make his living Tanner was forced to turn to the popular biblical subjects for which he is best known.[3]

In 1925, Howard University professor Alain Locke, a leading figure of the Harlem Renaissance, published an essay in *Survey Graphic* magazine devoted to the new black artists. Locke called for a revival of racial pride "expressed in economic independence, cultural and political militancy." In his view, African art would replace the classical art of Greece and Rome in the visual vocabulary of the New Negro artist. Locke saw this as the means whereby African-American artists could enter the artistic mainstream, which was already under the spell of the African-influenced masters of Europe. However, as Patton points out, "Locke reduced Africa to a cultural trope for the purpose of promoting racial authenticity . . . ignoring the real complexity of its culture."[4]

White critics such as Van Vechten seemed to be swept up by the exoticism they discerned in the work of the New Negro artists. Moreover, they were not above exploiting this "otherness" for their personal gain. In 1926, Van Vechten published a novel he called *Nigger Heaven*. The crude title shocked even Van Vechten's father, but the book was an enormous international success. It contained lightly disguised portraits of many of the leading lights of the new black artistic movement. Black critics such as W. E. B. DuBois thought *Nigger Heaven* was salacious; others were angered by Van Vechten's nerve in daring to write about the black experience at a time when black authors had difficulty finding major publishers. Van Vechten made no apologies for his novel, and the book was eventually translated into nine foreign languages. Re-issued years after Van Vechten's death, the novel was characterized by critic Paul Padgette as "creative and imaginative, . . . a phenomenal work to be published by a white author in the 1920s."[5]

If Van Vechten's reputation rested solely on his infamous novel and his promotion/exploitation of young black artists, he would probably be forgotten now, certainly worth little more than a footnote in the story of the Harlem Renaissance. But his most memorable achievement was still to come.

Six years after *Nigger Heaven* brought the new black art movement to the attention of the world, Van Vechten abandoned literature for a career as the unpaid court photographer of Harlem's black artists and performers. Van Vechten's photographs of African-American artists, performers, writers, and other notables, writes James Smalls, "assisted in the establishment of blackness as dignified and beautiful within the confines of a bourgeois western art tradition."[6] The collection of thousands of negatives and prints made by the former Iowan constitute the most complete inventory of black celebrity portraits made between 1932 and 1964. They are housed with the rest of Van Vechten's estate at Yale University. In addition, many vintage Van Vechten prints are now owned by the Smithsonian museums and other important art institutions.

Van Vechten's role in the development and, regrettably, the exploitation of black artists was and still is controversial. Re-examination of his career, his personal relationships with some of the stars of the New Negro movement, and his impact on their careers — which now seem larger and more important than his own work — continues to this day. Black critics such as Patton are willing to admit only that Van Vechten and his friends were "well intended."[7]

The second Iowan to make his presence felt among the artists of the new black movement was real estate investor William E. Harmon (1862–1928). In the last years of his life, Harmon created the Harmon Foundation, which operated in New York City from 1925 until 1967 and funded the William E. Harmon awards for "Distinguished Achievement among Negroes." Administered by Mary Beattie Brady, the Harmon Foundation became best known for its visual arts prizes and for a series of juried exhibitions (1926, 1927, 1928, and 1933) held in New York City under the direction of the Commission on Race Relations of the Federal Council of the Church of Christ in America. The Harmon Foundation also sponsored traveling exhibitions, which for the most part toured historically black colleges in the South.[8]

Like Van Vechten's patronage, the efforts of the Harmon Foundation created controversy. Although the white director of the foundation, Mary Beattie Brady, was advised by Alain Locke and other leaders of the New Negro artists' movement, the selection of pictures and the choice of prize winners were not always warmly accepted. Nevertheless, today the catalogs of the Harmon-sponsored exhibitions are among the most important documents of the first significant African-American art movement.

Contemporary art historians and critics, focusing their attention on the artists of the Harlem Renaissance, tend to ignore patrons such as Van Vechten and Harmon, whose support of black artists provided an important source of the funding and promotion that all artistic enterprises must have in order to survive. It should also be noted that Van Vechten, one of the most important cultural gatekeepers of his day, placed his reputation on the line for the black artists whose work he admired. At a time when the Ku Klux Klan was a national phenomenon and racism was considered respectable even in academia, Van Vechten's decision to champion the burgeoning aspirations of African-American artists could not have been an easy one.

Iowa and the Art of Africa

Alain Locke, intellectual leader of the New Negro fine arts movement, urged those who wished to capture a "true" African-American culture to become familiar with African art.[9] But the artist who wanted to carry out Locke's program in the 1920s would have been hard pressed to find a major art museum willing to show "primitive" African sculpture as part of its permanent collection. The works that had so astonished Picasso and other avant-garde artists in Paris in the early years of the twentieth century were still mostly relegated to museums of ethnology and anthropology.

Today, however, collections of African art, primarily wooden sculptures, can be found on permanent display at the Des Moines Art Center and the Museum of Art at the University of Iowa in Iowa City. The Brody Collection at the Des Moines Art Center and the Stanley Collection at the University of Iowa Museum of Art were the gifts of wealthy white families eager to share a passion for African art with their fellow Iowans. Catalogs dealing with objects in both collections have been published by their respective museums. Another small group of African works is held by the Blanden Art Museum in Fort Dodge. Taken as a whole, these collections are among the finest public exhibitions of art by black Africans in the Midwest.

Iowa and the Art of Haiti

If you wish to study the art of the Italian Renaissance, you would certainly want to visit Italy. The great art of imperial Spain is found at the Prado museum in Madrid, and France offers a host of fine museums that examine every period of French culture. But if you wish to see some of the major works of the black artists of Haiti, you need go no further than the public art museums of Waterloo and Davenport. During the past 30 years, museums in these cities have acquired a selection of paintings, sculptures, banners, and other works that now constitute the largest accumulation of Haitian art in the United States and the largest collection of Haitian art outside Haiti.

Unfortunately, the Haitian holdings of the Waterloo Center for the Arts and Davenport City Museum of Art are probably better known outside the borders of Iowa than within the state. *Tracing the Spirit,* an exhibition selected from the permanent collection of the Davenport Museum of Art, has been shown in Akron, Ohio; Naples and Coral Cables, Florida; Oklahoma City, Oklahoma; and Los Angeles, California.[10] *Haitian Art — Twenty Years of Collecting at the Waterloo Museum of Art* has been seen in the gallery of Purdue University in Indiana, the Zanesville Art Center in Ohio, and the Quincy Art Center in Illinois.[11] Both exhibitions were accompanied by handsome, colorful catalogs that show major works in the collections. The catalogs also contain

Iowa's remarkable Haitian collections are the products of the individual enthusiasms of local donors who visited the island and were enchanted by the rich visions of Haiti's artists.

scholarly essays on customs and aesthetics in the context of Haiti, the first black-ruled nation in the Western Hemisphere.

Iowa's remarkable Haitian collections are the products of the enthusiasm of local donors who visited the island and were enchanted by the rich visions of Haiti's artists. The Davenport exhibition catalog is dedicated to Dr. Walter E. Neiswanger, long-time museum trustee and founding donor of the Haitian collection. The larger Waterloo collection was established by major gifts of art given in 1977 by Dr. and Mrs. F. Harold Rueling. Many other patrons have since contributed to these holdings, including noted Haitian art authority Ute Stebich. The City of Waterloo has appropriated funds that allowed museum staff to travel to Haiti and bring back work by new artists.

Iowa and the Art of Richard Hunt

Fort Des Moines, the military camp at the edge of Iowa's capital city, has a unique place in U.S. history. It served as the site for the first training camp for African-American commissioned officers during World War 1 and for the training of the first Woman's Auxiliary Army Corps (WAAC) in 1942. Fort Des Moines was thus the initial setting for the overall racial and gender command integration of America's armed forces.

A monument celebrating the historical significance of Fort Des Moines has been commissioned by the board of the Fort Des Moines Memorial Park and Education Center. Richard H. Hunt, the artist selected to design and build the monument's heroic sculpture, is an internationally acclaimed artist and a Fellow of the American Academy of Arts and Sciences. A native of Illinois, Hunt has enjoyed an illustrious career that includes major commissions in many American cities. His smaller sculpture and graphic work can be found in several Iowa museums, including the Waterloo Museum of Art, the Des Moines Art Center, and the Blanden Art Museum in Fort Dodge. But none of these institutions owns one of his giant outdoor pieces, like that commissioned for the Fort Des Moines project.

The board's invitation to create this important historical monument is not the first time Hunt has been asked to design a large work in Iowa. In the late 1970s, Hunt was invited to Fort Dodge to discuss making a sculpture garden in a rural setting, five miles north of the city. His sketches for the project, published here for the first time, include large sculptures and an altered landscape. Unfortunately, the project was never realized.

Hunt's Fort Des Moines commission is historic in both subject matter and scale. It is among the largest outdoor sculpture

Richard Hunt. Scale model for Fort Des Moines sculpture. (courtesy Richard Hunt)

Richard Hunt. Two sketches for a sculpture garden in Fort Dodge. c. 1978. Ink on paper. (courtesy William Doan)

projects undertaken in Iowa and the first to commemorate an important event in twentieth-century African-American history.[12]

African-American Artists in Iowa

The painters, sculptors, graphic artists, dancers, and performance artists discussed in this chapter live or have lived and worked in Iowa during the twentieth century. Some are included because they received a significant part of their professional training within the state's borders. Others are mentioned because they created important works while residing in Iowa. Still others have spent most of their professional lives in Iowa, becoming part of the cultural history of the state while contributing to the traditions of their chosen media. The profiles that follow are not intended to be a complete list of all the professional artists of color who have lived and worked in Iowa, but taken together they comprise an overview that includes artists working in a variety of media and expressing a variety of viewpoints.

Elisabeth Catlett (b. 1919)

Elisabeth Catlett was the first student to earn a master of fine arts degree at the art school of the University of Iowa. Catlett's degree was conferred in 1940. The relationships of parents and children have interested Catlett during the length of her career, forming a major theme of her art. Her thesis project, a marble sculpture of a mother and child, won the first prize in sculpture at the 1941 American Negro Exposition in Chicago.[13]

In Iowa, Catlett was a student of the renowned painter Grant Wood. The ambitious young black artist and the aging white regionalist found their affinity in the rigor of his approach to the technique of painting. Catlett particularly remembered Wood's dictum: "You should paint what you know about." She realized that she knew most about black people, and it was at Iowa that she began to focus seriously on black subject matter.[14] Although Wood was best known as the painter of *American Gothic* and other semi-satirical midwestern portraits and scenes, he was also a master carpenter who encouraged his students in that craft. It was his knowledge of form and content that influenced Catlett when she took up sculpture.

The Harlem Renaissance was a recent memory when Catlett received her undergraduate degree, *cum laude*, at Howard University in 1938. The influence of Alain Locke, a member of the Howard faculty, and the social upheaval spurred by the disasters of the Great

Depression politicized Catlett and her art. While going to school in Washington, D.C., she participated in peaceful protests, going so far as to stand on the steps of the U.S. Supreme Court with a rope around her neck to dramatize the horror of lynching. Catlett continued to fight injustice during her short stint as head of the art department and teacher at Dillard University in New Orleans. She found imaginative ways for her students to see the art at the Delgado Museum, located in the middle of a park prohibited to blacks, and she was long remembered for confronting her own conservative college administration.[15]

During a trip to Chicago in 1941, Catlett met black muralist Charles White. Six months later, they married and began to seek their individual artistic careers in New York. Following World War 2, Catlett found herself pursued by the infamous Sen. Joseph R. McCarthy and his fellow red-baiters. Exhausted by the frustrations of the fight for justice and caught in a failing marriage, Catlett used a Rosenwald Foundation grant to move to Mexico, returning to New York only to complete her divorce from Charles White.[16] Catlett was hounded by the U.S. State Department, which branded her an "undesirable alien" after she took Mexican citizenship and refused to allow her to return to the United States to visit her ailing mother.[17]

These years of personal and political turmoil were prelude to a new intensity and maturity in the artist's work. In Mexico, Catlett established herself as a teacher and working artist who was nourished by the rich visual tradition of popular Mexican culture. The prints, paintings, and sculptures she subsequently created explored the history and experience of black women with singular depth and beauty of form.

Catlett also found fulfillment in her personal life. In 1947 she married artist Francisco Mora, with whom she raised three sons. Catlett and her husband moved to Cuernavaca in 1976, following her retirement from positions at the National University of Mexico. In her spacious studio, she continued to work on monumental sculptures for which she received worldwide praise.

In 1974, after vigorous protests led by Edward Spriggs, then executive director of the Studio Museum in Harlem, the U.S. government lifted Catlett's *persona non grata* standing so that she could once more travel in her homeland.[18]

Now hailed as one of the world's most famous and successful artists of African descent, Elisabeth Catlett is at last receiving favorable attention in the U.S. A major biographical study of her

Elisabeth Catlett, a student of Grant Wood early in her career (from Anna A. Bontemps, ed., Forever Free: Art by African American Women*)*

life and work was published in 1984, with a text by Samella Lewis, director of the Museum of African-American Art in Los Angeles. More recently, she was among the artists commissioned to create works celebrating the twenty-fifth anniversary of the Hirshhorn Museum and Sculpture Garden in Washington, D.C. A major retrospective exhibition of her work, with an accompanying catalog, was sponsored by the State University of New York. In addition, Morgan State University, a historically black college in Maryland, recently mounted an exhibition of her prints and published a catalog of the show. The text of "Lift Every Voice and Sing," sometimes called the "Negro national anthem," has been published with illustrations based on Catlett's portraits of black women and scenes of black history originally created with the Rosenwald grant during the 1940s.[19]

Catlett's sensitivity to her materials creates in her sculptures the swelling, somewhat abstracted forms that invest them with a sense of refinement. Her figures have dignity, carrying themselves with a monumental grace found in objects created by artists of earlier ages. Always a modernist in her three-dimensional work, Catlett makes use of a more literal style in her graphic art, but she shows the same sensitivity to media and materials in her prints as she does in her sculpture. Her print subjects are often dramatically composed and, in the popular Mexican tradition, they are accessible and highly charged with political meaning.

Leon N. Hicks (b. 1933)

Leon Hicks earned a master of arts in painting (1961) and a master of fine arts degree in printmaking (1963) from the University of Iowa. While in Iowa City he studied printmaking techniques with Mauricio Lasansky. Since leaving the state he has had a distinguished career as an artist, teacher, and historian of black culture.

Hicks taught printmaking at Florida A&M, Lincoln University, and — from 1974 to 1998 — at Webster University in St. Louis, Missouri. Recently retired from Webster, he moved to his native Florida, where his wife, Pauline Ellis Hicks, is head of the medical library at Florida A&M in Tallahassee. The artist's résumé also includes a teaching position at Concord College in Athens, West Virginia, where he was the only black faculty member as well as the only person of color in the town.

Hicks has studied art history at Stanford University and has received a grant from the National Endowment for the Humanities to study African-American art history. He regularly lectures on the art of the Harlem Renaissance. In 1992, he mounted an African-American Invitational Exhibition called *Beyond the Innocence*, for which he wrote the catalog essay. The exhibition was sponsored by the St. Louis Artists' Guild.

Like other black artists, Hicks has known the frustration of having his art defined in terms of his skin color. In his essay for *Beyond the Innocence*, Hicks wrote that "contemporary black African-American artists tend to express a new vision of the world in their artistic intents. It is represented by an ambitious preoccupation with the introverted aspects of their personal intents and this 'vision' is in opposition to the collective sensibilities of the African-American black masses. Their missions are for fulfillment within themselves as artists."[20]

Hicks himself evolved from the highly political black arts movement of the 1960s towards a more personal, non-objective mode of expression. However, during his last year at Webster, Hicks seemed to question the wisdom of his disengagement from the struggle. He was particularly disappointed that the school he had served for so many years had rejected all his recommendations for black faculty members. As at Athens, he was once again the only man of color on the faculty.

As Hicks's vision developed and his knowledge of the history of his medium expanded, his prints "abandoned the representational image," and began to exploit "the essential power of a minimal statement." Hicks called his new working process "generative aesthetics."[21] Hicks's most recent work is a major series of large copper plate burin engravings, completely abstract, displayed titled *Virtualscape/Installation*. The engraving plates were finished before a single proof image was made, a feat of technical virtuosity unique in this difficult and physically demanding medium. In the catalog essay that accompanied *Virtualscape/Installation*, Tom Lang notes that Hicks's early work includes "flawless draftsmanship, a boundless flair for the dramatic, and a particularly personal vision of the transformation of subject to content."[22] It is a measure of Hicks's astonishing confidence in his abilities that his most ambitious and fully realized series of prints — which he regards as a single work — was made in a medium that does not tolerate mistakes or accept corrections. The 30 large engravings that make up the series are accompanied by another massive print, 3 by 6 feet, a superb display of printmaking virtuosity.

It is a measure of Hicks's astonishing confidence that his most ambitious and fully realized series of prints — which he regards as a single work — was made in a medium that does not tolerate mistakes or accept corrections.

In addition to his careers as artists and teacher, Leon Hicks has also been a businessman, executive vice president of Hicks Etchprint, Inc., an art supply and equipment company, and a philanthropist. Profits from his company are plowed back into the community. Hicks has also used funds from print sales to establish the A. Quinn Jones Scholarship Fund.

Floyd L. Shepherd (b. 1939)

Floyd Shepherd is a native of Des Moines. He received an associate of arts degree from Grandview College in 1959, a bachelor of arts from Drake University in 1969, and a master of arts degree from Drake in 1976. He taught in the Des Moines public schools for more than 18 years. In 1986, he took sabbatical leave to study for a degree in counseling at the University of Missouri in St. Louis. Since 1988, he has been Adjunct Professor of Art at Des Moines Area Community College.

From 1992 until 1999, Shepherd operated Two Worlds, the only Des Moines art gallery featuring art and crafts by Africans and people of African descent. The gallery showed the work of several Iowans. Shepherd said that he created Two Worlds so local people of color "could have a place to buy African-American art."[23] He believed that "Iowa has not been kind to the African-American community," systematically ignoring and excluding their cultural contributions from exhibition in the state's cultural institutions. He was critical of the Des Moines Art Center for making only "token overtures" to artists of color. Although Two Worlds made only "a narrow margin of profit" at best, Shepherd felt that local African-Americans needed their "just due." Two Worlds paid homage to an important part of African-American culture otherwise unrepresented in Iowa's capital city.

As an artist, Shepherd believes that "if you live the experience, you can make a statement about that experience," and his personal imagery is based on his experiences. Shepherd's collage pictures, pasted and painted compositions created from clippings and color photocopies of contemporary people and events, weave together various facets of African-American culture and experience, unified by his vision of that experience — rhythmic, complex, and a little dark in feeling — even when the subject is nominally exuberant or joyful.

Jean Berry (b. 1938)

Jean Berry, born in Okmulgee, Oklahoma, received her B.F.A. in 1989 at Drake University, where she majored in drawing and sculpture. Subsequently, she worked with the Two Worlds gallery from 1993 to 1997 and also exhibited her own art in museums and galleries in many states.

Jean Berry. Christ Speaks to the Children *(Stations of the Cross series). Charcoal. 24" x 36". (courtesy Jean Berry)*

Floyd Shepherd, far left, Des Moines artist, gallery owner, and teacher (courtesy William Doan)

Jean Berry, surrounded by her work (courtesy Jean Berry)

Berry is the only woman of African descent profiled in the book *LIFEWORK: Portraits of Iowa Women Artists.*[24] In the book's essay about Berry and her work, author Dawn Bowman notes that the artist "enjoys the ardent support of her family." But it was the death of Berry's third child — her youngest daughter, Toni, at the age of 19 — that perhaps most profoundly affected her art and her life. Berry told Bowman that Toni's struggle with cancer, and the encouragement of her teacher Chaney Rosenbaum gave her the motivation to return to school at Drake.

Writing about her art, Berry says that she wants her work to "evoke strong responses from the people who see it."[25] She works in series, often choosing subject matter with special relevance to the black experience, such as the potent charcoal images she created for *Crisis of the Black Male, Contemporary*

Stations of the Cross, and *Black Fathers and Sons.* In her *Souljah Series,* Berry began to integrate color into her typical black and white imagery, using vivid ethnic patterns to clothe the women she depicted.

Berry, who is leaving her papers to the Iowa Women's Archive in Iowa City, has commented that "my age is an important factor in my confidence level. I don't have a lot of time, so I know I have to give it everything, right now."[26]

Jerry (Flakes) Burrell (1942–1978)

Jerry Burrell was born and lived most of his life in Des Moines. His father, Fred, worked in a packing plant. His mother, Priscilla, stayed home to raise the family's five children in the vibrant black neighborhood surrounding Center Street between 9th and 15th. Jerry showed an interest in art as a young boy, sending off his money for a series of paint-by-numbers kits. He soon realized that this was a money-making scam and began to follow an independent path to creating art.

Shortly after graduating from North High School, Burrell went to San Francisco where he stayed with his father's sister. He soon returned to Des Moines, where he moved into his family's basement and briefly took a job building lawnmowers at Western Tool. Burrell's first studio outside his basement room was at East 9th and Grand, across from the old Hill Brothers shoe store. Later he had a studio at the Black Theology Center at 11th and Forest. With Charles Boston and others, Burrell taught art classes to neighborhood youth.

Burrell became the undisputed leader of this inner-city art colony. He pursued his inner vision of black identity relentlessly, sleeping and eating very little, and painting most of his waking hours. He had little interest in money. His paints were leftovers he found or was given. His painting supports were also unconventional, including — in addition to paper and canvas — found pieces of plywood, planks, and once even a door. When he needed money, he would take one of his paintings to a friend like Al (Hinky) Brewer, who owned a barbershop on University Avenue, and sell it at a modest price. Thus his art, which came out of the Center Street community, usually remained there. Unfortunately, several murals — one in the old Community Center and another in Soul Village — were lost when the buildings were demolished or renovated during urban renewal in the mid-1960s.

Jerry (Flakes) Burrell, in front of his mural at the Hamilton Hill Center, Schenectady, New York, 1977 (courtesy Rose Burrell)

Burrell relocated to Schenectady, New York, in the 1970s. He died there a few years later from lead poisoning contracted from his habit of licking the tip of his paint brush, wet with lead-based house paints.

Jerry Burrell had no children by his first and only marriage, but he and Berniece Lewis had a son. Burrell's legacy lives on in his paintings and sculpture.[27]

Madai (b. 1955)

Timothy Taylor, known professionally as Madai, earned degrees in art and social work from Buena Vista University in Storm Lake. His pictures are included in the permanent collections of the Waterloo Municipal Museum of Art and the Blanden Art Museum in Fort Dodge. He has twice been appointed to the Blanden's board of trustees and currently serves as its president. He also serves as pastor of Agape Church of Christ — Wheel of Compassion Ministry in Fort Dodge.

The first person to influence Madai toward a career in the arts was his older brother, Herman. Madai recalled that Herman "was attending Malcolm X College in Chicago and was doing things with the visual arts."[28] At the age of 14, Madai became interested in the art Herman was developing and began to paint and draw, later adding collage to his repertory.

Spiritual themes are the heart of Madai's art. Primarily interested in works on paper, unique monoprints and collages, in several series he has developed a sophisticated abstract vocabulary to express his search for the divine. Madai's work as a social activist also finds expression in his art — including a series created in response to a brother's AIDS-related death. He has also produced two series of small collages on the subject of black incarceration rates in Iowa and the lack of black counselors and parole officers in the state's corrections system.

In his search for new and fresh visual experience, Madai has developed a hybrid technique that combines elements of steel-plate printing with painting.[29] The "ink" used in the process is oxidized metal, which is allowed to penetrate sheets of heavy paper over periods of time which may extend from days to weeks.[30] Paint — sometimes mixed with sawdust or other materials — is applied sparingly, almost randomly, once the impression of rusted metal has formed the basic image. In recent work, the artist has begun to make use of rusty wire from used political lawn signs to create complex linear patterns.

Madai (courtesy William Doan)

Madai's efforts to establish communication among artists of color resulted in two major group exhibitions, called *Visions of Color*, which were initiated at the Blanden Art Museum. The first of these, seen in 1992 at Fort Dodge, featured only artists of African descent. The second version of the show, produced in 1995, defined "color" in far broader terms. Among the black artists who participated in these shows were Jean Berry, Michael Chinn, Brenda Jones, Madai, Jean Marie Salem, and Fredrick Woodard.[31] Catalogues for both exhibitions were published and made available at the museums where *Visions of Color* was displayed.

Karen Mitchell (b. 1960)

Photographer Karen Mitchell, a native of Des Moines, attended journalism classes at Drake University. Her work as a photojournalist has carried her far in her profession. Early in 2000, Karen began work as deputy photo director of the New York bureau of the Associated Press. She accepted this new

Karen Mitchell's silverprint photograph of an exhausted Wynton Marsalis. 9" x 13" (courtesy Karen Mitchell)

challenge after four years as director of photography for the *Des Moines Register.*

The quality of Karen's work is a tribute to the support and encouragement of her parents. Her father, LeRoy Mitchell, taught art in the Des Moines public schools for many years and was especially influential in Karen's life. "He touched a lot of people," Karen recalls. "He's been dead 15 years, but people still tell me how he influenced them in his classes. I hope to touch people in the same way."

Now that Karen has a potential audience of tens of millions of readers every day, her own influence is bound to be felt. The standards she set for herself are best understood by seeing her pictures, such as her portrait of a weary trumpeter, Wynton Marsalis, exhausted by four hours of rigorous rehearsal for a concert in Rochester, New York. The brilliant, dapper musician has been captured in a rare moment of vulnerability. What the picture does not show is Karen's four-hour wait to seize an expressive moment revealing the physical and emotional price that the quest for perfection extracts from even the greatest artists. Such "selectivity makes an artist," she says.[32] Karen's ability to recognize and capture what a master photographer once called "the decisive moment" sets her apart from others in her profession. According to Karen, the camera may record the image, but "the person behind the picture makes art."

Brenda Jones (b. 1950)

Brenda Jones draws and paints metaphors and symbols, but human drama is never far from the center of her artistic universe. "Art has a lot to do with your environment, your knowledge, and your creative abilities. As a student at Drake, I attended Tyler School of Art in Rome, Italy. It was an opportunity to see Michelangelo's sculptures first-hand. [In Rome] I viewed a retrospective of Vassily Kandinsky's work and witnessed a prolific amount of creativity. This was a magnificent period. Years later, I moved to New York to learn, observe, and study not only great art work in museums and galleries, but also to absorb the cultural diversity of the city itself."[33]

Now teaching at Iowa State University in Ames, Jones passes on to her students the love of art first encouraged by her junior high school art teacher, Mylinda Pyle, when she was only 11. "This incredible woman nourished my love of history and the possibilities of having an art career," she recalls.[34] Today, Jones travels between

Ames and Rome, where she teaches in a school maintained by ISU's design department.

Her own art, Jones says, explores "human complexity and the implications of conscious thought."[35] Cages, masks, bones, and bodies recur in the artist's recent work. Both men and women are depicted, sometimes summoned from her training and imagination, sometimes the result of sessions when she draws from the model, perhaps a friend who is willing to endure a few hours of close scrutiny by the artist. Jones says that the meanings of her paintings sometimes change as they evolve. "I think what I am trying to do in the art is depict how I see society at this moment."[36]

Ruthie O'neil (b. 1940)

Ruthie O'neil has lived in Waterloo since she was 15, but her early years in Mississippi provided the source of her extraordinary yard art. She grew up in a large plantation house passed to her grandmother by the white family for whom she had worked. While friends and neighbors assumed the O'neil family had considerable wealth, they were pressed for cash and found it necessary to repair and re-use old and broken objects to furnish their home. The family marveled at young Ruthie's ability to transform discarded items into functional pieces. She attributes her skill to the example of her grandmother, who recycled well-worn hand-me-downs from her white friends. O'neil also found inspiration for her art in her own visions. "When I was a child, I dreamed about living up North and owning a home that I could decorate like I wanted. My bedroom [in Mississippi] *was* that 'home' where my imagination lived."[37]

Ruthie O'neil's dreams included a specially landscaped yard featuring the color purple. Years later, when she moved to Waterloo and acquired a home, she began to fulfill her folk-art dreams. For the past four decades, O'neil has collected and arranged dozens of disparate objects, most of which she has painted purple. Some of the objects found in O'neil's sculptured environment have been collected by the roadside. Others are objects from everyday life that have taken on new and highly decorative identities. Bathroom fixtures, toy trains, commercial garden decor, and carefully arranged plantings are complimented by rocks, bricks, boards, and discarded containers, often touched with O'neil's purple paint brush. They form a unique and original expression of her inner life.

Brenda Jones (courtesy William Doan)

Ruthie O'neil (below) at home with examples of her yard art in Waterloo (courtesy David Jackson)

African-American Heritage Museum and Cultural Center of Iowa, Cedar Rapids

Among the most recent developments in black art in Iowa is the African-American Heritage Museum and Cultural Center of Iowa in Cedar Rapids. Chartered in 1994, the African-American Heritage Foundation, Inc., has launched a state-wide fund drive to raise more than $3 million for the construction of a museum building. When completed, the museum and cultural center will show collections of African and African-American art, artifacts, and documents, which it has begun to collect. Lectures, performances, and workshops about people of African descent will also be sponsored by the center.

Non-Commercial Performance Art

The African tradition of movement, supremely athletic, full of energy and sophisticated rhythm, has been infused into American culture for almost 400 years. As racial barriers fell in the second half of the twentieth century, African-Americans brought their traditions of dance and sport into the cultural mainstream from which they had been excluded.

The artistic category here called "performance art" is meant to be inclusive of several forms of expression that are essentially athletic but also contain strong aesthetic elements. Sports such as figure skating, diving, and bodybuilding share with dance an aesthetic subjectivity utterly different from activities in which decisions are made by objective scores or timings. Of these four, only dance and bodybuilding exist at a high level in the African-American community of Iowa. Our state has welcomed Bill T. Jones, one of the most influential figures in world dance, who has created and performed two of his most important works within our borders. In Des Moines, while other dance companies came and went, the Gateway Dance Theatre persevered. In bodybuilding, the Mr. Iowa title has been dominated by black competitors and several of these men have reached national stature.

Bill T. Jones (b. 1952)

Iowa seems an unlikely place for the *avant garde* in any field, but the state has provided the setting for workshops and performances by the celebrated dancer and choreographer Bill T. Jones. A visitor to Iowa for many years, the co-founder and director of the Bill T. Jones/Arnie Zane Dance Company has used Iowans of all races and backgrounds as performers and participants in his unique, controversial, and sometimes highly emotional creations.

The Last Supper at Uncle Tom's Cabin, a long complex of dance movements and dramatic readings, was presented at

continued on page 517

The Gateway Dance Theater of Des Moines, rehearsing and performing, c. 1980 (David Penney photos courtesy Penny Furgerson)

Jerry (Flakes) Burrell. Untitled. *1978. Mixed housepaints on plywood. 36" x 48". (courtesy Roger Burrell)*

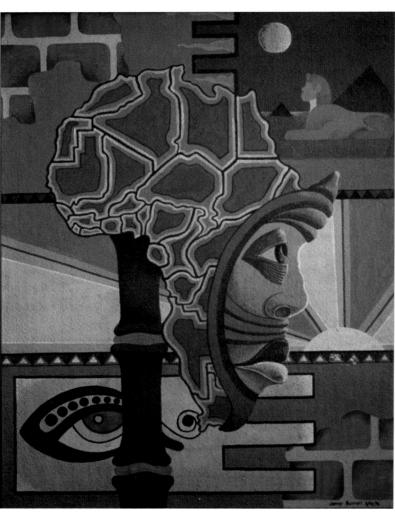

Jerry (Flakes) Burrell. Untitled. *1968. Mixed house paints on plywood. 24" x 30". (courtesy Jerry Burrell family)*

Jerry (Flakes) Burrell. Untitled. *1968. Mixed house paints on scrap board. 6" x 23". (courtesy John and Elaine Estes)*

Jerry (Flakes) Burrell. Images of Africa. *1973. Mixed house paints on plywood. (courtesy Priscilla Burrell)*

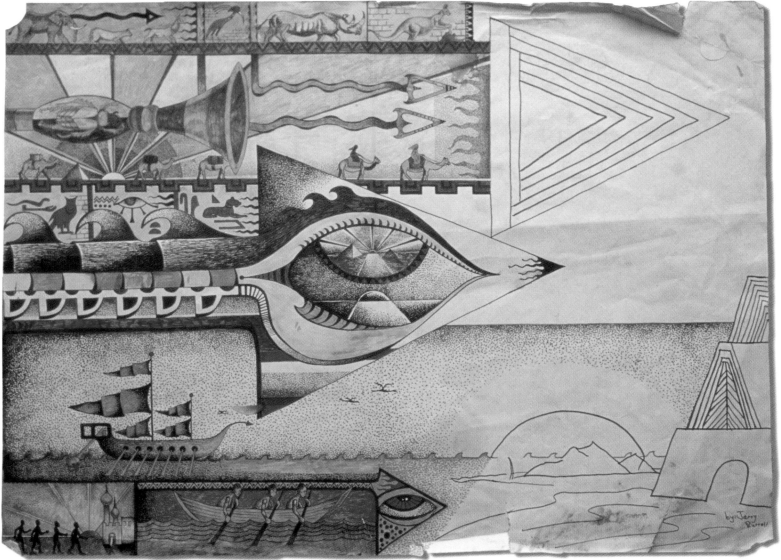

Jerry (Flakes) Burrell. Untitled. *n.d. Watercolor and pen on paper. 30" x 24". (courtesy Rose Burrell)*

Jerry (Flakes) Burrell. Untitled portrait. *1971. Mixed house paints. 11" x 17". (courtesy Jerry Burrell family)*

Jerry (Flakes) Burrell. Untitled. *n.d. Pen and pencil on paper board scrap. 17" x 11". (courtesy Rose Burrell)*

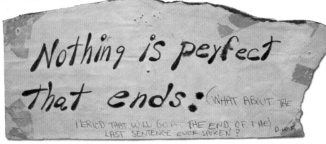

Nothing is perfect that ends: (WHAT ABOUT THE PERIOD THAT WILL GO AT THE END OF THE LAST SENTENCE EVER SPOKEN? D.W.R)

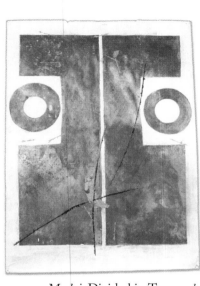

Madai. Divided in Two. *n.d.*
Mixed media on paper. 41" x 58".
(courtesy Madai)

Madai. Untitled poster. *n.d. Mixed media.*
21" x 28". Carried by Madai at a statehouse rally
calling attention to the incarceration of 24 percent
of the state's African-American adult men.
(courtesy Madai)

Madai. Suffering of the Mortal
Soul. *n.d. Mixed media on paper.*
43" x 54". (courtesy Madai)

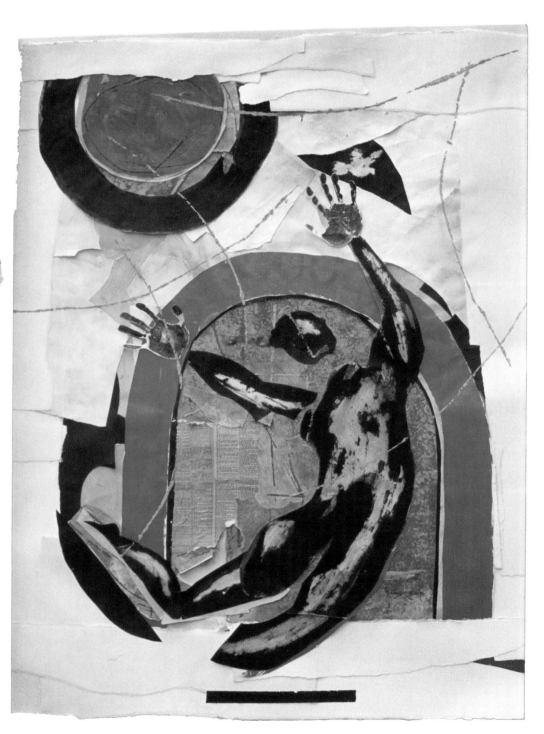

Madai. Outside In. *2000. Mixed media on paper and*
canvas. 57" x72". (courtesy Hal and Avril Chase)

Madai. Cry of the Dove. *1999.*
Mixed media on paper. 52" x 73". (courtesy Madai)

Madai. Hollowed Stirring. *n.d. Mixed media on paper.*
52" x 70". (courtesy Madai)

Madai. Cry of the Dove II. *1999. Mixed media on paper.*
52" x 73". (courtesy Madai)

Jean Berry. Adam. *1996. Oil stick on cardboard with hairspray. (courtesy Jean Berry)*

Jean Berry. Rib of. *1996. Oil stick on cardboard with hairspray. (courtesy Jean Berry)*

Jean Berry. Eve. *1996. Oil stick on cardboard with hairspray. (courtesy Jean Berry)*

Jean Berry. Serpentine's Fire _(Souljah series). n.d. Charcoal and pastel. 34" x 60". (courtesy Jean Berry)_

Jean Berry. Serpentine's Fire _(Souljah series). n.d. Charcoal and pastel. 34" x 60". (courtesy Jean Berry)_

Jean Berry. Ruth _(Souljah series). n.d. Charcoal and pastel. 34" x 60". (courtesy Jean Berry)_

James Harris. Black and Gold and White. *n.d. Acrylic on canvas. 82" x 48". (courtesy John and Elaine Estes)*

continued from page 508

Hancher Auditorium on the University of Iowa campus, with a cast that included a large number of local performers recruited as part of the corps. During the scene in which these Iowans appeared, they were given the option of removing their clothes; most availed themselves of the opportunity. Prior to the performance, protesters complained to law-enforcement officials, demanding that the state's attorney general or local police cancel the show. However, their complaints were found to be without merit.

The later and more easily accessible "Still/Here" was based, in part, on workshops with victims of AIDS and other terminal diseases. The stories and themes discussed in these meetings were woven into the final dance creation. A documentary, including scenes from Iowa, was created and shown on national educational television. During the autumn of 1994, when Jones's company was preparing *Still/Here* in Iowa, the choreographer was featured on the cover of *Time* magazine, which described his career and his personal battle with HIV/AIDS.

In addition to his own company, Bill T. Jones has created dances for Alvin Ailey's dance company — the premier modern black dance company in America — and the American Dance Theatre. Jones has received the so-called "genius" fellowship given by the MacArthur Foundation and two "Bessie" awards for his work.[38] Recently, Jones's health improved sufficiently to allow him to perform in public after years away from the stage due to the effects of HIV infection.

Gateway Dance Theatre

In 1972, Penny and Lee Burton Furgerson Jr. founded Des Moines's Gateway Dance Theatre as an alternative to ballet and conventional western dance studies. The Furgersons offered lessons to adults and children based on the dance styles of Africa, the Caribbean, and India. Outreach was an important part of their activities, and the company touched the lives of many who might not otherwise have had an opportunity to learn about their dance heritage.

A 1955 graduate of East Waterloo High School, Lee Furgerson attended classes at both the University of Iowa and Iowa State University. In addition to his job at Blue Cross/Blue Shield and his work with the Gateway Dance Theatre, Furgerson was also a member of the Iowa Advisory Committee to the U.S.

Penny Furguerson performing at the Des Moines Art Center (David Penney photo courtesy Penny Furgerson)

Rod Ketchens won his first Mr. Iowa title in 1987. (courtesy William Doan)

Kelly Gantt of Davenport, winner of Mr. Iowa and Muscle Mania competitions (courtesy William Doan)

Commission on Civil Rights and chaired the commission for several years.[39] He died of the effects of heart disease in October 1999 at the age of 61.

By that time, the Gateway Dance Theatre had performed locally and nationally, sometimes bringing ethnic dance to corners of Iowa that had not seen a live dance performance. Before and after Furgerson's death, the company was part of many public festivals and celebrations, including "I'll Make Me a World," the large-scale festival of African-American heritage held each year at the State Historical Society in Des Moines.

Bodybuilding

Bodybuilding shares with platform diving, water ballet, and figure skating elements of dance movement, theatrical performance, and well-developed athletic prowess. In Iowa, only bodybuilding has a significant following. Annual Mr. Iowa contests held in various parts of the state, under several different sponsors, often have black champions alone in the spotlight at the end of the evening show. Indeed, half the men claiming the Mr. Iowa title in the 1990s were of African descent. Considering the tiny population of black youth in Iowa, this record of achievement is astonishing. Those who have made exceptional contributions in this area of performance art include Rod Ketchens, Kelly Gantt, Randy Jackson Sr., and Darryl Mayfield.

As the careers of these exceptional athlete/artists indicate, by the turn of the twenty-first century, Mr. Iowa was not necessarily a sandy-haired farm boy. Five times out of ten, men of African descent have been crowned with this title. The strength, discipline, and graceful athleticism these men have presented to the public contrasts sharply with negative stereotypes that have plagued African-American males. Each time a black competitor steps onto the posing platform, often moving to the beat of African-American musicians, he is pitting his power and pride against a long history of racial prejudice and rejection. In bodybuilding, appearance is nearly everything. The strength and beauty of the black male — combined with a supreme sense of physical presence, honed in long hours, days, and years of practice, and a will to be the best — have been significantly rewarded.

Rod Ketchens (b. 1966)

Known among his friends as a quiet and gentle man, bodybuilder Rod Ketchens's stage routine is among the most colorful on the national scene. His stage performances are wildly dramatic, featuring a transformation from a masked monster drawn from horror films to his own smiling, friendly, and very muscular persona.

Ketchens, a native of Waterloo, was a long-time member of the Woodbury County Sheriff's Department in Sioux City. What began as weight training in his freshman year at Sioux City's Morningside College developed into a dream that he could become a professional. After he completed college and a decade in law enforcement, he decided to follow his dream and devoted himself full-time to a career as a physical trainer and bodybuilder by establishing RK Solid.

He began to compete in 1986, and he remembers his first year as a "a rocky one." Persistent and eager to learn, the novice bodybuilder placed in every show he entered. Ketchens won his first Mr. Iowa title in 1987, and by the mid-90s he had claimed his pro card and was nationally ranked. His picture began to appear in national bodybuilding magazines, and his massive physique and warm smile decorated product endorsements.[40] Ketchens continues to compete in national, professional physique contests and to present his dramatic routine as a guest poser at regional contests. In 1998, he began to produce his own annual contest in Sioux City as well.

Kelly Gantt (b. 1970)

Kelly Gantt, a young insurance claims investigator who lives with his wife and three children in Davenport, is the first Iowan to claim the most important amateur "natural" (drug-free) bodybuilding title in the United States. Gantt was the overall winner of Muscle Mania, held in California in 1997, the same year he claimed the Mr. Iowa title.

Gantt, who was born in Quincy, Illinois, in 1970 and moved with his family to Iowa City four years later, discovered weight training as an athlete in school. He attended college at St. Ambrose University in Davenport, where he earned a degree in management.

Although friends told him he would do well as a bodybuilder, Gantt was nervous about posing before an audience until he attended his first contest in 1994. There he won the overall title, the first in a string of victories, and from that moment he was "hooked."[41] His posing routine is measured, filled with large gestures that enhance the feeling of strength he projects and give the viewer time to appreciate his defined, symmetrical physique.

While he admits that "racism is still out there," Gantt does not think his career has suffered because of his African descent. His residence in a small Iowa city is perhaps a greater barrier to national attention than the color of his skin; Davenport is far away from bodybuilding centers such as Florida and California, where most bodybuilding magazines are published. As a natural bodybuilder, Gantt sometimes found himself competing against those who use illegal performance enhancing drugs. But this potential handicap did not hold him back.

Randy Jackson Sr. (b. 1959)

Randy Jackson began weight training in 1978 while he was in the U.S. Army, and began his career as a competitor in 1984. Since that time, he has won many titles, including the Mr. Iowa crown. He also coaches physical training and the martial arts in Waterloo.

Long experience on the posing platform has served Jackson well. He is able to blend the required muscle display poses with dance moves drawn directly from African-American popular dance forms. His performances are accompanied by contemporary black music. Like Gantt, Jackson is a natural — that is, drug-free — competitor. "I don't use steroids. I believe in being natural. I've

been that way all my life. That's why I'm able to compete in over a dozen shows a year."[42] Now eligible to compete in Masters competition, Jackson maintains a rigorous training schedule that includes appearances in major national contests, where he is posing against men who are two decades younger. Jackson's strong convictions about performance-enhancing drugs have formed the core of his message to children and adults. Jackson has even taken his philosophy to the inmates of Iowa's correctional facilities.[43]

Darryl Mayfield (b. 1964)

Darryl Mayfield dreamed of becoming a professional football player, but a serious hamstring injury early in his collegiate career ended his fantasy about life in the NFL. Athletics continued to play an important role in his life, however. In 1989, a year before he joined the Des Moines Police Department, he began to train seriously with weights.

As a law officer, Mayfield competed in the National Physique Committee Police and Fire Olympics in 1992, taking home the physique trophy. He also won the light heavyweight division at the 1993 Mid-States Classic, in Rockford, Illinois. Now competing as a heavyweight, Mayfield maintains his commitment to drug-free bodybuilding.[44] In 1996, he purchased the 5800 Fitness Club in Johnston, becoming the first African-American gym owner in central Iowa and one of the few black business owners in that affluent suburb of Des Moines.

A Rich Legacy

Thus throughout the 1900s and into the present century, painters, sculptors, photographers, and performance artists of African descent have found in Iowa a nurturing environment for their particular artistic gifts. For the most part, Iowa's black artists have enjoyed public recognition and respect for their aesthetic achievements. In several cases, they have also emerged as advocates in important social and cultural movements, expressing through their art the consciousness of the black community as a whole. Because of the relatively small number of black artists working in the state at any given time, it may be an exaggeration to speak of the African-American artistic presence as an Iowa "tradition." But certainly today's black artists are building on the rich legacy established over the past many decades by the bold work of their artistic forebears.

Randy Jackson Sr. (above) of Waterloo. Darryl Mayfield (below), bodybuilder and businessman, owns the 5800 Fitness Club in Johnston. (both photos courtesy William Doan)

Notes

1. James Smalls, "Public Faces, Private Thoughts," in *The Passionate Camera,* ed. Deborah Bright (London: Routledge, 1998), 78; Nathan Irvin Huggins, *Harlem Renaissance* (New York: Oxford Univ. Press, 1973).

2. Sharon F. Patton, *African-American Art* (New York: Oxford Univ. Press, 1998), 125. Patton is critical of both black and white patrons of the New Negro art movement for their willingness to "Africanize" the movement as a substitute for a home-grown black aesthetic.

3. Ibid., 98–99. Tanner is one of the few black artists well-represented in the collection of the Des Moines Art Center. At least one of Tanner's religious paintings is usually on display in the galleries devoted to the museum's permanent collection. Recently, the museum has added works by several contemporary black artists, including Carrie Mae eems, Glen Ligon, and Martin Puryear.

4. Ibid., 115–16.

5. Paul Padgette, *The Dance Photography of Carl Van Vechten* (New York: Schirmer Books, 1981), 2.

6. Smalls, 79.

7. Patton, 125.

8. Ibid., 119. Catalogs from the Harmon exhibitions are in the collection of the State Historical Society in Des Moines.

9. Ibid., 116.

10. Karen McCarthy Brown, *Tracing the Spirit: Ethnographic Essays on Haitian Art from the Collection of the Davenport Museum of Art* (Davenport: Davenport Museum of Art, 1995), 6.

11. Cammie Scully, *Haitian Art: Twenty Years of Collecting at the Waterloo Museum of Art* (Waterloo: Waterloo Museum of Art, 1997), 1.

12. *Museum Development Campaign* (Des Moines: Fort Des Moines Black Officers Memorial, Inc., 1997), 1. Hunt played an active role in the design of the complex that includes his sculpture.

13. Samella Lewis, *The Art of Elisabeth Catlett* (Claremont CA: Handcraft Studios, 1984), 192.

14. Ibid., 14.

15. Ibid., 15. Catlett's ingenious strategy for getting her students into the museum involved driving them to the very steps of the building, which was privately owned, so that they would not have to set one footstep on the soil of the segregated public park that surrounded the building.

16. Ibid., 16.

17. Ibid., 23–24.

18. Ibid., 24.

19. James Weldon Johnson, *Lift Every Voice and Sing,* with illustrations by Elisabeth Catlett (New York: Walker and Co., 1993). The book, with an introduction by Jim Haskins, includes song texts and music and the powerful Catlett illustrations, as well as biographical material about the author and the artist.

20. Leon N. Hicks, *Beyond the Innocence: An African-American Invitational Exhibition, January 19 through February 12, 1992* (St. Louis: St. Louis Artists' Guild, 1992).

21. Tom Lang, *Leon Hicks Virtualscape/ Installation* (St. Louis: Webster University, 1996), 7.

22. Ibid.

23. Interview with the artist, 1998. All quotes are from this interview.

24. Dawn Bowman, "Jean Berry," in *Lifework: Portraits of Iowa Women Artists,* ed. Marianne Abel and Carol Lauhon (Bettendorf: Lifework Arts Press, 1998), 49.

25. Jean Berry, "Jean Berry, Artist," artist's statement prepared for this book in 1999.

26. Bowman, 49.

27. The author thanks Hal Chase for this information, which is based on his interviews with Rose Burrell, Mar. 18, 2000; Priscilla Burrell, Mar. 20, 2000; Roger Burrell, Dec. 13, 2000; and Charles Boston, Dec. 11, 2000.

28. Ibid., 20.

29. Interview with the artist, 1999.

30. A documentary video, *Madai Makes a Picture,* produced by the Doan Family Foundation, Inc., in 1994, shows the artist's unusual and time-consuming technique. The documentary follows the progress of a single large work over a two-week period, from the first cutting of the paper until the final application of lines of paint.

31. Madai Taylor and Lisa Phillips, *Visions of Color* (Ames: Student Union Board of the Iowa State Memorial Union, 1995).

32. Interview with the artist, 1999.

33. Taylor and Phillips, 18.

34. Ibid.

35. Ibid.

36. Interview with the artist, 1999.

37. The author thanks David Jackson, curator of the African-American Historical Museum and Cultural Center of Iowa for this information about Ruthie O'neil, the subject of his dissertation at the University of Iowa.

38. Bill T. Jones and Susan Kuklin, *Dance* (New York: Hyperion, n.d.). Additional information is included in the video documentary titled *Still/ Here,* narrated by Bill Moyers, which aired on Iowa Public Television in January 1997. The documentary begins with scenes of the world premier performance on September 29, 1994, at Hancher Auditorium in Iowa City and includes other Iowa scenes.

39. *Tractor* (Summer 1999): 24.

40. William Doan, "Black Muscle Power — Iowa Style," *Iowa State Bystander* [1894–1994 Anniversary Edition: 100 Years of Black Achievement], 1994, 58.

41. Kelly Gantt interview, 1998.

42. Doan, 59.

43. Ibid.

44. Darryl Mayfield interview, 1999.

William Sayles Doan (b. 1940) attended the schools of Journalism and Speech at Northwestern University (1958–62).

He has produced and written film and video documentaries. He is the author of Photoflexion *(St. Martin's Press, 1985) and* A Book of Days *(Messenger Publishing, 1990). Doan's photographs can be found in many museum collections, including the Art Institute of Chicago and the State Historical Society of Iowa.*

He was an Iowa delegate to the national NAACP convention in 1971, and he is an associate member of ONYX. William Doan is the secretary of the Doan Family Foundation, established by his mother in 1981.

His book on the photographs of Al Urban will be published by Janssen in 2001.

A Des Moines Playhouse production of The Odd Couple *included Al Downey Jr. (courtesy Al Downey Jr.)*

The Joy Generators, a popular Des Moines–based band of the 1930s and 1940s (courtesy Betty June Hayes Dixon)

The Song of the River

African-American Music and Entertainment in Iowa

by Raymond Kelso Weikal

Tina Haas swings at Jazz in July. (Des Moines Metro Arts)

Prologue

Tell the story. Sing the truth.

The truth is that African-American music is an auditory delta. It's the trinity of a thousand bayous, a hundred creeks, and one river; it's the Mississippi, the Ohio, the Missouri, the Raccoon and Des Moines; it's the migrants thirsty for opportunity pushing north, pushing against the tide, against 300 years of enslavement and racism; it's the river that divides this one nation, black and white, past and future; it's the roiling vein of soil and blood, nutrients made of people's lives, intermingled, the bones of the enslaved and enslaver fed on by the same hungry trout; it's the twittering laugh, the thunderous roar, the windswept sigh, the still moan, the song of the river.

The truth is that when she sings, Tina Haas is a queen, her back straight, head tilted towards the sky, with a long drape of dark brown hair spilling across the caramel-colored skin of her neck. She sings a river of song: rhyme and rhythm and reason.

The sound shifts and turns, sometimes so soft the audience stills like repentant churchgoers when the preacher whispers; it builds with punched words and elongated phrases, jumping from lower to upper registers; it builds to a roar, a demand to *be heard*, carried by the band that starts to sway and the audience that all at once begins to boogie.

That Ms. Haas is African-American is obvious and not noteworthy. American pop culture has, since at least the 1920s, made almost cliché the image of the black female rhythm and blues singer with an imposing, sexy swagger and vocal dynamics. And Ms. Haas is an admitted imbiber and mimicker of that great tradition.

What may be surprising, though, is that she is a product of Iowa. Her voice, her drive, her dream have all been nurtured and shaped by the culture of that state. Her life is almost a microcosm of the black experience in Iowa: brought north from Missouri; raised on a farm; a mulatto, white and black; self-discovery in college; and maturity in the state that she calls home, Iowa.[1]

And Tina is only, and blessedly, the most recent in a tradition of African-American music-making that can be traced to the very earliest days of the state's settlement. This story begins with enslaved and free men making the long pioneer days go a bit faster by singing of better times.

The truth is that African-American music is an auditory delta. . . . It's the twittering laugh, the thunderous roar, the windswept sigh, the still moan, the song of the river.

Featuring "home talent" in a production titled Millie's Millions, *the Keosauqua Theatrical Troupe was one of dozens operating throughout Iowa in the early 1900s. (Van Buren County Historical Society)*

It continues during Reconstruction, when the frontier became less isolated and the people congregated, particularly in churches, where community was solidified by spirituality; it grew wider with the industrial revolution, when new technologies and greater urbanization created mass marketing and pop culture; given impetus by the Great War, it roared through the 1920s; in the Great Depression it offered solace and escape; during the Good War it took on the new beat of youth and progress, the voice of a generation determined to have its own. This voice gets stronger through the Forgotten War and the 10,000 Day War; it's a voice that is still heard today in the gospel choirs of the church, the jazz in the park, the rhythm and blues in the bars, and the rap on the radio.

African-American music has had a vital place in the history of Iowa. And it has affected, and has been affected by, both blacks and whites.

Tones Loud, Long and Deep

Ask virtually any African-American and he or she will tell you that music is central to the black experience. Black Iowans have been no different from African-Americans throughout the

Americas in the use and importance of music. It can be found on any occasion and place where black people congregated — work, play, worship, protest.

The importance of music in black life seems to have had its roots in the culture of an enslaved people that arose in America during the seventeenth, eighteenth, and nineteenth centuries. Music was one of the primary forms of expression in Africa — indeed, it remains so.[2] Africans developed a complex method of tonal and rhythmic arrangements and language that centered on the voice but was often accompanied by a variety of stringed instruments.

This music was one of many art forms that were part of the advanced civilizations on that continent before the advent of the slave trade in the 1490s; writing, weaving, metalworking, and drawing were also accomplished to a high order by Africans.[3] But with the crack of the trader's whip, the enslaved were bound in a world that offered them little opportunity for self-expression.

Soon after the introduction of enslaved Africans into North America, the first racist laws were passed that restricted the life of the newcomers.[4] The most important of these new restrictions was the denial of education, making it difficult for literature and writing to be used as means of expression. Consequently, black people turned to the human voice, the one thing that could not be enslaved. With memories of Africa shaped by and shaping the new rhythms and realities of life in colonial North America, they sang to create solidarity through the expression of shared experience. Misfortune borne by many seems less heavy. This was especially true for African-Americans.[5]

Deep River, my home is over Jordan, Deep River,

Lord, I want to cross over into camp ground;

Lord, I want to cross over into camp ground;

Lord, I want to cross over into camp ground;

Lord, I want to cross over into camp ground.[6]

The lyrics of that old gospel song tell it like it was. And is.

Frederick Douglass provides a rare glimpse into the form and importance of music in the world of the enslaved. "The slaves selected to go to the Great House Farm, for the monthly allowance for themselves and their fellow slaves, were peculiarly enthusiastic. While on their way, they would make the dense old woods, for miles around, reverberate with their wild songs, revealing at once the highest joy and deepest sadness. . . . They were tones loud, long and deep; they breathed the prayer and complaint of souls boiled over with the bitterest anguish. Every tone was a testimony against slavery, and a prayer to God for deliverance from chains."[7]

It was out of this culture that the first African-American settlers came to Iowa in the 1830s. While it is not possible at this point to locate specific examples, it is reasonable to believe that at least some of the 188 African-Americans who inhabited the state in 1840 were making music. The importance of music in African-American culture cannot be underestimated. Muddy Waters said that "the blues was born from behind a mule"; wherever one finds black people putting in a hard day of labor, one will find them singing about it.[8]

The deep old blues of the antebellum era was a form of individual storytelling. It was a black woman or man's way of letting the world know who they were, their experience, and what that meant. Music helped bring order through rhythm, meaning through rhyme. To a black person working in the strange land of frontier Iowa, music would likely have been a way of achieving acceptance and an important psychological defense. However, there are no known accounts of African-American music in Iowa before the Civil War. It can only be left to reason and imagination to think what place music must have held for the state's few hundred black people.

The picture of life for black people in Iowa grows clearer in the Reconstruction Era. While not as overtly racist as the old Confederacy, Iowa was predominately populated by northern European immigrants who had a distrust of the unknown. Racism was a fact of life for many black people, a general delineation of what an African-American could and could not do. However, music became one way of overcoming majority ignorance and intolerance. Well-performed songs can be contagious. A talent wrenches admiration from all but the most hardened hearts and can lead to greater assimilation in the community. For example, the black population of Keosauqua included "talented musicians . . . who were called upon to perform at festive occasions."[9]

Early in their enslaved existence, black people discovered the power of song as a subtle method of loosening the enslaver's grip. Plantation songs often mocked the ridiculous positions in which black people were placed in American society.[10] When chattel enslavement gave way to economic serfdom, African-Americans continued to use the old methods to convey messages created from their lives of new freedoms and old troubles.[11] They brought their songs with them as they moved west and north in increasing numbers. In Iowa, many African-Americans from the South were recruited to serve as strikebreakers in the coal mines of the southern part of the state.

A fantastic example of black people finding solidarity through music occurred at one of these mines. When a group of white strikers demanded that the African-American miners go back south, the workers "came out of the mines, sang a couple of plantation songs and then resumed work."[12] The irony that the black workers felt at that moment must have been enormous: white unions at that time did not allow black membership. In a very gracious way, those miners declared that if they couldn't play the game, they didn't have to follow the rules.

The largest settlement of black coal miners was in the company town of Buxton. Not surprisingly, the town produced a number of capable musicians, both women and men, some of whom traveled throughout Iowa and even put on one show at the State Fair.[13]

A history of Lee County published by the WPA in 1942 refers to the black dock workers of Keokuk who unloaded the boats stopped by the rapids on the Mississippi: "On warm summer evenings these Negroes would come ashore with their banjoes . . . and play and sing the old plantation melodies until after midnight. They were fresh from the south land, freed from the sorrows of slavery, yet with the old life so vivid in consciousness that they sang on the banks of Montrose and Keokuk with hearts full of old memories and new inspiration."[14]

Of note is the rememberer's reference to "new inspiration." The openness of the West must have had a singular effect on the new black population, after the cloister of enslavement. The song, then, had changed, shaped by this new environment.

Perhaps the most important institution of pre– and post– Civil War African-American society was the church. The Protestant and Catholic congregations of white America were often segregated at best, and exclusionary and excusatory instruments of enslavement at worst. Out of this arose the independent black church movement, led by such people as Richard Allen, Absolom Jones, and William White of the African Methodist Episcopal church. By the time the Civil War ended, membership in black

"They were tones loud, long and deep . . . the prayer and complaint of souls boiled over with the bitterest anguish. Every tone was a testimony against slavery, and a prayer to God for deliverance from chains."

—Frederick Douglass

*A mandolin group in Iowa, c.1900
(SHSI Iowa City)*

*An African-American minstrel group
performing on Main Street, Ruthven,
Iowa, c.1895 (SHSI Iowa City)*

churches had grown phenomenally, most notably among the Baptists.[15] The majority of black people that moved into the state came from the South, primarily Missouri.[16] They brought with them their style of worship, and consequently there were African-American congregations established in every major Iowa city. By 1906, 2,387 black people were attending 33 black Baptist and 37 black Methodist churches.[17]

In Des Moines, the first black church was Burns Methodist, established in 1865 at 4th and Vine.[18] This was followed by St. Paul AME in 1879; Maple Street Baptist, begun as a mission in 1886 and taking its present name in 1901; Corinthian Baptist in 1893 under the Rev. George W. Robinson; Rev. M. Toomey's Union Baptist in 1912; St. John's AME — later, Kyles AME — in 1916; and Mt. Olive Baptist, on South Union Street, in 1920.

Integral to any black worship service is music, primarily in the form of the song. The rise of the black church and its music marked an important change in African-American music in general. Along with a growing number of traveling minstrel and stage shows just before the Civil War and continuing to World War 1, the churches helped to codify black music, laying down the taxonomy and syntax of what would become the classic forms.

The earliest music in black churches were spirituals, a more formal arrangement of the plantation songs that Frederick Douglass recounted so vividly.[19] Marked by repetitive verses and complex shadings of moaned and hollered choruses, they often start softly, build to a crescendo, and quickly drop off at the end. The effect is similar to that of chanting or meditation, with the listener and singer — the two are supposed to be the same — being lifted up in a current of sound that rises like a wave before crashing in a torrent and ebbing back to the beginning.

The lyrics are very often metaphors that draw analogies between the persecution of the Israelites at the hands of the Egyptians and their own enslavement by Europeans. The songs lay down a basic description of experience, then point the congregation towards the promised land of freedom. This redemption often has double meaning, both of body and soul. The overriding theme is that time and righteousness are on their side, that no matter what is done to them, they can, at the very least, be assured of freedom through death and redemption through Christ in heaven.

Sinner, sinner you better pray,

Looks like my Lord a-comin' in de sky.

Or yo' soul be los' on de jedgment day,

Looks like my Lord a-comin' in de sky.

O little did I think he was so nigh,

Looks like my Lord a-comin' in de sky.

He spoke an' he made me laugh and cry,

Looks like my Lord a-comin' in de sky.[20]

The earliest existing pre–World War 1 editions of the *Iowa Bystander* reveal a proliferation of singing and performing groups centered on the church. A 1912 issue of the *Bystander* tells of one Coleridge Taylor, whose musical recital at Bethel AME in Keokuk was a "grand success . . . twenty dollars being received."[21]

Though the church was an important factor in the life of turn-of-the-century black Iowans, there were other, secular forms of entertainment. It was a dynamic time in American music: white and black music mixed in ways never before seen, in places like New Orleans, New York, and Memphis.[22] Musicians were combining European methods of musical notation and playing with African-American forms. In Iowa, African-Americans were introduced to the sounds of the traditional marching band. A marvelous photo in *Lee County, Iowa: A Pictorial History* reveals the overwhelmingly African-American makeup of the People's Institute Keokuk Band. Formed in the early 1900s, these volunteers met in the Black Lodge at 12th and Johnson in Keokuk. They would play for their own enjoyment and community events.[23]

In addition to musical distractions, prior to World War 1 Iowa was the destination of traveling vaudeville shows. In January 1912, S. H. Dudley played in Des Moines for five days. This popular vaudevillian was part of the Smart Set Company, "A Band of Genuine Disturbers of Gloom."[24] Shelburn Gardens, at 12th and Center, was the sight of an "Indian operetta" titled "The Feast of the Red Corn," on March 2, 1923. Performed under the auspices of the YWCA's Girls Work Committee, the local actresses included Lona Green (soprano), Lucile Green (mezzo-soprano), Marguerite Winn, Dorothy Manuel, Gloria Griffin, and Mary Woods.[25]

The importance of music in African-American life is nicely illustrated by the case of Mrs. Harriet Newsome. In the 1870s her father, a freedman, moved from Savannah, Missouri, and — with

Terry's "Uncle Tom's Cabin" theater troupe and band members, Little Sioux, Iowa, c.1919 (from Breeling, History of Little Sioux)

the help of a group of whites from College Springs — settled in the southern Iowa border town of Blanchard. The family he and his wife raised were the sole African-American residents. Apparently Mrs. Newsome's mother was the daughter of an African tribal king. She exhibited talent early, and was sent to study music with teachers in Wyoming and Massachusetts. From there she became an accomplished concert soprano and "dramatic reader," traveling with a variety of groups up and down the East Coast of the United States. When her mother fell ill in 1932, Mrs. Newsome returned home to care for her. She never left the small town after this, and she restricted herself to singing with the choir at her church. Mrs. Newsome's words reveal a faithful and optimistic person who believed in the power of music and fellowship to overcome racial barriers. She tells how the local white school principal made it clear that both blacks and whites were to be treated equally and together. "Singing is the way I pray some time, music is a mode of expression, of telling what life really means and stands for. I never get lonely. I don't have time for that. I've had a wonderful life . . . and these are wonderful people in this town."[26]

The dynamics of black church music in Iowa changed with World War 2. A rising secularization of spirituals and gospel music — caused by the birth of pop culture, the rising black middle class, and increasing educational opportunities — began to emerge.

John Deere

With the opening salvo of World War 1 in Europe, the demand for mass-produced goods drove an incredible growth and innovation in manufacturing. Drawn by the call for factory labor, huge numbers of black people moved north to seek jobs in the new industries.[27]

In Iowa, John Deere proved to be a powerful magnet: drummer Bobby Parker, guitarist Eddie (Pickin) Bowles, blues harpist Louis McTizic, and Waterloo gospel composer Randolph O. Dean all got work with John Deere.[28] These were people who had either experienced farm work or were only one generation removed from it; they may not have known Iowa from Norway, but they knew about its most famous manufacturer.

The importance of this should not be ignored. Through centuries of being constricted and persecuted by the dominant white society, black people had learned to be wary of traveling to places that might be unwelcome. Even a seemingly insignificant thing like the name on the side of a tractor could have made Iowa

enough of a known factor to pull in potential African-American immigrants.[29]

Musicologist and record producer Dick Waterman tells an enlightening story. Driving across the Midwest with legendary country blues guitarist Son House in the early 1960s as part of a tour he'd put together, it seems that the young white producer and the old black bluesman found very little to talk about, so they sat in silence for several hours. Then, just as they crossed the Mississippi into Davenport, House turned and said just two words: "John Deere."[30]

New economic opportunities during World War 1 led to an increase in political and social opportunities for black people. They were now living together in larger numbers and creating a new market for goods, services, and entertainment. Capitalists were especially quick to exploit and expand the popularity of African-American musicians. The importance of sound recordings and radio on black music can hardly be overstated. Before these technologies, the church was the greatest unifying element in black culture. With the growth of the entertainment industry, marketing decisions were being made by corporate executives, and the product was available to anyone with a corner store and enough money. No longer could the church act as the sole prescribing force in the life of an African-American.[31] This was true in Iowa as in the rest of the nation. Bobby Parker, a jazz drummer in Des Moines, says that most of his musical knowledge and interest came from listening to records in the 1920s and 1930s.[32]

In addition, the new age brought greater ease of travel, particularly with the massive growth of the railroad. Musicians from the music centers of New Orleans, St. Louis, New York, and Chicago could now tour across the country, even to states with small populations. Iowa was a beneficiary of this new network of entertainment.

With mass marketing came the need to find artists who would appeal to the greatest number of people. In the age of modernity, marketers had little desire to record spirituals, with their ancient, heavy melodies and dark themes. Instead, this time period witnessed the rise of gospel, classic blues, and jazz — upbeat, swinging modifications of the spiritual and old, rural blues.[33] These new musical forms became an even more overt form of racial identity for African-Americans.

It is curious enough that one of the Iowans most profoundly affected by this new sound and medium was a young white boy

In Iowa, John Deere proved to be a powerful magnet: drummer Bobby Parker, guitarist Eddie (Pickin) Bowles, blues harpist Louis McTizic, and Waterloo gospel composer Randolph O. Dean all got work with John Deere.

Jitterbug contest at the Billiken Club in Des Moines, 1940 (Don Ultang photo / Des Moines Register)

The Billiken Club featured jazz in the 1930s and 1940s. (SHSI Des Moines)

from Davenport. Leon (Bix) Beiderbecke, born in 1903, is cited among the great fathers of jazz. The foundation of Bix's talent was profoundly bifurcated. On the one hand was the long classical tradition of his strongly musical German family; it was his family that forced him to learn piano, though reading music was a skill he never mastered.[34] On the other hand were the jazz recordings of such groups as the New Orleans Rhythm Kings and the sounds coming from the riverboats that wound their way up, Mississippi from St. Louis and past Davenport.

Greatest 24-Hour City

Concurrent with the development of gospel, jazz, and blues as products of pop culture was a rising black middle class. In Iowa, one of the most important catalysts for this growing economic security in African-American life was the establishment of the first U.S. Army officer training camp for black officers at Fort Des Moines. Hundreds of African-Americans from all over the country came to Iowa, the majority being educated college students. This migration was accompanied by music. At a large recognition ceremony for the troops at the Drake University Stadium, singing was the primary entertainment. Black soldiers would march through the streets "singing marching songs, ragtime, or spirituals," which the white and black residents were reported to have "enjoyed."[35]

This huge influx of African-Americans in Iowa marks the period when Center Street emerged as a focal point of black life in Des Moines. The Center Street neighborhood was unique in providing African-American residents so many social opportunities in one place. The Billiken, the Sepia, the 1113 Club, the Nip, and the Watkins are just some of the nightclubs that existed on or near

Irene Myles grew up in Perry in the 1920s, traveled the country for many years with the Nat Towles Orchestra, and settled in Des Moines in 1973. Singing and playing piano in a trio that included drummer Bobby Parker, she delighted Des Moines audiences until her death in 1996. (courtesy Ron Gray)

American tradition with its yearly minstrel show. The program included songs such as "Swanee River" and "Are You from Dixie?" performed by members. This annual event was used to raise money for local "welfare work, Boy Scout, YMCA and YWCA camp funds, and other useful purposes." The president of the Monarchs was T. L. Howard, the manager of the Billiken Nite Club. The 1941 minstrel show included the Congo Rhythm Band, a popular group that dated back to at least 1933 as Jerry Hayes and His Joy Jenerators. "An operatic symphony to sizzling jungle notes!" one of their posters reads. "With a team of fine brown skinned dancing beauties!"[37]

Center Street Enthusiasm

The enthusiasm of the Center Street community is apparent in the sheer number of occasions for which dances were held. Election days, reunions, graduations, anniversaries, virtually any event could be seized upon as an excuse to throw a dance. If you were around Des Moines on November 7, 1922, at the Blue Circle Hall on 4th and Grand, you could both dance to Ray Dysart's Xylo Sax Harmony Band and receive election returns. The yearly Easter egg hunt was cause for a dance at the Billiken. At the same club, you could enjoy the "X-Mass Morning One O'clock Jump," the "Labor Day Jam Session," the "Pre–Labor Day Dawn Dance," or even the "Pre–Decoration Day Dawn Dance," with music by Arney Liddell's 14-piece Riverview Park Band.[38]

Of course, just in case that wasn't enough, the Billiken also held an annual Armistice Day dance.[39] Located at 12th and Center, the Billiken Club was one of the most important in the neighborhood. Owned by Azalia Mitchell, it seated up to 600 patrons.[40] Josephine Baker and Flip Benson played there as headliners. According to Bobby Parker and Mel Harper, many famous black entertainers who performed for white audiences downtown would later come to the Billiken or the Sepia to play in after-hours jam sessions.

Ernest (Speck) Redd and his band were one of the house bands that played at the Billiken on a regular basis. Born in Missouri and moving to Des Moines in 1942, Redd is considered to be one of the best jazz pianists ever to play in Iowa. He played a style of bluesy, uptempo jazz that was almost unique to the Midwest. Jay McShann of Kansas City was perhaps the most famous practitioner of this sound. The Speck Redd Band of the 1940s and 1950s consisted of Presell Frazier on drums and Francis Bates on bass.

Center, between 10th and 16th streets. In the 1920s and especially after the repeal of prohibition in the 1930s, the neighborhood was, according to several commentators, the pinnacle of Iowa's African-American community. Its streets brimmed with activity. And its music flowed like flood waters. Pam Williams, a child at the time, remembers hearing music pouring out of the clubs as she ran down the street. Mildred Crowder Mayberry claims that Des Moines was considered the "greatest 24-hour city" because of this community. The flurry of new clubs that opened after the repeal of prohibition left club owners desperate for players and willing not to ask too many questions. Bobby Parker was able to get a job as a jazz drummer in bars while underage.[36]

Social clubs abounded, providing a ready support network for musicians by throwing parties and picnics on every possible occasion. The Royal Dukes Club and the Merrymakers Club both held annual fundraising dances. In the 1930s and 1940s a group called the Monarchs kept alive a nineteenth-century African-

Redd played consistently up through the 1960s, before passing away in 1974. He also supplemented his income by teaching both jazz and classical piano.[41]

Two blocks east of the Billiken at 1014 Center was the Sepia Club. The club was opened in 1940 by Seymour and Howard Gray. The owners were also part of the house band, Seymour on bass and Howard on tenor saxophone. Also part of the house band — and the family — was alto sax man Rufus Spates, who was married to Howard and Seymour's sister, Edythe. Edythe Spates was the owner of a local beauty shop.[42]

Outside the Sepia Club, one would have seen a poster, printed locally by Robert Patten, advertising the night's entertainment by "Des Moines' Own Songthrush," Irene Myles.[43] (Early posters spell her last name as Miles; it is unclear whether she changed the spelling at some point, or whether it was just a misprint.) Stepping inside, one would be in a room that was often packed, particularly on weekend nights. Playing a grand piano and

singing songs like "Night and Day" or "East of the Sun" would be a beautiful young black woman. Most Des Moines residents who remember those days say she was simply the best.

Born Irene Myles Terry in Jefferson, Iowa, in 1921, her family soon moved to Perry, Iowa, where she grew up.[44] In 1937 she settled in Des Moines, quickly finding work as a singer at an Ingersoll Avenue establishment called the Old West End Coffee Shop. Her talent was too large to be missed, and she eventually toured with the Nat Towles Orchestra. She was so well known in Des Moines that posters from the 1930s and 1940s simply refer to her as "Irene." After spending several years touring the nation and living in Milwaukee, she returned to Iowa in 1973. Up until just a few months before her death of heart disease in 1996, she consistently played throughout metropolitan Des Moines. Bobby Parker, who had been a drummer for her since the 1930s, remembers "she was very professional. She even made us wear tuxes at the end." At her funeral at St. Paul AME Church of Des

Ernest (Speck) Redd played the blues-based Kansas City jazz made famous in the 1940s by Jay McShann. (courtesy Ernest [Butch] Redd)

Posters advertise acts appearing at the Billiken Club throughout the 1930s and 1940s. (SHSI Des Moines)

Moines, hundreds came to honor her and what she had accomplished.[45]

I remember the night I heard her sing at her regular gig in the restaurant of the Hotel Fort Des Moines. This was in the early 1990s, and by then her voice had the smoky timbre of a person who has seen much that life has to offer. She played simply and softly, only the right notes, and her singing was real, tragic and romantic without being overly dramatic. Current Des Moines-area singers Suzy Miget, Janey Hooper, and Tina Haas all cite Myles as one of their primary influences, not just musically but also personally. She always made it clear what motivated her to play. "It's the people. One night I played for two and a half hours straight because the people in the audience kept clapping. That night I worked too hard."[46]

Bobby Parker is one of a cadre of African-Americans in Des Moines who still have vivid memories of the great Center Street

era. Born in 1919 in Des Moines, Parker grew up in a family of musicians. His grandfather played several instruments, which he kept around the family home, a source of unending fascination for the young Bobby. He grew to love jazz by listening to band leaders such as Count Basie and Benny Goodman on a Memphis radio station he listened to late at night. His natural love of rhythm steered him away from the brass instruments and towards the drums, much to his parents' dismay. He grew up hearing his mother and sister sing and play piano at St. Paul's AME, where they were members, but jazz was in his veins. When prohibition was repealed in 1933 and tavern owners started calling him, desperately looking for musicians to entertain their new customers, he began what became a lifelong avocation. He played regularly with Ace Oliver, Jerry Hayes, and Ace's sister Ethel, in addition to Irene Myles. He remembers playing in 1936 and 1937 at a particularly wild place called the Casa Loma. He would skip school and play every night for four hours. He says that Ethel Oliver never practiced but would show up at a gig at the last possible moment and start playing, saying hardly a word. Of her brother Ace, Bobby says that he was "very good."

In 1939, Parker went to Omaha to play with the Lloyd Hunter Big Band, a 15-piece orchestra that toured the Midwest. Things were going fine until 1942, when the U.S. Army called for a few years of his time. He ended up serving in the China-Burma-India theatre of operations, driving a supply truck over the treacherous Burma Road from India, helping to keep the Chinese army equipped.

Returning to Des Moines after the war, he literally walked into a gig at the Watkins Hotel in 1946. The Oliver Cox Orchestra was set to begin for a series of gigs that night, but for some reason the drummer did not want to play. Bobby bought the drummer's kit on the spot and took over his place in the band, thereby reasserting his place on the Des Moines music scene. He remembers that the Watkins, Des Moines's first black-owned hotel, was a happening place at the time, mainly because of all the money the African-American population was making at the local munitions factory. He says that Owen Watkins, the owner, was "a taskmaster — pretty mean."

Parker also recalls that the social world in Des Moines was segregated as a fact, though not in law. He would often play at clubs in the white sections of town with all-white audiences, then return to Center Street to play after-hours jams in front of blacks

Lindy hoppers at a Des Moines night club, 1940s (Iowa Women's Archives)

and whites. The irony of discriminating against the very people providing one's entertainment has been a theme in American life since the turn of the century. Parker remembers that the club owners treated him well and remembers little overt racism as a rule. Still, when asked, he made clear that there were places that black people just did not go without first being invited by a white, whereas whites were always allowed to party on Center Street. In addition, white players made twice as much as he did for the same amount of work.[47] Lewis McTizic remembers that the after-hours club scene in Waterloo also was always an integrated one.[48]

Mel Harper has owned and operated several clubs in Des Moines since the 1950s, most recently Mel's Bar and Grill in West Des Moines. Every place Harper ever ran was always integrated, he emphatically points out, even though that wasn't the case in the downtown "white" bars. Robert A. Wright Sr., a Des Moines police officer who worked the Center Street beat from 1945 to 1954, recalls that back in the 1940s the music scene brought a lot of whites into the neighborhood, but then that slowly faded away. He distinctly remembers that Ray Johnson and Joyce Addudell were one of the last white couples to hang out on Center Street.[49]

Examples of black people being kept out of "white only" clubs can be found right up into the 1970s. In June 1979 several African-Americans were turned away from Woodfields, a disco in Iowa City.[50] They were unable to produce the three pieces of identification demanded of them by the bouncers, even though no white person had to meet the same requirement. Led by Robert Martin, a black resident of Iowa City, a lawsuit was pursued with the city's Human Relations Commission. "This is something right out of Alabama or Mississippi," Martin told *Des Moines Register* writer Jerald Heth at the time. After much legal wrangling, club owners Harry Ambrose and Daniel Lovetinksy had their liquor license suspended and were ordered to pay the seven African-Americans $400 each as restitution.[51]

One can only imagine how things worked 30 years previously, when human rights commissions were non-existent. Most African-Americans say that at that time there was an invisible but unquestioned line that separated the two communities. Indeed, this division was not always invisible. At Cornell College in Mt. Vernon, students and faculty had an annual minstrel show that included racist routines done in blackface. This tradition didn't end until the mid-1960s, when the faculty senate decided it might

be insensitive towards African-Americans.[52] A Des Moines City Council document from the 1960s clearly shows that there was concerted governmental discrimination against the black community in the state's capital city as well.[53]

Still, Iowa's music scene thrived, and much of it centered on the state's African-American communities. Bobby Parker remembers the great traveling acts of nationally known tours that came into Des Moines. He himself backed up jazz guitarist Charlie Christian at one time, and Des Moines also hosted such acts as Pearl Bailey, Count Basie, Cab Calloway, Duke Ellington, and Ella Fitzgerald. In 1939, internationally reknowned black mezzo-soprano Etta Moten played at Hoyt Sherman Auditorium and Josephine Baker played at the Billiken. Other visiting celebrities included Chuck Berry, Pee Wee Crayton, Earl (Fatha) Hines, the Ink Spots, Preston Love, and the Temptations.[54]

Numerous regionally known acts played in Des Moines on a fairly regular basis too. Judging from the number of times his

The Gray Brothers Orchestra of Iowa (courtesy Ron and Dorothy Gray)

Singer Paul Robeson performed at Hoyt Sherman Place in the 1930s. De facto segregation in public accommodations meant that black performers like Robeson typically stayed in the black neighborhoods of Des Moines and other Iowa cities. (SHSI Des Moines)

Iowa's Catherine Williams, in the chorus line of "The Singing Kid," a 1940 musical featuring Al Jolson and Cab Calloway. Like many talented performers, Catherine Williams left Iowa to pursue her career. (Iowa Women's Archives)

Howard and Seymour Gray, owners of the Sepia Club in Des Moines, c.1950 (courtesy Ron Gray and Dorothy Gray Looper)

band was advertised on local posters, Ray Dysart's Harmony Band from Minneapolis must have felt very much at home in Des Moines.[55] Jay McShann's band from Kansas City regularly entertained in the area as well.[56]

It would appear every major jazz player of the 1930s, 1940s, 1950s, and 1960s came to play in Des Moines. They most commonly played at either the Orpheum or the Paramount.[57] Because of de facto segregation, these performers often had to stay in the Center Street neighborhood, at such places as Mrs. Moore's rooming house.[58] This became an advantage for local residents, who were able to rub elbows with such great artists. Often, the visitors would stop by at the Billiken or Sepia to sit in with that night's band for a set or two. When they did this, they had a healthy pool of local musicians with whom to play. Singer Lucille Brooks, trombonist Eddie Barber, and saxophonists Walter Akins, H. Bowman, and Howard Gray were all ready to play, as was guitarist Johnny Clinton. Bass players Dudly Black, Mutt Gaiter, and Orville Cox, and pianists Buck Buckner and Margarite Butts were also available. Other pianists included Mary Clark at the Watkins Club and Al Collins of the Monte Carlo Novelty Band, as well as Milt Madison, Irene Myles, Ethel Oliver, and Sy Oliver, the last two members of a family of talented musicians from Buxton. In addition to Bobby Parker, a bandleader looking

for a drummer might call on Tony Anthony, who drove a cab during the day, or George Fletcher. Olonzo Hayes held down the beat for his brother Jerry's band, as did Gene Jackson for the Soul Brothers Band. Buck Perry, Big Al Richardson, and Les Wright also played drums.[59]

Local bands included the Wee Sisters, consisting of Adeyln Wilson, Evelyn Brooks, and Alma Baxter, who began performing in 1938. In 1940 the Wee Sisters had second billing to Shirley Temple at the Iowa State Fair. Bill Riley was so impressed at the time that he helped them get even more professional gigs. Eventually, they worked with and were helped by big band leader Fletcher Henderson.[60]

Most Considered Music an Avocation

Most of these players considered music to be an avocation. Undoubtedly, more of them would have followed Irene Myles and pursued professional opportunities had they been available. Some did so for periods of time, taking on day jobs when work in music was short. Such was the case with Parker, who played full-time in Omaha with a big band before returning to Des Moines to take work with John Deere.[61]

Quite simply, though, the market for jazz in Des Moines and Iowa was not big enough to support a large group of

professional musicians. Many young people who showed promise went elsewhere, to the major cities, where opportunities were more prevalent.

Indeed, Des Moines's proximity to Kansas City, St. Louis, and Chicago can be seen as an asset and a liability. It meant that Iowa became the destination of many professional acts traveling the national circuit, providing much-needed exposure to trends in African-American music. On the other hand, these cities lured away many of the most promising local musicians. Irene Myles, Bobby Parker, and Harriet Newsome left the state to find adequate music education and employment.[62]

Trumpeter Leroy (Snake) White is another example of how the bigger midwestern cities lured away the cream of Iowa's talent.[63] Born to a Buxton minister in 1907, White grew up in Perry but left for Des Moines when he was 17 to form a vocal group called "The Do-Dads of Diddy-Wa-Diddy" with three of his friends. They worked pick-up jobs in Riverview Park and the Center Street district, singing songs like "You Got to See Your Mama Every Night or You Can't See Mama at All."

But White was out to disprove his father's prediction that nothing would come of his love of jazz, so he alighted for Kansas City. There he paid his musical dues before becoming part of the Thirteen Original Blue Devils, one of a number of hardworking

uptempo jazz ensembles in the area.[64] These Kansas City groups became a sort of college for several future jazz greats, including a still relatively unknown Lester Young, with whom White worked. From there, White's career followed the steady arc of a working jazz musician in the 1930s and 1940s.[65]

White's musical career peaked in 1944, when he stopped touring and started arranging, eventually ending up with Desilu Productions. Clients in those years included Frank Sinatra, Duke Ellington, Earl (Fatha) Hines, and Ella Fitzgerald. But life on the road is a Faustian bargain, and he was told by a doctor in 1965 that he needed to give up a life that included too much alcohol or lose his life. He chose the former and decided to return to Perry, where he knew "the lights go out at nine o'clock."

The story doesn't end there. In 1985, White, with support from Perry resident Dorothy Walker, started the Roy White 17-piece Big Band. Symbolizing his renewed faith in Christianity, the band played a form of "gospel jazz," relying on a spectrum of local, part-time players. In December 1985, Roy White was back on stage, at Drake's Hall of the Performing Arts, moving up front to sing "Yes, God Is Good." He sang with so much exuberance, noted a reviewer, "that the audience clapped along and whistled when he finished."[66]

(Left to right)

Good times at the Sepia Club (courtesy Ron Gray and Dorothy Gray Looper)

Cliff Payton's Trio backing an unidentified guitar player at the WOC-TV studio: Cliff Payton, drums; Mallie William, sax; and Floyd Banister, piano (Putnam Museum)

The Wee Sisters began performing in 1938 and went on to work with Fletcher Henderson's big band. (Iowa Women's Archives)

Performances of the Jubilee Singers were broadcast over KXEL Waterloo in 1944. (Grout Museum)

Sister Rosetta Tharpe, whose gospel singing electrified Des Moines audiences, August 1946 (SHSI Des Moines)

On the March for His Cause

Through the first half of the twentieth century, a rift existed between religious and secular forces within the nation's African-American community, particularly in the arena of music. Blues, ragtime, and, less so, jazz were disparaged by black church leaders as the devil's music. Many secular players were made into pariahs, not to be associated with by the church-going middle-class of black America.[67]

The African-American population in Iowa doesn't seem to have had the same degree of animosity between their religious and secular realms. Bobby Parker and Mel Harper don't recall being at all rejected by their church-going neighbors. They and other local musicians seem to have had an easy relationship with work and worship. At the funeral of Irene Myles, for example, her pastor spoke movingly of his love for her music.[68]

This is not to say there was no competition between churches and clubs in Iowa after 1920. At least in central Iowa, the church appears to have made a concerted effort to respond to the new distractions of jazz and blues. Throughout the nation, the black church had begun to innovate a style that moved the music closer to the up-tempo, chorally complex forms that secular music had begun to explore. For church leaders, the important thing was that the interest of the community be maintained, especially among the youth.

To that end, Des Moines churches attempted to present a religious option to the secular options in the Center Street neighborhood. Week-long revivals took place on a regular basis. In 1943, the Union Baptist Church, at East 16th and University, conducted a revival and a musical simultaneously. The Brown Chapel AME Zion Church on Walker Street had an "old time revival" to attract attendees, advertising that "national gospel singer and pianist" Dorothy Austin would be the entertainment.[69]

Young people seem to have been on the mind of the leaders of Mt. Zion Baptist Church when they sponsored a "Big Spring Festival," with "games, good speaking by reasonable men, and food." During "Home Coming Week" in July 1942, Maple Street Baptist — at East 10th and Maple — had a "talent night, with sweet music." Maple Street Baptist was also the site of a February 1946 performance of "The Outcast of the Streets," a drama directed by Etella Coates.[70]

St. Paul's AME appears to have been an innovator as early as 1922, when the church presented a movie with an African-American cast called *The Poison Pool*. "Marimbaphone soloist" Enza

L. Morgan performed there in April 1923. St. Paul's helped to continue the turn-of-the-century tradition of African-American marching bands with its drum and bugle corps, run by the church's men's group, dubbed The Brotherhood, Inc. One can measure the importance of outreach by the number of organizations in a church dedicated to that purpose. An early St. Paul's church bulletin lists, among other things, a superintendent of young people; a senior and junior choir, and no less than 12 auxiliary organizations.[71]

Church music in Des Moines has been dominated by women. All five of St. Paul's organists were female, plus one of its three musical directors. At Corinthian Baptist in 1919, Dalza Hammitt was organist, assisted by Willa James. At least 9 out of St. Paul's 12 auxiliary presidents were women, plus the presidents of the junior choir and missions, and the superintendents of the Sunday school and young people. Three groups of stewardesses, with a total of 27 members, not counting the 3 women listed as stewards, and 15 of the church's class leaders were female.[72]

Corinthian Baptist had junior and senior choirs. St. Paul AME had a youth choir too. In addition to its annual spring music festival, one year St. Paul's also advertised a concert by Piney Woods School graduate Pruth McFarlin, whom it called "America's greatest Negro tenor."[73]

Regional interest in gospel was sufficient to convince some local talent to take a shot at full-time singing. A young Mildred Griffin, just out of high school, had pamphlets printed up by Robert Patten detailing her devotion to Christ and asking for opportunities to sing to congregations for a small gratuity.[74] Born in 1923, she was part of a Corinthian Baptist family, though her first recital was given at St. Paul's AME. Griffin is an example of how the church was making a concerted effort to win back young people.

In a letter that begins "Dear Minister," she writes that "the youth of the world needs to get a stronger hold on God's hand and get on the march for His cause." By the time of this pamphlet's printing, she had already performed in Ottumwa and Council Bluffs, Iowa; Chicago and Maywood, Illinois; Gary, Indiana; Omaha, Nebraska; and St. Louis, Missouri. Travel of this sort requires a network of support — money for expenses, housing, board, and so on — so her success indicates a church community that was anything but stagnant.

Eastern Iowa provides two important examples of how the church provided opportunities for musicians to practice their

talent. Waterloo's Charlesetta Dawson, born in Mt. Pleasant in 1955, began singing in the church at age two.[75] Honing her skills in church, she found herself directing a choir of her younger siblings, two brothers and two sisters. She says that even as a child she had the gift of hearing the elements of music, how to mix natural voices so that they sounded good. The entire family was musically inclined. Her mother played piano, and her father had a singing quartet of his own. In 1979, Dawson got her degree at UNI, and eventually she became the director of the Northern Iowa Gospel Choir. Moving on to elementary school teaching, she now uses her own unique methods to incorporate popular music into her daily lesson plans.

Randolph O. Dean, also of Waterloo, was born in Alabama in 1937 to a family of 11 brothers and sisters.[76] His early musical experience included the family choir formed by his parents. Dean moved to Waterloo in 1960 to work for John Deere. He would retire 33 years later. Soon after moving to Iowa, he joined the Mt. Carmel Missionary Baptist Church, where he became the choir director, a position he held for 30 years. He has been writing gospel for 40 years. Dean calls it a "God-given gift" and says that "lyrics just come into my head." He is inspired by phrases and verses from the scriptures, and he receives commissions from friends and

Gospel singer Martha Brooks of Fort Madison performed with bandleader Tommy Dorsey. (courtesy Rev. Brooks)

The Des Moines All-Women Band was a symbol of the pervasive influence of women in African-American music, particularly in the churches. (courtesy Eleanor Archer)

acquaintances for various events. Dean does not read music but works entirely by ear. His compact disc recording, titled *Hold On*, was well received by the national gospel circuit.

As the 1940s moved into the 1950s, black music moved to the sound of the big beat. Known as rhythm and blues, it was born of southern shouters like Lightnin' Hopkins, Howlin' Wolf, and T-Bone Walker. They literally had to scream the lyrics in order to be heard above the thundering rhythm section. Less manic were the smooth singing groups, inspired both by the crooners — Frank Sinatra and Nat King Cole — and their own church background. The most famous practitioners of this sound were the Ink Spots, who inspired the founders of a small independent label in Detroit called Motown.

The church, particularly the evangelical congregations, were quick to match this new style with the old truth. In Des Moines there was the True Friends, who performed from the 1940s through the 1960s. Members at various times included Victor Coleman, Garnett Canon, Al Williams, Robert Dixon Sr. and Robert Dixon Jr., Lester Jornech, Rev. Alex Crawford Jr., Robert Timms, Ronald McClain, Nedion and Grant Townsell, and Howard Flaggs. Des Moines in the early 1950s also had the female Joy Soft Gospel Singers: Rubey Spencer, Mary Jane Dixon, Crissey Diggs, Blanette Scales, and Elsie Miller. From the Union Baptist Church came

the Dixon Wonders, made up of siblings Laura, Robert, Edmonia, and Henrietta Dixon.[77]

The Richard Allen Chorus was started in 1952 at St. Paul's AME Church in Des Moines by Lauretta Reeves.[78] After playing piano in her teens for the church's Sunday school, Reeves decided the church needed a group willing to reach beyond the confines of the diocese. Her group was a success, eventually performing with such luminaries as Sidney Poitier, in addition to serving as a bridge over the racial gulf by singing for numerous white congregations.

In eastern Iowa, the Silverlite Gospel Singers, a Christian a capella group, was organized in the Cedar Rapids area.[79] The group included Henry Dawson, Louis Bragg, Lawrence Baker, James McGowan, Edward Brown, and Fred Martin. It was Martin who formed the group in 1952, after moving north from Texas, where he had already made a name for himself as a singer. All were members of Mt. Zion Church in Cedar Rapids, and they sang a combination of what Martin calls gospel and jubilee. They traveled throughout the South and Midwest: Louisiana, Arkansas, Texas, Illinois, and Nebraska. Though unable to pinpoint what exactly sets it apart, Martin insists that the gospel made in Iowa was unique from that made in other places. He believes the lack of an established gospel education system in Iowa allowed gospel singers to innovate and develop their own voice. His group made

The Silverlite Gospel Singers (far left), formed in 1952, were all members of the Mt. Zion Church in Cedar Rapids. Traveling throughout the South and Midwest, this a capella group sang gospel and jubilee music for more than 30 years. (Linn County Historical Society)

Vocal music groups were very popular in the years after World War 2. This group was part of a WOC/WHO broadcast. (SHSI Des Moines)

music for Christ for more than 30 years, finally bringing things to a close in 1986.

In a similar vein, and also based in Cedar Rapids, is Psalms. Begun in 1988, Psalms performs the whole gamut of African-American music, from early spirituals to contemporary pop-gospel. Led by keyboardist Ron Teague of Iowa City, with support from Vince Harrelson on bass and Marcus Beats on drums, the singers include Sharilyn Bell, Sandy Reed, Allen Bell, Paul Tillman, and Michael Cole. Doris Akers, an aunt to several of the members, is perhaps the nation's best-known black gospel singer and songwriter. The members of Psalms all say she is one of their greatest influences. In addition to work in churches, they perform at festivals, benefits, and reunions. Group members do not feel there is anything particularly unique about gospel in Iowa. They tend to divide the form by generations, saying that the younger one gets, the more beat in the music. Along with Louis McTizic, Psalms was part of the Iowa Sesquicentennial Festival in Washington, D.C.

In the western part of the state, Mt. Zion Pentecostal Church of Council Bluffs has made its contribution to gospel in Iowa in the form of the Reed Brothers — Chris, Hershal, and Jeff — a group of singers and composers who perform both gospel and Christian contemporary music. Playing by ear, they come from a family of singing preachers.[80]

Over the years, the True Friends of Des Moines (left) included Victor Coleman, Garnett Canon, Al Williams, Robert Dixon Sr., Robert Dixon Jr., Lester Jornech, Rev. Alex Crawford Jr., Robert Timms, Ronald McClain, Nedion and Grant Townsell, and Howard Flaggs. Pictured here is the group in 1950. (SHSI Des Moines)

Ottumwa soprano Ivory Winston became an acclaimed opera performer. (courtesy Gwen Sanders)

Religion and church music has played a considerable role in the life and career of Simon Estes, Iowa's most famous African-American native son. Simon Estes was born in 1938 to a Centerville family that would congregate in the family house at night, praying and singing hymns. Estes's ability to sing was recognized early, but his family insisted he focus on doing well in school. A good education was the best way to achieve the American dream, the Esteses believed. "Whatever else people can take away from you, they can't take away what's in your head."[81]

In high school, Estes was a successful choir singer and athlete. He credits sports with giving him the focus he needed for his singing career later. Despite living in a generally segregated community, he cites his family and his white friends, including his high school football coach, for creating a network of support that kept him from failing.

While working full-time and attending the University of Iowa in 1960, Estes became the first black member of the Old Gold Singers, a university ensemble. After a concert, Estes was approached by University of Iowa voice teacher Charles Kellis

about the possibility of singing opera. Estes responded, "What's opera?" A few days of imbibing the opera albums given to him by Kellis led him to conclude "this is the most beautiful stuff I've ever heard," and he set his sights on a career in opera. With support from Kellis, the Rockefeller Foundation, the NAACP, and other funds, Estes moved from Iowa to the Julliard School of Music in New York and finally to intensive operatic studies in Germany.

In Berlin in April 1965, Estes made his operatic debut in *Aida*, playing Verdi's Ramfis. He went on to continued success in both Germany and the Soviet Union, playing several roles; placing third in the Munich International Vocal Competition of 1965; and taking second in the First International Tchaikovsky Vocal Competition despite knowing no Russian and learning his piece virtually the night before.

Returning to the U.S. in 1967, his career took off, despite much institutional racism within the established opera community. The list of his singing credentials is extensive — including engagements with the San Francisco and Chicago Lyric Operas, playing the lead in a Zurich production of *Der Fliegende Hollander* by Richard Wagner, playing Porgy in a 1985 revival of *Porgy and Bess* at the New York Metropolitan Opera, appearing at Carnegie Hall, and recording several gospel albums for Phillips Records and an album of black spirituals on CD.

Returning regularly to Iowa for visits with his family and to sing at churches and with the Des Moines Symphony, Estes is a model of protest through action, of quietly disproving every false conception that a racist may try to pin on him by doing everything excellently. Despite this, only a small percentage of his work is done in the United States, a situation his former teacher Charles Kellis calls "ridiculous." Estes is well aware of this discrimination and doesn't shy away from pointing it out. "The fact is that Simon Estes is the only black man with a major career in the opera world today," he asserts. "I can assure you that it's not because I'm the first with a major talent, and, believe me, there are plenty of younger black singers with beautiful voices."

In a sense, Estes has fought racism in a way that seems characteristic to Iowa, going about his life with quiet passion, familial devotion, endurance, humility, and faith. In comments made as he endowed a University of Iowa scholarship, the singer declared, "I believe very strongly that we are put on this earth to help other people. Rather than leave money for these programs in my will when I die, I like to spread the wealth around now. When I was going to college we were very poor — poor economically, but very rich in love and respect. I worked my way through the University of Iowa, and I'd just like to make things easier for other young people."[82]

The Little Singer Girl

The Center Street neighborhood flourished until the early 1960s, when urban renewal tore the area in two. In the name of progress and without the consultation of black residents, an interstate highway was built through the middle of Des Moines. A major hospital complex expanded into the neighborhood. Half the Center Street community was cut off from the other half. Then the city started tearing down older buildings considered urban blight. Many of these buildings housed the very nightclubs and restaurants that formed the heart of the Center Street community. The neighborhood was destroyed and with it the hopes of many Des Moines black people in the promise of America. For this reason, a neighborhood historian titled her book *They Took Our Piece of the Pie*.[83]

Despite this, people like Bobby Parker and Irene Myles remained and kept playing. People like them would inspire a new generation of jazz artists in Des Moines. One young member of this new wave is Tina Haas. Like Irene Myles, who grew up in Perry, Ms. Haas was raised in a small town, Algona, in northwestern Iowa. She lived with her grandparents on their farm just outside of town. Her mother is black, and her father, who left the family soon after Tina's 1965 birth in Kansas City, is white. Her grandparents — Bill and Dorothy Boldridge — are part of a highly regarded family in the Algona area. Indeed, Algona's Boldridge Park is named after them.

Haas lived in Algona until she was 18 years old. Because of her multicultural heritage, and because she lived in rural Iowa, she grew up with a sense of both black and white worlds. The confusion in self-identity that this caused led her to music as a source of comfort. She recalls singing from the age of three, and remembers always considering it a gift. She was "the little singer girl." As a schoolgirl she would often run up to her room to sing to her assembled audience of stuffed animals. Comforted, she came to

The Four Notes, featuring Irene Myles on piano and Bobby Parker on the drums, pleased Des Moines night club patrons throughout the 1950s. (courtesy Bobby Parker)

(Opposite, above left to right)

Musical opportunities were not limited to Iowa's larger cities. This is the Estherville Men's Chorus with Leon (Speed) Blake. (courtesy Pete Obje)

Worldwide fame has not weakened the affection opera singer and Centerville native Simon Estes feels for Iowa. (Bystander)

think of songs as friends.

Despite the fact that her grandfather was a musician, both he and his wife discouraged their granddaughter from pursuing music as more than an avocation. Like the parents of Simon Estes, "they thought it was too impractical a way to make a living." This theme is perhaps a reflection of life in Iowa, where the traditions of a farm culture insist on pragmatic pursuits. Certainly, she was not the first Iowa musician encouraged by parents to find more practical vocations and to leave music strictly an avocation.

In high school, Haas started singing with the choir at the local Methodist church. Clearly talented as a singer, and unique as a person, the choir director often set her apart to sing leads and solos. Haas believes this was when she first discovered the joy of authentic hymn singing, how worshipping and praising as a group can lift up an individual soul. In addition, she gives much credit to her choir director at Algona High School, Deb Anderson. Haas says that Anderson taught her the joy of singing and how working toward artistic greatness can be its own reward. Ms. Anderson

Sonny Rollins blows his horn at Cornell College. (Cornell College Archives)

also used rehearsals for musicals to show Haas the importance of charisma on stage. Anderson was the person who really encouraged Haas to pursue music professionally.

During these years, she was primarily interested in the pop music she was hearing on the radio. Though pushed by those around her to "sing black," she rebuffed these efforts and listened to such acts as Stevie Nicks and Olivia Newton-John. It was when she found a collection of her aunt's and uncle's records from the 1960s that she really connected with her identity as a black person for the first time. Listening to the Temptations, the Four Tops, and the Supremes, she heard black people singing in ways that she wanted to sing, something different from the experience of singing at church and school. This knowledge came to fruition when she enrolled at Drake University in Des Moines. It was there that she became part of the Drake Gospel Choir. She overcame some initial discrimination on the part of others who did not perceive her as African-American and discovered real cohesion and unity of spirit in the act of making music with the group.

Haas dropped out of Drake after one year and took on her first professional music gig. Bob West, a trumpet professor at the university, took her into his jazz band and she sang with them from 1986 to 1990, making two recordings in the process.

After a lull, she returned to professional music in 1994, when she started singing at Mel's Bar and Grill with the jazz trio of Sam Salamone on sax, Jason Brewer on trumpet, and Frank Tribble on guitar. Until it closed in 2000, Mel's was a place where blacks and whites could come together in Des Moines to hear jazz and rhythm and blues. There Haas was first seen by Irene Myles. As a result of that meeting, Myles wrote what became Haas's signature tune — a growling, swinging melody called "Mean and Evil." Over the course of their friendship, Myles taught Haas that "jazz is you; it's about expressing your feelings and life through music, and vocal illustration." When she speaks of Myles, Haas sighs deeply and with a touch of awe at the remembrance.[84]

Tina Haas's experience at Drake University and Charlesetta Dawson's tenure with the Northern Iowa Gospel Choir illustrate the importance of Iowa colleges and universities in the dissemination of African-American music throughout the state. Festivals and programs like the annual Spring Music Festival at Cornell College were relatively rare opportunities for blues and jazz players of the day to pass on their knowledge through concerts and master classes. An outstanding example occurred in 1977, when jazz saxophonist Sonny Rollins came to Cornell. During a master class and a performance with the college's jazz band, Rollins struck the attendees "as gentle and humble a human being as you ever met, who rehearsed past the allotted times, who couched his suggestions to the student musicians in gentle terms and who afterwards congratulated several of them for doing a good job."[85]

At Grinnell College in the late 1950s, a young pianist from Chicago who was majoring in engineering started a jazz band that became a popular campus act. As a result, this man, Herbie Hancock, changed his major to music and began a career that made him one of the best-known names in modern jazz. His time in Iowa was short, but it seems to have had an impact. The enlightened atmosphere at Grinnell gave him the space to put together a group that could explore the new sounds that jazz trumpeter Miles Davis and saxophonist John Coltrane were bringing to the forefront. Focused on the exploration of tone, these musicians sought to get the right mix of color out of each piece. Their bands were often larger than the bebop groups of the 1940s: octets, nonets, or even larger, as in Hancock's band. In May 1958, the band presented "The Grinnell Jazz Colloquium," a concert of tunes by Count Basie, Stan Kenton, Ray Anthony, and Miles Davis, as well as an original by Hancock titled "Top Brass."[86] An op-ed piece in Grinnell's campus newspaper shows that the student musicians were well aware of what they were doing: "What you will hear this evening is representative of progressive, modern or cool jazz, call it what you will. These are new forms that have etched tremendous influence on contemporary music. But the contributions of the blues will not be wholly discounted."[87] Not long after leaving Grinnell in 1960, he got his first big break, an offer to play keyboard for Miles Davis.

At Grinnell in 1967, a group of six black students, predominantly from out of state and led by Milton Rolland and Gwendolyn Moore, began gathering to sing gospel tunes as a way of retaining their cultural identity.[88] This group eventually grew to become, in 1973, an official entity of the college's music department — The Young, Gifted and Black Gospel Choir. Over the years the group has toured across the state and nation, and in 1974 released a recording. Though initially an all-black organization, the choir now includes members from several different ethnic groups and takes its inspiration from a quote by W. E. B. DuBois that "sometime, somewhere, men will judge by their souls, and not by their skins."[89]

Herbie Hancock majored in music at Grinnell in the 1950s and began a career that made him one of the best-known names in modern jazz. Shown here performing in the courtyard of the Bucksbaum Center for the Fine Arts in 1999 (Grinnell College)

Jazz was popular on college campuses in the 1950s. Led by singer Sampson (Sam) Rice, these students at the University of Dubuque formed their own "mixed" band. (University of Dubuque Archives)

Eddie (Pickin) Bowles

"Eddie Bowles played the guitar and sang. I am 57 years old, and I recall sitting in front of his house in Cedar Falls with other neighborhood children to listen to him sing. I was five, or maybe a little older, and I remember how on hot summer evenings Eddie would play for us, his chair pushed back so it leaned against his house. Eddie also came to Miner School and sang and played his guitar for school programs.

"The neighborhood of 4th Avenue where we lived is now nearly gone as a result of flood-control buy-outs. When we lived there, the area was bordered by the Illinois Central Railroad on the south and the backwaters of the Cedar River on the north. The neighborhood was just four or five blocks long, with houses on each side. Most people living on 4th Avenue were poor and had large families. The homes were small, yet I recall many families with eight or ten children. There were no sidewalks, no curbs, no gas or water or sewer services until years later, in the 1960s or 1970s. We had outhouses, pumps outside or on the back porch, and oil burners or coal heaters. I do not recall the houses having furnaces.

"The people on the street worked at factory jobs or on the railroad. At the time I did not know we were 'poor people,' since we all had similar circumstances. Seems like everyone knew everyone else or was related to them in some way.

"Sarah and Eddie Bowles were the only black people I recall seeing when I was a child. The rest of the people were white, with one family having a mother who was a Cherokee Indian. I don't recall anyone treating Sarah and Eddie any differently than anyone else. But when I grew up and became aware of the segregation and discrimination that blacks in Waterloo suffered, I recall wondering why Sarah and Eddie lived on 4th Avenue. Who were they? What did Eddie do for a living? And why didn't they have kids like everyone else? I don't recall ever thinking of them as being old. They seemed to stay the same age year after year, from as far back as I can remember them until sometime in the 1970s."

— Linda Fobian, February 2001

Eddie (Pickin) Bowles had an incredible impact on those who knew him in Cedar Falls — especially his neighbors on 4th Avenue. (Waterloo Courier)

Man, It's the River

Eddie (Pickin) Bowles was born in Lafayette, Louisiana. There he was steeped in the mix of French, African, and spiritual music that makes up Cajun. Moving to New Orleans around 1910, he started playing guitar in local bands and at funerals. In 1914, he moved north with his wife Sarah to Cedar Falls, where he worked as a laborer and eventually got a job with John Deere. Shortly before he died in 1984, he reminisced about his life in music. "I've lived a long, long time, and when you live as long as I have, the loneliness gets in. But when I play [my] guitar, all the good memories make the loneliness go away. Ah, there are so many good memories hiding in that old guitar. I teach people who care about my music, and when I go I'll still be around from my music being played by others."[90]

The development of blues music in Iowa follows the pattern of Bowles's life — coming out of the agrarian South and moving to the North in the Great Migration. Like the spiritual, the blues incorporates the steady rhythm and repetition of African music. Unlike its musical parent, though, blues lyrics address secular matters.[91] Musicologist Harry Oster points out that this music is more concerned with social and economic troubles, focusing on the harsh reality of sharecropping existence — evil landowners, no-good men and women, and perpetual poverty.[92] Generally, the singer reaches some point where plans are stymied by forces beyond the singer's control, such as the boll weevil. Typically, a song's verses are tied up with a clever or ironic twist of language, often a double entendre that's a sexual metaphor. The spiritual dimension is usually confined to the singer's lamenting his own damned soul. The singer often wishes that he or she could reform, but inevitably fails. The attraction of the blues lies in the combination of irrepressible rhythm, vocal gymnastics, and lyrics that tell a story about the world that is realistic yet clever.

Big Bill Broonzy at Iowa State

As with other new forms of black music, African-Americans in Iowa came in contact with the blues primarily through the pop culture industry.[93] Blues musicians of the 1950s, such as Muddy Waters and Big Bill Broonzy, stuck to a circuit that included the Deep South and the bigger midwestern cities of Chicago, St. Louis, and Kansas City. Except for river towns such as Davenport and Clinton in the eastern part of the state, traveling blues performers rarely ventured into Iowa.

The fall of racial barriers and the rise of electric blues out of Chicago and Memphis after World War 2 meant that a number of famous blues acts started to play throughout the state, B.B. King, Buddy Guy, Ray Charles, Luther Allison, Larry McCray, and Gatemouth Brown among them. It was during this period of newfound freedom of movement and opportunity that Big Bill Broonzy ended up spending some time in Ames, Iowa.

The career of William Lee Conley Broonzy is a microcosm of the American bluesman's life in the twentieth century. Born to a family of Mississippi sharecroppers in 1893, in his youth Broonzy imbibed the sounds he heard from the many Delta blues men passing through the area.[94] In 1920, he moved north, pushing up the Mississippi like so many others in those days, searching for a promised land of economic opportunity. What he found was

I dreamed I was in the White House,
Settin' on the president's chair,
I dreamed he shake my hand
Said, "Old Bill, I'm glad you're here."

    But it was just a dream, man,
    Just a dream I had on my mind.
    When I woke up the next morning.
    Jim Crow did I find.

I dreamed I was in heaven,
Settin' down on the throne.
I dreamed I had an angel
Layin' back in my arms.

I dreamed I went out with an angel,
And I had a good time.
I dreamed I was satisfied
And nothin' to worry my mind.

    But it was just a dream, man,
    Just a dream I had on my mind.
    When I woke up the next morning,
    Not a pinfeather could I find.

— **"Just a Dream***,*" ***Big Bill Broonzy***[98]

Big Bill Broonzy's Life in Iowa

by Leonard Feinberg

Dr. Leonard Feinberg was a professor in the Department of English at Iowa State University for 35 years, retiring in 1981. He now resides in San Diego, California.

My wife, Lillian, and I knew Studs Terkel in Chicago. In 1950, when he was a radio host, he organized a group of musicians to go with him on tour around the Midwest: Big Bill Broonzy sang blues, Win Strake sang American folk songs, and another man sang Elizabethan music.

They came to Ames, Iowa, to give a concert in 1950, and since we knew Studs, we invited all of them to our house for dinner. That was the first time we met Big Bill Broonzy.

Several weeks later I got a letter addressed to "Mr. Finburg, Ames, Iowa." Ames was a smaller place at that time, so the letter was delivered to me. Bill wrote that the doctor told him he was getting sick from the smoke of the nightclubs where he was performing, and unless he got out of them he would die.

Bill had been brought up on a farm, and in his letter he asked, "Can you find me a job in Iowa on a farm?"

I talked with Shorty Schilletter, director of housing and employment at the university, to see if he could help us find a job for Big Bill on a farm.

Shorty couldn't get Bill a job on a farm, but found him a job as a janitor on campus and university housing (a little Quonset hut) to live in. Broonzy at that time was making $400 a week in Chicago, and all Shorty could offer him was $150 a month, so I didn't think Broonzy would take it. But Big Bill phoned me at midnight one night, which was ordinary time for him I suppose, and said, "Thank you. I'm coming."

A week later an old black Cadillac pulled up in front of our house. Bill unloaded it to stay temporarily at our house.

When he was done, he lay down on my son's bed and slept for 24 hours straight; he was that sick and tired. Shortly after that he started his job, and his wife joined him.

He often came over to our house for meals, and he played with our children. He asked if he could plant succotash in our garden —meaning could he plant the vegetables needed to make succotash — and he did.

After he recovered his health a little, he began to play on campus for fraternities and sororities and at our house for parties. One of the requirements before he played at our house was three glasses of whisky before he started.

A year later, in 1951, Bill was having Thanksgiving dinner at our house when he got a telegram, in care of me, from France.

Chicago, a boomtown ripe for new talent.

There he began to evolve a more formalized style that would help lay the foundation for the Chicago sound. Less than successful as a country blues performer, he took a cue from the dominant bluesman in that city at the time, Tampa Red, and took on musical partners. This band, the Memphis Five, forced him to slowly abandon the loose expository style of rural form; just the same, he never forgot that telling the story was the most important thing, that the instruments must never eclipse the story. After improving his guitar playing under Papa Charlie Jackson, Broonzy started tearing up the club and rent-party scene. Right up to the ascendancy of Leadbelly in the 1940s,

Broonzy was the godfather of blues in the city of big shoulders and even bigger blues men.

Broonzy never really lost touch with the reality of everyday, working-class life. In between times of plenty, he worked numerous blue-collar jobs. In 1950, during one of his periodic turnarounds, he played a concert in Ames. He fell ill and ended up staying in the hospital on the campus of Iowa State College.

As Leonard Feinberg explains (above), though Broonzy left Ames when he recovered, he was back a few weeks later, this time to stay for a while. Music historian Francis Davis has written that Broonzy "liked college life. He liked being able to say he had been to college."[95]

It was the 2000-year anniversary of the city of Paris, and guests were invited from all over the world to join the celebration. Bill was offered a couple hundred dollars a week to perform.

He read the telegram and threw it away, but my wife dug it out of the wastebasket immediately and tried to persuade him to go. "I don't go anywhere I can't see where I'm going to or where I'm coming from," Broonzy retorted.

Two weeks later he got another telegram, offering him twice the money, and this time we persuaded him to go.

Shortly after Bill arrived in Paris, he sent us a clipping from a French newspaper that read, "We are privileged to have with us a musician associated with a well-known American university." I suppose they thought he was a music professor or something.

While he was there, his hosts arranged for him to tour Europe and Africa. One of the places he went was Ethiopia.

When he got off the plane, he told the cab driver to take him to the best hotel in town because he was making good money at the time and could afford it.

So the cabby took him to the best hotel, but when Bill went to check in the desk clerk said, "We don't serve Negroes here." So the cabby took him to a fleabag that did serve him.

Bill came back to Ames in 1952, but only to pick up his things. The European tour had re-energized his career, and he was on the road again. In the course of his career, Big Bill Broonzy wrote 400 songs, but he couldn't read music.

He did it all by ear.

One of his songs was written in 1948 at the request of the Henry Wallace presidential campaign, and it went like this:

If you white,

you all right.

If you brown,

stick around.

If you black,

Git back,

git back,

git back.

Big Bill Broonzy with Tommy and Ellen Feinberg in Ames, 1951 (courtesy Leonard Feinberg)

Working as a janitor for the college, Broonzy impressed people in Ames with his charismatic features — a large, handsome man with a wide smile and huge voice. He seems to have been liked by everyone. As a teenager, Lou Thompson bought a guitar for $13.50, and would try to imitate the sounds that Big Bill made with his guitar while the two sat on the old statesman's couch. "I have to say it made a deep and lasting impression on me, and you're talking about 1953 or '54, so segregation was still very much a part of the South and he was a person who lived through probably some of the worst."[96]

In the mid-1950s, Broonzy hit the road again, to take advantage of another blues revival that was starting in the wake of the beat movement. It was his last. Throat cancer claimed his voice and the rest of his body in 1958. He died in Chicago, his adopted home.[97]

The players that came out of Chicago and Memphis in the 1950s sparked a blues scene that today is experiencing a genuine renaissance.[98] Louis McTizic of Waterloo is an outstanding example of an Iowa bluesman who came out of that time.[99] A stocky man with chiseled features, McTizic has a gravely voice that is at odds with his gentle personality. He loves to play. He gets energized as the crowd gets going, swaying and bouncing between band members, shouting out lyrics with verbal winks to the audience that eggs him on.

Blues singer Louis McTizic has lived in Waterloo since the 1950s. (courtesy Louis McTizic)

Born in rural Tennessee in 1936, McTizic's father was a local minister who hauled a piano to and from church every Sunday in order to sing and play. He remembers well the outdoor gatherings of family and neighbors to do "some singing." Listening at night to a clandestine radio, he heard the new sounds of blues records broadcast by a Memphis station. He learned guitar by ear while still a child, but was handicapped when he blew off his thumb and little finger in a hunting accident, an incident that causes him to chuckle when he tells it now. He started playing the blues harmonica because of its portability.

In 1957 he moved to Waterloo, where his sister lived. He felt comfortable in its small but vital black community. Many African-Americans from western Tennessee and northeastern Mississippi moved into the area, bringing the Memphis form of blues with them. Earl Hooker, a brilliant young blues guitar player from Memphis, also lived and played in Waterloo for a couple of years.

In Waterloo, McTizic formed the first of his many bands that would tour throughout Iowa and Illinois. In his view, the music being made in Waterloo was influenced mostly by the traditions people brought with them from the South. He talks fondly of the informal after-hours clubs and rent parties that made up the Waterloo blues scene in the 1950s, 1960s, and 1970s. He remembers that African-Americans from the big manufacturing plants like John Deere would bring their white friends to party with them. He can remember very little bad blood between blacks and whites at these parties, just good music and good times.

It's Tough Being a Female Blues Guitarist

McTizic is also a great bandleader, allowing his players the time and space to make tight ensemble blues. Etheleen Wright is one of two guitarists in the band. A quiet woman who is not afraid to tell the truth, she was already an accomplished bass player when she took up guitar to play with McTizic. As with so many others, music was for her a family affair. Her father was a pianist; her grandfather was a guitarist. She was raised by her grandmother, who took her to a Church of God in Christ, where enthusiastic "holy" playing and singing was encouraged. As a teen, she strayed to jazz and blues, eventually forming a group of her own called Etheleen Wright and the Mixers. In the mid-1970s she hooked up with McTizic. She says that it is tough being a female blues

548

guitarist — a medium dominated by men — but it just makes her practice harder.[100] Wright, like Tina Haas and others, has been forced by the limited market for black music in Iowa to be a general practitioner, delving into virtually every musical form.

Another bluesman who played in northern Iowa in the post-war period is singer Big Walter Smith, born in Oklahoma in 1930. In the 1960s, while living in Kansas City, he was called by a white band from Iowa, the Silvertones, to play at a local club for African-Americans. The band liked his singing so much that he was asked to join them and he agreed. They were to play at the Home Run Club in Cedar Rapids for six months, and then Smith was to return to Kansas City. Instead he ended up staying for three years. Smith remembers fondly the other band members, who included Damon Lee on guitar and harmonica and Joe Scheroman on bass, and feels that his influence helped make them better musicians. "They all improved greatly when they started backing me up." From Iowa, Smith moved even further north, to the Twin Cities in Minnesota, where he has enjoyed a successful career as a working blues singer. Among others, he has worked with Bobby Blue Bland, B.B. King, and Albert Collins.

Kevin Burt's musical roots were in Waterloo. Kevin's father was from Mississippi, where he was active in the local blues scene. He moved to Iowa to take a job with John Deere and later, when Kevin was two or three years old, he ran an after-hours club in the basement of their home. Kevin grew up listening to his father and brothers sing in the church choir, while he pursued his first love, football. This led to a successful high school career and a tryout with a Canadian Football League team. He just barely missed the cut and ended up moving to Iowa City after getting his degree at the University of South Dakota.

While working at the Evers Conners Rights and Resources Center for Independent Living, his boss, Ethel Madison, heard him singing along with a Luther Vandross song on the radio, something he had done all his life. She said, quite seriously, that he was good and he ought to consider singing with a band. She suggested trying out for the group in which her son played drums, advice that he followed. Out of that tryout in 1990 the Blues Instigators were formed, a group that eventually won the 1995 blues challenge of the Central Iowa Blues Society.[101]

Most followers of the Iowa blues scene consider the Blues Instigators to be one of Iowa's best bands. Their style covers the whole gamut of popular African-American music, from blues

Kevin Burt sings with the Instigators at the Mississippi Valley Blues Fest in Davenport, July 1996. Burt is accompanied by Matt Panek on guitar, Eric Madison on drums, and Dwayne Watford on bass guitar. (courtesy Jeff Schmatt / Rubicon Photo)

standards to rhythm and blues to soul. Burt struts and bellows like a commodore, using the traditional vocal techniques that can be traced back to the first African settlers in North America. His command of the stage is complete, and his easy way with the audience belies a serious student of the form. "Musicians are just like athletes," Burt says. "They work their way up, deciding at each level if they have the commitment necessary to continue on. If they do, they just do it."[102]

After a lull in the late 1950s and early 1960s, when blues was eclipsed by rhythm and blues and rock and roll, a resurgence began that lasted until the early 1970s. An important extension of the revival was the creation and proliferation of blues societies around Iowa and the nation. Groups such as the Central Iowa Blues Society of Des Moines, the South Skunk Blues Society in Newton, and Davenport's Mississippi Valley Blues Society put on

shows with professional blues musicians, support local acts with advertising, and use their newsletters as a source of education in African-American music. The membership in these groups is overwhelmingly white, but that is hardly surprising given the demographics of the state. What is also true is that these societies go out of their way to make sure that black artists are recognized and appreciated. For the members of these societies, the issue becomes expression: what are these artists saying, why are they saying it, and what does that mean?

Long Tradition of Bridging Racial Barriers

Many contemporary Iowa groups continue the long tradition of bridging racial barriers through blues and jazz. Guitarist and singer Taz Grant, perhaps the most famous bluesman in central Iowa, has had several white players in his

Taz Grant, originally from Chicago, has played his funk-rock-jazz-blues in Iowa since 1987. (courtesy Taz Grant)

The human race itself has a river to cross, the river of the tribe. The question of how to maintain one's identity while also living peacefully with those who are different has plagued the species for as long as humans have kept records.

Tina Haas sings during Jazz in July *in Des Moines. (Des Moines Metro Arts)*

band. Louis McTizic has a white guitar player; Kevin Burt's Instigators have a white guitarist and bass player. This seems to be part of a national development, as groups led by Larry McCray, Buddy Guy, B. B. King, and Robert Cray are all interracial. It is an example of how music is able to overcome what are perceived to be unbreakable barriers.

Radio has long been one of the most important reasons for the spread of black music in the United States. African-American music has been found on the radio in Iowa since at least 1941.[103] Program notes for WOI radio in that year list a show called *Today's Music* playing popular jazz artists of the day. Program director Doug Brown says that he has heard jazz on WOI for "as long as I can remember," since the mid-1940s. Public radio in Iowa continues to be an important means of disseminating African-American music throughout the state. Because they are not beholden to a profit margin, public radio stations are able to play a cross section of music that might not otherwise be heard. WOI-FM currently provides several hours a week of jazz, the only station in the central Iowa market to do so. As blues becomes more a part of mainstream American culture, some commercial stations have begun to devote one or two hours a week to the form.

In Iowa, KUCB in Des Moines was Iowa's principal black radio station. Started in 1981 by local activist Joeanna Cheatom, KUCB focused on black issues.[104] In addition to providing a necessary outlet for the concerns of Des Moines African-Americans, the station was one of the first to play rap and rhythm and blues. In 1978, KBBG was begun as a black-oriented radio station for the Waterloo/Cedar Falls area. The effort to launch the station was led by William Cribbs. "Education is what we're about," he said at the time. "Black lifestyles aren't accurately represented in the media because black people have been excluded from the decision-making positions."[105]

Coda

On a warm, clear evening in July, a man and women — both white — sit listening to a black woman sing her heart out. Around them is a congregation of dark and light-skinned people in shorts, T-shirts, and baseball caps who have come to this place just south of Drake University to hear Tina Haas sing. She is well supported by a white bass player and pianist and a black drummer. As she sways with the music, the lyrics flow pure, then twitter and pop, then swing up to the clouds, then down in to the gutter. The crowd smiles, some dancing and singing along. And for perhaps an hour, the people seem to genuinely unite. It is not a matter of forgetting; it's about celebrating. Understandably, Tina Haas is clearly overjoyed by this. She is an Iowan, bred in the small town and educated in the big city. She has been shaped by both the black and white world and has seen the good in both. Her vision is clear. "One of my purposes is to be a line-blurring person, a bridge to transcend the pain of racial hate, to get past the dividing line of pride and make it a sharing thing. If I have a dream, it's to one day see this nation turned into a white-black dialogue of celebration."[106]

It is and always will be true that spirituals, gospel, blues, and jazz have roots that are undeniably African. But like any art form, the greatness of the music lies in its ability to help humans everywhere connect with each other. As Iowa and the nation enter a new century, they find themselves with lingering and malignant signs of racism. I believe that the answer will not be found in race solidarity — so-called pride — but rather in the lifting up of all good things because they are good. The human race itself has a river to cross, the river of the tribe. The question of how to maintain one's identity while also living peacefully with those who are different has plagued the species for as long as humans have kept records. Perhaps a small lesson can be learned from the group of people who gathered that July evening to hear the truth sung with amazing grace.

I've known rivers: I've known rivers ancient as the world

and older than the flow of human blood in human veins.

My soul has grown deep like the rivers.

I bathed in the Euphrates when dawns were young.

I built my hut near the Congo and it lulled me to sleep.

I looked upon the Nile and raised the pyramids above it.

I heard the singing of the Mississippi when Abe Lincoln

went down to New Orleans, and I've seen its muddy bosom

turn all golden in the sunset.

I've known rivers: Ancient, dusky rivers.

My soul has grown deep like the rivers.[107]

Tell it.

Frank Tribble with his guitar and Julius Brooks on saxaphone are mainstays of Iowa's jazz scene. (Des Moines Metro Arts)

Notes

1. Tina Haas interviews, Sept. 25 and Oct. 23, 1996.

2. Eileen Southern, *The Music of Black Americans* (New York: Norton, 1983), 6.

3. John Hope Franklin and Alfred A. Moss Jr., *From Slavery to Freedom* (New York: McGraw-Hill, 1994), 22, 25.

4. Ibid., 56.

5. LeRoi Jones, *Blues People* (New York: Morrow, 1963), 28–29.

6. Miles Mark Fisher, *Negro Slave Songs in the United States* (New York: Citadel, 1981), 41.

7. Emory Elliott, et al., eds., *American Literature* (Engelwood Cliffs: Prentice-Hall, 1991), 1762.

8. Michael (Hawkeye) Herman interviews, Oct. 3, 1996, and Aug. 22, 1997.

9. Leola Bergmann, *The Negro in Iowa* (Iowa City: SHSI, 1948; repr. 1969), 36.

10. Fisher, 66.

11. Southern, 222.

12. Bergmann, 42.

13. Ibid., 43.

14. Ibid., 39.

15. Franklin and Moss, 100, 101–2, 231–32.

16. Bergmann, 32.

17. Ibid., 49.

18. Robert Patten Collection, SHSI Des Moines.

19. Southern, 167.

20. James Weldon Johnson and J. Rosamond Johnson, *American Negro Spirituals* (New York: Viking, 1969), 39.

21. *Iowa Bystander*, Jan. 5, 1912.

22. Jones, 71.

23. Jerry Sloat, *Lee County, Iowa: A Pictorial History* (Virginia Beach, VA; 1993).

24. *Iowa Bystander*, Jan. 12, 1912.

25. Patten Collection.

26. *DMR*, July 10, 1960.

27. Franklin and Moss, 340–41.

28. Bobby Parker interview, Feb. 15, 1997; Louis McTizic interview, May 21, 1997; Hal Martyn, "Eddie 'Pickin' Bowles Is Dead, but He'll Be around for a Long Time," unidentified newspaper clipping dated Oct. 6, 1984.

29. Herman interview.

30. Ibid.

31. Jones, 101.

32. Parker interview.

33. Jones, 101.

34. Gunther Schuller, *Early Jazz* (New York: Oxford Univ. Press, 1968), 187.

35. Bergmann, 57, 59.

36. Gayline Narcisse, *They Took Our Piece of the Pie* (Des Moines: Iowa Bystander Co., 1996); Parker interview.

37. Patten Collection.

38. Ibid.

39. Ibid.

40. Ibid.

41. Ibid.

42. Ibid.

43. Ibid.

44. Dawn Bormann, "Blues Singer Irene Myles Dead at 75," *DMR*, Oct. 24, 1996.

45. Jim Pollock, "A Soulful Tribute to Myles," *DMR*, Oct. 29, 1996.

46. Bormann, op. cit.

47. Parker interview.

48. McTizic interview.

49. Narcisse, op. cit.

50. Jerald Heth, "Suit Claims Bias by Disco against Blacks," *DMR*, June 26, 1979.

51. Ibid. See also "Disco's Liquor Permit Revoked," *DMR*, Aug. 2, 1979.

52. C. William Heywood memorandum on African-American history at Cornell College. Cornell College Archives.

53. Narcisse, op. cit.

54. Ibid. See also Patten Collection and Parker interview.

55. Patten Collection.

56. Narcisse, op. cit.

57. Ibid.

58. Ibid.

59. Ibid.

60. Patten Collection.

61. Parker interview.

Buxton Band (courtesy Mary Collier Graves)

62. Bergmann, 1; Parker interview; *DMR*, July 10, 1960.

63. Melinda Voss, "'Snake' White Finds an Angel for Gospel Jazz," *DMR*, Oct. 17, 1988.

64. Lee Hill Kavanaugh, "The Vine Comes Alive," *Midwest Jazz* 4 (Winter 1997): 17.

65. Voss, op. cit.

66. *DMR*, Nov. 9, 1986.

67. Bruce Cook, *Listen to the Blues* (New York: Scribners, 1973), 204–5.

68. Pollock, op. cit.

69. Patten Collection.

70. Ibid.

71. Ibid.

72. Ibid.

73. Ibid.

74. Ibid.

75. Clifford Weston interview, Iowa Sesquicentennial Files, SHSI Des Moines.

76. Ibid.

77. Patten Collection.

78. *DMR*, July 25, 1978.

79. Fred Martin interview, n.d.

80. Cynthia Schmidt interview, Iowa Sesquicentennial Files, SHSI Des Moines.

81. Eric Mortensen, "Simon Estes," undergraduate essay, Nov. 20, 1995. Simon Estes and Mary L. Swanson, *Simon Estes in His Own Voice* (Cumming IA: LMP, 1999).

82. Ibid.

83. Narcisse, op. cit.

84. Haas interviews.

85. Patrick Lackey, "Jazz Giant Rollins Right at Home at Grinnell," *DMR*, April 19, 1977.

86. *Scarlet and Black,* May 2, 1958, Herbie Hancock file, Grinnell College Archives.

87. Ibid.

88. Young, Gifted, and Black file, Grinnell College Archives.

89. Ibid.

90. Martyn, op. cit.

91. Jones, 61.

92. Harry Oster, *Living Country Blues* (Detroit: Folklore Associates, 1969).

93. Jones, 102.

94. Cook, 133.

95. Francis Davis, *The History of the Blues* (New York: Hyperion, 1995).

96. Mark Moran, "Big Bill Broonzy," WOI radio broadcast, Ames, Iowa, Aug. 18, 1997.

97. Ibid.

98. Alan Lomax, *The Land Where the Blues Began* (New York: Delta, 1993), 457.

99. McTizic interview.

100. Etheleen Wright interview, May 21, 1997.

101. Kevin Burt interview, Oct. 31, 1996.

102. Ibid.

103. WOI staff interview, Aug. 21, 1997.

104. Susan Caba, "KUCB Plans to Boost Power," *DMR*, June 15, 1983.

105. Jack Hovelson, "Black Station for Waterloo," *DMR*, May 4, 1978.

106. Haas interviews.

107. Langston Hughes, *The Collected Poems of Langston Hughes*, ed. Arnold Rampersad (New York: Knopf, 1994), 23.

The author acknowledges the following people for their help in the preparation of this chapter of Outside In: *Gaynelle Narcisse; Bobby Parker; Kevin (B. F.) Burt; Michael (Hawkeye) Herman; Onalee Green and the Cedar Falls Historical Society; Dr. Harry Oster, Ph.D.; Tina Haas; Fred Martin; Ann G. Kintner and Grinnell College; Louis McTizic; Eric R. Mortenson; Gaylene Narcisse; and Jack Lufkin and the staff of the State Historical Society of Iowa. The author would also like to thank: Hal Chase, for the vision, the chance, the drive, and the patience; all my friends and family, for their support; and Jesus Christ.*

The Bobby Dawson trio played at Johnny and Kay's in Des Moines, 1969. (courtesy Bobby Dawson)

Toni Ross and Vincent Saunders, neighbors and pals in Mason City (courtesy Meredith Saunders)

Neighboring

by James Alan McPherson

During the early summer of 1999, while I was reflecting on Philip Hubbard's *My Iowa Journey*, a memoir about the author's childhood and career as an official at the University of Iowa, and an account of Hubbard's struggle to advance human rights within the university community, a kind of explosion took place that shattered the calm and lazy glow of the season.[1] News began circulating that Ms. Linda Maxson, Dean of the College of Liberal Arts, had decided to "suspend" the world-famous International Writing Program, created in 1967 by Paul Engle, and suggested that future foreign participants in the program be re-assigned to Liberal Arts or International Programs. She cited lack of faculty and funding as the reason for this bureaucratic decision. A hue and cry was instantly raised in the Iowa community, on a website named "Save IWP" and in the *Daily Iowan,* the campus newspaper. By early July, more than 300 people had signed a petition calling for restoration of the program and sent it to Governor Vilsack. Dean Maxson and the University of Iowa administration immediately called for a public forum, during which the issues affecting the IWP were discussed by more than 100 participants. The administration apologized for having moved so quickly, and so silently, to restructure the program. They promised that everything possible would be done to save the IWP.

I had kept my distance on the controversy, although all that summer I kept running into people who expressed to me their concern about the program's fate. I spoke briefly with Lemuel Torrevillas and his wife, Rowena, longtime workers in the program, who were very sad about its possible demise. I spoke with clerks at the University of Iowa Credit Union and the Mercantile Bank, people met by chance on the street or in shops. They all expressed general affection for the program and for the international community it brought to Iowa City each fall. I also spoke with people who had an inside understanding of what had developed, people who had intimate understanding of what had happened behind the closed doors of the bureaucracy. Two separate understandings emerged from all these encounters. The first, which was current among those outside the official bureaucracy, was that support for the IWP had grown out of a genuine expression of "good will" or of "grace" or of the Iowa tradition of "neighboring."

Support for the International Writers Program had grown out of a genuine expression of "good will" or of "grace" or of the Iowa tradition of "neighboring."

*Elsie Woodsmall
and Rose Wells
were Lee Town
neighbors in Mount
Pleasant for more
than 30 years.
(Jerry Woodsmall
painting courtesy
Larry Woodsmall)*

From this perspective, money had never been the chief concern of the program. But from the official perspective of the bureaucracy, it had been, in fact, the chief concern. It seemed that some years before the arrival of Dean Maxson, the state legislature had determined to better rationalize its ties with the University of Iowa and its various programs. It had ordered a stricter accountability well before Ms. Maxson arrived on the Iowa campus. Also, following trends in the rest of the country, if not in the rest of the world, the corporate model had begun invading non-profit institutions with the result that what once had been warm and friendly networks of people who worked together to achieve mutually agreed-upon ends began to change. A new corps of impersonal bureaucrats had been integrated into such institutions, people responsible for the overseeing of very specific and limited parts of the over-all whole.

This bureaucratization of the *numen* — the life force that had once sustained the IWP — now was beginning to cannibalize and to attempt to rationalize ancient ideas about good will, about grace, about neighboring, about all non-bottom line concerns. Finally, there was the deep-seated assumption that the IWP had grown out of this country's efforts to win the Cold War; that the great number of foreign students who had been invited to Iowa City during the 1950s, and 1960s and 1970s and into the 1980s, when the forces of communism had been muscular, were now "free" of this potential infection. The fact that the U.S. Information Agency of the Department of State in Washington, D.C., had withdrawn its support from the IWP was proof of this. In the official view of things, the Cold War had been "won," and so all the apparatus that had been employed to continue that great effort should be thanked, but should also be taken off the government dole. It seems that Dean Maxson and the University of Iowa administration had been caught between the emotional preferences of local partisans of the IWP and the calculated decisions of people in Des Moines and in Washington, D.C., people at great distances from the University of Iowa campus. Consequently, they had been scapegoated.

As for me, during this heated period, I clung to my own memories.

The arrival of the International Writers in Iowa City each fall had been a delightful tradition, an opportunity for communal neighboring. There were the parties at the Engle home, high on a hilltop just behind, and to the right of, the Mayflower

Residence Hall where most of the visiting writers lived, on Dubuque Street. This proximity of residences made a rhetorical statement. Paul and his wife, Hualing, in their spacious home just above the Mayflower, acted as guardians of the multicultural flock of writers who roamed the halls of the Mayflower. Going to Paul's home many times to meet the writers, I could not help but make an analogy between the Engle home and the Pawnell home, further down Dubuque Street and also on a hilltop, that had been a station on the old Underground Railroad. Fugitive slaves were hid in the cellar of the Pawnell home. I liked to watch the writers, especially those from communist countries (China or Eastern Europe), as they grew more and more self-assured in their conversations, slowly daring more and more personal disclosures. They, much like the fugitive slaves in the cellars of the Pawnell home, were breathing in freedom from the cool Iowa air. There were the group trips to the John Deere Company, an Iowa benefactor of the program, to the Amana Colonies, for a touch of local color, and to other Iowa landmarks. There were the readings at which young American writers got opportunities to learn, at first hand, about the quality of life in distant lands. But most impressive of all was the annual reception given by the First National Bank (now the Mercantile Bank, thanks to a corporate merger) at the encouragement of its president, Bob Sirk. The yearly reception, open to the entire Iowa City community, always took place in all the rooms of the bank, and it affirmed Bob Sirk's roots as a small-town Iowan skilled in the tradition of neighboring.

Both Philip Hubbard's *My Iowa Journey* and Paul Engle's *A Lucky American Childhood* celebrate this tradition of neighboring.[2] It was an emotional and spiritual, not to mention practical, resource that was indigenous to the life in the small towns of Iowa during the early parts of the twentieth century. This resource grew out of a sense of interdependence, of communal obligation, of concern for the well being of a stranger. It was this tradition that led a ten-year-old Paul Engle, in Cedar Rapids, to accept employment from the newly arrived Goldstern family ("those damn Jews"). Orthodox Jews, the family employed Paul as a *shabbas goy* — a non-Jew who did on the Jewish sabbath, Saturday, the work that *Exodus* ordered Jews to not do. Paul earned 15 cents each Saturday for lighting fires in the Goldstern home. This initial gesture, grounded in "neighboring," led Paul to explore Jewish history and tradition in the U.S. and

later in Europe. It also led him, after his time as a Rhodes Scholar and after he began to write poems, to envision both the Writers' Workshop and, in 1967, the International Writers' Workshop, as no more than radical attempts at neighboring. Paul remained true to his sense of tradition. "I was a lucky kid," he reminds us, "living close to those remote people. They brought a strange, foreign quality into our modest midwest neighborhood . . . where all the families lived cheerfully together in the shared condition of hard work and little money. It was wonderful to be taken in as an honorary Jew by those whom I had at first feared."[3]

Philip Hubbard, in *My Iowa Journey*, recounts similar experiences of kindly intervention across racial and ethnic lines in his own home community near Des Moines. As a matter of fact, comparable stories could have been told by black fugitive slaves in the nineteenth century, especially Dred Scott; and in the twentieth century by George Washington Carver and the thousands of black college students from the South who came to Iowa to study when they could not attend state-supported schools at home.

It is an acknowledged fact that Iowa has a very proud tradition of helping the stranger, of neighboring, that has long been quietly celebrated by black Americans and especially by those international people, students as well as writers, who over the years have been welcomed here. To most of these people, especially those from totalitarian countries, the good experience of Iowa must have seemed like a blessing, a miracle. But to people like Paul Engle and Bob Sirk, who helped to minister to their needs, it was simply a matter of good neighboring, of affirming a meaning that helped defined the civil tradition of an agricultural state with norms of conduct grounded in the necessities, the practical necessities, of frontier life.

James Alan McPherson is the author of Crabcakes, Hue and Cry, Railroad, *and* Elbow Room, *for which he won the Pulitzer Prize in 1978.*

His essays and short stories have appeared in numerous periodicals — including the New York Times Magazine, Esquire, Atlantic Monthly, Newsday, Ploughshares, Iowa Review, *and* Doubletake — *and anthologies such as* Best American Short Stories, Best American Essays, *and* O. Henry Prize Winners.

McPherson has received a Guggenheim Fellowship and a MacArthur Fellowship. He is currently Professor of English at the Writers' Workshop at the University of Iowa in Iowa City.

Notes

1. Philip Hubbard, *My Iowa Journey: The Life Story of the University of Iowa's First Tenured African American Professor* (Iowa City: Univ. of Iowa Press, 1999).

2. Hubbard, op. cit.; Paul Engel, *A Lucky American Childhood* (Iowa City: Univ. of Iowa Press, 1996).

3. Engle, 161.

*"Four things are too
wonderful for me —
the way of an eagle in the sky,
a ship on the sea,
a snake on a rock,
and a man with a maid."*
— Philemon

*Like many of the
preceding chapters of*
Outside In,
*the following pages
reveal that the family is
the heartbeat of
African-American
history, that love is its
pulse, and that the beat
will go on — a rhythm
of life connecting past,
present, and future.*

*"Children's" wedding at Malone AME, Sioux City
(courtesy Frankie Williams)*

*Napoleon and Velona Walker
wedding (courtesy Velona Walker)*

*Anthony and Mary Reasby
wedding, Waterloo, 1936
(courtesy the Reasby family)*

The Reed-Atkinson wedding, Cedar Rapids, 1940 (Iowa Women's Archive)

*Frank and Ann Allen wedding,
1998 (courtesy April Arbuckle)*

Lee and Penny Furgerson family
(courtesy Penny Furgerson)

Minnie Doyle and her family, Albia, c.1900 (courtesy Dorothy Gray Looper)

Ye shall be fruitful . . .

Lacy Spriggs Sr. family
(courtesy Lacy Spriggs Sr.)

JoMoore Stewart family (courtesy Al Downey Sr.)

Sandra Miller (left) and Dixie Moore Spencer (right) grew up as sisters in Clara Miller's Marshalltown home. (courtesy Clara Miller)

(Left)Percy and Lileah Harris family, Cedar Rapids (courtesy Percy and Lileah Harris)

(Above) Max and Kittie Weston-Knauer family (courtesy Max and Kittie Weston-Knauer)

559

. . . and multiply.

*(Right) Sarah Jane Warren
and grandchildren,
Marshalltown, c.1940
(courtesy Helen I. Johnson)*

*(Far right)
William H. Matthews and
sons, Missouri Valley, 1920s
(courtesy Henry G. Matthews)*

Arthur and Victor Propes, Des Moines, c. 1940 (courtesy Victor Propes)

Miles Dawson and sons, Argyle, c. 1940 (courtesy Bobby Dawson)

A Family Album

*Rev. and Mrs. Baker, founders,
Second Baptist Church, Clarinda
(Nodaway Valley Historical Society)*

*Andrew and Hannah Anderson
lived in Buxton, c.1900.
(courtesy Dorothy Garrett Pryor)*

*Helen and Frank Johnson
of Marshalltown
(courtesy Helen I. Johnson)*

(Above) Harper family reunion, Fort Madison (courtesy Lois Harper Eichaker)

(Below) Furgerson family reunion, Cedar Rapids, 1998 (courtesy Penny Furgerson)

Whose kingdom shall have no end . . .

Afterword

by Dorothy Schweider

In a book published in 1996, *Iowa: The Middle Land*, I wrote that while much new scholarship on Iowa had appeared in the previous 20 years, there were still areas of Iowa's past that had been neglected. One of these was the history of African-Americans in the state. It is gratifying to note that the need no longer exists. With the publication of *Outside In: African-American History in Iowa, 1838-2000*, Iowa offers a stellar example to the rest of the nation regarding the way that African-American history ought to be done. From this point on, whenever scholars or laypersons want to know about any aspect of the black experience here, they need only look inside the covers of this book.

What about the Wider Context?

But while *Outside In* details in myriad ways the experiences of black Iowans through the years, what about the wider context? How does the black experience here relate to that of Iowans from other backgrounds? Can the appellation, "Iowa, the middle land," with its implications of economic and social moderation, a sense of centeredness, and a belief in family and community values, be used to describe the experiences of the state's African-Americans?

Clearly, the answer is yes. Even a brief perusal of Iowa history quickly shows that people came here in the nineteenth and twentieth centuries to improve their lives, both economically and socially. They carried along their cultural baggage — their religious beliefs and practices, their commitment to education for their progeny, their language, and typically a strong desire to improve their general well-being. These practices hold true whether the newcomers were migrating from eastern states or immigrating from foreign lands. And once here, they created new communities and new institutions as well as joining groups already formed. When one looks at the institutions and activities that all Iowans have valued through the years, one sees these same institutions and activities mirrored within the African-American experience. In fact, one has only to peruse the chapter titles of *Outside In* to see that the African-American experience in Iowa has not only been a major one, but has exemplified the ideals and values that all Iowans have held to be important.

More specially, the foregoing 21 essays make clear that African-Americans living in Iowa – living in both rural and urban landscapes – have been involved in, and have contributed to, all aspects of the state's economic development. The first generation of black men labored in many different occupations. In Des Moines, they worked for the Rock Island Railroad; in the Mississippi River towns, they labored in the hog-slaughtering plants; and in places like Buxton, Haydock, and Zookspur, they mined coal. Black women worked as well, often employed as domestics, cooks, or washerwomen. And black families worked the land in places like Fayette County.

Typically the earliest African-American workers had little choice but to accept menial positions. However, as the chapters in this book make abundantly clear, although they faced discrimination every step of the way, they continually pushed against these barriers. Through the years, they made great progress toward achieving not only economic but also social and political equality. These chapters also make clear that like Iowans in general, over some three or four generations, blacks have moved up the social and economic ladder. Today many descendants of these first workers are engaged as physicians, musicians, teachers, lawyers, and prominent businessmen rather than the unskilled workers of the past.

Along with work go family and community concerns. In all places where they have settled – large or small, rural or urban – blacks have formed kinship networks to provide solidarity and stability for their families, developed community institutions

Can the appellation, "Iowa, the middle land," with its implications of economic and social moderation, a sense of centeredness, and a belief in family and community values, be used to describe the experiences of the state's African-Americans?

(particularly religious ones), and contributed to the social, cultural, and religious life of the wider community. As the chapter on religion shows, wherever African-Americans have lived, their churches have been at the heart of their communities. Perhaps concern with family and community institutions have been most evident in Buxton, a coal-mining community in southeastern Iowa that existed from 1900 into the 1920s. Buxton, with its large black population and its economic and social equality for all ethnic and racial groups, allowed for a flowering of community institutions, fraternal organizations, and successful business establishments. Former residents referred to Buxton as a "black man's utopia" or, as one former resident put it, it was a "kind of heaven to me."

The result of all these experiences is evident in the foregoing chapters. Collectively they show there is not a single major area where African-Americans have not made their mark — and in the process improved the general climate and well-being of all Iowans. In fact, the courage, the tenacity, and the hard work has led to outstanding contributions in many different areas of Iowa's society. At the same time, it is also evident that the experiences of African-Americans parallel closely those of others who have come to call Iowa home. Certainly, the term "middle land" — with its implication of stability, centeredness, and moderation — encompasses the experiences of black Iowans as well as that of other Iowans.

Finally, there is another consideration about an even wider context. This volume will long be important to all Iowans because it presents an in-depth history of the black community here. But it should also serve an additional purpose: providing both a model and an inspiration for people in other states to produce a study of their African-American citizens. For those states that have not done so, and there are many, there is now a fine model to guide them. Perhaps this will be the major legacy of *Outside In*.

Emily Vermillion. George Washington Carver and Henry Agard Wallace. *1986. Oil on canvas. (Simpson College)*

"[Carver] was gentle and patient and gave me a feeling for growing plants which has not left me to this day. . . . He made botany something living . . . such botanists as Carver are exceedingly rare. There was in him both a creative urge and a sense of destiny which would not let him rest."
— **Henry A. Wallace on his mentor George Washington Carver, 1956**

Dorothy Schwieder is University Professor Emeritus of History at Iowa State University. For over 30 years at ISU she taught courses in the history of Iowa, American women, and the Midwest.

She has written numerous books and articles on Iowa and midwestern history. Her book, Growing Up with the Town: Family and Community on the Great Plains, *a history of her family and home town in South Dakota, will be published by the University of Iowa Press.*

Dr. Schwieder presently serves as chair of the State Historical Society of Iowa Board of Trustees and is on the Speakers Bureau for Humanities Iowa. She is married to Elmer Schwieder. The Schwieders have two children and two granddaughters.

Notes

1. Dorothy Schwieder, *Iowa: The Middle Land* (Ames: Iowa State Univ. Press, 1996), 355.

2. See Dorothy Schwieder, Joseph Hraba, and Elmer Schwieder, *Buxton: Work and Racial Equality in a Coal Mining Community* (Ames: Iowa State Univ. Press, 1987).

INDEX

565

Randy Jedele, District Chair of Communication for Des Moines Area Community College, earned his M.A. degree at Eastern Kentucky University. Mr. Jedele has indexed nearly two dozen books in various fields, including women's studies, religious studies, and language arts. In his leisure time, he enjoys traveling, gardening, cooking, and reading.

The Outside In *group gives thanks to the following volunteers for their assistance in preparing the index: John Arbuckle, Avril Chase, Rick Christman, Ted Clinkenbeard, Bruce Hann, Dan Ivis, Roslea Johnson, Audrey Mackaman, Kimberly Nelson, Dale Norris, Erma Payne, Barbara Chase Sanburg, Shirley Sandoval, Jim Stick, and Vanessa Veiock. And special thanks to Jan Winter and her assistant, Melva Schmidt, for the data input.*

Family photos can provide important clues to the styles, tastes and habits of a generation for the historical record. If you have photographs that you would like to be included with the Outside In collection at the State Historical Society, please contact Dr. Hal Chase at Des Moines Area Community College.

Paul and Susan Koch Bridgford have been graphic designers in printing, publishing, and advertising for more than 25 years. This is their first official collaboration. They live with their children Clare and Grant in Des Moines, where Paul is a free-lance artist and illustrator and Susan is the third generation to manage Koch Brother's printing — a 113-year-old family business.

A LAST WORD ABOUT THE PHOTOGRAPHS FOR OUTSIDE IN

Many of the images used in this book came from public and private collections and scrap books across the state. Because of their irreplaceable nature, they were photographed on-site by Hal Chase using a hand-held camera and available light. The quality of these images varies as dramatically as the condition of the originals.

To maintain the historic value of these photographs, the only retouch or manipulation was made to ensure that the quality of reproduction was as high as possible.

Each of the authors

contributed their work

to OUTSIDE IN for

no pay or royalties.

The 78th General Assembly

appropriated

for the project in 1999.

As of the publication date,

contributions

have been received from:

$ 90,000

78th General Assembly of Iowa

$ 35,000

Gardner and Florence Call Cowles
   Foundation, Inc.

$ 15,000

Prairie Meadows
   Racetrack and Casino

$ 10,000

Des Moines Register

George and Lois Harper Eichacker

Helen and James Hubbell Jr.

David and Elizabeth Kruidenier

Pioneer Hi-Bred International, Inc.

State Historical Society, Inc.

$ 5,000

Leola N. Bergmann

J.C. and Sue Rutledge Brenton

Hal and Avril Chase

Chrysalis Foundation

Cownie Charitable Trust

Des Moines Pioneer Club

Joseph M. Dorgan Memorial Trust

Firstar Bank Iowa, N.A.

Greater Des Moines Foundation

John R. and Zelda Z. Grubb

Iowa Women's Foundation

The Links Incorporated

NAACP — Des Moines Branch

$ 1,000

American Legion Foundation

Chase Investment Co., LLC

Barbara B. Clay

City of Des Moines

Mr. and Mrs. Mike Earley

Farmers and Merchants State Bank

Fred and Charlotte Hubbell

Thomas R. Hutchison

Iowa Girls High School
   Athletic Union

Mercy Medical Center

National Conference for
   Community and Justice, Inc.

Marvin A. Pomerantz

Watson Powell Jr.

John Ruan Foundation Trust

TruArt Color Graphics

United Negro College Fund – Iowa

Wells Fargo Bank Iowa, N.A.

Wells Fargo Home Mortgage

Wells Fargo Financial